FACTS ABOUT THE BRITISH PRIME MINISTERS

DERMOT ENGLEFIELD
JANET SEATON
ISOBEL WHITE

FACTS ABOUT THE BRITISH PRIME MINISTERS

Foreword by Prime Minister John Major

A COMPILATION OF
BIOGRAPHICAL AND HISTORICAL
INFORMATION

The H.W. Wilson Company
New York, 1995

For Dora, Barry and David

Printed in the United States of America

Library of Congress Cataloging-in-Publication Data

Englefield, Dermot J. T.

Facts about the British prime ministers: a compilation of biographical and historical information / Dermot Englefield, Janet Seaton, Isobel White; Foreword by John Major.

p. cm.

Includes index.

ISBN 0-8242-0863-3

1. Prime ministers—Great Britain—Biography—Juvenile literature. 2. Great Britain—Politics and government—Juvenile literature. [1. Prime ministers. 2. Great Britain—Politics and government.] I. Seaton, Janet. II. White, Isobel. III. Title.

DA28.4.E54 1994

941'.0099—dc20

[B]

94-33988

CIP

AC

CONTENTS

Age and Physical Appearance

Cultural and Vocational Background

Death and Burial

Miscellany

Political Career

Elections

Parliamentary Service

Office of Prime Minister

Miscellany

10 DOWNING STREET
LONDON SW1A 2AA

The office of Prime Minister is not yet three hundred years old, making it a relative stripling in constitutional terms. Yet, as this book makes clear, each of my predecessors has made their own particular mark on history. These do not always relate directly to political activities as the example of the Earl of Rosebery shows. I do not expect any future Prime Minister to come close to his record in winning the Derby three times.

As well as providing a mine of facts and dates for historians, the material in this book will tempt the reader to reach judgements on what distinguishes Prime Ministers from each other. This is no easy task. Asquith once said that "the office of Prime Minister is what its holder chooses to make it". The facts in this book illustrate that there is no blueprint for a Prime Minister, as a quick glance at the sections on Disraeli and Gladstone—both notable holders of the office—demonstrates.

I have no doubt that many readers will enjoy using the vast range of data in this book in many ways, from comparing Prime Ministers' star signs to measuring my predecessors' relative popularity by the number of statues which have been erected in their honour. For example, readers will discover which Prime Minister fought a duel in Battersea Park and which was President of the Society for Psychical Research!

Much painstaking work has clearly gone into the production of this fascinating book. I am very pleased to have been given the opportunity to provide the foreword to a work of reference which, I am sure, will be useful to people from all walks of life.

John Major

PREFACE

Facts About the British Prime Ministers is an attempt to set down in a relatively brief compass the salient historical, political and personal facts associated with each of the fifty people who have held this great office since 1721, when the position first assumed something like its present dimensions.

The information on each Prime Minister has been compiled and organised for handy reference. Part I, the main section, consists of chapters on each PM, arranged chronologically and all having the identical order and structure of presentation. Each chapter opens with a brief summary of a PM's career and significance. A section follows with personal and family information (parents, siblings, wife, and children). Next, Life and Career contains lists of elections fought; party, parliamentary and ministerial posts held; and Governments formed. This section also includes a chronology of important events and accomplishments of a PM's life. Each chapter closes with a section of background information covering education, non-parliamentary career, finances, hobbies, honours, anecdotes, residences, memorials, and select lists of publications by and about the PM.

Part II of the book selects certain categories of information from the chapters in Part I and rearranges and analyses them into 80 lists and tables to provide the reader with comparative views of the PMs in such topics as: length of service as PM; age at appointment; length of parliamentary service; place of birth and burial; longevity; ancestry; fathers' occupations; birth position in family; physical appearance; religion; schools and universities attended; sports and hobbies; military service; club memberships; residences; non-parliamentary occupations; wives; number of children; cause of death; chronological order of administrations; PMs who were also Speaker of the House; and many others.

In the process of our research, we have noted that standard reference books do not necessarily agree on the facts, nor do biographies. We have attempted to resolve discrepancies by returning to original sources. A Note on Sources appears on page xxv. Despite the considerable help we have received from individuals and institutions—noted below—any errors are the responsibility of the compilers, who would welcome corrections or possible additions if they could be sent to the publishers.

The preparation of this book has taken many years and the compilers/editors are indebted to a number of people for their support, advice and helpfulness.

First of all, we would like to thank a number of our colleagues at the House of Commons Library who capably drafted some of the main biographical entries. Their initials appear at the end of each entry they drafted and are as follows: PB

(Pam Ball), DC (Dora Clark), FC (Fintan Codd), GC (Gillian Cooper), HH (Helen Holden), EJ (Elizabeth Jones), JL (Julia Lyall), AP (Andrew Parker), CS (Chris Sear), and ZS (Zoe Smallwood).

Another colleague to whom we express our appreciation is Barry K. Winetrobe, who was most helpful in providing political analysis and advice, in addition to preparing some of the summaries which appear on the first page of each biographical entry.

We would also like to thank a number of librarians, archivists and curators who responded with generosity to our appeals for information in their records. These include Sheila Edwards, Librarian of the Royal Society; PD Hunter, Librarian of the Vaughan Library, Harrow School; Paul Quarrie, Keeper of the College Collections, Eton College; JCD Field, Librarian, Westminster School; Robin Harcourt Williams, Librarian and Archivist to the Marquess of Salisbury, Hatfield House; Brenda Burgess, Librarian of the Earl of Derby's Estate; Peter McKay, archivist to Compton Estates Management Services, Castle Ashby; Peter Day, Keeper of the Devonshire Collections, Chatsworth; Hanne Mason, Personal Assistant to the Marquess of Bute, Mount Stuart, Isle of Bute; Margaret Sanders, Information services Librarian, Worcester City Library; M. Tohill, Worcester County Record Office; Majorie Geary, Irish Library, Londonderry County Library Service; and Maura Corcoran, Oireachtas Library, Leinster House, Dublin.

We also thank Rev. Tom Pringle, Priest-in-Charge, Isle of Arran; DC Ward, Secretary, White's Club; Stephen Green, Curator, Marylebone Cricket Club and we acknowledge the help of Dr. Mark Pottle, Research Fellow, Wolfson College, Oxford.

We are grateful too to a number of former Prime Ministers, namely Rt. Hon. Lord Home of the Hirsel; Rt. Hon. Lord Wilson of Rievaulx; Rt. Hon. Sir Edward Heath, KG MP; and Rt. Hon. Lord Callaghan of Cardiff, all of whom showed great kindness in confirming certain facts.

To these former Prime Ministers themselves, we would add various members of the families of Prime Ministers who were very helpful and went to great trouble to answer specific questions. These include Anne, Countess Attlee; Clarissa, Countess of Avon; Earl Grey; Lord Eden of Winton; Lord Bonham-Carter; and Lord Oxford and Asquith.

With regard to the heraldry we are grateful for guidance from Sir Colin Cole, former Garter Principal King of Arms and in particular to Robert Harrison of the House of Lords Record Office whose expertise prevented more than one solecism. E.N. Taylor, Hon. FHS, very kindly prepared the Coats of Arms.

Finally, we would like to thank the publishers, in particular Bruce Carrick and Selma Yampolsky, for their patience and good temper in waiting while people in a country some thousands of miles away, while undertaking full time jobs, sought to draw together the varied history of these fifty individuals who have held the reins of power in the United Kingdom during the last two hundred and seventy-four years.

Dermot Englefield
Janet Seaton
Isobel White

Westminster, January 1995

INTRODUCTION

THE OFFICE OF PRIME MINISTER IN THE TWENTIETH CENTURY

The term Prime Minister was used on occasion in England as early as the seventeenth century, but it was the great 19th century historian Thomas Babbington Macaulay, who set the office of Prime Minister in context when he wrote: 'When there was a Lord Treasurer that great officer was generally Prime Minister but it was not until the time of Walpole that the first Lord of the Treasury was considered as head of the executive [or] government'. 'Head of the executive' describes the job of Prime Minister and distinguishes it from that of being a president, for the latter is both head of the executive and head of state. It follows, therefore, that the primary relationship of a British Prime Minister is with the head of state, the reigning sovereign.

THE SOVEREIGN AND THE PRIME MINISTER

The sovereign is formally the ultimate executive authority in the land, and hence military officers hold the Queen's commission and civil servants are servants of the crown. Therefore, it is the sovereign, now Queen Elizabeth II, who appoints a Prime Minister to be head of her Government, namely the person who is the leader of the political party which commands majority support in the House of Commons. In turn, the Prime Minister may advise the sovereign to dissolve Parliament (the sovereign does not always accept such advice) so that a General Election may be held in which the voters themselves can decide which political party (and therefore which party leader) will govern the country.

The sovereign has other relationships with the Prime Minister. At the opening of each session of Parliament, the Queen is driven to the House of Lords to read the Queen's Speech. This speech, actually written by her Government and approved in advance by the Cabinet, reports the activities and plans of the sovereign as 'Head of State' and announces the Government's legislative programme for the coming session of Parliament. At a more private level the Prime Minister normally goes to Buckingham Palace each Tuesday evening to have an audience with the Queen. Also, during the long summer recess of Parliament, when the Queen spends a considerable time at Balmoral Castle in Scotland, the Prime Minister will normally spend a weekend there in August or September again seeking to keep the Queen informed of Government and Parliamentary matters.

From the 1830s until 1917 the Prime Minister used to write a daily letter to the sovereign. Today, this task continues but is delegated to a Lord Commissioner of the Treasury, a Government whip in the House of Commons, who is also Vice-Chamberlain of the Royal Household and who writes to the Queen each day telling her of the day's events in Parliament. In addition, two or more red boxes of documents are sent every week from 10 Downing Street to Buckingham Palace for the Queen to read and, in some cases, sign. The relationship, therefore, between Prime Minister and sovereign is a practical and sustained one.

THE PARTY AND THE PRIME MINISTER

The road to appointment as Prime Minister requires that a person has already achieved leadership of a political party that can command the support of a majority in the House of Commons. Each political party elects its leadership, and the parties have different rules governing such elections. For instance, in the case of the Labour Party, from 1922 until 1981, the members of the Parliamentary Labour Party (i.e. the Labour Members of Parliament) used to elect a leader at the beginning of each session if the Labour Party was not in government. These elections were often uncontested, although on occasion more than one ballot has been required, as with the election of Clement Attlee in 1935, in order to reach the absolute majority of votes necessary to be elected as leader.

In 1981 the makeup of the Labour Party electoral college was changed from consisting only of members of the Parliamentary Labour Party to including the memberships of trade unions and socialist societies (which were given 40 percent of the votes); the constituency parties (with 30 percent) and the Parliamentary Labour Party (with 30 percent). Since 1981 it has been decided that constituency parties should themselves ballot their own membership on the basis of one-member-one-vote, that Members of the European Labour Party (i.e. Labour Members of the European Parliament) should be included with the Parliamentary Labour Party and finally that a nomination for leadership of the Parliamentary Labour Party should have the support of at least 20 percent of the Labour Members of Parliament. After the 1992 General Election, this meant that the support of at least 55 Labour Members of Parliament was needed for nomination as a candidate.

Following the death of John Smith in 1994, the Labour Party, using a further modified form of voting, elected Tony Blair as its leader and, therefore, Leader of Her Majesty's (loyal) Opposition. That title reminds us that the Leader of the Opposition is in fact Prime Minister-in-waiting, should the Conservative Government re-elected in 1992 fail to maintain its majority in the House of Commons.

The Conservative Party did not have an electoral process for choosing a leader until 1965. For instance, in 1957 when Anthony Eden resigned as Prime Minister and a new leader of the Party was needed, there was consultation by Lord Salisbury and the Lord Chancellor with members of the Cabinet, the Chairman of the Party and the Chairman of the 1922 Committee (a highly influential committee of Conservative backbench Members of Parliament, i.e. non-ministers, which was first formed in 1922). After these consultations, advice was given to the Queen, who herself also consulted the former Prime Minister, Winston Churchill. As a result of these consultations, Harold Macmillan emerged as the next Prime Minister. In 1963 when

Macmillan resigned there was wider consultation but still no ballot and Douglas-Home was chosen as party leader. By 1965, however, there was a balloting system in place and when Douglas-Home resigned (after losing the General Election in 1964), the system was used for the first time.

To win election it was necessary not only to have an overall majority of the votes of Conservative Members of Parliament but also an extra margin of 15 percent more votes than the candidate with the next highest number of votes.

The detail of party election processes is important in understanding how individual party members work their way up to becoming Prime Minister and it also shows that party leaders must keep in close touch with their supporters in Parliament. It is normal practice for the Conservative Party leader, whether as Prime Minister in Government or as Leader of the Opposition, to address members of the 1922 Committee in July, shortly before the summer recess. Indeed the leaders of both political parties are kept closely informed about party views and feelings, including those of individuals, by their Chief Whips. Party leaders frequently use the clublike facilities of the Houses of Parliament for talks with their party colleagues. The dramatic situation at the time of Margaret Thatcher's defeat in 1990 showed that, with leaders of both parties now subject to possible annual election, Prime Ministers must depend more than ever on the support of their political parties and parliamentary colleagues.

THE CABINET AND THE PRIME MINISTER

For many decades the Cabinet has varied between about 18 and 22 members. It is made up, first, of certain ministers who are members of the Cabinet almost ex officio, such as the Chancellor of the Exchequer, the Foreign Secretary, the Home Secretary, and now the Secretaries of State of major departments of Government.

In modern times these Cabinet Members have mostly been members of the House of Commons. A second, smaller group of Cabinet Members are those, like the Lord President of the Council, the Lord Privy Seal or the Chancellor of the Duchy of Lancaster, who do not have major departments of Government to run and who therefore are available in particular for Cabinet committee work. Finally, a Cabinet usually has two or three members of the House of Lords, including the Lord Chancellor and the Leader of the House of Lords.

All Cabinet members are appointed and, if need be, dismissed by the Prime Minister who acts as Chairman of the Cabinet.

The full Cabinet normally meets on Thursday mornings in the Cabinet room in 10 Downing Street. A further meeting may be held on Tuesday mornings and emergency meetings may on occasion be held at 10 Downing Street or if necessary, in the Prime Minister's room in the House of Commons.

Proceedings of the Cabinet are confidential, and the minutes of meetings are not made available to the public for thirty years. The convention of collective responsibility means that the Cabinet takes decisions unanimously. Any member who has a serious disagreement of principle with the policy of the Government is expected to resign. In addition to these Cabinet posts, the Government includes a further 80 or so ministers at two grades: Ministers of State and, below them, Under-Secretaries of State. These office holders also are appointed by the Prime Minister, whose powers and patronage are clearly very great, as he is able to offer a ministerial post to nearly one-third of his party sitting in the Commons.

The balance the Prime Minister needs to achieve within his Cabinet is a delicate one. His party will have a range of views on major policies, and to some degree these should be represented in the Cabinet. Cabinet Ministers are directly responsible to the House of Commons for the work of their departments, so they must be effective performers both in the House of Commons itself and, in recent years, under questioning by the Members of the House of Commons Departmental Select Committees. Of course, like all politicians today, Ministers must be able to handle the media. Major legislation will need to be carried through Parliament by these Ministers so a command of detail and a persuasive manner are needed. Finally, any Cabinet is likely to include rivals to the Prime Minister, who are ready to present themselves should there be a question over his abilities or the extent of his support within the party. It will be noted throughout this book that almost every Cabinet contains at least one future Prime Minister.

As already mentioned, much of the work of the Cabinet is undertaken in Cabinet Committees. Because of the confidentiality surrounding their proceedings, little information concerning the existence of Cabinet Committees was available until Prime Minister Thatcher, in reply to a 1979 Parliamentary Question, stated, 'I have established four Standing Committees of the Cabinet: a defence and overseas policy committee and an economic strategy committee, both under my chairmanship; a home and social affairs committee under the chairmanship of my right honorable friend the Home Secretary; and a legislation committee under the chairmanship of the Lord Chancellor.' Prime Minister Major has published full details of the Cabinet Committees of his Government.

It was only in 1916 under Prime Minister Lloyd George that a Secretariat was established for the Cabinet, initially the War Cabinet. Before then no formal records of Cabinet proceedings had been kept. In 1922 Prime Minister Bonar Law decided to continue the secretariat, and its first secretary, Maurice Hankey, retained the post until 1938. The Secretariat is based in the Cabinet Office, which is linked physically with 10 Downing Street and is mostly staffed with civil servants on attachment from other Departments of State. The Secretary to the Cabinet is also Head of the Home Civil Service and as such is the most senior British civil servant.

The Prime Minister has a number of areas of significant patronage, but clearly the most important is designating his Cabinet and the more junior Ministers of the Crown. There is much talk about the various styles of running Cabinet meetings—the economy of an Attlee or the sometimes bullying style of a Churchill, for instance—but getting difficult business through a Cabinet which is not always harmonious can clearly be a formidable test for any Prime Minister.

PARLIAMENT AND THE PRIME MINISTER

The most important relationship between Parliament and the Prime Minister is based on the PM's ability to maintain his majority in the House of Commons.

If the Government is defeated in a vote on a major policy issue, it does not resign immediately, but the Prime Minister tables or puts forward a motion of confidence in Government policies for debate in the House of Commons (the Opposition could put forward a vote of no confidence), and at the end of that debate there is a vote which the Prime Minister must win in order to continue in office. On 28 March 1979, Margaret Thatcher, as Leader of the Opposition, moved 'That this House has no confidence in Her Majesty's Government. At the end of the debate that night the

House voted 311 to 310 in favour of the motion. Prime Minister Callaghan then replied: 'Now that the House of Commons has declared itself, we shall take our case to the country'. In other words, the Government would resign and seek a fresh mandate at a General Election. More recently, Prime Minister Major's Government was defeated on an aspect of the Maastricht Treaty. The Prime Minister immediately tabled a motion for debate the next morning: 'That this House has confidence in the policy of Her Majesty's Government'. At the end of an all-day debate, Mr. Major won by 339 votes to 299, and so the Government survived.

Of course, the Prime Minister does not often live on such a knife-edge in sustaining a majority in the House of Commons. Usually, he has a working single-party majority, which may, however, be gradually eroded as by-elections result in defeats in Government-held seats.

The Prime Minister comes regularly to the House of Commons, with which he has a formal relationship not only as head of the Government, but also as one of its 651 Members. He does not take part in the House's committee work, (neither Standing Committee work, which considers legislation, nor Select Committee work, which mostly examines particular policies and their administration). His duties are confined to making formal statements to the House, to debating and to answering Parliamentary Questions, which are often critical and challenging.

In some degree the relationship of Parliament and the Prime Minister is a matter of individual temperament. Gladstone clearly enjoyed the give-and-take of questions in the House, and he answered far more questions and intervened in far more debates than Disraeli. During the first World War, Lloyd George found less time (and had less inclination) to attend sessions of the House of Commons than many of his 19th-century predecessors. This lower level of parliamentary activity on the part of the PMs continued for some years. Churchill enjoyed the cockpit of the House of Commons during his period as a Prime Minister under war- time pressures and both he, and to a lesser degree, Eden enjoyed debating. On the other hand, Harold Macmillan enjoyed making the grand speech but was less happy at Prime Minister's Question Time. Prime Minister Thatcher, especially during her final years, withdrew somewhat from the House of Commons, and one could speculate that this withdrawal played some part in isolating her from her parliamentary colleagues and thus contributed to her final fall. Whatever the personal inclinations of a Prime Minister, however, there are certain occasions, when the House must be addressed. Mention has been made of one such occasion, the Queen's Speech in the House of Lords, which sets out the Government's programme at the beginning of every parliamentary session. This speech is the prelude to a five-day debate on the Government's programme, during which the Prime Minister and other senior ministers have to explain and defend important aspects of the Government's policies to the House of Commons.

A second occasion when the Prime Minister's presence is required is when debates occur on really major constitutional issues. Should the House of Commons quite clearly wish the Prime Minister to speak on such an issue, it would be unlikely that he would fail to do so, for the House is very conscious of its dignity and of the Prime Minister's responsibility to it. Otherwise, increasing pressure on the Prime Minister's time precludes his being in the chamber for long except to make a speech or listen to the Leader of the Opposition replying, or help a ministerial colleague having a difficult time in the House of Commons—when it is usual for the Prime Minister to be found sitting next to that Minister, offering support. Compared with a century ago or even half a century ago, however, it is now rare for a PM to intervene in a debate.

Modern Prime Ministers now regularly attend a growing number of heads of government meetings. These include quarterly meetings of the European Council (the heads of government of the members of the European Union) and periodic meetings of G7 group, (the seven leading industrial nations). There are also visits to other countries and organisations such as the United Nations or NATO. In 1991 Prime Minister Major made 25 overseas visits covering a total of 57 days; in 1992, an election year, he made 27 visits covering a total of 47 days. On returning, in particular from international meetings, a PM comes to the House of Commons as soon as practicable to make a statement. The statement, together with answers to subsequent questions, can easily last an hour or more. But these statements are not confined in subject to overseas visits. The Prime Minister has a number of specific domestic responsibilities, for instance, as Minister for the Civil Service, and is required to make ministerial statements on this subject as well as others.

The final occasion when the Prime Minister must address the House of Commons is at Prime Minister's Question Time. During the second half of the nineteenth century, when the idea of a Question Time was being developed, Prime Minister's questions came at the end of questions to other ministers. Gladstone, for instance, might answer as many as seventy questions during a session; Disraeli about fifty questions. By the beginning of the twentieth century, because the growing number of Parliamentary Questions to Ministers meant fewer of the Prime Minister's questions could be dealt with in the allotted time, it was decided to start them earlier. That arrangement continued with occasional modifications until 1953, when because of his age and frailty, Churchill was required to answer Parliamentary Questions on only two days a week. Since a Procedure Committee report in 1961, Prime Minister's questions are taken on Tuesdays and Thursday from 3:15 to 3:30 pm, and are broadcast and televised.

What actually happens in connection with Prime Minister's questions is that a Member tables [asks] a question in very general terms to avoid having the question referred instead to a responsible departmental minister, e.g., agriculture or transport. The question, therefore, might read: "to ask the Prime Minister if he will list his engagements" for a particular date. The member's real question will be the supplementary one the Speaker will then invite him to ask. In the case of supplementary questions, in particular those from members of the Opposition, the Prime Minister will not know their subject until they are asked. Only ten questions a day are allowed to be tabled so that a draw of Members' names takes place. Often, not all ten questions can be answered between 3:15 and 3:30, so those not dealt with in the Chamber receive written replies. In the course of a session, a Prime Minister may have to reply to between 200 and 300 questions in the Chamber and a further 150 in writing. In addition, the Prime Minister might reply to another 1,000 questions from Members asking only for a written reply.

The range of subjects in Prime Minister's Question Time can be very wide, from a specific enquiry, probably instigated by a lobby, such as whether `turtle soup has been served at any official function at 10 Downing Street' or whether a particular book has been added to the library of 10 Downing Street, to questions about those national and international voluntary organisations to which the Prime Minister belongs or about any discussions on human rights he may have had during a recent visit with a foreign government.

To prepare for these Question Times, Prime Ministers all seem to set aside a significant period of time to work with their staff in Downing Street in particular on the day itself, to ensure that they are briefed on current affairs and developments. Now that Prime Minister's Question Times are televised to an audience that can reach millions, they have increasingly become adversarial occasions with members of the opposing parties frequently cheering their leader on: rallying the party behind him is one of the Party Leader's roles.

The Prime Minister also has more informal relations with Parliament, and these, for the most part, are conducted in the Houses of Parliament, although it should not be forgotten that he regularly entertains members of all parties at official functions at 10 Downing Street. The Prime Minister has a T-shaped room in the House of Commons, large enough to meet groups of Members—even the Cabinet if necessary—but intimate and relaxed enough for smaller gatherings of only a few individuals. When the House of Commons votes on a motion, the process takes about 15 minutes, during which the Prime Minister has the chance to rub shoulders with other Members and time for a word in a corridor or a lobby. The PM uses the facilities of the Members' Dining Room, where the Conservatives sit on the lefthand side and the Labour Members on the righthand side of the room. There is the even more informal setting of the Members' Tea Room, a good spot in which to catch up with gossip and put a finger on the pulse of the party. The House of Commons remains a physically small and often crowded institution, so that informal contacts are easily made, should a Prime Minister wish. Finally, the fact that the PM represents an electorate in his district of about 70,000, just like the other 650 Members of the House of Commons, helps him in his informal relationships with his colleagues in Parliament.

PATRONAGE AND THE PRIME MINISTER

Mention has already been made of the patronage powers of the Prime Minister, who appoints about one hundred ministers to their posts, nearly a third of the party's representation in the House of Commons. A different area of patronage is the Prime Minister's Honours List, in which the PM recommends to the sovereign the award of honours to individuals, which may range in importance from a peerage to different orders of the British Empire. Prime Minister Major has reduced what might be called the class structure of these honours. Individual merit gets greater emphasis than the rank of the post held.

The Prime Minister's patronage also extends to the appointment of senior civil servants. Prime Ministers vary in their involvement in selection, but most wish to approve the appointment of at least the most senior grade officials. Recommendations come forward from the Head of the Civil Service who is Cabinet Secretary and in regular contact with the Prime Minister.

An area of Prime Ministerial patronage less well known is the selection of bishops and archbishops. The constitutional position is clear: a bishopric is a Crown appointment because the sovereign is the Head of the Church, so it becomes the duty of the Prime Minister to offer her advice on the filling of such posts. Since the Reformation, and in particular since the Appointment of Bishops Act of 1533, there have been moments of tension in this matter between sovereign and Prime Minister but by the early eighteenth century it was generally agreed that the Prime Minister's recommendation would normally be accepted. Queen Victoria on occasion argued an appointment with a Prime Minister and even persuaded one to change his recommendation. In the twentieth century the Church of England set up a number of commissions to consider a greater role for itself in recommending the appointment of Bishops. As the established Church, the Church of England has 26 seats in the House of Lords, held by archbishops and bishops, giving them a role in Parliament.

Over a period of years, new procedures were proposed, debated and reviewed by the Church and various Governments. In 1976 it was agreed that the Queen would continue to make the appointments, following advice from her Prime Minister, but that a Church committee would forward two names to the Prime Minister with an order of preference. The Prime Minister can choose either name to recommend to the Queen or can reject both and ask the Church committee to come forward with other names. This particular area of Prime Ministerial patronage remains one of the more unusual corners of British constitutional arrangements.

THE PUBLIC AND THE PRIME MINISTER

In deciding who should be elected to head a political party and therefore become a potential Prime Minister, members of a party with power or influence over the selection give increasing weight to a candidate's performance vis à vis the public. The importance of this factor has grown greatly, in particular since World War II, because of the amazing revolution in communications.

It was probably Chamberlain, in his negotiations with Hitler during the late 1930s, who became the first Prime Minister to be thrust across the cinema screens of Britain, thus becoming a familiar figure as he brought messages of hope or despair directly to the public. Churchill's radio broadcasts during World War II remain the classic achievement of a Prime Minister who needed to win and maintain the support of the public for action. By today's standards, Attlee might be regarded as too private a person to make a good Prime Minister, although his rating as a Prime Minister by political historians seems steadily to rise.

Public opinion polling, which dates from the 1930s, almost invariably includes questions concerning the rating of the Prime Minister, as well as the Leader of the Opposition. The pressure of the media seems increasingly to raise questions of leadership ability, while for the benefit of the public every presumed weakness and sometimes strength is recorded and draws comment.

There is a direct link between the Prime Minister's office and the public via the Lobby journalists, who are briefed daily by the Prime Minister's press secretary. Briefings take place every Monday to Thursday morning at 10 Downing Street and in the afternoon at the House of Commons. On Friday morning there is a special briefing for the Sunday papers. The Prime Minister's press secretary post requires a difficult combination of discretion and liveliness.

Most Prime Ministers carefully ration themselves with regard to broadcast interviews for the public, bearing in mind that such an occasion may bring into play the Leader of the Opposition's right of reply in the form of a `counter' interview, generally the next day.

It is during the campaign for a General Election that a Prime Minister is required to communicate most directly with the public. The PM will have chosen the date and must therefore take very direct responsibility for the timing of the party's campaign. The three weeks or so of campaigning for a General Election bring a full load of daily press conferences, appearances, speeches, opinion polls and other political strategies, and behind all this the Prime Minister must continue to govern the country on behalf of the public from whom he is trying to win re-election.

THE CIVIL SERVICE AND THE PRIME MINISTER

As already mentioned, the Prime Minister will often choose to be involved in appointments to the most senior posts in the civil service. However, civil servants do not resign when a new Government takes over but, with professional political impartiality, remain in office to carry out the wishes of the new Prime Minister and his ministers.

Usually a more junior minister runs the day-to-day affairs of the civil service, which employs about half a million people, but important changes of policy or decisions will come before the Cabinet with the views of the Prime Minister. An interesting footnote to this arrangement is that in the buildup to a General Election, informal contacts take place between senior civil servants and the Leader of the Opposition and also members of the shadow cabinet, so that, in the event of a change of Government, the handover of responsibility will be as smooth and efficient as possible.

It has been suggested more than once that there should be a Prime Minister's Department to complement the Departments of State run by members of the Cabinet. But apart from the difficulty that a such department would not fit into No. 10 Downing Street, the fact that the Prime Minister's Office has a very small staff means that his personal involvement and support is both flexible and well informed. The 1992 costs of the PM's office—including not only 10 Downing Street and the Prime Minister's country house of Chequers but also charges for buildings and services, the use of aircraft and cars, postal services and the whole range of staff support needed—ran to slightly under £10,000,000. (The cost of his work as a Member of Parliament representing his electors is not included). The argument against establishing a full Department is that the PM's job is not to double check or rethink the work of his Cabinet colleagues or to present alternative reports and policy proposals but is rather to act as the managing director of a public company, and travelling light in terms of a personal bureaucracy is likely to sharpen his performance.

PRECEDENCE AND THE PRIME MINISTER

It is a strange fact that although the post of Prime Minister has functioned for over two and one-half centuries, its existence in law and in precedence has only recently been recognised. The carefully polished plate on the front door of No. 10 Downing Street bears only the legend `First Lord of the Treasury.' The first time the term `Prime Minister' was used in an Act of Parliament was in 1917. The term did not occur in the text of an Act until the Ministers of the Crown Act of 1937. The Prime Minister's precedence in England was established only slightly earlier, in 1905, when King Edward VII issued a warrant from Sandringham which included the words:

> 'Whereas We taking into Our Royal consideration that the precedence of Our Prime Minister has not been declared or defined by due authority, We deem it therefore expedient that the same should be henceforth established and defined.
>
> Know ye therefore that in the exercise of Our Royal Prerogative We do hereby declare Our Royal Will and Pleasure that in all times hereafter the Prime Minister of Us, Our Heirs and Successors shall have place and precedence next after the Archbishop of York. '

As long as the Prime Minister is a member of the House of Commons, which has always been the case since 1902, or becomes one on taking office, this Royal Warrant establishes the PM as the most senior commoner of England. In Scotland the PM holds a similar position, following immediately after the Moderator of the General Assembly of the Church of Scotland.

THE PRIME MINISTER AS HEAD OF THE GOVERNMENT

The Prime Minister's role as head of the sovereign's Government involves two final, time-consuming responsibilities. The first is to deal with fellow heads of government from other countries, who frequently wish to meet the PM and may issue him an invitation to visit their country. Number 10 Downing Street, therefore, is a regular point for scheduled visits and official entertaining during much of the year. Closely linked with this responsibility is the Prime Minister's role in foreign affairs. Sometimes this has involved strong personal relationships. Churchill and Roosevelt, Kennedy and MacMillan, Thatcher and Reagan—these personal friendships produced effective harmony in matters of policy, in particular when world crises have arisen. But with the increasingly frequent meetings of such important institutions as the European Council, and Group-of-Seven heads of government, and with the regular contacts within the Commonwealth, it is clear that at times the jobs of Prime Minister and Foreign Secretary draw very close.

THE RESIDENCES OF THE PRIME MINISTER

10 Downing Street

Certain addresses conjure up pictures of political power. 'The White House', for instance, suggests the great power of an elected leadership. 'The Kremlin' still suggests monolithic and secretive power. And what is suggested by the simple No. 10 Downing Street? It sounds rather domestic, just a house in a row in a side street, less grand than many, and therefore, perhaps, of limited political significance. Yet as the front door swings open numerous times each day, individuals and delegations of every sort—heads of state, political leaders, representatives of industry, ordinary petitioners—enter with the purpose of meeting the Prime Minister of the United Kingdom.

George Downing, a property speculator after whom Downing Street is named, was born in 1623, a nephew of John Winthrop, the Governor of Massachusetts. As a young man he crossed to the American colonies and studied at Harvard University, of which he was the second graduate. He returned to England in 1646 to make his fortune and after a varied and rather chequered career, he developed property he had acquired in a narrow street off Whitehall. Half a century later, George II offered his first Lord of the Treasury, Robert Walpole, a large property facing north over what is now Horse Guards called Bothmar House, together with a smaller house behind it in Downing Street. The two houses were knocked together and the main entrance was located on the Downing Street side because it offered a shorter drive to the Houses of Parliament.

After accepting the houses on behalf of his office as First Lord of the Treasury,

Robert Walpole lived there for nearly seven years until 1742, but for another twenty-one years no Prime Minister lived at No. 10. From 1785 until 1834, there were occasions when Prime Ministers chose not to live there. The Duke of Wellington, for instance, was presented with Apsley House at Hyde Park Corner, as a gift from a grateful nation, and moved there from the more modest quarters of No. 10 Downing Street.

Again, in the period 1834-1877 no Prime Minister lived in Downing Street, but then both Disraeli and Gladstone made it their residence, as did the Earl of Rosebery. Since Balfour (1902-1905), all Prime Ministers have lived at No. 10 with just two exceptions. For half of his time as Prime Minister, Harold Macmillan had to live at Admiralty House, because No. 10 and Nos. 11 and 12 Downing Street, were being rebuilt. When Prime Minister Wilson returned to power in 1974, he used 10 Downing Street for work, but did not live there.

For the Prime Ministers, 10 Downing Street plays three roles: a place to work, a place to receive visitors, and a personal residence. The ground floor, the main working area, includes an entrance hall, the Prime Minister's Principal Private Secretary's room, accommodation for others of the senior staff, and, most important, the Cabinet Room. The Cabinet Room, once lined with books, was where Winston Churchill drafted some of his famous war-time speeches. Up an elegant stairway, lined with portraits of Prime Ministers, a visitor reaches the first floor and the State Rooms, now frequently seen on television with visiting dignitaries shaking hands with the Prime Ministers. Like No. 10 itself, the State Rooms are not very large. They consist of three linked drawing rooms, a large dining room which can seat as many as sixty people, and a smaller dining room which seats about ten. Finally, on the floor above is the Prime Minister's private flat, adapted for such use at the end of the 1930s by the Chamberlains. The flat includes a drawing room, a small dining room, and six or seven bedrooms. The flat is furnished in what might be called a traditional English style, with many of the pieces and pictures on loan from important collections. Number 10 Downing Street forms a handsome setting for work and living, without the grandiose scale which so often marks the official residences of heads of government.

The staff of No. 10 Downing Street number a little over one hundred, including typists and doorkeepers. The Prime Minister has about six special advisers who are not civil servants, but who are there partly to lessen any feeling of isolation that the Prime Minister may feel, as well as offering immediate advice, on such matters as foreign affairs and economics.

The other staff, who are all civil servants, include five Private Secretaries: one for overseas affairs, two more for parliamentary affairs and one for home affairs, and a fifth for economic affairs. It is these staff members who, among their other duties, collect information from government departments and help the PM prepare for Question Time in the House of Commons on Tuesdays and Thursdays. The words 'close knit team' and 'domestic scale' are often used in describing the intimacy of working in No. 10, and it is obvious that the building itself plays an important role in shaping methods of work.

Chequers

No. 10 Downing Street is a town house in all respects. For most of the last two hundred and seventy-five years, most Prime Ministers have been wealthy and have had their own country houses to which they could escape the rigours of office. In 1909 Arthur Lee, later Viscount Lee of Fareham, acquired Chequers, a country house in Buckinghamshire, about 40 miles north west of London. In 1917, after making significant repairs and restoration, Lord Lee offered the property to the Prime Minister, then Lloyd George, as an official country house for the Prime Minister of the day. What lay behind the gift was Lee's view that in an increasingly democratic age Prime Ministers might well come from social backgrounds that did not include a country house to retire to for relaxation.

Prime Ministers have varied in their liking for Chequers. Neither Lloyd George nor Bonar Law, the first two Prime Ministers to use it, found it congenial, but Stanley Baldwin, a country-lover, certainly did, as did Neville Chamberlain.

Winston Churchill used it frequently during World War II, even though he had purchased his own country house, and it was from Chequers that he phoned President Roosevelt on 7 December 1941, pledging Britain's declaration of war on Japan following the attack on Pearl Harbour. Attlee enjoyed Chequers during the period 1945-1951. Macmillan, who had a country house in Sussex, allowed his senior Ministers the use of Chequers. Prime Minister Major has frequently retreated to his home in Huntingdonshire in preference to Chequers.

Dorneywood

In 1942 Lord Courtauld-Thomson gave his home, Dorneywood, also in Buckinghamshire, to the National Trust, but its use was to be an alternative residence for the Prime Minister of the day or a senior ministerial colleague whom he might nominate. In particular Lord Courtauld-Thomson sought through his gift to provide a place for the entertainment of visitors from overseas. Like Chequers, Dorneywood was carefully restored early in the twentieth century and furnished in a traditional style, described as 'cultivated taste between the wars'. With the agreement of the resident minister, some of the garden is opened to the public on a few days each year.

Chevening

The final house to be made available to the Prime Minister is Chevening, near Sevenoaks in Kent. From 1721 until 1968 it was the home of the Earls of Stanhope. The seventh Earl offered it as a country residence for the Prime Minister or one of a short list of Cabinet ministers or royalty whom he might chose or agree on. The Foreign Secretary of the day quite often uses Chevening as a residence, and the Government may hold meetings or conferences there. Recently it has become a custom for the annual Budget to be planned during a weekend at Chevening.

NOTES ON SOURCES

This work has been compiled from many sources, so many that it would be impossible to list them all. At the early stages of the project, however, we chose to rely on certain basic published sources, and this brief note seeks to draw attention to those that we found especially valuable and to explain our choices where appropriate.

GENERAL SOURCES

We found that Van Thal's *The Prime Ministers* (1974) gave an excellent overview of the career of each PM, but without the wealth of detail that we then sought to obtain.

Biographical reference works provided a starting point, although, as we found throughout this exercise, they often disagree even on basic data. We relied particularly on *The Dictionary of National Biography*, *Who's Who, Who Was Who* and Boase's *Modern English Biography*. We also used *Biographical Memoirs of Fellows of the Royal Society*. For peers, we consulted G E C's *Complete Peerage* and *Complete Baronetage*, together with Burke's and Debretts, with their equivalents for Scotland and Ireland.

Parliamentary sources were central to our purposes, and we had frequent recourse to *Hansard's Parliamentary Debates* and its predecessors, as well as the *Journals* of both Houses of Parliament. The authoritative History of Parliament Trust histories of the House of Commons at various periods proved invaluable, not only for biographical details, but for information about elections, office holders, and political events. *Dod's Parliamentary Companion*, *Vacher's Parliamentary Companion* and Stenton and Lees' *Who's Who of British MPs* were all equally important.

More general sources often provided vital facts in particular cases, and we made extensive use of *The Times, The Annual Register* and *The Gentleman's Magazine*. Many biographies were a disappointment as far as facts were concerned. More useful for our purposes, where they were available, were letters and diaries.

PERSONAL INFORMATION

We have generally chosen to refer to each PM by the name by which they were known while they were PM. We have listed the other names by which they may have been known throughout their life in Part II. Apart from their election results, we have tried to use the same name throughout each chapter.

We have given dates only for peerage creations in this section. Dates for inheritances can be derived from other data, usually the death of the father, and are usually noted in the section on Important Dates.

The illustrations of the coats of arms have been provided by E. N. Taylor. Mottoes and their translations have largely been based on Elvin's *Handbook of Mottoes* (2nd rev ed 1987).

The date of first entering Parliament is the date on which the subject became eligible to enter Parliament. For the House of Commons, this is the date on which the Member of Parliament was 'returned' (in effect the date on which the result of their election was declared). Until 1928 these dates were published from time to time as an official Parliamentary Paper, *The Official Return of Members to Parliament*. After 1928 the date is taken to be polling day. For the House of Lords, eligibility is created in a number of ways. The commonest is by the creation or inheritance of a peerage. In the case of peers who had only a Scottish rather than a UK title and who had to select 16 of their number to represent them in the House of Lords, Sainty's *A List of Representative Peers for Scotland 1707-1963, and for Ireland 1800-1961* (1968) was helpful, together with Fergusson's *The Sixteen Peers of Scotland 1707-1959* (1960).

No one may enter either House until he or she

becomes 21 years of age, so in cases where the subject was elected or inherited a peerage before reaching 21, we used the date of their 21st birthday. We have tried where appropriate to include the dates on which subjects actually took their seats.

The date appointed Prime Minister generally accords with Fryde's *Handbook of British Chronology* (3rd ed 1986), which we chose because he uses the date on which they kissed the monarch's hands, the definitive moment of the creation of a new ministry. We have not included abortive ministries such as that of Bath and Waldegrave, who did not kiss hands. Neither have we noted reappointments after successful General Elections or changes of sovereign.

The date on which someone ceased to be Prime Minister (or indeed any minister) is extremely difficult to find. We have tried to find the date on which the sovereign accepted the seals of office, rather than the date on which someone tried to give them up or announced his resignation. There may be a gap between appointments, particularly after a death in office, and these are noted in Part II.

Ceasing to be a Member of Parliament refers to the House of Commons. Members of the House of Lords can only leave completely (as opposed to obtaining temporary leave of absence) by renouncing their title, as Douglas-Home did. An MP may leave the House of Commons by inheriting or being awarded a peerage, by dying, by retiring at the end of a Parliament or by being defeated at a General Election. The date of leaving the House for retirements or for defeats of sitting Members is the date on which Parliament was dissolved. An MP may not resign, except by applying for a disqualifying office such as the Chiltern Hundreds. In these cases we have had to use the date on which the writ was moved for the consequential by- election, as we have been unable to discover the date on which the application was accepted. We have allocated our signs of the zodiac by reference to Linda Goodman's *Sun Signs* (1972).

LIFE AND CAREER

Dates of General Elections are taken from the *Official Return* and Craig's *British Electoral Facts 1832-1987* (5th ed 1989). Dates are expressed as months until the advent of the single polling day in 1918.

Election results after 1832 are taken from Craig's series *British Parliamentary Election Results* and its successors *Britain Votes*. Before 1832 the best source is the History of Parliament Trust series on *The House of Commons*, but for periods not yet covered by that series we have used *The Parliaments of England*, by Stooks Smith (2nd ed by Craig 1973). If all else fails, the *Official Return* at least confirms the winning candidate.

Irish constituencies can be confusing as they returned Members to the UK Parliament between 1800 and 1921, but otherwise had their own Parliament. Walker's *Parliamentary Election Results in Ireland 1801-1922* (1978) supplements the sources already mentioned.

Parties are cited using contemporary names. Party names change from time to time, and candidates may call themselves by any label they choose, so anomalies are inevitable. We have followed the usage in the sources on election results unless evidence in a particular case made this misleading. Abbreviations are explained in a separate list.

We have tried to find a maiden speech in every case, but where this has not been possible we have noted the first one we have been able to find as the first recorded speech. Reports of debates were not verbatim until 1909, and during parts of the eighteenth century the publication of reports of debates was actually forbidden by law, so this has not been an easy task. We have given the full reference wherever possible.

It was also difficult to ascertain exact dates for ministerial offices held. We have relied heavily on Haydn's *Book of Dignities* (1894), Cook's series *British Historical Facts*, and Butler's *British Political Facts* (6th ed 1986). More detailed sources included Thomson's *The Secretaries of State 1681-1782* (1968), Sainty's *Leaders and Whips in the House of Lords 1783-1964* (1964), and Carr-Gomm's *Handbook of the Administrations of Great Britain 1801-1900* (1901).

BACKGROUND

We used *The Dictionary of National Biography DNB* and the *Dictionary of British Portraiture* (1979) as guides to statues and portraits.

For letters and personal papers we used the Royal Commission on Historical Manuscripts' *Papers of British Cabinet Ministers 1782-1900* (1982) and Foster's *British Archives* (2nd ed 1989).

Our section on Further Reading is just a selection of the most useful works. It is not a comprehensive listing, although we have tried to include the standard biographies.

GLOSSARY

This list is a brief glossary of terms that might be unfamiliar to some of our readers. Further terms and details may be found in Wilding & Laundy's *Encyclopaedia of Parliament* (1970).

backbenchers Members of Parliament without posts who sit on the back benches of the Chamber of the House of Commons, the front bench being reserved for ministers and 'shadow' ministers.

by-election An election in a specific constituency to fill a vacancy.

Chiltern Hundreds A sinecure disqualifying office for which a Member of Parliament must apply if they wish to resign their seat.

constituency An area of the country represented by one or more Members of Parliament.

Debate on the Address Debate on general matters in both Houses immediately following the Queen's Speech (*q.v.*). Formal thanks are also given to the Sovereign for the speech, which opens each session of Parliament.

dissolution The ending of a Parliament by royal proclamation when the Sovereign agrees to the Prime Minister's request for a General Election.

division A vote on an issue where Members are counted as they pass through the lobbies outside the Chambers.

Father of the House The Member of Parliament with the longest unbroken service in the House of Commons.

First Reading First stage in the passage of a Bill in each House, usually without debate.

front bench Government Ministers sit on the front bench to the Speaker's right, and Opposition or 'shadow' ministers sit on the front bench to the Speaker's left. All other Members of Parliament are known as backbenchers.

General Election A simultaneous election in all constituencies for a new Parliament. Since 1918 voting has taken place on the same day, but earlier elections could take several weeks.

'Glittering Cabinets' Cabinets which contain one or more future and/or former Prime Ministers.

hereditary peer A peer whose title may be inherited, usually by the eldest son.

King's Speech See Queen's Speech

kissing hands The kissing of the Sovereign's hands by a new Prime Minister and other Ministers, a ceremony indicating formal assumption of the office.

Leader of the House The Minister responsible for the arrangement of Government business in the House.

life peer One whose peerage is granted only for life.

maiden speech The first speech a Member makes in the House.

motion A formal proposal put before the House for debate and vote.

opposition leader The Leader of the largest political party in the House of Commons not in government, known as 'Leader of Her Majesty's Loyal Opposition'.

Parliament A Parliament exists between one General Election and the next, a period which is divided into sessions.

Privy Council A group of advisers to the Sovereign. Ministers not already Privy Counsellors become so on joining the Cabinet.

Queen's Speech The sovereign's speech delivered in the House of Lords to both Houses at the beginning of each session of Parliament. It includes an outline of the Government's legislative programme for the session.

royal assent The sovereign has to agree to all Acts of Parliament before they can finally become law.

Scottish Representative Peer Before 1963, one who was elected as one of the sixteen peers of Scotland entitled to sit in the House of Lords.

Second Reading The stage at which a Bill is discussed in principle rather than in detail.

whip Weekly instructions circulated to Members by their Party's Whips, outlining forthcoming business and giving voting instructions. These instructions may be underlined three times for a "Three Line Whip," when attendance is expected.

whips The Members of both Houses assigned by their Party to ensure that members of that Party are present to vote on a motion before the House.

ABBREVIATIONS

b	born
BBC	British Broadcasting Corporation
Bt, Bart	Baronet
bur	buried
CB	Companion of the Order of the Bath
Co	Company; Country
CoCon	Coalition Conservative
Col	Column
CoLib	Coalition Liberal
Com	Communist
Con	Conservative
Co-op	Co-operative party
d	died
DCL	Doctor of Civil Law
diss	dissolved
div	divorced
DLitt	Doctor of Letters
DSC	Distinguished Service Cross
DSO	Distinguished Service Order
EEC	European Economic Community
excl	excluding
FBA	Fellow of the British Academy
FCO	Foreign and Commonwealth Office
FRS	Fellow of the Royal Society
GBE	Knight Grand Cross of the Order of the British Empire
GCB	Knight Grand Cross of the Order of the Bath
GCH	Knight Grand Cross of Hanover
GCMG	Knight Grand Cross of the Order of St. Michael & St. George
GCVO	Knight Grand Cross of the Royal Victorian Order
GLC	Greater London Council
HC Deb	House of Commons Debates
Hon	Honourable
HMC	Historical Manuscripts Commission
ILP	Independent Labour Party
Ind	Independent
IOM	Isle of Man
JP	Justice of the Peace
KC	King's Counsel
KCB	Knight Commander of the Bath
KCMG	Knight Commander of the Order of St. Michael & St. George
KG	Knight of the Garter
KT	Knight of the Thistle
Lab	Labour

Lib	Liberal
LLD	Doctor of Laws
LU	Liberal Unionist
m	married
MBE	Member of the Order of the British Empire
MC	Military Cross
MCC	Marylebone Cricket Club
MP	Member of Parliament
NATO	North Atlantic Treaty Organisation
nd	no date
NEC	National Executive Committee
NHS	National Health Service
NL	National Labour
p.a.	per annum
Parl Deb	Parliamentary Debates
Parl Hist	Parliamentary History
Parl Reg	Parliamentary Register
PC	Privy Counsellor
PM	Prime Minister
QC	Queen's Counsel
RA	Royal Academy
Rad	Radical
RAF	Royal Air Force
RAMC	Royal Army Medical Corps
RIBA	Royal Institute of British Architects
RN	Royal Navy
RtHon	Right Honourable
ScotNat	Scottish Nationalist
SDF	Social Democratic Federation
SDP	Social Democratic Party
SLP	Scottish Labour Party
SNP	Scottish National Party
Soc	Socialist
SPP	Scottish Prohibition Party
TUC	Trades Union Congress
unm	unmarried
VAD	Volunteer Aid Detachment
VE	Victory in Europe
WEU	Western European Union

FACTS ABOUT THE BRITISH PRIME MINISTERS

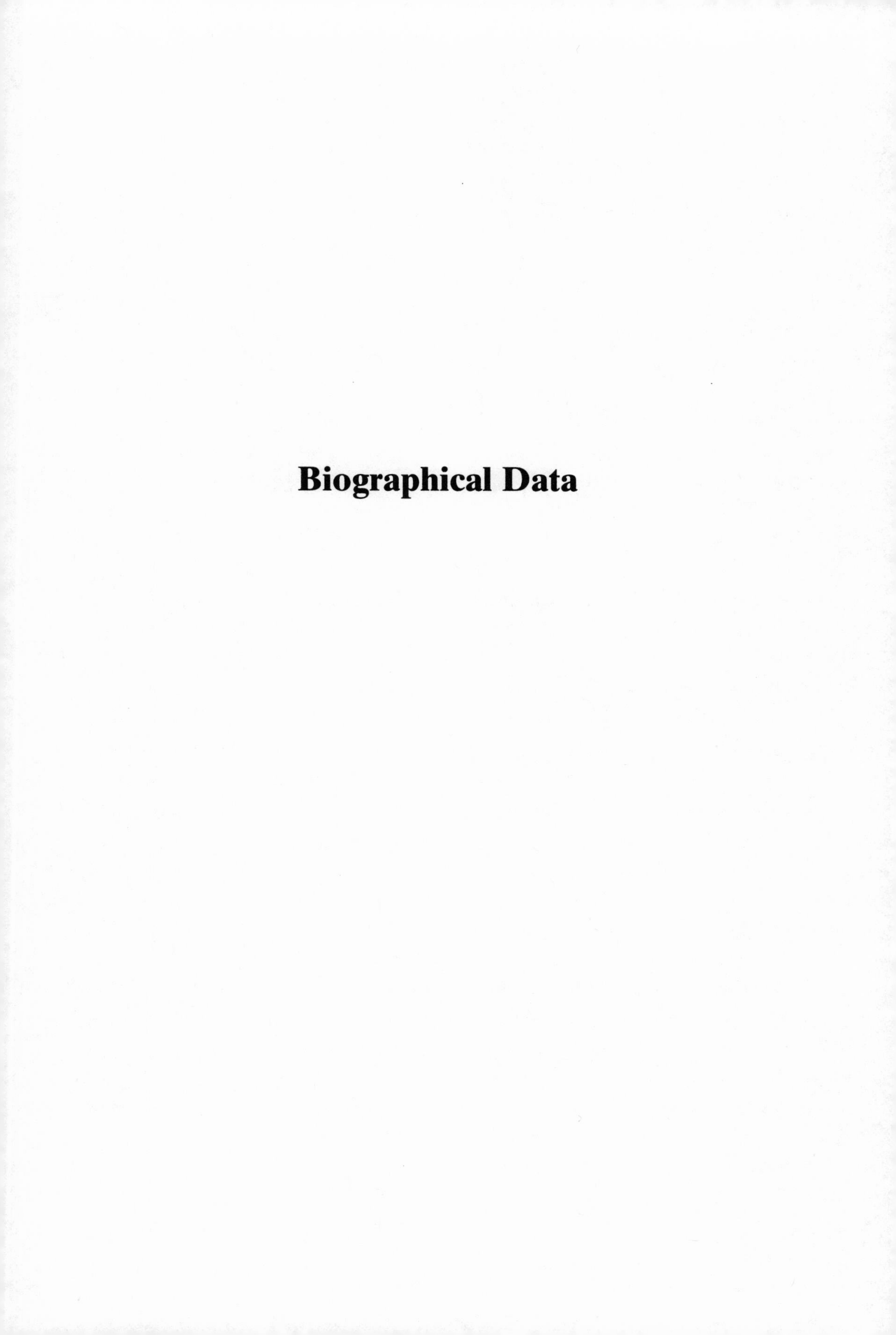

Biographical Data

Bettmann

Sir Robert Walpole

Lived 1676–1745
Political Party Whig
Prime Minister 3 April 1721–11 February 1742
Government Whig
Reigning Monarchs George I; George II

Fari quae sentiat Speak what you think

WALPOLE AS PRIME MINISTER

Generally recognised as the first British Prime Minister, Walpole still holds the record for the longest time as PM— almost 21 years. He entered Parliament in 1701 and held a series of ministerial offices, including Secretary at War and First Lord of the Treasury. When he was reappointed to the latter office in 1721 and Chancellor of the Exchequer, his Premiership can be said to begin. By choosing to remain in the Commons, he enhanced that House's political power in Parliament. His policies, especially his financial ones, were by and large popular and included the creation of a sinking fund to reduce the national debt, a reduction in the land tax, and the promotion of exports. However, he began to lose favour with George II, who became King in 1727, because of his 1737 compromise over Civil List payments, and the death in the same year of Queen Caroline, who had been a close friend. His illness following the declaration of war with Spain in 1739 led to widespread doubts about his ability to remain in office. He fought off a censure motion attacking his leadership in early 1741, but his Whig party was defeated in the election shortly afterward. Although he overcame another confidence vote over his handling of the Spanish war in 1742, he accepted a peerage in February that year and almost immediately resigned as PM.

PERSONAL INFORMATION

Names Robert Walpole
Peerages Baron Houghton, Viscount Walpole and 1st Earl of Orford, 6 Feb 1742
Nicknames 'Sir Bluestring', for accepting the Order of the Garter; 'Screen-Master General', for screening offenders from investigation in the South Sea Bubble affair
Born 26 Aug 1676
Birthplace Houghton, Norfolk
Religion Anglican
Ancestry English. His family were prominent Norfolk Whigs. His grandfather Edward took part in the restoration of Charles II (1660).
Dates and places of marriages 1) 30 Jul 1700, Knightsbridge Chapel, London 2) before 3 Mar 1738
Age at marriages 1) 24 years, 4 days 2) *c.* 62 years
Years married 1) 37 years, 21 days 2) *c.* 93 days
First entered Parliament 11 Jan 1701
Date appointed PM 3 Apr 1721
Age at appointment 44 years, 107 days
Date ceased to be PM 11 Feb 1742
Total time as PM 20 years, 314 days
Ceased to be MP 6 Feb 1742
Lived after last term as PM 3 years, 35 days
Date of death 18 Mar 1745
Place of death 5 Arlington St., London
Age at death 68 years, 204 days
Place of funeral Probably Houghton, Norfolk
Place of burial Houghton, Norfolk
Zodiac sign Virgo

FATHER

Sir Robert Walpole. He was known as 'Colonel' Walpole from his rank in the Norfolk Militia
Date and place of birth 18 Nov 1650, Norfolk
Occupation Norfolk landowner, farmer and MP for Castle Rising 1689–1700
Date of marriage 22 Feb 1671
Date of death 18 Nov 1700
Place of burial Houghton, Norfolk

MOTHER

Mary Burwell
Date of birth *c.* 1655
Profile She was a woman of some learning with extravagant tastes.
Date of marriage 22 Feb 1671
Date of death 14 Mar 1711
Place of burial Houghton, Norfolk

BROTHERS AND SISTERS

Robert Walpole was the third son and the fifth born of 17 children, 8 of whom died when they were very young.
Susan, b. 6 Jun 1672; d. before 1677
Mary, b. 8 Jun 1673; m. Sir Charles Turner (MP King's Lynn 1695–1728); d. Apr 1701
Edward, b. 23 Jun 1674; bur. 5 Feb 1697
Burwell, b. 6 Aug 1675; d. 30 Jun 1690 in the Battle of Beachy Head
John, b. 3 Sep 1677; d. young
Horatio (1st Baron Walpole of Wolterton), b. 8 Dec 1678; MP Lostwithiel 1710, Castle Rising 1710–15, Bere Alston 1715–17, East Looe 1718–22, Great Yarmouth 1722–34, Norwich 1734–56; d. 5 Feb 1757
Christopher, b. 20 Feb 1679; d. 22 Jun 1681
Elizabeth, b. 24 Mar 1681; bur. 9 May 1681
Elizabeth, b. 16 Oct 1682; bur. 10 Aug 1686
Galfridus, b. 15 Mar 1683; m. Constance Hays; MP Lostwithiel 1715–21, Postmaster General 1720–25; d. 6 Aug 1726
Anne, b. 6 Apr 1685; bur. 26 Apr 1685
Dorothy (Dolly), b. 18 Sep 1686; m. Charles, 2nd Viscount Townshend; d. 29 Mar 1726
Susan, b. 5 Dec 1687; m. Anthony Hamond; d. 1763
Mordaunt, b. 13 Dec 1688; bur. 24 Feb 1689
Charles, b. 30 Jun 1691; d. young
William, b. 7 Apr 1693; bur. 30 May 1694

FIRST WIFE

Catherine Shorter
Date of birth *c.* 1682
Mother Elizabeth Philipps
Father John Shorter of Bybrook, Kent
Father's occupation Baltic timber merchant
Age at marriage *c.* 18
Number of children 5
Date and place of death 20 Aug 1737, Chelsea, London
Place of burial Houghton, Norfolk
Years younger than PM *c.* 6 years
Profile Catherine Walpole enjoyed extravagance, frequently attending the opera, collecting exotic birds and buying expensive clothes and jewellery.

SECOND WIFE

Maria (Molly) Skerrett
Date and place of birth 5 Oct 1702, City of London
Mother Hester Pleydell
Father Thomas Skerrett of St. George's, Hanover Square
Father's occupation Merchant
Age at marriage 36
Number of children 2
Date of death 4 Jun 1738
Place of burial Houghton, Norfolk
Years younger than PM 25 years, 330 days
Profile Witty and beautiful, she lived at Walpole's house in Richmond Park before they were married. She is said to have inspired the character of Polly Peachum in John Gay's *The Beggars' Opera* and its sequel *Polly.*

CHILDREN

3 sons, 4 daughters
By his first wife Catherine:
Robert (Baron Walpole of Walpole), b. Mar. 1701; m. 2 Mar 1724, Margaret Rolle; Clerk of the Pells, Ranger of Richmond Park; d. 31 Mar 1751
Catherine, b. 1703; d. 9 Oct 1722
Mary, b. 1705; m. 14 Sep 1723, George, 3rd Earl of Cholmondeley (MP East Looe 1724–27, New Windsor 1727–33); d. 2 Jan 1732
Edward, b. 1706; unm.; MP Lostwithiel 1730–34, Great Yarmouth 1734–68; d. 12 Jan 1784
Horatio (Horace) (4th Earl of Orford), b. 5 Oct 1717; unm.; MP Callington 1741–54, Castle Rising 1754–57, King's Lynn 1757–68; d. 2 Mar 1797.
By his second wife Maria:
Maria, b. 1725; legitimised by her parents' marriage in 1738. Became Lady Maria Walpole in 1742 by a Patent of Precedence her father secured for her on his resignation as Prime Minister; m. 23 Feb 1746 Col. Charles

Churchill (MP Castle Rising 1715–45); a housekeeper at Windsor Castle, 1762–82; d. 1801

Of illegitimate birth:
Catherine Daye, mother unknown; d. Oct 1775

LIFE AND CAREER

PARLIAMENTARY ELECTIONS FOUGHT

*(*designates candidate elected)*

DATE Jan 1701. General Election
CONSTITUENCY Castle Rising
RESULT Thomas Howard* (Whig); Robert Walpole* (Whig)

DATE Oct 1701. General Election
CONSTITUENCY Castle Rising
RESULT Richard Jones, Earl of Ranelagh* (Tory); Robert Walpole* (Whig)

DATE Jul 1702. General Election
CONSTITUENCY King's Lynn
RESULT Sir Charles Turner* (Whig); Robert Walpole* (Whig)

DATE May 1705. General Election
CONSTITUENCY King's Lynn
RESULT Sir Charles Turner* (Whig); Robert Walpole* (Whig)

DATE 6 Mar 1708. By-election caused by Walpole's appointment as Secretary at War
CONSTITUENCY King's Lynn
RESULT Robert Walpole* (Whig)

DATE Apr 1708. General Election
CONSTITUENCY King's Lynn
RESULT Sir Charles Turner* (Whig); Robert Walpole* (Whig)

DATE 4 Feb 1710. By-election caused by his appointment as Treasurer of the Navy
CONSTITUENCY King's Lynn
RESULT Robert Walpole* (Whig)

DATE Oct 1710. General Election
CONSTITUENCY King's Lynn
RESULT Sir Charles Turner* (Whig); Robert Walpole* (Whig)

DATE Oct 1710. General Election
CONSTITUENCY Norfolk
RESULT Sir John Wodehouse* 3216; Sir Jacob Astley* (Tory) 3200; Ash Windham 2783; Robert Walpole (Whig) 2397

DATE 11 Feb 1712. By-election caused by Walpole's expulsion from the House of Commons and imprisonment in the Tower of London
CONSTITUENCY King's Lynn
RESULT Robert Walpole* (Whig); (Re-elected despite his ineligibility)

DATE Aug 1713. General Election
CONSTITUENCY King's Lynn
RESULT Sir Charles Turner*(Whig); Robert Walpole* (Whig)

DATE Jan 1715. General Election
CONSTITUENCY King's Lynn
RESULT Robert Walpole* (Whig); Sir Charles Turner* (Whig)

DATE 8 Nov 1715. By-election caused by Walpole's appointment as First Lord of the Treasury and Chancellor of the Exchequer
CONSTITUENCY King's Lynn
RESULT Robert Walpole* (Whig)

DATE 22 Jun 1720. By-election caused by Walpole's appointment as Paymaster of the Forces
CONSTITUENCY King's Lynn
RESULT Robert Walpole* (Whig)

DATE 10 Apr 1721. By-election caused by Walpole's appointment as First Lord of the Treasury and Chancellor of the Exchequer
CONSTITUENCY King's Lynn
RESULT Robert Walpole* (Whig)

DATE Mar 1722. General Election
CONSTITUENCY King's Lynn
RESULT Robert Walpole* (Whig); Sir Charles Turner* (Whig)

DATE 10 Jun 1723. By-election caused by Walpole's appointment as Secretary of State
CONSTITUENCY King's Lynn
RESULT Robert Walpole* (Whig)

DATE Aug 1727. General Election
CONSTITUENCY King's Lynn
RESULT Sir Charles Turner* (Whig); Sir Robert Walpole* (Whig)

DATE Apr 1734. General Election
CONSTITUENCY King's Lynn
RESULT Sir Charles Turner* (Whig); Sir Robert Walpole* (Whig)

DATE Apr 1741. General Election
CONSTITUENCY King's Lynn
RESULT Sir Robert Walpole* (Whig); Sir John Turner* (Whig)

PARTY ACTIVITY

Walpole held no party office, though he was de facto leader of the group of Whigs who, from Apr 1717 to Jun 1720, opposed Stanhope's Whig administration.

PARLIAMENTARY AND MINISTERIAL EXPERIENCE

First Recorded Speech His maiden speech is traditionally recorded as a failure, but no details survive. His first recorded speech in the House of Commons was on 24 Jan 1704 on the rights of electors. (*Parl. Hist.* vol 6, 1702–14 col 298–9)
Privy Counsellor 29 Sep 1714
Ministerial Offices Member of the Council of the Lord High Admiral Jun 1705–08; Secretary at War 25 Feb 1708–1710; Treasurer of the Navy 21 Jan 1710–Jan 1711; Paymaster of the Forces Oct 1714–15, Jun 1720–21; Leader of the House of Commons Sep 1714– Apr 1717, Feb 1721–Feb 1742; First Lord of the Treasury and Chancellor of the Exchequer 11 Oct 1715–10 Apr 1717, 3 Apr 1721–11 Feb 1742; Secretary of State, Northern Department 29 May–8 Dec 1723.

PARLIAMENTARY AND MINISTERIAL EXPERIENCE—*Continued*

Opposition Leader while PM William Pulteney

GOVERNMENTS FORMED

Administration 3 Apr 1721–11 Feb 1742

GENERAL ELECTION RESULTS

JAN 1715: Whigs 372; Tories 186. Total 558
Whig majority 86

MAR 1722: Whigs 389; Tories 169. Total 558
Whig majority 220

AUG 1727: Whigs 415; Tories 128; Opposition Whigs 15. Total 558
Government majority 272

APR 1734: Ministerial Whigs 330; Tories 145; Opposition Whigs 83. Total 558
Government majority 102

APR 1741: Ministerial Whigs 286; Tories 136; Opposition Whigs 131; Seats vacant 5. Total 558
Government majority 19

CABINET

Prime Minister, First Lord of the Treasury and Chancellor of the Exchequer Sir Robert Walpole

Lord Chancellor Earl of Macclesfield (1721–25); Lord King (1725–33); Lord Talbot (1733–37); Lord Hardwicke (1737–42)

Lord President Lord Carleton (1721–25); Duke of Devonshire (1725–30); Lord Trevor (1730); Earl of Wilmington (1730–42)

Lord Privy Seal Duke of Kingston (1721–26); Lord Trevor (1726–30); Earl of Wilmington (1730); Duke of Devonshire (1731–33); Viscount Lonsdale (1733–35); Earl of Godolphin (1735–40); Lord Hervey (1740–42)

Secretary of State (Northern Department) Viscount Townshend (1721–30) (Sir R. Walpole 29 May–8 Dec 1723 in Townshend's absence); Earl of Harrington (1730–42);

Secretary of State (Southern Department) Lord Carteret (1712–24); Duke of Newcastle (1724–42)

Master General of the Ordnance Duke of Marlborough (1721–22); Earl Cadogan (1722–25); Duke of Argyll and Greenwich (1725–40); Duke of Montagu (1740–42)

Secretary at War G. Treby (1721–24); H. Pelham (1724–30); Sir W. Strickland (1730–35); Sir W. Yonge (1735–42)

First Lord of the Admiralty Earl of Berkeley (1721–27); Viscount Torrington (1727–33); Sir C. Wager (1733–42)

IMPORTANT DATES IN PERSONAL AND POLITICAL LIFE

18 NOV 1700 Death of his father, whom he wanted to succeed as MP for Castle Rising. Thomas Howard approves Walpole's candidacy on 25 Nov.

11 JAN 1701 Enters Parliament as MP for Castle Rising.

JUN 1705 First appointment as member of Council of the Lord High Admiral.

DEC 1709 Participates in impeachment of Henry Sacheverell.

17 JAN 1712 Accused of corruption while Secretary at War, he is expelled from the House and committed to the Tower of London.

11 FEB 1712 Samuel Taylor elected to fill Walpole's seat; however Mayor of King's Lynn refuses to return Taylor. Walpole is returned instead, despite his ineligibility.

6 MAR 1712 The election is declared void and a new by-election ordered. Walpole is released from the Tower in July, after Parliament is prorogued.

31 AUG 1713 Re-elected for King's Lynn at the General Election.

29 SEP 1714 Sworn a Privy Counsellor.

APR 1715 Chairs committee of secrecy which recommends impeachment of Bolingbroke, Ormonde and Stafford.

11 OCT 1715 Appointed First Lord of the Treasury and Chancellor of the Exchequer.

10 APR 1717 Walpole resigns post in protest when Townshend is dismissed for voting against the Mutiny Bill. Walpole asserts the principle of collective ministerial responsibility, splitting the Whigs in Parliament.

DEC 1719 Walpole leads successful opposition to the Peerage Bill to limit the number of Peers.

MAY 1720 Despite Walpole's opposition, sale of government debts to the South Sea Company goes ahead. He makes a fortune by speculating in the stock, but when its value declines, public panic sets in. Recalled to sort out the crisis, he enhances his reputation.

3 APR 1721 Appointed First Lord of the Treasury and Chancellor of the Exchequer for the second time. Walpole's preeminence among his colleagues earns his position the title of Prime Minister.

22 AUG 1722 Bishop Francis Atterbury arrested as a traitor and imprisoned in the Tower of London. Using a Bill of Pains and Penalties to prosecute the bishop, Walpole gains favour with the King while strengthening his position as Prime Minister.

JUN 1723 George I awards peerage to Walpole's son Robert, who becomes Baron Walpole of Walpole. Walpole's refusal of the peerage for himself demonstrates his belief in the House of Commons as the true seat of power.

APR 1725 Spain and Austria sign the Treaty of Vienna. To safeguard trade, Secretary of State Townshend and the King arrange the Treaty of Hanover (signed Sep 1725) between England, France and Prussia.

MAY 1725 Impeachment of the Earl of Macclesfield, the Lord Chancellor, for corruption.

26 JUN 1726 Walpole made a Knight of the Garter and nicknamed 'Sir Bluestring' because of his humble origins

12 JUN 1727 Death of King George I.

NOV 1729 Treaty of Seville with Spain containing provision that confirms Gibraltar under British rule.

MAR 1733 Walpole's unpopular Excise Bill, proposing a tax increase on tobacco and wine imports, withdrawn. Walpole is burnt in effigy by celebrating London crowds.

1736 John Porteus, captain of the garrison in Edinburgh, fires on crowd of protestors, killing eight. Sentenced to death, Porteus is pardoned by Queen Caroline. When outraged Edinburgh residents hang him themselves, a serious defeat is inflicted on both Court and Government.

FEB 1737 Controversy over amount of Civil List payments to the King. Walpole bribes two MPs to vote for his compromise, the only instance in which bribery is proved against him; he thereafter steadily loses favour with the King.

21 JUN 1737 Licensing Act empowers Lord Chamberlain to censor plays.

20 AUG 1737 Death of Catherine, his first wife.

20 NOV 1737 Death of Queen Caroline heralds further decline in Walpole's influence with the King.

4 JUN 1738 Death in childbirth of his second wife, Maria, to whom he was devoted. It is an unexpected, bitter blow to Walpole.

FEB 1739 Walpole announces a Convention with Spain to settle their differences, but the terms of the agreement are fiercely opposed in Parliament.

19 OCT 1739 Despite Walpole's efforts to avert it, war is declared with Spain. He falls ill, and many people lose confidence in his ability to carry out his duties.

21 FEB 1740 Pulteney moves for the papers relating to the Convention of Pardo. Walpole faces the attack by turning the debate into an issue of confidence. He wins the vote comfortably.

17 FEB 1741 A censure motion charges Walpole with making himself 'sole and prime minister'. He argues that he is accountable for the conduct of the ministry as a whole, and the motion is defeated.

MAY 1741 Whigs split in General Election whose overall result depends on the outcome of several contested elections. Opposition wins an initial majority, but Walpole does not immediately resign.

21 JAN 1742 Walpole wins debate on motion of no confidence in the Government's conduct of war with Spain, but his position is not secure.

6 FEB 1742 Created Earl of Orford.

11 FEB 1742 Defeat finally inevitable, Walpole resigns as Prime Minister and goes to the House of Lords, where he soon secures a Patent of Precedence for his illegitimate daughter, who becomes Lady Maria Walpole.

MAR 1742 Committee appointed to inquire into the distribution of secret service money under his premiership; Bill introduced to indemnify witnesses who might testify against Walpole defeated in the Lords. The committee allege corruption, but the matter is not pursued.

NOV 1744 Despite failing health, he travels from Houghton to London at the request of the King, who wishes to consult him. His illness worsens as a result and he takes a remedy for the stone which lacerates his bladder, leading to his death.

BACKGROUND

PHYSICAL CHARACTERISTICS AND HEALTH

Tall with brown eyes, Walpole was handsome in his youth, but later on he became rather portly. and his legs swelled. His health was generally poor. He almost died from an attack of smallpox while he was a student at Cambridge, and throughout his life he suffered frequent attacks of gravel, stone and fever. In later life he had gout. Walpole died of a lacerated bladder, caused by a remedy he took for kidney stones.

EDUCATION

Primary 1682–90, Rev. Richard Ransome's elementary School, Great Dunham, Norfolk.

Secondary 1690–96, Eton. He entered a false age, 12 instead of 13, to qualify as a King's Scholar.

University 1696–98, King's College, Cambridge. He resigned his scholarship on 19 May 1698, following the death of his eldest brother, Edward.

Cultural and vocational background Schooled in the classics, he also studied French and history and attended Major Foubert's riding school in London.

Languages He studied Latin and French and had some knowledge of Italian, but was a poor linguist.

NON-PARLIAMENTARY CAREER

Early occupations As a younger son, he was destined for the Church, but when his eldest brother died he became manager of his father's estates. He was a member of Lincoln's Inn, but never became a barrister.

Other posts Deputy Ranger, Richmond Park; 1727, Ranger, Richmond Park; 1733, High Steward, Great Yarmouth; 1738, High Steward, King's Lynn

HONOURS

Freedom of Cities 1733, Norwich

Academic 1728, LLD from Cambridge

Other than peerage 27 May 1725, Knight of the Bath; 26 May 1726, Knight of the Garter

CLUBS

Kit-Cat Club (founder member), White's.

There is no evidence that Walpole was a Freemason, although a Masonic Lodge was held at Houghton Hall in 1731.

HOBBIES, SPORTS, PETS

His main interest was collecting paintings. He was also a connoisseur of wine, and brewed his own beer known as 'hogan', which was popular with his Norfolk house guests. He enjoyed field sports, especially hunting and beagling. Every November he held a hunting congress at Houghton. His love of hunting gave rise to the House of Commons custom of not sitting on Saturdays.

FINANCES

Walpole made a sizeable personal fortune from the sale of South Sea stock at 1,000 percent profit.

Income His income from official salaries has been estimated at £9,000 a year.

Spouses finances His first wife brought a dowry of £7, 000, of which he paid £4,500 to his father and the remaining £2,500 to his eldest son Robert to discharge a mortgage. His second wife had a personal fortune of £30,000. He assigned to her the income from several sinecures, amounting to £1,000 p.a. by 1735.

Pensions £4,000 a year on retirement, which he did not apply for until 1744.

Legacies On his father's death in 1700 he inherited nine manors in Norfolk and one in Suffolk, with an income in rents of over £2,000 a year. By 1740 this had risen to between £5,000 and £8,000 p. a.

Debts He died about £40,000 in debt, his creditors remaining unpaid as late as 1778. Houghton Hall had been mortgaged.

Will All his paintings at Chelsea were moved to Houghton Hall as heirlooms. The collection was sold in 1779 by his grandson, George, to Catherine the Great of Rus-

FINANCES—*Continued*

sia; it is now in the Hermitage in St. Petersburg. He left his youngest son Horace the house in Arlington Street and the sum of £5,000, together with an income of £1, 000 a year from his post of Collector of Customs (any surplus from the latter was to be shared with his brother Edward).

ANECDOTES

He was ridiculed as Peachum in Gay's *The Beggar's Opera*—Peachum espouses middle-class pieties even though he is a receiver of stolen goods—and as Flimnap in *Gulliver's Travels.*

George I is reported to have said that Walpole could turn stones into gold.

Although his Latin was good, he once lost a guinea to Pulteney by a blunder in a quotation from Horace. Pulteney held up the guinea in the House of Commons, saying, ''Tis the first money I've had from the Treasury these many years, and it will be the last.'

The Earl of Chesterfield described him thus: 'In private life, good-natured, cheerful, social, inelegant in his manners, loose in his morals, with a coarse strong wit.'

QUOTATIONS

'Every man has his price' was wrongly attributed to Walpole. He said, 'All these men have their price', indicating men who owed their places in the House of Commons to money or family connections.

'The balance of power' was from an address in the House of Commons on 13 Feb 1741.

My Lord Bath, you and I are now as insignificant men as any in England. (To Pulteney, Earl of Bath, on their elevation to the House of Lords).

RESIDENCES

Houghton Hall, King's Lynn, Norfolk
St. James's Square, London
Orford House, Chelsea, London
The Old Lodge, Richmond Park, London
10 Downing Street. He moved in 22 Sep 1735. This was 10 Downing Street's first use as the official residence of the Prime Minister.
5 Arlington Street, London (plaque)
Open to the public Houghton Hall, now owned by the National Trust, was built by Walpole in the period 1722–35 and described at the time as 'the most complete and sumptuous Palladian house in England'. It is situated in beautiful parkland and contains magnificent furniture, pictures and china.

MEMORIALS

STATUES AND BUSTS

Houghton Church, Norfolk; bust, British Museum; 1738, bust by Rysbrack, Houghton Hall, a copy of which is in the National Portrait Gallery.

PORTRAITS

1710–15, by Sir Godfrey Kneller, Houghton Hall; 1727, by John Wootton, Houghton Hall; 1740 by Jean Baptiste van Loo, Houghton Hall

OTHER MEMORIALS

Walpole, Massachusetts, and Orford, New Hampshire, were named after him.

BIBLIOGRAPHIC INFORMATION

LETTERS AND PERSONAL PAPERS

Many of his letters are printed in Coxe's *Memoirs of the Life of Sir Robert Walpole*. His papers belong to the Marquess of Cholmondeley and are deposited in Cambridge University Library.

PUBLICATIONS

Walpole published several political pamphlets: 1711, 'The Debts of the Nation Stated and Considered'; 1711, 'The Thirty-five Millions Accounted for'; 1712, 'The Case of Mr. Walpole, In a Letter from a Tory Member of Parliament to His Friend in the Country'; 1713, 'A Short History of the Parliament'; 1718, 'The Thoughts of a Member of the Lower House'; 1720, 'The South Sea Scheme Considered'; 1720, 'The Grand Accuser: The Greatest of All Criminals'; 1729, 'Observations upon the Treaty Between the Crowns of Great Britain, France and Spain'.

FURTHER READING

Black, J. *Robert Walpole and the Nature of Politics in Early Eighteenth-Century Britain.* London, 1990.
Coxe, W. *Memoirs of the Life of Sir Robert Walpole.* 3 vols. London, 1798.
Hill, B.W. *Sir Robert Walpole.* London, 1989.
Morley, J. *Walpole.* London, 1889.
Plumb, J.H. *Men and Places.* London, 1963.
—*Sir Robert Walpole: The Making of a Statesman.* London, 1956.
—*Sir Robert Walpole: The King's Minister.* London, 1960.

J.S.

Bettmann

Earl of Wilmington

Lived 1673–1743

Political Party Tory (until July 1698); Whig 1698–1743

Prime Minister 16 February 1742–2 July 1743

Government Whig

Reigning Monarch George II

Je ne cherche que un I seek but one

WILMINGTON AS PRIME MINISTER

The only Prime Minister to have sat in Parliament in the 17th century, Spencer Compton was originally elected as a Tory, but rapidly switched to the Whigs. He subsequently held various ministerial positions in Walpole's Government, as well as also being (unusually, to modern eyes) Speaker of the House of Commons from 1715 to 1727. In 1727, he was the new King's preferred choice for the premiership in place of Walpole, but he doubted his own ability to hold such a post. As compensation he was sent to the House of Lords as Earl of Wilmington and was successively Lord Privy Seal and Lord President of the Council under Walpole. Despite this he did not oppose the 1741 censure motion against his leader. After the failure of the King's attempts to put the opposition in power following Walpole's fall in 1742, Wilmington was made Prime Minister, an office he held for just over a year until his death. His brief premiership was dominated by foreign affairs. Wilmington's policy, directed by Lord Carteret, was to keep Great Britain in the War of the Austrian Succession, fighting the forces of Prussia, France, and Spain. A significant domestic policy of Wilmington's administration was the passage of a bill to curb public drunkenness by increasing the tax on spirits, making liquor more expensive.

PERSONAL INFORMATION

Names Spencer Compton
Peerages Baron Wilmington, 8 Jan 1728; 1st Earl of Wilmington and Viscount Pevensey, 14 May 1730
Born 1673
Birthplace Compton Wynyates, Warwickshire
Religion Anglican
Ancestry English. His family were illustrious and loyal supporters of the crown in Warwickshire.
First entered Parliament 3 Jun 1698
Date appointed PM 16 Feb 1742
Age at appointment *c.* 69 years
Date ceased to be PM 2 Jul 1743
Total time as PM 1 year, 136 days
Ceased to be MP 8 Jan 1728
Lived after last term as PM Died in office
Date of death 2 Jul 1743
Place of death St. James' Square, London
Age at death *c.* 70 years
Place of burial Compton Wynyates, Warwickshire

FATHER

James Compton, 3rd Earl of Northampton
Date of birth 19 Aug 1622
Occupation MP Warwickshire, 1640–43. Expelled from the House for voting against the attainder of the Earl of Strafford. Recorder of Coventry; Lord Lieutenant of Warwickshire; Colonel of a regiment of horse and later of foot; Constable of the Tower; a Lord of Trade.
Dates of marriages 1) 5 Jul 1647, Lady Isabella Sackville (d. 14 Oct 1661); 2) 29 Jan 1663, Mary Noel
Date of death 15 Dec 1681
Place of burial Compton Wynyates, Warwickshire

MOTHER

Mary Noel
Date of marriage 29 Jan 1663
Date of death 22 Aug 1719
Place of burial Compton Wynyates, Warwickshire

BROTHERS AND SISTERS

Wilmington was the third son and the youngest of five children. He had a half sister (Alathea) from his father's first marriage.
From his father's first marriage:
A male child, b. May 1649; d. 22 May 1649
William, b. 27 May 1653; d. Sep 1661
Anne, b. 14 Jul 1655; d. 1660
Isabella, b. 16. Dec 1656; d. 3 Mar 1657
James, b. 1659; d. Aug 1662
Alathea, b. 1660; m. Sir Edward Hungerford; d. 1678
From his father's second marriage:
George (4th Earl of Northampton), b. 16 Oct 1664; m. 1) 1686 Jane Fox (d. 10 Jul 1721); 2) 2 Jul 1726 Elizabeth Thorold (d. 15 Jan 1750); Lord Lieutenant of Warwickshire, Constable of the Tower, Master of the King's Leash; d. 15 Apr 1727
Juliana, b. 1665; d. young
Mary, b. *c.* 1669; m. Charles Sackville, 6th Earl of Dorset (MP East Grinstead 1660–75); d. 6 Aug 1691
James, bap. 8 Jul 1672; d. 20 Aug 1672

MARRIAGE

Wilmington was unmarried, but some sources say that he had illegitimate children, of whom one daughter married James Glen, a Governor of South Carolina.

LIFE AND CAREER

PARLIAMENTARY ELECTIONS FOUGHT

*(*designates candidate elected)*

DATE Nov 1695. General Election
CONSTITUENCY East Grinstead
RESULT Sir Thomas Dyke* (Tory); John Conyers* (Tory); Lord Orrery; Spencer Compton (Tory)

DATE 3 Jun 1698. By-election caused by the death of Charles Cornwallis.
CONSTITUENCY Eye
RESULT Spencer Compton* (Tory)

DATE Jul 1698. General Election
CONSTITUENCY Eye
RESULT Spencer Compton* (Tory); Sir Joseph Jekyll* (Whig)

DATE Jan 1701. General Election
CONSTITUENCY Eye
RESULT Spencer Compton* (Whig), Sir Joseph Jekyll* (Whig)

DATE Oct 1701. General Election
CONSTITUENCY Eye
RESULT Spencer Compton* (Whig); Sir Joseph Jekyll* (Whig)

DATE Jul 1702. General Election
CONSTITUENCY Eye
RESULT Spencer Compton* (Whig); Sir Joseph Jekyll* (Whig)

DATE May 1705. General Election
CONSTITUENCY Eye
RESULT Spencer Compton* (Whig); Sir Joseph Jekyll* (Whig)

DATE Apr 1708. General Election
CONSTITUENCY Eye
RESULT Spencer Compton* (Whig), Sir Joseph Jekyll* (Whig)

DATE Aug 1713. General Election
CONSTITUENCY East Grinstead
RESULT Spencer Compton* (Whig); John Conyers* (Tory)

DATE Jan 1715. General Election
CONSTITUENCY East Grinstead
RESULT Spencer Compton* (Whig); John Conyers* (Tory)

DATE Jan 1715. General Election
CONSTITUENCY Sussex
RESULT James Butler* (Whig) 1964; Spencer Compton** (Whig) 1898; Charles Eversfield (Whig) 1113; B. Ashburnham 1008

***Elected both for East Grinstead and the county of Sussex; he chose to sit for Sussex.*

DATE Mar 1722. General Election
CONSTITUENCY East Grinstead
RESULT Spencer Compton* (Whig); John Conyers* (Tory)

DATE Mar 1722. General Election
CONSTITUENCY Sussex
RESULT Spencer Compton** (Whig); Henry Pelham* (Whig)*

***Elected both for East Grinstead and the county of Sussex; he chose to sit for Sussex.*

DATE Aug 1727. General Election
CONSTITUENCY Sussex
RESULT Sir Spencer Compton* (Whig); Henry Pelham* (Whig)

PARLIAMENTARY AND MINISTERIAL EXPERIENCE

First Recorded Speech 17 Mar 1715, on being chosen Speaker. (*Parl. Hist.* vol 7 1714–22, col. 40–42)
Privy Counsellor 6 Jul 1716
Ministerial Offices Paymaster of the Queen's Pensions, 26 Apr 1707–14; Treasurer to Prince George of Denmark, 26 Apr 1707–08; Treasurer to the Prince of Wales, Mar 1715–27; Paymaster General, Oct 1722–30; Lord Privy Seal, 8 May–Dec 1730; Lord President of the Council, 31 Dec 1730–42; First Lord of the Treasury and Leader of the House of Lords, 16 Feb 1742–2 Jul 1743
Opposition Leader while PM William Pulteney, Earl of Bath
Speaker of the House 17 Mar 1715–17 Jul 1727

GOVERNMENTS FORMED

Administration 16 Feb 1742–2 Jul 1743

GENERAL ELECTION RESULT
APR 1741: Ministerial Whigs 286; Tories 136; Opposition Whigs 131; Seats vacant 5. Total 558.
Government majority 19

CABINET
Prime Minister and First Lord of the Treasury Earl of Wilmington
Lord Chancellor Lord Hardwicke
Lord President Earl of Harrington
Lord Privy Seal Earl Gower
Secretary of State (Northern Department) Lord Carteret
Secretary of State (Southern Department) Duke of Newcastle
Chancellor of the Exchequer S. Sandys
Commissioner of the Forces and Master General of the Ordnance Duke of Argyll (1742)
Commissioner of the Forces Earl of Stair (1743)
Master General of the Ordnance Duke of Montagu (1743)
Paymaster of the Forces H. Pelham
First Lord of the Admiralty Earl of Winchilsea

IMPORTANT DATES IN PERSONAL AND POLITICAL LIFE

15 DEC 1681 Death of his father. His elder brother George inherits his title.
25 JAN 1687 Admitted as a barrister to the Middle Temple.
28 FEB 1690 Matriculates, Trinity College, Oxford.
3 JUN 1698 First elected to Parliament in a by-election at Eye, Suffolk, after standing unsuccessfully at East Grinstead in 1695.
1705 Appointed Chairman of the Committee charged with drawing up the articles of the Union with Scotland.
1705–08 Chairman of the Committee of Privileges and Elections.
26 APR 1707 Appointed Paymaster of the Queen's Pensions and Treasurer to Prince George of Denmark.
14 DEC 1709 Member of the Committee appointed to draw up articles of impeachment against Sacheverell. Walpole also on the Committee.
21 SEP 1710 Parliament dissolved, but Wilmington fails to find a seat after he is dropped by his patron, Lord Cornwallis. He is out of Parliament until the next General Election.
28 AUG 1713 Elected as MP for East Grinstead.
1714 Counsel for Dr. Bentley, Master of Trinity College, Cambridge, at his trial before the Bishop of Ely.
17 MAR 1715 Elected Speaker of the House.
MAR 1715 Appointed Treasurer to the Prince of Wales.
6 JUL 1716 Sworn a Privy Counsellor.
22 AUG 1719 Death of his mother.
9 OCT 1722 Re-elected as Speaker.
OCT 1722 Appointed Paymaster General, an office he was to hold until 1730. The practice of holding ministerial office at the same time as the Speakership of the House of Commons was subsequently discontinued.
12 JUN 1727 Death of King George I. On the accession of George II, Wilmington is asked to draw up the King's first speech to the Privy Council. Feeling unequal to the task, he asks Walpole to write it for him. In spite of Wilmington's being the King's favourite for the post of Prime Minister, Walpole keeps the position. Wilmington admits that he does not think he can do the job.
17 AUG 1727 Elected for the county of Sussex, but Walpole advises the King to make him a Peer to compensate for not becoming Prime Minister, and he is created Baron Wilmington on 8 Jan 1728.
8 MAY 1730 Appointed Lord Privy Seal under Walpole.
14 MAY 1730 Becomes Viscount Pevensey and Earl of Wilmington.
31 DEC 1730 Appointed Lord President of the Council.
12 JUN 1733 Made a Knight of the Garter.
FEB 1741 Despite being one of Walpole's ministers, he does not oppose Lord Carteret's motion for his removal.
28 JAN 1742 Walpole defeated on the Chippenham election petition, and the King sends for Pulteney, the leader of the Opposition, to form an administration. His efforts, however, fail.
16 FEB 1742 Wilmington is appointed First Lord of the Treasury, and, thus, Prime Minister
16 JUN 1742 The Place Act receives Royal Assent. It excludes certain officers from becoming members of Parliament, an attempt to reduce corruption.
22 MAR 1743 The Spirituous Liquors Act increases the duties on spirits. An unpopular measure, it is designed to curb increases in public drunkenness.
27 JUN 1743 King George II defeats the French at the Battle of Dettingen, but the War of the Austrian Succession continues until 1748. Foreign policy dominates the political agenda.
2 JUL 1743 Dies in office.

BACKGROUND

PHYSICAL CHARACTERISTICS AND HEALTH

Contemporary accounts suggest that he was rather taller and broader than average. Little is known about his health, although in later life he suffered from kidney stones.

EDUCATION

Secondary St. Paul's School, Westminster
University Trinity College, Oxford 1690 (aged 15)
Cultural and vocational background In 1698 he finished his education by travelling abroad. During this time he was elected MP for Eye.

NON-PARLIAMENTARY CAREER

Early occupations In 1687 he was admitted as a barrister to the Middle Temple.
Other posts 1722, Treasurer of Chelsea Hospital; 1732, Governor of Charter House

HONOURS

Academic 1730, DCL from Oxford
Other than peerage 27 May 1725, Knight of the Bath; 12 Jun 1733, Knight of the Garter

CLUBS

Kit-Cat Club

HOBBIES AND SPORTS

He was fond of good food. He was interested in botany and collected exotic plants. He also collected coins and medallions.

FINANCES

Income He earned a great deal of money as Paymaster General between 1722 and 1730, although the actual amount is not known.
Will His estates and personal property passed to his nephew James, 5th Earl of Northampton. According to one source he left no will.

ANECDOTES

'The most formal solemn man in the world, but a great lover of private debauchery'. (H. Walpole. *Memoirs of the Reign of George II* Vol. 1, 1846, p. 178.)

'A plodding, heavy fellow, with great application, but no talents, and vast complaisance for a Court, without any address . . . His only pleasures were money and eating; his only knowledge forms and precedents; and his only insinuation bows and smiles.' (Hervey, *Memoirs of the Reign of George II,* 1884 ed., Vol. 1, p. 33.)

'See yon old, dull important Lord
Who at the long'd for money board
Sits first, but does not lead;
His younger brethren all things make;
So that the Treasury's like a snake,
And the tail moves the head.'
(C. Hanbury Williams. 'New Ode to a Great Number of Great Men Newly Made'. *Works* 1822.)

QUOTATIONS

As Speaker, on whether Members had a right to be heard: 'No Sir, you have a right to speak, but the House have a right to judge whether they will hear you.' (*Hatsell's Precedents* 1818, Vol. II, p. 108.)

On the Duke of Newcastle: 'He always loses half an hour in the morning which he is running after the rest of the day without being able to overtake it.'

RESIDENCES

Compton Wynyates, Warwickshire
Compton Place, Eastbourne, Sussex
22 St. James's Square, London
A house in Chiswick

MEMORIALS

PORTRAITS

c. 1710, by Sir Godfrey Kneller, National Portrait Gallery; before 1727, by Sir Peter Lely, Palace of Westminster

OTHER MEMORIALS

Wilmington, Delaware; Wilmington, Massachusetts, and Wilmington, North Carolina, were all named after him.

BIBLIOGRAPHIC INFORMATION

LETTERS AND PERSONAL PAPERS

The family papers are in the possession of the Marquess of Northampton at Castle Ashby, Northamptonshire.

FURTHER READING

Caulfield, J. *Memoirs of the celebrated persons composing the Kit-cat Club.* London, 1821.
Compton, W.B. *History of the Comptons of Compton Wynyates.* London, 1930.

J.S.

Bettmann

Henry Pelham

Lived 1694–1754
Political Party Whig
Prime Minister 27 August 1743–6 March 1754
Government Whig
Reigning Monarch George II

Vincit amor patriae The love of my country surpasses all

PELHAM AS PRIME MINISTER

Henry Pelham was the son of a long-serving MP, and younger brother of the Duke of Newcastle, his successor as PM. He was first elected to Parliament in 1717. He became a minister in 1720, and was a close ally of Walpole. Pelham was influential as a mediator between the PM and Newcastle, and persuaded his brother not to resign from Walpole's Government in 1741 over the Spanish war. He refused to take over from Walpole in 1742 out of friendship for the fallen PM, but became Premier after Wilmington's death the following year. He remained in office for over 10 years, partly due to his ability to unite different political factions in a 'broad-bottom' Government, and was the only Member of the House of Commons in his Cabinet. His premiership saw attempts at social and fiscal reform, not all of which were successful. In Scotland, Bonnie Prince Charlie's Jacobite Rebellion of 1745 was put down. In foreign affairs, the War of the Austrian Succession was concluded in 1748, bringing peace with France and trade with Spain. He overcame several political crises, including a brief resignation in 1746 over the King's attempts to replace him, and a dispute with Newcastle in 1750. His health suffered from 1748 on, and he tried to retire in 1751, only to be dissuaded by the King. He died in office in 1754.

PERSONAL INFORMATION

Names Henry Pelham
Nickname King Henry the Ninth
Born 25 Sep 1694
Birthplace probably Laughton, Sussex
Religion Anglican
Ancestry English. He came from a Norman family who settled in Hertfordshire. They later acquired lands in Sussex, where they became established.
Date of marriage 29 Oct 1726
Age at marriage 32 years, 34 days
Years married 27 years, 128 days
First entered Parliament 28 Feb 1717
Date appointed PM 27 Aug 1743. (There was a gap of seven weeks since the death of the previous PM.)
Age at appointment 48 years, 336 days
Dates ceased to be PM 1) 11 Feb 1746 (resigned but was reinstated 14 Feb 1746) 2) 6 Mar 1754
Total time as PM 10 years, 191 days (ignoring the hiatus)
Ceased to be MP 6 Mar 1754
Lived after last term as PM Died in office
Date of death 6 Mar 1754
Place of death Arlington Street, Piccadilly, London
Age at death 59 years, 161 days
Place of funeral At his request there was no funeral
Place of burial Laughton, Sussex
Zodiac sign Libra

FATHER

Thomas, 1st Baron Pelham
Date of birth 1653
Occupation MP East Grinstead 1678–79; Lewes 1679–1701; Sussex 1702–05
Dates of marriages 1) 26 Nov 1679, Elizabeth Jones (1664–7 Oct 1681) 2) 21 May 1686, Lady Grace Holles
Date of death 23 Feb 1712
Place of burial Laughton, Sussex

MOTHER

Lady Grace Holles
Date of birth c. 1668
Date of marriage 21 May 1686
Date of death 13 Sep 1700
Place of burial Laughton, Sussex

BROTHERS AND SISTERS

Henry Pelham was the third son and ninth of eleven children.
From his father's first marriage:
Lucy, b. 1 Oct 1680; bur. 2 May 1689
Elizabeth, b. *c.* 7 Oct 1681; m. Charles, Viscount Townshend; (He later married Walpole's sister.) d. 11 May 1711
From his father's second marriage:
Grace, b. 3 Apr 1687; m. George Naylor (MP Seaford 1706–10 and 1713–22); d. Apr 1710
Frances, b. Dec 1688; m. Christopher Wandesford, Viscount Castlecomer (MP Morpeth 1710–13, Ripon 1715–19); d. 27 Jun 1756
Mary, b. 31 Jan 1690; bur. 12 Dec 1702
Gertrude, b. 6 Jan 1691; m. David Polhill (MP Kent 1710, Bramber 1723–27, Rochester 1727–41 and 1742–54)
John, bur. 18 Feb 1692
Lucy, b. 1692; m. Henry Clinton, 7th Earl of Lincoln (Lord of the Bedchamber 1714–27, Joint Paymaster General of the Forces 1715–20) d. 20 Jul 1736
Thomas, (Duke of Newcastle) (*q.v.*), b. 21 Jul 1693; Prime Minister 1754–56, 1757–62; d. 17 Nov 1768
Margaret, b. 1696; m. Sir John Shelley (MP Arundel 1727–41, Lewes 1743–47); d. 24 Nov 1758

WIFE

Lady Catherine Manners
Date of birth c. 1700
Mother Catherine Russell
Father John, 2nd Duke of Rutland
Father's occupation MP Derbyshire 1701, Leicestershire 1701–02, 1710–11, Grantham 1705–10; Lord Lieutenant of Rutland, 1712–15, and of Leicestershire 1714–21
Age at marriage c. 26 years
Number of children 8
Date and place of death 17 Feb 1780, Whitehall, London
Place of burial Laughton, Sussex
Years younger than PM c. 6 years
Profile She was the Keeper of Greenwich Park.

CHILDREN

2 sons, 6 daughters
Catherine, b. 24 Jul 1727; m. 16 Oct 1744, Henry Clinton, 9th Earl of Lincoln, later 2nd Duke of Newcastle; d. 27 Jul 1760
Frances, b. 18 Aug 1728; d. 10 Jan 1804
Lucy, b. *c.* 1729; d. 6 Feb 1740
Thomas, b. 31 Oct 1729; d. 28 Nov 1739
Dorothy, b. 1734; d. young
Grace, b. Jan 1735; m. 12 Oct 1752, Lewis Monson Watson, 1st Lord Sondes; d. 31 Jul 1777
Henry, b. 8 Apr 1736; d. 27 Nov 1739
Mary, b. 22 Sep 1739

LIFE AND CAREER

PARLIAMENTARY ELECTIONS FOUGHT

*(*designates candidate elected)*

DATE 28 Feb 1717. By-election caused by the appointment of Sir William Ashburnham as Commissioner of the Alienation Office
CONSTITUENCY Seaford
RESULT Henry Pelham* (Whig)

DATE 7 Jun 1720. By-election caused by Pelham's appointment as Treasurer of the Chamber
CONSTITUENCY Seaford
RESULT Henry Pelham* (Whig)

DATE 10 Apr 1721. By-election caused by Pelham's appointment as one of the Lords Commissioners of the Treasury
CONSTITUENCY Seaford
RESULT Henry Pelham* (Whig)

DATE Mar 1722. General Election
CONSTITUENCY Sussex
RESULT Spencer Compton* (Whig); Henry Pelham* (Whig)

DATE 16 Apr 1724. By-election caused by Pelham's appointment as Secretary at War

CONSTITUENCY Sussex
RESULT Henry Pelham* (Whig)

DATE Aug 1727. General Election
CONSTITUENCY Sussex
RESULT Spencer Compton* (Whig); Henry Pelham* (Whig)

DATE 21 May 1730. By-election caused by Pelham's appointment as Paymaster General of the Land Forces
CONSTITUENCY Sussex
RESULT Henry Pelham* (Whig)

DATE Apr 1734. General Election
CONSTITUENCY Aldborough
RESULT Henry Pelham* (Whig); William Jessop* (Whig)

DATE Apr 1734. General Election
CONSTITUENCY Sussex
RESULT Henry Pelham** (Whig) 2,271; James Butler* (Whig) 2,053; Sir Cecil Bishopp 1,704; John Fuller 1, 581
***Elected both for Aldborough and the county of Sussex, he chose to sit for Sussex.*

DATE Apr 1741. General Election
CONSTITUENCY Sussex
RESULT Henry Pelham* (Whig); James Butler* (Whig)

DATE 15 Dec 1743. By-election caused by Pelham's appointment as First Lord of the Treasury
CONSTITUENCY Sussex
RESULT Henry Pelham* (Whig)

DATE Jun 1747. General Election
CONSTITUENCY Sussex
RESULT Henry Pelham* (Whig); John Butler* (Whig)

PARLIAMENTARY AND MINISTERIAL EXPERIENCE

First Recorded Speech 6 May 1720, on the establishment of insurance companies. (*Parl. Hist.* vol. 7, 1714–22, p. 648–49)
Privy Counsellor 1 Jun 1725
Ministerial Offices Treasurer of the Chamber 25 May 1720–22; Lord of the Treasury 3 Apr 1721–24; Secretary at War 3 Apr 1724–8 May 1730; Paymaster General 8 May 1730–43; Leader of the House of Commons Feb 1742–6 Mar 1754; First Lord of the Treasury 25 Aug 1743–6 Mar 1754; Chancellor of the Exchequer 12 Dec 1743–6 Mar 1754
Opposition Leaders while PM William Pulteney, Earl of Bath 1742–46; Frederick, Prince of Wales 1746–51; Duke of Bedford 1751–54

GOVERNMENTS FORMED

Administration (The 'Broad Bottom' ministry) 27 Aug 1743–6 Mar 1754

GENERAL ELECTION RESULTS

APR 1741: Ministerial Whigs 286; Tories 136; Opposition Whigs 131; Seats vacant 35. Total 558
Government majority 19
JUN 1747: Ministerial Whigs 351; Tories 115; Opposition Whigs 92. Total 558.
Government majority 144

CABINET
Prime Minister and First Lord of the Treasury Henry Pelham
Lord Chancellor Earl of Hardwicke
Lord President Earl of Harrington (1743–45); Duke of Dorset (1745–51); Earl of Granville (1751–54)
Lord Privy Seal Earl of Cholmondeley (1743–44); Earl of Gower (1744–54)
Chancellor of the Exchequer Lord Sandys (Aug–Dec 1743); H. Pelham (Dec 1743–Mar 1754)
Secretary of State (Northern Department) Lord Carteret (1743–44); Earl of Harrington (1744–46); Earl of Chesterfield (1746–48); Duke of Newcastle (1748–54)
Secretary of State (Southern Department) Duke of Newcastle (1743–48); Duke of Bedford (1748–51); Earl of Holdernesse (1751–54)
First Lord of the Admiralty Earl of Winchilsea (1743–44); Duke of Bedford (1744–48); Earl of Sandwich (1748–51); G. Anson (1751–54)
*Secretary of State for Scotland** Marquess of Tweeddale (1743–46)
Master General of the Ordnance Duke of Montagu (1743–49); (Office not in Cabinet 1749–54)
Lord Chamberlain Duke of Grafton
Keeper of the Great Seal of Scotland Duke of Argyle
Master of the Horse Duke of Richmond (1743–51); Duke of Devonshire (1751–54)
Paymaster General *W. Pitt (1746–54);
**Office not always in Cabinet*

IMPORTANT DATES IN PERSONAL AND POLITICAL LIFE

13 SEP 1700 His mother dies shortly before his sixth birthday.
6 SEP 1710 Enrolls at Hart Hall, Oxford, but does not graduate.
22 JUL 1715 Distinguishes himself in battle during the Jacobite Rebellion
1715–17 Completes his education by travelling abroad.
28 FEB 1717 First elected to Parliament for the Cinque Ports constituency of Seaford in Sussex. Sir William Ashburnham accepts a sinecure to make way for him.
6 MAY 1720 His first recorded speech, moving an address of thanks to the King for his offer to finance the establishment of insurance companies. The motion is seconded by Walpole.
25 MAY 1720 Appointed Treasurer of the Chamber, the first of many ministerial posts he was to hold.
3 APR 1721 Appointed a Lord of the Treasury, under Walpole. Walpole becomes both mentor and friend to Pelham.
3 APR 1724 Appointed Secretary at War.
1 JUN 1725 Sworn a Privy Counsellor.
29 OCT 1726 He marries Lady Catherine Manners, daughter of the Duke of Rutland. Her dowry enables him to buy half of the family estates in Lincolnshire, and his brother Thomas gives him some of the family's land in Sussex, making him financially secure for the first time.
8 MAY 1730 Appointed Paymaster General. His many ministerial posts give him an unusual degree of experience of government.
MAR 1733 He defends Walpole from attack by a crowd in the House of Commons lobby after a debate on the controversial Excise Bill. He threatens the mob with his sword, and they disperse.
28 NOV 1739 His elder son Thomas dies of an epidemic sore throat, the day after his younger son Henry had died of the same illness, which became known for a time as 'Pelham's fever'.
13 FEB 1741 Speaks strongly in defence of Walpole on a motion to have him removed. His friendship with Wal-

IMPORTANT DATES IN PERSONAL AND POLITICAL LIFE—*Continued*

pole is central to his success, and he often mediates between Walpole and his own brother Thomas, the Duke of Newcastle.

OCT 1741 He persuades his brother not to resign in protest at the ending of the war with Spain, preventing a damaging split in the Walpole administration.

18 FEB 1742 After Walpole's resignation he becomes what is now called Leader of the House but refuses to accept either of the offices Walpole had held, not wanting to profit by his friend's fall.

25 AUG 1743 After Wilmington's death he is appointed First Lord of the Treasury and thus Prime Minister. In spite of the King's dislike of the Pelhams, Henry Pelham is appointed Prime Minister because of his ability to unite different factions within a 'broad-bottom' ministry. His skill in persuading people of opposing views to work together brings a period of unusual stability and harmony to British politics.

12 DEC 1743 Appointed additionally to the post of Chancellor of the Exchequer.

24 NOV 1744 Pelham and the Duke of Newcastle, among others, complain to the King about Carteret's conduct of foreign policy, and obtain Carteret's dismissal. This considerably strengthens Pelham's position.

8 JAN 1745 Britain, Austria, the Netherlands and Saxony sign the Quadruple Alliance.

18 MAR 1745 He is saddened by the death of Walpole, who had always given him sound political advice.

25 JUL 1745 The second Jacobite Rebellion begins when Charles Edward Stuart lands in Scotland and proclaims his father, James, King of Scotland and England.

26 AUG 1745 The convention of Hanover is signed between Britain and Prussia.

11 FEB 1746 The Cabinet crisis. Pelham and most of the Cabinet resign upon learning that the King wants to replace him with the Earls of Granville (Carteret) and Bath (Pulteney). Pelham and his colleagues are reinstated three days later.

16 APR 1746 Defeat of the Jacobite forces at Culloden.

6 MAY 1746 Pelham brings Pitt into the Cabinet as Paymaster General, thereby giving office to one of his ablest rivals.

28 JUL 1746 The Earls of Kilmarnock, Cromartie and Balmerino are tried and later sentenced to death for their part in the Jacobite Rebellion, although Cromartie is later reprieved.

17 JUN 1747 At the King's suggestion, both Houses of Parliament pass an Act awarding a free pardon to anyone involved in the Jacobite Rebellion who is now prepared to give his allegiance to the King.

20 JUN 1747 Pelham calls a snap election a year earlier than necessary under the Septennial Act. Catching the Opposition by surprise, the Whigs are returned with an increased majority.

18 OCT 1748 The Treaty of Aix-la-Chapelle brings peace with France and ends the War of the Austrian Succession. The war has been a military and financial failure for Britain.

28 NOV 1749 Pelham's measure reassigning the mounting national debt to the Bank of England helps to establish a coherent system of national finance.

JUL 1750 A treaty with Spain reestablishes trade on a peaceful basis after years of disputes.

NOV 1750 A serious argument develops between Pelham and his brother, the Duke of Newcastle, who wants to remove the Duke of Bedford as Secretary of State for the Southern Department. Pelham resists, fearing that such a move will intensify Bedford's opposition.

20 MAR 1751 Frederick, Prince of Wales, falls ill and suddenly dies. Without his leadership the Opposition factions become scattered and ineffectual.

30 MAR 1751 Pelham, harrassed and wearied by his official duties, wants to retire to a sinecure, but is dissuaded by the King, who realises that Pelham's remaining in office can ensure stable government.

22 MAY 1751 Regency Act allows the Princess of Wales to become Regent if necessary, a measure designed to prevent power falling into the hands of the Duke of Cumberland, a prominent opponent of the Ministry. A Bill is passed adopting the Gregorian calendar, which moves the beginning of the year from 25 Mar to 1 Jan. The new calendar abolishes 11 days between the 2nd and 14th Sep 1752, which causes a public outcry.

15 JUN 1751 Cabinet changes bring the Earl of Granville back into the Cabinet as Lord President of the Council. The Duke of Bedford finally leaves office, becoming chief spokesman for the Opposition forces.

JUN 1753 He supports legislation to naturalise Jews, but the Jewish Naturalisation Act has to be repealed in the following session because of public opposition.

7 JUN 1753 The Earl of Hardwicke's Marriage Bill proposes marriage licences for any marriage where banns had not been read in the parish church. In spite of vociferous opposition, it is eventually passed.

JUN 1753 An Act passed establishing the British Museum. Funds are to be raised by means of a lottery, an expedient Pelham only reluctantly approves.

6 MAR 1754 Dies after an illness.

BACKGROUND

PHYSICAL CHARACTERISTICS AND HEALTH

He had blue eyes. He is said to have eaten too much and exercised too little. In August 1748 he had his first serious illness, a bad attack of shingles, and his health suffered from then onwards. In July 1753 he was afflicted with an inflammatory disease, erysipelas. He went to stay in Scarborough but the disease was not cured. He returned to London, had a relapse, and died on 6 Mar 1754.

EDUCATION

Primary With his brother Thomas, the future Duke of Newcastle (*q.v.*) he began his education under the private instruction of a resident tutor, Richard Newton, who later became famous as the Principal of Hart Hall, Oxford, and as an educational reformer.

Secondary Westminster School.

University Hart Hall, Oxford, matriculated on 6 Sep 1710 at the age of 15, but did not graduate.

Cultural and vocational background He travelled in Europe, leaving England in 1715 and returning in late Oct 1717. He had been elected MP for Seaford in his absence.

NON-PARLIAMENTARY CAREER

Military service He served as a volunteer during the Jacobite rising in 1715. On 22 Jul 1715 he was made Captain of a troop of dragoons in Brigadier Dormer's regiment. He distinguished himself at the battle at Preston, Lancashire, where the rebels were defeated.

HONOURS

17 Apr 1746, Fellow of the Royal Society

CLUBS

White's

FINANCES

As a younger son he remained financially dependent on his elder brother Thomas, Duke of Newcastle, who gave him £1,000 annually until 1726, when Pelham married. He was a moderate man, who neither made a fortune nor incurred debt. He died poor.

Income He did not take full advantage of his position as Paymaster General, a normally lucrative post.

Spouse's finances His wife brought him a dowry of £30, 000, which enabled him to obtain the family estates in Lincolnshire. On his marriage his brother gave him half the family lands in Sussex.

Pensions His widow was granted an annual pension of £1,000

Legacies Inherited £5,000 on the death of his father in 1712.

ANECDOTES

'Mr. Pelham died in Mar, 1754; and our tranquility, both at home and abroad, expired with him. He had acquired the reputation of an able and honest minister, had a plain, solid understanding, improved by experience in business, as well as by a thorough knowledge of the world; and without being an orator, or having the finest parts, no man in the House of Commons argued with more weight, or was heard with greater attention.

'He was a frugal steward to the public, averse to continental extravagance and useless subsidies; preferring a tolerable peace to the most successful war; jealous to maintain his personal credit and authority; but nowise inattentive to the true interest of his country.' (Earl of Waldegrave. *Memoirs from 1754 to 1758*, 1821.)

'Mr Pelham is dead! All that calm, that supineness, of which I have lately talked to you so much is at an end! There is no heir to such luck as his. The whole people of England can never agree a second time upon the same person for the residence of infallibility.' (Toynbee, Mrs. P. ed. *Letters of Horace Walpole*, 1903.)

'His knowledge was rather useful than extensive; his understanding more solid than brilliant. His abilities did not burst forth with that splendor which has distinguished the opening career of many statesmen, but were gradually developed by experience and practice, and seemed to grow equal to the occasions by which they were called into action. He was slow and cautious in deciding, yet firm and persevering, when his resolution was once formed; though he knew the proper time and occasion to bend to popular prejudice, or public opinion. Instead of declining under the weight of years, his energies continued to increase; and, at no period did he better assume the spirit and authority of a great minister, than in that which immediately preceded his dissolution'. (Coxe, W. *Memoirs of the Administration of Henry Pelham*, 1829.)

QUOTATIONS

In April 1747 the House of Lords fined and imprisoned those that had published reports of their debates, despite a ban. When it was proposed that the Commons follow the same course, Pelham replied, 'Let them alone; they make better speeches for us than we can make for ourselves'.

RESIDENCES

Esher Place, Surrey. Only the old gatehouse, Wolsey's Tower, still stands.

Arlington St., Piccadilly, London.

MEMORIALS

PORTRAITS

c. 1751, by W. Hoare, National Portrait Gallery; *c.* 1752, by J. Shackleton, National Portrait Gallery

BIBLIOGRAPHIC INFORMATION

LETTERS AND PERSONAL PAPERS

Many letters are reprinted in Coxe. His correspondence with Lord Essex (1732–36) and with the Duke of Newcastle and others (1716–54) is in the British Museum.

The Pelham Papers, which Coxe used, are now lost. Some papers in the possession of the Duke of Newcastle are now in Nottingham University Library, others are in the possession of the Sussex Archaeological Society.

FURTHER READING

Coxe, W. *Memoirs of the Administration of Henry Pelham* 2 vols. London, 1829.

Lower, M.A. *Historical and Genealogical Notices of the Pelham Family*. London, 1873.

Nulle, S.H. *Thomas Pelham-Holles, Duke of Newcastle: His Early Political Career 1693–1724*. Philadelphia, 1931.

Owen, J.B. *The Rise of the Pelhams*. London, 1957.

Pelham, Mrs E.G. *and* McLean, D. *Some Early Pelhams*. Hove, Sussex, 1931.

Wilkes, J.W. *A Whig in Power: The Political Career of Henry Pelham*. Evanston, Ill., 1964.

J.S.

Bettmann

Duke of Newcastle

Lived 1693–1768

Political Party Whig

Prime Minister 16 March 1754–11 November 1756
29 June 1757–26 May 1762

Government Whig

Reigning Monarchs George II; George III

Vincit amor patriae The love of my country exceeds everything

NEWCASTLE AS PRIME MINISTER

Brother of Henry Pelham, his predecessor as PM, Newcastle was the first PM to spend his entire parliamentary career in the Lords, having taken his seat shortly after becoming 21. He was an influential election broker, controlling many constituencies, and his connection by marriage to the Marlboroughs further enhanced his influence. He was part of Walpole's inner group from 1722 and his power grew as Walpole's declined following the death of Queen Caroline in 1737. He championed Britain's entry into the war of the Austrian succession in 1741 despite Walpole's opposition. Newcastle took over as PM on Pelham's death in 1754. His first term was dominated by foreign affairs, including the beginning of a long military conflict around the world with France in the Seven Years War. Early reverses, such as Braddock's defeat at the Monongahela and the loss of Minorca, led to his resignation in 1756. He returned to office the following year, having secured Pitt's support. Newcastle's influence declined from 1760 with the accession of George III, and Pitt's resignation a year later. His final year as PM saw parliamentary battles over the financing of the war in Europe. Following his resignation in 1762, his influence declined as his allies deserted him or were purged from the Government, although he joined Rockingham's Government in 1765 as Lord Privy Seal.

PERSONAL INFORMATION

Names Thomas Pelham-Holles

He added the name of Holles in 1711 as required by the will of his uncle John Holles, who left him the bulk of his estates. In adult life he signed himself 'Holles-Newcastle.'

Peerages Baron Pelham of Laughton, Viscount Haughton; Earl of Clare 19 Oct 1714; Marquess of Clare, Duke of Newcastle upon Tyne 11 Aug 1715; Duke of Newcastle under Lyme 17 Nov 1756, Baron Pelham of Stanmer 4 May 1762

Nicknames Permis, in mockery of his sheepish way of prefacing what he said at court with the words 'Est-il permis?'; Hubble-Bubble, in reference to his fussing and his habit of hurrying everywhere.

Born 21 Jul 1693

Birthplace London

Religion Anglican

Ancestry English. He and his brother Henry Pelham (*q.v.*) came from a Norman family who settled in Hertfordshire and later acquired lands in Sussex, where they became established.

Date and place of marriage 2 Apr 1717, London

Age at marriage 23 years, 255 days

Years married 51 years, 229 days

First entered Parliament Became entitled to sit in the House of Lords on coming of age on 21 Jul 1714; took his seat on 1 Aug 1714

Dates appointed PM 1) 16 Mar 1754; 2) 29 Jun 1757

Age at appointment 1) 60 years, 238 days; 2) 63 years, 344 days

Dates ceased to be PM 1) 11 Nov 1756; 2) 26 May 1762

Total time as PM 1) 2 years, 240 days; 2) 4 years, 330 days; a total of 7 years, 205 days

Lived after last term as PM 6 years, 175 days

Date of death 17 Nov 1768

Place of death Newcastle House, Lincoln's Inn Fields, London

Age at death 75 years, 119 days

Place of funeral & burial Laughton, Sussex

Zodiac sign Cancer

FATHER

Thomas, 1st Baron Pelham

Date of birth 1653

Occupation MP East Grinstead 1678–79; Lewes 1679–1701; Sussex 1702–05

Dates of marriages 1) 26 Nov 1679, Elizabeth Jones (1664–81); 2) 21 May 1686, Lady Grace Holles

Date of death 23 Feb 1712

Place of burial Laughton, Sussex

MOTHER

Lady Grace Holles

Date of birth *c.* 1668

Date of marriage 21 May 1686

Date of death 13 Sep 1700

Place of burial Laughton, Sussex

BROTHERS AND SISTERS

Thomas Pelham was the elder of two sons and the eighth of eleven children.

From his father's first marriage:

Lucy, b. 1 Oct 1680; bur. 2 May 1689

Elizabeth, b. *c.* 7 Oct 1681; m. Charles, Viscount Townshend. (He later married Walpole's sister); d. 11 May 1711

From his father's second marriage:

Grace, b. 3 Apr 1687; m. George Naylor (MP Seaford 1706–10 and 1713–22); d. Apr 1710

Frances, b. Dec 1688; m. Christopher Wandesford, Viscount Castlecomer (MP Morpeth 1710–13, Ripon 1715–19); d. 27 Jun 1756

Mary, b. 31 Jan 1690; bur. 12 Dec 1702

Gertrude, b. 6 Jan 1691; m. David Polhill, (MP Kent 1710, Bramber 1723–27, Rochester 1727–41 and 1742–54)

John, bur. 18 Feb 1692

Lucy, b. 1692; m. Henry Clinton, 7th Earl of Lincoln (Lord of the Bedchamber 1714–27, Joint Paymaster General of the Forces 1715–20); d. 20 Jul 1736

Henry (*q.v.*), b. 25 Sep 1694; Prime Minister 1743–54; d. 6 Mar 1754

Margaret, b. 1696; m. Sir John Shelley (MP for Arundel 1727–41, Lewes 1743–47); d. 24 Nov 1758

WIFE

Lady Henrietta (Harriet) Godolphin

Date of birth *c.* 1701

Mother Henrietta Churchill, later Duchess of Marlborough

Father Francis, 2nd Earl of Godolphin

Father's occupation MP Helston 1701–08; Oxfordshire 1708–10; Tregony 1710–12. Cofferer of the Household, Warden of the Stannaries, Lord Lieutenant of Oxfordshire, Lord of the Bedchamber, Groom of the Stole, Privy Counsellor, Governor of the Scilly Isles, Lord Privy Seal.

Age at marriage about 16 years

Number of children None. Harriet became pregnant shortly after their marriage in 1717 but had a miscarriage, and never conceived again.

Date and place of death 17 Jul 1776, Twickenham Park, London

Place of burial Laughton, Sussex

Years younger than PM *c.* 8 years

Profile She enjoyed painting, sewing and music. She studied the harpsichord and played the guitar. She entertained and visited her friends, and indulged in gambling, of which she kept meticulous accounts although her losses were small. Like her husband she was a hypochondriac, and she regularly took the waters at Bath. She took little part in public life, but helped the Duke to keep accounts of his finances. She is said to have been plain, but her husband was apparently, and unfashionably, entirely faithful to her.

LIFE AND CAREER

PARLIAMENTARY ELECTIONS FOUGHT

None. He was a Peer. His extensive ownership of land in 11 counties enabled him to influence elections in many seats. He was also renowned for his lavish election parties at which he entertained local voters.

PARTY ACTIVITY

Membership of group or faction In 1763 he joined the Wildman's Club, a group of Opposition Whigs. He did not attend meetings very frequently.

PARLIAMENTARY AND MINISTERIAL EXPERIENCE

First Recorded Speech 14 Apr 1716 in favour of the Septennial Bill. (*Parl. Hist.* vol. 7, 1714–22, col 300)
Privy Counsellor 16 Apr 1717
Ministerial Offices Lord Chamberlain 14 Apr 1717–14 Apr 1724; Secretary of State, Southern Dept. 14 Apr 1724–6 Feb 1748; Secretary of State, Northern Dept 6 Feb 1748–Mar 1754; Leader of the House of Lords Feb 1748–Nov 1756, Jul 1757–26 May 1762; First Lord of the Treasury 16 Mar 1754–16 Nov 1756; 29 Jun 1757–26 May 1762; Lord Privy Seal 25 Aug 1765–30 Jul 1766.
Opposition Leader while PM William Pitt, Earl of Chatham (1754–56); There was no discernible Opposition during Newcastle's second administration.

GOVERNMENTS FORMED

First Administration 16 Mar 1754–11 Nov 1756

GENERAL ELECTION RESULT
APR 1754: Government Whigs 368; Tories 106; Opposition Whigs 42; Doubtful 26; Seats vacant 16. Total 558
Overall majority 194
CABINET
Prime Minister and First Lord of the Treasury Duke of Newcastle
Chancellor of the Exchequer H.B. Legge (1754–55); Sir G. Lyttleton (1755–56)
Secretary of State (Northern Department) Earl of Holdernesse
Secretary of State (Southern Department) Sir T. Robinson (1754–55); H. Fox (1755–56)
First Lord of the Admiralty Lord Anson
Lord President of the Council Earl Granville
Lord Privy Seal Lord Gower (1754–55; 1755–56); Duke of Marlborough (1755)
Lord Chancellor Earl of Hardwicke
Paymaster General W. Pitt (1754–55); Earl of Darlington and Viscount Dupplin (1755–56)

Second Administration 29 Jun 1757–26 May 1762

GENERAL ELECTION RESULT
MAR 1761: Not analysed
CABINET
Prime Minister and First Lord of the Treasury Duke of Newcastle
Chancellor of the Exchequer H.B. Legge (1757–61); Viscount Barrington (1761–62)
Secretary of State (Northern Department) Earl of Holdernesse (1757–61); Earl of Bute (1761–62)
Secretary of State (Southern Department) W. Pitt (1757–61); Earl of Egremont (1761–62)
First Lord of the Admiralty Lord Anson
Lord President of the Council Earl Granville
Lord Privy Seal Earl Temple (1757–61); Duke of Bedford (1761–62)
Lord Keeper of the Great Seal (afterwards *Lord Chancellor*) Lord Henley
Master General of the Ordnance Duke of Marlborough (1757–59); Lord Ligonier (1759–62)
Paymaster General H. Fox
President of the Board of Trade Earl of Halifax (1757–61); Lord Sandys (1761–62)
Chancellor of the Duchy of Lancaster Lord Edgecumbe (1757–58); Earl of Kinnoull (1758–62)
Treasurer of the Navy G. Grenville
Secretary at War Viscount Barrington (1757–61); C. Townshend (1761–62)
Lord Chamberlain Duke of Devonshire

IMPORTANT DATES IN PERSONAL AND POLITICAL LIFE

15 JUL 1711 Death of his uncle John Holles, Duke of Newcastle, who leaves him the bulk of his estate, providing that he change his name to Pelham-Holles, which he does.

23 FEB 1712 On the death of his father, he succeeds to the title of Baron Pelham of Laughton, with three guardians to guide him during his minority.

AUG 1713 First General Election at which he tries to exercise his power of patronage. His uncle's will leaving him the Yorkshire estates and the right to choose their MPs is disputed by his widowed aunt, and he fails to secure the election of his nominees.

13 JUL 1714 The protracted dispute over his uncle's will settled.

1 AUG 1714 Takes his seat in the House of Lords, shortly after coming of age.

19 OCT 1714 Created Viscount Haughton of Haughton, Nottinghamshire and Earl of Clare in Suffolk.

JAN–FEB 1715 The first successful operation of his power of patronage. He is said to have secured the election of fourteen Members of Parliament in the General Election.

11 AUG 1715 Created Marquess of Clare and Duke of Newcastle upon Tyne.

6 SEP 1715 Beginning of the Jacobite Rebellion. As Lord Lieutenant of Middlesex, Westminster and Nottinghamshire he is required to muster militia in each county.

14 APR 1716 In the debate on the Second Reading of the Septennial Bill, proposing that Parliaments should last for seven years instead of three, Newcastle speaks in favour because it is expensive to maintain his patronage of parliamentary seats.

2 APR 1717 Newcastle marries Lady Harriet Godolphin, daughter of the Duke of Marlborough. Association with the Marlboroughs brings him additional prestige and influence.

14 APR 1717 Appointed to his first ministerial office as Lord Chamberlain of the Household.

16 APR 1717 Sworn a Privy Counsellor.

28 NOV 1717 Becomes godfather to Prince George William, son of the Prince of Wales, at the King's invitation. The ensuing row between the King and the Prince, who was not consulted, culminates in the latter being banished to Leicester House, which becomes a focus for political opposition.

30 APR 1718 Installed as a Knight of the Garter at Windsor.

18 FEB 1719 A Private Act finally accomplishes the division of the property bequeathed to him by his uncle.

11 MAY 1719 The King goes to Hanover, leaving power in the hands of a commission of 13 Lord Justices, including Newcastle. This is the first of many occasions on which he holds this high office.

7 JUL 1721 Newcastle's debts are so bad (a total of £88, 572) that a Deed of Trust is established to manage their repayment.

MAR–APR 1722 The first General Election after the passing of the Septennial Act, one of the most corrupt. Newcastle lavishly entertains voters and influential people.

19 APR 1722 Death of the Earl of Sunderland, who had plotted against the Pelhams, advances Newcastle's career. He becomes part of the ruling group with Walpole and Townshend.

14 APR 1724 Succeeds Carteret as Secretary of State for the Southern Department in Walpole's Cabinet.

29 OCT 1726 Newcastle's brother Henry Pelham marries Lady Catherine Manners. Her dowry enables Henry to buy some of Newcastle's Lincolnshire estates for £30, 000. Newcastle also gives him some of the family's estates in Sussex.

20 NOV 1737 Death of Queen Caroline heralds the decline of Walpole's power and the rise of Newcastle's.

1738 Another Deed of Trust is necessary to pay his debts and to provide him with a current income.

13 FEB 1741 Speaks against Carteret's motion for the removal of Walpole, which is defeated.

1741 Britain enters the War of the Austrian Succession, representing triumph of Newcastle's policy over Walpole, who wanted to avoid war.

MAY 1741 Despite Newcastle's great patronage the General Election is a disaster for Walpole's ministry. The Whigs are split, and he has an overall majority of only 19.

OCT 1741 Threatens to resign over the ending of the war with Spain and the King's declaration of the neutrality of Hanover, which are contrary to his policy. His brother Henry Pelham and the Earl of Hardwicke persuade him to stay.

17 NOV 1741 The Pelham Family Settlement enables lands that had been entailed under his uncle's will to be sold to pay off his debts.

11 FEB 1742 Walpole resigns. Newcastle helps to form the Wilmington administration and continues to serve as Secretary of State for the Southern Department.

25 MAY 1742 Newcastle speaks strongly against the Bill to indemnify those who might give evidence to the inquiry into Walpole's conduct, arguing that it is contrary to natural justice. He finds himself in agreement with Carteret.

25 AUG 1743 His brother Henry Pelham becomes Prime Minister. They are close friends and consult each other frequently, although they do not always agree.

24 NOV 1744 Newcastle and Pelham complain to the King about Carteret's conduct of foreign policy, leading to his resignation. This greatly increases the Pelhams' importance.

11 FEB 1746 Newcastle and Pelham and most of the Cabinet resign in protest at the King's plans to ask Carteret to form a ministry. Carteret tries to do so but fails, and Pelham's ministry resumes office three days later.

20 JUN 1747 Pelham outmanoeuvres his opponents by calling a General Election a year earlier than the Septennial Act requires. Newcastle's influence helps to elect 15 MPs, and the ministry is returned with a majority of 144.

NOV 1750 Newcastle tries to persuade Pelham to get rid of the Duke of Bedford, but Pelham refuses, fearing it will drive Bedford into the arms of the Opposition: one of the brothers' most serious disputes.

14 JUN 1751 The Duke of Bedford is dismissed, and as Pelham has predicted, he becomes a focus for the forces of opposition. The reshuffle also brings back his old adversary Carteret (Earl Granville) as Lord President of the Council, a post he continues to hold when Newcastle becomes Prime Minister.

6 MAR 1754 The sudden death of his brother Henry Pelham comes as a great shock.

16 MAR 1754 Becomes Prime Minister.

APR–MAY 1754 His brother's unexpected death on the eve of the General Election leaves Newcastle no choice but to carry out his brother's plans, which are well advanced. The Government secures a majority of 194.

MAY 1754 French aggression against Britain in the American colonies causes alarm. Newcastle cannot decide what to do, but eventually sends troops to defend British interests.

JUL 1754 The French victory over Washington in Ohio forces the British to take action.

MAY 1755 Despite peace negotiations, French reinforcements arrive in North America, resulting in the escalation of hostilities between Britain and France.

30 SEP 1755 Britain concludes a treaty with Russia to provide support if Hanover is attacked.

16 JAN 1756 Convention of Westminster, a treaty with Prussia to oppose attacks in Germany. This bilateral action demonstrates Newcastle's sole preoccupation with British interests and his failure to understand how other countries will react.

18 MAY 1756 Britain declares war on France, thus beginning the Seven Years' War. France has also landed on Minorca, challenging Britain there as well as in the American colonies. Britain sends a fleet under Admiral Byng, but the loss of Minorca is felt as a national humiliation for which Newcastle is blamed. A weak and insecure leader, Newcastle tries to put the blame on others, but largely fails.

20 JUN 1756 An incident known as the 'Black Hole of Calcutta' occurs in India when the Nawab of Bengal attacks Calcutta and imprisons 146 people in a narrow cell on a very hot night. Only 23 survive. This is seen as a further foreign humiliation.

SEP 1756 On a visit to Lady Catherine Pelham at Greenwich he is attacked by an angry mob and forced to take refuge in the Greenwich Observatory.

13 OCT 1756 Fox resigns following bitter criticism in the House of Commons of the conduct of the war.

20 OCT 1756 Newcastle reluctantly tells the King that he is prepared to resign, having failed to persuade Pitt to join the Government.

11 NOV 1756 Newcastle resigns, leaving Pitt to form a new administration with the Duke of Devonshire at its head.

13 NOV 1756 Created Duke of Newcastle under Lyme. To ensure the survival of the Newcastle name he devises a remainder to his nephew, the 9th Earl of Lincoln.

5 APR 1757 The King decides to dismiss Pitt, and invites Newcastle to form an administration. Newcastle, however, refuses to serve without the support of the Prince of Wales and his followers, including Pitt.

3 MAY 1757 A House of Commons Committee of Inquiry into the loss of Minorca concludes that all the appropriate orders had been given, thus clearing Newcastle's name.

29 JUN 1757 Newcastle returns to office as Prime Minister for the second time, having succeeded in obtaining Pitt's support. Pitt becomes Secretary of State for the Southern Department.

26 JUL 1757 The French invade Hanover. The Duke of Cumberland is defeated at Hastenbeck and signs the

IMPORTANT DATES IN PERSONAL AND POLITICAL LIFE—*Continued*

Convention of Klosterseven, which removes Hanover from the war.

11 APR 1758 Britain signs a treaty with Prussia which provides for the payment of an annual subsidy. This subsidy becomes increasingly unpopular.

2 JUN 1758 Pitt's Bill to liberalise the law of habeas corpus rejected by the House of Lords. Pitt furious with Newcastle, who had supported the peers' action.

13 SEP 1759 Wolfe's victory at Quebec over the French settles Canada's fate. Towards the end of the year Holdernesse informs Pitt that Newcastle is meddling in diplomacy behind his back. Pitt rebukes Newcastle severely and removes his contact, Joseph Yorke, from the negotiations between Britain and France.

31 JUL 1760 Hanover regained by the victory at Warburg.

25 OCT 1760 Death of George II. George III does not trust Newcastle. His favourite is the Earl of Bute, whose rise in power is matched by the decline of Pitt's and Newcastle's.

DEC 1760 The King warns Newcastle that he cannot use public money to influence voters in the impending General Election. Newcastle uses his own money, unaware that the Earl of Bute is able to use the King's money to strengthen his own support.

JAN 1761 Newcastle is pleased with the outcome of the General Election, despite the financial restrictions. He estimates his supporters number 291, his opponents 108 and other doubtfuls 113, but he underestimates the forces that are gathering to oppose him.

MAR 1761 Legge opposes the payment of the annual subsidy to Prussia. Newcastle has him replaced by Lord Barrington. He also acquiesces in the replacement of Holdernesse by Bute as Secretary of State for the Northern Department, a move which allows his rival to further his political ambitions.

5 OCT 1761 Pitt resigns, unable to persuade his colleagues of the necessity of declaring war on Spain. His departure further reduces Newcastle's influence.

DEC 1761 War declared with Spain.

APR 1762 Newcastle yields to pressure not to renew the Prussian subsidy.

3 MAY 1762 He tries to persuade the King of the need to raise £2 million for the war effort in Europe, but the King states that £1 million is enough.

4 MAY 1762 Created Baron Pelham of Stanmer.

5 MAY 1762 Prussia and Russia sign a peace treaty which signals the ending of the Seven Years' War.

7 MAY 1762 Faced with opposition from some of his Treasury colleagues to his proposal to raise £2 million, he reluctantly accepts the plan for £1 million and announces his intention to resign.

26 MAY 1762 Newcastle finally hands over the seals of his office. He refuses the offer of a pension, saying that it has been an honour to serve the Royal Family.

31 OCT 1762 The King dismisses the Duke of Devonshire from his post as Lord Chamberlain, in the belief that he is acting under Newcastle's influence. Newcastle is outraged and presses his supporters in office to resign, which some of them do. Fox retaliates by dismissing all those who owe their position to the Pelhams. This becomes known as the 'purge of the Pelhamite innocents.'

23 DEC 1762 Newcastle is further humiliated by being stripped of all his Lord Lieutenancies and honorary offices.

MAR 1763 Newcastle makes an agreement with Pitt to act together to oppose Bute.

6 MAR 1764 Death of his great friend Lord Hardwicke. As a consequence he becomes more moderate in his opposition.

2 OCT 1764 Death of the Duke of Devonshire, another good friend and political adviser. At about this time, Pitt breaks off his agreement with Newcastle, making him increasingly isolated.

22 MAR 1765 The Stamp Act passed to impose a tax on the American colonies. Newcastle predicts it will cause discontent.

30 JUN 1765 Whig leaders meet at Claremont and vote to try to form an administration, even without Pitt.

15 JUL 1765 Appointed Lord Privy Seal in the new Rockingham ministry. He is also given responsibility for ecclesiastical appointments. He hopes to be consulted as an elder statesman but Rockingham tends to follow the advice of his younger Cabinet colleagues. He is restored as Lord Lieutenant of Nottinghamshire and Steward of Sherwood Forest.

8 JAN 1766 He offers to resign if that will enable Pitt to join the ministry, but to his relief he is not asked to do so.

11 MAR 1766 Newcastle gives one of his best parliamentary performances in the debate on the repeal of the Stamp Act and its concomitant Bill on the right of Parliament to legislate for the colonies.

30 JUL 1766 A loss of Royal support for the ministry causes a general lack of confidence, and Newcastle resigns as Lord Privy Seal. The King offers him a pension of £4,000 p.a., but he proudly refuses. He remains keenly interested in politics and often speaks in the House of Lords.

DEC 1767 Suffering from a persistent cold and cough he decides to go to Bath with his wife to take the waters. Feeling no better, however, he returns to Claremont, but his condition worsens. He has probably suffered a stroke.

APR 1768 He recovers a little in the early part of the year but his political strength is waning, and he can only help the return of seven MPs in the General Election.

17 NOV 1768 He collapses and dies shortly afterwards.

BACKGROUND

PHYSICAL CHARACTERISTICS AND HEALTH

Newcastle was taller than average. He had a high forehead, dark grey eyes and a hooked nose. He usually wore court dress and the blue ribbon of a Knight of the Garter. He was a hypochondriac, worrying constantly about his health. He employed his own apothecary. He had an aversion to unaired beds. He had a tendency to over-indulge in eating and drinking at the banquets and parties he often gave. He wore pince-nez glasses and in later life he lost his teeth. In 1767 he suffered a stroke from which he never fully recovered.

EDUCATION

Primary With his brother Henry Pelham he began his education under the private instruction of a resident tutor, Richard Newton, who later became famous as the Principal of Hart Hall, Oxford, and as an educational reformer.
Secondary Westminster School, London.
University Clare Hall, Cambridge. He matriculated in 1710, but did not graduate.
Qualifications He studied Classics. In later life as Chancellor of Cambridge University he established two annual Chancellor's Medals to encourage classical literature, which were awarded from 1752 to 1765.
Languages French.

NON-PARLIAMENTARY CAREER

Other posts 1714–62, Lord Lieutenant of Nottingham, Middlesex and Westminster; Steward of Sherwood Forest and Folewood Park; 1715, Vice Admiral of the coast of Sussex; 1737, High Steward of Cambridge University; 1749, Chancellor of Cambridge University; 1760, Lord Lieutenant of Sussex; 1765, Lord Lieutenant of Nottingham, Steward of Sherwood Forest, and Recorder of Nottingham.

HONOURS

Freedom of cities 1760, Bristol
Academic 1728, LLD from Cambridge; 1749, Chancellor of Cambridge University
Other than peerage Mar 1718, Knight of the Garter; 26 Oct 1749, Fellow of the Royal Society

CLUBS

Hanover Club (founder member, 1713); Kit-Cat Club; White's

HOBBIES AND SPORTS

He liked music and went to the opera. He was a patron of the arts, including at one time Richard Steele, founder of the *Tatler* and the *Spectator*. He wrote poetry (none survives) and built up libraries at Newcastle House and Claremont. He took an interest in the gardens at Claremont, where he grew melons and pineapples. He employed a French chef there, and was overly fond of food and drink, indulging especially at his election parties. He also enjoyed hunting and shooting.

FINANCES

All Newcastle's inheritances were free of debt, but he spent recklessly to support his grand ducal lifestyle. He entertained lavishly and spent generously at election times in the pursuit of political advantage. He was not, however, corrupt and never enriched himself at the public's expense.
Income Lord Chamberlain of the Household £1,200 p.a.; Secretary of State, Southern Department £5,780 p.a.; First Lord of theTreasury £5,680 p.a.; Lord Privy Seal £2,600 p.a.
Spouse's finances His wife brought a dowry of £22,000, which was paid by the Duchess of Marlborough. He agreed to pay her an annuity of £1,400.
Pensions In 1766 the King offered him a pension of £4, 000 p.a. but he refused it.
Legacies In July 1711 Newcastle inherited the bulk of the vast estate of his uncle John Holles, Duke of Newcastle, which was valued at between £25,000 and £40,000 a year. His uncle's widow and his cousin Harriet contested the will, and after much litigation an arbitrator was appointed. The settlement gave Harriet the whole of the Cavendish estate. He got lands worth £20,000 and was exempted from paying Harriet her portion of £20,000. His aunt lost her case, but the settlement was not agreed until 13 Jul 1714 and the delay caused him financial problems.
On the death of his father in 1712 he inherited the Pelham estates in Sussex, with their annual rent-roll of £4,000 and timber resources later valued at £9,000.
Debts He was constantly in debt. In 1720 he lost about £6,000 in financial speculation on shares in the South Sea Bubble. In 1721 his total debts were estimated at £88,572, and a Deed of Trust was established to pay them off. However, his heavy expenses in the General Election of 1722 plunged him deeper into debt. By 1734 his debts amounted to £137,000. In 1738 another Deed of Trust was set up to pay his debts and to provide him with an income. His gross annual income from land was about £27,000. In 1751 Claremont was mortgaged. On his death his debts amounted to £114,000.
Will He made his will on 29 Feb 1768. It provided that all his just debts should be paid. The Sussex estates were left to Thomas Pelham, and everything else to the Duchess.

ANECDOTES

'He was a Secretary of State without intelligence, a Duke without money, a man of infinite intrigue, without secrecy or policy, and a Minister despised and hated by his master, by all parties and Ministers, without being turned out by any.' (Horace Walpole. *Memoirs of the Reign of George II* Ed. Lord Holland, 1846. vol. 1, p. 166.)

'The public put him below his level: for though he had no superior parts, nor eminent talents, he had a most indefatigable industry, a perseverance, a court craft, and a servile compliance with the will of his sovereign for the time being.' (Lord Chesterfield, cited by Sir Lewis Namier. *England in the Age of the American Revolution*. 2nd ed. 1961 p. 7.)

QUOTATIONS

I shall not, therefore, think the demands of the people a rule of conduct, nor shall ever fear to incur their resentment in the prosecution of their interest. I shall never flatter their passions to obtain their favour, or gratify their revenge for fear of their contempt. (*Parl. Hist.* vol 12, 1741–43 col. 699)

We know that the brightest character may easily be darkened by calumny. (*loc. cit.*)

RESIDENCES

He inherited land and property in eleven counties, but his main residences were:
Newcastle House, Lincoln's Inn Fields, London
Halland House, Sussex
Bishopstone Place, Seaford, Sussex
Claremont House, Esher, Surrey
Nottingham Castle

MEMORIALS

PORTRAITS

c. 1721, by Sir Godfrey Kneller, National Portrait Gallery; *c.* 1752, by William Hoare, National Portrait Gallery

BIBLIOGRAPHIC INFORMATION

LETTERS AND PERSONAL PAPERS

Newcastle's letters can be found in the following sources:

Coxe, W. *Memoirs of the Administration of Henry Pelham.* 2 vols. London, 1829.
Bateson, M. *A Narrative of the Changes in the Ministry 1765–67.* London, 1898.
Lodge, R. *The Private Correspondence of Chesterfield and Newcastle, 1744–1746.* London, 1930.
Yorke, P.C. *The Life and Correspondence of Philip Yorke, Earl of Hardwicke.* 3 vols. Cambridge, 1913.
McCann, T.J. *The Correspondence of the Dukes of Richmond and Newcastle 1724–1750.* Lewes, 1984.

Most of the Newcastle papers are in the British Library; there are also some in the University of Nottingham Library.

FURTHER READING

Browning, R. *The Duke of Newcastle.* New Haven, 1975.
Kelch, R.A. *Newcastle: A Duke without Money.* London, 1974.
Lower, M.A. *Historical and Genealogical Notices of the Pelham Family.* London, 1873.
Nulle, S.H. *Thomas Pelham-Holles, Duke of Newcastle: His Early Political Career 1693–1724.* Philadelphia, 1931.
Turberville, A.S. *The House of Lords in the XVIIIth Century.* Oxford, 1927.
Williams, B. *Carteret and Newcastle.* London, 1966.

J.S.

Bettmann

Duke of Devonshire

Lived 1720–1764
Political Party Whig
Prime Minister 16 November 1756–29 June 1757
Government Whig
Reigning Monarch George II

Cavendo tutus (a play on the name Cavendish) Safe by being cautious

---

DEVONSHIRE AS PRIME MINISTER

William Cavendish was an MP for 10 years before entering the House of Lords as Lord Cavendish in 1751. He became a minister almost immediately, and was a successful Lord Lieutenant and Governor-General of Ireland. George II asked Devonshire to form a ministry following Newcastle's resignation in 1756, although in reality Pitt dominated the political scene. Devonshire's brief period in office was notable for the court martial of Admiral Byng for his failure to relieve Minorca, and for difficulties with the Duke of Cumberland over the defence of Hanover. The latter dispute provoked a political crisis in early 1757 leading to the reconstitution of the Government, with Newcastle replacing Devonshire as Prime Minister. Devonshire remained in the Government as Lord Chamberlain, but the influence of Bute and the Tories increased as that of Newcastle and Devonshire declined. When Devonshire refused to attend Privy Council meetings following Bute's appointment as PM, George III dismissed him from ministerial office and from the Privy Council.

PERSONAL INFORMATION

Names William Cavendish
Peerages Marquess of Hartington; Lord Cavendish of Hardwick; 4th Duke of Devonshire
Born 1720
Religion Anglican
Ancestry English. He came from a noble family of wealthy Whigs who had helped to establish the House of Hanover on the British throne.
Date and place of marriage 27 Mar 1748, Lady Burlington's House, Pall Mall, St. James's, London
Age at marriage c. 28 years
Years married 6 years, 256 days
First entered Parliament 19 May 1741
Date appointed PM 16 Nov 1756
Age at appointment c. 36 years
Date ceased to be PM 29 Jun 1757
Total time as PM 225 days
Ceased to be MP 13 Jun 1751
Lived after last term as PM 7 years, 95 days
Date of death 2 Oct 1764
Place of death Spa, Germany
Age at death c. 44 years
Place of burial All Saints' Church, Derby

FATHER

William Cavendish, 3rd Duke of Devonshire
Date of birth 26 Sep 1698
Occupation MP Lostwithiel 1721–24, Grampound 1724–27, Huntingdonshire 1727–29; Lord President of the Council; Lord Privy Seal; Lord Steward of the Household; Lord Lieutenant of Ireland
Date of marriage 27 Mar 1718
Date of death 5 Dec 1755
Place of burial All Saints' Church, Derby

MOTHER

Catherine Hoskins
Date of birth c. 1698
Profile The daughter of a Surrey squire, she did not share her husband's privileged background. Nevertheless she was a gay and convivial companion, providing a happy home life.
Date of marriage 27 Mar 1718
Age when PM took office c. 58 years
Date of death 8 May 1777
Place of burial All Saints' Church, Derby

BROTHERS AND SISTERS

Devonshire was the eldest son and second of seven children.

Caroline (Countess of Bessborough), b. 22 May 1719; m. William Ponsonby, Viscount Duncannon and Earl of Bessborough (MP Newtownards 1725–27; Co. Kilkenny 1727–28; Derby 1742–54; Saltash 1754–56; Harwich 1756–58); d. 20 Jan 1760
Elizabeth, b. 24 Apr 1723; m. John Ponsonby, brother of William, Earl of Bessborough (MP Newtown, Co. Down, 1739–42; Speaker of the Irish House of Commons)
Rachel, b. 7 Jun 1727; m. Horatio Walpole, 2nd Baron Walpole of Wolterton (Sir Robert Walpole's nephew); d. 7 May 1805
George Augustus, b. 8 Apr 1728; unm.; MP Weymouth and Melcombe Regis 1751–54; Derbyshire 1754–80, 1781–94; Comptroller of the Household 1761–62; Privy Counsellor 1762; d. 2 May 1794
Frederick, b. 17 Aug 1729; unm.; Field Marshall and Colonel 34th Foot; MP Derbyshire 1751–54; Derby 1754–80; d. 21 Oct 1803
John, b. 22 Oct 1732; unm.; MP Weymouth and Melcombe Regis 1754–61; Knaresborough 1761–68; York 1768–84; Derbyshire 1794–96; Lord of the Treasury 1765–66; Privy Counsellor 1782; Chancellor of the Exchequer 1782, 1783; d. 18 Nov 1796

WIFE

Charlotte Elizabeth Boyle, Baroness Clifford
Date and place of birth 27 Oct 1731, Chiswick, Middlesex
Mother Lady Dorothy Savile
Father Richard Boyle, 3rd Earl of Burlington, 4th Baron Clifford, 4th Earl of Cork
Father's occupation Peer
Age at marriage 16 years, 152 days
Number of children 4
Date and place of death 8 Dec 1754, Uppingham, Rutland
Place of burial All Saints' Church, Derby
Years younger than PM c. 11 years

CHILDREN

3 sons, 1 daughter
William (Lord Clifford), b. 14 Dec 1748; m. 1) 5 Jun 1774, Georgiana Spencer (1757–1806); 2) 19 Oct 1809, Mrs. Elizabeth Foster; Lord High Treasurer of Ireland; Governor of County Cork; an army colonel; Lord Lieutenant of Derbyshire; KG, DCL; d. 29 Jul 1811
Dorothy, b. 27 Aug 1750; m. 8 Nov 1766, William Cavendish-Bentinck, 3rd Duke of Portland (*q.v.*); d. 3 Jun 1794
Richard, b. 19 Jun 1752; unm.; MP Lancaster 1773–80, Derbyshire 1780–81; d. 7 Sep 1781
George Augustus Henry (Earl of Burlington), b. 31 Mar 1754; m. 27 Feb 1782, Lady Elizabeth Compton; MP Knaresborough 1775–80, Derby 1780–96, Derbyshire 1797–1831; d. 4 May 1834

LIFE AND CAREER

PARLIAMENTARY ELECTIONS FOUGHT

*(*designates candidate elected)*

DATE Apr 1741. General Election
CONSTITUENCY Derbyshire
RESULT William Cavendish* (Whig); Sir Nathaniel Curzon* (Tory)

DATE Jun 1747. General Election
CONSTITUENCY Derbyshire
RESULT William Cavendish* (Whig); Sir Nathaniel Curzon* (Tory)

PARLIAMENTARY AND MINISTERIAL EXPERIENCE

Maiden Speech On 16 Nov 1742 he moved the Address on the King's Speech (*Parl. Hist.* vol 12, 1741–43, col. 853)

Privy Counsellor Sworn 12 Jul 1751; dismissed 3 Nov 1762; appointed Privy Counsellor in Ireland 4 Jul 1761 but not sworn

Ministerial Offices Master of the Horse Jul 1751–55; Lord Treasurer of Ireland 2 Mar 1754–2 Oct 1764; First Lord of the Treasury and Leader of the House of Lords 16 Nov 1756–29 Jun 1757; Lord Chamberlain of the Household May 1757–31 Oct 1762

GOVERNMENTS FORMED

Administration 16 Nov 1756–29 Jun 1757

GENERAL ELECTION RESULT

APR 1754: Government Whigs 368; Tories 106; Opposition Whigs 42; Doubtful 26; Seats vacant 16. Total 558.
Overall majority 194

CABINET

Prime Minister and First Lord of the Treasury Duke of Devonshire

Chancellor of the Exchequer H.B. Legge (1756–57); Lord Mansfield (1757)

Secretary of State (Northern Department) Earl of Holdernesse

Secretary of State (Southern Department) W. Pitt

First Lord of the Admiralty Earl Temple (1756–57); Earl of Winchilsea (1757)

Lord President of the Council Earl Granville

Lord Privy Seal Earl Gower

Paymaster General Earl of Darlington; Viscount Dupplin

Secretary at War Viscount Barrington

Treasurer of the Navy G. Grenville

IMPORTANT DATES IN PERSONAL AND POLITICAL LIFE

19 MAY 1741 Elected MP for the first time for Derbyshire

16 NOV 1742 Moves the loyal address of the House of Commons in reply to the King's Speech at the opening of Parliament.

27 MAR 1748 Marries Lady Charlotte Elizabeth Boyle, daughter and heiress of the 3rd Earl of Burlington. Devonshire's marriage brings him extensive estates in England and Ireland and greatly increases his political influence.

13 JUN 1751 Succeeds to his father's barony as Lord Cavendish of Hardwicke. His brother Frederick succeeds him as MP for Derbyshire, and his brother George Augustus also enters Parliament as MP for Weymouth & Melcombe Regis.

JUL 1751 Appointed to his first ministerial post as Master of the Horse.

12 JUL 1751 Sworn a Privy Counsellor

2 MAR 1754 Appointed Lord Treasurer of Ireland

8 DEC 1754 His wife dies of smallpox.

27 MAR 1755 Appointed Lord Lieutenant and Governor-General of Ireland, where he is a popular and able administrator.

5 DEC 1755 His father dies and he succeeds to the title as 4th Duke of Devonshire.

MAY 1756 Devonshire returns from Ireland.

13 OCT 1756 In the furore over the loss of Minorca, his friend Henry Fox resigns as Secretary of State for the Southern Department, making Newcastle's position as Prime Minister very precarious and he tells the King that he can no longer carry on.

28 OCT 1756 The King asks Devonshire to form a ministry.

11 NOV 1756 Newcastle resigns.

16 NOV 1756 Devonshire appointed First Lord of the Treasury and thus becomes Prime Minister.

18 NOV 1756 Made a Knight of the Garter.

2 DEC 1756 Parliament meets to hear the King's Speech, which had been written by Pitt. Pitt himself is confined to his bedchamber with gout, and very little business is transacted in the House.

16 DEC 1756 Cabinet discusses sending troops to America. Pitt's target is to have 17,000 men there by April.

28 DEC 1756 Start of the trial of Admiral Byng on charges that he failed in his duty to relieve Minorca.

27 JAN 1757 Byng's court martial ends, and two days later death sentence is pronounced, although the judges recommend clemency because they believe him guilty of an error of judgement rather than cowardice.

17 FEB 1757 Pitt makes his first appearance in the House as Minister to convey a message from the King asking for money to subsidise Hanover. House agrees to send troops for its protection under the command of the Duke of Cumberland.

28 FEB 1757 Court Martial Bill passes its stages in the House of Commons and is sent to the House of Lords. Its purpose is to allow the judges who had participated in the court martial of Admiral Byng to ignore their oaths of secrecy and explain what their sentence means. The House of Lords examines the judges and concludes there has been no malpractice. Byng's execution, which had been postponed to allow Parliament to consider the Bill, is fixed for 14th Mar.

14 MAR 1757 Admiral Byng shot at Portsmouth. Pitt's efforts to save him had angered the King.

6 APR 1757 Cumberland refuses to take up his command in Germany while Pitt is in office, so the King decides to dismiss Pitt, whom he had always disliked. Legge, Grenville and several others resign in protest, and there is no effective government for almost two months.

16 JUN 1757 The Earl of Hardwicke summons a conference with Pitt, the Duke of Newcastle and the Earl of Bute to try to form a new ministry. Pitt finally drops his opposition to working with the Duke of Newcastle, and after much negotiation all the offices in a new ministry are agreed, with the Duke of Newcastle at their head.

29 JUN 1757 The new ministry kisses hands. Devonshire, who had been more of a figurehead than an active leader, agrees to stay in the Cabinet as Lord Chamberlain.

25 OCT 1760 George II dies. The new King distrusts the Duke of Newcastle, and favours the Earl of Bute.

27 OCT 1760 At a Privy Council meeting, Devonshire persuads Newcastle not to retire and continues to support him.

25 MAR 1761 Earl of Bute made Secretary of State for the Northern Department. His political power increases at the expense of that of Devonshire and Newcastle.

22 SEP 1761 Devonshire's son William is one of the six eldest sons of peers chosen to support the King's train at the Coronation.

26 MAY 1762 Newcastle resigns and Bute becomes Prime Minister. Devonshire declines to attend meetings of the Privy Council.

IMPORTANT DATES IN PERSONAL AND POLITICAL LIFE—*Continued*

OCT 1762 The King summons Devonshire to a Cabinet Council to discuss the peace terms with Spain, but he refuses to attend. The King dismisses him from his post as Lord Chamberlain on the 31st.

3 NOV 1762 The King personally erases Devonshire's name from the list of Privy Counsellors.

23 DEC 1762 The King dismisses the Dukes of Newcastle and Grafton and Lord Rockingham from their Lord Lieutenancies as part of his purge of the Whigs.

30 DEC 1762 Devonshire resigns from his Lord Lieutenancy in protest at the treatment of his friends.

AUG 1764 His health deteriorates, and he goes to take the waters at Spa in Germany

2 OCT 1764 Devonshire dies in Spa.

BACKGROUND

PHYSICAL CHARACTERISTICS AND HEALTH

Devonshire was tall, with a long narrow face and a fresh complexion. He was considered to be one of the best-looking young men in London. Towards the end of his life he was in poor health. He had a fever in 1761 which left him weak and unable to attend Privy Council meetings in May and June. He fell ill again in February 1762. He suffered from palsy. He had tried the waters at Bath, but to no avail. In 1764 he suffered a stroke and went to Spa in Germany to recuperate, where he died on 2 October at the comparatively young age of 44.

He was charming, polite and affable. Garrick spoke of his 'great prudery in dress and detestation of approaching within a mile of the *bon ton*'.

EDUCATION

Secondary As nothing seems to be known about Devonshire's education, he is assumed to have had private tuition.

Cultural and vocational background Devonshire travelled in Europe for some time before his election in 1741.

NON-PARLIAMENTARY CAREER

Military service In the 1745 Jacobite rebellion Devonshire and Sir Nathaniel Curzon, who were the MPs for Derbyshire, became colonels of two companies, each with 600 volunteers.

Other posts 1754–64, Governor of County Cork; 1755–56, Lord Lieutenant and Governor General of Ireland; 1755–62, Lord Lieutenant of Derbyshire; 1760, Governor of St. Bartholomew's Hospital, London.

HONOURS

Other than peerage 18 Nov 1756, Knight of the Garter; 12 Nov 1761, Fellow of the Royal Society; 9 Dec 1762, Fellow of the Society of Arts

CLUBS

White's; Jockey Club (founder member)

HOBBIES AND SPORTS

Devonshire was one of the founders of the Jockey Club and won a Jockey Club Plate in 1754 while he was Master of the Horse.

FINANCES

Devonshire came from a very wealthy family, but the extent of his fortune is not known.

Spouse's finances His wife, Lady Charlotte Boyle, brought to the marriage immense estates in Yorkshire, Derbyshire, Ireland and London, including Bolton Abbey and Burlington House, Piccadilly.

Will His son William inherited a fortune which amounted to some £35,000 p.a.

ANECDOTES

'I do not know any man so fitted to make a wife happy: with so great a vocation for matrimony, that I verily believe if it had not been established before his time, he would have had the glory of the invention.' (Lady Mary Montagu, writing in 1748.)

'Lord Hartington and his father the Duke of Devonshire were the fashionable models of goodness, though their chief merit was a habit of caution. The Duke outside was unpolished; his inside was unpolishable.' (Horace Walpole. *Memoirs of the reign of George II.*)

QUOTATIONS

2 Nov 1760, Every King must make use of human means to attain human ends or his affairs will go to ruin. (*Devonshire Diary* p. 52)

22 Apr 1761, I thought it absolutely necessary that . . . the King's servants should all appear of one mind, for nothing would so much retard the making or prejudice the peace itself as our enemie's (sic) perceiving that we were not agreed among ourselves. (*Devonshire Diary*, p. 94)

RESIDENCES

He owned many great houses, the most important being his main home, *Chatsworth House*, Derbyshire.

He also owned:

Bolton Abbey, Yorkshire

Lismore Castle, County Waterford, Ireland

Chiswick House, Middlesex

Burlington House, Piccadilly, London

Open to the public

Chatsworth House. It was one of the first stately homes to be officially opened to the public. Devonshire employed Capability Brown to landscape the gardens at a cost of £40,000.

The gardens of *Lismore Castle*, County Waterford, Ireland, are also open to the public.

MEMORIALS

PORTRAITS

1741, by William Hogarth (Yale Center for British Art, New Haven, Connecticut, USA)

OTHER MEMORIALS

Cavendish, Vermont, was named after him.

BIBLIOGRAPHIC INFORMATION

LETTERS AND PERSONAL PAPERS

Devonshire's political correspondence is in the Devonshire collection at Chatsworth House. His 'Memoranda on State of Affairs,' covering 1759–62, are published in *The Devonshire Diary (see below).*

FURTHER READING

Bickley, F. *The Cavendish Family.* London, 1911.
Brown, P.D. and Schweizer, K.W. *The Devonshire Diary.* London, 1982. (Camden Society, Fourth series vol. 27).
Cox, J. C. *Three Centuries of Derbyshire Annals.* 2 vols. London, 1890.
Cox, J. Charles and Hope, W.H. St. John. *The Chronicles of the Collegiate Church or Free Chapel of All Saints, Derby.* London, 1881.
Grove, J. *The Lives of All the Earls and Dukes of Devonshire.* London, 1764.
Pearson, J. *Stags and Serpents: The Story of the House of Cavendish and the Dukes of Devonshire.* London, 1983.

J.S.

Bettmann

Earl of Bute

Lived 1713–1792
Political Party Tory
Prime Minister 26 May 1762–8 April 1763
Government Tory
Reigning Monarch George III

Avito viret honore He flourishes through the honour of his ancestors

---

BUTE AS PRIME MINISTER

The first Scottish-born British Prime Minister—and the first Tory to hold that office—Bute sat in the House of Lords as an elected Scottish representative peer over a period of 43 years, (with a 20 year gap from 1741 to 1761). When he became tutor to the future George III, it proved to be the foundation of his political career. A series of royal appointments followed. In May 1762, he was appointed First Lord of the Treasury in succession to Newcastle. During his brief administration, Bute obtained parliamentary approval for the 1763 Treaty of Paris, which ended the Seven Years War and confirmed Great Britain's expanded colonial possessions in Canada, the West Indies, and India. He then resigned from office as he had promised when appointed. However, he continued to interfere in the affairs of his successor, George Grenville, and to act as George III's advisor, although he failed to have Grenville ousted. The King's removal in 1765 of Bute's brother from a Scottish office at Grenville's instigation ended Bute's royal advisory role.

PERSONAL INFORMATION

Names John Stuart
Peerages 3rd Earl of Bute
Nicknames John Thistle; Jack Boot (a pun on his name). The jackboot and the petticoat, symbolising Bute and his alleged paramour Princess Augusta were often burned during riots.
Born 25 May 1713
Birthplace Parliament Square, Edinburgh
Religion Episcopalian
Ancestry Scottish. His family traced their ancestry from King Robert II, who appointed his son, Sir John Stewart, as Sheriff of Bute in 1385. The island of Bute is still the family seat.
Date of marriage 24 Aug 1736
Age at marriage 23 years, 91 days
Years married 55 years, 199 days
First entered Parliament Elected a Scottish Representative Peer on 14 Apr 1737 and took his seat in the House of Lords on 24 Jan 1738.
Date appointed PM 26 May 1762
Age at appointment 49 years, 1 day
Date ceased to be PM 8 Apr 1763
Total time as PM 317 days
Ceased to be an elected Peer 1 Sep 1780
Lived after last term as PM 28 years, 337 days
Date of death 10 Mar 1792
Place of death South Audley St., Grosvenor Square, London
Age at death 78 years, 290 days
Place of funeral A funeral procession went from South Audley St. to Rothesay, Isle of Bute
Place of burial Rothesay, Isle of Bute
Zodiac sign Gemini

FATHER

James Stuart, 2nd Earl of Bute
Date of birth 1657
Occupation He was a Scottish Representative Peer from 1715 to his death and a Lord of the Bedchamber. He was Lord Lieutenant of Buteshire.
Date of marriage 19 Feb 1711
Date of death 28 Jan 1723
Place of burial Rothesay, Isle of Bute

MOTHER

Anne Campbell
Dates of marriages 1) 19 Feb 1711; 2) 19 Sep 1731, Alexander Fraser of Strichen
Date of death 9 Oct 1736

BROTHERS AND SISTERS

The Earl of Bute was the eldest son and the second of eight children.
Elizabeth, b. 6 Mar 1717; d. Jun 1725
James Stuart Mackenzie, b. 13 Nov 1718; m. his cousin Elizabeth Campbell; MP Argyllshire 1742–47, Buteshire 1747–54, Ayr Burghs 1754–61, Ross-shire 1761–80. Envoy to Turin 1758–61, PC 1761, Keeper of the Privy Seal of Scotland 1763–5, 1766–1800; d. 6 Apr 1800
Archibald, d. 30 May 1728
Anne, m. James, Lord Ruthven; d. 2 Dec 1786
Mary, m. Sir Robert Menzies of that Ilk, Bt; d. 30 Dec 1773
Jean, m. William Courtenay; d. 24 Jan 1802
Grace, m. John Campbell of Stonefield (Lord Stonefield); d. 5 Jun 1783

WIFE

Mary Wortley Montagu. (Baroness Mount Stuart)
Date and place of birth 10 Mar 1718 Pera, Constantinople
Mother Lady Mary Pierrepont
Father Edward Wortley Montagu
Father's occupation MP Huntingdon, 1705–13, 1722–34; Westminster 1715–22; Peterborough 1734–61. Lord of the Treasury 1714–15; Ambassador to Turkey 1716–18.
Age at marriage 18 years, *c.* 177 days
Number of children 11
Date and place of death 6 Nov 1794, Isleworth, Middlesex
Place of burial Wortley, Yorkshire
Years younger than PM *c.* 5 years
Profile Said to be plain but dutiful, she had no formal education. She was loyal to her husband, to whom she was devoted. Intelligent and witty, in later life she corresponded frequently with her mother, Lady Mary Wortley Montagu, and sent boxes of books to her in Italy. After her mother's death, she became offended by her popular reputation as an author and burned her mother's diary to avoid further unseemly interest.

CHILDREN

5 sons, 6 daughters
Mary, b. 20 Jan 1740; m. 7 Sep 1761, James Lowther, Earl of Lonsdale (MP Cumberland 1757–61, 1762–68, 1774–84, Westmoreland 1761–62, Cockermouth 1769–74) d. 5 Apr 1824
Jane, b. 13 Apr 1742; m. 1 Feb 1768, George, Earl Macartney (MP Cockermouth 1768–69, Ayr Burghs 1774–76, Bere Alston 1780–81); d. Feb 1828
John (Viscount Mount Stuart, Baron Cardiff, First Marquess of Bute), b. 30 Jun 1744; m. 1) 12 Nov 1766, Charlotte Jane Windsor (1746–1800) 2) 17 Sep 1800, Frances Coutts; MP Bossiney 1766–76; Viscount Mount Stuart 20 May 1766; Envoy to Turin 1779–83; Ambassador to Spain 1783, 1795–96, Privy Counsellor 1779; d. 16 Nov 1814
Anne, b. Aug 1746; m. 1) 2 Jul 1764, (div. 16 Mar 1779) Hugh Percy, 2nd Duke of Northumberland (MP Westminster 1763–76); 2) Baron von Poellnitz; d. 1822
James Archibald, b. 19 Sep 1747; m. 8 Jun 1767, Margaret Cunynghame; MP Ayr Burghs 1768–74, Buteshire 1774-80, 1784-90, 1806-07, Plympton Erle 1780–84, Bossiney 1790–96, 1797–1802; Lieut-Col. of 92nd Highland regiment of Foot, 1779; d. 1 Mar 1818
Augusta, b.10 Jan 1749; m. Captain Andrew Corbet, of the Horse Guards; d. 5 Feb 1778
Caroline, b. 28 May 1750; m. 1 Jan 1778, John Dawson, 1st Earl of Portarlington; d. 20 Jan 1813
Charles Stuart, b. Jan 1753; m. 20 Apr 1778, Louisa Vere Bertie; MP Bossiney 1776–90, Ayr Burghs 1790–94, Poole 1796–1801; Lieut-Gen. of British Forces 1798; Governor of Minorca, 1799: d. 25 Mar 1801
William Stuart, b. 12 Mar 1755; m. 3 May 1796, Sophia Margaret Juliana Penn; Canon of Christ Church, Oxford; Bishop of St. David's 1793; Archbishop of Armagh 1800; d. 6 May 1822
Louisa, b. 12 Aug 1757; unm.; a poet; d. 4 Aug 1851
Frederick, b. Sep 1758; MP Ayr Burghs 1776–80, Buteshire 1796–1802; d. 17 May 1802

LIFE AND CAREER

PARLIAMENTARY ELECTIONS FOUGHT

Scottish Peers did not all attend the House of Lords, but elected sixteen of their number to represent them. Bute was elected a Scottish Representative Peer on 14 Apr 1737, 5 May 1761, 26 Apr 1768 and 15 Nov 1774, and thus was in Parliament from 1737–41, and 1761–80.

PARLIAMENTARY AND MINISTERIAL EXPERIENCE

Maiden speech Said to have been made on 19 Jan 1762, but his first recorded speech was on 5 Feb 1762, on the war with Spain. (*Parl. Hist.* vol 15, 1753–64, col 1218)
Privy Counsellor 27 Oct 1760
Ministerial Offices Secretary of State, Northern Dept 25 Mar 1761–26 May 1762; First Lord of the Treasury and Leader of the House of Lords 26 May 1762– 8 Apr 1763
Opposition Leader while PM Duke of Newcastle

GOVERNMENTS FORMED

Administration 26 May 1762–8 Apr 1763

GENERAL ELECTION RESULT
MAR 1761: Not analysed
CABINET
Prime Minister and First Lord of the Treasury Earl of Bute
Chancellor of the Exchequer Sir F. Dashwood
Secretary of State (Northern Department) Earl of Egremont
Secretary of State (Southern Department) G. Grenville
Lord Chancellor Lord Henley
Lord President of the Council Lord Granville
Lord Privy Seal Duke of Bedford
First Lord of the Admiralty Earl of Halifax
Master General of the Ordnance Lord Ligonier
Paymaster General H. Fox
Lord Chamberlain Duke of Devonshire (May-Oct 1762) Duke of Marlborough (Nov 1762-Apr 1763)

IMPORTANT DATES IN PERSONAL AND POLITICAL LIFE

28 JAN 1723 Bute's father dies and he is left in the guardianship of his mother and two Campbell uncles.
24 AUG 1736 Marries Mary Wortley Montagu against her mother's wishes.
14 APR 1737 Elected as a Scottish Representative Peer at a by-election caused by the death of the Earl of Orkney.
24 JAN 1738 Takes his seat in the House of Lords as a Scottish Representative Peer.
27 APR 1741 Gives up his seat in the Lords at Dissolution, and retires to Bute for five years. Does not return to take part in the House of Lords for twenty years.
1746 Buys a half share in Kenwood House, London, from his uncle, the 3rd Duke of Argyll, but gives it up in 1754, when he moves to a house in South Audley Street, off Grosvenor Square, London.
1747 By chance he is introduced to Frederick, Prince of Wales, at Egham races when he is asked to make up a foursome at cards. His friendship with the Prince lays the foundation of his future career.
1751 Frederick's death increases his influence in the Royal Household as the Prince's widow comes to rely on his advice.
1754 Buys a house on Kew Green, London, and builds an extension to house his botanical library. Its garden has a gate into the grounds of Kew Palace, where he is helping Princess Augusta to create Kew Gardens.
1755 Princess Augusta appoints him 'finishing tutor' to the future George III. Bute's close relationship with and influence over both George and Princess Augusta cause deep and lasting resentment and hostility with the public.
MAY 1755 As Princess Augusta's political adviser, he arranges an alliance between the opposition forces of Leicester House and Pitt, against the Duke of Newcastle.
13 NOV 1755 At the opening of Parliament the opposition attacks the King's speech in the debate, causing Newcastle to dismiss Pitt and his supporters from the positions with which he had tried to secure their loyalty.
15 NOV 1756 Bute appointed Groom of the Stole in Prince George's Household. Prince George has repeatedly asked Newcastle to give Bute such a position, but the King and Newcastle resist and only relent when George refuses to accept any appointments to his Household unless Bute is among them.
25 OCT 1760 Death of King George II. On hearing the news Prince George writes to Bute promising to do nothing until he hears from him.
27 OCT 1760 Made a Privy Counsellor.
19 NOV 1760 King George III delivers his first speech to Parliament, containing the words 'I glory in the name Briton'. 'Briton' had been suggested by Bute instead of 'Englishman'.
25 MAR 1761 Bute appointed Secretary of State for the Northern Department.
3 APR 1761 Bute's wife created Baroness Mount Stuart of Wortley, Yorkshire.
3 NOV 1761 Elected again as a Scottish Representative Peer in May, Bute reappears in the House of Lords after an absence of over 20 years.
9 NOV 1761 Mobbed by a hostile crowd on his way to a Guildhall banquet.
1762 Commissions Robert Adam to build a mansion between Berkeley Square and Piccadilly to be known as Bute House, but in 1765 it is sold unfinished to the Earl of Shelburne, who renames it Lansdowne House.
4 JAN 1762 Bute obliged to declare war with Spain.
19 JAN 1762 Makes a particularly pompous maiden speech to the House of Lords.
5 FEB 1762 Opposes Duke of Bedford's motion for the withdrawal of troops from Germany.
26 MAY 1762 Succeeds Newcastle as First Lord of the Treasury.
JUN 1762 John Wilkes starts *The North Briton* to attack Bute Administration.
OCT 1762 Bute seeks to persuade Whigs to approve his peace treaty in the House, and succeeds in tempting Henry Fox away from his party to become Leader of the House of Commons.
3 NOV 1762 Duke of Bedford signs preliminary treaty at Fontainebleau, ending the war with France and Spain known as the Seven Years War.
9 DEC 1762 Both Houses of Parliament pass motions approving the treaty.
23 DEC 1762 Bute begins general proscription of the old Whigs. Newcastle, Grafton and Rockingham dismissed from their Lord Lieutenancies.

1763 Buys a 1000-acre estate at Luton Hoo in Bedfordshire, for about £100,000. Capability Brown landscapes the gardens and Robert Adam is the architect of a large mansion.

10 FEB 1763 Definitive Treaty of Paris signed. Britain retains or makes gains in Canada, India and the West Indies, acquires Florida and recovers Minorca.

22 MAR 1763 Bill published imposing a very unpopular tax on cider.

28 MAR 1763 In spite of fierce opposition, Bute speaks unequivocally in favour of the cider tax in the House of Lords, and it receives Royal Assent the following day.

8 APR 1763 Bute resigns office, having always said that he would only stay until peace was achieved. He is relieved to relinquish a position in which he has not had the support of colleagues and which has brought him into great disfavour with the public. He fears that his own unpopularity could tarnish the King. He recommends George Grenville as his successor.

AUG 1763 Grenville shows resentment of Bute's interference; Bute advises the King to dismiss him.

28 SEP 1763 Having failed to persuade Pitt to replace Grenville, Bute resigns as Keeper of the Privy Purse and leaves London for Luton Hoo.

MAY 1765 The Duke of Cumberland fails to form an alternative administration. Grenville forces the King to renounce Bute's influence and to dismiss Bute's brother, James Stuart Mackenzie, as Lord Privy Seal in Scotland. This ends Bute's role as the King's personal adviser, although he still visits Princess Augusta.

10 JUL 1765 The King dismisses the Grenville Administration, and the Marquess of Rockingham becomes Prime Minister.

FEB 1766 Bute votes against the Government twice on the American question.

17 MAR 1766 Bute speaks and votes against the Third Reading of the Bill to repeal the Stamp Act, differing with the King for the first time on any political issue.

JUL 1766 The King again asks Pitt to form a Government, and this time he consents. It contains many of Bute's former adherents but ignores Bute himself. Bute writes letter of protest to the King, but to no avail.

MAR 1768 Bute is still deeply unpopular. Mobs rioting in favour of John Wilkes attack his town house, breaking the windows in Lady Bute's room as she lies in bed.

26 APR 1768 Bute re-elected as a Scottish Representative Peer, but later that year he goes to Italy, where he spends more than a year travelling under the name of Sir John Stuart.

JUL 1769 Returns to England in good health, but soon falls ill. In November, goes abroad again until June 1771.

1771 A fire guts his magnificent library at Luton Hoo.

8 FEB 1772 The death of Princess Augusta leaves him 'without a single friend near the royal person.'

1773 Buys a site near Christchurch, Hampshire, and builds Highcliffe, overlooking the sea.

15 NOV 1774 Bute is again elected a Scottish Representative Peer.

1778 Negotiations take place to lure Bute out of retirement and into alliance with Pitt. Bute is reluctant and Pitt (now the Earl of Chatham) dies in May, but when the correspondence is made public, causing an uproar, the controversy makes Bute ill again.

1 SEP 1780 Retires from Parliament because of age at its Dissolution.

1785 Bute's book *Botanical Tables* published.

NOV 1790 Slips and falls while collecting plants on the cliffs at Highcliffe in Hampshire. Sprains his ankle, which is slow to heal.

10 MAR 1792 Death of Bute, thought to be partly a result of his fall.

BACKGROUND

PHYSICAL CHARACTERISTICS AND HEALTH

Bute was tall, slim and very handsome. He was also vain, being particularly proud of his shapely legs. In his youth he loved to dress up and take part in plays. In later years his extreme unpopularity began to affect his health. He couldn't sleep, and suffered from 'bilious fevers.' After his resignation in 1763 he went to Harrogate for a month's cure, and in 1768 he went to Italy, where his health improved. In 1790 he fell twenty-eight feet down cliffs near his Hampshire home while collecting plants, and this is thought to have contributed to his death.

EDUCATION

Secondary 1720–28, Eton.

University 1728–32, University of Leiden, the Netherlands.

Qualifications Degree in civil and public law from the University of Leiden

Cultural and vocational background He did not make the Grand Tour, but went to Groningen and Leiden in the Netherlands in 1728. Leiden was renowned as a centre of botanical teaching.

NON-PARLIAMENTARY CAREER

Early occupations He was passionately interested in botany, and spent most of the first nine years of his married life on Bute studying botany, agriculture and architecture.

Other posts 1737, A Commissioner of Police for Scotland; 16 Oct 1750, A Lord of the Bedchamber to Frederick, Prince of Wales; Oct 1756–25 Mar 1761, Groom of the Stole to Prince George; Jun 1761, Ranger of Richmond Park; Aug 1761, Governor of Charterhouse; 1763, Keeper of the Privy Purse; Jun 1765, Trustee of the British Museum; Dec 1780, President of the Society of Antiquaries of Scotland. He was also a Commissioner of Chelsea Hospital and an honorary director of Kew Gardens, London.

HONOURS

Academic 1761 Chancellor of Marischal College, Aberdeen; Honorary Fellow of the Royal College of Physicians, Edinburgh.

Other than peerage 10 Jul 1738, Knight of the Thistle; 27 May 1762, Knight of the Garter (having previously resigned the Order of the Thistle)

CLUBS

White's

HOBBIES AND SPORTS

In his youth he was involved in amateur theatricals with his relatives. He frequently played the part of Lothario. Interested in botany, he had a shrub (Stewartia) named after him during his lifetime. Many botanical books were dedicated to him. He collected botanical plants and plant drawings and astronomical, philosophical and mathematical instruments and had a gallery of Dutch and Flemish paintings. He helped Princess Augusta to create Kew Gardens.

FINANCES

He was not well off, but in 1761 his wife's inheritance made him a wealthy man. He became a patron of the arts, including science and literature. He obtained a pension of £300 p.a. for Dr. Johnson, and appointed Robert Adam, the architect as Surveyor of the King's Works.

Spouse's finances His wife's father, who was a miser, tried to prevent their marriage by withholding her dowry of £20,000, but when he died in 1761 he left Lady Bute his whole fortune of some £1,300,000. She became Baroness Mount Stuart of Wortley. Eighteen months later her mother died and she inherited again. She had a life interest in land at Wortley that was worth £17,000 p.a.

ANECDOTES

'Lord Bute is a very unfit man to be a Prime Minister of England. First, he is a Scotchman; secondly, he is the King's friend; and thirdly he is an honest man'. (Bishop Warburton, quoted in Coats, p.27)

'Always upon stilts, he had an extraordinary appearance of wisdom, both in his look and manner of speaking; for whether the subjects be serious or trifling he is equally pompous, slow and sententious' (Earl Waldegrave. *Memoirs, 1754–8*, 1821 p.38.)

'As the Earl of Bute lived esteemed and respected, he has died most sincerely and justly lamented, leaving few equals behind him for knowledge, sense and dignity of mind'. (*Gentleman's Magazine* obituary, 1792 vol, i, p.285)

QUOTATIONS

28 Mar 1763, A noble duke knows the difficulty to choose proper taxes. (During a debate on the cider tax, *Parl Hist* vol 15, 1753 -64, col 1313)

RESIDENCES

Mount Stuart, Isle of Bute
Kenwood House, London
Kew Green, London
South Audley Street, Grosvenor Square, London
Bute House, Piccadilly, London
Luton Hoo, Bedfordshire
Highcliffe, Christchurch, Hampshire

Open to the public *Kenwood House*, an elegant mansion designed by Robert Adam, containing the Iveagh Bequest collection of paintings; *Luton Hoo* is open to the public, but the house was gutted by fire in 1843 and substantially remodelled in Edwardian style.

MEMORIALS

PORTRAITS

1763, by Sir Joshua Reynolds; 1773, by Sir Joshua Reynolds, National Portrait Gallery; n.d., attributed to Allan Ramsay, Scottish National Portrait Gallery

OTHER MEMORIALS

After his death, *Butea superba*, a genus of tropical trees was named after him. *Stewartia*, an American shrub, was named after him between 1742 and 1746 by Linnaeus.

BIBLIOGRAPHIC INFORMATION

LETTERS AND PERSONAL PAPERS

Most of Bute's personal papers are in the family archives at Mount Stuart, Isle of Bute. Some papers and letters to Bute are in the Central Library, Cardiff.

PUBLICATIONS

1785, *Botanical Tables, Containing the Different Familys of British Plants . . .* 9 vols. London;

1787, *The Tabular Distribution of British Plants.* (Attributed to Bute).

FURTHER READING

Almon, J. *The History of the Late Minority.* London, 1766.
Coats, A. M. *Lord Bute: an Illustrated Life of John Stuart, third Earl of Bute 1713-1792.* Aylesbury, 1975.
Lovat-Fraser, J. A. *John Stuart, Earl of Bute.* Cambridge, 1912.
McKelvey, J.L. *George III and Lord Bute: the Leicester House Years* Durham, North Carolina, 1973.
Schweizer, K.W. *Lord Bute: Essays in Reinterpretation* Leicester, 1988.
Wortley, Mrs E. S. *A Prime Minister and His Son.* From the correspondence of the 3rd Earl of Bute and of Lieut. Gen. Sir Charles Stuart. London, 1925.

J.S.

Bettmann

George Grenville

Lived 1712–1770
Political Party Whig
Prime Minister 16 April 1763–10 July 1765
Government Whig
Reigning Monarch George III

Pro deo, patria et amicis For God, my country and my friends

GEORGE GRENVILLE AS PRIME MINISTER

A member of a political family (his sister married Chatham, and one of his sons became Prime Minister), George Grenville entered Parliament in 1741. His maiden speech supported the censure movement against Walpole in January 1742, and his parliamentary reputation grew rapidly thereafter. He entered Pelham's Government in 1744. His 'Cobhamite' faction, including Pitt, were dismissed by the Newcastle administration in 1755, only to be brought back into the Government the following year. Grenville moved closer to Bute, and his fortunes blossomed when George III became King in 1760. He entered Newcastle's second administration in 1761, and also served under Bute, although his career suffered for a time because of his opposition to Bute's peace negotiations with France. He became PM the following year, but Bute remained an important political influence, especially with the King. Grenville's Government had to deal with the alleged seditious libel of the MP John Wilkes and also the introduction of the Stamp Act in 1776, which required the American colonies to pay for their own defence. When English weavers rioted to protest imported silk, the King blamed Grenville for the violence. Insulted when the PM tried to remove the Queen from the regency list because of her friendship with Bute, King George succeeded in replacing Grenville in 1765.

PERSONAL INFORMATION

Names George Grenville
Nickname Gentle Shepherd, arising from his speech on the cider tax in 1763 in which he repeatedly asked where else a tax could be laid. Opposition MPs began to sing the hymn, 'Gentle Shepherd, Tell Me Where.'
Born 14 Oct 1712
Birthplace Westminster, London
Religion Anglican
Ancestry English. The Grenvilles were descended from a Norman family which had held land in Buckinghamshire since the 12th century. They were always acquiring more land, draining marshes and making other improvements to their holdings.
Date of marriage May 1749
Age at marriage c. 36
Years married c. 3 years
First entered Parliament 4 May 1741
Date appointed PM 16 April 1763
Age at appointment 50 years, 184 days
Date ceased to be PM 10 Jul 1765
Total time as PM 2 years, 85 days
Ceased to be MP 13 Nov 1770
Lived after last term as PM 5 years, 126 days
Date of death 13 Nov 1770
Place of death Bolton St., Piccadilly, London
Age at death 58 years, 30 days
Place of burial Wotton, Buckinghamshire
Zodiac sign Libra

FATHER

Richard Grenville
Date of birth 23 March 1678
Occupation MP Wendover, 1715–22; Buckingham, 1722–27
Date of marriage 25 Nov 1710
Date of death 17 Feb 1727
Place of burial Wotton, Buckinghamshire

MOTHER

Hester Temple (Countess Temple)
Date of birth c. 1690
Date of marriage 25 Nov 1710
Date and place of death 6 Oct 1752, Wotton, Buckinghamshire
Place of burial Wotton, Buckinghamshire

BROTHERS AND SISTERS

George Grenville was the second son of seven children.
Richard (Earl Temple, Lord Cobham), b. 26 Sep 1711; m. Anne Chambers; MP Buckingham 1734–41, 1747–52; Buckinghamshire 1741–47; First Lord of the Admiralty 1756–57; Lord Privy Seal 1757–61; d. 11 Sep 1779
Henry, b. 4 Apr 1714; d. 1 May 1716
James, b. 12 Feb 1715; m. Mary Smyth; MP Old Sarum 1742–47; Bridport 1747–54; Buckingham 1754–68; Horsham 1768–70; d. 14 Sep 1783
Henry, bap. 15 Sep 1717; m. Margaret Banks; MP Bishop's Castle 1759–61, Thirsk 1761–65, Buckingham 1768–74; Governor of Barbados 1746–56; Ambassador to Constantinople 1761–65; d. 22 April 1784
Thomas, b. 4 April 1719; unm.; MP Bridport 1746–47; a naval captain, he was killed in action; d. 3 May 1747
Hester (Baroness Chatham), b. 8 Nov 1720; m. William Pitt, Earl of Chatham (*q.v.*); d. 3 Apr 1803

WIFE

Elizabeth Wyndham
Date of birth c. 1716
Mother Lady Catherine Seymour
Father Sir William Wyndham
Father's occupation MP Somerset 1710–40
Number of children 11, 2 of whom died in infancy
Date and place of death 5 Dec 1769, Wotton, Buckinghamshire
Place of burial Wotton, Buckinghamshire
Years younger than PM c. 4 years
Profile She was a devoted wife, looking after the family estates while her husband busied himself with national politics. Smallpox had scarred her face and she had a slight stammer, but nevertheless she was considered, 'the first prize in the marriage lottery of our century.'

CHILDREN

4 sons, 5 daughters
Maria Hester, d. in infancy, 16 Dec 1751
Richard Percy, b. 12 March 1752; d. 7 Jul 1759
George (Earl Temple, Marquess of Buckingham), b. 18 Jun 1753; m. 16 April 1775, Lady Mary Elizabeth Nugent (Baroness Nugent); Teller of the Exchequer 1764–1813; MP Buckinghamshire 1774–79; Lord Lieutenant of Ireland 1782–83, 1787–89; Secretary of State for Foreign Affairs Dec 1783; d. 11 Feb 1813
Charlotte, b. 14 Sep 1754; m. 21 Dec 1771, Sir Watkin Williams-Wynn (MP Denbighshire 1774–89, Shropshire 1772– 74) d. 29 Sep 1832
Thomas, b. 31 Dec 1755; unm.; MP Buckinghamshire 1779–84, 1813–18; Aldeburgh 1790–96; Buckingham 1796–1809; Envoy to Paris 1782, Minister Extraordinary to Vienna 1793, President of the Board of Control 1806, First Lord of the Admiralty 1806–07; d. 17 Dec 1846
Elizabeth, b. 24 Oct 1756; m. 12 Apr 1787, John, 1st Earl of Carysfort (MP East Looe 1790, Stamford 1790–1801; Commissioner of the Board of Control); d. 2. Dec 1842
William Wyndham (Lord Grenville) (*q.v.*), b. 24 Oct 1759; Prime Minister 1806-07; d. 12 Jan 1834
Hester, b. 23 Nov 1760; m. 10 May 1782 Hugh, 1st Earl Fortescue (MP Beaumaris 1784–85); d. 13 Nov 1847
Catharine, b. 1761; m. 19 Jun 1780 Richard, 2nd Baron Braybrooke (MP Grampound 1774–80, Buckingham 1780–82, Reading 1782–97); d. 6 Nov 1796

LIFE AND CAREER

PARLIAMENTARY ELECTIONS FOUGHT

*(*designates candidate elected)*

DATE Apr 1741. General Election
CONSTITUENCY Buckingham

RESULT George Denton* (Whig); George Grenville* (Whig)

DATE 28 Dec 1744. By-election caused by Grenville's appointment as a Lord of the Admiralty
CONSTITUENCY Buckingham
RESULT George Grenville* (Whig)

DATE Jun 1747. General Election
CONSTITUENCY Buckingham
RESULT Richard Grenville* (Whig); George Grenville* (Whig)

DATE Apr 1754. General Election
CONSTITUENCY Buckingham
RESULT George Grenville* (Whig); James Grenville* (Whig)

DATE 7 Dec 1756. By-election caused by Grenville's appointment as Treasurer of the Navy
CONSTITUENCY Buckingham
RESULT George Grenville* (Whig)

DATE Mar 1761. General Election
CONSTITUENCY Buckingham
RESULT George Grenville* (Whig); James Grenville* (Whig)

DATE 7 Jun 1762. By-election caused by Grenville's appointment as Secretary of State for the Northern Department
CONSTITUENCY Buckingham
RESULT George Grenville* (Whig)

DATE 30 Nov 1762. By-election caused by Grenville's appointment as a Lord of the Admiralty
CONSTITUENCY Buckingham
RESULT George Grenville* (Whig)

DATE 25 Apr 1763. By-election caused by Grenville's appointment as First Lord of the Treasury
CONSTITUENCY Buckingham
RESULT George Grenville* (Whig)

DATE Mar 1768. General Election
CONSTITUENCY Buckingham
RESULT George Grenville* (Whig); Henry Grenville* (Whig)

PARTY ACTIVITY

Membership of group or faction In his early days as an MP he was a member of his uncle's faction, whose members were known as 'Cobham's cubs.' After his premiership he led a group of Whig supporters known as Grenvillites.

PARLIAMENTARY AND MINISTERIAL EXPERIENCE

Maiden Speech 21 Jan 1742. Said to have been made on 21 Jan 1742 in the debate criticising Walpole's conduct of the war.

First Recorded Speech 10 Dec 1742 on payments to the Hanoverian troops. (*Parl Hist* vol 12, 1741–43, cols 1051–1053)

Opposition offices He was appointed to a Committee of Public Accounts in May 1742, but it was never actually set up.

Privy Counsellor 21 Jun 1754

Ministerial Offices Lord of the Admiralty, 27 Dec 1744–Jun 1747; Lord of the Treasury, Jun 1747–Mar 1754; Treasurer of the Navy, Mar 1754–20 Nov 1755, Nov 1756–9 Apr 1757, Jun 1757–May 1762; Leader of the House of Commons Oct 1761–Oct 1762, Apr 1763–Jul 1765; Secretary of State, Northern Department, 27 May–9 Oct 1762; First Lord of the Admiralty, Oct 1762–Apr 1763; First Lord of the Treasury and Chancellor of the Exchequer 16 Apr 1763–10 Jul 1765

Opposition Leader while PM Duke of Newcastle

GOVERNMENTS FORMED

Administration 16 Apr 1763–10 Jul 1765

GENERAL ELECTION RESULT
MAR 1761: Not analysed

CABINET
Prime Minister, First Lord of the Treasury and Chancellor of the Exchequer G. Grenville
Lord President of the Council Earl Granville (Apr–Sep 1763); Duke of Bedford (1763–65)
Lord Privy Seal Duke of Marlborough
Lord Chancellor Lord Henley (Earl of Northington)
Secretary of State (Northern Department) Earl of Halifax (Apr–Sep 1763); Earl of Sandwich (1763–65)
Secretary of State (Southern Department) Earl of Egremont (Apr–Aug 1763); Earl of Halifax (1763–65)
Lord Chamberlain Earl Gower
First Lord of the Admiralty Lord Egmont
Master General of the Ordnance Marquess of Granby
Paymaster General of the Forces Lord Holland
Secretary at War W. Ellis
First Lord of Trade Lord Hillsborough

IMPORTANT DATES IN PERSONAL AND POLITICAL LIFE

4 MAY 1741 Elected to Parliament for Buckingham. His uncle Richard, Viscount Cobham, had arranged for his selection and return for his pocket borough, which had 13 electors.

21 JAN 1742 His maiden speech in favour of Pulteney's motion to investigate Walpole's conduct of the war impresses the House.

MAY 1742 Grenville elected to a Committee to investigate public accounts, but the motion to set it up is defeated. Nevertheless, election to the committee confirms Grenville's high standing in the House of Commons.

11 JAN 1744 Acts as chief spokesman for his uncle, Viscount Cobham, who heads a faction on the opposition side in the debate on the subsidy to be paid for the Hanoverian troops. His speech against the motion is praised, although the motion is carried.

27 DEC 1744 Grenville appointed to his first ministerial post as a Lord of the Admiralty.

FEB 1746 King tries to persuade the Earls of Granville and Bath to form an administration. Grenville, like most of the Cabinet and other leading office holders, hands in his resignation. They all resume office again, however, when the King's attempt fails.

JUL 1746 He is passed over for promotion to the Treasury in favour of Henry Bilson Legge, to whom Grenville is senior. He becomes increasingly embittered as a result.

DEC 1746 Supports the election of his brother Thomas as MP for Bridport. The number of Grenville brothers in the House increases to four with Thomas's election.

19 FEB 1748 Grenville introduces a Bill to move the summer assizes from Aylesbury to Buckingham, but it is seen as an attempt to inflate a local squabble into a national debate, making him unpopular.

MAY 1749 Marries Elizabeth Wyndham, the granddaughter of the Duke of Somerset, after postponing the wed-

IMPORTANT DATES IN PERSONAL AND POLITICAL LIFE—*Continued*

ding in hopes of receiving a large legacy. The Duke continues to disapprove of the match and leaves Elizabeth a very small allowance in his will.

13 SEP 1749 Death of Viscount Cobham, his uncle and political mentor. His mother inherits his titles and becomes Countess Temple on 18 October, when his brother Richard becomes Earl Temple.

NOV 1749 His wife falls ill, and they go to Bath for nine months while she convalesces.

6 OCT 1754 Death of his mother, Countess Temple.

6 MAR 1754 Pelham's death represents another setback to his political career. He hopes to get a better post under Newcastle, but is reappointed as a Treasurer of the Navy. He is bitter that William Pitt, soon to marry his sister Hester, does not fight harder on his behalf.

20 NOV 1755 Newcastle dismisses the Cobhamites from office, including Pitt and Grenville. They now begin to work together in opposition against subsidising the troops in Hanover.

JUN 1756 The loss of Minorca arouses public anger and dismay. Several Ministers, including Fox, the Leader of the House, desert Newcastle by resigning, leaving Newcastle with no alternative but to turn to the Cobhamites for support. Pitt tries to form an administration but Devonshire has to lead it. Grenville is disappointed again as he retains his post as Treasurer of the Navy.

24 JAN 1758 Grenville promotes a Bill to reform the payment of seamen's wages. It becomes law in April.

WINTER 1758 His eldest son Richard, aged six, falls ill. Grenville stays with him when he can, and is distraught when Richard dies on 7 Jul 1759.

1759 Grenville increasingly estranged from Pitt, who he thinks is spending far too much on the war, and increasingly friendly with Bute and the Leicester House faction. Having used his time as Treasurer of the Navy to become financially independent of his elder brother, Grenville establishes a reputation in the House of Commons as a procedural expert.

25 OCT 1760 Death of George II brings the conduct of the war to the forefront of political debate. The new King, with Bute and Grenville, urges peace, whereas Pitt and Newcastle are strongly in favour of continuing.

18 NOV 1760 At Pitt's request, Grenville writes the King's speech for the opening of Parliament.

11 FEB 1761 Becomes a member of the Cabinet, though still as Treasurer of the Navy.

MAR 1761 His rival Legge dismissed as Chancellor of the Exchequer, but Grenville is disappointed again, as the office goes to Lord Barrington. Grenville decides that it is his destiny to become Speaker, but Bute and the King dissuade him. As some compensation for Grenville, Bute arranges for his private secretary, Charles Jenkinson, to keep Grenville informed of events. This knowledge puts him in a powerful position.

2 OCT 1761 Pitt, Temple and James Grenville announce their intention to resign following the Cabinet's refusal to declare war on Spain, which had just signed a treaty with France.

3 OCT 1761 Bute summons Grenville from Wotton to London and offers him the post of Secretary of State for the Southern Department, which Pitt had held. Grenville refuses, believing that he would have no political or family support, and instead proposes his brother-in-law, Lord Egremont.

13 OCT 1761 Bute offers Grenville the position of Leader of the House. Grenville accepts, feeling that he is isolated already. His brother Temple, however, goes so far as to cut Grenville's sons out of his will. Grenville repeatedly seeks assurances of support from the King and his senior Ministers. Eventually the King agrees to show his confidence in Grenville by giving his brother-in-law Lord Thomond a position in the Royal Household.

2 JAN 1762 Newcastle's Government forced to declare war on Spain to curb her claims to territory in North America. Newcastle has raised money to finance the war on the continent. Grenville and Bute, wanting to reduce the Prussian subsidy, argue that that money should be spent on the war with Spain.

APR 1762 Newcastle outvoted on this issue at Cabinet meetings.

7 MAY 1762 Newcastle tells the King he will resign. Five days later the House of Commons agree without a division to finance the Spanish war.

26 MAY 1762 Newcastle resigns, and Bute becomes Prime Minister. Bute offers Grenville the post of Chancellor of the Exchequer, but Grenville refuses, wanting instead to become Secretary of State for the Northern Department. Bute at first objects because Grenville's brother-in-law Lord Egremont is at the Southern Department, but he relents and Grenville is appointed on the following day.

10 OCT 1762 Bute negotiates with France for peace without consulting the Cabinet. Grenville opposes him and does not use his position as Leader of the House to rally support. Bute therefore decides to demote him to First Lord of the Admiralty. Grenville swallows his pride and accepts the post because he needs the money. Since the break with his brother, Earl Temple, the previous year, he has had no private income. Fox becomes Leader of the House.

MAR 1763 Grenville speaks in favour of the proposed cider tax, asking where else the tax can be laid. Opposition MPs ridicule him by singing 'Gentle Shepherd, tell me where', causing great amusement. The experience ruins Grenville's confidence.

25 MAR 1763 To Grenville's surprise, Bute asks him to take over as Prime Minister. In fact Fox has already refused the position on health grounds. Grenville accepts, even though Bute has arranged most of the posts in the new ministry. Suspecting that Bute wants to remain in power behind the scenes, Grenville succeeds in outmanoeuvring him.

16 APR 1763 Grenville accepts the seals of office knowing that Bute still craves involvement in political affairs. However, he grows increasingly suspicious of the King, who consults Bute behind his back.

23 APR 1763 John Wilkes publishes issue no. 45 of the *North Briton*, containing a virulent attack on the King's prorogation speech.

26 APR 1763 The Earl of Halifax issues a general warrant for the arrest of all associated authors and printers. Wilkes, MP for Aylesbury, is arrested with the others on 30 Apr.

6 MAY 1763 The court hearing releases Wilkes, deciding that he is protected from arrest by parliamentary privilege. The Government decides to move against him before his appeal for damages, due to be heard on 6 December.

1 JUN 1763 The King sends Bute to canvass Opposition leaders about forming a new ministry. Grenville goes to the King, demanding that Bute be kept out of matters of state. The King asks for ten days to consider his proposal, but in the meantime Bute's attempts fail.

21 AUG 1763 The King summons Grenville and tells him that he has his full confidence. That day Grenville's brother-in-law, Lord Egremont, dies suddenly, leaving the Secretaryship of the Southern Department vacant.

26 AUG 1763 The King tells Grenville he is bringing in Pitt to replace Egremont. This convinces Grenville that Bute and the King are conspiring to undermine him.

27 AUG 1763 The King fails to persuade Pitt to take office.

28 AUG 1763 Once again the King assures Grenville of his full support. Grenville insists that Bute be kept out of political affairs.

15 NOV 1763 At the opening of the new session Grenville has a majority on the King's message that Wilkes should answer the charges against him in the King's Bench Court.

24 NOV 1763 Lord North moves a motion that parliamentary privilege not cover seditious libels.

6 DEC 1763 Wilkes's appeal for damages is heard before the Court of Common Pleas in Westminster Hall. Chief Justice Pratt releases him and declares general warrants illegal.

20 JAN 1764 Wilkes expelled from the House of Commons, but he is already in France.

10 FEB 1764 The Government wins the vote on an Opposition motion to repeal the cider tax.

17 FEB 1764 The House holds a memorable debate on the legality of general warrants.

21 FEB 1764 Wilkes found guilty of being the author of the *North Briton.*

9 MAR 1764 Grenville's budget speech announces his plans for the Stamp Act, to raise revenue in the American colonies to finance their own defence. After the debate in which he is criticised for not consulting the colonists, he agrees to delay the introduction of the measure for one year. The Budget resolutions are eventually passed as the Plantation Act.

1764 The Currency Act prohibits the issue of paper money in the Southern colonies.

6 FEB 1765 Grenville presents the stamp duty resolutions to the House but fails to mention the many petitions against them. Despite this there is no real Opposition campaign against the measure.

22 MAR 1765 The Stamp Act receives Royal Assent.

MAR 1765 The King ill with recurrent coughs and fevers; it is thought that he may die within the year. He himself proposes a Regency Bill, but it does not specify the name of the Regent.

24 APR 1765 The King specifies that the Regent should be either the Queen or another member of the Royal Family. Intended to allay suspicions that Bute might be made Regent, this measure only arouses more controversy because of the close friendship between Bute and the Queen. When Ministers decide to remove the Queen's name, the King takes it as an insult.

13 MAY 1765 The Committee on the Regency Bill reinserts the Queen's name.

15 MAY 1765 The Regency Bill receives Royal Assent.

15 MAY 1765 Riots by silk weavers because of the Government's failure to restrict the imports of silk. Grenville is blamed for the riots by the King, who again tries—and fails—to persuade Pitt to form an administration. Earl Temple also refuses office, as he has lately been reconciled with his brother George.

21 MAY 1765 The King summons Grenville and asks him to continue in office. Grenville, however sets conditions: Bute is to be excluded from the King's counsels; Bute's brother, James Stuart Mackenzie is to be removed as Lord Privy Seal of Scotland and thereby from his power over Scottish patronage; and Lord Holland to be removed from his post as Paymaster General. The King agrees.

JUN 1765 The King tries again to form a new administration under Pitt, without success. Eventually, however, the Duke of Cumberland arranges a new ministry without Pitt, headed by the Marquess of Rockingham.

10 JUL 1765 After a difficult two years, Grenville finds himself once more in Opposition, although this time he is surrounded by a group of about 70 supporters.

17 DEC 1765 Grenville proposes an amendment to the Debate on the Address, expressing disgust at the colonial protests against the Stamp Act. However, he has misjudged the mood of the House and has to withdraw it.

6 FEB 1766 Grenville, in a debate against the repeal of the Stamp Act, asks the House to call upon the King to enforce the law. Rockingham's Cabinet supports the principle that Britain has the right to tax the colonies but has concluded that the Stamp Act is unenforceable, and that it would be better to repeal it than to bring the law into disrepute by trying to enforce it. Grenville and his supporters are heavily defeated in the voting.

JUL 1766 Rockingham leaves office, but when Pitt (now Earl of Chatham), not Grenville, is invited to form an administration. Grenville's political reputation suffers a severe blow.

18 NOV 1766 The House debates an Order in Council forbidding the export of grain. Grenville had campaigned against it as unconstitutional. The Government admit as much, but argue that action to alleviate the shortage of bread is necessary. By arguing on procedural rather than practical grounds Grenville loses some support.

26 JAN 1767 A Committee of Supply debate the Army estimates. Grenville tries to move an amendment that the colonies pay the costs of the armies stationed there. Many agree with the principle, but fail to support the amendment.

JUL 1767 The Duke of Grafton invites him to join the new ministry he is trying to assemble, but Grenville declines, believing the Duke is trying to divide and weaken the opposition factions by tempting key individuals into office.

MAR 1768 Grenville plays an active part in the General Election campaign, but his influence is waning. Nineteen of his supporters have not been re-elected, although he has gained nine new ones, giving him a reduced group of 31 supporters in the House.

MAY 1768 The election of John Wilkes for Middlesex at the General Election in March sparks off pro-Wilkes riots in London, giving Grenville an excuse to attack the Government for its handling of events.

28 JAN 1769 Grenville opposes the Government's motion calling for Wilkes's expulsion from the House as a matter of principle, believing it constitutionally wrong. He loses many of his supporters as a result.

5 DEC 1769 His wife dies after a serious illness.

28 FEB 1770 Grenville introduces a Bill to reform the House of Commons' handling of disputed election cases. It passes through all its stages quickly and is given Royal Assent on 12 April, becoming one of his greatest achievements.

13 NOV 1770 Having been ill since the summer, Grenville dies in London on the day of the opening of Parliament.

BACKGROUND

PHYSICAL CHARACTERISTICS AND HEALTH

Grenville was thin and carried himself stiffly erect. He suffered from recurring respiratory illness which caused him to spend months at a time away from London. In 1742 he went to the South of France for the sake of his health, in 1743 to Scotland and in 1748 to Bath. He died of a blood disorder.

EDUCATION

Secondary 1725–28, Eton
University 1730–33, Christ Church, Oxford

NON-PARLIAMENTARY CAREER

Early occupations He studied for a career in the law: 1729, Inner Temple; 1734, Lincoln's Inn; 1735, called to the Bar.

CLUBS

White's

FINANCES

The Grenville family were prosperous landowners but as a younger son George Grenville remained financially dependent on his elder brother Richard for much of his life. His financial abilities were put to good use in his ministerial positions. His legal studies were paid for by his uncle, Viscount Cobham, who left the bulk of his wealth to Richard. Richard leased to him the house at Wotton and gave him an allowance until their estrangement in 1761. They were not reconciled until May 1765.

Income As a Lord of the Admiralty in 1744 he earned about £1,000 p.a. Three years later as a Lord of the Treasury his salary was about £1,400 p.a.

Spouse's finances His wife Elizabeth had hoped to inherit a substantial sum from her grandfather the Duke of Somerset, but he disapproved of her marriage and left her a very small allowance. Her dowry, however, amounted to £20,000.

Legacies His father died in 1727, leaving him £3,000, which was administered by his elder brother. His uncle Viscount Cobham also left him a generous legacy on his death in 1749.

Debts He lent money to his relations, rather than borrowing it.

Will He left the £20,000 of his wife's dowry to his daughters on their marriage. He also owned 35,000 acres in East Florida which was held in trust for his children. The income from the property provided annuities for each of them.

ANECDOTES

'Mr. Grenville was, confessedly, the ablest man of business in the House of Commons, and, though not popular, of great authority there from his spirit, knowledge, and gravity of character.' (Horace Walpole. *Memoirs of the reign of George III*; edited by Sir Denis Le Marchant vol. IV, p. 188)

'He was a man born to public business, which was his luxury and amusement. An Act of Parliament was in itself entertaining to him, as was proved when he stole a turnpike bill out of somebody's pocket at a concert and read it in a corner in despite of all the efforts of the finest singers to attract his attention.' (Thomas Pitt, quoted by Lord Camelford in *Family characters and anecdotes*. Fortescue MSS.)

QUOTATIONS

2 Dec 1755, Nations are pretty much like old gamesters: they compare the chance they have of gaining with the chance they have of losing, and they never venture when they plainly see that the odds are against them.

24 Jan 1758, It is the common artifice of false patriots to use the people as a scaling ladder to preferment; and, when they are firmly seated on the pinnacle of power, they spurn at the means of their promotion.

RESIDENCES

Wotton, Buckinghamshire
Upper Brook Street, London
Great George Street, London
10 Downing Street, London
Bolton Street, Piccadilly, London

MEMORIALS

STATUES AND BUSTS

1768, by Laurity Holm; by Nollekens, Brasenose College, Oxford

PORTRAITS

1764, by William Hoare, Christ Church Oxford; 1764–67, by Sir Joshua Reynolds, John Bass Museum, Miami, Florida

BIBLIOGRAPHIC INFORMATION

LETTERS AND PERSONAL PAPERS

The main sources are the Grenville Papers in the British Library, which are described *The Grenville Papers* and *Additional Grenville Papers* (see below).

Some Grenville papers are in the Stowe Collection in the Huntingdon Library, San Marino, California. There are also some papers in the Bodleian Library, Oxford.

FURTHER READING

Cornish, R. T. *George Grenville 1712-1770: a Bibliography*. Westport, Connecticut, 1992.

Lawson, P. *George Grenville: A Political Life*. Oxford, 1984.

Lipscomb, G. *The History and Antiquities of the County of Buckingham*. 4 vols. London, 1847.

Smith, W. J. *The Grenville Papers: Being the Correspondence of Richard Grenville Earl Temple and the Rt. Hon. George Grenville, Their Friends and Contemporaries*. 4 vols. London: 1852.

Tomlinson, J.R.G. *Additional Grenville Papers 1763–1765*. Manchester, 1962.

Wiggin, L.M. *The Faction of Cousins: A Political Account of the Grenvilles 1733–1763*. New Haven, 1958.

J.S.

Bettmann

Marquess of Rockingham

Lived 1730–1782

Political Party Whig

Prime Minister 13 July 1765–30 July 1766; 27 March –1 July 1782

Government Whig

Reigning Monarch George III

En Dieu est tout In God is everything

ROCKINGHAM AS PRIME MINISTER

Rockingham spent his entire parliamentary career in the House of Lords. He resigned from his various non-ministerial offices in 1762 in protest at Devonshire's removal from the Privy Council, but from the factional intrigues that ensued, he ultimately emerged as Prime Minister in July 1765. This first period in office was dominated by the Stamp Act controversy, and came to an end when the King replaced him with Chatham. The 'Rockingham Whigs', in Government and Opposition, displayed the first signs of a modern political party, not only by promoting a political programme, but also seeking to carry it through in office, even to the extent of overturning existing policies of his predecessors. He opposed North's American policy, preferring to grant the colonists their independence. In 1782 Rockingham succeeded North as Prime Minister in alliance with Shelburne. His second brief premiership was marked by the repeal of the Declaratory Act in 1720, which made laws passed by the Westminster Parliament binding on Ireland, and by continuing military reverses in North America. Other than Walpole himself, he was the only Prime Minister since 1721 never to have served in any other PM's cabinet. Rockingham was a noted gambler and a lover of horseracing, and suggested the name for what became the 'St Leger,' one of Britian's classic horseraces.

PERSONAL INFORMATION

Names Charles Watson-Wentworth
Peerages Styled Viscount Higham 1739–46, and Earl of Malton 1746–50; Earl of Malton 17 Sep 1750; 2nd Marquess of Rockingham
Born 13 May 1730
Ancestry English. His family was descended from the Watsons of Rockingham Castle, Northamptonshire, who became prominent Yorkshire Whigs
Date and place of marriage 26 Feb 1752, Golden Square, St. James's, Westminster, London
Age at marriage 21 years, 289 days
Years married 30 years, 49 days
First entered Parliament Became entitled to sit in the House of Lords on coming of age on 13 May 1751; took his seat on 21 May 1751
Dates appointed PM 1) 13 Jul 1765; 2) 27 Mar 1782
Age at appointment 1) 21 years, 8 days; 2) 51 years, 318 days
Dates ceased to be PM 1) 30 Jul 1766; 2) 1 Jul 1782
Total time as PM 1) 1 year, 17 days; 2) 96 days; a total of 1 year, 113 days
Lived after last term as PM Died in office
Date of death 1 Jul 1782
Place of death Wimbledon, London
Age at death 52 years, 49 days
Place of funeral York
Place of burial York Minster
Zodiac sign Taurus

FATHER

Thomas Watson-Wentworth, Marquess of Rockingham
Date and place of birth 13 Nov 1693, Tidmington, Worcestershire
Occupation MP Malton 1715–27, Yorkshire 1727–28; then a Peer
Date of marriage 22 Sep 1716
Date of death 14 Dec 1750
Place of burial York Minster

MOTHER

Lady Mary Finch
Date and place of birth 1701, Burley on the Hill, Rutland
Profile All that is known is that she was dark and very tall.
Date of marriage 22 Sep 1716
Date of death 30 May 1761
Place of burial York Minster

BROTHERS AND SISTERS

Rockingham was the fifth son and eighth child in a family of ten.
William, bap. 25 Apr 1718; bur. 3 May 1718
Thomas, bap. 18 Jan 1720; d. Aug 1734
Anne, m. William, 3rd Earl Fitzwilliam (MP Peterborough 1741–42); d. 29 Aug 1769
Daniel, bap. 9 Jun 1724; bur. 9 Apr 1730
Mary, bap. 13 Oct 1725; bur. 15 Oct 1725
Mary, b. 18 Jul 1727; m. John Milbanke
William (Viscount Higham), bap. 2 Sep 1728; d. 16 Aug 1739
Charlotte, b. 11 Feb 1732; unm.; d. 1810
Henrietta-Alicia, b. 7 Dec 1737; m. William Sturgeon

WIFE

Mary Bright
Date of birth 1736
Mother Margaret Norton
Father Thomas Bright (d. 1739)
Stepfather Sir John Ramsden
Father's and Stepfather's occupation Both were landowners
Age at marriage 16
Number of children None
Date and place of death 19 Dec 1804; Hillingdon House, Uxbridge, Middlesex
Place of burial York Minster
Years younger than PM *c.* 6 years
Profile She acted as her husband's secretary and political adviser. Newcastle said of her 'The little woman has her influency.' She was also musical, playing the harpsichord.

CHILDREN

None

LIFE AND CAREER

PARLIAMENTARY ELECTIONS FOUGHT

None. He was a Peer.

PARTY ACTIVITY

Party Leadership Rockingham led his own party, the Rockingham Whigs.

PARLIAMENTARY AND MINISTERIAL EXPERIENCE

First Recorded Speech Although Rockingham replied to a procedural point on 20 Jan 1766 he made his first recorded speech on 28 May 1766 in the debate on the Bill to introduce a window tax.
Privy Counsellor 10 Jul 1765
Ministerial Offices Leader of the House of Lords 13 Jul 1765 –30 Jul 1766; First Lord of the Treasury 13 Jul 1765–30 Jul 1766, 27 Mar– 1 Jul 1782
Opposition Leaders while PM Duke of Bedford, George Grenville

GOVERNMENTS FORMED

First Adminstration 13 Jul 1765–30 Jul 1766

GENERAL ELECTION RESULT
MAR 1761: Not analysed

CABINET
Prime Minister and First Lord of the Treasury Marquess of Rockingham
Chancellor of the Exchequer W. Dowdeswell

Lord President of the Council Earl of Winchilsea & Nottingham
Lord Chancellor Lord Henley (later Earl Northington)
Secretary of State (Northern Department) Duke of Grafton (Jul 1765–May 1766) H. S. Conway (May–Jul 1766)
Secretary of State (Southern Department) H. S. Conway (Jul 1765–May 1766) Duke of Richmond (May–Jul 1766)
President of the Board of Trade Earl of Dartmouth
First Lord of the Admiralty Lord Egmont
Lord Privy Seal Duke of Newcastle
Chancellor of the Duchy of Lancaster Lord Strange
Master General of the Ordnance Marquess of Granby
Treasurer of the Navy Viscount Howe
Secretary at War Viscount Barrington
Paymaster General C. Townshend

Second Adminstration 27 Mar–1 Jul 1782

GENERAL ELECTION RESULT
SEP 1780: Government 260; Opposition 254; Others 144. Total 558.
CABINET
Prime Minister and First Lord of the Treasury Marquess of Rockingham
Chancellor of the Exchequer Lord John Cavendish
Lord President of the Council Lord Camden
Lord Chancellor Lord Thurlow
Secretary of State (Home Department) Earl of Shelburne
Secretary of State (Foreign Affairs) C. J. Fox
President of the Board of Trade Lord Grantham
First Lord of the Admiralty Viscount Keppel
Lord Privy Seal Duke of Grafton
Chancellor of the Duchy of Lancaster Lord Ashburton
Master General of the Ordnance Duke of Richmond
Commander in Chief General Conway

IMPORTANT DATES IN PERSONAL AND POLITICAL LIFE

14 DEC 1750 Rockingham's father dies, leaving him a very wealthy young man.

21 MAY 1751 Takes his seat in the House of Lords and soon becomes a Lord of the Bedchamber to George II.

26 FEB 1752 Marries Mary Bright, a wealthy 16-year-old heiress.

1753 He establishes the Rockingham Club at York to promote his influence over candidates in Yorkshire seats, having failed in July to get his protege Sir George Savile accepted for one of the county seats.

15 NOV 1753 At the opening of the new session of Parliament he is invited to move the Address, but refuses, demonstrating his shyness and lack of ambition.

OCT 1756 Loyalty to the old King leads him to decline an invitation to become Master of the Horse to the Prince of Wales.

6 MAY 1760 The King makes him a Knight of the Garter, almost before his political career has begun.

26 MAY 1762 Newcastle resigns, marking the end of the 'old Whig' era, at least for a time.

3 NOV 1762 On the day that the new King strikes Devonshire's name from the list of Privy Counsellors, Rockingham and others resign their offices in protest.

23 DEC 1762 In the ensuing backlash Rockingham is dismissed from his Lord Lieutenancies. Many of his supporters also resign their local offices.

16 APR 1763 Bute's replacement as Prime Minister by George Grenville marks a gradual return to Whig principles.

OCT 1763 Grenville fails to win enough support to become a Governor of Charterhouse, and Rockingham is appointed.

MAR 1765 Lord John Cavendish persuades Rockingham to accompany him to see Pitt with a view to strengthening the unfocused opposition to the Grenville administration.

MAY 1765 The Regency crisis reinforces the King's determination to remove Grenville, but Pitt cannot be persuaded to form a new ministry. Eventually the Duke of Cumberland's negotiations lead to Rockingham's first ministry.

10 JUL 1765 Rockingham becomes a Privy Counsellor.

13 JUL 1765 He is appointed Prime Minister and First Lord of the Treasury, his first ministerial post. Edmund Burke is his private secretary.

31 OCT 1765 Death of the Duke of Cumberland, who has consistently attended Cabinet meetings, although he does not hold office. Rockingham's leadership becomes more positive.

1 NOV 1765 The Stamp Act, which had been passed in March under Grenville, comes into force amid fierce protests against it in the American colonies. Although Rockingham's ministry at first tries to enforce the act, it becomes impossible to do so. The Duke of Cumberland had advocated using troops to quell opposition, but his death makes the Act's repeal inevitable, and a ministerial committee is set up to examine the problem and report to the Cabinet.

14 JAN 1766 Pitt makes a strong speech in favour of repealing the Stamp Act, arguing that Parliament should only impose external, not internal, taxes on the colonies.

20 JAN 1766 Rockingham speaks briefly in the House on a procedural point.

27 JAN 1766 The House of Commons receives petitions from American colonists against the Stamp Act. They challenge Parliament's right to impose taxation on the colonies at all. Pitt supports their arguments but he is vehemently opposed by the majority of the House.

3–6 FEB 1766 Five resolutions forming the basis of American policy are passed in the Commons but defeated in the Lords, which damages Rockingham's reputation.

24 FEB 1766 The Committee of the Whole House to consider the American papers takes evidence on the Stamp Act question, and particularly on the economic effects of the crisis. Its report recommends that the Act be repealed, and that an Act be passed confirming the dependency of the American colonies.

4 MAR 1766 Two Bills embodying the Committee's proposals pass through the Commons. The ministry's majority in the Lords is small on 11 Mar, but by 18 Mar both the Repeal Act and the Declaratory Act receive Royal Assent.

21 APR 1766 A new window tax is proposed to replace the revenue lost by the repeal of Bute's highly unpopular cider tax. It arouses little excitement in the Commons but faces opposition in the Lords, where on 28 May Rockingham makes a rare speech in favour of the measure.

22 APR 1766 Resolutions are passed in the Commons declaring general warrants illegal, continuing Rockingham's policy of reversing measures passed by his predecessors.

28 APR 1766 The Duke of Grafton resigns, convinced that the ministry is too weak without Pitt. But Rockingham refuses to include him since Pitt persists in his efforts to undermine Rockingham. Grafton's departure gravely wounds public confidence in the ministry.

IMPORTANT DATES IN PERSONAL AND POLITICAL LIFE—*Continued*

23 MAY 1766 After many refuse the offer of Grafton's Cabinet post, the Duke of Richmond agrees to replace him. Rockingham has avoided asking for help from any of Bute's followers, but his failure to come to terms with political realities leads directly to his downfall.

6 JUL 1766 Northington offers his resignation as Lord Chancellor. Pitt had responded positively to overtures from the King's intermediaries about forming a new ministry, and Northington hopes to provoke Rockingham into threatening to resign. In this Northington is disappointed.

9 JUL 1766 The King informs Rockingham and his colleagues that a new ministry is to be formed under Pitt. Many of the senior Ministers resign, but Rockingham hopes that many of his supporters will continue in office to pursue his policies.

30 JUL 1766 Rockingham resigns from office, and Pitt, now Earl of Chatham, becomes Prime Minister.

NOV 1766 The Rockingham supporters who have stayed in office feel slighted by Chatham. Rockingham threatens Chatham that if they are not given more patronage they will resign. Only four actually resign, demonstrating Rockingham's lack of power in Opposition.

JUL 1767 Grafton negotiates with him to form a new administration, but divisions within the Whigs cause the plan to fail. Rockingham takes little further part in public affairs while Chatham remains in office.

MAR 1768 The General Election is a success for the Rockingham Whigs. They are estimated to have 57 Members of the House of Commons.

9 MAY 1769 Rockingham and Grenville both attend a political dinner of the Society of Supporters of the Bill of Rights, a group founded by supporters of Wilkes. The Wilkes affair begins to unite opposition forces.

22 JAN 1770 Rockingham moves a resolution to set up a Committee of the Whole House on the State of the Nation. Chatham supports this.

28 JAN 1770 Grafton resigns from office, fatally weakened by the death of Charles Yorke, one of Rockingham's supporters whom the King has tried to persuade to support the failing Minister.

APR 1770 Edmund Burke publishes *Thoughts on the Causes of the Present Discontents* which defines 'party' in favourable terms and lends credibility to the Rockingham Whigs.

NOV 1770 Rockingham spends nearly three months at Bath with his wife, who has suffered a severe attack of jaundice. His absence contributes to the lack of cohesion among the Opposition. After Grenville's death on the 13th his supporters disperse instead of joining the Rockingham Whigs.

8 FEB 1771 A backbench MP, Colonel George Onslow, demands that the Government enforce the law against the printing of parliamentary debates, a practice which is rapidly increasing. His ridicule in the press forces the House to summon the printers but they defy the House. The Government can only imprison the city magistrates who had defended the printers.

30 MAR 1771 Rockingham and others pay a token visit to the imprisoned Lord Mayor. In debate they support the House's right to maintain the secrecy of debates while doubting the efficacy of exercising it.

20 JAN 1775 Rockingham supports Chatham's motion for the recall of troops from Boston, where the 'Boston Tea Party' has demonstrated the colonists' opposition to the payment of import duty. Generally Rockingham opposes North's conciliatory approach towards the Americans, preferring to grant their independence. He takes little part in the House while the war continues.

MAR 1778 He speaks out in favour of the immediate granting of American independence, but motions criticizing the conduct of the war are defeated.

11 MAY 1779 Rockingham moves an address on Irish grievances, an issue which is to figure prominently during his next administration. The Irish want free trade, but the arguments continue until trade concessions are finally made in December.

30 DEC 1779 Rockingham attends the first meeting of the Yorkshire Movement, petitioning for the reform of public finance.

28 JUN 1780 North's administration having been weakened by events both inside the House and elsewhere, he approaches Rockingham to try to arrange a coalition. Rockingham's terms, however, cannot be met. The King refuses to consider accepting the principle of American independence.

SEP 1780 North hopes that a General Election will catch the Opposition unprepared, but his supporters are returned with a slightly reduced majority.

25 NOV 1781 News of General Cornwallis's defeat and surrender at Yorktown reaches England. The ensuing parliamentary debates put North in an impossible position. He becomes convinced of the necessity of conceding independence, but knows that the King will never agree.

20 MAR 1782 North resigns, with the King's reluctant agreement.

27 MAR 1782 Rockingham is appointed Prime Minister for the second time, in an uneasy alliance with Shelburne and his supporters.

8 APR 1782 Despite growing unrest in Ireland, William Eden's motion to repeal the Declaratory Act which is accomplished two days later, that allows the King to make laws binding in Ireland is lost.

16 APR 1782 At a special meeting of the Irish Parliament Grattan demands legislative and judicial independence for Ireland.

15 MAY 1782 The Cabinet finally decides on the repeal of the Declaratory Act, thus satisfying Irish demands.

23 MAY 1782 The Cabinet tries to make progress towards peace in the colonies by resolving that their negotiator Thomas Grenville (son of George Grenville) propose American independence as an unconditional first step. At the same time Shelburne briefs his own negotiator, Richard Oswald, that the Cabinet's offer of independence is conditional on achieving peace. This position is the one that would find most favour with the King.

MAY–JUN 1782 Two important Acts which reduce political corruption are passed: Clerke's Act, which disqualifies government contractors from sitting in the Commons; and Crewe's Parliament Act, which disenfranchises customs and excise officers.

14 JUN 1782 Burke's Civil List Bill to regulate royal expenditure, pensions and offices has its Second Reading in the Commons. The King has opposed it, but allows it to pass at the end of the session in July.

23 JUN 1782 Rockingham, who has been ill on and off since taking office in March, now falls seriously ill. Shelburne begins to make overtures to Pitt, amongst others, with a view to forming his own Government if Rockingham dies.

26 JUN 1782 Fox, the Secretary of State for Foreign Affairs, is angry that the Cabinet's original unconditional offer of independence to the colonies is being undermined. He raises the matter again in Cabinet, but they reverse their earlier decision. Fox threatens to resign.

30 JUN 1782 Fox tries to clarify the position at a further Cabinet meeting. However, the Cabinet again denies that the offer of independence is unconditional, and Fox announces that he will resign.

1 JUL 1782 Rockingham dies, clearing the way for Shelburne.

BACKGROUND

PHYSICAL CHARACTERISTICS AND HEALTH

Rockingham was a tall, thin, dignified man. His skin was sallow and he did not enjoy good health. Several childhood illnesses left him a weak, nervous character and his famous shyness prevented him from being a frequent or an effective speaker in the House. He died of influenza.

EDUCATION

Primary 1738 Westminster School

Secondary Eton

University Some sources say he went to St. John's College, Cambridge, but this cannot be substantiated.

Cultural and vocational background He was sent to Geneva in 1746 but in 1748 he returned to make a tour of England. He then did a Grand Tour of France, Italy, Austria and Germany, buying many works of art for Wentworth Woodhouse.

Languages French and Italian

NON-PARLIAMENTARY CAREER

Military service In 1745 he became Colonel of a regiment of volunteers formed by his father. When they were disbanded he went to join the Duke of Cumberland's forces at Carlisle, using a false name and pass, as he was only 15 years old.

Other posts 1751, Lord Lieutenant of the North and West Ridings of Yorkshire (dismissed 1762; re-appointed 1765); 1755, Vice Admiral of Yorkshire (dismissed 1763; re-appointed 1766); 1751–62 Lord of the Bedchamber; 1763, Trustee of Westminster School; Governor of Charterhouse; 1766, High Steward of Hull

HONOURS

Other than peerage 7 Nov 1751 Fellow of the Royal Society; 13 Feb 1752 Fellow of the Society of Antiquaries; 6 May 1760 Knight of the Garter

CLUBS

White's. He was a founder member of the Jockey Club.

HOBBIES AND SPORTS

Rockingham loved betting and horseracing. According to Walpole, as a young man he once ran a race from Norwich to London between 5 geese and 5 turkeys. He suggested the name 'St. Leger', which in 1778 became the famous Doncaster St. Leger horserace. He owned several racehorses. One of them, Whistlejacket, was painted by Stubbs. He also played chess.

FINANCES

Rockingham's family was one of the largest landowners in the country. He constantly tried to expand and improve his estates, with such success that he was elected a Fellow of the Royal Society for his services in agriculture.

Income In 1751 he was earning £14,000 a year from rents. By 1761 this had almost doubled, to £24,000 a year.

Spouse's finances Mary Bright was reputed to be one of the wealthiest heiresses in the north of England, but the Bright estates were burdened with debts and mortgages. Mary's parents took responsibility for many of the debts so that she could obtain an income from the estates on her marriage. In return Rockingham gave Mary £500 p.a. pin money, £2,000 and a further £1,000 as a jointure after his death.

Legacies He inherited huge estates from his father.

Will His estates passed to his nephew William, 4th Earl Fitzwilliam, who then assumed the additional surname of Wentworth.

ANECDOTES

He once failed to attend one of his own Cabinet meetings. He described his behaviour to Newcastle with these words: 'I have been guilty of a strange forgetfulness tonight in having totally forgot that there was to be a meeting by appointment, at the Duke of Grafton's. I did not recollect it till I came home and heard that they had just sent here for me'. This may have given rise to a popular saying of the day: 'The Ministry sleeps, and the Minister's Rocking'em'.

QUOTATIONS

31 Oct 1776, *Englishmen*, whatever their local situation may be, know no obedience to any thing but the laws. (*Almon's Debates* vol 5, p. 4)

9 Mar 1778, The King can have no interests, no dignity, no views whatever, distinct from those of his people. (*Almon's Debates*, vol 10, p. 294)

RESIDENCES

Wentworth Woodhouse, Yorkshire

Badsworth Hall, Yorkshire.

He also owned extensive property at Malton; Yorkshire; Milton; Great Harrowden, Northamptonshire, and County Wicklow, Ireland.

Grosvenor Square, London.

MEMORIALS

STATUES AND BUSTS

The mausoleum in Wentworth Park contains a statue by Nollekens. Busts by the same sculptor are at Althorp, Northamptonshire and Goodwood, West Sussex.

PORTRAITS

1766–8, by Sir Joshua Reynolds, Fitzwilliam Museum, Cambridge; 1768, from the studio of Reynolds,

MEMORIALS—*Continued*

National Portrait Gallery, London, and Mansion House, York.

OTHER MEMORIALS

The town of Rockingham, Vermont, and Rockingham County, New Hampshire, were named after him. 'Rockingham ware' china takes its name from being made on his estate at Swinton, Yorkshire.

BIBLIOGRAPHIC INFORMATION

LETTERS AND PERSONAL PAPERS

Extracts from Rockingham's correspondence are printed in Albemarle. Sheffield City Library has a collection of Rockingham papers.

FURTHER READING

Albermarle, G.T. *Memoirs of the Marquess of Rockingham and His Contemporaries.* 2 vols. London, 1852.

Guttridge, G. H. *The Early Career of Lord Rockingham 1730–1765.* Berkeley, California, 1952.

Langford, P. *The First Rockingham Administration 1765–1766.* London, 1973.

O'Gorman, F. *The Rise of Party in England: The Rockingham Whigs 1760–82.* London, 1975.

J.S.

Bettmann

Earl of Chatham

Lived 1708–1778
Political Party Whig
Prime Minister 30 July 1766–14 October 1768
Government Whig
Reigning Monarch George III

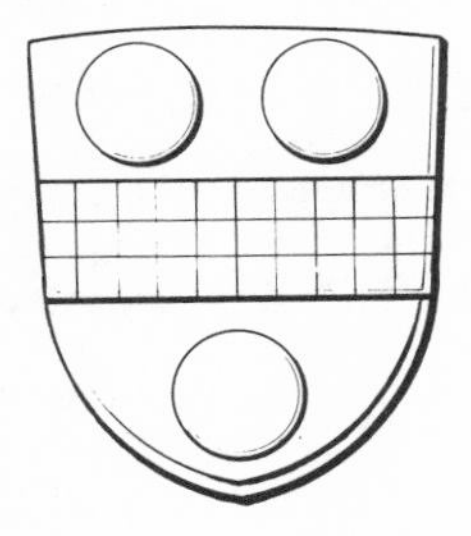

Benigno numine By divine providence

CHATHAM AS PRIME MINISTER

Although Prime Minister for only a little over two years, William Pitt, Earl of Chatham, dominated much of mid-18th century British politics. When he was passed over for promotion by Newcastle, he became rapidly estranged from the Government, and was dismissed in late 1755. However by the end of 1756 he was Prime Minister in all but name in Devonshire's Government, although he antagonised many and was dismissed by the King in the following year. His public popularity ensured his rapid return to the political scene in what was in effect a Chatham-Newcastle ministry, where he presided over the military successes of the Seven Years War (1756-1763). The accession of George III in 1760 strengthened Bute's peace faction, leading to Chatham's resignation the following year over the Government's refusal to make war on Spain. Ill health and the King's refusal of his terms led Chatham to reject several royal overtures to form a ministry, until he finally succeeded Rockingham in 1766. He decided immediately to govern from the Lords (becoming Earl of Chatham), thereby depriving himself of his power base as the 'Great Commoner.' Grafton, as First Lord of the Treasury, increasingly had to take control of the Government due to Chatham's deteriorating health. After his resignation, Chatham devoted much of his remaining political career to the growing crisis in the North American colonies, the topic of his parliamentary speech in 1778, which precipitated his fatal collapse.

PERSONAL INFORMATION

Names William Pitt
Peerages Viscount Pitt of Burton Pynsent & Earl of Chatham, 4 Aug 1766
Nicknames The Great Commoner; Pitt the Elder
Born 15 Nov 1708
Birthplace Golden Square, Westminster, London
Religion Anglican
Ancestry English. His family were respectable public officeholders with property in Dorset and Hampshire. Their name and fortune was made by Chatham's grandfather, Thomas Pitt, an East India trader who became Governor of Madras. Most of his children married into the peerage.
Date and place of marriage 16 Nov 1754, Argyle Street, London
Age at marriage 46 years, 1 day
Years married 23 years, 176 days
First entered Parliament 18 Feb 1735
Date appointed PM 30 Jul 1766
Age at appointment 57 years, 257 days
Date ceased to be PM 14 Oct 1768
Total time as PM 2 years, 76 days
Ceased to be MP 4 Aug 1766
Lived after last term as PM 9 years, 209 days
Date of death 11 May 1778
Place of death Hayes Place, Bromley, Kent
Age at death 69 years, 177 days
Last words To his son: 'Leave your dying father, and go to the defence of your country.'
Place of funeral & burial Westminster Abbey
Zodiac sign Scorpio

FATHER

Robert Pitt
Date and place of birth 1680, India (possibly Madras)
Occupation MP Old Sarum, 1705–10, 1713–22; Salisbury 1710–13; Okehampton 1722–27. Clerk of the Household to the Prince of Wales.
Date of marriage Jun 1703
Date of death 21 May 1727
Place of burial Died in Paris

MOTHER

Lady Harriet Villiers
Date of birth c. 1682
Profile She was tall, slim and beautiful. She had a sense of humour and an understanding nature. Her reputation was virtuous.
Date of marriage Jun 1703
Date of death 21 Oct 1736
Place of burial Died in Paris

BROTHERS AND SISTERS

Chatham was the second son and fourth of seven children.

Thomas, b. 1705; m. 1) Christian Lyttleton, 2) Maria Murray; MP Okehampton 1727–54, Old Sarum 1754–55, Mar–Jul 1761; d. 17 Jul 1761
Harriet, m. Sir William Corbet (MP Montgomery 1728–41, Ludlow 1741–48); d. young after making a 'private marriage'.
Catherine, m. Robert Nedham (MP Old Sarum 1734–41, later Viscount Kilmorey)
Elizabeth, b. 1710; m. John Hannan; d. 1770
Ann, b. 1712; Maid of Honour to the Queen; d. 1781
Mary, b. 1725; d. 1787

WIFE

Hester Grenville
Date and place of birth 8 Nov 1720, Wotton, Buckinghamshire
Mother Hester, Countess Temple
Father Richard Grenville
Father's occupation MP Wendover, 1715–22; Buckingham, 1722–27
Age at marriage 34 years, 8 days
Number of children 5
Date and place of death 3 Apr 1803, Burton Pynsent, Somerset
Place of burial Westminster Abbey
Years younger than PM 11 years, 358 days
Profile She was tall and graceful, with auburn hair. Her manner was sweet and charming, and she enjoyed country life. Sister of George Grenville (*q.v.*) she was created Baroness Chatham in 1761 in recognition of her husband's political service.

CHILDREN

3 sons, 2 daughters
Hester, b. 18 Oct 1755; m. 19 Dec 1774, Charles, Lord Mahon (MP Chipping Wycombe 1780–86); d. 18 Jul 1780
John (2nd Earl of Chatham), b. 9 Oct 1756; m. 10 Jul 1783, Lady Mary Elizabeth Sydney; Master General of the Ordnance 1801–06, 1807–10; Lieutenant General 1802; General 1812; First Lord of the Admiralty 1788–94; Lord Privy Seal 1794–96; Lord President of the Council 1796–1801; Governor of Plymouth 1805–07; Governor of Jersey 1807–20; Governor of Gibraltar 1820; d. 24 Sep 1835
Harriot, b. 18 Apr 1758; m. 28 Sep 1785, Hon. Edward James Eliot (MP St. Germans 1780–84, Liskeard 1784–97; a Lord of the Treasury 1792–93); she acted as her brother William's hostess at 10 Downing Street from 1785–86; d. 24 Sep 1786
William (*q.v.*), b. 28 May 1759; Prime Minister 1783–1801, 1804–06; d. 23 Jan 1806
James Charles, b. 24 Apr 1761; Naval captain; d. 13 Nov 1780

LIFE AND CAREER

PARLIAMENTARY ELECTIONS FOUGHT

*(*designates candidate elected)*

DATE 18 Feb 1735. By-election caused by Thomas Pitt's decision to sit for Okehampton
CONSTITUENCY Old Sarum
RESULT William Pitt* (Whig)

DATE Apr 1741. General Election
CONSTITUENCY Old Sarum

RESULT William Pitt* (Whig); George Lyttleton* (Whig)

DATE 26 Feb 1746. By-election caused by Pitt's appointment as Joint Vice Treasurer of Ireland
CONSTITUENCY Old Sarum
RESULT William Pitt* (Whig)

DATE 12 May 1746. By-election caused by Pitt's appointment as Paymaster General
CONSTITUENCY Old Sarum
RESULT William Pitt* (Whig)

DATE Jun 1747. General Election
CONSTITUENCY Seaford
RESULT William Pitt* (Whig) 49; William Hay* (Whig) 49; William Hall Gage (Whig) 23; Charles Sackville, Earl of Middlesex (Whig) 19

DATE Apr 1754. General Election
CONSTITUENCY Aldborough
RESULT William Pitt* (Whig); Andrew Wilkinson* (Whig)

DATE 7 Dec 1756. By-election caused by the appointment of James Grenville as a Lord of the Treasury
CONSTITUENCY Buckingham
RESULT William Pitt* (Whig)

DATE 11 Dec 1756. By-election caused by Sir George Lyttleton being called to the House of Lords
CONSTITUENCY Okehampton
RESULT William Pitt** (Whig)
***Elected both for Buckingham and Okehampton, Pitt chose to sit for Okehampton.*

DATE 9 Jul 1757. By-election caused by Robert Henley's appointment as Lord Keeper of the Seal
CONSTITUENCY Bath
RESULT William Pitt* (Whig)

DATE Mar 1761. General Election
CONSTITUENCY Bath
RESULT Viscount Ligonier* (Whig); William Pitt* (Whig)

PARTY ACTIVITY

In Mar 1742 he was selected as a member of a secret Committee of Inquiry into Walpole's use of the Civil List money. The inquiry was allowed to lapse in the autumn.
Membership of group or faction Boy Patriots

PARLIAMENTARY AND MINISTERIAL EXPERIENCE

Maiden Speech 22 Apr 1735. He spoke against the Place Bill. (*HMC Egmont MSS* II, p. 171)
Privy Counsellor 28 May 1746
Ministerial Offices Joint Vice Treasurer of Ireland, 22 Feb–6 May 1746; Paymaster General, 6 May 1746–20 Nov 1755; Secretary of State (Southern Dept.)& Leader of the House of Commons, 4 Dec 1756–6 Apr 1757, 27 Jun 1757–5 Oct 1761; Lord Privy Seal, 30 Jul 1766–Feb 1768, 21 Mar–14 Oct 1768
Opposition Leader while PM Marquess of Rockingham

GOVERNMENTS FORMED

Administration 30 Jul 1766–14 October 1768

GENERAL ELECTION RESULT
MAR 1761: Not analysed

GENERAL ELECTION RESULT
MAR 1768: Not analysed

CABINET
Prime Minister & Lord Privy Seal Earl of Chatham
First Lord of the Treasury Duke of Grafton
Chancellor of the Exchequer C. Townshend (1766–Sep 1767); Lord Mansfield (Sep–Oct 1767); Lord North (Oct 1767–1768)
Lord President of the Council Earl of Northington (1766–Dec 1767); Earl Gower (Dec 1767–1768)
Lord Chancellor Lord Camden
Secretary of State (Northern Dept.) H.S. Conway (1766–Jan 1768); Viscount Weymouth (1768)
Secretary of State (Southern Dept.) Earl of Shelburne
President of the Board of Trade Earl of Hillsborough (Aug–Dec 1766; 1768) Viscount Clare (Dec 1766–Jan 1768)
Secretary of State for the Colonies Lord Hillsborough (1768) (Office created Jan 1768)
First Lord of the Admiralty Sir E. Hawke
Chancellor of the Duchy of Lancaster Lord Strange
Master General of the Ordnance Marquess of Granby
Treasurer of the Navy Viscount Howe
Secretary at War Viscount Barrington
Paymasters General Lord North, G. Cooke (1766–Dec 1767); G. Cooke, T. Townshend (Dec 1767–1768)

IMPORTANT DATES IN PERSONAL AND POLITICAL LIFE

1710 His grandfather Thomas Pitt returns from India having been dismissed from his post as Governor of Madras. Brings with him the 'Pitt Diamond,' which makes the family's fortune when sold at a large profit.
1726–28 Enters Trinity College, Oxford, where he begins to suffer from gout and gets into debt. He leaves without taking a degree and goes to the University of Utrecht for several months.
9 FEB 1731 Cornet in his uncle Lord Cobham's regiment, the King's Own Regiment of Horse.
1733–4 Chatham travels in Europe, mainly France and Switzerland.
18 FEB 1735 First elected to Parliament at a by-election for Old Sarum, his family's pocket borough.
22 APR 1735 Maiden speech, made against the Place Bill, which would disqualify certain officials from sitting in the House of Commons.
29 APR 1736 A sarcastic speech on Pulteney's motion to congratulate the King on the marriage of the Prince of Wales angers Walpole to the point of having Pitt dismissed from his regiment.
SEP 1737 Appointed Groom of the Bedchamber to the Prince of Wales. His brother-in-law George Lyttleton becomes the Prince's Private Secretary.
1738 Makes an official visit to Bath and is presented with the Freedom of the City.
MAR 1739 Speaks forcefully against Walpole's proposed convention with Spain. Terming it 'nothing but a stipulation for national ignominy', he demonstrates his growing powers of oratory.
MAR 1742 Sits on a Committee of Inquiry into Walpole's use of Civil List money.
OCT 1744 Sarah, Duchess of Marlborough dies, leaving him £10,000 for his political activities in opposing Walpole.
NOV 1744 Henry Pelham and the Duke of Newcastle force the King to get rid of Carteret, but there is no offer of a place for Chatham in the changed ministry.

IMPORTANT DATES IN PERSONAL AND POLITICAL LIFE—*Continued*

APR 1745 Resigns as Groom of the Bedchamber. His career now depends on improving his relations with the King, and distancing himself from opposition forces is the first step.

22 FEB 1746 Appointed Joint Vice Treasurer of Ireland, a post which entitles him to enter the Privy Council of Ireland, a modest beginning to his ministerial career.

6 MAY 1746 The Paymaster General, Thomas Winnington, dies, and his place is taken by Chatham, giving him a Cabinet post.

28 MAY 1746 Admitted to the Privy Council.

JUN 1747 Chatham can no longer stand for Old Sarum because his brother Thomas supports the Opposition. He stands in Seaford for the ministry, and defeats the opposition candidates there.

6 MAR 1754 Henry Pelham dies. Although Chatham cannot hope to become Prime Minister, he anticipates promotion as a reward for his loyal services. The Duke of Newcastle becomes PM, but does nothing for him. He is greatly offended, and writes to the Duke on 24 Mar expressing his indignation.

APR 1754 Selected for Newcastle's borough of Aldborough, Yorkshire. Whatever his disappointments, he still aspires to high office. At the General Election he is indeed re-elected to Parliament.

SEP 1754 Engaged to Hester Grenville, sister of George Grenville, soon to be Prime Minister. Although she is twenty-three years his junior, Chatham has known her for many years through his association with the Grenville family.

14 NOV 1754 On the day of the opening of Parliament he presents a Bill for the relief of Chelsea Pensioners, who received their pension a year in arrears. It passes in December.

16 NOV 1754 Marries Lady Hester Grenville by special licence and goes to Wickham in Kent for a short honeymoon.

13 NOV 1755 Having ceased to support the ministry, he makes a brilliant speech denouncing the proposed German subsidies.

20 NOV 1755 Chatham and Legge dismissed from office. A potential financial disaster is averted when Chatham's brother-in-law, Lord Temple, agrees to lend him £1,000 a year.

4 DEC 1756 After Newcastle's ministry has tottered to a close, Chatham becomes Secretary of State for the Southern Department and Leader of the House of Commons under the Duke of Devonshire.

7–11 DEC 1756 Acceptance of office necessitates a fresh election, and Pitt stands at two by-elections at Buckingham and Okehampton. Elected for both, he chooses to sit for Okehampton.

6 APR 1757 Dismissed from office for a second time. This time his popularity as a man of principle is demonstrated by the number of cities that vote to give him their freedoms.

27 JUN 1757 The King forced to reappoint him as Secretary of State with sole charge of the direction of war and foreign affairs.

9 JUL 1757 Re-elected for Bath, which he prefers to Okehampton.

6 SEP 1757 Chatham's expedition to 'alarm the coasts of France' sets sail after lengthy obstacles and delays. In spite of his genius for both strategy and tactics, he has great difficulty in persuading his colleagues that an attack on the French coast will damage French confidence in America and elsewhere and give England the initiative in the war.

7 OCT 1757 The expedition returns empty-handed, a terrible disappointment. He had fought hard to resist plans to send these forces to Germany to relieve the Duke of Cumberland, and their failure adds to a number of reversals in other theatres of war.

25 NOV 1758 English forces capture Fort Duquesne from the French, marking a series of successes in the North American campaign.

27 NOV 1758 General Forbes informs Chatham that he has renamed Fort Duquesne 'Pittsburg' in his honour.

18 SEP 1759 The surrender of Quebec signals the inevitable defeat of the French forces in Canada, crowning a year of military victories for English forces in Germany, North America and the East Indies. Chatham has fulfilled his promise to 'save the country,' and is hailed as 'The Great Commoner.' His popularity has never been greater.

19 NOV 1760 George III's first speech to Parliament, largely written by his favourite, the Earl of Bute, contains criticisms of the conduct of the war which Chatham has to fight to have removed. Bute continues to advocate peace, but Chatham wants to press home his military advantage.

SEP 1761 Chatham proposes war with Spain, but the King, Bute and most of his Cabinet colleagues refuse to support him.

5 OCT 1761 Chatham and Temple resign on the war issue. The King, with Bute's eager backing, offers Chatham the governorship of Canada or Chancellorship of the Duchy of Lancaster. He refuses, hinting that rewards for his relatives would be welcome, and accepts a pension of £3,000 for his own lifetime and for that of his wife Hester and his son John. This, and Hester's becoming Baroness Chatham, lampooned as 'Lady Cheat'em', make Chatham unpopular for a time.

17 OCT 1761 Chatham writes to the town clerk of the City of London setting the record straight about the reasons for his resignation; the letter appears in the *Public Ledger*, instantly restoring his popularity.

9 NOV 1761 On his way to the Lord Mayor's dinner at the Guildhall he is cheered by the crowds, who are more delighted to see him than they are by the King and Queen. Bute is jeered.

4 JAN 1762 Bute is obliged to declare war on Spain.

9 NOV 1762 Despite a bad attack of gout Chatham speaks vehemently against the proposed peace treaty with France and Spain. Some of his three-hour long speech has to be delivered from a sitting position, and he is too ill to stay for the division.

8 APR 1763 Bute resigns and is replaced by Grenville.

21 AUG 1763 The death of Lord Egremont, a leading member of Grenville's Cabinet, leads to negotiations with Chatham and Bedford to try to strengthen the ministry.

25 AUG 1763 Chatham is offered the premiership but wants places for his Whig friends. The King refuses his terms, so Grenville remains in office.

17 FEB 1764 Supports a motion condemning general warrants as illegal.

JAN 1765 Sir William Pynsent, a complete stranger, leaves him his Somerset estate of Burton Pynsent, valued at £40,000. Chatham is too ill with gout to see it for six months.

MAY 1765 Determined to get rid of Grenville, the King sends the Duke of Cumberland to Hayes to ask Chatham to join a new ministry. In poor health and aware that he is the King's last resort, he refuses.

10 JUL 1765 Grenville replaced by Rockingham.

14 JAN 1766 Chatham reappears in the House to denounce the Stamp Act, which had been passed during his absence the previous year, drawing a distinction between the right to legislate and the right to levy taxes. Grenville rejects his argument, and Pitt again restates his views in a memorable speech full of passionate oratory. After this performance Rockingham and Grafton ask him to join the ministry but he refuses, perhaps because of ill health.

7 JUL 1766 The King dismisses Rockingham and invites Chatham to advise 'how an able and dignified ministry may be formed.' He cannot refuse.

30 JUL 1766 Becomes Prime Minister and Lord Privy Seal, a less onerous office than the more usual one of First Lord of the Treasury.

4 AUG 1766 Created Viscount Pitt of Burton Pynsent and Earl of Chatham. His acceptance of a peerage is controversial and arguably his biggest mistake. The office of Lord Privy Seal could only be held by a peer at this time, and he feels that a title will give him dignity. However, the fact that he now leads from the Lords rather than the Commons weakens the ministry and divorces him from his power base.

24 SEP 1766 Chatham places a ban on the export of grain by means of an Order in Council to solve the problem of food riots. This action is felt to be unconstitutional.

11 NOV 1766 His maiden speech in the House of Lords defends his measures in statesmanlike terms.

NOV 1766 Chatham asks Lord Edgcumbe to become a Lord of the Bedchamber instead of Treasurer of the Household to make way for his protege John Shelley. Edgcumbe refuses and is dismissed. Since Edgcumbe is a Rockingham supporter, Rockingham seizes his chance of toppling the ministry by urging other Rockinghamites to resign in protest. Several do so, but Chatham is able to fill their places.

27 FEB 1767 Townshend's Budget is overturned by a successful Rockinghamite motion to reduce land tax from the usual 4 shillings in the pound to 3. With his ministry in difficulties, Chatham collapses on his way to London and spends the next 18 months completely out of touch with politics, suffering a mental breakdown.

JUN 1767 Townshend introduces measures to tax the colonists in order to pay for their own defences, although this is contrary to Chatham's policy, but the ministry is now out of his control.

3 JUL 1767 Grafton and Northington are given permission to open negotiations with opposition groups. Rockingham hopes to form an alliance with Bedford and his supporters to replace the Chatham ministry, but the King is reluctant to see Chatham go.

17 AUG 1767 Chatham gives Hester the authority to act on his behalf in all his affairs, which shows the seriousness of his illness.

DEC 1757 Grafton reconstructs the ministry.

23 JAN 1768 The King urges Chatham to stay in office.

2 FEB 1768 The privy seal is put in commission so that urgent business can be dealt with. It is later to be returned to him.

11 MAR 1768 Parliament dissolved for a General Election.

9 OCT 1768 Grafton informs Lady Chatham that the Earl of Shelburne has decided to resign, prompting Chatham a few days later to ask the King's permission to resign.

14 OCT 1768 His resignation is accepted.

7 JUL 1769 Chatham has an audience with the King. He had resumed control of his affairs in January, but tells the King that he has decided to retire to the country.

22 JAN 1770 Despite his intentions, he returns to the House on this and several other occasions over the following 18 months to speak in support of Opposition motions. Although he speaks well, he cannot sustain a role as a leading Opposition figure.

28 JAN 1770 Lord North replaces Grafton as PM.

22 NOV 1770 His power as a threat to those abroad is illustrated by a powerful speech on a motion for the production of papers relating to the seizure of Port Egmont in the Falkland Islands.

22 JAN 1771 The Spanish return Port Egmont to the British.

26 MAY 1774 Speaks against the repressive measures being proposed in the wake of the Boston Tea Party.

20 JAN 1775 Proposes a motion that the troops should be recalled from Boston. It is heavily defeated.

1 FEB 1775 Introduces a Bill 'for settling the troubles in America' which includes recognising the representative Congress of Philadelphia. When it fails to get even a First Reading he suffers a relapse and is seriously ill for the next two and a quarter years.

18 APR 1775 First shots fired in the American War of Independence.

30 MAY 1777 Chatham struggles to the House to plead for a cessation of hostilities in America. 'You cannot conquer the Americans. I might as well talk of driving them before me with this crutch.'

AUG 1777 Chatham falls from his horse and is confined to bed for a time.

20 NOV 1777 At the opening of Parliament Chatham speaks eloquently against the employment of Indian 'savages' against the Americans.

2 DEC 1777 News of the surrender of Burgoyne and his army at Saratoga reaches London. North asks the King to let him resign, but is refused.

6 FEB 1778 France signs a treaty with America, recognising independence.

MAR 1778 North begs the King to appoint Chatham in his place, but the King insists that although an approach can be made, he will never deal with Chatham directly. Chatham replies that he wishes to speak to the King and to form his own ministry, but the King refuses to take the matter further. North withdraws, still protesting that a change in the ministry is essential.

7 APR 1778 Chatham comes to the House for the last time. He opposes Richmond's proposal to give the colonies their independence and urges the House not to fear war with France. His last words in the House are said to have been, 'If the Americans defend independence they shall find me in their way.' As he rises to speak a second time he collapses and is carried out of the Chamber. The House adjourns as a mark of respect.

11 MAY 1778 He dies at Hayes.

7–8 JUN 1778 His body lies in state in the Painted Chamber of the Palace of Westminster.

9 JUN 1778 Buried in Westminster Abbey.

BACKGROUND

PHYSICAL CHARACTERISTICS AND HEALTH

Chatham was a tall, thin man. He held himself erect, and was an imposing figure with his flashing eyes and long hooked nose. He dressed elegantly, and was both vain and proud.

His poor health was dominated by two hereditary problems, gout and acute depression. There was a history of mental instability on his mother's side of the family, and as he grew older he suffered increasingly from severe bouts of depression. The unexpected loss of his second wife was a great source of sadness to him. In 1777 he suffered a slight stroke which caused him to fall from his horse. On 7 Apr 1778 he collapsed during his last speech in the House of Lords and died a few weeks later.

EDUCATION

Secondary 1719–26 Eton

University 1726–28 Trinity College, Oxford (left before graduating) 1728 University of Utrecht

Cultural and vocational background 1733–34, He made a private tour of France and Switzerland

Languages He wrote Latin verse while at Oxford. Later he spoke good French.

NON-PARLIAMENTARY CAREER

Military service He became a Cornet in the King's Own Regiment of Horse, 9 Feb 1731. He was dismissed in 1736.

Other posts 1737–45 Groom of the Bedchamber to the Prince of Wales.

HONOURS

Freedom of cities 1738, Bath; 1757, City of London, Bedford, Chester, Exeter, Newcastle on Tyne, Norwich, Salisbury, Stirling, Tewkesbury, Worcester, Yarmouth etc.; 1761, Dublin.

Other than peerage 26 Jan 1744 Fellow of the Royal Society.

CLUBS

White's

HOBBIES AND SPORTS

As a young man he played cricket. In later years he took up horse riding. He was interested in military history. He developed a passion for the expensive hobby of landscape gardening.

FINANCES

Despite his income and some generous legacies, he was constantly in debt. He enjoyed spending large amounts of money on his estates, particularly on the landscaping of Burton Pynsent. Although in need of money he refused to profit from the 'perks' of the job as Paymaster General. In later years his wife managed his affairs, but shielded him from the consequences of his extravagant lifestyle.

Income Pitt earned about £400 a year as Groom of the Bedchamber. Later, as Lord Privy Seal his salary was £3,000 a year, rising to £4,000 as Paymaster General.

Spouse's finances Hester Grenville brought £14,000 worth of Reduced Bank Annuities as her part of the marriage settlement.

Pensions After his resignation the King granted a pension of £3,000 p.a. to him, his wife (who was created Baroness Chatham) and their son John.

Legacies In 1726 his grandfather left him £100 p.a. which was doubled on his mother's death. In 1744 the Duchess of Marlborough left him £10,000 for his political activities. In 1765 Sir William Pynsent left him his estate at Burton Pynsent and a generous £3,000 a year.

Debts He got into debt at Oxford and in later life was rarely out of it. In 1744 the Duke of Bedford granted him an annuity of £300, and after his dismissal from office in 1755 his brother, Lord Temple, gave him an annuity of £1,000. In 1767 he gave power of attorney over his affairs to his wife, and by 1775 both Hayes and Burton Pynsent were heavily mortgaged and friends were lending them large sums. On his death Parliament voted £20,000 to pay off his debts.

ANECDOTES

'A Minister that inspires great actions must be a great minister and Lord Chatham will always appear so, by comparison with his predecessors and successors.' (Horace Walpole, 1778)

'England has been a long time in labour, but she has at last brought forth a man.' (Frederick the Great)

'Once, when Secretary of State, he was staying with a friend near London whose grounds he had undertaken to adorn and in the evening was summoned suddenly to London. He at once collected all the servants with lanterns, and sallied forth to plant stakes in the different places that he wished to mark for plantations'. (Quoted in Rosebery *Chatham*).

QUOTATIONS

The atrocious crime of being a young man . . . I shall neither attempt to palliate nor deny. (1741, Speech in the House of Commons)

Unlimited power is apt to corrupt the minds of those who possess it. (1770, Speech in the House of Lords)

If I were an American, as I am an Englishman; while a foreign troop was landed in my country, I never would lay down my arms—never—never—never! (1777, Speech in the House of Lords)

You may ravage, you cannot conquer. It is impossible. You cannot conquer the Americans. (1777, Speech in the House of Lords)

The parks are the lungs of London. (Quoted by William Windham MP, 1808)

RESIDENCES

South Lodge, Enfield Chase, Middlesex

Hayes Place, Bromley, Kent (Sold to Thomas Walpole in 1765 but repurchased two years later)

10 St. James's Square (Later occupied by two other Prime Ministers, the Earl of Derby and William Gladstone). Now called Chatham House (plaque).

Burton Pynsent, Somerset

North End House, Hampstead, London (now called Wildwood House)

He also had a house in Bath.

MEMORIALS

STATUES AND BUSTS

1766, by J. Wilton, Crawford School, Cork; 1782, by John Bacon, Sr., Guildhall, London; 1784, by John Bacon, Jr., Westminster Abbey, London; n.d., by MacDowell, Palace of Westminster, London.

PORTRAITS

1766, by William Hoare, Guildhall, Bath; 1772, after Richard Brompton, National Portrait Gallery; 1779, by J. S. Copley: 'The collapse of the Earl of Chatham in the House of Lords, 7 Jul 1778,' National Portrait Gallery

OTHER MEMORIALS

The original Blackfriars Bridge, London was called 'Pitt Bridge' for a short period. Pittsburgh, Pennsylvania, originally Fort Duquesne, was named in his honour, as were Pittsfield, Massachusetts; Pittsboro, North Carolina; Pittsylvania, Virginia; Chatham County, Virginia, and Chatham Strait, Arkansas. 10 St. James's Square is now called Chatham House.

BIBLIOGRAPHIC INFORMATION

LETTERS AND PERSONAL PAPERS

The Chatham papers are in the Public Record Office.

Chatham's letters have been published in: Taylor, W. S. and Pringle, J. H. *Correspondence of William Pitt, Earl of Chatham*. 4 vols. London, 1838–40; Kimball, G. S. *Correspondence of William Pitt when Secretary of State with Colonial Governors* . . . 2 vols. New York, 1906.

PUBLICATIONS

Some Latin verses were published in *Pietas Universitatis Oxoniensis in obitum serenissimi Regis Georgii I*. 1727.

FURTHER READING

Ayling, S. *The Elder Pitt, Earl of Chatham*. London, 1976.

Black, J. *Pitt the Elder*. Cambridge, 1992.

Brooke, J. *The Chatham Administration 1766–1768*. London, 1956.

Brown, P.D. *William Pitt, Earl of Chatham: the Great Commoner*. London, 1978.

Lever, Sir T. *The House of Pitt*. London, 1947.

Plumb, J. H. *Chatham*. London, 1965.

Rosebery, Archibald Philip Primrose, 5th Earl of. *Chatham: His Early Life and Connections*. London, 1910.

Sherrard, O. A. *Lord Chatham*. 3 vols. London, 1952–58.

Tunstall, B. *William Pitt, Earl of Chatham*. London, 1938.

Williams, B. *The Life of William Pitt, Earl of Chatham*. 2 vols. London, 1913.

J.S.

Bettmann

Duke of Grafton

Lived 1735–1811
Political Party Whig
Prime Minister 14 October 1768–28 January 1770
Government Whig
Reigning Monarch George III

Et decus et pretium recti Both the honour and the reward of rectitude.

GRAFTON AS PRIME MINISTER

Grafton's first ministerial post was in Rockingham's Government in 1765, from which he resigned the following year over the PM's refusal to bring Pitt into his ministry. He became First Lord of the Treasury when Pitt was appointed Prime Minister in July 1766, and somewhat reluctantly had to take control of the Government at the age of 31 because of the ill-health of the PM (now in the Lords as the Earl of Chatham). Much of 1767 was spent in efforts to reconstruct Chatham's failing Government, and in October of the following year Grafton became Prime Minister when Chatham finally resigned. His short period of office was taken up with the American colonial situation, concerning which he believed that all duties on the colonies should be removed—except that on tea. His administration also had to deal with the repeated attempts of John Wilkes, who had been convicted of seditious libel, to take his seat in Parliament. Grafton's ministry broke up in January 1770, although he agreed to serve as Lord Privy Seal under Lord North in 1771, a post he gave up in 1775 following disagreement over North's American policy.

PERSONAL INFORMATION

Names Augustus Henry Fitzroy
Peerages Styled Earl of Euston, 1747–57; 3rd Duke of Grafton
Nicknames Royal Oak; The Turf Macaroni
Born 28 Sep 1735
Religion Unitarian
Ancestry English. His ancestor, the first Duke, was one of three illegitimate sons of King Charles II by Barbara, Duchess of Cleveland. His family was often in royal service. They had lands in Suffolk.
Dates and places of marriages 1) 29 Jan 1756, 13 St. James's Square, Westminster, London (Div. 23 Mar 1769); 2) 24 Jun 1769, Woburn Abbey, Bedfordshire
Age at marriages 1) 20 years, 123 days; 2) 33 years, 269 days
Years married 1) 13 years, 53 days, 2) 41 years, 263 days
First entered Parliament 10 Dec 1756
Date appointed PM 14 Oct 1768
Age at appointment 33 years, 16 days
Date ceased to be PM 28 Jan 1770
Total time as PM 1 year, 106 days
Ceased to be MP 6 May 1757
Lived after last term as PM 41 years, 45 days
Date of death 14 Mar 1811
Place of death Euston Hall, Suffolk
Age at death 75 years, 167 days
Place of burial Euston, Suffolk
Zodiac sign Libra

FATHER

Lord Augustus Fitzroy
Date of birth 16 Oct 1716
Occupation MP Thetford 1739–41; Naval captain
Date of marriage Mar 1734
Date of death 28 May 1741
Place of burial Died in Jamaica

MOTHER

Elizabeth Cosby
Place of birth Possibly New York, where her father William was governor.
Dates of marriages 1) Mar 1734; 2) after 1741, James Jeffreys
Date of death 21 Dec 1788

BROTHERS AND SISTERS

Grafton was the second of three sons.
Charles, b. 1734; d. 1735 or 36
Charles (Baron Southampton), b. 25 Jun 1737; m. 27 Jul 1758, Anne Warren; MP Orford 1759–61, Bury St. Edmunds 1761–74, Thetford 1774–80; General in the Army (1793); held various posts in the Royal Household; d. 21 Mar 1797

FIRST WIFE

Anne Liddell
Date of birth 1738
Mother Anne Delmé
Father Henry Liddell, Baron Ravensworth
Father's occupation MP Morpeth, 1734–47, then a Peer
Age at marriages 1) *c.* 18 years 2) *c.* 31 years, m. 26 Mar 1769, John Fitzpatrick, Earl of Upper Ossory
Number of children 1) 5, 2 of whom d. in infancy; 2) 4
Date and place of death 24 Feb 1804, Grosvenor Square, London.
Place of burial Grafton, Northamptonshire
Years older than PM *c.* 3 years
Profile In Jan 1765 she and the Duke were separated. She had a son by John Fitzpatrick in 1768, and married him as soon as her marriage to the Duke had been dissolved by an Act of Parliament on 23 Mar 1769.

SECOND WIFE

Elizabeth Wrottesley
Date of birth 1 Nov 1745
Mother Lady Mary Leveson-Gower
Father Sir Richard Wrottesley
Father's occupation MP Tavistock 1747–54; Clerk Comptroller of the Green Cloth 1749–54; Chaplain to George III 1763; Dean of Worcester 1765–9.
Age at marriage 23 years 235 days
Number of children 13
Date and place of death 25 May 1822, Lower Brook Street, Middlesex
Years younger than PM 10 years, 3 days
Profile She was said to be 'not handsome, but quiet and reasonable, having a very amiable character.' In 1769 Grafton described her as someone 'whose merit as a wife, tenderness and affection as mother of a numerous family, and exemplary conduct thro' life, need not be related.'

CHILDREN

7 sons, 9 daughters
By his first wife Anne:
Georgiana, b. 8 May 1757; m. 4 Jun 1778, John Smyth (MP Pontefract 1783–1807); d. 18 Jan 1799
George Henry (4th Duke of Grafton), b. 14 Jan 1760; m. 16 Nov 1784, Lady Charlotte Maria Waldegrave; MP Thetford 1782–84, Cambridge University 1784–1811; Lord Lieutenant, Vice Admiral and Custos Rotulorum of Suffolk; d. 28 Sep 1844
Charles, b. 14 Jul 1764; m. 1) 20 Jun 1795 Frances Mundy (d. 9 Aug 1797) 2) 10 Mar 1799, Lady Frances Anne Stewart; MP Bury St. Edmunds 1787–96, 1802–18; an Army General; d. 20 Dec 1829
By his second wife Elizabeth:
Henry, b. 19 Apr 1770; m. 2 Oct 1800, Caroline Pigot; Prebendary and Canon of Westminster, London; d. 7 Jun 1828
Charlotte, b. 14 Aug 1771
Augustus, served in the Navy; d. 1801
Frederick, b. 16 Sep 1774
Elizabeth, b. 19 Oct 1775; m. 4 Jul 1811, her first cousin William Fitzroy; d. 31 Mar 1839
Louisa, b. 13 Jul 1777; d. 16 Feb 1804
Augusta, b. 19 Feb 1779; m. 19 Nov 1811, Rev. George-Frederick Tavel; d. 29 Jun 1839
Frances, b. 1 Jun 1780; m. 25 Nov 1800, Francis-Almeric Spencer, Lord Churchill (MP Oxfordshire 1801–15)
Caroline, b. 15 Jul 1781; d. 28 May 1803
William, b. 1 Jun 1782; m. 22 Aug 1816, Georgiana Raikes; MP Thetford 1806–12; an Admiral; d. 13 May 1857
Harriet, b. 8 Apr 1784; d. 14 Apr 1804
John-Edward, b. 24 Sep 1785; MP Thetford 1812–18, Bury St. Edmunds 1820–26; d. 28 Dec 1856

CHILDREN—*Continued*

Isabella, b. 17 Nov 1786; m. 14 Aug 1812, Barrington-Pope Blachford (MP Newtown, Isle of Wight, 1807–16)

LIFE AND CAREER

PARLIAMENTARY ELECTIONS FOUGHT

*(*designates candidate elected)*

DATE 10 Dec 1756. By-election caused by William Murray's appointment as Attorney General
CONSTITUENCY Boroughbridge
RESULT Augustus Henry Fitzroy* (Whig)

DATE 21 Dec 1756. By-election caused by William Stanhope being called to the House of Lords
CONSTITUENCY Bury St. Edmunds
RESULT Augustus Henry Fitzroy** (Whig)
*****Elected both for Boroughbridge and Bury St. Edmunds, he chose to sit for the family borough of Bury St Edmunds.*

PARTY ACTIVITY

Membership of group or faction He was a leader of the 'Young Friends' of the Duke of Newcastle in opposition to Bute and Grenville.

PARLIAMENTARY AND MINISTERIAL EXPERIENCE

Maiden Speech 9 Dec 1762, in the House of Lords, on the preliminary terms of the Peace of Paris.
Privy Counsellor 10 Jul 1765
Ministerial Offices Secretary of State, Northern Department 12 Jul 1765–14 May 1766; First Lord of the Treasury Jul 1766–28 Jan 1770; Leader of the House of Lords Aug 1766–28 Jan 1770; Lord Privy Seal 12 Jun 1771–9 Nov 1775, 27 Mar 1782–2 Apr 1783

GOVERNMENTS FORMED

Administration 14 Oct 1768–28 Jan 1770

GENERAL ELECTION RESULT
MAR 1768: Not analysed

CABINET
Prime Minister and First Lord of the Treasury Duke of Grafton
Chancellor of the Exchequer Lord North
Lord President of the Council Earl Gower
Lord Privy Seal Earl of Bristol
Secretary of State (Northern Department) Viscount Weymouth (Oct 1768); Earl of Rochford (Oct 1768–1770)
Secretary of State (Southern Department) Earl of Shelburne (Oct 1768); Viscount Weymouth (Oct 1768–1770)
Secretary of State for the Colonies Lord Hillsborough
First Lord of the Admiralty Sir E. Hawke
Master General of the Ordnance Marquess of Granby
Joint Postmasters-General Lord Sandwich; Lord le Despencer
Lord Chancellor Lord Camden (1768–Jan 1770); C. Yorke (Jan 1770)

IMPORTANT DATES IN PERSONAL AND POLITICAL LIFE

28 MAY 1741 His father dies in Jamaica as a result of a fever caught in the battle at the siege of Carthagena, where he commanded the *Orford.* Grafton and his brother Charles are brought up by their grandfather.

1753 Graduates from Cambridge and tours Europe with a Swiss companion.

29 JAN 1756 Marries Anne Liddell, the daughter of Baron Ravensworth.

1756 Appointed a Lord of the Bedchamber to the Prince of Wales.

10 DEC 1756 He is returned unopposed for Boroughbridge in Yorkshire, one of the Duke of Newcastle's pocket boroughs. Later the same month he is also returned unopposed for Bury St. Edmunds, his family's borough. Not surprisingly he chooses to sit for Bury St. Edmunds.

6 MAY 1757 Succeeds his grandfather as 3rd Duke of Grafton, and also becomes Lord Lieutenant of Suffolk at only twenty-one years old.

14 NOV 1760 Grafton comes to the first of a series of agreements with the Davers family that his nominee for the Bury St. Edmunds seat will not be opposed, provided he finds an alternative seat for the Davers family representative.

JUNE 1761 Grafton and his wife go abroad for the sake of his wife's health, returning the following year.

9 DEC 1762 Grafton makes his first speech on the preliminary terms of the Peace of Paris. Unfortunately it goes unrecorded, but he describes it himself as, 'too declamatory, and directed chiefly against Lord Bute. The violence of my language was easily excused in a young man speaking from his heart.'

3 MAY 1763 Grafton attempts to visit Wilkes, imprisoned in the Tower of London for publishing what are said to be 'seditious libels' against Parliament, and writes to him.

11 JAN 1765 He and his wife are separated.

10 JUL 1765 Made a Privy Counsellor.

12 JUL 1765 Appointed to his first ministerial post, Secretary of State for the Northern Department, at the age of 29.

28 APR 1766 He decides to resign because he thinks the ministry is too weak without Pitt, and Rockingham has made it clear that he will never invite Pitt to join it. He relinquishes the seals on 14th May.

30 JUL 1766 The King, having dismissed Rockingham, invites Pitt to form an administration. Grafton accepts the post of First Lord of the Treasury with reluctance, because he does not feel he can do the job.

4 AUG 1766 Pitt accepts a peerage, becoming Earl of Chatham. Grafton is dismayed as he knows that the Commons will be more difficult to manage if the Chief Minister is in the House of Lords.

1 NOV 1766 Wilkes, who has been declared an outlaw, writes to Grafton, asking him to plead his case with the King. Grafton shows the letter both to the King and to Chatham, but takes no other action.

JAN–FEB 1767 Grafton makes repeated attempts to get Chatham to take decisions about the Government's dealings with the East India Company, but without success.

24 APR 1767 A letter from Charles Townshend openly refers to Mrs. Haughton (or Horton), otherwise known as Nancy Parsons, a woman of loose morals with whom Grafton is living.

3 JUL 1767 The King agrees that Grafton should approach the adherents of the Duke of Bedford with a view to strengthening the ministry.

7 JUL 1767 Grafton sees Rockingham, who thinks (mistakenly) that he is being asked to lead a new ministry.

23 JULY 1767 Grafton reports Rockingham's desires to the King, who assures Grafton that he does not want Rockingham. Grafton is forced to turn to the Bedford faction, ensuring that the policy balance will tip towards greater hostility to America.

17 AUG 1767 Chatham's illness has become so serious that he gives his wife Hester power of attorney over his affairs. Grafton is left in charge of the ministry.

SEP 1767 He encourages North to become Chancellor of the Exchequer, which he does on 7th October.

DEC 1767 Grafton reconstructs the ministry, although Chatham is nominally still in charge.

JAN 1768 Grafton manages to split the Southern Department so that American affairs are dealt with by a new minister, the Secretary of State for the Colonies. This has the desired effect of forcing Shelburne to resign in protest later that year.

11 MAR 1768 Parliament is dissolved for a General Election.

28 MAR 1768 Polling begins for Middlesex, where Wilkes has decided to stand. There are riots in his support and he is elected.

APR 1768 Grafton appears at the opera with Mrs. Haughton.

10 MAY 1768 The new Parliament assembles, but the majority is no greater than before. This is blamed on Grafton's indolence.

23 AUG 1768 His wife has a son by John Fitzpatrick, whom she marries the following year.

14 OCT 1768 The King reluctantly accepts Chatham's resignation. Grafton officially becomes Prime Minister.

19 OCT 1768 Shelburne resigns and is replaced by Viscount Weymouth.

29 NOV 1768 Elected Chancellor of Cambridge University.

21 JAN 1769 First appearance of Junius, a scathing critic of Grafton's administration, who writes a series of letters attacking him and supporting Chatham's return.

27 FEB 1769 The Government secures an agreement with East India Company concerning the taxation of their profits.

23 MAR 1769 His divorce from Anne Liddell is finalised, following an Act of Parliament.

15 APR 1769 The House overturns the election of John Wilkes and declares Colonel Luttrell duly elected for Middlesex, despite only having polled 216 votes against 1,143 for Wilkes. The first six months of the year are dominated by the Wilkes affair. Wilkes, who had been convicted of publishing 'seditious libels' some years before, stands for Parliament at Middlesex. He is elected and reelected several times, and each time the House expels him and declares him ineligible to stand, which increases his popularity. Grafton's mishandling of this affair is an embarrassment and weakens his administration.

1 MAY 1769 Cabinet discussion of the port duties levied on the American colonies. Grafton wants to repeal all of the duties, but the Cabinet decides to retain the duty on tea.

24 JUN 1769 Marries his second wife, Elizabeth Wrottesley.

1 JUL 1769 Installed as Chancellor of Cambridge University, giving £500 to the town for improvements.

AUTUMN 1769 Grafton is criticised for neglecting his duties. He has 'diverted himself in the country, coming to town but once a week, or once a fortnight, to sign papers at the Treasury; and as seldom to the King,' according to Horace Walpole (*Memoirs of the reign of George III*). Junius continues his campaign against Grafton, accusing him of illegally cutting wood in Whittlebury and Salcey Forests. Grafton is, in reality, entitled to do so by virtue of his position as Ranger. The administration's credibility begins to crumble.

20 SEP 1769 Made a Knight of the Garter.

END 1769 Chatham begins to recover from his illness, and his supporters rally to him.

9 JAN 1770 Parliament reassembles after the Christmas break.

17 JAN 1770 Camden is dismissed as Lord Chancellor because of his lack of support for the administration, and Granby resigns as Master General of the Ordnance. On the same day the King persuades the reluctant Charles Yorke to accept the office of Lord Chancellor.

20 JAN 1770 Yorke dies. This is probably the last straw for Grafton, who has been struggling to keep the administration together.

28 JAN 1770 Grafton resigns as First Lord of the Treasury, and is succeeded by Lord North.

12 JUN 1771 North persuades Grafton to take office again as Lord Privy Seal.

8 NOV 1775 Grafton speaks out against the Address to the King, advocating the repeal of all legislation affecting America passed since 1763.

9 NOV 1775 The King asks Grafton to give up the Great Seal, which he does.

11 MAY 1778 Death of Earl of Chatham.

3 FEB 1779 Grafton replies to the King's invitation to join the Cabinet that he will not act without the support of the Marquess of Rockingham.

6 NOV 1780 A heated dispute between Grafton and the Earl of Pomfret is discussed in the House of Lords concerning threats that have been made to Pomfret and his family by a man who Pomfret thinks is backed by Grafton. Grafton denies any involvement in the affair and Pomfret is severely censured for his intemperate behaviour.

20 MAR 1782 North resigns from office.

27 MAR 1782 Rockingham becomes Prime Minister. Grafton accepts the office of Lord Privy Seal for the second time.

1 JUL 1782 Rockingham dies. The Earl of Shelburne succeeds him and Grafton continues in office.

16 FEB 1783 The Duke of Rutland is given a place in the Cabinet. Grafton is angered that he and the rest of the Cabinet have not been consulted, and they decide to resign.

19 FEB 1783 Grafton sees the King and offers to resign the Seal.

24 FEB 1783 Faced with growing discontent in his Cabinet, Shelburne goes to the King to offer his resignation, advising him to send for Chatham.

2 APR 1783 After months of fruitless negotiations, a new administration is finally formed under the Duke of

IMPORTANT DATES IN PERSONAL AND POLITICAL LIFE—*Continued*

Portland. Grafton leaves office, resolving to spend more time with his pack of hounds at Whittlebury and his horses at Newmarket.

1789 Grafton publishes a tract advocating greater attention to public worship. He is a regular attender at the Unitarian Chapel in Essex Street, off the Strand, London.

30 MAY 1797 Makes a rare contribution to debate by speaking on the Duke of Bedford's motion of no confidence.

14 MAR 1811 Grafton dies.

BACKGROUND

PHYSICAL CHARACTERISTICS AND HEALTH

Although not tall, Grafton appeared elegant and graceful. In later life he was described as: 'an elderly gentleman, of spare form, middle stature, straight silver hair, a prominent nose, and a countenance of much severity; and dressed in a light-coloured tight-fitting coat, long black boots and a small three-cornered hat.' (Albemarle, *Memoirs of the Marquess of Rockingham*, 1852)

He was shy and disliked ceremonial. Occasionally he would fall asleep at Cabinet meetings.

EDUCATION

Primary A private school in Hackney, London.
Secondary Westminster School
University 1751–53 Peterhouse, Cambridge
Qualifications 1753 M.A.
Cultural and vocational background Between 1753 and 1754 Grafton did the Grand Tour, visiting France, Switzerland, Italy, Germany and Holland.

NON-PARLIAMENTARY CAREER

1756–58 Lord of the Bedchamber to the Prince of Wales; 1757–63, 1769–90 Lord Lieutenant of Suffolk; 1768 Chancellor of Cambridge University; 1778 Recorder of Thetford and Coventry; Ranger of Whittlebury and Salcey Forests; High Steward of Dartmouth; 1793 Trustee of the British Museum.

HONOURS

Academic He declined the degree of LLD usually conferred on Chancellors of the University of Cambridge because he disliked 'subscribing to the Articles of the Church of England.'
Other than peerage 20 Sep 1769, Knight of the Garter

CLUBS

Jockey Club (founder member), Brooks's, White's

HOBBIES AND SPORTS

He loved hunting and had a pack of hounds at Wakefield Lodge in Northamptonshire. He also bred racehorses, winning the Derby three times and the Oaks twice. He often went to the races at Newmarket, and his seat at Euston was a regular rendezvous for Jockey Club members. He enjoyed farming, and collecting and talking about books.

FINANCES

Pensions He was proud never to have taken 'a place or a pension.'
Legacies As a descendant of Charles II he inherited a special annuity.

ANECDOTES

Horace Walpole compared Grafton to 'an apprentice, thinking the world should be postponed to a whore and a horse race.'

Grenville said, 'The account of the Cabinet Council meeting being put off, first for a match at Newmarket, and secondly because the Duke of Grafton had company at his house, exhibits a lively picture of the present administration.'

Horace Walpole presents the following portraits of Grafton: 'Richmond and Grafton were much of an age; each regarded himself as Prince of the Blood; and emulation soon created a sort of rivalship between them. . . . The Duke of Grafton was low, but manly, and with much grace in his address. The passions of both were strong, but of the first, ardent; of the latter, slow and inflexible. His temper was not happy . . . Both were thought avaricious . . . The Duke of Grafton had a grace and dignity in his utterance that commanded attention, and dazzled in lieu of matter; and his temper being shy and reserved, he was supposed to be endued with more steadiness than his subsequent conduct displayed. Neither of them wanted obstinacy; but their obstinacy not flowing from system, it was in both a torrent more impetuous in its course than in its duration.'

'The ductility and congenial indolence of the Duke of Grafton, accompanied with much respect and good breeding, fixed his Majesty in preferring him to all men whom he *could* employ: and though the Duke not long afterwards fell into a connection of very ill-odour at Court, *yet* the tedious tyranny of Grenville, and the inveteracy of Rockingham to Bute, were so much more dreaded that Grafton did not cease to be almost a favourite.'

QUOTATIONS

Wisdom is at no time more conspicuous, nor more amiable, than in the acknowledgement of error. (30 May 1797, Speech in the House of Lords, on the Duke of Bedford's motion of no confidence).

RESIDENCES

Euston Hall, Thetford Suffolk
Wakefield Lodge, Whittlebury Forest, Northamptonshire.
Open to the public Euston Hall, a fine 18th-century house with a famous collection of paintings is open during the summer months.

MEMORIALS

PORTRAITS

1762, by Pompeo Batoni, National Portrait Gallery; 1776, by R. E. Pine, Euston Hall, Suffolk; 1805, by John Hoppner, Euston Hall, Suffolk

OTHER MEMORIALS

Grafton, Vermont; Grafton and Grafton County, New Hampshire, were named after him. Euston Road, Grafton Street and Fitzroy Square are all London streets named after the family.

BIBLIOGRAPHIC INFORMATION

LETTERS AND PERSONAL PAPERS

Many letters are reprinted in his *Autobiography.* His papers are in Suffolk Record Office, Bury St. Edmunds.

PUBLICATIONS

1789, *Hints submitted to the serious attention of the clergy, mobility and gentry by a layman*; 1797, *The serious reflections of a rational Christian from 1788 to 1797* (published anonymously)

FURTHER READING

Anson, Sir W. R. *Autobiography and Political Correspondence of Augustus Henry Third Duke of Grafton K.G.*; ed. Sir W. R. Anson. London, 1898.

J.S.

Bettmann

Lord North

Lived 1732–1792
Political Party Tory until 1783; Whig 1783–92
Prime Minister 28 January 1770–27 March 1782
Government Tory
Reigning Monarch George III

La vertu est la seule noblesse Virtue is the only nobility

LORD NORTH AS PRIME MINISTER

North, a hard working and sound administrator, for some twelve years acted as Prime Minister, Chancellor of the Exchequer, and leader of the House of Commons. His membership of the Commons and friendship with the King, together with his equitable temperament and his essentially moderate policies helped ensure support for him. However, he believed that ministers should be personally responsible for their departments and confided to the King that he did not really have the leadership qualities to be head of an administration. In turn, the King played on North's sense of duty, persuading him to continue in office, whereby the King was assured of an orderly House of Commons. His first years as Prime Minister were dominated by the American problem, where ultimately, and too late, he sought to follow conciliatory tactics. Rightly he appreciated that the real clash was about power, rather than just taxation. The defeat of the British at Saratoga in 1777 insured his last years as Prime Minister would increasingly be regarded a failure. The anti-Catholic (Gordon) riots in 1780, in which rioters agitated for repeal of the Catholic Relief Act, reflected his unsatisfactory domestic policy. After the King finally accepted his resignation in 1782, he continued to be influential through the Fox-North Coalition, which supported Prime Minister Portland under whom he served as Home Secretary. He was a member of the House of Lords for his last two years.

PERSONAL INFORMATION

Names Frederick North
Peerages Earl of Guilford, Lord North of Kirtling and Baron Guilford
Nicknames Boreas (the north wind), Lord-deputy North
Born 13 Apr 1732
Birthplace Albemarle St., Piccadilly, London
Religion Anglican
Ancestry English. His family had belonged to the peerage since the 16th century and were traditionally Tories. His father became a Whig and supported the Hanoverian Kings, settling in Oxfordshire.
Date and place of marriage 20 May 1756, St. James's, Westminster, London
Age at marriage 24 years 37 days
Years married 36 years 77 days
First entered Parliament 15 Apr 1754
Date appointed PM 28 Jan 1770
Age at appointment 37 years, 290 days
Date ceased to be PM 27 Mar 1782
Total time as PM 12 years, 58 days
Ceased to be MP 4 Aug 1790
Lived after last term as PM 10 years, 138 days
Date of death 5 Aug 1792
Place of death 41 Grosvenor Square, London
Age at death 60 years, 114 days
Last words He thanked his family for their kindness to him since his blindness, and assured them that he felt no pain.
Place of funeral Oxford, Oxfordshire
Place of burial All Saints' Church, Wroxton, Oxfordshire
Zodiac sign Aries

FATHER

Francis, 1st Earl of Guilford
Date of birth 13 Apr 1704
Occupation MP Banbury 1727–29. Became a Peer in 1729. He was Lord of the Bedchamber to Frederick, Prince of Wales, a governor to Prince George and Treasurer to the Queen Consort.
Dates of marriages 1) 17 Jun 1728, Lady Lucy Montagu (d. 7 May 1734); 2) 24 Jan 1736, Elizabeth Legge, Dowager Viscountess of Lewisham (d. 21 Apr 1745); 3) 13 Jun 1751, Lady Katherine Watson (d. 17 Dec 1766)
Age when PM took office 65 years 290 days
Date of death 4 Aug 1790
Place of burial All Saints' Church, Wroxton, Oxfordshire

MOTHER

Lady Lucy Montagu
Date place of birth *c.* 1709
Date of marriage 17 Jun 1728
Date of death 7 May 1734
Place of burial All Saints' Church, Wroxton, Oxfordshire

BROTHERS AND SISTERS

North was the eldest of six children.
From his father's first marriage:
Lucy, b. Apr 1734; m. Thomas Bradley, a tradesman, whereupon her father denied her existence; d. 7 Jun 1790.
From his father's second marriage:
Louisa, b. 23 Mar 1737; m. Lord Willoughby de Broke (a Lord of the Bedchamber); d. 2 Apr 1798
Frances, b. *c.* 1737; d.*c.* 1746
Brownlow, b. 17 Jul 1741; m. Henrietta Maria Bannister; Bishop of Coventry and Lichfield 1771, Worcester 1774, Winchester 1781; d. 12 Jul 1820
Charlotte, b. 1742; d. 1746
Elizabeth Legge's children from her previous marriage:
Arthur Legge, b. 1727; d. 6 Oct 1729
William Legge (2nd Earl of Dartmouth), b. 20 Jun 1731; m. Frances Catherine Gunter Nicoll; First Lord of Trade 1765–66, 1772–75; Secretary for the Colonies, 1772–75, Lord Privy Seal 1775–82; d. 15 Jul 1801
Anne Legge; m. James Brudenell, 5th Earl of Cardigan (MP Shaftesbury 1754–61, Hastings 1761–68, Great Bedwyn 1768, Marlborough 1768–80, Constable of Windsor Castle); d. 12 Nov 1786
Elizabeth Legge; m. Colonel Whitshed Keene (MP Wareham 1768–74, Ludgershall 1774, Montgomery 1774–1818, a Lord of the Admiralty)

WIFE

Anne Speke
Date and place of birth 1740; Dillington House, Ilminster, Somerset
Mother Dame Anne Drake
Father George Speke, of White Lackington, Somerset.
Father's occupation Landowner and MP for Milborne Port 1722–27, Taunton 1727–34, Wells 1735–47
Age at marriage *c.* 16
Number of children 7
Date and place of death 17 Jan 1797; Bushey Park, Middlesex.
Place of burial All Saints' Church, Wroxton, Oxfordshire
Years younger than PM *c.* 8 years
Profile A daughter described her: 'plain in her person but had excellent good sense . . . a singular mildness and placidity of temper with humour and conversational powers by no means contemptible.' She was Ranger of Bushey Park from 1771 until she died.

CHILDREN

4 sons, 3 daughters
George Augustus (3rd Earl of Guilford), b. 11 Sep 1757; m. 1) 24 Sep 1785, Maria Frances Mary Hobart (d. Apr 1794); 2) 28 Feb 1796, Susan Coutts; MP Harwich 1778–84; Wootton Bassett 1784–90; Petersfield 1790; Banbury 1790–92. Comptroller of the Queen's Household 1781–83; Under Secretary, Home Office 1783; d. 20 Apr 1802
Catherine Anne, b. 16 Feb 1760; m. 26 Sep 1789, Sylvester Douglas, Lord Glenbervie (MP Fowey 1795–96, Midhurst 1796–1800, Plympton Erle 1801–02, Hastings

CHILDREN—*Continued*

1802–06; First Commissioner of Woods, Forests and Land Revenues); d. 6 Feb 1817

Francis (4th Earl of Guilford), b. 25 Dec 1761; m. 19 Jul 1810, Maria Boycott; Army Officer; patron of the stage; d. 11 Jan 1817

Anne, b. 8 Jan 1764; m. 20 Jan 1798, John Baker-Holroyd, Earl of Sheffield (MP Coventry 1780–84, Bristol 1790–1802; Member of the Board of Trade); d. 18 Jan 1832

Frederick (5th Earl of Guilford), b. 7 Feb 1766; Chamberlain of the Exchequer 1779–1826; MP Banbury 1792–94; d. 14 Oct 1847

Charlotte, b. Dec 1770; m. 2 Apr 1800, Hon. John Lindsay; d. 25 Oct 1849

Dudley, b. 31 May 1777; d. 18 Jun 1777

LIFE AND CAREER

PARLIAMENTARY ELECTIONS FOUGHT

*(*designates candidate elected)*

DATE Apr 1754. General Election
CONSTITUENCY Banbury
RESULT Lord North* (Tory)

DATE 4 Jun 1759. By-election caused by North's appointment as a Lord of the Treasury
CONSTITUENCY Banbury
RESULT Lord North* (Tory)

DATE Mar 1761. General Election
CONSTITUENCY Banbury
RESULT Lord North* (Tory)

DATE 17 Nov 1766. By-election caused by North's appointment as Joint Paymaster of the Forces
CONSTITUENCY Banbury
RESULT Lord North* (Tory)

DATE 30 Nov 1767. By-election caused by North's appointment as Chancellor of the Exchequer.
CONSTITUENCY Banbury
RESULT Lord North* (Tory)

DATE Mar 1768. General Election
CONSTITUENCY Banbury
RESULT Lord North* (Tory)
DATE Oct 1774. General Election
CONSTITUENCY Banbury
RESULT Lord North* (Tory)

DATE 9 Jun 1778. By-election caused by North's appointment as Lord Warden of the Cinque Ports
CONSTITUENCY Banbury
RESULT Lord North* (Tory)

DATE Sep 1780. General Election
CONSTITUENCY Banbury
RESULT Lord North* (Tory)

DATE 9 Apr 1783. By-election caused by North's appointment as Home Secretary
CONSTITUENCY Banbury
RESULT Lord North* (Tory)

DATE Mar 1784. General Election
CONSTITUENCY Banbury
RESULT Lord North* (Tory)

DATE Jun 1790. General Election
CONSTITUENCY Banbury
RESULT Lord North* (Tory)

PARTY ACTIVITY

He was an assiduous Committee member, sitting on 48 in 1758–59, 31 in 1759–60, 23 in 1760–61 and 13 in 1761–62.

Membership of group or faction The King's Friends

PARLIAMENTARY AND MINISTERIAL EXPERIENCE

Maiden Speech 1 Dec 1757. He seconded the Address to the Throne at the opening of Parliament (*Parl Hist* vol 15, col 837, ref only).

Privy Counsellor 10 Dec 1766.

Ministerial Offices Lord of the Treasury 2 Jun 1759–10 Jul 1765; Joint Paymaster of the Forces 19 Aug 1766–1767; Chancellor of the Exchequer 7 Oct 1767–27 Mar 1782; Leader of the House of Commons Jan 1768–27 Mar 1782; First Lord of the Treasury 28 Jan 1770–27 Mar 1782; Home Secretary 2 Apr–22 Dec 1783

Opposition Leader while PM Marquess of Rockingham

GOVERNMENTS FORMED

Administration 28 Jan 1770–27 Mar 1782

GENERAL ELECTION RESULTS

MAR 1768: Not analysed

OCT 1774:

Supporters of the Administration 321; Others 237. Total 558.

Majority 84

SEP 1780: Government 260; Opposition 254; Others 144. Total 558.

CABINET

Prime Minister, First Lord of the Treasury and Chancellor of the Exchequer Lord North

Lord President of the Council Earl Gower (1770–Nov 1779); Earl Bathurst (Nov 1779–1782)

Lord Chancellor Earl Bathurst (Jan 1771–Jun 1778); Lord Thurlow (Jun 1778–1782)

Secretary of State (Southern Department) Viscount Weymouth (Jan–Dec 1770; Nov 1775–Nov 1779); Earl of Rochford (Dec 1770–Nov 1775); Earl of Hillsborough (Nov 1779–1782)

Secretary of State (Northern Department) Earl of Rochford (Jan–Dec 1770); Earl of Sandwich (Dec 1770–Jan 1771); Earl of Halifax (Jan–Jun 1771); Earl of Suffolk & Berkshire (Jun 1771–Mar 1779); Viscount Weymouth (Mar–Oct 1779); Viscount Stormont (Oct 1779–1782)

President of the Board of Trade Earl of Hillsborough (1770–Aug 1772); Earl of Dartmouth (Aug 1772–Nov 1775); Lord Sackville-Germain (Nov 1775–Nov 1779); Earl of Carlisle (Nov 1779–Dec 1780); Lord Grantham (Dec 1780–1782)

Secretary of State for the Colonies Lord Harwich (1770–Aug 1772); Earl of Dartmouth (Aug 1772–Nov 1775); Lord Sackville-Germain (Nov 1775–Feb 1782); W. Ellis (1782).

First Lord of the Admiralty Sir E. Hawke (1770–Jan 1771); Earl of Sandwich (Jan 1771–1782)

Lord Privy Seal Earl of Halifax (1770–Jan 1771); Earl of Suffolk & Berkshire (Jan–Jun 1771); Duke of Grafton (Jun 1771–Nov 1775); Earl of Dartmouth (Nov 1775–1782)

Chancellor of the Duchy of Lancaster Lord Strange (1770–Jun 1771); Earl of Clarendon (Jun 1771–1782)

Master General of the Ordnance Marquess of Granby 1770–Oct 1772); Viscount Townshend (Oct 1772–1782)

Treasurer of the Navy Sir G. Elliot (1770–Jun 1777); Lord Mendip (Jun 1777–1782)

Secretary at War Viscount Barrington (1770–Dec 1778); C. Jenkinson (Dec 1778–1782)

IMPORTANT DATES IN PERSONAL AND POLITICAL LIFE

21 MAR 1750 MA at Trinity College, Oxford. Next few years spent travelling in Europe with his step-brother William, 2nd Earl of Dartmouth.

15 APR 1754 First elected to Parliament for the family borough of Banbury.

20 MAY 1756 Marries Anne Speke, daughter of a Somerset landowner.

1 DEC 1757 Makes maiden speech.

17 JAN 1758 Pitt offers him a position at the Court of Turin, but after consulting his father, North refuses it.

2 JUN 1759 Takes up his first ministerial post as a Lord of the Treasury under Newcastle, a distant cousin. When Newcastle resigns in 1762, North stays in office.

24 NOV 1763 North, managing the Government's case against MP John Wilkes, moves the motion that parliamentary privilege not cover cases of seditious libel. This attempt to suppress scathing attacks in Wilkes' weekly *North Briton* only strengthens the campaign for individual rights.

24 JAN 1764 Speaks against the repeal of the cider tax, causing Sir William Pynsent to cut North's wife out of his will.

10 JUL 1765 North retires from office when Rockingham comes to power.

24 MAY 1766 Rockingham offers North the Vice Treasurership of Ireland. Refuses the post after some hesitation.

19 AUG 1766 North appointed Joint Paymaster of the Forces under Chatham.

10 DEC 1766 North made a Privy Counsellor.

4 MAR 1767 Chatham offers him the positions of Chancellor of the Exchequer and Leader of the House, but North refuses.

7 OCT 1767 Accepts the post of Chancellor after the death in September of the incumbent, Charles Townshend.

JAN 1768 North becomes Leader of the House of Commons.

MAR 1768 At the General Election Wilkes is elected for Middlesex.

17 FEB 1769 North has Wilkes declared ineligible, paving the way for the Government's candidate, Colonel Luttrell.

1 MAY 1769 The Cabinet approves North's motion to retain the duty on tea in the colonies by a majority of one.

28 JAN 1770 North becomes Prime Minister after the resignation of the Duke of Grafton, his cousin.

5 MAR 1770 House of Commons debates and approves decision to retain the tea duty, which had become a symbol of British sovereignty.

15 MAR 1770 North restrains the House from prosecuting the Lord Mayor of London and others, who had presented an insulting petition to the King entitled 'The Remonstrance of the City of London.' He requests that Remonstrance and the King's reply merely be laid before the House, thereby defusing the situation and strengthening the Government's position.

MAR 1771 North becomes embroiled in attempts to prevent London printers from publishing reports of debates in the House of Commons; after an angry mob attacks his carriage on the way to Parliament, North has to be rescued by Opposition MPs.

14 JUN 1771 His wife is appointed Ranger of Bushey Park, a sinecure including a house and a salary.

18 JUN 1772 North made a Knight of the Garter, one of the few commoners to be so honoured since Walpole.

3 OCT 1772 North unanimously elected Chancellor of Oxford University. His investiture later that month is attended by Benjamin Franklin, a mark of Franklin's respect for North.

26 APR 1773 House of Commons debates a Bill to allow the East India Company to export tea to America free of external duties.

MAY 1773 North supports a motion of censure of Clive's conduct in India; later changes his mind.

16 DEC 1773 Growing unrest in the colonies culminates in the Boston Tea Party: colonists attack and destroy shipments of tea from the East India Company. North asserts Parliament's right to legislate for the colonies.

14 MAR 1774 North introduces the first of his measures attempting to enforce the authority of the Crown, the Boston Port Bill, which passes by a large majority.

15 APR 1774 North introduces two further measures, the Massachusetts Government Bill and the Massachusetts Justice Bill. Despite opposition, both pass within weeks.

26 MAY 1774 The Quebec Bill allowing French majority to worship as Roman Catholics, but denying them full political rights, passes Second Reading.

20 FEB 1775 Faced with increasing opposition in America, North changes tactics and proposes conciliation. His motion provides that Britain not levy taxes on the colonies if they could support themselves on their own taxation. Change of heart too late to avoid war.

19 APR 1775 First shots are fired in a skirmish at Lexington, Massachusetts.

4 MAY 1775 A petition arrives from the New York Assembly offering to pay duties but insisting on the right to levy their own taxes. Commons reject this denial of Parliament's rights. The American War of Independence is under way.

25 JUL 1775 Battle of Bunker Hill, Boston.

20 NOV 1775 North introduces Prohibitory Bill to suppress all American trade by seizure of their shipping. Bill authorises the dispatch of a Peace Commission to negotiate with the rebellious colonists.

4 JUL 1776 American Declaration of Independence signed.

12 JUL 1776 Peace Commissioners arrive in New York.

SEP 1776 Breaks his arm in a fall from his horse.

SEP 1777 King grants North up to £20,000 to pay his debts.

17 OCT 1777 Burgoyne surrenders British forces at Saratoga.

16 JUN 1778 Appointed Lord Warden of the Cinque Ports, thus easing his financial difficulties.

NOV 1779 Lords Gower and Weymouth resign their posts in protest at the Administration's failure to deal with unrest in Ireland.

13 DEC 1779 North introduces measures to relax restrictions on Irish trade.

IMPORTANT DATES IN PERSONAL AND POLITICAL LIFE—*Continued*

6 APR 1780 North opposes Dunning's resolution against growing influence of the Crown, but it passes.

7 JUN 1780 A crowd threatens him in Downing Street during the anti-Catholic Gordon riots.

19 OCT 1781 Cornwallis surrenders at Yorktown.

27 FEB 1782 Conway's motion condemning the continuation of the war with America passes.

15 MAR 1782 North narrowly survives two motions of no confidence.

20 MAR 1782 North has begged the King many times to let him resign, and this time the King agrees, granting him a pension of £4,100 p.a.

14 FEB 1783 Meets with Fox to discuss joint tactics.

17 & 21 FEB 1783 Followers of North and Fox defeat Shelburne's ministry in two divisions in the House of Commons.

24 FEB 1783 Shelburne resigns, although his resignation is not accepted until 26 March.

2 MAR 1783 King offers North, via his father, the Earl of Guilford, a Cabinet post and a say in the formation of a new ministry. North refuses office, but agrees to consultations.

3 & 4 MAR 1783 King offers a Fox-North coalition ministry if an independent peer can be found to lead it. Fox and North declare they will only serve under the Duke of Portland. After further overtures to Pitt the King agrees to a new ministry.

2 APR 1783 The Fox-North coalition takes office under the leadership of the Duke of Portland. North becomes Home Secretary.

17 DEC 1783 During a debate on the India Bill about the influence of the King on his ministers, North speaks out strongly in defence of ministerial responsibility.

18 DEC 1783 Portland administration dismissed.

APR 1784 After General Election North still leads a sizeable number of supporters in the new Parliament.

MAY 1785 North attacks Pitt's proposals to allow equality of trade between Britain and Ireland claiming such equality would undermine Britain's trading position.

1787 Onset of blindness.

1 DEC 1788 Makes a rare appearance in the House to take a full part in debates on the Regency Bill.

4 AUG 1790 Succeeds his father as 2nd Earl of Guilford.

25 NOV 1790 North is led to his place in the House of Lords.

1 APR 1791 North's maiden speech in the Lords attacks Pitt's Russian policy.

6 MAR 1792 His last speech opposes the repeal of taxes.

5 AUG 1792 Dies of dropsy.

BACKGROUND

PHYSICAL CHARACTERISTICS AND HEALTH

North bore a striking resemblance to the King, which caused speculation that he was his half-brother. Like the King, he was of medium height, with light hair, bushy eyebrows and large grey eyes. Horace Walpole's description of him was unflattering: 'two large prominent eyes that rolled about to no purpose (for he was utterly short-sighted), a wide mouth, thick lips and an inflated visage gave him the air of a blind trumpeter.' (*Memoirs of the Reign of George III*, IV p 78). Always overweight, he became obese in later life. In Sep 1776 he was thrown from his horse in Bushey Park and broke his right arm. In 1787 he began to go blind, and on 15 Nov 1790 he had to be led to his seat in the Lords as 2nd Earl of Guilford. He died of dropsy.

EDUCATION

Secondary 1742–48 Eton

University 1749 Trinity College, Oxford

Qualifications 1750 Master of Arts

Cultural and vocational background After university he and his stepbrother, the Earl of Dartmouth, travelled in Europe. In 1752 North spent a year at the University of Leipzig studying the German constitution. North and Dartmouth visited Vienna, Milan and Paris, and returned to England at the end of 1753.

Languages North spoke fluent French and knew German and Italian.

NON-PARLIAMENTARY CAREER

Other posts 1771 Elder Brother of Trinity House; 1772 Chancellor of Oxford University; 1773 Master of Trinity House; 1774 Lord Lieutenant of Somerset; 1776 Governor of the Levant Company; 1778 Lord Warden of the Cinque Ports

HONOURS

Freedom of cities 1782 Exeter

Academic 1769 LLD Cambridge; 1772 DCL Oxford

Other than peerage 18 Jun 1772 Knight of the Garter; 26 Feb 1776 Fellow of the Society of Arts

CLUBS

White's, Brooks's

HOBBIES AND SPORTS

In his youth he enjoyed dancing, which he had learned while travelling in Europe.

FINANCES

North was dogged by debt until his father died in 1790. During the 1765–66 parliamentary session he had to rent out his house in Grosvenor Square and go to live with his mother-in-law, Lady Drake. His father was wealthy but ignored North's pleas for assistance. By the time the Earl of Guilford died North had only two years left to enjoy his inheritance.

Income In 1756–57 his income fluctuated between £2, 000 and £2,200 p.a. His salary as a Lord of the Treasury was £1,400 p.a. By 1767 his income had risen to £2,500 but he was in debt. In 1777 his estates were worth £2, 500 p.a.

Spouse's finances His wife was related to Sir William Pynsent of Somerset who was going to leave her £200, 000. North's vote in favour of the cider tax caused Pynsent to leave it to Chatham instead.

Pensions The King granted him an annuity of £4,100 on his resignation.

Legacies His father's death in 1790 left him well off. He is also rumoured to have received a legacy of £2,000

from a Mr. Vernon of Jamaica, and £60,000 from Beau Brummel's father.

Debts By 1777 he was £18,000 in debt, at a time when his salaries amounted to £7,000 p.a. In September 1777 the King gave him £20,000 to pay his debts. When he left office in 1782 the King held him responsible for £19, 274 of election debts, which he was unable to pay.

Will Dated 21 Jul 1792, his will was largely family bequests. Lady North received £500 p.a. each from the Oxfordshire and Kent estates. His children were well provided for.

ANECDOTES

North had the habit of sleeping, or appearing to sleep in the Chamber of the House of Commons as a means of avoiding arguments. Once, an opponent stopped his tirade to complain that North was asleep. North opened his eyes and said 'I wish to God I were.'

At Covent Garden one evening an acquaintance asked who was 'that plain-looking lady in the box opposite.' North replied that it was his wife, whereupon his companion said that he had meant the lady next to her. 'That, sir, is my daughter: we are considered to be three of the ugliest people in London,' he replied cheerfully.

When he was blind an old opponent, Colonel Isaac Barré, who was also blind, came to visit him. North greeted him warmly: 'Though you and I have had our quarrels in the past, I wager there are no two men in England who would be happier to see one another today.'

QUOTATIONS

Men may be popular without being ambitious, but there is hardly an ambitious man who does not try to be popular. (Quoted by C. D. Smith).

RESIDENCES

41 Grosvenor Square, Piccadilly, London
Dillington House, Somerset
10 Downing Street
Grove House, Tunbridge Wells, Kent
Bushey House, Bushey Park, Middlesex
Wroxton Abbey, Oxfordshire
Waldershare Park, Kent

MEMORIALS

STATUES AND BUSTS

By John Bacon, Bodleian Library, Oxford; by William Behnes, Eton College, Berkshire.

PORTRAITS

By Nathanial Dance, National Portrait Gallery; from the studio of Reynolds, Petworth, West Sussex; 1779, by J. S. Copley, Library of the Boston Athenaeum, Boston, Mass.

OTHER MEMORIALS

Several London streets were named after him: North Court, near Tottenham Court Road; North Mews, Gray's Inn Road; and Guilford Street, Bloomsbury. Guilford, North Carolina, was named in his honour.

BIBLIOGRAPHIC INFORMATION

LETTERS AND PERSONAL PAPERS

The main collections of papers relating to the North family are in the British Library; the Bodleian Library, Oxford; and Kent County Archives Office, Maidstone, Kent. Some correspondence can be found in: Fortescue, Sir John. *Correspondence of George III, 1760–1783*. 6 vols., London, 1927.

FURTHER READING

Butterfield, H. *George III Lord North and the People 1779–80*. London, 1949.
Cannon, J. *Lord North: The Noble Lord in the Blue Ribbon*. London, 1970.
Christie, I. R. *The End of North's Ministry 1780–1782*. London, 1958.
Lucas, R. *Lord North*. 2 vols. London, 1913.
Pemberton, W. B. *Lord North*. London, 1938.
Smith, C. D. *The Early Career of Lord North the Prime Minister*. London, 1979.
Thomas, P. D. G. *Lord North*. London, 1976.
Valentine, A. *Lord North*. 2 vols. Norman, Oklahoma, 1967.

J.S.

National Portrait Gallery

Earl of Shelburne

Lived 1737–1805
Political Party Whig
Prime Minister 4 July 1782–26 March 1783
Government Whig
Reigning Monarch George III

Virtute non verbis By valour not by boasting

SHELBURNE AS PRIME MINISTER

After serving in the military, he was elected to the House of Commons, but never sat there, succeeding to a seat in the House of Lords at the age of twenty-four. He was a supporter of Chatham, sharing many of his views and not placing much value on political party. During the 1770s he showed great independence including keeping the Rockingham Whigs at a distance. Although he accepted principles of free trade promoted by Adam Smith, he balked at the idea of independence for the American colonists. He was clever but did not receive the trust of his colleagues. He appointed a Cabinet with the best of talents rather than one of strong party allegiance, believing that Ministers should be personally responsible to the Sovereign. The King, therefore, turned to him to hold the Rockingham Whigs in the administration in check. Naturally some resignations ensued on his appointment, including those of Fox and Cavendish. Shelburne's drive for efficiency in government was not very successful. But the main issue was securing peace with the American colonists. The terms that satisfied him were rejected in the House of Commons by a small majority. Not having cultivated a supporting party in the House of Commons and with declining support from the King, he had to resign after just eight months in office.

PERSONAL INFORMATION

Names William Fitzmaurice (1737–51); William Petty (1751–61)
Peerages Styled Viscount Fitzmaurice (1753–61); 2nd Earl of Shelburne, Viscount Fitzmaurice, Baron Dunkeron, Lord Wycombe; Earl Wycombe of Chipping Wycombe, Viscount Calne and Calstone, Marquess of Lansdowne, 6 Dec 1784
Nicknames Malagrida; The Jesuit in Berkeley Square
Born 2 May 1737
Birthplace Bride Street, Dublin, Ireland
Religion Dissenter
Ancestry Irish. His father came from the Fitzmaurices, a great adventuring family who had been ruling the county of Kerry since the 12th century. His grandfather was the 1st Earl of Kerry. In 1751 his father assumed the name of Petty on succeeding to his uncle's estates.
Dates and places of marriages 1) 3 Feb 1765, Chapel Royal, St. James's, London; 2) 19 Jul 1779, St. George's; Bloomsbury, London
Age at marriages 1) 27 years, 275 days; 2) 42 years, 78 days
Years married 1) 5 years, 337 days; 2) 10 years, 41 days
First entered Parliament 2 Jun 1760 (Elected, but never took his seat in the House of Commons)
Date appointed PM 4 Jul 1782
Age at appointment 45 years, 63 days
Date ceased to be PM 26 Mar 1783
Total time as PM 266 days
Ceased to be MP 10 May 1761
Lived after last term as PM 22 years, 72 days
Date of death 7 May 1805
Place of death Lansdowne House, Berkeley Square, London
Age at death 68 years, 5 days
Place of funeral Presumably at High Wycombe, Buckinghamshire
Place of burial All Saints' Church, High Wycombe, Buckinghamshire
Zodiac sign Taurus

FATHER

John Fitzmaurice (assumed the name of Petty in 1751); Baron Dunkeron, Viscount Fitzmaurice, 1st Earl of Shelburne, Baron Wycombe
Date of birth 1706
Occupation Landowner and politician. He was a Member of the Irish Parliament for County Kerry from 1743–51, MP for the family borough of Chipping Wycombe 1754–60, then a Peer.
Date of marriage 16 Feb 1734
Date of death 10 May 1761

MOTHER

Mary Fitzmaurice (his cousin)
Profile According to Shelburne, she was 'one of the most passionate characters I ever met with, but good natured and forgiving, with a boundless love of power . . . If it had not been for her continual energy my father would have passed the remainder of his life in Ireland and I might at this time be the chief of some little provincial faction'.
Date of marriage 16 Feb 1734
Date of death 9 Dec 1780

BROTHERS AND SISTERS

Shelburne was the elder son and probably first of five children.
Thomas, b. Jul 1742; m. 21 Dec 1777, Mary O'Brien, daughter of the Earl of Inchiquin; MP Calne 1762–74, Chipping Wycombe 1774–80; a scholar and friend of Dr. Johnson, he became a linen merchant; d. 28 Oct 1793
Female child, d. young
Anne, d. young
Mary, d. young

FIRST WIFE

Lady Sophia Carteret
Date of birth 26 Aug 1745
Mother Sophia Fermor
Father John Carteret, Earl Granville
Father's occupation Peer
Age at marriage 19 years, 162 days
Number of children 2
Date of death 5 Jan 1771
Place of burial Bowood, Wiltshire
Years younger than PM 8 years, 116 days
Profile An amiable, virtuous woman.

SECOND WIFE

Lady Louisa FitzPatrick
Date of birth 1755
Mother Evelyn Leveson-Gower
Father John FitzPatrick, 1st Earl of Upper Ossory
Father's occupation MP Bedfordshire, 1753–58, then a Peer
Age at marriage c. 24 years
Number of children 2
Date and place of death 7 Aug 1789, Lansdowne House, Berkeley Square, London
Years younger than PM c. 18 years
Profile Jeremy Bentham, who played chess and billiards with her, paid tribute to her beauty, her reserve and her kindness.

CHILDREN

3 sons, 1 daughter
By his first wife, Lady Sophia:
John Henry (2nd Marquess of Lansdowne), b. 6 Dec 1765; m. 27 May 1805, Lady Maria Arabella Gifford (a widow); MP Chipping Wycombe 1786–1802, then a Peer; d. 15 Nov 1809
William Granville, bap. 7 Nov 1768; d. 27 Jan 1778
By his second wife, Lady Louisa:
Henry (Petty-Fitzmaurice from 1818) (3rd Marquess of Lansdowne, 4th Earl of Kerry), b. 2 Jul 1780; m. 30 Mar 1808, Louisa Emma Fox-Strangways, daughter of the 2nd Earl of Ilchester; MP Calne 1802–06, University of Cambridge 1806–07, Camelford 1807–09; Chancellor of the Exchequer 1806–07; Home Secretary 1827–28, Lord President of the Council 1830–34, 1835–41, 1846–52; Minister without portfolio 1852– 58; d. 31 Jan 1863
Louisa, b. 8 Dec 1781; d. young

LIFE AND CAREER

PARLIAMENTARY ELECTIONS FOUGHT

*(*designates candidate elected)*

DATE 2 Jun 1760. By-election caused by his father's elevation to the peerage
CONSTITUENCY Chipping Wycombe
RESULT William Petty, Viscount Fitzmaurice* (Whig)

DATE 1761. General Election (Irish Parliament)
CONSTITUENCY Kerry
RESULT William Petty, Viscount Fitzmaurice* (Whig), John Blenerhasset*

DATE Mar 1761. General Election
CONSTITUENCY Chipping Wycombe
RESULT William Petty, Viscount Fitzmaurice* (Whig); Robert Waller* (Whig)

PARTY ACTIVITY

Membership of group or faction Pittites, Chathamites

PARLIAMENTARY AND MINISTERIAL EXPERIENCE

Maiden Speech 5 Feb 1762, in favour of withdrawing the troops from Germany. (*Chatham Papers*)
Privy Counsellor 20 Apr 1763
Ministerial Offices President of the Board of Trade 20 Apr–2 Sep 1763; Secretary of State for the Southern Department 30 Jul 1766–19 Oct 1768; Secretary of State for Home, Irish & Colonial Affairs 27 Mar–4 Jul 1782; Leader of the House of Lords Mar 1782–Apr 1783; First Lord of the Treasury 4 Jul 1782–26 Mar 1783
Opposition Leader while PM Lord North

GOVERNMENTS FORMED

Administration 4 Jul 1782–26 Mar 1783

GENERAL ELECTION RESULT
SEP 1780:
Government 260; Opposition 254; Others 144. Total 558

CABINET
Prime Minister and First Lord of the Treasury Earl of Shelburne
Chancellor of the Exchequer W. Pitt
Lord President of the Council Lord Camden
Lord Chancellor Lord Thurlow
Home Secretary T. Townshend (Lord Sydney)
Foreign Secretary and President of the Board of Trade Lord Grantham
First Lord of the Admiralty Viscount Keppel (Jul 1782–Jan 1783); Viscount Howe (Jan–Feb 1783)
Lord Privy Seal Duke of Grafton
Chancellor of the Duchy of Lancaster Lord Ashburton
Master General of the Ordnance Duke of Richmond

IMPORTANT DATES IN PERSONAL AND POLITICAL LIFE

11 MAR 1755 Matriculates at Christ Church, Oxford, where he studies 'natural law and the law of nations; some history . . .'.

1757 He leaves university without taking a degree and goes into the army. His father buys him a commission in the 20th Regiment of Foot.

JUN 1758 He transfers into the 3rd Regiment of Foot-Guards.

1 AUG 1759 He distinguishes himself at the Battle of Minden during the Seven Years War.

2 JUN 1760 While still abroad on active service he is elected to the House of Commons for the family borough of Chipping Wycombe, Buckinghamshire.

16 OCT 1760 He plays a prominent part in the Battle of Kloster Kampen.

4 DEC 1760 He is rewarded for his military service by promotion to the rank of Colonel and an appointment to the post of aide-de-camp to the King.

28 MAR 1761 He is again returned as Member of Parliament for Chipping Wycombe at the General Election, but never takes his seat. On his father's death in May he inherits a peerage, becoming Earl of Shelburne and Baron Wycombe.

APR 1761 Shelburne applies for the Comptrollership of the Household but the King refuses his request.

3 NOV 1761 He takes his seat in the House of Lords as Baron Wycombe.

5 FEB 1762 He signs a protest to the King calling for troops to be withdrawn from Germany, which damages his relations with Bute. This is probably the occasion of his maiden speech.

25 MAR 1763 Bute proposes Shelburne as Secretary of State for Trade, but Grenville objects that he is too young and inexperienced. Bute then offers him the lesser post of President of the Board of Trade. Shelburne at first tries to make his acceptance conditional on being given equal status with the Secretary of State, but he backs down and accepts the post unreservedly when this is refused. His petulant ambitiousness makes him unpopular with his colleagues.

20 APR 1763 Sworn a member of the Privy Council and appointed President of the Board of Trade and foreign plantations in Grenville's ministry.

JUN 1763 Annoyed by his constant disagreements with Egremont, the Secretary of State, he writes to Bute, threatening to resign. Bute persuades him to remain.

2 SEP 1763 Resigns as President of the Board of Trade after becoming involved, at Bute's behest, in an intrigue designed to replace Grenville by Pitt. Despite assuring the King of his continued support Shelburne soon attaches himself to Pitt and joins the ranks of the Opposition.

8 DEC 1763 The King dismisses him from his post as aide-de-camp because of his speech on 29 Nov in the debate about the Wilkes *North Briton* case, in which he had spoken against the resolution that 'privilege of Parliament does not extend to the case of writing and publishing seditious libels.' Shelburne retires to look after his country estates.

25 APR 1764 He takes his seat in the Irish House of Lords as Earl of Shelburne.

3 FEB 1765 He marries Lady Sophia Carteret, only child of Lord Granville.

26 MAR 1765 Appointed Major-General.

11 JUL 1765 Refuses Rockingham's offer of the Presidency of the Board of Trade, being strongly opposed to a number of the measures the Government is promoting, above all to the Stamp Act and the imposition of internal taxes on the American colonies.

20 JUL 1766 Shelburne is offered the post of Secretary of State for the Southern Department by Pitt. He assumes office on 30 Jul.

8 AUG 1766 An Order in Council greatly increases his Department's responsibilities by transferring the adminis-

tration of the colonies to it from the Board of Trade. He adopts a conciliatory approach but is constantly undermined by his Cabinet colleagues.

JUN 1767 His failure to prevent Charles Townshend's imposition of duties on tea and other imports into the American colonies drives him to despair.

JAN 1768 Grafton removes Shelburne's responsibilities for the American colonies, determined to pursue a policy of coercion against them.

19 OCT 1768 Shelburne finally resigns as Secretary of State, spending his next two years joining Chatham in attacking the ineffectual Grafton administration.

5 JAN 1771 Death of his wife Sophia.

11 MAY 1771 Shelburne goes abroad with his friend Isaac Barré, visiting France and Italy. In Paris he meets Abbé Morellet, a liberal thinker who becomes a great influence in his life.

26 MAY 1772 He becomes a Lieutenant-General.

JUN 1772 Shelburne employs Dr. Joseph Priestley as his librarian and archivist at Bowood. Priestley has been a Unitarian preacher and is a noted scientific researcher. He provides valuable companionship.

17 JUN 1773 Shelburne speaks at length on the East India Company Regulation Bill. His knowledge of Indian affairs greatly impresses the House.

20 JAN 1775 He supports Chatham's motion for the withdrawal of troops from Boston, where Townshend's ill-advised policy on tea duties has fanned the fires of colonial discontent. He condemns 'the madness, injustice and infatuation of coercing the Americans into a blind and servile submission'.

5 MAR 1778 Of the American Conciliatory Bills he says, 'The moment that the independence of America is agreed to by our Government, the sun of Great Britain is set, and we shall no longer be a powerful or respectable people'.

11 MAY 1778 Chatham dies. Shelburne takes over the leadership of his supporters, the Chathamites.

19 JUL 1779 Marries his second wife, Lady Louisa FitzPatrick, second daughter of John, 1st Earl of Upper Ossory.

22 MAR 1780 Fights a duel in Hyde Park at 5 a.m. with Lieutenant-Colonel Fullarton over an imagined slight suffered by the latter. Their first shots miss. By the second Shelburne is wounded in the groin. The public gives him vociferous support. Several towns confer their freedom on him.

27 MAR 1782 Shelburne becomes Secretary of State for the Home Department in the new Rockingham administration.

1 JUL 1782 Death of the Marquess of Rockingham.

4 JUL 1782 Shelburne is appointed First Lord of the Treasury and proceeds, with difficulty, to form a ministry. Fox and some other Rockingham supporters resign from their posts.

13 NOV 1782 Following sustained efforts by Shelburne, a provisional peace treaty between Great Britain and the US is signed in Paris.

20 JAN 1783 Preliminary articles of peace with France and Spain are agreed.

22 FEB 1783 A motion in the House of Commons censuring the peace terms is carried by 207 votes to 190. Shelburne offers his resignation on the 24th, convinced that the King is undermining his position.

26 MAR 1783 Shelburne's resignation is accepted. Once more he retires to the country, never to take office again.

2 APR 1783 Portland agrees to head a new coalition which includes Fox and Lord North. Shelburne travels abroad, visiting France and Germany.

6 DEC 1784 Shelburne is created Viscount Calne and Calstone, Earl Wycombe and Marquess of Lansdowne, but is not offered a ministerial post.

1 MAR 1787 Speaks in favour of the commercial treaty with France, but in general he prefers to avoid Parliament and London, entertaining a wide variety of intellectual guests at his Bowood home.

7 AUG 1789 Death of his second wife, Louisa.

1792 With the failure of Pitt's Russian policy and rioting in Birmingham, the King invites Shelburne to give his views on the state of the country. Shelburne replies at some length, but there is no response.

30 MAY 1797 He speaks in favour of parliamentary reform, one of his fundamental principles.

1801 The illness of the King prompts plans for a Regency. Lord Moira approaches Shelburne to find out if he would take office in a new ministry, but the King's recovery makes it unnecessary.

17 MAR 1801 Addington forms a new ministry.

23 MAY 1803 Shelburne's last speech in the House of Lords urges the Government to make peace with France.

7 MAY 1805 Shelburne dies in London.

BACKGROUND

PHYSICAL CHARACTERISTICS AND HEALTH

Representations of Shelburne show a heavily built man of medium height with strongly marked features, thick eyebrows and an apparently florid complexion.

His health seems to have been generally good. Towards the end of his life he wrote in a letter to his friend Morellet, 'The dampness and uncertainty of this climate disagrees with me every year more. You used to tell me that you were ten or twelve years older than me, but I can now tell you that I am ten or twelve years older than you'.

EDUCATION

Primary None. His autobiography states: 'From the time I was 4 years old till I was 14 my education was neglected to the greatest degree'.

Secondary In his autobiography he says, 'I was first sent to an ordinary publick school, I was then shut up with a tutor'.

University 1755, Christ Church, Oxford

Qualifications He left Oxford in 1757 without taking a degree

NON-PARLIAMENTARY CAREER

Military service In 1757 his father bought him a commission in the 20th Regiment of Foot, then commanded by Colonel James Wolfe. During the Seven Years War he took part in the expedition to Rochefort and other raids on the French coast. In June 1758 he transferred into the 3rd Regiment of Foot Guards. He distinguished himself under Lord Granby at the Battle of Minden in 1759, and again under Prince Ferdinand of Brunswick at Kloster Kampen in 1760. On his return to England

NON-PARLIAMENTARY CAREER—*Continued*

he was rewarded with the rank of Colonel and the post of aide-de-camp to the new King, George III. In 1765 he was made a Major-General, in 1772 Lieutenant-Colonel, and a General in 1783.

HONOURS

Freedom of cities He was awarded several freedoms, but it is not known which ones.
Other than peerage 19 Apr 1782, Knight of the Garter; 22 Mar 1798, Fellow of the Society of Arts

CLUBS

Boodle's, White's

HOBBIES AND SPORTS

He was a generous patron of literature and the fine arts. He built up a substantial library at Bowood House and employed a leading radical thinker, Dr. Joseph Priestley, as his librarian and paid companion from 1772 to 1780.

He acquired important collections of manuscripts and state papers, many from the Cecils; also the papers of Sir Julius Caesar, Master of the Rolls of James I and Charles I. He was also an assiduous collector of maps, charts, coins and medals. He enjoyed playing chess.

He was interested in the good management of his estates and employed Capability Brown to lay out his country seat at Bowood Park. Jeremy Bentham reported that the establishment at Bowood included a leopard, a spaniel and four cats.

FINANCES

One of the principal sources of the Petty family fortunes was the marriage of Shelburne's grandfather Thomas Fitzmaurice to Anne Petty, who with energy and intelligence so improved the family position that its style of living and financial strength was 'superior to any family whatever in Ireland'. Furthermore, under the terms of Henry Petty's will, his estates and property passed to Shelburne's father, Anne Petty's 5th son, on condition that he change his name from Fitzmaurice to Petty.
Income At his death in 1805 his estates in England and Ireland were estimated to yield an income of over £35, 000 per year.
Spouse's finances Shelburne's first wife, Lady Sophia Carteret, brought him large estates including Lansdowne Hill near Bath, from which he later took his title of Marquess.
Legacies He inherited the Petty estates on the death of his father.
Will He left £10,000 p. a. and the sum of £100,000 to his son Henry.

ANECDOTES

'Lord Shelburne used to catch hold of the most imperfect scrap of an idea and filled it up in his own mind, sometimes correctly, sometimes erroneously. His manner was very imposing, very dignified, and he talked his vague generalities in the House of Lords in a very emphatic way, as if something good were at the bottom, when in fact there was nothing at all'. (Jeremy Bentham)

A contemporary satire on his oratory began:

Lost and obscur'd in Bowood's humble bow'r,
No party tool-no candidate for pow'r
I came, my lords, an hermit from my cell,
A few blunt truths in my plain style to tell. (*Rolliad*)

Goldsmith is said to have remarked to Shelburne, 'Do you know that I never could conceive the reason why they call you Malagrida, for Malagrida was a very good sort of man'.

Gainsborough is said to have flung away his pencil after a second attempt to draw a likeness of him, and exclaimed, 'Damn it! I never could see through varnish, and there's an end'.

QUOTATIONS

1762, It will appear from history that a partiality to continental states has always been destructive to the interest of this country. (Speech on the Duke of Bedford's motion on the withdrawal of troops from Germany)

1775, The madness, injustice and infatuation of coercing the Americans into a blind and servile submission. (Speech in support of Chatham's motion for the withdrawal of troops from Boston)

1783, I avow that monopoly is always unwise, but if there is any nation under heaven who ought to be the first to reject monopoly, it is the English. (Speech defending the provisional treaties he had negotiated with the American States *Parl. Hist.*)

RESIDENCES

Lixnaw, County Kerry, Ireland
Bowood House, Bowood Park, Wiltshire
Lansdowne House, Berkeley Square, London
Wycombe Abbey, Buckinghamshire
Open to the public Bowood Park. Bowood House was built in the 18th century. Shelburne added a wing to it and laid out the grounds under the advice of Capability Brown and Hamilton of Pain's Hill.

MEMORIALS

PORTRAITS

1786, by Sir Joshua Reynolds, Bowood, Wiltshire

OTHER MEMORIALS

In 1783 the town of Roseway in Nova Scotia was named Shelburne in honour of his pro-American policies. Shelburne in Vermont, Massachusetts and New Hampshire were also named after him.

BIBLIOGRAPHIC INFORMATION

LETTERS AND PERSONAL PAPERS

Some of Shelburne's papers are in the British Library, but the great majority of them are in the William L. Clements Library, University of Michigan. A few papers are still in the possession of the family.

PUBLICATIONS

1791, a paper on sepulchral monuments

FURTHER READING

Fitzmaurice, Lord *Life of William Earl of Shelburne.* 2nd revised edition. 2 vols., London, 1912.
Norris, J. *Shelburne and Reform.* London, 1963.

J.S.

Christ Church College

Duke of Portland

Lived 1738–1809
Political Party Whig
Prime Minister 2 April 1783–18 December 1783; 31 March 1807–4 October 1809
Governments 1) Coalition: Whig/Tory; 2) Tory
Reigning Monarch George III

Craignez honte Fear shame

PORTLAND AS PRIME MINISTER

With only limited ministerial experience Portland was appointed Prime Minister to act as a figurehead for the Fox-North coalition. He had the support of the King, but George III was awaiting a chance to appoint Pitt Prime Minister. Portland showed independence in putting together his Cabinet but his India Bill, seeking administrative reforms, while passed by the House of Commons, was defeated in the House of Lords at the instigation of the King. Portland was dismissed after only eight months. After being out of office for eleven years he joined Pitt's administration as Home Secretary, 1794–1801, and subsequently Addington's and then again Pitt's administration as Lord President of the Council, 1801–1805. In early 1807 he was appointed by the King to replace the unfavoured Grenville as Prime Minister. Again Portland became the nominal head of a tolerated but difficult and fractious Cabinet. The Canning-Castlereagh dispute, culminating in a duel, was beyond the rather isolated Portland's power to control. Failing health led to his inevitable resignation at over seventy-one years of age.

PERSONAL INFORMATION

Names William Henry Cavendish Bentinck
Peerages 3rd Duke of Portland, Marquess of Titchfield, Earl of Portland, Viscount Woodstock, Baron Cirencester
Born 14 Apr 1738
Religion Anglican
Ancestry The Bentincks originated in Oversijssel, Netherlands. Hans William Bentinck was a close associate of William of Orange, and came to England with William in 1688–89, after which he was given extensive estates and the title of Portland. He married an Englishwoman and his heirs married into the great English families of Gainsborough and Oxford.
Date and place of marriage 8 Nov 1766, Burlington House, Piccadilly, London
Age at marriage 28 years, 208 days
Years married 27 years, 207 days
First entered Parliament 28 Mar 1761
Dates appointed PM 1) 2 Apr 1783; 2) 31 Mar 1807
Age at appointment 1) 44 years, 353 days; 2) 69 years, 351 days
Dates ceased to be PM 1) 18 Dec 1783; 2) 4 Oct 1809
Total time as PM 1) 260 days; 2) 2 years, 187 days, a total of 3 years, 82 days
Ceased to be MP 1 May 1762
Lived after last term as PM 26 days
Date of death 30 Oct 1809
Place of death Bulstrode, Buckinghamshire
Age at death 71 years, 199 days
Place of funeral and burial St. Marylebone, London
Zodiac sign Aries

FATHER

William Bentinck, 2nd Duke of Portland
Date of birth 1 Mar 1709
Occupation A Peer. Harleian Trustee at the British Museum 1753–62. Fellow of the Royal Society, 1739. Knight of the Garter, 20 Mar 1741. He was wise, gentle, kindly and retiring, but politically unambitious and inconspicuous.
Date of marriage 11 Jul 1734
Date of death 1 May 1762
Place of burial Westminster Abbey, London

MOTHER

Margaret Cavendishe Harley
Date of birth 11 Feb 1715
Profile The only daughter and heir of Edward Harley, 2nd Earl of Oxford, she was active, energetic and accomplished at 'turning'—wood, jet, ivory and amber. She had a passion for collecting, was interested in animals, botany, entomology and therapeutics. She enjoyed the society of famous men. In later life she suffered neuralgic pains and her health deteriorated.
Date of marriage 11 Jul 1734
Age when Prime Minister took office 70 years, 51 days
Date of death 17 Jul 1785
Place of burial Westminster Abbey, London

BROTHERS AND SISTERS

Portland was the eldest son and the third of six children.

Elizabeth (Marchioness of Bath), b. 27 Jul 1735; m. Thomas Thynne, 3rd Viscount Weymouth, later Marquess of Bath, 22 May 1759; Lady of the Bedchamber to Queen Charlotte, 1761–93; Mistress of the Robes, 1793–1818; d. 12 Dec 1825
Henrietta (Countess of Stamford), b. 8 Feb 1737; m. George Harris, Lord Grey of Grooby, later the 5th Earl of Stamford (1768) and Earl of Warrington (1796); d. 4 Jun 1827
Margaret Cavendishe, b. 26 Jul 1739; d. 23 Apr 1756
Frances Cavendishe, b. 9 Apr 1741; d. Mar 1743
Edward Charles, b. 3 Mar 1744; m. Elizabeth, daughter of Richard Cumberland, the dramatist; MP Lewes 1766–68, Carlisle 1768–74, Nottingham 1775–96 and Clitheroe, 1746–1802; d. 8 Oct 1819

WIFE

Lady Dorothy Cavendish
Date of birth 27 Aug 1750
Age at marriage 16 years, 73 days
Number of children 6
Mother Charlotte Elizabeth, Baroness Clifford
Father William Cavendish, 4th Duke of Devonshire (*q.v.*)
Father's occupation Prime Minister 1756–57
Date of death 3 Jun 1794
Place of burial St. Marylebone, London
Years younger than Prime Minister 12 years, 135 days
Profile She was taught privately by John Bruckner, pastor at the Church of Walloon Lutherans at Norwich. Cold and particular, her standards were very strict. Portland and the Prince of Wales were estranged between 1785 and 1787 as she would not receive Mrs. Fitzherbert, the Prince of Wales's wife. She died suddenly of 'mortification of the bowels'.

CHILDREN

4 sons, 2 daughters
William Henry Cavendish (Marquess of Titchfield); b. 24 Jun 1768; m. 4 Aug 1795 Henrietta Scott; MP Petersfield, Hants 1790–91, Buckingham 1791–1809; Lord Lieutenant of Middlesex, 1794–1842; succeeded his father as 4th Duke of Portland Oct 1809; a Lord of the Treasury, Mar–Sep 1809; Privy Counsellor Apr 1827; Lord Privy Seal Apr–Jul 1827; Lord President of the Council Aug 1827–Jan 1828; d. 27 Mar 1844.
William Edward Cavendish, b. 14 Sep 1774; m. 19 Feb 1803, Lady Mary Acheson, daughter of the 1st Earl of Gosford;. following a career in the army 1791–1802; Governor at Madras for the East India Company and Governor of India 1827–35; MP Glasgow 1837; d. 17 Jun 1839
Charlotte; b. 3 Oct 1775; m. the grandson of the 5th Earl of Warwick, Mar 1793
Mary, b. 13 Mar 1778; unm.
William Charles Augustus Cavendish, b. May 1780; m. 1) Georgina Seymour; 2) Anne, daughter of Marquess of Wellesley; a Lieutenant-Colonel in the Army
William Frederick Cavendish, b. 2 Nov 1784; m. Lady Mary Lowther, daughter of 1st Earl of Lonsdale; a Major-General in the Army

LIFE AND CAREER

PARLIAMENTARY ELECTIONS FOUGHT

*(*designates candidate elected)*
DATE Mar 1761. General Election
CONSTITUENCY Weobley, Herefordshire
RESULT William Henry Cavendish* (Whig) (He ceased being an MP on 1 May 1762, when he succeeded his father and went to the House of Lords)

PARTY ACTIVITY

Party Leadership Leader of the Whigs, Apr 1783–Jul 1794
Other offices Member in 1774 of a Westminster Committee to protest against the waste of public money and to promote reform.

PARLIAMENTARY AND MINISTERIAL EXPERIENCE

First recorded speech 8 Apr 1783, on the date when Lord North would be made a Peer. (Debrett. *Parliamentary Register*, vol 28, 1782–1783 c 104)
Privy Counsellor 10 Jul 1765
Ministerial Offices Lord Chamberlain of the Household, 12 Jul 1765–Dec 1766; Lord Lieutenant of Ireland, 8 Apr–15 Sep 1782, First Lord of the Treasury, 2 Apr –18 Dec 1783, 31 Mar 1807–4 Oct 1809; Leader of the House of Lords, 2 Apr–18 Dec 1783; Home Secretary, 11 Jul 1794–30 Jul 1801; Lord President of the Council, 30 Jul 1801–14 Jan 1805

GOVERNMENTS FORMED

First Administration 2 Apr–18 Dec 1783

GENERAL ELECTION RESULT
SEP 1780: Government 260; Opposition 254; Others 144. Total 558.
CABINET
Prime Minister and First Lord of the Treasury Duke of Portland
Chancellor of the Exchequer Lord J. Cavendish
Lord President of the Council Viscount Stormont
Home Secretary Lord North (Apr–Dec 1783); Earl Temple (Dec 1783)
Foreign Secretary C. J. Fox
First Lord of the Admiralty Viscount Keppel
Lord Privy Seal Earl of Carlisle
Chancellor of the Duchy of Lancaster Lord Ashburton (Apr–Aug 1783); Earl of Derby (Aug–Dec 1783)

Second Administration 31 Mar 1807–4 Oct 1809

GENERAL ELECTION RESULTS:
OCT 1806: Government 349; Neutral 208; Opposition 92; Independent 9. Total 658.
MAY 1807: Government 388; Opposition 224; Independent 29; Doubtful 17. Total 658
CABINET
Prime Minister and First Lord of the Treasury Duke of Portland
Chancellor of the Exchequer and Chancellor of the Duchy of Lancaster S. Perceval
Lord President of the Council Earl Camden
Lord Chancellor Lord Eldon
Home Secretary Lord Hawkesbury
Foreign Secretary G. Canning
President of the Board of Trade Earl Bathurst
Secretary of State for War and Colonies Viscount Castlereagh
President of the Board of Control R. Dundas (Apr 1807–Jul 1809); Earl of Harrowby, (Jul–Oct 1809)
First Lord of the Admiralty Lord Mulgrave
Lord Privy Seal Earl of Westmoreland
Master General of the Ordnance Earl of Chatham
Secretary at War Sir J. M. Pulteney (Apr 1807–Jun 1809); Lord Gower (Jun–Oct 1809)

IMPORTANT DATES IN PERSONAL AND POLITICAL LIFE

28 MAR 1761 Elected unopposed as MP for Weobley, Herefordshire.
1 MAY 1762 Succeeds his father as the 3rd Duke of Portland, and therefore gives up his seat in the House of Commons, never having made a speech.
1764 Has a brief love affair with Maria, Countess of Waldegrave, who is later to marry the Duke of Gloucester.
1765–1766 Portland enters into another love affair, with Anne Liddell, Duchess of Grafton, who is separated from her husband. Despite her increasing ardour, it is an unsuitable liaison for a young Duke with political ambitions, and he ends the affair by announcing his engagement to Lady Dorothy Cavendish in Mar 1766. This affair may have been the reason for the antagonism between Portland and Grafton in later life.
10 JUL 1765 Admitted to the Privy Council
12 JUL 1765 Appointed Lord Chamberlain of the Household under the Marquess of Rockingham. He finds the work very tiring.
30 JUL 1766 Rockingham resigns as Prime Minister. Portland remains as Lord Chamberlain in an administration nominally headed by the Duke of Grafton, but effectively run by the Earl of Chatham. The supporters of Rockingham who remain in the Government consider resigning, but decide not to as they feel that this is what Chatham really wants.
DEC 1766 With his personal antipathy towards Grafton, and his growing dislike of the increasingly domineering Earl of Chatham (whom he calls the 'Great Commoner'), Portland's position becomes untenable. The Rockinghamites meet again, and decide that Portland should resign, along with the Earl of Bessborough and Scarborough and Lord Monson, in an attempt to force Chatham to change his ways or resign. It does not succeed, and Portland spends the next 18 years in Opposition.
1766–1776 Portland now turns his attentions to electioneering, securing the return of two of his friends for Wigan in 1768. He is prepared to spend vast amounts of money, bringing him into conflict with Sir James Lowther, 'the petty tyrant of the north'. Portland decides to oppose Lowther's candidates with two of his own, who are successful in the 1768 election. Lowther wins a seat in the County, but after allegations of corruption by Portland, Lowther's election is overturned on petition, and Portland's candidate is returned in his place. These election battles, later called 'the severest ever recorded', cost Portland over £30,000.
AUG 1767 In a bid to destroy Portland's influence in Carlisle before the election, Lowther challenges Portland's right to own Inglewood Forest and the Manor of Carlisle in Cumbria. The reversion of the Honour of Penrith had been granted in perpetuity to the 1st Earl of Portland in 1696, but the two lands in question had not

IMPORTANT DATES IN PERSONAL AND POLITICAL LIFE—*Continued*

been specifically mentioned. Lowther applies to Lord North, Surveyor-General, for the right to lease the lands, which is granted to him on 7 Aug 1767. Portland applies to the Treasury Board for a decision.

22 DEC 1767 The Treasury Board accepts North's recommendation and Lowther is allowed to lease the lands. Portland fights on, with much public support, as it is felt that everyone's property would be endangered if Lowther is allowed to win.

17 FEB 1768 Rockingham's supporters decide to use this issue as a battleground with the Government, and accordingly Sir George Savill MP introduces a Bill declaring that a period of sixty years' possession of crown land entitles the possessor to full ownership. The Bill is deferred until the next session when it is enacted, but as it is not retrospective, Portland is unable to retrieve his land. Lowther shows his determination by beginning to evict Portland's tenants.

11 FEB 1771 A Bill introduced by Sir William Meredith, designed to make Savill's Bill retrospective, is defeated on its Third Reading. Lowther, meanwhile, instigates a lawsuit against Portland to try to prove the case.

NOV 1771 After a lengthy trial, Lowther loses his case on a technicality. Lowther then tries to get Portland to prove that, although Lowther's case is invalid, Portland's own claim is valid.

19 APR 1775 The first shots in the American War of Independence are fired at Lexington.

JUN 1775 Portland is robbed by a highwayman, losing £20-£30 and his gold watch.

4 JUL 1776 American Declaration of Independence.

13–14 AUG 1776 It is finally decided by jury that Portland has a right to the lands in Cumbria he had disputed with Lowther. The long trial and constant harassment over the previous ten years cost Portland a fortune and virtually bankrupts him.

1776 Following his father's death in 1762, Portland's mother had continued to live at Welbeck, despite owning Bulstrode where Portland continues to live. Portland and the Duchess argue often about the terms, until Portland agrees to pay the Duchess a lease of £16,000 p.a., despite having an income of less than this figure.

17 OCT 1777 The war in America continues until the surrender at Saratoga. France then intervenes, and the House of Lords decide to go into Committee to discuss the situation. An Opposition motion to make Portland the chairman is defeated by 58 to 33.

1780 With the war going from bad to worse, negotiations start to include certain members of the Opposition. When it becomes clear that Shelburne and Rockingham have to be included as well, negotiations collapse.

8 APR 1782 Portland is appointed Lord Lieutenant of Ireland in Rockingham's second administration, following North's resignation on 20 Mar 1782.

14 APR 1782 Portland arrives in Dublin.

1 JUL 1782 Death of Marquess of Rockingham. Portland is elected Leader in succession to Rockingham, despite the real power-base being that of Fox and North.

15 SEP 1782 Portland resigns as Lord Lieutenant of Ireland. He originally decided to resign on the death of Rockingham, but is persuaded to stay on for a short while by the new Prime Minister, Shelburne. He does not return to England until the middle of October, in order to recover from a riding accident in which he has dislocated a collarbone and fractured a rib.

24 FEB 1783 Shelburne resigns after defeats in the House of Commons. The King agrees to accept a Fox-North coalition as long as someone else can be found to lead the Government. Despite hoping that William Pitt the Younger would take the position, he finally agrees to accept Portland as the new Prime Minister.

2 APR 1783 Portland becomes Prime Minister. The King is less than pleased with this arrangement, and awaits his chance to get rid of Portland.

JUN 1783 The King objects to the new Government's proposals to give the Prince of Wales, on his coming of age, an income double that received by George III himself in similar circumstances, as well as paying off his debts. George III threatens to make the affair public, whereupon Portland has to persuade the Prince to accept half the original sum. Portland's position is precarious.

DEC 1783 The India Bill, designed to reform the governing of India, is passed by the Commons on 9 Dec. Portland speaks on the Second Reading in the Lords on 15 Dec, but progress is disrupted by the King's refusal to quash rumours that he is violently opposed to the Bill, despite an approach from Portland. The Bill is defeated by 19 votes on 17 Dec.

18 DEC 1783 Portland's ministry is dismissed by the King, who sends out messengers to collect the seals of office, rather than bothering with an audience. Portland remains in opposition until 1794.

1787 Despite having fought so hard to keep his lands in Cumbria, Portland's financial position is so bad that he is forced to sell them to his brother-in-law, the 5th Duke of Devonshire.

27 SEP 1792 Portland is appointed Chancellor of the University of Oxford. He also refuses the Garter, as it has been offered by Pitt and Portland does not want to reduce his own influence by seeming to agree with the Whig's long-term enemy.

3 JUN 1794 His wife dies.

11 JUL 1794 Over the previous few years, Portland had begun to distance himself from Fox's Whigs over Fox's attitude towards the Government and its conduct of the war with France and started supporting Pitt. Portland is urged to join Pitt's Government, and on 11 Jul he is appointed Home Secretary.

SEP 1794 The Foreign Secretary, Lord Grenville, suggests that in order to ensure that Parliament support the continuing war with France, the Government should avow that the French system of government in itself is not a bar to peace. Portland, who detests the revolutionary government, objects, saying that he is not prepared 'to become a party to the renunciation of the existing monarchy in France'.

1794–95 Food shortages lead to serious riots and the suggestion of a voluntary restriction of consumption. Portland, along with other members of the Privy Council, agrees and refuses to eat bread of more than a certain fineness in order to save wheat.

29 OCT 1795 Missiles are thrown at the King, who is convinced that his life is in danger. The Government, alarmed at the increasing unrest, introduces two Bills, one for the protection of the King and one to prevent seditious meetings. Portland also arranges for considerable numbers of troops to be quartered on the outskirts of London. Despite his new powers, however, Portland is generally restrained in his use of the new Acts.

JAN 1795 Portland, having responsibility for Ireland, sends his friend Lord Fitzwilliam to Dublin as Lord Lieutenant. Fitzwilliam promptly attempts to grant full equality of rights to Roman Catholics, whereupon Portland repudiates his friend's suggestion, and a meeting of the Cabinet on 23 Feb recalls Fitzwilliam. The Irish feel that Portland has betrayed them. The resulting unrest leads to the Irish rebellion of 1798.

23 MAY 1798 The Irish rebellion breaks out, but is quickly put down because of preventative measures instituted by Portland's department.

MAR 1800 Both Houses of the Irish Parliament approve Union with the British Parliament. Portland has authorized the new Lord Lieutenant, Cornwallis, to use whatever means might be necessary to pass the measure, including bribery. Cornwallis therefore promises to create a large number of new Irish peerages, but Portland decides in June that Cornwallis has offered too many, infuriating Cornwallis.

14 MAR 1801 Pitt resigns as Prime Minister, as the King opposes Pitt's attempt to introduce Catholic emancipation. Portland, who has supported the King against Pitt, remains as Home Secretary under the new Prime Minister, Addington.

30 JUL 1801 Portland is moved to the Lord Presidency of the Council to make way for Lord Pelham as Home Secretary. The loss of income from this change of position causes serious financial problems for Portland.

10 MAY 1804 Pitt replaces Addington as Prime Minister, Portland remains as Lord President.

14 JAN 1805 Portland resigns to allow Addington to return to the Cabinet in his place; he remains in the Cabinet without portfolio until Pitt dies on 23 Jan 1806. Portland retires to Bulstrode, an old man suffering badly from gout, hoping for a peaceful retirement.

22 MAR 1806 Portland is cut for the stone, an operation to remove kidney stones, performed without anaesthetic. Portland's stoical, silent acceptance of the pain impresses all.

5 MAR 1807 Having obtained the King's approval for a Bill allowing Roman Catholics to hold commissions in the army up to the rank of Colonel, Grenville's Government introduces a Bill that opens up all commissions in the army to Roman Catholics. Grenville, faced with the King's anger, agrees to withdraw the Bill, but wants to be allowed to announce in Parliament the benefits that would have accrued from the measure. The King, however, has been in correspondence with Portland, who supports him, and knows that Portland will be prepared to serve once again, despite his ill health. Grenville's Ministry of All the Talents is dismissed.

31 MAR 1807 Portland becomes Prime Minister for the second time, insisting that he is still a Whig, despite heading a Tory Government. Portland promptly dissolves Parliament, and the ensuing election confirms his position. Portland, however, is too old and ill to run a Government, and leaves his Cabinet to do what they like. He hardly ever speaks in the Lords throughout his premiership.

5 JUL 1807 Grenville had left a legacy of military failure, with Napoleon's conquest of the continent and the British dominion over Buenos Aires (Jun 1806) being overthrown by a local rebellion. In Jun 1807, 7,000 British soldiers march on Buenos Aires, but withdraw following combat on 5 Jul 1807. The British commander, General Whitelocke, is courtmartialled. Portland's ministry thus begins under an air of gloom that is never to be dissipated.

2 SEP 1807 The unprovoked bombardment of Copenhagen by the British navy invokes hostile criticism of the Government.

AUG 1808 Following the overrunning of Portugal and Spain by Napoleon, the British send troops to the peninsula, but are unable to halt Napoleon's progress.

24 MAR 1809 Canning, the Foreign Secretary, writes to Portland accusing other members of the Cabinet of inefficiency in the running of the Peninsular war and threatens to resign. Without naming him, it is clear that Canning means Castlereagh, the Secretary of State for War and the Colonies. Portland, forced to choose between the two, decides to sack Castlereagh, but is unwilling to carry it out. Unfortunately, several members of the Cabinet discover the manouevres, while Castlereagh remains in complete ignorance of the problem. Portland is thus faced with a Cabinet whose members are split in allegiance between Canning and Castlereagh and which effectively ceases to function.

CIRCA 15 AUG 1809 Portland has an apoplectic seizure on the journey from London to Bulstrode. He only makes a partial recovery in the next few weeks and decides to resign.

SEP 1809 Canning announces his intention to resign, which leads Castlereagh to discover what had been going on. Furious, he demands satisfaction, and on 21 Sep 1809, he and Canning fight a duel. Both men soon resign.

4 OCT 1809 Portland formally resigns and is replaced by Spencer Perceval.

30 OCT 1809 Portland dies following a second apoplectic seizure.

BACKGROUND

PHYSICAL CHARACTERISTICS AND HEALTH

Portland was a tall, dignified and handsome man, with a strong profile and clear complexion. He hated public speaking, and found it difficult to make decisions, and was so retiring that he hardly ever spoke in Parliament during his second premiership.

Portland's health was good until his old age, although he occasionally suffered from gout. He was cut for the stone in 1806, and the problems soon returned, so that he was in severe pain throughout 1807. Despite this, and despite realising that it would probably kill him, he accepted his second appointment as Prime Minister. Throughout this period, he was too old and infirm to be anything other than a figurehead.

EDUCATION

Primary Private education until 1747
Secondary 1747–54, Westminster School
University 1755–57, Christ Church College, Oxford
Qualifications 1 Feb 1757, Master of Arts
Cultural and vocational background Portland undertook the Grand Tour from 1757–61, visiting Italy, Hamburg, Prussia and Warsaw. He returned when his father, worried by the large debts he was incurring, decided to restrict his income.

NON-PARLIAMENTARY CAREER

Other posts 1764–1809 Harleian Trustee of the British Museum; 1786 High Steward of Bristol; 27 Sep 1792–

NON-PARLIAMENTARY CAREER—*Continued*

1809 Chancellor of the University of Oxford; 1794 Recorder of Nottingham; 1795–1809 Lord Lieutenant of Nottingham; 1797–1809 Elder brother of Trinity House; 1807–09 Master of Trinity House

HONOURS

Academic 7 Oct 1792, DCL
Other than peerage 5 Jun 1766, Fellow of the Royal Society; 2 Feb 1774, Fellow of the Society of Antiquaries; 16 Jul 1794, Knight of the Garter

CLUBS

White's, Brooks's (founding member)

HOBBIES AND SPORTS

Portland's main interest was art. Among other things, he bought the Barberini Vase, now in the British Museum and known as the Portland Vase.

FINANCES

Portland's finances were convoluted throughout his life and he was usually deep in debt. He was profligate and unable to live within his means, and while on the Grand Tour he had to write begging letters to both his sisters, and to his father, who reluctantly paid his debts. On succeeding his father in 1762, he found himself unable to manage his estates efficiently. In a time of poor harvests, his income could not match his spending, and he insisted on making many improvements to his estates. He spent vast amounts of money electioneering, including over £30,000 in Carlisle in 1768 and also had protracted and expensive legal battles with Sir James Lowther over the ownership of Inglewood Forest, Cheshire. He was also forced to pay £16,000 p.a. to his mother as rent for Welbeck, despite an estimated income of about £9,000. The death of his mother in 1785, and the income of £12,000 p.a. from her estates, saved him from bankruptcy. Generous to a fault, he often bailed his equally profligate brother out of trouble, as well as lending large sums to friends: George Byng, Lord Tennison, at one time owed Portland over £36,000.
Income Estimated at £9,000 p.a. in 1762 on his marriage; gained a further £12,000 p.a. from his mother's estates after her death.
Legacies Inherited Bulstrode from his father, and the Cavendish estates from his mother.
Will Proved 1809, leaving everything to his son, William Henry Cavendish.

ANECDOTES

Portland was very shy, and became painfully embarrassed when speaking in public. He was barely able to make a speech in the House of Lords owing to nerves and a horror of the forthcoming ordeal. The Earl of Malmesbury, writing on Portland's reaction when urged to break with Fox in 1792, said, 'Although I have often seen him benumbed and paralysed, never saw him, or anyone else, so completely so before . . . Nothing could be so painful'.

It was said that 'he possessed in an eminent degree the talent of dead silence'.

Malmesbury also wrote 'I have often been with him when I thought he would have died in his chair; and his powers of attention were so weakened that he could neither read a paper, nor listen for a while, without becoming drowsy or falling asleep'.

QUOTATIONS

On accepting office for a second time, Portland, recognising his age and infirmity, said: 'My fears are not that the attempt to perform this duty will shorten my life, but that I shall neither bodily nor mentally perform it as I should'.

RESIDENCES

Burlington House, Piccadilly, London
Bulstrode, Buckinghamshire
10 Downing Street
Welbeck Abbey, Nottinghamshire

MEMORIALS

PORTRAITS

1792, by Sir Thomas Lawrence, owned by Bristol Corporation; 1794–97, by George Romney, Christ Church College, Oxford; 1814, by Benjamin West, Examination Schools, Oxford; 1814, by Matthew Pratt, National Gallery of Art, Washington D.C.

OTHER MEMORIALS

Portland Place, London W1, is named after Portland, landlord of the area when it was laid out in 1778. The Portland Vase, in the British Museum.

BIBLIOGRAPHIC INFORMATION

LETTERS AND PERSONAL PAPERS

Portland's political, personal and family correspondence is kept in the Library of Nottingham University. Some papers from his second premiership of 1807–09 are kept in the Public Record Office.

FURTHER READING

Turberville, A.S., *A History of Welbeck Abbey and Its Owners*, 2 Vols, 1755–1879, London 1934.

C.S.

Bettmann

William Pitt

Lived 1759–1806
Political Party Tory
Prime Minister 19 December 1783–14 March 1801; 10 May 1804–23 January 1806
Government Tory
Reigning Monarch George III

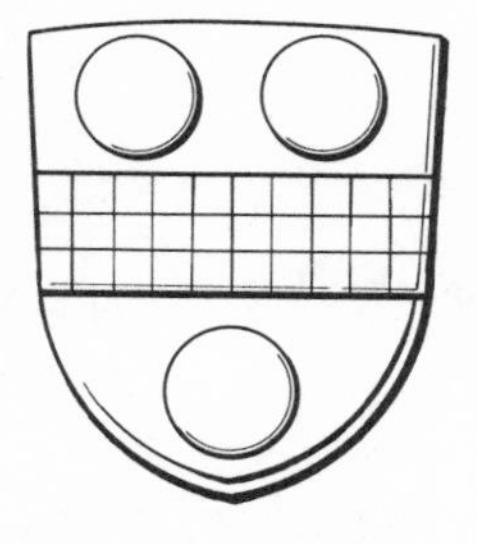

Benigno numine By benign providence

PITT AS PRIME MINISTER

Pitt died before the age of forty-seven, having spent almost nineteen years as Prime Minister. His was a career that resembled no other. He was son of a Prime Minister who coached him for the office, and had him educated to be a barrister. Pitt was elected to the House of Commons aged twenty-one and became Chancellor of the Exchequer just eighteen months later. Within another eighteen months he accepted the office of Prime Minister, after refusing it twice. He supported parliamentary reform and free trade. His Cabinet, made up of peers only, was not impressive but Pitt himself was very effective—undertaking the King's business, reforming national finances notably excise duties and replacing expensive sinecures with peerages. He won elections in 1784 and 1790. He was less successful as a war leader, as his idea of a grand alliance against France expired by 1795. By changing the administration of India, Canada and the emerging Australia, he helped develop imperial alternatives to the now-independent United States. His policy of union with Ireland led to a clash with the King in 1800, as Pitt sought to link union with gradual Catholic Emancipation, and he therefore resigned. From May 1804 he was once more Prime Minister but with a weaker Administration, again attempting to form a coalition against Napoleon. He grew increasingly ill and died in office at the beginning of 1806.

PERSONAL INFORMATION

Names William Pitt
Nickname Pitt the Younger
Born 28 May 1759
Birthplace Hayes, Kent
Religion Anglican
Ancestry English. His family was long-established and well-connected on both sides, and included several notable landowners, Members of Parliament and public servants. His father, created Earl of Chatham (*q.v.*) in 1766, was Prime Minister from 1766–68. The family seat was in Hayes, Kent.
First entered Parliament 8 Jan 1781
Dates appointed PM 1) 19 Dec 1783; 2) 10 May 1804
Age at appointment 1) 24 years, 205 days; 2) 44 years, 348 days
Dates ceased to be PM 1) 14 Mar 1801; 2) 23 Jan 1806
Total time as PM 1) 17 years, 85 days; 2) 1 year, 258 days; a total of 18 years, 343 days
Ceased to be MP 23 Jan 1806
Lived after last term as PM Died in office
Date of death 23 Jan 1806
Place of death Bowling Green House, Putney Heath, London
Age at death 46 years, 240 days
Last words Variously cited as 'Oh, my country! How I leave my country!', 'Oh my country! How I love my country!', and (by oral tradition) 'I think I could eat one of Bellamy's veal pies'.
Place of funeral Lay in state in the Painted Chamber, Westminster, London, from 20–21 Feb 1806. Funeral took place on 22 Feb at Westminster Abbey, London.
Place of burial Westminster Abbey, London
Zodiac sign Gemini

FATHER

William Pitt (1st Earl of Chatham) (*q.v.*)
Date and place of birth 15 Nov 1708, Westminster, London
Occupation Prime Minister 1766–68
Date of marriage 16 Nov 1754
Date of death 11 May 1778
Place of burial Westminster Abbey, London

MOTHER

Hester Grenville
Date and place of birth 8 Nov 1720, Wotton, Buckinghamshire
Profile The sister of two eminent statesmen, George Grenville (*q.v.*) and Richard, Earl Temple, she was created Baroness Chatham in 1761 in recognition of her husband's political service.
Date of marriage 16 Nov 1754
Age when Prime Minister took office 1) 63 years, 41 days
Date of death 3 Apr 1803
Place of burial Westminster Abbey, London

BROTHERS AND SISTERS

Pitt was the second son and fourth of five children.
Hester, b. 19 Oct 1755; m. 18 Dec 1774, Charles, Viscount Mahon (MP Chipping Wycombe 1780–86); d. 18 July 1780
John (2nd Earl of Chatham), b. 9 Oct 1756; m. 10 Jul 1783, Lady Mary Elizabeth Sydney; Master General of the Ordnance 1801–06, 1807–10; Lieutenant General 1802; General 1812; First Lord of the Admiralty 1788–94; Lord Privy Seal 1794–96; Lord President of the Council 1796–1801; Governor of Plymouth 1805–07; Governor of Jersey 1807–20; Governor of Gibraltar 1820; d. 24 Sep 1835
Harriot, b. 18 Apr 1758; m. Sep 1785, Hon. Edward James Eliot (MP St. Germans 1780–84, Liskeard 1784–97; a Lord of the Treasury 1782–93); she acted as Pitt's hostess at 10 Downing Street from 1785–86; d. 24 Sep 1786
James Charles, b. 24 Apr 1761; Naval Captain; d. 13 Nov 1780

MARRIAGE

Pitt was unmarried.

LIFE AND CAREER

PARLIAMENTARY ELECTIONS FOUGHT

*(*designates candidate elected)*

DATE Sep 1780. General Election
CONSTITUENCY Cambridge University
RESULT James Mansfield* 277, John Townshend* 247, Thomas Villiers, Lord Hyde 206, Richard Croftes 150, William Pitt (Tory) 142

DATE 8 Jan 1781. By-election after William Lowther, returned for two seats in the General Election, chose to sit for Carlisle.
CONSTITUENCY Appleby
RESULT William Pitt* (Tory)

DATE 5 Aug 1782. By-election following Pitt's appointment as Chancellor of the Exchequer
CONSTITUENCY Appleby
RESULT William Pitt* (Tory)

DATE 3 Jan 1784. By-election following Pitt's appointment as Prime Minister.
CONSTITUENCY Appleby
RESULT William Pitt* (Tory)

DATE Mar 1784. General Election
CONSTITUENCY Cambridge University
RESULT William Pitt* (Tory) 351, George Henry Fitzroy, Earl of Euston* 299, Lord John Townshend 278, James Mansfield 181

DATE Jun 1790. General Election
CONSTITUENCY Cambridge University
RESULT William Pitt* (Tory) 510, George Henry Fitzroy, Earl of Euston* 483, Lawrence Dundas 207

DATE 18 Dec 1792. By-election following Pitt's appointment as Lord Warden of the Cinque Ports
CONSTITUENCY Cambridge University
RESULT William Pitt* (Tory)

DATE May 1796. General Election
CONSTITUENCY Cambridge University
RESULT William Pitt* (Tory); George Henry Fitzroy, Earl of Euston*

DATE Jun 1802. General Election

CONSTITUENCY Cambridge University
RESULT William Pitt* (Tory); George Henry Fitzroy, Earl of Euston*

DATE 17 May 1804. By-election following Pitt's appointment as Prime Minister.
CONSTITUENCY Cambridge University
RESULT William Pitt* (Tory)

PARTY ACTIVITY

Membership of group or faction Upon entering Parliament, Pitt joined the Opposition Shelburne group and, in 1804, towards the end of his political career, was again drawn into active opposition, against Addington. In an age of intrigue, however, Pitt was remarkable for his determination to be independent of both King and Party, and his general political detachment was to earn him a small personal following in the House of Commons.

PARLIAMENTARY AND MINISTERIAL EXPERIENCE

Maiden Speech 26 Feb 1781. Debate on Edmund Burke's motion for the reintroduction of the Bill for Economical Reform. (Debrett, J. (ed). *The Parliamentary Register.* 2nd series, vol 19, c. 17–22)
Privy Counsellor 10 Jul 1782
Ministerial Offices Chancellor of the Exchequer, 13 Jul 1782–5 Apr 1783, 27 Dec 1783–21 Mar 1801, 10 May 1804–23 Jan 1806; First Lord of the Treasury and Leader of the House of Commons 19 Dec 1783–17 Mar 1801; 10 May 1804–23 Jan 1806
Opposition Leaders while Prime Minister Charles James Fox (1783–1801); Fox, Lord Grenville and Henry Addington (1804–06)

GOVERNMENTS FORMED

First Administration 19 Dec 1783–14 Mar 1801 (Mince Pie Administration)

GENERAL ELECTION RESULTS
SEP 1780: Government 260; Opposition 254; Others 144. Total 558
MAR 1784: Not analysed.
Government majority 120.
JUN 1790: Supporters of the Administration 340; Opposition 183; Independent 29; Doubtful 6. Total 558
Majority 122
MAY 1796: Supporters of the Administration 340; Opposition 183; Independent 29; Doubtful 10. Total 558 Majority 290

CABINET
Prime Minister, First Lord of the Treasury and Chancellor of the Exchequer W. Pitt
Lord President of the Council Earl Gower (1783–Nov 1784); Lord Camden (Dec 1784–Jul 1794); Earl Fitzwilliam (Jul–Dec 1794); Earl of Mansfield (Dec 1794–Sep 1796); Earl of Chatham (Sep 1796–1801)
Lord Chancellor Lord Thurlow (1783–Jan 1792) (Seal in commission June 1792–Jan 1793)
Home Secretary Lord Sydney (1783–Jun 1789); W. Grenville (Lord Grenville 1790) (Jun 1789–Jun 1791); H. Dundas (Jun 1791–Jul 1794); Duke of Portland (Jul 1794–1801)
Secretary of State, Foreign Office Marquess of Carmarthen (Duke of Leeds 1789) (1783–Jun 1791); Lord Grenville (Jun 1791–1801)
*President of the Board of Trade** Lord Hawkesbury (Earl of Liverpool 1796) (Aug 1786–1801)
Secretary of State for War and Colonies (Transferred from Home Office 1794); H. Dundas (July 1794–1801)
President of the Board of Control H. Dundas (Jun 1793–1801)
First Lord of the Admiralty Earl Howe (1783–Jul 1788); Earl of Chatham (Jul 1788–Dec 1794); Earl Spencer (Dec 1794–1801)
Lord Privy Seal Duke of Rutland (1783–Nov 1784) (Seal in commission Mar–Nov 1784); Earl Gower (Marquess of Stafford 1786) (Nov 1784–Jul 1794); Duke of Marlborough (Jul–Dec 1794); Earl of Chatham (Dec 1794–Feb 1798)
*Chancellor of the Duchy of Lancaster** Lord Hawkesbury (Earl of Liverpool 1796) (Sep 1786–1801)
Master-General of the Ordnance Duke of Richmond (Jan 1784–Feb 1795); C. M. Cornwallis (Feb 1795–1801)
*Treasurer of the Navy** H. Dundas (Jan 1784–Jun 1800);
Secretary at War Sir G. Yonge (1783–Jul 1794); W. Windham (Jul 1794–1801)
Ministers without Portfolio Earl of Mansfield; Earl Camden (Jun 1798–1801)
Commander-in-Chief Lord Amherst (Jan 1793–1801)
**Office not always in Cabinet*

Second Administration 10 May 1804–23 Jan 1806

GENERAL ELECTION RESULT
JUN 1802: Supporters of the Administration 467; Old Opposition 124; New Opposition 25; Independent 19; Doubtful 23. Total 658
Majority 276

CABINET
Prime Minister, First Lord of the Treasury and Chancellor of the Exchequer W. Pitt
Lord President of the Council Duke of Portland (1804–Jan 1805); H. Addington (Viscount Sidmouth 1805) (Jan–Jul 1805); Earl Camden (Jul 1805–1806)
Lord Chancellor Lord Eldon
Home Secretary Earl of Liverpool
Foreign Secretary Lord Harrowby (1804–Jan 1805); Lord Mulgrave (Jan 1805–1806)
President of the Board of Trade Earl of Liverpool (May–Jun 1804); Duke of Montrose (Jun 1804–1806)
Secretary of State for War and Colonies Earl Camden (1804–Jun 1805); Viscount Castlereagh (Jun 1805–1806)
President of the Board of Control Viscount Castlereagh
First Lord of the Admiralty Viscount Melville (1804–Apr 1805); Lord Barhan (Apr 1805–1806)
Lord Privy Seal Earl of Westmoreland
Chancellor of the Duchy of Lancaster Lord Mulgrave (1804–Jan 1805); Earl of Buckinghamshire (Jan–Jul 1805); Lord Harrowby (Jul 1805–1806)
Master-General of the Ordnance Earl of Chatham

IMPORTANT DATES IN PERSONAL AND POLITICAL LIFE

SPRING 1776 Pitt graduates with an MA, without examination, from Pembroke Hall, now College, Cambridge.
11 MAY 1778 His father, the Earl of Chatham, dies.
12 JUN 1780 Pitt is called to the Bar and subsequently joins the Western Circuit.
20 JUL 1780 His elder sister Hester dies after childbirth.

IMPORTANT DATES IN PERSONAL AND POLITICAL LIFE—*Continued*

16 SEP 1780 Pitt fails to gain election for Cambridge University, coming last of the field of five candidates, but securing nearly 14 percent of the votes cast.

13 NOV 1780 His younger brother James dies at sea.

23 JAN 1781 Pitt takes his seat in the House of Commons, as Member of Parliament for Appleby, through the influence of the northern boroughmonger, Sir James Lowther, later 1st Earl of Lonsdale.

26 FEB 1781 Pitt makes his widely acclaimed maiden speech in the House of Commons on the subject of reform of the economy. Remarkable for its debating style and the power and eloquence with which it is delivered, the speech prompts Burke to exclaim, 'He is not a chip off the old block: he is the old block itself'.

20 MAR 1782 Lord North announces his resignation as Prime Minister. Pitt subsequently declines the offer of the Vice-Treasurership of Ireland under the Rockingham Ministry, having previously declared that he would 'never accept of a subordinate position' in government.

7 MAY 1782 In a masterly speech before a crowded House of Commons, Pitt moves for a Select Committee to consider the question of Parliamentary representation, calling for a 'moderate and substantial reform'. The motion is defeated by 161 to 141.

6 JUL 1782 Pitt is appointed Chancellor of the Exchequer by Rockingham's successor, Shelburne.

FEB 1783 Pitt's overtures to Fox, authorised by Shelburne with the aim of gaining Fox's support for the Government, are rebuffed. According to tradition, the two men are never to speak in private again.

21 FEB 1783 Shelburne resigns after his Ministry's defeat by supporters of Fox and North in two divisions in the House of Commons. Pitt, conscious that he lacks a majority in the House, subsequently declines the King's repeated invitations to form a government.

31 MAR 1783 Pitt announces his resignation as Chancellor of the Exchequer, declaring that he is 'unconnected with any party whatever', and can act independently.

2 APR 1783 The Fox-North Coalition takes office under the Duke of Portland.

7 MAY 1783 On the anniversary of his first speech on the subject, Pitt again unsuccessfully moves for a measure of parliamentary reform.

12 SEP–22 OCT 1783 Pitt visits France with his friends Edward Eliot and William Wilberforce.

DEC 1783 Sensing an opportunity to bring down the coalition, the King intervenes to secure the defeat in the House of Lords of Fox's India Bill, designed to regulate the affairs of the East India Company.

18 DEC 1783 The King dismisses the Portland administration.

19 DEC 1783 Pitt is appointed first Lord of the Treasury and Chancellor of the Exchequer. He is not yet 25 years of age.

12–23 JAN 1784 Pitt's 'mince pie administration', so called as it was not originally envisaged to last beyond Christmas, suffers a series of defeats in the House of Commons in the face of Fox's determined opposition. The breach between the two men, fuelled by their contrasting personalities has been made almost inevitable by Fox's antipathy towards the King, who reciprocates the hatred and favours Pitt, and by Fox's coalition with North, which Pitt, hostile towards North and aloof from faction, has refused to join. Pitt, nevertheless, steadfastly refuses demands for his resignation.

JAN 1784 Pitt enhances his standing in the country and frustrates the Opposition by declining the sinecure of the Clerk of the Pells, worth £3,000 p.a. and in his own gift, offering it instead to the Shelburnite Colonel Isaac Barré.

28 FEB 1784 Pitt receives the Freedom of the City of London at the Hall of the Grocer's Company. He and his carriage come under attack by a mob on his return from the ceremony, lending Pitt further support in the country at large.

1 MAR 1784 Fox's resolution demanding Pitt's dismissal is carried in the House of Commons by 12 votes, his majority beginning to wane as independent Members, sensing the popular mood, revert to their traditional support of the Government.

24 MAR 1784 Pitt asks the King to dissolve Parliament, Fox's majority in the House having fallen to one when a similar motion was debated on the 8th. Parliament is formally dissolved the following day.

3 APR 1784 At the General Election, Pitt is returned for Cambridge University, the seat which he continues to represent for the rest of his life.

13 AUG 1784 Pitt's India Bill, by which much of the effective control of the East India Company passes to the Board of Control, of which Pitt is the senior member, is enacted.

3 MAR 1785 A proposed scrutiny, on the grounds of corruption, of the Westminster election in which Fox has been returned is abandoned after the Government is defeated on the issue by 38 votes.

18 APR 1785 Pitt moves for leave to bring in his moderate Parliamentary Reform Bill, which seeks the purchase, with the electors' consent, of 36 small boroughs, the redistribution of the resulting 72 seats among London and the counties and a modest extension of the franchise. The motion is defeated by 74 votes, effectively postponing the reform of Parliament for nearly half a century.

17 AUG 1785 Pitt withdraws his Irish resolutions, which seek an equalisation of duties in trade between England and Ireland in return for the latter's contribution towards the cost of naval defences, because of opposition among English industrialists, and in the House of Commons and Irish Parliament.

AUG 1785 Pitt purchases Holwood House in Kent, further contributing towards his personal financial problems.

26 MAY 1786 A Bill is enacted to implement the Sinking Fund. The purpose of the Fund, along with Pitt's tax reforms, which had brought a reduction in individual taxation and the imposition of new or increased direct taxes, is to reduce the National Debt, which had reached an unprecedented level of approximately £250 million. An annual surplus of £1 million is to be allocated to the purchase of stock and allowed to accumulate as compound interest for 28 years, when it is to produce an annual income of £4 million.

21 SEP 1786 Pitt undergoes an operation at 10 Downing Street to remove a facial cyst. He chastises the surgeon, John Hunter, for exceeding his estimated time of six minutes for the operation by half-a-minute.

24 SEP 1786 His sister Harriot dies at 10 Downing Street after childbirth.

26 SEP 1786 A commercial treaty with France is signed at Versailles.

MAY 1787 Articles of impeachment of Warren Hastings, former Governor-General of India, are approved, Pitt and Wilberforce having voted the preceding June with

Fox, Burke and Sheridan on a motion concerning Hastings's treatment of the Zamindar of Benares.

13 FEB 1788 Impeachment proceedings begin in Westminster Hall, London. Hastings is to be honourably acquitted of all charges seven years later, and awarded a pension of £4,000 p.a. and a loan of £50,000.

APR–AUG 1788 Treaties establishing a triangular 'Triple Alliance' between Britain, Prussia and Holland are signed. The treaties are intended to limit French influence.

NOV 1788–FEB 1789 The King's temporary mental illness precipitates the 'Regency Crisis', during which Pitt, in the face of opposition from the Whigs and the Prince of Wales, successfully moves for severe restrictions to be placed on the Prince's exercise of the royal authority. The King's subsequent recovery is the cause of national celebration.

1788 Pitt refuses an offer of £100,000 from the City of London merchants and bankers to meet his debts. He has already declined financial assistance from the King.

14 JUL 1789 The storming of the Bastille in Paris marks the start of the French Revolution.

MAY–NOV 1790 Exploiting Britain's alliance with Prussia, Pitt mounts a successful diplomatic campaign against Spain in the dispute over Nootka Sound, Vancouver Island, leading to Spanish renunciation of claims to sovereignty of the Pacific Coast.

FEB–JUL 1791 Pitt makes unsuccessful diplomatic moves for the restoration to Turkey of Ochakov (Odessa), on the Black Sea, by Catherine II of Russia. In April, the Duke of Leeds resigns as Foreign Secretary over the conduct of the issue, to be replaced by Grenville.

JUN 1791 Pitt's Canada Act, by which Canada is divided into the predominantly English Lower and predominantly French Upper Province, becomes law.

2 APR 1792 Pitt makes one of the greatest speeches of his career in support of Wilberforce's motion to abolish slavery, the third occasion on which the House of Commons has debated the issue since 12 May 1789. The motion is defeated by Dundas's successful proposal for gradual abolition.

21 MAY 1792 In fear of insurrection spreading from revolutionary France to Britain, a Royal Proclamation is issued against 'divers wicked and seditious writings'. Similarly, two years later, the Habeas Corpus Act, which normally prevented detention without trial, is suspended, remaining so until 1801.

AUG 1792 Having declined the King's offer of the Garter in 1790, when he asked that the honour be conferred instead upon his brother, Pitt accepts the royal invitation to become Lord Warden of the Cinque Ports.

1 FEB 1793 France declares war on Britain and Holland. The allies' military weakness and unpreparedness is later ameliorated by treaties with Russia, Prussia, Austria, Spain, Sardinia and Naples. Although each is motivated by different aims, the alliance is advocated by Pitt in the hope of using Britain's naval strength to capture French possessions in the West Indies.

27 AUG 1793 Lord Hood's blockading fleet takes possession of the town of Toulon, its arsenal and fleet. Four months later, however, it is to be lost to the superior military strength of France, which also forces the allies' humiliating retreat in Flanders.

26 NOV 1793 7,000 troops, under the command of Vice Admiral Sir John Jervis, sail to the West Indies, and capture the Islands of Martinique, St. Lucia, Marie Galantes and Guadeloupe.

11 JUL 1794 Pitt strengthens his Cabinet and secures a political triumph when the 'Portland Whigs', Lord Grenville, Lord Dundas, the Duke of Portland, Earl Spencer, Earl Fitzwilliam and William Windham join the Government. The Flanders campaign nevertheless continues to give cause for concern.

1796 Pitt negotiates for peace, prompted by the disintegration of the alliance, the failure of military intervention, the threat to the West Indies conquests from the troops' yellow fever and native rebellion, and domestic unrest stemming from the rise in the price of bread.

25 DEC 1796 A French invasion of Ireland, mounted by 43 vessels carrying some 15,000 troops commanded by Lazare Holhe, is abandoned only because gales off Bantry Bay drive the fleet to sea. This accentuates Pitt's failure to conduct a coherent war policy.

JAN 1797 Pitt renounces without giving reasons his possible marriage to Eleanor Eden, eldest daughter of Lord Auckland, and the only woman with whom his name is seriously linked. He declares only that there are 'decisive and insurmountable' obstacles to the match. His withdrawal has been the subject of much conjecture, although the lack of interest in women which he tends to show throughout his life may well explain Pitt's disinclination to marry.

16 APR 1797 The Navy mutinies at Spithead in protest against inefficient and corrupt administration and poor pay. The mutiny later spreads to Plymouth, Weymouth, Yarmouth and the Nore.

JUL–SEP 1797 At Pitt's behest, Lord Malmesbury conducts peace negotiations with France at Lille.

MAY–JUN 1798 Rebellion breaks out in Ireland, prompted by fear of British coercion in the South, and in anticipation of French assistance. Lacking organisation, it fails, but Pitt, morally committed to Catholic emancipation and convinced of the need for union of the two Parliaments, is determined to offer the Catholic majority the prospect of reform.

27 MAY 1798 Pitt fights a duel on Putney Heath, London, with George Tierney, the radical member of Parliament for Southwark, following exchanges in the House of Commons debate on naval manning. Neither man is injured.

1 AUG 1798 Nelson's celebrated victory over the French in the battle of the Nile assists Pitt's formation of the Second Coalition against France, which, by the end of the year, comprises Britain, Portugal, Naples, Russia and the Porte, and soon afterwards, Austria.

25 DEC 1799 First Consul Bonaparte writes personal letters to George III and the Emperor Francis II, proposing an end to the war.

3 FEB 1800 Pitt defends his rejection of Bonaparte's overtures in a masterly speech in the House of Commons, the Government's policy being approved by a majority of more than 200.

2 JUL 1800 The Act of Union with Ireland is enacted, having been passed in May and confirmed by the Irish Parliament in June. The first Parliament of Great Britain and Ireland is to meet on 22 Jan 1801, with 100 extra Irish seats.

3 FEB 1801 Pitt tenders his resignation because of the King's opposition to his policy on Catholic emancipation. The King's subsequent illness delays the formation of a new Government under Henry Addington, and causes Pitt to promise that he will never again press the Irish question during the reign. During much of the following two years, he does not attend Parliament, but re-

IMPORTANT DATES IN PERSONAL AND POLITICAL LIFE—*Continued*

sides at Walmer Castle, Kent, and suffers increasing ill-health.

17 MAR 1802 Following six months of negotiations at Amiens, a peace treaty with France is signed.

28 MAY 1802 Three weeks after the House of Commons votes by a large majority that Pitt has 'rendered great and important services to the country and deserves the thanks of the House', his 43rd birthday is celebrated by a dinner attended by more than 800 guests, for which George Canning writes the song 'The Pilot that Weathered the Storm'.

MAR 1803 Pitt rejects Addington's proposition that he should return to government as Chancellor of the Exchequer, with his elder brother Lord Chatham as First Lord of the Treasury and Prime Minister, declaring that he will return, at the command of the King, as Prime Minister or nothing else.

23 MAY 1803 Pitt makes a notable speech against the Government in the House of Commons debate on Britain's declaration of war on France of 18 May, but shows clear signs of his growing physical debility.

SUMMER 1803 Lady Hester Stanhope, Pitt's lively niece, comes to live at Walmer at her uncle's request, a surprisingly successful, mutually beneficial arrangement.

10 MAY 1804 Pitt returns to office as Prime Minister, following Addington's resignation in the face of mounting opposition led by Pitt, Fox and Grenville. His second administration is to be weaker than the first, Grenville, Windham and Spencer refusing to join a Government from which Fox has been excluded by the King.

14 JAN 1805 Faced by opposition from factions led by Fox, Grenville and Addington and with the aim of strengthening his majority in the House, Pitt seeks and secures reconciliation with Addington, whom he appoints Lord President of the Council. Addington is to resign in July.

8 APR 1805 The House of Commons votes to impeach Pitt's old friend, Lord Melville, formerly Henry Dundas, First Lord of the Admiralty; the Speaker, Charles Abbot, having voted in favour of censure. Pitt reels at this outcome, and sits on the Government front bench 'with tears trickling down his cheeks'.

SUMMER 1805 Pitt engineers the Third Coalition, with Russia, Sweden and Austria, against France. It is to collapse, in spite of Nelson's success at Trafalgar, following the victories of Napoleon at Ulm in October and at Austerlitz in December.

9 NOV 1805 Pitt, his health deteriorating, delivers his final public speech, at the Lord Mayor's Banquet, in the Guildhall, London.

23 JAN 1806 Pitt dies at Bowling Green House, probably due to renal failure and cirrhosis of the liver.

BACKGROUND

PHYSICAL CHARACTERISTICS AND HEALTH

Pitt stood about six feet tall, a thin, angular man of stiff bearing. His long face, framed in his youth by auburn hair, was enlivened by bright eyes, while his nose was, according to Romney 'Turned up at all mankind'. He had a deep, rich and melodic voice, but the awkwardness of his gestures belied his statesmanship and skill as an orator. Rosebery referred to his 'Sawing the air with windmill arms sometimes almost touching the ground'.

Pitt was never robust, and throughout his life he experienced debilitating episodes of gout, sickness and severe headaches, aggravated by his heavy consumption of port. Henry Addington remarked, 'Mr. Pitt liked a glass of port very well, and a bottle better'. Ironically, it was the former's father, Dr. Anthony Addington, who had prescribed the young Pitt a bottle of port a day as a remedy for the gout which struck him while at Cambridge. Pitt's health deteriorated during periods of stress and adversity, and by the 1790s, his face was showing signs of both the mental strain of office and physical disease. On his return to the House of Commons in May 1803, the Whig Thomas Creevy noted, 'I really think Pitt is done: his face is no longer red, but yellow; his looks are dejected; his countenance I think much changed and fallen, and every now and then he gives a hollow cough. Upon my soul, hating him as I do, I am almost moved to pity to see his fallen greatness'.

Pitt's death has been variously attributed to exhaustion, anxiety and depression. Reilly concludes that it was advanced disease rather than overwork which hastened his decline: 'Pitt suffered from gout, crystallized in the kidneys, and alcoholism, and his death was due to renal failure, probably accompanied by cirrhosis of the liver'.

EDUCATION

Primary and secondary Educated at home, under the tutelage of the Reverend Edward Wilson, who was engaged in 1765.

University 1773–1776 Pembroke Hall (now College), Cambridge

Qualifications 1776, Master of Arts (without examination)

Cultural and vocational background In Sep 1783, Pitt travelled to France with his friends Edward Eliot and William Wilberforce, and the following month was presented to King Louis XVI and Queen Marie Antoinette at Fontainebleau. While there he also met Benjamin Franklin. He returned to England later in October, and was never to leave the country again.

Languages Pitt was highly accomplished in the classical languages, and was described by Lord Grenville as the 'Best Greek scholar' with whom he had ever conversed. Of the modern languages, he spoke only French.

NON-PARLIAMENTARY CAREER

Early occupations Pitt trained as a lawyer at Lincoln's Inn, and was called to the Bar in June 1780. He joined the Western Circuit in early August.

Military service 1803–06 Colonel of the Cinque Ports Volunteers and Trinity House Reserve Volunteers.

Other posts 1790 High Steward, Cambridge University; 1790–1806 Master of the Corporation of Trinity House; 1792 Lord Warden of the Cinque Ports; 1792 Constable of Dover Castle

HONOURS

Freedom of cities 1784 London

CLUBS

Brooks's, White's, Goosetree's, Western Circuit club, London

HOBBIES AND SPORTS

Like his father, Pitt was a keen gardener, and indulged his self-confessed 'passion for planting' at Holwood, carrying out extensive work on the grounds. He enjoyed country pursuits such as riding and shooting, and hunted occasionally. He is also said to have played chess. Holwood was filled with Greek and Latin literature, in which Pitt had an academic interest but there is conflicting evidence as to whether he read widely for pleasure.

FINANCES

Pitt's personal finances were both complex and confused. Rarely out of debt, he demonstrated an indifference to his predicament which contrasts strongly to the close attention he paid to national financial affairs. At the age of 21 he began to engage in the convoluted borrowing which was to be characteristic of his future financial transactions, when he and his brother mortgaged the leases of two sets of rooms at Lincoln's Inn, in return for a loan of £1,500 at five percent interest. It was, however, the purchase of Holwood House in Aug 1785, on a mortgage of £4,000, which was to bring about Pitt's effective bankruptcy. Not only did he live beyond his means, but evidence suggests that he was systematically cheated by servants and tradesmen. Despite offers of assistance and the sale of Holwood in 1802 for £1,500, Pitt died substantially in debt.

Income Until the sale of Hayes Place in 1785, which yielded him nearly £4,400, Pitt's annual income amounted to approximately £600, half of which came from his brother John, the new Lord Chatham, the other half from his mother, paid out of an allowance made to her by her eldest son. As First Lord of the Treasury he was paid £5,622 p.a. (gross) and as Chancellor of the Exchequer, £1,800. From late 1793, as Lord Warden of the Cinque Ports, he received an additional gross sum of £4,382 p.a. This increased his net official income from £6,900 to just short of £10,000 p.a.

Legacies Pitt's father bequeathed him £3,500, which could not be paid due to the extent of Chatham's debts.

Debts By 1801, Pitt's debts were estimated at £46,000. He refused both the King's offer of assistance, and a gift of £100,000 from the City of London merchants and bankers. He did, however, finally agree to his friends organising a private fund, which eventually yielded £11, 500. Nevertheless, this was insufficient to ease his predicament, and on his death, his debts were found to be £40,000. On 3 Feb 1806, Parliament voted to settle this sum from public funds.

Will Proved on 27 Feb 1806. Pitt's will acknowledged his debts, and recognised that he owed 'more than I can leave behind me'. His wish that provision be made for his niece, Hester Stanhope and her sisters was fulfilled by the resolution of the House of Commons of 3 Feb.

ANECDOTES

Pitt's public demeanour was generally cold, stiff and reserved. A contemporary, Sir Nathaniel William Wraxall, wrote the following upon his appointment as Prime Minister: 'From the instant that Pitt entered the doorway [of the Commons] he advanced up the floor with a quick and firm step, his head erect and thrown back, looking neither to the right nor the left, not favouring with a nod or a glance any of the individuals seated on either side, among which many who possessed £5,000 a year would have been gratified even by so slight a mark of attention. It was not thus that Lord North or Fox treated Parliament . . . ' (Wraxall, *Posthumous Memoirs*)

Pitt's austere image belied his behaviour in private. While he declared to Wilberforce that he was 'the shyest man alive' (Reilly, p. 135), he exhibited warmth towards family and friends, enjoyed the company of children and was known to indulge in boyish horseplay, often associated with his drinking.

Wraxall recorded the following incident from 1784: 'Returning by way of frolic very late at night on horseback to Wimbledon from Addiscombe, the seat of Mr. Jenkinson [later Lord Liverpool] near Croydon, where the party had dined, Lord Thurlow, who was then Chancellor, Pitt and Dundas found the turnpike gate situated between Tooting and Streatham thrown open. Being elevated above their normal prudence and having no servant near them, they passed through the gate at a brisk pace without stopping to pay the toll, regardless of the remonstrances or threats of the keeper of the turnpike who, running after them and believing them to belong to some highwaymen who had recently committed depradations on that road, discharged the contents of his blunderbuss at their backs. Happily he did no injury'. (Wraxall, *Posthumous Memoirs*)

Pitt's intellectual prowess combined with his irreverence to dramatic effect in an early encounter with Edward Gibbon, author of the *Decline and Fall of the Roman Empire*, at a dinner held in Lincoln's Inn in 1780. The host James Bland Burges recorded that Pitt engaged in a brilliant political debate with the historian who "finding himself driven into a corner from which there was no escape made some excuse for rising from the table and left the room'. He refused to return, declaring 'That young gentleman is, I have no doubt, extremely ingenious and agreeable, but I must acknowledge that his style of conversation is not exactly what I am accustomed to, so you must positively excuse me . . . ' And away he went, in high dudgeon." (Quoted by Ehrman, pp. 22–3)

Pitt was generally held to be indifferent to women, although in the 1780s his name was linked to Jane, Duchess of Gordon, who acted as hostess at Downing Street for a number of years. She was a lively, coarse and unconventional woman, as conveyed by a contemporary:

> The Duchess triumphs in her manly mien,
> Loud is her accent and her phrase obscene.

When she and Pitt met again after not having seen each other for a long period, she enquired, 'Well, Mr. Pitt, do you talk as much nonsense now as you used to do when you lived with me?' He replied 'I do not know, Madam, whether I talk so much nonsense, I certainly do not hear as much'. (Reilly, pp. 250–1)

QUOTATIONS

If . . . this ill-omened marriage is not already solemnised, I know a just and lawful impediment, and in the name of the public safety I here forbid the Banns. (On the Coalition, House of Commons, 1783)

Necessity is the plea for every infringement of human freedom. It is the argument of tyrants; it is the creed of slaves. (House of Commons, 18 Nov 1783)

On every principle by which men of justice and honour are actuated, it is the foulest and most atrocious deed which the history of the world has yet had occasion to attest. (On the execution of Louis XVI of France, House of Commons, 1 Feb 1793)

There is no principle of the law of nations clearer than this, that, when in the cause of war any nation acquires new possessions, such nation has only temporary right to them, and they do not become property till the end of the war. (House of Commons, 30 Dec 1796)

We will not leave the monster to prowl the world unopposed. He must cease to annoy the abode of peaceful men. If he retire to the cell, whether of solitude or repentance, thither we will not pursue him, but we cannot leave him on the throne of power. (On the war against France, House of Commons, 7 Jun 1799)

We must recollect . . . what it is we have at stake, what it is we have to contend for. It is for our property, it is for our liberty, it is for our independence, nay, for our existence as a nation; it is for our character, it is for our very name as Englishmen, it is for everything dear and valuable to man on this side of the grave'. (22 Jul 1803)

England has saved herself by her exertions, and will, I trust, save Europe by her example. (Guildhall, London, 9 Nov 1805)

Roll up that map [of Europe]; it will not be wanted these ten years. (Following Napoleon's victory at Austerlitz, Jan 1806)

RESIDENCES

Hayes Place, Hayes, Kent
Holwood, near Bromley, Kent (See also Pitt's Cottage, below),
Burton Pynsent, near Langport, Somerset
Stone Buildings, Lincoln's Inn, London
10 Downing Street,
Walmer Castle near Deal, Kent
12 Park Place, London
15 Johnston Street, Bath, Avon,
14 York Place (now 120 Baker Street), London (Plaque)
Bowling Green House, Putney Heath, London
Open to the public Walmer Castle and Garden, a 16th-century coastal defence fortress, official residence of the Lords Warden of the Cinque Ports from 1792 (an English Heritage property); Pitt's Cottage, Westerham, Kent, now a restaurant and tea room. According to tradition, Pitt took this cottage while supervising alterations being carried out at Holwood.

MEMORIALS

STATUES AND BUSTS

1831, by Francis Chantrey, Hanover Square, London; 1815, by Joseph Nollekens, Senate House, Cambridge; 1813, by Richard Westmacott, above the west door of Westminster Abbey, London; by J. C. Bubb, inscription by Canning, Guildhall, London; by P. MacDowell, St. Stephen's Hall, Palace of Westminster, London

PORTRAITS

By John Hoppner (replica, 1805), National Portrait Gallery; 1789, by James Gillray, National Portrait Gallery; 1793, by Karl Anton Hickel, group portrait, 'William Pitt Addressing the House of Commons', National Portrait Gallery; by Thomas Lawrence, Windsor Castle

BIBLIOGRAPHIC INFORMATION

LETTERS AND PERSONAL PAPERS

The main collections of papers relating to Pitt are in the British Library; Cambridge University Library; the Public Record Office; Suffolk Record Office, Ipswich; Kent County Archives Office, Maidstone, Kent; and the John Rylands Library, University of Manchester. The William L. Clements Library, University of Michigan, Ann Arbor, Michigan, also houses a sizeable collection of his letters. Much correspondence can also be found in Aspinall, A., ed. *The Later Correspondence of George III*. 5 vols. Cambridge, 1962–70; Stanhope, P. H., 5th Earl. *Life of the Right Honourable William Pitt*. 4 vols. London, 1861–2. The most comprehensive collection of Pitt's speeches is Hathaway, W.S., ed. *The Speeches of the Right Honourable William Pitt in the House of Commons*. 4 vols., London, 1806; Extracts from the above are contained in Coupland, R., ed. *The War Speeches of William Pitt the Younger*. 3rd ed., Oxford, 1940.

FURTHER READING

Ehrman, J. *The Young Pitt*. 3 vols., London, 1983–85
Harvey, A.D. *William Pitt the Younger, 1759–1806: a bibliography*. Bibliographies of British Statesmen, no. 1. Westport, 1989.
Jarrett, D. *Pitt the Younger*. London, 1974
Reilly, R. *Pitt the Younger, 1759–1806*. London, 1978.
Rose, J. H. *William Pitt and the Great War*. London, 1911.
—. *William Pitt and the National Revival*. London, 1911.
Rosebery, Lord. *Pitt*. London, 1899.
Stanhope, P. H., 5th Earl. *Life of the Right Honourable William Pitt*. 4 vols., London, 1861–62.

G.C.

Bettmann

Henry Addington

Lived 1757–1844
Political Party Tory
Prime Minister 17 March 1801–10 May 1804
Government Tory
Reigning Monarch George III

Libertas sub Rege pio Liberty under a pious King

ADDINGTON AS PRIME MINISTER

A doctor's son, Addington was a young companion of Pitt and a mediocre performer in the House of Commons to which he was elected in 1784. But he was industrious and learnt House procedures, so that in 1789 Pitt secured him the Speakership, an office he reformed and enhanced over a period of nearly twelve years. When Pitt resigned he supported Addington as next Prime Minister. Addington, claiming his ambition was peace and that peace was essential for England pleased everyone by agreeing to the Treaty of Amiens in 1802. A successful election followed and as his own Chancellor of the Exchequer he introduced a very effective Budget in 1803. War was again declared on France in 1803 but the administration of the subsequent Military Service Act encouraging volunteers was bungled and the Administration's reputation damaged. Addington was not an inspiring performer in the House of Commons and certainly no replacement for Pitt who increasingly took up the role of Opposition. With France looking less threatening Addington's majority in the House of Commons fell away and he resigned before it disappeared. His political career continued for another thirty years, however, and he became Lord Privy Seal and then Lord President under Grenville, Lord President under Spencer Perceval, and for a long period Home Secretary under Lord Liverpool.

PERSONAL INFORMATION

Names Henry Addington
Peerages Viscount Sidmouth, 12 Jan 1805
Nickname The Doctor
Born 30 May 1757
Birthplace Bedford Row, Holborn, London
Religion Anglican
Ancestry English. His family were yeoman farmers who originated in Fringford, Oxfordshire. His father became a doctor, initially in Reading, Berkshire, where he ran a lunatic asylum, then in London, where his practice included many of the gentry, including King George III.
Dates and places of marriages 1) 17 Sep 1781; 2) 29 Jul 1823, St. George's, Hanover Square, London
Age at marriage 1) 24 years, 110 days; 2) 66 years, 60 days
Years married 1) 29 years, 279 days; 2) 18 years, 271 days
First entered Parliament 5 Apr 1784
Date appointed PM 17 Mar 1801
Age at appointment 43 years, 291 days
Date ceased to be PM 10 May 1804
Total time as PM 3 years, 54 days
Ceased to be MP 11 Jan 1805
Lived after last term as PM 39 years, 281 days
Date of death 15 Feb 1844
Place of death White Lodge, Richmond, Surrey
Age at death 86 years, 261 days
Last words 'Mary Anne' (His daughter, who was present at the time)
Place of funeral and burial St. Mary's Church, Mortlake, Surrey
Zodiac sign Gemini

FATHER

Dr. Anthony Addington
Date and place of birth 13 Dec 1713, Fringford, Oxfordshire
Occupation Physician
Date of marriage 22 Sep 1745
Date of death 22 Mar 1790
Place of burial St. Michael's, Fringford, Oxfordshire

MOTHER

Mary Hiley
Profile Inconsequential but affectionate, she did much to alleviate the harsh and bleak atmosphere generated by Addington's father.
Date of marriage 22 Sep 1745
Date of death 7 Nov 1778
Place of burial St. Michael's, Fringford, Oxfordshire

BROTHERS AND SISTERS

Addington was the eldest son, and fourth of six children.
Anne, b. 1747; m. William Goodenough MD, brother of the Bishop of Carlisle; d. 12 Jun 1806
Eleanor, b. 1749; m. James Sutton (MP Devizes 1765–80; Sutton stepped down as MP to allow Addington to stand in his place); d. 1827
Elizabeth, b. 1754; m. William Hoskins of North Perrot, Somerset; d. 1827
John Hiley (known as Hiley), b. 1759; m. Mary Unwin; MP Truro 1787–90, Winchelsea 1794–96, Wendover 1796–1802, Bossiney 1802, Harwich 1803–18; Lord of Treasury 1800–01, 1802–1803, Secretary of Treasury 1801–02, Joint Paymaster General 1803–04, Commissioner for India 1806–07, Under-Secretary of State for Home Affairs 1812–18; d. 11 Jun 1818
Charlotte, b. 1761; m. Charles Bragge (a barrister, MP Monmouth 1790–96, Bristol 1796–1812, Bodmin 1812–18, Harwich 1818–23; held a number of ministerial posts); d. 1839

FIRST WIFE

Ursula Mary Hammond
Date of birth 14 May 1760
Father Leonard Hammond, of Cheam, Surrey
Father's occupation Businessman
Age at marriage 21 years 126 days
Number of children 8, one of whom died in infancy.
Date and place of death 23 Jun 1811, Portman Square, London
Place of burial St. Mary's Church, Mortlake, Surrey
Years younger than PM 2 years 349 days
Profile She was described by her son-in-law, Hon. George Pellew: 'meek and retiring . . . her piety and purity . . . the delicacy and refinement of her character . . . revealed themselves'. She was co-heiress to her father, and brought an income of £1000 a year to her marriage. Very loyal to Addington, King George III said, when Pitt fell out with Addington, that Mrs. Addington was far more vengeful than Addington could be.

SECOND WIFE

Hon Mary Anne Townsend
Date of birth *c.* 1783
Mother Anne Maria Eagnall
Father William Scott, Lord Stowell
Father's occupation Lawyer, MP Downton 1790–1801, Oxford University 1801–21. Appointed as a judge of the Admiralty, and to the Privy Council in 1798, he was a life-long friend of Addington.
Age at marriage *c.* 40
Number of children None
Date and place of death 26 Apr 1842 White Lodge, Richmond
Place of burial Sonning Church, Sonning, Berkshire
Years younger than PM *c.* 26 years
Profile Widow of Thomas Townsend of Honington Hall, Warwickshire, she was gentle, kind and intelligent, and more sophisticated than Addington's first wife. She was also generous, giving land to Berkshire Hospital, and a new market cross to Devizes. A sculptor said, 'her face was more full of lively sweetness than any he ever saw.' She was not very healthy, however, and in the last years of her life she was half paralysed and in almost constant pain.

CHILDREN

4 sons, 4 daughters; 1 son died in infancy
By his first wife, Ursula Mary:
Mary Anne, b. *c.*1782, unm.; devoted to her father, she stayed with him all his life, nursing him through his final illness; d. 1844
Henry, b. 30 Sep 1786; unm.; Clerk of the Pells, Jul 1802. He went to Christ Church, Oxford, in Oct 1803, but under the strain of studying suffered a complete mental

and physical breakdown in Mar 1805 from which he never recovered; d. 30 Jul 1823
Charles Anthony, b. *c.* Jun 1789; d. Aug 1789
William Leonard (2nd Viscount Sidmouth), b. 13 Nov 1794; m. 20 Apr 1820, Mary Young; entered the Church, but deserted Anglicanism for the Clapham sect and then the Irvingites, where he became an 'Angel'; Rector of Poole 1821–44; d. 25 Mar 1864
Frances, m. 20 Jun 1820 Rev. George Pellew; d. 27 Feb 1870
Charlotte, m. 1838 Rev. Horace Gore Currie
Harriet, m. 1838 Thomas Barker Wall
By his second wife, Mary Anne: None

LIFE AND CAREER

PARLIAMENTARY ELECTIONS FOUGHT

*(*designates candidate elected)*

DATE Mar 1784. General Election
CONSTITUENCY Devizes
RESULT Sir James Tylney Long* (Tory), Henry Addington* (Tory)

DATE Jun 1790. General Election
CONSTITUENCY Devizes
RESULT Henry Addington* (Tory), Joshua Smith* (Tory)

DATE May 1796. General Election
CONSTITUENCY Devizes
RESULT Henry Addington* (Tory), Joshua Smith* (Tory)

DATE 25 Feb 1801. By-election caused by Addington's acceptance of the Chiltern Hundreds and his resignation as Speaker
CONSTITUENCY Devizes
RESULT Henry Addington* (Tory)

DATE 21 Mar 1801. By-election caused by Addington's appointment as Prime Minister
CONSTITUENCY Devizes
RESULT Henry Addington* (Tory)

DATE Jun 1802. General Election
CONSTITUENCY Devizes
RESULT Henry Addington* (Tory)

PARTY ACTIVITY

Membership of group or faction Addington was never formally the leader of a party, but he was able to command a majority as Prime Minister as the acknowledged successor of Pitt. He headed a group of up to 68 MPs after his resignation as Prime Minister, but this support had virtually disappeared by 1812.

PARLIAMENTARY AND MINISTERIAL EXPERIENCE

Maiden Speech 24 Jan 1786. He seconded the Address to the Throne at the opening of Parliament (*Parl. Hist.* vol 25, cols 999-1000).
Privy Counsellor 23 Jun 1789
Ministerial Offices First Lord of the Treasury and Leader of the House of Commons 17 Mar 1801–10 May 1804; Chancellor of the Exchequer 21 Mar 1801–10 May 1804; Lord President of the Council 14 Jan–4 Jul 1805, 8 Oct 1806-25 Mar 1807, 8 Apr-11 Jun 1812; Lord Privy Seal 5 Feb–8 Oct 1806; Home Secretary 11 Jun 1812–17 Jan 1822; Minister without Portfolio 17 Jan 1822–29 Nov 1824
Opposition Leader while PM Charles James Fox
Speaker of the House 8 Jun 1789–10 Feb 1801

GOVERNMENTS FORMED

Administration 17 Mar 1801–10 May 1804

GENERAL ELECTION RESULTS
MAY 1796: Supporters of the Administration 424; Opposition 95; Independent 29; Doubtful 10. Total 558
Majority 290
JUN 1802: Supporters of the Administration 467; Old Opposition 124; New Opposition 25; Independent 19; Doubtful 23. Total 658
Majority 276

CABINET
Prime Minister, First Lord of the Treasury and Chancellor of the Exchequer Henry Addington
Lord Chancellor Lord Eldon
Lord President of the Council Earl of Chatham (Mar–Jun 1801); Duke of Portland (Jun 1801–1804)
Lord Privy Seal Earl of Westmoreland
Home Secretary Duke of Portland (Mar–Jun 1801); Lord Pelham (Jun 1801–June 1803); C. Yorke (Aug 1803–1804)
Foreign Secretary Lord Hawkesbury
Colonial Secretary Lord Hobart
First Lord of the Admiralty Earl St. Vincent
Master General of the Ordnance Earl of Chatham (Jun 1801–04)
President of the Board of Control Viscount Lewisham (1801–Jul 1802); Lord Castlereagh (Jul 1802–04)
Chancellor of the Duchy of Lancaster Earl of Liverpool (1801–Nov 1803); Lord Pelham (Nov 1803–04)

IMPORTANT DATES IN PERSONAL AND POLITICAL LIFE

24 FEB 1778 Addington awarded BA from Brasenose College, Oxford.
17 SEP 1781 Marries Ursula Mary Hammond, daughter of a businessman from Cheam, Surrey.
5 APR 1784 Enters Parliament as MP for Devizes, Wiltshire.
24 JAN 1786 Reluctantly makes his maiden speech.
8 JUN 1789 Elected Speaker on the instigation of his childhood friend, William Pitt (The Younger), winning the vote over Sir Gilbert Elliot by 215–142. Appointed to the Privy Council on 23 June 1789.
10 MAR 1790 Debate on the payment of a salary to the Speaker gives Addington £6000 per year.
1 FEB 1793 France declares war on Britain.
END OF 1793 Pitt suggests that Addington should follow Dundas as Home Secretary. Addington prefers to remain Speaker, and refuses.
23 APR 1795 The nine-year impeachment of Warren Hastings for impropriety in his conduct in India ends with Hastings's acquittal. As Speaker, Addington formulates the constitutional principle that an impeachment pro-

IMPORTANT DATES IN PERSONAL AND POLITICAL LIFE—*Continued*

cess cannot be ended by the dissolution of Parliament, thus ensuring that the Monarch cannot save his favourites from being impeached by dissolving Parliament.

4 DEC 1797 When Pitt's Budget fails to provide enough funds to maintain the war with France. Addington suggests a 'voluntary contribution', whereby taxpayers may pay a higher rate than that for which they had originally been assessed. When this becomes law, Addington gives £2000, about one-fifth of his income. The appeal stirs patriotic feelings to such an extent that about £2, 800,000 is raised over the year of the appeal.

29 APR 1798 Appointed Commander of the Woodley Cavalry, a volunteer regiment.

12 FEB 1799 Addington makes a speech in the House (unusual for a Speaker) on the Bill of Union with Ireland, detailing the problems that union would bring, following consultation with John Foster, Speaker of the Irish House. Although he supports union, Addington opposes Catholic emancipation, the effects of which he fears. The Act of Union is passed in 1800.

10 FEB 1801 Addington resigns as Speaker in order to become Prime Minister. Pitt has resigned as Prime Minister because he is unable to persuade the King to agree to Catholic emancipation. With Pitt's approval, the King asks Addington, Pitt's friend, to become Prime Minister.

17 MAR 1801 Following a delay owing to an illness of George III, Addington becomes Prime Minister.

2 APR 1801 Nelson destroys the Danish fleet at Copenhagen in order to break up the Northern League. Addington supports Nelson, but his main aim is to secure peace with France, Britain no longer being able to afford the ongoing war. He rescinds an Order enabling the Royal Navy to arrest French fishermen, which leads the French diplomat, M. Otto, to return to London. Lord Hawkesbury, Addington's Foreign Secretary, and Otto conduct talks throughout the summer and autumn of 1801.

1802 Throughout 1802, Pitt gradually becomes dissatisfied with his position, and begins to turn against Addington.

25 MAR 1802 The Treaty of Amiens is signed, ending the war with France. Various territories, including Malta, are to be returned to France, while the French are to evacuate Italy. Having brought peace, Addington finds his reputation at its highest point in his premiership.

5 APR 1802 Addington's first Budget repeals Pitt's income tax based on reported income given by the individual tax-payer, which is very inefficient. Addington decides to overhaul the whole system. Addington's Budget does much to tidy up the nation's finances.

JUL 1802 Appoints his son to the sinecure of Clerk of the Pells, worth £3000 p.a. Despite having first offered the post to several others, including Pitt, he is accused of nepotism.

JUL 1802 A General Election strengthens Addington's hand in the Commons. Although the parties are represented at close to their pre-election levels, this is seen as a victory, considering the difficulties of the Administration's first year.

OCT 1802 Addington moves into White Lodge, Richmond Park, Surrey. George III grants it to him for life when he resigns as Prime Minister in 1804.

OCT 1802 Napoleon organizes an insurrection in Switzerland. Addington promises the Swiss money and moral support if they choose to fight and delays the evacuation of British troops from various colonies. Unable and unwilling to take further action, however, Addington appears weak.

JAN 1803 Addington tentatively opens negotiations with Pitt designed to incorporate him into the Administration, but Pitt rejects the position of Chancellor of the Exchequer in March 1803 on the grounds that he is only prepared to return to the Government as Prime Minister. Addington then suggests a Government with Pitt under Pitt's own brother, Lord Chatham, while Pitt insists that Lord Grenville should become Prime Minister. When neither side backs down, the split between the two is complete.

JAN–MAY 1803 Napoleon demands the immediate evacuation of Malta by Britain, as promised in the Treaty of Amiens, but the British Ambassador refuses, owing to Napoleon's interference in Switzerland. Last-minute negotiations collapse, making a resumption of war inevitable.

18 MAY 1803 War declared on France.

23/24 MAY 1803 Debate on the resumption of war with France. Addington's speech fails to inspire, while Pitt demonstrates his abilities as an orator. It becomes clear that Addington will eventually have to stand down in favour of Pitt.

3 JUN 1803 Pitt refuses to back the Government on a censure motion, thus making public the split between Addington and Pitt. Although Addington wins the vote by 335–58, the public begins to turn against him.

13 JUN 1803 Addington's Budget re-introduces income tax, but now to be collected at the source. It proves much more effective than Pitt's version. Although Pitt attacks it during a debate in July, he will keep it in the same form in his own Budget in 1805.

JUL 1803 The Military Service Act is passed, allowing volunteers to enrol for the war with France. The response, however, is so enthusiastic, with over 300,000 volunteers, that the Government, unable to cope, is forced to forbid further enrollment in certain areas by August, which seriously damages its public esteem.

23 JUL 1803 A small uprising in Ireland catches the Government unawares, and leads to the murder of the Chief Justice, Lord Kilwarden. Although most of the rebels are caught and executed, the bad impression created adds to the growing disenchantment with Addington throughout the country.

OCT 1803 Addington refuses the Order of the Garter.

DEC 1803 The imminence of invasion by France keeps opposition in Parliament to a minimum, but as this threat disappears, opposition begins to grow, with Pitt actively opposing the Government.

15 MAR 1804 The Government's majority on a debate on the Navy is only 71, with Pitt voting against. Pitt's strength is seen later, when he votes with the Government on the Volunteer Consolidation Bill, and the Opposition can only muster 56 votes.

16 APR 1804 A vote on the Irish Militia Augmentation Bill reduces the Government's majority to 21. It rises to 52 on 23 Apr in a debate on defence of the country, but falls to 37 on 25 Apr on the Army of Reserve Suspension Bill.

30 APR 1804 Following Pitt's precedent in 1801, Addington introduces the Budget even though he has indicated that he will resign as Prime Minister. As it is a safe Budget, approved by Pitt, there is no discussion of it following the speech.

10 MAY 1804 Addington sees the drop in his majority as a rejection by the House of Commons, and despite being still able to muster a majority, he resigns. Pitt returns as Prime Minister. Addington refuses a peerage, much to the annoyance of George III.

11 JAN 1805 Despite still leading a large faction in the Commons, Addington is persuaded to enter the House of Lords as Viscount Sidmouth, and accordingly resigns his seat at Devizes. He also accepts a position in the Cabinet as Lord President of the Council on 14 Jan.

15 JAN 1805 Takes his seat in the House of Lords.

10 JUL 1805 Resigns from the Cabinet, refusing to agree with Pitt's wish to impeach Lord Melville over funds that disappeared when Melville was Treasurer of the Navy.

AUG 1805 Addington devastated when his son Henry suffers a complete mental and physical breakdown from which he never recovers.

23 JAN 1806 Pitt dies. He and Addington had become socially reconciled over the previous months, but never returned to the closeness of their earlier years. Addington writes: 'May everlasting happiness await him. To me it is a comfort not to be expressed, that I have been enabled at this crisis to show, not merely attention, but the affection that has never been extinguished.'

5 FEB 1806 Addington enters Grenville's administration as Lord Privy Seal, moving to the Lord Presidency of the Council on 8 Oct 1806.

25 MAR 1807 Opposing the extension of the law to Britain (already existing in Ireland) allowing Roman Catholics to hold military commissions up to the rank of Colonel, Addington resigns, and faced with similar opposition from the King, the rest of the Government soon follows.

AUTUMN/WINTER 1807 Addington's health breaks down. He does not resume public life until early 1808 and does not make a complete recovery until the end of 1809.

16 MAR 1808 Addington argues that the Orders in Council, which had caused the US to cease trade with Britain and Europe, should be amended to exempt the US from the threat of having their ships seized by the Royal Navy.

27 MAY 1808 He opposes Grenville's motion to extend the franchise to certain classes of Irish Catholics.

21 MAY 1811 Addington introduces the Dissenting Ministers Bill, in order to tighten up the rules on who can obtain a licence to preach. It is defeated without a division.

23 JUN 1811 Addington's wife Ursula Mary, dies after a short illness. He struggles to overcome the greatest tragedy in his life. Nicholas Vansittart is to write three months later that he is 'in deep affliction, and feeble health, and anxious only for retirement.' Addington does not adhere to this feeling regarding retirement, however.

8 APR 1812 Appointed Lord President of the Council.

11 MAY 1812 Spencer Perceval, the Prime Minister, is assassinated and replaced by Lord Liverpool.

11 JUN 1812 Addington appointed Home Secretary and lays before Parliament evidence of threatened revolts by Luddites. Although the worst of the Luddite troubles has passed, many reports of impending disturbances, often greatly exaggerated, continue to come in. Secret committees at both Houses are set up, and Justices of the Peace are given more power.

JAN 1813 Seventeen Luddites condemned to death at York for the murder of William Horsfall. In order to discourage other potential revolutionaries, Addington refuses to consider leniency, and they are hanged. For the next few years, the country remains relatively free from domestic troubles.

18 JUN 1815 Napoleon finally defeated at the Battle of Waterloo.

1815–16 With the decline of war industries, the resumption of trade within Europe, and the subsequent application of tariffs to trade with Britain, the flood of soldiers returning from the war are unable to find jobs, and unrest increases. Addington refuses to help, however, claiming it is not the Government's job to intervene in such problems.

FEB 1817 Following reports from secret committees of both Houses on the increased unrest, Addington suspends Habeas Corpus (the suspension is lifted in Feb 1818) and introduces Bills to prevent seditious meetings and to penalise attempts to seduce the loyalties of the armed forces.

JUNE 1817 Following an attempted insurrection in Derbyshire and the subsequent execution of three of the ringleaders, Addington issues a circular to all Lord Lieutenants instructing them to hold anybody charged with seditious libel. His authority is undermined, however, when a test case overturns this circular.

11 JUN 1818 Hiley, Addington's brother and long-time supporter, dies.

16 AUG 1819 A bad harvest in 1818 has given fresh impetus to the growing agitation for reform. The 'Peterloo Massacre' follows a meeting at St. Peter's Field, Manchester, when inexperienced yeomen are ordered by the local magistrates to arrest the main speaker, Henry Hunt, and in the ensuing panic 11 people are killed. Addington's reputation suffers because of his support for the actions of the magistrates, despite an outcry in the country and the attacks of the Opposition.

DEC 1819 To crack down on further disturbances, Addington introduces the 'Six Acts' which restrict meetings; impose heavy penalties on publishers of seditious libel; and apply the Four penny tax, intended for newspapers, to pamphlets.

29 JAN 1820 Death of George III and succession of George IV.

23 FEB. 1820 The 'Cato Street Conspiracy', an attempt to blow up the Cabinet by a group led by Arthur Thistlewood, is foiled under Addington's personal supervision.

AUG 1820 A Secret Committee of the House of Lords involving Addington is set up to enquire into the actions of Queen Caroline, whom George IV hopes to divorce. The 'trial' lasts 80 days, during which angry crowds support the Queen, blaming Addington for the proceedings. Although the trial is inconclusive, the problem ends when the Queen dies in the summer of 1821.

17 JAN 1822 Addington resigns as Home Secretary, but remains in the Cabinet without a portfolio.

29 JUL 1823 Addington is married for the second time, to the Hon. Mary Anne Townsend.

31 JUL 1823 Henry, Addington's eldest son, dies after a long illness.

29 NOV 1824 Resigns from the Cabinet for the last time.

SUMMER 1825 He uses his first period of leisure for travel, and tours Belgium, Germany and France with his daughters. The following year, he tours Holland and France.

4 APR 1829 Addington's last speech in the House of Lords, opposing the Catholic Emancipation Bill.

7 OCT 1831 He votes against the first Reform Bill and also against the second Reform Bill on 13 Apr 1832, which effectively marks the end of his public life. He occasionally votes after this time, but not on anything major.

IMPORTANT DATES IN PERSONAL AND POLITICAL LIFE—*Continued*

26 APR 1842 Following a long illness, Mary Anne, Lady Sidmouth dies. Addington's sight begins to fail, and he becomes increasingly feeble.

15 FEB 1844 Dies of influenza.

BACKGROUND

PHYSICAL CHARACTERISTICS AND HEALTH

According to Samuel Bamford (*Passages in the Life of a Radical*, 1844), Addington was 'a tall, square and bony figure . . . his forehead was broad and prominent, and from their cavernous orbits looked mild and intelligent eyes.' Sir Nathaniel Wraxhall *(Posthumous Memoirs of His Own Time*, 1836) said that he was 'tall and well proportioned, his countenance pleasing, his features fine, and his manners mild, calm, grave, calculated to conciliate mankind.'

Generally a healthy man, he had several periods of poor health, particularly between 1805–06, when he was diagnosed as having 'congestion of the liver' causing back pain and langour. Something of a hypochondriac, he was convinced he was going to die, and brooded on his symptoms, describing them in great detail to all his friends.

Between 1807–09, he suffered from erysipelas, an inflammation of the skin. He took to his bed in Nov 1807 and did not return to public life until early in 1808. His erysipelas was not healed until Sir Lucas Pepys prescribed a 'bracing mode of treatment' which cleared it at the end of 1809.

In his later years he rarely went out, unable to walk far, and he began to lose his sight (although he did not go completely blind). By the end of his life, he had lost most of his attentiveness, and had become very feeble. He died of influenza.

EDUCATION

Primary 1762–68 Rev. William Gilpin's School, Cheam, Surrey

Secondary 1768–73 Winchester; 1773–74 Private tuition under Dr. Goodenough, Ealing

University 1774–79 Brasenose College, Oxford

Prizes and awards 1779 Chancellor's Medal for English Essay

Qualifications 1778 Bachelor of Arts; 1780 Master of Arts

Cultural and vocational background Addington decided to stay at Oxford for a year after completing his BA in 1778, and then left to take up the study of Law in Lincoln's Inn. He appears to have neglected his studying for at least a year, and spent the summer with his brother-in-law James Sutton at Devizes in 1780. It was at this point that he first got to know the constituency he was to inherit from Sutton in 1784.

Languages He was accomplished in Greek while at school.

NON-PARLIAMENTARY CAREER

Early occupations Following his graduation from Oxford in 1779, Addington spent several years studying for the Bar, to which he was called on 11 May 1784.

Military service Addington was Commander of the Woodley Cavalry, Berkshire, from 29 April 1798–Dec 1806. Addington spent almost all his free time in the next two years, drilling and training the men. He was very proud of their turn-out, and took great pride in presenting them to the King in July 1799.

Other posts 1784–1844 Recorder of Devizes; 1798 High Steward of Reading; 1802–44 Governor of the Charter House; 1806–07, 1812–15 Ranger of Richmond Park; 1815–44 Deputy-Ranger of Richmond Park; 1813–42 Lord High Steward of Westminster; 1818 Commissioner for building new churches; 1818–44 Elder Brother of Trinity House

HONOURS

Freedom of cities 1819 City of London

Academic 16 June 1814 DCL Oxford

Other than peerage 24 Mar 1791 Fellow of the Society of Arts

CLUBS

White's

HOBBIES AND SPORTS

A very austere and grave man, Addington had few hobbies. At school he played cricket and quoits, but in adult life his only hobbies were riding and writing poetry.

FINANCES

Before his marriage, Addington had no money of his own, but his wife's income from her father meant that they had few major financial problems. As Speaker his income was such that he was able to give £2000, under his own scheme of a 'voluntary contribution' to help with the running of the war in France. Following his resignation as Prime Minister Addington was offered a pension that he felt able to refuse, but the succeeding years brought more financial worries to the point where, in 1822, he felt he had to accept a pension from the King. His financial problems were, however, solved in 1823 when he married a wealthy widow.

Income In his first year as Speaker, Addington's income was approximately £1200, mainly from fees on Bills and other proceedings of the House. In 1790, a vote in the Commons led to Addington being given a salary of £6000 p.a., and in 1798 his overall income was about £10,000 p.a. From 1805–23, he received his son's income of £3000 p.a. as Clerk of the Pells, following his son's breakdown. Addington used half of this to look after his son.

Spouse's finances Addington's first wife received about £1000 p.a. from her father, and was co-heiress when he died. Addington's second wife received a jointure from her deceased first husband's family, which was relinquished when she received her inheritance on the death of her father, Lord Stowell, in 1836.

Pensions Addington accepted a pension of £3000 p.a. from the King in 1822, which he gave up on his second marriage.

Will Proved April 1844, and he was succeeded by his son, William

ANECDOTES

Addington was a notably poor orator, not making his maiden speech until two years had passed, and was a reluctant speaker from then on. Harriet, Lady Bessborough, wrote: 'Hare says he heard but one sentence in Mr. Addington's speech the other night. He woke from his sleep and heard: "For as this is that which was said to . . . ". Hare was quite satisfied and turned to sleep out the rest.'

When Addington announced his first Cabinet, it was notable for the absence of any of the more talented politicians of the day. John Hookham Frere said that his father 'went through all the members of the new Cabinet, and rubbing his hands at the end, said: "Well, Thank God, we have at last got a ministry without one of those confounded men of genius in it."'

At the time of the trial of Queen Caroline (1820), Addington and Lord Castlereagh, seen as the authors of the proceedings, were reviled and threatened by mobs wherever they went. They disregarded these threats, however, and walked about the streets as usual without any attendants. One day in Parliament Street, a large mob got up around them and started hooting violently at them. 'Here we go', said Addington, 'the two most popular men in England.' 'Yes' replied Castlereagh, 'through a grateful and admiring multitude.'

Addington was introduced to so many adminstrations in order to please George III that Canning said that he was like the smallpox that everyone was obliged to have once in their lives.

QUOTATIONS

In youth, the absence of pleasure is pain, in old age, the absence of pain is pleasure.(Quoted in Pellew, Vol III, p. 475)

RESIDENCES

7 Clifford Street, London
Paper Buildings, Lincoln's Inn, London
Southampton Street, Bloomsbury, London
47, Lower Brook Street, London
Woodley Estate, Sonning, Reading, Berkshire
Palace Yard, Westminster (as Speaker)
10 Downing Street
White Lodge, Richmond Park, Richmond, Surrey

MEMORIALS

STATUES AND BUSTS

1831, by William Behnes, National Portrait Gallery

PORTRAITS

c.1803, by Sir William Beechey, National Portrait Gallery; 1833, by George Richmond, National Portrait Gallery; 1793–5, by Karl Anton Kickel, National Portrait Gallery; 1823, by Sir George Hayter, National Portrait Gallery.

BIBLIOGRAPHIC INFORMATION

LETTERS AND PERSONAL PAPERS

The main collection of papers relating to Addington are in the Devon Record Office, Exeter, with a much smaller collection of letters in the Gloucestershire Record Office, Gloucester.

Addington's correspondence was extensively used in the book by Pellew, but severely edited to spare the feelings of the family.

FURTHER READING

Farnsworth, A. *Addington - Author of the Modern Income Tax*. London, 1951.

Hughes, E. I. *The First Viscount Sidmouth: A Résumé*. 1968.

Pellew, G. *The Life & Correspondence of Rt Hon Henry Addington, First Viscount Sidmouth*. 3 vols. London, 1847.

Ziegler, P. *Addington*. London, 1965.

C.S.

Bettmann

Lord Grenville

Lived 1759–1834
Political Party Whig
Prime Minister 11 February 1806–25 March 1807
Government Whig
Reigning Monarch George III

Repetens exempla suorum Following the example of his ancestors

---

GRENVILLE AS PRIME MINISTER

After early Ministerial office in 1791 Grenville, at the age of thirty-one, became Pitt's Foreign Secretary for a decade. Hardworking rather than imaginative his instinct was to follow not lead. With his own clearly established priorities, he was regarded as a successful Foreign Secretary. After Pitt's death in office the King lacking candidates turned unenthusiastically to Grenville to be his next Prime Minister. With similar lack of enthusiasm Grenville accepted. He formed a broadly based Administration from three of the four major factions, with Fox as his Foreign Secretary—a 'Ministry of All the Talents'. He instituted reforms in the Treasury's accounting practices, reorganised the armed forces, and reformed the governing of Scotland to ensure support of Scottish MPs. With Fox he successfully moved a resolution in the House of Commons abolishing the slave trade. This vigorous start was not maintained. Fox died and Grenville lost Pittite support, although he increased his majority at the General Election of 1806. When his administration sought to extend military commissions to Catholics, he clashed with the King to whom he refused reassurances not to raise the subject again. He resigned barely a year after taking office, but remained politically active for another fifteen years.

PERSONAL INFORMATION

Names William Wyndham Grenville
Peerages Baron Grenville of Wotton-under-Bernewood
Nickname Bogey
Born 24 Oct 1759
Birthplace Wotton House, Buckinghamshire
Religion Anglican
Ancestry English. The Grenvilles were the descendants of a branch of a Norman family, which settled in England, and became substantial landowners. Through the marriage in 1710 of Richard Grenville and Hester Temple, whose wealthy, well-connected family lived at Stowe, Buckinghamshire, they further increased their prosperity and inherited an earldom.
Date and place of marriage 18 Jun 1792, Hanover Square, London
Age at marriage 32 years, 268 days
Years married 41 years, 188 days
First entered Parliament 19 Feb 1782
Date appointed PM 11 Feb 1806
Age at appointment 46 years, 110 days
Date ceased to be PM 25 Mar 1807
Total time as PM 1 year, 42 days
Ceased to be MP 25 Nov 1790
Lived after last term as PM 26 years, 293 days
Date of death 12 Jan 1834
Place of death Dropmore Lodge, Burnham, Buckinghamshire
Age at death 74 years, 80 days
Place of funeral Burnham, Buckinghamshire
Place of burial St. Peter's Church, Burnham, Buckinghamshire
Zodiac sign Scorpio

FATHER

George Grenville (*q.v.*)
Date and place of birth 14 Oct 1712, Westminster, London
Occupation Prime Minister 1763–65
Date of marriage May 1749
Date of death 13 Nov 1770
Place of burial Wotton, Buckinghamshire

MOTHER

Elizabeth Wyndham
Date of birth *c.* 1716
Profile She was the daughter of Sir William Wyndham, a Somerset squire, who became the leader of the Hanoverian Tories in the Commons. A devout Anglican, she devoted herself to raising her large family, supporting her husband in his political career and supervising her children's education. She looked prematurely aged as a result of smallpox, suffered from a stammer, and during the last years of her life showed great courage in the face of a long and painful illness.
Date of marriage May 1749
Date of death 5 Dec 1769
Place of burial Wotton, Buckinghamshire

BROTHERS AND SISTERS

Grenville was the third son and sixth of nine children, two of whom died in infancy.

Maria Hester, d. in infancy 16 Dec 1751
Richard Percy, b. 12 Mar 1752; d. 7 Jul 1759
George (Earl Temple, Marquess of Buckingham), b. 18 Jun 1753; m. 16 Apr 1775, Lady Mary Elizabeth Nugent; Teller of the Exchequer 1764–1813; MP Buckinghamshire 1774–79; Lord Lieutenant of Ireland 1782–83, 1787–89; Secretary of State for Foreign Affairs Dec 1783; d. 11 Feb 1813
Charlotte, b. 14 Sep 1754; m. 21 Dec 1771 Sir Watkin Williams-Wynn (MP Shropshire 1772–74, Denbighshire 1774–89); d. 29 Sep 1832
Thomas, b. 31 Dec 1755; unm.; MP Buckinghamshire 1779–84, 1813–18, Aldeburgh 1790–96, Buckingham 1796–1809; Envoy to Paris 1782; Minister Extraordinary to Vienna 1793; President of the Board of Control 1806; First Lord of the Admiralty 1806–07; d. 17 Dec 1846
Elizabeth, b. 24 Oct 1756; m. 1787, Lord Carysfort (created Earl of Carysfort 1789; Joint Master of the Rolls 1789–1801; MP East Looe 1790; Stamford 1790–1801; Envoy to Berlin 1800-02; Privy Counsellor 1806; Joint Paymaster General and a Commissioner of the Board of Control 1806–07); d. 21 Dec 1842
Hester, b. 23 Nov 1760; m. 10 May 1782, Lord Fortescue (MP Beaumaris 1784–85); d. 13 Nov 1847
Catherine, b. 1761; m. 1782, Richard Aldworth Neville, Lord Braybrooke (MP Grampound 1774–80, Buckingham 1780–82, Reading 1782–97); d. 6 Nov 1796

WIFE

Anne Pitt
Date and place of birth 10 Sep 1772, Hanover Square London
Mother Anne Wilkinson
Father Thomas Pitt, 1st Baron Camelford
Father's occupation MP Old Sarum 1761–63, 1774–83, Okehampton 1768–74; a Lord of the Admiralty 1763–65; FSA 1784; created Lord Camelford, Baron of Boconnoc, Cornwall 1784
Age at marriage 19 years, 312 days
Number of children None
Date and place of death 13 Jun 1864, 35 South Street, Grosvenor Square, Middlesex
Years younger than PM 12 years, 322 days
Profile Her father versed her carefully in what he deemed the 'great essentials of character . . . religion and virtue', and impressed upon her the importance of reading, history and foreign languages. She was a slight, not unattractive woman, whose clothes tended to 'simplicity and neatness rather than to finery and ostentation'. Described also as 'charming . . . sensible, well-informed, unaffected', she was devoted to her husband, with whom she enjoyed a happy marriage, and a number of mutual interests, including gardening. She became heiress to her brother, the 2nd Baron Camelford in March 1804.

LIFE AND CAREER

PARLIAMENTARY ELECTIONS FOUGHT

*(*designates candidate elected)*

DATE 19 Feb 1782. By-election caused by Richard Aldworth Neville's appointment as agent to the regiment of the militia of the County of Buckinghamshire
CONSTITUENCY Buckingham
RESULT William Wyndham Grenville* (Whig)

DATE 5 Jan 1784. By-election caused by Grenville's appointment as Joint Paymaster of the Land Forces
CONSTITUENCY Buckingham
RESULT William Wyndham Grenville* (Whig)

DATE Mar 1784. General Election
CONSTITUENCY Buckinghamshire
RESULT William Wyndham Grenville* (Whig) 2,261; John Aubrey* 1,740; Ralph Verney 1,716

DATE 19 Jun 1789. By-election caused by Grenville's appointment as Home Secretary
CONSTITUENCY Buckinghamshire
RESULT William Wyndham Grenville* (Whig)

DATE Jun 1790. General Election
CONSTITUENCY Buckinghamshire
RESULT William Wyndham Grenville* (Whig); Sir Ralph Verney, Bt.; Earl Verney of the Kingdom of Ireland*

PARTY ACTIVITY

Grenville was an assiduous committee member and chairman, participating in inquiries into such subjects as the East India Company, and national income and expenditure.

Membership of group or faction Upon first entering Parliament, Grenville joined the opposition led by Rockingham, Shelburne and Fox. The Grenvilles, as a family interest, were soon to become separated from the Rockingham party, however, and transferred their support to the King's friends. Grenville's subsequent allegiance to Pitt yielded in 1803–1804 to cooperation with Fox and, by 1806, the Grenvilles were one of six leading political groups competing for office. Following his premiership, Grenville became nominal head of the main party in opposition to the administrations of Portland, Perceval and Liverpool.

PARLIAMENTARY AND MINISTERIAL EXPERIENCE

Maiden Speech 20 Dec 1782, House of Commons, on the Irish question. Grenville himself considered his maiden speech to be a lengthier contribution made on 22 Jan 1783 on the Renunciation Bill. (Debrett, J. ed. *The Parliamentary Register.* 2nd series, vol 26, col 131, 139–141

Opposition offices Nominal leader of the Opposition, 1807–17

Privy Counsellor 15 Sep 1782 (Ireland); 31 Dec 1783

Ministerial Offices Chief Secretary for Ireland, 15 Aug 1782–2 May 1783; Paymaster General, 26 Dec 1783–7 Mar 1784; Member of the Board of Trade 5 Mar 1784–23 Aug 1786; Joint Paymaster General 7 Mar 1784–4 Sep 1789; Commissioner of the Board of Control 31 Aug 1784–28 Mar 1790; Vice President of the Board of Trade 23 Aug 1786–8 Aug 1789; Home Secretary, 5 Jun 1789–8 Jun 1791; President of the Board of Control 12 Mar 1790 –28 Jun 1793; Leader of the House of Lords, Nov 1790–20 Feb 1801, 11 Feb 1806–25 Mar 1807; Foreign Secretary, 8 Jun 1791–20 Feb 1801; First Lord of the Treasury 11 Feb 1806–25 Mar 1807

Opposition Leader while PM Lord Hawksbury (later Earl of Liverpool)

Speaker of the House 5 Jan–5 Jun 1789

GOVERNMENTS FORMED

Administration 11 Feb 1806–25 Mar 1807 (All the Talents)

GENERAL ELECTION RESULTS

JUN 1802: Supporters of the Administration 467; Old Opposition 124; New Opposition 25; Independent 19; Doubtful 23. Total 658
Majority 276

OCT 1806: Supporters of the Administration 349; Opposition 92; Neutral 208; Independent 9. Total 658
Majority 40

CABINET

Prime Minister and First Lord of the Treasury Lord Grenville
Chancellor of the Exchequer Lord H. Petty
Lord President of the Council Earl Fitzwilliam (Feb–Oct 1806); Viscount Sidmouth (Oct 1806–07)
Lord Chancellor Lord Erskine
Home Secretary Earl Spencer
Foreign Secretary C. J. Fox (Feb–Sep 1806); Viscount Howick (Sep 1806–07)
President of the Board of Trade Lord Auckland
Secretary of State, War and Colonies W. Windham
President of the Board of Control Lord Minto (Feb–Jul 1806); T. Grenville (Jul–Oct 1806); G. Tierney (Oct 1806–07)
First Lord of the Admiralty C. Grey (Viscount Howick Apr 1806); T. Grenville (Sep 1806–07)
Lord Privy Seal Viscount Sidmouth (Feb–Oct 1806); Lord Holland (Oct 1806–07)
Chancellor of the Duchy of Lancaster Earl of Derby
Master-General of the Ordnance Earl of Moira
Treasurer of the Navy R. B. Sheridan
Secretary at War R. Fitzpatrick
Master of the Mint Lord Spencer (Feb–Oct 1806); C. Bathurst (Oct 1806–1807)
Lord Chief Justice of the King's Bench Lord Ellenborough
Minister without Portfolio Earl Fitzwilliam (Oct 1806–1807)

IMPORTANT DATES IN PERSONAL AND POLITICAL LIFE

1780 Grenville graduates from Oxford University, and proceeds, in April, to study law at Lincoln's Inn. A political career soon beckons, however, and he is never called to the Bar.

19 FEB 1782 At the instigation of his elder brother, Earl Temple, Grenville enters Parliament as Member for the family borough of Buckingham, and immediately joins the opposition led by Rockingham, Shelburne and Fox, against North's conduct of the American war.

20 FEB 1782 Grenville votes with the Opposition for an enquiry into naval administration. North subsequently resigns following further defeats and a marginal victory on a vote of no confidence.

15 AUG 1782 Not having achieved office under the ensuing Rockingham ministry, Grenville is appointed Chief Secretary to his brother Temple, Lord-Lieutenant of Ireland, and a month later sworn as a member of the Irish Privy Council, under Rockingham's successor, Shelburne.

20 DEC 1782 Grenville speaks in the House of Commons for the first time to propose his plans for the settlement of the Irish question.

22 JAN 1783 He speaks at greater length, in what he considers his maiden speech, seconding Townshend's motion for leave to introduce the Renunciation Bill, designed to establish the 'right claimed by the people of Ireland to be bound only by laws enacted by his majesty and the parliament of that kingdom in all cases whatever'. The Bill is enacted in April.

JUN 1783 Grenville resigns office upon the appointment of Lord Northington as Lord-Lieutenant of Ireland, replacing Temple.

AUG 1783 He relinquishes his studentship at Christ Church College and declines to proceed to an MA, a decision described by the Dean as the product of a 'delicate and honourable mind'.

26 DEC 1783 Following the collapse of the Fox-North coalition, which had taken office under the Duke of Portland in April, Grenville is appointed Paymaster General in the first administration of his cousin William Pitt the Younger, and five days later becomes a member of the Privy Council.

5 MAR 1784 Grenville is appointed to the Board of Trade, and subsequently made Joint Paymaster General with Constantine, 2nd Baron Mulgrave.

21 APR 1784 After a particularly fierce contest, Grenville is returned for Buckinghamshire in the General Election.

31 AUG 1784 He is appointed to the newly-constituted Board of Control for Indian Affairs.

19 MAY 1785 Grenville makes a long, powerful speech in support of Pitt's propositions concerning trade between the United Kingdom and Ireland.

SUMMER 1785–AUTUMN 1786 Grenville plays a prominent role in the successful trade negotiations with France, further enhancing his reputation.

9 MAR 1786 At Pitt's behest, he is made chairman of a House of Commons committee formed to report on national income and expenditure. On the basis of its report, Pitt introduces his plans for a sinking fund, credit for which Grenville later claims 'a larger share than I believe anybody knows'.

23 AUG 1786 Grenville is appointed Vice-President of the Board of Trade.

SUMMER–EARLY AUTUMN 1787 He acts as Pitt's envoy in the Hague and Paris, successfully negotiating a diplomatic settlement of the Dutch constitutional crisis, which threatens European peace.

LATE 1787–1788 Grenville acts as an unofficial adviser to his brother, since 1784, the Duke of Buckingham, upon the latter's appointment as Lord-Lieutenant of Ireland.

AUG 1788 Grenville is granted the reversion to the Chief Remembranceship of the Exchequer, a sinecure worth approximately £2,400 p. a. in fees.

5 JAN 1789 On the sudden death of the incumbent, and with an urgency forced by the regency crisis, Grenville is elected Speaker of the House of Commons by 215 votes to 144, becoming the youngest occupant of the post since the time of Edward III.

16 JAN 1789 Grenville makes a notable, lengthy speech in support of the Government's proposals for the exercise of royal authority during the King's illness.

MAY 1789 Grenville participates in the debate on the slave trade resolutions, during which he declares that Wilberforce's speech entitles him 'to the thanks of the house, of the people of England, of all Europe, and of the latest posterity'.

5 JUN 1789 Grenville resigns the Speakership and, on the same day, is appointed Home Secretary, in the place of Lord Sydney.

12 MAR 1790 Having earlier resigned the offices of Joint Paymaster General and of Vice-President of the Board of Trade, Grenville succeeds Sydney as President of the Board of Control.

25 NOV 1790 On the first day of the new Parliament he is created Baron Grenville of Wotton-under-Bernewood in the County of Buckingham, fulfilling an ambition held since 1786. At Pitt's request he now assumes responsibility for the conduct of the Government's business in the House of Lords.

13 DEC 1790 Grenville makes his maiden speech as a peer during a debate on the convention with Spain, establishing himself as a commanding, highly respected speaker in the Upper House.

8 JUN 1791 Upon the resignation of Francis, 5th Duke of Leeds, over the conduct of the Ochakov crisis, Grenville is appointed Foreign Secretary, a position for which his industriousness and academic accomplishments eminently suit him.

13 DEC 1791 Grenville is appointed Ranger of St. James's and Hyde Parks, another sinecure, worth approximately £1,200 p. a. He subsequently exchanges this for a further sinecure, the Auditorship of the Exchequer, from which his income is to amount to some £4,000 p.a.

18 JUL 1792 Grenville marries Anne Pitt, whose paternal grandfather was Chatham's elder brother. Three months later they move into Dropmore, which Grenville had purchased earlier the same year.

11 FEB 1793 France declares war on Britain, vindicating Grenville's fears for European security and stability after the Revolution of 1789.

1793–1795 Having previously advocated neutrality as a means of avoiding conflict, Grenville now supports Prussia and Austria in their campaign against France through diplomatic negotiations with the Mediterranean and Baltic powers.

22 MAY 1794 In fear of revolutionary activity spreading to Britain, Grenville moves the First Reading of the Habeas Corpus Suspension Bill. Two years later, and with a similar motivation, he is to introduce the Treasonable Practices Bill and the Seditious Meetings Bill.

1796 Grenville advocates the adoption of a firm stance in the conduct of negotiations with France, which are to resume in the summer of 1797. In 1799, he is to reject Bonaparte's peace proposals with similar vigour.

FEB 1801 Grenville and Pitt resign office in the face of the King's opposition to Catholic emancipation. Grenville, with his expertise in Irish affairs, his advocacy of conciliation with the Irish Catholics and his position as Leader of the House of Lords, has been pre-eminent in the development of Cabinet policy on Ireland, following the decision in 1798 to proceed with the union of the two Parliaments.

NOV 1801 His confidence in Addington's conduct of foreign policy decreasing, Grenville speaks forcefully in opposition to the terms of peace with France, which he considers 'fraught with degradation and humiliation',

IMPORTANT DATES IN PERSONAL AND POLITICAL LIFE—*Continued*

and votes against the Address, which is nevertheless carried by 114 to 10.

1802–1804 Grenville gradually abandons his independent stance of 1801 and, disappointed by Pitt's response to his proposal for a pact between those out of office, turns to Fox with whom he cooperates at the head of a new combined Opposition to last for the next 14 years.

1804 Following Addington's resignation in the face of a diminishing majority in the House of Commons, Grenville declines office under Pitt without Fox, whom the King refuses to admit. This completes the political separation between the cousins, and Grenville's commitment to the Opposition alliance gathers strength during the ensuing months.

27 JAN 1806 Following the death of Pitt four days earlier, and the remaining Cabinet's reluctance to carry on in office under a new head, the King invites Grenville to form a Government 'without exclusion'.

11 FEB 1806 Grenville is appointed Prime Minister and First Lord of the Treasury, Fox, Secretary of State for Foreign Affairs and Lord Sidmouth, Lord Privy Seal in his 'Ministry of All the Talents'. The administration is heralded by some as 'a Fox or a Sidmouth Government with a trace of Grenville', but this belies Grenville's strong influence upon it. He soon sets to work on his 'defensive and husbanding system', instigating administrative reforms in the Treasury and its accounting practices, and in the sphere of Scottish civil justice, and devising new financial mechanisms to meet the increasing costs of war.

7 MAY 1806 Grenville introduces in the House of Lords the Foreign Slave Trade Bill, designed to reduce British participation in the trade by two-thirds to three-quarters by giving statutory force to Pitt's proclamation of August 1805. During the Third Reading debate, nine days later, Grenville further states that 'an event most grateful to his feelings' would be 'to witness the abolition of a traffic that is an outrage to humanity, and that trampled on the rights of mankind'.

JUN 1806 Grenville and Fox successfully move resolutions in both Houses of Parliament for the abolition of the slave trade, Grenville having performed the critical functions of lobbying in the House of Lords on behalf of the measure, and persuading Sidmouth of its merits. The following February, he is to move in an eloquent speech the Second Reading of the Bill that carries the resolutions into effect.

13 SEP 1806 Fox dies, necessitating a reconstruction of the Ministry. During the summer Grenville had faced increasing opposition over the conduct of the Government's affairs in the House of Commons and its taxation and military reforms. His subsequent failure either to gain support of leading Opposition Members, or to secure the elevation of his brother Thomas to retain his personal influence and satisfy Buckingham, causes Grenville to recast the administration in a manner which lends it neither strength nor authority.

OCT 1806 The failure of the Paris peace negotiations, in tandem with the outbreak of the Franco-Prussian War, renders Grenville vulnerable at home. With a view to strengthening his ministry, he seeks and gains the King's agreement to the dissolution of Parliament.

OCT–NOV 1806 Grenville sees his majority increase by between 20 and 30 in the ensuing General Election.

5 MAR 1807 In the face of Dublin's Catholic leaders' threat to petition the new Parliament for full Catholic relief, an action which would be certain to divide the ministry, Lord Howick, later Earl Grey, who has succeeded Fox as Foreign Secretary, introduces the Roman Catholic Army and Navy Service Bill. The measure, which would enable Catholics to hold commissions in both services, is held by the King and Sidmouth to extend the provisions of the Irish Act of 1793, and neither will, therefore, accept it.

15 MAR 1807 Faced with the alternatives of proceeding with the Bill and alienating the King, or modifying the measure and placing his administration in an impossible position, Grenville decides to drop the Bill. He does, however, request the King's permission to speak openly on the subject of Catholic claims in Parliament and to offer such advice to the monarch 'as the course of circumstances shall appear to require'.

17 MAR 1807 The King demands a positive assurance from his Ministers that they will not press the issue on him again, an undertaking which Grenville, by now anxious that the Government be dismissed allowing him to retire as he wishes, is unable to give.

25 MAR 1807 Following the King's announcement that he intends to seek an alternative administration, Grenville surrenders his seal of office. On the same day, ironically, the Bill abolishing the slave trade gains Royal Assent—the one lasting testimony to his ministry. During the following ten years he is to be the leader of the main body of opposition to the Portland, Perceval and Liverpool administrations.

29 SEP 1809 Grenville declines Perceval's invitation to join the Government in a coalition with Grey upon resignation of the Duke of Portland. His differences with Perceval on the Irish question were such that his agreement to the proposition would be considered 'a dereliction of public principle'.

14 DEC 1809 After a hard-fought contest, Grenville is elected Chancellor of Oxford University, in place of the Duke of Portland, who had died the previous October. He is duly installed on 10 Jan 1810.

FEB 1812 Following the Regency crisis of the previous year, during which Grenville has failed to secure office for the Opposition, both he and Grey refuse to accept the Prince's request to join the Government, claiming their differences are 'too many and too important to admit of such a union', and that they are 'firmly persuaded of the necessity of a total change in the present system of government' in Ireland.

MAY–JUN 1812 Together with Grey, Grenville enters into unsuccessful negotiations first with Lord Wellesley, and then with the Earl of Moira, over the formation of a coalition government.

23 MAY 1812 Grenville splits with Grey and other Foxite Whigs in his support of the Government in the debate on the renewal of the war against Napoleon.

1813 Grenville actively participates in the framing of Grafton's Catholic Bill, and demonstrates his advocacy of free trade in his opposition to the East India Company charter on 'enlarged' rather than 'partisan' grounds. He also strongly supports Romilly's Shoplifting Bill in a speech which, the sponsor claims, 'for strength of reasoning, for the enlarged view of a great statesman, for dignity of manner and force of eloquence . . . was one of the best speeches that I have ever heard delivered in Parliament'.

1814 Grenville returns to another of his major long-held interests when he makes a forceful speech in favour of the abolition of the international slave trade.

NOV 1814–MAR 1815 Grenville speaks in the House of Lords on at least 25 occasions in opposition to the Corn Laws, in defence of free trade, and as a proponent of a return to monetary orthodoxy, which he hopes will induce an economic revival.

23 MAY 1815 A split begins to develop between Grenville and his personal followers on the one hand and Grey and the majority of the party on the other, prompted by Grenville's support for the renewal of the war with France and the reimposition of the Bourbons on a divided France. Grenville defends his decision to vote with the Government on the grounds that Napoleon 'the common enemy of Europe' has broken the compact that the allies had made with France in the first Treaty of Paris.

19 FEB 1816 The Opposition's internal division again becomes apparent in a debate on the settlement as a whole, in which Grenville fails to persuade Grey of the legitimacy of the restoration of the Bourbons which the latter claims is the product of 'force and force alone'. The split deepens, owing to Grenville's unwillingness to challenge the Government over its economic policies.

FEB 1817 Grenville's position as leader of the Opposition becomes untenable when he endorses the Government's decision to suspend Habeas Corpus, declining to support Grey in his view that the civil disorder then prevalent can only be alleviated by retrenchment and parliamentary reform. Grenville is to announce later in the session that his political career has come to a close.

JUN 1819 Despite their personal rift, Grenville offers support to Grey for his Roman Catholic Relief Bill.

30 MAR 1819 Grenville makes one of his most elaborate, widely respected speeches during the debate on Lord Lansdowne's motion on the state of the country, when he advocates the re-establishment of the rule of law as a means of signalling a determination to deal with the causes of civil unrest.

DEC 1821 With a view to strengthening his ministry, Lord Liverpool makes overtures to the Grenville party. Grenville, by now having almost retired from active politics, has no desire for office but sponsors an arrangement by which his nephews, Charles Williams Wynn and the Marquess of Buckingham, receive a Cabinet post and dukedom, respectively.

FEB 1822 Grenville makes his penultimate speech in the House of Lords, in support of Lord Donoughmore's Catholic Bill.

21 JUN 1822 Declaring himself to be 'one of those who had always been favourable to the concession of the Catholic claims', he makes his final speech during the Second Reading debate on Portland's Roman Catholic Peers Bill, also an unsuccessful measure, to enable Catholic peers to sit in the House of Lords.

1823 Grenville suffers a paralytic stroke from which he is never to recover fully . Another follows four years later.

12 JAN 1834 Grenville dies at Dropmore, having suffered a further debilitating attack the previous year.

BACKGROUND

PHYSICAL CHARACTERISTICS AND HEALTH

Grenville was a man of average height, but was distinguished by his disproportionately large head, prominent eyes and square build. Wraxall commented upon his 'ponderous physical formation', further noting that 'Nature had bestowed upon him no exterior advantages. His person was heavy and devoid of elegance or grace, his address cold and formal, his manners destitute of suavity. Even his eloquence partook of these defects'. He became increasingly stout with age, a tendency seized upon by contemporary humourists, as in the following verse published in 1795:

> . . . Nature in all her dispensations wise,
> who form'd his head-piece of so vast a size,
> hath not, 'tis true, neglected to bestow
> its due proportions on the part below;
> and hence the reason, that to secure the State
> his top and bottom, may have equal weight.

It was largely these characteristics which, together with his ungainliness, rather unkempt appearance, and need to wear glasses by his mid-twenties, lent him the nickname of 'Bogey' or goblin, first coined in the 1784 Parliament.

Throughout most of his life Grenville enjoyed extremely good health and, while he always slept badly, he tended to succumb only to an annual cold. His failing eyesight caused him great concern, however, dampening his joy at his installation as Chancellor of Oxford in 1810, and causing him considerable difficulty in reading by 1818. In early 1823, Grenville's health deteriorated suddenly, however, when he suffered the first of a series of strokes from which he was never to regain his strength. Three years later, by which time he was also afflicted by gout, his brother Tom reported that he required assistance to rise from his chair and that 'his occasional walks up and down the garden be all abandoned for a little wheeling chair in which his servants push him along the gravel walks'. Another stroke was to follow in 1827, and by the time of the third in 1833, he had already been complaining for some time of a decrease in 'firmness of mind'. He died in January 1834 'without pain or struggle so that his last breath was scarcely perceptible'.

EDUCATION

Primary Preparatory school at East Hill, Wandsworth, London

Secondary 1770–76, Eton

University 1776–80, Christ Church College, Oxford

Prizes and awards 1779, Chancellor's prize for Latin verse

Qualifications 1780, Graduated B.A.

Cultural and vocational background Grenville was highly gifted academically and demonstrated a keen, lifelong interest in, and extensive knowledge of, classical literature, English and mathematics. In retirement he printed an annotated Homer, and wrote *Nugae Metricae*, a volume of translations into Latin from Greek, Italian and English. He also edited the letters of his uncle, Lord Chatham.

Languages In addition to being highly accomplished in classical languages, Grenville demonstrated a very good knowledge of such modern foreign languages as French, writing several critiques of French translations.

NON-PARLIAMENTARY CAREER

Early occupations Grenville trained as a lawyer, entering Lincoln's Inn in 1780, but his political interests prevailed, and he was never called to the Bar.

Other posts 1788, Chief Remembrancer of the Exchequer 1791–94, Ranger of St. James's and of Hyde Park; 1793–1834, Elder Brother of Trinity House; 1794–1834, Auditor of the Exchequer; 1807–34, Trustee of the British Museum; 1810–34, Chancellor of the University of Oxford; High Steward of Bristol; Governor of the Charter House

HONOURS

Academic 1809, DCL

Other than peerage 18 Mar 1784, Fellow of the Society of Antiquaries; 23 Apr 1818, Fellow of the Royal Society

CLUBS

Goosetree's, White's

HOBBIES AND SPORTS

Grenville collected china, prints and pictures, and very much enjoyed landscaping and gardening. His private study at Dropmore was filled with classical and English literature, which he read voraciously. A list which he maintained of his reading in 1803 reveals an impressive range and depth of interest, and included the Greek version of the New Testament (read twice), the last ten books of the *Odyssey* (also read twice), the poetry of a large number of other classical poets, and a quantity of French and English historical tracts.

FINANCES

Grenville enjoyed sound personal finances throughout most of his life, vindicating Lord Rosebery's remark that 'Never indeed was family so well provided for during an entire century as the Temple-Grenville's. As a young man his income was certainly adequate, at least until 1783, although he had no easily disposable capital. Prior to his marriage he estimated his capital at nearly £34,000, and enjoyed a healthy personal income, which was to increase considerably during the next nine years. It was his marriage to Anne Pitt in 1792 which brought him the financial independence he always sought; her father, who owned sizeable estates in the south west, supplied £20,000 as a dowry, and £11,000 upon his death. In 1792, Grenville also purchased Dropmore for £3,000, to which he made £14, 000 of alterations during the first three years. Further land purchases followed, increasing his property in Buckinghamshire to 26,000 acres by 1815, from which he derived a rental income of £2,200 p.a. Grenville's outgoings on his various properties together with the depressed economic climate did impose certain financial strains upon him during the decade following his premiership. However, the completion of improvements at Dropmore, his leasing and subsequent sale of Camelford House, and increased income from Boconnoc, saw him restored to sound circumstances, which he enjoyed for the remainder of his life.

Income Grenville received a salary of £4,000 p.a. as Chief Secretary for Ireland, and £2,000 as Paymaster General. His income as Speaker was estimated at £2, 700 for his 151 days in office. In 1792 he estimated his personal income as £1,300 p. a., excluding his £1,200 for the Rangership and £5,500 as Secretary of State. In 1795 his public income rose to £7,700 at which level it remained until 1801. In 1811–12, his income dropped to its lowest level since the 1790s, but subsequently increased.

Spouse's finances Grenville's wife's resources increased substantially following the death of her father in 1793 and that of her mother and brother in 1803 and 1804. Her inheritance included the substantial property of Boconnoc in Cornwall together with Camelford House in central London and estates in Dorset, Wiltshire and Norfolk. Grenville was to sell the property in the latter two counties in order to pay off Anne's inherited legacies and debts, leaving the couple with £13,000 net.

Legacies Under the terms of his father's will, Grenville received £300 p. a. plus any additional sums which accrued from a property of 35,000 acres in East Florida which George Grenville purchased sometime after 1763. Between 1770 and 1785 this amounted to an average figure of £1,300 p. a., rising to around £2,700 p. a. between mid-1781 and June 1782.

Will Proved February 1834. His widow inherited his estate.

ANECDOTES

Grenville's public demeanour was characterised by aloofness, reserve and austerity. Lord Liverpool wrote of him in April 1807 'Lord Grenville is the most extraordinary character I ever knew. He has talents of uncommon industry, but he never sees a subject with all its bearings, and consequently his judgement can never be right. He is not an ill-tempered man, but he has no feelings for anyone, not even for those to whom they are most due. He is in his outward manner offensive to the last degree. He is rapacious with respect to himself and his family, but a great economist with respect to everyone and everything else'.

As indicated by Liverpool, the common perception of Grenville's character contrasted sharply with the warmth and affection he demonstrated towards his family. His letters to his wife usually began with 'My dearest angel' and ended 'God bless you my dearest wife' or 'My dear little woman'. Lord Mornington, writing to him in October 1792, remarked upon certain improvements that marriage had engendered in him: 'I cannot tell you with how much pleasure I saw your menage. I told Pitt that matrimony had made three very important changes in you which could not but affect your old friends, 1) a brown lapelled coat instead of the eternal blue single breasted, 2) strings in your shoes, 3) very good perfume in your hair powder'.

QUOTATIONS

1780, I have treasured up in my mind a saying of Lord Cobham's which was repeated to me frequently by my uncle, after having been confirmed to him, as he said by all his experience, this was that there is nothing within the compass of a reasonable man's wish which he may not be sure of attaining provided he will use the proper means.

1780, Dependence . . . that greatest curse of nature.

1783, I do not like to stand forth so conspicuous in public questions, which I had always rather follow than lead. . . . (To Pitt in response to request to move the terms of peace for the Government)

1788, I suppose there never was a situation in which any set of men ever had, at once, so many points to decide, so essentially affecting their own honour, character and future situation. I hope God, Who has been pleased to afflict us with this severe and heavy trial, will enable us to go through it honestly, conscientiously, and in a manner not dishonourable to our characters. (On the Regency Crisis)

1794, The existence of the two systems of government was fairly at stake, and in the words of St. Just, whose curious speech I hope you have seen, that it is perfect blindness not to see that in the establishment of the French republic is included the overthrow of all other governments of Europe. (On the war against France)

1803, I can hardly keep wondering at my own folly in thinking it worthwhile to leave my books and garden, even for one day's attendance in the House of Commons.

1807, [He longed] daily and hourly . . . 'for the moment when my friends will allow me to think that I have fully discharged (by a life of hitherto incessant labour) every claim that they, or the country can have upon me . . . I want one great and essential quality for my station, and every hour increases the difficulty . . . I am not competent to the management of men. I never was so naturally and toil and anxiety more and more unfit me for it'.

1807, I feel very repugnant to any course of active opposition having been most unaffectedly disinclined to take upon myself the task in which I have been engaged and feeling no small pleasure in an honourable release, I could not bring myself to struggle to get my chains on again. (In response to Howick's request to attend a meeting to discuss measures of opposition)

1807, The deed is done and I am again a free man, and to you I may express what it would seem like affectation to say to others, the infinite pleasure I derive from emancipation. (On his resignation)

RESIDENCES

Wotton House, Wotton Underwood, Aylesbury, Buckinghamshire
Buckingham House, Pall Mall, London
17 St. James's Square, London
Dropmore Park, Heathfield Road, Burnham, Buckinghamshire
Cleveland Row (Stornoway House), London
Camelford House, London
Boconnoc House, Boconnoc, Lostwithiel, Cornwall

MEMORIALS

STATUES AND BUSTS

1810, by Joseph Nollekens, Royal Collection

PORTRAITS

1781, by George Romney, Eton College, Windsor, Berkshire; *c.* 1800, by John Hoppner, National Portrait Gallery, and in North Carolina Museum of Art, Raleigh, North Carolina; 1810, by Thomas Phillips, in robes of the Chancellor of Oxford University, Royal College of Surgeons, Lincoln's Inn Fields, London; 1812, by William Owen, in robes, Christ Church College, Oxford; by T. A. Dean, engraving from lost portrait by J. Jackson, British Museum, London; by M. Gauci, lithograph from drawing by Grenville's niece, Lady Charlotte Proby, British Museum, London; by George Jones, group portrait, 'Reception of the Prince Regent in Oxford, June 1814', Magdalen College, Oxford; by Sir George Hayter, group portrait 'The Trial of Queen Caroline, 1872', National Portrait Gallery

BIBLIOGRAPHIC INFORMATION

LETTERS AND PERSONAL PAPERS

The main collection of papers relating to Grenville is in the National Library of Wales, Aberystwyth, Dyfed; Buckinghamshire Record Office, Aylesbury, Buckinghamshire; the National Library of Scotland, Edinburgh; the British Library and the Public Record Office. The Henry E. Huntingdon Library, San Marino, California, houses a substantial collection of letters written principally to his elder brother, the 1st Marquess of Buckingham.

Much correspondence can also be found in Arthur Aspinall's *Correspondence of George, Prince of Wales, 1770–1812*; *Later Correspondence of George III*; and *Letters of George IV, 1812–1830*.

There is no collected edition of Grenville's speeches, although one of his House of Commons speeches and at least ten of his House of Lords speeches were published as pamphlets.

PUBLICATIONS

Grenville published a substantial number of works including: 1784, *Thoughts on the present East India Bill: passed into law, August 1784*; 1788, *Consideration on the establishment of a Regency*; 1790, *Conduct of the Parliament of 1784*; 1801, *Letters of Sulpicius*, [on the armed neutrality]; 1804–05, *Letters written by the late Earl Chatham to his nephew, Thomas Pitt, Esq.*; 1810, *Vis electrica*, (poem printed in *Poemata Praemiis Cancellarii Academicis Donata et in Thearro Sheldoniano Recitata*); 1824, *Nugae metricae*; 1828, *Essay on the supposed advantages of a Sinking Fund, part the first*; 1829, *Oxford and [John] Locke*; 1830, *Dropmore.*

FURTHER READING

Harvey, A. D. *Lord Grenville, 1759–1834: A Bibliography*. Bibliographies of British Statesmen, no. 2. Westport, 1989.

Jupp, P. *Lord Grenville, 1759–1834*. Oxford, 1985.

G.C.

Bettmann

Spencer Perceval

Lived 1762–1812
Political Party Tory
Prime Minister 4 October 1809–11 May 1812
Government Tory
Reigning Monarchs George III; (Prince Regent)

Sub cruce candida Under the white cross

PERCEVAL AS PRIME MINISTER

Perceval brought the rigour of the professional lawyer to the practice of government. Industrious, organised, and able, he held successively the two senior posts of Solicitor-General and Attorney-General. Pitt was his hero and patron, and while he was a conservative in the ordering of society, opposing government intervention on principle, his high moral standards as an enthusiastic Anglican ensured his support for Wilberforce's anti-slavery campaign. Appointed Prime Minister in 1809 with little likelihood of holding the position for long he had great difficulty forming an Administration and continued to be his own Chancellor of the Exchequer. While his 1810 Budget was successful, criticism of the Bank of England caused a prolonged financial crisis and increasing inflation caused by the war worsened economic problems. He took a firm line against growing restlessness of the population while not interesting himself in the causes of the unrest. Abroad, lack of military success and inability to conclude the war successfully brought increased pressure on his administration. The King's deteriorating health led to the successful passing of the Regency Bill and Perceval was also successful in curtailing financial support for the Prince Regent. The general situation was improving when he was murdered in the lobby of the House of Commons.

PERSONAL INFORMATION

Names Spencer Perceval
Nickname Little P
Born 1 Nov 1762
Birthplace Audley Square, London
Religion Anglican
Ancestry Irish. The Percevals were related to the Earls of Egmont. An early family history traced their line back to 9th- century Normandy, but this is now discredited.
Date and place of marriage 10 Aug 1790, East Grinstead, Sussex
Age at marriage 27 years, 283 days
Years married 21 years, 276 days
First entered Parliament 9 May 1796
Date appointed PM 4 Oct 1809
Age at appointment 46 years 338 days
Date ceased to be PM 11 May 1812
Total time as PM 2 years, 221 days
Ceased to be MP 11 May 1812
Lived after last term as PM Died in office
Date of death 11 May 1812
Place of death Lobby of the House of Commons
Age at death 49 years, 193 days
Last words Oh, I am murdered
Place of funeral Perceval's body lay in Downing Street until 16 May, when the funeral procession left for Charlton, Kent.
Place of burial St. Luke's, Charlton, Kent
Zodiac sign Scorpio

FATHER

John Perceval, 2nd Earl of Egmont
Date and place of birth 24 Feb 1711, Westminster, London
Occupation MP Dingle (Ireland) 1731–48, Westminster 1741–47, Weobley 1747–54, Bridgwater 1754–62; Lord of the Bedchamber to the Prince of Wales 1748–51; P.C. 1755, Joint Postmaster-General 1762–63; First Lord of the Admiralty 1763–66
Dates of marriages 1) 15 Feb 1737 Lady Catherine Cecil (d. 16 Aug 1752) 2)26 Jan 1756 Catherine Compton
Date of death 4 Dec 1770
Place of burial St Luke's Church, Charlton, Kent

MOTHER

Catherine Compton
Date and place of birth 4 Jun 1731, Cintra, near Lisbon, Portugal
Profile Related to the Earls of Northampton, she was created Baroness Arden of Lohort, Ireland, in her own right on 23 May 1770.
Date of marriage 26 Jan 1756
Date of death 11 Jun 1784
Place of burial St Luke's Church, Charlton, Kent

BROTHERS AND SISTERS

Perceval was the second son and fifth of nine children. He had seven half brothers and sisters.
From his father's first marriage:
John James (3rd Earl of Egmont), b. 29 Jan 1738; m. Isabella, daughter of Lord Nassau Paulett of Powlett; MP Bridgwater 1762–69; Lt. Col. in the Guards; d. 25 Feb 1822
Cecil Parker, b. 19 Oct 1739; d. while at Eton, 4 Mar 1753
Philip Tufton, b. 10 Mar 1741; Captain, Royal Navy; d. 12 Apr 1795
Edward, b. 21 Apr 1744; Captain, Royal Dragoon Guards; d. 26 Feb 1829
Frederick Augustus, b. 11 Feb 1749; d. 21 Jan 1757
Catherine, b. 20 Feb 1746; m. Thomas Wynn, Baron Newborough (MP Caernarvonshire 1761–74, St Ives 1775–80, Beaumaris 1796–1807); d. Jun 1782
Margaret, b. 10 Oct 1748; d. 23 Jan 1750
From his father's second marriage:
Charles George (Lord Arden), b. 1 Oct 1756; m. Margaretta Elizabeth Wilson, sister of Spencer Perceval's wife Jane; MP Launceston 1780–90, Warwick 1790–96, Totnes 1796–1802; Lord of the Admiralty 1783–1801; Master of the Mint 1801–02; Commissioner of the India Board 1801-03; Lord of the Bedchamber 1804–12; d. 5 Jul 1840
Mary, b. 15 Jul 1758; m. Andrew Berkeley Drummond; d. 18 Sep 1839
Anne, b. 15 Dec 1759; d. 1 Aug 1772
Charlotte, b. 31 Jan 1761; d. 19 Feb 1761
Elizabeth, b. 12 Dec 1763; unm.; d. 4 Apr 1846
Henry, b. 26 Jun 1765; d. 27 Jul 1772
Frances, b. 4 Dec 1767; m. John Mitford, Baron Redesdale (MP Bere Alston 1788–99, East Looe 1799–1802); d. 22 Aug 1817
Margaret, b. 17 Mar 1769; m. Thomas Walpole; d. 12 Dec 1854

WIFE

Jane Spencer-Wilson
Date of birth 7 Jul 1769
Mother Jane Weller
Father Sir Thomas Spencer-Wilson, Bt.
Father's occupation Colonel of the 50th Regiment of Foot, MP Sussex, 1774–80.
Age at marriages 1) Spencer Perceval, 20 years 35 days 2) Sir Henry William Carr, *c.* 45 years
Number of children 12
Date of death 26 Jan 1844
Place of burial St Luke's, Charlton, Kent
Years younger than PM 6 years, 248 days
Profile Her father, a Sussex landowner, objected to her marriage to the impecunious Spencer Perceval. While on a visit to relatives in East Grinstead she married him, dressed for the ceremony in her riding habit.

CHILDREN

6 sons, 6 daughters
Jane, b. 23 Oct 1791; m. 20 Mar 1821 Edward Perceval; d. 13 Jan 1824
Frances (Fanny), b. 1792
Maria, b. Feb 1794; bur. 6 Aug 1807
Spencer, b. 11 Sep 1795; m. 3 Jul 1821 Anna Eliza Macleod; MP Ennis 1818–20; Newport, Isle of Wight 1827–31, Tiverton 1831–32; Teller of the Exchequer 1813–34; Under Secretary of State for Home Affairs 1827; Clerk of Ordnance 1828–30; d. 16 Sep 1859
Frederick James, b. 1796; m. 1) 1827 Mary Barker (d. 24 Apr 1843); 2) 1844 Emma Gilbert; Magistrate
Henry, b. *c.* 1796
Dudley Montague, b. 22 Oct 1800; Deputy Teller of the Exchequer 1828–34; d. 2 Sep 1856
Isobella, b. 10 Dec 1801; m. 1835, Spencer Horatio Walpole (MP Midhurst 1846–56, Cambridge University 1856–82); d. 1886
John Thomas, b. Feb 1803

CHILDREN—*Continued*

Louisa, b. 11 Mar 1804
Frederica, d. Jul 1875
Ernest Augustus

LIFE AND CAREER

PARLIAMENTARY ELECTIONS FOUGHT

*(*designates candidate elected)*

DATE 9 May 1796. By-election caused by the resignation of Charles Compton
CONSTITUENCY Northampton
RESULT Spencer Perceval* (Tory)

DATE May 1796. General Election
CONSTITUENCY Northampton
RESULT Spencer Perceval* (Tory) 720; Edward Bouverie* (Whig) 512; William Walcot 474

DATE 21 Feb 1801. By-election caused by Perceval's appointment as Solicitor General
CONSTITUENCY Northampton
RESULT Spencer Perceval* (Tory)

DATE 19 Apr 1802. By-election caused by Perceval's appointment as Attorney General
CONSTITUENCY Northampton
RESULT Spencer Perceval* (Tory)

DATE Jun 1802. General Election
CONSTITUENCY Northampton
RESULT Spencer Perceval* (Tory); Edward Bouverie* (Whig)

DATE Oct 1806. General Election
CONSTITUENCY Northampton
RESULT Spencer Perceval* (Tory); Edward Bouverie* (Whig)

DATE 1 Apr 1807. By-election caused by Perceval's appointment as Chancellor of the Exchequer
CONSTITUENCY Northampton
RESULT Spencer Perceval* (Tory)

DATE May 1807. General Election
CONSTITUENCY Northampton
RESULT Spencer Perceval* (Tory); Edward Bouverie* (Whig)

PARTY ACTIVITY

Membership of group or faction Pittite Tories 1796–1800

PARLIAMENTARY AND MINISTERIAL EXPERIENCE

Maiden Speech 20 May 1797, on mutinies in sea and land forces. (*Parl. Hist.* vol. 33, col. 810)
Opposition office Leader of the Opposition 1806
Privy Counsellor 26 Mar 1807
Ministerial Offices Solicitor General 14 Jan 1801–15 Apr 1802; Attorney General 15 Apr 1802–12 Feb 1806; Chancellor of the Exchequer 26 Mar 1807–11 May 1812; Leader of the House of Commons 31 Mar 1807–11 May 1812; Chancellor of the Duchy of Lancaster 30 Mar 1807–11 May 1812; First Lord of the Treasury 4 Oct 1809–11 May 1812; Commissioner of the Treasury for Ireland 1810–11 May 1812.
Opposition Leader while PM George Ponsonby (nominally Earl Grey)

GOVERNMENTS FORMED

Administration 4 Oct 1809–11 May 1812

GENERAL ELECTION RESULT
MAY 1807: Government 388; Opposition 224; Independent 29; Doubtful 17. Total 658

CABINET
Prime Minister, First Lord of the Treasury, Chancellor of the Exchequer and Chancellor of the Duchy of Lancaster S. Perceval
Lord President of the Council Earl Camden (Oct 1809–Apr 1812), Viscount Sidmouth (Apr–May 1812)
Lord Chancellor Lord Eldon
Home Secretary R. Ryder
Foreign Secretary Earl Bathurst (Oct–Dec 1809) Lord Wellesley (Dec 1809-Mar 1812), Viscount Castlereagh (Mar-May 1812)
President of the Board of Trade and Master of the Mint Earl Bathurst
Secretary for War and Colonies Earl of Liverpool
President of the Board of Control R. Dundas (Viscount Melville) (Nov 1809–Apr 1812), Earl of Buckinghamshire (Apr–May 1812)
First Lord of the Admiralty Lord Mulgrave (Apr 1807–May 1810), C. P. Yorke (May 1810–Mar 1812), Viscount Melville (Mar–May 1812)
Lord Privy Seal Earl of Westmoreland
Master General of the Ordnance Earl of Chatham (Apr 1807–May 1810), Earl of Mulgrave (May 1810–May 1812)
Secretary at War Viscount Palmerston
Ministers without Portfolio Duke of Portland (Oct–Nov 1809), Earl of Harrowby (Nov 1809–May 1812), Earl Camden (Apr–May 1812)

IMPORTANT DATES IN PERSONAL AND POLITICAL LIFE

4 DEC 1770 His father dies when he is only eight years old.
14 JAN 1780 Enters Trinity College, Cambridge.
11 JUN 1784 Death of Perceval's mother Catherine, Baroness Arden. She is succeeded by Perceval's elder brother Charles who is a constant source of support to him.
10 AUG 1790 Perceval marries Jane Spencer-Wilson against her father's wishes. Her elder sister had married his elder brother Charles in 1787.
1790 Having worked at the Bar in the Midland Circuit with much diligence for some years, he obtains the post of Deputy Recorder of Northampton with the help of his grandfather, Lord Northampton.
MAR 1791 He is given two sinecures in the Mint: Surveyor of the Meltings and Clerk of the Irons. The income from these greatly improves his finances.
APR 1791 Publishes an anonymous pamphlet about the constitutional questions arising from the impeachment of Warren Hastings, said to have brought him to the favourable notice of Pitt.

1792–94 He is retained by the Crown at the important trials of Thomas Paine and Horne Tooke. In 1794 he is appointed Counsel to the Board of Admiralty.

4 FEB 1796 Perceval becomes a King's Counsel. In January Pitt had offered him the post of Chief Secretary of Ireland, but Perceval refused, saying that he had to continue at the Bar to provide for his family.

9 MAY 1796 First elected to Parliament at a by-election, where he is returned unopposed for one of the Northampton seats.

30 MAY 1796 After the dissolution of Parliament he retains his seat despite a contest.

20 MAY 1797 Makes his maiden speech in support of Pitt's proposal to increase the penalties against persons convicted of inciting mutinies in the forces.

AUG 1798 Appointed Solicitor General to the Queen and solicitor to the Board of Ordnance.

14 JAN 1801 Pitt having resigned, Addington forms a new ministry. Finding himself short of debating strength, he makes Perceval, whose clever style is admired, his Solicitor General. This is Perceval's first ministerial post. He relinquishes the Court of Kings Bench and practises only in that of Chancery.

15 APR 1802 Resigns as Solicitor General on being promoted to Attorney General. In that capacity he successfully conducts two important prosecutions: one for high treason (Despard), the other for libel against Napoleon Bonaparte (Peltier).

6 JUN 1803 His sister Frances marries John Mitford, Baron Redesdale, Lord Chancellor of Ireland and a vehement opponent of Catholic emancipation.

10 MAY 1804 Perceval continues as Attorney General in Pitt's second administration, always defending it strongly against factional attacks.

24 MAY 1804 Appears for the Crown in prosecuting Cobbett for libels.

8 APR 1805 The results of the inquiry into fraud and financial abuses in the Navy Department are discussed. The Treasurer of the Navy, Lord Melville, is severely criticised. His unsatisfactory answers eventually lead to a motion for his impeachment on 11 Jun.

30 APR 1805 An evangelical Christian, Perceval introduces a Bill to give bishops power to enforce residence in all clergy livings worth less than £400 a year, and to compel the payment of a salary to resident curates in livings worth over that amount. It is defeated.

23 JAN 1806 Pitt dies in office.

12 FEB 1806 Perceval resigns as Attorney General and returns to the back benches, where he continues to influence Tory party policy, becoming a fierce critic of Grenville and Fox.

14 APR 1806 Perceval re-introduces his Bill to force non-resident clergy to pay salaries to curates left in charge, but it fails again.

29 MAY 1806 The King sets up a Commission to inquire into allegations of misconduct of the Princess of Wales. Perceval is the chief legal adviser on the Princess's side. The Commission dismisses the most serious charges but finds her guilty of 'grossly indelicate conduct'. Perceval helps to arrange her reconciliation with the King, and is accused by his opponents of trying thereby to further his own ambitions.

OCT 1806 After the death of Fox, Perceval is invited to join the Government, but he refuses. He is re-elected for Northampton at the General Election.

5 MAR 1807 Perceval strongly opposes the government Bill to make concessions to the Catholics in Ireland, and contributes significantly to the downfall of Grenville's administration on 19 Mar.

26 MAR 1807 Appointed Chancellor of the Exchequer under Portland, at a salary of £1,323 p.a. He wanted the post of Attorney General or even Home Secretary, which are better paid, but agrees to the Exchequer when he is offered the Chancellorship of the Duchy of Lancaster in addition, which is to be for life, with an extra salary. However, after Parliamentary protests, the Duchy is only his 'at the King's pleasure'. He also becomes Leader of the House of Commons on 31 Mar.

29 APR 1807 Perceval drafts the King's speech at the dissolution of Parliament.

MAY 1807 The General Election strengthens Portland's majority. It is to be Perceval's last contest.

26 JUN 1807 The new Parliament meets to hear another King's Speech written largely by Perceval.

7 JUL 1807 Following Napoleon's successes at Eylau and Friedland, the Treaty of Tilsit is signed. It is thought to contain secret threats to besiege Britain.

6 SEP 1807 The Danes surrender after the Government orders a pre-emptive strike against the Danish fleet at Copenhagen.

11 NOV 1807 There is fierce opposition in Parliament both to the action against Denmark and to the Orders in Council subsequently drafted by Perceval, designed to impose retaliatory trade restrictions on neutral countries. His Bill is eventually passed on 11 Mar 1808.

FEB 1808 Perceval's Budget has to cover expenditures of *c.* £49 million. War taxes are estimated to produce only £20 million, and after other duties and taxes and with lottery income of £350,000 a total of £8 million has to be borrowed.

12 APR 1808 Perceval's third Bill to enforce the payment of curates meets with great opposition in Parliament, in spite of his pamphlet explaining the aims of the measure.

8–10 MAR 1809 A three-day debate takes place on a motion calling for the removal of the Duke of York as Commander-in-Chief. This arises from the practice of the Duke's mistress of taking payments for arranging appointments and promotions. Perceval's three-hour speech responding to the debate is widely acclaimed. A few days later the Duke of York resigns.

AUG–SEP 1809 The illness of the Duke of Portland adds to the weakness of his administration, which splits into factions. Canning gathers supporters in his bid to take over as Prime Minister, but Perceval is also a serious candidate.

4 OCT 1809 The King decides to appoint Perceval as Prime Minister, describing him as 'the most straightforward man he has almost ever known.'

OCT 1809 Perceval has great difficulty in filling posts in his Cabinet, and has to keep the office of Chancellor of the Exchequer himself, being unable to find a replacement.

23 JAN 1810 Parliament meets to debate the King's Speech. Opposition criticisms of the conduct of the war in Spain and the disastrous Walcheren expedition are refuted in a long speech by Perceval. The Opposition amendment is soundly defeated.

26 JAN 1810 Another Opposition attack comes in a motion calling for an inquiry into the Walcheren expedition. This time the Government is defeated by 195 votes to 186.

28 JAN 1810 The Government is defeated in three successive divisions on the composition of the Finance Committee, which is largely made up of friends of Perceval.

IMPORTANT DATES IN PERSONAL AND POLITICAL LIFE—*Continued*

31 MAR 1810 The findings of the Walcheren inquiry are debated and the Government narrowly survives four divisions. Nevertheless the reputation of the Earl of Chatham, who had commanded the expedition, is fatally damaged and he later resigns.

6 APR 1810 A warrant is signed for the arrest of Sir Francis Burdett, an MP who had supported the rights of people and the press to watch and report proceedings in the House of Commons. He is sent to the Tower of London, amid widespread rioting in his support. He is eventually released in June, after Parliament has gone into recess.

16 MAY 1810 Despite his misgiving, Perceval's Budget proposals are well received. The report of the Bullion Committee, however, criticises the Bank of England and precipitates a financial crisis which lasts for over a year.

18 OCT 1810 King George III becomes deeply distressed by the terminal illness of his favourite daughter, Princess Amelia. The first signs of the return of his insanity are observed.

19 DEC 1810 Perceval informs the Prince of Wales that the Cabinet has agreed on the terms of a Regency Bill which includes several restrictions on the Regent's powers. Angered by this, the Prince leads the opposition to Perceval's proposals.

4 FEB 1811 The Regency Bill is passed, a personal triumph for Perceval, although the Prince immediately begins to plan changes in the Cabinet. The King's health gradually begins to improve, however, and the Prince eventually decides to confirm Perceval in office.

19 JUL 1811 Inflation has been the inevitable consequence of war. Perceval, therefore, sponsors a Bill to make bank notes legal tender, marking the end of the exchange crisis.

DEC 1811 The Prince Regent had been pressing for a large grant from Parliament for the maintenance of the Royal Household. After lengthy negotiations Perceval persuades him to accept a smaller settlement financed from the civil list, making an important constitutional point.

17 JAN 1812 Wellesley, who had openly supported the Prince Regent, offers his resignation as Foreign Secretary.

31 JAN 1812 Charles Yorke resigns from the Admiralty because of ill-health and an aversion to serving the Prince Regent.

7 FEB 1812 Perceval has an audience with the Prince to discuss offering Opposition leaders places in a coalition government. Their acceptance is so unlikely that Perceval is again confirmed in office as the best candidate available.

28 APR 1812 The Government agrees to an inquiry into the Orders in Council which have been imposed as a war measure to restrict trade with France, but are now producing adverse effects on the economy and on relations with America.

11 MAY 1812 On his way to take part in the Committee of the Whole House debate on the Orders in Council, Perceval is shot in the lobby of the House of Commons. His assassin, John Bellingham, gives himself up immediately. He had been trying to obtain government compensation for debts incurred while in Russia, but without success.

12 MAY 1812 An inquest is held into Perceval's death, and a verdict of wilful murder is returned. His body is returned to Downing Street. Later that day the House of Commons meets and agrees to vote an annuity to Perceval's wife Jane and a grant for the support of his children.

15 MAY 1812 John Bellingham is tried at the Old Bailey and condemned to death.

16 MAY 1812 Perceval's funeral cortege leaves Downing Street. He is buried in the family vault in St Luke's, Charlton.

18 MAY 1812 John Bellingham is executed.

JUN 1812 A classical memorial to Perceval is placed in Westminster Abbey.

BACKGROUND

PHYSICAL CHARACTERISTICS AND HEALTH

Perceval was thin, rather pale and small. His complexion was sallow, some even called it 'sepulchral'. Although his build was slight he seems to have suffered no serious health problems. After two years in office, however, the strain of continual political crises was beginning to tell. He looked frail and anxious.

EDUCATION

Secondary 1774–79, Harrow
University 1780–81, Trinity College, Cambridge
Prizes and awards College Declamation Prize for English
Qualifications 1782, M.A.
Languages He wrote Latin poetry.

NON-PARLIAMENTARY CAREER

Early occupations He was called to the Bar in 1786 and practised on the Midland Circuit. He became Deputy Recorder of Northampton in 1790 and then began to receive important Crown briefs. He took silk in 1796. He was a regular speaker at the Crown and Rolls debating society, in which only MPs and barristers could participate.

Military service 1794–1803, joined the London and Westminster Light Horse Volunteers.

Other posts 1790, Deputy Recorder of Northampton; 1790–96, Commissioner of Bankrupts; 1791, Surveyor of Meltings and Clerk of Irons in the Mint; 1794–1800, Counsel to the Admiralty and the Navy; 1798, Solicitor General to the Queen; Solicitor to the Board of Ordnance; 1800–07, Counsel to Cambridge University

CLUBS

White's

HOBBIES AND SPORTS

He was a devoted family man and liked nothing better than playing games with his children. He opposed gambling and hunting on principle and considered them a waste of money. He spent some time in the study of prophecy.

FINANCES

At the time of his marriage in 1790 he was a 'briefless' barrister with an income of £200, and took lodgings over a carpet shop in Bedford Row, London. He was entirely dependent on his income from the law. By 1804 his fee income had increased to £10,000 p.a. He was reluctant to accept ministerial office because of the consequent drop in salary.

Income His income rose steadily from £200 in 1790, to £2,600 in 1800, and reached a peak of £9,723 in 1804. From October 1809 until his death he refused to accept the salary due to him as Chancellor of the Exchequer.

Pensions In 1812 Parliament voted an annuity of £2,000 for life to Perceval's wife Jane. After her death £1,000 p.a. would go to her heir. A sum of £50,000 was granted for the support of the children. Lord Arden paid Jane an additional pension.

Debts While out of office in 1806 he was forced to borrow money from his brother, Lord Arden.

ANECDOTES

At Cambridge he insisted on paying the salary of an office to a defeated candidate because he had forgotten to cast a promised vote. (Quoted in Gray, p. 6)

He was a young man 'with strong and invincible prejudices on many subjects' who had read little and who was 'of a conversation barren of instruction.' Yet 'by his excellent temper, his engaging manners, and his sprightly conversation he was the delight of all that knew him'. (Sir Samuel Romilly, quoted in Gray, p. 9)

'He is not a ship of the line, but he carries many guns, is tight-built, and is out in all weathers'. (Grattan, quoted in Gray, p. 468)

'Perceval had the sweetest of all possible tempers, and was one of the most conscientious men I ever knew; the most instinctively obedient to the dictates of conscience; the least disposed to give pain to others; the most charitable and truly kind and generous creature I ever knew'. (William Wilberforce, *Memoirs*, vol. 4, p. 26)

QUOTATIONS

I have nothing to say to the nothing that has been said. (During a debate on corrupt electoral practices).

Inadvertence is certainly never felt by me as an excuse. (In a letter to Wilberforce)

RESIDENCES

Charlton House, near Woolwich, Kent
Bedford Row, London
Belsize House, Hampstead, London
59 & 60 Lincoln's Inn Fields, London
Elm Grove, Ealing, Middlesex
10 Downing Street

MEMORIALS

STATUES AND BUSTS

1813, a marble bust by Joseph Nollekens, Wellington Museum, London; 1818, a marble bust by Joseph Nollekens, Belton House, Lincolnshire; 1818, by Sir Francis Chantrey, Northampton Town Hall, Northants.

PORTRAITS

1812, a death mask taken by Joseph Nollekens, from which G. F. Joseph painted several portraits. One is in the National Portrait Gallery, London; another in Trinity College, Cambridge.

BIBLIOGRAPHIC INFORMATION

LETTERS AND PERSONAL PAPERS

Perceval's papers are in the British Museum.

PUBLICATIONS

1791, *A review of the arguments in favour of the continuance of impeachments nothwithstanding a dissolution*; 1792, *The duties and powers of public officers with respect to violations of the public peace*; 1800, *Observations intended to point out the application of a prophecy in the eleventh chapter of the Book of Daniel to the French Power*; 1808, *A letter to the Rev. Dr. Mansel on the Curate's Bill*; 1809, *Six letters on the subject of Dr. Milner's explanation.*

FURTHER READING

Gillen, M. *Assassination of the Prime Minister*. London, 1972.

Gray, D. *Spencer Perceval: The Evangelical Prime Minister, 1762–1812*. Manchester, 1963.

Treherne, P. *The Right Honourable Spencer Perceval*. London, 1909.

Walpole, S. *The Life of the Rt. Hon. Spencer Perceval*, 2 vols. London, 1874.

Williams, C.V. *The Life and Administration of the Right Hon. Spencer Perceval . . .* London, 1812.

J.S.

Bettmann

Earl of Liverpool

Lived 1770–1828
Political Party Tory
Prime Minister 8 June 1812–9 April 1827
Government Tory
Reigning Monarchs George III; (Prince Regent); George IV

Palma non sine pulvere The palm is not obtained without labour

---

LIVERPOOL AS PRIME MINISTER

Liverpool's comprehensive education for the Prime Ministership included holding the posts of Foreign Secretary and War Secretary. An excellent administrator and judge of people he sought to centralise Cabinet government, keeping much policy in his own hands through an inner Cabinet. His first great achievement was, with the aid of Wellington in the field, to conclude the war with France. His second was to contain public discontent with the dislocations brought about by the end of the war. During the 1820s, he was converted to Free Trade and gradually rebuilt prosperity. He supported some social legislation and had clear and concrete views on Parliamentary reform. On the other hand he totally opposed a Bill for the enfranchisement of Catholics introduced in 1821. He had disagreements with George IV and Canning, his Foreign Secretary, with whose policy he agreed, was a difficult colleague. In 1825 passage by the House of Commons of another Bill on Catholic emancipation tempted him to resign, but he continued as Prime Minister when the emancipation Bill was defeated in the House of Lords. Prematurely exhausted, he resigned in 1827 and died eighteen months later.

PERSONAL INFORMATION

Names Robert Banks Jenkinson
Peerages Baron Hawksbury (15 Nov 1803); 2nd Earl of Liverpool
Born 7 Jun 1770
Birthplace London
Religion Anglican
Ancestry English, although his maternal grandmother was part-Indian. His family had made their way in trade and then land purchase in Oxfordshire and Gloucestershire. A number were MPs.
Dates and places of marriages 1) 25 Mar 1795, Wimbledon, Surrey; 2) 24 Sep 1822, Hampton Court Palace, Surrey
Age at marriages 1) 24 years, 291 days; 2) 52 years, 109 days
Years married 1) 26 years, 79 days; 2) 6 years, 71 days
First entered Parliament 7 Jun 1791 (his coming of age; first elected on 18 Jun 1720 while under 21)
Date appointed PM 8 Jun 1812
Age at appointment 42 years, 1 day
Date ceased to be PM 9 Apr 1827
Total time as PM 14 years, 305 days
Ceased to be MP 15 Nov 1803
Lived after last term as PM 1 year, 239 days
Date of death 4 Dec 1828
Place of death Coombe House, Kingston upon Thames, Surrey
Age at death 58 years, 180 days
Place of funeral Hawksbury, Gloucestershire
Place of burial Parish Church, Hawksbury, Gloucestershire
Zodiac sign Gemini

FATHER

Charles Jenkinson, 1st Earl of Liverpool
Date and place of birth 26 Apr 1727, Winchester, Hampshire
Occupation MP Cockermouth 1761–67; Appleby 1767–72; Harwich 1772–74; Hastings 1774–80; Saltash 1780–86. A politician and administrator, he was leader of the 'King's Friends' in the Commons, and held a number of ministerial posts, including Secretary at War during the North administration.
Dates of marriages 1) 9 Feb 1769, Amelia Watts (d. 7 Jul 1770); 2) 22 Jun 1782, Catherine Cope (née Bisshopp) (d. 1 Oct 1827)
Date of death 17 Dec 1808
Place of burial Parish Church, Hawksbury, Gloucestershire

MOTHER

Amelia Watts
Date of birth *c.* 1751
Profile She died at the age of 19, shortly after childbirth.
Date of marriage 9 Feb 1769
Date of death 7 Jul 1770
Place of burial Parish Church, Hawksbury, Gloucestershire

BROTHERS AND SISTERS

Liverpool was the only child of his father's first marriage, and eldest of three from his father's second marriage.
From his father's second marriage:
Charles Cecil Jenkinson (3rd Earl of Liverpool), b. 29 May 1784; m. Julia Evelyn Medley; MP Sandwich 1807–12, Bridgnorth 1812–18, East Grinstead 1818–28; junior minister in departments of Home, War and Colonies; d. 3 Oct 1851
Charlotte, b. *c.* 1783; m. Hon. James Walter Grimston, 1st Earl of Verulam (MP St. Albans, 1802–08); d. 16 Apr 1863

FIRST WIFE

Lady Louisa Theodosia Hervey
Date of birth 19 Feb 1767
Mother Elizabeth Davers
Father Frederick Augustus, 4th Earl of Bristol
Father's occupation Bishop of Derry
Age at marriage 28 years, 34 days
Number of children None
Date and place of death 12 Jun 1821 Fife House, Whitehall, London
Place of burial Parish Church, Hawksbury, Gloucestershire,
Years older than PM 3 years 108 days
Profile After her parents' separation when she was in her teens, Louisa led a dull and isolated life with her mother in Suffolk. Her marriage to Liverpool was destined to be childless, and she devoted herself to charitable work, while enjoying the social side of her husband's career. They were a devoted couple.

SECOND WIFE

Mary Chester
Date and place of birth 24 Jun 1777 Chicheley, Buckinghamshire
Mother Catherine Legge
Father Rev. Charles Chester (formerly Bagot)
Father's occupation Minister of religion (Anglican)
Age at marriage 45 years, 92 days
Date and place of death 18 Oct 1846, Norbiton Hall, Surrey
Place of burial Kingston upon Thames, Surrey
Years younger than PM 7 years, 17 days
Profile Described by Lady Erne as, 'a person of more than ordinary merit', Mary Chester had been a longtime friend of Liverpool's first wife.

CHILDREN

None

LIFE AND CAREER

PARLIAMENTARY ELECTIONS FOUGHT

*(*designates candidate elected)*
DATE Jun 1790. General Election
CONSTITUENCY Rye
RESULT Robert Banks Jenkinson** (Tory); Charles Long* (Tory)

DATE Jun 1790. General Election
CONSTITUENCY Appleby

PARLIAMENTARY ELECTIONS FOUGHT—*Continued*

RESULT Robert Banks Jenkinson** (Tory); Richard Ford* (Tory)
**Elected both for Rye and Appleby, he chose to sit for Rye.*

DATE 28 Jun 1793. By-election caused by Jenkinson's appointment as a Commissioner for the Affairs of India
CONSTITUENCY Rye
RESULT Robert Banks Jenkinson* (Tory)

DATE May 1796. General Election
CONSTITUENCY Rye
RESULT Robert Banks Jenkinson* (Tory); Robert Dundas* (Tory)*

DATE 13 Mar 1799. By-election caused by Jenkinson's appointment as Master of the Mint
CONSTITUENCY Rye
RESULT Robert Banks Jenkinson* (Tory)

DATE 25 Feb 1801. By-election caused by Jenkinson's appointment as Secretary of State for Foreign Affairs
CONSTITUENCY Rye
RESULT Robert Banks Jenkinson* (Tory)

DATE Jun 1802. General Election
CONSTITUENCY Rye
RESULT Robert Banks Jenkinson* (Tory); Thomas Davis Lamb* (Tory)

PARLIAMENTARY AND MINISTERIAL EXPERIENCE

Maiden Speech 29 Feb 1792 He spoke against a motion censuring the Government for actions in increasing the size of the Navy to combat the Russian invasion of Turkey. (*Parl. Hist.* vol 29, col 918)
Opposition office Leader of the Opposition, Jan 1806–Mar 1807
Privy Counsellor 13 Mar 1799
Ministerial Offices Commissioner of the Board of Control 28 Jun 1793–28 Mar 1799; Master of the Mint 14 Feb 1799–Feb 1801; Member of the Board of Trade 14 Mar–17 Jul 1799; Foreign Secretary 20 Feb 1801–12 May 1804; Leader of the House of Lords Nov 1803–Feb 1806, Mar 1807–Apr 1827; Home Secretary 12 May 1804–4 Feb 1806, 25 Mar 1807–30 Oct 1809; Secretary of State for War and Colonies 31 Oct 1809–10 Jun 1812; First Lord of the Treasury 8 Jun 1812– 9 Apr 1827
Opposition Leaders while PM George Ponsonby 1808–17; George Tierney 1817–21; (nominally Earl Grey)

GOVERNMENTS FORMED

Administration 8 Jun 1812–9 Apr 1827

GENERAL ELECTION RESULTS
MAY 1807: Government 388; Opposition 224; Independent 29; Doubtful 17. Total 658
OCT 1812: Government 400; Opposition 196; Doubtful 37; Independent 24; Neutral 1. Total 658
JUN 1818: Government 411; Opposition 198; Independent 32; Grenvillite 11; Doubtful 5; Neutral 1. Total 658
MAR 1820: Not analysed
JUN 1826: Not analysed
CABINET
Prime Minister and First Lord of the Treasury 2nd Earl of Liverpool
Chancellor of the Exchequer N. Vansittart (1812–Jan 1823); F. J. Robinson (Jan 1823–1827)
Lord President of the Council Earl of Harrowby
Lord Chancellor Lord Eldon
Home Secretary Viscount Sidmouth (1812–Jan 1822); R. Peel (Jan 1822–27)
Foreign Secretary Viscount Castlereagh (1812–Sep 1822); G. Canning (Sep 1822–27)
President of the Board of Trade Earl Bathurst (Jun–Sep 1812); Earl of Clancarty (Sep 1812–Jan 1818); F. J. Robinson (Sep 1818–Jan 1823); W. Huskisson (Jan 1823–1827)
Secretary for War and Colonies Earl Bathurst
President of the Board of Control Earl of Buckinghamshire (1812–Jun 1816); G. Canning (Jun 1816–Jan 1821); C. Bathurst (Jan 1821–Feb 1822); C. W. Williams Wynn (Feb 1822–1827)
First Lord of the Admiralty Viscount Melville
Lord Privy Seal Earl of Westmorland
Chancellor of the Duchy of Lancaster C. Bathurst ((1812–Aug 1812); Earl of Buckinghamshire (Aug 1812–Feb 1823); N. Vansittart (Feb 1823–1827)
Master General of the Ordnance Earl of Mulgrave (1812–Jan 1819); Duke of Wellington (Jan 1819–1827)
Treasurer of the Navy F. J. Robinson (Feb 1818–Feb 1823); W. Huskisson (Feb 1823–1827)
Master of the Mint W. Wellesley Pole (Sep 1814–Oct 1923) (Oct 1823–1827 Office not in Cabinet)
Minister Without Portfolio Earl Camden (Jun–Dec 1812); Earl of Mulgrave (Jan 1819–May 1820)
**Office not always in Cabinet*

IMPORTANT DATES IN PERSONAL AND POLITICAL LIFE

JUL 1789 Liverpool, on a grand tour of the Continent, witnesses the storming of the Bastille in Paris on 14 Jul.
MAY 1790 He takes an MA from Christ Church College, Oxford.
18 JUN 1790 First elected to Parliament at the age of 20 for both the pocket borough of Appleby and the Treasury borough of Rye. He chooses Rye, but does not take his seat while under age. Instead he continues his travels in Europe.
29 FEB 1792 Having taken his seat in the House of Commons, he makes his maiden speech.
8 MAR 1792 Although still only 21 years of age, he is invited to attend a ministerial meeting at 10 Downing Street.
JUN 1792 He resumes his travels on the Continent through Holland to France, where he makes detailed, but unofficial, observations on the political situation there, in numerous letters to his father.
28 JUN 1793 Appointed to the Board of Control set up by Pitt's India Act.
APR 1794 At Pitt's instigation, Jenkinson becomes Colonel of the Cinque Ports Regiment of Fencible Cavalry.
25 MAR 1795 He marries Lady Louisa Hervey. His father considers him too young, at 24 years, to marry, particularly to someone without personal wealth.
1 JUN 1796 His father is created Earl of Liverpool; he is styled Lord Hawksbury, a courtesy title by which he is known until his father's death on 17 Dec 1808.
14 FEB 1799 Appointed as Master of the Mint.
13 MAR 1799 He is presented to the King and sworn in as a member of the Privy Council.
20 FEB 1801 After Pitt's resignation, and the start of the Addington administration, he is appointed Foreign Sec-

retary, with immediate responsibility for peace negotiations with France.

26 MAR 1802 Treaty of Amiens signed, ending the war with France.

18 MAY 1803 Despite the Treaty, relations with France remain tense, and war is declared once more.

15 NOV 1803 Elevated to the peerage as Baron Hawksbury, he becomes Leader of the House of Lords.

12 MAY 1804 Appointed Home Secretary in Pitt's second administration.

21 OCT 1805 Victory and death of Nelson at the Battle of Trafalgar.

JAN 1806 During Pitt's serious illness, he is virtually in charge of the Government, and draws up the King's speech at the opening of Parliament.

22 JAN 1806 Death of Pitt.

25 JAN 1806 George III presses him to accept appointment as Prime Minister, but he refuses. The King appoints him Lord Warden of the Cinque Ports.

FEB 1806 During Grenville's Ministry of All the Talents, he is Leader of the Opposition, his only period out of Government office from 1793 until his final illness in 1827.

25 MAR 1807 He returns as Home Secretary in the Portland administration.

17 DEC 1808 He succeeds his father as 2nd Earl of Liverpool.

31 OCT 1809 Under the new administration of Spencer Perceval, Liverpool is appointed Secretary of State for War and Colonies.

OCT 1810 He takes a leading part in the constitution of a Regency necessitated by the mental incapacity of George III, despite fears that the Prince of Wales might remove Perceval's administration from office.

FEB 1811 Regency Bill passed by Parliament.

11 MAY 1812 Spencer Perceval is assassinated; negotiations between the Cabinet and the Prince Regent fail to find an immediate successor.

21 MAY 1812 Government defeated on a censure motion by 174 votes to 170; protracted negotiations continue.

8 JUN 1812 Liverpool is appointed Prime Minister and First Lord of the Treasury with the authority to form a stronger administration.

18 JUN 1812 United States declares war with Great Britain, over a number of maritime grievances.

21 JUN 1813 Wellington's victory at Vitoria during the Peninsular War breaks the back of French military power in Spain.

JAN 1814 Liverpool prepares to make peace with Napoleon, on favourable terms, amidst growing anti-Napoleonic fervour in Britain.

APR 1814 Napoleon abdicates and returns to Elba.

9 JUN 1814 Liverpool, the King of Prussia and Viscount Castlereagh are invested as Knights of the Garter at a special ceremony at Carlton House.

28 JUL 1814 The definitive Treaty of Peace with France, signed on 30 May, is greeted with overwhelming approval in Parliament.

NOV 1814 Liverpool decides to wind up the war with the United States.

24 DEC 1814 Treaty of Peace with the United States is signed at Ghent.

15 MAR 1815 Liverpool makes his first important speech as Prime Minister on economic affairs, introducing new Corn Laws to improve the agricultural situation in the post-war period.

1 MAR 1815 Napoleon escapes from Elba; Liverpool sends his half-brother, Cecil, to Paris to report on the morale of the French government and army.

18 JUN 1815 Battle of Waterloo: total defeat of the French. In July Napoleon surrenders and is exiled to St. Helena.

18 MAR 1816 Government defeated by 238 votes to 201 on its policy to continue with an income tax to aid recovery from the expenses of the war. Instead, £5-6 million has to be borrowed from the Bank of England. Throughout the year, bad harvests and stagnation in manufacturing lead to rioting.

MAY 1818 Liverpool secures £1 million of public funds to finance a church building programme.

JUL 1819 The report of the Milan Commission, investigating the conduct of Princess Caroline, estranged wife of the Prince Regent, is submitted to the Cabinet. The Prince Regent had for some time wished to divorce her, but Liverpool remains unconvinced of the wisdom of this, because of the inevitable salacious publicity.

16 AUG 1819 The 'Peterloo' massacre: against a background of increasing public discontent and calls for parliamentary reform, a meeting is held at St. Peter's Fields, Manchester, at which 11 people are killed and hundreds injured.

NOV 1819 In response to Peterloo and other public disorder, six Bills are speedily introduced to curtail seditious meetings and newspapers, to prevent military-style training, to seize arms and to deal with other related matters.

29 JAN 1820 Death of George III; the Prince Regent ascends to the throne as George IV.

23 FEB 1820 The Cato Street Conspirators, who had plotted to assassinate the Cabinet, are arrested and condemned as traitors to be executed on 1 May.

5 JUL 1820 Following a report by a Secret Committee which recommended legislative action on Queen Caroline, a Bill of Pains and Penalties is introduced, including a clause for the dissolution of the marriage.

10 NOV 1820 The Bill passes its 3rd Reading in the Lords by a majority of only nine, which leads Liverpool to withdraw it, fearing it could not be passed in the Commons.

APR 1821 The Commons passes, for the first time, a Bill for the enfranchisement of Roman Catholics. It is rejected by the Lords; Liverpool, a long-time opponent of the measure, speaks against it.

19 JUL 1821 Coronation of George IV; Caroline is refused admission to the ceremony; she dies on 7 Aug.

APR-JUN 1822 Liverpool tries to strengthen his Cabinet, but meets with resistance from the King. It is a time of great strain to Liverpool's nerves, as his wife, to whom he is devoted, is seriously ill and dies on 12 Jun.

AUG 1822 The suicide of Lord Londonderry, the Foreign Secretary, mandates further Cabinet reorganisation for Liverpool. After a battle of words with the King, Canning is finally accepted to take over the post.

24 SEP 1822 Liverpool marries Mary Chester, an old friend of his first wife.

JAN 1823 A time of greater prosperity begins, and Liverpool attempts to reduce taxation to ease distress, particularly among landowners. Optimism and the well-being of the nation becomes a continuing theme in the King's speeches and budget proposals over the next two years.

MAR 1825 Prosperity leads to great speculation in stocks and shares, which drains the Bank of England and brings about a great monetary crisis. Relief comes in December after an issue of Exchequer bills is authorized.

IMPORTANT DATES IN PERSONAL AND POLITICAL LIFE—*Continued*

21 APR 1825 When a Bill for Catholic emancipation is passed by the Commons, Liverpool is ready to resign. He is persuaded to continue in office when the Bill is rejected by the Lords by 48 votes.

MAY 1826 Following the end of a run of good harvests and a depression in manufacturing industries, Liverpool secures Parliament's approval for a revision of the Corn Laws.

17 FEB 1827 Liverpool, at home at Fife House, opening his morning post, suffers a severe cerebral haemorrhage, which leaves him temporarily paralysed.

9 APR 1827 His incapacity leads to his retirement as Prime Minister; in July he has another stroke.

4 DEC 1828 Liverpool dies, having suffered a further stroke.

BACKGROUND

PHYSICAL CHARACTERISTICS AND HEALTH

Liverpool was tall, but not robust, and had a particularly long neck. This, and his naturally melancholy expression, combined to give him an inelegant and lanky appearance. He filled out somewhat in middle age, but always retained a rather unstylish air.

He became prone to vascular complaints, and from his early fifties suffered from a form of thrombophlebitis in his left leg, which continued to cause discomfort throughout the rest of his life.

On 17 Feb 1827 he suffered a severe cerebral haemorrhage, which left him temporarily paralysed. His condition fluctuated before he suffered another stroke in Jul 1827. He lingered on as a shadow of his former self until he died after further spasms and convulsions on 4 Dec 1828, at the age of 58.

EDUCATION

Primary Albion House, Parsons Green, Fulham, London

Secondary 1783–87 Charterhouse

University 1787–89, 1790 Christ Church College, Oxford

Qualifications 1790 Master of Arts

Cultural and vocational background After two years at university, he travelled to France, where he witnessed the storming of the Bastille on 14 Jul 1789. He returned to England to gain his MA before continuing on the Grand Tour, visiting Rome, Naples and Florence. He returned to England in June 1791, before taking his seat in the House of Commons.

Languages He spoke fluent French, and studied Latin and Greek.

NON-PARLIAMENTARY CAREER

Military service During his early Parliamentary career, he volunteered for military service, and in 1794 became Colonel of the Cinque Ports Regiment of Fencible Cavalry. In 1796 he was quartered in Dumfries, and furnished a guard at the funeral of the poet Robert Burns.

Other posts 1806, Lord Warden of the Cinque Ports; 1812, Master of Trinity House; 1816, High Steward of the Borough of Kingston upon Thames; 1824, Trustee of the National Gallery; 1826, Trustee of the British Museum.

HONOURS

Freedom of cities 1825 Bristol

Academic 1826 Hon. LL.D Cambridge

Other than peerage 22 May 1794, Fellow of the Royal Society; 3 Jun 1813, Fellow of the Society of Arts; 9 Jun 1814, Knight of the Garter

CLUBS

White's

HOBBIES AND SPORTS

Liverpool had a great interest in the arts, and commissioned both statues and paintings. He founded the National Gallery in 1824.

He was also very interested in literature, and built up an extensive library which was sold at Christie's after his death. It included works on history, English antiquities, law, divinity, languages, and travel, as well as his greatest interest—politics and political history.

FINANCES

While his father was alive, Liverpool relied upon his official salaries and his father's generosity for his income. Although comfortably off throughout his life, he was not considered by his contemporaries to be particularly wealthy. His considerable official expenses—for travel, secretarial staff and official entertainment—had to be met from his official salary.

Income After his father's death in 1808, his total income amounted to about £23,000. His salary as Master of the Mint 1799–1801 was £3,000; as Lord Warden of the Cinque Ports 1806–28, £3,000; as First Lord of Treasury, £4,000.

Spouse's finances His first wife, Louisa, had a £5,000 legacy left to her on the death of her father.

Legacies He inherited an income of around £15,000 on the death of his father, including the rental of two estates in Gloucestershire, Hawksbury and Eastwood.

Will Dated 21 Sep 1821 to 20 Aug 1827, his personal estate on death amounted to some £120,000. Of this two-fifths was given away in bequests or charged with life annuities; £45,500 went to his half-brother as residuary legatee.

ANECDOTES

Pitt described Liverpool's maiden speech in the House of Commons, when he was only 21 years old, in the following terms: 'Not only a more able first speech than had ever been heard from a young member, but one so full of philosophy and science, strong and perspicuous language, and sound and convincing arguments, that it would have done credit to the most practised debater and most experienced statesman that ever existed'.

In his youth he was very keen on doing voluntary military service, and on encouraging others to follow suit. As a joke, George Canning, a friend at Oxford, had a pack of posters printed and delivered to Liverpool at a dinner party, with a note saying that they were already on display all over London. The poster read:

Tight lads, who would wish for a fair opportunity,
Of defying the Frenchman, with perfect impunity,
Tis the bold Colonel Jenkinson calls you to arm,
And solemnly swears you shall come to no harm.

Liverpool was mortified at this and burst into floods of tears, causing a temporary rift in the friendship of the two men.

QUOTATIONS

29 Feb 1792, On peace our greatness as a nation completely and almost wholly depends.

15 Mar 1815, Not to protect the agricultural interest would be in reality to discourage it.

10 May 1821, (I consider) the right of election as a public trust, granted not for the benefit of the individual, but for the public good.

RESIDENCES

Conduit Street, London
Coombe House, near Kingston upon Thames, Surrey (also known as *Coombe Wood*)
Fife House, Whitehall, London (which Liverpool used as his official residence in preference to 10 Downing Street)
Walmer Castle, near Deal, Kent
Open to the public Walmer Castle—one of the coastal castles built by Henry VIII, and the official residence of the Lords Warden of the Cinque Ports

MEMORIALS

PORTRAITS

c. 1796, by Sir Thomas Lawrence, National Portrait Gallery; *c.* 1820, by Sir Thomas Lawrence, Windsor Castle; *c.* 1826, by Sir Thomas Lawrence, National Gallery.

OTHER MEMORIALS

Liverpool Road, Islington, London N1 and Liverpool Street in the City of London EC2 were named after him (and subsequently Liverpool Street Station). Liverpool Arms Public House, Kingston upon Thames, Surrey.

BIBLIOGRAPHIC INFORMATION

LETTERS AND PERSONAL PAPERS

The main collections of papers relating to the Liverpool family are in the British Library, and in the William R. Perkins Library, Duke University, Durham, North Carolina.
Many of his letters are reprinted in Yonge.

FURTHER READING

Cookson, J.E. *Lord Liverpool's Administration 1815–1822.* Edinburgh, 1975.
Gash, N. *Lord Liverpool: The Life and Political Career of Robert Banks Jenkinson, Second Earl of Liverpool, 1770–1828.* London, 1984.
Petrie, C. *Lord Liverpool and his times.* London, 1954.
Yonge, C. D. *The Life and Administration of the Second Earl of Liverpool.* 3 vols. London, 1868.

P.B.

Historical Pictures

George Canning

Lived 1770–1827

Political Party Tory

Prime Minister 12 April 1827–8 August 1827

Government Tory/Whig Coalition

Reigning Monarch George IV

Ne cede malis: sed contra Yield not to misfortunes: on the contrary, meet them with fortitude

---

GEORGE CANNING AS PRIME MINISTER

Canning was a Whig by background so that when he sought the friendship and, indeed, patronage of the Tory Pitt his integrity became suspect. Witty, sharp, and entertaining there was a danger, some thought, that he was too clever. Pitt ensured him advancement through the Foreign Office and the Board of Control and in turn Canning remained loyal to Pitt. First appointed Foreign Secretary under Portland in 1808 he held no really senior post again until he succeeded Castlereagh as Foreign Secretary in 1822. He was in the Cabinet, however, from 1816 to 1821. Canning believed in British independence from Europe, supporting a balance of power on the European continent together with a strong British navy. He also wished to strike out for new markets in South America, 'calling the New World into existence to redress the balance of the Old', as he expressed it. In domestic matters however he was a firm Tory suppressing any hint of rebellion among the people and opposing repeal of the Test Act against dissenters and the reform of Parliament. He did, however, consistently support Catholic emancipation. When Liverpool became ill Canning moved quickly to secure the King's invitation to form a Government, but had great difficulty, as Tory mistrust surfaced again. After a little over one hundred days in office he died.

PERSONAL INFORMATION

Names George Canning
Nicknames The Cicero of the British Senate; The Zany of Debate
Born 11 Apr 1770
Birthplace Marylebone, London
Religion Anglican
Ancestry Irish. His family originally had a seat at Foxcole in Warwickshire but Canning was descended from a branch of the family which had settled in Ulster and had been granted the manor of Garvagh in Londonderry, N. Ireland, by James I in 1618.
Date and place of marriage 8 Jul 1800, Brooke St., London
Age at marriage 30 years, 88 days
Years married 27 years, 31 days
First entered Parliament 28 Jun 1793
Date appointed PM 12 Apr 1827
Age at appointment 57 years, 1 day
Date ceased to be PM 8 Aug 1827
Total time as PM 119 days
Ceased to be MP 8 Aug 1827
Lived after last term as PM Died in office
Date of death 8 Aug 1827
Place of death Chiswick House, Middlesex
Age at death 57 years, 119 days
Last words Spain and Portugal
Place of funeral and burial Westminster Abbey, London
Zodiac sign Aries

FATHER

George Canning
Date and place of birth 1736, Garvagh, Londonderry
Occupation He was a barrister, called to the Bar at the Middle Temple. He wrote articles, pamphlets and poetry and did some translating. He briefly set up as a wine merchant but the business failed.
Date of marriage 21 May 1768
Date of death 11 Apr 1771
Place of burial St. Marylebone Church, London

MOTHER

Mary Ann Costello
Date and place of birth c. 1749, Connaught, Ireland
Profile She was a great beauty who went on the stage when left destitute after the death of her husband, at first in London and later touring the country. She lived with a fellow actor, Samuel Reddish. She later tried selling an eye ointment she had invented but this failed. She retired from the stage in 1801.
Dates of marriages 1) 21 May 1768, George Canning (d. 11 Apr 1771); 2)11 Feb 1783, Richard Hunn
Date of death 10 Mar 1827
Place of burial Bath, Somerset

BROTHERS AND SISTERS

Canning was the first son and second and only surviving child of his father's three children. He had 10 half-brothers and sisters.
girl, b. 1769; d. 1769
boy, b. 23 Dec 1771; d. young
Illegitimate children of his mother and Samuel Reddish:
William, d. young
Twin to William, d. young
Samuel, m. Dorothy Ashby; a collector of HM Customs at Falmouth; lived in Jamaica for a while and died insolvent
Charles, b. 1778; m. Beatrice Charlotte Manning; Captain in the 22nd Bengal Native Infantry; d. 8 Jun 1810
Daughter, twin to Charles, b. 1778; spoke the epilogue on stage at a performance for her mother's benefit at Exeter Mar 1783
From his mother's second marriage:
Richard, b. before 1792
Mary; m. Richard Thompson of HM Customs House; d. 1823
Maria, b. *c.* 1788; m. Humphrey Noad; d. 3 Mar 1860
Frederick, b. 1789; m. Frances Emma Pickmore; captain in the Royal Navy; d. 13 Oct 1852
Ann, twin to Frederick, b. 1789; d. 1794

WIFE

Joan Scott (Viscountess Canning)
Date of birth 14 Mar 1776
Mother Margaret Dundas
Father Major General John Scott
Father's occupation MP Caithness 1754–61, Tain Burghs 1761–68, Fife, 1768–75. A soldier, he became a Colonel of the 26th Regiment of Foot in 1762 and a Major General in 1770.
Age at marriage 24 years, 116 days
Number of children 4
Date and place of death 15 Mar 1837, 10 Grosvenor Square, London
Place of burial Westminster Abbey, London.
Years younger than PM 5 years, 341 days
Profile She preferred to stay in the background rather than be a society hostess. She acted as Canning's secretary, copying his letters and playing a supportive role. Canning adored her and trusted her judgement on everything, discussing all his public as well as private concerns with her. Although publicly a self-effacing figure she was a strong personality at home, well able to match her husband's dominant character. She published a pamphlet after Canning's death defending his Portuguese policy and vigorously attacking Wellington's foreign policy, which she saw as a betrayal of everything Canning had achieved. She was created Viscountess Canning on 22 Jan 1828.

CHILDREN

3 sons 1 daughter
George Charles, b. 25 Apr 1801; d. 31 Mar 1820
William Pitt, b. 16 Dec 1802; Post Captain in the Navy; d. 25 Oct 1828
Harriet, b. 13 Apr 1804; m. 8 Apr 1825, Ulick John de Burgh (1st Marquess of Clanricarde); d. 8 Jan 1876
Charles John (2nd Viscount and 1st Earl Canning), b. 14 Dec 1812; m. 5 Sep 1835, Hon. Charlotte Stuart; MP Warwick 1836–37; Under Secretary of State for Foreign Affairs 1841; Chief Commissioner for Woods and Forests 1846; Postmaster General 1853–55; Governor General and then Viceroy of India 1856–62; d. 17 Jun 1862

LIFE AND CAREER

PARLIAMENTARY ELECTIONS FOUGHT

*(*designates candidate elected)*

DATE 28 Jun 1793. By-election caused by resignation of Sir Richard Worsley, Bt.
CONSTITUENCY Newtown, Isle of Wight
RESULT George Canning* (Tory)

DATE May 1796. General Election
CONSTITUENCY Wendover
RESULT John Hiley Addington* (Tory); George Canning* (Tory)

DATE 26 Mar 1799. By-election caused by Canning's appointment as one of the Commissioners for the Affairs of India
CONSTITUENCY Wendover
RESULT George Canning* (Tory)

DATE 5 Jun 1800. By-election caused by Canning's appointment as Joint Paymaster General of the Forces.
CONSTITUENCY Wendover
RESULT George Canning* (Tory)

DATE Jun 1802. General Election
CONSTITUENCY Tralee
RESULT George Canning* (Tory)

DATE 4 Jun 1804. By-election caused by Canning's appointment as Treasurer of the Navy
CONSTITUENCY Tralee
RESULT George Canning* (Tory)

DATE Oct 1806. General Election
CONSTITUENCY Newtown, Isle of Wight
RESULT Sir Robert Barclay, Bt.* (Tory); George Canning* (Tory)

DATE 1 Apr 1807. By-election caused by Canning's appointment as Foreign Secretary.
CONSTITUENCY Newtown, Isle of Wight
RESULT George Canning* (Tory)

DATE May 1807. General Election
CONSTITUENCY Hastings
RESULT George Canning* (Tory); Sir Abraham Hume, Bt.* (Tory)

DATE Oct 1812. General Election
CONSTITUENCY Liverpool
RESULT George Canning* (Tory) 1631; Isaac Gascoyne* (Tory) 1532; Henry Peter Brougham (Whig) 1131; Thomas Creevey (Whig) 1068; Banastre Tarleton (Tory) 11

DATE 12 Jun 1816. By-election caused by Canning's appointment as First Commissioner for the Affairs of India
CONSTITUENCY Liverpool
RESULT George Canning* (Tory) 1280; Thomas Leyland (Rad) 738

DATE Jun 1818. General Election
CONSTITUENCY Liverpool
RESULT George Canning* (Tory) 1654; Isaac Gascoyne* (Tory) 1444; William Philip Molyneaux, Earl of Selton, (Whig) 1280; Arthur Heywood (Whig) 8; George Williams (Whig) 2; John Bolton (Tory) 1; Ralph Benson (Tory) 1; Sir William Barton (Tory) 1; John Bridge Aspinall (Tory) 1

DATE Mar 1820. General Election
CONSTITUENCY Liverpool
RESULT George Canning* (Tory) 1635; Isaac Gascoyne* (Tory) 1532; Peter Crompton (Rad) 345; Thomas Leyland (Rad) 125.

DATE 10 Feb 1823. By-election caused by resignation of Nicholas Vansittart
CONSTITUENCY Harwich
RESULT George Canning* (Tory)

DATE Jun 1826. General Election
CONSTITUENCY Newport, Isle of Wight
RESULT George Canning* (Tory); William Henry John Scott* (Tory)

DATE 20 Apr 1827. By-election caused by resignation of Augustus Frederick Ellis
CONSTITUENCY Seaford
RESULT George Canning* (Tory)

PARTY ACTIVITY

Membership of group or faction Pittites

PARLIAMENTARY AND MINISTERIAL EXPERIENCE

Maiden Speech He spoke during a debate on a treaty with the King of Sardinia, granting him a subsidy to help him fight against the French. (*Parl. Hist.* vol 30, 31 Jan 1794, col 1317–29.)
Privy Counsellor 28 May 1800
Ministerial Offices Under Secretary of State for Foreign Affairs, 6 Jan 1796–29 Mar 1799; Commissioner of the Board of Control for India 30 Mar 1799–15 Mar 1801; Joint Paymaster General of the Forces 5 Jul 1800–15 Mar 1801; Treasurer of the Navy 26 May 1804–Feb 1806; Foreign Secretary 25 Mar 1807–Oct 1809, 16 Sep 1822–Apr 1827; President of the Board of Control 20 Jun 1816–15 Jan 1821; Leader of the House of Commons 16 Sep 1822–8 Aug 1827; First Lord of the Treasury 12 Apr 1827–8 Aug 1827; Chancellor of the Exchequer 20 Apr 1827–8 Aug 1827
Opposition Leaders while PM Earl Grey; Viscount Althorp

GOVERNMENTS FORMED

Administration 12 Apr 1827–8 Aug 1827

GENERAL ELECTION RESULT
JUN 1826: Not analysed.

CABINET
Prime Minister, First Lord of the Treasury and Chancellor of the Exchequer G. Canning
Lord President of the Council Earl of Harrowby
Lord Chancellor Lord Lyndhurst
Home Secretary W. Sturges Bourne (Apr–Jul 1827); Marquess of Lansdowne (Jul–Aug 1827)
Foreign Secretary Viscount Dudley and Ward
President of the Board of Trade W. Huskisson
Secretary of State for War and Colonies Viscount Goderich
President of the Board of Control C. W. Williams-Wynn
First Lord of the Admiralty Duke of Clarence
Lord Privy Seal Duke of Devonshire (Apr–Jul 1827); Earl of Carlisle (Jul–Aug 1827)
Chancellor of the Duchy of Lancaster N. Vansittart
Master General of the Ordnance Marquess of Anglesey
Treasurer of the Navy W. Huskisson
Secretary at War Viscount Palmerston

Master of the Mint G. Tierney
Minister without Portfolio Marquess of Lansdowne (May–Jul 1827); Duke of Portland (May–Aug 1827)

IMPORTANT DATES IN PERSONAL AND POLITICAL LIFE

22 JUN 1791 Takes his BA at Christ Church College, Oxford, and goes on a short tour of The Netherlands in place of the Grand Tour.

SEP 1791 Commences his studies as a law student at Lincoln's Inn.

15 AUG 1792 Pitt, at their first meeting, becomes Canning's hero. Canning changes his alliance from the Whigs to the Tory party. He feels some of the Whigs have become increasingly radical, showing sympathy with revolutionary developments in France and supporting the idea of parliamentary reform at home, both of which Canning opposes. Canning's ambition, his patriotic desire to serve his country and his need for money, which can only be earned by holding office, all draw him towards the Tories. He boldly writes to the Prime Minister asking for an interview. Pitt subsequently promises to find him a seat.

28 JUN 1793 Elected to Parliament for the first time as Member for Newtown, Isle of Wight.

31 JAN 1794 He makes his maiden speech.

5 JUL 1794 Receives his MA from Oxford.

6 JAN 1796 Takes up his first appointment as Parliamentary Under-Secretary of State for Foreign Affairs.

25 MAY 1796 He is elected as one of two MPs for Wendover, Bucks., in the General Election.

SEP 1797 He is appointed Receiver General of the Alienation Office, a sinecure which brings him an annual salary of up to £700.

20 NOV 1797 The first issue of *The Anti-Jacobean* or *Weekly Examiner* is published by Canning and others. A pro-Government satirical magazine, it is to run until 9 Jul 1798 and includes poems and articles by Canning.

30 MAR 1799 Canning leaves the Foreign Office and becomes one of the Commissioners of the Board of Control for India.

28 MAY 1800 He is made a Privy Counsellor.

5 JUL 1800 He takes up an appointment as Joint Paymaster-General of the forces.

8 JUL 1800 He marries Joan Scott. The marriage is blissfully happy and also makes him financially independent as she possesses £100,000.

15 MAR 1801 Following the fall of Pitt he resigns all his offices except the Receiver Generalship of the Alienation Office out of loyalty to the former Prime Minister. He refuses to serve under Addington whom he regards as inadequate and an unworthy successor to Pitt.

27 MAY 1802 He introduces a motion to control the slave trade in Trinidad.

24 JUL 1802 In the General Election Canning is elected for Tralee Borough, Co. Kerry, Ireland.

29 MAY 1804 He is appointed Treasurer of the Navy by Pitt.

6 JAN 1805 Canning tenders his resignation after Pitt appoints Addington (now Viscount Sidmouth) Lord President of the Council. He feels unable to serve in the same Cabinet as a man whose administration he had attacked vigorously and publicly between 1801 and 1804. Pitt refuses Canning's resignation but offers him the Irish First Secretaryship instead. Canning considers this for seven days and then decides to remain in the Cabinet as Treasurer of the Navy out of loyalty to Pitt.

6 FEB 1806 Canning makes a speech in Parliament praising his mentor Pitt after the latter's death.

1 JUL 1806 Grenville offers Canning a post in the Cabinet in the Ministry of All Talents. Canning refuses this and all Grenville's subsequent offers.

3 NOV 1806 Elected as one of the two Members for Newtown, Isle of Wight at the General Election.

25 MAR 1807 Appointed Foreign Secretary by the Duke of Portland, his brother-in-law.

5 MAY 1807 Elected as one of two Members for Hastings in the General Election.

28 JUL 1807 At Canning's initiative, a British fleet is sent to Denmark to capture the Danish fleet, which Canning suspects is to be used by Napoleon for an attack on England. The expedition succeeds.

22 OCT 1807 A Convention of friendship and amity with Portugal is signed by Canning and Souza, the Portuguese ambassador, in London in the face of French aggression.

14 JAN 1809 A Treaty of peace, friendship and alliance with Ferdinand VII of Spain is signed in London. It had been negotiated by Frere (diplomatic representative to Spain) on Canning's instructions.

4 APR 1809 Canning writes to the Prime Minister, the Duke of Portland, expressing unhappiness at the composition and performance of the Cabinet; indeed he feels so strongly about what he regards as Castlereagh's mishandling of the War Office that he feels he can no longer work with him. In discussion with Portland he threatens to resign from the Foreign Office unless Castlereagh is moved. Portland agrees but the decision is postponed. Castlereagh himself is, naturally, not informed.

21 SEP 1809 Canning fights a duel with Castlereagh when the latter challenges him after discovering Canning's attempt to move him from the War Office. Canning is wounded in the thigh.

9 OCT 1809 Canning gives up the seals of office as Foreign Secretary, the King having refused his offer to become Prime Minister following Portland's death.

18 MAR 1812 Canning refuses an offer from Perceval to join the Cabinet.

22 JUN 1812 Canning carries a motion in favour of Catholic emancipation through the House of Commons by 235 votes to 106.

27 JUL 1812 Canning refuses the Foreign Secretaryship offered to him by the Earl of Liverpool and Viscount Castlereagh on the grounds that he considers it humiliating to serve under Castlereagh as Leader of the House.

16 OCT 1812 He is elected for Liverpool at the General Election.

10 JUL 1814 The Earl of Liverpool agrees to appoint Canning Ambassador to Portugal.

NOV 1814 Canning sails for Lisbon as Ambassador Extraordinary and Minister Plenipotentiary.

10 APR 1815 Canning resigns as Ambassador but his resignation is deferred until June. He returns to London in the autumn.

20 JUN 1816 Appointed President of the Board of Control.

31 MAR 1820 Canning is greatly distressed by the death of his beloved eldest son, George Charles, who had been in continual bad health since childhood.

12 DEC 1820 Canning resigns as President of the Board of Control, having refused to take part in the proceedings against Queen Caroline, a personal friend.

APR 1822 Appointed Governor-General of India. He is prevented from taking up the post by Castlereagh's suicide.

IMPORTANT DATES IN PERSONAL AND POLITICAL LIFE—*Continued*

18 SEP 1822 Canning assumes the office of Foreign Secretary and Leader of the House of Commons following Castlereagh's suicide.

10 FEB 1823 Elected as Member of Parliament for Harwich, Essex.

30 APR 1823 Canning speaks in a debate on a censure motion in the Commons when he defends his policy of British neutrality over the French invasion of Spain following diplomatic failure to prevent war. The motion is defeated by 372 votes to 20.

15 MAY 1823 Canning introduces amendments to a motion on the abolition of slavery, emphasising the primary importance of improving the condition of slaves and looking forward to their emancipation as soon as possible. The amendments are passed.

12 OCT 1823 Discussions between Canning and Polignac, the French Ambassador, lead to the Polignac Memorandum, setting down each country's attitude to Spanish American independence. The French commit themselves to non-interference in South America.

16 MAR 1824 Canning introduces an Order in Council protecting slaves in Trinidad, St. Lucia and Demerara from ill treatment, enlarging their rights and improving their status. It is passed without division.

23 JUL 1824 Canning persuades the Cabinet to recommend to the King that Britain negotiate a commercial treaty with Buenos Aires which would effectively amount to diplomatic recognition.

31 DEC 1824 Canning writes to British ministers in Mexico and Colombia, authorising them to negotiate commercial treaties and also informs the Spanish government of his resolve to recognise immediately Colombia, Mexico and Buenos Aires as independent states.

4 APR 1826 A protocol with Russia concerning British mediation between Ottoman Porte (Turkey) and the Greeks is signed at St. Petersburg by Wellington, acting under Canning's instructions.

13 JUN 1826 Canning is elected as one of two Members of Parliament for Newport, Isle of Wight, at the General Election.

9 DEC 1826 At Canning's insistence, the Cabinet agrees to send troops to the aid of Portugal, which is being invaded from Spain by supporters of Dom Miguel, who claims the Portuguese throne.

1 MAR 1827 Canning introduces the Corn Bill in the Commons, incorporating Huskisson's sliding scale of duties levied on foreign corn.

10 APR 1827 The King sends for Canning and asks him to try to assemble a new administration formed on the same principles as that of the Earl of Liverpool, who has been incapacitated by a stroke.

12 APR 1827 Canning kisses the King's hands, becoming Prime Minister and First Lord of the Treasury. Seven members of the Cabinet (Wellington, Peel, Westmorland, Bexley, Melville, Eldon and Bathurst) resign.

19 APR 1827 Canning opens negotiations with Lord Lansdowne, leader of the Whigs, in order to form a coalition with the Whigs.

20 APR 1827 Elected as Member of Parliament for Seaford and appointed Chancellor of the Exchequer.

26 APR 1827 Canning reaches an agreement with Lord Lansdowne and the Duke of Devonshire. Lord Lansdowne agrees to urge the Whigs to support the Government and join it if invited.

7 MAY 1827 Canning announces the formation of a committee of finance to consider the state of the revenue.

28 MAY 1827 Canning opposes Lord John Russell's motion to disenfranchise the borough of Penhryn and redistribute its seats to Birmingham and Manchester but the motion passes in the Commons.

1 JUN 1827 Canning introduces the Budget, which is passed without division.

12 JUN 1827 The Government is defeated in the Lords after an amendment to the Corn Bill introduced by Wellington at the Committee stage is retained at the Report stage. The Bill is dropped.

18 JUN 1827 Canning introduces the Corn Amendment Bill as a temporary measure, intending to introduce a new Bill in the following session; the new Bill is passed.

21 JUN 1827 Canning makes his last speech in the House of Commons on the Corn Amendment Bill.

6 JUL 1827 Treaty with France and Russia, based on the Protocol signed with Russia in April 1826, for the pacification of Greece (in which the three powers agree to mediate between the Turks and the Greeks) signed in London.

6 AUG 1827 Convention of commerce with the USA signed in London, together with a convention concerning the north-west coast of America continuing the temporary 1818 agreement over rival British and American claims to Oregon.

8 AUG 1827 Canning dies at Chiswick House where he has been staying in an attempt to regain his deteriorating health.

BACKGROUND

PHYSICAL CHARACTERISTICS AND HEALTH

Stratford Canning described George Canning at 25: 'his features alternately expressive of deep thought and lively wit, his mild yet penetrating eyes, his full but rather scornful lip, the handsome contour of his thin and slightly freckled face . . . his dark well-shorn chin bore witness to the colour of his hair which before he wore powder a raven might have envied.' (In Lane-Poole *The Life of Stratford Canning*)

In 1812 (when he was 42) he was described by Cyrus Redding as ' a handsome man in feature, compact in person, moulded between activity and strength . . . he was bald as the first Caesar.' (In *Fifty Years Recollections*, I, pp. 177–178)

He suffered indifferent health as a young man with frequent minor illnesses. In 1804 he badly injured his leg after a fall while out riding. In later life his health worsened, with frequent attacks of gout causing him severe pain. His right hand was sometimes so badly affected he could hardly write. He was exhausted by his work as Foreign Secretary and Leader of the House. He fell dangerously ill with a bowel complaint in 1825 and later experienced severe pain in the chest and rheumatism.

In January 1827 he caught a severe cold at the Duke of York's funeral from which he never fully recovered. In his last illness he was in excruciating pain from inflammation of the liver and lungs.

EDUCATION

Primary 1778–82, Hyde Abbey School, Winchester
Secondary 1782–87, Eton
University 1787–91, Christ Church College, Oxford
Prizes and awards 1789 Chancellor's Prize for Latin verse
Qualifications 1791, Bachelor of Arts; 1794 Master of Arts
Cultural and vocational background He could not afford a Grand Tour after graduating and so went on a short tour of The Netherlands and Brussels in the summer of 1791.
Languages He worked hard at learning French while at university but was never very fluent. He admitted he could not write it and his opponents claimed he could not speak it.

NON-PARLIAMENTARY CAREER

Early occupations He entered Lincoln's Inn in September 1791 but was never called to the Bar. He gave up the law shortly after entering Parliament.
Other posts 1797, Receiver-General of the Alienation Office; 1814–15, Ambassador Extraordinary and Plenipotentiary to Portugal; 1822 Appointed Governor-General of India but never took up the post; Governor of Charterhouse School, Godalming

HONOURS

Academic 16 Jun 1814, Hon. DCL, Oxford
Other than peerage 12 Jan 1826, Fellow of the Royal Society

CLUBS

White's

HOBBIES AND SPORTS

He liked the theatre and wrote poetry (mainly satirical) which was published. He was an excellent conversationalist. He loved practical jokes and parlour games. He dabbled in farming in Lincolnshire.

FINANCES

Canning was born into poverty, as his father had been disinherited. When his wealthy uncle took charge of his education a small Irish estate (Kibrahan, Co. Kilkenny) was settled on Canning which gave him a meagre fluctuating income throughout his life. He struggled financially until he was appointed to a Government post in 1796 which gave him a salary. His marriage made him financially independent but he subsequently spent the majority of his wife's fortune on property (including a Lincolnshire farm which lost money), election costs, paying off debts incurred before marriage and later his second son's gambling debts, and general expenses. He was shocked to discover how much of her fortune had gone by 1821 and accepted the post of Governor- General of India in order to recoup his finances, as the salary was £25,000 p.a.
Income His Irish estate gave him an income of £200 p.a. on average. In 1791 his income from his grandfather's legacy was £86 p.a. His post as Receiver-General of the Alienation Office paid him up to £700 p.a. His salary as Under Secretary of State was £1,500 p.a. in 1796 rising to £2,000 in 1799. His salary as Treasurer of the Navy was £4,000 p.a. As Ambassador to Lisbon he received £14,000 p.a. In 1821 his income was £2,200 for the year including £980 from his Lincolnshire farm and £360 from the Irish estate.
Spouse's finances His wife possessed *c.* £100,000 on her marriage inherited from her father who had made a fortune gambling.
Pensions He received a pension of £500 when he left office in 1801. It was rumoured that he made it over to his mother.
Legacies His grandfather left him £3,000 on his 21st birthday, 11 Apr 1791.
Debts In 1792 he asked Rev. William Leigh for a loan of £300 to pay off various debts. He had a number of debts on marriage.
Will Dated 20 Sep 1809, it left his entire estate to his wife who was named joint executor with the Duke of Portland. A codicil provided for his mother, who, however, in the natural course of events, predeceased him.

ANECDOTES

Canning once attended a church service, following which the clergyman asked his opinion of the sermon. Canning said, 'You were brief'.

'Yes', said the clergyman, 'you know I avoid being tedious'.

'But you *were* tedious', said Canning.

In 1826 Lord Liverpool complained to Mr. Arbuthnot: 'I have not the strength and nerves to bear Mr. Canning's perpetual notes. He sends me a dozen of them a day; every trifle, a remark from one of his secretaries, a pamphlet, a paragraph in a newspaper, is cause for his firing off a note; and I live in continual dread every time the door opens that it is to bring a note from Mr. Canning, till I am driven half distracted'. Mrs. Arbuthnot, who recorded the above conversation in her diary, added 'Mr. Pitt used to say that Mr. Canning was like a mistress, always affronted and always writing notes'.

In 1826 Canning sent Charles Bagot, Ambassador in the Netherlands, a despatch notifying him that an additional levy of 20 percent had been levied on Dutch vessels and goods. It was accompanied by another despatch in a cipher which Bagot did not possess. When Canning eventually supplied him wih a new cipher code Bagot and his second secretary sat up all night deciphering the despatch which read:

In matters of commerce the fault of the Dutch,
Is giving too little and asking too much;
With equal protection the French are content
So we'll lay on Dutch bottoms just 20 percent.
(chorus) 20 percent 20 percent
(chorus of English Customs House Officers)
We clap on Dutch bottoms just 20 percent
(chorus of French Douaniers)
Vous trapperez Falck avec 20 percent.

Bagot replied: 'You have fretted me to fiddlesticks, and I have a great mind not to give you the satisfaction of ever knowing how completely your mystification of me has succeeded'.

ANECDOTES—*Continued*

A contemporary recounted Wellington's memories of Canning: He thought him the finest speaker he had ever heard; though he prided himself extremely upon his compositions, he would patiently endure any criticisms upon such papers as he submitted for the consideration of the Cabinet; and would allow them to be altered in any way that was suggested . . . it was not so, however, in conversation and discussion. Any difference of opinion or dissent from his views threw him into an ungovernable rage, and on such occasions he flew out with a violence which, the Duke said, had often compelled him to be silent that he might not be involved in bitter personal altercation.

QUOTATIONS

1796, The happiness of constant occupation is infinite. (Letter to Lord Boringdon)

1802, Away with the cant of 'measures not men' the idle supposition that it is the harness and not the horses that draw the chariot along. No, Sir, if the comparison must be made, if the distinction must be taken, men are everything, measures comparatively nothing. (Speech in the Commons attacking the Addington ministry.)

1823, For 'alliance' read 'England' and you have the clue to my policy. (Letter to J. H. Frere)

1823, I am compelled to confess that, in the conduct of public affairs, the good object of my contemplation is the interest of England . . . intimately connected as we are with the system of Europe, it does not follow that we are therefore called upon to mix ourselves on every occasion, with a restless and meddling activity, in the concerns of the nations which surround us. (Speech at Plymouth)

1826, I consider it to be the duty of a British statesman in internal as well as external affairs, to hold a middle course between extremes; avoiding alike extravagancies of despotism or the licentiousness of unbridled freedom. (Speech in the Commons)

1826, Contemplating Spain, such as our ancestors had known her, I resolved that if France had Spain it should not be Spain with the Indies. I called the New World into existence to redress the balance of the Old. (Speech in the Commons)

RESIDENCES

2 Paper Buildings, Inner Temple
Charles Street, St. James's Square
37 Conduit Street, London
South Hill, nr. Bracknell, Bucks
24 Bruton Street, London
50 Berkeley Square, London (plaque)
Hinckley, Leicestershire
Gloucester Lodge, Old Brompton, Middlesex
A5 Albany, London
Long Sutton, Lincolnshire
10 Downing Street
100 Marine Parade, Brighton

MEMORIALS

STATUES AND BUSTS

1819, marble bust by Sir Francis Chantrey, Palace of Westminster; 1821, marble bust by Sir Francis Chantrey, National Portrait Gallery; 1867, by Richard Westmacott, north-west corner of Parliament Square, originally erected at the west end of New Palace Yard, Palace of Westminster on 2 May 1832; 1834, by Sir Francis Chantrey, Plateia Kanningos (Canning Square), Athens, Greece, to commemorate his service to Greek independence.

PORTRAITS

c. 1798, by John Hoppner, Provost's Lodge, Eton College, Berkshire; by Sir Thomas Lawrence, Christ Church College, Oxford; 1825, by Sir Thomas Lawrence, National Portrait Gallery; *c.* 1825, by Sir Thomas Lawrence (finished by Richard Evans), National Portrait Gallery; 1829, by C. Turner after Sir Thomas Lawrence, Palace of Westminster; by William Saye after Sir Thomas Lawrence, Palace of Westminster

OTHER MEMORIALS

Canning Passage and Place, Kensington, London, and Canning's Oak at Clivedon, Buckinghamshire, are named after him. He used to sit near the oak for hours looking at the view of the Thames. Four public houses are named after him in Fenton (Staffordshire), Hartbury (Gloucestershire), London SW2 and London SE5. The town of Canning, Arkansas, in the United States is named in his honour.

BIBLIOGRAPHIC INFORMATION

LETTERS AND PERSONAL PAPERS

The majority of Canning's papers are in Leeds Archive Department. Some remain in the possession of the Earl of Harewood. Other papers are in the William L. Clements Library, University of Michigan. A notebook relating to Spain and Greece is in the Public Record Office.

Published editions of letters and speeches: Stapleton, E. T. *Some Official Correspondence of George Canning*, 2 vols. London, 1887; Kaye, T. *Speeches of the Right Hon. George Canning Delivered on Public Occasions in Liverpool, with a Portrait of Mr. Canning.* London, 1825; Thierry, R. *The Speeches of the Right Honourable George Canning with a Memoir of His Life.* 6 vols. London, 1828.

PUBLICATIONS

1786, While at Eton he produced a weekly journal entitled *The Microcosm*; 1797–98, Various contributions to *The Anti-Jacobin* or *Weekly Examiner* including 'The friend of humanity and the knife-grinder', 'Mrs. Brownrigg the Prentice-cide', 'The Progress of Man', parts 2 and 3, 'The Song of Rogero' and 'New Morality'; 1802, 'The pilot that weathered the storm', poem to commemorate Pitt's birthday; 1809, 'Austrian State Papers', was one of various articles he contributed to *The Quarterly Review*; 1823, *The Poetical Works of the Rt. Hon. George Canning MP, Secretary of State for Foreign Affairs.*

FURTHER READING

Dixon, P. *Canning: Politician & Statesman*. London, 1976.
Gale, F. R. 'Mrs. Canning's Children' in *Notes & Queries*, vol. 157, 21 Sep 1929, p. 203.
Hill, F. H. *George Canning*. London, 1887.
Hinde, W. *George Canning*. London, 1989.
Marshall, D. *The Rise of George Canning*. London, 1938.
Petrie, C. *George Canning* 2nd ed. London, 1946.
Temperley, H.W.V. *Life of Canning*. London, 1905.

J.L.

Historical Pictures

Viscount Goderich

Lived 1782–1859

Political Party Tory 1806–1830; Whig 1830–1836; Conservative 1836–1859

Prime Minister 31 August 1827–8 January 1828

Government Tory/Whig Coalition

Reigning Monarch George IV

Foy est tout Faith is everything

GODERICH AS PRIME MINISTER

Goderich built up a sound reputation before becoming Prime Minister having been President of the Board of Trade and a mostly successful Chancellor of the Exchequer. He entered the House of Lords just a few weeks before taking up the Prime Ministership after over twenty years in the House of Commons. Goderich was not a firm leader of an Administration, doubtless the reason the King invited him to form one in the first place, and he found his Cabinet colleagues disloyal and lacking in rigour. His Chancellor of the Exchequer Herries and Secretary of War Huskisson in particular were a source of trouble and in Cabinet they failed to settle down to constructive work. It became clear that the qualities that had made him a satisfactory departmental minister were not adequate to run a fractious Cabinet. Even the one overseas success of his Prime Ministership, the winning of the battle of Navarino against the Turks and the Egyptians, drew confused Cabinet reaction, as sympathy for the Greeks was contradicted by fears of Russian moves against a defeated Turkey. Amidst this disarray Goderich resigned after only a few months in office, although some years later he returned to serve briefly in the Cabinet of Earl Grey.

PERSONAL INFORMATION

Names Frederick John Robinson
Peerages Viscount Goderich of Nocton 28 Apr 1827; Earl of Ripon 13 Apr 1833
Nicknames Prosperity Robinson; Goody (or Goosey) Goderich; The Blubberer
Born 30 Oct 1782
Religion Anglican
Ancestry English. An ancestor was knighted in 1633 and his son Metcalfe Robinson acquired an estate at Newby and was made a baronet in 1660. Goderich's grandfather was a diplomat and Cabinet minister and was created 1st Baron Grantham in Lincolnshire in 1761.
Date and place of marriage 1 Sep 1814, Lambeth, London
Age at marriage 31 years, 306 days
Years married 24 years, 149 days
First entered Parliament 13 Nov 1806
Date appointed PM 31 Aug 1827
Age at appointment 44 years, 305 days
Date ceased to be PM 8 Jan 1828
Total time as PM 130 days
Ceased to be MP 28 Apr 1827
Lived after last term as PM 31 years, 20 days
Date of death 28 Jan 1859
Place of death Putney Heath, London
Age at death 76 years, 90 days
Place of funeral and burial Nocton, Lincolnshire
Zodiac sign Scorpio

FATHER

Thomas Robinson, 2nd Baron Grantham
Date and place of birth 30 Nov 1738, Vienna, Austria
Occupation MP Christchurch 1761–70. He succeeded to the peerage in 1770. He became a junior Lord of Trade, Vice-Chamberlain of the Household, Ambassador to Spain, First Lord of Trade and Plantations and Foreign Secretary.
Date of marriage 17Aug 1780
Date of death 20 Jul 1786
Place of burial Chiswick, London

MOTHER

Lady Mary Jemina Grey Yorke
Date of birth 9 Feb 1757
Profile She was very patriotic but confessed she did not understand politics. She loved her garden and theatre. She was a painter and sketcher, especially of castles, as she was interested in architectural styles.
Date of marriage 17 Aug 1780
Age when PM took office 70 years, 203 days
Date of death 7 Jan 1830

BROTHERS AND SISTERS

Goderich was the second of three sons.
Thomas Philip (later Weddell, 3rd Baron Grantham), b. 8 Dec 1781; m. Henrietta Frances Cole, daughter of the Earl of Enniskillen; a landowner considered in 1845 to be one of the wealthiest men in Britain; d. 14 Nov 1859
Philip, b. Oct 1783, d. young

WIFE

Lady Sarah Albinia Louisa Hobart
Date of birth 22 Feb 1793
Mother Margaretta Adderley (née Bourke)
Father Robert Hobart, 4th Earl of Buckinghamshire
Father's occupation Served in the army; MP Portarlington 1784–90, Armagh 1790–97, Bramber 1788–90 and Lincoln 1790–96; Chief Secretary to the Lord Lieutentant for Ireland; Governor of Madras; Secretary of State for War and the Colonies; President of the Board of Control and Chancellor of the Duchy of Lancaster.
Age at marriage 21 years, 191 days
Number of children 3
Date and place of death 9 April 1867, Grantham House, Putney Heath, London
Place of burial Nocton, Lincolnshire
Years younger than PM 10, years 115 days
Profile She was insecure and neurotic with a morbid anxiety about her husband's safety. A notorious hypochondriac, she was obsessed with her health while her religious zeal led to her nickname of Bessy Holyoake. In later years she established an elementary school and rebuilt Nocton Church.

CHILDREN

2 sons, 1 daughter
Eleanor Henrietta Victoria, b. 22 May 1815; d. 31 Oct 1826
Hobart Frederick, b. Sep 1816; d. Sep 1816
George Frederick Samuel (Earl de Grey of Wrest, 4th Baron Grantham, 2nd Earl and 1st Marquess of Ripon), b. 24 Oct 1827; m. 8 Apr 1851, Henrietta Anne Theodosia Vyner; MP Hull 1852–53, Huddersfield 1853–57, West Riding of Yorkshire 1857–59; Under-Secretary of State for India 1861; Secretary of State for War 1863; Secretary of State for India 1866; Lord President of the Council 1868; Viceroy of India 1880–84; First Lord of the Admiralty 1886; Colonial Secretary 1892–95 and Lord Privy Seal 1905–08; d. 9 Jul 1909

LIFE AND CAREER

PARLIAMENTARY ELECTIONS FOUGHT

*(*designates candidate elected)*
DATE Oct 1806. General Election
CONSTITUENCY Carlow Borough
RESULT Frederick Robinson* (Tory)

DATE May 1807. General Election
CONSTITUENCY Ripon
RESULT Frederick Robinson* (Tory); George Gipps* (Tory)

DATE 30 Jun 1810. By-election caused by Goderich's appointment as one of the Lord Commissioners of the Admiralty
CONSTITUENCY Ripon
RESULT Frederick Robinson* (Tory)

DATE Oct 1812. General Election
CONSTITUENCY Ripon
RESULT Frederick Robinson* (Tory); George Gipps* (Tory)

PARLIAMENTARY ELECTIONS FOUGHT—*Continued*

DATE 12 Nov 1813. By-election caused by Goderich's appointment as Joint Paymaster General of the Land Forces
CONSTITUENCY Ripon
RESULT Frederick Robinson* (Tory)

DATE 3 Feb 1818. By-election caused by Goderich's appointment as Treasurer of the Navy
CONSTITUENCY Ripon
RESULT Frederick Robinson* (Tory)

DATE Jun 1818. General Election
CONSTITUENCY Ripon
RESULT Frederick Robinson* (Tory); George Gipps* (Tory)

DATE Mar 1820. General Election
CONSTITUENCY Ripon
RESULT Frederick Robinson* (Tory); George Gipps* (Tory)

DATE 11 Feb 1823. By-election caused by Goderich's appointment as Chancellor of the Exchequer
CONSTITUENCY Ripon
RESULT Frederick Robinson* (Tory)

DATE Jun 1826. General Election
CONSTITUENCY Ripon
RESULT Frederick Robinson* (Tory); Lancelot Shadwell* (Tory)

PARTY ACTIVITY

1807, Member of an election committee; 1809, Member of a committee investigating the Walcheren expedition; 1817, Member of a committee investigating the nature and causes of unrest in Britain; 1819, Member of the finance committee studying the currency situation; 1841, Member of a committee considering the revision of the Corn Laws.
Membership of group or faction Canningites; Stanleyites; Peelites

PARLIAMENTARY AND MINISTERIAL EXPERIENCE

Maiden Speech 11 Apr 1808. He spoke on the Reversion of Offices Bill about hereditary sinecures. (*Parl. Deb.* 1st series vol 11 col 24)
Privy Counsellor 13 Aug 1812
Ministerial Offices Under-Secretary of State for War and the Colonies 27 Apr–Sep 1809; A Lord of the Admiralty 12 Jun 1810–3 Oct 1812; Member of the Board of Trade 13 Aug–29 Sep 1812; Vice-President of the Board of Trade 29 Sep 1812–Jan 1818; A Lord of the Treasury 3 Oct 1812–Nov 1813; Joint Paymaster-General of the Land Forces 9 Nov 1813–Aug 1817; President of the Board of Trade 24 Jan 1818–Jan 1823, 3 Sep 1841–14 May 1843; Treasurer of the Navy 12 Feb 1818–Jan 1823; Chancellor of the Exchequer 12 Jan 1823–Apr 1827; Secretary of State for War and the Colonies 28 Apr–Aug 1827, 22 Nov 1830–2 Apr 1833; Commissioner for the Affairs of India 17 May–Aug 1827; Leader of the House of Lords Apr 1827–Jan 1828; First Lord of the Treasury 31 Aug 1827–21 Jan 1828; Lord Privy Seal 4 Apr 1833–4 Jun 1834; President of the Board of Control 17 May 1843–June 1846
Opposition Leader while PM Earl Grey (nominal)

GOVERNMENTS FORMED

Administration 31 Aug 1827–8 Jan 1828

GENERAL ELECTION RESULT
JUN 1826: Not analysed

CABINET
Prime Minister and First Lord of the Treasury Viscount Goderich
Chancellor of the Exchequer J. C. Herries
Lord President of the Council Duke of Portland
Lord Chancellor Lord Lyndhurst
Home Secretary Marquess of Lansdowne
Foreign Secretary Viscount Dudley and Ward
President of the Board of Trade C. Grant
Secretary of State for War and the Colonies W. Huskisson
President of the Board of Control C. W. Williams-Wynn
First Lord of the Admiralty Duke of Clarence
Lord Privy Seal Earl of Carlisle
Chancellor of the Duchy of Lancaster Lord Bexley
Master-General of the Ordnance Marquess of Anglesey
Treasurer of the Navy C. Grant
Secretary at War Viscount Palmerston
Master of the Mint G. Tierney
1st Commissioner of Woods and Forests W. Sturges Bourne

IMPORTANT DATES IN PERSONAL AND POLITICAL LIFE

EASTER 1802 He receives his MA at Cambridge and shortly afterwards enters Lincoln's Inn as a law student.
1804 Appointed private secretary to the 3rd Earl of Hardwicke, the Lord Lieutenant of Ireland. He holds the post until Hardwicke resigns in Mar 1806.
13 NOV 1806 Elected to Parliament for the first time as Member for Carlow Borough, Ireland.
9 MAY 1807 In the General Election he is elected as Member for Ripon, which he represents until 1827.
MAY 1807 Robinson accompanies Lord Pembroke to Vienna on a diplomatic mission.
11 APR 1808 He makes his maiden speech during a debate on hereditary sinecures.
19 JAN 1809 At the opening of the Parliamentary session he moves the Address, strongly supporting the war in Spain.
27 APR 1809 Castlereagh offers him a post as Under-Secretary of State in the War and Colonies Office which he accepts.
SEP 1809 He feels bound to give up his office when Castlereagh resigns. The following month the new Prime Minister Perceval offers him a post in the Treasury or Admiralty but he declines.
23 JUN 1810 Appointed a Lord of the Admiralty by his cousin Charles Yorke, the new First Lord of the Admiralty.
13 AUG 1812 Becomes a Privy Counsellor.
29 SEP 1812 Appointed Vice-President of the Board of Trade by Lord Liverpool.
3 OCT 1812 He leaves the Admiralty to take a seat on the Treasury board instead.
9 NOV 1813 Appointed joint Paymaster-General of the Land Forces having resigned his seat at the Treasury.
27 DEC 1813 He accompanies Castlereagh on a diplomatic mission around Europe which ends in negotiations for the Treaty of Paris following the Napoleonic Wars. He returns to London the following May.
1 SEP 1814 He marries Lady Sarah Hobart.

1 MAR 1815 At the Prime Minister's request, but with reluctance, he introduces the Corn Bill, a protectionist measure to prevent wheat being imported until the price rises above 80 shillings per quarter.

6 MAR 1815 A mob attacks his house in fury over the Corn Bill, but he and his wife had left for her father's house. The mob makes a second attack the following day, but are repulsed by soldiers inside the house. Two people are killed. The incident causes him to break down in tears when he makes a statement about it in the Commons which leads to him being nicknamed the 'Blubberer.'

MAY–JUN 1815 He attends various conferences with US representatives concerning trade, which lead to the Commercial Convention of 3 Jul 1815.

24 JAN 1818 He enters the Cabinet as President of the Board of Trade.

12 FEB 1818 Appointed Treasurer of the Navy in addition to his other post, which gives him a salary.

27 AUG 1818 He conducts further negotiations with the Americans over trade in the West Indies but they break down.

1 APR 1822 He introduces two Bills removing many restrictions on ships trading in the West Indies. They become law on 24 Jun 1822.

21 JAN 1823 He succeeds Nicholas Vansittart as Chancellor of the Exchequer.

21 FEB 1823 He brings in his first Budget. He has an estimated surplus of £7,147,214. £5,000,000 of this goes into the Sinking Fund to pay off part of the National Debt and the rest is used for tax reductions, including cutting the Window Tax by one half. His prediction of a coming period of prosperity earns him the nickname 'Prosperity Robinson.'

23 FEB 1824 He brings in his second Budget, reducing or abolishing many duties on foreign goods. Austria's repayment of part of a British loan results in a surplus, which he uses for grants to build new churches, restore Windsor Castle and found the National Gallery.

28 FEB 1825 He introduces his third Budget, cutting duties further and again reducing the House Tax and the Window Tax.

10 FEB 1826 Following a major commercial crisis in December 1825 he introduces the Promissory Notes Bill, preventing the issue of notes of a smaller value than £5. He is forced to compromise a week later and allows the Bank of England to continue to issue small notes until 10 Oct. The compromise considerably damages his reputation.

13 MAR 1826 In his fourth Budget presentation, he reviews principal alterations in taxation, and assures the House of Commons that the crisis is over.

4 MAY 1826 He defends his policies during a debate on a motion that an Address be made to the Crown calling for an inquiry on the causes of distress in the country.

31 OCT 1826 His daughter Henrietta dies, aged 11, after a painful illness. He is grief-stricken.

14 DEC 1826 He writes to Lord Liverpool requesting a move to the House of Lords. He also asks to be appointed to a less burdensome office due to anxiety over his wife's health. Liverpool refuses.

28 APR 1827 He is appointed Secretary of State for War and the Colonies and becomes Viscount Goderich of Nocton.

17 MAY 1827 He is appointed a Commissioner for the affairs of India and takes up duties as leader of the House of Lords.

8 AUG 1827 Following Canning's death the King sends for Goderich and asks him to take over as Prime Minister. The next day the King sends a letter setting out his views on the Government which include a ban on considering parliamentary reform or Catholic emancipation and a refusal to allow any more Whigs into the Cabinet. Goderich agrees to the King's demands but asks that Catholic emancipation be made an 'open question' as it had been in Canning's time. The King agrees to this but subsequently sends Goderich a list of 'suggestions' regarding the composition of the Cabinet.

17 AUG 1827 Treaty of amity and commerce with Brazil signed in Rio de Janeiro.

31 AUG 1827 Goderich kisses hands as Prime Minister.

3 SEP 1827 Goderich yields to pressure from the King and appoints Herries Chancellor of the Exchequer, to the disgust of the Whigs in the Cabinet. This weakens his standing with his colleagues.

28 SEP 1827 Following Turkish rejection of the proposed armistice in the Greek War of Independence laid down in the Treaty of London, Goderich summons the Cabinet to discuss the Greek situation. They decide to impose a limited blockade around Greece and to avoid open battle. After some delay these instructions are sent to Admiral Codrington, commander of the fleet in that area, but he does not receive them until 8 November. In the meantime Stratford Canning, ambassador to Constantinople, orders a total blockade of Greece, acting on his own initiative.

29 SEP 1827 Convention with US concerning boundaries signed in London.

20 OCT 1827 At Navarino Bay the British fleet meets the Turkish and Egyptian forces. A shot is fired and a full-scale battle ensues, during which the Turkish forces are destroyed.

NOV 1827 In a series of meetings the Cabinet are divided over how to respond to the Greek situation in the absence of any official Turkish reaction.

NOV 1827 A quarrel arises between Herries and Huskisson over the proposed appointment of Lord Althorp as chairman of a finance committee to be established after Parliament opens.

11 DEC 1827 Huskisson, Lansdowne and Goderich write to the King stressing the opposition to the Government from members of both parties and threatening resignation unless Lords Wellesley and Holland are admitted to the Cabinet and either the Duke of Wellington or Lord Hill is appointed Master-General of the Ordnance. The King rejects Holland (a Whig) and considers the letter Goderich's resignation.

17 DEC 1827 The King offers Lord Harrowby the Prime Ministership, which he refuses. On Harrowby's advice the King decides to retain Goderich for the time being and agrees to admit Lord Holland to the Cabinet.

19 DEC 1827 Following a meeting between the leading members of the Cabinet, Lyndhurst, Lansdowne, Dudley and Huskisson, the Cabinet pledge their support to Goderich as Prime Minister.

21 DEC 1827 Herries writes to Goderich concerning the dispute over the formation of the finance committee and threatens resignation.

29 DEC 1827 Huskisson, convinced of a plot against him, again offers his resignation. Subsequently, Lansdowne indicates that he would resign if Huskisson leaves the Government.

8 JAN 1828 Having failed to heal the divisions in his Cabinet, Goderich resigns as Prime Minister.

21 JAN 1828 Wellington becomes Prime Minister.

IMPORTANT DATES IN PERSONAL AND POLITICAL LIFE—*Continued*

22 NOV 1830 Goderich is appointed Secretary of State for War and the Colonies under Earl Grey's Whig administration.

27 MAR 1833 Under pressure from Lord Grey and other colleagues he reluctantly gives up the Colonial Office and accepts the post of Lord Privy Seal. He is duly sworn into office seven days later.

13 APR 1833 He is created Earl of Ripon.

25 JUN 1833 He introduces Lord Stanley's Bill to abolish slavery in the colonies in the House of Lords, breaking down several times, but succeeding in carrying various resolutions.

JAN 1834 He refuses to attend Cabinet meetings following Grey's repeated failure to give him a better post. Eventually Grey placates him by promising him another office in the future. However this never materialises.

27 MAY 1834 He resigns along with Stanley, Graham and the Duke of Richmond in opposition to Irish Church reform.

14 JUL 1834 A fire destroys Nocton Hall, his home in Lincolnshire. He lives at the Steward's house at Nocton and at his houses in Carlton Gardens and Putney Heath while the house is restored.

DEC 1836 He is reconciled with Peel and returns to the Conservative Party.

3 SEP 1841 Appointed President of the Board of Trade by Peel.

18 APR 1842 He moves the Second Reading of the Corn Importation Bill, fixing a new scale of duties.

5 JUL 1842 He explains the provisions of the Customs Bill, which revises the system of tariffs to abolish prohibitory duties, to the Lords.

17 MAY 1843 Appointed President of the Board of Control for India.

25 MAY 1846 He moves the Second Reading in the Lords of the Bill to abolish the Corn Laws and subsequently moves the Committee Stage and then the Third Reading.

JUN 1846 He resigns all his offices following the fall of Peel's Government.

14 MAY 1847 Makes his last speech in the Lords on Irish affairs.

28 JAN 1859 He dies at Putney Heath, having been ill for two months.

BACKGROUND

PHYSICAL CHARACTERISTICS AND HEALTH

Goderich had blue eyes, blonde hair and a fair complexion but was not regarded as handsome. He had a tendency to corpulence. When Chancellor of the Exchequer he was ill before his first budget, possibly through nerves. During the few months of his Prime Ministership his health appears to have deteriorated. He was described as exhausted and depressed in Dec 1827 and a Cabinet colleague thought he might collapse. However in May 1828 he was feeling well and, according to a contemporary, 'looked happier and fatter than when Prime Minister.' His health began to worsen again in the late 1830s and by 1843 he was so ill that Gladstone, as his deputy, was virtually running the Board of Trade for him. In his later years he was physically infirm and exhibited signs of senility. In his last illness his son reported that he was suffering from influenza.

EDUCATION

Primary Sunbury
Secondary 1796–99 Harrow
University 1799–1802 St. John's College, Cambridge
Prizes and awards 1801 Sir William Browne's medal for the best Latin ode
Qualifications 1802 MA
Cultural and vocational background He was unable to go on the Grand Tour due to the Napoleonic Wars. He was very scholarly and well-read. He was particularly interested in the ancient Greek and Roman civilisations and admired Coleridge. He was a devout Christian.

NON-PARLIAMENTARY CAREER

Early occupations He entered Lincoln's Inn 7 May 1802 but was never called to the Bar. He ceased to be a member of the Inn 6 November 1809. He acted as private secretary to the 3rd Earl of Hardwicke who was serving as Lord Lieutenant of Ireland 1803–06.
Military service Captain in Yorkshire Hussar Regiment of Yeomanry Cavalry 1803–14 (sinecure)
Other posts 1821 Justice of the Realm; 1824 Trustee of the National Gallery; 1827 Governor of the Charterhouse School, Surrey; 1830s Commissioner for Chelsea Hospital; 1830–33 President of the Royal Geographical Society; 1834–45 President of the Royal Society of Literature.

HONOURS

Academic 1839 DCL, Oxford University
Other than Peerage 17 Apr 1828, Fellow of the Royal Society

CLUBS

Alfred, White's

HOBBIES AND SPORTS

He wrote poetry. He seems to have inherited his mother's love of flowers and gardens but also enjoyed hunting and shooting.

FINANCES

As a younger son he was landless and practically penniless in his own right until his mother died in 1830. He was dependent on his mother, brother and wife and his income from various governmental positions. When his father-in-law died in 1816 his wife's inheritance brought financial security.

Income He was paid £1,000 p.a. as a Lord of the Admiralty, £2,000 p.a. as Joint Paymaster-General of the Forces, and approximately £5,300 p.a. (plus fees of *c.* £800) as Chancellor of the Exchequer.
Spouse's finances His wife was the sole heiress of her father and inherited all his unentailed estates when he died in 1816.
Pensions He was described as being 'too rich' to compete for a pension in 1825.

Legacies He received Grantham House and £50,000 from his mother when she died in 1830. He received a share of the Ripon properties left to him and his brother by Miss Lawrence (a distant relative) in 1845.

Will His will was signed in 1850, with a codicil added in 1856. His property was divided between his wife and his son. There were several minor legacies to his servants, including his dead daughter's old nurse. The codicil provided for the maintenance of the children of a dead servant.

ANECDOTES

1814, While at Chaumont, France, on a diplomatic mission with Castlereagh, Goderich rummaged through the papers on his desk 'like a general going through important dispatches.' His colleagues nicknamed him the 'Grand Duke of Phussandbussle' and left a letter to him on his desk using this nickname. Thereafter, Robinson often called himself the 'Grand Duke.'

1826, John Wilson Croker MP, fellow member of the Alfred Club, wrote: 'Everyone knows the story of a gentleman's asking Lord North who "that frightful woman was!" and his lordship's answering "that is my wife". The other, to repair the blunder, said "I do not mean her, but that monster next to her." "Oh" said Lord North, "that monster is my daughter." With this story Fred Robinson, in his usual absent enthusiastic way, was one day entertaining a lady whom he sat next to at dinner, and lo! the lady was Lady Charlotte Lindsay—the monster in question.

Robinson once sat next to Lord Lyndhurst in Chancery Court listening to two lawyers arguing their cases. As he left he whispered to Lord Lyndhurst: "well I don't know how the case may be decided; but in my opinion, Mr. Hart has so completely answered Mr. Bell that he has not a leg to stand on." Lyndhurst replied "I am sorry I cannot agree with you, for they are both on the same side."'

QUOTATIONS

1 Mar 1813, I cannot forget that the principle of our constitution is jealousy. It is jealous of the Crown, jealous of the aristocracy, jealous of the democracy, and the Roman Catholics have no right to complain, if it is jealous of them. (Speech in the Commons during debate on Catholic emancipation)

4 Oct 1841, The science of Government whether legislative or executive, was, in fact, neither more nor less than a perpetually recurring struggle with difficulties. (Speech in the Lords)

7 Feb 1843, There was no one good in this life that had not with it some concomitant evil. (Speech in the Lords on the ill-effects of the introduction of machinery)

RESIDENCES

Charles Street, St. James's Square, London
Old Burlington Street, London
Nocton Hall, Sleaford, Lincolnshire
Somerset House, Strand, London
Blackheath, Kent
10 Downing Street
Pembroke House, Whitehall
1 Eastern Terrace, Brighton
1 Carlton Gardens, London
Grantham House, Putney Heath, Surrey

MEMORIALS

PORTRAITS

c. 1823, by Sir Thomas Lawrence, National Portrait Gallery

BIBLIOGRAPHIC INFORMATION

LETTERS AND PERSONAL PAPERS

His correspondence with George IV and Cabinet colleagues 1826–35 is in Buckinghamshire Record Office, Aylesbury. Most of his other surviving papers are in the British Library.

PUBLICATIONS

1810. *A Sketch of the Campaign in Portugal.*

FURTHER READING

Jones, W. D. *'Prosperity' Robinson: the Life of Viscount Goderich 1782–1859.* London, 1967.

J.L.

Bettmann

Duke of Wellington

Lived 1769–1852

Political Party Tory

Prime Minister 22 January 1828–16 November 1830; 17 November 1834–9 December 1834

Governments Tory

Reigning Monarchs George IV; William IV

Virtutis fortuna comes Fortune is the companion of valour

WELLINGTON AS PRIME MINISTER

Until the age of fifty Wellington led an enormously successful soldier's life although he also had varied House of Commons, ministerial, and diplomatic experience. He was already a household name when appointed Prime Minister after Goderich's resignation. His was not the world of party politics: conservative in temperament and highly principled, he sought to return government to the stable days of Liverpool. The election of O'Connell as MP for Clare in Ireland in 1828, hastened his inclusion of Catholic emancipation in the 1829 King's speech, a significant achievement. However problems, including a bad winter in 1829–30, unemployment and economic difficulties, and the King's death resulted in national tension and loss of support for the Tories. The General Election of 1830 suggested growing support for reform, but Wellington spoke uncompromisingly against it, was defeated in the House of Commons, and resigned. He held office again for a few days in 1834 and was frequently a member of the Cabinet in the 1830s and 1840s. His resignation as Prime Minister after nearly three years seemed to have been a willing one, as he left a post he realised did not suit him.

PERSONAL INFORMATION

Names Arthur Wellesley (Wesley until 1798)
Peerages Baron Douro of Wellesley, 4 Sep 1809; Viscount Wellington of Talavera and of Wellington, 4 Sep 1809; Earl of Wellington, 28 Feb 1812; Marquess of Wellington, 3 Oct 1812; Marquess of Douro and Duke of Wellington, 11 May 1814
Nicknames The Iron Duke; Conkey; (Old) Nosey; The Great Captain; The Achilles of England; Europe's Liberator; Saviour of the Nations; The Best of Cut-throats; The Beau; Old Hookey; Douro; The Peer; Arty; The Eagle
Born 1 May 1769
Birthplace 6, Merrion St., Dublin
Religion Anglican
Ancestry Anglo-Irish. His family, originally English, was granted land in Ireland by Henry VIII. Their name was Colley. His grandfather, a member of the Irish Parliament, was adopted by his uncle Garrett Wesley, took his name, and inherited the Wesley estates in County Meath including Dangan Castle. The Wesleys were wealthier than the Colleys and claimed their ancestor came over as a standard-bearer to Henry II.
Date and place of marriage 10 Apr 1806, the Longford's town house in Rutland Square, Dublin
Age at marriage 36 years, 344 days
Years married 15 years, 14 days
First entered Parliament 30 Apr 1790 (Irish Parliament); 1 Apr 1806 (British Parliament)
Dates appointed PM 1) 22 Jan 1828; 2) 17 Nov 1834
Age at appointments 1) 58 years, 266 days; 2) 65 years, 200 days
Dates ceased to be PM 1) 16 Nov 1830; 2) 9 Dec 1834
Total time as PM 1) 2 years, 298 days; 2) 22 days; a total of 2 years, 320 days
Ceased to be MP 4 Sep 1809
Lived after last term as PM 17 years, 280 days
Date of death 14 Sep 1852
Place of death Walmer Castle, Walmer, Kent
Age at death 83 years, 136 days
Last words Yes, if you please (when asked if he would like some tea)
Place of funeral and burial St. Paul's Cathedral, London
Zodiac sign Taurus

FATHER

Garrett Wesley (or Wellesley), 2nd Baron and 1st Earl of Mornington, 1st Viscount Wellesley of Dangan
Date and place of birth 19 Jul 1735, Dangan Castle, near Dublin
Occupation MP Trim (in the Irish Parliament), 1757–58. He was a composer and musician, president and conductor of a musical academy in Dublin and Professor at Trinity College, Dublin
Date of marriage 6 Feb 1759
Date of death 22 May 1781
Place of burial Grosvenor Chapel, South Audley St., London

MOTHER

Anne Hill
Date of birth 23 Jun 1742
Profile Contemporaries considered that she lacked judgement and finish. She occupied herself making shell flowers.
Date of marriage 6 Feb 1759
Age when PM took office 85 years, 191 days
Date of death 10 Sep 1831
Place of burial Grosvenor Chapel, South Audley St., London

BROTHERS AND SISTERS

Wellington was the fifth son and sixth of nine children.
Richard (1st Baron Wellesley, 2nd Earl of Mornington, 1st Marquess Wellesley), b. 20 Jun 1760; m. 1) Hyacinthe Roland; 2) Marianne Paterson; MP Trim 1780–81, Beeralston 1784–86, Saltash 1786–87, Windsor 1787–96, Old Sarum 1796–97; Governor General of India; Ambassador to Spain; Foreign Secretary; Lord Lieutenant of Ireland; d. 26 Sep 1842
Arthur, d. young
William, (later Wellesley-Pole, 1st Baron Maryborough, 3rd Earl of Mornington), b. 20 May 1763; m. Katherine Elizabeth Forbes; MP Trim, East Looe, 1790–94, Queen's County, 1801–21; Clerk of the Ordnance; Secretary to the Admiralty; Chief Secretary for Ireland; Master of the Mint; Postmaster General; d. 22 Feb 1845
Francis, d. young
Anne, b. 1768; m. 1) Hon. Henry Fitzroy, 2) Culling Charles Smith; d. 16 Dec 1844
Gerald Valerian, b. 7 Dec 1770; m. Emily Mary Cadogan; Rector of Stratfield Saye and of Chelsea; Chaplain to the Royal Household, Prebendary of Durham and Dean of Windsor; d. 24 Oct 1848
Mary, b. 1772; d. 1794
Henry (1st Baron Cowley), b. 20 Jan 1773; m. 1) Lady Charlotte Cadogan (div.); 2) Lady Georgiana Cecil; Ambassador to Spain, Vienna and Paris; MP Trim 1795, Eye 1807–09; Secretary to the Treasury; d. 27 Apr 1847

WIFE

Hon. Catherine Sarah Dorothea Pakenham
Date and place of birth Jan 1772, Pakenham Hall (now Tullynally Castle)
Mother Catherine Rowley
Father Edward Michael Pakenham, 2nd Baron Longford
Father's occupation Irish landowner; MP County Longford, 1765–66; a Post-Captain in the Royal Navy.
Age at marriage 34 years
Number of children 2
Date and place of death 24 Apr 1831, Apsley House, 149 Piccadilly, London
Place of burial Stratfield Saye, Hampshire
Years younger than PM *c.* 3 years
Profile She was very bookish. When young she was full of gaiety and charm. She later became over-emotional, melancholy and depressed, self-critical, anxious and opinionated. She was frail and often tired. She was an inept household manager. Tender-hearted and easily moved by 'hard luck' stories she gave away a lot of money indiscriminately. She hero-worshipped Wellington and gushed over him. After the Battle of Salamanca when the captured French eagles [standards] were brought to her she embraced them screaming, 'They are mine, they are mine' and fainted away. A contemporary described her as amiable, unaffected and simple-minded. She was shy, dressed badly and was very short-sighted.

CHILDREN

2 sons

CHILDREN—*Continued*

Arthur Richard (2nd Duke of Wellington), b. 3 Feb 1807; m. 18 Apr 1839, Lady Elizabeth Hay; MP Aldborough 1830–31, Norwich 1837–52; Lieutenant-General in the army; Lord-Lieutenant of Middlesex and Master of the Horse, 1853–58. d. 13 Aug 1884

Lord Charles Wellesley, b. 16 Jan 1808; m. 9 Jul 1844, Hon. Augusta Sophia Anne Pierrepont; MP South Hampshire 1847, Windsor 1852; Major-General in the army; Chief Equerry and Clerk Marshall to Queen Victoria; d. 9 Oct 1858

LIFE AND CAREER

PARLIAMENTARY ELECTIONS FOUGHT

*(*designates candidate elected)*

DATE Apr 1790. General Election (Irish Parliament)
CONSTITUENCY Trim
RESULT Hon. Arthur Wesley* (Tory)

DATE 1 Apr 1806. By-election caused by resignation of Thomas Lamb
CONSTITUENCY Rye
RESULT Sir Arthur Wellesley* (Tory)

DATE 15 Jan 1807. By-election caused by the resignation of Sir Christopher Hawkins
CONSTITUENCY Mitchell
RESULT Sir Arthur Wellesley* (Tory)

DATE 21 Apr 1807. By-election caused by Wellington's appointment as Chief Secretary for Ireland
CONSTITUENCY Mitchell
RESULT Sir Arthur Wellesley* (Tory)

DATE May 1807. General Election
CONSTITUENCY Newport, Isle of Wight
RESULT Henry John Temple, Viscount Palmerston* (Tory); Sir Arthur Wellesley** (Tory)

DATE May 1807. General Election
CONSTITUENCY Tralee
RESULT Sir Arthur Wellesley* (Tory)

***Elected both for Newport and Tralee, he chose to sit for Newport*

PARTY ACTIVITY

Party Leadership Leader of the Conservative Party in the Lords, Jan 1828–Jul 1846.

PARLIAMENTARY AND MINISTERIAL EXPERIENCE

Maiden Speech 1) In Irish Parliament, 10 Jan 1793. He seconded the Address to the Throne (*Parl. Reg., Ireland* 4th S. 5th P., Geo. III, v. 13, p. 5); 2) In British Parliament, 22 Apr 1806. He defended his brother's Indian administration against an attack by James Paull, MP. (*Parl Deb.*, 1st ser, vol 6, col 863-864)

Opposition offices Leader of the Opposition in the Lords, 1835–41

Privy Counsellor 8 Apr 1807

Ministerial Offices Chief Secretary for Ireland 3 Apr 1807–Apr 1809; Master-General of the Ordnance 1 Jan 1819–Apr 1827; First Lord of the Treasury 22 Jan 1828–16 Nov 1830, 17 Nov -9 Dec 1834; Leader of the House of Lords 22 Jan 1828–16 Nov 1830, 17 Nov 1834–Apr 1835, 3 Sep 1841–Jul 1846; Foreign Secretary 17 Nov 1834–Apr 1835; Minister without Portfolio 3 Sep 1841–Jun 1846

Opposition Leader while PM Earl Grey

GOVERNMENTS FORMED

First Administration 22 Jan 1828–16 Nov 1830

GENERAL ELECTION RESULT
JUN 1826: Not analysed

CABINET

Prime Minister and First Lord of the Treasury Duke of Wellington
Chancellor of the Exchequer H. Goulburn
Lord President of the Council Earl of Bathurst
Lord Chancellor Lord Lyndhurst
Home Secretary R. Peel
Foreign Secretary Earl of Dudley (Apr 1827–Jun 1828); Earl of Aberdeen (Jun 1828–Nov 1830)
President of the Board of Trade C. Grant (Sep 1827–Jun 1828); W. V. Fitzgerald (Jun 1828–Feb 1830); J. C. Herries (Feb–Nov 1830)
Secretary of State for War and the Colonies W. Huskisson (Sep 1827–May 1828); Sir G. Murray (May 1828–Nov 1830)
President of the Board of Control G. W. Williams Wynn (Feb 1822–Jul 1828); Viscount Melville (Jul–Sep 1828); Lord Ellenborough (Sep 1828–Nov 1830)
First Lord of the Admiralty Duke of Clarence (Apr 1827–Sep 1828); Viscount Melville (Sep 1828–Nov 1830)
Lord Privy Seal Lord Ellenborough (Jan 1828–Jun 1829); Earl of Rosslyn (Jun 1829–Nov 1830)
Chancellor of the Duchy of Lancaster Earl of Aberdeen (Jan–Jun 1828); C. Arbuthnot (Jun 1828–Nov 1830)
Master-General of the Ordnance Marquess of Anglesey (Apr 1827–Apr 1828); Viscount Beresford (Apr 1828–Nov 1830)
Treasurer of the Navy W. Fitzgerald
Secretary at War Viscount Palmerston (Jan–May 1828); H. Hardinge (May 1828–Nov 1830)
Master of the Mint J. C. Herries

Second Administration 17 Nov–9 Dec 1834

GENERAL ELECTION RESULT
DEC 1832: Liberal 479; Conservative 179. Total 658 Majority 300

CABINET

Prime Minister, First Lord of the Treasury, and Foreign Secretary Duke of Wellington
Lord Chancellor Lord Lyndhurst
No others were appointed.

IMPORTANT DATES IN PERSONAL AND POLITICAL LIFE

7 MAR 1787 Wellington enters the army as an Ensign in the 73rd Foot.

25 DEC 1787 He becomes a Lieutenant in the 76th Foot. The following month he is transferred to the 41st in Dublin and later to the 12th Light Dragoons. On arrival in Dublin he also takes up the post of aide-de-camp to

the Marquess of Buckingham, the Lord-Lieutenant of Ireland, retaining the post until March 1793.

30 APR 1790 He is elected to the Irish Parliament as Member for Trim despite being under age. He represents the constituency until 1797.

30 JUN 1791 He is promoted to Captain in the 58th Foot. Subsequently he transfers to the 18th Light Dragoons.

30 APR 1793 He is promoted to Major of the 33rd Foot. He had purchased his promotion with a loan from his brother. In September he is promoted again to the rank of Lieutenant-Colonel.

JUN 1794–APR 1795 He sees active service for the first time when his regiment is posted to the Netherlands in an attempt to defend the Low Countries against the French. The expedition fails and the troops are withdrawn when the French overrun the Netherlands but Wellington has learned a lot about military tactics.

3 MAY 1796 He is promoted to Colonel and shortly afterwards sails for India to join his regiment.

MAR–MAY 1799 He fights in the 4th Mysore War against the local Muslim ruler Tippoo Sultan. This climaxes with the assault on and fall of Seringapatam at which Tippoo is killed. Following the war Wellington is appointed Governor of Seringapatam. The following year he defeats the remains of Tippoo's army under Dhoondiah Waugh.

29 APR 1802 He is promoted to Major General.

AUG–DEC 1803 He fights in the 2nd Mahratta War against Scindiah of Gwalior, a local chief, winning victories at Assaye and Argaum before taking the garrison of Gawilghur, which victory heralds the end of the war.

1 SEP 1804 He is created a Knight of the Bath for his services in India.

10 SEP 1805 On his return to London he reports to the Foreign Secretary, Castlereagh. In Castlereagh's ante-room he meets Lord Nelson for the first and only time. Nelson is to die commanding the fleet at the Battle of Trafalgar a month later.

30 JAN 1806 He is appointed Colonel of the 33rd Regiment.

1 APR 1806 He is elected as MP for Rye.

10 APR 1806 He marries Catherine Pakenham in Dublin.

22 APR 1806 He makes his maiden speech defending his brother's policy as Governor-General of India against an attack by James Paull, MP.

15 JAN 1807 He is elected MP for Mitchell, Cornwall.

3 APR 1807 He is appointed Chief Secretary for Ireland.

MAY 1807 He is elected MP for Newport, Isle of Wight, and for Tralee, County Kerry. He opts to serve for Newport.

31 JUL–30 SEP 1807 He is sent on the Copenhagen Expedition to capture the Danish fleet, which Napoleon has threatened to take over and use against the British. After a short and successful campaign, Copenhagen surrenders. Wellington receives the formal thanks of Parliament.

OCT 1807 The French declare war on Portugal. The Peninsular War is underway.

MAY 1808 Following the French occupation of Spain, Madrid revolts against the French army. The following month the Portuguese also begin a revolt. Spanish and Portuguese delegations arrive in London asking for assistance. An expeditionary force is sent out under the temporary command of Wellington. It begins landing at Mondego Bay in Portugal on August 1.

17 AUG 1808 Wellington defeats the French at the Battle of Rolica and three days later defeats them again at Vimeiro. However, Lieutenant General Sir Harry Burrard, (who has assumed command of the expeditionary force) forbids Wellington to capitalise on his success by marching on Lisbon, much to Wellington's disgust. Instead Wellington is obliged to sign the armistice, known as the Convention of Cintra, which gives generous terms to the defeated French army.

OCT 1808 Wellington returns home, leaving Sir John Moore in command of the army. He is blamed by many for signing the deeply unpopular Convention of Cintra and is examined by the military inquiry set up to inquire into the Convention. The inquiry approves the Convention. Wellington is exonerated.

16 JAN 1809 The British troops, who had retreated to Corunna when Napoleon entered Madrid in December, beat off the French at the Battle of Corunna and are successfully evacuated, but Sir John Moore is killed.

22 APR 1809 Wellington, assuming command after Moore's death (resigning as Chief Secretary for Ireland), lands with the British army at Lisbon and proceeds to drive the French Marshal Soult out of Oporto. The French army retreats into Spain.

28 JULY 1809 Wellington and his troops, having crossed into Spain, defeat the French at the Battle of Talavera. As a reward he is created Baron Douro of Wellesley and Viscount Wellington of Talavera.

13 AUG 1809 Wellington is obliged to retreat into Portugal as his army is facing starvation and disease. During the autumn he gives orders for the building of earthworks to defend Lisbon. These become known as the Lines of Torres Vedras.

10 JUL 1810 The French take the fortress at Ciudad Rodrigo after a short siege and invade Portugal. They subsequently besiege and take Almeida.

27 SEP 1810 Wellington defeats Marshal Massena at Bussaco and then retreats behind the Lines of Torres Vedras for the autumn and winter. Massena is unable to breach the lines and eventually retreats into Spain.

3–5 MAY 1811 Wellington, having pursued Massena from Portugal, defeats a relieving French army at Fuentes de Onoro and then takes Almeida.

31 JUL 1811 He is made a General (with local rank only).

19 JAN 1812 He captures Ciudad Rodrigo after a siege. In March and April he besieges and captures Badajoz but at heavy cost. He weeps when he hears the number of casualties.

28 FEB 1812 He is created an Earl.

22 JUL 1812 Wellington routs the French under Marmont at the Battle of Salamanca and enters Madrid the following month. For his reward he is created a Marquess in Britain, Generalissimo of the Spanish Armies, and a Member of the Order of the Golden Fleece in Spain.

19 SEP 1812 He begins to besiege Burgos but the siege fails the following month and he is forced to retreat into Portugal for the winter.

21 JUN 1813 Having advanced again from Portugal Wellington defeats the French at Vittoria and proceeds to drive Soult and his army across the Pyrenees. Following Vittoria, he is made a Field Marshal.

10 NOV 1813 Having crossed the border into France Wellington defeats Soult at Nivelle, at Nive in December and again at Orthez the following February.

31 MAR 1814 The Allies enter Paris. Wellington, however, does not hear the news until after the Battle of Toulouse.

6 APR 1814 Napoleon abdicates at Fontainebleau. Wellington does not hear the news for another six days.

IMPORTANT DATES IN PERSONAL AND POLITICAL LIFE—*Continued*

10 APR 1814 In the final battle of the Peninsular War Wellington narrowly defeats Soult's troops at the Battle of Toulouse.

3 MAY 1814 He is created Duke of Wellington.

24 MAY–8 JUN 1814 Castlereagh sends him on a diplomatic mission to Madrid to try to persuade the reactionary government in Spain to follow a more liberal course.

23 JUN 1814 He returns to Britain to a hero's welcome and is voted £400,000 by Parliament.

28 JUN 1814 Wellington takes his seat in the House of Lords.

22 AUG 1814 He takes up residence in Paris as Ambassador to France.

FEB–MAR 1815 He represents Britain at the Congress of Vienna. The Congress hears on 7 March that Napoleon has escaped from the island of Elba and returned to France. The Treaty of Chaumont (the alliance of Austria, Britain, Prussia and Russia against Napoleon) is renewed and Wellington is appointed Commander-in-Chief of the allied armies, setting out for Brussels to take charge.

16 JUN 1815 The French army under Marshal Ney attacks Wellington's troops at Quatre Bras while troops under Napoleon attack the Prussian army under the command of Marshal Blucher at Ligny. The allies are able to hold their ground against the French.

18 JUN 1815 Wellington's armies defeat the French at the Battle of Waterloo.

7 JUL 1815 Allied troops enter Paris. Wellington remains in command of the army of occupation until November 1818. During that time he is appointed Allied Referee on French reparations and attends the Congress of Aix-la-Chappelle.

1 JAN 1819 On his return to Britain he is appointed Master-General of the Ordnance and enters the Cabinet.

OCT–NOV 1822 He is the British representative at the Congress of Verona.

FEB–MAY 1826 He is sent on a mission to Russia to negotiate with the new Tsar to try and prevent war between Russia and the Ottoman Empire against Greece.

22 JAN 1827 He accepts the post of Commander-in-Chief of the army following the death of the Duke of York. In April, following Lord Liverpool's stroke, Canning, rather than Wellington, is asked by the King to form an administration and sends Wellington a letter (which Wellington regards as insulting in tone) informing him of this fact. Wellington, feeling he is being snubbed by Canning and the King, resigns but is re-appointed Commander-in-Chief after Canning dies in August and Goderich becomes Prime Minister.

22 JAN 1828 He kisses hands as Prime Minister following Goderich's resignation.

14 FEB 1828 He is obliged to resign the post of Commander-in-Chief when people protest his holding that position at the same time as that of Prime Minister.

26 FEB 1828 The Government is defeated in the Commons when the House votes in favour of repealing the Corporation and Test Acts—which demand that all members of corporations be Anglicans. As a result the Government itself repeals the Acts—the first stage of Catholic emancipation.

31 MAR 1828 Charles Grant, President of the Board of Trade, introduces the Corn Bill proposing a sliding scale of duties on imports of foreign corn. Despite fierce opposition from some members of the Commons and Lords, it eventually passes without amendment on 26 Jun.

19 MAY 1828 Huskisson, despite being in the Cabinet, refuses to vote with the Government on a Bill to redistribute a disenfranchised seat. He offers his resignation the next day, and it is accepted. Subsequently Wellington gets rid of the other Canningites in the Cabinet.

5 JUL 1828 At a by-election in County Clare, Ireland, Daniel O'Connell is elected an MP. As a Catholic he is not able to take up his seat, but his election raises again the question of Catholic emancipation. The threat of rebellion in Ireland causes Wellington to broach the subject of Catholic emancipation with the King.

5 MAR 1829 The Catholic Emancipation Bill is introduced in the Commons. It passes both Houses with Opposition support and receives Royal Assent on 13 April 1829.

21 MAR 1829 Wellington fights a duel with Lord Winchilsea who has savagely attacked him over Catholic emancipation. The combatants deliberately miss each other in firing and honour is satisfied.

26 JUN 1830 Wellington is confirmed as Prime Minister on the accession of the new King, William IV.

2 NOV 1830 In response to an attack by Grey in the Lords, Wellington defiantly and totally rejects any idea of further parliamentary reform, causing an uproar in and out of Parliament and seriously weakening the Government. Wellington is forced to issue orders for the defence of Apsley House against feared mob attacks. In fact, his house is not stoned at this time, but in Apr 1831 and again in Oct 1831.

16 NOV 1830 Wellington's Government resigns after being defeated in the Commons on a motion relating to the Civil List, forestalling a debate on an Opposition motion concerning parliamentary reform.

24 APR 1831 Wellington's wife dies.

7 MAY 1832 The third Reform Bill, introduced by Lord Grey, the new Prime Minister, is defeated by the Lords in Committee. The next day Grey demands that more peers be created in order to pass the Bill. When the King refuses, Grey resigns and the King asks Wellington to form a Government and bring in an alternative reform measure.

17 MAY 1832 Grey's Government resumes. Wellington, having failed to stop Grey's Reform Bill due to his inability to form an alternative ministry, reluctantly agrees with the King to make enough peers abstain from voting to let the Bill through. It receives Royal Assent on 7 Jun 1832. Wellington is afterwards surrounded by an angry mob while riding around London and has to be escorted by the police.

17 NOV 1834 Lord Melbourne's Government having fallen, the King sends for Wellington and asks him to form a Government. Wellington recommends that the King send for Peel, who is in Rome, but agrees to act as a 'caretaker' Prime Minister until Peel returns. He is appointed First Lord of the Treasury and Secretary of State.

10 DEC 1834 Peel becomes Prime Minister on his return from Rome and Wellington remains in the Cabinet as Foreign Secretary.

7 APR 1835 Wellington is out of office on the fall of Peel's Government. He is Leader of the Opposition in the Lords for the next 6 years.

3 SEP 1841 When Peel becomes Prime Minister for the second time Wellington is appointed Cabinet Minister without Portfolio, remaining so until Peel's Government falls in June 1846.

15 SEP 1842 He is appointed Commander-in-Chief of the army again and holds the office until his death.

28 MAY 1846 Out of loyalty to Peel he persuades the Lords to support the Bill repealing the Corn Laws, although he disapproves of it.

14 SEP 1852 He dies suddenly at Walmer Castle and lies in state at Walmer until 10 Nov, and then in Chelsea Hospital until 17 Nov.

BACKGROUND

PHYSICAL CHARACTERISTICS AND HEALTH

Wellington had an enormous aquiline nose, which led to many nicknames, and penetrating blue eyes. When young he wore his naturally curly hair short and never used powder. He was always neat and particular in his dress. He was 5'9" tall, and slim. As he grew older he became very thin and stooped.

Wellington experienced bad health as a child and as a young man. In India he suffered from fevers and Malabar itch (a form of ringworm). He was subject to attacks of rheumatism and lumbago from 1804 onwards. He was singularly lucky in avoiding serious injury during his military career.

Increasing deafness in 1822 led him to a quack doctor, who syringed his ear with caustic, causing intense inflammation and nearly killing him. Thereafter he was permanently deaf in one ear and was stricken by fits of dizziness or fainting. He had always said that health was a function of will power but after this episode he was subject to severe attacks of illness for several years.

He had several seizures (apparently minor strokes) in the late 1830s and 1840s. On 14 Sep 1852 he suffered a series of seizures and died shortly afterwards.

EDUCATION

Primary Diocesan School, Trim, County Meath, Ireland; Brown's Seminary, King's Road, Chelsea

Secondary 1781–84, Eton; 1784–85, tutored privately by the Rev. Henry Michell in Brighton; 1785, tutored privately in Brussels

Professional 1786, Royal Academy of Equitation, Angers, Anjou, France

Cultural and vocational background Wellington had a musical upbringing, listening to his father and playing the violin.

Languages Wellington learned French while at Brussels and Angers.

NON-PARLIAMENTARY CAREER

Early occupations He was land agent for his brother's Dangan estates in the early 1790s.

Military service He entered the army as an Ensign in the 73rd Highland Regiment on 7 Mar 1787, and was shortly afterwards appointed aide-de-camp to the Lord-Lieutenant of Ireland, a post he held until 1793. He was created a Lieutenant in the 76th Regiment on 25 Dec 1787 and transferred to the 41st Regiment the following month. He was stationed in Ireland until 1794, during which time he was promoted to Captain in the 38th Foot (30 June 1791), transferred to the 18th Light Dragoons and then promoted to Major in the 33rd Foot (30 Apr 1793) and finally to Lieutenant-Colonel (30 Sep 1793). He commanded a brigade in Flanders during the defence of the Low Countries from Jun 1794–Apr 1795. On 3 May 1796 he was promoted to Colonel and in Jun 1796 he sailed for India where he was stationed for the next eight years. During that time he fought successfully in the 4th Mysore War (Mar–May 1799) and the 2nd Mahratta War (Aug–Dec 1803). He was promoted to Major-General on 29 Apr 1802. In Dec 1805 he commanded a brigade on the Elbe but without fighting, returning home in Feb 1806 having been appointed Colonel of the 33rd Regiment on 30 Jan 1806. In February 1806 he was posted to Hastings. He went on the Copenhagen Expedition (Jul–Sep 1807) to capture the Danish fleet. He was promoted to Lieutenant-General on 25 Apr 1808. When the Peninsular War broke out he was placed in temporary command of the expeditionary force to Portugal (12 Jul 1808) but was superseded after the Battle of Vimeiro (21 Aug 1808) and was recalled to Britain. In Apr 1809 he was sent back to Portugal where he successfully commanded the army during the remainder of the Peninsular War until Apr 1814, winning many notable battles. He was created Marshal General of the Portuguese Army on 6 Jul 1809, a General (with local rank only) on 3 Jul 1811, Generalissimo of the Spanish Armies (22 Sep 1812), Colonel of the Royal Regiment of Horse Guards (1 Jan 1813) and Field Marshal (21 Jun 1813). In Mar 1815 he was appointed Commander of the Allied Armies for the renewed campaign against Napoleon and won the Battle of Waterloo on 18 Jun 1815. He was Commander-in-Chief of the Army of Occupation from Oct 1815 to Nov 1818, and Commander-in-Chief of the British Army from Jan to Apr 1827, Aug 1827 to Feb 1828, and from Aug 1842 until his death. He was also Colonel of the Grenadier Guards and Colonel-in-Chief of the Rifle Brigade.

Other posts 1799–1800, Governor of Seringapatam; 1814, Diplomatic mission to Madrid; 1814–15, Ambassador to France; 1815, First Plenipotentiary to the Congress of Vienna; 1817, Allied Referee on French reparations; 1818, Joint Plenipotentiary to Congress of Aix-la-Chapelle; 1819–26, Governor of Plymouth; 1820–52, Lord- Lieutenant of Hampshire; 1821, 1831, 1838, Lord High Constable at the coronation of George IV, William IV, and Victoria; 1821–22, Plenipotentiary at the Congress of Verona; 1826, Diplomatic mission to Russia; 1826–52, Constable of the Tower of London; 1826–52, Lord Lieutenant of the Tower Hamlets; 1826, Special Ambassador to St. Petersburg; 1829–52, Lord Warden of the Cinque Ports and Constable of Dover Castle; 1829, Elder Brother of Trinity House; 1830, Governor of the Charterhouse School; 1834–52, Chancellor of the University of Oxford; Commander of the Royal Military College and Military Asylum; 1837–52, Master of Trinity House; 1850–52, Chief Ranger and Keeper of the Royal Parks.

HONOURS

Freedom of cities 1814, Hertford; 1814, St. Albans; 1829, Doncaster

Academic 1814, Honorary Doctor of Law, Oxford University; 1835, Honorary Doctor of Laws and Literature, Cambridge University; Visitor of Worcester College, Oxford

Foreign 1811, Count of Vimeiro (Portugal); 1811, Grand Cross of the Tower and Sword of Portugal; 1812, Duke of Ciudad Rodrigo (Spain); Grandee of the First Class (Spain); Marquess of Torres Vedras (Portugal); Duke of Vittoria (Portugal); Order of St. Ferdinand; Order of the Golden Fleece (Spain); 1814, Order of Maria Theresa of Austria; Order of the Sword of Sweden; Order of the Black Eagle of Prussia; Order of St. George (Russia); 1815, Prince of Waterloo (Netherlands); Order of St. Alexander Nevski (Russia); Order of St. Andrew (Russia); Order of William of the Netherlands; Order of the Annunciation of Savoy (Sardinia); Order of the Elephant of Denmark; Order of the Rue Crown of Saxony; Order of Fidelity (Baden); Order of the Lion (Baden); Order of Saint Esprit of France; Order of Maximilian-Joseph of Bavaria; 1817, Order of St. Hermengilde (Spain); Order of Charles III (Spain); Order of St. Janarius (Naples); Order of St. Ferdinand (Naples); Order of the Golden Lion of Hesse Cassel; Order of Merit of Würtemberg

Other than peerage 25 Feb 1805, Knight of the Bath; 4 Mar 1813, Knight of the Garter; 2 Jan 1815, Grand Cross of the Bath; 25 Nov 1847, Fellow of the Royal Society

CLUBS

He was initiated as a Freemason at Trim Lodge *c.* 1791 but never went to any lodge again.

Kildare Street Club, Ireland; Guard's Club; Athenaeum (founding member); Oriental (founding member); Crockford's Gambling Club; White's; Army and Navy; United Services; City of London; Carlton

HOBBIES AND SPORTS

When young he read widely and played cards and the violin, but he gave these up to concentrate on his military career.

At 16 he owned a terrier called Vick. He enjoyed hunting. His horses included Elmore (his favorite hunter) and his charger Copenhagen.

He loved inventing and buying new gadgets.

He seems to have been well-read, and was particularly interested in theological, philosophical and topographical works. He bought works of art and appeared to admire the Dutch school of painting but he had little feel for the intellectual life of his time.

FINANCES

As a young man he was heavily dependent on his soldier's pay, which was insufficient for his needs, and a small family allowance. However, by the time he left India he had amassed a modest fortune of £43,000 (largely through prize money in the wars and his allowance as Governor of Mysore).

In recognition of his achievements in the Peninsular War he was voted several grants by Parliament: in 1812 £100,000, in 1814 a £15,000 annuity or up to £400,000 in lieu, and in 1815 £200,000 for the purchase of estates. He received £60,000 prize money after Waterloo but gave back two-thirds to the Treasury.

Wellington never used his position to advance his money interests. He re-invested his rents annually to improve his estates. When his steward at Stratfield Saye bought him a new farm at less than it was worth, Wellington made him pay the ex-owner the difference. He also had estates in Portugal, Spain and Belgium which seem to have been badly managed. His Stratfield Saye agent was dishonest and lost him a lot of money. Wellington gave generously to those in need and reduced the rents of hard-pressed tenants.

Income When he first joined the army he had an income of £125 p.a. and was paid 10s a day as an aide-de-camp. As a Captain he received 17s 6d daily and as a Lieutenant-Colonel, 30s daily. 0 . . . n 1807 his salary as Chief Secretary of Ireland was £6,566 p. a. He was entitled to an army salary from five countries when in command of the allied forces in Europe (e.g., £8,000 p.a. as a Spanish Generalissimo). He was entitled to a salary of £2,973 12s 6d as Lord Warden of the Cinque Ports but he refused it.

Spouse's finances She gave away money indiscriminately, left bills unpaid and used her allowance to pay off her brother's debts, to Wellington's fury. He refused to raise her allowance from £500 to £670 p.a. in 1822. In 1827 she admitted to having debts of £10,000 which were then paid off by Wellington but she was found to have further undisclosed debts totalling £10,000 when she died in 1831.

Pensions He refused a pension from Portugal in 1811 or 1812. When he was made a Viscount he was given a pension of £2,000 which went up to £4,000 when he became an Earl. He also had an annuity of 2,000 florins from the Low Countries.

Debts He began to get into debt in 1791 which led to Lord Longford's refusal to let him marry his sister in 1793. After this humiliation Wellington always had a lifelong horror of debt. He gave up cards to prevent his debts getting worse but by 1796 he was heavily in debt to his brother Richard and owed £955 14s 18d to his brother's agent, John Page. Although unable to reduce his debts during his early years in India, by the time he returned he had accumulated enough money to pay them off. In old age he denied that he had ever been in debt.

Will In his will written in 1818, he left the bulk of his property to his eldest son Arthur, and his heirs or to his younger son Charles if Arthur died without a male heir, or to a succession of nephews if neither son had a male heir. A clause asked the executors to purchase an estate for the Duchess of Wellington and his son Charles who also received an annuity.

ANECDOTES

The Duke loved children. One day he came across a small boy sitting by the side of the road sobbing and asked him what the matter was. The boy replied that he had to go away to school the next day and was worried about his pet toad as there was nobody to look after it. The Duke promised to attend to the matter personally. A week or so later the boy received a letter at his school: 'Field Marshal the Duke of Wellington presents his compliments to Master —— and has the pleasure to inform him that his toad is well'.

Wellington was sitting in his office one day when a man rushed in crying 'I must kill you'. Wellington did not raise his head from his papers. He merely said 'Does it have to be today?' The intruder looked confused. 'Well they didn't tell me . . . but soon, surely', he replied. 'Good', said Wellington briskly. 'A little later on then, I'm busy at the moment'. The man withdrew and was seized by the police who had been informed that there was an escaped lunatic on the rampage.

At Vienna, Wellington was obliged to sit through Beethoven's *Battle of Victoria* (or *Wellington's Victory*). Afterwards a Russian envoy asked him if the music had been anything like the real thing. 'By God, no', said Wellington, 'if it had been like that I'd have run away myself'.

During the Battle of Waterloo, an officer sent a message that he could see Napoleon among the French forces, his guns were ready and he requested permission to fire. Wellington forbade him, saying 'It is not the business of generals to shoot one another'.

QUOTATIONS

I don't know what effect these men will have upon the enemy, but, by God, they terrify me. (On a new draft of soldiers sent out during the Peninsular War)

Jun 1815, (Pointing at a British private) There! It all depends upon that article whether we do the business or not. Give me enough of it and I am sure. (To Thomas Creevey shortly before the Battle of Waterloo)

1815, By God! I don't think it would have been done if I had not been there. (Comment after the Battle of Waterloo)

1815, Nothing except a battle lost can be half so melancholy as a battle won. (Comment after the Battle of Waterloo)

Oct 1818, Nobody cares a damn about the House of Lords: the House of Commons is everything in England and the House of Lords nothing. (To Thomas Creevey in Brussels)

1828, There, there is the business of the country which I have not time to look at—all my time being employed in assuaging what gentlemen call their feelings. (To John Wilson Croker MP after he had been made Prime Minister)

1828, One man wants one thing and one another: they agree to what I say in the morning, and then in the evening they start with some crotchet which deranges the whole plan. I have been accustomed to carry on things in quite a different manner: I assembled my officers and laid down my plan and it was carried into effect without any more words.

1832, I never saw so many shocking bad hats in my life. (On seeing the first reformed House of Commons)

Don't quote Latin; say what you have to say, and then sit down. (Advice to a new MP)

There is no mistake; there has been no mistake; and there shall be no mistake.

All the business of war, and indeed all the business of life, is to endeavour to find out what you don't know from what you do; that's what I called guessing what was at the other side of the hill. (To John Wilson Croker)

RESIDENCES

Dangan Castle, County Meath, Ireland
11 Harley Street, London
Chief Secretary's Lodge, Phoenix Park, Dublin
4 Hamilton Place, Piccadilly, London
Hôtel de Charost, rue du Faubourg St. Honoré, Paris
Mont-Saint-Martin, near Cambrai, France
Apsley House, Piccadilly, London
Stratfield Saye House, Hampshire
10 Downing Street
Walmer Castle, Walmer, Kent
Open to the public 1) *Apsley House*, built in the 1770s by Robert Adam and enlarged in 1828 when a Corinthian portico was added. It houses the Wellington Museum. 2) *Stratfield Saye*, built in the reign of Charles I. It contains a Wellington exhibition, including many of his possessions. In the spacious grounds are a wild fowl sanctuary, gardens and Copenhagen's grave. 3) *Walmer Castle*, Official residence of the Lords Warden of the Cinque Ports. Wellington's rooms have been preserved unaltered. The original Wellington boot is on display.

MEMORIALS

STATUES AND BUSTS

1813, by Joseph Nollekens, Apsley House, London; 1844, by Sir Francis Chantrey, at the Royal Exchange, London; 1844, by Baron Carlo Marochetti, Glasgow; 1846, by Matthew Coles Wyatt, Aldershot; 1852, by George Gammon Adams, Apsley House; 1852, by John Francis, National Portrait Gallery; 1852, by Thomas Campbell, Dalkeith Place, Edinburgh; 1852, by Edward Hodges Bailey, Palace of Westminster, London

PORTRAITS

c. 1812, by Francisco Goya, National Portrait Gallery, London; *c.* 1812, by Francisco Goya, Apsley House, London; 1814, by Sir Thomas Lawrence, Apsley House, London; 1814, by Sir Thomas Lawrence, Windsor Castle, Berkshire; 1839, by B. R. Haydon, Liverpool College, Liverpool; *c.* 1840, by Andrew Morton, Wallace Collection, London; 1851–52, by John Lucas, Palace of Westminster

OTHER MEMORIALS

Nearly 40 avenues, streets, squares, etc., and 30 pubs are named after him in London alone as well as 17 streets given his family name Wellesley. His battles are also commemorated (e.g., Waterloo Station) as are his homes Apsley and Walmer.

Abroad many of his battlefields are marked by tablets or monuments. The elm tree which had been his command post at Waterloo became known as the Wellington tree. In 1838 two chairs were made from its wood for Wellington himself and Queen Victoria.

A Wellington monument by Smike is in Phoenix Park, Dublin, and a statue of Achilles in his honour (made from metal from guns captured during his battles) is in Hyde Park, London.

A pillar in his honour is near Wellington in Somerset.

Wellington College (a public school) was founded in his honour.

MEMORIALS—*Continued*

There is an avenue of Wellingtonias (trees, Sequoia gigantica) at Stratfield Saye.

The 33rd Regiment, which he commanded, was later renamed the Duke of Wellington's Regiment.

The dish of beef in a pastry crust, Beef Wellington, is named after him.

Above the Village of Khandalla in the Western Ghat is a jutting peak, which became known as 'the Duke's nose'. A mountain in Tasmania is named after him.

The capital city of New Zealand and Wellington, Maine, are named after him.

Wellington boots are named after him.

BIBLIOGRAPHIC INFORMATION

LETTERS AND PERSONAL PAPERS

Many of his papers are in Southampton University Library. The British Library has a large collection of his letters. The remainder of his papers are scattered around the country and abroad including collections at the India Office, the Public Records Office, Kew, the National Library of Scotland, and Bodleian Library, Oxford. Published editions are as follows: 1834–39, Gurwood, J., ed, *The Dispatches of Field Marshal the Duke of Wellington, KG, During His Various Campaigns from 1799 to 1818.* 13 vols. New edition, 13 vols. 1837–39. Second Edition, 8 vols. 1844–47; 1858–72, Wellington, 2nd Duke of, ed. *Supplementary Despatches and Memoranda of Field Marshal Arthur Duke of Wellington, KG,* 15 vols. 1858–72; 1867–80, Wellington, 2nd Duke of, ed. *Despatches, Correspondence and Memoranda of Field Marshal Arthur Duke of Wellington, KG from 1818 to 1832,* 8 vols.; 1976, Brooke, J. and Gandy, J. eds. *Wellington I: Political Correspondence, 1833–November 1834,* HMC; Olney, R. J. and Melvin, J. eds. *Wellington II: Political Correspondence, November 1834–April 1835,* HMC; 1861, Raikes, H. ed. *Private Correspondence of Thomas Raikes with the Duke of Wellington and Other Distinguished Contemporaries*; 1874, Colchester, Lord, ed. *History of the Indian Administration of Lord Ellenborough in His Correspondence with the Duke of Wellington*; 1890, Herrick, C. T., ed. *The Letters of the Duke of Wellington to Miss J., 1834–1851,* Second Edition, 1924; 1903, Weigall, Lady R., ed. *Correspondence of Lady Burghersh with the Duke of Wellington*; 1927, Burghclere, Lady, ed. *A Great Man's Friendship: Letters of the Duke of Wellington to Mary, Marchioness of Salisbury, 1850–1852*; 1948, Webster, C. K., ed. 'Some letters of the Duke of Wellington to his brother William Wellesley-Pole'. *Camden Miscellany 18,* Royal Historical Society, Camden, 3rd Series, 79; 1952, Wellington, Duke of, ed. *Selection from the Private Correspondence of the First Duke of Wellington,* Roxburghe Club; 1954, Wellington, Duke of, ed. *My Dear Mrs. Jones: The Letters of the First Duke of Wellington to Mrs. Jones of Pantglas*; 1965, Wellington, Duke of, ed. *Wellington and His Friends.*

PUBLICATIONS

Memorandum of Russian Campaign of 1812; *Comment on Clausewitz's criticism of the Waterloo campaign*

FURTHER READING

Aldington, R. *Wellington. Being an Account of the Life and Achievements of Arthur Wellesley, 1st Duke of Wellington.* London, 1946.

Bryant, A. *The Great Duke: or The Invincible General.* London, 1971.

Fortescue, J. *Wellington.* London, 1925.

Guedalla, P. *The Duke.* London, 1931.

James, L. *The Iron Duke: A Military Biography of Wellington.* London, 1992.

Longford, E. *Wellington: Pillar of State.* London, 1972.

---. *Wellington: The Years of the Sword.* London, 1969.

Thompson, N. *Wellington After Waterloo.* London and New York, 1986.

J.L.

Historical Pictures

Earl Grey

Lived 1764–1845
Political Party Whig
Prime Minister 22 November 1830–9 July 1834
Government Whig
Reigning Monarch William IV

De bon vouloir servir le roy To serve the King with right good will

GREY AS PRIME MINISTER

Although Grey's credentials for Prime Ministership were sound—twenty years in the House of Commons and over twenty years in the House of Lords—his ministerial experience was limited. His political views were firmly Whig and he opposed both the Irish union in 1800 and religious discrimination against Catholics. He first took office briefly under Grenville in 1806 and then succeeded Fox as Foreign Secretary for a few months until the fall of Grenville. It was then nearly a quarter century before he returned to office, as Prime Minister. Although not supported by a Whig Cabinet, Grey attempted with great skill and taking infinite pains to secure a Reform Bill. He succeeded at the third attempt. His steadiness, good judgement, and firm but tactful handling of the King were to be of lasting importance. Other domestic measures included an act limiting working hours and, based on the findings of a Royal Commission, a Poor Law Amendment Act. He supported his able Foreign Secretary Palmerston in securing the abolition of slavery in the British Empire and wound up the East India Company as a commercial venture an important step in the development of sound administration in India. At seventy and with the reform question resolved Grey resigned.

PERSONAL INFORMATION

Names Charles Grey
Peerages Earl Grey, Viscount Howick and Baron Grey of Howick
Born 13 Mar 1764
Birthplace Falloden, Northumberland
Religion Anglican
Ancestry English. He came from a long-established Northumbrian family who had owned land at Howick since 1319.
Date and place of marriage 18 Nov 1794, Hertford Street, London
Age at marriage 30 years, 250 days
Years married 50 years, 126 days
First entered Parliament 6 Jul 1786
Date appointed PM 22 Nov 1830
Age at appointment 66 years, 254 days
Date ceased to be PM 9 Jul 1834
Total time as PM 3 years, 229 days
Ceased to be MP 14 Nov 1807
Lived after last term as PM 11 years, 8 days
Date of death 17 Jul 1845
Place of death Howick Hall, Northumberland
Age at death 81 years, 126 days
Place of funeral and burial Howick, Northumberland
Zodiac sign Pisces

FATHER

Sir Charles Grey, 1st Baron Grey, 1st Viscount Howick and 1st Earl Grey
Date and place of birth 23 Oct 1729, Howick, Northumberland
Occupation Soldier who served in the American War of Independence and the French Wars, during which he was commander-in-chief in charge of amphibious operations in the West Indies. He reached the rank of General. Later, became Governor of Dunbarton and then of Guernsey.
Date of marriage 8 Jun 1762
Date of death 14 Nov 1807
Place of burial Howick, Northumberland

MOTHER

Elizabeth Grey
Date of birth c 1745
Date of marriage 8 Jun 1762
Date of death 26 May 1822
Place of burial Howick, Northumberland

BROTHERS AND SISTERS

Grey was the second son and second of 9
Henry, d. Jun 1764
Elizabeth, b. 1765; m. Samuel Whitbread (MP Bedford 1790–1815); with her sister, inherited her mother's estate; d. 28 Nov 1846
Henry George, b. 25 Oct 1766; m. Charlotte des Voeux; General in the army and Colonel of the 13th Light Dragoons; d. 11 Jan 1845
George, b. 10 Oct 1767; m. Mary Whitbread; Navy Captain, Resident Commander of Portsmouth dockyard and Marshall in Barbados; 3 Oct 1828
Thomas, b. 1770; Lieutenant-Colonel of the 12th Foot regiment at the Cape of Good Hope; d. *c.* Apr 1797
William, b. 20 Oct 1777; m. Maria Shirrett; Lieutenant-Colonel in the army, served in the French wars in the Low Countries; d. 10 Aug 1817
Edward, b. 25 Mar 1782; m. 1) Charlotte Croft; 2) Elizabeth Adair; 3) Eliza Innes; Bishop of Hereford; d. 24 Jul 1837
Hannah Althea, b. 1785; m. 1) Captain Bettesworth; 2) Edward Ellice (MP Coventry 1818–26, 1830–63; Secretary at War 1833–34); inherited her mother's estate with her sister; d. 28 Jul 1832

WIFE

Mary Elizabeth Ponsonby
Date of birth 4 Mar 1776
Mother Hon. Louisa Molesworth
Father William Brabazon Ponsonby, 1st Baron Ponsonby of Imokilly
Father's occupation MP Cork City 1764–76, Bandon 1776–83, Co. Kilkenny 1783–1800 (Irish Parliament; 1801–06 (British Parliament); Joint Postmaster-General for Ireland 1784–89 and Governor of Co. Kilkenny.
Age at marriage 18 years, 259 days
Number of children 16
Date and place of death 26 Nov 1861; Eaton Square, London
Place of burial Howick Hall, Northumberland
Years younger than PM 11 years, 357 days
Profile She was a cheerful and good-humoured woman who was devoted to her husband and children and liked to knit. Her letters indicate a keen interest in politics and current affairs.

CHILDREN

7 daughters, 10 sons
By his wife Mary Elizabeth:
daughter, b. 1795; d. 1795
Louisa Elizabeth, b. 7 Apr 1797; m. 9 Dec 1816, John George Lambton, MP (1st Earl of Durham); Lady of the Bedchamber to Queen Victoria 1837–38; d. 26 Nov 1841.
Elizabeth, b. Jul 1798; m. 1826, John Croker Bulteel (MP Devon South 1832–35); d. 1880
Caroline, b. Aug 1799; m. 15 Jan 1827, Hon. Captain George Barrington (MP Sunderland 1832–33; a Lord of the Admiralty); created a Lady of the Royal Order of Victoria and Albert; d. 28 Apr 1875
Georgiana, b. Feb 1801; d. 1900
Henry (3rd Earl Grey), b. 28 Dec 1802; m. 9 Aug 1832, Maria Copley; MP, Winchelsea 1826–30, Higham Ferrers 1830–31, Northumberland 1831–32, North Northumberland 1832–41, Sunderland 1841–45; Under-Secretary of State at the Colonial Office 1830–34, at the Home Office 1834, Secretary of State at War 1835–39 and Secretary of State for War and Colonies 1846–1852; Lord Lieutenant of Northumberland 1847–77; d. 9 Oct 1894
Charles, b. 15 Mar 1804; m. 26 Jul 1836, Caroline Elizabeth Farquhar; General in the army; MP, Chipping Wycombe 1831–37, and later equerry and Private Secretary to the Prince Consort 1849–61 and Queen Victoria 1866–70; d. 31 Mar 1870
Frederick William, b. 23 Aug 1805; m. 20 Jul 1846, Barbarina Charlotte Sullivan; became an Admiral; d. 2 May 1878
Mary, b. 3 May 1807; m. 30 Jul 1829, Sir Charles Wood, 1st Viscount Halifax (MP Great Grimsby 1826–31, Wareham 1831, Halifax 1832–65, Ripon 1865–66, First

Lord of the Admiralty 1855–58, Lord Privy Seal 1870–74); d. 6 Jul 1884
William, b. *c.* May 1808; d. 1815
George, b. 16 May 1809; m. 20 Jan 1845, Jane Frances Stuart; Admiral; d. 3 Oct 1891
Thomas, b. 29 Dec 1810; d. 1826
John, b. 2 Mar 1812; m. 1) Jul 1836, Lady Georgiana Hervey; 2) 11 Apr 1874, Helen Mary Spalding; Rector of Houghton-le-Spring and a Canon of Durham; d. 11 Nov 1895
Francis Richard, b. 31 Mar 1813; m. 12 Aug 1840, Lady Elizabeth Howard; Rector of Morpeth and an Honorary Canon of Newcastle; d. 22 Mar 1890
Henry Cavendish, b. 16 Oct 1814; Captain in the Army; d. 5 Sep 1880
William George, b. 15 Feb 1819; m. 20 Sep 1858, Thesa Catherine Stedink; diplomatic clerk in the Foreign Office; Secretary of the Legation at Paris; d. 19 Dec 1865
Illegitimate child by Georgiana, Duchess of Devonshire:
Lady Eliza Courtney, b. 20 Feb 1792; m. Colonel Robert Ellice; d. 1859

LIFE AND CAREER

PARLIAMENTARY ELECTIONS FOUGHT

*(*designates candidate elected)*

DATE 6 Jul 1786. By-election caused by Lord Algernon Percy inheriting a peerage
CONSTITUENCY Northumberland
RESULT Charles Grey* (Whig)

DATE Jun 1790. General Election
CONSTITUENCY Northumberland
RESULT Charles Grey* (Whig), Sir William Middleton, Bt.* (Whig)

DATE May 1796. General Election
CONSTITUENCY Northumberland
RESULT Thomas Richard Beaumont* (Tory), Charles Grey* (Whig)

DATE Jun 1802. General Election
CONSTITUENCY Northumberland
RESULT Thomas Richard Beaumont* (Tory), Charles Grey* (Whig)

DATE 21 Feb 1806. By-election caused by Grey's appointment as First Commissioner of the Admiralty
CONSTITUENCY Northumberland
RESULT Charles Grey* (Whig)

DATE Oct 1806. General Election
CONSTITUENCY Northumberland
RESULT Charles Grey, Viscount Howick* (Whig), Thomas Richard Beaumont* (Tory)

DATE May 1807. General Election
CONSTITUENCY Northumberland
RESULT Thomas Richard Beaumont* (Tory), Lord Percy* (Whig), Charles Grey, Viscount Howick (Whig) - withdrew before final poll

DATE May 1807. General Election
CONSTITUENCY Appleby
RESULT James Ramsey Cuthbert* (Whig), Charles Grey, Viscount Howick* (Whig)

DATE 20 Jul 1807. By-election caused by Richard Fitzpatrick's decision to serve for Bedfordshire
CONSTITUENCY Tavistock
RESULT Charles Grey, Viscount Howick* (Whig)

PARTY ACTIVITY

Party Leadership Leader of Whig Party 1807–26 (1807–17 with Grenville); 1827–34
Membership of group or faction Foxites; Society of the Friends of the People

PARLIAMENTARY AND MINISTERIAL EXPERIENCE

Maiden Speech 21 Feb 1787. He attacked the Free Trade Treaty recently negotiated with the French. (*Parl. Hist.* vol 26, col 471–80)
Opposition offices Leader of the Opposition 1806–26, 1827–30
Privy Counsellor 5 Feb 1806
Ministerial Offices First Lord of the Admiralty 11 Feb–Sep 1806; Foreign Secretary 24 Sep 1806–Mar 1807; First Lord of the Treasury and Leader of the House of Lords 22 Nov 1830–9 Jul 1834
Opposition Leader While PM Duke of Wellington

GOVERNMENTS FORMED

Administration 22 Nov 1830–9 Jul 1834

GENERAL ELECTION RESULT
JUL 1830: Not analysed
APR 1831: Not analysed
DEC 1832: Liberal 479; Conservative 179. Total 658 Majority 300
CABINET
Prime Minister and First Lord of the Treasury Earl Grey
Lord Chancellor Lord Brougham and Vaux
Lord President of the Council Marquess of Lansdowne
Lord Privy Seal Lord Durham (1830–Apr 1833); Earl of Ripon (Apr 1833–Jun 1834); Earl of Carlisle (Jun–Jul 1834)
Home Secretary Viscount Melbourne
Foreign Secretary Viscount Palmerston
Secretary of State for War and the Colonies Viscount Goderich (1830–Apr 1833); E. G. Stanley (Apr 1833–Jun 1834); T. Spring-Rice (Jun–Jul 1834)
Chancellor of the Exchequer Viscount Althorp
First Lord of the Admiralty Sir J. Graham (1830–Jun 1834); Lord Auckland (Jun–Jul 1834)
President of the Board of Control C. Grant
Chancellor of the Duchy of Lancaster Lord Holland
Minister Without Portfolio Earl of Carlisle (1830–Jun 1834)
*Postmaster General** Duke of Richmond (Dec 1830–Jul 1834)
*Paymaster General** Lord John Russell (June 1831–Jul 1834)
*Chief Secretary of Ireland** E. G. Stanley (Jun 1831–Mar 1833)
*President of the Board of Trade** C. P. Thompson (Jun–Jul 1834)
*Master of the Mint** J. Abercromby (Jun–Jul 1834)

—Administration 22 Nov 1830–9 Jul 1834— *Continued*

*Secretary at War** E. Ellice (Jun–Jul 1834)
[*Office not always in Cabinet]

IMPORTANT DATES IN PERSONAL AND POLITICAL LIFE

1784 Grey leaves Trinity College, Cambridge, without a degree and spends most of the next three years on a grand tour of Europe.

6 JUL 1786 Elected to Parliament for the first time at a by-election to serve for the county of Northumberland.

27 FEB 1787 He makes his maiden speech attacking the recently negotiated Free Trade Treaty with France.

SPRING 1787 Appointed to the committee drawing up articles of impeachment against Warren Hastings, former Governor-General of Bengal. Subsequently he is appointed to the committee of managers of the Warren Hastings trial as the youngest member and speaks in the trial on 25 Feb 1788.

NOV 1788–FEB 1789 George III's madness causes the Whigs to hope for office under the Prince of Wales, who is sympathetic to their cause, and to disagree over who should hold which office. Grey wants to become Chancellor of the Exchequer, which is considered rather ambitious for one so inexperienced. He later lowers his sights to Secretary at War. The King recovers, however, leaving the Opposition with no hope of office and bitterly divided among themselves.

12 APR 1791 Grey moves a series of resolutions attacking the Government, which is trying to pressure the Russian government into withdrawing from the Turkish outpost of Ochakov and attempting, with its allies, to restrict Russian expansionism generally. The resolutions are defeated.

6 MAY 1791 The two leading Whigs, Fox and Burke, split during an opposition debate on the Canada Bill; Grey sides with Fox.

11 APR 1792 Grey attends a dinner at Lord Porchester's to launch the Society of the Friends of the People, a group of moderate, liberal Whigs who reject both the extremes of reactionary Conservatism and radicalism and the ideas of Burke. The Society is dedicated to overthrowing Pitt's administration and is also in favour of parliamentary reform, a cause with which Grey's name is increasingly linked. The Society contributes to the split in the Whig Party by exposing its divisions.

6 MAY 1793 Grey presents a motion calling for parliamentary reform. The motion is defeated by 282 votes to 41.

JUL 1794 A large number of Whigs, led by the Duke of Portland split from Fox and join the Government in coalition with Pitt. Fox is left with 50 supporters in the Commons (including Grey) and a handful in the Lords.

8 NOV 1794 Grey marries Mary Elizabeth Ponsonby, thus allying himself with a prominent Whig family.

26 MAY 1797 He proposes his second reform motion in the Commons, which is defeated by 256 votes to 91. After this Fox, Grey and their supporters, seeing that the chance of achieving reform is hopeless, secede from Parliament. Grey does not speak in Parliament again until Feb 1799.

7 FEB 1799 He makes the first of many speeches in the Commons opposing the Union Bill, calling for a more liberal policy towards Ireland and an end to religious discrimination against Catholics.

1801 The Foxite Whigs return to Parliament after their secession but Grey, disillusioned, sees little chance of office and attends Parliament very sparingly for the next few years, preferring to remain in Northumberland with his family.

23 JUN 1801 Grey's father is created a baron. Grey is furious as he will be obliged to give up his seat in the Commons and enter the Lords when his father dies.

17 JUL 1801 Grey and his family move into Howick House which has been offered to them as a residence by his uncle Sir Henry Grey. They live there for the rest of Grey's life. Grey loves Howick and dislikes leaving it to come to London.

29 NOV 1802 Fox writes to Grey, urging him to take a more active role in politics again in the hope that Addington (who has succeeded Pitt as Prime Minister) will give him a place in his ministry, thus helping to keep Pitt out of power. Grey refuses office and to take on the leadership of the Foxite party but wishes to attempt to preserve the fragile peace between Britain and France, although he thinks his attempts will fail and that true peace is unlikely.

JAN 1804 Fox is approached by Grenville and his followers asking for an alliance in opposition to the current Government, aiming to replace it with a broadly based ministry. Fox wishes Grey to play a leading role in the opposition, but Grey advocates caution and declines to commit himself to concerted parliamentary action.

MAY 1804 On the fall of Addington's ministry Pitt becomes Prime Minister again. He makes overtures to the Foxites to be part of his Government but the King refuses to have Fox in the Cabinet and Grey and the other Foxites decline to take office without Fox.

5 FEB 1806 Grey is made a Privy Counsellor.

11 FEB 1806 Following Pitt's death and the formation of a new ministry (All the Talents) under Grenville, Grey takes office for the first time as First Lord of the Admiralty. Fox is Foreign Secretary.

11 APR 1806 Grey's father is created an Earl and a Viscount. Grey takes his father's second title (Viscount Howick) as a courtesy title but continues to sit in the Commons, as, technically, he is still a commoner.

25 APR 1806 Grey introduces proposals to increase the pay of the navy which has not changed since Queen Anne's reign. He also raises allowances for navy pensioners and for improving conditions at Greenwich hospital.

24 SEP 1806 After the death of Fox, Grey succeeds him as Foreign Secretary and as leader of the Whigs.

1806–7 The peace negotiations with France collapse. Grey makes proposals to energise Spain and Portugal against Napoleon and plans an offensive in the Mediterranean. An expedition is sent to Constantinople to force the Turks to allow Russia access to the Mediterranean. Unfortunately the commander of the expeditionary force disobeys orders and the expedition fails.

FEB 1807 Against his wishes Grey is forced to accept the majority view in the Cabinet and agrees to send instructions to his commanders in South America to attack Buenos Aires in order to block French ambitions in Latin America. The expedition fails.

23 FEB 1807 The Slave Trade Abolition Bill passes in the Commons. Grey makes the principal speech and is chiefly responsible for guiding it through the Commons.

5 MAR 1807 Grey moves for leave to bring in a Bill to allow Catholics to be promoted to the rank of General in the army and the equivalent rank in the navy. He has explained the proposals to the King, who appears not to have understood them. On realising how wide a measure it is, the King insists that the Government withdraw the Bill.

15 MAR 1807 The Cabinet agrees to drop the Bill promoting Catholics in the army and navy but when the King insists that they promise not to bring in any more measures to aid the Catholics they refuse and the Government falls. Grey is to be out of office for the next 24 years.

MAY 1807 Grey returns to Northumberland to fight the General Election only to find that the Duke of Northumberland has put up his son, Lord Percy, as an alternative candidate. Mindful of the fact that his father is unlikely to live much longer and he will soon be elevated to the Lords, Grey withdraws from the contest before the poll and is subsequently elected for Appleby.

20 JUL 1807 He is elected for Tavistock at a by-election.

14 NOV 1807 Grey's father dies and he succeeds to the Earldom. He is forced to give up his seat in the Commons and reluctantly enters the House of Lords.

30 MAR 1808 Grey's uncle dies, leaving Grey all his property.

23 SEP 1809 The new Prime Minister, Perceval, offers to negotiate with Grey and Lord Grenville with a view to the Whigs joining the Government in a coalition. Grey however refuses on the grounds that too few Cabinet places are offered to the Whigs and that it is irresponsible to insist on Catholic emancipation at this time.

JAN 1811 When the Prince Regent assumes power, negotiations are opened between the Prince and Grenville and Grey regarding the possible formation of a new Whig administration, but break down over conflicts about appointments to various offices. The Government under Perceval remains in office.

23 MAY 1812 Following Perceval's assassination, Grey and Grenville are approached by Marquess Wellesley (Wellington's older brother and formerly Foreign Secretary) to negotiate a new administration, but decline on the grounds that they would be in a minority in the Cabinet on most issues and because of personal dislike of other members of the Cabinet, especially Canning. Grey has never forgiven Canning for taking office in 1807, when, despite claiming to be in favour of Catholic emancipation, he had accepted the post of Foreign Secretary in a Government that had promised the King it would not bring in any pro-Catholic measures. Grey thinks this hypocritical and regards Canning as a political adventurer.

24 FEB 1817 In a speech in the Lords Grey attacks the suspension of the Habeas Corpus Act which Grenville supports. The two men had been gradually drifting apart and after this they give up trying to work together and split; Grey is left to lead a small minority against the Government. Grenville and his supporters sit on the cross-benches until joining Lord Liverpool's Government in 1821.

3 NOV 1820 Grey makes one of his finest speeches in the Lords denouncing the Bill of Pains and Penalties (an attempt to divorce the new King George IV and Queen Caroline). When the Bill is dropped George IV's resentment means that Grey has forfeited any chance of gaining office during his reign. However it makes him popular in the country.

26 JUN 1830 George IV dies and is succeeded by his brother William IV who has no prejudice against Grey. The General Election leaves Wellington's Government in a weaker position than before.

2 NOV 1830 In reply to the King's speech, Grey calls for parliamentary reform. Wellington's reply totally rules out any reform measure, causing uproar in and outside Parliament and leading to radical demonstrations and unrest. The Government is seriously weakened.

16 NOV 1830 Wellington's Government resigns after being defeated on a proposal on the Civil List. The King sends for Grey and asks him to form a Government.

22 NOV 1830 Grey kisses hands as Prime Minister.

NOV 1830 At their first Cabinet meeting the new Government consider how to tackle the riots and other symptoms of unrest affecting the country. Special Commissions are appointed to try those arrested and magistrates are encouraged to pass stiff sentences.

11 DEC 1830 Grey sets up a sub-committee consisting of Lord Durham, Lord Duncannon, Lord John Russell, and Sir J. Graham to look into the question of parliamentary reform and submit draft proposals to the Cabinet.

20 DEC 1830 A protocol is signed in London by Britain, France, Austria, Russia and Prussia recognising Belgian independence. Throughout his ministry Grey's foreign policy is directed to preserving Belgian independence from France and Holland through diplomatic channels.

14 JAN 1831 The Committee reports to Grey with drafts for three Bills for England and Wales, Scotland, and Ireland. The proposals include giving the franchise to all households whose property is rated at £20 p. a. (later dropped to £10), five-year Parliaments, disenfranchisement of non-residents in the boroughs, two-day polls, more polling stations, registration of electors, the total disenfranchisement of all boroughs with less than 2,000 inhabitants and the partial disenfranchisement of boroughs with less than 4,000 inhabitants, most of the spare seats to go to towns with over 10,000 inhabitants, and a secret ballot (later dropped).

1 MAR 1831 Lord John Russell introduces the first version of the Reform Bill to the House of Commons. It disenfranchises 60 boroughs completely and 47 partially. This leaves 168 seats disenfranchised, most of which are redistributed. Borough franchise is given to £10 householders and the county franchise to £10 copyholders, £50 leaseholders and 40s freeholders.

22 MAR 1831 The Reform Bill passes its Second Reading by only one vote (302-301).

19 APR 1831 The Government is defeated in Committee by eight votes on an amendment to the Reform Bill insisting that the number of Members for England and Wales not be reduced. Seeing he is not going to get the Bill through the Commons Grey asks the King to dissolve Parliament. A General Election is called, resulting in a landslide victory for those in favour of reform.

27 MAY 1831 Grey is created a Knight of the Garter.

6 JUL 1831 The Second Reform Bill passes its Second Reading in the new House of Commons by a majority of 136. It consequently passes its Third Reading and is sent to the Lords in September.

8 OCT 1831 The Lords throw out the Second Reform Bill on the Second Reading despite a brilliant speech by Grey. Riots and civil unrest follow throughout the country.

12 DEC 1831 The Third Reform Bill is introduced into the Commons. It passes its Second Reading on 17 Dec 1831.

3 JAN 1832 Having secured the agreement of the majority of his Cabinet Grey tries to persuade the King to create more peers if necessary in order to get the Reform Bill through the Lords.

15 JAN 1832 The King writes to Grey agreeing to create more peers as a last resort with the following condi-

IMPORTANT DATES IN PERSONAL AND POLITICAL LIFE—*Continued*

tions: Only three new titles will be created; the other peerages will be created by calling up the eldest sons of peers into the Lords and by bringing Scottish and Irish peers into the English peerage.

FEB 1832 Grey sets up a Royal Commission to look into the Poor Law, leading to the introduction of the Poor Law Amendment Bill.

14 APR 1832 The Lords give the Reform Bill its Second Reading by a nine vote majority.

7 MAY 1832 The Government is defeated by 35 votes at the Committee stage of the Reform Bill on a motion postponing consideration of disenfranchisement clauses of the Bill. The Government resigns the next day when William IV refuses Grey's request to create 50 to 60 new peers to get the Bill through the Lords. The King asks them to stay in office until a new ministry is formed and sends for Wellington to ask him to form a Tory Government.

15 MAY 1832 Wellington gives up the attempt to form a Government. The King asks Grey to resume Government, and three days later promises to create more peers if necessary to get the Reform Bill through.

4 JUN 1832 Wellington persuades 100 Tory peers to abstain on the Third Reading of the Reform Bill in the Lords and it passes by 106 votes to 22. It receives Royal Assent three days later and becomes law.

28 AUG 1833 Two Acts are passed giving the Scottish electorate the right to elect their own representatives at local government level.

28 AUG 1833 An Act abolishing slavery throughout the British Empire is passed. Former slave owners receive compensation.

28 AUG 1833 An Act is passed winding up the East India Company as a commercial concern and making it instead a Corporation which governs India under certain revised conditions, including a declaration that all offices be open to the natives regardless of creed or colour.

29 AUG 1833 Royal Assent is given to a Factory Act which limits the working hours of children and young people and introduces factory inspection.

17 APR 1834 The Poor Law Amendment Bill is introduced to the House of Commons, implementing the main recommendations of the Royal Commission set up the previous year and establishing poor law unions, responsible for the building of workhouses. It is still going through Parliament when Grey resigns, finally becoming law in August 1834.

6 MAY 1834 During a debate on the Irish Tithes Bill Lord John Russell states publicly that the revenues of the Church of Ireland are larger than required for religions and moral instruction of members of that church and, thus, the endowments of the Church of Ireland should be used for other purposes. This speech exposes the deep divisions in the Cabinet over this issue and as a result Stanley, Graham, Richmond and Ripon resign.

21 JUN 1834 Lord Wellesley, now Lord Lieutenant of Ireland, writes to Grey on the advice of Littleton, the new Irish Secretary, concerning the Bill to renew the Irish Coercion Act which is before Parliament. He advises Grey to drop the clauses concerning restrictions on public meetings, over which there has been considerable disagreement in the Cabinet. Grey however insists on retaining those clauses. Littleton had consulted Daniel O'Connell secretly and given O'Connell the impression that if he did not oppose the Bill the public meeting clauses would be dropped. When the clauses are included in the Bill, O'Connell, feeling he has been duped, reveals to the House the gist of Littleton's conversations. The Opposition demands the production of Wellesley's letter. Althorp feels compelled to resign as Leader of the House. Weary of office, Grey decides to resign with him.

9 JUL 1834 Grey announces his resignation to the Lords, having informed the King of his intentions the previous day. The Tories fail to form an administration, but Grey refuses to return to office, feeling his political career is over. Melbourne succeeds him as Prime Minister. Grey returns to Howick for the rest of his life.

APR 1835 He is invited by his colleagues to return to Government as Prime Minister or Foreign Secretary but he declines.

SUMMER 1843 His health begins to fail.

17 JUL 1845 He dies peacefully at Howick.

BACKGROUND

PHYSICAL CHARACTERISTICS AND HEALTH

Grey was tall, slim and strikingly handsome. Lord Melbourne commented on his high forehead and small, intelligent but cold eyes. In later years he went bald and wore spectacles.

At preparatory school he suffered from many illnesses, which may have been of a nervous origin. In later years he was subject to fits of depression.

In Jan 1804 he ruptured a sinew in his right leg and was unable to walk for a week. In middle life he suffered from agonising stomach pains, probably due to an ulcer, but in later years these grew less troublesome. In Jan 1839 his wife's portrait fell off the wall on to his head and he was confined to bed for a month.

His health began to decline in the summer of 1843, when he may have had a slight stroke. His speech deteriorated and his eyesight was permanently damaged. He had circulation problems with his legs which was diagnosed as gout, but which may have been gangrene. He was in permanent pain for the last 18 months of his life and finally suffered an attack of erysipelas in his arm on 17 July 1845, lapsed into a coma and died.

EDUCATION

Primary 1770–73 Preparatory School at Marylebone, London

Secondary 1773–81 Eton

University 1781–84 Trinity College, Cambridge; left without taking a degree

Prizes and awards He won several prizes for English composition and declamation at Cambridge.

Cultural and vocational background He went on the Grand Tour of France, Germany and Switzerland 1784–86 at first alone and then with Henry, Duke of Cumberland.

Languages He learned Italian on the Grand Tour.

NON-PARLIAMENTARY CAREER

Other posts 1831–45 Elder Brother of Trinity House; 1831–45 Trustee of the National Gallery; Governor of the Charterhouse School; Vice-President of the Marine Society

HONOURS

Freedom of cities 1834, Edinburgh
Other than peerage 27 May 1831 Knight of the Garter

CLUBS

Brooks's, Whig Club, White's

HOBBIES AND SPORTS

Grey loved the countryside and enjoyed riding, shooting and walking. He laid out many walks at Howick and planted trees in the grounds. He kept dogs, including one called Viper, his companion in old age. He read aloud to his family in the evening. He played cribbage.

FINANCES

Grey inherited nothing from his parents. His uncle Sir Henry Grey financed his Grand Tour and first election to the House of Commons in 1786. Although he inherited Sir Henry's estates in 1808 Grey was never a rich man. In 1797 he said he couldn't afford to keep an establishment in London. In 1801 when his uncle invited him and his family to come and live in Howick, Grey warned his wife that they would not be well off.

Grey's children caused him to spend a great deal of money. In 1823 he complained about the cost of buying his second son Charles's army promotion. In 1826 he spent £14,000 trying to get his eldest son Henry elected in Northumberland and was concerned about the burdens on his estate and the 'scanty portions' he would leave to his children. In Feb 1827 one of the estate properties had to be sold for £40,000 to cover Henry's election costs. In 1828 he spent £1,400 to buy Charles his promotion to army major. In 1830 he complained he was 'wretchedly poor' when he paid for Charles's promotion to Lieutenant-Colonel and for his son John's extravagances.

Legacies He inherited the Howick estate from his uncle Sir Henry Grey.

Will Dated 14 Jan 1842, it left the bulk of his estate to his eldest son Henry with generous provisions for his other children and his wife (who in addition was left his London house or the means of buying a residence if he had no London house when he died) and such of the contents of his home in Howick as she desired.

ANECDOTES

Grey was notoriously unwilling to leave Howick and the countryside and come up to London. His colleagues lost patience. In 1808 Turney wrote to him: 'Have you a reason which you can publicly assign for staying away? The death of your uncle has removed the old one, a scanty income. What new one have you got which you can state? You must show yourself in the field as the leader of a party or you must cease to be so'.

In 1807 Grey lost his seat because of the Duke of Northumberland's influence. He never forgave the Duke. One of his grandsons remembered: 'Lord Grey was very kind to his grandchildren. His son, Uncle Francis, asked him to let the boys come to Alnwick. They were given ten shillings, which they spent on a hatchet each, and, as they walked home they cut notches in all the Duke of Northumberland's gates. They were dragged up to Grandpapa by Uncle Francis and he told him they had spoilt all the Duke of Northumberland's gates.

"No boys, did you really?" answered Lord Grey. "Here is ten shillings more, and if there are any gates that are not notched go and cut them".'

Grey's friend Thomas Creevey MP described Grey in retirement: 'Just as I was in the midst of writing the last sentence Lord Grey stalked into the great library, his spectacles aloft upon his forehead and I saw at once he was for jaw so I abandoned my letter for you and joined him. It would do you good to see me send him to bed every night at half after eleven o'clock which is half an hour beyond his usual time. This I do regularly and it amuses him much. He looks about for his book, calls his dog Viper and out they go, he having been all day as gay as possible and not an atom of that gall he was subject to in earlier life . . . The same tranquillity and cheerfulness, amounting almost to playfulness, instead of subsiding have rather increased during my stay and have never been interrupted by a single moment of thoughtfulness or gloom. He could not have felt more pleasure from carrying the Reform Bill than he does apparently when he picks up half-a-crown from me at cribbage. A curious stranger would discover no out-of-the-way talent in him, no powers of conversation, a clever man in *discussion* certainly, but with no fancy and no judgement (or very little) in works either of fancy or art. A most natural, unaffected, upright man, hospitable and domestic; far surpassing any man one knows in his noble appearance and beautiful simplicity of manner and equally surpassing all his contemporaries as a splendid public speaker. Take him all in all I never saw his fellow; nor can I see any imitation of him on the stocks'.

QUOTATIONS

25 Apr 1800, No man can subscribe more cordially than I do to the maxim that in government practical good is infinitely preferable to speculative perfection. (Speech in the Commons *Parl Hist* Vol 35 c 57–72)

Apr 1832, Mark my words, within two years you will find that we have become unpopular, for having brought forward the most aristocratic measure that ever was proposed in Parliament. (In conversation with Lord Sidmouth about the Reform Bill).

Summer 1834, The only way with newspaper attacks is, as the Irish say, 'to keep never minding'. This has been my practice through life. (In conversation during his final months as Prime Minister).

RESIDENCES

Falloden, Northumberland
Howick Hall, Howick, Northumberland
Hertford Street, Mayfair, London
Ham Common, London
Portman Square, London
Government House, Devonport

RESIDENCES—*Continued*

Hanover Square, London
10 Downing Street
East Sheen
Berkeley Square, London
Open to the public The Howick Hall grounds with a natural, informal woodland garden and a rhododendron garden are open.

MEMORIALS

STATUES AND BUSTS

1827, a marble bust by Thomas Campbell, Palace of Westminster; statue by E. H. Bailey, Newcastle

PORTRAITS

c. 1781, by George Romney, Eton College; 1793, by Sir Thomas Lawrence, Howick; c. 1820, attributed to Thomas Philips, National Portrait Gallery; c. 1827, by Sir Thomas Lawrence, Howick; c. 1828, by Sir Thomas Lawrence, National Portrait Gallery (on loan to the Palace of Westminster)

OTHER MEMORIALS

Grey Street in Newcastle-Upon-Tyne and Earl Grey Street in Edinburgh were named after him; Earl Grey tea is named after him; there is a pub in Edinburgh named after him.

BIBLIOGRAPHIC INFORMATION

LETTERS AND PERSONAL PAPERS

The majority of his papers are at Durham University's Department of Paleography and Diplomatic (Grey of Howick collection).

Other letters are at the Royal Archives, Windsor Castle, Staffordshire Record Office, the British Library, Gloucestershire Record Office, and the Borthwick Institute, York University.

Some material is published in: Grey, C. *Some Account of the Life and Opinions of Charles, 2nd Earl Grey*, 1861; Grey, Earl ed *The Reform Act*, 1832. *The Correspondence of the Late Earl Grey with His Majesty King William IV and with Sir Herbert Taylor from Nov 1830 to Jun 1832*. 2 vols, 1867; Le Strange, G. ed *Correspondence of Princess Lieven and Earl Grey*. 2 vols, 1890; Trevelyan, GM *Lord Grey of the Reform Bill Being the Life of Charles, Second Earl Grey*, London, 1920.

FURTHER READING

Derry, J. W. *Charles, Earl Grey: Aristocratic Reformer*. Oxford, 1992

Grey, C. *Some Account of the Life and Opinions of Charles, Second Earl Grey*. London, 1861.

Smith, E. A. *Lord Grey 1764–1845*. Oxford, 1990.

Trevelyan, G. M. *Lord Grey of the Reform Bill, Being the Life of Charles, Second Earl Grey*, London, 1920.

J. L.

Bettmann

Lord Melbourne

Lived 1779–1848

Political Party Whig

Prime Minister 16 July 1834–14 November 1834
18 April 1835–30 August 1841

Governments Whig

Reigning Monarchs William IV; Victoria

Virtute et fide By valour and faith

MELBOURNE AS PRIME MINISTER

A Whig by family tradition, Melbourne was in the House of Commons 1806–1812 and 1816–1829 before joining the House of Lords on his father's death. A sceptical but tolerant character, he had an easy and informal manner which helped him when Secretary for Ireland 1827–8 while his conventional law and order conservatism was shown when he was Home Secretary 1830–34. On Grey's resignation in 1834, the King appointed him Prime Minister as the least bad choice and, except for five months following November 1834, he remained Prime Minister for seven years. Without any strong political convictions he held together a difficult and divided Cabinet and sustained support in the House of Commons through a very uneasy alliance of Whigs, Radicals and also Irish under O'Connell. His was not a reforming Government, despite the important Municipal Corporations Act of 1835 which ensured the growing middle class secured control of urban local goverment. Melbourne preserved the transitional caretaker note of keeping order, raising taxes and conducting foreign policy. In 1837 when Victoria became Queen, Melbourne undertook her political education in a remarkable friendship between a sovereign and her Prime Minister—a contrast to his rather unconventional personal life. The outbreak of rebellion in Jamaica led him to resign in 1839 only to take up office again when Peel refused to form a Government. However, his Parliamentary support was declining and in 1840 it grew difficult to hold the Cabinet together, in particular regarding foreign policy with France. He was defeated in the House of Commons, prompted by the Queen to call an election against his will, and finally resigned in August 1841.

PERSONAL INFORMATION

Names William Lamb
Peerages 2nd Viscount Melbourne of Kilmore and Baron Melbourne (UK)
Born 15 Mar 1779
Birthplace Melbourne House, Piccadilly, London
Religion Anglican
Ancestry English. The family fortune had been made three generations earlier by Peniston Lamb, a lawyer from Nottinghamshire. His nephew and heir, Matthew Lamb, increased the fortune and acquired a baronetcy. He also married an heiress, Charlotte Coke, of Melbourne Hall, Derbyshire.
Date and place of marriage 3 Jun 1805, St George's, Hanover Square, London
Age at marriage 26 years, 80 days
Years married 22 years, 237 days
First entered Parliament 31 Jan 1806
Dates appointed PM 1) 16 Jul 1834; 2) 18 Apr 1835
Age at appointments 1) 55 years, 123 days; 2) 56 years, 34 days
Dates ceased to be PM 1) 14 Nov 1834; 2) 30 Aug 1841
Total time as PM 1) 121 days; 2) 6 years 134 days; a total of 6 years, 255 days
Ceased to be MP 22 Jul 1828
Lived after last term as PM 7 years, 86 days
Date of death 24 Nov 1848
Place of death Brocket Hall, Hertfordshire
Age at death 69 years, 255 days
Place of funeral and burial Hatfield Church
Zodiac sign Pisces

FATHER

Peniston Lamb, 1st Viscount Melbourne, created an Irish Baron in 1770; Lord Melbourne of Kilmore and an Irish Viscount in 1781; created an English Peer in 1815
Date of birth 29 Jan 1745
Occupation MP Ludgershall 1768–84; Malmesbury 1784–90; Newport, Isle of Wight, 1790–93; appointed gentleman of the bedchamber to the Prince of Wales 1783–96
Date of marriage 13 Apr 1769
Date of death 22 Jul 1828
Place of burial Hatfield Church

MOTHER

Elizabeth Milbanke
Date of birth 1749
Profile Lady Melbourne was ambitious as well as beautiful and intelligent. After her marriage she became one of the leading society hostesses in London. She was known to have had several liaisons and there were rumours that her second son, William, was fathered by Lord Egremont. Melbourne denounced the rumours in later life, but Egremont always took a great interest in him.
Date of marriage 13 Apr 1769
Date of death 6 Apr 1818
Place of burial Hatfield Church

BROTHERS AND SISTERS

Melbourne was the second son and second child in a family of six children.
Peniston, b. 3 May 1770; Captain in the Hertfordshire Yeoman Cavalry, 1794; MP Newport, Isle of Wight 1793–96, Hertfordshire 1802–05; d. 24 Jan 1805
Frederick James, (3rd Viscount Melbourne and Baron Beauvale 1839), b. 17 Apr 1782; m. 1841, Countess Alexandrina Julia, daughter of the Count of Maltzahn, the Prussian minister at Vienna; Diplomat, Ambassador to Portugal and Austria; d. 29 Jan 1853
George, b. 11 Jul 1784; MP Westminster 1819–20, Dungarvan 1822–34; Under-Secretary of State for Home Affairs Nov 1830–2 Jan 1834; d. 2 Jan 1834
Emily Mary b. 21 Apr 1787; m. 1) 1805, 5th Earl Cowper (d. 22 Jun 1837); 2) 16 Dec 1839, 3rd Viscount Palmerston (*q.v.*); d. 11 Sep 1869
Harriet, b. 1789; d. 1803

WIFE

Lady Caroline Ponsonby
Date of birth 13 Nov 1785
Mother Lady Henrietta Frances, daughter of John, 1st Earl Spencer
Father Frederick Ponsonby, 3rd Earl of Bessborough
Father's occupation Peer
Age at marriage 19 years, 202 days
Number of children 1
Date and place of death 26 Jan 1828, Melbourne House, Whitehall, London
Place of burial Hatfield Church
Years younger than PM 6 years, 241 days
Profile Lady Caroline had no systematic education; she spent some of her childhood in Italy and later went to live with her cousins at Devonshire House. When she was ten her grandmother, Lady Spencer, took care of her and became alarmed at Caroline's eccentric behaviour. She consulted a doctor who advised that Caroline should not be strictly disciplined. As a result she effectively ran wild and could not write or spell until she was in her teens.

Despite her lack of formal education, Lady Caroline Lamb was a good linguist, fluent in French, Italian and Greek. She was artistic and loved both music and painting, especially watercolours. She wrote poetry and three novels, *Glenarvon*, published in 1816, *Graham Hamilton*, 1822 and *Ada Reis: A Tale*, 1823.

Although Lady Caroline was not conventionally beautiful, her animated conversation often made her seem so. She was impulsive and excitable, sometimes to the verge of hysteria and often flew into terrible rages.

In 1812 she met Lord Byron who described her as 'the cleverest, most agreeable, absurd, amiable, perplexing, dangerous, fascinating little being.' She in turn noted in her diary that he was 'mad, bad and dangerous to know.' Their love affair lasted until the summer of 1813 but Caroline's passionate infatuation with the poet continued. The affair had been public and notorious and its death throes were undignified. Melbourne decided finally to separate from his wife in 1814 but the separation did not occur until 1825. In 1824 Caroline accidentally met Byron's funeral procession; her instability worsened and she spent the last few years of her life either at Brocket Hall in Hertfordshire or in Brighton.

CHILDREN

1 son

George Augustus Frederick, b. 28 Aug 1807; Augustus was mentally handicapped; he led an almost vegetable existence after childhood and had to be cared for constantly, often by Melbourne, who was devoted to him; d. 26 Nov 1836

LIFE AND CAREER

PARLIAMENTARY ELECTIONS FOUGHT

*(*designates candidate elected)*

DATE 31 Jan 1806. By-election caused by the elevation of Hon. Charles Kinnaird to the House of Lords.
CONSTITUENCY Leominster
RESULT William Lamb* (Whig)

DATE Oct 1806. General Election
CONSTITUENCY Haddington Burghs (Scotland)
RESULT William Lamb* (Whig)

DATE May 1807. General Election
CONSTITUENCY Portarlington (Ireland)
RESULT William Lamb* (Whig)

DATE 16 Apr 1816. By-election caused by the resignation of George Ponsonby
CONSTITUENCY Peterborough
RESULT William Lamb* (Whig)

DATE Jun 1818. General Election
CONSTITUENCY Peterborough
RESULT William Elliot* (Whig); William Lamb* (Whig)

DATE 29 Nov 1819. By-election caused by the elevation of Hon. Thomas Brand to the House of Lords
CONSTITUENCY Hertfordshire
RESULT William Lamb* (Whig)

DATE Mar 1820. General Election
CONSTITUENCY Hertfordshire
RESULT Sir John Saunders Sebright, Bt.* (Whig); William Lamb* (Whig)

DATE 24 Apr 1827. By-election caused by the appointment of George Canning as PM
CONSTITUENCY Newport, Isle of Wight
RESULT William Lamb* (Whig)

DATE 7 May 1827. By-election caused by the resignation of William Russell
CONSTITUENCY Bletchingley
RESULT William Lamb* (Whig)

PARTY ACTIVITY

Party Leadership Leader of the Whigs 1834–42.

PARLIAMENTARY AND MINISTERIAL EXPERIENCE

Maiden Speech 19 Dec 1806, He spoke in reply to the King's speech. (*Parl Deb.* !st ser, vol 8, col 35-41)

Privy Counsellor 30 Apr 1827; 16 Jul 1827 (Ireland)

Ministerial Offices Chief Secretary for Ireland 29 Apr 1827–May 1828; Home Secretary 22 Nov 1830–16 Jul 1834; First Lord of the Treasury and Leader of the House of Lords 16 Jul 1834–14 Nov 1834, 18 Apr 1835–30 Aug 1841

Opposition Leaders while PM 1) 1834, Duke of Wellington (House of Lords); Sir Robert Peel (House of Commons); 2) 1835–41, Duke of Wellington (House of Lords); Sir Robert Peel (House of Commons)

GOVERNMENTS FORMED

First Administration 16 Jul 1834–14 Nov 1834

GENERAL ELECTION RESULT

DEC 1832: Whigs 441; Tories 175; Others 42. Total 658
Whig Majority 225 (excl. the Speaker)

CABINET

Prime Minister and First Lord of the Treasury Lord Melbourne
Lord Chancellor Lord Brougham & Vaux
Lord President of the Council Marquess of Lansdowne
Lord Privy Seal Earl of Mulgrave
Chancellor of the Exchequer Viscount Althorp
Home Secretary Viscount Duncannon
Foreign Secretary Viscount Palmerston
Secretary for War and the Colonies T. Spring Rice
First Lord of the Admiralty Lord Auckland
President of the Board of Trade C. Poulett Thomson
President of the Board of Control C. Grant
Master of the Mint J. Abercromby
Chancellor of the Duchy of Lancaster Lord Holland
Secretary at War Viscount Howick
First Commissioner of Woods and Forests Sir J.C. Hobhouse
Paymaster General Lord J. Russell

Second Administration 18 Apr 1835–30 Aug 1841

GENERAL ELECTION RESULT

JAN 1835 Whigs 385; Tories 273; Total 658
Whig Majority 113 (excl. the Speaker)

CABINET

Prime Minister and First Lord of the Treasury Lord Melbourne
Lord Chancellor Lord Cottenham (1836–41)
Lord President of the Council Marquess of Lansdowne
Lord Privy Seal Lord Duncannon (1835–Jan 1840); Earl of Clarendon (1840–41)

Second Administration 18 Apr 1835–30 Aug 1841—*Continued*

First Commissioner of Woods and Forests Lord Duncannon
Chancellor of the Exchequer T. Spring Rice (1835–39); Sir F. T. Baring (1839–41)
Home Secretary Lord J. Russell (1835–39); Marquess of Normanby (1839–41)
Foreign Secretary Viscount Palmerston
Secretary for War and Colonies Lord Glenelg (1835–39); Marquess of Normandy (Feb–Aug 1839); Lord J. Russell (1839–41)
First Lord of the Admiralty Lord Auckland (Apr–Sep 1835); Earl of Minto (1835–41)
President of the Board of Trade C. Poulett Thomson (Apr–Aug 1839); H. Labouchere (1839–41)
President of the Board of Control Sir J. C. Hobhouse
Chancellor of the Duchy of Lancaster Lord Holland (1835–40); Earl of Clarendon (1840–Jun 1841); Sir G. Grey (1841)
Secretary at War Viscount Howick (1835–39); T. B. Macaulay (1839–41)
*Chief Secretary for Ireland** Viscount Morpeth (1839–41)
[*Office not always in Cabinet]

IMPORTANT DATES IN PERSONAL AND POLITICAL LIFE

1799 Melbourne leaves Cambridge and studies in Glasgow for two years.
1804 Called to the Bar and works briefly on the Northern Circuit.
24 JAN 1805 Death of his elder brother Peniston. Now heir to his father's estates, Melbourne abandons his legal career.
3 JUN 1805 Marries Lady Caroline Ponsonby.
31 JAN 1806 First enters Parliament as MP for Leominster.
19 DEC 1806 Maiden speech in reply to the King's speech at the opening of Parliament.
28 AUG 1807 His only child, Augustus, is born.
25 MAY 1810 Speaks in the House of Commons advocating the emancipation of Catholics.
FEB 1812 Refuses to accept a post in Spencer Perceval's Tory administration as a Lord of the Treasury.
1812 Lady Caroline Lamb's notorious affair with Lord Byron begins. It is to end in the summer of 1813, although Caroline continued to write to Byron and made efforts to see him.
SEP 1812 Melbourne does not stand at the General Election and remains out of the House of Commons for almost four years.
1815 Lady Caroline's brother Frederick seriously wounded at the Battle of Waterloo. The Lambs go to him and live in Brussels during June and August.
16 APR 1816 Elected MP for Peterborough.
MAY 1816 Lady Caroline Lamb's autobiographical novel, *Glenarvon*, published, creating a sensation in fashionable society and greatly embarrassing Melbourne and his family.
6 APR 1818 Death of his mother, Lady Melbourne
29 JAN 1820 Death of George III.
1825 Melbourne and Lady Caroline are formally separated.
JUN 1826 Fearing defeat, Melbourne decides not to seek reelection as MP for Hertfordshire at the General Election.
29 APR 1827 Canning becomes PM and appoints Melbourne Chief Secretary for Ireland; a seat is found for him as MP for Newport, Isle of Wight, and then exchanged for Bletchingley.
8 AUG 1827 Death of Canning. Lord Goderich becomes PM for a short time but resigns early in 1828.
1827 Melbourne meets Lady Elizabeth Branden. Their affair is to last about five years.
26 JAN 1828 Death of Lady Caroline Lamb.
APR 1828 Wellington is PM and although Melbourne had continued in his post as Chief Secretary for Ireland he now resigns along with Palmerston and Dudley, following the quarrel between the PM and Huskisson over the corrupt borough of East Retford. The Government wants the seat abolished and the franchise transferred to the adjoining country districts. Huskisson argues that it should go to Birmingham, which is under-represented.
MAY 1828 A court case brought by Lord Branden against Melbourne alleging that he had seduced his wife is dismissed, but Melbourne has to pay substantial amounts to Branden to ensure that the action goes no further.
22 JUL 1828 Death of his father, the 1st Viscount Melbourne.
1 FEB 1829 Melbourne takes the oath and sits in the House of Lords for the first time.
13 APR 1829 The Catholic Relief Bill receives the Royal Assent. Melbourne has always favoured the emancipation of Catholics and the new Act enables them to be admitted by a new oath to Parliament and to nearly all civil and political offices.
26 JUN 1830 Death of George IV and accession of William IV.
16 NOV 1830 Wellington resigns as PM.
22 NOV 1830 Melbourne becomes Home Secretary in Grey's administration.
1830–31 Agrarian troubles. As Home Secretary, Melbourne has to lay down firm measures to contain these.
1831 Beginning of Melbourne's friendship with Mrs. Caroline Norton.
7 JUN 1832 The Reform Bill receives the Royal Assent.
1834 Transportation of the Tolpuddle Martyrs. They are six agricultural labourers from Dorset who have tried to unionise their fellow labourers. They are convicted on charges of administering illegal oaths and sentenced to transportation to Australia. Melbourne deals calmly with the unionists' deputations sent to plead with him and the ensuing protests and demonstrations. The sentence of the six is remitted in 1836, and they are given permission to return to England.
2 JAN 1834 Death of George Lamb, Melbourne's brother and his Under-Secretary for Home Affairs.
16 JUL 1834 Melbourne becomes PM after Grey resigns. 'He is the only man to be Prime Minister', Lord Durham says, 'because he is the only one of whom none of us would be jealous.' It is essentially a caretaker administration.
16 OCT 1834 Destruction of the Houses of Parliament by fire.
14 NOV 1834 William IV, whose sympathies lie with the Tories, dismisses Melbourne as PM despite the Whig majority in the House of Commons.
10 DEC 1834 Sir Robert Peel becomes PM.
JAN 1835 General Election. Although the Tories win about another 80 seats they remain in a minority in the House of Commons.
8 APR 1835 After a series of defeats in the Commons, Peel resigns.

18 APR 1835 Melbourne becomes PM for the second time.

1835 Municipal Corporations Act passes: a reform measure intended to wipe out corruption and incompetence in local government.

1836 Dissenters' Marriage Act. This measure allows dissenters to be married in their own chapels.

22 JUN 1836 George Norton brings a civil suit for damages against Melbourne because of his friendship with his wife. Melbourne and Caroline Norton are found not guilty of an adulterous relationship.

26 NOV 1836 Death of his son Augustus.

20 JUN 1837 Death of William IV and accession of Victoria.

JUL 1837 General Election. Whigs remain in power. Melbourne spends a great deal of time advising the young Queen and takes on the role of her private secretary.

1838 Rebellion breaks out in Canada. Lord Durham becomes Governor General and is given special powers.

1838–39 The Government is discredited by the Hastings affair. Lady Flora Hastings, a Lady-in-Waiting to the Queen's mother and a member of a Tory family, is suspected of being pregnant, although unmarried. These suspicions are shared by the Queen, but prove to be unfounded, although Lady Flora has to submit to medical examinations to clear her name. The Tories rally behind the family, attacking the Government and there is criticism of Victoria.

7 MAY 1839 Melbourne resigns as PM after a very close vote in the Commons on a measure to suspend the constitution in Jamaica, where a rebellion has broken out.

11 MAY 1839 Melbourne resumes office as PM after Peel has refused to form an administration because Victoria declines to give up any of her Ladies of the Bedchamber, most of whom were members of Whig families. Melbourne is reluctant to place the inexperienced Queen in a difficult position, and although constitutionally wrong, he continues his administration to prevent the Queen's wishes being overruled. The Bedchamber Question leaves the Government weakened and further discredited.

10 FEB 1840 Victoria marries her cousin, Albert of Saxe-Coburg.

1840 The Syrian question leads to a crisis in relations with France and to conflict within Melbourne's Cabinet. The Treaty of London allied Britain with Austria, Prussia and Russia to attempt to force Mehemet Ali, the Turkish Sultan's Viceroy of Egypt out of Syria, where he had assumed control. The French are left out of the alliance and French relations with Britain deteriorate sharply. The Cabinet are divided on how to avoid war with France, but Melbourne manages to hold his administration together until the crisis is over, despite accusations of indecisiveness and prevarication.

27 MAY 1841 The Government is defeated in the House of Commons on a vote of no confidence proposed by Peel. Parliament is dissolved and the Whigs are defeated at the General Election.

30 AUG 1841 Melbourne resigns as PM following the defeat of the Whigs at the General Election and in both Houses of Parliament on votes following the Address.

23 OCT 1842 He suffers a severe stroke from which he never fully recovers; he resigns from the leadership of the party.

24 NOV 1848 Melbourne dies at Brocket Hall in Hertfordshire.

BACKGROUND

PHYSICAL CHARACTERISTICS AND HEALTH

Melbourne was a tall, dark, handsome man, but tended to be overweight (he always ate and drank a great deal). A contemporary described him as having 'a sweet countenance and an expression of refined, easy, careless good humour.' He had a knack of falling asleep when and wherever he felt like it and a habit of absentmindedly talking to himself. He was often troubled by gout and by 1835 was sometimes crippled by it for a week at a time. As Melbourne grew older he suffered much from lumbago and acute attacks of indigestion. As his health deteriorated he became subject to insomnia and depression. In October 1842 he had a stroke from which he never fully recovered.

EDUCATION

Primary 1785–88, Melbourne boarded with a private tutor, the Reverend Thomas Marsham, Curate of Hatfield.

Secondary 1788–96, Eton

University 1796–99, Trinity College, Cambridge; 1799–1801, Studied under Professor Millar in Glasgow

Prizes and awards 1798, He won the Trinity College declamation prize with an oration on *The Progressive Improvements of Mankind.*

Qualifications 1799, MA

Cultural and vocational background Melbourne spent his year in Glasgow studying and debating religion, politics and the law. When he returned to London he immediately became part of the society in which his mother was firmly established as a leading hostess. Her guests included politicians and Royalty; Melbourne was soon fully occupied with social engagements until he embarked on serious study for his legal career in Nov 1802.

Languages Latin, Greek and French

NON-PARLIAMENTARY CAREER

Early occupations Melbourne had been entered at Lincoln's Inn on 21 Jul 1797. He moved into Chambers in Dec 1801 and began to study in earnest for a legal career in Nov 1802. He was called to the Bar in the Michaelmas term 1804 and worked briefly on the Northern Circuit. His career was ended by the death of his elder brother, which left him heir to the peerage and the family estates and fortune.

Military service Captain, Hertfordshire Voluntary Infantry, 1803; Major, 1804

Other posts Elder Brother of Trinity House, 1836–48

HONOURS

Other than peerage 1841, Melbourne refused to accept the Order of the Garter on leaving office saying. 'I wish to quit office without having any honour conferred upon me; the Queen's confidence towards me is sufficiently known without any public mark of this nature. I have always disregarded these honours, and there would be an inconsistency in my accepting this'; 25 Feb 1841, Fellow of the Royal Society.

CLUBS

Brooks's, White's

HOBBIES AND SPORTS

Melbourne was a sociable man who loved conversation. He read a great deal throughout his life, studying theological works and Elizabethan drama; he had a passion for Shakespeare and could recite long passages from the plays. Although he generally took very little exercise, he enjoyed a day's shooting and was an excellent shot.

FINANCES

After the death of his elder brother, Melbourne became heir to the family estates which included Brocket Hall in Hertfordshire, Melbourne Hall in Derbyshire, Melbourne House in Whitehall, London, and coalfields in Derbyshire and Nottinghamshire. By 1842 he became increasingly concerned about his financial position. His income had decreased by one third mainly because he had run his houses in London and the country extravagantly. He sold Melbourne House in Whitehall to economise and bought a house in South Street, Mayfair. He was generous and lavish, in 1847 he was still paying Lady Branden £800–£1,000 a year as well as making presents to Mrs. Norton.

Income In 1835 it was £21,000 p.a.

Pensions He was refused a state pension in his later years as he still had a considerable fortune.

Legacies Inherited a substantial fortune as well as the family estates from his father in 1828.

Debts Borrowed £10,000 at 3 percent interest in 1848 from Queen Victoria to meet commitments.

Will His heir was his brother Frederick James Lamb, 3rd Viscount Melbourne.

ANECDOTES

1827, When Canning proposed Melbourne for the post of Chief Secretary for Ireland, William IV said 'William Lamb, William Lamb—put him anywhere you like'.

28 May 1828, When Melbourne resigned as Chief Secretary for Ireland, his sister Emily Cowper wrote to their brother Frederick Lamb: 'William is very well satisfied to resign, is as usual in very good spirits and stands higher in character with all parties than anybody else in England, so that I think we shall still see him some day Prime Minister . . . '

Melbourne's handwriting was notoriously bad. While Home Secretary he wrote to order the transfer of a regiment of infantry. Anglesey replied: 'It must be acknowledged that your 50s and your 80s are fatally alike. However, I soon discovered my error . . . and the 50th, instead of the 80th, is upon the move'.

1836, 'Although Melbourne may be *trop camarade* for a Prime Minister in some things, yet it is this very familiar, unguarded manner, when it is backed by perfect integrity and quite sufficient talent, that makes him perfectly invaluable and invulnerable'. (Talleyrand)

1838, Melbourne ate and drank to excess; in 1838 Lady Lyttelton observed that nothing would remove him from office, 'unless he contrives to displace himself by dint of consommés, truffles, pears, ices and anchovies, which he does his best to revolutionize his stomach with every day.'

Melbourne's relationship with Queen Victoria was one of trusted friend and mentor; he was almost paternal in his attitude towards her and she in turn relied heavily on her Prime Minister. She noted in her journal that he was 'very straightforward, honest, clever and good' and that 'he alone inspires me with that feeling of great confidence and I may say security, for I feel so safe when he speaks to me and is with me'. Melbourne took on the role of her private secretary and spent a great deal of time in attendance on the young Queen.

QUOTATIONS

1812, It is impossible that anybody can feel the being out of Parliament more keenly for me than I feel it for myself. It is actually cutting my throat. It is depriving me of the great object of my life. . . .

1834, After he had been dismissed as PM by William IV he said to Holland, 'I hardly ever felt so much relaxed or in better spirits in my life. I know by experience that after a time one gets tired of being out and longs for office, but at first nothing can be more delightful.'

1835, Nothing induces a man to keep his own temper so much as the observation that others either have lost or are likely to lose theirs.

To Queen Victoria: 'No woman should touch pen and ink . . . they have too much passion and too little sense'.

If a thing is very urgent you can always find time for it; but if a thing can be put off, why then you put it off.

RESIDENCES

Brocket Hall, Hertfordshire
Melbourne Hall, Derbyshire
Melbourne House, Piccadilly, London
Melbourne House, Whitehall, London (now known as *Dover House* and used by the Scottish Office)
South Street, Mayfair, London

Melbourne refused to live at 10 Downing Street while he was PM, preferring to stay at his house in South Street, Mayfair.

Open to the public Melbourne Hall and gardens

MEMORIALS

STATUES AND BUSTS

1838, bust by R. Moody, Royal Collection; 1838, bust by John Francis, Royal Collection; 1841, bust by Sir Francis Chantrey, Royal Collection

PORTRAITS

1796, by John Hoppner, Royal Collection; *c.* 1805, by Sir Thomas Lawrence, National Portrait Gallery; 1836, by Sir Edwin Landseer, National Portrait Gallery; 1839, 'Queen Victoria and Lord Melbourne riding at Windsor' by Sir Francis Grant. Royal Collection; 1844, by John Partridge, National Portrait Gallery

BIBLIOGRAPHIC INFORMATION

LETTERS AND PERSONAL PAPERS

Most of Melbourne's papers are in either the Royal Archives at Windsor Castle or Hertfordshire Record Office. Some of his political correspondence is held by the Broadlands Archives Trust.

Lord Melbourne's Papers. Ed. Lloyd C. Sanders. London, 1889.

FURTHER READING

Cecil, D. *Melbourne*. London, 1965.
Marshall, D. *Lord Melbourne*. London, 1976.
Torrens, W. McC. *Memoirs of the Right Honorable William, Second Viscount Melbourne*. 2 vols. London, 1878.
Ziegler, P. *Melbourne*. London, 1976.

I.W.

Bettmann

Sir Robert Peel

Lived 1788–1850

Political Party Conservative

Prime Minister 10 December 1834–8 April 1835
30 August 1841–29 June 1846

Governments Conservative

Reigning Monarchs William IV; Victoria

Industria By industry

PEEL AS PRIME MINISTER

Peel was Chief Secretary for Ireland at age 24 and then Home Secretary a decade later. Clever, with a practical axiomatic style, he sought to analyse problems and then follow up with action. Coming from a successful industrial background, being an enlightened landlord, he was interested in helping the working classes and underpinning the emerging middle class. He thereby helped his country avoid the revolutionary dramas that swept through much of continental Europe in 1848. As Home Secretary he founded the Metropolitan Police in 1829 (the Peelers) and with difficuty carried through the Catholic Relief Bill in 1829. Following the 1834 election, when Peel explained his policies to his Tamworth constituents—the Tamworth Manifesto— he was invited to form his first administration, which lasted just four months. In his second administration he reintroduced income tax and certain more conciliatory measures toward Ireland and, finally, both on principle and under pressure of approaching famine in Ireland repealed the Corn Laws. This split the Conservative Party which Peel had led since 1834 and he and his supporters, the Peelites, were subject to attacks from the rising Conservative star Disraeli. In 1846 Peel resigned as Prime Minister claiming in a famous speech that while maintaining Tory principles, he had ameliorated the lot of labour.

PERSONAL INFORMATION

Names Sir Robert Peel (2nd baronet)
Nickname Orange Peel
Born 5 Feb 1788
Birthplace Chamber Hall, near Bury, Lancashire
Religion Anglican
Ancestry Peel came from a Lancashire family of farmers and weavers, who had become textile manufacturers.
Date and place of marriage 8 Jun 1820, 45 Upper (West) Seymour Street, near Hyde Park, London
Age at marriage 32 years, 124 days
Years married 30 years, 24 days
First entered Parliament 15 Apr 1809
Dates appointed PM 1) 10 Dec 1834; 2) 30 Aug 1841
Age at appointments 1) 46 years, 308 days; 2) 53 years, 206 days
Dates ceased to be PM 1) 8 Apr 1835; 2) 29 Jun 1846
Total time as PM 1) 119 days; 2) 4 years, 303 days; a total of 5 years, 57 days
Ceased to be MP 2 Jul 1850
Lived after last term as PM 4 years, 3 days
Date of death 2 Jul 1850
Place of death 4 Whitehall Gardens, London
Age at death 62 years, 147 days
Place of funeral and burial Drayton Bassett Parish Church, Staffordshire
Zodiac sign Aquarius

FATHER

Sir Robert Peel, 1st Baronet
Date and place of birth 25 Apr 1750, Peelfold, Oswaldtwistle, Lancashire
Occupation Landowner and one of the most successful cotton mill owners in the country; in 1802 he employed about 15,000 people. MP Tamworth 1790–1820, he was made a Baronet in 1800. Peel was concerned for the welfare of the children who worked in his factories and in 1802 he introduced the Health and Morals of Apprentices Bill which laid down measures designed to protect the children in the cotton mills. It was the first piece of legislation of its kind.
Dates of marriages 1) 8 Jul 1783, Ellen Yates (d. 1803); 2) 17 Oct 1805, Susanna Clerke
Date of death 3 May 1830
Place of burial Drayton Bassett Parish Church, Staffordshire

MOTHER

Ellen Yates
Date of birth 1766
Profile Ellen Yates was the daughter of Peel's partner in his cotton business, William Yates. She was an energetic woman with a pleasant temperament who died not long after the birth of her eleventh child.
Date of marriage 8 Jul 1783
Date of death 28 Dec 1803
Place of burial Drayton Bassett Parish Church, Staffordshire

STEPMOTHER

Susanna Clerke
Date of marriage 17 Oct 1805
Date of death 10 Sep 1824

BROTHERS AND SISTERS

Peel was the eldest son and third of eleven children.
From his father's first marriage:
Mary, b. 1785; m. George Dawson (MP Co. Derry, 1815–30, Harwich 1830–32; an Irish landowner and an old college friend of Peel) d. Jan 1848
Elizabeth, b. 1786; m. Rev. William Cockburn (Dean of York); d. 16 Jun 1828
William Yates, b. 3 Aug 1789; m. Lady Jane Moore, daughter of the 2nd Earl of Mountcashell; MP Bossiney, 1817–18, Tamworth 1818–30, Yarmouth, Isle of Wight, 1830–31, Cambridge University 1831–32, Tamworth 1835–37 and 1847; Commissioner of the Board of Control 1826; Under-Secretary for the Home Department 1828; Lord of the Treasury 1830 and 1834–35; d. 1 Jun 1858
Edmund, b. 8 Aug 1791; m. Emily Swinfen; Owned mills at Fazeley and was Chairman of the Trent Valley Railway Company; MP Newcastle-under-Lyme 1831, 1835–37; d. 1 Nov 1850
John, b. 22 Aug 1798; m. Augusta Swinfen; Entered the church. Peel bought him a living in Handsworth, Warwickshire; d. 20 Feb 1875
Jonathan, b. 12 Oct 1799; m. Alice Jane, daughter of the Marquess of Ailsa; MP Norwich 1826, Huntingdon 1831–68; Surveyor-General of the Ordnance 1841–46; Secretary of State for War 1858–59 and 1866; Major-General in the Army 1854, Lieutenant-General 1859; d. 13 Feb 1879
Lawrence, b. 1801; m. Lady Jane Lennox, daughter of the Duke of Richmond; Private Secretary to Peel at the Home Office 1822; d. 10 Dec 1888
Harriet Eleonora, b. Apr 1803; m. Robert Henley Eden, Lord Henley; d. 7 May 1869
Eleonora, d. 1803 (in childhood)
Anne, d. Aug 1799 (in childhood)
From his father's second marriage: None.

WIFE

Name Julia Floyd
Date and place of birth 19 Nov 1795, India
Mother Rebecca Juliana Darke (d. 1 Feb 1802); Stepmother: Lady Denny (m. Sir John Floyd Jul 1805)
Father General Sir John Floyd, Bt, K.B.
Father's occupation Officer in the Army
Age at Marriage 24 years, 202 days
Number of children 7
Date and place of death 28 Oct 1859, 4 Whitehall Gardens, London
Place of burial Drayton Bassett Parish Church, Staffordshire
Years younger than PM 7 years, 288 days
Profile

Lady Peel was a beautiful but temperamental woman. As she grew older she became more nervous and emotional. Her life centred on her family and her husband in particular to whom she was completely devoted. She was not very interested in politics nor was she noted as a society hostess but was always supportive of Peel, corresponding with him constantly when they were apart. She was distraught at his death and, on refusing a peerage which had been offered her soon after by Lord John Russell, she declared that 'the solace (if

WIFE—*Continued*

any such remains for me) for the deplored bereavement I sustain will be that I bear the same unaltered honoured name that lives for ever distinguished by his virtues and his services'.

CHILDREN

5 sons, 2 daughters

Julia, b. 30 Apr 1821; m. 1) 14 Jul 1841, Viscount Villiers, later 6th Earl of Jersey (d. 1859); 2) Charles Brandling; d. 14 Aug 1893

Robert, (G.C.B. 3rd Baronet); b. 4 May 1822; m. 17 Jan 1856 Lady Emily Hay, daughter of 8th Marquess of Tweeddale; Diplomatic Service 1844–50; MP Tamworth 1850–80, Huntingdon 1884–85, Blackburn 1885–86; Junior Lord of the Admiralty 1855–57; Chief Secretary for Ireland 1861–65; d. 9 May 1895

Frederick (Rt. Hon. Sir Frederick Peel K.C.M.G.), b. 26 Oct 1823; m. 1) 1857 Elizabeth Emily Shelley (d. 1865); 2) 1879 Janet Pleydell-Bouverie; MP Leominster 1849–52; Bury 1852–57 and 1859–65; Under-Secretary of State for the Colonies 1851–52 and Dec 1852–55; Under-Secretary of State of War 1855–57; 1860, financial Secretary to the Treasury; Chief Railway Commissioner; d. 6 Jun 1906

William, (Sir William Peel K.C.B.), b. Nov 1824; Captain in the Royal Navy. Won the V.C; Served in the Crimea and was Commander of the Naval Brigade during the Indian Mutiny; d. 27 Apr 1858

John Floyd, b. 24 May 1827; m. 1851 Annie Jenney; Captain, Scots Fusilier Guards; d. 21 Apr 1910

Arthur Wellesley (Viscount Peel of Sandy); b. 3 Aug 1829; m. 14 Aug 1862 Adelaide Dugdale; MP Warwick 1865–85; Warwick & Leamington 1885–95. Secretary for the Poor Law Board 1868–71; Parliamentary Secretary to the Board of Trade 1871–73; Liberal Chief Whip and Parliamentary Secretary to the Treasury 1873–74; Under- Secretary of State for the Home Department Apr–Dec 1880. Speaker of the House of Commons 1884–95; created Viscount Peel 1895; d. 24 Oct 1912

Eliza, b. Apr 1832; m. 25 Sep 1855 Hon. Francis Stonor, son of Lord Camoys; d. Apr 1883

LIFE AND CAREER

PARLIAMENTARY ELECTIONS FOUGHT

(**designates candidate elected)*

DATE 15 Apr 1809. By-election caused by the resignation of Quinton Dick
CONSTITUENCY Cashel
RESULT Robert Peel* (Con)

DATE Oct 1812 General Election
CONSTITUENCY Cashel
RESULT Robert Peel* (Con)

DATE Oct 1812. General Election
CONSTITUENCY Chippenham
RESULT Charles Brooke* (Lib); Robert Peel** (Con)

***Elected both for Cashel and Chippenham, he chose to sit for Chippenham.*

DATE 10 Jun 1817. By-election caused by the resignation of Speaker Charles Abbot (later Lord Colchester) because of ill-health
CONSTITUENCY Oxford University
RESULT Robert Peel* (Con)

DATE Jun 1818. General Election
CONSTITUENCY Oxford University
RESULT Sir William Scott* (Con); Robert Peel* (Con)

DATE Mar 1820. General Election
CONSTITUENCY Oxford University
RESULT Sir William Scott* (Con); Robert Peel* (Con)

DATE 12 Feb 1822. By-election caused by Peel's appointment as Home Secretary
CONSTITUENCY Oxford University
RESULT Robert Peel* (Con)

DATE Jun 1826. General Election
CONSTITUENCY Oxford University
RESULT Robert Peel* (Con); Thomas G.B. Estcourt* (Con)

DATE 4 Feb 1828. By-election caused by Peel's appointment as Home Secretary
CONSTITUENCY Oxford University
RESULT Robert Peel* (Con)

DATE 28 Feb 1829. By-election caused by Peel's resignation over the issue of Catholic emancipation
CONSTITUENCY Oxford University
RESULT Robert H. Inglis Bt.* (Con) 755; Robert Peel (Con) 699

DATE 2 Mar 1829. By-election caused by the resignation of Sir M.M. Lopes Bt.
CONSTITUENCY Westbury
RESULT Robert Peel* (Con)

DATE Jul 1830. General Election
CONSTITUENCY Tamworth
RESULT Lord C.V.F. Townshend* (Lib); Robert Peel* (Con)

DATE Apr 1831. General Election
CONSTITUENCY Tamworth
RESULT Lord C.V.F. Townshend* (Lib); Sir Robert Peel* (Con)

DATE Dec 1832. General Election
CONSTITUENCY Tamworth
RESULT Lord C.V.F. Townshend* (Lib); Sir Robert Peel* (Con)

DATE Jan 1835. General Election
CONSTITUENCY Tamworth
RESULT Sir Robert Peel* (Con); W.Y. Peel* (Con)

DATE Jul 1837. General Election
CONSTITUENCY Tamworth
RESULT Sir Robert Peel* (Con) 387; E. H. A'Court* (Con) 245; J. Townshend (Lib) 185

DATE Jun 1841. General Election
CONSTITUENCY Tamworth
RESULT Sir Robert Peel* (Con) 365; E. H. A'Court* (Con) 241; J. Townshend (Lib) 147

DATE 13 Sep 1841. By-election caused by Peel's appointment as Prime Minister
CONSTITUENCY Tamworth
RESULT Sir Robert Peel* (Con)

DATE Jul 1847. General Election
CONSTITUENCY Tamworth

RESULT Sir Robert Peel* (Con); W.Y. Peel* (Con)

PARTY ACTIVITY

Party Leadership Leader of the Conservative Party 1834–46

PARLIAMENTARY AND MINISTERIAL EXPERIENCE

Maiden Speech 23 Jan 1810. Peel seconded the reply to the King's speech at the opening of Parliament. He spoke for forty minutes and the speech was widely acclaimed. (HC Deb, 1st ser, vol XV, col 39-43)
Privy Counsellor 13 Aug 1812; 5 Sep 1812 (Ireland)
Ministerial Offices Under- Secretary of State for War and the Colonies, Jun 1810–Aug 1812; Chief Secretary for Ireland, 4 Aug 1812–3 Aug 1818; Home Secretary, 17 Jan 1822–10 Apr 1827; Home Secretary and Leader of the House of Commons, 26 Jan 1828–15 Nov 1830; Chancellor of the Exchequer 10 Dec 1834–8 Apr 1835; First Lord of the Treasury and Leader of the House of Commons 10 Dec 1834–8 Apr 1835, 30 Aug 1841–29 Jun 1846
Opposition leaders while PM 1834–35, Lord John Russell; 1841–46, Lord John Russell

GOVERNMENTS FORMED

First Administration 10 Dec 1834–8 Apr 1835

GENERAL ELECTION RESULT
DEC 1832: Whigs 441; Tories 175; Others 42. Total 658
Whig majority 225 (excl. the Speaker)
CABINET
Prime Minister, First Lord of the Treasury and Chancellor of the Exchequer Sir R. Peel
Home Secretary H. Goulburn
Foreign Secretary Duke of Wellington
Lord Chancellor Lord Lyndhurst
Secretary of State for War and the Colonies Earl of Aberdeen
Secretary at War J. C. Herries
Lord Privy Seal Lord Wharncliffe
First Lord of the Admiralty Earl de Grey
President of the Board of Trade A. Baring (Lord Ashburton)
Lord President of the Council Earl of Rosslyn
President of the Board of Control Lord Ellenborough
Paymaster General Sir E. Knatchbull
Master-General of the Ordnance Sir G. Murray

Second Administration 30 Aug 1841–29 Jun 1846

GENERAL ELECTION RESULT
JUN 1841: Conservative 367; Liberal 271; Others 20. Total 658
Conservative majority 77 (excl. the Speaker)
CABINET
Prime Minister and First Lord of the Treasury Sir R. Peel
Lord Chancellor Lord Lyndhurst
Chancellor of the Exchequer H. Goulburn
Home Secretary Sir J. Graham
Foreign Secretary Earl of Aberdeen
Colonial Secretary Lord Stanley (1841–45); W. E. Gladstone (1845–46)
President of the Board of Trade Earl of Ripon (1841–43); W. E. Gladstone (1843–45); Marquess of Dalhousie (1845–46)
President of the Board of Control Earl of Ellenborough (Sep–Oct 1841); Lord Fitzgerald & Vesey (1841–43); Earl of Ripon (1843–46)
Paymaster General Sir E. Knatchbull (1844–45); Lord Ashburton (1845–46)
Lord Privy Seal Duke of Buckingham (1841–42); Duke of Buccleuch (1842–46); Earl of Haddington (Jan–Jun 1846)
Lord President of the Council Lord Wharncliffe (1841–Jan 1846); Duke of Buccleuch (Jan–Jun 1846)
First Lord of the Admiralty Earl of Haddington (1841–46); Earl of Ellenborough (Feb–Jun 1846)
*Secretary at War** Sir H. Hardinge (1841–44): S. Herbert (1845–46)
Commander-in-Chief (but without Civil Office) Duke of Wellington
*Chancellor of the Duchy of Lancaster** Lord G. Somerset (1844–46)
*First Commissioner of Woods and Forests** Earl of Lincoln (1845–46)
[* Office not always in Cabinet]

IMPORTANT DATES IN PERSONAL AND POLITICAL LIFE

MAR 1809 Leaves Oxford University
14 APR 1809 Peel returned as MP for Cashel in Tipperary, Ireland.
23 JAN 1810 Maiden speech, seconding the reply to the King's speech at the opening of Parliament. It was 40 minutes long and applauded by all who heard it.
JUN 1810 Peel appointed Under Secretary for War and the Colonies in Spencer Perceval's administration.
4 AUG 1812 Lord Liverpool becomes Prime Minister following the assassination of Perceval. Appoints Peel Chief Secretary for Ireland.
13 AUG 1812 Peel sworn a Privy Counsellor and the following month arrives in Dublin to take up his new post.
OCT 1812 Peel returned as MP for both Cashel and Chippenham at the General Election. He decides to sit for Chippenham.
MAY 1813 Daniel O'Connell dubs Peel 'Orange Peel' in a speech attacking him as Chief Secretary for Ireland.
23 JUN 1814 Introduction of the Peace Preservation Bill, designed to strengthen the Irish police force by giving the Lord Lieutenant powers to appoint special constables under a magistrate to restore law and order in disturbed areas.
8 JUL 1814 Peel proposes a renewal of the Insurrection Act in Ireland; by the end of the month both the Peace Preservation Bill and this measure have been passed by Parliament.
29 AUG 1815 O'Connell issues a direct challenge to Peel and they agree to meet at Ostend for a duel. It never takes place, however, as O'Connell is arrested after his arrival in London.
9 MAY 1817 Debate on Catholic emancipation in the House of Commons. Peel makes a powerful speech opposing emancipation and gains for himself a national reputation.
10 JUN 1817 Peel elected MP for Oxford University at by-election caused by the resignation of Charles Abbot, Speaker of the House of Commons.
3 AUG 1818 Resigns as Chief Secretary for Ireland; having held the post for six years he is anxious to have a period of respite.
1819 Peel is Chairman of the Parliamentary Committee of Enquiry into the return of the gold standard—the

IMPORTANT DATES IN PERSONAL AND POLITICAL LIFE—*Continued*

Currency Committee. The Bill that follows from the Committee's report lays the foundations of the currency system in Britain for the rest of the century.

8 JUN 1820 Marries Julia Floyd.

28 NOV 1821 Peel accepts offer of the post of Home Secretary in Liverpool's administration.

17 JAN 1822 Receives Home Secretary's seals of office from King George IV.

14 MAR 1822 Peel proposes that a House of Commons Select Committee be established to look into the policing of the metropolis. He chairs the Committee himself.

17 JUN 1822 The Committee reports that an effective system of policing cannot be reconciled with a free society. Peel, however, remains convinced of the need for an efficient police force.

23 MAR 1825 Burdett's Bill to emancipate Catholics is introduced. Peel opposes the Bill but it continues through its stages successfully. Peel decides his position is untenable and at the end of April offers his resignation. The Bill is defeated in the House of Lords, however, and he stays on as Home Secretary.

1825 Jury Act. This is Peel's first consolidation measure and first major reform of the criminal law. It consolidates 85 Acts relating to juries.

9 MAR 1826 Introduction of measures to consolidate the law on theft, and to reform the administration of justice. The latter becomes law by the end of the session but Peel has second thoughts about his criminal justice Bill and it is held over until 1827 when four Bills are introduced to deal with the laws on theft and malicious injury to property and to repeal old statutes which have been rendered obsolete. A further Bill reforming aspects of the criminal law will be introduced in May 1827; by the end of the session all of them are on the statute book.

1826 A trade depression and an industrial slump bring widespread unrest in the factories. Working hours are reduced, and wages lowered, resulting in unemployment, riots and crime. As Home Secretary Peel uses military force with restraint to control the situation.

MAR 1827 Lord Liverpool, the Prime Minister resigns because of ill health. Peel tells George IV that he cannot serve under Canning, opposed as they are on the issue of Catholic emancipation. He resigns when Canning becomes Prime Minister on 10 Apr 1827.

1 MAY 1827 Peel explains his resignation to the House of Commons and denies any personal hostility towards Canning.

8 AUG 1827 Death of Canning. Viscount Goderich becomes Prime Minister but his administration is short-lived.

22 JAN 1828 The Duke of Wellington becomes Prime Minister; Peel takes office as Home Secretary and Leader of the House of Commons.

28 FEB 1828 Peel proposes a Committee of Enquiry into the state of the police and the increase in crime in London.

11 JUL 1828 The Committee recommend the establishment of a general police force for London (except for the City) under the immediate direction of the Home Secretary.

1829 Metropolitan Police Improvement Act. By September the Metropolitan police are on duty for the first time. They are called 'Bobbies' or 'Peelers', a tribute to the man who founded the force.

1829 To settle the Catholic emancipation question, Peel agrees, after a personal request from Wellington, to steer through Parliament the necessary legislation. His complete turnabout on this issue shocks his supporters and is never forgotten.

FEB 1829 Peel resigns his seat as MP for Oxford University because of the Catholic question. He stands again but is defeated. A seat is obtained for him after the 'resignation' of the Member for Westbury, Sir Manasseh Lopes.

13 APR 1829 The Catholic Relief Bill receives the Royal Assent. The Act enables Catholics to be admitted by a new oath to Parliament and to be eligible for nearly all civil and political offices.

3 MAY 1830 Death of his father. Peel inherits the baronetcy.

26 JUN 1830 Death of George IV and accession of William IV.

15 NOV 1830 Wellington's Government is defeated in the House of Commons on a vote on the Civil List and resigns the following day.

22 NOV 1830 Lord Grey becomes Prime Minister.

JUL–OCT 1834 Melbourne becomes Prime Minister following Lord Grey's resignation. Four months later, however, Melbourne and his administration are dismissed by William IV. Wellington takes office as Prime Minister but tells the King that the PM must be in the House of Commons and that the only man for the position is Peel. Peel, on holiday in Italy, is eventually tracked down.

25 NOV 1834 In Rome Peel is given William IV's letter commanding him to return home and head the new administration.

10 DEC 1834 Peel becomes Prime Minister for the first time.

18 DEC 1834 Peel issues his 'Tamworth Manifesto', ostensibly an address to his constituents but actually a statement of the principles and aims of his new administration.

30 DEC 1834 Parliament dissolved.

JAN 1835 General Election. The Conservatives gain some seats but do not have a majority.

FEB 1835 An Ecclesiastical Commission is set up to look into the income, patronage and organisation of the Church of England.

8 APR 1835 Peel resigns as Prime Minister. He has been unable to run business smoothly in the Commons. The Government has been defeated several times and finally resigns after defeat on a motion on the appropriation of the surplus revenues of the Irish Church.

18 APR 1835 Melbourne takes office as Prime Minister.

NOV 1836 Peel elected Rector of Glasgow University.

20 JUN 1837 Death of William IV and accession of Victoria.

7 MAY 1839 Melbourne resigns after a very close vote on the Bill to suspend the constitution in Jamaica following unrest in that country. Queen Victoria summons Peel and asks him to form an administration. The Queen refuses to give up her Ladies of the Bedchamber, most of whom have close Whig connections. Peel is unable to persuade her to do otherwise and Melbourne returns to office.

27 MAY 1841 The Government is defeated by one vote on a motion of no confidence.

JUN 1841 Parliament dissolved.

30 AUG 1841 Peel becomes Prime Minister for the second time following a Conservative victory at the General Election and Lord Melbourne's subsequent resignation.

11 MAR 1842 Peel announces the reintroduction of income tax.

1842 Frequent outbreaks of civil disorder as a result of unemployment and poverty.

20 JAN 1843 Peel's private secretary, Edward Drummond, shot in the back in Whitehall and dies of his injuries. The murderer had mistaken him for Peel.

NOV 1843 Queen Victoria and Prince Albert stay with Peel at Drayton Manor.

JUL 1844 Bank Charter Act regularizes the issue of notes and the central Banking functions of the Bank of England.

14 FEB 1845 Budget introduced by Peel. Tariffs greatly reduced and income tax renewed for a further three years.

NOV–DEC 1845 Peel holds a series of Cabinet meetings to discuss suspension of the Corn Laws. The potato crop has failed in Britain and Ireland and Peel wants to introduce measures which will gradually remove all duties on foreign corn imports over a period. The Cabinet is reluctant to support such a policy.

5 DEC 1845 Unable to unite the Cabinet Peel announces his decision to resign.

6 DEC 1845 Queen Victoria agrees that Lord John Russell should form the next Government; Peel will support him over the repeal of the Corn Laws.

20 DEC 1845 Lord John Russell fails to form a new administration and Peel resumes office. Lord Stanley resigns from the Cabinet but the other members of the Government unite behind Peel.

27 JAN 1846 Peel outlines his proposals for tariff reform to the House of Commons, including the reduction or abolition of a long list of duties and a progressive reduction until abolition in 1849 of the duty on corn.

28 FEB 1846 Twelve days of debate in the House of Commons on tariff reform come to an end. The Government motion is approved but two thirds of the Conservatives had voted against Peel.

25 JUN 1846 The Corn Bill passes its Third Reading in the House of Lords. In the Commons the Government is defeated on the Second Reading of the Irish Crimes Bill (the 'Coercion' Bill).

29 JUN 1846 Peel resigns as Prime Minister. He makes his famous resignation speech in the Commons later that day and is cheered by crowds all the way from his home in Whitehall Gardens to the Palace of Westminster.

28 JUN 1850 Last speech in the House of Commons on foreign policy.

29 JUN 1850 Falls from his horse on Constitution Hill. The horse stumbles on top of him, aggravating his injuries.

2 JUL 1850 Peel dies at Whitehall Gardens, London.

BACKGROUND

PHYSICAL CHARACTERISTICS AND HEALTH

Peel was a tall handsome man with blue eyes and reddish hair. Although his nose was curved and his complexion somewhat florid he was physically striking in appearance. He was a fastidious man and was always well dressed. He had great physical strength and stamina, especially in his youth, possibly because of his sporting activities. Although his health was generally good he suffered from inflammation of the eyes in 1821 (a condition which later recurred and was caused by the long years of work as Chief Secretary for Ireland). In 1837 he had his first attack of sciatica which he typically tried to cure by going grouse shooting. In the 1820's Peel had had a shooting accident while experimenting with a new type of cartridge; the noise had damaged his left ear and he suffered from a continual buzzing sound in his head which became worse when he was tired. The condition became chronic and caused him much distress over the years.

EDUCATION

Primary Peel had lessons at home with the Reverend James Hargreaves, Curate of Bury until he was ten. When the family moved to Drayton Manor he studied at a small school under the Reverend Francis Blick, Vicar of Tamworth, until he went to Harrow.

Secondary 1800–04, Harrow

University 1805–09, Christ Church, Oxford

Qualifications 1808, Double first class degree in classics and mathematics and physics; 1814, MA

NON-PARLIAMENTARY CAREER

Early occupations In Jun 1809 Peel entered Lincoln's Inn and began to prepare himself for a legal career.

Other posts 1827, Trustee of the National Gallery; 1837, Rector of Glasgow University; 1830–35, High Steward of the Borough of Tamworth; 1830–35, Elder Brother of Trinity House

HONOURS

Freedom of cities 1837 Burgh of Lanark; 1837 Glasgow

Academic 1817, DCL Oxford

Other than peerage Other than becoming a Privy Counsellor and on 5 Dec 1822, a Fellow of the Royal Society, Peel accepted no other honour throughout his career. He even left a note at his death stating that it was his wish that no member of his family should accept an honour on behalf of his own services in politics. He was also sparing in dispensing honours to others when he held ministerial office.

CLUBS

Alfred; Pitt's; White's; Union; Carlton

HOBBIES AND SPORTS

From his youth Peel enjoyed country sports, especially shooting. He was an excellent shot and throughout his life regularly attended shoots. At Oxford he took part in cricket and boat racing.One of his greatest hobbies was collecting paintings, mainly the classical Dutch and Flemish artists. He was the patron of Sir Thomas Lawrence who painted a series of portraits for Peel including one of his wife. Peel's other interests included reading. He had a fine library in his house in Whitehall Gardens and read widely in the areas of history, law and economics. He was also interested in science and agricultural reform, and played chess.

FINANCES

Peel was a rich man but he did not hoard his wealth. He spent his money on works of art, his properties, acquiring land and entertaining. He also made many donations to charitable causes particularly in his constituency of Tamworth where he founded a free school for poor boys and provided funds for the first public library and reading room in the town.

Income His salary as Chief Secretary for Ireland was £5, 000 per annum; after 1830 his gross annual income was probably over £40,000.

Legacies The estate of the 1st Baronet, Peel's father, amounted to nearly one and a half million pounds. A third went to Peel's brothers and sisters but the main Tamworth estate was inherited by Peel himself.

Will Peel's personal fortune was about £120,000 (more than half in land) apart from the entailed estate.

ANECDOTES

1788, There is an unconfirmed story that at Peel's birth his father fell on his knees and dedicated the child to the service of his country and at the christening publicly expressed the hope that he would follow in Pitt's footsteps. Peel himself related another incident when his father said to him 'Bob, you dog, if you are not Prime Minister some day, I'll disinherit you'.

Although he was a reserved man, Peel could be moved to unreasonable anger by personal criticism. He was twice on the brink of fighting a duel; the first time in 1815 with Daniel O'Connell who had attacked him as Chief Secretary for Ireland and the second in 1837 with Captain John Townshend who had claimed that Peel had used unfair influence at an election in Tamworth.

Peel gave his name to the 'Peelites', a group of yonger men who were committed to carrying on his principles after he left office. The Metropolitan Police were also known as 'Bobbies' or 'Peelers' after their founder.

Peel was a close friend of Queen Victoria and Prince Albert. When Peel died Victoria wrote that her husband 'feels he has lost a second father.'

QUOTATIONS

9 Mar 1826, In a speech in the House of Commons Peel referred to his 'legitimate ambition to leave behind me some record of the trust I have held, which may outlive the fleeting discharge of the mere duties of ordinary routine, and that may perhaps confer some distinction on my name, by connecting it with permanent improvements in the judicial institutions of the country.'

1 May 1827, I may be a Tory. I may be an illiberal—but . . . Tory as I am, I have the further satisfaction of knowing that there is not a single law connected with my name which has not had as its object some mitigation of the criminal law; some prevention of abuse in the exercise of it; or some security for its impartial adminstration. (Speech in the House of Commons)

29 Jun 1846, But it may be that I shall leave a name sometimes remembered with expressions of goodwill in the abodes of those whose lot it is to labour, and to earn their daily bread by the sweat of their brow, when they shall recruit their exhausted strength with abundant and untaxed food, the sweeter because it is no longer leavened by a sense of injustice. (Resignation as Prime Minister, speech in the House of Commons)

28 Jun 1850, Constitutional liberty will be best worked out by those who aspire to freedom by their own efforts. (Last speech on foreign policy, House of Commons)

RESIDENCES

Drayton Manor, near Tamworth, Staffordshire
11 Little Scotland Yard, London
36 Great George Street, London
12 Stanhope Street, off Park Lane, London
4 Whitehall Gardens, London

Open to the public Drayton Manor Park. The house that Peel had built in the 1830s was destroyed, but the area is now a pleasure park.

MEMORIALS

STATUES AND BUSTS

1835, bust by Sir Francis Chantrey, Royal Collection; 1851, by M. Noble, National Portrait Gallery; 1851, by E.H. Baily, Bury, Lancashire; 1852, by John Gibson, Westminster Abbey, London; 1852–54, by M. Noble, St. George's Hall, Liverpool; 1876–77, by M. Noble, Parliament Square, London

PORTRAITS

1826, by Sir Thomas Lawrence; 1838, by John Linnell, National Portrait Gallery; by H. W. Pickersgill, National Portrait Gallery; *c.* 1844, by F. X. Winterhalter, Royal Collection

BIBLIOGRAPHIC INFORMATION

LETTERS AND PERSONAL PAPERS

Most of Peel's papers are in the British Library; some correspondence with artists is in the Fitzwilliam Museum, Cambridge and various notebooks and cheque books are in the Surrey Record Office, Kingston upon Thames.

PUBLICATIONS

1856–57 Peel's, autobiographical memoranda on the Catholic emancipation in 1829 and the repeal of the Corn Laws in 1846 were published after his death in *Memoirs by the Rt. Hon. Sir Robert Peel.* Ed. Earl Stanhope and Edward Cardwell, 2 volumes.

FURTHER READING

Gash, N. *Mr. Secretary Peel: the Life of Sir Robert Peel to 1830.* 2nd ed. London, 1985.

—. *Sir Robert Peel: the Life of Sir Robert Peel after 1830.* 2nd ed. London, 1986.

—. *Peel.* London, 1976. [A condensed version of *Mr. Secretary Peel* and *Sir Robert Peel.*]

Parker, C.S. *Sir Robert Peel . . . From his Private Correspondence.* London, 1891.

I.W.

Bettmann

Lord John Russell

Lived 1792–1878

Political Party Liberal

Prime Minister 30 June 1846–21 February 1852
29 October 1865–26 June 1866

Governments Liberal

Reigning Monarch Victoria

Che sara sara What will be will be

RUSSELL AS PRIME MINISTER

Third son of the Duke of Bedford, Russell entered the House of Commons aged 22. He was soon identified as a reformer and his early work included drafting and introducing the Reform Bill. By 1834 he was the recognised leader of the House of Commons Liberals in opposition and in 1845 of the Liberal Party. He supported Peel's repeal of the Corn Laws and when in 1846 Peel was defeated, Russell, with the support of the Peelites, became Prime Minister. The 1847 General Election strengthened his position but he continued to lack an overall majority. His problems included the famine in Ireland where, after starting well, he failed to secure adequate Parliamentary funds to alleviate the famine. He did achieve improvements to the Poor Law, better pay for teachers and the granting of representative government for New South Wales, thereby setting a pattern for the future. His administration responded to problems rather than seeking like Peel's to be strong, but his majority was unsteady and gradually faded away. His Cabinet included Palmerston, an experienced and independent minded Foreign Secretary who finally overstepped the mark and was dismissed only, in February 1852, to bring down Russell's first administration by defeating the Government on the Militia Bill. Between 1852 and 1865 Russell held office as Foreign Secretary under Aberdeen and later Palmerston and Colonial Secretary under Palmerston, an usually active political career and he then returned as Prime Minister after Palmerston's death in 1865. He immediately sought to introduce a further Reform Bill to extend the franchise but a Cabinet lacking his innate radicalism and courage failed to support him and his second administration lasted only eight months.

PERSONAL INFORMATION

Names Lord John Russell
Peerages Viscount Amberley of Amberley, County Gloucester, and of Ardsalla, County Meath, and Earl Russell of Kingston Russell, County Dorset 30 Jul 1861
Nicknames Finality Jack; Johnny; The Widow's Mite
Born 18 Aug 1792
Birthplace Hertford Street, Mayfair, London
Religion Anglican
Ancestry English. Younger son of the 6th Duke of Bedford. The title dated from the 16th century.
Dates and places of marriages 1) 11 Apr 1835, St. George's, Hanover Square, London; 2) 20 Jul 1841, Minto, County Roxburgh, Scotland
Age at marriages 1) 42 years, 236 days; 2) 48 years, 336 days
Years married 1) 3 years, 204 days; 2) 36 years, 312 days
First entered Parliament 18 Aug 1813 (his coming of age; first elected on 4 May 1813 while under 21)
Dates appointed PM 1) 30 Jun 1846; 2) 29 Oct 1865
Age at appointments 1) 53 years, 316 days; 2) 73 years, 72 days
Dates ceased to be PM 1) 21 Feb 1852; 2) 26 Jun 1866
Total time as PM 1) 5 years, 236 days; 2) 240 days; a total of 6 years, 111 days
Ceased to be MP 30 Jul 1861
Lived after last term as PM 11 years, 336 days
Date of death 28 May 1878
Place of death Pembroke Lodge, Richmond Park, Surrey.
Age at death 85 years, 273 days
Last words Told his wife that he fell back on the faith of his childhood.
Place of funeral & burial Chenies, Buckinghamshire
Zodiac sign Leo

FATHER

Lord John Russell, 6th Duke of Bedford
Date of birth 6 Jul 1766
Occupation Ensign, 3rd Foot Guards 1783–85. MP Tavistock 1788–90 and 1790–1802. Lord Lieutenant of Ireland 1806–07. Recorder, Bedford 1789–1839.
Dates of marriages 1) 21 Mar 1786, Hon. Georgiana Elizabeth Byng (d. 1801); 2) 23 Jun 1803, Lady Georgiana Gordon
Date of death 20 Oct 1839
Place of burial Chenies, Buckinghamshire

MOTHER

Hon. Georgiana Elizabeth Byng, daughter of 4th Viscount Torrington
Date of marriage 21 Mar 1786
Date of death 11 Oct 1801
Place of burial Chenies, Buckinghamshire

STEPMOTHER

Lady Georgiana Gordon
Date and place of birth 18 Jul 1781, Gordon Castle, Scotland
Date of marriage 23 Jun 1803
Age when PM took office 58 years, 334 days
Date of death 24 Feb 1853
Place of burial Nice, France

BROTHERS AND SISTERS

Russell was the third of three sons by the 6th Duke of Bedford's first wife; he had four half brothers from his father's second marriage.
From his father's first marriage:
Francis, (Marquess of Tavistock and 7th Duke of Bedford), b. 13 May 1788; m. Lady Anna Maria Stanhope; MP Peterborough 1809–12, Bedfordshire 1812–32; Lord Lieutenant of Bedfordshire 1859–61; d. 14 May 1861
Lord George William, b. 8 May 1790; m. Elizabeth Anne Rawdon; Soldier: A.D.C. to William IV 1830–37 and Victoria 1837–41, Major-General 1841, MP Bedford 1812–31; d. 16 Jul 1846
From his father's second marriage:
Wriothesley, b. 11 May 1804; m. Elizabeth Laura Henrietta Russell; Rector of Chenies, Buckinghamshire, and Canon of Windsor; d. 6 Apr 1886
Edward, b. 24 Apr 1805; m. Mary Ann Taylor; Admiral; d. 8 Feb 1860
Charles James Fox, b. 10 Feb 1807; m. Isabella Clarissa Davies; Lt. Col. 52nd Regiment; MP Bedfordshire 1832–48, Serjeant at Arms to the House of Commons 1848–75; d. 29 Jun 1894
Alexander George, b. 16 Dec 1821; m. Anne Emily Worsley; General in the Army, Colonel, Rifle Brigade; d. 10 Jan 1907

FIRST WIFE

Lady Adelaide Ribblesdale, née Lister
Date and place of birth 12 Sep 1807, Armitage Park, County Stafford
Mother Mary Grove
Father Thomas Lister
Number of children 4 by first marriage to Lord Ribblesdale; 2 by second marriage to Lord John Russell
Age at marriage 27 years, 211 days
Years younger than PM 15 years, 25 days
Date and place of death 1 Nov 1838, Brighton
Place of burial Chenies, Buckinghamshire

SECOND WIFE

Lady Frances Anna Maria Elliot-Murray-Kynynmound
Date and place of birth 15 Nov 1815, Minto, County Roxburgh, Scotland
Age at marriage 25 years, 247 days
Number of children 4
Mother Mary Brydone
Father Gilbert Elliot-Murray-Kynynmound, 2nd Earl of Minto
Date and place of death 17 Jan 1898, Pembroke Lodge, Richmond Park, Surrey
Place of burial Cremated at Woking, buried at Chenies, Buckinghamshire
Years younger than PM 23 years, 89 days

Profile

Lady Russell was twenty-three years younger than her husband and took on the responsibilities of his stepchildren and daughters by his first wife. She always had a great influence on him as did her father, the 2nd Earl of Minto. She was as shy as her husband and never rose to the role of a political hostess, but Russell was happiest when at home with his family and he and his wife shared simple tastes. Lady Russell's health was not good and nearly always gave way in a political crisis.

CHILDREN

3 sons, 3 daughters
By his first wife, Lady Adelaide:

Lady Georgiana Adelaide, m. 15 Aug 1867, Archibald Peel (nephew of Sir Robert Peel, the Prime Minister); d. 25 Sep 1922

Lady Victoria, b. 21 Oct 1838; m. 16 Apr 1861, Henry Montagu Villiers (Bishop of Durham); d. 9 May 1880

By his second wife Lady Frances:

John (Viscount Amberley) b. 10 Dec 1842; m. 8 Nov 1864, Katherine Louisa Stanley; MP Nottingham 1866–68; d. 9 Jan 1876

George Gilbert William, b. 14 Apr 1848; Lieutenant, 9th Lancers; d. 27 Jan 1933

Francis Albert Rollo, b. 11 Jul 1849; m. 1) 21 Apr 1885, Alice Sophia Godfrey (d. 12 May 1886); 2) 28 Apr 1891, Gertrude Ellen Cornelia Joachim; d. 30 Mar 1914

Mary Agatha, b. Mar 1853; d. 23 Apr 1933

LIFE AND CAREER

PARLIAMENTARY ELECTIONS FOUGHT

*(*designates candidate elected)*

DATE 4 May 1813. By-election caused by the death of the Hon. Richard Fitzpatrick
CONSTITUENCY Tavistock
RESULT Lord John Russell* (Lib)

DATE Jun 1818. General Election
CONSTITUENCY Tavistock
RESULT Lord John Russell* (Lib); Lord William Russell* (Lib)

DATE Mar 1820. General Election
CONSTITUENCY Huntingdonshire
RESULT W. H. Fellowes* (Con); Lord John Russell* (Lib)

DATE Jun 1826. General Election.
CONSTITUENCY Huntingdonshire
RESULT Lord Mandeville* (Con) 968; W. H. Fellowes* (Con) 911; Lord John Russell (Lib) 858

DATE 19 Dec 1826. By-Election caused by Viscount Duncannon choosing to sit for Kilkenny
CONSTITUENCY Bandon
RESULT Lord John Russell* (Lib)

DATE Jul 1830. General Election
CONSTITUENCY Bedford
RESULT William Henry Whitbread* (Lib) 515; Captain Frederick Polhill* (Con) 491; Lord John Russell (Lib) 490

DATE Apr 1831. General Election
CONSTITUENCY Devonshire
RESULT Lord Ebrington* (Lib); Lord John Russell* (Lib)

DATE Dec 1832. General Election
CONSTITUENCY Devon, Southern
RESULT Lord John Russell* (Lib) 3,782; J. C. Bulteel* (Lib) 3,684; Sir J.B.Y. Buller Bt. (Con) 3,217

DATE Jan 1835. General Election
CONSTITUENCY Devon, Southern
RESULT Sir J.B.Y. Buller Bt.* (Con); Lord John Russell* (Lib)

DATE 7 May 1835. By-election caused by Russell's appointment as Secretary of State for the Home Department
CONSTITUENCY Devon, Southern
RESULT M.E.N. Parker* (Con) 3,755; Lord John Russell (Lib) 3,128

DATE 19 May 1835. By-election caused by the resignation of C.R. Fox.
CONSTITUENCY Stroud
RESULT Lord John Russell* (Lib)

DATE Jul 1837. General Election
CONSTITUENCY Stroud
RESULT G.P. Scrope* (Lib) 698; Lord John Russell* (Lib) 681; J. Adams (Con) 297

DATE Jun 1841. General Election
CONSTITUENCY City of London
RESULT J. Masterman* (Con) 6,339; Sir M. Wood Bt* (Lib) 6,315; G. Lyall* (Con) 6,290; Lord John Russell* (Lib) 6,221; M. W. Attwood (Con) 6,212; J. Pattison (Lib) 6,070; W. Crawford (Lib) 6,065; J. Pirie (Con) 6, 017

DATE 8 Jul 1846. By-election caused by Russell's appointment as Prime Minister and First Lord of the Treasury.
CONSTITUENCY City of London
RESULT Lord John Russell* (Lib)

DATE Jul 1847. General Election
CONSTITUENCY City of London
RESULT Lord John Russell* (Lib) 7,137; J. Pattison* (Lib) 7,030; Baron L. N. de Rothschild* (Lib) 6,792; J. Masterman* (Con) 6,722; Sir G. G. de H. Larpent Bt. (Lib) 6,719; R.C.L. Bevan (Con) 5,268; J. Johnson (Con) 5,069; J. W. Freshfield (Con) 4,704; W. Payne (Lib) 513

DATE Jul 1852. General Election
CONSTITUENCY City of London
RESULT J. Masterman* (Con) 6,195; Lord John Russell* (Lib) 5,537; Sir J. Duke Bt* (Lib) 5,270; Baron L. N. de Rothschild* (Lib 4,748; R. W. Crawford (Lib) 3,765

DATE 3 Jan 1853. By-election caused by Russell's appointment as Secretary of State for Foreign Affairs
CONSTITUENCY City of London
RESULT Lord John Russell* (Lib)

DATE 14 Jun 1854. By-election caused by Russell's appointment as Lord President of the Council
CONSTITUENCY City of London
RESULT Lord John Russell* (Lib)

DATE 3 Mar 1855. By-election caused by Russell's appointment as Secretary of State for the Colonies.
CONSTITUENCY City of London
RESULT Lord John Russell* (Lib)

PARLIAMENTARY ELECTIONS FOUGHT—*Continued*

DATE Mar 1857. General Election
CONSTITUENCY City of London
RESULT Sir J. Duke Bt.* (Lib) 6,664; Baron L. N. de Rothschild* (Lib) 6,398; Lord John Russell* (Lib) 6, 308; R. W. Crawford* (Lib) 5,808; R. Currie (Lib) 4,519

DATE Apr 1859. General Election
CONSTITUENCY City of London
RESULT R. W. Crawford* (Lib); Sir J. Duke Bt* (Lib); Baron L. N. Rothschild* (Lib) Lord John Russell* (Lib)

DATE 27 Jun 1859. By-election caused by Russell's appointment as Secretary of State for Foreign Affairs.
CONSTITUENCY City of London
RESULT Lord John Russell* (Lib)

PARTY ACTIVITY

Party Leadership Leader of the Liberal Party 1845–55
Other offices Leader of the Liberal Party in the House of Commons 1834–55; in the House of Lords 1865–68

PARLIAMENTARY AND MINISTERIAL EXPERIENCE

Maiden Speech 12 May 1814. He spoke against the enforced union of Norway with Sweden. (*Parl. Deb.* 1st ser, vol 27, col 862)
Privy Counsellor 22 Nov 1830
Ministerial Offices Paymaster General of the Forces 16 Dec 1830–9 Jul 1834; Home Secretary 18 Apr 1835–30 Aug 1839; Leader of the House of Commons 18 Apr 1835–30 Aug 1841, 30 Jun 1846– 21 Feb 1852, 19 Dec 1852–30 Jan 1855; Colonial Secretary 30 Aug 1839–30 Aug 1841, 23 Feb–13 Jul 1855; First Lord of the Treasury 30 Jun 1846–21 Feb 1852, 29 Oct 1865–26 Jun 1866; Foreign Secretary 28 Dec 1852–21 Feb 1853, 18 Jun 1859– 29 Oct 1865; Lord President of the Council 12 Jun 1854–24 Jan 1855; Leader of the House of Lords 29 Oct 1865–26 Jun 1866.
Opposition Leaders while PM 1) 1846–52: Lord George Bentinck (1846–47); Lord Granby (Feb–March 1848; (No formal leaders March 1848–Feb1849); Triumvirate: B. Disraeli, Lord Granby, J.C. Herries (Feb 1849–Feb 1852 2) 1865–66: 14th Earl of Derby

GOVERNMENTS FORMED

First Administration 30 Jun 1846–21 Feb 1852

GENERAL ELECTION RESULT
JUN 1841: Conservative 367; Liberal 271; Others 20. Total 658
Conservative majority 77 (excl. the Speaker)
JUL 1847: Conservative 324; Liberal 293; Others 39. Total 658
No overall majority

CABINET
Prime Minister and First Lord of the Treasury Lord J. Russell
Lord Chancellor Lord Cottenham (1846–50); Lord Truro (1850–52)
Lord President of the Council Marquess of Lansdowne
Lord Privy Seal Earl of Minto
Home Secretary Sir G. Grey
Foreign Secretary Viscount Palmerston (1846–51); Earl Granville (1851–52)
Secretary for War and the Colonies Earl Grey
Chancellor of the Exchequer Sir C. Wood
President of the Board of Control Sir J. C. Hobhouse (1846–52); F. Maule (Feb 1852)
First Lord of the Admiralty Earl of Auckland (1846–49); Sir F. T. Baring (1849–52)
*Chief Secretary for Ireland** H. Labouchere (1846–47);
Chancellor of the Duchy of Lancaster Lord Campbell (1846–50); Earl of Carlisle (1850–52)
*Paymaster-General** T. B. Macaulay (1846–48); Earl Granville (1851–52)
Postmaster General Marquess of Clanricarde
President of the Board of Trade Earl of Clarendon (1846–47); H. Labouchere (1847–52)
First Commissioner of Woods etc. *Viscount Morpeth (1846–48)
First Commissioner of Works Lord Seymour
[*Office not always in Cabinet]

Second Administration 29 Oct 1865–26 Jun 1866

GENERAL ELECTION RESULT
JUL 1865: Liberal 370; Conservative 288. Total 658
Liberal majority 81 (excl. the Speaker)

CABINET
Prime Minister and First Lord of the Treasury Lord J. Russell
Lord Chancellor Lord Cranworth
Lord President of the Council Earl Granville
Lord Privy Seal Duke of Argyll
Home Secretary Sir G. Grey
Foreign Secretary Earl of Clarendon
Secretary of State for War Earl de Grey & Ripon (1865–66); Marquess of Hartington (Feb–Jun 1866)
Secretary of State for the Colonies E. Cardwell
Secretary of State for India Sir C. Wood (1865–66); Earl de Grey & Ripon (Feb–Jun 1866)
Chancellor of the Exchequer W. E. Gladstone
First Lord of the Admiralty Duke of Somerset
*Chancellor of the Duchy of Lancaster** G. J. Goschen (Jan–Jun 1866)
President of the Poor Law Board C. P. Villiers
Postmaster-General Lord Stanley of Alderley
President of the Board of Trade T. M. Gibson
[*Office not always in Cabinet]

IMPORTANT DATES IN PERSONAL AND POLITICAL LIFE

1812 Leaves Edinburgh University without taking his degree.
4 MAY 1813 Elected MP for the first time for Tavistock at the age of 20.
12 MAY 1814 Maiden speech against the enforced union of Norway with Sweden.
FEB 1817 Resigns as MP on grounds of ill health.
18 JUN 1818 Re-elected as MP for Tavistock.
25 APR 1822 First major speech on parliamentary reform.
26 FEB 1826 Moves repeal of the Test and Corporation Acts. His motion carries and the subsequent repeal of the Acts allows non-conformists to become MPs.
16 DEC 1830 Russell appointed Paymaster General in Earl Grey's administration.
1 MAR 1831 Moves First Reading of the Reform Bill. Russell's popularity and standing date from this speech.
21 MAR 1831 The Bill is carried on the Second Reading by 302 to 301, but the Government is defeated during its Committee Stage.
JUN 1831 Russell becomes a member of the Cabinet, still as Paymaster General.

24 JUN 1831 Russell reintroduces the Reform Bill after the General Election. It is carried by a large majority in the Commons, but it is defeated in the House of Lords in Oct 1831.

12 DEC 1831 Introduction of the Third Reform Bill.

7 MAY 1832 Third Reform Bill also defeated in the House of Lords. Grey's administration resigns but the Tories are not able to form a Government and the Whigs are reinstated.

4 JUN 1832 Reform Bill read a third time in the House of Lords; receives the Royal Assent on 7 Jun. Reform Bills are also passed for Scotland and Ireland.

16 JUL 1834 Lord Melbourne becomes Prime Minister following the resignation of Earl Grey.

NOV 1834 Lord Althorp, leader of the Whigs in the House of Commons, succeeds to the peerage on the death of his father. The vacancy is offered to Russell but William IV objects and dismisses Melbourne as PM despite the Whig majority in the House of Commons. Peel becomes Prime Minister and Russell is now recognized leader of the Whigs in the Commons.

8 APR 1835 Peel resigns as PM. Melbourne takes office and Russell becomes Home Secretary in the new administration.

11 APR 1835 Marries Lady Adelaide Ribblesdale.

7 MAY 1835 Russell defeated at Devon, Southern when seeking re-election as Home Secretary. He is subsequently elected for Stroud.

16 JAN 1836 First of the Runnymede Letters published in the *Times* attacking Russell. Although published anonymously they were actually written by Disraeli.

20 JUN 1837 Death of William IV and accession of Victoria.

20 NOV 1837 Russell declares in a speech on the Address that it is impossible for him to take part in further measures of electoral reform. This earns him the hostility of the Radicals and the nickname 'Finality Jack.'

1 NOV 1838 Death of his first wife.

2 FEB 1839 Russell threatens to resign because of Glenelg's administration of the Colonial Office. Normanby becomes Colonial Secretary.

7 MAY 1839 Melbourne resigns as PM after a very close vote in the Commons on a measure to suspend the constitution in Jamaica where a rebellion has broken out. Peel is asked to form an administration but refuses after Victoria declares that she wishes to keep all her Whig Ladies of the Bedchamber.

11 MAY 1839 Melbourne resumes office as PM.

30 AUG 1839 Russell is appointed Colonial Secretary.

20 OCT 1839 Death of his father, the 6th Duke of Bedford. His brother Francis inherits the peerage.

20 JUL 1841 Russell marries again. His second wife, Lady Frances Elliot, daughter of the 2nd Earl of Minto, is 23 years younger than he.

30 AUG 1841 Peel becomes PM following the Conservative victory at the General Election.

22 NOV 1845 Russell's famous 'Edinburgh Letter' (addressed to his constituents in the City of London but written from Edinburgh) in which he calls for the total repeal of the Corn Laws.

5 DEC 1845 Peel has already proposed this measure to his Cabinet but has been unable to carry them with him. He resigns but Russell is unable to form an administration. Peel returns to office and repeals the Corn Laws with Russell's support.

25 JUN 1846 Peel's Government is defeated on the Second Reading of the Irish Crimes Bill (the 'Coercion' Bill) and four days later Peel resigns.

30 JUN 1846 Russell becomes PM for the first time.

1846 The Irish potato crop fails, resulting in the deaths of around one million Irish in the first two years of Russell's administration. The Government grants relief money for soup kitchens and finances public works to create employment.

1847 Education Act improves teachers' pay and conditions and grants money to nonconformist schools.

JUL 1847 General Election; the state of the parties is confused, with the Conservatives split between the Protectionists and the Peelites. Amongst the Liberals is a group of Radicals. Russell cannot command a regular party majority despite his wooing of the Peelites.

1847 Russell's appointment of Dr. Hampden as Bishop of Hereford causes controversy within the Church.

1848 Two Budgets introduced within ten days; the first by Russell, the second by the Chancellor of the Exchequer, Wood.

MAR 1848 Russell goes to St. Leonards in Sussex to try to regain his deteriorating health.

1848 Encumbered Estates Act frees land for sale in Ireland; many of the new owners are Catholics.

1850 Australian Colonies Act creates Victoria and gives New South Wales representative government.

1850 Continuous friction with Lord Palmerston, the Foreign Secretary, who is apt to act independently from the Government.

30 OCT 1850 'Durham Letter', in which Russell is critical of a recent Papal Bull creating Roman Catholic Bishops in England. The letter meets with hostility from High Church Anglicans and Catholics but leads to the Ecclesiastical Titles Act which renders illegal the assumption of titles by Roman Catholic priests in England.

22 FEB 1851 Government defeated on new Reform measures. Russell resigns as PM but Lord Stanley finds it impossible to form a new adminstration and Russell resumes office on 3 Mar.

2 DEC 1851 Napoleon carries out coup détat in Paris and the next day Palmerston, without consulting his colleagues, tells the French ambassador that he approves of the Emperor's actions.

17 DEC 1851 Tired of the continual friction with Palmerston, Russell dismisses him. Earl Granville is made Foreign Secretary.

20 FEB 1852 Palmerston moves an amendment to the Militia Bill; the Government loses the vote.

21 FEB 1852 Russell and his Cabinet resign.

23 FEB 1852 Derby has shortlived administration as PM.

19 DEC 1852 Following the defeat of Derby's Government Aberdeen forms a coalition ministry of Liberals and Peelites. Russell takes office as Foreign Secretary.

21 FEB 1853 Unable to carry the burden of two offices, Russell resigns from the Foreign Office in favour of Clarendon and continues as Leader of the House of Commons and as a member of the Cabinet without ministerial office.

DEC 1853 Russell proposes a new Reform Bill, which has to be postponed because of lack of Cabinet support.

28 MAR 1854 Declaration of war by England and France on Russia; the beginning of the Crimean War.

24 JAN 1855 Russell resigns from the Cabinet because he is unable to defend the Government against a motion critical of its conduct of the war.

29 JAN 1855 Aberdeen's Government is defeated on this motion.

6 FEB 1855 Palmerston becomes PM. Russell does not join the Government at first, but goes as British representative to the Vienna Conference.

IMPORTANT DATES IN PERSONAL AND POLITICAL LIFE—*Continued*

23 FEB 1855 Russell accepts post of Colonial Secretary.

13 JUL 1855 Resigns from the Government.

1856–1857 Lives in Lausanne, Switzerland, and Italy for a while.

20 FEB 1858 Derby made PM after the defeat of Palmerston's Government on the Conspiracy Bill.

12 JUN 1859 Palmerston takes office again after Derby's administration is defeated on a no confidence amendment to the Address when Parliament meets after the General Election of Apr 1859. Russell becomes Foreign Secretary.

1861 From the beginning of the American Civil War Russell maintains a strict neutrality between the opposing sides.

30 JUL 1861 Created Earl Russell at the end of the Parliamentary session.

18 OCT 1865 Death of Palmerston.

29 OCT 1865 Russell takes over as PM.

26 JUN 1866 He resigns as PM after the Government is defeated by the combined forces of the Conservatives and those Whigs opposed to reform on an amendment to his new Reform Bill.

3 DEC 1868 He refuses Gladstone's offer of a seat in the Cabinet 'without other responsibility.'

9 JAN 1876 Death of his eldest son, Viscount Amberley.

28 MAY 1878 Dies at Pembroke Lodge, Richmond, Surrey.

BACKGROUND

PHYSICAL CHARACTERISTICS AND HEALTH

Lord John Russell was born two months premature and was always of small stature. He suffered a lot of ill health as a child and throughout his life, resigning as an MP in 1817 because of poor health and having to recuperate at St. Leonards in 1848 while Prime Minister. Russell suffered continually from coughs and colds, and was also subject to fainting fits. Fully grown, Russell stood 5 feet 4 3/4 inches and weighed about 112 lb. A contemporary, Charles Sumner, described him in 1838 speaking in the House of Commons: 'In person diminutive and rickety, he reminded me of a pettifogging attorney . . . He wriggled around, played with his hat, and seemed unable to dispose of his hands or his feet; his voice was small and thin, but not withstanding all this, a House of five hundred members was hushed to catch his smallest accents.'

EDUCATION

Primary 1800–01, School at Sunbury, run by Dr. Moore

Secondary 1803–04 Westminster School; 1804–05, Educated at Woburn by a private tutor, Dr. Cartwright; 1805–08, studied under Rev. John Smith, Vicar of Woodnesborough, near Sandwich.

University 1809–12 University of Edinburgh. Russell left without taking his degree.

Cultural and vocational background 1808, Visited Portugal and Spain; 1810 and 1812–13, Russell again visited the continent and in 1815 spent some months in Italy; 1826, visited Paris, Geneva, Genoa, Florence and Rome

Languages Latin, Greek, French and some Spanish

NON-PARLIAMENTARY CAREER

Early occupations Russell's early aspirations were to be a writer and poet.

Military service 1813 Captain in the Bedfordshire Militia.

Other posts 1836, Ecclesiastical Commissioner; 1849, Elder Brother, Trinity House; 1854, Charity Commissioner; 1855, Trustee of the British Museum; 1859, President of the Statistical Society; 1861, President of the British and Foreign School Society

HONOURS

Freedom of cities 1841, Borough of Selkirk; 1845, Edinburgh; 1846, Glasgow

Academic 1845, LL.D Edinburgh; 1846, Lord Rector of Glasgow University; 1863, Lord Rector of Aberdeen University

Other than peerage 6 May 1847, Fellow of the Royal Society; 8 May 1862, Knight of the Garter; 25 March 1869, Grand Cross of the Order of St. Michael and St. George

CLUBS

Grillion's; Reform*

*(Russell was one of the original members)

HOBBIES AND SPORTS

Russell was happiest when at home with his family. He enjoyed reading and travelling and spent much time on his own writings. He was not particularly interested in sport, but he did attend an occasional shoot.

FINANCES

Russell was never a wealthy man. He was not particularly careful with money but his lifestyle was modest. His father ensured that he had an income of about £2, 000 from the family estates and paid his election expenses. These were subsequently paid by his brother, the 7th Duke of Bedford.

Income £2,000 p.a. from his father's estate. In 1857, his brother the 7th Duke of Bedford, started to pay him an annuity of £2,000 p.a.

Legacies His father left him an additional legacy of £10, 000 on his death in 1839. An old friend, Lady Holland, left him £1,000 and a life interest in her Lambeth estate on her death in 1845 i.e. between £1200 and £1500 p.a. Inherited the Ardsalla Estate on his brother's death in 1861.

Debts Russell's financial situation became notorious after he testified to a Select Committee in 1850 that he had never been in debt before he was Prime Minister.

ANECDOTES

People were always surprised by Lord John Russell's small stature. Sydney Smith countered this in the 1830s: 'Before this Reform agitation commenced Lord John was over six feet high. But, engaged in looking after your interests, fighting the peers, the landlords, and the rest of your natural enemies, he has been so constantly kept in hot water that he is boiled down to the proportions in which you now behold him.'

Russell was never businesslike about his affairs and frequently mislaid papers or forgot to give official boxes to messengers. Letters were abrupt, unfinished or mistakenly sent to the wrong recipient. Colleagues would arrive for an appointment at Downing Street to find he had gone out. In 1852 Lord Minto told him 'You are the best of Prime Ministers, but you would have been a bad Postmaster General: the calculation of time and space being evidently beyond your powers.'

Sydney Smith said of him: 'I believe Lord John Russell would perform the operation for the stone, build St. Peter's, or assume—with or without ten minutes' notice—the command of the Channel fleet; and no one would discover by his manner that the patient had died, the church tumbled down, and the Channel fleet been knocked to atoms.'

His father wrote to him in 1838, 'There are circumstances in which you give great offence to your followers . . . in the House of Commons by not being courteous to them, by treating them superciliously, and de haut en bas, by not listening with sufficient patience to their solicitations or remonstrances'.

QUOTATIONS

A proverb is one man's wit and all men's wisdom. (Attributed)

A spur in the head is worth two in the heel. (Attributed)

1831, It is impossible that the whisper of a faction should prevail against the voice of a nation. (Letter to Thomas Atwood after the rejection of the Reform Bill)

24 Jun 1831, When I am told, that the government of a country does not affect the condition of its people, I say, look to Ireland. (Speech in the House of Commons)

17 March 1847, I cannot look with indifference to the statement that the great proportion of the people of this country have only to work, to sleep, to eat and to die. In my opinion, it is the duty of the state to endeavour that you should have a population, in the first place, aware of the doctrines of religion; that, in the next place, they should be able to cultivate domestic habits and domestic affections; and that, in the third place, they should be likely to look up to the laws and government of the country as their protectors from undue inflictions upon the young of this country . . . (Speech in the House of Commons on factory legislation)

1878, I have made mistakes, but in all I did my object was the public good. (To his wife)

RESIDENCES

Hundreds Farm, Woburn
66 South Audley Street, London
11 Old Burlington Street, London
19 Half Moon Street, London
Wilton Crescent, London
39 Chesham Place, London
*Pembroke Lodge**, Richmond, Surrey
10 Downing Street
(**Pembroke Lodge* was offered to the Russells by Queen Victoria in 1847. They lived here for the rest of their lives.)

MEMORIALS

STATUES AND BUSTS

By Sir J. E. Boehm, Westminster Abbey

PORTRAITS

1851, by G. F. Watts, National Portrait Gallery; 1853, by Sir Francis Grant

BIBLIOGRAPHIC INFORMATION

LETTERS AND PERSONAL PAPERS

Russell's papers are in the Public Record Office.

PUBLICATIONS

Russell's major works are:

1819, *The Life of William Lord Russell*; 1820, *Essays and Sketches of Life and Character, by a Gentleman who has left his lodgings*; 1821, *An Essay on the History of the English Government and Constitution from the reign of Henry VIII to the present time*; 1822, *The Nun of Arrouca* (a novel); 1822, *Don Carlos*; or *Persecution*, a tragedy in five acts; 1824, *Memoirs of the Affairs of Europe from the Peace of Utrecht* vol. 1 (vol. II, 1829); 1828, *The establishment of the Turks in Europe*: an historical discourse; 1859–66, *The Life and Times of Charles James Fox;* 1875, *Recollections and Suggestions 1813–1873.*

FURTHER READING

Prest, J. *Lord John Russell.* London, 1972.
Walpole, S. *The Life of Lord John Russell.* 2 vols. London, 1889.

I.W.

Bettmann

Earl of Derby

Lived 1799–1869

Political Party Whig (1822–37); Conservative (1837–69)

Prime Minister 23 February 1852–17 December 1852
20 February 1858–11 June 1859
28 June 1866–25 February 1868

Governments Conservative

Reigning Monarch Victoria

Sans changer Without changing

DERBY AS PRIME MINISTER

Derby was appointed Chief Secretary for Ireland at the age of 31. He brought forward the Irish Education Bill and reformed the Irish tithe system. After being appointed Colonial Secretary in 1833, he introduced measures to abolish slavery. Moving from his Whig background to join Peel's Government he became leader of the Conservative Party in 1846. In 1851 he entered the House of Lords and was appointed Prime Minister in 1852. His majority depended upon the support of the Peelites. His Chancellor, Disraeli, was anathema to the Peelites and they refused to support his Budget, thereby bringing down Derby's first administration. He led the Conservative opposition first against Aberdeen and then against Palmerston, and, when the latter fell in 1858, the Queen asked Derby to form his second administration. Although a minority Government, it passed the important India Bill, transferring that country from the East India Company to the Crown, and the Jews Relief Act of 1858, which enabled Jews to sit in Parliament. Next year Derby was defeated in the House of Commons on a vote of confidence and again Palmerston took over the Government. Derby continued to lead the Conservative Party while Disraeli continued to lead the Conservatives in the House of Commons. In 1866 Russell found his party divided over a Reform Bill and resigned. Derby then became the first Prime Minister to hold office a third time. He successfully passed a watered-down Reform Bill in 1867, and resigned as Prime Minister for health reasons in 1868.

PERSONAL INFORMATION

Names Edward George Geoffrey Smith Stanley
Peerages Lord Stanley of Bickerstaffe, 4 Nov 1844, and 14th Earl of Derby
Nicknames Scorpion Stanley; The Rupert of Debate
Born 29 Mar 1799
Birthplace Knowsley Hall, Prescot, Lancashire
Religion Anglican
Ancestry Lancashire landowners. The 2nd Baron Stanley was created Earl of Derby by Henry VII in reward for his support at the Battle of Bosworth in 1485.
Date and place of marriage 31 May 1825, Marylebone, London
Age at marriage 26 years, 81 days
Years married 44 years, 145 days
First entered Parliament 30 Jul 1822
Dates appointed PM 1) 23 Feb 1852; 2) 20 Feb 1858; 3) 28 Jun 1866
Age at appointments 1) 52 years, 331 days 2) 58 years, 328 days 3) 67 years, 91 days
Dates ceased to be PM 1) 17 Dec 1852; 2) 11 Jun 1859; 3) 25 Feb 1868
Total time as PM 1) 292 days; 2) 1 year, 111 days; 3) 1 year, 242 days; a total of 3 years, 280 days
Ceased to be MP 4 Nov 1844
Lived after last term as PM 1 year, 240 days
Date of death 23 Oct 1869
Place of death Knowsley Hall, Prescot, Lancashire
Age at death 70 years, 208 days
Last words When asked how he was, Derby replied 'Bored to utter extinction'.
Place of funeral and burial Knowsley Church, Knowsley, Lancashire
Zodiac sign Aries

FATHER

Edward Smith Stanley, 13th Earl of Derby
Date and place of birth 21 Apr 1775, London
Occupation Landowner in Lancashire, famous for his private zoological collection at Knowsley. MP Preston 1796–1812, Lancashire 1812–32. President of the Linnaean Society 1828–33 and President of the Zoological Society 1831–51.
Date of marriage 30 Oct 1798
Date of death 30 Jun 1851
Place of burial Ormskirk Church, Ormskirk, Lancashire

MOTHER

Charlotte Margaret Hornby
Date of birth 20 Oct 1778
Profile Charlotte Hornby was the 13th Earl's first cousin and daughter of the Rev. Geoffrey Hornby, Rector of Winwick, Lancashire.
Date of marriage 30 Oct 1798
Date of death 16 Jun 1817
Place of burial Ormskirk Church, Ormskirk, Lancashire

BROTHERS AND SISTERS

Derby was the eldest son and first of seven children.

Charlotte Elizabeth, b. 11 Jul 1801; m. 16 Dec 1823 Edward Penrhyn; d. 15 Feb 1853
Henry Thomas, b. 9 Mar 1803; m. 11 Sep 1835 Anne Woolhouse; MP Preston 1832–37; d. 2 Apr 1875
Emily Lucy, b. 2 Mar 1804; d. 13 Nov 1804
Louise Emily, b. 1 Jun 1805; m. 18 Apr 1825 Lt.-Col. Samuel Long; d. 11 Dec 1825
Eleanor Mary, b. 3 May 1807; m. Jun 1835 Reverend Frank George Haywood (Rector of Winwick)
Charles James Fox, b. 25 Apr 1808; m. 10 Dec 1836 Frances Augusta Campbell; Lt.-Col. Grenadier Guards; Colonel 3rd Bn. the Lancs Militia; d. 13 Oct 1884

WIFE

Emma Caroline Bootle-Wilbraham
Date of birth 17 Mar 1805
Mother Mary Elizabeth Taylor
Father Edward Bootle-Wilbraham, 1st Lord Skelmersdale
Father's occupation Tory MP Westbury 1795–96; Newcastle-under-Lyme 1796–1812; Clitheroe 1812–18; Dover 1818–28. Created Baron Skelmersdale, of Skelmersdale, County of Lancaster, 1828.
Age at marriage 20 years, 45 days
Number of children 3
Date and place of death 26 Apr 1876, 15 Cromwell Road, South Kensington, London.
Place of burial Knowsley Church, Knowsley, Lancashire.
Years younger than PM 5 years, 355 days
Profile Emma was Derby's closest confidante and friend; she occasionally acted as his personal secretary. She hosted innumerable political parties for him although Lord Redesdale described these as 'of a dullness as depressing as a London fog'.

CHILDREN

2 sons, 1 daughter
Edward Henry (15th Earl of Derby), b. 21 Jul 1826; m. 5 Jul 1870, Mary Catherine Gascoyne-Cecil, widow of the Marquess of Salisbury; MP King's Lynn 1848–69; Under Secretary of State for Foreign Affairs 1852; Secretary of State for the Colonies 1858, 1882–85; President of the Board of Control 1858, 1882-85; Secretary of State for India 1858–59; Secretary of State for Foreign Affairs 1866–68, 1874–78; Secretary of State for the Colonies 1882–85; d. 21 Apr 1893
Frederick Arthur (16th Earl of Derby, Baron Stanley of Bickerstaffe and Baron Stanley of Preston), b. 15 Jan 1841; m. 31 May 1864, Constance Villiers, daughter of the 4th Earl of Clarendon; Officer in the Grenadier Guards; MP Preston 1865–68, Lancashire, North 1868–85, Lancashire, Blackpool 1885–86; Lord of the Admiralty 1868; Financial Secretary to the War Office 1874–77 and to the Treasury 1877–78; Militia ADC to Queen Victoria 1877–1901 and to King Edward VII 1901–08; Secretary of State for War 1878–80 and for the Colonies 1885–86; President of the Board of Trade 1886–88. Governor General of Canada 1888–1893; d. 14 Jun 1908
Lady Emma Charlotte, b. 25 Dec 1835; m. 11 Oct 1860, Col. Hon. Sir W.P.M. Chetwynd Talbot, Derby's private secretary and brother of the 18th Earl of Shrewsbury; d. 23 Aug 1928

LIFE AND CAREER

PARLIAMENTARY ELECTIONS FOUGHT

*(*designates candidate elected)*

DATE 30 Jul 1822. By-election caused by the resignation of Joseph F. Barham
CONSTITUENCY Stockbridge
RESULT Hon. Edward G. G. Smith Stanley* (Whig)

DATE Jun 1826. General Election
CONSTITUENCY Preston
RESULT Hon. Edward G. G. Smith Stanley* (Whig) 2, 944; John Wood* (Whig) 1,974; Captain Barrie, R.N. (Tory) 1,653; William Cobbett (R) 995

DATE Jul 1830. General Election
CONSTITUENCY Preston
RESULT Hon. Edward G. G. Smith Stanley* (Whig) 2, 996; John Wood* (Whig) 2,389; Henry Hunt (R) 1,308

DATE 7 Dec 1830. By-election caused by Derby's appointment as Chief Secretary for Ireland
CONSTITUENCY Preston
RESULT Henry Hunt* (R) 3,730; Hon. Edward G. G. Smith Stanley (Whig) 3,392.

DATE 10 Feb 1831. By-election caused by appointment of Sir R. H. Vivian, Bt., as Commander of the Forces in Ireland
CONSTITUENCY Windsor
RESULT Hon. Edward G. G. Smith Stanley* (Whig)

DATE Apr 1831. General Election
CONSTITUENCY Windsor
RESULT John Ramsbottom* (Whig); Hon. Edward G. G. Smith Stanley* (Whig)

DATE Dec 1832. General Election
CONSTITUENCY Lancashire, Northern
RESULT J. W. Patten* (Tory); Hon. Edward G. G. Smith Stanley* (Whig)

DATE 12 Apr 1833. By-election caused by Derby's appointment as Secretary of State for War and the Colonies
CONSTITUENCY Lancashire, Northern
RESULT Hon. Edward G. G. Smith Stanley* (Whig)

DATE Jan 1835. General Election
CONSTITUENCY Lancashire, Northern
RESULT J. W. Patten* (Tory); Lord Stanley* (Whig)

DATE Jul 1837. General Election
CONSTITUENCY Lancashire, Northern
RESULT J. W. Patten* (Tory); Lord Stanley* (Tory)

DATE Jun 1841. General Election
CONSTITUENCY Lancashire, Northern
RESULT J. W. Patten* (Tory); Lord Stanley* (Tory)

DATE 21 Sep 1841. By-election caused by Derby's appointment as Secretary of State for War and the Colonies.
CONSTITUENCY Lancashire, Northern
RESULT Lord Stanley* (Tory)

PARTY ACTIVITY

Party Leadership Leader of the Conservative Party 1846–68
Membership of group or faction Leader of the 'Derby Dilly'

PARLIAMENTARY AND MINISTERIAL EXPERIENCE

Maiden Speech 30 Mar 1824 on the Manchester Gas Light Bill. (*HC Deb* 2nd ser, vol 11, col 11-13)
Privy Counsellor 22 Nov 1830; 10 Jan 1831 (Ireland)
Ministerial Offices Junior Lord of the Treasury, 1827; Under Secretary of State for War and the Colonies, 1828; Chief Secretary for Ireland, 29 Nov 1830–29 Mar 1833; Secretary of State for War and the Colonies, 3 Apr 1833–27 May 1834, 3 Sep 1841–23 Dec 1845; First Lord of the Treasury and Leader of the House of Lords 23 Feb–17 Dec 1852, 20 Feb 1858–11 Jun 1859, 28 Jun 1866–25 Feb 1868
Opposition Leaders while PM 1) 1852, 3rd Marquess of Lansdowne (House of Lords); Lord John Russell (House of Commons); 2) 1858–59, Earl Granville (House of Lords); Lord Palmerston (House of Commons); 3) 1866–68, Earl Russell (House of Lords); W. E. Gladstone (House of Commons).

GOVERNMENTS FORMED

First Administration 23 Feb 1852–17 Dec 1852

The 'Who? Who?' Cabinet, so called because when Derby gave out the names of his cabinet ministers, the Duke of Wellington, deaf and surprised by the unfamiliar names, kept saying 'Who? Who?'.

GENERAL ELECTION RESULTS
JUL 1847: Conservative 324; Liberal 293; Irish Repealers 36; Chartists 1; Others 2. Total 656
No overall majority
JUL 1852: Conservative 330; Liberal 324. Total 654.
Conservative majority 7 (excl. the Speaker)

CABINET
Prime Minister and First Lord of the Treasury Earl of Derby
Lord Chancellor Lord St. Leonards
Lord President of the Council Earl of Lonsdale
Lord Privy Seal Marquess of Salisbury
Home Secretary S. Walpole
Foreign Secretary Earl of Malmesbury
Secretary of State for War and the Colonies Sir J. Pakington
Chancellor of the Exchequer B. Disraeli
President of the Board of Control J. C. Herries
Postmaster General Earl of Hardwicke
President of the Board of Trade J. W. Henley
First Lord of the Admiralty Duke of Northumberland
First Commissioner of Works Lord John Manners

Second Administration 20 Feb 1858–11 Jun 1859

GENERAL ELECTION RESULTS
MAR 1857: Liberal 377; Conservative 264; Others 13. Total 654
Liberal majority 100
APR 1859: Liberal 357; Conservative 297. Total 654.
Liberal majority 59 (excl. the Speaker)

CABINET
Prime Minister and First Lord of the Treasury Earl of Derby
Lord Chancellor Lord Chelmsford
Lord President of the Council Marquess of Salisbury
Lord Privy Seal Earl of Hardwicke

Home Secretary S. Walpole (Feb 1858–Mar 1859); T. H. S. Sotheron Estcourt (Mar–Jun 1859)
Foreign Secretary Earl of Malmesbury
Secretary of State for War J. Peel
Secretary of State for the Colonies Lord Stanley (Feb–Jun 1858); Sir E. Bulwer-Lytton (Jun 1858–Jun 1859)
Secretary of State for India Lord Stanley (Sep 1858–Jun 1859)
Chancellor of the Exchequer B. Disraeli
First Lord of the Admiralty Sir J. Pakington
President of the Board of Control Earl of Ellenborough (Mar–Jun 1858); Lord Stanley (Jun–Aug 1858) (Board of Control abolished 2 Aug 1858)
President of the Board of Trade J. W. Henley (Feb 1858–Mar 1859); Earl of Donoughmore (Mar–Jun 1859)
First Commissioner of Works Lord John Manners

Third Administration 28 Jun 1866–25 Feb 1868

GENERAL ELECTION RESULT
JUL 1865: Liberal 369; Conservative 289. Total 658
Liberal majority 79 (excl. the Speaker)

CABINET
Prime Minister and First Lord of the Treasury Earl of Derby
Lord Chancellor Lord Chelmsford
Lord President of the Council Duke of Buckingham (1866–67); Duke of Marlborough (1867–68)
Lord Privy Seal Earl of Malmesbury
Home Secretary S. Walpole (1866–67); G. Hardy (1867–68)
Foreign Secretary Lord Stanley
Secretary of State for War J. Peel (1866–67); Sir J. Pakington (1867–68)
Secretary of State for the Colonies Earl of Carnarvon (1866–67); Duke of Buckingham (1867–68)
Secretary of State for India Viscount Cranborne (1866–67); Sir S. Northcote (1867–68)
Chancellor of the Exchequer B. Disraeli
First Lord of the Admiralty Sir J. Pakington (1866–67); H. T. L. Corry (1867–68)
Chief Secretary for Ireland Lord Naas
*President of the Poor Law Board** G. Hardy (1866–67);
Minister without Portfolio S. Walpole (1867–68)
President of the Board of Trade Sir S. Northcote (1866–67); Duke of Richmond (1867–68)
First Commissioner of Works Lord John Manners
[*Office not always in Cabinet]

IMPORTANT DATES IN PERSONAL AND POLITICAL LIFE

1820 Derby leaves Christ Church College, Oxford, without taking his degree.

30 JUL 1822 Enters Parliament for the first time as a Whig MP for Stockbridge, a rotten borough. The seat is bought for him by his grandfather, the 12th Earl of Derby.

30 MAR 1824 Makes his maiden speech on the Manchester Gas Light Bill. Hansard records it as a 'speech of much clearness and ability', and Sir J. Mackintosh, the speaker after Derby said the speech 'must have given the highest satisfaction to all who heard it . . . no man could have witnessed with greater satisfaction than himself an accession to the talents of the House, which was calculated to give lustre to its character and strengthen its influence'.

JUN 1824 Derby sails from Liverpool to New York to travel in the United States and Canada.

31 MAY 1825 Marries Emma Caroline Bootle-Wilbraham.

26 JUN 1826 Returned as MP for Preston, a seat previously held by his father for many years. He describes himself at this time as 'an old constitutional Whig'.

1827–1828 Holds ministerial office for two brief periods in 1827 and 1828. He is appointed a junior Lord of the Treasury under Canning and then takes office as Under Secretary for the Colonies in Goderich's administration.

29 NOV 1830 Appointed Chief Secretary for Ireland in Lord Grey's administration. He is defeated at the subsequent by-election in December by Henry 'Orator' Hunt, but returned as MP for Windsor two months later.

1831 Irish Education Act. As Chief Secretary Derby brings in this measure, which creates the Irish Board of National Education under which children of all denominations are admitted to the schools receiving government grants. The system allows for religious teaching of a non-controversial nature.

1832 Several measures are passed reforming the Irish tithe system.

27 FEB 1833 Derby makes his famous speech in the House of Commons defending the Irish Coercion Bill, a successor to the Insurrection Acts.

3 APR 1833 Cabinet changes following the resignation of Lord Durham, the Lord Privy Seal, lead to Derby's appointment as Colonial Secretary.

14 MAY 1833 Derby introduces five resolutions calling for the emancipation of the slaves of the British Empire within one year. In June he presents the Abolition of Slavery Bill. This measure is to give the slaves their freedom on 1 Aug 1834.

6 MAY 1834 There is disagreement in the Cabinet about the revenues of the Irish Church. Derby is opposed to any alienation of Church property, but Lord John Russell thinks the Church's income is excessive and that it should be investigated and the surplus appropriated for secular purposes. When Russell points out in the Commons that Derby does not speak for the whole party on this issue, Derby comments, 'Johnny has upset the coach'.

27 MAY 1834 When Henry George Ward introduces a resolution calling for the redistribution of the Irish Church revenues, Derby resigns before a debate on the motion fully reveals the split in the Government. The 'Derby Dilly', a faction led by Derby with Sir James Graham and the Duke of Richmond as supporters, is formed. They adopt a policy statement, the 'Knowsley Creed', the main tenets of which are church and municipal reform. Gradually Derby grows closer to Peel, and three years later in Dec 1837 he joins the Tory party.

3 SEP 1841 Appointed Secretary of State for War and the Colonies in Peel's second administration, Derby takes on the responsibility for the 'Opium Wars' with China.

AUG 1842 Treaty of Nanking. The Chinese Emperor cedes Hong Kong to the British. Derby suggests that it should be ruled by a Governor and Council, and also that it should be a free port.

4 NOV 1844 Derby is called to the House of Lords as Lord Stanley of Bickerstaffe. This is at his own request. His health is failing and he is weary of life in the House of Commons. There is also a need for an active Government man in the upper House.

1845 Derby is criticised for his handling of problems in New Zealand stemming from conflict between the Maoris and the settlers. The Governor, Fitzroy, is eventually recalled for failing to follow Derby's instructions.

IMPORTANT DATES IN PERSONAL AND POLITICAL LIFE—*Continued*

NOV 1845 Derby disagrees with Peel over the repeal of the Corn Laws. Peel's reversal of policy on this issue leads to a split in the Cabinet.

5 DEC 1845 Peel resigns as Prime Minister, unable to unite his Cabinet over the Corn Laws issue. Russell fails in his attempts to form a Government; Peel resumes office. Unable to support Peel's policy on the Corn Laws, Derby resigns from the Cabinet.

23 DEC 1845 He now becomes a focus for the Protectionists and declares that he will oppose the Bill to repeal the Corn Laws when it reaches the House of Lords.

25 MAY 1846 Derby speaks for three hours in support of the Corn Laws but the vote goes against the Protectionists.

27 JUN 1846 Peel resigns as Prime Minister after the passing of the Corn Bill, leaving the Conservative Party deeply divided. Lord John Russell becomes Prime Minister.

1848 Derby becomes Leader of the Conservative Party.

2 JUL 1850 Death of Peel, following a riding accident.

22 FEB 1851 The Peelites refuse to support Derby when he attempts to form a Government after Lord John Russell resigns because he has declared his intention to reinstate a duty on foreign corn. Russell later resumes office.

30 JUN 1851 Death of his father, the 13th Earl of Derby.

21 FEB 1852 The Russell administration falls after Palmerston and the Conservatives combine forces to defeat the Government on the Militia Bill.

23 FEB 1852 Derby takes office as Prime Minister for the first time. He is compelled to form his Cabinet with loyal Conservatives so inexperienced that the ministry is dubbed the 'Who? Who? Cabinet'.

JUL 1852 General Election. Derby gains about another 25 supporters, but not enough to make him independent of the Peelites.

17 DEC 1852 Derby's administration collapses after Disraeli's Budget is defeated by the combined forces of the Whigs, Peelites, Radicals and Irish. Aberdeen becomes Prime Minister, leading a coalition Government.

30 JAN 1855 Aberdeen's administration falls after criticism of the Government's handling of the Crimean War. Derby cannot secure a majority in the House of Commons to take over as Prime Minister and Palmerston leads the next Government.

20 FEB 1858 Derby forms his second administration after the defeat of Palmerston's Government over the Conspiracy Bill. It is once more a minority Government, dependent on the divisions among the opposition for survival.

1858 India Bill. This measure transfers control of India from the East India Company to the Crown, administered by a Secretary of State assisted by a Council.

23 JUL 1858 Jews Relief Act receives Royal Assent. This measure ends the disabililty of Jews from sitting in Parliament.

MAR 1859 The Government brings forward proposals for electoral reform, but the Bill is defeated. Derby seeks and is granted a dissolution of Parliament.

APR 1859 General Election. The Government is still in a minority position despite gaining some 25 seats.

11 JUN 1859 A no confidence amendment to the Address is carried and Derby resigns. Palmerston becomes Prime Minister.

1862 Derby publishes privately his *Translations of Poems, Ancient and Modern.*

1862 Derby becomes chairman of the Central Executive Committee which coordinates the work of the relief committees during the Lancashire cotton famine, caused by the American Civil War, which halts the supply of cotton from the Southern states to Lancashire.

1864 His translation of the *Iliad* is published. It is well received and the first edition sells out in a week.

JUL 1865 General Election. The Whigs are again returned to power under Palmerston. Disraeli is discouraged and offers to retire from leading the Conservatives in the Commons. Derby refuses to consider anyone else as leader of the Tories in the Lower House.

18 OCT 1865 Death of Palmerston. Lord John Russell becomes Prime Minister for the second time.

JUN 1866 Russell's administration is divided over the Reform Bill. The anti-reform Whigs splinter off and join the Conservative opposition.

26 JUN 1866 Russell resigns and two days later, 28 Jun, Derby becomes Prime Minister for the third time.

25 FEB 1867 Disraeli introduces the Reform Bill in the House of Commons. The 'Ten Minute Bill' has been hastily amended to drop the proposals for household suffrage in the face of Cabinet opposition. The Bill is not well received and with many Conservatives joining the Opposition's demands for a more radical measure, Derby decides to reinstate the household suffrage proposals.

18 MAR 1867 A new Reform Bill is introduced in the House of Commons.

9 AUG 1867 The Reform Bill, which Derby describes as 'taking a leap in the dark', receives Royal Assent.

25 FEB 1868 Derby resigns as Prime Minister because of ill health and Disraeli succeeds him.

APR–JUL 1868 Derby is active in the House of Lords where he is the unofficial leader of the Conservative Peers.

17 JUN 1869 His last major speech, against the Bill to disestablish the Irish Church.

23 OCT 1869 Derby dies at Knowsley.

BACKGROUND

PHYSICAL CHARACTERISTICS AND HEALTH

Derby's bearing was that of a man with natural authority, although he was not tall. He had aristocratic features but was not described as particularly handsome. His youthful appearance was commented on. He had brown wavy hair, a firm chin and full lips, and had inherited his mother's aquiline nose. In later life he frequently wore clothes that were long out of fashion and he usually sported a large black satin cravat. Derby had a tenor voice of great beauty which contributed to his oratorical skills.

In his late thirties Derby first suffered an attack of the gout which was to plague him for the rest of his life. The attacks had so increased in severity and frequency by 1858 that Disraeli commented 'nothing disheartens a party as much as an invalid chief, and they are always afraid he is going to die and break up the ministry'. At the end of his Second Administration in 1859 Derby was not sorry to resign; he was worn out by office and by his illness. By 1867 his health was so bad that there were hints that his mental state was also affected, but this may have been due to the opium which was frequently administered to him. His death two years later followed a period when he was never free of the pain of chronic gout.

EDUCATION

Secondary 1811–17, Eton
University 1817–20, Christ Church, Oxford
Prizes and awards 1819, Chancellor's Latin verse prize for his poem *Syracuse*
Qualifications Derby did not take his degree.
Cultural and vocational background 1824, Derby travelled for eight months in Canada and the United States. The tour included visits to New York State, New England, Pennsylvania, West Virginia, Ohio, New Orleans and Washington.
Languages Latin and Greek: he later translated the *Iliad*; French and German

NON-PARLIAMENTARY CAREER

Other posts 1834–86, Lord Rector of the University of Glasgow; 1835–66, Sloane Trustee of the British Museum; 1852–69, Chancellor of the University of Oxford; 1852–69, Elder Brother of Trinity House; 1848, Steward of the Jockey Club

HONOURS

Academic 1852, DCL Oxford
Other than peerage 28 Jun 1859, Knight of the Garter; 15 Dec 1859, Fellow of the Royal Society; 25 Mar 1869, Knight Grand Cross of St. Michael and St. George

CLUBS

Jockey Club

HOBBIES AND SPORTS

Derby was an excellent classical scholar; he translated the *Iliad* into blank verse and this was published in 1864. He also translated French and German poetry and other classical works.

Throughout his life he was passionately interested in sport; particularly country sports such as shooting partridges and wildfowl, but his main hobby was horse racing. He was said to be the life and soul of the great race meetings until 1863 when he finally sold his stud. He was a member of the Jockey Club.

Derby had a reputation for being a gambler and for being easily distracted from politics by his other interests.

FINANCES

Lord Derby was a wealthy man, with estates principally in Lancashire and Cheshire. There were also extensive estates in Limerick, Ireland. Derby's annual income was estimated to be £60,000 although Disraeli once stated that it was almost double this at £110,000. Derby was also involved in business ventures and he always managed his estates efficiently. He was the owner of racehorses and it is estimated that his income from this amounted to about £94,000 over twenty-two years.
Income Estimated to be £60,000 per year.
Legacies Inherited his estates from his father, the 13th Earl of Derby.
Debts Inherited the burden of a debt of about £500,000, which had come about largely because of the expense of his father's zoological collection at Knowsley.
Will Derby's will was proved at under £250,000. The annual value of his estates at this time were said to be just under £170,000. His wife was awarded £6,000 a year for life and an immediate payment of £3,000. His younger son, Frederick Arthur received £125,000. After other smaller legacies, the remainder went to his heir, the 15th Earl.

ANECDOTES

Although Derby had a reputation for being diverted from political matters by his passions for racing and shooting, the Earl of Malmesbury recorded in his *Memoirs* that Derby could 'sit down at once to write the longest and most important paper right off, in a delicate hand and without a single erasure'.

Derby's powers of oratory were famous. Lord Campbell described him as ' . . . a host in himself. He has marvellous acuteness of intellect and consummate power in debate. There is no subject which he cannot master thoroughly and lucidly explain. His voice and manner are so good that no one can hear him without listening to him'.

In *New Timon* (1845) Bulwer-Lytton wrote of him:

'One after one the Lords of Time advance,
Here Stanley meets—how Stanley scorns the glance!
The brilliant chief, irregularly great,
Frank, haughty, rash, the Rupert of Debate'.

Disraeli said of him in Jul 1874 when he unveiled Derby's statue in Parliament Square, London: 'He abolished slavery, he educated Ireland, he reformed Parliament'.

G. C. H. G. Lennox wrote to Disraeli of Derby: 'as a leader of a party he is more hopeless than ever—devoted to whist, billiards, racing, betting . . . ' (undated letter)

QUOTATIONS

24 Feb 1857, In a speech in the House of Lords, Derby attacked Palmerston's policy on China: ' . . . I am an advocate in a cause which I believe to be that of policy, of justice and humanity. I am an advocate for weakness against power, for perplexed and bewildered barbarism against the arrogant demands of overweening, self-styled civilisation. I am an advocate for the feeble defencelessness of China against the overpowering might of Great Britain'.

16 Mar 1857, My notions may perhaps be old-fashioned and contrary to the enlightenment of the day, but they are the opinions to which I have steadfastly adhered through no inconsiderable period of my life, and I cannot change them now. . . . I intend to maintain inviolate the great institutions of the country: I intend to support as far as my feeble voice can go, the prerogatives of the Crown, the independence and hereditary character of your Lordships' House and the rights of the people. I intend to support the doctrines

QUOTATIONS—*Continued*

and rights of property of that Established Church of which I have always been an attached member . . . . (Speech in the House of Lords)

1 Mar 1858, My Lords, there can be no greater mistake than to suppose that a Conservative ministry necessarily means a stationary ministry. We live in an age of constant progress, moral, social and political . . . our constitution itself is the result of a series of perpetual changes. Like the venerable old country houses of England, it has been framed from time to time by successive occupants, with no great regard for architectural uniformity or regularity of outline, but adding a window here, throwing out a gable there, and making some fresh accommodation in another place, as might appear to suit, not the beauty of the external structure, but the convenience and comfort of the inhabitants. My Lords, in politics, as in everything else, the same course must be pursued—constant progress, improving upon the old system, adapting our institutions to the altered purposes they are intended to serve, and by judicious changes meeting the demands of society. (Speech in the House of Lords at the beginning of his second administration.)

1867, One of Derby's supporters visited him and complained that the Reform Bill was too radical. Derby replied: 'Don't you see how it has dished the Whigs?'

6 Aug 1867, After the Third Reading of the Reform Bill in the House of Lords Derby commented on the measure: 'No doubt we are making a great experiment and taking "a leap in the dark" but I have the greatest confidence in the sound sense of my fellow-countrymen, and I entertain a strong hope that the extended franchise which we are now conferring upon them will be the means of placing the institutions of this country on a firmer basis, and that the passing of this measure will tend to increase the loyalty and contentment of a great portion of Her Majesty's subjects'.

17 Jun 1869, My Lords, I am now an old man, and like many of your Lordships, I have already passed the three score years and ten. My official life is entirely closed; my political life is nearly so; and, in the course of nature, my natural life cannot now be long. That natural life commenced with the bloody suppression of a formidable rebellion in Ireland, which immediately preceded the Union between the two countries. And may God grant that its close may not witness a renewal of the one and the dissolution of the other!' (His last speech in the House of Lords on the Bill to disestablish the Irish Church)

RESIDENCES

Knowsley Hall, Prescot, Lancashire

Limerick, Ireland, Derby built a house on the family estates and lived there for a time after his marriage.

10 St. James's Square, London; the house was previously lived in by the Elder Pitt and later by W.E. Gladstone. (plaque)

23 St. James's Square, London; Derby did not live at 10 Downing Street.

Open to the public Knowsley Hall is not open to the public, but in 1970 a safari park set in 600 acres of Knowsley Park was opened by the 18th Earl of Derby.

MEMORIALS

STATUES AND BUSTS

Parliament Square, London; Miller Square, Preston, Lancashire

PORTRAITS

By G. H. Harlow, Eton College, Berkshire; 1844, by Frederick Richard Say, National Portrait Gallery, London; 1858, by Sir Francis Grant, Examination Schools, Oxford

OTHER MEMORIALS

In 1870 the Derby (Classical) Scholarship, tenable for a year and worth £150, was founded to commemorate Derby's connection with Oxford University.

BIBLIOGRAPHIC INFORMATION

LETTERS AND PERSONAL PAPERS

The papers are in the possession of the present Earl of Derby, Knowsley Hall, Prescot, Merseyside.

PUBLICATIONS

1830, *Journal of a Tour in America 1824–1825*; 1837, *Conversations on the Parables for the Use of Children*; 1862, *Translations of Poems, Ancient and Modern*; 1864, Translation of the *Iliad*.

FURTHER READING

Bagley, J. J. *The Earls of Derby 1485–1985*. London, 1985.

Derby, Fifteenth Earl of. *Disraeli, Derby and the Conservative Party. The political journals of Lord Stanley 1849–1869*. Ed., J. R. Vincent. Hassocks, Sussex, 1978.

Jones, W. D. *Lord Derby and Victorian Conservatism*. Oxford, 1956.

Kebbel, T.E. *Life of the Earl of Derby, K.G.*. 2nd ed. London, 1893. (The Statesmen Series, Ed. L. C. Sanders)

Saintsbury, G. *The Earl of Derby*. London, 1892. (The Prime Ministers of Queen Victoria Series, Vol. VII, Ed. S. J. Reid)

I.W.

Bettmann

Earl of Aberdeen

Lived 1784–1860
Political Party Conservative
Prime Minister 19 December 1852–30 January 1855
Government Coalition
Reigning Monarch Victoria

Fortuna sequatur Let Fortune be attendant

ABERDEEN AS PRIME MINISTER

Unusually for a Prime Minister, Aberdeen never sat in the House of Commons. At the age of 22 he entered the House of Lords and a few years later started a successful career in diplomacy which prepared him for two effective periods as Foreign Secretary, 1828–30 and 1841–46. He supported Peel and became leader of the Peelites in 1850. Two years later when Derby's Government was defeated, Aberdeen agreed to try to form a coalition Government of Peelites, Whigs and radicals. In addition he needed the support of Irish members in the House of Commons. His Cabinet included Russell as Foreign Secretary, Palmerston as Home Secretary and Gladstone as Chancellor of the Exchequer, and controlling it proved too much of a challenge for the former diplomat Aberdeen, a conciliator rather than a decisive leader. Foreign affairs, and in particular the drift toward war with Russia, dominated Aberdeen's Prime Ministership. Responsibility for failing to conduct the Crimean War efficiently was pinned on Aberdeen personally and a motion in the House of Commons proposing a Committee of Enquiry to consider the conduct of the war led to Aberdeen's resignation. He had also failed to carry a Reform Bill, although other legislation concerned with taxation, the Civil Service and legal matters was passed early in his administration, which showed his ability to be a reforming Prime Minister. However, his essentially unsuccessful career suggests clearly the need for Prime Ministers, if they are to be effective, to have real powers of leadership.

PERSONAL INFORMATION

Names George Hamilton-Gordon (formerly Gordon. In Nov 1818 he obtained a royal licence to assume the surname Hamilton as a 'memorial of his respect for the memory of his late father-in-law, John James Hamilton, Marquess of Abercorn, K.G. deced.' [*London Gazette*, 1818])
Peerages 4th Earl of Aberdeen; Viscount Gordon of Aberdeen, 1 Jun 1814
Born 28 Jan 1784
Birthplace Edinburgh, Scotland
Religion Anglican although he attended Presbyterian services and was sympathetic towards this church.
Ancestry Scottish. The Gordons claimed descent from Bertrand de Gourdon who killed Richard Coeur de Lion in 1199. De Gourdon's children settled in Scotland at the beginning of the 13th century and the family rose to eminence in the 16th and 17th centuries.
Dates and places of marriages 1) 28 Jul 1805, Bentley Priory, Stanmore, Middlesex; 2) 8 Jul 1815, Bentley Priory, Stanmore, Middlesex
Age at marriages 1) 21 years, 181 days; 2) 31 years, 161 days
Years married 1) 6 years, 216 days; 2) 18 years, 49 days
First entered Parliament Elected a Scottish Representative Peer on 4 Dec 1806 and took his seat in the House of Lords on 17 Dec 1806.
Date appointed PM 19 Dec 1852
Age at appointment 68 years, 326 days
Date ceased to be PM 30 Jan 1855
Total time as PM 2 years, 42 days
Ceased to be elected Peer 1 Jun 1814
Lived after last term as PM 5 years, 319 days
Date of death 14 Dec 1860
Place of death Argyll House, St. James's, London
Age at death 76 years, 321 days
Place of funeral St. John the Evangelist Church, Great Stanmore, Middlesex
Place of burial Abercorn family vault, St. John the Evangelist Church, Great Stanmore, Middlesex
Zodiac sign Aquarius

FATHER

George Gordon, Lord Haddo
Date of birth 28 Jan 1764
Occupation Heir to the 3rd Earl of Aberdeen. Grand Master of Freemasons 1784–86.
Date of marriage 18 Jun 1782
Date of death 2 Oct 1791
Place of burial Methlick Church, Methlick, Aberdeenshire

MOTHER

Charlotte (Charles) Baird
Profile Charlotte never recovered from the shock of her husband's early death. She quarrelled with her father-in-law, the 3rd Earl of Aberdeen, soon afterwards and went to live in London with her children. She died at Clifton four years later.
Date of marriage 18 Jun 1782
Date of death 8 Oct 1795

BROTHERS AND SISTERS

Aberdeen was the eldest son and first of seven children.
William of Ellon, b. 18 Dec 1784; Vice-Admiral, Commander in Chief at the Nore 1854–57; a Lord of the Admiralty 1841–46; MP Aberdeenshire 1820–54; d. 3 Feb 1858
Sir Alexander, b. 1786; soldier; a Lieutenant-Colonel and favourite aide-de-camp of the Duke of Wellington, he was killed at the Battle of Waterloo; a monument was erected by the family at Waterloo, and a replica of it at Haddo; d. 18 Jun 1815
Sir Charles, b. 5 Jul 1790; Lieutenant-Colonel of the Forty-Second Highlanders; d. 30 Sep 1835
Alicia, b. 1790; Lady of the Bedchamber to Princess Sophia Matilda; d. 24 Apr 1847
Sir Robert GCB, GCH, b. 1791; diplomat; Envoy Extraordinary to Brazil 1826; Ambassador to the Ottoman Empire 1828 and to Austria 1841–47; d. 8 Oct 1847
John, b. posthumously in 1792; Admiral; d. 8. Nov 1869

FIRST WIFE

Catherine Elizabeth Hamilton
Date of birth 10 Jan 1784
Mother Catherine Copley
Father John James Hamilton, First Marquess of Abercorn
Father's occupation Peer and landowner
Age at marriage 21 years, 199 days
Number of children 4, one of whom died in infancy
Date and place of death 29 Feb 1812, Argyll House, St. James's, London
Place of burial Great Stanmore, Middlesex
Years older than PM 18 days
Profile Catherine Hamilton was a noted beauty: charming, lively and spontaneous. Aberdeen fell deeply in love with her and never recovered from her early death. His son Arthur said that with her death, 'the sunshine went out of his life forever'.

SECOND WIFE

Harriet, Dowager Viscountess Hamilton, née Douglas
Date of birth 8 Jun 1792
Mother Frances Lascelles
Father Hon. John Douglas, son of James, 14th Earl of Morton
Age at marriage 23 years, 30 days
Number of children 3 by her marriage to Viscount Hamilton; 5 by her marriage to Aberdeen
Date and place of death 26 Aug 1833, Argyll House, St. James's, London
Place of burial Stanmore, Middlesex
Years younger than PM 8 years, 132 days
Profile Harriet was the widow of his first wife's brother. Their father-in-law, the Marquess of Abercorn, engineered the marriage as a solution to the problem of finding a suitable stepfather for his grandson and heir. The marriage was not very successful; Aberdeen still

mourned Catherine, and Harriet never captured his heart in the way his first wife had done. She was not Catherine's intellectual equal. Indeed, Aberdeen told his brother Alexander in 1810 that she was 'certainly one of the most stupid persons I ever met with'.

Harriet was jealous of Aberdeen's relationship with his three daughters by Catherine. She did not attempt to conceal her resentment and at times behaved maliciously towards them, to her husband's distress. She loathed Haddo and refused to go there and from 1819 they began to spend time apart. Nevertheless, he was grief-stricken when she died in 1833, aged only 41.

CHILDREN

4 sons, 4 daughters
By his first wife, Catherine:
Jane, b. 11 Feb 1807; d. 18 Aug 1824
Caroline Katherine, b. 28 Mar 1808; d. 24 Jul 1818
Alice, b. 12 Jul 1809; d. 29 Apr 1829
By his second wife, Harriet:
George John James, (5th Earl of Aberdeen and 2nd Viscount Aberdeen), b. 28 Sep 1816; m. 5 Nov 1840, Mary Baillie; MP Aberdeenshire, 1854–60; d. 22 Mar 1864
Sir Alexander, b. 11 Dec 1817; m. 9 Dec 1852, Caroline Emilia Mary Herschel; MP Aberdeenshire, 1875–85; Knight of the Legion of Honour and the Medjidie; Equerry to both Prince Albert and Queen Victoria; Colonel of the First Battalion of the Prince of Wales's Leinster Regiment, later a General; d. 19 May 1890
Frances, b. 1818; d. 20 Apr 1834
Douglas, b. 13 Mar 1824; m. 15 Jul 1851, Lady Ellen Susan Anne Douglas, daughter of the 16th Earl of Morton; Clergyman; Chaplain in Ordinary to Queen Victoria; Hon. Chaplain to King Edward VII; Canon of Salisbury; d. 6 Dec 1901
Arthur, (GCMG, DCL, First Baron Stanmore of Great Stanmore, Middlesex 1893), b. 26 Nov 1829; m. 24 Sep 1865, Rachel Emily Shaw-Lefevre; Private Secretary to his father as PM, 1852–55; MP Beverley 1854–57. Lieutenant Governor of New Brunswick 1861–66; Governor of Trinidad 1866–70, Mauritius 1871–74, Fiji 1875–80 and New Zealand 1880–82; High Commissioner and Consul-General for the Western Pacific 1877–83; Governor of Ceylon 1883–90; wrote a biography of his father for the series *The Prime Ministers of Queen Victoria*; d. 30 Jan 1912

LIFE AND CAREER

PARLIAMENTARY ELECTIONS FOUGHT

Scottish Peers did not all attend the House of Lords, but elected sixteen of their number to represent them. Aberdeen was elected a Scottish Representative Peer on 4 Dec 1806, 9 Jun 1807 and 13 Nov 1812. On 1 Jun 1814 his viscountcy entitled him to sit in the House of Lords in his own right.

PARTY ACTIVITY

Party Leadership Leader of the Scottish Conservative Party 1838

Other offices 1819, Elected to the 'Secret Committee' of the House of Lords appointed to examine the resumption of cash payments by the Bank of England; since 1797 the issue of gold coinage had been suspended in favour of paper money. 1826, Appointed to the Royal Commission set up to enquire into the state of the Scottish universities.

Membership of group or faction After the death of Sir Robert Peel, Aberdeen became the leader of those Conservatives who had supported the repeal of the Corn Laws, the Peelites.

PARLIAMENTARY AND MINISTERIAL EXPERIENCE

Maiden Speech 13 Apr 1807 in a debate on the change of administration. (*Parl. Deb.* 1st ser, vol IX, col 352-4)

Privy Counsellor 22 Jul 1814

Ministerial Offices Chancellor of the Duchy of Lancaster 22 Jan– 2 Jun 1828; Secretary of State for Foreign Affairs 2 Jun 1828–16 Nov 1830, 3 Sep 1841–29 Jun 1846; Secretary of State for War and the Colonies 20 Dec 1834–8 Apr 1835; First Lord of the Treasury and Leader of the House of Lords 19 Dec 1852–30 Jan 1855

Opposition Leader While PM Aberdeen's was a Coalition Government

GOVERNMENTS FORMED

Administration 19 Dec 1852–30 Jan 1855

GENERAL ELECTION RESULT

JUL 1852: Conservative 330; Liberal 324. Total 654
Conservative majority 7 (excl. the Speaker)

CABINET

Prime Minister and First Lord of the Treasury Earl of Aberdeen
Lord Chancellor Lord Cranworth
Lord President of the Council Earl Granville (1852–54); Lord J. Russell (1854–55)
Lord Privy Seal Duke of Argyll
Home Secretary Viscount Palmerston
Foreign Secretary Lord J. Russell (1852–53); Earl of Clarendon (1853–55)
Secretary of State for War and the Colonies Duke of Newcastle (1852–54); (War and Colonies were separated into two departments 10 Jun 1854)
Secretary of State for War Duke of Newcastle (1854–55)
Secretary of State for the Colonies Sir G. Grey (1854–55)
Chancellor of the Exchequer W. E. Gladstone
First Lord of the Admiralty Sir J. Graham
President of the Board of Control Sir C. Wood
*Chancellor of the Duchy of Lancaster** Earl Granville (1854–55)
Minister without Portfolio Marquess of Lansdowne (1852–53); Lord J. Russell (1853–54)
Secretary at War S. Herbert
First Commissioner of Works Sir W. Molesworth
[*Office not always in Cabinet]

IMPORTANT DATES IN PERSONAL AND POLITICAL LIFE

2 OCT 1791 Aberdeen's father dies following a fall from his horse. His mother is to die four years later. Scottish law allows orphans to name their 'curators' or guardians when they reach the age of 14. Aberdeen appoints William Pitt (*q.v.*) and Henry Dundas, later Lord Melville.

1794 At the age of 10 Aberdeen goes to Harrow.

IMPORTANT DATES IN PERSONAL AND POLITICAL LIFE—*Continued*

OCT 1800 Aberdeen goes to St. John's College, Cambridge. He only studies there for two sessions but receives his MA in 1804, noblemen being able to obtain a degree without sitting an examination.

30 AUG 1801 Death of his grandfather, the 3rd Earl of Aberdeen. He thus succeeds to the earldom at the age of 17. Later this year he sets off on a tour of the continent.

1802 He visits Paris, where he meets Napoleon.

1803 In Athens he excavates the amphitheatre on the hill called the Pynx. The reliefs he finds there come to Britain with the Elgin Marbles and are now in the British Museum.

1804 On his return home Aberdeen founds the Athenian Society and two years later writes about Troy for the *Edinburgh Review.* Byron later refers to him as 'The travell'd thane, Athenian Aberdeen.'

28 JAN 1805 He comes of age and inherits his Scottish estates, which he visits for the first time since he had left as a child. He is shocked at their condition and how his countrymen live, in contrast to life in the south of England, where he has been living.

28 JUL 1805 Marries Lady Catherine Hamilton.

23 JAN 1806 Death of Pitt, Aberdeen's former guardian. He is deeply upset, not only at the loss of a friend and mentor, but also by the blow to his political career, as Pitt had promised Aberdeen an English peerage which would have given him a seat in the House of Lords.

4 DEC 1806 Aberdeen canvasses heavily to gain support for his election as Scottish Representative Peer. He is successful and takes his seat on 17 Dec 1806.

13 APR 1807 He makes his maiden speech during the debate on the change of administration when the Duke of Portland succeeds Lord Grenville as PM.

1807 Aberdeen is offered the post of Ambassador to Russia which he turns down. He also rejects the offer of appointment as British Minister to Sicily, probably because of his father-in-law's opposition to this posting.

16 MAR 1808 He is made a Knight of the Thistle.

28 APR 1808 Elected a Fellow of the Royal Society.

1809 Aberdeen again turns down the post of Ambassador to Russia.

29 FEB 1812 Death of his first wife, Catherine, from tuberculosis. She had never been robust and had been weakened by a miscarriage the previous year. Aberdeen is devastated by her death and mourns her for the rest of his life.

6 AUG 1813 Aberdeen leaves London on a special mission to Emperor Francis I of Austria, sent by Castlereagh, the Foreign Secretary in Lord Liverpool's administration. His instructions are to reopen relations with Austria and reestablish a British presence in the councils of the European powers at the end of the Napoleonic wars.

28 SEP 1813 He is appointed Ambassador Extraordinary and Minister Plenipotentiary to Vienna.

3 OCT 1813 Aberdeen signs the treaty of alliance with Austria at Toplitz.

16 OCT 1813 Aberdeen witnesses the aftermath of the Battle of Leipzig.

5 FEB 1814–19 MAR 1814 With Lord Cathcart and Sir Charles Stewart Aberdeen represents Great Britain at the Chatillon Conference.

1 MAR 1814 The Treaty of Chaumont brings about the Grand Alliance of Austria, Russia, Prussia and Britain.

31 MAR 1814 The fall of Paris.

11 APR 1814 Napoleon abdicates as Emperor of France.

30 MAY 1814 The Treaty of Paris is signed. Aberdeen leaves Paris the next day. He is reported to have brought the treaty home in his own carriage.

1 JUN 1814 As a reward for his diplomatic work he is created Viscount Gordon of Aberdeen, a peer of the United Kingdom,

22 JUL 1814 Admitted to the Privy Council

8 JUL 1815 He is married, for the second time, to Harriet, Dowager Viscountess Hamilton, the widow of his first wife's brother.

18 JAN 1818 Death of his father-in-law, Lord Abercorn. Aberdeen changes his name as a mark of respect to incorporate Abercorn's surname Hamilton and is known as Hamilton-Gordon from this time. He now has the responsibility of administering the Abercorn estates until his stepson James comes of age. For the next ten years looking after his own and the Abercorn estates almost fully occupies his time.

24 JUL 1818 Death of his daughter Caroline from tuberculosis.

18 AUG 1824 Death of his daughter Jane.

22 JAN 1828 Accepts the post of Chancellor of the Duchy of Lancaster in Wellington's first administration and also undertakes to assist the Earl of Dudley at the Foreign Office.

2 JUN 1828 Aberdeen is appointed Foreign Secretary when Dudley and the other Canningites resign from Wellington's Cabinet.

1828 The most pressing problem when Aberdeen takes office is the Eastern question: the Greek struggle for independence from the Ottoman Empire. Aberdeen is sympathetic towards the Greeks and wishes to help them as much as possible within the constraints of preserving European stability. The problem seems to be settled after the Conference of London in Feb 1830, but the issue is still not completely resolved at the end of Wellington's administration.

SEP 1828 Aberdeen demonstrates his reluctance to become involved in the internal problems of another power over the Portuguese succession crisis: Donna Maria, heiress to the Portuguese throne, is on her way to Portugal from Brazil when she learns at Gibraltar of a coup d' état by her uncle Miguel. Donna Maria's supporters ask the British for help but Wellington's Government refuses, pursuing a policy of strict neutrality. By 1830 the problem is whether Miguel should be recognised as King by Britain; this is still also unresolved at the end of Wellington's premiership.

29 APR 1829 Aberdeen's daughter Alice dies in his arms at Bentley Priory. She had suffered ill-health for some years. His grief for the last of his daughters by Catherine causes him to shut himself away in the Foreign Office completely alone for some days.

10 JUN 1829 Argentina proclaims Louis Vernet, a Hamburg merchant, governor of the Falkland Islands. Aberdeen protests to Buenos Aires about the breach of British sovereignty. Grey and Palmerston later enforce this by sending a naval detachment in Jan 1833.

26 JUN 1830 Death of George IV and accession of William IV.

15 NOV 1830 Resignation of Wellington's Government after defeat on a motion about the Civil List. Grey becomes Prime Minister.

26 AUG 1833 Death of his second wife, Harriet.

20 APR 1834 Death of the only daughter of his second marriage. Aberdeen had nursed Frances with devotion during several years of ill-health.

20 DEC 1834 Appointed Secretary of State for War and the Colonies in Sir Robert Peel's shortlived first administration which is to end 8 Apr 1835. During this period Aberdeen has to deal with problems in Canada, South Africa and the West Indies.

FEB 1840 Francois Guizot, who wins Aberdeen's respect and trust, comes to London as the French Ambassador.

MAY 1840 Aberdeen introduces his Non-Intrusion Bill in an attempt to avert the impending schism in the Scottish Church. It is later withdrawn.

5 NOV 1840 Aberdeen's eldest son, Lord Haddo, marries Mary Baillie. Aberdeen immediately warms to his daughter-in-law, who becomes one of his closest confidantes.

3 SEP 1841 In Peel's second administration Aberdeen again takes office as Secretary of State for Foreign Affairs during a dispute with America over the north-east boundary between Maine and New Brunswick. The King of the Netherlands acts as arbiter in the dispute but the Americans reject his compromise solution. Lord Ashburton, sent by Aberdeen as special envoy to Washington, negotiates a treaty by which the disputed territory between the United States and the British Provinces is divided.

9 AUG 1842 The treaty is signed and Lord Palmerston bitterly attacks it as 'capitulation.'

1843 Queen Victoria visits the French royal family at Chateau d'Eu in Normandy, accompanied by Aberdeen, who has many long conversations with Guizot, now Prime Minister of France. From this time the two governments began to speak of the 'entente cordiale' between them; this is the French translation of Aberdeen's words 'a cordial, good understanding.'

1844 Despite the 'entente', however, relations with France deteriorate sharply with the crisis in Tahiti. Britain had been reluctant to take the island under its protection even though there were a number of British missionaries, led by George Pritchard, resident there. The French sent missionaries of their own in the 1830s and in 1842 Admiral Dupetit Thouars forced the Tahitians to accept a French protectorate. By 1844 Tahiti is in turmoil; Pritchard has been arrested for opposing the French and ill treated before being sent home. Feelings run high in both countries but Aberdeen strives to avoid a war over such an issue and negotiates a settlement whereby the French pay compensation to Pritchard.

18 SEP 1845 Aberdeen offers to resign because of differences in the Cabinet over foreign and defence policy, especially in relation to France. Peel refuses to accept his resignation, however, and the Prime Minister and Foreign Secretary agree to differ on defence policy.

15 JUN 1846 The Oregon Treaty. In 1842 the American colonists in the south of Oregon had made claims to exclusive possession of the territory. By 1845 American settlers are swamping the British and eventually Aberdeen, faced with problems elsewhere in the world, concedes almost everything at stake by signing the treaty.

29 JUN 1846 Peel resigns as PM after the passing of the Bill to reform the Corn Laws. Aberdeen had always supported Peel on this and other economic issues even though they differ on foreign policy.

2 JUL 1850 Death of Sir Robert Peel. Aberdeen is recognised as the leader of the Conservatives who had supported Peel's repeal of the Corn Laws. They are known as the Peelites.

22 FEB 1851 Lord John Russell's administration is defeated over the new electoral reform measures. Russell resigns as PM but resumes office after Derby fails to form a government. The administration lasts for only another year.

23 FEB 1852 Lord Derby takes office as PM. His Government collapses in December after Disraeli's Budget is defeated by the combined forces of the Whigs, Peelites, Radicals and Irish.

1852 During the summer Lord John Russell has made the first overtures towards the Peelites. The election in July had not secured an overall majority for Lord Derby's Conservatives and during the following months there is much discussion between the opposition parties as to how they can cooperate to take power. The Duke of Newcastle advocates Aberdeen as the only person who can head a coalition government and suggests that it be called a 'liberal' government. Aberdeen agrees; he can cooperate with Russell as a 'liberal conservative' but he will never consider joining with him as a Whig.

19 DEC 1852 Queen Victoria invites Aberdeen to form a Government. Aberdeen declares that 'the new government should not be a revival of the old Whig Cabinet with the addition of some Peelites, but should be a Liberal Conservative government in the sense of that of Sir Robert Peel.' Aberdeen sees his role as bringing a coalition into being, and once it is secure he intends to retire. The Government is to be a minority one, which can only secure a majority in the House of Commons with the support of the Irish.

29 DEC 1852 First meeting of Aberdeen's Cabinet, which includes 7 Peelites, 5 Whigs and 1 Radical. Lord John Russell is Foreign Secretary and Lord Palmerston Home Secretary.

21 FEB 1853 Lord John Russell resigns as Foreign Secretary, unable to combine the leadership of the House of Commons with the Foreign Office. The Earl of Clarendon becomes Foreign Secretary in his place.

18 APR 1853 The Chancellor of the Exchequer, W. E. Gladstone, presents the Budget in a much acclaimed five-hour speech. Aberdeen declares that it has strengthened his administration.

1853 The India Act, providing for some administrative reform in India and establishing competetive examinations for the Indian Civil Service, is passed.

29 APR 1853 The House of Lords defeats the Bill to admit Jews to Parliament, despite Aberdeen's support for the measure.

1853 During the summer Lord John Russell drafts measures for electoral reform. Aberdeen is optimistic that he can get the Cabinet's support for this despite Palmerston's avowed opposition to any reform.

JUL 1853 Vienna Conference of the four powers, Great Britain, France, Austria and Prussia, to find a peaceful settlement to the dispute between Turkey and Russia. The Russians accept the formula for peace, the Vienna Note, but on 20 Aug the Turks, who have drawn up a proposal of their own, known as 'the Turkish Ultimatum' reject it.

OCT 1853 Turkey declares war on Russia against the advice of her allies, Britain and France.

30 NOV 1853 The Russians, contradicting their declared aim of not seeking to worsen the situation, destroy a Turkish naval squadron at Sinope on the Black Sea. Aberdeen, who has always believed that the Russians could be trusted, can no longer hold out against those members of his Cabinet who advocate a more aggressive policy to protect Turkey.

DEC 1853 The British fleet is ordered into the Black Sea.

IMPORTANT DATES IN PERSONAL AND POLITICAL LIFE—*Continued*

6 JAN 1854 The Russian fleet is warned by the allies to return to Sebastopol.

13 FEB 1854 Russell introduces the Reform Bill into the House of Commons. It is immediately apparent that it will be fiercely opposed and although Aberdeen wants to proceed with the measure, he cannot command the support of his Cabinet, and with war imminent the Bill is abandoned.

27 FEB 1854 An ultimatum is sent to Russia by Britain and France.

28 MAR 1854 War with Russia (The Crimean War) is declared.

31 MAR 1854 In a debate in the House of Lords, Derby attacks Aberdeen as being responsible for the Crimean War. 'I believe this war would never have taken place', he says, ' . . . if at the particular time of these particular difficulties arising, the noble Earl opposite had not been the Minister at the head of the government'. Aberdeen's reply and whole handling of this critical debate are disastrous. A few weeks later, when he makes some ill-advised comments about the motives of the Tsar, Queen Victoria and his colleagues in Parliament are appalled. Clarendon tells him that his speech has 'jarred against public opinion'.

APR 1854 Aberdeen's son Alexander leaves for the Crimea with the Guards. He is to write frequently, giving his father first-hand information about the campaign.

SEP 1854 The allied armies land in the Crimea.

17 OCT 1854 The siege of Sebastopol begins.

DEC 1854 The Russians bring massive reinforcements to Sebastopol. The British forces suffer greatly. Food is short as the weather has made it difficult to get supplies through. Men and horses are dying of cold, starvation and disease. Many years of underfunding and poor organisation are behind the Army's troubles, but the public, outraged at newspaper reports of the conditions in the Crimea, blame the Government.

23 JAN 1855 When Parliament meets, John Roebuck proposes a Committee of Enquiry to look into the conduct of the Crimean War. Lord John Russell resigns from the Cabinet the same day, unwilling to defend the Government's record.

29 JAN 1855 Roebuck's motion is carried by 305 to 148.

30 JAN 1855 Aberdeen tenders his resignation to the Queen at Windsor. Lord Palmerston becomes Prime Minister.

15 MAY 1855 Aberdeen is summoned before the 'Sebastopol Committee' set up as a result of Roebuck's motion. The Committee reports in June with a moderate report which refrains from censure of individuals, despite its criticism of the Government's policy with regard to the Crimea.

OCT 1857 Queen Victoria visits Aberdeen at Haddo, a public demonstration of the high regard in which she holds her former Prime Minister.

26 JUL 1858 Aberdeen makes his last speech in the House of Lords on the abolition of the slave trade.

1859 His health starts to fail.

14 DEC 1860 Aberdeen dies at Argyll House, St. James's, London.

BACKGROUND

PHYSICAL CHARACTERISTICS AND HEALTH

Aberdeen was of average height with dark curly hair. As a young man he resembled his cousin, the poet Lord Byron. Many regarded him as handsome, although with age he became heavy and awkward. The personal tragedies he suffered in the 1830s took their toll and in 1839 his hair turned white and then fell out.

Aberdeen suffered from headaches throughout his life, which he attributed to an accident in France in 1813 when his carriage overturned and he suffered concussion. In May 1842 he wrote to his brother Robert, 'For the last six weeks or two months I have been tormented with a continual noise and confusion in the head which has now become much worse, and is more like carrying about with me Niagara than anything else'. He offered his resignation as Foreign Secretary at this time on the grounds of ill health but Sir Robert Peel refused to accept it.

In later years he developed sciatica, which made travelling difficult, and deafness, which may have contributed towards his poor performance in the House of Lords as Prime Minister.

EDUCATION

Primary Preparatory schools in Barnet and Parsons Green, London

Secondary 1795–1800, Harrow

University 1800–02, St. John's College, Cambridge

Qualifications 1804, MA

Cultural and vocational background 1801–04, he toured the Continent, spending much of the time in Greece.

Languages Latin, Greek, French

NON-PARLIAMENTARY CAREER

Early occupations Diplomat. In 1813 he was appointed Ambassador Extraordinary and Minister Plenipotentiary to Austria. He declined the offer of the permanent position of Ambassador to Austria in 1814.

Other posts 1812, Trustee of the British Museum; 1812, President of the Society of Antiquaries; 1845, Ranger of Greenwich Park; 1846, Lord Lieutenant of the County of Aberdeen; 1847, Chancellor of King's College, Aberdeen; 1858, Elder Brother of Trinity House

HONOURS

Academic 1817, Lord Rector of King's College, Aberdeen

Foreign 1813, Grand Cross of St. Stephen of Austria

Other than peerage 16 Mar 1808, Knight of the Thistle; 7 Feb 1855, Knight of the Garter (Aberdeen was given the rare honour of being permitted to hold the two Orders at the same time) 28 Apr 1808, Fellow of the Royal Society

CLUBS

White's; Aberdeen was also a Freemason.

HOBBIES AND SPORTS

Aberdeen was a scholar and connoisseur. He had a deep interest in classical studies and archaeology, and was a keen collector of classical antiquities. In May 1805 he was elected to the Society of Dilettanti and remained an active member until the 1820s. He was also a member and later President of the Society of Antiquaries. In later life his interests turned to science, especially botany.

He became interested in agricultural matters as a result of attempting to improve his Scottish estates. He did a lot of forestry work himself and it was estimated that during his life about 14 million trees were planted on the estates. He started new drainage systems in the late 1840s and experimented with livestock, particularly Shorthorn cattle and South Downs sheep.

Aberdeen was not a great sportsman, but he enjoyed shooting pheasants and partridges and deer stalking on the Haddo estate. He enjoyed other hunting pursuits as well, and his otter hounds were renowned.

FINANCES

Aberdeen was not very wealthy and occasionally his financial situation was precarious. His grandfather had provided small sums of money for all his grandchildren in his will but Aberdeen's brothers and sister all turned to him for help at various times.

The Aberdeen estates were extensive, more than 50, 000 acres, but the land was very poor being mainly bog and stones. He had about 1,000 tenants who were more like peasants than agricultural workers. In 1801 when Aberdeen succeeded to the Earldom the income from the estates was just over £10,000 a year. By 1821 this had more than doubled after his many improvements to the land; he cleared and drained much of it and introduced new farming methods. While Prime Minister he had little time to devote to his own affairs which suffered from the neglect; he also missed his official salary once he was out of office.

Income Aberdeen's income rarely rose above £20,000 p.a. This was the income of a wealthy man in Scotland, but not in England.

Legacies 1818, His father-in-law, Lord Abercorn, left him a substantial amount of money in his will.

Debts Aberdeen inherited large debts from both his father and his grandfather, about £30,000. He was still paying off some of the 3rd Earl's debts in the 1830s.

ANECDOTES

Lord Byron led the criticism of Aberdeen and the Earl of Elgin about their removal of classical antiquities from the original sites. In *English Bards and Scotch Reviewers*, 1809, Byron referred not only to 'the travelled Thane, Athenian Aberdeen' but also declared,

> Let Aberdeen and Elgin still pursue
> The Shade of fame through regions of virtu;
> Waste useless thousands on their Phidean freaks;
> Misshapen monuments and maim'd antiques;
> And make their grand saloons a general mart
> For all the mutilated blocks of art.

Sir James Graham wrote in his *Diary*, 23 Dec 1852, about Aberdeen's Coalition Government: 'It is a powerful team, but it will require good driving. There are some odd tempers and queer ways among them, but on the whole they are gentlemen, and they will have a perfect gentleman at their head, who is honest and direct, and who will not brook insincerity in others'.

Disraeli wrote scathingly of Aberdeen in the *Press*, 4 Jun 1853, 'His mind, his education, his prejudices are all of the Kremlin school. Now that he is placed in a prominent position, and forced to lead English gentlemen, instead of glozing and intriguing with foreign diplomatists, not a night passes that his language or his demeanour does not shock and jar upon the frank and genial spirit of our British Parliament. His manner, arrogant and yet timid—his words, insolent and yet obscure—offend even his political supporters. His hesitating speech, his contracted sympathies, his sneer, icy as Siberia, his sarcasms, drear and barren as the Steppes, are all characteristic of the bureau and the chancery, and not of popular and aristocratic assemblies animated by the spirit of honour and the pride of gentlemen. If war breaks out—and the present prospect is that war will break out—this dread calamity must be placed to the account of this man, and of this man alone'.

Aberdeen had refused to rebuild the Parish Church of Methlick. After his death a text from Chronicles was found written by him on several different scraps of paper:

> And David said to Solomon, My Son, as for me, it was in my mind to build an house unto the name of the Lord, my God: but the word of the Lord came to me, saying, Thou hast shed blood abundantly, and hast made great wars: thou shalt not build an house unto my name, because thou hast shed much blood upon the earth in my sight.

QUOTATIONS

4 Apr 1845, My lords, I consider war to be the greatest folly, if not the greatest crime, of which a country could be guilty, if lightly entered into; and I agree entirely with a moral writer who has said that if a proof were wanted of the deep and thorough corruption of human nature, we should find it in the fact that war itself was sometimes justifiable. (Speech in the House of Lords)

2 Sep 1852, I think it clear that all government in these times must be a government of progress; conservative progress, if you please; but we can no more be stationary, than reactionary. (Letter to Henry Goulburn)

7 Jun 1853, On the Crimean War: 'As we are drifting fast towards war, I should think the Cabinet ought to see where they are going'. (Letter to the Earl of Clarendon)

12 Feb 1854, I still say that war is not inevitable, unless, indeed, we are determined to have it, which, perhaps, for aught I know, may be the case. (Letter to the Earl of Clarendon)

3 Mar 1854, My conscience upbraids me the more, because seeing as I did from the first, all that was to be apprehended, it is possible that by a little more energy and vigour, not on the Danube, but in Downing Street, it might have been prevented. (Letter to Lord John Russell)

1855, I have never entertained the least doubt of the justice of the war in which we are at present engaged.

7 Feb 1855, I do not know how I shall bear being out of office. I have many resources and many objects of interest; but after being occupied with great affairs, it is not easy to subside to the level of common occupations. (To his daughter-in-law, Mary)

RESIDENCES

Haddo House, Methlick, Aberdeenshire, Scotland
Argyll House, St. James's, London
Bentley Priory, Stanmore, Middlesex
Buchan Ness, Aberdeenshire, Scotland
The Ranger's House, Blackheath, London (In 1945 Queen Victoria appointed him to the sinecure post of Ranger of Greenwich Park which gave him the use of the house. He lived there occasionally but during his lifetime it was the usual residence of his son, Lord Haddo.

Open to the public
Haddo House, Methlick, Aberdeenshire. Owned by the National Trust for Scotland, it is a Georgian house designed in 1781 by William Adam.
The Ranger's House, Blackheath, London. Owned by English Heritage.

MEMORIALS

STATUES AND BUSTS

c. 1865, bust by William Theed, Jr., Royal Military Academy, Sandhurst; 1874, bust by Matthew Noble, commissioned by a group of Aberdeen's friends, bearing the Greek inscription 'Most Just', Westminster Abbey, London; effigy by Sir. J. E. Boehm, Great Stanmore Church, Middlesex

PORTRAITS

1808, by Sir Thomas Lawrence, Haddo House, Methlick, Aberdeenshire; 1828, by Sir Thomas Lawrence, Private Collection; *c.* 1839, by Sir Martin Archer Shee, Scottish National Portrait Gallery, Edinburgh; *c.* 1847, by Sir John Partridge, National Portrait Gallery

BIBLIOGRAPHIC INFORMATION

LETTERS AND PERSONAL PAPERS

Aberdeen's papers are in the British Library.

Selections from the correspondence of the Earl of Aberdeen, edited by Sir Arthur Gordon, 13 vols, privately printed 1854–85; *The correspondence of Lord Aberdeen and Princess Lieven*, edited by E. Jones Parry, Royal Historical Society, Camden Third Series, lx, ixii, 2 vols, 1938–39.

PUBLICATIONS

1805, Review of Sir William Gell's book, *The Topography of Troy*, in the *Edinburgh Review*, with William Drummond; 1806, Review of M. L. Dutens's book *Recherches sur le Tems, le plus récule de l'Usage des Voûtes chez les Anciens*, in the *Edinburgh Review*; 1809, Preface to Rev. G. D. Whittington's *Ecclesiastical Antiquities of France*; 1812, Introduction to William Wilkin's edition of Vitruvius's *De Architectura*; 1822, revised edition of the above as *An Inquiry into the Principles of Beauty in Grecian Architecture: with an Historical View of the Rise and Progress of the Art in Greece.*

FURTHER READING

Balfour, Lady F. *The Life of George Fourth Earl of Aberdeen KG, KT.* 2 vols. London, 1922.
Chamberlain, M. E. *Lord Aberdeen. A Political Biography.* London, 1983.
Gordon, Sir A. *The Earl of Aberdeen.* London, 1983. [The Prime Ministers of Queen Victoria series, S. J. Reid, ed.]
Iremonger, L. *Lord Aberdeen. A Biography of the Fourth Earl of Aberdeen KG, KT., Prime Minister 1852–1855.* London, 1978.

I.W.

Bettmann

Viscount Palmerston

Lived 1784–1865

Political Party Tory, 1806–1826; Canningite, 1826–1830; Whig, 1830–1855; Liberal, 1855–1865

Prime Minister 6 February 1855–19 February 1858;
12 June 1859–18 October 1865

Governments Liberal

Reigning Monarch Victoria

Flecti non frangi To be bent not to be broken

PALMERSTON AS PRIME MINISTER

First elected at the age of 26, Palmerston was to wait until he was 70 before he formed his first administration in 1855. Meanwhile he built up a remarkable record of ministerial service, holding posts for much of the period 1807–1855, including long periods as Secretary for War and also as Foreign Secretary. His policy was to further British interests, including trade, by making neither friends nor enemies. Although his style could be impulsive, hot tempered and at times high handed, he sustained a certain popularity with the people, who saw him as a winner. When Aberdeen failed and resigned in 1855 the forceful Palmerston, despite his age, was the obvious successor and his successful conclusion to the Crimean war set a seal on his early achievement. Defeated in the House of Commons over his agressive China policy, he promptly called and won a General Election in 1857. A year later he was again defeated in the Commons during the Conspiracy to Murder Bill and resigned. In 1859 the modern Liberal Party was born, led by Palmerston, and shortly afterwards Derby, defeated in the House of Commons, resigned enabling Palmerston to form his second administration. Much of the next six years was concerned with foreign policy in all quarters of the world including the American Civil War, China, Lebanon and Syria, Brazil, and his failure to defend Denmark against Bismarck. This latter problem led to his censure in Parliament in 1865 but he called a General Election, won it, and then died before Parliament reassembled.

PERSONAL INFORMATION

Names Henry John Temple
Peerages Viscount Palmerston of Palmerston, Co. Dublin, and Baron Temple of Mount Temple, Co. Sligo
Nicknames Pam; Lord Cupid; Lord Pumicestone; Old Pam
Born 20 Oct 1784
Birthplace 4 Park Street, Westminster, London (Now 20 Queen Anne's Gate)
Religion Anglican
Ancestry The Temples were an old English family. Sir John Temple had been awarded land in Ulster by Cromwell, which he kept on the ascension of Charles II. This land was lost under James II and regained under William III. By Palmerston's time the lands were extensive, including estates in Ireland, and Broadlands in Hampshire. The first Viscount Palmerston, of Co. Dublin, was created in 1723.
Date and place of marriage 16 Dec 1839, St. George's, Hanover Sq., London
Age at marriage 55 years, 57 days
Years married 26 years, 306 days
First entered Parliament 8 May 1807
Dates appointed PM 1) 6 Feb 1855; 2) 12 Jun 1859
Age at appointments 1) 71 years, 109 days; 2) 75 years, 235 days
Dates ceased to be PM 1) 19 Feb 1858; 2) 18 Oct 1865
Total time as PM 1) 3 years, 13 days; 2) 6 years, 128 days; a total of 9 years, 141 days
Ceased to be MP 18 Oct 1865
Lived after last term as PM Died in office
Date of death 18 Oct 1865
Place of death Brocket Hall, Hertfordshire
Age at death 81 years, 363 days
Last words Thinking he was signing a treaty, he said 'That's Article 98, now go on to the next'. (An apparently erroneous quotation is 'Die, my dear doctor, that's the last thing I shall do'.)
Place of funeral and burial Westminster Abbey, London
Zodiac sign Libra

FATHER

Henry Temple, 2nd Viscount Palmerston
Date and place of birth 4 Dec 1739
Occupation MA Clare Hall, Cambridge 1759. MP East Looe, 1762–68, Southampton, 1768–74; Hastings, 1774–84; Boroughbridge, 1784–90; Newport, Isle of Wight, 1790–96; Winchester, 1796–1800. A Lord of the Board of Trade, 1765–66; a Lord of the Admiralty, 1766–67; a Lord of the Treasury, 1777–82. FSA 7 Mar 1776; FRS 7 Nov 1776.
Dates of marriages 1) 6 Oct 1767, Frances Poole (d. 1 Jan 1769); 2) 5 Jan 1783, Mary Mee
Date of death 16 Apr 1802
Place of burial Romsey Church, Romsey, Hampshire

MOTHER

Mary Mee
Date of birth 1754
Profile The daughter of a wealthy merchant from Dublin, she led an active social life, and her love of the theatre introduced her to society. Lord Glenberries called her 'a good-natured, obliging woman'; Phiner Ward, on the other hand, called her 'fawning and mean'. She was devastated by her husband's death.
Date of marriage 5 Jan 1783
Date of death 20 Jan 1805
Place of burial Romsey Church, Romsey, Hampshire

BROTHERS AND SISTERS

Palmerston was the second but eldest surviving of five children.
From his father's first marriage:
A daughter, b. 17 May 1769
From his father's second marriage:
Hon. Frances, b. 18 Feb 1786. m. 1820 Admiral William Bowles, CB; d. Nov 1838
Hon. Sir William, KCB, b. 17 Jan 1788; unm.; Minister plenipotentiary at Naples; d. Aug 1856
Mary, b. 15 Jan 1789; d. 1790
Elizabeth, b. 30 Mar 1790; m. 1811 Rt. Hon. Lawrence Sulivan (a Commissioner of the Royal Military Asylum); d. 1837.

WIFE

Amelia (Emily) Mary, Lady Cowper
Date of birth 21 Apr 1787
Mother Elizabeth, Lady Melbourne
Father Sir Peniston Lamb, 1st Lord Melbourne. (It was, however, widely believed that her real father was the Earl of Egremont.)
Father's occupation The son of an attorney, Sir Peniston was a squire in Hertfordshire until his elevation to the peerage as Lord Melbourne of Kilmore. A wealthy man, he became a Lord of the Bedchamber to the Prince of Wales in 1784. Bourne calls him 'a sulk and a soak', who only got on through the ambition of his wife. MP Ludgershall 1768–84, Malmesbury 1784–90, Newport, Isle of Wight 1790–93.
Age at marriage 1) 18 years, 90 days to Peter Nassau, Lord Cowper (d. 22 Jun 1837); 2) 52 years, 239 days to Palmerston
Number of Children 3
Date and place of death 11 Sep 1869, Brocket Hall, Hertfordshire
Place of burial Westminster Abbey, London
Years younger than PM 22 years, 183 days
Profile She was educated at home with her sister, Harriet. Gay and beautiful, she was very popular in society, where she was seen as kind and even-tempered, but at times arrogant and weak. She had a succession of lovers, including Palmerston, as she was bored by her first husband, a reserved, cultivated and good-mannered man, but also very dull, with a 'slow pronunciation and a slow gait and pace', who took to drink in later life. Her brother, the 2nd Viscount Melbourne and future PM, said she was 'a remarkable woman, a devoted mother, an excellent wife—but not chaste, not chaste'.

LIFE AND CAREER

PARLIAMENTARY ELECTIONS FOUGHT

*(*designates candidate elected)*

DATE 7 Feb 1806. By-election caused by the death of William Pitt.
CONSTITUENCY Cambridge University
RESULT Lord Henry Petty* (Whig) 331; John Charles Spencer, Viscount Althorp, (Whig) 145; Henry John Temple, Viscount Palmerston (Tory) 128

DATE Oct 1806. General Election
CONSTITUENCY Horsham
RESULT Francis John Wilder* (Whig) 44; Love Parry Jones* (Whig) 44; James Edward Harris (Tory) 29; Henry John Temple, Viscount Palmerston (Tory) 29 (As the result was unclear, a double return was made, allowing Westminster to make the decision on petition. The Committee appointed to consider the case reported on 20 Jan 1807, declaring Wilder and Jones as the MPs.)

DATE May 1807. General Election
CONSTITUENCY Cambridge University
RESULT George Henry Fitzroy, Earl of Euston* (Whig) 324; Sir Vicary Gibbs* (Tory) 312; Henry John Temple, Viscount Palmerston (Tory) 310; Lord Henry Petty (Whig) 265

DATE May 1807. General Election
CONSTITUENCY Newport, Isle of Wight
RESULT Henry John Temple, Viscount Palmerston (Tory)*; Sir Arthur Wellesley* (Independent)

DATE 29 Jan 1810. By-election caused by Palmerston's appointment as Secretary at War
CONSTITUENCY Newport, Isle of Wight
RESULT Henry John Temple, Viscount Palmerston* (Tory) (Took the Chiltern Hundreds, 25 Mar 1811)

DATE 27 Mar 1811. By-election caused by the elevation of Lord Euston to the House of Lords
CONSTITUENCY Cambridge University
RESULT Henry John Temple, Viscount Palmerston* (Tory) 451; John Henry Smyth* (Whig) 345

DATE Oct 1812. General Election
CONSTITUENCY Cambridge University
RESULT Henry John Temple, Viscount Palmerston* (Tory); John Henry Smyth* (Whig)

DATE Jun 1818. General Election
CONSTITUENCY Cambridge University
RESULT Henry John Temple, Viscount Palmerston* (Tory); John Henry Smyth* (Whig)

DATE Mar 1820. General Election
CONSTITUENCY Cambridge University
RESULT Henry John Temple, Viscount Palmerston* (Tory) John Henry Smyth* (Whig)

DATE Jun 1826. General Election
CONSTITUENCY Cambridge University
RESULT Sir J.S. Copley* (Tory) 772; H.J. Temple, Viscount Palmerston* (Whig) 631; W. J. Bankes (Tory) 508; H. Goulburn (Tory) 437

DATE Jul 1830. General Election
CONSTITUENCY Cambridge University
RESULT Henry John Temple, Viscount Palmerston* (Whig); William Cavendish* (Whig)

DATE 30 Nov 1830. By-election caused by Palmerston's appointment as Secretary of State for Foreign Affairs
CONSTITUENCY Cambridge University
RESULT Henry John Temple, Viscount Palmerston* (Whig)

DATE May 1831. General Election
CONSTITUENCY Cambridge University
RESULT Henry Goulburn* (Tory) 805; William Yates Peel* (Tory) 804; William Cavendish (Whig) 630; Henry John Temple, Viscount Palmerston (Whig) 610

DATE 18 Jul 1831. By-election caused by the resignation of Charles Tennyson, who chose to sit for Stamford
CONSTITUENCY Bletchingley
RESULT Henry John Temple, Viscount Palmerston*(Whig)

DATE Dec 1832. General Election
CONSTITUENCY Hampshire, Southern
RESULT Henry John Temple, Viscount Palmerston* (Whig) 1,627; Sir George Staunton, Bt. (Whig) 1,524; J. W. Fleming (Con) 1,266

DATE Jan 1835. General Election
CONSTITUENCY Hampshire, Southern
RESULT J. W. Fleming* (Con) 1,746; H. C. Compton* (Con) 1,689; Henry John Temple, Viscount Palmerston (Whig) 1,504; Sir George Staunton, Bt. (Whig) 1,450

DATE 1 Jun 1835. By-election caused by the retirement of James Kennedy
CONSTITUENCY Tiverton
RESULT Henry John Temple, Viscount Palmerston* (Whig)

DATE Jul 1837. General Election
CONSTITUENCY Tiverton
RESULT John Heathcoat* (Whig) 323; Henry John Temple, Viscount Palmerston* (Whig) 246; B. B. Dickinson (Con) 180

DATE Jun 1841, General Election
CONSTITUENCY Tiverton
RESULT John Heathcoat* (Whig); Henry John Temple, Viscount Palmerston* (Whig)

DATE Jun 1841. General Election
CONSTITUENCY Liverpool
RESULT Viscount Sandon* (Con) 5,979; C. Cresswell* (Con) 5,792; Sir J. Walmsley (Whig) 4,647; Henry John Temple, Viscount Palmerston (Whig) 4,431

DATE 10 Jul 1846. By-election caused by Palmerston's appointment as Secretary of State for Foreign Affairs
CONSTITUENCY Tiverton
RESULT Henry John Temple, Viscount Palmerston* (Whig)

DATE Jul 1847. General Election
CONSTITUENCY Tiverton
RESULT John Heathcoat* (Whig) 148; Henry John Temple, Viscount Palmerston* (Whig) 127; G. J. Harney (Chartist) 0

DATE Jul 1852. General Election
CONSTITUENCY Tiverton
RESULT John Heathcoat* (Whig); Henry John Temple, Viscount Palmerston* (Whig)

DATE 3 Jan 1853. By-election caused by Palmerston's appointment as Secretary of State for Home Affairs
CONSTITUENCY Tiverton
RESULT Henry John Temple, Viscount Palmerston* (Whig)

PARLIAMENTARY ELECTIONS FOUGHT—*Continued*

DATE 12 Feb 1855. By-election caused by Palmerston's appointment as Prime Minister
CONSTITUENCY Tiverton
RESULT Henry John Temple, Viscount Palmerston* (Whig)

DATE Mar 1857. General Election
CONSTITUENCY Tiverton
RESULT John Heathcoat* (Lib); Henry John Temple, Viscount Palmerston* (Lib)

DATE Apr 1859. General Election
CONSTITUENCY Tiverton
RESULT Hon. George Denman* (Lib); Henry John Temple, Viscount Palmerston* (Lib)

DATE 27 Jun 1859. By-election caused by Palmerston's appointment as Prime Minister
CONSTITUENCY Tiverton
RESULT Henry John Temple, Viscount Palmerston* (Lib)

DATE 28 Mar 1861. By-election caused by Palmerston's appointment as Constable of Dover Castle and Warden of the Cinque Ports
CONSTITUENCY Tiverton
RESULT Henry John Temple, Viscount Palmerston* (Lib)

DATE Jul 1865. General Election
CONSTITUENCY Tiverton
RESULT Henry John Temple, Viscount Palmerston* (Lib) 261; J. W. Walron* (Lib) 220; Hon. George Denman (Lib) 217

PARTY ACTIVITY

Party Leadership Leader of the Liberal Party, Feb 1855–Oct 1865

PARLIAMENTARY AND MINISTERIAL EXPERIENCE

Maiden Speech 3 Feb 1808, He spoke in defence of the Government's decision to order the Navy to bombard Copenhagen, to stop Napoleon seizing the Danish fleet. (*Parl. Deb.* 1st ser, vol 10, col 300–301
Privy Counsellor 1 Nov 1809
Ministerial Offices Lord of the Admiralty, 6 Apr 1807–26 Oct 1809; Secretary at War, 27 Oct 1809–26 May 1828; Secretary of State for Foreign Affairs, 22 Nov 1830–17 Nov 1834; 18 Apr 1835–30 Aug 1841; 6 Jul 1846–26 Dec 1851; Secretary of State for Home Affairs, 28 Dec 1852–6 Feb 1855; First Lord of the Treasury, 6 Feb 1855–19 Feb 1858, 12 Jun 1859–18 Oct 1865
Opposition Leader while PM Benjamin Disraeli, Leader of the Conservative Party

GOVERNMENTS FORMED

First Administration 6 Feb 1855–19 Feb 1858

GENERAL ELECTION RESULTS
JUL 1852: Conservative 330; Liberal 324.Total 654
Conservative majority 7 (excl. the Speaker)
MAR 1857: Liberal 377; Conservative 264; Others 13. Total 654
Liberal majority 100

CABINET
Prime Minister and First Lord of the Treasury Viscount Palmerston
Lord Chancellor Lord Cranworth
Lord President of the Council Earl Granville
Lord Privy Seal Duke of Argyll (Feb–Nov 1855); Earl of Harrowby (Dec 1855–Feb 1858); Marquess of Clanricarde (Feb 1858)
Home Secretary Sir G. Grey
Foreign Secretary Earl of Clarendon
Secretary of State for War Lord Panmure
Secretary of State for the Colonies S. Herbert (Feb 1855); Lord J. Russell (Feb–Jul 1855); Sir W. Molesworth (Jul–Nov 1855); H. Labouchere (Nov 1855–Feb 1858)
Chancellor of the Exchequer William Gladstone (Feb–Mar 1855); Sir G. C. Lewis, (Mar 1855–Feb 1858)
First Lord of the Admiralty Sir J. Graham (Feb–Mar 1855); Sir C. Wood, (Mar 1855–Feb 1858)
President of the Board of Control Sir C. Wood (Feb -Mar 1855); R. V. Smith, (Mar 1855–Feb 1858)
Chancellor of the Duchy of Lancaster Earl Granville (Feb–Mar 1855); Earl of Harrowby (Mar -Dec 1855); M. T. Baines (Dec 1855–Feb 1858)
Minister without Portfolio Marquess of Lansdowne
Postmaster-General Viscount Canning (Feb–Nov 1855); Duke of Argyll (Nov 1855–Feb 1858)
President of the Board of Trade E. Cardwell (Feb–Mar 1855); Lord Stanley of Alderley (Mar 1855–Feb 1858)
First Commissioner of Works Sir W. Molesworth (Feb–Jul 1855); Sir B. Hall (Jul 1855–Feb 1858)

Second Administration 12 Jun 1859–18 Oct 1865

GENERAL ELECTION RESULTS
APR 1859: Liberal 357; Conservative 297; Total 654.
Liberal majority 59 (excl. the Speaker)
JUL 1865: Liberal 370; Conservative 288; Total 658.
Liberal majority 81 (excl. the Speaker)

CABINET
Prime Minister and First Lord of the Treasury Viscount Palmerston
Lord Chancellor Lord Campbell (Jun 1859–Jun 1861); Lord Westbury (Jun 1861–Jul 1865); Lord Cranworth (Jul–Oct 1865)
Lord President of the Council Earl Granville
Lord Privy Seal Duke of Argyll
Home Secretary Sir G. C. Lewis (Jun 1859–Jul 1861); Sir G. Grey (Jul 1861–Oct 1865)
Foreign Secretary Lord J. Russell
Secretary of State for War S. Herbert (Jun 1859–Jul 1861); Sir G. C. Lewis (Jul 1861–Apr 1863); Earl de Grey and Ripon (Apr 1863–Oct 1865)
Secretary of State for the Colonies Duke of Newcastle (Jun 1859–Apr 1864); E. Cardwell (Apr 1864–Oct 1865)
Secretary of State for India Sir C. Wood
Chancellor of the Exchequer W.E. Gladstone
First Lord of the Admiralty Duke of Somerset
Chief Secretary for Ireland E. Cardwell (Jun 1859–Jul 1861); Sir R. Peel (Jul 1861–Oct 1865)
Chancellor of the Duchy of Lancaster Sir G. Grey (Jun 1859–Jul 1861); E. Cardwell (Jul 1861–Apr 1864); Earl of Clarendon (Apr 1864–Oct 1865)

IMPORTANT DATES IN PERSONAL AND POLITICAL LIFE

16 APR 1802 Palmerston's father dies of throat cancer, leaving Palmerston under the guardianship of the Earls of Malmesbury and Chichester.

7 FEB 1806 Palmerston stands for the Tories at Cambridge University in a by-election caused by the death of Pitt. He comes third.

4 NOV 1806 He stands for Horsham, paying Lady Irvin £1, 500 for the privilege. As the result is unclear, all four candidates are declared elected. On petition, Palmerston is unseated.

6 APR 1807 Palmerston appointed a junior Lord of the Admiralty.

8 MAY 1807 Palmerston loses Cambridge University once again, but is elected for Newport, Isle of Wight. The seat is in the gift of Sir Leonard Holmes, who is so wary of outside influences on the Isle of Wight that he makes it a condition of the gift that Palmerston should not set foot in the constituency.

3 FEB 1808 Palmerston makes his maiden speech, backing the Government on their decision to bombard Copenhagen.

28 OCT 1809 The Duke of Portland resigns as Prime Minister. His replacement, Spencer Perceval, offers Palmerston the position of Chancellor of the Exchequer. He refuses, worried by his lack of experience, but accepts the extra-Cabinet position of Secretary at War.

1810 Palmerston becomes embroiled in an argument as to who has ultimate responsibility for the army: the Secretary at War or the Commander in Chief. After a dispute, King George III agrees, on Perceval's advice, that Palmerston is senior.

1810 After affairs with Sarah Sophia, Lady Jersey, and Dorothy de Lieven, Palmerston begins an affair with Emily, Lady Cowper, that is to last until they marry, after the death of her husband, in 1839. It is widely believed that Palmerston is the father of some of her children.

25 MAR 1811 A new writ is moved for Newport, Palmerston having taken the Chiltern Hundreds.

27 MAR 1811 Palmerston is finally elected MP for Cambridge University.

1 MAR 1813 He speaks in the House of Commons in favour of Catholic emancipation.

3 JUL 1815 On Palmerston's suggestion, it is agreed that any soldier who had served at Waterloo will be able to count it as two years service for the purposes of pay and pensions.

8 MAR 1816 Complaints arise about expenditure on the army not being reduced after the end of the French war. Palmerston maintains that the army needs to be kept in readiness because of its increased responsibilities.

1 APR 1818 Lieutenant Davis, a deranged ex-officer with a grievance about a pension, shoots at Palmerston on the stairs at the War Office, giving him a slight wound on the back. Palmerston pays for a barrister for Davis, who is sent to Bedlam, the insane asylum.

1821 Determined to reduce expenditure at the War Office, Palmerston draws up a plan to reduce administrative costs by £18,000.

23 MAR 1822 Charles Smith, a poacher caught on Palmerston's estates, is executed. Palmerston is strongly criticised by radicals in the Commons as he has refused to intervene, arguing that it is not right to use private influence to affect the outcome of a case.

NOV 1822 Palmerston is offered the post of Governor General of India. He turns it down.

30 APR 1823 In Palmerston's first speech on foreign affairs since his maiden speech, he refuses to offer the Spanish any false hopes of help after the French invasion of Spain.

1823 He proposes on two occasions to Lady Georgiana Fane, the younger sister of Sarah, Lady Jersey. Aware of his affair with her sister, she turns him down. He is to try again in Jul 1825, only to be refused once more.

14 AUG 1827 Palmerston is promised the Chancellorship of the Exchequer. He refuses, not wanting to face a by-election, but he agrees to take it in the new session. In the face of the King's opposition, Canning does not honour this agreement, and offers Palmerston first the Governorship of Jamaica, then the Governor Generalship of India. He refuses both posts.

26 MAY 1828 Palmerston resigns from Wellington's Government, following a quarrel over the redistribution of two constituencies. He is joined by the remnants of Canning's supporters in the Government, Canning having died in Aug 1827.

22 NOV 1830 He returns to the Government under Earl Grey as Secretary of State for Foreign Affairs and chairs an international conference on the future of Belgium, following the Belgian uprising against the Dutch on 28 Aug 1830. Palmerston wants Belgium to become an independent and neutral country to stop French designs on the area.

27 JAN 1831 The articles of peace are signed, agreeing to the principle of Belgian independence. The Belgians elect Duc de Nemours, the son of French King Louis-Philippe, as King of Belgium. Palmerston fears this will mean war with France and gets the conference to agree to reject any candidate from the ruling families of the five main countries involved. The Dutch, meanwhile, invade Belgium, and France, in turn, invades to stop the Dutch. Under pressure from Palmerston, an act of separation is signed on 13 Nov 1832, and following the defeat of the Dutch, Belgium becomes independent.

FEB 1831 Revolts break out in Italy and the Papal states. Austria and France become involved, and Palmerston tries to pressure the various parties into solving their difficulties. However, he is unable to commit forces and therefore fails.

MAY 1831 Palmerston loses his seat at Cambridge University in the first election after the First Reform Bill. He finds a seat at Bletchingley instead.

4 JUN 1832 The Second Reform Bill is passed. Palmerston is unenthusiastic, but is prepared to help its passage.

8 JUL 1833 The Treaty of Unkiar Skelessi between Russia and Turkey includes a secret clause allowing only Russian ships into the Dardanelles. Palmerston protests, antagonising the Russians, which leads to the Muchengratz declaration of Oct 1833, when Austria, Prussia and Russia declare their opposition to revolution.

22 APR 1834 As a counterbalance to the Muchengratz declaration, Palmerston sets up the Quadruple Alliance between Britain and France, agreeing to support the Liberal governments of Spain and Portugal. Palmerston becomes seen as the champion of constitutional freedom in Europe.

18 APR 1835 Palmerston is appointed Foreign Secretary, despite having lost his seat in Hampshire. He pays the sitting MP for Tiverton £2,000 to resign, and is returned unopposed.

18 MAY 1836 Palmerston continues to try to exclude French influence from Spain and Portugal by persuading Queen Maria of Portugal to marry Prince Ferdinand of Saxe-Coburg Gotha, instead of the French Duc de Nemours, arguing that an alliance between France and Portugal would be against British interests.

IMPORTANT DATES IN PERSONAL AND POLITICAL LIFE—*Continued*

22 JUN 1837 Emily Cowper's husband dies. Palmerston immediately proposes, but she keeps him waiting for over two years before accepting.

JUL 1839 The Opium War with China starts. It finishes at the end of the year with victory for Britain, and at the peace negotiations (concluded in Aug 1842) Palmerston insists on harsh terms, including the cession to Britain of an island off the Chinese coast and the legalization of the opium trade.

1839–1840 Palmerston tries to oust Mehemet Ali as Viceroy of Egypt, whose independence threatens the stability of the Middle East. France supports Egypt, while Russia supports Egypt's long-standing enemy, Turkey. Mehemet had invaded Syria in 1833, and Palmerston tries to require Mehemet to withdraw from Syria. Despite France's refusal to take part, Palmerston signs the Treaty of London on 15 Jul 1840, whereby Britain, Russia, Austria and Prussia agree to force Mehemet to leave Syria. Palmerston's policy proves successful when Mehemet is expelled from Syria.

NOV 1840 Palmerston demands the release of Alexander McLeod, who has boasted about being involved in the burning of the U.S. ship *Caroline* in Dec 1837 and is to be tried in the U. S. for murder. Palmerston maintains that the attack on the *Caroline* had been undertaken on behalf of the British government. He prepares to send the fleet to the U.S. if McLeod is executed; the U. S. government, not wishing to provoke Palmerston, pays for the best lawyers available to defend McLeod, who is acquitted. Palmerston believes that his firmness is the only way to deal 'with such cunning fellows as these Yankees'.

30 AUG 1841 Melbourne's Government resigns after a disastrous election and defeats in both Houses of Parliament on votes following the Address. Palmerston also resigns.

29 AUG 1842 The Treaty of Nanking ends the Opium Wars by agreeing to Palmerston's terms, even though he is no longer in office. Hong Kong, which Palmerston calls 'a barren island with barely a house upon it,' is ceded to the British.

1841–1846 Palmerston spends his first long period away from office indulging in his favourite pastimes of hunting, riding and racing his horses. He also travels extensively, and frequently attacks the Government in the Commons.

16 JUL 1844 Palmerston makes a three-hour speech in the Commons denouncing the slave trade.

1845 Palmerston is elected an honorary member of the Jockey Club.

6 JUL 1846 Palmerston returns to office as Foreign Secretary under Lord John Russell.

OCT 1846 Radical Septembrists in Portugal seize Oporto following the annulment of the constitution and the imposition of an unelected government by Queen Maria. She appeals to Palmerston for help, and he reluctantly agreed to send the British fleet to blockade Tagus. When peace negotiations fail in May 1847, Palmerston, backed by Spain and France, orders the British to march against the Septembrist Junta, causing them to surrender. The constitution is restored, but Queen Maria's government remains in power.

MAR 1848 As revolution breaks out on mainland Europe, Palmerston gloats at the downfall of many of his old rivals. He is at all times determined to pursue British interests, and is in favour of the Spanish revolution, while being wary of those in France and Italy.

JAN 1850 Palmerston orders British ships to blockade Greek ports and seize Greek ships, following the refusal of the Greek government to compensate Don Pacifico, a Portuguese Jew but a British subject living in Athens, after an anti-Semitic mob has burnt his house. Despite protests abroad, Palmerston's line, that a British subject would always be protected, is very popular with the public. He makes his famous 'Civis Romanus Sum' speech on 25 Jun 1850.

19 DEC 1851 Russell dismisses Palmerston for declaring his approval of Louis Napoleon's coup in Paris. The public is very angry at this dismissal, but the establishment rejoices that 'Palmerston is smashed.' He is so angry that he refuses to deliver the seals of office to the Queen when ordered to do so on 26 Dec, leaving for Broadlands instead.

20 FEB 1852 Russell resigns after Palmerston's amendment to the Government's Militia Bill is passed by 13 votes. Lord Derby, now Prime Minister, offers Palmerston the position of Chancellor, but he turns it down, as he supports free trade and the Tories are in favour of protection. Needing Palmerston's support, Derby comes out in favour of free trade, but Palmerston still refuses a position in the Government, although he backs Derby in Parliament.

17 DEC 1852 Derby resigns when his Government is defeated on the supplementary budget by the combined forces of the Whigs, Peelites, Radicals and Irish.

28 DEC 1852 Palmerston becomes Home Secretary under Lord Aberdeen.

20 AUG 1853 Palmerston passes the Factories Act in an attempt to make working lives better. Critics however, feel that he has not gone far enough. Palmerston also passes the Smoke Abatement Act, to improve life in London, and the Penal Servitude Act, which stops transportation to Van Diemen's Land (Tasmania).

DEC 1853 Palmerston resigns from Aberdeen's Cabinet, ostensibly over the Government's policy in the East, but more probably because of Russell's proposals for a further Reform Bill. He withdraws his resignation on 23 Dec, suggesting that there had been a misunderstanding.

1854 Palmerston passes the Youthful Offenders Act, to send young offenders to schools rather than prison, and persuades the Government to agree to pardon Irish and Chartist deportees in Van Diemen's Land.

28 MAR 1854 Britain and France declare war on Russia following the Russian war with Turkey.

SEP 1854 The British army invades the Crimea, but the war does not go well.

JAN 1855 The Government resigns when forced to instigate a Committee of Inquiry into the conduct of the war.

6 FEB 1855 Failing to find anyone else, Queen Victoria is forced to appoint Palmerston as Prime Minister. His first act is to agree to the Committee of Inquiry, causing the resignation of William Gladstone, Sidney Herbert and Sir James Graham.

SEP 1855 During 1855, the Crimean war proceeds with mixed fortunes, although Palmerston has improved the supply of goods and services to the army. The fighting ends with the surrender of Sebastopol and peace talks begin.

26 FEB 1856 At a Peace Congress in Paris, an armistice is signed. Palmerston wanting to be tough, demands the ceding of Bessarabia, neutralisation of the Black Sea, independence for Circassia, and Turkish control of the Crimea, but concerted opposition from the French forces Palmerston to compromise: Russia cedes a small area of Bessarabia and demilitarises the Black Sea, but keeps most of its land.

OCT 1856 China seizes a British registered ship, the *Arrow*. Bowling, Governor of Hong Kong, orders the bombardment of Canton. Palmerston tells the Cabinet that he supports Bowling's action, even though Chinese mobs hunt down Britons as a result of the bombardment.

3 MAR 1857 Palmerston is defeated in the House of Commons by 263 to 247 over his China policy, but then calls an election which he wins with a majority of 100.

10 MAY 1857 The outbreak of the Indian mutiny causes many people in Great Britain to call for the widespread extermination of Hindus and Moslems. There is an outcry when Lord Canning, the Governor General, is perceived as being too lenient. Palmerston, however, supports Canning, and the public reaction turns in Palmerston's favour, as the mutiny is put down.

14 JAN 1858 An Italian republican named Orsini throws a bomb at Napoleon III. Although the assassination attempt fails, it emerges that Orsini has links with London. The French protest, and Palmerston introduces the Conspiracy to Murder Bill to appease them.

FEB 1858 Palmerston introduces the Government of India Bill to transfer the administration of India from the East India Company to the Crown.

18 FEB 1858 He is defeated on an amendment to the Conspiracy to Murder Bill criticising him.

21 FEB 1858 Palmerston resigns and enters opposition.

NOV 1858 Palmerston visits Napoleon III at Compiègne, hoping it will ease Anglo-French relations if he is to return to power.

6 JUN 1859 The Liberal Party is formed at a meeting of 274 members of the Parliamentary Liberal Party at Willis's Rooms in St. James's Street, London. They demonstrate the unity of the various factions of the Liberal Party, led by Palmerston and supported by Lord John Russell and John Bright.

11 JUN 1859 Lord Derby's Government, having lost its majority in the April General Election, is defeated on a vote of no confidence and resigns. After being turned down by Lord Grenville, Victoria turns to Palmerston once more, and he becomes Prime Minister on 12 Jun.

12 JUL 1859 The peace of Villafranca between Austria and France is signed, following the battle of Solferino. Palmerston condemns the Treaty, and uses the increasing anti-French feeling in the country as an excuse to re-arm and to build fortifications on the South coast. It means, however, that he can now support the cause of Italian liberation.

APR–MAY 1860 Gladstone, the Chancellor of the Exchequer, introduces a Bill to abolish tax on paper duties after a Budget surplus of £5 million is announced. Palmerston wants to use the money for national defence, but allows it to be included in the Budget. As it is an open secret that Palmerston opposes the measure, the Conservatives fight it vigorously, and on 21 May 1860 it is defeated by 193 to 104 in the House of Lords, the first time the Lords had rejected a finance Bill for over 200 years. The action is referred to the Committee of Privileges, which condemns it, but Palmerston effectively defuses the crisis by refusing to reintroduce the Bill straight away. It does pass the following year.

MAY 1860 Garibaldi invades Sicily and conquers Naples. Palmerston's policy is to remain neutral, despite misgivings.

MAY 1860 Palmerston tries to prevent the French from extending their interests in Lebanon and Syria, attempting to stop French troops going to the aid of the Maronites who are being massacred by Moslems in Lebanon, as he believes that the Turkish government can do this without outside intervention. The French insist and go ahead, although Palmerston gets them to agree for a stipulated period. British influence in the area declines sharply as a result.

AUG 1860 A combined British and French expedition marches on Peking to force compliance with the 1842 Treaty of Nanking, leading to the burning of the Emperor's Summer Palace. Palmerston welcomes the chance to 'bring John Chinaman to his bearings'.

27 MAR 1861 Palmerston is appointed Warden of the Cinque Ports.

12 APR 1861 Outbreak of the American Civil War. Palmerston supports the Southern states, although refusing to recognise the sovereignty of the Confederacy. He is prepared to go to war with the U.S. over the capture of a British passenger ship, the *Trent*, by a federal ship, the *San Jacinto*, as the *Trent* has two Southern envoys, Mason and Slidell, on board. U.S. forces concede to pressure from Palmerston and release Mason and Slidell, not wishing to go to war with Britain.

JUL 1862 Palmerston allows a Confederate warship, the *Alabama*, to be built secretly at Birkenhead. After protests, he tries to prevent its departure, but is too late. Seven years after Palmerston's death, Britain is to pay the U.S. £15,500,000 in compensation for the damage caused by the *Alabama*.

OCT 1861 A joint British, French and Spanish force lands in Mexico to force Mexico to pay its debts. After the invasion, Palmerston discovers Napoleon's plan to place the Archduke Maximilian on the Mexican throne, which he supports.

7 OCT 1862 Gladstone makes a speech praising the South, stating that Jefferson Davis has 'made a nation'. Sir George Lewis, the Secretary for War denies that this means that the Government intends to recognise the Confederacy. Palmerston, despite sympathy for the Confederate cause, believes that Gladstone and Lewis are unwise to refer to the situation in speeches.

EASTER 1863 Installed as Lord Rector of Glasgow University. He later visits Edinburgh, cheered by large crowds, and impressing onlookers by climbing to the top of Arthur's Seat to demonstrate his continuing health and energy.

1863 Brazil breaks off diplomatic relations with Britain. The British navy has patrolled the Brazilian coast since 1845 in order to stop the slave trade. They abuse their powers by seizing three Brazilian trading ships in retaliation for the arrest of a British officer. Palmerston refuses to apologise, or to compensate the traders. He eventually agrees, under pressure from his Cabinet, to let King Leopold of Belgium mediate. Palmerston is very annoyed when Leopold favours Brazil, believing that Leopold has been bribed.

JUL 1863 Palmerston supports Denmark over ownership of Schleswig-Holstein, but refuses to interfere when Prussia under Bismarck and Austria invade in February 1864, despite appeals from the Danish government.

25 JUN 1864 Despite agreeing in Cabinet to send the fleet to aid Denmark, in a statement in the Commons on 27 Jun Palmerston makes it clear that the Danes will not

IMPORTANT DATES IN PERSONAL AND POLITICAL LIFE—*Continued*

be helped. Confidence in Palmerston is seriously shaken, and the Government loses a vote of censure in the Lords by nine votes. After a bitter debate, the Government wins in the Commons by 313 to 295 in early July. Palmerston, however, is seen to have been humiliated.

JUL 1865 Palmerston's majority in the House of Commons increases after a General Election, with Palmerston extremely popular with the people.

18 OCT 1865 Palmerston never sees Parliament recalled. He catches a chill when out for a drive in his carriage, which brings on a violent fever, and after rallying somewhat, he dies. Despite his wish to be buried at Romsey, the Cabinet insist on a state funeral in Westminster Abbey.

BACKGROUND

PHYSICAL CHARACTERISTICS AND HEALTH

Palmerston was a delicate child, who suffered from erysipelas, an inflammation of the skin. He grew up to be 5'10", with dark hair, a fresh complexion, and good looks, with tremendous energy and good health. He rode regularly, and was a great believer in the benefits of exercise. Despite lacking a few teeth because of hunting accidents, he was very attractive to women, and had a large number of affairs. As he grew older, he was occasionally overweight with a receding hairline, but apart from an attack of cholera in April 1833, he remained in good health into his sixties. However, at this time he often became worn down by the stresses of his job, was frequently tired, and suffered bad headaches, gout and boils. He aged rapidly in the 1850s, and became increasingly deaf. His eyesight began to fail and his ill-fitting false teeth were noticeable. He remained active, however, and although he was frequently too ill to work in the 1860s, he still walked and rode wherever possible. He caught a chill in October 1865 after insisting on riding in an open carriage, and died on 18 Oct.

EDUCATION

Primary Palmerston had various tutors, including Therese Menier, a French governess, and Gaetano Ravizzotti, appointed in 1793.

Secondary 1795–1800, Harrow School

University 1800–03; Edinburgh University; 1803–06, St. John's College, Cambridge University

Qualifications MA Cambridge, 27 Jan 1806

Cultural and vocational background Tour of Europe with his parents, 1792–94

Languages French, Italian

NON-PARLIAMENTARY CAREER

Military service Honorary Colonel of the 1st Cinque Ports Artillery Volunteers; Lieutenant Colonel, Hampshire Militia

Other posts Lord Warden of the Cinque Ports 27 Mar 1861–65; Lord Rector of Glasgow University, 1863–65; Elder Brother of Trinity House, 1860–65; Master of Trinity House, 1862–65; Governor/Constable of Dover Castle, 1861–65

HONOURS

Academic 1862, DCL Oxford; 1864, LLD Cambridge

Foreign Knight of the Tower & Sword of Portugal

Other than peerage Grand Cross of the Order of the Bath, 1832; Knight of the Garter, 12 Jul 1856

CLUBS

Brooks's; Traveller's; Arthur's; White's; Athenaeum; Watiers; Alfred's; Jockey; Almick's

HOBBIES AND SPORTS

Palmerston was very keen on dancing and swimming, but his main love was riding and hunting. As a keen race-horse owner, he won the Cesarewitch in 1841, and the Ascot stakes in 1853. He was a patron of literature and the arts, although he was noted as only a dutiful visitor to galleries and the opera.

FINANCES

Throughout his life, Palmerston was worried about his financial affairs, and had a constant battle to keep his income up with his expenditure. His main income came from the vast estates left him by his father in Dublin, Sligo, Hampshire and Yorkshire, as well as houses in Hanover Square, Sheen and Broadlands. Paying off the mortgage on Broadlands left him with an annual payment of £1,500, on top of which he had to pay annual annuities and allowances which totalled £1,800 by 1820. His income, meanwhile, was £8,000 p.a. in 1803 and £14,000 p.a. in 1811. He also had a large amount of stock, worth £18,000 in 1811, but he speculated wildly and lost over £5,000 in the 1820s. Also in the 1820s he spent a considerable amount of money becoming a director of the Welsh Slate Company and the Devon & Cornwall Mining Company, the latter of which caused endless trouble for no profit; his shares in the former, meanwhile, were worth over £44, 000 at his death. He also spent a great deal of money on improvements to his estates. To finance his expenditure, he rented out the house in Hanover Square, sold Temple Grove for over £12,000 in 1808 and took out a number of mortgages, including one of £14,000 in 1818, and one of £10,000 in 1823. In later life his financial position improved, but he never shook off his reputation of being constantly in debt.

Income Palmerston's War Office salary was £2,480 p.a.; as Foreign Secretary his salary was £6,000 p.a., but this was reduced to £5,000 after a cost cutting drive in 1831.

Spouse's finances His wife was the widow of Lord Cowper, who left her his estates of Brocket Hall, Hertfordshire.

Legacies Palmerston's father had been heavily in debt, and left a mortgage of £10,000 on Broadlands, as well as substantial legacies of £20,000 to his other children, which left a deficit of £28,000. Luckily, none of the children took their full amount, allowing the mortgage to be paid off.

Debts Palmerston was often in debt, and was sued 20 times between 1811 and 1844 by various creditors, as he seemed to feel it unnecessary to pay bills, often of small amounts, the lowest being £2.12.0.

Will Dated 22 Nov 1864, proved 22 Dec 1865, leaving under £120,000. He left his estates to his widow, and the remainder to her second son, Hon. William Francis Cowper.

ANECDOTES

During a debate on China on 16 Mar 1857, Lord Derby, referring to Palmerston's many changes in political direction, said that he was 'a political chameleon which offers a different hue and colour to the spectator according to the side from which he gazes. I defy any man, even the most ardent of his supporters, to say, when he professes confidence in the noble Viscount, what upon any great domestic question of the day is the policy to which he pledges himself'.

The Palmerstons were noted for being unpunctual. He often arrived late for banquets, and made Queen Victoria wait for dinner when she visited him at Brocket Hall. It was said at the time that 'the Palmerstons always miss the soup'. Before visiting Paris in 1846, Lord Brougham took Lady Palmerston aside 'to tell her that when they dined at the Tuileries she would see a large deep bowl with a ladle in it which would be of immense interest to her. It was a silver soup tureen'.

Palmerston's reputation as a ladies' man lasted into his late seventies. In Jun 1863, he was visited at the House of Commons by Mrs. O'Kane, wife of an Irish Radical journalist. She later claimed that they committed adultery, whereupon her husband petitioned for divorce, citing Palmerston as co-respondent and claiming £20,000 in damages. The case was dismissed but was a subject of gossip around the country for weeks. The story considerably enhanced Palmerston's popularity in the country, and it was even said that Palmerston had encouraged the story because he hoped to call a General Election.

QUOTATIONS

30 Apr 1823, To have talked of war and to have meant neutrality, to have threatened an army and to have retreated behind a state paper, to have brandished the sword of defiance in the hour of deliberation and to have ended with a penful of protests on the day of battle would have been the conduct of a cowardly bully. (Speech, House of Commons, on French invasion of Spain)

14 Jul 1840, It seems pretty clear that, sooner or later, the Cossack and the Sepoy, the man from the Baltic and he from the British Isles will meet in the centre of Asia. It should be our business to take care that the meeting should take place as far off from our Indian possessions as may be convenient and advantageous to us. But the meeting will not be avoided by our staying at home to receive the visit. (Letter to John Hobhouse)

28 Jul 1843, A wise government in its home policy considers the reasonable wants of the people; in its foreign policy it is prepared to resist the unjust demands and the unreasonable views of foreign powers. The present government inverts this method; it is all resistance at home, all concession abroad. (Speech, House of Commons)

1 Mar 1848, We have no eternal allies and we have no perpetual enemies. Our interests are eternal and perpetual and those interests it is our duty to follow. (Speech, House of Commons)

5 Mar 1848, Large republics seem to be essentially and inherently aggressive. (Letter to Lord Normanby)

26 Jun 1850, As the Roman, in days of old, held himself free from indignity when he could say 'Civis Romanus Sum', so also a British subject in whatever land he may be, shall feel confident that the watchful eye and the strong arm of England will protect him against injustice and wrong. (Speech, House of Commons)

Dec 1850, I believe weakness and irresolution are, on the whole, the worst faults that statesmen can have. A man of energy may make a wrong decision, but, like a strong horse that carries you rashly into a quagmire, he brings you by his sturdiness out on the other side.

5 Mar 1857, You may call it coalition, you may call it the accidental and fortuitous concurrence of atoms . . . but I say that when Gentlemen are in the habit of finding themselves in the same lobby, it is not unnatural to suppose that they may, under certain circumstances, be ready to unite them-selves together for forming an administration and become responsible for the opinions which they severally entertain. (On rumours of a coalition with Disraeli)

23 Aug 1859, England is one of the greatest powers in the world, no event or series of events bearing on the balance of power, or on probabilities of peace or war can be matters of indifference to her, and her right to have and to express opinions on matters thus bearing on her interests is unquestionable. (Letter to Queen Victoria)

RESIDENCES

Broadlands, Romsey, Hampshire
4 Carlton Gardens, London (plaque)
20 Queen Anne's Gate, London (plaque)
94 Piccadilly, London (plaque)
North Audley St., London
5 Carlton House Terrace, London
12 Stanhope St., London
9 Stanhope St., London
Open to the public *Broadlands*, Romsey, Hampshire

MEMORIALS

STATUES AND BUSTS

1876, by Thomas Woolner, Parliament Square, London; by Matthew Noble, Romsey market place

PORTRAITS

1802, by Thomas Heaphy, National Portrait Gallery; *c.* 1810–20, by Sir Thomas Lawrence, Broadlands; 1833, by Sir G. Hayter, Broadlands *c.* 1850, by John Partridge, House of Commons; 1858, by F. Cruikshank, Broadlands; 1865, by W. Barraud, Broadlands; by Sally Chappell (photograph), Victoria & Albert Museum; by John Partridge (Palmerston at 45), National Portrait Gallery;

OTHER MEMORIALS

Memorial in Westminster Abbey by Robert Jackson; Medallion portrait in Portland Stone in spandrels

MEMORIALS—*Continued*

of the arches of Grosvenor Hotel, 101 Buckingham Palace Road, London.

Many roads and public houses are named after Palmerston.

BIBLIOGRAPHIC INFORMATION

LETTERS AND PERSONAL PAPERS

Connell, B. ed. *Regina v Palmerston: The Correspondence between Queen Victoria and her Foreign and Prime Minister, 1837–1865*. London, 1862. Guedalla, P. ed. *The Palmerston Papers: Correspondence of Lord Palmerston with Mr. Gladstone, 1851–1865*. London, 1828. Lieven, Princess, Lord Sudley, ed. *Lieven-Palmerston Correspondence, 1828–1856*. London, 1943. Francis, G. H. *Opinions and policy of Rt. Hon. Viscount Palmerston as Minister, Diplomatist and Statesman [Speeches]*. London, 1852.

Most of Palmerston's personal papers were placed in the Broadlands Archives Trust in 1960. The Hampshire Record Office, Winchester, holds a large number of letters, papers, diaries and other material. The British Library holds various manuscripts relating to Palmerston's ministerial work.

PUBLICATIONS

Contributions to the *New Whig Guide*.

FURTHER READING

Airlie, M, Countess of. *Lady Palmerston and Her Times*. London, 1922.

Argyll, 9th Duke of. *Viscount Palmerston, KG*. 1862.

Ashley, Rt. Hon. A.E.M. *Life of Palmerston, 1846–1865*, 2 vols. London, 1876.

Bourne, K. *Palmerston: The Early Years*. London, 1982.

Bulwer, Rt. Hon. Sir H. L. *The Life of Henry John Temple, Viscount Palmerston*, Vols. I–III by Bulwer, Vols. IV–V by Ashley. London, 1870–1876.

Connell, B.. *Portrait of a Whig Peer*. London, 1957.

Guedalla, P. *Palmerston*. London, 1926.

Judd, D. *Palmerston*. London, 1975.

Pemberton, W. B. *Lord Palmerston*. London, 1954.

Ridley, J. *Lord Palmerston*. London, 1970.

Southgate, D. *The Most English Minister . . . The Policies and Politics of Palmerston*. London, 1966.

C.S.

Bettmann

Benjamin Disraeli

Lived 1804–1881

Political Party Independent Radical 1832–1835; Conservative 1835–1881

Prime Minister 27 February 1868–1 December 1868; 20 February 1874–21 April 1880

Governments Conservative

Reigning Monarch Victoria

Forti nihil difficile All is easy to the brave

DISRAELI AS PRIME MINISTER

Disraeli was first elected to Parliament as a Tory in 1837. He sought office under Peel unsuccessfully and then turned against him. Following Peel's resignation in 1846 the way became clearer for Disraeli's advancement. From 1848 he was effectively, if not formally, leader of the Tory opposition and then in 1852 Derby appointed him Chancellor of the Exchequer. An unsuccessful Budget contributed to the fall of the Tory government but he was an effective Opposition Leader in the House of Commons during Palmerston's Prime Ministership. Derby, Prime Minister again in 1866, once more appointed Disraeli his Chancellor of the Exchequer. When Derby resigned in 1868 because of ill health, Disraeli was invited to form his first administration, although it was only a caretaker Government. During its nine months a number of reforming acts were passed, including the Capital Punishment Within Prisons Act, which abolished public executions, and various Parliamentary reform acts. 1868–1874 was a difficult period for Disraeli both politically and personally—his wife died in 1872. Still the organisation of the party was reformed and the Conservative victory in the 1874 General Election led to Disraeli's second administration. Social reform was marked by acts covering trade unions, public health, factories, the sale of food and drugs, etc. In 1879 after persistent ill health, he moved to the House of Lords as Earl of Beaconsfield to lead the Government from there. Foreign policy became ever more central to his concerns, in particular the Eastern Question following Turkish atrocities against the Bulgarians. He was regarded as a success at the Congress of Berlin which closed the Russo-Turkish war. Despite this the Liberals won the 1880 General Election. Disraeli resigned and then led the opposition from the House of Lords for his last year.

PERSONAL INFORMATION

Names Benjamin Disraeli
Peerages Viscount Hughenden of Hughenden and 1st Earl of Beaconsfield, 12 Aug 1876
Nicknames Dizzy
Born 21 Dec 1804
Birthplace 6 Kings Road, Bedford Row, London (Now 22 Theobalds Road).
Religion Born Jewish but was baptised into the Church of England on 31 Jul 1817 at St. Andrew's Church, Holborn, London.
Ancestry Italian Sephardi Jewish origin; his grandfather emigrated from Italy in 1748.
Date and place of marriage 28 Aug 1839, St. George's Church, Hanover Square, London
Age at marriage 34 years, 250 days
Years married 33 years, 109 days
First entered Parliament 27 Jul 1837
Dates appointed PM 1) 27 Feb 1868; 2) 20 Feb 1874
Age at appointments 1) 63 years, 68 days; 2) 69 years, 61 days
Dates ceased to be PM 1) 1 Dec 1868; 2) 21 Apr 1880
Total time as PM 1) 278 days; 2) 6 years, 61 days; a total of 6 years, 339 days
Ceased to be MP 12 Aug 1876
Lived after last term as PM 363 days
Date of death 19 Apr 1881
Place of death 19 Curzon Street, London
Age at death 76 years, 119 days
Last words I had rather live but I am not afraid to die.
Place of funeral and burial Hughenden Church, Buckinghamshire
Zodiac sign Sagittarius

FATHER

Isaac D'Israeli
Date and place of birth 11 May 1766, 5 Great St. Helens, London
Occupation Scholar and author; his famous work was *Curiosities of Literature*, 6 vols. 1791–1834.
Date of marriage 10 Feb 1802
Date and place of death 19 Jan 1848, Bradenham House, Buckinghamshire
Place of burial Bradenham, Buckinghamshire

MOTHER

Maria Basevi
Date of birth *c.* 1776
Date of marriage 10 Feb 1802
Date and place of death 21 Apr 1847, Bradenham House, Buckinghamshire
Place of burial Bradenham, Buckinghamshire

BROTHERS AND SISTERS

Benjamin Disraeli was the eldest son and second of five children.
Sarah b. 29 Dec 1802; d. 19 Dec 1859
Naphtali, b. 5. Nov 1807; d. 1807
Raphael (Ralph), b. 9 May 1809; m. 1861, Katherine Trevor; Clerk Assistant in the House of Lords 1875; his son, Coningsby, inherited Disraeli's title and estate; d. 18 Oct 1898
Jacobus (James), b. 21 Jan 1813; m. Isabella Anne Cave; farmer at the Manor Farm, Bradenham; County Court Treasurer 1852; Commissioner of the Inland Revenue 1858; d. 23 Dec 1868

WIFE

Mary Anne Wyndham Lewis née Evans, Viscountess Beaconsfield, 30 Nov 1868
Date and place of birth 11 Nov 1792; Saudons, Bramptford, Speke, near Exeter
Mother Eleanor Viney
Father Lieutenant John Evans, RN
Father's occupation Lieutenant in the Royal Navy
Age at marriage 46 years, 240 days
Number of children None
Date and place of death 15 Dec 1872, Hughenden, Buckinghamshire
Place of burial Hughenden Church, Buckinghamshire.
Years older than PM 12 years, 40 days
Profile She was poorly educated and twelve years Disraeli's senior and at the time of their marriage there was much gossip that he had married her for her money. Stories abound about her eccentric ways and her overwhelming solicitude for her husband. She once crushed her hand badly in a carriage door but remained silent during the journey because she feared it would upset Disraeli before he made an important speech.

Some saw her as rather empty-headed, talkative and outspoken but there was no doubt about Disraeli's devotion to her and his reliance on her support. After her death he paid tribute to her: 'There was no care which she could not mitigate, and no difficulty which she could not face. She was the most cheerful and the most courageous woman I ever knew.'

CHILDREN

None

LIFE AND CAREER

PARLIAMENTARY ELECTIONS FOUGHT

*(*designates candidate elected)*

DATE 26 Jun 1832. By-election caused by the resignation of Sir Thomas Baring
CONSTITUENCY Wycombe
RESULT Hon. Charles Grey* (Whig) 23; Benjamin Disraeli (Independent Radical) 12

DATE Dec 1832. General Election

CONSTITUENCY Wycombe
RESULT Hon. R.J. Smith* (Lib) 179; Hon. Charles Grey* (Lib) 140; Benjamin Disraeli (Independent Radical) 119

DATE Jan 1835. General Election
CONSTITUENCY Wycombe
RESULT Hon. R.J. Smith* (Lib) 289; Hon. Charles Grey* (Lib) 147; Benjamin Disraeli (Independent Radical) 128

DATE 29 Apr 1835. By-election caused by the appointment of Henry Labouchere as Vice-President of the Board of Trade and Master of the Mint
CONSTITUENCY Taunton
RESULT Henry Labouchere* (Lib) 452; Benjamin Disraeli (Con) 282

DATE Jul 1837. General Election
CONSTITUENCY Maidstone
RESULT Wyndham Lewis* (Con) 782; Benjamin Disraeli* (Con) 668; T.P. Thompson (Lib) 559; T.E. Perry (Lib) 25

DATE Jun 1841. General Election
CONSTITUENCY Shrewsbury
RESULT George Tomline* (Con) 793; Benjamin Disraeli* (Con) 785; Sir L.P.J. Parry (Lib) 605; C. Temple (Lib) 578

DATE Jul 1847. General Election
CONSTITUENCY Buckinghamshire
RESULT Hon. C.C. Cavendish* (Lib); Benjamin Disraeli* (Con); C.G. du Pre* (Con)

DATE 12 Mar 1852. By-election caused by Disraeli's appointment as Chancellor of the Exchequer
CONSTITUENCY Buckinghamshire
RESULT Benjamin Disraeli* (Con)

DATE Jul 1852. General Election
CONSTITUENCY Buckinghamshire
RESULT C.G. du Pre* (Con) 2,000; Benjamin Disraeli* (Con) 1,973; Hon. C.C. Cavendish* (Lib) 1,403; J. Lee (Lib) 656

DATE Mar 1857. General Election
CONSTITUENCY Buckinghamshire
RESULT Hon. C.C. Cavendish* (Lib); Benjamin Disraeli* (Con); C.G. du Pre* (Con)

DATE 8 Mar 1858. By-election caused by Disraeli's appointment as Chancellor of the Exchequer.
CONSTITUENCY Buckinghamshire
RESULT Benjamin Disraeli* (Con)

DATE Apr 1859. General Election
CONSTITUENCY Buckinghamshire
RESULT Hon. W.G. Cavendish* (Lib); Benjamin Disraeli* (Con); C.G. du Pre* (Con)*

DATE Jul 1865. General Election
CONSTITUENCY Buckinghamshire
RESULT Benjamin Disraeli* (Con); C.G. du Pre* (Con); R.B. Harvey* (Con)

DATE 13 Jul 1866. By-election caused by Disraeli's appointment as Chancellor of the Exchequer
CONSTITUENCY Buckinghamshire
RESULT Benjamin Disraeli* (Con)

DATE Nov 1868. General Election
CONSTITUENCY Buckinghamshire
RESULT Benjamin Disraeli (Con); C.G. du Pre* (Con); N.G. Lambert* (Lib)

DATE Jan 1874. General Election
CONSTITUENCY Buckinghamshire
RESULT Benjamin Disraeli* (Con) 2,999; Sir. R.B. Harvey* (Con) 2,902; N.G. Lambert* (Lib) 1,720; W. Talley (Con) 151

DATE 17 Mar 1874. By-election caused by Disraeli's appointment as Prime Minister and First Lord of the Treasury
CONSTITUENCY Buckinghamshire
RESULT Benjamin Disraeli* (Con)

PARTY ACTIVITY

Party Leadership Leader of the Conservative Party 1868–81.
Membership of group or faction Young England Group 1842–44

PARLIAMENTARY AND MINISTERIAL EXPERIENCE

Maiden Speech 7 Dec 1837. He spoke on Irish elections. (*HC Deb.*, 3rd ser, vol 39, col 802–7)
Privy Counsellor 27 Feb 1852
Ministerial Offices Chancellor of the Exchequer 27 Feb–17 Dec 1852; Chancellor of the Exchequer and Leader of the House of Commons 26 Feb 1858–11 Jun 1859, 6 Jul 1866–27 Feb 1868; First Lord of the Treasury 27 Feb -1 Dec 1868, 20 Feb 1874–21 Apr 1880; Lord Privy Seal 12 Aug 1876–4 Feb 1878; Leader of the House of Lords Aug 1876–21 Apr 1880
Opposition Leaders while PM 1) 1868, W. E. Gladstone 2) 1874–5, W. E. Gladstone; 1875–6, Lord Hartington; 1876–80, Earl Granville (House of Lords)

GOVERNMENTS FORMED

First Administration 27 Feb 1868–1 Dec 1868

GENERAL ELECTION RESULT
JUL 1865: Liberal 370; Conservative 288. Total 658 Liberal majority 81 (excl. the Speaker)
CABINET
Prime Minister and First Lord of the Treasury B. Disraeli
Lord Chancellor Lord Cairns
Lord President of the Council Duke of Marlborough
Lord Privy Seal Earl of Malmesbury
Home Secretary G. Hardy
Foreign Secretary Lord Stanley
Secretary of State for War Sir J. Pakington
Secretary of State for the Colonies Duke of Buckingham
Secretary of State for India Sir S. Northcote
Chancellor of the Exchequer G.W. Hunt
First Lord of the Admiralty H.T.L. Corry
*Chief Secretary for Ireland** Lord Naas (Feb-Sep 1868)
Minister without Portfolio S. Walpole
President of the Board of Trade Duke of Richmond
First Commissioner of Works Lord J. Manners
[*office not always in Cabinet]

Second Administration 18 Feb 1874–21 Apr 1880

GENERAL ELECTION RESULT
JAN 1874: Conservative 350; Liberal 242; Others 60. Total 652
Conservative majority 49 (excl. the Speaker)
CABINET
Prime Minister and First Lord of the Treasury B. Disraeli
Lord Chancellor Lord Cairns

Second Administration 18 Feb 1874–21 Apr 1880—*Continued*

Lord President of the Council Duke of Richmond
Lord Privy Seal Earl of Malmesbury (1874–76); B. Disraeli (1876–78); Duke of Northumberland (1878–80)
Home Secretary R. A. Cross
Foreign Secretary Earl of Derby (1874–78); Marquess of Salisbury (1878–80)
Secretary of State for War G. Hardy (1874–78); F. A. Stanley (1878–80)
Secretary of State for the Colonies Earl of Carnarvon (1874–78); Sir M. Hicks Beach (1878–80)
Secretary of State for India Marquess of Salisbury (1874–78); Viscount Cranbrook (1878–80)
Chancellor of the Exchequer Sir S. Northcote
First Lord of the Admiralty G. W. Hunt (1874–77); W. H. Smith (1877–80)
*Chief Secretary for Ireland** Sir M. Hicks Beach (1876–80)
Postmaster General Lord J. Manners
President of the Board of Trade Viscount Sandon (1878–80)
[*office not always in Cabinet]

IMPORTANT DATES IN PERSONAL AND POLITICAL LIFE

JAN 1825 First appearance of *The Representative*, a daily newspaper he founds with his publisher and friend, John Murray. It lasts only a few months.

APR 1826 Publication of his first novel, *Vivien Grey*.

26 JUN 1832 Stands for Parliament for the first time as an Independent Radical at a by-election at Wycombe but fails to get elected.

1833 Meets Lady Henrietta Sykes and enters a liaison with her that is to continue for three years. Sir Francis Sykes seems to condone the relationship, but the visits of all three to Bradenham cause great scandal in Buckinghamshire.

10 JUL 1834 Meets the former Tory Lord Chancellor, Lord Lyndhurst, who becomes his political patron.

JAN 1835 Commits himself to the Tory party after his third defeat at Wycombe standing as an Independent Radical. Loses the by-election at Taunton in April but is now an official Tory party candidate.

APR–MAY 1835 Quarrels publicly with Daniel O'Connell following reports in the press that Disraeli had referred to him as 'an incendiary and traitor'. Disraeli challenges O'Connell to a duel but the police intervene and he is bound over to keep the peace.

AUG 1835 Joins the attacks by peers on the Municipal Corporations Bill by writing (anonymously) 14 leading articles in the *Morning Post*.

DEC 1835 *A Vindication of the English Constitution in a Letter to a Noble and Learned Lord by Disraeli the Younger* published, marking his progress as a political thinker.

JAN–MAY 1836 Writes a series of 19 open letters in the *Times* under the pseudonym 'Runnymede' lampooning individual members of the Government.

1836 Parts from Lady Henrietta Sykes in the autumn.

27 JUL 1837 Returned as MP for the first time, for Maidstone, at the General Election.

7 DEC 1837 Maiden speech on the subject of Irish elections. He is shouted down but ends his speech with the words 'I sit down now but the time will come when you will hear me.'

18 DEC 1837 Speaks for the first time after his maiden speech, on the Copyright Bill. He had been advised to be dull and the speech is successful.

12 JUL 1839 In the debate on the Poor Law he expresses sympathy with the Chartists.

28 AUG 1839 Marries Mary Anne Wyndham Lewis.

JUN 1840 Is one of only five MPs who protest at the harsh treatment of the Chartist leaders.

JUN 1841 Disraeli elected MP for Shrewsbury at the General Election, but the election does not go smoothly for him; legal proceedings about his alleged bribery of electors continue for some months.

30 AUG 1841 Peel becomes PM. Desperate for office, Disraeli writes to him but is still not made a member of the Government.

1842 The 'Young England' set, mainly a group of young aristocrats who had been at Eton and Cambridge together and first entered Parliament in 1841, emerges, led by George Smythe. Members include Lord John Manners, Alexander Baillie-Cochrane and Disraeli. They establish themselves during the 1843 session, but the group gradually disintegrates towards the end of 1844.

28 FEB 1845 Makes his famous speech in the House of Commons, attacking Peel for his lack of regard for the views of his party: 'The Right Honourable Gentleman caught the Whigs bathing and walked away with their clothes. He has left them in the full enjoyment of their liberal position, and he is himself a strict conservative of their garments'.

1845 Becomes Deputy Lieutenant of Buckinghamshire.

JAN 1846 A 'protectionist' group of MPs is set up to coordinate opposition to Peel within the Conservative Party. Bentinck, Disraeli and Stafford O'Brien lead the group in attacks on Peel over the Corn Laws.

15 MAY 1846 Disraeli viciously and mercilessly attacks Peel in the debate on the Corn Importation Bill, a performance which finally wipes out the memory of his disastrous maiden speech. When accused by Peel of touting for office he denies it (a lie), banking on the hope that Peel will not have his letter of 1841 on hand (he doesn't).

29 JUN 1846 Peel resigns after defeat on the Irish Coercion Bill. With Peel no longer leader of the Conservatives, Disraeli's career can advance.

JUL–SEP 1847 General Election. The parties are fairly evenly divided and Russell's administration continues. Disraeli decides to stand for Buckinghamshire following his purchase of Hughenden Manor. After the election he sits on the Opposition front bench with Peel.

16 DEC 1847 He supports Russell's motion that the House should consider the removal of the civil disabilities of Jews, following the election of Baron Lionel de Rothschild as Liberal Member for the City of London. Disraeli is heard in frosty silence during the debate; to many his speech seems blasphemous. He consistently supports Jewish emancipation Bills over the next ten years.

21 SEP 1848 Sudden death of his friend and leader of the Tories in the House of Commons, Lord George Bentinck.

DEC 1848 The leader of the Conservative Party, Lord Stanley, attempts to bypass Disraeli for the leadership of the Tories in the House of Commons, supporting Herries, who refuses to take on the leadership. A committee of three with equal powers is then proposed: Disraeli, Herries and Granby. Disraeli is now effectively Leader of the Opposition.

1851 The beginning of Disraeli's friendship with Mrs. Brydges Williams of Mount Braddon, Torquay, a widow of over 80 with Jewish origins. The Disraelis visit her in Torquay and Disraeli writes to her frequently until her death in 1863. His letters vividly portray life in London and at Hughenden.

23 FEB 1852 Following Russell's resignation, the Earl of Derby becomes PM and Disraeli is made Chancellor of the Exchequer in the 'Who? Who?' cabinet.

JUL 1852 General Election. Again no party has an overall majority and Derby continues in office.

3 DEC 1852 Presenting his first Budget, Disraeli speaks for five hours. Gladstone replies forcefully, thus beginning the 'great Parliamentary duel' between the two. The Government is defeated in the vote on the Budget and Derby resigns.

30 DEC 1852 Gladstone succeeds Disraeli as Chancellor in the new administration led by Aberdeen and an argument ensues between the two concerning the furniture in the official Downing Street residence and the Chancellor's robe which Disraeli refuses to give up.

7 MAY 1853 First issue of his weekly newspaper, *The Press* which runs for five years. Disraeli retains anonymity as a contributor. When he returns to office in 1858 the paper is sold.

6 FEB 1855 Following the resignation of Aberdeen Palmerston becomes PM after Derby declines office, much to Disraeli's fury if Palmerston will not serve with the Conservatives.

MAR 1857 General Election. Palmerston continues as PM following a Liberal victory.

19 FEB 1858 Palmerston's Government is defeated on the Second Reading of a Bill to amend the law of conspiracy.

21 FEB 1858 Derby takes office as PM and Disraeli is again appointed Chancellor of the Exchequer.

28 FEB 1859 Reform Bill introduced. The Government is defeated by a Liberal alliance against the Bill.

APR 1859 General Election. Conservative representation increases but not sufficiently to give them an overall majority in the House of Commons.

12 JUN 1859 Palmerston becomes PM after the defeat of the Government over the Italian question.

19 DEC 1859 His sister, Sarah Disraeli, dies.

11 JUN 1860 Following criticism of his leadership in the press Disraeli considers resignation. Sir William Miles, a leading Conservative and MP for Somerset East, dissuades him.

25 MAR 1863 Elected a trustee of the British Museum.

26 JUN 1866 Lord Russell resigns as PM following a Whig-Tory alliance against his Reform Bill. Derby becomes PM and Disraeli becomes Chancellor of the Exchequer, appointing 'Monty' Corry as his Private Secretary. Monty becomes devoted to him and indispensable after Mary Anne's death.

23–25 JUL 1866 Hyde Park riots: a mass meeting in favour of electoral reform has been forbidden but crowds break down the railings near Marble Arch and continue to demonstrate for two days.

26 FEB 1867 Introduction of Reform Bill; the 'Ten Minutes Bill' finally agreed to in a frantic last-minute Cabinet meeting. This Bill is withdrawn on 4 Mar and a new one introduced on 18 Mar.

15 AUG 1867 The Reform Bill receives the Royal Assent.

NOV 1867 Mary Anne is seriously ill and Disraeli too is ill, with gout.

27 FEB 1868 Becomes PM for the first time after Derby's resignation because of ill health. 'I have climbed to the top of the greasy pole,' he declares, but it is to be a caretaker administration.

23 MAR 1868 Gladstone introduces his resolution for the Disestablishment of the Church of Ireland.

1 MAY 1868 The resolution is carried, and Disraeli offers his resignation, which is refused by Queen Victoria. It is agreed, however, that Parliament should be dissolved in the autumn once the new electoral register is ready.

MAY–NOV 1868 Measures passed during this short administration include the first nationalisation measure, an Act empowering the Post Office to buy up all the telegraph companies; the abolition of public executions under the Capital Punishment Within Prisons Act; and, to complete the work of parliamentary reform, the Registration of Voters Act: the Irish and Scottish Reform Acts; the Boundary Act and the Corrupt Practices Act.

NOV 1868 General Election. Liberal victory.

1 DEC 1868 Disraeli resigns as PM without meeting Parliament. On leaving office he asks the Queen to bestow a peerage on his wife, who becomes Viscountess Beaconsfield.

2 MAY 1870 Publication of *Lothair*, which proves an enormous success.

15 DEC 1872 His wife dies.

12 MAR 1873 An alliance of Conservatives and Irish Catholics defeat the Government over a Bill to establish a Roman Catholic University in Dublin.

13 MAR 1873 The Government resigns and Queen Victoria invites Disraeli to form an administration, but he refuses to lead a minority government and Gladstone continues in office.

JAN 1874 Conservative victory in the General Election.

20 FEB 1874 Disraeli becomes PM for the second time.

1875 Major measures of social reform passed, including two Trade Union Acts; the Public Health Act; the Artisans' Dwellings Act; the Agricultural Holdings Act; the Factory Act and the Sale of Food and Drugs Act. The Conspiracy and Protection of Property Act legalizes peaceful picketing.

JUN 1876 Turkish atrocities against the Bulgarians are in the news, but Disraeli doubts the veracity of the *Daily News* reports.

11 AUG 1876 Makes his last speech in the House of Commons.

12 AUG 1876 Bowing to persistent ill-health Disraeli leaves the House of Commons to lead from the Lords; he is created Earl of Beaconsfield. Sir Stafford Northcote becomes Party Leader in the House of Commons.

SEP 1876 Gladstone attacks the Government's foreign policy in his pamphlet 'The Bulgarian Horrors and the Question of the East'. The publication polarises public opinion, with bitterness on both sides.

DEC 1876–JAN 1877 Conference of Constantinople.

24 APR 1877 Russia declares war on Turkey. Derby, the Foriegn Secretary, leaks information to the Russian ambassador, Shuvalov, widening the rift between himself and Disraeli.

28 JAN 1878 Derby and the Colonial Secretary Carnarvon resign from the Cabinet over plans to authorise a note of credit and send warships through the Dardanelles.

31 JAN 1878 Armistice signed at Adrianople.

3 MAR 1878 Treaty of San Stephano signed by Russia and Turkey, creating Bulgaria.

13 JUN 1878 Congress of Berlin, attended by Disraeli and Salisbury. Bismarck comments, 'Der alte Jude, das ist der Mann' (The old Jew—that's the man).

13 JUL 1878 Treaty of Berlin. Disraeli and Salisbury accept the Order of the Garter on their return to London.

IMPORTANT DATES IN PERSONAL AND POLITICAL LIFE—*Continued*

Disraeli announces that they have brought 'Peace with honour'.

MAR 1880 General Election. Liberal victory.

21 APR 1880 Disraeli resigns as PM and becomes Leader of the Opposition from the House of Lords.

19 APR 1881 Death of Disraeli. Protocol prevents the Queen from attending his funeral but she visits the grave later and also has a marble monument erected in Hughenden Church; its inscription ends with a quotation from Proverbs: 'Kings love him that speaketh right'.

BACKGROUND

PHYSICAL CHARACTERISTICS AND HEALTH

Disraeli had dark hair and eyes, an olive complexion and a well defined nose. He wore his hair in ringlets with a curl in the middle of his forehead. He was short-sighted and used an eye-glass. In 1867 Sir John Skelton described him as 'the potent wizard himself, with his olive complexion and coal-black eyes, and the mighty dome of his forehead'.

Disraeli loved clothes and was always something of a dandy. Henry Bulmer described him at a dinner party in 1880 as wearing 'green velvet trousers, a canary coloured waistcoat, low shoes, silver buckles, lace at his wrists, and his hair in ringlets . . . '

In his early twenties Disraeli suffered a nervous breakdown. It was three years before he fully recovered. While abroad in 1831 he contracted venereal disease and had to undergo a six week course of mercury treatment on his return to England. In later life he suffered from gout and asthma. In 1877 he consulted a homeopath, Joseph Kidd, who decided he was suffering from Bright's Disease. Despite Kidd's help, chronic bronchitis eventually led to his death.

EDUCATION

Primary c. 1808–16, Miss Roper's school in Islington, then the Reverend John Potticany's school in Elliot Place, Blackheath, London.

Secondary 1817–21, Higham Hall School in Walthamstow. The headmaster was the Reverend Eli Cogan, a Unitarian minister.

Professional 18 Nov 1824, Admitted as a student to Lincoln's Inn;. 30 Apr 1827, Name entered as a prospective bencher; 25 Nov 1831, Withdrew from Lincoln's Inn

Cultural and vocational background 1824, Six weeks Grand Tour to Belgium and the Rhine Valley; 1826, Grand Tour for two months to Switzerland, Italy and France; 1830–31, Grand Tour of the Near East: Gibraltar, Spain, Malta, Corfu, Albania, Greece, Turkey, the Holy Land and Egypt.

Languages He spoke French, badly.

NON-PARLIAMENTARY CAREER

Early occupations 10 Nov 1821 Articled to Swain, Stevens, Maples, Pearse and Hunt of 6 Frederick's Place, Old Jewry, London. He abandoned his career in law some ten years later and concentrated on his writing career.

Other posts 1836, Magistrate; 1845, Deputy Lieutenant of Buckinghamshire; 1863, Trustee of the British Museum

HONOURS

Freedom of cities 1867, Edinburgh; 1878, City of London

Academic 1853, DCL, Oxford; 1867, LLD, Edinburgh; 1871, Lord Rector of Glasgow University

Other than peerage 10 Feb 1876, Fellow of the Royal Society; 22 Jul 1878, Knight of the Garter

CLUBS

Carlton; Coventry; Crockford's; Athenaeum. The latter, of which his father was a founding member, blackballed him at first but accepted him as a member in 1841. He said of them 'I hate clubs, not being fond of male company.'

HOBBIES AND SPORTS

Disraeli was a gourmet. He enjoyed collecting rare books and also loved planting and conserving trees. 'I have a passion for trees and books' he once said. He occasionally went fishing. His pets were a peacock and two swans called Hero and Leander. He also played chess.

FINANCES

Disraeli was heavily in debt for most of his life. In 1824–25 he speculated on the Stock Exchange and incurred heavy losses. An extravagant lifestyle and a series of contested elections did not help. Both Mary Anne and his father helped to pay off some of the more pressing debts but he never revealed their full extent to his family. By 1848 his debts amounted to about £40,000 following the purchase of Hughenden. In 1863, Andrew Montagu, a West Yorkshire Squire who wanted to use some of his wealth to help the Conservative Party, bought up all Disraeli's debts and charged him a reasonable rate of interest. By his death his financial position was good and the executors easily paid off the mortgage on Hughenden.

Income His income from his books varied. *Vivien Grey* (1826) brought him £200 and *The Young Duke* (1831) £500. *Lothair* (1870) realised over £6,000 and its success brought about the publication of a collected edition of his works, bringing him a further £1,000.

Spouse's finances Mary Anne had a house in London and an income of between £4–5,000 a year during her lifetime.

Pensions 1859, He received a Cabinet pension of £2,000 a year on leaving office as Chancellor of the Exchequer.

Legacies 1848, Disraeli received approximately £10,000 from his father's will; 1863, over £30,000 from Mrs Brydges Williams's will; 1869, £5,000 from his brother James's will.

Debts 1841, Debts were about £20,000; by 1848 they amounted to about £40,000.

Will The will was proved at £63,000 originally and then increased to £84,000.

ANECDOTES

1834, Disraeli met Lord Melbourne who asked him what he wanted to be. Disraeli replied that he wanted to be Prime Minister. 'No chance of that in our time,' said Melbourne, 'Nobody can compete with Stanley . . . '

1835, Daniel O'Connell, the Irish Roman Catholic leader, attacked Disraeli in the House of Commons. When he referred to Disraeli's Jewish ancestry, the latter replied, 'Yes, I am a Jew, and when the ancestors of the right honourable gentleman were brutal savages in an unknown island, mine were priests in the temple of Solomon'.

Disraeli was a critical gourmet. At a public dinner the food took so long to come from the kitchen to the banqueting hall that it was quite cold by the time it reached the table. Sipping champagne after the meal he commented, 'Thank God for something warm'.

Princess Marie Louise, a grand-daughter of Queen Victoria, recounted the story of a young lady at dinner one evening with Gladstone and on the following with Disraeli. When asked what impressions the two politicians had made upon her, she replied. 'When I left the dining room after sitting next to Mr. Gladstone I thought he was the cleverest man in England. But after sitting next to Mr. Disraeli I thought I was the cleverest woman in England'.

Disraeli was devoted to his wife, Mary Anne. It was a happy marriage and in later years he used to tease her saying that he had only married her for her money. 'But if you had to do it again, you'd do it for love,' she would reply. He dedicated his book *Sybil* to her: 'a perfect wife'.

Disraeli had a close relationship with Queen Victoria. She once paid him the honour of visiting him at Hughenden. On his deathbed he declined another royal visit. 'No it is better not. She will only ask me to take a message to Albert'.

QUOTATIONS

7 Dec 1837, Though I sit down now, the time will come when you will hear me. (On being shouted down when making his maiden speech in the House of Commons)

16 Feb 1844, Thus you have a starving population, an absentee aristocracy, and an alien church, and in addition the weakest executive in the world. That is the Irish question. (Speech in the House of Commons)

17 Mar 1845, A conservative government is an organized hypocrisy. (Debate in the House of Commons on the Corn Laws)

11 Feb 1851, Justice is truth in action. (Speech in the House of Commons)

16 Dec 1852, England does not love coalitions. (Speech in the House of Commons on the opposition to his Budget)

25 Nov 1864, Party is organized opinion. (Speech at Oxford)

3 Apr 1872, I believe that without party Parliamentary government is impossible. (Speech at Manchester)

1876, I am dead: dead, but in the Elysian fields. (On his elevation to the House of Lords.)

16 Jul 1878, Lord Salisbury and myself have brought you back peace—but a peace I hope with honour. (On his return from the Congress of Berlin)

When I want to read a novel, I write one.

RESIDENCES

6 King's Road, Bedford Row London (now 22 Theobalds Road)
6 Bloomsbury Square, London
Bradenham House, Buckinghamshire
35 Duke Street, London
31a Park Street, London
1 Grosvenor Gate, London (Now 29 Park Lane)
Hughenden Manor Buckinghamshire
Edward's Hotel, George Street, Hanover Square, London
2 Whitehall Gardens, London
10 Downing Street
1 Seamore Place, London
19 Curzon Street, London (plaque)

Open to the public *Hughenden Manor* which Disraeli purchased in 1847 was acquired by the National Trust in 1947.

MEMORIALS

STATUES AND BUSTS

1883, by Sir J. E. Boehm, Westminster Abbey; 1883, by Mario Raggi, Parliament Square; 1883, by Count Gleichen, Palace of Westminster; 1883, by C. B. Birch, St. George's Hall, Liverpool; 1884, by H.T. Margetson, Moorgate, Ormskirk; 1887, by T. Rawcliffe, Queen's Park, Bolton

PORTRAITS

1828, by Daniel Maclise, Hughenden Manor; 1851, by Sir Francis Grant, Hughenden Manor; 1862, by T.J. Barker, Hughenden Manor; 1869, by Charles Lucy, Victoria and Albert Museum, London; 1877, by T. Blake Wirgman, Western Park, Salop; 1877, by Heinrich Von Angeli, Royal Collection; 1880, by Henry Wiegall, Burghley House, Northamptonshire; 1881, by Sir John Everett Millais, National Portrait Gallery.

OTHER MEMORIALS

The day of his death, 19 Apr, was named Primrose Day after his favourite flower. Out of this grew the Primrose League, a political organisation, which exists today and declares its principles to be 'the maintenance of religion; of the unity of the Commonwealth, and the improvement of the condition of the people'.

MEMORIALS—*Continued*

The Disraeli lecture series, St Stephen's Constititutional Club. The first lecture was given on 13 Nov 1985 by Rt Hon Norman Tebbit MP.

BIBLIOGRAPHIC INFORMATION

LETTERS AND PERSONAL PAPERS

The Disraeli Papers are on permanent loan from the National Trust to the Bodleian Library, Oxford. There is an unpublished list of the papers available at the Library.

Home Letters Written in 1830 and 1831. Ed. R. Disraeli, 1885.

Lord Beaconsfield's Correspondence with His Sister 1832–1852. Ed. R. Disraeli, 1886.

Lord Beaconsfield's Letters, 1830–1852 (2 previous volumes plus additions), 1887.

The Letters of Disraeli to Lady Bradford and Lady Chesterfield. Ed. Marquess of Zetland, 1929.

Letters from Benjamin Disraeli to Frances Anne, Marchioness of Londonderry, 1837–1861. Ed. Marchioness of Londonderry, 1938.

Benjamin Disraeli Letters. Vol I 1815–34. Vol II 1835–37. Vol III 1838–41. Vol IV 1841–47. Ed. J.A.W. Gunn, J. Matthews et al., Toronto, 1982–89.

PUBLICATIONS

Disraeli was a prolific letter writer and novelist. The publication of *Lothair* in 1870 was an immense success; a novel by an ex-Prime Minister was a unique event. His novels were: 1826, *Vivien Grey*; 1828, *The Voyage of Captain Popanilla*; 1831, *The Young Duke*; 1832, *Contarini Fleming, a psychological autobiography*; 1833, *The Wondrous Tale of Alroy and the Rise of the Iskander*; 1837, *Henrietta Temple, a Love Story*; 1837, *Venetia*; 1844, *Coningsby, or the New Generation*; 1845, *Sybil, or the Two Nations*; 1847, *Tancred, or the New Crusade*; 1870, *Lothair*; 1880, *Endymion.*

He wrote many articles for newspapers and periodicals and also a biography of his friend Lord George Bentinck, published in 1852. In 1834 *The Revolutionary Epick*, a poem, was published and his tragic play *The Count of Alarcos* appeared in 1839. The latter was performed at the Theatre Royal, London in 1868 when Disraeli was Prime Minister.

FURTHER READING

Blake, R. *Disraeli.* London, 1966.

Bradford, S. *Disraeli.* London, 1982.

Hibbert, C. *Disraeli and His World.* London, 1978.

Monypenny, W.F. and Buckle, G.E. *The Life of Benjamin Disraeli, Earl of Beaconsfield.* 6 vols. London, 1910–20.

Pearson, H. *Dizzy: the Life and Nature of Benjamin Disraeli, Earl of Beaconsfield.* London, 1951.

Weintraub, S. *Disraeli: A Biography* London, 1993.

I.W.

Bettmann

William Ewart Gladstone

Lived 1809–1898

Political Party Conservative 1832–1859; Liberal 1859–1898

Prime Minister 3 December 1868–17 February 1874;
23 April 1880–9 June 1885;
1 February 1886–20 July 1886;
15 August 1892–2 March 1894

Governments Liberal

Reigning Monarch Victoria

Fide et virtute With faith and virtue

GLADSTONE AS PRIME MINISTER

Over sixty years of public life saw Gladstone move from the ranks of the Tories to the Liberals in the 1850s. He was President of the Board of Trade under Peel and Chancellor of the Exchquer under Aberdeen and again under Palmerston and Russell, contributing significantly to the development of this office. His serious moral upbringing and his 1850 visit to Naples to witness its problems moved him toward Liberal values. He then found a cause nearer home—Ireland—and also a voice and a presence that carried his views beyond Parliament to the people. His first administration passed an Act to disestablish the Church of Ireland and his first Irish Land Act, but he was defeated on the Irish University Bill. He ran his Cabinet as 'primus inter pares' supporting his colleagues as their respective departments carried through reforms. Under his second administration an Act was passed to strengthen the coercion powers of the Irish Viceroy, together with a second Irish Land Act. He extended the franchise, but overseas, the revolt in Sudan led to the loss of British control and the death of Gordon at Khartoum. His 1885 Budget was defeated and Gladstone resigned as Prime Minister. During his short third administration in 1886 he introduced an Irish Home Rule Bill and again during his fourth administration in 1892, but he failed to have it passed on each occasion. The fall of Parnell, leader of the Irish Home Rule Party, was a serious blow at the time of his last attempt. He was a man of great breadth of vision but also a person with burning causes, such as the Eastern Question of the Turks in the Balkans, which led to divisions in his Cabinet. His legacy included a seriously damaged and divided Liberal Party

PERSONAL INFORMATION

Names William Ewart Gladstone
Nicknames G.O.M. (Grand Old Man); The People's William
Born 29 Dec 1809
Birthplace 62 Rodney Street, Liverpool.
Religion Anglican
Ancestry Scottish. His father migrated to Liverpool from Leith in 1787.
Date and place of marriage 25 Jul 1839, Hawarden Parish Church, Flint.
Age at marriage 29 years, 208 days
Years married 58 years, 298 days
First entered Parliament 14 Dec 1832
Dates appointed PM 1) 3 Dec 1868; 2) 23 Apr 1880; 3) 1 Feb 1886; 4) 15 Aug 1892
Age at appointments 1) 58 years, 340 days; 2) 70 years, 116 days; 3) 76 years, 34 days; 4) 82 years, 230 days
Dates ceased to be PM 1) 17 Feb 1874; 2) 9 Jun 1885; 3) 20 Jul 1886; 4) 2 Mar 1894
Total time as PM 1) 5 years, 76 days; 2) 5 years, 47 days; 3) 169 days; 4) 1 year, 199 days; a total of 12 years, 126 days
Ceased to be MP 8 Jul 1895
Lived after last term as PM 4 years, 78 days
Date of death 19 May 1898
Place of death Hawarden Castle, Flint
Age at death 88 years, 141 days
Last words Amen
Place of funeral & burial Westminster Abbey. Gladstone's body lay in state in Westminster Hall 25–28 May 1898.
Zodiac sign Capricorn

FATHER

Sir John Gladstone
Date and place of birth 11 Dec 1764, Leith, Scotland
Occupation Sir John Gladstone made his fortune from trade, especially with America and the West Indies, where he owned sugar plantations. He was MP for Lancaster 1818–20, Woodstock 1820–26 and Berwick 1826–27
Dates of marriages 1) 1792 Jane Hall (d. 1798); 2) 29 Apr 1800, Anne Mackenzie Robertson
Date of death 7 Dec 1851
Place of burial St Andrew's Chapel, Fasque, Kincardineshire, Scotland.

MOTHER

Anne Mackenzie Robertson
Place of birth Dingwall, Ross-shire, Scotland.
Profile Anne Gladstone was a frail and delicate woman, an evangelical Episcopalian who involved herself in many charitable and philanthropic works.
Date of marriage 29 Apr 1800
Date of death 23 Sep 1835
Place of burial Fettercairn Church, near Fasque. Later interred in St Andrew's Chapel, Fasque.

BROTHERS AND SISTERS

William Ewart Gladstone was the fourth son and fifth child of six.
From his father's first marriage: none
From his father's second marriage:
Anne Mackenzie, b. 24 Dec 1802; Although she died young Anne had a great influence on Gladstone who later described her as a 'perfect saint'; d. 19 Feb 1829
Thomas (2nd Bt), b. 25 Jul 1804; MP Queenborough 1830, Portarlington 1832–35, Leicester 1835–37; d. 22 Mar 1889
Robertson, b. 15 Nov 1805; joined his father in business; Mayor of Liverpool 1842; d. 23 Sep 1875
John Neilson, b. 18 Jan 1807; Captain in the Royal Navy; MP Walsall 1841, Ipswich 1842–47, Devizes 1852–57 and 1859–63; d. 6 Feb 1863
Helen Jane, b. 28 Jun 1814; unm.; shocked Gladstone by her alcoholism, drug addiction and conversion to Roman Catholicism; d. 16 Jan 1880

WIFE

Catherine Glynne
Date and place of birth 6 Jan 1812, Hawarden Castle, Flint
Mother Mary Neville
Father Sir Stephen Richard Glynne
Father's occupation Landowner
Age at marriage 27 years, 200 days
Number of children 8
Date and place of death 14 Jun 1900, Hawarden Castle, Flint
Place of burial Gladstone's grave in Westminster Abbey
Years younger than PM 2 years, 8 days
Profile The Glynnes were a historic Whig family. Catherine's mother, daughter of Lord Braybrooke, was closely related to four Prime Ministers; George Grenville, Lord Grenville, Lord Chatham and William Pitt.

Catherine was taught French and Italian by a governess at Hawarden. Her sports included riding, swimming and archery.

Catherine was vague and untidy in contrast to Gladstone who was punctual and methodical. She was a relaxed, good humoured person who disliked formal entertaining; her life centred firmly on her family. Tension between the couple usually arose out of exasperation for each other's contrasting habits; she once exclaimed 'If you weren't such a great man you would be a terrible bore!'

Gladstone told her everything about his political life and wrote to her frequently when they were apart. She was often unconventional and oblivious to public opinion especially in the help she gave to her husband in his work with prostitutes.

CHILDREN

4 sons, 4 daughters

William Henry, b. 3 Jun 1840; m. 30 Sep 1875, Hon. Gertrude Stuart; MP Chester 1865–68; Whitby 1868–80; Worcestershire, East 1880–85; d. 4 Jul 1891

Stephen Edward, b. 4 Apr 1844; m. 29 Jan 1885, Annie Wilson; Rector of Hawarden 1872–1904, Barrowby, Grantham, Lincolnshire 1904–11, Rural Dean of Mold 1884–92; d. 23 Apr 1920

Agnes b. 18 Oct 1842; m. 27 Dec 1873, Very Reverend E.C. Wickham (Dean of Lincoln); d. 9 May 1931

Catherine Jessy, b. 27 Jul 1845; d. 9 Apr 1850 of meningitis

Mary, b. 23 Nov 1847; m. 2 Feb 1886, Reverend Harry Drew (Rector of Hawarden); secretary to both her parents until their deaths, she lived with them both before and after her marriage; d. 1 Jan 1927

Helen, b. 28 Aug 1849; Vice Principal of Newnham College, Cambridge 1882–96. Warden of Women's University Settlement 1901–6; d. 19 Aug 1925

Henry Neville (Lord Gladstone of Hawarden), b. 2 Apr 1852; m. 30 Jan 1890, Hon. Maud Rendel; Private Secretary to his father; Senior Partner of Ogilvy, Gillanders & Co. of London and Liverpool and of Gillanders, Arbuthnot & Co. of Calcutta; Director of Peninsular and Oriental Steam Navigation Company; Lord Lieutenant of Flintshire; Treasurer of the National Library of Wales; d. 28 Apr 1935

Herbert John (Viscount Gladstone of Lanark), b. 7 Jan 1854; m. 2 Nov 1901 Dorothy Paget; MP Leeds 1880–85, Leeds, West 1885–1910; Private Secretary to his father for a time; a Lord of the Treasury 1881–85; Deputy Commissioner of the Board of Works 1885; Financial Secretary, War Office 1886; Under Secretary, Home Office 1892–95; First Commissioner of Works 1894–95; Chief Whip to the Liberal Party 1899–1905; Home Secretary 1905–10; First Governor-General and High Commissioner of South Africa 1910–14; Head of War Refugees Organisation 1914–19; d. 6 Mar 1930

LIFE AND CAREER

PARLIAMENTARY ELECTIONS FOUGHT

*(*designates candidate elected)*

DATE Dec 1832. General Election
CONSTITUENCY Newark-on-Trent
RESULT W.E. Gladstone* (Con) 887; W.F. Handley* (Con) 798; T. Wilde (Lib) 726

DATE Jan 1835. General Election
CONSTITUENCY Newark-on-Trent
RESULT W.E. Gladstone* (Con); T. Wilde* (Lib)

DATE Jul 1837. General Election.
CONSTITUENCY Newark-on-Trent
RESULT W.E. Gladstone* (Con); T. Wilde* (Lib)

DATE Jul 1837. General Election
CONSTITUENCY Manchester
RESULT C.P. Thomson* (Lib) 4,158; M. Philips* (Lib) 3,759; W.E. Gladstone (Con) 2,224

DATE Jun 1841. General Election
CONSTITUENCY Newark-on-Trent
RESULT W.E. Gladstone* (Con) 633; Lord John Manners* (Con) 630; T.B. Hobhouse (Lib) 394

DATE 14 Sep 1841. By-election caused by Gladstone's appointment as Vice-President of the Board of Trade and Master of the Mint
CONSTITUENCY Newark-on-Trent
RESULT W.E. Gladstone* (Con)

DATE Jul 1847. General Election
CONSTITUENCY Oxford University
RESULT Sir R.H. Inglis* (Con) 1,700; W.E. Gladstone* (Con) 997; C.G. Round (Con) 824

DATE Jul 1852. General Election
CONSTITUENCY Oxford University
RESULT Sir R.H. Inglis* (Con) 1,369; W.E. Gladstone (Con) 1,108; R.B. Marsham (Con) 758

DATE 20 Jan 1853. By-election caused by Gladstone's appointment as Chancellor of the Exchequer
CONSTITUENCY Oxford University
RESULT W.E. Gladstone* (Con) 1,022; D.M. Perceval (Con) 898

DATE Mar 1857. General Election
CONSTITUENCY Oxford University
RESULT W.E. Gladstone* (Con); Sir W. Heathcote* (Con)

DATE 12 Feb 1859. By-election caused by Gladstone's appointment as Lord High Commissioner to the Ionian Islands
CONSTITUENCY Oxford University
RESULT W.E. Gladstone* (Con)

DATE Apr 1859. General Election
CONSTITUENCY Oxford University
RESULT W.E. Gladstone* (Con); Sir W. Heathcote* (Con)

DATE 1 Jul 1859. By-election caused by Gladstone's appointment as Chancellor of the Exchequer.
CONSTITUENCY Oxford University
RESULT W.E. Gladstone* (Lib) 1,050; Marquess of Chandos (Con) 859

DATE Jul 1865. General Election.
CONSTITUENCY Oxford University
RESULT Sir W. Heathcote* (Con) 3,236; G. Hardy* (Con) 1,904; W.E. Gladstone (Lib) 1,724

DATE Jul 1865. General Election
CONSTITUENCY Lancashire, Southern
RESULT Hon. A.F. Egerton* (Con) 9,171; C. Turner* (Con) 8,806; W.E. Gladstone* (Lib) 8,786; W.J. Leigh (Con) 8,476; H.Y. Thompson (Lib) 7,703; J.P. Heywood (Lib) 7,653

DATE Nov 1868. General Election.
CONSTITUENCY Lancashire, South-Western
RESULT R.A. Cross* (Con) 7,729; C. Turner* (Con) 7,676; W.E. Gladstone (Lib) 7,415; H.R. Grenfell (Lib) 6,939

DATE Nov 1868. General Election
CONSTITUENCY Greenwich
RESULT D. Salomons* (Lib) 6,684; W.E. Gladstone* (Lib) 6,386; Sir H.W. Parker (Con) 4,704; Viscount Mahon (Con) 4,372

DATE 21 Dec 1868. By-election caused by Gladstone's appointment as Prime Minister and First Lord of the Treasury

PARLIAMENTARY ELECTIONS FOUGHT—*Continued*

CONSTITUENCY Greenwich
RESULT W.E. Gladstone* (Lib)

DATE Jan 1874. General Election
CONSTITUENCY Greenwich
RESULT T.W. Boord* (Con) 6,193; W.E. Gladstone* (Lib) 5,968; J.E. Liardet (Con) 5,561; J.B. Langley (Lib) 5,255

DATE Mar 1880. General Election.
CONSTITUENCY Leeds
RESULT W.E. Gladstone* (Lib) 24,622; J. Barran* (Lib) 23,647; W.L. Jackson* (Con) 13,331; W. St. J. Wheelhouse (Con) 11,965

DATE Mar 1880. General Election
CONSTITUENCY Edinburghshire
RESULT W.E. Gladstone** (Lib) 1,579; Earl of Dalkeith (Con) 1,368

***Elected both for Leeds and Edinburghshire, he chose to sit for Edinburghshire.*

DATE 10 May 1880. By-election caused by Gladstone's appointment as Prime Minister, First Lord of the Treasury and Chancellor of the Exchequer
CONSTITUENCY Edinburghshire
RESULT W.E. Gladstone* (Lib)

DATE Nov 1885. General Election
CONSTITUENCY Edinburghshire
RESULT W.E. Gladstone* (Lib) 7,879; C. Dalrymple (Con) 3,248

DATE 10 Feb 1886. By-election caused by Gladstone's appointment as Prime Minister, First Lord of the Treasury and Lord Privy Seal
CONSTITUENCY Edinburghshire
RESULT W.E. Gladstone* (Lib)

DATE Jul 1886. General Election.
CONSTITUENCY Edinburghshire
RESULT W.E. Gladstone** (Lib)

DATE Jul 1886. General Election
CONSTITUENCY Leith District of Burghs
RESULT W.E. Gladstone* (Lib)

*** Elected both for Edinburghshire and Leith District of Burghs, he chose to sit for Edinburghshire.*

DATE Jul 1892. General Election
CONSTITUENCY Edinburghshire
RESULT W.E. Gladstone* (Lib) 5,845; A.G. Wauchope (Con) 5,155

DATE 24 Aug 1892. By-election caused by Gladstone's appointment as Prime Minister, First Lord of the Treasury and Lord Privy Seal
CONSTITUENCY Edinburghshire
RESULT W.E. Gladstone* (Lib)

PARTY ACTIVITY

Party Leadership Leader of the Liberal Party 1865–75, 1880–94

PARLIAMENTARY AND MINISTERIAL EXPERIENCE

Maiden Speech 3 Jun 1833. He defended his father's interests in West Indies sugar plantations in a speech of about fifty minutes which was well received. (*Parl. Deb.* 3rd ser, vol XVIII, col 330–7)

Privy Counsellor 3 Sep 1841

Ministerial Offices Junior Lordship at the Treasury 26 Dec 1834–27 Jan 1835; Under Secretary for the Colonies 27 Jan–8 Apr 1835; Vice-President of the Board of Trade 3 Sep 1841–15 May 1843; President of the Board of Trade 15 May 1843–3 Feb 1845; Colonial Secretary 23 Dec 1845–27 Jun 1846; Chancellor of the Exchequer 28 Dec 1852–22 Feb 1855, 18 Jun 1859–26 Jun 1866, 30 Aug 1873–17 Feb 1874, 28 Apr 1880–16 Dec 1882; Leader of the House of Commons 29 Oct 1865–26 Jun 1866; First Lord of the Treasury and Leader of the House of Commons 3 Dec 1868–17 Feb 1874, 23 Apr 1880–9 Jun 1885, 1 Feb–20 Jul 1886, 15 Aug 1892–2 Mar 1894; Lord Privy Seal 17 Feb–20 Jul 1886, 20 Aug 1892–2 Mar 1894.

Opposition Leaders while PM 1) 1868–74, Benjamin Disraeli; 2) 1880–85, Sir S. Northcote; 3) 1886, Sir M. Hicks Beach; 4) 1892–94, A.J. Balfour

GOVERNMENTS FORMED

First Administration 3 Dec 1868–17 Feb 1874

GENERAL ELECTION RESULT
NOV 1868: Liberal 387; Conservative 271. Total 658
Liberal majority 115 (excl. the Speaker)

CABINET
Prime Minister and First Lord of the Treasury W.E. Gladstone
Lord Chancellor Lord Hatherley (1868–72); Lord Selborne (1872–74)
Lord President of the Council Earl de Grey and Ripon (1868–73); H.A. Bruce (1873–74)
Lord Privy Seal Earl of Kimberley (1868–70); Viscount Halifax (1870–74)
Home Secretary H.A. Bruce (1868–73); R. Lowe (1873–74)
Foreign Secretary Earl of Clarendon (1868–70); Earl Granville (1870–74)
Secretary of State for War E. Cardwell
Secretary of State for the Colonies Earl Granville (1868–70); Earl of Kimberley (1870–74)
Secretary of State for India Duke of Argyll
Chancellor of the Exchequer R. Lowe (1868–73); W.E. Gladstone (1873–74)
First Lord of the Admiralty H.C.E. Childers (1868–71); G.J. Goschen (1871–74)
*Vice-President of the Committee of the Privy Council on Education in England and Wales** W.E. Forster (1870–74)
Chief Secretary for Ireland C.S. Fortescue (1868–71); Lord Hartington (1871–74)
*Chancellor of the Duchy of Lancaster** H.C.E. Childers (1872–73); J. Bright (1873–74)
President of the Local Government Board J. Stansfeld (1871–74)
President of the Poor Law Board (Later became the Local Government Board) G. J. Goschen (1868–71); J. Stansfeld (1871)
*Postmaster-General** Lord Hartington (1868–71)
President of the Board of Trade J. Bright (1868–71); C.S. Fortescue (1871–74)
[* Office not always in Cabinet]

Second Administration 23 Apr 1880–9 Jun 1885

GENERAL ELECTION RESULT
MAR 1880: Liberal 352; Conservative 237; Others

63. Total 652
Liberal majority 51 (excl. the Speaker)

CABINET

Prime Minister and First Lord of the Treasury W.E. Gladstone
Lord Chancellor Lord Selborne
Lord President of the Council Earl Spencer (1880–83); Lord Carlingford (1883–85)
Lord Privy Seal Duke of Argyll (1880–81); Lord Carlingford (1881–85); Earl of Rosebery (1885)
Home Secretary Sir W.V. Harcourt
Foreign Secretary Earl Granville
Secretary of State for War H.C.E. Childers (1880–82); Lord Hartington (1882–85)
Secretary of State for the Colonies Earl of Kimberley (1880–82); Earl of Derby (1882–85)
Secretary of State for India Lord Hartington (1880–82); Earl of Kimberley (1882–85)
Chancellor of the Exchequer W.E. Gladstone (1880–82); H.C.E. Childers (1882–85)
First Lord of the Admiralty Earl of Northbrook
*Chief Secretary for Ireland** W.E. Forster (1880–82)
*Lord Lieutenant of Ireland** Earl Spencer (1882–85)
Chancellor of the Duchy of Lancaster J. Bright (1880–82); Earl of Kimberley (1882); J.G. Dodson (1882–84); G.O. Trevelyan (1884–85)
President of the Local Government Board J.G. Dodson (1880–82); Sir C. Dilke (1882–85)
*Postmaster-General** G.J. Shaw-Lefevre (1884–85)
President of the Board of Trade J. Chamberlain
*First Commissioner of Works** Earl of Rosebery (1885)
[* Office not always in Cabinet]

Third Administration 1 Feb– 20 Jul 1886

GENERAL ELECTION RESULT

NOV 1885: Liberal 319; Conservative 249; Others 102. Total 670
No overall majority

CABINET

Prime Minister, First Lord of the Treasury and Lord Privy Seal W.E. Gladstone
Lord Chancellor Sir F. Herschell
Lord President of the Council Earl Spencer
Home Secretary H.C.E. Childers
Foreign Secretary Earl of Rosebery
Secretary of State for War H. Campbell-Bannerman
Secretary of State for the Colonies Earl Granville
Secretary of State for India Earl of Kimberley
Chancellor of the Exchequer Sir W.V. Harcourt
First Lord of the Admiralty Marquess of Ripon
Chief Secretary for Ireland J. Morley
President of the Local Government Board J. Chamberlain (Feb–Apr 1886); J. Stansfeld (Apr–Jul 1886)
*Secretary for Scotland** G.O. Trevelyan (Feb–Apr 1886)
President of the Board of Trade A.J. Mundella
[* Office not always in Cabinet]

Fourth Administration 15 Aug 1892– 2 Mar 1894

GENERAL ELECTION RESULT

JUL 1892: Liberal 272; Conservative 313; Others 85. Total 670
No overall majority

CABINET

Prime Minister, First Lord of the Treasury and Lord Privy Seal W.E. Gladstone
Lord Chancellor Lord Herschell
Lord President of the Council Earl of Kimberley
Home Secretary H.H. Asquith
Foreign Secretary Earl of Rosebery
Secretary of State for War H. Campbell-Bannerman
Secretary of State for the Colonies Marquess of Ripon
Secretary of State for India Earl of Kimberley
Chancellor of the Exchequer Sir W.V. Harcourt
First Lord of the Admiralty Earl Spencer
Vice-President of the Committee of the Privy Council on Education in England and Wales A.H.D. Acland
Chief Secretary for Ireland J. Morley
Chancellor of the Duchy of Lancaster J. Bryce
President of the Local Government Board H.H. Fowler
Postmaster-General A. Morley
Secretary for Scotland G.O. Trevelyan
President of the Board of Trade A.J. Mundella
First Commissioner of Works G.J. Shaw-Lefevre

IMPORTANT DATES IN PERSONAL AND POLITICAL LIFE

10 OCT 1828 Becomes a student at Christ Church College, Oxford.

16 MAY 1831 His speech at the Oxford Union against the Reform Bill, argues that electoral reform would mean revolution.

1831 Double first degree in classics and mathematics.

1832 Grand Tour of Europe.

14 DEC 1832 Returned as MP for the first time for Newark-on-Trent under the patronage of the Duke of Newcastle, Gladstone sits with the Conservative opposition in the House of Commons.

3 JUN 1833 Maiden speech during the Committee stage of a Bill to emancipate slaves throughout the Empire; defends his father against accusations about the treatment of slaves on his plantations in the West Indies made by Lord Howick..

26 DEC 1834 Junior Lord of the Treasury in Sir Robert Peel's administration.

17 JAN 1835 Meets Disraeli for the first time at dinner with Lord Lyndhurst, the Lord Chancellor; later recalls having been taken aback by Disraeli's foppish dress.

27 JAN 1835 Under-Secretary of State for the Colonies.

8 APR 1835 Out of office following resignation of Peel's Government.

8 JUN 1839 Engagement to Catherine Glynne.

25 JUL 1839 Marries Catherine at Hawarden; Lord Lyttelton marries her younger sister Mary at the same ceremony.

JAN 1840 Begins his work of rescuing and rehabilitating prostitutes in London.

3 SEP 1841 Reluctantly accepts post of Vice- President of the Board of Trade in Peel's Government saying his lack of knowledge of trade makes him unfit for the position.

9 APR 1842 Dines with Queen Victoria for the first time at Buckingham Palace. He comments on the absence of a chaplain and failure to say grace.

18 SEP 1842 In a shooting accident he loses top joint of the forefinger of his left hand.

15 MAY 1843 Peel appoints him President of the Board of Trade and member of the Cabinet.

9 AUG 1844 Gladstone carries the first general Railway Bill through Parliament. The Railway Act ensures that Rail Companies provide some accommodation on trains for poorer people; fares are not to exceed a penny a mile for third class passengers on these 'Parliamentary trains'.

IMPORTANT DATES IN PERSONAL AND POLITICAL LIFE—*Continued*

3 FEB 1845 Resigns from the Cabinet disagreeing with grant to Maynooth College in Dublin where Roman Catholic clergy are trained.

23 DEC 1845 Peel invites Gladstone to join the Government again as Colonial Secretary; he has to stand for re-election on taking office but the Duke of Newcastle, opposed to the Government's policy over the Corn Laws, refuses to support him. Gladstone is without a seat in the House of Commons for nearly two years but remains a member of Peel's Cabinet.

JUN 1846 Gladstone's sister Helen placed under restraint by the Lunacy Commission. She has had a long history of instability and drug (opium) addiction.

1847 Liquidation of the Oak Farm Company, owned by Sir Stephen Glynne, Gladstone's brother-in-law. Liabilities of about £450,000 are secured on Hawarden. Gladstone works to improve finances of the estate and enters an agreement with Sir Stephen for joint occupation of Hawarden and sharing of running expenses.

16 DEC 1847 Joins Disraeli in speaking and voting for Lord John Russell's motion to allow Jews to take the oath on becoming a member of the House of Commons by deleting the words 'on the faith of a Christian' from the oath.

1848 Gladstone called out as a Special Constable during outbreaks of Chartist troubles . He founds Church Penitentiary Association for the Reclamation of Fallen Women with Bishops Wilberforce and Bloomfield.

16 DEC 1852 Replies to Disraeli's Budget speech. The Budget is rejected and Lord Derby resigns as PM immediately.

19 DEC 1852 Lord Aberdeen forms a coalition government.

28 DEC 1852 Gladstone becomes Chancellor of the Exchequer in Aberdeen's administration.

18 APR 1853 His first Budget is based on economy in public expenditure and continues the unpopular income tax.

OCT 1853 Turkey declares war on Russia.

6 MAR 1854 Gladstone increases the income tax from 7d to 10½d in anticipation of the Crimean War.

6 FEB 1855 Lord Palmerston becomes Prime Minister.

22 FEB 1855 Gladstone resigns from the Government, disagreeing with Palmerston's decision to accept Roebuck's proposed Committee of Inquiry into the conduct of the Crimean War.

8 NOV 1858 Leaves England to become Lord High Commissioner Extraordinary to the Ionian Islands until Mar 1859. There had been outbreaks of violence there as the islands (a British Protectorate since 1815) want union with Greece.

12 JUN 1859 Palmerston forms his second administration. Gladstone again takes office as Chancellor of the Exchequer; in his first Budget he raises income tax from 5d to 9d.

10 FEB 1860 Gladstone's second Budget follows a commercial treaty with France; the number of articles subject to customs duty are reduced considerably. Taxes on food are reduced and income tax is increased to 10d on incomes above £150 and to 7d on lower incomes. One of his greatest achievements, the Budget helps to reduce the cost of living, and his reputation soars. He had also proposed repeal of the excise duty on paper but this meets opposition, and the House of Lords rejects the Paper Bill.

8 FEB 1861 Gladstone introduces the Post Office Savings Bank Bill to enable small savings to be invested through postal and money order offices.

11 APR 1861 Budget reduces income tax on higher incomes to 9d and ensures that from 1861 all financial legislation from a Budget will be incorporated into a single Finance Bill, thus achieving the repeal of excise duty on paper, because the Lords do not dare to reject a whole Budget. The measure makes books, pamphlets and newspapers cheaper.

1862 Gladstone and his wife provide relief work on the Hawarden estate for workers in the Lancashire cotton industry who have been thrown out of work because ports of the Southern States have been blockaded in the American Civil War, preventing the export of cotton.

1863 Gladstone tries to tax the incomes of charities. A loud public outcry ensues and a deputation headed by the Duke of Cambridge, the Archbishops of York and Canterbury and the Earl of Shaftesbury appeal against his argument that all money is a trust from God and should therefore all be taxed alike. His proposal is decisively defeated by the House of Commons.

11 MAY 1864 During the Second Reading of a Private Member's Bill to lower the franchise qualification in towns, Gladstone says, 'I venture to say that every man who is not presumably incapacitated by some consideration of personal unfitness or of political danger is morally entitled to come within the pale of the constitution.' This is seen as coming close to advocating universal suffrage. The Radicals are delighted; the Queen and Palmerston horrified.

18 JUL 1865 Loses his seat at Oxford University in the General Election.

22 JUL 1865 Returned as Member for Lancashire, Southern at a later poll in the same General Election.

29 OCT 1865 Following the death of Palmerston, Lord John Russell becomes PM for the second time and invites Gladstone to lead the House of Commons and to continue in office as Chancellor of the Exchequer.

12 MAR 1866 Introduces the Representation of the People Bill which proposes to lower the property qualifications for voters. The Bill is opposed not only by Conservatives but also by some Liberals.

3 MAY 1866 Gladstone's Budget repeals duties on timber and pepper; he warns that British coalfields may be exhausted by 1966.

26 JUN 1866 He announces the Government's resignation to the House of Commons after a vote against Russell's new Reform Bill. Lord Derby becomes PM, although he does not have a majority in the Commons.

JUL 1866 Gladstone upsets Queen Victoria by refusing to support the purchase of gun-metal for the Prince Consort's memorial in Kensington Gardens.

18 NOV 1868 Returned as Member for Greenwich following his defeat at South-West Lancashire in the General Election.

23 NOV 1868 Publication of *A Chapter of Autobiography.*

3 DEC 1868 Gladstone becomes PM for the first time following the Liberal victory at the General Election.

26 JUL 1869 Bill for the Disestablishment of the Irish Church becomes law.

AUG 1870 Legislation includes the Irish Land Act and the Education Act (introduced by W. E. Forster), which introduced public elementary education.

1871 Gladstone troubled by the 'royalty question'. An outbreak of republican feeling arises from the fall of the French monarchy, the Queen's neglect of her public duties and public offence at the Prince of Wales's pleasure-seeking way of life. Relations between Gladstone and Queen Victoria become strained and eventually mutually antipathetic.

17 AUG 1871 The Army Regulation Bill abolishing purchase of commissions in the army is passed.

13 FEB 1873 Introduction of the Irish University Bill proposing a new university at Dublin open to both Catholics and Protestants.

13 MAR 1873 Following the Government's defeat on the Second Reading of the Irish University Bill, Gladstone resigns. Disraeli refuses to take office and, as both party leaders are unwilling to advise a dissolution of Parliament, Gladstone resumes office.

17 FEB 1874 Resigns as PM following the Conservative victory at the General Election. Disraeli becomes PM.

NOV 1874 Publication of his pamphlet 'The Vatican Decrees in their Bearing on Civil Allegiance'; 150,000 copies are sold, earning him £2,000.

FEB 1875 He retires as Leader of the Liberal Party when the House reassembles, but continues to sit on the Opposition front bench. Publication of 'Vaticanism: an answer to reproofs and replies'.

MAR 1875 Gladstone sells 11 Carlton House Terrace and some of his collection of pictures and porcelain. He takes a less expensive house at 73 Harley Street.

6 SEP 1876 Publication of his pamphlet 'The Bulgarian Horrors and the Question of the East', attacking the Government's foreign policy. During the Eastern Crisis Gladstone's opinion of Disraeli deepens to hatred.

7 MAY 1877 Moves the first of his five resolutions on the Eastern Question in the House, speaking for two and a half hours.

NOV 1879 Gladstone's Midlothian campaign, a fortnight's tour of the country prior to the General Election. He makes five major speeches indoors and many brief ones outside. He is received ecstatically, moving public opinion against Disraeli by the power of his oratory.

6 APR 1880 Gladstone returned as Member for both Leeds and Edinburghshire at the General Election. He chooses to sit for Edinburghshire, and his son Herbert is later elected to fill the vacant seat at Leeds. His son William is also elected to Parliament for Worcestershire East.

21 APR 1880 Following the Liberal victory in the General Election Disraeli resigns without waiting for Parliament to meet.

22 APR 1880 Queen Victoria asks Lord Hartington to form a Government, but he persuades her, with the help of Lord Granville, to send for Gladstone.

23 APR 1880 Gladstone becomes Prime Minister for the second time; he decides to combine the offices of Prime Minister and Chancellor of the Exchequer.

10 JUN 1880 His Budget repeals the malt tax to help farmers during agricultural depression. Income tax is raised from 5d to 6d and the tax on beer increased.

1 FEB 1881 Coercion Bill passed by the Commons after a sitting lasting 41 hours. The Viceroy in Ireland is given powers to detain people for as long as thought necessary. The Bill is passed despite a great deal of Parliamentary obstruction by Irish MPs.

7 APR 1881 Gladstone fights for the Irish Land Bill, which occupies 58 sittings in the Commons, becoming law on 22 Aug 1881.

19 APR 1881 Death of Disraeli. Gladstone does not attend the funeral but makes a dignified and careful speech in the Commons proposing a national memorial in Westminster Abbey.

1881 The Bradlaugh case. Charles Bradlaugh has been expelled repeatedly from the House of Commons over a period of five years because of his atheism and consequent inability to swear the oath of allegiance. Despite his antipathy towards Bradlaugh, Gladstone introduces a Bill to enable non-believers to affirm (Quakers and Jews are already able to do this). The Bill is lost but eventually Bradlaugh moves his own Affirmation Bill in 1888.

6 MAY 1882 Murder of Lord Frederick Cavendish, Chief Secretary for Ireland, and his permanent Under-Secretary, T.H. Burke, in Phoenix Park, Dublin. An even more severe Coercion Bill is introduced as a result.

JUL 1882 Egyptian crisis. The British Army occupies Egypt following nationalist riots. The opening of the Suez Canal in 1869 has increased Egypt's political importance.

16 DEC 1882 Gladstone resigns as Chancellor of the Exchequer. H.C.E. Childers takes over this office.

NOV 1883 Revolt in Sudan against Egyptian rule. The Mahdi defeats the Egyptian army; General Gordon sent to Sudan.

FEB 1884 Gordon reaches Khartoum and sends home details of his plans to defeat the Mahdi. Although Gordon had been instructed only to arrange an evacuation, jingoism in England forces Gladstone to send an expeditionary force to his aid.

28 FEB 1884 Introduction of the Representation of the People Bill to give the same voting rights to householders in the counties as those enjoyed by their counterparts in the boroughs. The Conservatives and the Lords oppose the Bill unless this extension of the franchise is accompanied by a redistribution of seats. The Bill is lost at the prorogation of Parliament.

6 NOV 1884 Second Representation of the People Bill introduced.

1 DEC 1884 The Redistribution of Seats Bill is introduced.

6 DEC 1884 Royal Assent given to the Representation of the People Bill.

26 JAN 1885 Fall of Khartoum. General Gordon and his forces are massacred two days before Lord Wolseley's relief expedition arrives. Universal outrage follows when news of this reaches London early in February.

30 MAR 1885 The Russians move into Afghanistan. To divert attention away from the Sudan, Gladstone has British forces in Afghanistan made ready for action, but the Russians withdraw.

8 JUN 1885 The Government is defeated on the Budget by an alliance of Conservatives and Irish Nationalists.

9 JUN 1885 Gladstone resigns; Lord Salisbury becomes PM.

12 JUN 1885 The Redistribution Bill is passed by the House of Lords.

13 JUN 1885 Queen Victoria offers Gladstone an earldom, which he declines.

NOV 1885 General Election. Lord Salisbury continues in office, in alliance with the Irish Nationalists.

17 DEC 1885 Herbert Gladstone reveals to the Press his father's support for a policy of home rule in Ireland.

21 JAN 1886 In the Queen's speech at the opening of Parliament, the Government's intention to preserve the union between Great Britain and Ireland is announced.

27 JAN 1886 Gladstone and the Irish Nationalists join forces to defeat the Government.

28 JAN 1886 Lord Salisbury resigns.

1 FEB 1886 Gladstone takes office as PM for the third time at the age of 76, combining it with the office of Lord Privy Seal.

IMPORTANT DATES IN PERSONAL AND POLITICAL LIFE—*Continued*

26 MAR 1886 Joseph Chamberlain and Sir George Trevelyan resign from the Government over Gladstone's Home Rule proposals.

8 APR 1886 Introduction of the Home Rule Bill, which is debated for 16 days during the next 2 months.

8 JUN 1886 The Home Rule Bill is defeated by 30 votes on the Second Reading. Gladstone asks the Queen to dissolve Parliament. During the election campaign Gladstone's motives and character are savagely attacked by the *Times* as well as by his political opponents. Lord Randolph Churchill accuses him of being 'an old man in a hurry.'

20 JUL 1886 Gladstone resigns as PM following the Conservative victory at the General Election.

25 JUL 1888 The Gladstones celebrate their golden wedding anniversary.

NOV 1890 The alliance between the Liberals and the Irish Nationalists ends, following the public scandal when Parnell is cited as co-respondent in W. H. O'Shea's divorce suit against his wife. Gladstone had urged Parnell to retire temporarily from public life to let the storm die down but he had refused.

2 OCT 1891 Announces his 'Newcastle Programme' at Newcastle-on-Tyne; it includes Home Rule for Ireland, disestablishment of the Church in Scotland and Wales, 'one man, one vote' and triennial Parliaments.

JUL 1892 Liberal majority at the General Election.

11 AUG 1892 Lord Salisbury resigns as PM after a vote of no confidence.

15 AUG 1892 Gladstone becomes PM for the fourth time, and again combines it with being Lord Privy Seal.

13 FEB 1893 Introduction of the Home Rule Bill.

8 SEP 1893 House of Lords rejects the Home Rule Bill.

JAN 1894 Gladstone refuses to accept increased Naval estimates, despite strained relations with France. Finding himself isolated in the Cabinet, he resigns as PM on 2 Mar 1894, remaining an MP until the General Election of Jul 1895.

24 MAY 1894 Undergoes operation for cataract.

24 SEP 1896 His last public speech, at Liverpool, protesting against the massacres of Armenians in Turkey.

19 MAY 1897 Dies at Hawarden. His body lies in state in Westminster Hall before burial in Westminster Abbey.

BACKGROUND

PHYSICAL CHARACTERISTICS AND HEALTH

Gladstone was well above the contemporary average height for adult males. He was just over 5′10″ and weighed nearly 168 pounds in 1859. As a young man he was considered handsome with pale, rather delicate features and brown curly hair. His eyes were frequently commented on. At the time of his maiden speech in 1833 George Keppel (Whig Member for East Norfolk) noted his 'earnest intelligent countenance and large, expressive, black eyes.' He also had a good voice. Although never a dandy he was always neatly dressed.

Throughout his life Gladstone took great care to keep himself fit; his exercise was mainly serious walking. He was always a good sleeper. Generally his health was robust and when Sir Andrew Clark, his doctor, examined him at the age of 72 he declared him 'sound from head to toes and built in the most beautiful proportion'. He added that because of his careful habits Gladstone had a good chance of living to be 100. His eyesight was always poor however and in 1894 he underwent an operation for cataract. At times of crisis he was prone to sudden bouts of illness; these were possibly a physical reaction to mental stress. He died from cancer which had started behind the cheekbone and gradually spread.

EDUCATION

Primary c. 1816, Preparatory school at Seaforth Vicarage, four miles from Liverpool. The tutor was the Reverend William Rawson.

Secondary 1821–27, Eton

University 1828–31, Christ Church, Oxford. He read Classics but in 1830 started to study mathematics as well. In 1830 Gladstone was president of the Union for a term.

Prizes and awards 1829, Elected a student of Christ Church; this was a tribute, as these studentships were usually awarded to the family and friends of the Dean and Canons.

Qualifications 1831, Double First in Classics and Mathematics

Cultural and vocational background 1832, Grand Tour of Europe with his brother Lieutenant John Gladstone RN. They visted Brussels, Lyons, Turin, Florence, Rome, Naples, Venice and Milan.

NON-PARLIAMENTARY CAREER

Early occupations In Jan 1833 Gladstone entered Lincoln's Inn but six years later he requested that his name be removed from the list as he had given up his intention of being called to the Bar.

HONOURS

Freedom of cities 1877, Dublin; 1883, Kirkwall; 1892, Liverpool

Academic Honorary Fellow of All Souls College Oxford; 1860, Lord Rector of Edinburgh University; 1877, Lord Rector of Glasgow University; 1897, Honorary degree from the new Welsh University at Aberystwyth

Other than Peerage 13 Jan 1881, Fellow of the Royal Society

CLUBS

Oxford and Cambridge; Carlton (from 1833–60); Grillion's dining club; 'The Club'—a distinguished dining society; Reform (resigned in 1874)

HOBBIES AND SPORTS

Gladstone read a great deal, especially theological and classical works and made translations of both. He was a good singer and possessed a fine baritone voice. He collected paintings and porcelain, and played chess.

His sporting activites were riding and walking. The latter was his favourite form of exercise; even at the age of sixty-three he was still recording a walk of thirty-three miles in Scotland in his diary. He also had a curious passion for chopping down trees.

FINANCES

Gladstone was one of the most generous and charitable men of his generation. He spent about £83,000 during his life on rescue work with prostitutes. He also spent £267,000 of his own money on his brother-in-law's estate at Hawarden which the Gladstones shared with Sir Stephen Glynne until his death in 1874. The property then passed to Gladstone's wife for her lifetime, although the title deeds were made over to their eldest son William. The estate was then 6,966 acres, worth £18,195 a year. During the 1880s Gladstone distributed £120,000 to members of his family and spent £30,000 founding the Hostel and Library of St. Deiniols. As a result he left only about £50,000 in his will. He always regarded wealth as a trust from God; to be used for God's purposes.

Income Most of Gladstone's income came from his assets and from money inherited from his father.

Spouse's finances On marriage Catherine brought Gladstone £8,666, her share under her father's settlement; also £950 in cash and a twentieth share in Oak Farm Iron Company stock. Her wedding presents were valued at £600.

Legacies It is estimated that Gladstone's total fortune from his father was about £151,000.

Will Gladstone's heir was his grandson, William Glynne Charles Gladstone, who inherited Hawarden Castle. Gladstone had disposed of much of his money during the 1880s and left only £50,000.

ANECDOTES

When Gladstone was 16, he decided to start keeping a daily account of his expenditure of time. He continued this until Dec 1896; there are 41 volumes of his diary.

In the 1840s Gladstone began his lifelong work of rescuing and trying to rehabilitate prostitutes. He walked the streets of London at night and waited for them to accost him; he would then suggest they accompany him home for food and shelter. Many malicious rumours were spread about this work, which caused great anxiety among his supporters.

Communication at Hawarden was by means of a private language, 'Glynnese', a kind of slang: 'quite an old shoe' meant 'an old friend'; 'over the moon', 'high spirits' and 'a face', 'an uninvited or self-invited guest'. Gladstone did not often use the language but Mrs. Gladstone used it whenever possible. Lord Lyttelton published a glossary to it in 1857.

In 1853 one of Gladstone's first acts as Chancellor of the Exchequer was to order the Foreign Office to stop using large thick sheets of double notepaper when single, thinner sheets would do.

Gladstone's relationship with Lord Palmerston was never an easy one and often came close to the breaking point. He later said that he never attended a Cabinet meeting between 1859 and 1865 without taking the precaution of carrying a letter of resignation in his pocket.

Benjamin Jowett said of him that no one of such great simplicity had ever been found in so exalted a station.

Henry Labouchère said that while he had no objection to Gladstone's habit of concealing the ace of trumps up his sleeve, he did object to his reiterated claim that it had been put there by Almighty God.

In a letter to Lord Clarendon in 1860 the Honourable Emily Eden said of Gladstone ' . . . if he were soaked in boiling water and rinsed until he were twisted into a rope, I do not suppose a drop of fun would ooze out.'

Relations between Queen Victoria and Gladstone were never very harmonious. Just before he became PM for the second time in 1880 she wrote to Sir Henry Ponsonby that she 'will sooner abdicate than send for or have anything to do with that half-mad fire-brand who would soon ruin everything and be a dictator'.

She also commented, 'He speaks to me as if I were a public meeting.'

Disraeli said of him: 'He has not a single redeeming defect.'

QUOTATIONS

11 May 1864, I venture to say that every man who is not presumably incapacitated by some consideration of personal unfitness or of political danger, is morally entitled to come within the pale of the constitution.

27 Apr 1866, You cannot fight against the future. Time is on our side. The great social forces which move onward in their might and majesty. . . . are against you. They are marshalled on our side. (Speech on the Reform Bill)

Dec 1878, I am a firm believer in the aristocratic principle—the rule of the best. I am an out-and-out inegalitarian. (To John Ruskin)

29 Nov 1879, No Chancellor of the Exchequer is worth his salt who is not ready to save what are meant by candle-ends and cheese-parings in the cause of his country. (Speech at Edinburgh)

7 Oct 1881, The resources of civilization are not yet exhausted. (Speech in Leeds on conflict in Ireland)

28 Jun 1886, All the world over, I will back the masses against the classes. (Speech at Liverpool)

RESIDENCES

62 Rodney Street, Liverpool
Seaforth House, near Liverpool
92 Jermyn Street, London
Albany, off Piccadilly, London
13 Carlton House Terrace, London
Hawarden Castle, Flint
*11 Carlton House Terrace, London (plaque)
73 Harley Street, London
Dollis Hill, Willesden, London (Lent by Lord Aberdeen)
4 Whitehall Gardens, London and
1 Carlton Gardens, London (both owned by Stuart Rendel, father of his daughter-in-law Maud.)

*Gladstone lived at 11 Carlton House Terrace while PM. He used 10 Downing Street as an office.

MEMORIALS

STATUES AND BUSTS

1869, by J.A. Acton, St. George's Hall, Liverpool; 1878, by W. Theed, Manchester; *c.* 1894, by E.O. Ford,

MEMORIALS—*Continued*

National Liberal Club, London; 1900, by F.W. Pomeroy, Central Lobby, Palace of Westminster; 1902, by T. Brock, RA, Westminster Abbey; 1905, by Sir W.H. Thornycroft, The Strand, Aldwych, London

PORTRAITS

c. 1833, by Joseph Severn, Reform Club, London; *c.* 1840, by W. H. Cobley, Museum and Art Gallery, Newark-on-Trent; 1841, by William Bradley, Eton College, Berkshire; 1855, by Philip Westcott RA, National Liberal Club, London; 1859, by G. F. Watts, National Portrait Gallery, London; *c.* 1869, by Charles Lucy, Victoria and Albert Museum, London; 1875, by Lowes Dickinson RA, Liverpool College; 1879, by Sir J. E. Millais, National Portrait Gallery, London; 1879, by W. T. Roden, City Art Gallery, Birmingham; *c.* 1879, by Franz-Seraph Von Lenbach, Scottish National Portrait Gallery; 1885, by Sir J. E. Millais, Christ Church, Oxford; 1888, by H. J. Thaddeus, Reform Club, London; 1890, by A. E. Emslie, National Portrait Gallery, London; 1890, by Percy Bigland, Walker Art Gallery, Liverpool; *c.* 1892, John Colin Forbes, National Liberal Club, London; *c.* 1893, by S. P. Hall, National Portrait Gallery, London; 1893, by Prince Pierre Troubetskoy, National Portrait Gallery, London

BIBLIOGRAPHIC INFORMATION

LETTERS AND PERSONAL PAPERS

Most of Gladstone's political papers and correspondence are in the British Library. His personal correspondence and family papers are at St. Deiniol's Library, Hawarden and Lambeth Palace Library, London.

The Gladstone Diaries vol 1 and 2 1825–1839, Ed. M.R.D. Foot; vol 3 and 4 1840–1854, Ed. M.R.D. Foot and H.C.G. Matthew; vol 5 and 6 1855–1868, vol 7 Jan 1869–Jun 1871, vol 8 Jul 1871–Dec 1874, vol 9 Jan 1875–Dec 1880, vol 10 Jan 1881–June 1883, vol 11 Jul 1883–Dec 1886, Ed. H.C.G. Matthew, OUP, 1968–90.

PUBLICATIONS

1838, *The Church in Its Relations with the State*; 1840, *Church Principles Considered in Their Results*; 1845, *Remarks upon Recent Commercial Legislation*; 1845, *A Manual of Prayers from the Liturgy, Arranged for Family Use*; 1851, Translation of *The Roman State 1815–1850* by Farini (Vols. I and II); 1852, *An Examination of the Official Reply of the Neapolitan Government*; 1858, *Studies in Homer and the Homeric Age*; 1861, Translations by Lord Lyttelton and the Rt. Hon. W.E. Gladstone; 1868, *A Chapter of Autobiography*; 1869, *Juventus Mundi, the Gods and Men of the Heroic Age*; 1874, *The Vatican Decrees in Their Bearing on Civil Allegiance: A Political Expostulation*; 1875, *Vaticanism: An Answer to Replies and Reproofs*; 1876, *The Bulgarian Horrors and the Question of the East*; 1876, *The Church of England and Ritualism*; 1876, *A Biographical Sketch of Lord Lyttelton*; 1876, *Homeric Synchronism: An Inquiry into the Time and Place of Homer*; 1877, *Lessons in Massacre*; 1878, *A Literary Primer on Homer*; 1879, *Gleanings of Past Years 1843–79* (7 volumes); 1886, *The Irish Question, History of an Idea, Lessons of the Election*; 1890, *The Impregnable Rock of Holy Scripture*; 1890, *Landmarks of Homeric Study, Together with an Essay on the Points of Contact Between the Assyrian Tablets and the Homeric Text*; 1895, *The Psalter with a Concordance*; 1896, *The Works of Bishop Butler*.

Apart from the books and pamphlets listed above, Gladstone was a prolific writer of journal articles on political, religious and classical topics. Most of these he republished in *Gleanings of Past Years* in 1879.

FURTHER READING

Feuchtwanger, E. J. *Gladstone*. 2nd ed., London 1989.
Magnus, P. *Gladstone: a biography*. London, 1954.
Matthew, H.C.G. *Gladstone 1809–1874*. Oxford, 1986.
Morley, J. *The Life of William Ewart Gladstone* 2 vols. London, 1905–06.
Shannon, R. *Gladstone*. Volume I 1809–1865. London, 1982.

I.W.

Bettmann

Marquess of Salisbury

Lived 1830–1903

Political Party Conservative

Prime Minister 23 June 1885–28 January 1886;
25 July 1886–11 August 1892;
25 June 1895–11 July 1902

Governments Conservative

Reigning Monarchs Victoria; Edward VII

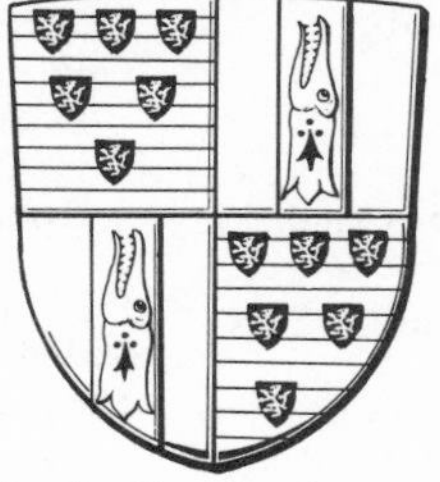

Sero sed serio Late but in earnest

SALISBURY AS PRIME MINISTER

Salisbury was elected MP at the age of 23 after a protracted world tour learning about problems in the Empire. He published his rigorous conservative ideas in articles in the *Quarterly Review.* He held the post of Secretary of State for India twice and this was followed by promotion to Foreign Secretary under Disraeli where he shared in the Prime Minister's success at the Congress of Berlin in 1878. Their friendship warmed so that Salisbury became leader of the opposition when he entered the House of Lords in 1878. From 1882–1902 he was either joint leader or leader of the Conservative Party. Salisbury became Prime Minister with some reluctance. His first administration included legislation on housing the working class. In his second administration he included important reforming acts, introducing elected county councils to improve local government and providing for free elementary education. Abroad, Rhodesia was established and a settlement with regard to Africa reached with the other imperial powers of France, Germany and Portugal. Until 1890 Salisbury acted as Foreign Secretary, bringing great experience to the office when foreign affairs were crucial. In 1895 he formed his third and last administration. The Empire in the form of Kenya, Uganda, Nigeria, etc., flourished although Salisbury was opposed to too much Whitehall interference. One area where he was not successful was the Cape Colony in South Africa. The subsequent Boer War split his Cabinet and led to his resignation in 1902. A reserved, distant, and aristocratic figure, he became an able public speaker and held the office of Prime Minister effectively.

PERSONAL INFORMATION

Names Robert Arthur Talbot Gascoyne-Cecil
Peerages 3rd Marquess of Salisbury, 9th Earl of Salisbury, Viscount Cranborne and Baron Cecil of Essendom
Born 3 Feb 1830
Birthplace Hatfield House, Hertfordshire
Religion Anglican
Ancestry Descended from the first Lord Salisbury who was the son of Lord Burghley, Minister of Queen Elizabeth I.
Date and place of marriage 11 Jul 1857, St Mary Magdalene, Munster Square, Paddington, London
Age at marriage 27 years, 158 days
Years married 42 years, 132 days
First entered Parliament 22 Aug 1853
Dates appointed PM 1) 23 Jun 1885; 2) 25 Jul 1886; 3) 25 Jun 1895
Ages at appointments 1) 55 years, 140 days; 2) 56 years, 172 days; 3) 65 years, 142 days
Dates ceased to be PM 1) 28 Jan 1886; 2) 11 Aug 1892; 3) 11 Jul 1902
Total time as PM 1) 219 days; 2) 6 years, 17 days; 3)7 years, 16 days; a total of 13 years, 252 days
Ceased to be MP 12 Apr 1868
Lived after last term as PM 1 year, 42 days
Date of death 22 Aug 1903
Place of death Hatfield House, Hertfordshire
Age at death 73 years, 200 days
Place of burial Hatfield Church, Hertfordshire
Zodiac sign Aquarius

FATHER

James Brownlow William Gascoyne-Cecil, 2nd Marquess of Salisbury
Date and place of birth 17 Apr 1791, 20 Arlington Street, London
Occupation Landowner; MP Weymouthg 1813-17, Hertford 1817–23; Lord Privy Seal 1852; Lord President of the Council 1858–59.
Dates of marriages 1) 2 Feb 1821 Frances Mary Gascoyne (d. 15 Oct 1839); 2) 29 Apr 1847 Lady Mary Catherine Sackville-West
Date of death 12 Apr 1868
Place of burial Hatfield Church, Hertfordshire

MOTHER

Frances Mary Gascoyne
Date and place of birth 25 Jan 1802, 10 Great Stanhope Street, London
Profile Heiress to large estates in Lancashire and Essex, she was one of the two women in whom the Duke of Wellington had complete confidence. According to Maxwell's *Life of Wellington*, in her case "no whisper of reproach was ever uttered. From first to last there existed between her and the Duke an ideally helpful friendship and a camaraderie of common interest."
Date of marriage 2 Feb 1821
Date of death 15 Oct 1839
Place of burial Hatfield Church, Hertfordshire

STEPMOTHER

Lady Mary Catherine Sackville-West
Date and place of birth 23 Jul 1824, Bourn, Cambridgeshire
Dates of marriages 1) 29 Apr 1847, 2nd Marquess of Salisbury (d. 12 Apr 1868); 2) 5 Jul 1870, 15th Earl of Derby, eldest son of 14th Earl of Derby (*q.v.*)
Date of death 6 Dec 1900
Place of burial Knowsley, Lancashire

BROTHERS AND SISTERS

Salisbury was the third son and fifth child of six by the 2nd Marquess's first wife.
From his father's first marriage:
James Emilius William Evelyn, (Viscount Cranborne), b. 29 Oct 1821; unm.; although he went blind at an early age he was a historical essayist and a member of the Société de L'histoire de France, the Société de L'histoire de Belgique and the Institut Génevois; d. 14 Jun 1865
Lady Mildred Arabella Charlotte, b. 24 Oct 1822; m. 7 Jul 1842, Alexander Beresford-Hope (MP Maidstone 1841–52, Stoke 1865–68, Cambridge 1868–87); d. 18 Mar 1881
Lord Arthur George Villiers Gascoyne-Cecil, b. 15 Dec 1823; d. 25 Apr 1825
Lady Blanche Mary Harriet, b. 5 Mar 1825; m. 15 Aug 1843 James Maitland Balfour; mother of A. J. Balfour (*q.v.*); d. 16 May 1872
Lord Eustace Brownlow Henry Cecil, b. 24 Apr 1834; Lieut. Col., Coldstream Guards; Surveyor-General of the Ordnance 1874–80; MP South Essex 1865–68, West Essex 1868–85; d. 3 Jul 1921

From his father's second marriage:
Sackville Arthur, b. 16 Mar 1848; d. 29 Jan 1898
Mary Arabella Arthur, b. 26 Apr 1850; m. 25 Jan 1872, 10th Earl of Galloway; d. 18 Aug 1903
Arthur, b. 3 Jul 1851; d. 16 Jul 1913
Lionel, b. 21 Mar 1853; d. 13 Jan 1901
Margaret Elizabeth, b. 30 Oct 1854; d. 11 Mar 1919

WIFE

Georgina Caroline Alderson
Date of birth 6 Apr 1827
Mother Georgina Drewe
Father Sir Edward Hall Alderson
Father's occupation Judge
Age at marriage 30 years, 96 days
Number of children 8
Date and place of death 20 Nov 1899, Hatfield House, Hertfordshire
Place of burial Hatfield Church, Hertfordshire
Years older than PM 2 years, 303 days
Profile Georgina, Marchioness of Salisbury, was more gregarious than her husband, possessing a sharp, ready wit and a forceful personality. In her youth, she studied church history, ecclesiology and medieval architecture. Throughout her life she read widely and was a writer of

verses and short stories. She was also a keen horsewoman and traveller.

Early on in Salisbury's career she would wait for him in the Ladies' Gallery of the House of Commons until the end of the day's business. She ran the family homes and assumed responsibility for the poor on the Hatfield estate. She also helped to organise a ragged school near her house in London and taught there for a time. Salisbury came to rely heavily on her advice and support in his political career as well as at home, and he greatly valued her judgement of character.

CHILDREN

5 sons, 3 daughters

Beatrix Maud, b. 11 Apr 1858; m. 27 Oct 1883, William Waldegrave Palmer, 2nd Earl of Selborne KG; d. 27 Apr 1950

Gwendolen, b. 3 Jul 1860; biographer of her father; d. 28 Sep 1945

James Edward Hubert, (4th Marquess of Salisbury), KG, PC, GCVO, CB, DL, JP; b. 23 Oct 1861; m. 17 May 1887, Lady Cicely Alice Gore; MP North East Lancashire 1885–92; Rochester 1893–1903; Under-Secretary of State for Foreign Affairs 1900–03; Lord Privy Seal 1903–05; President of the Board of Trade 1905; Lord President of the Council and Deputy Leader of the House of Lords 1922–24; Chancellor of the Duchy of Lancaster 1922; Lord Privy Seal 1924–29; Leader of the House of Lords 1925–31; d. 4 Apr 1947

Rupert Ernest William; b. 9 Mar 1863; m. 16 Aug 1887, Lady Florence Mary Bootle-Wilbraham; Rector of Hatfield and Bishop of Exeter; d. 23 Jun 1936

Edgar Algernon Robert, (Viscount Cecil of Chelwood), PC, KC, QC, JP b. 14 Sep 1864; m. 22 Jan 1889, Lady Eleanor Lambton; Barrister; Under-Secretary of State for Foreign Affairs 1915–18; Minister of Blockade 1916–18; Assistant Secretary of State for Foreign Affairs 1918–19; Lord Privy Seal 1923–24; Chancellor of the Duchy of Lancaster 1924–27; one of the founders of the League of Nations; d. 24 Nov 1958

Fanny Georgina Mildred, b. 1 Feb 1866; d. 24 Apr 1867

Edward Herbert, KCMG, DSO, b. 12 Jul 1867; m. 18 Jun 1894, Violet Georgina Maxse; Colonel in the Grenadier Guards; Under-Secretary for War in Egypt; Under-Secretary for Finance, Agent-General for the Sudan and Financial Adviser to the Egyptian Government; d. 13 Dec 1918

Hugh Richard Heathcote, (Baron Quickswood), b. 14 Oct 1869; Assistant Private Secretary to Secretary of State for Foreign Affairs (his father) 1891–92; MP Greenwich 1895–1906, Oxford University 1910–37; Provost of Eton 1936–44; d. 10 Dec 1956

LIFE AND CAREER

PARLIAMENTARY ELECTIONS FOUGHT

*(*designates candidate elected)*

DATE 22 Aug 1853. By-election caused by the resignation of J.C. Herries
CONSTITUENCY Stamford
RESULT Lord Robert Cecil* (Con)

DATE Mar 1857. General Election
CONSTITUENCY Stamford
RESULT Lord Robert Cecil* (Con); Sir F. Thesiger* (Con)

DATE Apr 1859. General Election
CONSTITUENCY Stamford
RESULT Lord Robert Cecil* (Con); Sir S.H. Northcote Bt.* (Con)

DATE Jul 1865. General Election
CONSTITUENCY Stamford
RESULT Viscount Cranborne* (Con); Sir S.H. Northcote Bt.* (Con)

DATE 12 Jul 1866. By-election caused by Salisbury's appointment as Secretary of State for India and Hay's as a Lord Commissioner of the Treasury
CONSTITUENCY Stamford
RESULT Viscount Cranborne* (Con): Sir J.C.D. Hay Bt.* (Con)

PARTY ACTIVITY

Party Leadership Leader of the Conservative Party 1881–1902; (1881–85 Joint Leader with Sir Stafford Northcote)

PARLIAMENTARY AND MINISTERIAL EXPERIENCE

Maiden Speech 7 Apr 1854 (*Parl. Deb.* 3rd ser, vol 132, col 711-4). He opposed the Second Reading of the Oxford University Bill.

Privy Counsellor 6 Jul 1866

Ministerial Offices Secretary of State for India 6 Jul 1866–8 Mar 1867, 21 Feb 1874–1 Apr 1878; Secretary of State for Foreign Affairs 2 Apr 1878–21 Apr 1880, 23 Jun 1885–28 Jan 1886, Jan 1887–11 Aug 1892, 25 Jun 1895–12 Nov 1900; Leader of the House of Lords Jun 1885– Feb 1886, Aug 1886–11 Aug 1892, 25 Jun 1895–11 Jul 1902; First Lord of the Treasury 25 Jul 1886–11 Aug 1892; Lord Privy Seal Nov 1900– 11 Jul 1902

Opposition Leaders while PM 1) 1885–86, Earl Granville (House of Lords); W E Gladstone (House of Commons); 2) 1886–92, Earl Granville (House of Lords); Earl of Kimberley (House of Lords); W. E. Gladstone (House of Commons); 3) 1895–1902, Earl of Rosebery (House of Lords); Earl of Kimberley (House of Lords); Sir W. Harcourt (House of Commons); Sir H. Campbell-Bannerman (House of Commons)

GOVERNMENTS FORMED

First Administration 23 Jun 1885–28 Jan 1886

GENERAL ELECTION RESULT

MAR 1880: Liberal 352; Conservative 237; Others 63. Total 652

Liberal majority 51 (excl. the Speaker)

CABINET

Prime Minister and Foreign Secretary Marquess of Salisbury
First Lord of the Treasury Earl of Iddesleigh
Lord Chancellor Lord Halsbury
Lord President of the Council Viscount Cranbrook
Lord Privy Seal Earl of Harrowby
Home Secretary Sir R.A. Cross
Secretary of State for War W.H. Smith
Secretary of State for the Colonies F.A. Stanley
Secretary of State for India Lord R. Churchill
Chancellor of the Exchequer Sir M. Hicks Beach

—First Administration 23 Jun 1885–28 Jan 1886—*Continued*

First Lord of the Admiralty Lord G. Hamilton
*Vice-President of the Committee of the Privy Council on Education in England and Wales** E. Stanhope (Jun–Sep 1885)
*Chief Secretary for Ireland** W.H. Smith (Jan 1886)
Lord Lieutenant of Ireland Earl of Carnarvon
Lord Chancellor of Ireland Lord Ashbourne
Postmaster-General Lord J. Manners
Secretary for Scotland Duke of Richmond (Jun–Aug 1885); E. Stanhope (Aug 1885–Jan 1886)
[*Office not always in Cabinet]

Second Administration 25 Jul 1886–11 Aug 1892

GENERAL ELECTION RESULT
JUL 1886: Conservative 393; Liberal 192; Others 85. Total 670
Conservative majority 115 (excl. the Speaker)

CABINET
Prime Minister and First Lord of the Treasury Marquess of Salisbury
Lord Chancellor Lord Halsbury
Lord President of the Council Viscount Cranbrook
*Lord Privy Seal** Earl of Cadogan (Apr 1887–Aug 1892)
Home Secretary H. Matthews
Foreign Secretary Earl of Iddesleigh (1886–1887); Marquess of Salisbury (Jan 1887–Aug 1892)
Secretary of State for War W. H. Smith (Aug 1886–Jan 1887); E. Stanhope (Jan 1887–Aug 1892)
Secretary of State for the Colonies E. Stanhope (Aug 1886–Jan 1887); Sir H. T. Holland (Jan 1887–Aug 1892)
Secretary of State for India Viscount Cross
Chancellor of the Exchequer Lord R. Churchill (Aug 1886–Jan 1887); G. J. Goschen (Jan 1887–Aug 1892)
First Lord of the Admiralty Lord G. Hamilton
*President of the Board of Agriculture** H. Chaplin (Sep 1889–Aug 1892)
*Chief Secretary for Ireland** Sir M. Hicks Beach (Aug 1886–Mar 1887); A. J. Balfour (Mar 1887–Nov 1891)
Lord Chancellor for Ireland Lord Ashbourne
Chancellor of the Duchy of Lancaster Viscount Cranbrook (3–16 Aug 1886); Lord John Manners (Aug 1886–Aug 1892)
*President of the Local Government Board** C.T. Ritchie (Apr 1887–Aug 1892)
Minister without Portfolio Sir M. Hicks Beach (Mar 1887–Feb 1888)
*Secretary for Scotland** A. J. Balfour (Nov 1886–Mar 1887)
President of the Board of Trade Sir F. A. Stanley (Aug 1886–Feb 1888); Sir M. Hicks Beach (Feb 1888–Aug 1892)
[*Office not always in Cabinet]

Third Administration 25 Jun 1895–24 Oct 1900

GENERAL ELECTION RESULT
JUL 1895: Conservative 411; Liberal 177; Others 82. Total 670
Conservative majority 153 (excl. the Speaker)

CABINET
Prime Minister and Foreign Secretary Marquess of Salisbury
First Lord of the Treasury A.J. Balfour
Lord Chancellor Earl of Halsbury
Lord President of the Council Duke of Devonshire
Lord Privy Seal Viscount Cross
Home Secretary Sir M. White Ridley
Secretary of State for War Marquess of Lansdowne
Secretary of State for the Colonies J. Chamberlain
Secretary of State for India Lord G. Hamilton
Chancellor of the Exchequer Sir M. Hicks Beach
First Lord of the Admiralty G. Goschen
President of the Board of Agriculture W. Long
*President of the Board of Education** Duke of Devonshire (Mar–Oct 1900)
Lord Lieutenant for Ireland Earl of Cadogan
Lord Chancellor for Ireland Lord Ashbourne
Chancellor of the Duchy of Lancaster Viscount Cross (Jun–Jul 1895); Lord James of Hereford (Jul 1895–Oct 1900)
President of the Local Government Board H. Chaplin
Secretary for Scotland Lord Balfour of Burleigh
President of the Board of Trade C.T. Ritchie
First Commissioner of Works A. Akers-Douglas
[*Office not always in Cabinet]

Fourth Administration 24 Oct 1900–11 Jul 1902

GENERAL ELECTION RESULT OCT 1900 Conservative 402; Liberal 183; Labour 2; Others 83. Total 670
Conservative majority 135 (excl. the Speaker)
Prime Minister and Lord Privy Seal Marquess of Salisbury
First Lord of the Treasury A.J. Balfour
Lord Chancellor Earl of Halsbury
Lord President of the Council Duke of Devonshire
Home Secretary C.T. Ritchie
Foreign Secretary Marquess of Lansdowne
Secretary of State for War W. St.J. Broderick
Secretary of State for the Colonies J. Chamberlain
Secretary of State for India Lord G. Hamilton
Chancellor of the Exchequer Sir M. Hicks Beach
First Lord of the Admiralty Earl of Selborne
President of the Board of Agriculture R.W. Hanbury
President of the Board of Education Duke of Devonshire
Chief Secretary for Ireland G. Wyndham
Lord Lieutenant for Ireland Earl of Cadogan
Lord Chancellor for Ireland Lord Ashbourne
Chancellor of the Duchy of Lancaster Lord James of Hereford
President of the Local Government Board W. Long
Postmaster-General Marquess of Londonderry
Secretary for Scotland Lord Balfour of Burleigh
President of the Board of Trade G.W. Balfour
First Commissioner of Works A. Akers-Douglas

IMPORTANT DATES IN PERSONAL AND POLITICAL LIFE

1847 Becomes a student at Christ Church, Oxford.
JUL 1851–MAY 1853 Visits South Africa, Australia and New Zealand.
1853 Elected to a fellowship of All Souls College, Oxford.
22 AUG 1853 Elected as MP for the first time for Stamford.
7 APR 1854 Maiden speech in the House of Commons.
11 JUL 1857 Marries Georgina Alderson, despite his father's disapproval.
1858 Writes *Theories of Parliamentary Reform* for that year's volume of 'Oxford Essays'.
14 JUN 1865 Death of his elder brother James. Becomes Viscount Cranborne and his father's heir.
6 JUL 1866 Secretary of State for India in Lord Derby's third administration. Sworn a Privy Counsellor.

8 MAR 1867 Resigns from the Government because of his opposition to the extension of the franchise in the Reform Bill.

30 MAR 1868 His last speech in the House of Commons. He opposes Gladstone's proposal for the disestablishment of the Irish Church.

12 APR 1868 Succeeds to the title on the death of his father.

7 MAY 1868 Takes his seat in the House of Lords for the first time.

12 NOV 1869 Becomes Chancellor of Oxford University.

FEB 1874 General Election. Disraeli becomes PM with a substantial Conservative majority.

21 FEB 1874 Secretary of State at the India Office. His relationship with Disraeli not unclouded, but it improves towards the end of the administration.

DEC 1876 Sent as British representative to the Six Powers' conference on the Eastern question in Constantinople. The conference ends in failure but Salisbury makes a good impression on the other European leaders.

1 APR 1878 Following the resignation of Lord Derby, Salisbury becomes Foreign Secretary. Before he is formally gazetted (on 2 Apr 1878) he issues the 'Salisbury Circular', a memorandum to the other European powers on why the Treaty of San Stefano (between Russia and Turkey) should not be allowed to stand.

13 JUN–13 JUL 1878 Congress of Berlin. Salisbury attends with Disraeli. They return bringing 'peace with honour' following the signing of the treaty settling the Balkan problems.

30 JUL 1878 Made a Knight of the Garter.

MAR 1880 General Election. W.E. Gladstone becomes PM following the Liberal victory.

19 APR 1881 Death of Disraeli.

9 MAY 1881 Salisbury becomes Leader of the Opposition in the House of Lords, Sir Stafford Northcote in the House of Commons. They are 'dual leaders' of the Conservative Party in the country.

OCT 1883 Article in the *Quarterly Review* on the dangers of radicalism; although anonymous, Salisbury is recognised as the author.

18 JUN 1885 Gladstone's Government falls after a vote on the Budget.

23 JUN 1885 Salisbury reluctantly accepts office as PM and decides to combine it with that of Foreign Secretary.

JUL 1885 Introduces a Bill that embodies the main recommendations of the Royal Commission on the Housing of the Working Classes.

DEC 1885 General Election. No party obtains an overall majority.

27 JAN 1886 The Government is defeated when Liberals and Parnellites vote against an agricultural measure.

28 JAN 1886 Salisbury resigns as PM.

15 MAY 1886 Makes a controversial speech against Home Rule for Ireland.

25 JUL 1886 Following the General Election, called over the Irish question, the Conservatives are the largest party in the House of Commons and Salisbury takes office again as PM. He forms his second administration on a majority formed by an alliance of the Conservatives and Liberal Unionists in the House of Commons.

DEC 1886 Lord Randolph Churchill, the Chancellor of the Exchequer, resigns after a series of differences with Salisbury.

21 JUN 1887 Queen Victoria's Golden Jubilee.

1888 Local Government Act transferring the administration of the counties to elected county councils.

1889 The British South Africa Company is granted a Royal Charter to colonise what will eventually become Rhodesia, whose capital city is named Salisbury.

1890–91 Disagreements with Germany, Portugal and France over the African territories are settled, demonstrating Salisbury's great diplomatic skills.

1891 Free Education Act abolishing fees for elementary education.

JUL 1892 General Election results in small Liberal majority over the Conservatives.

11 AUG 1892 Salisbury resigns; Gladstone becomes PM.

1894 Salisbury becomes President of the British Association.

25 JUN 1895 After Rosebery's Liberal Government is defeated on a vote on the Army Estimates, Salisbury forms a coalition government with Devonshire and Chamberlain until the General Election.

JUL 1895 General Election gives the Conservatives a majority. Once again Salisbury combines the offices of Prime Minister and Foreign Secretary.

DEC 1895 Dispute with the United States over the boundary between British Guiana and Venezuela.

1896 Becomes Lord Warden of the Cinque Ports.

1897 Workmen's Compensation Act, making the employer liable for accidents at work.

21 JUN 1897 Queen Victoria's Diamond Jubilee.

1898 Local Government for Ireland Act.

19 MAY 1898 Death of Gladstone.

JUN 1898 Convention with France settles boundary disputes in West Africa.

21 MAR 1899 France relinquishes claims to lands in the Sudan.

OCT 1899 Outbreak of the Boer War.

20 NOV 1899 Death of Lady Salisbury.

MAY 1900 Relief of Mafeking.

OCT 1900 'Khaki' General Election. Conservatives return to power with a reduced majority.

12 NOV 1900 In failing health, Salisbury hands over the Foreign Office to Lord Lansdowne.

22 JAN 1901 Death of Queen Victoria.

31 MAY 1902 End of Boer War. Treaty of Vereeniging.

11 JUL 1902 Salisbury resigns as PM on the grounds of ill health. His nephew, A. J. Balfour, becomes PM.

22 AUG 1903 Dies at Hatfield House, Hertfordshire.

BACKGROUND

PHYSICAL CHARACTERISTICS AND HEALTH

Salisbury was a frail child, prone to depression and somnambulism. Throughout his life he suffered attacks of what he called 'nerve storms', fits of depression during which the least noise or physical contact was unbearable. He was a tall, stooping man, about six foot four and large in frame. He was short-sighted and so indifferent to his appearance that, while Prime Minister, he was refused entry to the Casino in Monte Carlo because of his scruffy dress.

EDUCATION

Primary 1836 Short spell at a boarding school near Hatfield. Prior to this he had been tutored privately by a local clergyman.

Secondary 1840–45, Eton. He was eventually removed because of persistent bullying and was again tutored privately at Hatfield before going to Oxford.

University 1847–49, Christ Church, Oxford

Qualifications BA, 1850. Obtained a fourth class degree in mathematics; MA, 1853; DCL (By diploma) 1869

Cultural and vocational background 1851–52 Visited South Africa, Australia, and New Zealand

NON-PARLIAMENTARY CAREER

Early occupations Until the death of his elder brother in 1865 made him heir to the Cecil family fortune he supplemented his income by writing regular articles for *Bentley's Review* and the *Quarterly Review.* He entered Lincoln's Inn 13 Apr 1850. He became a landowner and farmer after the death of his father.

Other Posts 1856 Trustee of the National Portrait Gallery; 1868 Chairman of the Great Eastern Railway; 1869 Chancellor of the University of Oxford; 1884–1903 Grand Master of the Primrose League; 1885 Elder Brother of Trinity House; 1894 President of the British Association; 1896 Lord Warden of the Cinque Ports

HONOURS

Academic 1888, LLD (Cambridge); 1894, Hon. Studentship of Christ Church, Oxford

Other than peerage 28 Jan 1869, Fellow of the Royal Society; 30 Jul 1878, Knight of the Garter; 22 Jul 1902, Grand Cross of the Royal Victorian Order

CLUBS

Carlton

HOBBIES AND SPORTS

By nature a solitary man, Salisbury was a voracious reader especially in the classics, although Sir Walter Scott and Jane Austen were his favourite novelists. Throughout his life he studied theology, history and science; he became interested in chemistry and provided himself with a laboratory at Hatfield. He experimented with the introduction of electricity and by 1883 his house was the first private home in England to be equipped with electric lighting. It was also one of the first to have a telephone.

Salisbury enjoyed walking around his estates; after he inherited Hatfield he developed an interest in farming. In his later years he used a tricycle for exercise.

FINANCES

After his marriage Salisbury had to turn to journalism to make enough money to support his family. His father had opposed his marriage to Georgina Alderson and refused to increase his allowance. Salisbury's financial position was not secure until 1865, when the death of his elder brother left him heir to the family estates. In the early 1880s these amounted to just over 20,000 acres worth £33,413 a year. The estates were principally in Hertfordshire, but Salisbury also owned land in Dorset, Lancashire, Middlesex, Essex, Bedfordshire, Norfolk and Wiltshire.

Income Income from the estates amounted to £33,413 in the early 1880s.

Spouse's finances Georgina Alderson was the daughter of a judge; she had no fortune of her own.

Will His heir was his eldest son, James Edward Hubert Gascoyne-Cecil, 4th Marquess of Salisbury

ANECDOTES

As Foreign Secretary Salisbury became famous for his trust of the 'man on the spot' in overseas countries. He had a horror of distant bureaucratic control.

Disraeli said of him to Lady Gwendolen Cecil, 'Courage is the rarest of all qualities to be found in public men. Your father is the only man of real courage that it has been my lot to work with'.

When Salisbury reformed his administration after the General Election in 1900, it contained so many of his relatives that it was nicknamed the 'Hotel Cecil'. The expression 'Bob's your uncle' is supposed to have originated after Salisbury appointed his nephew A. J. Balfour as Chief Secretary for Ireland in 1887.

QUOTATIONS

1877, No lesson seems to be so deeply inculcated by the experience of life as that you never should trust experts.

1886, I have four departments—the Prime Minister's, the Foreign Office, the Queen and Randolph Churchill; the burden of them increases in that order.

1888, We are part of the community of Europe and we must do our duty as such.

1896, Our first duty is towards the people of this country, to maintain their interests and their rights; our second is to all humanity. (Guildhall Banquet)

c. 1896, By office boys for office boys (Of the newly established *Daily Mail* newspaper)

1897, The federated action of Europe is our sole hope of escaping from the constant terror and calamity of war.

RESIDENCES

Hatfield House, Hertfordshire
Park Crescent, London
Fitzroy Square, London
Childwall Hall, near Liverpool, Lancashire
Cranborne Manor, Wiltshire
Villa at Puys, near Dieppe, France
Villa at Beaulieu, on the Riviera, France
Arlington Street, London
Open to the public
Hatfield House, Hertfordshire (built 1607–12)

MEMORIALS

STATUES AND BUSTS

By Sir G. Frampton, outside Hatfield Park Gates; by H. Hampton, Foreign Office; 1902–03, by G. Frampton, Oxford Union Society Debating Hall; 1875, by W. Theed, Jr., Hatfield House

PORTRAITS

1872, by G. Richmond, Hatfield House; 1882–83, by Millais, National Portrait Gallery; 1884, by Watts,

National Portrait Gallery; 1887, by G. Richmond, Windsor; 1893, by Sir H. Von Herkaner, Carlton Club

OTHER MEMORIALS

Monument near the West Door of Westminster Abbey. Designed by Goscombe John. Voted by Parliament. Salisbury, Rhodesia was named after him.

BIBLIOGRAPHIC INFORMATION

LETTERS AND PERSONAL PAPERS

His letters and papers are in the archives of the Marquess of Salisbury, Hatfield House, Hatfield, Hertfordshire.

PUBLICATIONS

Salisbury was a regular contributor to the *Quarterly Review* 1860–83.

FURTHER READING

Cecil, D. *The Cecils of Hatfield House.* London, 1973.
Cecil, Lady G. *Life of Robert, Marquess of Salisbury 1830–1892.* 4 vols. London, 1921–23.
Kennedy, A. L. *Salisbury 1830–1903; Portrait of a Statesman.* London, 1953.
Taylor, R. *Lord Salisbury.* London, 1975.

I.W.

Christ Church College, Oxford

Earl of Rosebery

Lived · 1847–1929
Political Party Liberal
Prime Minister 5 March 1894–22 June 1895
Government Liberal
Reigning Monarch Victoria

Fide et fiducia By fidelity and confidence

ROSEBERY AS PRIME MINISTER

Rosebery, like Aberdeen, never sat in the House of Commons. A liberal, he was, nevertheless a staunch upholder of the British Empire. He first became a public figure when he effectively managed Gladstone's Midlothian campaign. In 1881 he became Under Secretary at the Home Office with special responsibility for Scotland, but he was not convinced that Gladstone showed real interest in Scottish affairs and resigned after two years. He then travelled the world promoting his Imperial policy and made the celebrated speech 'The British Empire is a Commonwealth of Nations'. Although he returned to be Foreign Secretary in Gladstone's last administration he accepted the position only on his own terms. When Gladstone resigned in 1894 Rosebery was the Queen's choice to succeed, not Gladstone's. He found it difficult to lead a Government from the House of Lords. He was increasingly at odds with his Chancellor of the Exchequer Sir William Harcourt and and was castigated in the Commons for blocking Irish home rule. In little over a year the Government fell apart for lack of leadership in the Cabinet, and following a vote of censure in June 1895, he resigned. While not a successful Prime Minister Rosebery achieved his declared ambitions: to marry an heiress, own a racehorse that won the Derby, and be Prime Minister.

PERSONAL INFORMATION

Names Archibald Philip Primrose
Peerages 5th Earl of Rosebery, Viscount of Rosebery, Viscount of Inverkeithing, Lord Primrose and Dalmeny, Lord Dalmeny and Primrose in the peerage of Scotland, also Baron Rosebery (UK)
Born 7 May 1847
Birthplace 20 Charles Street, Berkeley Square, London
Religion Anglican
Ancestry Scottish
Date and place of marriage 20 Mar 1878, Christ Church Mayfair and the Registrar's office, Mount Street, London
Age at marriage 30 years, 317 days
Years married 12 years, 244 days
First entered Parliament Became entitled to sit in the House of Lords on coming of age on 7 May 1868; took his seat on 22 May 1868.
Date appointed PM 5 Mar 1894
Age at appointment 46 years, 302 days
Date ceased to be PM 22 Jun 1895
Total time as PM 1 year, 109 days
Lived after last term as PM 33 years, 333 days
Date of death 21 May 1929
Place of death The Durdans, Epsom, Surrey
Age at death 82 years, 14 days
Last words He asked to hear the music of the Eton Boating Song as he died.
Place of funeral St. Giles' Cathedral, Edinburgh
Place of burial Dalmeny, Scotland
Zodiac sign Taurus

FATHER

Archibald Primrose, Lord Dalmeny
Date and place of birth 2 Oct 1809, Barnbougle Castle, Scotland
Occupation Liberal MP for Stirling Burghs 1833–47; Lord of the Admiralty 1835–41; Vice-Lieutenant of Linlithgowshire 1844
Date of marriage 20 Sep 1843
Date and place of death 23 Jan 1851, Dalmeny, Scotland
Place of burial Dalmeny, Scotland

MOTHER

Catherine Lucy Wilhelmina Stanhope
Date of birth 1 Jun 1819
Profile Lady Dalmeny was beautiful and intelligent. She read widely and was renowned for her conversation.
Dates of marriages 1) 20 Sep 1843, Lord Dalmeny (d. 1851); 2) 2 Aug 1854, Henry George Vane, 4th Duke of Cleveland
Age when PM took office 74 years, 278 days
Date and place of death 18 May 1901, Wiesbaden, Germany
Place of burial Staindrop, County Durham

BROTHERS AND SISTERS

Rosebery was the eldest son and third of four children.
Mary Catherine Constance, b. 1844; m. 8 Oct 1885, Henry Hope of Luffness; d. 3 Sep 1935
Constance Evelyn, b. 1 May 1846; m. 15 Jul 1867, Henry, 2nd Lord Leconfield; 27 Jun 1939
Everard Henry, 8 b. Sep 1848; Colonel, Grenadier Guards; Military Attache, Vienna; d. 8 Apr 1885

WIFE

Hannah de Rothschild
Date of birth 1851
Mother Juliana Cohen
Father Meyer Amschel de Rothschild
Father's occupation Baron of the Austrian Empire; MP Hythe 1859–74; sportsman and successful racehorse owner; collector of works of art
Age at marriage 27 years
Number of children 4
Date and place of death 19 Nov 1890, Dalmeny, Scotland
Place of burial Jewish cemetery at Willesden, London
Years younger than PM 3 years
Profile Although Hannah was an only child and heiress, her education was much neglected. She was a shy, kind woman devoted to her husband. At the time of her marriage she was much distressed by criticism levelled at her in the Jewish press but there was never any suggestion that she would give up her religion. Her adoration of Rosebery was always apparent to others although there are many stories about his impatience with her. She possessed both common sense and tact; her judgement of character was good. Rosebery did not realise how much he relied on her love and support until after her premature death from typhoid. He was slow to recover from the depression that followed his bereavement and he never remarried.

CHILDREN

2 sons, 2 daughters
Sybil Myra Caroline, b. Sep 1879; m. 28 Mar 1903, Sir Charles Grant; d. 25 Feb 1955
Margaret Etrenne Hannah, b. 1 Jan 1881; m. 20 Apr 1899, Robert, Marquess of Crewe; Lady of the Imperial Order of the Crown of India (1911) and Chevalier of the Legion of Honour, France (1947); d. 13 Mar 1967
Albert Edward Harry Meyer Archibald, (6th Earl of Rosebery), b. 8 Jan 1882; m. 1) 15 Apr 1909, Dorothy Alice Margaret Augusta Grosvenor (div. 1919); 2) 24 Jan 1924, Eva Isabel Marian Strutt; MP Midlothian 1906–10; landowner and racehorse breeder; d. 30 May 1974
Neil James Archibald, b. 14 Dec 1882; m. 7 Apr 1915, Lady Victoria Stanley; MP Wisbech 1910–17; Parliamentary Under-Secretary at the Foreign Office Feb–May 1916; Parliamentary Military Secretary at the Ministry of Munitions Sep–Dec 1916; Joint Parliamentary Secretary at the Treasury Dec 1916–Mar 1917; Captain, Royal Buckinghamshire Yeomanry. Killed in action at Gaza, 17 Nov 1917

LIFE AND CAREER

PARTY ACTIVITY

Party Leadership Leader of the Liberal Party 1894–96
Membership of group or faction 1902 President of the Liberal League. Asquith, Grey and Fowler were Vice-

PARTY ACTIVITY—*Continued*

Presidents.

PARLIAMENTARY AND MINISTERIAL EXPERIENCE

Maiden Speech 9 Feb 1871, Seconded the Address to Her Majesty in the House of Lords, following the opening of Parliament. (*HL Deb.* vol 204, 3rd ser col 22–8)

Privy Counsellor 26 Aug 1881

Ministerial Offices Under Secretary of State, Home Office, 8 Aug 1881–7 Jun 1883; First Commissioner of the Board of Works, 13 Feb–9 Jun 1885; Lord Privy Seal, 5 Mar–9 Jun 1885; Foreign Secretary, 6 Feb–20 Jul 1886; 18 Aug 1892–11 Mar 1894; First Lord of the Treasury, Lord President of the Council and Leader of the House of Lords 5 Mar 1894–22 Jun 1895

Opposition Leaders while PM Marquess of Salisbury (in the House of Lords); A.J. Balfour (in the House of Commons)

GOVERNMENTS FORMED

Administration 5 Mar 1894–22 Jun 1895

GENERAL ELECTION RESULT

JUL 1892: Conservative 313; Liberal 272; Others 85. Total 670

No overall majority

CABINET

Prime Minister, First Lord of the Treasury and Lord President of the Council Earl of Rosebery
Lord Chancellor Lord Herschell
Lord Privy Seal Lord Tweedmouth
Home Secretary H.H. Asquith
Foreign Secretary Earl of Kimberley
Secretary of State for War H. Campbell-Bannerman
Secretary of State for the Colonies Marquess of Ripon
Secretary of State for India H.H. Fowler
Chancellor of the Exchequer Sir W.V. Harcourt
First Lord of the Admiralty Earl Spencer
Vice-President of the Committee of the Privy Council for Education in England and Wales A.H.D. Acland
Chief Secretary for Ireland J. Morley
Chancellor of the Duchy of Lancaster Lord Tweedmouth
President of the Local Government Board G.J. Shaw Lefevre
Postmaster-General A. Morley
Secretary for Scotland G.O. Trevelyan
President of the Board of Trade J. Bryce

IMPORTANT DATES IN PERSONAL AND POLITICAL LIFE

OCT 1867 Refuses to stand as candidate for Darlington, having not yet committed himself to a political party.

4 MAR 1868 Death of his grandfather. Becomes 5th Earl of Rosebery and takes his seat in the House of Lords on 22 May.

1869 Buys his first racehorse, Ladas, in breach of the university rules at Oxford. When faced with the choice of either his horse or his degree, he leaves Oxford.

1870 Elected to the Jockey Club. Spends nearly three months in France and Italy.

9 FEB 1871 Seconds the Address to her Majesty in the House of Lords following the opening of Parliament. The speech is well received.

1871 Becomes President of the United Industrial School in Edinburgh.

FEB 1872 Declines Gladstone's offer of the post of Lordship in Waiting.

MAY 1873 Accepts Lord-Lieutenancy of Linlithgow after much persuasion from family and friends.

SEP 1873 Visits USA and Canada.

NOV 1874 Visits USA again, and Cuba.

OCT–NOV 1876 Third visit to USA.

20 MAR 1878 Marries Hannah de Rothschild.

25 APR 1880 Refuses Gladstone's offer of the post of Under-Secretary of State at the India Office, fearing that his help during the Midlothian Campaign would be seen as personal ambition rather than devotion to Party.

14 JUL 1880 He again refuses the post of Under-Secretary at the India Office, partly because of physical exhaustion. He had come close to a complete breakdown earlier in the year.

8 AUG 1881 Takes office as Under-Secretary of State at the Home Office, with special responsibility for Scottish affairs.

27 JUN 1882 Complains to Gladstone about the lack of Parliamentary time given to Scottish affairs.

DEC 1882 Expresses concern to Gladstone over the whole system for managing Scottish business; Gladstone, however, is preoccupied with the Irish question.

7 JUN 1883 Resigns as Under-Secretary at the Home Office following criticism that the Under-Secretary is a peer and that there has been no progress on the proposals for a separate Minister for Scotland.

30 JUL 1883 Writes to Gladstone saying that he will not rejoin the Government except as a member of the Cabinet.

1 SEP 1883 Leaves for a tour of the USA and Australia. During this visit to Australia he makes his famous speech at Adelaide on 18 Jan 1884 about the British Empire as a commonwealth of nations.

20 JUN 1884 Proposes that a Select Committee be appointed to look at the efficiency of the House of Lords, but his motion is defeated.

NOV 1884 Gladstone asks him to accept office as First Commissioner of the Board of Works with a seat in the Cabinet. Rosebery declines at first, partly because of his poor health and partly because of his doubts about the Government's policy on Egypt.

FEB 1885 Following the fall of Khartoum, Rosebery puts himself at Gladstone's disposal and takes office as Commissioner of the Board of Works with a seat in the Cabinet as Lord Privy Seal on 13 Feb 1885.

8 APR 1885 Death of his brother, Everard Primrose.

6 FEB 1886 Rosebery accepts the office of Foreign Secretary in Gladstone's third administration. Queen Victoria terms it the 'only really good appointment' in the whole Government.

OCT 1886 Visits India where he writes a sonnet about the Taj Mahal.

18 JAN 1889 Elected to the new London County Council as one of four City members. He is immediately elected chairman.

16 JUL 1890 Resigns as Chairman of the London County Council.

19 NOV 1890 Death of Hannah, Lady Rosebery, from typhoid.

1891 Publication of his book on Pitt.

1892 Elected to the London County Council as one of two members for East Finsbury. He resumes the chairmanship until 27 Jun 1892.

18 AUG 1892 Becomes Foreign Secretary again in Gladstone's fourth administration.

17. NOV 1893 He intervenes in the coal strike and chairs the Conference of Federated Coal-Owners and the Miners' Federation.

2 MAR 1894 Gladstone resigns as PM after disagreement in the Cabinet over the Naval estimates.

5 MAR 1894 Rosebery becomes PM.

12 MAR 1894 He makes his first speech in the House of Lords as PM provoking an uproar in the Party when he comments that home rule for Ireland can come only when England, 'the predominant member of the three Kingdoms' agrees to it.

13 MAR 1894 The day following Rosebery's controversial speech, Labouchere moves an amendment to the Address critical of the powers of the House of Lords. The Address is negatived and a new one substituted.

12 APR 1894 Signing of the Anglo-Belgian Treaty leasing territory in the Upper Nile to the King of the Belgians.

16 APR 1894 Sir William Harcourt introduces his Budget which reforms death duties. Rosebery is critical of this measure.

6 JUN 1894 Wins the Derby with his horse Ladas II.

20 JUN 1894 The National Liberal Federation meets at Leeds. Resolutions are passed against the House of Lords, including one that called for an end to the Lords' right of veto.

25 OCT 1894 Rosebery makes a speech at the Cutlers' Feast in Sheffield on foreign policy. He declares that the 'little England' party is dead.

27 OCT 1894 In a speech at Bradford he says that the next election will be fought over the question of House of Lords reform.

19 FEB 1895 Rosebery threatens to resign because of lack of support from his party in Parliament.

21 FEB 1895 He withdraws his resignation after protestations of loyalty from his Cabinet.

APR 1895 He suffers an attack of influenza. Added to his chronic insomnia this brings about a severe illness. He resumes his official duties much too soon and has a relapse which prompts rumours that he will retire.

29 MAY 1895 Wins the Derby with Sir Visto.

21 JUN 1895 The Government is defeated on a formal motion to reduce the Secretary for War's salary by £100. This is a censure on the low supply of cordite ammunition. The Secretary for War, Campbell-Bannerman, feels obliged to resign and the Government with him.

22 JUN 1895 Rosebery visits Queen Victoria at Windsor and formally resigns.

8 OCT 1896 Resigns as Leader of the Liberal Party in the interest of party unity.

28 MAY 1897 Pallbearer at Gladstone's funeral.

1901 The Liberal Imperial Council formed of Rosebery's supporters.

17 JUL 1901 Writes to the *Times* restating his determination not to return to party politics.

FEB 1902 The Liberal League is formed with Rosebery as President. H.H. Asquith, Sir Edward Grey and Sir Henry Fowler are Vice-Presidents.

1910 Puts forward motions proposing reform of the House of Lords. He speaks against the Parliament Bill but later supports the Government.

DEC 1916 He refuses office in the second Coalition Government.

17 NOV 1917 Death of his son, Neil, in action in Gaza.

NOV 1918 Rosebery suffers a stroke and is left partially crippled.

21 MAY 1929 Dies at the Durdans, Epsom.

BACKGROUND

PHYSICAL CHARACTERISTICS AND HEALTH

Lord Rosebery was of average height and sturdy build. He had slightly prominent blue eyes. A childhood accident left him with a scar on his forehead. His voice was strong, pleasant and melodious. In dress he was elegant and dapper.

From his late twenties onwards he suffered from insomnia. This became a severe problem from the age of forty until his death. In Nov 1918 he suffered a stroke which left him permanently crippled.

EDUCATION

Primary 1855, Bayford House boarding school near Hertford, *c.* 1858, Mr. Lee's School at Brighton

Secondary 1860–65, Eton

University 1866, Entered Christ Church, Oxford

Qualifications He left Oxford without taking his degree when the university authorities objected to his owning a racehorse. Given the choice of either selling his horse or leaving, he impulsively abandoned his studies.

Cultural and vocational background Rosebery travelled widely as a student. He visited Italy and Russia in 1868. In 1870 he spent three months in Italy and during the early 1870s he visited America three times. Despite not taking his degree he was considered one of the most widely read young men of his generation.

NON-PARLIAMENTARY CAREER

Other posts 1873, Lord Lieutenant of Linlithgow; 1881–1929, Member of the Council on Scottish Education; 1883, Trustee of the British Museum; 1884, Lord Lieutenant of Midlothian; 1889–90, 1892, Chairman of the London County Council; 1901, Member of the Board of the Great Northern Railway; 1901, Elder Brother of Trinity House

HONOURS

Freedom of cities 1872, Burgh of Queensberry; 1884, Dundee; 1884, Aberdeen; 1888, Wick; 1890, Glasgow; 1894, Bristol; 1897, Stirling; 1899, Bath

Academic 1878, Lord Rector of Aberdeen University; 1880, Lord Rector of Edinburgh University; 1899, Lord Rector of Glasgow University; 1911, Lord Rector of St. Andrews University;
LLD: 1879, Glasgow; 1881, Aberdeen; 1882, Edinburgh; 1888, Cambridge; DCL: 1893, Oxford; 1876, F. S.A.; 1902, Chancellor of the University of London; 1908, Chancellor of Glasgow University

Foreign 1910, Order of St. Stephen of Hungary

Other than peerage 10 Jun 1886, Fellow of the Royal Society; 21 Nov 1892, Order of the Garter; 28 Jun 1895, Order of the Thistle; 1874, Hon. Colonel 8th Battalion

HONOURS—*Continued*

Royal Scots; 1915, Captain General Royal Company of Archers

CLUBS

White's, Atheneum, Brooks's, City Liberal.

He was blackballed by the Travellers' Club.

HOBBIES AND SPORTS

Horseracing was his passion although he was not a good horseman himself. He was elected to the Jockey Club in Nov 1870. Between 1875 and 1928 he won every great race except the Ascot Gold Cup. He won the Derby three times with Ladas II in 1894, Sir Visto in 1895 and Cicero in 1905.

Rosebery was noted as one of the best shots in Britain. He also enjoyed sailing and was elected to the Royal Yacht Squadron.

Collecting books was another of his passions and Barnbougle was the repository for his collection of rare Scottish books and pamphlets, 3,000 of which were presented to the National Library of Scotland in 1927.

FINANCES

As a young man he gambled heavily. Later in life his extravagances were his hobbies of collecting books, pictures and old silver and his lifelong passion for horses. His generosity was famous but he did not seek publicity for his good works. He made numerous benefactions, among them the financing of a social centre in the East End of London that was equipped with a swimming pool.

Income In 1868, after he had succeeded to the title, probably over £30,000 p.a. His estates were some 15,568 acres in Midlothian, 5,680 acres in Linlithgow, 2,057 acres in Norfolk and the shale mines near Dalmeny.

Spouse's finances His marriage to Hannah de Rothschild brought him estates in England, including 5,473 acres in Buckinghamshire and 495 in Hertfordshire, as well as Mentmore House. At her death Hannah left £719, 876.

ANECDOTES

Rosebery was a good raconteur and wit, happiest in the company of a few close friends. His mood could change quickly. Churchill said of him that 'He could cast a chill over all and did not hesitate to freeze and snub.'

25 Jun 1886, Gladstone said of him; 'I say to the Liberal Party that they see the man of the future.'

It was said that his three declared ambitions were to marry an heiress, to own a Derby winner and to be Prime Minister of England.

Mar 1890, Jowett of Balliol wrote to Margot Tennant that he thought Rosebery 'very able, shy, sensitive, ambitious, the last two qualities rather at war with each other—very likely a future PM.'

1895, Gladstone summed up his character: 'I can say three things of him: 1) He is one of the very ablest men I have ever known; 2) He is of the highest honour and probity; 3) I do not know whether he really has common sense.'

QUOTATIONS

Rosebery said of himself as Premier, 'I never did have power.'

He once commented that the only two people who had thoroughly frightened him were Queen Victoria and Prince Bismarck.

18 Jan 1884, Does this fact of your (Australia) being a nation . . . imply separation from the Empire? God forbid! There is no need for any nation, however great, leaving the Empire, because the Empire is a Commonwealth of Nations. (Speech in Adelaide, Australia)

1899, There are two supreme pleasures in life. One is ideal, the other real. The ideal is when a man receives the seals of office from his Sovereign. The real pleasure comes when he hands them back.

RESIDENCES

2 Berkeley Square, London

The Durdans, Epsom, Surrey (Rosebery purchased the Durdans in 1872)

Dalmeny House and *Barnbougle Castle* on the Firth of Forth, Scotland

38 Berkeley Square, London

Mentmore, Buckinghamshire

Postwick Hill, near Norwich, Norfolk

10 Downing Street

Villa Delahante at Posilipo, near Naples (Rosebery purchased the Villa in 1897. In 1909 he made it over to the Foreign Office as a summer retreat for the Embassy at Rome.)

Open to the public. Mentmore is open to the public, although privately owned.

MEMORIALS

PORTRAITS

1866, by Henry Weigall, Christ Church, Oxford; 1886, by J.H. Lorimer, Eton College, Berkshire

BIBLIOGRAPHIC INFORMATION

LETTERS AND PERSONAL PAPERS

His personal papers are collected in the National Library of Scotland.

PUBLICATIONS

1862, A volume of verse, privately printed; 1891, *Pitt*, Macmillan's 'Twelve English Statesmen' series, Ed. John Morley; 1900, *Napoleon: The Last Phase*; 1906, *Lord Randolph Churchill*; 1910, *Chatham: His Early Life and Connections*.

Rosebery wrote many essays and appreciations. Most of these were gathered into two volumes, *Miscellanies*, Ed. John Buchan.

FURTHER READING

Marquess of Crewe, *Lord Rosebery*. 2 vols. London, 1931.

Raymond, E.T. *The Man of Promise—Lord Rosebery: A Critical Study*. London, 1923.

Rhodes, J.R. *Rosebery: A Biography of Archibald Philip, Fifth Earl of Rosebery*. London, 1963.

I.W.

Bettmann

Arthur James Balfour

Lived 1848–1930
Political Party Conservative
Prime Minister 12 July 1902–4 December 1905
Government Conservative
Reigning Monarch Edward VII

Virtus ad aethera tendit Virtue reaches to heaven

BALFOUR AS PRIME MINISTER

Elected MP in 1874 at the age of 26, Balfour took office in his uncle's (Lord Salisbury's) administration in 1885. From 1887–1891 he was Chief Secretary for Ireland. Salisbury then appointed him leader in the House of Commons, and Balfour became his spokesman and sounding board in the Commons. In 1902 Balfour succeeded his uncle as Prime Minister. He believed in maintaining the Empire and he was shocked by government inefficiencies revealed in the conduct of the just-concluded Boer War. He threw his considerable energies behind the problems of national defence, establishing an effective Defence Committee of the Cabinet (with himself in the chair) and supported the development of the navy. Although he opposed Home Rule for Ireland, he was instrumental in the Irish Land Purchase Act designed to help tenants purchase land. Active in foreign affairs he negotiated skillfully during the Russo-Japanese war and took a positive stance concerning emerging Anglo-American cooperation. In domestic matters he was particularly concerned with education, and he promoted the Education Act of 1902, which provided state aid for voluntary schools. During his administration a number of new universities were founded, including Manchester, Liverpool, and Sheffield, and he always supported the role of modern technology in developing industry and hence exports and trade. In December 1905, he failed to secure party unity on fiscal matters and resigned after three years in office, fruitful though they were. During the next twenty years he held many senior posts, including Foreign Secretary 1916–1919, when he made the celebrated Balfour Declaration in 1917 to 'establish in Palestine a national home for the Jews'. As Lord President in 1921 he represented Britain at the Washington Conference on Naval Limitation and joined Baldwin's Cabinet as late as 1925, adding to an unusual record of sustained post Prime Ministerial service.

PERSONAL INFORMATION

Names Arthur James Balfour
Peerages 1st Earl of Balfour, Viscount Trapain of Whittingehame, East Lothian, 5 May 1922
Nickname Bloody Balfour
Born 25 Jul 1848
Birthplace Whittingehame, East Lothian, Scotland
Religion Church of Scotland, but he was also a communicant in the Church of England
Ancestry Balfour's father was a Scottish landowner. The estate at Whittingehame had been purchased by his paternal grandfather, who had made a fortune as a contractor in India.
First entered Parliament 30 Jan 1874
Date appointed PM 12 Jul 1902
Age at appointment 53 years, 352 days
Date ceased to be PM 4 Dec 1905
Total time as PM 3 years, 145 days
Ceased to be MP 5 May 1922
Lived after last term as PM 24 years, 105 days
Date of death 19 Mar 1930
Place of death Fisher's Hill, near Woking, Surrey
Age at death 81 years, 237 days
Place of funeral and burial Whittingehame, East Lothian, Scotland
Zodiac sign Leo

FATHER

James Maitland Balfour
Date of birth 5 Jan 1820
Occupation MP Haddington 1841–47; Chairman of the North British Railway
Date of marriage 15 Aug 1843
Date of death 23 Feb 1856

MOTHER

Lady Blanche Mary Harriet Gascoyne-Cecil
Date of birth 5 Mar 1825
Profile Lady Blanche was the sister of Lord Robert Cecil, third Marquess of Salisbury (*q.v.*)
Date of marriage 15 Aug 1843
Date of death 16 May 1872
Place of burial Whittingehame, East Lothian, Scotland

BROTHERS AND SISTERS

Balfour was the eldest son and third of eight children.

Eleanor Mildred, b. 11 Mar 1845; m. 1876, Henry Sidgwick; Principal Newnham College, Cambridge, 1892–1910; d. 10 Feb 1936
Evelyn Georgiana Mary, m. 1871, John, 3rd Lord Rayleigh; d. 7 Apr 1934
Cecil Charles, b. 22 Oct 1849; shunned by the family as an inveterate gambler; forged a cheque in Balfour's name and went to Australia; d. 5 Apr 1881
Alice Blanche, b. 1850; kept house for Balfour both at Whittingehame and in London; d. 12 Jun 1936
Francis Maitland, b. 10 Nov 1851; Professor of Animal Morphology at Cambridge; d. 19 Jul 1882
Gerald William (2nd Earl of Balfour), b. 9 Apr 1853; MP Leeds, Central Division 1885–1906; Chief Secretary for Ireland 1895–1900; President of the Board of Trade 1900–05; President of the Local Government Board 1905; d. 14 Jan 1945
Eustace James Anthony, b. 8 Jun 1854; Architect and territorial soldier; d. 14 Feb 1911

MARRIAGE

Balfour was unmarried.

LIFE AND CAREER

PARLIAMENTARY ELECTIONS FOUGHT

*(*designates candidate elected)*

DATE Jan 1874. General Election
CONSTITUENCY Hertford
RESULT A.J. Balfour* (Con)

DATE Mar 1880. General Election
CONSTITUENCY Hertford
RESULT A.J. Balfour* (Con) 564; E.E. Bowen (Lib) 400

DATE 30 Jun 1885. By-election caused by Balfour's appointment as President of the Local Government Board
CONSTITUENCY Hertford
RESULT A.J. Balfour* (Con)

DATE Nov 1885. General Election
CONSTITUENCY Manchester, East
RESULT A.J. Balfour* (Con) 4,536; A. Hopkinson (Lib) 3,712

DATE Jul 1886. General Election
CONSTITUENCY Manchester, East
RESULT A.J. Balfour* (Con) 4,160; J.H. Crosfield (Lib) 3,516

DATE 11 Aug 1886. By-election caused by Balfour's appointment as Secretary for Scotland
CONSTITUENCY Manchester, East
RESULT A.J. Balfour* (Con)

DATE Jul 1892. General Election
CONSTITUENCY Manchester, East
RESULT A.J. Balfour* (Con) 5,147; Professor J.E.C. Munro (Lib) 4,749

DATE 1 Jul 1895. By-election caused by Balfour's appointment as First Lord of the Treasury.
CONSTITUENCY Manchester, East
RESULT A.J. Balfour* (Con)

DATE Jul 1895. General Election
CONSTITUENCY Manchester, East
RESULT A.J. Balfour* (Con) 5,386; Professor J.E.C. Munro (Lib) 4,610

DATE Oct 1900. General Election
CONSTITUENCY Manchester, East
RESULT A.J. Balfour* (Con) 5,803; A.H. Scott (Lib) 3,350

DATE Jan 1906. General Election
CONSTITUENCY Manchester, East
RESULT T.G. Horridge* (Lib) 6,403; A.J. Balfour (Con) 4,423

DATE 27 Feb 1906. By-election caused by the resignation of Hon. A.G.H. Gibbs.
CONSTITUENCY City of London
RESULT A.J. Balfour* (Con) 15,474; T.G. Bowles (Free Trader) 4,134

DATE Jan 1910. General Election
CONSTITUENCY City of London
RESULT A.J. Balfour* (Con) 17,907; Sir F.G. Banbury, Bt* (Con) 17,302; Sir H. Bell, Bt (Lib) 4,623

DATE Dec 1910. General Election
CONSTITUENCY City of London
RESULT A.J. Balfour* (Con); Sir F.G. Banbury, Bt* (Con)

DATE 14 Dec 1918. General Election
CONSTITUENCY City of London
RESULT A.J. Balfour* (Coalition Con); Sir F.G. Banbury, Bt* (Coalition Con)

PARTY ACTIVITY

Party Leadership Leader of the Conservative Party 1902–11
Membership of group or faction 1880, Member of the Fourth Party with Lord Randolph Churchill, John Gorst and Sir Henry Drummond Wolff.

PARLIAMENTARY AND MINISTERIAL EXPERIENCE

Maiden Speech 10 Aug 1876 on Indian silver currency. (*HC Deb* 3rd ser, vol 231, col 1033-4)
Opposition Offices Leader of the Opposition 1905-11
Privy Counsellor 24 Jun 1885 (Great Britain); 9 Mar 1887 (Ireland)
Ministerial Offices President of the Local Government Board 24 Jun 1885–Feb 1886; Secretary for Scotland 5 Aug 1886– Mar 1887; Chief Secretary for Ireland 7 Mar 1887–9 Nov 1891; First Lord of the Treasury and Leader of the House of Commons Oct 1891–Aug 1892, 29 Jun 1895–4 Dec 1905; Lord Privy Seal 12 Jul 1902–11 Oct 1903; First Lord of the Admiralty 25 May 1915–10 Dec 1916; Foreign Secretary 10 Dec 1916–23 Oct 1919; Lord President of the Council 23 Oct 1919–24 Oct 1922, 27 Apr 1925–7 Jun 1929
Opposition Leader while PM Sir Henry Campbell-Bannerman

GOVERNMENTS FORMED

Administration 12 Jul 1902–4 Dec 1905

GENERAL ELECTION RESULT
OCT 1900: Conservative 402; Liberal 183; Labour 2; Others 83. Total 670
Conservative majority 135 (excl. the Speaker)

CABINET
Prime Minister and First Lord of the Treasury A.J. Balfour
Lord Chancellor Lord Halsbury
Lord President of the Council Duke of Devonshire (1902–03); Marquess of Londonderry (1903–05)
Lord Privy Seal A.J. Balfour (1902–03); Marquess of Salisbury (1903–05)
Home Secretary A. Akers-Douglas
Foreign Secretary Marquess of Lansdowne
Secretary of State for War W.St.J. Brodrick (1902–03); H. Arnold-Foster (1903–05)
Secretary of State for the Colonies J. Chamberlain (1902–03); A. Lyttelton (1903–05)
Secretary of State for India Lord G. Hamilton (1902–03); W.St.J. Brodrick (1903–05)
Chancellor of the Exchequer C.T. Ritchie (1902–03); J.A. Chamberlain (1903–05)
First Lord of the Admiralty Earl of Selborne (1902–05); Earl Cawdor (Mar-Dec 1905)
President of the Board of Agriculture R.W. Hanbury (1902–03); Earl of Onslow (1903–05); A.E. Fellowes (Mar-Dec 1905)
President of the Board of Education Marquess of Londonderry
Chief Secretary for Ireland G. Wyndham (1902–05); W. Long (Mar–Dec 1905)
Lord Chancellor for Ireland Lord Ashbourne
President of the Local Government Board W. Long (1902–5); G. W. Balfour (Mar–Dec 1905)
Postmaster General J.A. Chamberlain (1902–03); Lord Stanley (1903–05)
Secretary for Scotland Lord Balfour of Burleigh (1902–03); A.G. Murray (1903–05); Marquess of Linlithgow (Feb-Dec 1905)
President of the Board of Trade G.W. Balfour (1902–05); 4th Marquess of Salisbury (Mar-Dec 1905)

IMPORTANT DATES IN PERSONAL AND POLITICAL LIFE

1866 Becomes a student at Trinity College, Cambridge. During the summer he had toured Italy with his sister Eleanor.
1869 Graduates from Cambridge and inherits his estate on his 21st birthday.
30 JAN 1874 Elected MP for Hertford at the General Election.
21 MAR 1875 After the death of May Lyttleton, whom he had hoped to marry, he goes on a world tour with her brother Spencer.
10 AUG 1876 Maiden speech on Indian silver currency.
1878 Introduces two Bills to reform the Burial Laws to allow Nonconformists to be buried in Anglican churchyards with their own form of service. Neither Bill is passed.
MAR 1878 Becomes his uncle's private secretary and accompanies Lord Salisbury to the Congress of Berlin.
1879 Publication of *A Defence of Philosophic Doubt.*
1880 After the General Election he becomes associated with the 'Fourth Party' led by Lord Randolph Churchill.
5 APR 1881 His brother Cecil is killed in a riding accident in Australia.
23 JUN 1885 Lord Salisbury becomes Prime Minister and appoints his nephew to the post of President of the Local Government Board.

IMPORTANT DATES IN PERSONAL AND POLITICAL LIFE—*Continued*

28 NOV 1885 Balfour elected as MP for Manchester East at the General Election. He is to sit for this constituency until 1906.

25 JUL 1886 Lord Salisbury becomes Prime Minister again and appoints Balfour to the newly created office of Secretary for Scotland.

17 NOV 1886 Becomes a member of the Cabinet.

7 MAR 1887 After the resignation of Sir Michael Hicks Beach, Balfour becomes Chief Secretary for Ireland. His appointment is greeted with some amazement, but his firmness in dealing with disorder earns him respect as well as the nickname 'Bloody Balfour'. He oversees the Criminal Law (Ireland) Amendment Act 1887 and the proclaiming of the Irish National League. More constructive measures follow, including the Irish Land Purchase Act of 1888 and the establishment of the Congested Districts Board in 1890.

OCT 1891 Balfour becomes Leader of the House of Commons and First Lord of the Treasury.

JUL 1892 Liberal victory at the General Election. Balfour leads the Opposition in the House of Commons.

JUL 1895 Leader of the House of Commons and First Lord of the Treasury again in Salisbury's third administration.

1895 Publication of *The Foundations of Belief.*

OCT 1900 'Khaki' General Election. The Conservatives return to power. Balfour is again appointed First Lord of the Treasury in Salisbury's fourth administration.

22 JAN 1901 Death of Queen Victoria.

11 JUL 1902 Salisbury resigns because of ill health and Balfour becomes PM.

18 DEC 1902 Education Act passed. Balfour had introduced the Bill in March and it was carried mainly by his efforts in the face of immense opposition. The Act provides State aid for voluntary schools and brings them under the local education authorities. The Nonconformists oppose the measure and there is especial resistance to it in Wales.

DEC 1902–MAR 1903 Creation of the Committee of Imperial Defence to improve cooperation between the armed services and to provide a consultative forum for debate on defence matters outside of party politics.

14 AUG 1903 Irish Land Act: to finance a scheme to enable tenants to buy their land in Ireland.

14 SEP 1903 Dissension in the party over tariff reform leads to the resignations of C.T. Ritchie and Lord Balfour of Burleigh from the Cabinet. Lord George Hamilton's resignation follows.

18 SEP 1903 Joseph Chamberlain resigns from the Cabinet to fight for tariff reform outside the Government.

2 OCT 1903 Duke of Devonshire resigns over the same issue.

15 AUG 1904 Licensing Act provides for a reduction in the number of public house licences to help combat the problem of alcoholism.

6 MAR 1905 George Wyndham resigns as Secretary of State for Ireland after his Under-Secretary had become involved in plans for a scheme of devolution for Ireland.

AUG 1905 Anglo-Japanese Treaty renewed. The Treaty recognizes each country's interests in China and Japan's interests in Korea.

4 DEC 1905 Balfour resigns as PM after failing to achieve party unity on fiscal policy. Campbell-Bannerman forms a Liberal Government.

JAN 1906 Loses his seat at Manchester East at the General Election.

27 FEB 1906 After the sitting MP is persuaded to retire, Balfour is returned as Member for the City of London in a by-election.

JAN 1910 General Election following the House of Lords' rejection of Lloyd George's Budget. Balfour describes the Lords' actions as 'Abundantly justified'.

6 MAY 1910 Death of King Edward VII.

JUN 1910 Constitutional Conference called between Party leaders to seek a compromise over the question of reform of the House of Lords.

DEC 1910 General Election. Minority Liberal Government formed by Asquith.

7 OCT 1911 Halsbury Club formed. It is critical of Balfour.

8 NOV 1911 Resigns as Leader of the Conservative Party and is succeeded by Andrew Bonar Law.

1914 Member of the administrative committee of the Prince of Wales Fund for the Relief of Distress.

4 AUG 1914 Britain declares war on Germany.

OCT 1914 Asquith invites Balfour to become a full member of the Committee of Imperial Defence, later the War Council.

MAY 1915 Balfour becomes First Lord of the Admiralty in the coalition government.

3 JUN 1916 Receives the Order of Merit.

7 DEC 1916 Lloyd George becomes PM and Balfour takes office as Foreign Secretary.

APR-JUN 1917 Heads a diplomatic mission to the United States. He receives a warm welcome in Washington, where he spends four weeks and addresses Congress.

2 NOV 1917 Issues the Balfour Declaration supporting a Jewish homeland in Palestine.

11 NOV 1918 End of World War I.

14 DEC 1918 First General Election since 1910. The Coalition Government is returned to office and Balfour continues as Foreign Secretary.

JAN 1919 Attends the Peace Conference in Paris.

24 OCT 1919 Balfour resigns as Foreign Secretary but retains his place in the Cabinet as Lord President of the Council.

NOV 1921 Represents Britain at the Washington conference on naval limitation.

3 MAR 1922 Made Knight of the Garter.

5 MAY 1922 Created Earl of Balfour, Viscount Trapain.

1922 During the summer Balfour takes office temporarily as Foreign Secretary while Curzon is abroad, recuperating from illness.

AUG 1922 Issues the Balfour Note, recommending a general cancellation of war debts.

MAR 1925 Joins Baldwin's Cabinet as Lord President of the Council.

OCT 1926 Chairs the Inter-Imperial Relations Committee at the Imperial Conference.

24 JUL 1928 The British Academy gives a lunch in honour of his eightieth birthday.

25 JUL 1928 Both Houses of Parliament present him with a Rolls Royce motor car.

MAY 1929 After the General Election Ramsay MacDonald becomes PM. Balfour travels to Bognor Regis to give up his seals of office as Lord President of the Council to George V.

19 MAR 1930 Dies after a long period of illness at his brother Gerald's house, Fisher's Hill, near Woking.

BACKGROUND

PHYSICAL CHARACTERISTICS AND HEALTH

In his youth Balfour was delicate and unable to enjoy the sports he pursued with such enthusiasm in later life. He had imperfect vision but only began to wear spectacles when he was a student at Cambridge. Later in life he habitually wore pince-nez glasses. He was over six feet tall and slender with long legs. He had brown eyes set wide apart, a short nose and large mouth. His private secretary for five years, Sydney Parry, described him on their first meeting in 1897: 'a long and somewhat languid figure uncoiling itself from an armchair beside the fireplace—a figure so well dressed that one noticed nothing except possibly a pair of very white spats: a gentle, rather tired voice; an extraordinarily pleasant manner.'

Throughout his life he was subject to periodic breakdowns in his health even though he was always careful to conserve his energy: he slept well, and often did not rise until late in the day. He appeared languid and weary which belied his inner strength. He suffered from sea-sickness which was a particular problem when he was Chief Secretary for Ireland and had to make frequent crossings to that country. In 1922 Balfour saw a doctor who had last examined him when he was Prime Minister and who declared that his health was now better than it had been then. However, he suffered increasingly from deafness and phlebitis. In March 1928 he suffered a mild stroke; his death in 1930 was due to circulatory failure.

EDUCATION

Primary 1859–61, Preparatory School at the Grange, Hoddesdon, Hertfordshire

Secondary 1861-66, Eton

University 1866–69, Trinity College, Cambridge. Read Moral Sciences.

Qualifications 1869, Second class Honours Degree

Cultural and vocational background 1866, toured Italy during the summer with his sister Eleanor; 1875, toured America, Australia, New Zealand and the Far East with Spencer Lyttelton.

Languages French

NON-PARLIAMENTARY CAREER

Other posts Elder Brother of Trinity House; 1894, President of the Society for Psychical Research; 1903–12, Grand Master of the Primrose League; 1904–1905, President of the British Association

HONOURS

Academic 1886, Lord Rector of St Andrew's University; 1890, Lord Rector of Glasgow University; 1891, Chancellor of Edinburgh University; 1919, Chancellor of Cambridge University; LL.D. Edinburgh, St Andrew's, Cambridge, Dublin, Glasgow, Manchester, Liverpool, Birmingham, Leeds, Sheffield, Bristol; D.C.L. Oxford and Durham; Litt. D. Cardiff

Foreign LL.D. Athens; D. Ph. Cracow; D.C.L. Columbia; 1919 Elected an 'Associé Etranger' of the Académie des Sciences Morales et Politiques.

Other than peerage Fellow of the British Academy; 12 Jan 1888, Fellow of the Royal Society; 3 Jun 1916, Order of Merit; 3 Mar 1922, Knight of the Garter

CLUBS

Carlton, Travellers', Athenaeum, White's

HOBBIES AND SPORTS

Balfour's hobbies were more than just pastimes; he had real passions for sport, music, his philosophical studies and his interest in machinery and technology. Golf and tennis, initially the old game of court tennis while he was at Cambridge and later the more familiar lawn tennis, were his favourite sports. Between 1891 and 1914 he would devote a whole month of each year to playing golf. He enjoyed music, attending concerts in the homes of his friends. His love of art led to a friendship with the artist Burne-Jones and his fascination with machinery led to a delight in cycling in the late 1890s. He read very widely in all fields, in literature and science, as well as philosophy, and bought a great number of books. He also played chess. Balfour moved in the social circles which spent the weekends at house parties in the great country houses such as Hatfield and Cliveden; his conversational skills were always much in demand on such occasions.

FINANCES

It was acknowledged that when he inherited his estate on his twenty-first birthday he was one of the richest young men in the country, worth over £1 million. In 1900 his income from investments together with his salary was £15,284 and his annual expenditure was £7, 058. However, he did not manage his financial affairs with great care and this, together with some imprudent financial speculations, led to debts in his later years.

Income In 1900 it amounted to £15,284

Debts His debts increased during old age, due partly to mismanagement of the estates of Whittingehame and partly to the Depression and unsuccessful financial speculation.

ANECDOTES

'Arthur Balfour is a young man of great ability and character, a high and the best type of an English gentleman, in my opinion, the future leader of the Tory party'. (W.E. Gladstone, 1882)

Balfour did not read newspapers. In Sep 1893 he admitted to his sister, Lady Rayleigh that he had 'not looked at a paper for weeks, never read them, knew he ought to . . . '

Sir Edward Hamilton wrote of him, 'He must be the first Prime Minister who in accordance with modern ways is called by his Christian name by the bulk of his colleagues'.

Lloyd George said 'I could work with Balfour but his underlying sense of class superiority is the trouble with him. He is kind and courteous, but makes you feel that he believes he is a member of a superior class'. (1908)

In the late 1880s and early 1890s he was a member of an aristocratic clique called the Souls. The group were interested in art, literature and philosophy and were given their name by Lord Charles Beresford who said they always seemed to be talking about their souls.

QUOTATIONS

Conservative prejudices are rooted in a great past and Liberal ones in an imaginary future.

19 May 1891, It is unfortunate, considering that enthusiasm moves the world, that so few enthusiasts can be trusted to speak the truth. (letter to Mrs. Drew)

2 Nov 1917, His Majesty's Government view with favour the establishment in Palestine of a national home for the Jewish people, and will use their best endeavours to facilitate the achievement of this object, it being clearly understood that nothing shall be done which may prejudice the civil and religious rights of existing non-Jewish communities in Palestine, or the rights and political status enjoyed by Jews in any other country. (Letter to Lord Rothschild)

RESIDENCES

Whittingehame, East Lothian, Scotland
Strathconan, Ross-shire, Scotland
4 Carlton Gardens, London
10 Downing Street

MEMORIALS

STATUES AND BUSTS

Bust by Onslow Ford, Whittingehame

PORTRAITS

c. 1870, by George Richmond, Whittingehame; 1890, by Ellis Roberts, Whittingehame; 1908, by P.A. László, Whittingehame; 1908, by J.S. Sargent, Carlton Club; 1923, by Sir William Rothenstein, Whittingehame; 1927, by Sir James Guthrie, Whittingehame; by P.A. László, Trinity College, Cambridge; by Fiddes Watt, Eton College

BIBLIOGRAPHIC INFORMATION

LETTERS AND PERSONAL PAPERS

British Library (political and philosophical papers); Whittingehame (personal and some political papers); Public Record office (small collection).

PUBLICATIONS

1878, *A Defence of Philosophic Doubt*; 1893, *Essays and Addresses*; 1895, *The Foundations of Belief*; 1920, *Essays Speculative and Political*; 1930, *Chapters of Autobiography* (Published posthumously, Ed. Blanche Dugdale)

FURTHER READING

Dugdale, B. *Arthur James Balfour, First Earl of Balfour, K.G., O.M.,F.R.S. etc.* 2 vol. London, 1939.

Egremont, M. *Balfour: A Life of Arthur James Balfour.* London, 1980.

Mackay, R.F. *Balfour: The Intellectual Statesman.* Oxford, 1985.

Young, K. *Arthur James Balfour: The Happy Life of the Politician, Prime Minister, Statesman and Philosopher, 1848–1930.* London, 1963.

I.W.

Bettmann

Sir Henry Campbell-Bannerman

Lived 1836–1908
Political Party Liberal
Prime Minister 5 December 1905–5 April 1908
Government Liberal
Reigning Monarch Edward VII

Ne obliviscaris Do not forget (Campbell) *Patriae fidelis* Faithful to my country (Bannerman)

CAMPBELL-BANNERMAN AS PRIME MINISTER

'CB' as he was universally known in later life was elected Liberal member for Stirling in 1868. He travelled widely in Europe, where he ranked as a cosmopolitan, but did not visit North America or the Empire. He did service as a middle ranking minister in the War Office but his performance in Parliament was not distinguished. He was consistent in his belief in Irish Home Rule. He became first official Prime Minister by Royal Warrant and pursued a liberal agenda, denouncing British 'barbarism' in the conduct of the Boer war. He gained self-government for Transvaal and the Orange Free State. At home he passed the Trade Disputes Bill and welcomed the first generation of Labour members. He favoured local control of education and women's suffrage and sought to improve the physical environment of the poor, especially in the growing cities. These measures were part of his broader vision of liberalism: 'men are best governed who govern themselves'. For his work on foreign policy, he drew an accolade from the Foreign Office as 'the best Prime Minister this office has ever had to deal with.' He was able to dominate the House of Commons, but age and health were against him. He suffered heart attacks in June 1907 and in April 1908, when he had to resign.

PERSONAL INFORMATION

Names Henry Campbell-Bannerman, formerly Henry Campbell (Bannerman added in 1871)
Nickname CB
Born 7 Sep 1836
Birthplace Kelvinside, near Glasgow, Scotland
Religion Church of Scotland
Ancestry Scottish
Date and place of marriage 13 Sep 1860, All Souls Church, Langham Place, London
Age at marriage 24 years, 6 days
Years married 45 years, 351 days
First entered Parliament 20 Nov 1868
Date appointed PM 5 Dec 1905
Age at appointment 69 years, 89 days
Date ceased to be PM 5 Apr 1908
Total time as PM 2 years, 122 days
Ceased to be MP 22 Apr 1908
Lived after last term as PM 17 days
Date of death 22 Apr 1908
Place of death 10 Downing Street, London
Age at death 71 years, 228 days
Last words 'This is not the end of me'
Place of burial Meigle Churchyard, Perthshire, Scotland
Place of funeral Westminster Abbey
Zodiac sign Virgo

FATHER

Sir James Campbell
Date and place of birth 3 Jun 1790, Port of Mentieth, Perthshire (registered under the name of MacOran)
Occupation Businessman and local politician. He was the leader of the Conservative Party in Glasgow and stood unsuccessfully for Parliament in 1837 and 1841. He became Lord Provost of Glasgow in 1840 and was knighted in 1841.
Date of marriage 1822
Date of death 10 Sep 1876

MOTHER

Janet Bannerman
Profile Daughter of Henry Bannerman, a Manchester merchant.

BROTHERS AND SISTERS

Campbell-Bannerman was the second son and youngest of six children
Jane, b. 1823; d. 1842
James Alexander, b. 20 Apr 1825; m. 1854, Anne Morton Peto; MP Universities of Glasgow and Aberdeen 1880–1906; Privy Counsellor 1898; d. 9 May 1908
Louisa, b. 1833; m. James A. Bannerman of Manchester; d. 1873
Helen, d. 1836
Mary, b. 1835; d. 1835

WIFE

(Sarah) Charlotte Bruce
Date of birth 1832
Mother Charlotte Forbes
Father Major-General Sir Charles Bruce, K.C.B.
Father's occupation Soldier
Age at marriage *c.* 28 years
Number of children None
Date and place of death 30 Aug 1906, Marienbad, Bohemia
Place of burial Meigle Churchyard, Perthshire, Scotland
Years older than PM *c.* 4 years
Profile Charlotte Campbell-Bannerman was a shy woman who suffered from ill-health for most of her life. She almost certainly had diabetes, a condition for which there was no treatment at that time. As a result of her illness she was overweight and this exacerbated her lack of self-confidence and dislike of London society.

Although she was not an intellectual she was an intelligent woman and a shrewd judge of character. She was heavily dependent on her husband, but her influence over him was considerable; he often referred to her as his 'higher authority' or as his 'final court of appeal'. Charlotte Campbell-Bannerman always took an interest in political affairs and CB's work; she was ambitious for him and fiercely loyal, taking hard any slight against him. When he was Financial Secretary to the Admiralty she accompanied him on his visits to the dockyards and was particularly interested in the conditions of the women workers who were mainly employed in the sail lofts.

Throughout their lives they were inseparable companions, sharing the same interests, especially a love of all things French, and the same sense of humour. They invented nicknames for CB's political colleagues so that they could talk discreetly in front of their servants.

When she became critically ill she would not be nursed by anyone except her husband. He exhausted himself by sitting up with her during the nights, although he had his duties as Prime Minister. CB was broken by her death in 1906 and he died just over a year later.

CHILDREN

None

LIFE AND CAREER

PARLIAMENTARY ELECTIONS FOUGHT

*(*designates candidate elected)*

DATE 30 Apr 1868. By-election caused by resignation of L. Oliphant
CONSTITUENCY Stirling District of Burghs
RESULT J. Ramsay* (Lib) 565; H. Campbell (Lib) 494

DATE Nov 1868. General Election
CONSTITUENCY Stirling District of Burghs
RESULT H. Campbell* (Lib) 2,201; J. Ramsay (Lib) 1,682

DATE Jan 1874. General Election
CONSTITUENCY Stirling District of Burghs
RESULT H. Campbell-Bannerman* (Lib)

DATE Mar 1880. General Election
CONSTITUENCY Stirling District of Burghs
RESULT H. Campbell-Bannerman* (Lib)

DATE Nov 1885. General Election
CONSTITUENCY Stirling District of Burghs
RESULT H. Campbell-Bannerman* (Lib)

DATE 10 Feb 1886. By-election caused by Campbell-Bannerman's appointment as Secretary of State for War

CONSTITUENCY Stirling District of Burghs
RESULT H. Campbell-Bannerman* (Lib)

DATE Jul 1886. General Election
CONSTITUENCY Stirling District of Burghs
RESULT H. Campbell-Bannerman* (Lib) 2,440; J. Pender (Liberal Unionist) 1,471

DATE Jul 1892. General Election
CONSTITUENCY Stirling District of Burghs
RESULT H. Campbell-Bannerman* (Lib) 2,791; W.T. Hughes (Liberal Unionist) 1,695

DATE 25 Aug 1892. By-election caused by Campbell-Bannerman's appointment as Secretary of State for War
CONSTITUENCY Stirling District of Burghs
RESULT H. Campbell-Bannerman* (Lib)

DATE Jul 1895. General Election
CONSTITUENCY Stirling District of Burghs
RESULT Sir H. Campbell-Bannerman* (Lib) 2,783; S.C. Macaskie (Con) 1,656

DATE Oct 1900. General Election
CONSTITUENCY Stirling District of Burghs
RESULT Sir H. Campbell-Bannerman* (Lib) 2,715; O.T. Duke (Liberal Unionist) 2,085

DATE Jan 1906. General Election
CONSTITUENCY Stirling District of Burghs
RESULT Sir H. Campbell-Bannerman* (Lib)

PARTY ACTIVITY

Party Leadership 1899–1908, Leader of the Liberal Party

PARLIAMENTARY AND MINISTERIAL EXPERIENCE

Maiden Speech 17 Jun 1869, Supported amendments to the Endowed Hospitals etc.(Scotland) Bill (*Parl Deb* 3rd ser, vol 197, col 155–7)
Opposition Offices Leader of the Opposition 1899-1905
Privy Counsellor 29 Nov 1884
Ministerial Offices Financial Secretary at the War Office 15 Nov 1871–Feb 1874, 28 Apr 1880–10 May 1882; Parliamentary and Financial Secretary to the Admiralty 10 May 1882–23 Oct 1884; Chief Secretary for Ireland 23 Oct 1884–Jun 1885; Secretary of State for War 6 Feb 1886–Jul 1886, 18 Aug 1892–Jun 1895; First Lord of the Treasury and Leader of the House of Commons 5 Dec 1905–3 Apr 1908
Opposition Leader while PM A.J. Balfour

GOVERNMENTS FORMED

Administration 5 Dec 1905–5 Apr 1908

GENERAL ELECTION RESULT
OCT 1900: Conservative 402; Liberal 183; Labour 2; Others 83. Total 670
Conservative majority 135 (excl. the Speaker)
CABINET
Prime Minister and First Lord of the Treasury Sir H. Campbell-Bannerman
Lord President of the Council Earl of Crewe
Lord Chancellor Sir R. Reid
Lord Privy Seal Marquess of Ripon
Chancellor of the Exchequer H. Asquith
Foreign Secretary Sir E. Grey
Home Secretary H. Gladstone
First Lord of the Admiralty Lord Tweedmouth
President of the Board of Agriculture and Fisheries Earl Carrington
Secretary of State for the Colonies Earl of Elgin
President of the Board of Education A. Birrell (1905–07); R. McKenna (1907–08)
Secretary of State for India J. Morley
Chief Secretary for Ireland J. Bryce (1905–07); A. Birrell (1907–08)
Chancellor of the Duchy of Lancaster Sir H. Fowler
President of the Local Government Board J. Burns
Postmaster-General S. Buxton
Secretary for Scotland J. Sinclair
President of the Board of Trade D. Lloyd George
Secretary of State for War R. Haldane
*First Commissioner of Works** L. Harcourt (1907–08)
[*Office not always in Cabinet]

IMPORTANT DATES IN PERSONAL AND POLITICAL LIFE

1858 Takes his degree at Trinity College, Cambridge; joins family firm, J. & W. Campbell, warehousemen and drapers, in Glasgow.
1860 Becomes partner in the family firm.
13 SEP 1860 Marries Charlotte Bruce in London.
30 APR 1868 Stands for Parliament for first time at by-election for the Stirling Burghs. Defeated by John Ramsay, another Liberal.
20 NOV 1868 General Election. CB returned as Member for the first time for seat he had lost earlier in the year.
1871 Death of his uncle, Henry Bannerman, who leaves him a life interest in his estate at Hunton near Maidstone, provided that he assume the name Bannerman, either alone or as an addition to his surname.
15 NOV 1871 Appointed Financial Secretary at the War Office.
JAN 1874 General Election. Conservative victory.
10 SEP 1876 Death of his father, Sir James Campbell
MAR 1880 General Election. Liberal victory. Gladstone becomes Prime Minister and CB again appointed Financial Secretary at the War Office.
10 MAY 1882 Appointed Parliamentary and Financial Secretary to the Admiralty.
23 OCT 1884 Becomes Chief Secretary for Ireland after Trevelyan resigns the post because of the breakdown of his health. CB had initially refused the post, doubting his ability to carry out the duties required and because of doubts about the policy of coercion. With Charlotte's encouragement however, he telegraphs his acceptance to Gladstone.
29 NOV 1884 Sworn as a member of the Privy Council.
MAR 1885 Introduces Bill to extend elementary education in Ireland.
8 JUN 1885 Government defeated on a vote on the Budget; Gladstone resigns as Prime Minister. Although CB has only been Chief Secretary for Ireland for a few months, his political reputation is enhanced by his performance in office.
1 FEB 1886 Gladstone named Prime Minister for the third time; CB appointed Secretary of State for War with a place in the Cabinet. CB supports Home Rule for Ireland.
JUL 1886 With the Liberal defeat in the General Election, Lord Salisbury becomes Prime Minister.
1888 CB serves as Chairman of the House of Commons Committee on naval expenditure and a member of Royal Commission on administration of the naval and military government departments.

IMPORTANT DATES IN PERSONAL AND POLITICAL LIFE—*Continued*

15 AUG 1892 Gladstone becomes PM for the fourth time after Liberal victory in General Election. CB is again appointed Secretary of State for War and member of the Cabinet Committee formed to draft the Home Rule Bill.

13 FEB 1893 Introduction of the Home Rule Bill.

2 MAR 1894 Gladstone resigns as PM following the crisis over naval estimates. CB had argued against Gladstone's demands for cuts. Lord Rosebery becomes PM.

8 APR 1895 Speaker Peel resigns. CB lets it be known that he would like the post, as his health is not good enough to permit him to consider becoming party leader. Rosebery and the Cabinet insist that he remain in the Government.

21 JUN 1895 Government defeated on a vote to reduce CB's salary as Secretary of State for War, a censure motion based on the low supply of cordite ammunition. Although CB feels obliged to resign, the Cabinet decides it cannot continue without him.

22 JUN 1895 Lord Rosebery resigns as PM.

1 JUL 1895 CB awarded GCB in recognition of his work as Secretary of State for War in reforming military administration.

8 OCT 1895 Rosebery resigns as leader of the Liberal Party.

1897 CB becomes a member of the House of Commons Select Committee appointed to inquire into the Jameson Raid in South Africa.

6 FEB 1899 A Liberal Party meeting held at the Reform Club unanimously elects CB as leader of the Liberals in the House of Commons.

OCT 1900 'Khaki' General Election. Conservative majority; Lord Salisbury continues in office as PM.

22 JAN 1901 Death of Queen Victoria.

14 JUN 1901 Speaking at a dinner given to him and Harcourt by National Reform Union, CB denounces the 'methods of barbarism' employed in the war against the Boers in South Africa by the British. Despite splits in party opinion over this issue, he continues to speak out about the situation.

9 JUL 1901 CB calls meeting of all Liberal MPs at the Reform Club, attempting to restore Party unity and confirm his own support. There is a unanimous vote of confidence in his continued leadership. He expresses no objection to free expression of opinions but refuses to tolerate any separate organisation within the Party.

19 FEB 1902 At a meeting of the National Liberal Federation in Leicester CB urges Lord Rosebery, the former Party leader, to declare a firm position. Two days later in a letter to the *Times* Rosebery states his opposition to CB's policies and declares his intention to remain outside the main Liberal Party.

27 FEB 1902 The Liberal League is formed with Rosebery, Asquith, Fowler and Grey as its main supporters.

31 MAY 1902 End of the Boer War.

4 DEC 1905 Balfour resigns as PM; the Conservative Party is divided over fiscal policy.

5 DEC 1905 CB takes office as PM. A Royal Warrant gives him the title of Prime Minister, in the first official use of that title for the office. The Prime Minister now ranks fourth in the nation, after the Archbishops of Canterbury and York and the Lord Chancellor. There are several attempts to persuade CB to lead from the House of Lords but he is determined not to take a peerage and be a figurehead Prime Minister.

JAN 1906 General Election. Electoral landslide for the Liberal Party.

13 FEB 1906 The Cabinet decide to send a committee—the Ridgeway Commission—to the Transvaal. Despite the Commission's insistence on continued British predominance in the region, CB remains determined to give the Boers self-government.

30 MAR 1906 CB supports Second Reading of W. Hudson's Bill allowing trade unions to operate freely within the law.

9 APR 1906 Introduction of the Education Bill to put all schools paid for out of rates under control of local authorities.

19 MAY 1906 CB receives deputation of suffragettes led by Emily Davies. Agitation for women's voting rights is increasing; CB is in sympathy with women's suffrage but the Liberal Party is divided on this issue.

31 JUL 1906 House of Commons votes to grant self-government to the Transvaal.

30 AUG 1906 Death of his wife Charlotte at Marienbad. Edward VII attends her funeral there. A second funeral is held later at Meigle.

19 DEC 1906 House of Lords insist on amendments to the Education Bill rejected by the Commons, and the Bill is lost.

8 MAR 1907 Women's Enfranchisement Bill. CB supports the Bill but his opponents prevent it from being enacted.

23 JUN 1907 CB suffers a heart attack.

24 JUN 1907 Despite illness, he makes an effective speech proposing that the Commons should have the power to override the Lords as a last resort.

5 APR 1908 After a period of recurrent heart attacks, CB resigns. H.H. Asquith takes over as PM.

22 APR 1908 CB dies at 10 Downing Street.

27 APR 1908 His funeral takes place in Westminster Abbey.

BACKGROUND

PHYSICAL CHARACTERISTICS AND HEALTH

T.P. O'Connor described CB as having a 'broad and somewhat short and typical Scotch face . . . stout, robust, well-knit figure . . . large eyes—light blue or grey, and open, lucid, fearless, and steady.'

CB was always very neatly dressed and was particular about his appearance. He was short-sighted but avoided wearing glasses, so that he had to close one eye to read his notes when making a speech.

His health was indifferent for many years. He was susceptible to colds, chills and influenza. In 1889 he suffered lung trouble. Exhausted after nursing his wife during the final weeks of her illness, he suffered a series of heart attacks which eventually proved fatal.

EDUCATION

Secondary 1845–47, Glasgow High School

University 1851, Glasgow University (did not take a degree); 1854–58, Trinity College, Cambridge

Prizes and awards 1853, Gold Medal for Greek at Glasgow University

Qualifications 1858, Third class degree in Classical Tripos, Cambridge University

Cultural and vocational background 1850, Campbell-Bannerman went on a grand tour of Europe lasting nearly a year with his elder brother James. They visited France, Switzerland, Italy, Sicily, Austria, Germany, Holland and Belgium.

Languages CB was fluent in French and Italian, less so in German.

NON-PARLIAMENTARY CAREER

Early occupations In 1858 Campbell-Bannerman joined the family firm in Glasgow, J and W Campbell, warehousemen and drapers. In 1860 he was made a partner.

Military service 1st Lancashire Rifle Volunteers.

Other posts Elder Brother of Trinity House, 1907.

HONOURS

Freedom of cities 1907, Glasgow; 1907, Montrose; 1907, Peebles; 1907, Edinburgh

Academic 1883, LLD, Glasgow University; 1906, DCL, Oxford University; 1907, LLD, Cambridge University

Other than peerage 1 Jul 1895, Knight of the Order of Bath

CLUBS

Athenaeum; Brooks's; Oxford and Cambridge; Reform

HOBBIES AND SPORTS

CB loved travelling in Europe; from 1872 onwards he spent two months of the year abroad. Charlotte and he would journey in leisurely fashion to spend five or six weeks at the spa of Marienbad in Bohemia. They had a passion for France and read a lot of French literature, furnished their homes with French furniture and enjoyed French food.

CB had no interest in sport. He took very little exercise and in London never walked if he could avoid it. He did walk around his estates in the country, however, and had a collection of walking sticks for this purpose. He enjoyed billiards but said of chess that it was 'not a game but a disease! When I see people with their eyes straining for long minutes together, staring at a board with every symptom of acute mental distress, I can only pity them.'

His pets included horses and French bulldogs of which he once had a kennel of about 30. He also had a Grey African parrot, bought the year he entered Parliament, which outlived him.

FINANCES

CB complained that people assumed he was wealthier than he actually was. He was never very rich but lived comfortably and maintained houses in Scotland, London and Kent. He was precise in managing his financial affairs and always kept a careful note of his personal expenditure. He also prepared the annual accounts for his estate in Kent.

Income CB drew an income from the family business in Glasgow as well from the estate in Kent.

Legacies In 1871 CB inherited Castle Belmont, Perthshire, and a life interest in his uncle's estate at Hunton near Maidstone in Kent. The property included a number of farms and a house called Gennings which CB used until 1887.

Debts During the last years of his life CB's expenses were heavy and he had to borrow £2,000 and later £700 from his brother James to make ends meet.

Will CB's heir was James Hugh Campbell, grandson of his elder brother. The property amounted to £38,000 net; a life interest in Belmont in Scotland was left to Mrs. Morton Campbell, James Campbell's mother, who had acted as his official hostess after Charlotte's death.

ANECDOTES

CB had a reputation for taking life easily; he had a regular routine which he disliked having disrupted even by affairs of state. He lived in London for the first five months of the year, then returned to Scotland in June or July to attend to his constituency business and in August travelled to Marienbad for a five or six week holiday. He returned to London at the end of October for a month before going to spend Christmas in Scotland.

In 1894 Sir William Harcourt wrote to CB, then Secretary of State for War, remonstrating about his absence from London: 'Christmas now being over . . . I really hope you will awake to the fact that there is an institution called HM's Government . . . I am extremely sorry that anyone should be put to inconvenience and most of all you. Scotland is a far cry, but then as a compensation it occupies more than half the Government, and till we get Home Rule for Scotland it is almost inevitable that Ministers should be occasionally in London.'

Sir Henry Lucy described CB thus in the 1890s: 'He does not take a prominent part in debate in the House, but in private circles he delights and adorns, he is known as a man bubbling over with natural humour.'

His secretary Arthur Ponsonby wrote of him: 'Just as one imagined he was inattentive, ready to take the line of least resistance or do nothing or yield, suddenly one came up against a rock, an obstinate determination, a perfectly clear and set conviction, which entirely upset everyone's calculations.'

After CB's death Asquith paid tribute to him in the House of Commons: 'In politics I think he may fairly be described as an idealist in aim and an optimist by temperament. Great causes appealed to him. He was not ashamed, even on the verge of old age, to see visions and to dream dreams . . . He never put himself forward, yet no one had greater tenacity of purpose. He was the least cynical of mankind, but no one had a keener eye for the humours and ironies of the political situation.' (1908)

QUOTATIONS

14 Jun 1901, When is a war not a war? When it is carried on by methods of barbarism in South Africa. (At a dinner given by the National Reform Union.)

23 Jul 1906, La duma est morte: vive la duma! (On learning that the Czar had dissolved the newly instituted Russian Parliament, the Duma.)

3 Apr 1908, After signing his letter of resignation to Edward VII, CB said to his private secretary: 'There's the last kick. My dear fellow, I don't mind. I've been Prime Minister for longer than I deserve.'

RESIDENCES

6 Claremont Gardens, Glasgow
60 Queen's Gate, London
117 Eaton Square, London
6 Grosvenor Place, London
**Gennings*, Kent
Castle Belmont, near Meigle, Perthshire
29 Belgrave Square, London
10 Downing Street, which he described as a 'rotten old barrack of a house'.

*In 1871 CB was left a life interest in the property of Hunton near Maidstone by his uncle Henry Bannerman. His uncle's widow remained there until her death in 1873. CB settled at *Gennings*, another house on the estate and spent several weeks there each year until 1887 when he sold the property.

MEMORIALS

STATUES AND BUSTS

By Paul Montford, Stirling, Scotland;a bust by Paul Montford, Westminster Abbey,

PORTRAITS

By Sir James Guthrie, Scottish National Portrait Gallery; by Brenda Morgan, National Liberal Club.

BIBLIOGRAPHIC INFORMATION

LETTERS AND PERSONAL PAPERS

Campbell-Bannerman's political and personal papers are in the British Library.

Early Letters of Sir Henry Campbell-Bannerman to his Sister Louisa, 1850–1. Ed. Lord Pentland. London, 1925.

FURTHER READING

Spender, J. A. *The Life of the Right Hon. Sir Henry Campbell- Bannerman, G.C.B.* 2 vols. London, 1923.
Wilson, J. *CB: A Life of Sir Henry Campbell-Bannerman.* London, 1973.

I.W.

Bettmann

H.H. Asquith

Lived 1852–1928
Political Party Liberal
Prime Minister 5 April 1908–5 December 1916
Governments Liberal, 5 April 1908–25 May 1915; Coalition 25 May 1915– 5 December 1916
Reigning Monarchs Edward VII; George V

Sine macula macla A mascle without a stain

ASQUITH AS PRIME MINISTER

During his first twenty-two years in Parliament Asquith was Home Secretary under Gladstone and, much later, Chancellor of the Exchequer under Campbell-Bannerman. His appointment as Liberal Prime Minister in 1908 meant the post was held for the first time by a member of the professional middle class. Asquith had a strong character with an excellent mind and north country determination. His first six and a half years of peace-time Premiership were mostly successful. He supported laying the foundation of the welfare state, believing that the state could be an instrument for positive development. He oversaw the Parliament Act of 1911, modifying the powers of the House of Lords after their Lordships had rejected the Budget of 1909, the 'People's Budget'. He absorbed the political changes caused by the rise of the Labour Party, becoming, therefore, a link between the nineteenth and twentieth centuries. With the outbreak of the 1914–1918 war his touch gradually became less sure. In May 1915 he formed a Coalition Cabinet to prosecute the war more effectively, in which Lloyd George was a very successful Minister of Munitions. With this able Cabinet, Asquith's indecisiveness became more apparent; he was more of a referee than an inspiring war leader. In 1916 Lloyd-George proposed a small War Council to improve efficiency. An alliance of Lloyd George and

Bonar Law outmanoeuvred Asquith when he insisted on chairing the Council. Following a hostile press campaign, Asquith resigned and the more dynamic Lloyd George became Prime Minister. Subsequently Asquith, as chairman of part of the Liberal Party, played an important role in supporting Ramsay MacDonald's first Labour Government in 1924.

PERSONAL INFORMATION

Names Herbert Henry Asquith (Known as Herbert until his second marriage, after which the few people who used his Christian name preferred Henry)
Peerages 1st Earl of Oxford and Asquith, 9 Feb 1925
Nicknames Old Boy; Pip-Emma; The Sledgehammer
Born 12 Sep 1852
Birthplace Croft House, Morley, Lancashire
Religion Nonconformist
Ancestry English. His father was a cloth manufacturer, spinning and weaving wool; his mother the daughter of a wool stapler from Huddersfield.
Dates and places of marriages 1) 23 Aug 1877, Didsbury Parish Church, Manchester; 2) 10 May 1894, St. George's Church, Hanover Square, London
Age at marriages 1) 24 years, 345 days; 2) 41 years, 232 days
Years married 1) 14 years, 31 days; 2) 33 years, 279 days
First entered Parliament 9 Jul 1886
Date appointed PM 5 Apr 1908
Age at appointment 55 years, 198 days
Date ceased to be PM 5 Dec 1916
Total time as PM 1) 7 years, 50 days; 2) 1 year, 194 days; a total of 8 years, 244 days
Ceased to be MP 9 Oct 1924
Lived after last term as PM 11 years, 72 days
Date of death 15 Feb 1928
Place of death The Wharf, Sutton Courtney, Berkshire
Age at death 75 years, 163 days
Place of funeral and burial Sutton Courtney Parish Church, Berkshire (now Oxfordshire); memorial service at Westminster Abbey.
Zodiac sign Virgo

FATHER

Joseph Dixon Asquith
Date and place of birth 10 Feb 1825, Morley, Yorkshire
Occupation Woollen cloth manufacturer
Date and place of marriage 18 Sep 1850, Cramsden Street Chapel, Huddersfield
Date of death 16 Jun 1860

MOTHER

Emily Willans
Date and place of birth 4 May 1828, Huddersfield, Lancashire
Profile Although a chronic invalid, who suffered from asthma and bronchitis, she was a cultivated woman with a biting turn of phrase and humour, well able to express herself in both speech and writing. She had a strong bent for foreign languages.
Date of marriage 18 Sep 1850
Date of death 12 Dec 1888

BROTHERS AND SISTERS

Asquith was the second son of five children.
William Willans, b. 23 Jun 1853; unm.; his growth was stunted due to a sporting injury at the age of 16; went to Oxford after Asquith; a schoolmaster at Clifton; d. 7 Nov 1918
(Emily) Evelyn, b. 20 May 1855; m. 1878 Reverend W. Wooding; d. 16 Dec 1937
Edith Margaret, b. 25 May 1859; d. 12 Jun 1859
Lilian Josephine, b. 6 May 1860; d. 31 Mar 1865

FIRST WIFE

Helen Kelsall Melland
Date and place of birth 30 Oct 1854, Deeplish Hill, Castleton, Lancashire
Mother Anne Heap Kelsall
Father Frederick Melland
Father's occupation Doctor
Age at marriage 23 years, 44 days
Number of children 5
Date and place of death 11 Sep 1891; Lamlash, Isle of Man
Place of burial Lamlash, Isle of Man
Years younger than PM 2 years, 31 days
Profile She was an unworldly and unambitious woman; calm and quietly assured with a strong, clear mind. Haldane said, 'Hers was a beautiful and simple spirit'. Asquith referred to her as 'Always perfect, loyal, sympathetic, devoted; not without pride in such successes as I had, but not the least anxious for me to "get on", never sanguine or confident, and as a rule inclined to take a less hopeful view of things. . . . She was the gentlest and best of companions'.

SECOND WIFE

Emma Alice Margaret (Margot) Tennant
Date of birth 2 Feb 1864
Mother Margaret Edith Abraham
Father Sir Charles Tennant
Father's occupation A wealthy Liberal baronet, one of the most prominent figures in the chemical industry; MP Glasgow 1879–80, Selkirk and Peebles 1880–86
Age at marriage 30 years, 105 days
Number of children 2
Date and place of death 28 Jul 1945, London
Place of burial Sutton Courtney Parish churchyard, Berkshire (now Oxfordshire)
Years younger than PM 12 years, 154 days
Profile She was educated by governesses and tutors at home until the age of 15 when, after a short period at finishing school in London, she went to study in Dresden. She was a leader of fashion, an extrovert socialite and successful hostess who entertained writers and painters as well as politicians. Though witty, she often sounded rude and haughty and tended to be indiscreet. She had an extravagant lifestyle ('I hope to leave nothing but debts'.) and was exhausting and uninhibited, spontaneous and stimulating. She transformed Asquith's life, bringing him into the centre of a more glittering social world.

On her marriage she coped admirably with Asquith's ready-made family of five children. Margot suffered some years of ill health following the birth of her first baby in May 1895; the baby died, and she was prostrate for three months. All her pregnancies were difficult and she lost two other children at birth in 1899 and 1907. She was plagued by sleeplessness and her ill health continued for so long that 'in the year 1908, when my husband became Prime Minister, I went to St. Paul's Cathedral and prayed that I might die rather than hamper his life as an invalid'. However, she continued her social life, and later recovered her health.

CHILDREN

5 sons, 2 daughters
By his first wife, Helen:
Raymond, b. 6 Nov 1878; m. 25 Jul 1907, Katherine Horner; barrister; Jan 1913 adopted as Liberal candidate for Derby; Dec 1914 enlisted into Queen's Westminster Rifles; d. 15 Sep 1916
Herbert, b. 11 Mar 1881; m. 28 Jul 1910, Lady Cynthia Charteris; barrister, poet and author; president of Oxford Union Society 1901; served in First World War, 1915–18; d. 5 Aug 1947
Arthur Melland, b. 24 Apr 1883; m. 30 Apr 1918, Hon. Betty Manners; Brigadier General, Royal Naval Division, 1914; d. 25 Aug 1939
(Helen) Violet, (Baroness Asquith of Yarnbury), b. 15 Apr 1887; m. 30 Nov 1915, Sir Maurice Bonham-Carter; created life peeress, Baroness Asquith of Yarnbury, 1964; politically knowledgeable and an accomplished public speaker; a governor of the BBC, 1941–66; President of the Liberal Party, 1947–65; President of the Royal Institute of International Affairs, 1964–69; d. 19 Feb 1969
Cyril, b. 5 Feb 1890; m. 12 Feb 1918, Anne Pollock; judge, Lord Chief Justice of Appeal in Ordinary; d. 24 Aug 1954
By his second wife, Margot:
Elizabeth Charlotte Lucy, b. 26 Feb 1897; m. 30 Apr 1919, Prince Antoine Bibesco; author of short stories, plays, novels and poetry; d. 7 Apr 1945
Anthony, b. 9 Nov 1902; unm.; film director; d. 20 Feb 1968

LIFE AND CAREER

PARLIAMENTARY ELECTIONS FOUGHT

*(*designates candidate elected)*

DATE Jul 1886. General Election
CONSTITUENCY Fife, Eastern
RESULT H.H. Asquith* (Lib) 2,863; J.B. Kinnear (Con) 2,489.

DATE Jul 1892. General Election
CONSTITUENCY Fife, Eastern
RESULT H. H. Asquith* (Lib) 3,743; J. Gilmour, Snr. (Con) 3,449.

DATE Jul 1895. General Election
CONSTITUENCY Fife, Eastern
RESULT H.H. Asquith* (Lib) 4,332; J. Gilmour, Snr. (Con) 3,616.

DATE Oct 1900. General Election
CONSTITUENCY Fife, Eastern
RESULT H.H. Asquith* (Lib) 4,141; A.H.B. Constable (Con) 2,710

DATE Jan 1906. General Election
CONSTITUENCY Fife, Eastern
RESULT H.H. Asquith* (Lib) 4,723; J. Gilmour, Jr. (Con) 3,279

DATE Jan 1910. General Election
CONSTITUENCY Fife, Eastern
RESULT H.H. Asquith* (Lib) 5,242; A. Sprot (Con) 3,183

DATE Dec 1910. General Election
CONSTITUENCY Fife, Eastern
RESULT H.H. Asquith* (Lib) 5,149; A. Sprot (Con) 3,350

DATE Dec 1918. General Election
CONSTITUENCY Fife, Eastern
RESULT A. Sprot* (Con) 8,996; H.H. Asquith (Lib) 6,994; W. P. Morgan (Ind/Prog) 591

DATE 12 Feb 1920. By-election caused by death of Sir J. M. McCallum
CONSTITUENCY Paisley
RESULT H.H. Asquith* (Lib) 14,736; J.M. Biggar (Lab/Co-op) 11,902; J.A.D. McKean (Con) 3,795

DATE 15 Nov 1922. General Election
CONSTITUENCY Paisley
RESULT H.H. Asquith* (Lib) 15,005; J.M. Biggar (Lab/Co-op) 14,689

DATE 6 Dec 1923. General Election
CONSTITUENCY Paisley
RESULT H.H. Asquith* (Lib) 9,723; J.M. Biggar (Lab/Co-op) 7,977; A.D.M. Shaw (Con) 7,758; D.D. Cormack (Ind Lab) 3,685

DATE 29 Oct 1924. General Election
CONSTITUENCY Paisley
RESULT E.R. Mitchell* (Lab) 17,057; H.H. Asquith (Lib) 14,829

PARTY ACTIVITY

Party Leadership Leader of the Liberal Party, 5 Apr 1908–15 Oct 1926
Membership of group or faction 1888–The Articles Club; 1885–1902, Imperial Federation League; 1902–28, Liberal League (formerly Imperial Federation League)

PARLIAMENTARY AND MINISTERIAL EXPERIENCE

Maiden Speech 24 Mar 1887. During debate on a motion to give precedence over all other business to the Irish Crimes Bill (*HC Deb* vol 312, col 1393–1400)
Opposition Offices Leader of the Opposition, 1916–18, 1920–22
Privy Counsellor 18 Aug 1892; 17 May 1916 (Ireland)
Ministerial Offices Home Secretary, 18 Aug 1892–29 Jun 1895; Chancellor of the Exchequer, 10 Dec 1905–4 Apr 1908; Secretary of State for War, 30 Mar–4 Aug 1914; First Lord of the Treasury and Leader of the House of Commons 5 Apr 1908–5 Dec 1916
Opposition Leaders while PM 1) A.J. Balfour (Con) 1902–11; A. Bonar Law, (Con) 1911–15; A. Henderson (Lab) 1908–10, 1914–15; G. Barnes (Lab) 1910; R. MacDonald, 1911–14. 2) A. Bonar Law (Con); A. Henderson (Lab).

GOVERNMENTS FORMED

First Administration 5 Apr 1908–9 Feb 1910

GENERAL ELECTION RESULT

JAN 1906: Liberal 399; Conservative 156; Irish Nationalist 82; Labour 29; Others 4. Total 670
Liberal majority 129 (excl. the Speaker)

CABINET

Prime Minister and First Lord of the Treasury H. H. Asquith
Lord President of the Council Lord Tweedmouth (Apr–Oct 1908); Viscount Wolverhampton (Oct 1908–10)
Lord Chancellor Lord Loreburn
Chancellor of the Exchequer D. Lloyd George
Home Secretary H. J. Gladstone
Foreign Secretary Sir E. Grey
Secretary of State for the Colonies Earl of Crewe
Secretary of State for War R. B. Haldane
Secretary of State for India Lord Morley
First Lord of the Admiralty R. McKenna
Chief Secretary for Ireland A. Birrell
Lord Privy Seal Marquess of Ripon, (Apr–Oct 1908); Earl of Crewe, (Oct 1908–1910)
President of the Board of Education W. Runciman
President of the Board of Trade W. S. Churchill
President of the Local Government Board J. Burns
President of the Board of Agriculture Earl Carrington
Postmaster-General S. Buxton
Chancellor of the Duchy of Lancaster Viscount Wolverhampton (Apr–Oct 1908); Lord Fitzmaurice (Oct 1908–Jun 1909); H. Samuel (Jun 1909–10)
Secretary for Scotland J. Sinclair
First Commissioner of Works L. Harcourt

Second Administration 9 Feb–19 Dec 1910

GENERAL ELECTION RESULT

JAN 1910: Liberal 274; Conservative 272; Irish Nationalist 82; Labour 40; Others 2. Total 670
No overall majority

CABINET

Prime Minister and First Lord of the Treasury H. H. Asquith
Lord President of the Council Viscount Wolverhampton, (Feb–Jun 1910); Earl Beauchamp (Jun–Nov 1910)
Lord Chancellor Lord Loreburn
Chancellor of the Exchequer D. Lloyd George
Home Secretary W. S. Churchill
Foreign Secretary Sir E. Grey
Secretary of State for the Colonies Earl of Crewe
Secretary of State for War R. B. Haldane
Secretary of State for India Viscount Morley
First Lord of the Admiralty R. McKenna
Chief Secretary for Ireland A. Birrell
Lord Privy Seal Earl of Crewe
President of the Board of Education W. Runciman (Feb 1910–Oct 1911); J. Pease (Oct–Nov 1911)
President of the Board of Trade S. Buxton
President of the Local Government Board J. Burns
President of the Board of Agriculture Earl Carrington
Postmaster-General H. Samuel
Chancellor of the Duchy of Lancaster J. Pease
Secretary for Scotland Lord Pentland (previously J. Sinclair)
First Commissioner of Works L. Harcourt

Third Administration 19 Jan 1910–25 May 1915

GENERAL ELECTION RESULT

DEC 1910: Liberal 272; Conservative 271; Irish Nationalist 84; Labour 42; Others 1. Total 670
No overall majority

CABINET

Prime Minister and First Lord of the Treasury H. H. Asquith
Lord President of the Council Viscount Morley of Blackburn, (Dec 1910–Aug 1914); Earl of Beauchamp (Aug 1914–May 1915)
Lord Chancellor Lord Loreburn (Dec 1910–Jun 1912) Viscount Haldane (Jun 1912–May 1915)
Chancellor of the Exchequer D. Lloyd George
Home Secretary W. S. Churchill (Dec 1910–Oct 1911) R. McKenna (Oct 1911–May 1915)
Foreign Secretary Sir E. Grey
Secretary of State for the Colonies L. Harcourt
Secretary of State for War R. B. Haldane (Dec 1910–Jun Jun 1912); J. Seely (Jun 1912–Mar 1914); H. H. Asquith (Mar–May 1914)
Secretary of State for India Earl of Crewe (Dec 1910–Mar 1911); Viscount Morley, (Mar–May 1911; May 1911–15)
First Lord of the Admiralty R. McKenna, (Dec 1910–Oct 1911); W. S. Churchill (Oct 1911–May 1915)
Chief Secretary for Ireland A. Birrell
Lord Privy Seal Earl of Crewe (Dec 1910–Oct 1911); Earl of Carrington (Oct 1911–Feb 1912); Marquess of Crewe (Feb 1912–May 1915)
President of the Board of Education W. Runciman (Dec 1910–Oct 1911); J. Pease (Oct 1911–May 1915)
President of the Board of Trade S. Buxton (Dec 1910–Feb 1914); J. Burns (Feb–Aug 1914); W. Runciman (Aug 1914–May 1915)
President of the Local Government Board J. Burns (Dec 1910–Feb 1914); H. Samuel (Feb 1914–May 1915)
President of the Board of Agriculture Earl Carrington, (Dec 1910–Oct 1911); W. Runciman (Oct 1911–Aug 1914); Lord Lucas (Aug 1914–May 1915)
Postmaster General H. Samuel (Dec 1910–Feb 1914); C. Hobhouse (Feb 1914–May 1915)
Chancellor of the Duchy of Lancaster J. Pease (Dec 1910–Oct 1911); C. Hobhouse (Oct 1911–Feb 1914); C. Masterman (Feb 1914–Feb 1915); E. Montague (Feb–May 1915)
Secretary for Scotland Lord Pentland, (Dec 1910–Feb 1912); T. McKinnon-Wood (Feb 1912–May 1915)
First Commissioner of Works Earl Beauchamp, (Jan 1910–Aug 1914); Lord Emmott (Aug 1914–May 1915)

Fourth Administration 25 May 1915–5 Dec 1916

COALITION GOVERNMENT

CABINET

Prime Minister and First Lord of the Treasury H. H. Asquith (Lib)
Minister without Portfolio Marquess of Landsdowne (Con)
Lord President of the Council Marquess of Crewe (Lib)
Lord Chancellor Baron Buckmaster (Lib)
Lord Privy Seal Earl Curzon (Con)
Chancellor of the Exchequer R. McKenna (Lib)
Minister of Munitions D. Lloyd George (Lib), (May 1915–Jul 1916); E. Montagu (Lib), (Jul–Dec 1916)
Home Secretary Sir J. A. Simon (Lib), (May 1915–Jan 1916); Sir H. Samuel (Lib), (Jan–Dec 1916)
Foreign Secretary Sir E. Grey (Lib)

Secretary of State for War Earl Kitchener, (May 1915–Jul 1916); D. Lloyd George (Lib), (Jul–Dec 1916)
Secretary of State for the Colonies A. Bonar Law (Con)
Secretary of State for India A. Chamberlain (Con)
First Lord of the Admiralty A. J. Balfour (Con)
Chief Secretary for Ireland A. Birrell (Lib), (May 1915–May 1916); H. Duke (Con) (Jul–Dec 1916) [Office vacant May 1916–Jul 1916]
President of the Board of Education A. Henderson (Lab), (May 1915–Aug 1916); Marquess of Crewe (Lib), (Aug–Dec 1916)
President of the Board of Agriculture Earl Selborne (Con), (May 1915–Jul 1916); Earl Crawford (Con), (Jul–Dec 1916)
President of the Local Government Board W. Long (Con)
President of the Board of Trade W. Runciman (Lib)
Chancellor of the Duchy of Lancaster W. S. Churchill (Lib), (May–Nov 1915); H. Samuel (Lib), (Nov 1915–Jan 1916); E. Montagu (Lib), (Jan–Jul 1916); T. McKinnon-Wood (Lib), (Jul–Dec 1916)
Secretary for Scotland T. McKinnon-Wood (Lib), (May–Jul 1916); H. Tennant (Lib), (Jul–Dec 1916)
First Commissioner of Works L. Harcourt (Lib)
Attorney General Sir E. Carson (Con), (May–Nov 1915); Sir F. Smith (Con), (Nov 1915–Dec 1916)

IMPORTANT DATES IN PERSONAL AND POLITICAL LIFE

16 JUN 1860 Asquith's father dies.

JAN 1864 Asquith and his brother go to live in London with their uncle, who returns to the north within a year, leaving the boys attending the City of London School and living as paying guests with a family in Pimlico.

1869 Asquith wins classical scholarship at Balliol College, Oxford.

SPRING, 1874 Awarded First Class degree in Greats at Balliol and elected to one of only two prize fellowships at the college in the autumn.

JUN 1876 Called to the Bar at Lincoln's Inn.

23 AUG 1877 Marries Helen Melland, daughter of a Manchester doctor.

1883 Prepares Memorandum on the law and history of the Parliamentary Oath for the Attorney General, which makes him better known.

9 JUL 1886 Elected Member of Parliament for East Fife, at General Election.

24 MAR 1887 His maiden speech during debate on the Irish Crimes Bill makes a profound impression, establishing Asquith as having leadership qualities.

FEB 1889 Acts as junior counsel to Sir Charles Russell before Parnell Commission.

5 FEB 1890 Appointed Queen's Counsel. Asquith's political and professional life begins to blossom.

1 SEP 1891 Wife dies of typhoid while on family holiday on Isle of Man.

JUL–AUG 1892 Conservative Government is defeated in the General Election and Gladstone returned as Liberal Prime Minister.

18 AUG 1892 Asquith appointed Home Secretary, his first ministerial post, and so becomes a Privy Counsellor.

5 MAR 1894 Gladstone resigns and Lord Rosebery becomes Prime Minister.

10 MAY 1894 Second marriage—to Margot Tennant; the wedding is a great social event, attended by most of the Cabinet.

JUL–AUG 1895 Liberals lose General Election and Asquith returns to his practice at the Bar. Lord Salisbury becomes Prime Minister of a minority Conservative Government.

11 OCT 1899 Boer War begins. Disagreements between Asquith and Campbell-Bannerman over policy concerning the war lead to a split in the delicate unity of the Liberal Party.

22 JAN 1901 Queen Victoria dies.

31 MAY 1902 Boer War ends with Treaty of Vereeniging.

12 JUL 1902 Lord Salisbury resigns as Prime Minister, succeeded by Arthur Balfour.

1–7 SEP 1905 The Relugas Compact. Asquith, Haldane and Grey meet at Relugas in Scotland while on holiday and agree that unless Campbell-Bannerman stands down as Leader of the Liberal Party to make way for Asquith, all three will refuse to serve under him.

5 DEC 1905 Campbell-Bannerman appointed Prime Minister, leading a Liberal Government, after the resignation of Balfour.

10 DEC 1905 Asquith becomes Chancellor of the Exchequer.

JAN–FEB 1906 Liberal landslide at the General Election, in which they win 377 seats.

18 APR 1907 Asquith presents his second Budget, which differentiates between earned and unearned income for tax purposes, paving the way for old age pensions the following year.

5 APR 1908 The King, who is staying in Biarritz, France, accepts Campbell-Bannerman's resignation due to ill health. Instead of returning to London, however, the King summons Asquith to Biarritz to invite him to form a ministry.

8 APR 1908 Asquith's acceptance of office is announced. He returns to England two days later.

30 APR 1908 First speech as Premier, at Reform Club, during which Asquith defines his political faith.

7 MAY 1908 Asquith's third Budget sees old age pensions safely established.

29 APR 1909 Lloyd George's 'People's Budget'.

JAN 1910 Rejection of 'People's Budget' by the House of Lords causes a major constitutional crisis and leads to the calling of a General Election.

14 APR 1910 Parliament Bill to curb the powers of the House of Lords introduced.

28 APR 1910 The 1909 Budget is passed by the House of Lords.

6 MAY 1910 Death of King Edward VII, succeeded by George V.

7 JUN 1910 Asquith summons a Constitutional Conference of party leaders, but they are unable to reach agreement.

25 NOV 1910 A resolution defining the powers of the House of Lords subsequently forms the basis of the Parliament Act of 1911.

28 NOV 1910 Parliament is dissolved and a General Election called.

11 APR 1912 Asquith introduces third Irish Home Rule Bill.

11 NOV 1912 Government defeated on an amendment to Financial Resolution of Government of Ireland Bill.

8 APR 1914 Asquith appointed Secretary of State for War.

7 JUL 1914 Government wins guillotine on Budget with 22 Liberal abstentions, leading to abandonment of Revenue Bill.

4 AUG 1914 First World War breaks out.

18 SEP 1914 Irish Home Rule Bill receives Royal Assent but is suspended until the end of the war.

NOV 1914 Asquith sets up War Council within the Cabinet for the conduct of the war.

IMPORTANT DATES IN PERSONAL AND POLITICAL LIFE—*Continued*

12 MAY 1915 Venetia Stanley, with whom Asquith has an intense friendship and to whom he has written almost daily for a period of years, tells him she is to marry Edwin Montagu, a member of the Cabinet.

17 MAY 1915 Asquith agrees to the formation of a Coalition Government together with the Conservatives; Coalition forms 25 May.

11 NOV 1915 Asquith forms new small war council to include himself, Balfour, Lloyd George, Bonar Law and McKenna, but excluding Kitchener.

20 APR 1916 Dublin Easter Rebellion; Sir Roger Casement is taken prisoner.

2 MAY 1916 Introduces Conscription Bill.

19 JUL 1916 Asquith tells Cabinet of his decision that Casement should be hanged.

15 SEP 1916 Asquith's son Raymond killed in the Battle of the Somme.

DEC 1916 Lloyd George campaigns for the direction of the war to be taken out of the hands of the Government and entrusted to a War Council of four, with himself as chairman, and Asquith, as Prime Minister, exercising little real control. The Unionists, under Sir Edward Carson, transfer their allegiance to Lloyd George and this, together with confusion and misunderstanding between Asquith and his Liberal colleagues, compounded by Bonar Law, leads to Asquith's resignation.

5 DEC 1916 Asquith sends his resignation to the King.

7 DEC 1916 Lloyd George becomes Prime Minister.

MAY 1917 Asquith refuses post of Lord Chancellor under Lloyd George, as he feels he cannot serve in a Lloyd George government, and thinks it right to preserve his independence for the sake of the Liberal Party.

28 DEC 1918 Loses his seat in so-called 'Coupon Election' but remains Leader of the Liberal Party.

12 FEB 1920 Elected as Member of Parliament for Paisley at by-election.

SPRING, 1920 Forced to move out of Cavendish Square by fall in income.

1 MAR 1920 Takes his seat in House of Commons to a 'Most feeble reception'.

19 OCT 1922 Lloyd George resigns, the coalition comes to an end and Conservative Andrew Bonar Law becomes Prime Minister on 23 Oct.

NOV 1922 The two Liberal factions fight the General Election separately.

1923 Asquith publishes his first book, *The Genesis of War*, to stave off financial problems.

23 JAN 1924 First Labour Government comes to power with Ramsay MacDonald as Prime Minister, needing Liberal votes to keep him in office.

29 OCT 1924 General Election timed to defeat the Liberals; Asquith loses his seat.

20 JAN 1925 Asquith accepts a peerage.

15 OCT 1925 Resigns leadership of Liberal Party.

22 MAR 1927 Last speech in Parliament—during House of Lords debate on the need for national economy.

30 JUL 1927 *The Times* launches a fund to help the now-impoverished Asquith.

15 FEB 1928 Asquith dies, having been incapacitated by his third stroke in Jan 1928.

BACKGROUND

PHYSICAL CHARACTERISTICS AND HEALTH

Asquith was of rather stocky build, but he was not particularly heavy and had clean-cut features. When young his hair was fair and neat. He was indifferent to clothes—his second wife Margot referred to his being 'unfashionably dressed' on their first meeting. For a brief period after their marriage his clothes were smarter, but he soon abandoned any attempt at elegance. By 1902 his hair had turned grey, his face had become full-cheeked and heavy-jowled and he had put on much more weight. He assumed a look of dignified, benevolent slovenliness, which is how he was best remembered.

He enjoyed robust health and was rarely unwell. Apart from a fortnight's illness in Oct 1915 he suffered no ill health during his term as Prime Minister. He was not ill enough to be confined to bed again until 1922, and then only for 3 days. However, in Jun 1926 he suffered a stroke, followed by a second early in 1927. He recovered and continued to be fairly active, although he played no more golf. Towards the end of the year his health deteriorated quickly and a third stroke followed in January 1928. As a result he became an invalid and was at times confused, though at other times his mind was perfectly clear and he received visitors with pleasure.

EDUCATION

Primary 1860–61, Huddersfield College; 1861–63, Moravian School, Fulneck, Leeds, Yorkshire

Secondary 1864–70, City of London School

University and professional 1870–74, Balliol College, Oxford; 1875–76, read law as student in chambers of Charles Bowen in the Temple

Prizes and awards 1869, awarded The Craven Classical Scholarship at Balliol; 1874, elected Fellow of Balliol

Qualifications 1874, First Class degree in Greats

Cultural and vocational background Asquith was an outstanding classical scholar with little interest in mathematics and the sciences. He was very widely read and had an excellent intellect which enabled him to deal with official business with extraordinary speed and skill.

Languages Latin and Greek

NON-PARLIAMENTARY CAREER

Early occupations Barrister from 1876, he also lectured and wrote articles for *The Spectator* and *The Economist*. He became a Queen's Counsel in February 1890.

HONOURS

Freedom of cities 1925, Leeds, London; 1927, York

Academic 1904, DCL Oxford; 1905, Rector of Glasgow University; 1907, LL.D Edinburgh and Glasgow Universities; 1908, Hon. Fellow, Oxford; 1908, Rector of Aberdeen University; 1909, LL.D Leeds University; 1911, LL.D St. Andrews University; 1912, LL.D Bristol University; 1913, DCL Durham University; 1921, LL.D McGill University.

Other than peerage 5 Nov 1908, Fellow of the Royal Society; 20 Dec 1919, awarded 3 medals by the King for services as Prime Minister during the war: 1914 War Star; 1914–1918 War Medal; 1918 Victory Medal; 1 Jun 1925, Order of the Garter

CLUBS

Reform; Athenaeum

HOBBIES AND SPORTS

He enjoyed a wide and varied social life, and often played golf, bridge and chess and read widely. He was a great letter writer, able with no effort to write a quick 500-word comment on his recent doings during a spare half-hour between important meetings or even during one of them. After 1918 he developed a strong interest in contemporary painting and sculpture, and often went to new plays, films and musicals of any note.

FINANCES

Throughout most of his career Asquith remained dependent on his professional earnings as a barrister; in the early years these were not great. His second marriage brought him extra income, but his wife was extravagant and he himself enjoyed a free-spending lifestyle even when he did not have the money to support it. When the Liberals lost the election in 1895 he returned to his work as a barrister. When he ceased to be Prime Minister his income fell and in 1920 he had to move out of Cavendish Square to the cheaper Bedford Square. At this time he began to write articles and in the following years published several books to boost his income. In 1927 his financial position was so bad that *The Times* launched a public fund on his behalf.

Income 1892-5 His post as a Minister yielded £5,000 p.a. His second marriage in 1894 brought him another £5, 000. Between 1895 and 1905 his income fluctuated between £5,000 and £10,000 p.a. No salary was attached to the post of Prime Minister, but as First Lord of the Treasury he received £5,000 p.a.

Spouse's finances Margot received £5,000 p.a. on her marriage. In 1927 she made £8,000 from her books and £10,000 from her other writings. After Asquith's death Lord Beaverbrook periodically gave her money and she supplemented her income with journalism.

Pensions None

Debts In May 1927, Asquith's debts amounted to about £15,000.

Will Asquith left £9,345, £300 of which, together with his personal effects, went to his widow (as she had been provided for by her father). Apart from a few small legacies, the residue went into a trust for his children by his first marriage.

ANECDOTES

'In cabinet he was markedly silent. Indeed he never spoke a word in council if he could get his way without it. He sat, like the great judge he was, hearing with trained patience the case deployed on every side, now and then interjecting a question or brief comment, searching or pregnant, which gave matters a turn towards the goal he wished to reach. . . . ' (Winston Churchill, 1937)

Henry Campbell-Bannerman, when Prime Minister (1905–08), referred to Asquith as 'The Sledgehammer' because of his power in debate: he would pile argument upon argument in flowing, lucid sentences, crushing his opponents by weight of logic.

'Asquith worries too much about small points. If you were buying a large mansion he would come to you and say "Have you thought there is no accommodation for the cat"?' (Lloyd George, in a letter to Lord Riddell, 1915)

' . . . Without appearing to notice, Mr. Asquith saw everything down to petty points of routine and detail which most people, I suspect, never dreamt of his observing. Thus at golf he would know the whereabouts of his opponent's ball in the rough better than the caddie.

On the eve of the Royal Dinner at 10 Downing Street to celebrate the King's coronation, he put his finger on two weak spots in the organisation, one of which had to do with the working of the ventilator in a room where a play was to be given later in the evening.' (Vaughan Nash, Asquith's private secretary for many years, c. 1931)

'That he should have enjoyed society, and taken so much of it during his life might seem incongruous in him until we realise that he took it as a rest: amiable people, pretty women, bright lights, friendly festivity and remarks flying about which he could catch and reply to by employing an eighth of his intellect afforded effective distraction: it was a refreshment. Henry James, coming back once from a luncheon party at Downing Street during the [1st World] war, remarked on "the extraordinary, the admirable, rigid, intellectual economy" which the Prime Minister practised on such occasions'. (Asquith's friend Desmond McCarthy writing in 1928 in a review of *Memories and Reflections*)

QUOTATIONS

1910, We had better wait and see. (used repeatedly in the House of Commons)

4 Apr 1914, The Army will hear nothing of politics from me, and in return I expect to hear nothing of politics from the Army. (Ladybank speech)

3 Jul 1914, In public politics as in private life, character is better than brains, and loyalty more valuable than either; but I shall have to work with the material that has been given to me. (Conversation with his wife)

24 Jul 1914, Happily there seems to be no reason why we should be anything but spectators [of the approaching war] (Letter to Venetia Stanley)

9 Nov 1914, We shall never sheathe the sword which we have not lightly drawn until Belgium receives in full measure all and more than all that she has sacrificed, until France is adequately secured against the menace of aggression, until the rights of the smaller nationalities of Europe are placed upon an unassailable foundation, and until the military domination of Prussia is wholly and finally destroyed. (Speech at the Guildhall, London)

21 Jan 1920 After writing to you and writing my cabinet letter [i.e., to the King, in those days the only written account of the business] and disposing of a lot of smaller things, I walked across after 6 to the Athenaeum, and took up a novel *Sir Perryworn's Wife* (a good title), which with judicious skipping I read from cover to cover. . . . I found it readable and soothing. [He

QUOTATIONS—*Continued*

would have been back in Downing Street by 8 p.m.] (Letter to Venetia Stanley)

1920, I confess I think the Prime Minister is underpaid. I was in office myself continuously for 11 years—two years as Chancellor of the Exchequer, and for the best part of 9 years as Prime Minister. I do not suppose my experience is in the least unique, but I was a much poorer man when I left office than when I entered. (Evidence to Select Committee on Remuneration of Ministers)

15 Apr 1923, Youth would be an ideal state if it came a little later in life. (*Observer*)

The War Office kept three sets of figures— one to mislead the public, another to mislead the Cabinet, and the third to mislead itself. (Alistair Horne, *The Price of Glory*, Ch. 2, 1962)

RESIDENCES

90 Mount Street, Mayfair, London
Eton House, John Street, Hampstead, London, (now called *Keats Grove*)
20 Cavendish Square, Mayfair, London (plaque)
10 Downing Street
44 Bedford Square, Bloomsbury, London
The Wharf, Sutton Courtney, Abingdon, Berkshire (now Oxfordshire)

MEMORIALS

STATUES AND BUSTS

1921, bust by Lady Kathleen Kennet, Tate Gallery, London; by Leonard Merrifield, completed by Gilbert Bays, Jun 1948, in the Members' Lobby, House of Commons, unveiled by Winston Churchill, Dec 1950; bust by Clair Sheridan, Oxford Union, Oxford.

PORTRAITS

1920, by Reginald Campbell, House of Commons, London; 1918, by Sir John Lavery, Reform Club, London; 1909, by Sir William Orpen, Lincoln's Inn, London; 1909, by Solomon J. Solomon, National Liberal Club, London; 1912, by George Fides Watt, Balliol College, Oxford; c. 1920, by Sir James Guthrie, National Portrait Gallery, London (version also in Scottish Portrait Gallery); 1914, by Sir James Guthrie, in group portrait, National Portrait Gallery, London.

OTHER MEMORIALS

In Statesman's Aisle, North Transept, Westminster Abbey

BIBLIOGRAPHIC INFORMATION

LETTERS AND PERSONAL PAPERS

The Asquith papers and correspondence are in the Bodleian Library, Oxford.

PUBLICATIONS

1923, *The Genesis of War*, 1924, *Studies and Sketches*; 1926, *Fifty Years of Parliament*; 1928, *Memories and Reflections 1852–1927*.

FURTHER READING

Asquith, Lady C. *Diaries 1915–1918*. London, 1968.
Asquith, H. *Moments of Memory*. London, 1937.
Bennett, D. *Margot: A Life of the Countess of Oxford and Asquith*. London, 1984.
Brock, M and E, eds. *H. H. Asquith: Letters to Venetia Stanley*. Oxford, 1982.
Jenkins, R. *Asquith*. London, 1964. (3rd rev. ed., 1986)
---. *Mr. Balfour's Poodle*. London, 1954.
Jolliffe, J. *Raymond Asquith: Life and Letters*. London, 1980.
Koss, S. *Asquith*. London, 1976.
Oxford and Asquith, M., Countess of. *The Autobiography of Margot Asquith*, 2 vols. London, 1922.
Spender, J. A. and Asquith, C. *Life of Henry Herbert Asquith, Lord Oxford and Asquith*, 2 vols. London, 1932.

D.C.

Bettmann

David Lloyd George

Lived 1863–1945
Political Party Liberal
Prime Minister 6 December 1916–19 October 1922
Government Coalition
Reigning Monarch George V

Y gwir yn erbyn y byd The truth against the world

LLOYD GEORGE AS PRIME MINISTER

Lloyd George was a man of great energy and unconventional outlook, character and policies. He was also complex and ambitious and, as Asquith's Chancellor, stimulated radical social policies, in particular through his 'People's Budget' of 1909. The outbreak of the 1914–1918 war offered him the necessary challenge and under Asquith he set up the Ministry of Munitions in 1915, running it with energy and success. Subsequently, seeing Asquith's inadequacy in pursuing the war he teamed up with Unionist leader Bonar Law to topple Asquith and became Prime Minister in December 1916. He appointed Law his Chancellor of the Exchequer, and transformed the national war effort not only with his energy and powers of communication but also by bringing in business men to improve efficiency and by revolutionising the cabinet system and its secretariat. He inspired the nation and became a great war leader, but Premiership depended on Unionist support and he remained to an extent a prisoner of the traditional military. Working with the Unionists he scored a personal triumph in the November 1918 election and spent much of the next six months negotiating the Treaty of Versailles. Late in 1919 he restored the system of a full peace-time Cabinet, retaining its secretariat. At home he supported for a time a radical housing policy and, more long lasting, extended unemployment insurance. However the economic situation deteriorated and abroad his attempts at the Genoa conference of 1922 to round off the 1914-1918 war failed. In October 1922 he decided to fight another election on the Coalition ticket but the Unionists withdrew their support and Lloyd George, the last Liberal Prime Minister, promptly resigned. As a sad coda, from 1926 to 1931 he was leader of the fast-declining Liberal party.

PERSONAL INFORMATION

Names David Lloyd George
Peerages 1st Earl Lloyd-George of Dwyfor & Viscount Gwynedd of Dwyfor in the County of Caernarvon (1 Jan 1945)
Nicknames The Welsh Wizard; The Man Who Won the War; The Goat
Born 17 Jan 1863
Birthplace 5 New York Place, Chorlton-upon-Medlock, Manchester, England
Religion Baptist
Ancestry Welsh. Son, grandson and great-grandson of yeoman farmers from Pembrokeshire, Wales
Dates and places of marriages 1) 24 Jan 1888, Methodist Chapel, Pencaenwydd, near Criccieth, Wales; 2) 23 Oct 1943, Guildford Registry Office, Surrey, England
Age at marriages 1) 25 years, 7 days; 2) 80 years, 279 days
Years married 1) 52 years, 361 days; 2) 1 year, 154 days.
First entered Parliament 10 Apr 1890
Date appointed PM 6 Dec 1916
Age at appointment 53 years, 325 days
Date ceased to be PM 19 Oct 1922
Total time as PM 5 years, 317 days
Ceased to be MP 1 Jan 1945
Lived after last term as PM 22 years, 158 days
Date of death 26 March 1945
Place of death Ty Newydd, Llanystumdwy, Wales
Age at death 82 years, 68 days
Last words A few days before he died he opened his eyes and said: 'The sign of the cross, the sign of the cross.'
Place of funeral and burial Lloyd George's body was borne on a simple farm cart from his house, Ty Newydd, to the spot by the River Dwyfor where he had chosen to be buried under a large boulder and where his funeral service was conducted.

FATHER

William George
Date and place of birth 1820, Trecoed, near Jordanstown, Pembrokeshire
Occupation He studied at Battersea Teachers Training College, London and spent 6 years as a schoolmaster in Liverpool. He taught later at Haverfordwest and Pwllheli. He retired from teaching due to ill health and shortly after the birth of David in 1863 he took over the tenancy of a small farm at Bulford in Pembrokeshire.
Dates of marriages 1) 20 Apr 1841 to Anne George (d. within a few years of marriage); 2) 16 Nov 1859 to Elizabeth Lloyd
Date of death 7 Jun 1864
Place of burial Trewrdan Cemetery, near Trecoed, Pembrokeshire

MOTHER

Elizabeth Lloyd
Date and place of birth 1 Oct 1828, Llanystumdwy, Caernarvonshire
Date of marriage 16 Nov 1859
Profile Before marriage she had been first a domestic servant and then a lady's companion.
Date of death 19 Jun 1896

BROTHERS AND SISTERS

David Lloyd George was the eldest son and third of four children

From his father's first marriage: None

From his father's second marriage:

Girl, unnamed, d. 1860 a few days after birth, which was recorded on the fly-leaf of the Lloyd's family bible

Mary Ellen, b. 8 Nov 1861; m. Captain Philip Davies; played a useful part in the social life and activities of Criccieth; d. 8 Aug 1909; a tablet was put up in her memory in Criccieth Public Library.

William, b. 23 Feb 1865; m. 23 Jul 1910, Anita Williams; a solicitor in partnership with David Lloyd George; wrote a biography, *My Brother and I*, 1958; d. Jan 1967

FIRST WIFE

Margaret Owen
Date of birth 4 Nov 1866
Mother Mary
Father Richard Owen
Father's occupation Farmer
Age at marriage 21 years, 81 days
Number of children 5
Date and place of death 20 Jan 1941, Criccieth, Caernarvonshire
Place of burial Cemetery in Criccieth, Caernarvonshire
Years younger than PM 3 years, 291 days
Profile She was educated at a girl's school in Dolgelly, Wales. During World War I she raised millions of pounds for charities and was awarded a DBE in 1920. She became the first woman Justice of the Peace in Wales in 1928.

SECOND WIFE

Frances Louise Stevenson
Date of birth 7 Oct 1888
Mother Louise Augustine Armainino
Father John Stevenson
Father's occupation Secretary to a firm of French import agents
Age at marriage 55 years, 16 days
Number of children 1
Date of death 5 Dec 1972
Profile She attended Clapham High School and Royal Holloway College, London University. After obtaining a classics degree, she became a teacher, and got to know Lloyd George when she was appointed as private tutor to his youngest child Megan in 1911. She acted as Lloyd George's personal secretary from 1913 until their marriage in 1943. She was appointed CBE in 1918.

CHILDREN

2 sons, 4 daughters
By his first wife Margaret:
Richard (2nd Earl Lloyd George of Dwyfor), b. 15 Feb, 1889; m. 1) 1917, Roberta McAlpine; divorced 1932; 2) 1935, Mrs. Winifred Calvé; engineer at Pearson & Son Oil Enterprises in Mexico and Central America; wrote biographies of both his parents—*Dame Margaret* in 1947, and *Lloyd George* in 1960; d. 1 May 1968
Mair Eluned, b. 2 Aug 1890, d. 29 Nov 1907. She died after an operation for appendicitis at the age of 17, while still a schoolgirl. One of her classmates was Frances Stevenson, later to become Lloyd George's secretary, mistress, and eventually his second wife.
Olwen Elizabeth, b. 3 Apr 1892; m. 19 Jun 1917, Thomas Carey Evans; VAD in World War I; at the age of 87 wrote a memoir of her father and her childhood; d. 2 Mar 1990
Gwilym (1st Viscount Tenby of Bulford, 1957), b. 4 Dec 1894; m. 14 Jun 1921, Edna Jones; MP Pembrokeshire, 1922–24 and 1929–50, Newcastle-upon-Tyne, 1951–57; Minister of Fuel and Power, 1942–45; Minister of Food, 1951–54; Home Secretary, 1954–57; d. 14 Feb 1967
Megan Afton (Lady Megan Lloyd-George), b. 22 Apr 1902; MP Anglesey, 1929–51, Carmarthen 1957–66; Deputy Leader of the Liberal Party, 1949–51; Companion of Honour, May 1966; d. 14 May 1966
By his second wife Frances:
Jennifer, b. 4. Oct 1929. Letters between Lloyd George and Frances Stevenson published in 1975 appear to provide proof that she was their natural child, although during their lifetime she was assumed to be Frances Stevenson's adopted daughter.

LIFE AND CAREER

PARLIAMENTARY ELECTIONS FOUGHT

(designates candidate elected)

DATE 10 Apr 1890. By-election caused by death of E. Swetenham
CONSTITUENCY Caernarvon District of Boroughs
RESULT D. Lloyd George* (Lib) 1,963; H.J.E. Nanney (Con) 1,945

DATE Jul 1892. General Election
CONSTITUENCY Caernarvon
RESULT D. Lloyd George* (Lib) 2,154; Sir. J.H. Puleston, (Con) 1,958

DATE Jul 1895. General Election
CONSTITUENCY Caernarvon
RESULT D. Lloyd George* (Lib) 2,265; H.J.E. Nanney (Con), 2,071

DATE Oct 1900. General Election
CONSTITUENCY Caernarvon
RESULT D. Lloyd George* (Lib) 2,412; H. Platt, (Con), 2,116

DATE Jan 1906. General Election
CONSTITUENCY Caernarvon
RESULT D. Lloyd George* (Lib) 3,221; R.A. Naylor (Con), 1,997

DATE Jan 1910. General Election
CONSTITUENCY Caernarvon
RESULT D. Lloyd George* (Lib) 3,183; H.C. Vincent (Con), 2,105

DATE Dec 1910. General Election
CONSTITUENCY Caernarvon
RESULT D. Lloyd George* (Lib) 3,112; A. L. Jones (Con), 1,904

DATE Dec 1918. General Election
CONSTITUENCY Caernarvon
RESULT D. Lloyd George* (Co Lib) 13, 993; A. Harrison (Ind) 1,095

DATE 15 Nov 1922. General Election
CONSTITUENCY Caernarvon
RESULT D. Lloyd George* (Nat Lib)

DATE 6 Dec 1923. General Election
CONSTITUENCY Caernarvon
RESULT D. Lloyd George* (Lib) 12,499; A.L. Jones (Con), 7,323

DATE 29 Oct 1924. General Election
CONSTITUENCY Caernarvon
RESULT D. Lloyd George* (Lib) 16,058; A.E. Zimmern (Lab), 3401

DATE 30 May 1929. General Election
CONSTITUENCY Caernarvon
RESULT D. Lloyd George* (Lib) 16,647; J.B. Davies (Con) 7,514; T.A. Rhys (Lab) 4536

DATE 27 Oct 1931. General Election
CONSTITUENCY Caernarvon
RESULT D. Lloyd George* (Lib) 17,101; F.P. Gowlay (Con), 11,714

DATE 14 Nov 1935. General Election
CONSTITUENCY Caernarvon
RESULT D. Lloyd George* (Lib), 19,242; A.R.P. Du Cros (Con), 9,633

PARTY ACTIVITY

Party Leadership Liberal Leader in the House of Commons, Oct 1926–Nov 1931
Other offices Chairman of Parliamentary Liberal Party from Dec 1924
Membership of group or faction After the 1931 General Election there were three Liberal groups in the House of Commons. Lloyd George led a small family group of 4 Independent Liberals. He and the others rejoined the Liberal Party in Nov 1935.

PARLIAMENTARY AND MINISTERIAL EXPERIENCE

Maiden speech 13 Jun 1890, He spoke in favour of temperance reform and against a measure which he thought would delay this, the Local Taxation (Custom & Excise Duties) Bill. (*HC Deb*, vol 345, col 871–874)
Privy Counsellor 11 Dec 1905
Ministerial Offices President of the Board of Trade, 11 Dec 1905–12 Apr 1908; Chancellor of the Exchequer, 12 Apr 1908–25 May 1915; Minister of Munitions, 25 May 1915–12 Jun 1916; Secretary of State for War, 12 Jun–6 Dec 1916; First Lord of the Treasury 6 Dec 1916–19 Oct 1922

PARLIAMENTARY AND MINISTERIAL EXPERIENCE—*Continued*

Father of the House 18 Nov 1929–1 Jan 1945

GOVERNMENTS FORMED

First Administration 6 Dec 1916–14 Dec 1918

GENERAL ELECTION RESULT

DEC 1910: Liberal 272; Conservative 271; Irish Nationalist 84; Labour 42; Others 1. Total 670
No overall majority

CABINET

From 6 Dec 1916–31 Oct 1919 there was an inner War Cabinet of between 5 and 7 ministers. Lloyd George, Earl Curzon and Bonar Law were members throughout. The other members were: A. Henderson (Lab), 10 Dec 1916–12 Aug 1917; V. E. Milner (Con), 10 Dec 1916–18 Apr 1918; J. Smuts (South African Defence Minister), 22 Jun 1917– 10 Jan 1919; G. Barnes (Lab), 29 May–3 Aug 1917, 13 Aug 1917–10 Jan 1919; A. Chamberlain (Con), 18 Apr 1918–31 Oct 1919; Sir E. Geddes, (Con) 10 Jan 1919–31 Oct 1919.

Prime Minister and First Lord of the Treasury D. Lloyd George
Lord President of the Council Earl Curzon
Lord Chancellor Lord Finlay
Lord Privy Seal Earl of Crawford
Chancellor of the Exchequer A. Bonar Law
Foreign Secretary A. Balfour
Home Secretary Sir G. Cave
First Lord of the Admiralty Sir E. Carson (Dec 1916–Jul 1917); Sir E. Geddes (Jul 1917–Jan 1919)
President of the Board of Agriculture and Fisheries R. Protheroe
Secretary of State for the Colonies W. Long
President of the Board of Education H. Fisher
Secretary of State for India A. Chamberlain (Dec 1916–Jul 1917); E. Montagu (Jul 1917–Jan 1919)
Chief Secretary for Ireland Sir. H. Duke, (Dec 1916–May 1918); E. Shortt (May 1918–Jan 1919)
Minister of Labour J. Hodge (Dec 1916–Aug 1917); G. Roberts (Aug 1917–Jan 1919)
Chancellor of the Duchy of Lancaster Sir. F. Cawley (Dec 1916– Feb 1918); Lord Beaverbrook (Feb–Nov 1918) (and Minister of Propaganda/Information); Lord Downham (Nov 1918–Jan 1919)
President of the Local Government Board Lord Rhondda (Dec 1916–Jun 1917); W. Hayes Fisher (Lord Downham) (Jun 1917–Nov 1918); Sir A. Geddes (Nov 1918–Jan 1919)
Minister of Munitions Supply C. Addison (Dec 1916–Jul 1917); W. Churchill (17 Jul 1917–Jan 1919)

Second Administration 14 Dec 1918–19 Oct 1922

GENERAL ELECTION RESULT

DEC 1918: Conservative 382; Liberal 163; Labour 57; Others 105. Total 707
Coalition majority 283 (excl. the Speaker)

CABINET

Prime Minister and First Lord of the Treasury D. Lloyd George
Lord President of the Council Earl Curzon (Jan 1919–Oct 1919; A. Balfour (Oct 1919–Oct 1922)
Lord Chancellor Lord Birkenhead
Lord Privy Seal A. Bonar Law (Jan 1919–Mar 1921); A. Chamberlain (Mar 1921–Oct 1922)
Chancellor of the Exchequer A. Chamberlain (Jan 1919–Apr 1921); Sir R. Horne (Apr 1921–Oct 1922)
Foreign Secretary A. Balfour (Jan–Oct 1919); Earl Curzon, (Oct 1919–Oct 1922)
Home Secretary E. Shortt
First Lord of the Admiralty W. Long (Jan 1919–Feb 1921); Lord Lee (Feb 1921–Oct 1922)
President of the Board of Agriculture (renamed Ministry on 15 Aug 1919) R. Protheroe (Jan–Aug 1919); Lord Lee (Aug 1919–Feb 1921); Sir A. Griffith Boscawen (Feb 1921– Oct 1922)
*Attorney General** Sir G. Hewart (Nov 1921–Mar 1922)
Secretary of State for the Colonies Viscount Milner (Jan 1919–Feb 1921); W. Churchill (Feb 1921–Oct 1922)
President of the Board of Education H. Fisher
Minister of Health (Department under Board of Education until Jun 1919) C. Addison (Jun 1919–Apr 1921); Sir A. Mond (Apr 1921–Oct 1922)
Secretary of State for India E. Montagu (Jan 1919– Mar 1922); Viscount Peel (Mar–Oct 1922)
*Lord Lieutenant of Ireland** Viscount French (Earl of Ypres) (Oct 1919–Apr 1921)
Chief Secretary for Ireland I. Macpherson (Jan 1919–Apr 1920); Sir M. Greenwood (Apr 1920–Oct 1922)
Minister of Labour Sir R. Horne (Jan 1919–March 1920); T. McNamara (Mar 1920–Oct 1922)
President of the Local Government Board C. Addison (Jan– Jun 1919) (*then Ministry of Health*)
[*Office not always in Cabinet]

IMPORTANT DATES IN PERSONAL AND POLITICAL LIFE

7 JUN 1864 Lloyd George's father dies when he is 17 months old. His mother takes her young family from Pembrokeshire to live with her brother Richard (known as Uncle Lloyd), the village shoemaker at Llanystumdwy, Caernarvonshire, North Wales.

SEP 1866 From the age of 3 years Lloyd George attends the village school in Llanystumdwy. This is the only formal education he receives.

8 DEC 1877 While still at school Lloyd George passes the preliminary examination of the Law Society.

JUL 1878 On leaving school he becomes articled to the firm of Breese, Jones & Casson, Solicitors of Portmadoc.

28 NOV 1881 Becomes a member of Portmadoc Debating Society.

APR 1884 Takes his final law examinations in London and while there he visits the House of Commons and hears Gladstone speak.

27 MAY 1884 Obtains a 3rd class honours degree.

JAN 1885 Starts his own solicitor's practice in Criccieth. Later joined in partnership by his brother William, in May 1887.

24 JAN 1888 Marries Margaret Owen.

JAN 1889 Elected Alderman of Caernarvonshire County Council.

OCT 1889 At a meeting of the Welsh National Council Lloyd George seconds a resolution in favour of disestablishment of the Welsh Church.

10 APR 1890 First elected to Parliament as Liberal MP for Caernarvon District of Boroughs after a by-election caused by the death of the sitting Conservative MP.

13 JUN 1890 His maiden speech, on the issue of temperance reform, made during the passage of the Local Taxation (Customs & Excise Duties) Bill, is a great success. He writes to his Uncle Lloyd, 'there is hardly a Liberal,

London or even provincial paper which does not say something complimentary about it.'

AUG 1892 The Conservative Government is defeated at the General Election and Gladstone is returned as Liberal Prime Minister.

1898 Forms Welsh National Liberal Council.

11 OCT 1899 Boer War begins. Lloyd George enters a fervent campaign against the war in speeches both inside Parliament and outside and arouses strong antagonism from supporters of the war.

2 JAN 1901 Queen Victoria dies, succeeded by Edward VII.

8 DEC 1901 Lloyd George due to make a speech at Birmingham Town Hall, in the constituency of pro-war Colonial Secretary Joseph Chamberlain. Despite barricades a huge mob of Chamberlain supporters surges into the Town Hall, all the windows are broken, and Lloyd George's words are drowned by boos, catcalls and cries of 'Pro Boer! Traitor! Kill him!' He escapes the angry crowd disguised as a policeman. One man is killed and many injured in the riots surrounding the event.

8 MAY 1902 During the Second Reading of the Education Bill Lloyd George makes a powerful speech against the privileges the Bill would grant the Church of England. The Bill is to bring under one authority schools run by both Nonconformist Churches and the Established Church.

31 MAY 1902 Boer war ends with the signing of the Treaty of Vereeniging.

11 DEC 1905 Campbell-Bannerman appoints Lloyd George President of the Board of Trade, and he becomes a Privy Counsellor.

29 NOV 1907 The death of his eldest daughter Mair at the age of 17 after an operation is his great sorrow. She had been his favourite child.

5 APR 1908 Asquith becomes Prime Minister after Campbell-Bannerman's resignation because of ill-health and on 12 Apr Lloyd George is appointed Chancellor of the Exchequer.

28 MAY 1908 Introduces Old Age Pensions Bill.

10 NOV 1908 Appointed Constable of Caernarvon Castle.

29 APR 1909 Lloyd George introduces his first Budget, known as the 'People's Budget.' It provokes bitter criticism from the Conservatives and the House of Lords, who see it as an attack on the land-owning classes. In order to raise additional revenue for old age pensions and new Dreadnought battleships for the Navy, the Budget increases income tax and death duties, introduces super-tax on incomes over £5,000 and brings in new taxes on land values and ownership of mineral rights.

30 NOV 1909 The 'People's Budget' is vetoed by the House of Lords by 350 votes to 75. Asquith asks the King to dissolve Parliament and a General Election is decreed for the new year.

14 APR 1910 The Parliament Bill, to curb the powers of the House of Lords, is introduced.

28 APR 1910 The 1909 Budget is passed by the House of Lords.

6 MAY 1910 Death of King Edward VII, succeeded by George V. Because of his political inexperience, and the need to resolve the problems concerning the House of Lords, Lloyd George proposes the setting up of a Constitutional Conference, to meet between June and November.

7 JUN 1910 The Constitutional Conference is convened by Asquith, but no agreement is reached.

25 NOV 1910 A Resolution defining the powers of the House of Lords forms the basis of the Parliament Act of 1911.

13 JUL 1911 As Constable of Caernarvon Castle Lloyd George attends the investiture of Prince Edward (later King Edward VIII) as Prince of Wales. He had personally coached the Prince in the few sentences of Welsh he speaks at the ceremony.

10 AUG 1911 Resolution on payment of Members is carried.

16 DEC 1911 The National Insurance Act introduces a system of compulsory insurance for sickness benefits and medical treatment which operates until the introduction of the National Health Service in 1948.

12 APR 1912 Welsh Disestablishment Bill, introduced by Home Secretary McKenna, is closely supervised by Lloyd George.

JAN 1913 Frances Stevenson becomes his secretary and his mistress. She remains his personal secretary and his lover for the next 30 years, until their marriage in Oct 1943.

JUN 1913 The Marconi Shares Scandal. The report of a Select Committee of Inquiry exonerates Lloyd George and the Attorney-General Rufus Isaacs of charges of corruption and improper speculation in the purchase of shares from the Marconi Company, but the affair adds to the hostility the Conservatives feel for Lloyd George.

4 AUG 1914 World War I begins.

19 SEP 1914 Lloyd George makes his first major speech on the War at the Queen's Hall, London.

17 NOV 1914 Introduces his first War Budget, which doubles income tax and increases tea and beer duties.

25 MAY 1915 In the first Coalition Government, formed by Asquith, he becomes head of the newly created Ministry of Munitions and greatly increases production.

5 JUN 1916 Kitchener, the War Minister, is drowned when the cruiser on which he is travelling to Russia is torpedoed. Lloyd George is appointed his successor on 12 Jun. While in this post he criticises the conduct of the war by the Government, with the support of the Conservatives under the leadership of Bonar Law and of Carson, the Ulster leader. They present Asquith with a plan for a small War Committee under the chairmanship of Lloyd George. This plan is ultimately rejected by Asquith and leads to Lloyd George's resignation as War Minister on 5 Dec.

5 DEC 1916 Asquith resigns as Prime Minister on the same day Lloyd George resigns as War Minister. Bonar Law is asked to form a government but declines as Asquith refuses to serve under him. This provides an opportunity for Lloyd George, who has the support of the Conservatives including both Bonar Law and Balfour.

7 DEC 1916 Lloyd George succeeds Asquith as Prime Minister.

1 NOV 1917 The Balfour Declaration on a national homeland for Jews receives Lloyd George's enthusiastic support and he delivers the draft to the leaders of Britain's Jews.

6 FEB 1918 The Representation of the People Act, giving the vote to women over 30, receives the Royal Assent.

8 AUG 1918 The Education Act raises school-leaving age to 14.

11 NOV 1918 Lloyd George announces from 10 Downing Street the signing of the armistice at 5 a.m. that morning and the cessation of hostilities on all fronts from 11 a.m. Lloyd George heads the British Empire Delegation.

IMPORTANT DATES IN PERSONAL AND POLITICAL LIFE—*Continued*

18 JAN 1919 Opening of Paris Peace Conference, leading to the signing of the Treaty of Versailles on 28 Jun 1919, and the establishment of the League of Nations.

10 JAN 1920 The Treaty of Versailles ratified.

31 MAR 1920 Formal disestablishment of the Welsh Church.

20 MAY 1920 National Health Insurance Act receives Royal Assent.

9 AUG 1920 Unemployment Insurance Act extends provisions of the 1911 Act to an additional 8 million people and provides weekly benefits of 15 s. for men and 12 s. for women.

6 DEC 1921 The Irish Treaty signed, dividing Ireland into the Irish Free State and Northern Ireland.

APR–MAY 1922 The Genoa Conference, Lloyd George's supreme effort to unite the nations of Europe.

JUN 1922 Sale of honours scandal. After Conservative criticism of the quality and quantity of knighthoods and peerages bestowed by Lloyd George in return for contributions to Liberal Party funds he agrees to appoint a Royal Commission to examine the procedure for awarding honours.

SEP–OCT 1922 The Chanak crisis. War with Turkey is averted by Lloyd George after Mustapha Kemal attempts to invade the neutral zone at Chanak. However, fears of war provide Lloyd George's opponents with a pretext for ending his premiership.

19 OCT 1922 At a meeting at the Carlton Club a majority of Conservative MPs vote, 187 to 87, to end the Coalition. Lloyd George resigns as Prime Minister, succeeded by Andrew Bonar Law (Conservative) on 23 Oct. The Liberal Party is never again to form a government.

SEP 1923 Lloyd George visits Canada and the USA. He addresses many meetings and receives a tumultuous welcome everywhere.

28 APR 1925 In his Budget statement the Chancellor, Winston Churchill, announces Britain's return to the Gold Standard—the restoration of pre-war parity of the pound sterling with the gold sovereign. This decision is severely condemned by Lloyd George in denunciatory speeches over the next few months, and is a contributing factor to the General Strike of May 1926.

4 MAY 1926 National Strike begins, organised by TUC at request of the miners, in support of shorter hours and higher pay. It lasts 9 days.

OCT 1926 The differences between Lloyd George and Asquith over the General Strike finally separate them and Asquith, now Lord Oxford, resigns as Leader of the Liberal Party, succeeded by Lloyd George.

1928 Publication of *Britain's Industrial Future.*

5 JUN 1929 Formation of minority Labour Government by Ramsay MacDonald.

AUG 1931 Lloyd George undergoes operation for removal of his prostate gland. At around the same time the Labour Government falls, and Ramsay MacDonald forms a National Government, which Lloyd George's illness prevents him from joining.

OCT 1931 The Conservative members of the National Government press for a General Election, which takes place on 17 Oct. The Liberal Party splits into 3 factions, with Lloyd George leading a tiny group of four Independent Liberals, including his son Gwilym and daughter Megan.

1933 Between 1933 and 1936 his 4 volumes of *War Memoirs* are published.

17 JAN 1935 On his 72nd birthday Lloyd George launches a programme for a 'new deal,' a revival of bold economic remedies he had first prescribed in 1929, and now under the auspices of a Council of Action for Peace and Reconstruction.

SEP 1936 Lloyd George visits Hitler at his mountain retreat at Berchtesgaden, Bavaria.

3 SEP 1939 Beginning of World War II.

3 MAY 1940 One of his last interventions in a debate in the House of Commons is an attack on Neville Chamberlain's handling of the war. Chamberlain resigns 2 days later and Winston Churchill becomes Prime Minister.

JUN 1940 Churchill, now Prime Minister, invites Lloyd George to join his Coalition Government but his offer is refused.

20 JAN 1941 Death of his wife Dame Margaret at Criccieth. A blizzard prevents Lloyd George being at her side when she dies—his car is stuck in a snow drift.

7 MAY 1941 Lloyd George's last speech in the House of Commons during a debate on the war situation, concerning assistance to Greece.

23 OCT 1943 Lloyd George marries Frances Stevenson at Guildford Registry Office—she had been his personal secretary and mistress for 30 years.

1944 His health begins to fail, and cancer is diagnosed.

1 JAN 1945 Elevated to the peerage as Earl Lloyd-George of Dwyfor and Viscount Gwynedd of Dwyfor.

26 MAR 1945 Dies at Ty Newydd, Llanystumdwy, North Wales.

BACKGROUND

PHYSICAL CHARACTERISTICS AND HEALTH

In his memoir of his father, published in 1960, Lloyd George's eldest son Richard described him from a photograph taken when he was 17: 'It is a remarkably handsome face, almost satanically handsome in a Byronic way. And how impeccable his sartorial style—the snug cravat, the romantic high collar, the smoothly draped collar. For a poor country youth his care for and sense of his personal appearance were extraordinary'.

Richard later described his father in old age: 'He was weather- beaten from his farming life and travels, and the tan set off a silvery mane strikingly and quite beautifully. He had a chevalier-like distinction, and the weather-beaten features contrasting with the ethereal head gave extra facets to his personality. With an attractive woman he was as much to be trusted as a Bengal tiger with a gazelle.'

'I recall the sensitive face, with deep furrows between the eyes—the broad brow, the beautiful profile—straight nose, neat insolent chin. And a complexion as young and fresh as a child's', Frances Stevenson remarked on first meeting with Lloyd George.

He was rather short but with a powerful body and broad shoulders. His hair was turning white, and he wore it rather long—in later years almost like a mane. He had a fine head and piercing blue eyes. (*Mowat* p. 37)

EDUCATION

Primary Llanystumdwy Village School

Secondary Lloyd George was taught French and Latin at home by his Uncle Lloyd, from specially purchased textbooks. These languages were not taught at the village school and knowledge of them was a requirement of the Law Society's Examinations, law being Lloyd George's chosen profession.

Qualifications 1884, passed final examinations of the Law Society with honours.

Cultural and vocational background Lloyd George did very well at school and received advanced tuition from David Evans, the excellent headmaster of the village school. In 1909 Mr. Evans said of his former pupil, by now Chancellor of the Exchequer, 'No teacher ever had a more apt pupil. He was always particularly good at sums, and now he is doing the big sum which we all have to pay'. He was also good at geography, which contributed to his love of travel. He visited Argentina and Uruguay in 1896, Italy in 1897, North Africa and the Levant in 1898, Canada in 1899 and Switzerland and Austria in 1902.

Languages He was bi-lingual in Welsh and English, and had been taught French and Latin by his Uncle Lloyd.

NON-PARLIAMENTARY CAREER

Early occupations At the age of 16 he was articled to a firm of solicitors, Breece, Jones & Casson, in Portmadoc, with whom he worked from Jul 1878 until the end of 1884. He then set up on his own as a solicitor and took his younger brother William into partnership. William ran the firm when Lloyd George entered Parliament.

Other posts 1908, Constable of Caernarvon Castle.

HONOURS

Freedom of cities 1908, Caernarvon; Cardiff

Academic 1908, DL University of Wales; DCL University of Oxford; 1910, Hon. Fellow of Jesus College, Oxford; 1917, LLD University of Glasgow; 1918, LLD University of Edinburgh; 1919, DCL University of Durham; D. Litt University of Sheffield; 1920, Lord Rector of Edinburgh University; LLD University of Cambridge; 1921, LLD University of Birmingham.

Foreign 1920, Grand Cordon of the Legion of Honour (France); Order of St. Maurice and St. Lazarus (Italy)

Other than peerage 5 Aug 1919, Order of Merit

CLUBS

Reform, National Liberal

HOBBIES AND SPORTS

Lloyd George enjoyed travelling and motoring in Continental Europe, especially mountaineering in Switzerland. He played golf, liked fishing, and was a great storyteller and mimic. He loved singing hymns round a piano and appreciated classical music, in particular opera, choral and church music. He was fond of pets and always had a dog—usually an Airedale. He had a black cat called Juan, a tame white pigeon called Doodie, and in his latter years Blanco, a white cat. After leaving political office Lloyd George spent most of his time at his estate in Surrey, named *Bron-y-De* at Churt, near Hindhead, where he farmed extensively, growing fruit and vegetables and raising poultry and pigs.

FINANCES

When Lloyd George first entered Parliament the solicitor's firm he had set up and which was now managed by his brother William provided him with an income.

His personal finances improved when he achieved ministerial office in Oct 1905.

Income As a member of the Cabinet and later Prime Minister, from Dec 1905–Oct 1922, his salary was £5, 000 p.a. His pay as an MP from Oct 1922–Dec 1944 varied between £360 and £600 p.a.

Will His estate was not large. Properties at Churt and Surrey were left to his younger son Gwilym, his daughters Lady Olwen Carey-Evans and Lady Megan Lloyd-George and his secretary Ann Parry. His house in Llanystumdwy and his papers were left to his widow Frances, Countess Lloyd-George. £1,000 was left to his secretary A. J. Sylvester. His heir Richard was not provided for.

ANECDOTES

1935, In his volume of memoirs *Down the Years*, Sir Alister Chamberlain recalls a dinner in Paris in March 1919, when Balfour asked Lloyd George what the new House of Commons was like—'I'll tell you', said Lloyd George, his eyes sparkling with fun and a smile spreading rapidly over his face. 'I made a speech to them. I addressed myself at first to the opposition benches in front of me. They were very cold and hostile, I couldn't get a cheer. This, said I to myself, is not the House of Commons; it's the Trades Union Congress. So I turned as one does in such circumstances to the benches behind me, but neither was that the House of Commons. It was the Associated Chambers of Commerce'.

Once, as an experiment, Lloyd George had his moustache shaved off. 'With the moustache gone, so altered was he in appearance that when he entered the House of Commons clean shaven, the constable on the members' entrance door challenged him, and the Speaker failed to recognise him when he rose to address the House'. (Sylvester, p. 14)

'Churchill was perhaps the greater man but George was more fun,' Beaverbrook said, comparing Britain's leaders in the two World Wars. (Morgan, p. 7)

'My father was probably the greatest natural Don Juan in the history of British politics.' (Richard, 2nd Earl, *Lloyd George*, p. 42)

Lloyd George was much amused when in Jun 1918 a small girl called out to him 'Hullo! Are you Charlie Chaplin?' With his splendid mane of white hair surmounted by a bowler hat, bushy moustache, wing collar and walking stick there were certain points of similarity.

'How can I convey to the reader, who does not know him, any just impression of this extraordinary figure of our time, the syren, this goat-footed bard, this half-human visitor to our age from the hag-ridden magic

ANECDOTES—*Continued*

and enchanted woods of Celtic antiquity?' (Quoted by J. M. Keynes in *Essays in Biography*)

QUOTATIONS

26 Jun 1907, A mastiff? It is the right honourable gentleman's [Mr. Balfour's] poodle. It fetches and carries for him. It barks for him. It bites anybody that he sets it on to. (Speech in House of Commons referring to the House of Lords)

A fully equipped duke costs as much to keep up as two dreadnoughts; and dukes are just as great a terror and they last longer. (Speech at Newcastle)

19 Sep 1914, The great peaks of honour we had forgotten—Duty, Patriotism, and clad in glittering white—the great pinnacle of Sacrifice, pointing like a rugged finger to heaven. (Speech at Queens Hall, London)

23 Nov 1918, What is our task? To make Britain a fit country for heroes to live in. (Speech at Wolverhampton)

I never believed in costly frontal attacks either in war or politics if there were a way round. (From his *War Memoirs*, 1934)

2 Jul 1935, A politician was a person with whose politics you did not agree. When you did agree, he was a statesman. (Speech at Central Hall Westminster)

1944, Negotiating with de Valera . . . is like trying to pick up mercury with a fork. (Quoted in *Eamon de Valera* by M. J. MacManus)

RESIDENCES

5 New York Place, Chorlton-upon-Medlock, Manchester. [This was his birthplace. Now demolished, a plaque commemorating the event is fixed to the wall of a Council house on the site]

Highgate, Llanystumdwy, Caernarvonshire, Wales

3 Routh Road, Wandsworth, London (plaque)

Brynawelon, Criccieth, Caernavonshire

179 Trinity Road, Balham, London

10 Downing Street

Bron-y-de, Churt, near Farnham, Surrey (destroyed by fire)

Ty Newydd, Llanystumdwy, Caernarvonshire

Open to the public *Highgate*, his boyhood home in Llanystumdwy is the Lloyd George Museum. *Ty Newydd* was acquired by a trust in 1989 and in 1990 became the Taliesin Centre, where courses in creative writing are given in English and Welsh.

MEMORIALS

STATUES AND BUSTS

In the square in Caernarvon; 1921, bust National Museum of Wales; busts and bas-relief by Sir. W. Goscombe John, Ceirog Memorial Institute; busts by Lady Kathleen Kennet, Imperial War Museum and National Museum of Wales; bas-relief by Dora Ohlfsen, National Library of Wales, Aberystwyth; 1963, by Uli Nimpsch, Members' Lobby of the House of Commons

PORTRAITS

1927, by Sir William Orpen, National Portrait Gallery; by Sir Max Beerbohm, National Portrait Gallery; 1935, by Sir John Lavery, National Museum of Wales; 1917, by Christopher Williams, National Museum of Wales and National Liberal Club; 1909, by Sir Luke Fildes, incorporated Law Society; 1907, by Augustus John, Aberdeen Art Gallery; 1907, cartoon by 'Spy' in *Vanity Fair*, entitled 'A Nonconformist Genius'; 1931, by Philip de Laslzo, Members' Tea Room, House of Commons

OTHER MEMORIALS

In Westminster Abbey. British Rail named a locomotive after him. In 1919 a new strain of raspberry was named after him. It was used for breeding purposes.

BIBLIOGRAPHIC INFORMATION

LETTERS AND PERSONAL PAPERS

The main collection of Lloyd George's papers, housed in the Beaverbrook Library from 1967–75, is now in the House of Lords Record Office.

Many of his family letters and other material relating to his life are deposited in the National Library of Wales, Aberystwyth.

PUBLICATIONS

1918, *The Great Crusade*; 1923, *Is It Peace?*; 1928, *Britain's Industrial Future*; 1932, *The Truth About Reparations and War Debts*; 1933–1936 *War Memoirs*, 4 vols.; 1938, *The Truth About the Peace Treaties*, 2 vols.

FURTHER READING

Beaverbrook, Lord *Decline and Fall of Lloyd George*. London, 1963.

Campbell, J. *Lloyd George: the Goat in the Wilderness, 1922–1931*. London, 1977.

Carey-Evans, O. *Lloyd George Was My Father*. London, 1985.

Constantine, S. *Lloyd George*. London, 1992.

Cregier, D. M. *Bounder from Wales*. Columbia, Missouri, 1976.

Du Parq, H. *Life of David Lloyd George*. 4 vols. London, 1912–1913.

George, W. *My Brother and I*. London, 1958.

George, W. R. P. *The Making of Lloyd George*. London, 1976.

Gilbert, B. B. *David Lloyd George: The Architect of Change 1863–1912*. London, 1987.

—*David Lloyd George: A Political Life. The Organiser of Victory 1912–1916*. London, 1992.

Grigg, J. *The Young Lloyd George*. London, 1973.

—*Lloyd George: The People's Champion, 1902–1911*. London, 1978.

—*Lloyd George: From Peace to War 1912–1916. London, 1985.*

Jones, T. *Lloyd George*. London, 1951.

Lloyd-George, F. *The Years That Are Past*. London, 1967.

Lloyd-George, R. *Lloyd George*. London, 1960.

McCormick, D. *Mask of Merlin*. London, 1963.

Morgan, K. O. *David Lloyd George: Welsh Radical as World Statesman*. Cardiff, 1963.

Mowat, C. L. *Lloyd George*. London, 1964.

Owen, F. *Tempestuous Journey: Lloyd George, His Life and Times*. London, 1954.

Rowland, P. *Lloyd George*. London, 1975.

Sylvester, A. J. *The Real Lloyd George*. London, 1947.

Taylor, A. J. P., ed. *My Darling Pussy: The Letters of Lloyd George and Frances Stevenson 1913–1941.*London, 1975.

Thomson, M. *David Lloyd George, The Official Biography.* London, 1948.

Wrigley, C. *Lloyd George.* Oxford, 1992.

C.F.

Bettmann

Andrew Bonar Law

Lived 1858–1923
Political Party Conservative
Prime Minister 23 October 1922–20 May 1923
Government Conservative
Reigning Monarch George V

BONAR LAW AS PRIME MINISTER

Born in Canada, Bonar Law was of Scottish background and only reached the House of Commons in early middle age after a successful business career in Glasgow. In November 1911 he became leader of the Unionist party as a compromise candidate and took a very strong line against Irish Home Rule. When war came, he supported the Government in the national war effort but in May 1915 insisted that Asquith should establish a Coalition Government. Eighteen months later, and still dissatisfied with Asquith when the latter resigned, Law failed to form an alternative government and recommended Lloyd George to the King. Under Lloyd George's Coalition Government he was a successful Chancellor of the Exchequer from 1916 to 1919 and supported him at the 1918 election, which was a personal triumph for Lloyd George and a reaffirmation of the strength of Law's Unionist party. During the Premier's absences concerning the Treaty of Versailles he acted as deputy Prime Minister but agreed to withdraw his party's support of Lloyd George as criticism of him grew within the Unionist party. When Lloyd George resigned he became Prime Minister in October 1922. He believed in minimum government interference and steady work rather than his predecessor's more agitated style. His Cabinet control was firm, helped by being a good listener and a stringent, even tart, commentator. He delegated to ministers but kept the Cabinet secretariat under Hankey. He was opposed to the arrangements for repaying the US war debts negotiated by Baldwin but under pressure agreed not to resign on the issue. However a terminal illness had been diagnosed, and seven months after becoming Prime Minister he was forced to resign and died shortly afterwards.

PERSONAL INFORMATION

Names Andrew Bonar Law
Nicknames The Unknown Prime Minister; The Gilded Tradesman
Born 16 Sep 1858
Birthplace Kingston (now Rexton), near Richibucto, New Brunswick, Canada
Religion Presbyterian
Ancestry His father was an Ulsterman from Portrush, Northern Ireland, and his mother, whose father was a Glasgow iron-merchant, was a native of Halifax, Nova Scotia.
Date and place of marriage 24 Mar 1891, West Free Church, Helensburgh, near Glasgow
Age at marriage 32 years, 188 days
Years married 18 years, 220 days
First entered Parliament 4 Oct 1900
Date appointed PM 23 Oct 1922
Age at appointment 64 years, 37 days
Date ceased to be PM 20 May 1923
Total time as PM 209 days
Ceased to be MP 30 Oct 1923
Lived after last term as PM 162 days
Date of death 30 Oct 1923
Place of death 24 Onslow Gardens, London
Age at death 65 years, 44 days
Place of funeral and burial He was cremated at Golders Green on 3 Nov 1923 and his ashes were taken to St. Columba's, Pont Street, London. His funeral took place on 5 Nov 1923 at Westminster Abbey. It was the first occasion since Gladstone's death in 1898 that a Prime Minister was buried in Westminster Abbey. The pall-bearers included the Prince of Wales, the Speaker, the Prime Minister (Baldwin), Asquith, Beaverbrook, Balfour, and Ramsay MacDonald.
Zodiac sign Virgo

FATHER

Rev. James Law
Date and place of birth 1822 Portrush, nr. Coleraine, Northern Ireland
Occupation A Presbyterian Minister, he had been educated at Glasgow University, was minister at Coleraine briefly and in 1845 went to New Brunswick, Canada, where he was minister in Kingston and Richibucto for 32 years.
Dates of marriages 1) *c.* 1850 Elizabeth Kidston (d. 16 Mar 1861); 2) *c.* 1865, Sophia Wood (d. May 1914)
Date of death 6 Oct 1882
Place of burial Graveyard of Kirk of Ballywillan, Portrush, Northern Ireland

MOTHER

Elizabeth Anne Kidston
Date and place of birth 1825, Halifax Nova Scotia
Profile She was delicate, and brought courage and steadfastness to her role as minister's wife and mother of five children in the austere and arduous conditions of mid-19th century Canada. She had a sweet kindliness of character.
Date of death 16 Mar 1861
Place of burial Church at Kingston (Rexton) New Brunswick, Canada

STEPMOTHER

Sophia Wood
Profile School teacher
Date of death May 1914

BROTHERS AND SISTERS

Bonar Law was the youngest boy in a family of four sons and one daughter, and he also had two younger half-sisters by his father's second wife, Sophia.
From his father's first marriage:
Robert, b. *c.* 1853; m. Isobel Brown; a successful farmer and merchant, also a heavy drinker; d. 23 Jan 1902
William Kidston, b. *c.* 1854; m. 1886, Fanny Emily Lyons; a doctor, with a medical practice in Coleraine, Northern Ireland; d. 9 Apr 1926
John (Jack), b. *c.* 1856; a tea planter in Ceylon, later a partner in the firm of William Jacks & Co. of Glasgow. He managed a branch in Middlesbrough from 1888; d. between 1916 and 1919
Mary, b. 1860; unm.; kept house for Bonar Law after the death of his wife. He depended on her for counsel during his 12 years of supremacy in the Conservative Party; d. 1929
From his father's second marriage:
Janet, b. 1866; unm.
Elizabeth, b. 1868; married and settled in Bath, England

WIFE

Annie Pitcairn Robley
Date of birth *c.* 1866
Father Harrington Robley
Father's occupation Ship broker
Age at marriage *c.*24 years
Number of children 6
Date and place of death 31 Oct 1909, Leeds
Place of burial Helensburgh, near Glasgow
Years younger than PM 8
Profile Mrs. Law was a person of spontaneity, sweetness and charm who was universally loved and to whom her husband was devoted. She brought up a family of six children and organised the twice-yearly moves between Glasgow and London for the first six years Law was an MP. Her death at the age of 43 after a gall-bladder operation was a loss from which Law never recovered.

CHILDREN

4 sons, 2 daughters
James Kidston, b. 20 Sep 1893; served with the Royal Securities Corporation; commissioned in the Royal Fusiliers and joined the Flying Corps during World War I; with an Observation Squadron in France, killed in action; d. 21 Sep 1917
Isabel Harrington, b. 1896; m. 3 June 1920, Maj. Gen. Sir Frederick Hugh Sykes (Chief of Air Staff Apr 1918–Feb 1919; MP Sheffield Hallam, 1922–28; Nottingham, Central 1940–45; Governor of Bombay 1928–33); devoted to her father, she cared for him during his last illness when her own son was only a few months old; d. 1969
Charles John, b. 21 Feb 1897; joined 3rd King's Own Scottish Borders at outbreak of World War I, sent to Egypt and listed missing in action at the Battle of Gaza; d. 19 Apr 1917
Harrington Robley, born *c.* 1899; Lieut. Commander in the Royal Navy during World War II; senior blind-flying instructor in the Fleet Air-Arm;. d. 31 May 1958

CHILDREN—*Continued*

Richard Kidston (1st Baron Coleraine of Haltemprice, East Riding) b. 27 Feb 1901; m. 26 Jan 1929, Mary Virginia Nellis; MP Hull, S.W. 1931–45; S. Kensington 1945–50; Hull, Haltemprice 1950–54; Minister of State at the Foreign Office, with Cabinet rank, 1943–45; Minister of Education May–June 1945; d. 15 Nov 1980

Catherine Mary, b. 1905; m. 1) 1926, Kent Colwell (marriage dissolved 1941); 2) 15 Nov 1961, 1st Baron Archibald

LIFE AND CAREER

PARLIAMENTARY ELECTIONS FOUGHT

*(*designates candidate elected)*

DATE Oct 1900. General Election
CONSTITUENCY Glasgow, Blackfriars & Hutchesontown,
RESULT A.B. Law* (Con) 4,130; A.D. Provand (Lib) 3, 140

DATE 18 Jan 1906. General Election
CONSTITUENCY Glasgow, Blackfriars & Hutchesontown
RESULT G.N. Barnes* (Lab) 3,284; A.B. Law (Con) 2, 974; A.D. Provand (Lib) 2,058

DATE 15 May 1906. By-election caused by resignation of Dr. F.R. Harris.
CONSTITUENCY Camberwell, Dulwich
RESULT A.B. Law* (Con) 6,709; D. Williamson (Lib) 5, 430

DATE Jan 1910. General Election
CONSTITUENCY Camberwell, Dulwich
RESULT A.B. Law* (Con) 8,472; H.E.A. Cotton (Lib) 6, 054

DATE Dec 1910. General Election
CONSTITUENCY Manchester, North-West
RESULT Sir G. Kemp* (Lib) 5,559; A.B. Law (Con) 5,114

DATE 27 Mar 1911. By-election caused by the resignation of T.M. Sandys
CONSTITUENCY Lancashire, Bootle
RESULT A.B. Law* (Con) 9,976; M. Muspratt (Lib) 7,782

DATE 14 Dec 1918. General Election
CONSTITUENCY Glasgow, Central
RESULT A.B. Law* (Co Con) 17,653; D.J.M. Quin (Ind Lab) 4,736

DATE 15 Nov 1922 General Election
CONSTITUENCY Glasgow, Central
RESULT A.B. Law* (Con) 15,437; E.R. Mitchell (Lab) 12, 923; Sir G. Paish (Lib) 2,518

PARTY ACTIVITY

Party Leadership Leader of the Conservative Party 13 Nov 1911–21 Mar 1921

PARLIAMENTARY AND MINISTERIAL EXPERIENCE

Maiden Speech Law's speech, delivered during the debate on the Address, was a reply to a bitter attack by Lloyd George upon punitive measures taken by the British Army against Boer farmers. (*HC Deb* vol 89, 19 Feb 1901, col 527–30

Opposition offices Leader of the Opposition 13 Nov 1911–25 May 1915

Privy Counsellor 22 Jun 1911

Ministerial Offices Parliamentary Secretary to Board of Trade 8 Aug 1902–18 Dec 1905; Secretary of State for the Colonies 25 May 1915–10 Dec 1916; Leader of the House of Commons 10 Dec 1916–23 Mar 1921, 23 Oct 1922–20 May 1923; Chancellor of the Exchequer 10 Dec 1916–10 Jan 1919; Lord Privy Seal 1 Jan 1919–23 Mar 1921; First Lord of the Treasury 23 Oct 1922–20 May 1923

Opposition Leader while PM James Ramsay MacDonald (Lab)

GOVERNMENTS FORMED

Administration 23 Oct 1922–20 May 1923

GENERAL ELECTION RESULT

14 DEC 1918: Conservative 382; Liberal 163; Labour 57; Others 105. Total 707
Coalition majority 283 (excl. the Speaker)

15 NOV 1922: Conservative 344; Labour 142; Liberal 115; Others 14. Total 615
Conservative majority 74 (excl. the Speaker)

CABINET

Prime Minister and First Lord of the Treasury A.B. Law
Chancellor of the Exchequer S. Baldwin
Home Secretary W. C. Bridgeman
Foreign Secretary Marquess Curzon
Secretary of State for the Colonies Duke of Devonshire
Secretary of State for India Viscount Peel
Secretary for Scotland Viscount Novar
First Lord of the Admiralty L. S. Amery
Lord President of the Council Marquess of Salisbury
Secretary for War Earl of Derby
President of the Board of Trade Sir P. Lloyd-Greame
Lord Chancellor Viscount Cave
Minister of Agriculture and Fisheries Sir R. Sanders
President of the Board of Education E. Wood
Minister of Health Sir A. Griffith-Boscawen (Oct 1922–Mar 1923); N. Chamberlain (Mar–May 1923)
Minister of Labour Sir A. Montague Barlow

IMPORTANT DATES IN PERSONAL AND POLITICAL LIFE

16 MAR 1861 Law's mother dies when he is two years old. His mother's sister, Janet Kidston, comes to Canada from Glasgow to keep house for Rev. James Law and his children.

1865 After the remarriage of his father, Law's aunt Janet Kidston takes him from Canada to Scotland to live with relatives of his late mother.

1870–1873 Attends Gilbertfield School in Hamilton near Glasgow, and later Glasgow High School where he achieves academic success.

1875 He leaves school at 16 and goes to work in the Glasgow office of his Kidston cousins' merchant bank, which merges with the Clydesdale Bank in the 1880s.

1878 Law joins the Glasgow Parliamentary Debating Association, where he becomes familiar with parliamentary procedure and masters the art of debate and speechmaking.

1885 He joins the firm of William Jacks and Co., iron merchants of Glasgow, as a junior partner.

24 MAR 1891 Marries Annie Pitcairn Robley.

1896 Mrs. Charles Kidston, his cousin's widow, dies and leaves Law £30,000, which enables him to start considering a career in politics.

1898 He is offically adopted as prospective Conservative candidate for Blackfriars & Hutchesontown division of Glasgow.

11 OCT 1899 Boer War begins.

4 OCT 1900 First elected to Parliament as Conservative MP for Blackfriars & Hutchesontown division of Glasgow, in what the Liberals are to call the 'Khaki Election'. The Conservatives had used Liberal opposition to the Boer War to gain support.

22 JAN 1901 Death of Queen Victoria and accession of Edward VII.

19 FEB 1901 Law makes his maiden speech during the debate on the Address. Although controversial—he replies to a bitter attack by Lloyd George against measures taken by the British Army against the Boers—it is ignored by journalists who concentrate on another maiden speech made the previous day by Winston Churchill.

22 APR 1902 Law makes a major speech in the Commons in favour of corn duty, which is widely praised and leads to his first ministerial appointment a few months later.

31 MAY 1902 The Boer War ends, with the signing of the Treaty of Vereeniging.

8 AUG 1902 Appointed Parliamentary Secretary to the Board of Trade by Balfour. During his three years in this post Law first emerges as an important figure in the Conservative Party, proving an effective speaker, with a phenomenal memory, never needing notes.

4 DEC 1905 Balfour resigns as Prime Minister because of divisions within the Conservative Party over free trade and tariff reform, and is succeeded by Sir Henry Campbell-Bannerman.

18 JAN 1906 Law loses his Glasgow seat in the General Election.

15 MAY 1906 He is returned at a by-election as the Member for Dulwich.

5 APR 1908 Asquith becomes Prime Minister after Campbell-Bannerman's resignation because of ill-health.

31 OCT 1909 The death of his wife Annie after a gall-bladder operation leaves him desolate.

17 JAN 1910 Law retains his Dulwich seat at the General Election, which had been called by Asquith in the wake of problems caused by the House of Lords rejection of Lloyd George's 1909 'People's Budget'.

6 MAY 1910 Death of King Edward VII and accession of King George V.

SEP 1910 Law renews his acquaintance with Max Aitken (later Lord Beaverbrook) whom he had first met two years previously. Both of Canadian birth, they become life-long friends. Beaverbrook is to act as pall-bearer at Law's funeral.

DEC 1910 Another General Election is called in the face of proposals for reform of the House of Lords. Law is persuaded to give up his seat at Dulwich and fight for the marginal seat of Manchester North West as a Tariff Reform candidate. He loses by 445 votes to the Liberal Candidate.

27 MAR 1911 A safe Conservative seat is found for Law at Bootle when the sitting MP resigns because of ill-health, causing a by-election. He wins the seat by 2,194 votes.

22 JUN 1911 Appointed a Privy Counsellor in George V's coronation honours.

10 AUG 1911 A resolution on payment of Members is carried.

11 AUG 1911 The Parliament Act, to curb the powers of the House of Lords, is carried by 131 votes to 114.

13 NOV 1911 Law is elected Leader of the Conservative Party in the House of Commons after the resignation of Balfour.

23 NOV 1911 He addresses a conference of the National Union of Conservatives denouncing home rule for Ireland.

26 JAN 1912 In one of his first speeches as Party Leader, at the Albert Hall, Law makes a memorable attack on the Liberal Government, especially over the question of the disestablishment of the Church in Wales.

12 FEB 1912 At a meeting at Law's house a decision is made to amalgamate the Conservative Central Office, the Conservative National Union and the Liberal Unionist Council into a single organisation.

9 APR 1912 He addresses a large demonstration outside Belfast against Irish Home Rule.

11 APR 1912 Asquith introduces the third Irish Home Rule Bill, to which Bonar Law replies 5 days later in terms of uncompromising hostility.

29 JUL 1912 Law addresses a rally at Blenheim Palace to further denounce Irish Home Rule.

1913 Member of the Committee of Imperial Defence, a small group advising the Prime Minister.

18 JUL 1913 Law sums up for the Opposition during a debate on a Conservative motion regretting the actions of Lloyd George and Rufus Isaacs (Chancellor and Attorney-General respectively) over the Marconi Shares Scandal. They had been suspected of improper speculation in the purchase of shares from the Marconi Company, and although they are subsequently exonerated by a Committee of Inquiry, Law feels the House should put on record its disapproval of what has happened. He attacks the Ministers for their lack of candour about their dealings.

3 AUG 1914 Outbreak of World War I.

18 SEP 1914 The Irish Home Rule Bill receives Royal Assent. A suspensory Bill simultaneously provides that it should remain in abeyance until after the end of the War. Law leaves the House of Commons in protest and goes to Belfast in order to renew and extend pledges of the Unionist Party to Ulster.

25 MAY 1915 Law becomes Secretary of State for the Colonies in Asquith's Coalition Government.

16 JUN 1915 Trial begins in Edinburgh of the firm of William Jacks & Co., in which Law had been a partner. They are accused of trading with the enemy in time of war. The two defendants are found guilty and receive brief jail terms. Law is deeply distressed at what he considers their harsh treatment for a technical breach of the laws, and is cheered in the House of Commons when he rises in reply to a question about the case and states the facts about his connection.

5 DEC 1916 Because Asquith refuses to accept the plan for a small War Committee, proposed by Lloyd George with the support of Bonar Law and the Ulster Leader Carson, Lloyd George resigns as War Minister and on the same day, Asquith resigns as Prime Minister. Bonar Law is invited to form a Government, but he had made a pact with Lloyd George that he would only accept if Asquith agreed to serve under him. Asquith's refusal causes him to recommend to the King that Lloyd George become Prime Minister.

10 DEC 1916 Law is appointed Chancellor of the Exchequer and Leader of the House of Commons by Lloyd George, the new Prime Minister. Law is also a member of Lloyd George's War Cabinet of 5.

IMPORTANT DATES IN PERSONAL AND POLITICAL LIFE—*Continued*

11 JAN 1917 In a speech at the Guildhall Law announces a new War Loan, which raises over £1000 million by the closing date of 16 Feb.

19 APR AND 21 SEP 1917 His two eldest sons, James and Charles, are killed in World War I.

2 MAY 1917 Law introduces the 5th War Budget.

OCT 1917 Law launches a campaign for National War Bonds to provide the nation with a continuous flow of money until the end of the war.

22 APR 1918 The 6th War Budget is introduced by Bonar Law.

11 NOV 1918 Signing of the Armistice ends World War I.

DEC 1918 On the eve of the General Election the Prime Minister Lloyd George and Bonar Law issue a joint letter: 'Two paths are closed, the one leading to a complete severance of Ireland from the British Empire, and the other to a forcible submission of the six counties of Ulster to a Home Rule Parliament against their will.'

10 JAN 1919 Appointed Lord Privy Seal and Leader of the House of Commons in Lloyd George's Coalition Government.

DEC 1919 Elected Lord Rector of Glasgow University.

30 MAR 1920 Second Reading of a fourth and final Irish Home Rule Bill supported by Law. He receives a great ovation when he replies to Asquith's attack upon the Bill.

11 MAR 1921 He delivers address as Lord Rector of Glasgow University.

17 MAR 1921 Law resigns as Leader of the House and of the Conservative Party owing to ill-health. He recouperates in the South of France and returns in the autumn to recommend the Irish Treaty.

6 DEC 1921 The Irish Treaty, which divides Ireland into the Irish Free State and Northern Ireland, is concluded.

15 DEC 1921 Law speaks in support of the Government during second day of debate on the Irish Treaty, although he views it with some scepticism. He is greeted with applause and the Treaty is carried by 401 to 58.

19 OCT 1922 Growing disillusionment with Lloyd George's premiership leads to a meeting of Conservative MPs at the Carlton Club. They vote 187 to 87 to end the Coalition and fight the next election as an independent group. Lloyd George resigns and Bonar Law is asked by King George V to form a government.

23 OCT 1922 Bonar Law is unanimously elected Leader of the Conservative Party and formally appointed Prime Minister and First Lord of the Treasury.

15 NOV 1922 The Conservative Party wins the General Election with a majority of 75.

27 NOV 1922 The Second Reading of the Irish Free State Bill.

9–11 DEC 1922 Law presides over a conference of Allied Prime Ministers in London, which is adjourned to Paris until Jan 1923.

JAN 1923 The American Debt Settlement problem—the debt owed to the US by Britain for munitions supplied during the War—almost causes Law's resignation. He does not want to accept the terms of the settlement negotiated by Baldwin but finally bows to the wishes of his colleagues.

FEB 1923 Law issues a short New Year's Honours List containing the names of only those of unimpeachable respectability. He delays issuing his list until the Royal Commission on Honours, forced on his predecessor Lloyd George, has issued its report.

APR 1923 When Parliament re-assembles after Easter, Law is often unable to speak because of pain in his throat, and Baldwin has to act as his mouthpiece.

17 MAY 1923 Cancer of the throat is diagnosed, but Law is not told of his incurable illness.

20 MAY 1923 Law resigns as Prime Minister because of his failing health, and is succeeded by Stanley Baldwin.

30 OCT 1923 Dies peacefully in his sleep.

BACKGROUND

PHYSICAL CHARACTERISTICS AND HEALTH

Law was above average height, with light hair and blue eyes. He wore a moustache. He spoke with a soft Scottish Canadian accent which sounded unusual in the House of Commons of that day.

By a very early age he had become a teetotaller and never touched alcohol except on doctor's orders for the rest of his life. He cared nothing for the pleasures of the table and left as soon as his meal was finished to indulge his love of tobacco, smoking cigars and pipes incessantly.

Max Aitken, Lord Beaverbrook, described Law as, 'A sombre raven among the glittering birds of paradise'.

EDUCATION

Primary Local schoolhouse in Kingston (now Rexton), New Brunswick, Canada

Secondary Gilbertfield School, Hamilton, Lanarkshire; Glasgow High School

University Law left school at 16, before he had matriculated, but he enrolled at Glasgow University for certain courses of study specially arranged for young businessmen (from 8 am–10 am)

Prizes and awards May 1873, First Prize for Greek in the Junior Class at Gilbertfield; Sep 1874, First Prize for French in the Junior Class of the Senior Division at Glasgow High School

Cultural and vocational background He was an avid reader, and admired the works of Walter Scott, Dickens, Gibbon and Carlyle. He had an encyclopaedic knowledge of the works of Carlyle and claimed to Austen Chamberlain that he had read Gibbon's *Decline and Fall* three times before he was 21. His favourite book was Carlyle's *Sartor Resartus* and to some extent the influence of Carlyle may have contributed to Law's Conservatism.

Languages Law read French and German and spoke French.

NON-PARLIAMENTARY CAREER

Early occupations On leaving school at the age of 16 Law joined the family firm of merchant bankers (William, Richard and Charles Kidston, first cousins of his mother). He worked for 10 years in the Glasgow office, commuting by train the 20 or so miles from Helensburgh.

In 1885 he joined the Glasgow firm of William Jacks & Co., Iron Merchants, as a junior partner, and remained there until he entered Parliament in 1900.

Other posts Chairman of the Scottish Iron Trade Association; JP for Dunbartonshire

HONOURS

Freedom of cities Bootle
Academic 1919, Lord Rector of Glasgow University; 1920, LL.D. Cambridge University; LL.D. Glasgow University

CLUBS

Carlton

HOBBIES AND SPORTS

Bonar Law enjoyed playing lawn tennis and with friends founded a tennis club at Helensburgh. He was also a keen golfer and after his marriage spent nearly every holiday near a golf course. He was devoted to indoor games, especially billiards, whist, bridge and chess—at which he excelled.

FINANCES

Bonar Law was able to consider entering Parliament partly because of the legacies totalling £60,000 he received from his relatives Catherine and Janet Kidston and also because he retained the directorships of his businesses—the Clydesdale Bank and Williams Jacks & Co. of Glasgow. He sustained heavy losses at the end of his life owing to the collapse of Williams Jacks & Co. Law knew how to make money and was successful in doing so, but there is no doubt his substantial legacies were of great assistance.
Income £6,000 p.a. during his first 10 years in Parliament, of which £4,500 came from investments and the remainder from directorships. After 1915 his income was £10,000 p.a.
Legacies He received two legacies of £30,000 each from his cousin Catherine Kidston and his aunt Janet Kidston, the first in 1896 and the second ten years later.
Will His estate totalled £71,324 (£61,213 after deduction of estate duty)

ANECDOTES

Although Bonar Law was generally regarded as a rather sombre figure, with no interest in the arts, music or dancing, it is recorded that during his engagement to Annie Robley he attended a fancy dress ball dressed as a sailor, while his fiancée was disguised as a Swiss peasant. His choice of costume was surprising as he was not a good sailor and suffered sea-sickness crossing to Ireland.

'It is fitting that we should have buried the Unknown Prime Minister by the side of the Unknown Soldier'. (H. H. Asquith, on the interment of Law's ashes in Westminster Abbey, Nov 1923)

Stanley Baldwin, in a letter to Lord Beaverbrook on 18 Dec 1928, said of him 'The most characteristic thing to those who knew him would be a ginger cake and a glass of milk, to which I brought him home pretty nearly every night for about four years.'

'I told Bonar that . . . I had been to a Mozart concert and the music was wonderful. Bonar remarked: "I don't care for music". As we motored along there was the Mediterranean blue sea on one side and the . . . Alpes Maritimes on the other. "Look, Bonar, what a wonderful scene that is". "I don't care for scenery", remarked Bonar. Presently we came to a bridge . . . I said to Bonar: "Look, Bonar, aren't those handsome women?" "I don't care for women", remarked Bonar very drily. "Then what the hell do you care for?" I asked. Then in his very soft voice, and quieter still, Bonar replied, "I like bridge".' (David Lloyd George)

'The fools have stumbled on their best man by accident' was the comment made by Lloyd George when Bonar Law was elected Leader of the Conservative Party in 1911.

Law was described thus in a letter by Lord Derby to George V, on 16 Nov 1911: 'He is a curious mixture. Never very gay, he has become even less so since the death of his wife . . . But still he has a great sense of humour—a first class debator—and a good though not a rousing platform speaker. He has all the great qualities of a great leader except one—and that is he has no personal magnetism and can inspire no man to real enthusiasm'.

Bonar Law cared nothing for art and music: theatre and opera bored him to distraction. When he received an honorary degree at Cambridge in 1920 special arrangements were made for him to be spared the music in King's Chapel.

Lord Beaverbrook, Law's great friend, said about his hospitality: 'The food on Bonar's table was always quite execrable. Its sameness was a penance and its quality a horror to me.' Beaverbrook's devotion to Law is best illustrated by his reply to Frances Stevenson's question 'You did love Bonar, didn't you Max?' (recounted in her 1976 autobiography) He replied unhesitatingly: 'I loved him more than anyone else in the world.'

QUOTATIONS

13 Nov 1911, If I am a great man then a good many great men of history are frauds. (In reply to Max Aitken on his election to leadership of Conservative Party)

27 Nov 1911, If, therefore, war should ever come between these two countries [Great Britain and Germany] which Heaven forbid! it will not, I think, be due to irresistible natural laws, it will be due to the want of human wisdom. (Speech in House of Commons)

26 Jan 1912, An example of destructive violence to which there is no parallel since the Long Parliament. (Speech at Albert Hall, London, on the record of Asquith's Government)

9 Apr 1912, I am afraid I shall have to show myself very vicious, Mr. Asquith, this session. I hope you will understand. (to Asquith, at the beginning of the 1912 session of Parliament)

[They [the present Liberal Government] have turned the House of Commons into an exchange where everything is bought and sold. In order to retain for a little longer the ascendancy of their party, to remain a few months longer in office, they have sold the Constitution, they have sold themselves. (Speech at Belfast)

29 Jul 1912, I can imagine no length of resistance to which Ulster can go in which I should not be prepared to support them, and in which, in my belief, they would not be supported by the overwhelming majority of the British people. (Speech at Blenheim Palace)

QUOTATIONS—*Continued*

1922, George will always be his own Party. (of David Lloyd George)

RESIDENCES

The Old Manse of St. Andrews, Kingston (now Rexton) New Brunswick, Canada
Ferniegair, Helensburgh, nr. Glasgow
Seabank, Helensburgh, nr. Glasgow
Kintillo, Helensburgh, nr. Glasgow
Pembroke Lodge, London
11 Downing Street
24 Onslow Gardens (plaque), London
10 Downing Street

MEMORIALS

PORTRAITS

By Sir James Guthrie, National Portrait Gallery, London; by René de l'Hôpital, Carlton Club, London; by J. B. Anderson, Constitutional Club, London; by J. B. Anderson, Conservative Club, Glasgow; cartoon by 'Spy', cartoon *Vanity Fair*

OTHER MEMORIALS

A cairn was raised to Law's memory in the Main Street of Rexton, New Brunswick, in 1925.

BIBLIOGRAPHIC INFORMATION

LETTERS AND PERSONAL PAPERS

Bonar Law's papers are now in the House of Lords Record Office.

FURTHER READING

Blake, R. *The Unknown Prime Minister*. London, 1955.
Taylor, M. A. *The Strange Case of Andrew Bonar Law* London, 1932.

C.F.

Bettmann

Stanley Baldwin

Lived 1867–1947
Political Party Conservative
Prime Minister 22 May 1923–22 January 1924; 4 November 1924–4 June 1929; 7 June 1935– 28 May 1937
Governments 1) Conservative; 2) Conservative; 3) National
Reigning Monarchs George V; Edward VIII; George VI

Per deum meum transilio murum With the help of my God I leap over the wall

BALDWIN AS PRIME MINISTER

Baldwin, like his predecessor, was a successful businessman first elected to Parliament in early middle age. He became Prime Minister after eight years as a backbencher and seven years as a minister, latterly Chancellor of the Exchequer. He believed in well-tried methods and traditional remedies. His first Premiership followed the resignation of Law for health reasons but within months Baldwin called a General Election on the issue of Free Trade, lost it and MacDonald became first Labour Prime Minister. But within a year, following a Government defeat, Baldwin was returned as Prime Minister with a solid majority. His 1924-1929 Government was concerned with housing and social welfare, seeking to bind the country and its classes together. Baldwin himself sought to act as a conciliator. Good at taking advice, he would support his Cabinet colleagues rather than impose his own ideas. At the General Strike of 1926, he held a firm conservative line while leaving action to Churchill and others. In 1927, partly under pressure from his own party, he pursued his anti-labour policy through the amendment of the Trade Disputes Act of 1906, restricting certain powers of the unions. Defeated at the 1929 election, in 1931 he joined MacDonald's first National Government and became Prime Minister again in 1935. He regarded the League of Nations with sympathetic scepticism and under MacDonald supported the idea of Dominion Status for India. At the 1935 election, which was fought mostly on domestic issues, Baldwin achieved a comfortable majority. His final achievement as Prime Minister was his adroit handling of the Abdication Crisis in 1936 when Edward VIII announced his intention of marrying an American divorcée, in violation of the principles of the Church of England, of which he was the head. Edward abdicated and his brother became King George VI. Baldwin failed to respond energetically enough to the emerging threat from Germany (occupation of the Rhineland in 1936), despite rearmament being an issue in the 1935 election campaign.

PERSONAL INFORMATION

Names Stanley Baldwin
Peerages Earl Baldwin of Bewdley and Viscount Corvedale, 8 Jun 1937
Born 3 Aug 1867
Birthplace Lower Park House, Bewdley, Worcestershire
Religion Anglican
Ancestry British. His father's family had been for centuries Shropshire yeomen who had settled as ironmasters within the Worcestershire border. His mother was one of the children of a Wesleyan minister of Highland stock who had settled in Northern Ireland after 1745.
Date and place of marriage 12 Sep 1892, St. Margaret's Church, Rottingdean, Sussex
Age at marriage 25 years, 40 days
Years married 52 years, 278 days
First entered Parliament 2 Mar 1908
Dates appointed PM 1) 22 May 1923; 2) 4 Nov 1924; 3) 7 Jun 1935
Age at appointments 1) 55 years, 292 days; 2) 57 years, 93 days; 3) 67 years, 308 days
Dates ceased to be PM 1) 22 Jan 1924; 2) 4 Jun 1929; 3) 28 May 1937
Total time as PM 1) 245 days; 2) 4 years, 212 days; 3) 1 year, 355 days; a total of 7 years, 82 days
Ceased to be MP 8 Jun 1937
Lived after last term as PM 10 years, 189 days
Date and place of death 14 Dec 1947, Astley Hall, Stourport-on-Severn, Worcestershire
Age at death 80 years, 133 days
Last words I am ready.
Place of funeral and burial Worcester Cathedral, Worcestershire
Zodiac sign Leo

FATHER

Alfred Baldwin
Date and place of birth 4 Jun 1841, Stourport-on-Severn, Worcestershire
Occupation MP Bewdley or West Division of Worcestershire, 1892–1908; Ironmaster; Chairman of Baldwin's Ltd., The Metropolitan Bank (of England and Wales), and The Great Western Railway
Date of marriage 9 Aug 1866
Date of death 13 Feb 1908
Place of burial All Saints Church, Wilden, near Stourport-on-Severn, Worcestershire

MOTHER

Louisa Macdonald
Date and place of birth 25 Aug 1845, Wakefield, Yorkshire
Profile Author of short story (written 1865) later published in the *Victoria Magazine*, of four novels, a volume of ghost stories (*The Shadow on the Blind and Other Ghost Stories*, 1895) and several books of poems and tales for children.
Date of marriage 9 Aug 1866
Age when PM took office 77 years, 270 days
Date of death 16 May 1925
Place of burial All Saints Church, Wilden, near Stourport-on-Severn, Worcestershire

BROTHERS AND SISTERS

Baldwin was an only child.

WIFE

Lucy Ridsdale
Date and place of birth 19 Jan 1869, Lancaster Villa, Aldridge Road Villas, Paddington, London
Mother Esther Lucy Thacker
Father Edward Lucas Jenks Ridsdale of The Dene, Rottingdean, Sussex
Father's occupation Master of the Mint
Age at marriage 22 years, 237 days
Number of children 7
Date and place of death 17 Jun 1945, Astley Hall, Stourport-on-Severn, Worcestershire
Place of burial Worcester Cathedral, Worcestershire
Years younger than PM 1 year, 169 days
Profile She was lively, outgoing, fond of playing sports, such as cricket and hockey. Sociable, she enjoyed parties and dancing. She was highly supportive of her husband, a practical homemaker and lived through her children, relations and friends. She had high moral standards and was involved in good works.

CHILDREN

4 daughters, 3 sons (the first stillborn)
Diana Lucy, b. 8 Apr 1895; m. 1) 24 Nov 1919, Captain Richard Gordon Munro, (div. 1934); 2) 24 Feb 1934, Captain George Durant Kemp-Welch
Leonora (Lorna) Stanley, b. 10 Jul 1896; m. 20 Jun 1922, Captain Hon. Sir Arthur Jared Palmer Howard (MP St. George's Westminster 1945–50)
Pamela Margaret (Margot), b. 16 Sep 1897; m. 2 Apr 1919, Captain Sir Herbert Maurice Huntington-Whiteley, 2nd Bt. (RN)
Oliver Ridsdale (2nd Earl Baldwin of Bewdley, Viscount Corvedale), b. 1 Mar 1899; unm.; author, journalist; served in World War I (Lieutenant, Irish Guards) and World War II (Major in Intelligence Corps); MP Dudley, 1929–31 and Paisley 1945–47; Governor of Leeward Islands, 1948–50; d. 10 Aug 1958
Esther Louisa (Betty), b. 16 Mar 1902
Arthur Windham (3rd Earl Baldwin of Bewdley, Viscount Corvedale), b. 22 Mar 1904; m. 25 Aug 1936, Joan Elspeth Tomes; served in World War II (RAF); Director of Great Western Railway and of Equitable Life Assurance Society; author; d. 5 Jul 1976

LIFE AND CAREER

PARLIAMENTARY ELECTIONS FOUGHT

*(*designates candidate elected)*

DATE Jan 1906. General Election
CONTITUENCY Kidderminster
RESULT E. B. Barnard* (Lib) 2,354; S. Baldwin (Con) 2,083

DATE 2 Mar 1908. By-election caused by death of Alfred Baldwin
CONTITUENCY Bewdley
RESULT S. Baldwin* (Con)

DATE Jan 1910. General Election
CONTITUENCY Bewdley
RESULT S. Baldwin* (Con) 6,618; J. L. Brooks (Lib) 2,370

DATE Dec 1910. General Election
CONTITUENCY Bewdley
RESULT S. Baldwin* (Con)

DATE 14 Dec 1918. General Election
CONTITUENCY Bewdley
RESULT S. Baldwin* (Con)

DATE 19 Apr 1921. By-election caused by Baldwin's appointment*as President of the Board of Trade
CONTITUENCY Bewdley
RESULT S. Baldwin* (Con) 14,537; H. Mills (Ind Lab) 1,680

DATE 15 Nov 1922. General Election
CONTITUENCY Bewdley
RESULT S. Baldwin* (Con) 11,192; S. Hancock (Lib) 5,748

DATE 6 Dec 1923. General Election
CONTITUENCY Bewdley
RESULT S. Baldwin* (Con) 12,395; S. Hancock (Lib) 6,026

DATE 29 Oct 1924. General Election
CONTITUENCY Bewdley
RESULT S. Baldwin* (Con)

DATE 30 May 1929. General Election
CONTITUENCY Bewdley
RESULT S. Baldwin* (Con) 16,593; S. B. Carter (Lib) 7,186; S. Hancock (Lab) 2,575

DATE 27 Oct 1931. General Election
CONTITUENCY Bewdley
RESULT S. Baldwin* (Con)

DATE 14 Nov 1935. General Election
CONTITUENCY Bewdley
RESULT S. Baldwin* (Con)

PARTY ACTIVITY

Party Leadership Leader of the Conservative Party, 1923–37

Other offices Baldwin served as a lay member of the Enemy Aliens Tribunal, Jun 1915–Sep 1917. He was appointed Parliamentary Private Secretary to Andrew Bonar Law, Chancellor of the Exchequer, in Dec 1916.

Membership of group or faction Member of the Unionist Business Committee, a Conservative 'ginger group' of backbench MPs

PARLIAMENTARY AND MINISTERIAL EXPERIENCE

Maiden Speech 22 Jun 1908, spoke on the Second Reading of the Coal Mines Bill from the viewpoint of an employer and a manufacturer. (*HC Deb*, vol 190, col 1433–1438)

Opposition offices Leader of the Opposition, 1924 and 1929–31.

Privy Counsellor 11 Jun 1920; 2 Aug 1927 (Canada)

Ministerial Offices Junior Lord of the Treasury, 29 Jan–18 Jun 1917; Financial Secretary to the Treasury, 18 Jun 1917–1 Apr 1921; President of the Board of Trade, 1 Apr 1921–24 Oct 1922; Chancellor of the Exchequer, 24 Oct 1922–27 Aug 1923; First Lord of the Treasury and Leader of the House of Commons 22 May 1923– 22 Jan 1924, 4 Nov 1924–5 Jun 1929, 7 Jun 1935–28 May 1937; Lord President of the Council, 25 Aug 1931–7 Jun 1935; Lord Privy Seal, 29 Sep 1932–31 Dec 1933.

Opposition Leaders while PM 1923–24, James Ramsay MacDonald; 1924–29, James Ramsay MacDonald; 1935–37, Clement Attlee

GOVERNMENTS FORMED

First Administration 22 May 1923–22 Jan 1924

GENERAL ELECTION RESULT

15 NOV 1922: Conservative 344; Labour 142; Liberal 115; Others 14. Total 615
Conservative majority 74 (excl. the Speaker)

CABINET

Prime Minister and First Lord of the Treasury S. Baldwin
Lord President of the Council Marquess of Salisbury
Lord Chancellor Viscount Cave
Lord Privy Seal Lord R. Cecil
Chancellor of the Exchequer S. Baldwin (May–Aug 1923); N. Chamberlain (Aug 1923–Jan 1924)
*Financial Secretary to the Treasury** Sir W. Joynson-Hicks (May–Aug 1923)
Foreign Secretary Marquess Curzon
Home Secretary W. Bridgeman
First Lord of the Admiralty L. Amery
Minister of Agriculture and Fisheries Sir R. Sanders
Secretary of State for Air Sir S. Hoare
Secretary of State for the Colonies Duke of Devonshire
President of the Board of Education E. Wood
Minister of Health N. Chamberlain (May–Aug 1923); Sir W. Joynson-Hicks (Aug 1923–Jan 1924)
Secretary of State for India Viscount Peel
Minister of Labour Sir A. Montague-Barlow
Postmaster-General Sir L. Worthington-Evans
Secretary for Scotland Viscount Novar
President of the Board of Trade Sir P. Lloyd-Greame
Secretary of State for War Earl of Derby
[*Office not always in Cabinet]

Second Administration 4 Nov 1924–4 Jun 1929

GENERAL ELECTION RESULT

29 OCT 1924: Conservative 412; Labour 151; Liberal 40; Others 12. Total 615
Conservative majority 210 (excl. the Speaker)

CABINET

Prime Minister and First Lord of the Treasury S. Baldwin
Lord President of the Council Marquess Curzon (1924–Apr 1925); Earl of Balfour (Apr 1925–29)

Second Administration 4 Nov 1924–4 Jun 1929—*Continued*

Lord Chancellor Viscount Cave (1924–Mar 1928); Lord Hailsham (Viscount) (Mar 1928–29)
Lord Privy Seal Marquess of Salisbury
Chancellor of the Exchequer W. Churchill
Foreign Secretary Sir A. Chamberlain
Home Secretary Sir W. Joynson-Hicks
First Lord of the Admiralty W. Bridgeman
Minister of Agriculture and Fisheries E. Wood (1924–Nov 1925); W. Guinness (Nov 1925–29)
Secretary of State for Air Sir S. Hoare
*Attorney General** Sir D. Hogg (Lord Hailsham) (1924–Mar 1928)
Secretary of State for Dominion Affairs L. Amery (Jun 1925–29)
Secretary of State for Colonial Affairs L. Amery
President of the Board of Education Lord E. Percy
Minister of Health N. Chamberlain
Secretary of State for India Earl of Birkenhead (1924–Oct 1928); Viscount Peel (Oct 1928–29)
Minister of Labour Sir A. Steel-Maitland
Chancellor of the Duchy of Lancaster Viscount Cecil of Chelwood (Nov 1924–Oct 1927); Lord Cushendun (Oct 1927–29)
Secretary for Scotland Sir J. Gilmour
President of the Board of Trade Sir P. Lloyd-Greame (changed name to Sir P. Cunliffe-Lister, 27 Nov 1927)
Secretary of State for War Sir L. Worthington-Evans
First Commissioner of Works Viscount Peel (1924–Oct 1928); Marquess of Londonderry (Oct 1928–29)
[*Office not always in Cabinet]

Third Administration 7 Jun–14 Nov 1935 (National Government)

GENERAL ELECTION RESULT

27 OCT 1931: Conservative 522; Labour 52; Liberal 36 (of whom 4 opposed the National Government); Others 5. Total 615
National Government majority 492 (excl. the Speaker)

CABINET

Prime Minister and First Lord of the Treasury S. Baldwin
Lord President of the Council J. MacDonald
Lord Chancellor Viscount Hailsham
Lord Privy Seal Marquess of Londonderry
Chancellor of the Exchequer N. Chamberlain
Foreign Secretary Sir S. Hoare
Home Secretary Sir J. Simon
First Lord of the Admiralty Sir B. Eyres-Monsell (Viscount Monsell)
Minister of Agriculture and Fisheries W. Elliot
Secretary of State for Air Sir P. Cunliffe-Lister (Viscount Swinton)
Secretary of State for the Colonies M. MacDonald
Secretary of State for Dominion Affairs J. Thomas
President of the Board of Education O. Stanley
Minister of Health Sir K. Wood
Secretary of State for India Marquess of Zetland
Minister of Labour E. Brown
Minister without Portfolio for League of Nations Affairs A. Eden
Secretary of State for Scotland Sir G. Collins
President of the Board of Trade W. Runciman
Secretary of State for War Viscount Halifax
First Commissioner of Works W. Ormsby-Gore

Fourth Administration 15 Nov 1935–28 May 1937 (National Government)

GENERAL ELECTION RESULT

14 NOV 1935: Conservative 429; Labour 154; Liberal 21; Others 11. Total 615
National Government majority 242 (excl. the Speaker)

CABINET

Prime Minister and First Lord of the Treasury S. Baldwin
Lord President of the Council J. R. MacDonald
Lord Chancellor Viscount Hailsham
Lord Privy Seal Viscount Halifax
Chancellor of the Exchequer N. Chamberlain
Foreign Secretary Sir S. Hoare (Nov–Dec 1935); A. Eden (Dec 1935–37)
Home Secretary Sir J. Simon
First Lord of the Admiralty Sir B. Eyres-Monsell (Viscount Monsell) (Dec 1935–Jun 1936); Sir S. Hoare (Jun 1936–37)
Minister of Agriculture and Fisheries W. Elliot (Dec 1935–Oct 1936); W. Morrison (Oct 1936–37)
Secretary of State for Air Sir P. Cunliffe-Lister (Viscount Swinton)
Secretary of State for the Colonies J. Thomas (Nov 1935–May 1936); W. Ormsby-Gore (May 1936–37)
*Minister for Co-ordination of Defence** Sir Thomas Inskip (Mar 1936–37)
Secretary of State for Dominion Affairs M. MacDonald
President of the Board of Education O. Stanley
Minister of Health Sir K. Wood
Secretary of State for India Marquess of Zetland
Minister of Labour E. Brown
Minister Without Portfolio Lord E. Percy (Jun 1935–Mar 1936)
Minister Without Portfolio for League of Nations Affairs A. Eden (Nov–Dec 1935)
Secretary of State for Scotland Sir G. Collins (Nov 1935–Oct 1936); W. Elliot (Oct 1936–37)
President of the Board of Trade W. Runciman
*Minister of Transport** Lord Hore-Belisha (Oct 1936–37)
Secretary of State for War A.D. Cooper
First Commissioner of Works W. Ormsby-Gore (Nov 1935–Jun 1936); Earl Stanhope (Jun 1936–37)
[*Office not always in Cabinet]

IMPORTANT DATES IN PERSONAL AND POLITICAL LIFE

1888 Baldwin takes a BA in history at Trinity College, Cambridge, and spends the next few years working in the family business, E.P. & W. Baldwin, later Baldwins Ltd., iron and steel manufacturers of Wilden, near Stourport-on-Severn, Worcestershire.

12 SEP 1892 Marries Lucy, daughter of E.L.J. Ridsdale, former Master of the Mint.

JAN 1906 Unsuccessfully contests Kidderminster at the General Election.

2 MAR 1908 On the death of his father, Alfred, MP for Bewdley, Stanley Baldwin is adopted for and elected to the seat. At the same time he inherits the bulk of his father's fortune of £250,000.

22 JUN 1908 Makes his maiden speech in the House.

1915 Member of Government committees on War Office contracts and on post-war trade problems stemming from German economic penetration. He also is a member of a Conservative ginger group of backbenchers, the

Unionist Business Committee, seeking a more efficient prosecution of the war.

JUN 1915–SEP 1917 Serves on the Enemy Aliens Tribunal, a judicial committee set up to review the cases of enemy aliens arrested and interned under the Defence of the Realm Act.

DEC 1916 Appointed Parliamentary Private Secretary to Andrew Bonar Law, Chancellor of the Exchequer.

29 JAN 1917–18 JUN 1917 Baldwin holds the post of a Junior Lord of the Treasury (unpaid), to act in effect as Under Secretary to the Chancellor of the Exchequer, the Financial Secretary to the Treasury at the time, Hardman Lever, having no seat in the House of Commons.

18 JUN 1917 Appointed Financial Secretary to the Treasury in Lloyd George's Coalition Government.

24 JUN 1919 Baldwin writes an anonymous letter to *The Times* urging the wealthy to impose a voluntary tax on themselves to help relieve the national burden. He invests £150,000 (20% of his estate) in government war loan stock and then destroys the stock certificates, thus making a £150,000 gift to the Treasury. Few follow his example, however.

11 JUN 1920 Made a Privy Counsellor.

1 APR 1921 Baldwin appointed President of the Board of Trade, and a member of the Cabinet, succeeding Sir Robert Horne who becomes Chancellor of the Exchequer.

31 MAY 1921 Baldwin introduces the Safeguarding of Industries Bill to give a measure of protection to British goods.

19 OCT 1922 At the Carlton Club party meeting Baldwin and other Conservatives, realising that the party leaders are prepared to face a General Election under Lloyd George, rebel and carry a resolution that the Conservatives should fight as an independent party with its own leader and its own programme. He seconds Bonar Law's election as Leader.

24 OCT 1922 Appointed Chancellor of the Exchequer.

15 NOV 1922 Baldwin is again returned for Bewdley at the General Election.

31 JAN 1923 Following Baldwin's trip to Washington to arrange for the settlement of the American debt, the Cabinet approves the terms he has secured.

16 FEB 1923 During Bonar Law's illness Baldwin comes to lead the House of Commons. In a speech on the Address he reveals his recipe for 'salvation for this country . . . Faith, Hope, Love and Work', leaving a deep impression on the House.

16 APR 1923 Baldwin introduces his first Budget.

20 MAY 1923 Bonar Law, a dying man, resigns as Prime Minister.

22 MAY 1923 Baldwin becomes Prime Minister.

28 MAY 1923 He is elected Leader of the Conservative Party.

26 JUN 1923 In a statement on air defence, Baldwin lays down the principle that Britain must not be left in a position of inferiority in air strength to any country within bombing range.

27 AUG 1923 Baldwin is replaced by Neville Chamberlain as Chancellor of the Exchequer.

19 SEP 1923 Baldwin meets Poincaré, the French premier, for informal talks in Paris on his way back from holiday in Aix-les-Bains. They issue a communique of surprising warmth, considering their differing views about the occupation of the Ruhr and the payment of reparations.

13 NOV 1923 Baldwin announces he has decided to dissolve Parliament at once and hold a General Election on the tariff issue.

6 DEC 1923 Baldwin is re-elected at Bewdley in the General Election and the Conservatives are returned with 258 seats against Labour's 191 and the Liberals' 158.

15 JAN 1924 The Government is defeated at the end of the debate on the Address.

16 JAN 1924 Baldwin resigns as Prime Minister and George V invites Ramsay MacDonald, as Leader of the next largest party in the Commons, to form an administration.

11 FEB 1924 Baldwin is re-elected to the leadership of the Conservative parliamentary party.

8 OCT 1924 The Labour Government is defeated in the House after the Attorney General drops the prosecution of John Campbell, acting editor of the Communist *Worker's Weekly* which has published an article appealing to members of the armed forces not to fire on fellow workers either in the military or in the class war.

29 OCT 1924 In the General Election Baldwin is returned unopposed at Bewdley. The Conservatives win 412 seats, Labour 151 and the Liberals 40.

4 NOV 1924 Baldwin becomes Prime Minister for the second time.

6 MAR 1925 He opposes the Bill introduced by the Conservative backbencher, Frederick Macquisten, the Trade Union (Political Fund) Bill, to oblige all trade unionists wishing to pay the political levy henceforth to contract in. Baldwin thinks this will not help industrial relations and makes a powerful speech, ending with the prayer 'Give peace in our time, O Lord'.

31 JUL 1925 In a difficult industrial situation, Baldwin pleads for conciliation. When the miners are on the eve of forcing a general stoppage Baldwin resorts to a Royal Commission and a subsidy.

1 DEC 1925 Baldwin, together with the Foreign Secretary, Austen Chamberlain, signs the Locarno Treaty for Great Britain. Under the Treaty the five signatories, the United Kingdom, France, Belgium, Italy and Germany, guarantee the inviolability of the German-Belgian and German-French frontiers as fixed by the Treaty of Versailles.

3 DEC 1925 Baldwin and others sign an Amending Agreement supplementing the Articles of the Treaty (of 1921) which settle a boundary dispute with the Irish Free State Government.

MAR 1926 The Samuel Report on the coal industry opposes nationalisation, but advocates some wage reduction on condition that both sides accept a policy of reorganisation. The Government accepts the report and leaves owners and miners to settle the details between them.

4 MAY 1926 The owners and miners fail to reach an agreement and a General Strike begins.

12 MAY 1926 End of the General Strike.

OCT 1926 Baldwin presides at his second Imperial Conference in London.

AUG 1927 Baldwin visits Canada with the Prince of Wales and makes a series of speeches interpreting Great Britain to Canada.

JUL 1928 Franchise extended to women of 21 and upwards on the same terms as men.

11 MAY 1929 Parliament dissolved.

30 MAY 1929 General Election. Baldwin returned for Bewdley but in the House the Liberals, with 59 seats, hold the balance between Labour's 287 and the Conservatives' 260.

5 JUN 1929 Baldwin resigns.

OCT–NOV 1929 Baldwin rebukes in the House of Commons newspaper attacks on his Indian policy instigated

IMPORTANT DATES IN PERSONAL AND POLITICAL LIFE—*Continued*

by newspaper proprietors Lords Beaverbrook and Rothermere, who are running an Empire Free Trade campaign, with which Baldwin is in only partial agreement.

SPRING, 1930 Relations between Baldwin and the press lords deteriorate still further after Rothermere demands that he be acquainted by Baldwin 'with the names of at least eight, or ten, of his most prominent colleagues in the next Ministry'.

MAR 1930 Baldwin becomes Chancellor of Cambridge University.

24 JUN 1930 At a party meeting in the Caxton Hall Baldwin replies with force and passion to the press lords' 'preposterous and insolent demand' and is given a vote of confidence with only one dissentient and an enthusiastic welcome when he enters the House of Commons later in the day.

30 OCT 1930 The campaign against Baldwin continues, and he is forced to confront it again in the same hall. By 462 votes to 116, however, he is confirmed in the leadership.

12 MAR 1931 Baldwin continues to promote views on India and Empire free trade at variance with those of many in the party, notably Churchill and the 'Diehards' but succeeds in rallying fellow MPs behind him in the debate in the House on India when he expresses his strong support for Viceroy Lord Irwin's policy of eventual Dominion status for India.

17 MAR 1931 In a speech at the Queen's Hall, in support of Duff Cooper, a Conservative candidate for Parliament, Baldwin replies fiercely to the press lords.

25 AUG 1931 The costs of unemployment insurance and the dole mount rapidly. The May Committee appointed to overhaul public expenditure propose drastic reductions, which divide and break up the Labour Government. A National Government is formed, MacDonald remaining Prime Minister. Baldwin becomes Lord President.

27 OCT 1931 General Election. Baldwin is returned unopposed for Bewdley. Conservatives win 522 seats and dominate the National Government. Baldwin does not wish to press his own claims to be Prime Minister and is content to serve as Lord President for four years, a position with influence in the Cabinet and of authority over his party.

SPRING, 1932 The Japanese invasion of Manchuria demonstrates the impotence of the League of Nations in the Far East.

29 FEB 1932 The Import Duties Bill receives Royal Assent. This imposes a general tariff and sets up an Import Duties Advisory Committee, marking a definite return to the protectionist era for which Baldwin has always yearned.

JUL–AUG 1932 Baldwin presides at the Imperial Economic Conference in Ottawa. Free trade members of the coalition who had threatened resignation as early as Jan 1932 can no longer 'agree to differ' and resign.

JAN 1933 Hitler is appointed German Chancellor.

25 OCT 1933 The generally pacifist and pro-disarmament feeling in the country is demonstrated in the East Fulham by-election by a marked turnover of votes to Labour. Later, Baldwin, in a speech to the House on 12 Nov 1936, looking back on this event, is to assert that his party would never have won a mandate for rearmament in the subsequent General Election, given the feeling in the country.

30 JUL 1934 Although Baldwin had told the House that the power and range of aircraft had abolished the old frontiers, he sounds no urgent alarm at the growth of German air power in introducing a measure of rearmament. His advisers are slow to give credence to reports of German rearmament. Baldwin deprecates panic and sees 'no risk in the immediate future of the peace being broken'.

NOV 1934 Baldwin admits that looking ahead 'there is ground for very grave anxiety' but maintains that 'It is not the case that Germany is rapidly approaching equality with us'. By May 1935 he feels that the estimate of the future situation with regard to air power has been 'completely wrong'.

4 DEC 1934 At a Conservative Central Council meeting Baldwin makes it clear that he accepts the White Paper of 1933 and the report of the Joint Select Committee (Nov 1934) on the future of India.

24 JAN 1935 Government of India Bill which provided for a measure of self government for India is presented.

11 FEB 1935 Second Reading of the Bill. Baldwin rallies his party to his views.

16 MAY 1935 Ramsay MacDonald, deserted by his old friends and associates, dependent on reluctant Conservative support and betraying increasing signs of declining powers, resigns.

7 JUN 1935 George V appoints Baldwin as Prime Minister.

28 JUN 1935 In a peace ballot held by the League of Nations Union 10.5 million people (90% of those who vote) are in favour of an all-round reduction of armaments by international agreement.

2 AUG 1935 The Government of India Bill receives Royal Assent.

14 NOV 1935 Baldwin is returned unopposed at Bewdley. The Conservatives gain 429 seats to Labour's 154 and the Liberals' 21.

8 DEC 1935 Foreign Secretary Hoare and French Prime Minister Laval initial in Paris an agreement for a proposed settlement of the Abyssinian War by a cession of Ethiopian territory to Italy. A surprised Baldwin acquiesces but subsequent public hostility to the pact in the UK forces him to disavow his Foreign Secretary.

20 JAN 1936 Death of George V.

3 MAR 1936 The Government publishes the White Paper *Statement Relating to Defence* which introduces the first real measure of expansion.

7 MAR 1936 Hitler reoccupies the Rhineland.

6 APR 1936 Faced with criticism of his leadership from within his own party, Baldwin is forced to obtain a vote of confidence in the House.

SUMMER, 1936 Baldwin becomes increasingly overwhelmed by domestic and international problems. By June he is showing signs of nervous exhaustion. At the end of July his doctor, Lord Dawson of Penn, orders three months' complete rest.

12 OCT 1936 Baldwin returns to 10 Downing Street. He deals with the Abdication Crisis arising from the decision of the new king, Edward VIII, to marry Mrs. Wallis Simpson, an American divorceé.

2 DEC 1936 Edward VIII renounces the throne and is succeeded by his brother, George.

5 MAY 1937 Baldwin is now in his seventieth year. He nominates Neville Chamberlain as his successor. His last set speech in the House is an appeal for peace in the mining industry, threatened with stoppage.

27 MAY 1937 He announces the Government's proposal to increase from £400 to £600 the salaries of MPs.

28 MAY 1937 Baldwin tenders his resignation. George VI makes him a Knight of the Garter.

8 JUN 1937 He becomes an Earl. He is worn out and suffering from increasing deafness. He resolves to make no political speeches.

1939 Baldwin visits Toronto and New York and delivers addresses on democracy and citizenship.

3 SEP 1939 Britain declares war on Germany. World War II begins.

1939 Baldwin withdraws to Astley Hall, his Worcestershire home, where he lives quietly, reading, listening to the radio, delving into family archives. He is often in pain from arthritis and limps with the aid of a stick. He appears seldom in public, aware of the widespread belief that he is to blame for all that has happened since 1931.

12 SEP 1942 He and Lucy celebrate their golden wedding anniversary.

17 JUN 1945 Death of Lady Baldwin.

14 DEC 1947 Death of Stanley Baldwin.

BACKGROUND

PHYSICAL CHARACTERISTICS AND HEALTH

Baldwin was of medium height, broad-shouldered, with sandy hair, parted in the middle and well smoothed-down, blue eyes, broad hands and a musical voice which carried well. In his sixties he could still walk several hours a day but in later years he suffered from arthritis and required the aid of a stick. He also became quite deaf.

On several occasions he was left in a state of nervous exhaustion after periods of strain or crisis.

The official cause of Baldwin's death was certified as coronary thrombosis.

EDUCATION

Primary 1877–81, Hawtrey's Preparatory School, near Slough, Berkshire

Secondary 1881–85, Harrow School, Middlesex

University 1885–88, Trinity College, Cambridge, where he read history. In the late 1880s/early 1890s he studied metallurgy for a term at Owens College (later the University of Manchester).

Qualifications 1888, BA degree (Third Class in History Tripos); 1892, MA

Languages Baldwin spoke French with a good accent and wrote it fluently. His German was passable and he could read Russian without difficulty.

NON-PARLIAMENTARY CAREER

Early occupations After Cambridge Baldwin entered the family business, E. P. & W. Baldwin, manufacturers of iron and steel, based at Wilden, near Stourport-on-Severn, Worcestershire. He frequently travelled to subsidiary companies in South Wales and Birmingham. In 1890 he visited the firm associates in Canada and the USA. Baldwin became a parish and county councillor (Worcestershire County Council-Hartlebury Division, 1898–1907) and a magistrate.

Military service Baldwin spent about two months between Aug and Oct 1888 training as an officer in the Artillery Volunteers but he never saw active service.

Other posts 1923–26, Lord Rector of the University of Edinburgh; 1925, a Trustee of Rhodes House, Oxford; 1925, Grand Master of the Primrose League; 1926, President of the Classical Association; 1927, a Trustee of the British Museum; 1927, an Elder Brother of Trinity House; 1928, Vice President of the London Library; 1928–31, Lord Rector of the University of Glasgow; 1929–47, Chancellor of the University of St. Andrews; 1930–47, Chancellor of the University of Cambridge; 1930–35, First Chairman of the Pilgrim Trust (remained a Trustee); 1930, Governor of Harrow School; 1930–33, a Trustee of the National Gallery; 1933, a Governor of Charterhouse School; 1936, a Member of the Imperial War Graves Commission; 1936, Hon. Master of the Bench, Inner Temple; 1937, Chairman of Imperial Relatives Trust; 1938–39, President of the MCC; 1939, High Steward of Tewkesbury; 1940, Chairman of the Garton Foundation

HONOURS

Freedom of cities London; Leeds; Bewdley, Worcestershire; Edinburgh; Winchester; Kidderminster; Aberystwyth; Inverness; Salisbury

Academic 1923, LL.D Cambridge, LL.D St. Andrews, 1925, DCL Oxford, DCL Durham LL.D Durham 1927, LL.D Edinburgh, LL.D Birmingham; 1933, LL.D London, LL.D Queen's, Belfast; 1934, LL.D Liverpool, Leeds

Foreign 1930 Member of the Académie des Sciences Morales et Politiques (Institut de France) 1934, LL.D Columbia, Canada, LL.D Toronto, Canada, LL.D McGill, Canada;

Other than peerage 3 Nov 1927, Fellow of the Royal Society; 28 May 1937, Knight of the Garter.

CLUBS

Carlton; United University; Athenaeum; Travellers'

HOBBIES AND SPORTS

Baldwin, all through his life, loved and found time to read novels. He particularly enjoyed Thomas Hardy, Rudyard Kipling, Joseph Conrad, Edgar Wallace and Mary Webb. He also read works by T. S. Eliot and Helen Waddell. He was very fond of the countryside, notably his native Worcestershire and that around Aix-les-Bains in France, which he visited each year on holiday. He was an enthusiastic walker, well into his sixties. As a younger man he played tennis and skiied. He enjoyed watching cricket and listening to music. He took a great interest in the pigs kept on the farm at his home, Astley Hall. He was a member of the Oddfellow's and the Foresters' friendly societies.

FINANCES

Stanley Baldwin inherited the bulk of his father's fortune on Alfred Baldwin's death in 1908. The latter was worth £250,000 by then. On 24 June 1919 Baldwin, in an anonymous letter to *The Times*, signed FST (i.e., Financial Secretary to the Treasury), pledged £120,000, or 20% of the estimated value of his estate (£580,000), to the purchase of £150,000 of the War Loan for cancellation. By so doing he sought to repay

FINANCES—*Continued*

what he had made during World War I and show his gratitude for the sacrifices of others. In the 1920s the value of Baldwin's Ltd. shares fell and for several years no dividends were paid. Stanley Baldwin came to depend more and more on his ministerial salary.

Income Estimated to be about £50,000 (mainly from securities) in 1914; in 1917 he began to receive a ministerial salary; in 1937 his income was £15,000–£20,000 (including his Prime Minister's pension). In 1940 his income was £18,000 (£15,000 of which was from securities).

Spouse's finances Lucy Baldwin had about £8,000 p.a. of her own (in 1928).

Pensions Stanley Baldwin was given a Prime Minister's pension of £2,000 p.a. in 1937.

Legacies He inherited the bulk of his father's estate, worth £250,000 in 1908.

Debts In 1917 he had an overdraft of £60,000. He had given away about £40,000 during World War I to war charities and to pay the friendly society contributions of every serviceman in his constituency. In Feb 1917 he borrowed £50,000 to put into war bonds.

Will Baldwin left more than £250,000. His property was divided between his two sons. His political papers were left to Cambridge University Library.

ANECDOTES

Baldwin's wife, Lucy, to encourage him during difficult times such as early in 1931 when there was some disquiet in the Conservative Party about his leadership, in particular his views on India, called him 'Tiger Baldwin'.

Baldwin's daughter, Lady Lorna Howard, told a story that illustrates the relationship between her father and the workers at the family plant: 'An embarrassed newlywed employee came to Baldwin and told him he had broken the bridal bed. Baldwin said it could be repaired free at the family ironworks, but the man feared it would make him the laughing stock of all his mates. So the broken bed was brought to the back door of Baldwin's house at night, wheeled through the hall the following morning, and taken across the road for repair as if it were Baldwin's own'.

During a by-election speech in 1931 Baldwin attacked the press lords in these words: 'The proprietors of the national newspapers are aiming at power, and power without responsibility, the prerogative of the harlot throughout the ages'. When the Duke of Devonshire, a stalwart of the Conservative party, heard a report of this speech he remarked, 'That's done it. He's lost us the tarts' vote now'.

QUOTATIONS

16 Feb 1923, Four words, of one syllable each, are words which contain salvation for this country and for the whole world. They are 'Faith', 'Hope', 'Love' and 'Work'. (Speech in debate on the Address)

29 May 1924, A platitude is simply a truth repeated until people get tired of hearing it. (Speech in debate on Committee of Supply)

17 Mar 1931, The papers conducted by Lord Rothermere and Lord Beaverbrook are not newspapers in the ordinary acceptance of the term. They are engines of propaganda, for the contantly changing policies, desires, personal wishes, personal likes and dislikes of two men . . . What the proprietorship of these papers is aiming at is power, and power without responsibility—the prerogative of the harlot throughout the ages. (Speech in support of Duff Cooper's election to the Commons)

10 Nov 1932, I think it is well also for the man in the street to realise that there is no power on earth that can protect him from being bombed. Whatever people may tell him, the bomber will always get through. . . . The only defence is in offence, which means that you have to kill more women and children more quickly than the enemy if you want to save yourselves. (Speech in debate on international affairs)

30 Jul 1934, Let us never forget this; since the day of the air, the old frontiers are gone. When you think of the defence of England you no longer think of the chalk cliffs of Dover; you think of the Rhine. (Speech in debate on armaments)

RESIDENCES

Lower Park House, Bewdley, Worcestershire
Wilden House, Near Stourport-on-Severn, Worcestershire
Dunley Hall, Near Stourport-on-Severn, Worcestershire
Astley Hall, Stourport-on-Severn, Worcestershire
27 Queen's Gate, South Kensington, London
93 Eaton Square, Belgravia, London (plaque)
11 Downing Street
10 Downing Street
Chequers
10 or 11 Upper Brook Street, Mayfair, London
60 or 69 Eaton Square, Belgravia, London
Fosse Wold, Stow-on-the-Wold, Gloucestershire (Baldwin's name was on the deed, but he did not live there)

MEMORIALS

STATUES AND BUSTS

c. 1925, by Lady Kathleen Kennet, in possession of the Baldwin family; 1925, by Sir Alfred Gilbert, in store at the library at Stourport, Worcestershire; 1927, by Newbury Trent at Harrow School, Middlesex.

PORTRAITS

1926, by Glyn Philpot; 1928, by Sir Oswald Birley in possession of 4th Earl Baldwin and on loan to the House of Commons, where it hangs in the Members' Tea Room; 1928, by Sir William Rothenstein, National Portrait Gallery; 1930, by Winifred Cécile Dongworth, National Portrait Gallery, (miniature); 1933, by Reginald Grenville Eves, National Portrait Gallery; 1933, by W. T. Monnington, Trinity College, Cambridge; 1938, by Sir Oswald Birley, Carlton Club, London; 1942, by Francis Dodd, National Portrait Gallery; 1942, by Francis Dodd, Rhodes House, Oxford

OTHER MEMORIALS

Plaque in the public gardens in Aix-les-Bains, France, erected by the municipality 'en souvenir des nombreux séjours'

Simple sandstone memorial in a roadside garden near Astley House, Stourport-on-Severn, Worcestershire.

BIBLIOGRAPHIC INFORMATION

LETTERS AND PERSONAL PAPERS

Baldwin bequeathed his political papers and correspondence, together with his press cutting books, consisting in all of 233 volumes, to Cambridge University.

The Baldwin Papers are housed in the Cambridge University Library and are described by A.E.B. Owen of the Library in his *Handlist of the Political Papers of Stanley Baldwin, First Earl Baldwin of Bewdley*, Cambridge, 1973.

Baldwin's private correspondence is in the possession of the family.

PUBLICATIONS

1926, *On England and Other Addresses*; 1928, *Our Inheritance: Speeches and Addresses*; 1935, *This Torch of Freedom: Speeches and Addresses*; 1937, *Service of Our Lives*; 1939, *An Interpreter of England.*

FURTHER READING

Baldwin, A. W. (3rd Earl Baldwin of Bewdley). *My Father: The True Story*. London, 1955.

—. *The Macdonald Sisters*. London, 1960.

Baldwin, O. (2nd Earl Baldwin of Bewdley). *The Questing Beast*. London, 1932.

Ball, S. *Baldwin and the Conservative Party: The Crisis of 1929–1931*. New Haven and London, 1988.

Blake, R. 'Baldwin and the Light' in *The Baldwin Age*. Ed. John Raymond. London, 1960.

Bryant, A. *Stanley Baldwin*. London, 1937.

Green, J. *Mr. Baldwin: A Story in Post-War Conservatism*. London, 1933.

Hyde, H. M. *Baldwin: The Unexpected Prime Minister*. London, 1973.

Jenkins, R. *Baldwin*. London, 1987.

Middlemass, K. and Barnes, J. *Baldwin. A Biography*. London, 1969.

Somervell, D. C. *Stanley Baldwin. An Examination of Some Features of Mr. G. M. Young's Biography*. London, 1953.

Young, G. M. *Stanley Baldwin*. London, 1952.

Young, K. *Stanley Baldwin*. London, 1976.

H.H.

Bettmann

Ramsay MacDonald

Lived 1866–1937

Political Party Labour; National Labour

Prime Minister 22 January 1924–4 November 1924; 5 June 1929–7 June 1935

Governments 1) Labour; 2) Labour; 3) National

Reigning Monarch George V

RAMSAY MACDONALD AS PRIME MINISTER

Ramsay MacDonald arrived from obscure Scottish origins to become the first Labour Prime Minister at the age of 57. Sober, industrious, intelligent but also eloquent, he joined the independent Labour Party in 1890 and entered Parliament in 1906. He wrote a series of books from 1905 to 1913 defining 'socialism' and, having a strong evolutionary sense, he envisaged the transformation from liberalism to socialism via parliamentary democracy. His attitude to the 1914-1918 war left him branded as a pacifist and he was defeated at the 1918 General Election. The 1922 election returned MacDonald to Parliament and, again becoming chairman of the Labour Party, he showed it to be the natural opposition in Parliament. In 1924, with the help of Asquith, he became Prime Minister and turned his attention to housing and education. As his own Foreign Secretary he took particular interest in reparations between France and Germany and held a cautious view of the new Soviet Union. Departing within a year, he showed patience during the 1924–29 Conservative Government and then won the most seats in the 1929 election. Two years after his second Government was formed, the crash of 1931 forced MacDonald to resign but the King asked him to form a National Government. This he did, thereby losing the support of many in his party. MacDonald then called an election asking for a 'doctor's mandate' to save the country and won a huge majority. While he was Prime Minister, he left domestic matters to colleagues, but he continued to be active in foreign affairs and defence, which was growing in importance. He resigned and exchanged posts with Baldwin in 1935.

PERSONAL INFORMATION

Names James Ramsay MacDonald (This is the form by which he was known for most of his life. On his birth certificate, however, his name appears as 'James McDonald Ramsay, child of Anne Ramsay')
Born 12 Oct 1866, Lossiemouth, Morayshire
Religion Scottish Presbyterian
Ancestry Scottish. His father, John Macdonald, was a Highlander from the Black Isle of Ross, who worked as head ploughman on a farm in Alves, near Elgin. His mother, Anne Ramsay, had worked on the same farm. After James's birth she worked in the fishing ports along the Morayshire coast and as a dressmaker to support herself and her son.
Date and place of marriage 23 Nov 1896, St. Mary Abbot's, Kensington, London
Age at marriage 30 years, 42 days
Years married 14 years, 289 days
First entered Parliament 16 Jan 1906
Dates appointed PM 1) 22 Jan 1924; 2) 5 Jun 1929
Age at appointments 1) 57 years, 102 days; 2) 62 years, 236 days
Dates ceased to be PM 1) 4 Nov 1924; 2) 7 Jun 1935
Total time as PM 1) 287 days; 2) 6 years, 2 days; a total of 6 years, 289 days
Ceased to be MP 9 Nov 1937
Lived after last term as PM 2 years, 155 days
Date of death 9 Nov 1937
Place of death On the liner Reina del Pacifico on a holiday voyage to South America. MacDonald died during the crossing of the Atlantic between La Rochelle, France and Bermuda.
Age at death 71 years, 28 days
Place of funeral Funeral service in Westminster Abbey, London. Cremation at Golders Green Crematorium, London.
Place of burial Spynie Churchyard, near Lossiemouth, Morayshire
Zodiac sign Libra

FATHER

John Macdonald
Occupation Ploughman

MOTHER

Anne Ramsay
Occupation Seamstress
Date of death 11 Feb 1910
Place of burial Spynie Churchyard, near Lossiemouth, Morayshire

BROTHERS AND SISTERS

His mother had no more children. It is not known whether his father had any other children.

WIFE

Margaret Ethel Gladstone
Date and place of birth 20 Jul 1870; 17 Pembridge Square, Bayswater, London
Mother Margaret King
Father Dr. John Hall Gladstone, FRS
Father's occupation Scientist; Professor of Chemistry at the Royal Institution; a founder of the YMCA.
Age at marriage 26 years, 126 days
Number of children 6
Date and place of death 8 Sep 1911, 3 Lincoln's Inn Fields, London
Place of burial Cremated at Golder's Green Crematorium, London. Buried in Spynie Churchyard, near Lossiemouth, Morayshire.
Years younger than PM 3 years, 281 days
Profile Before her marriage, she had been involved in social work in Hoxton, East London, and elsewhere. After 1896, as well as bringing up six children, she maintained her interest in social work and came to play an increasingly active role in founding the Women's Labour League. She held regular gatherings of friends and those active in the labour and socialist movements.

She travelled abroad with her husband on fact-finding visits to India (1897), South Africa (1902), Canada and Australasia (1906) and India (1909).

CHILDREN

3 sons, 3 daughters
Alister Gladstone, b. 18 May 1898; m. 1) 1922, Edith Katherine (Tina) Hart (div. 1936); 2) 1937, Doreen Mayberta Banaz; architect; d. 22 Mar 1993
Malcolm John, b. 17 Aug 1901; m. Dec. 1946, Mrs. Audrey Fellowes Rowley; MP Bassetlaw, 1929–31 and 1931–35, Ross and Cromarty 1936–45; Secretary of State for Dominion Affairs 1935–38; Secretary of State for Colonies 1935 and 1938–40; Minister of Health 1940–41; High Commissioner in Canada 1941–46; Governor General of Malayan Union and Singapore May–Jul 1946; Governor General of Malaya, Singapore and British Borneo 1946–48; High Commissioner in India 1955–60; Governor General then High Commissioner in Kenya 1963–65; special representative of UK Government in Africa 1967–69; d. 11 Jan 1981
Ishbel Allan, b. 2 Mar 1903; m. Mr. Peterkin; Jan 1936, bought the Plough Inn, a pub in Buckinghamshire
David Ramsay, b. 4 Jul 1904; d. 3 Feb 1910
Joan Margaret, b. 28 Apr 1908; m. Sep 1932, Dr. Mackinnon; went to medical school in 1927
Sheila, b. 7 Dec 1910, m. Mr. Lochhead; d. 22 Jul 1994

LIFE AND CAREER

PARLIAMENTARY ELECTIONS FOUGHT

*(*designates candidate elected)*
DATE Jul 1895. General Election
CONSTITUENCY Southampton
RESULT T. Chamberlayne* (Con) 5,924; Sir J.S.B Simeon* (Lib Unionist) 5,390; Sir F.H. Evans (Lib) 5,181; H.G. Wilson (Lib/Lab) 4,178; J. R. MacDonald (ILP) 867.
DATE Oct 1900. General Election
CONSTITUENCY Leicester
RESULT H. Broadhurst (Lib/Lab)* 10,385; Sir J.F.L. Rolleston* (Con) 9,066; W. Hazell (Lib) 8,528; J.R. MacDonald (Lab) 4,164
DATE Jan 1906. General Election
CONSTITUENCY Leicester

PARLIAMENTARY ELECTIONS FOUGHT—*Continued*

RESULT H. Broadhurst* (Lib/Lab) 14,745; J.R. MacDonald* (Lab) 14,685; Sir J.F.L. Rolleston (Con) 7,504
DATE Jan 1910. General Election
CONSTITUENCY Leicester
RESULT E. Crawshay-Williams* (Lib) 14,643; J.R. MacDonald* (Lab) 14,337; J.F. Fraser (Con) 8,548; E.A.A. Bayley (Con) 8,192
DATE Dec 1910. General Election
CONSTITUENCY Leicester
RESULT E. Crawshay-Williams* (Lib) 13,238; J.R. MacDonald* (Lab) 12,998; A. W. Wilshere (Con) 7,547.
DATE 14 Dec 1918. General Election
CONSTITUENCY Leicester, West
RESULT J. F. Green* (Nat Dem & Lab) 20,570; J.R. MacDonald (Lab) 6,347.
DATE 2 Mar 1921. By-election caused by the resignation of Will Crooks
CONSTITUENCY Woolwich, East
RESULT R. Gee* (Con) 13,724; J.R. MacDonald (Lab) 13,041.
DATE 15 Nov 1922. General Election
CONSTITUENCY Aberavon
RESULT J.R. MacDonald*(Lab) 14,318; S.H. Byass (Con) 11,111; J. Edwards (Nat Lib) 5,328
DATE 6 Dec 1923. General Election
CONSTITUENCY Aberavon
RESULTS J.R. MacDonald* (Lab) 17,439; S.H. Byass (Con) 13,927
DATE 29 Oct 1924. General Election
CONSTITUENCY Aberavon
RESULT J.R. MacDonald* (Lab) 17,724; W.H. Williams (Lib) 15,624
DATE 30 May 1929. General Election
CONSTITUENCY Seaham
RESULT J.R. MacDonald* (Lab then N Lab) 35,615; W.A. Fearnley-Whittingstall (Con) 6,821; H.A. Haslam (Lib) 5,266; H. Pollitt (Com) 1,431
DATE 27 Oct 1931. General Election
CONSTITUENCY Seaham
RESULT J.R. MacDonald* (Nat Lab) 28,978; W. Coxon (Lab) 23,027; G. Lumley (Con) 677
DATE 14 Nov 1935. General Election
CONSTITUENCY Seaham
RESULT E. Shinwell* (Lab) 38,380; J.R. MacDonald (Nat Lab) 17,882
DATE 31 Jan 1936. By-election caused by the death of A.N. Skelton
CONSTITUENCY Combined Scottish Universities
RESULT J.R. MacDonald* (Nat Lab) 16,393; Prof. A. D. Gibb (SNP) 9,034; D.C. Thomson (Lab) 3,597.

PARTY ACTIVITY

Party Leadership 21 Nov 1922–Aug 1931, Chairman and Leader of the Parliamentary Labour Party; 28 Sep 1931 expelled from Labour party.
Other offices 1896, Member of the National Administrative Council of the Independent Labour Party; 1900–06, Secretary of the Labour Representation Committee; 1906–09, Chairman of the Independent Labour Party; 1906–12, Secretary of the Labour Party National Executive Committee; 6 Feb 1911–5 Aug 1914, Chairman of the Parliamentary Labour Party; 1912–24, Treasurer of the Labour Party National Executive Committee; Oct–Dec 1917, Member of joint Labour Party National Executive Committee-Trade Union Congress Parliamentary Committee sub-committee on the international situation
Membership of group or faction 1885, member of the Social Democratic Federation in Bristol; 1886, Fabian Society; Sep 1914, helped to found the Union of Democratic Control, seeking to influence foreign policy

PARLIAMENTARY AND MINISTERIAL EXPERIENCE

Maiden speech 5 Mar 1906, attacking the examination syllabus for factory inspectors. (*HC Deb*, vol 153, col 119–125)
Opposition Offices Leader of the Opposition 1922-24, 1924-29
Privy Counsellor 22 Jan 1924
Ministerial Offices First Lord of the Treasury, Foreign Secretary and Leader of the House of Commons 22 Jan–4 Nov 1924; First Lord of the Treasury and Leader of the House of Commons 5 Jun 1929–7 Jun 1935; Lord President of the Council 7 Jun 1935–28 May 1937
Opposition Leaders while PM 1924, Stanley Baldwin; 1929–31, Stanley Baldwin; 1931–35, George Lansbury

GOVERNMENTS FORMED

First Administration 22 Jan–4 Nov 1924

GENERAL ELECTION RESULT
6 DEC 1923: Conservative 258; Labour 191; Liberal 158; Others 8. Total 615
No overall majority
CABINET
Prime Minister, First Lord of the Treasury and Foreign Secretary J.R. MacDonald
Lord President of the Council Lord Parmoor
Lord Chancellor Viscount Haldane
Lord Privy Seal J. Clynes
Chancellor of the Exchequer P. Snowden
Home Secretary A. Henderson
First Lord of the Admiralty Viscount Chelmsford
Minister of Agriculture and Fisheries N. Buxton
Secretary of State for Air Lord Thomson
Secretary of State for the Colonies J. Thomas
President of the Board of Education C. Trevelyan
Minister of Health J. Wheatley
Secretary of State for India Lord Olivier
Minister of Labour T. Shaw
Chancellor of the Duchy of Lancaster J. Wedgwood
Postmaster-General V. Hartshorn
Secretary for Scotland W. Adamson
President of the Board of Trade S. Webb
Secretary of State for War S. Walsh
First Commissioner of Works F. Jowett

Second Administration 5 Jun 1929–24 Aug 1931

GENERAL ELECTION RESULT
30 MAY 1929: Labour 287; Conservative 260; Liberal 59; Others 9. Total 615
No overall majority
CABINET
Prime Minister and First Lord of the Treasury J.R. MacDonald
Lord President of the Council Lord Parmoor
Lord Chancellor Lord Sankey
Lord Privy Seal J. Thomas (1929–Jun 1930); V. Hartshorn (Jun 1930–Mar 1931); T. Johnston (Mar–Aug 1931)

Chancellor of the Exchequer P. Snowden
Foreign Secretary A. Henderson
Home Secretary J. Clynes
First Lord of the Admiralty A. Alexander
Minister of Agriculture and Fisheries N. Buxton (1929–Jun 1930); C. Addison (Jun 1930–Aug 1931)
Secretary of State for Air Lord Thomson (1929–Oct 1930); Lord Amulree (Oct 1930–Aug 1931)
Secretary of State for the Colonies Lord Passfield
Secretary of State for Dominion Affairs Lord Passfield (1929–Jun 1930); J. Thomas (Jun 1930–Aug 1931)
President of the Board of Education Sir C. Trevelyan (1929–Mar 1931); H. Lees-Smith (Mar–Aug 1931)
Minister of Health A. Greenwood
Secretary of State for India W. Benn
Minister of Labour Miss M. Bondfield
Secretary of State for Scotland W. Adamson
President of the Board of Trade W. Graham
*Minister of Transport** H. Morrison (Mar–Aug 1931)
Secretary of State for War T. Shaw
First Commissioner of Works G. Lansbury
[*Office not always in Cabinet]

Third Administration 24 Aug 1931–27 Oct 1931

GENERAL ELECTIONS RESULT
30 MAY 1929: Labour 287; Conservative 260; Liberal 59; Others 9. Total 615
No overall majority
CABINET
Prime Minister and First Lord of the Treasury J.R. MacDonald
Lord President of the Council S. Baldwin
Lord Chancellor Lord Sankey
Chancellor of the Exchequer P. Snowden
Foreign Secretary Marquess of Reading
Home Secretary Sir H. Samuel
Secretary of State for the Colonies J. Thomas
Secretary of State for Dominion Affairs J. Thomas
Minister of Health N. Chamberlain
Secretary of State for India Sir S. Hoare
President of the Board of Trade Sir P. Cunliffe-Lister

Fourth Administration 27 Oct 1931–7 Jun 1935

GENERAL ELECTION RESULT
27 OCT 1931: Conservative 473; National Labour 13; Liberal National 35; Liberal 33; Independent Liberal 4; Labour 52; Others 5.
National Government majority 493
CABINET
Prime Minister and First Lord of the Treasury J.R. MacDonald
Lord President of the Council S. Baldwin
Lord Chancellor Viscount Sankey
*Lord Privy Seal** Viscount Snowden (Oct 1931–Sep 1932); S. Baldwin (Sep 1932–Dec 1933)
Chancellor of the Exchequer N. Chamberlain
Foreign Secretary Sir J. Simon
Home Secretary Sir H. Samuel (Oct 1931–Sep 1932); Sir J. Gilmour (Sep 1932–35)
First Lord of the Admiralty Sir B. Eyres-Monsell
Minister of Agriculture and Fisheries Sir J. Gilmour (Oct 1931–Sep 1932); W. Elliot (Sep 1932–35)
Secretary of State for Air Marquess of Londonderry
Secretary of State for the Colonies Sir P. Cunliffe-Lister
Secretary of State for Dominion Affairs J. Thomas
President of the Board of Education Sir D. Maclean (Oct 1931–Jun 1932); Lord Irwin (Viscount Halifax) (Jun 1932–35)
Minister of Health Sir E. Young
Secretary of State for India Sir S. Hoare
Minister of Labour Sir H. Betterton (Oct 1931–Jun 1934); O. Stanley (Jun 1934–35)
*Postmaster General** Sir K. Wood (Dec 1933–35)
Secretary of State for Scotland Sir A. Sinclair (Oct 1931–Sep 1932); Sir G. Collins (Sep 1935–35)
President of the Board of Trade W. Runciman
Secretary of State for War Viscount Hailsham
First Commissioner of Works W. Ormsby-Gore
[*Office not always in Cabinet]

IMPORTANT DATES IN PERSONAL AND POLITICAL LIFE

EARLY SUMMER 1885 MacDonald takes up a post in Bristol as assistant to the Rev. Mordaunt Crofton who is setting up a Boys' and Young Men's Guild. He joins the Social Democratic Federation there.

EARLY 1886 After a few months back in Lossiemouth, he goes to London to look for work, finding clerical jobs, first at the National Cyclists' Union, then at Cooper, Box & Co.

LATE 1887/EARLY 1888 He attends evening classes in science at the Birkbeck Institute, preparing to win a science scholarship at the South Kensington Museum, but is forced by ill-health to abandon his studies and return home to Lossiemouth.

EARLY 1888 Returns to London to take up a post as private secretary to Thomas Lough, prospective Liberal candidate for West Islington, where he is elected in 1892.

LATE 1880S/EARLY 1890S MacDonald becomes involved with political organisations, such as the London General Committee of the Scottish Home Rule Association; the St. Pancras Parliament, a debating group; the Fabian Society; the Fellowship of the New Life, a socialist sect, of which he becomes secretary; the Rainbow Circle, a discussion group.

JUL/AUG 1893 Adopted as the Labour Electoral Association's parliamentary candidate for Dover.

15 JUL 1894 He applies to join the newly formed Independent Labour Party.

17 JUL 1894 Having ceased to be parliamentary candidate for Dover, MacDonald is adopted as the ILP's parliamentary candidate for Southampton and fights the 1895 General Election, polling only 867 votes.

1894 MacDonald joins the Executive Committee of the Fabian Society.

23 NOV 1896 Marries Margaret Gladstone, daughter of Dr. John Gladstone, FRS, and active in social work in the East End of London.

1896 He joins the National Administrative Council of the ILP.

AUG 1897 The MacDonalds visit the USA, travelling to New York and Chicago.

1899 MacDonald is involved in drafting the resolution by which the Trade Union Congress convenes a special congress to devise plans for returning more Labour Members to the next Parliament.

1900 He is among those responsible for setting up the Labour Representation Committee, of which he becomes secretary. MacDonald holds this post until 1912.

28 SEP–24 OCT 1900 He stands, unsuccessfully, as Labour candidate for Leicester at the General Election.

IMPORTANT DATES IN PERSONAL AND POLITICAL LIFE—*Continued*

1901 He serves on the London County Council, representing Central Finsbury, until 1904.

AUG 1902 The MacDonalds visit South Africa to investigate the aftermath of the Boer War which had ended in June.

12 JAN–7 FEB 1906 MacDonald is returned as Labour Member for Leicester at the General Election. Like almost all the successful Labour candidates he owes his return to an electoral arrangement made with the Liberals.

5 MAR 1906 Makes his maiden speech, attacking the examination syllabus for factory inspectors.

LATE 1906 The MacDonalds visit Canada, Australia and New Zealand.

1906 MacDonald succeeds Philip Snowden as Chairman of the ILP, a post he is to hold until 1909.

SEP–DEC 1909 The MacDonalds visit India.

18 JAN 1910 In the General Election following the House of Lords' rejection of the Liberal Government's Finance Bill, MacDonald is again returned for Leicester.

FEB 1910 Death of his youngest son, David, and his mother, Anne Ramsay, within about ten days of each other.

6 DEC 1910 Retains his seat at Leicester in the General Election.

6 FEB 1911 MacDonald becomes Chairman of the Parliamentary Labour Party.

8 SEP 1911 Death of his wife, Margaret.

DEC 1912 Visits India as a member of the Royal Commission on the Indian Public Services, headed by Lord Islington.

4 AUG 1914 Britain declares war on Germany.

5 AUG 1914 MacDonald resigns his chairmanship of the Parliamentary Labour Party, which declines to support his proposal that Labour Members oppose the Government's demand for a war credit of £100,000,000.

13 AUG 1914 In an article in the *Labour Leader* he analyses the causes of the war and what he sees as the failure of British foreign policy.

SEP 1914 MacDonald is largely instrumental in founding the Union of Democratic Control, including liberals as well as socialists, the object of which is to secure a democratic foreign policy.

DEC 1914 He makes two visits to Belgium, the first as a volunteer member of a British ambulance corps attached to the Belgian army, the second as an official visitor.

MAY 1915 MacDonald, with others in the Parliamentary Labour Party, rejects Asquith's invitation to join the Government.

4 SEP 1915 A series of attacks on MacDonald's attitude to the origins and conduct of the war by Horatio Bottomley culminates in *John Bull.*

6 JAN 1916 MacDonald speaks against conscription at a Labour Party conference called to discuss the Party's attitude to the Government's proposals to introduce compulsory military service.

SEP 1916 A resolution that MacDonald's conduct in opposing British foreign policy has endangered the character and interests of the Moray Golf Club is carried at a special meeting of members. MacDonald is never to play on the Lossiemouth links again.

JUN 1917 MacDonald, having welcomed the Kerensky revolution in Russia in March, obtains the British Cabinet's permission to visit the Provisional Government in Petrograd, but the National Seamen's and Firemen's Union opposes the visit and prevents him from sailing from Aberdeen.

SEP–OCT 1917 Serves on the sub-committee to propose a new constitution for the Labour Party, which is adopted in Feb 1918.

OCT–DEC 1917 MacDonald is a National Executive Committee representative on a joint NEC-TUC Parliamentary Committee sub-committee on the international situation, which formulates a war aims memorandum, adopted by the Labour Party in December.

FEB 1918 He joins a Labour Party deputation to Paris to secure the support of French socialists for the British war aims memorandum.

14 DEC 1918 At the General Election MacDonald is defeated at West Leicester by over 14,000 votes.

MAR 1919 On his way back from the International Socialist conference in Berne, MacDonald travels to Paris seeking, with others from the Second International, to bring pressure to bear on the peace conference.

APR 1920 He persuades the ILP conference not to affiliate to the Communist Third International.

JUL–AUG 1920 He visits Berlin and, with a deputation from the Second International, the Menshevik Republic of Georgia.

NOV 1920 He becomes joint secretary of the Second International, now with its headquarters in London.

2 MAR 1921 MacDonald is defeated by a narrow majority at a by-election at East Woolwich, his opponents stressing his war record.

15 NOV 1922 At the General Election MacDonald is returned for Aberavon, with a majority of 3,207.

21 NOV 1922 Elected Chairman of the Parliamentary Labour Party, MacDonald becomes official Leader of the Opposition since the Labour Members now outnumber the Liberals.

6 DEC 1923 MacDonald is returned for Aberavon at the General Election. The Labour Party is again more powerful than the Liberals and the two together are strong enough to defeat the Conservative Government.

21 JAN 1924 Following the King's speech on 15 January, a Labour Party amendment to the Address is carried.

22 JAN 1924 MacDonald becomes Prime Minister and is sworn of the Privy Council. He also takes the office of Foreign Secretary.

JUL–AUG 1924 Following negotiations with M. Herriot, the French Prime Minister, MacDonald accepts the Experts' Report on German Reparations, which is put into operation following the Allied Conference in London.

5 AUG 1924 Pressure from some of its backbenchers contributes to the Government's announcing that a series of treaties, including the guarantee of a loan, will be signed with Soviet Russia.

8 OCT 1924 The abandonment of the prosecution of John Campbell, charged with inciting the armed forces to mutiny in the Communist *Workers' Weekly* leads to the Government being defeated on a motion calling for an inquiry into the case.

29 OCT 1924 In the ensuing General Election MacDonald is again returned for Aberavon but the Labour Party is adversely affected by the publication, four days before polling day, of the so-called Zinoviev letter, suggesting that the Government has been swayed by extremist influences. Labour loses over 40 seats and Stanley Baldwin becomes Prime Minister.

AUTUMN 1925 At the Labour Party conference in Liverpool MacDonald secures the approval of a resolution that the Communists are to have no part in the Labour Party.

MAY 1926 General strike. MacDonald, disliking direct action, tries to avert the strike, fails and finally acquiesces in it.

30 MAY 1929 MacDonald is returned for Seaham in the General Election. For the first time Labour is the largest single party in the House of Commons and MacDonald becomes Prime Minister for the second time.

1929 After conversations with the American ambassador, General Dawes, and a visit to President Hoover in the United States, the first to be made by a Prime Minister of Great Britain, MacDonald is able to bring about a revival of the Naval Conference. It meets in London to discuss naval disarmament in Great Britain, the United States and Japan.

NOV 1930–JAN 1931 He chairs the first Indian Round Table conference on dominion status for India.

31 JUL 1931 Publication of the report of the Economy Committee set up under the chairmanship of Sir George (later Lord) May. At a time of universal economic depression, unemployment, the cost of benefits and the rate of government borrowing rise in Great Britain. The report, which estimates a deficit of £120, 000,000 by Apr 1932, is followed by a flight of foreign investors from the pound and a serious drain on British gold reserves. MacDonald's Cabinet cannot agree on reductions of expenditure, particularly on unemployment insurance, necessary to balance the budget.

23 AUG 1931 MacDonald reports to King George V that his colleagues cannot agree and tenders the resignation of the Labour Government.

24 AUG 1931 A conference of the three party leaders— MacDonald, Stanley Baldwin for the Conservatives and Sir Herbert Samuel for the Liberals— leads to an all-party Government led by MacDonald. A number of his former colleagues and followers no longer support him, however.

28 SEP 1931 He and Philip Snowden are expelled from the Labour Party at its annual conference in Scarborough.

27 OCT 1931 MacDonald holds Seaham by a large majority and almost all the seats (554) are captured by National Government candidates at the General Election.

22 JAN 1932 Snowden and the free-trade Liberals are retained by the 'agreement to differ' on tariffs but leave the coalition after the preferential tariff agreements are reached at Ottawa in July that year.

APR 1932 He presides at a Four Power Conference in London and attends the Disarmament Conference in Geneva.

JUN–JUL 1933 MacDonald summons a World Economic Conference in London, but it is doomed by the refusal of the US government to agree to the stabilisation of currency.

MAR–JUN 1934 MacDonald's visits to Paris and Rome do much to bring about a consultative pact between Great Britain, France, Italy and Germany.

MAR 1935 MacDonald drafts the White Paper on National Defence, which heralds a programme of rearmament.

7 JUN 1935 MacDonald, increasingly incapacitated by illness and tiredness, resigns the premiership and assumes the sinecure office of Lord President of the Council in the Cabinet formed by Stanley Baldwin.

14 NOV 1935 MacDonald is defeated as National Labour candidate for Seaham at the General Election.

31 JAN 1936 He is returned for the Scottish universities at a by-election.

28 MAY 1937 Baldwin resigns as Prime Minister and MacDonald ceases to be a minister.

9 NOV 1937 MacDonald dies suddenly on a holiday voyage to South America.

BACKGROUND

PHYSICAL CHARACTERISTICS AND HEALTH

MacDonald was above average height and generally considered handsome. He had large eyes and thick, waving, dark brown (later white) hair.

In 1927 he had a mysterious throat infection while on a visit to the United States and almost died. He was admitted to hospital in Philadelphia in April and spent about a month there.

The events of August and September 1931 placed great physical and emotional strain on MacDonald and on 9 and 22 Sep he suffered some sort of collapse from nervous exhaustion.

In 1932 he underwent two operations for glaucoma—in February in his left eye; in May in his right eye.

In the last two years of his premiership MacDonald suffered increasingly from eye-strain, headaches, insomnia, tiredness and depression. He was, of course, in his late sixties by then. In June 1934 he was advised to take three months' rest and spent the summer quietly in Scotland, Canada and Newfoundland.

On 6 Nov 1937 he was knocked down by a bicycle in La Rochelle, France. On 9 Nov he died of heart failure on board the liner Reina del Pacifico, in mid-Atlantic.

EDUCATION

Primary To 1875, Free Kirk school in Lossiemouth; 1875–81, Church of Scotland school in Drainie.

Secondary 1881–85, He was the pupil-teacher at the Church of Scotland school in Drainie. As well as providing MacDonald with a small salary, this arrangement enabled him to gain a secondary education up to university entrance level.

University 1887–88, He attended evening classes at the Birkbeck Institute, London, in science and took courses on botany, agriculture, experimental physics and mathematics.

In 1888 he prepared to sit the examination for a science scholarship at the South Kensington Museum, London. However, nervous exhaustion prevented his taking the exam.

Cultural and vocational background After leaving Scotland in 1885 MacDonald continued to educate himself by reading; attending evening classes; joining socialist groups, such as the Social Democratic Federation in Bristol and the Socialist Union, the St. Pancras Parliament, the South Place Ethical Society, and the Fellowship of the New Life in London, for whom he wrote and lectured.

EDUCATION—*Continued*

Languages Spoke a little French.

NON-PARLIAMENTARY CAREER

Early occupations From 1881–85 MacDonald was the pupil teacher at the Church of Scotland school in Drainie, near Lossiemouth. On leaving Scotland he spent several months working for the Rev. Mordaunt Crofton and his Boys' and Young Men's Guild. Early in 1886 he went to London and found a job for a few weeks, addressing envelopes, at the National Cyclists' Union. He then took up a post as an invoice clerk at Cooper, Box & Co. in the City. Early in 1888 MacDonald was engaged as a private secretary by Thomas Lough, tea merchant, secretary of the Home Rule Union and prospective Liberal candidate for West Islington, where he was elected in 1892. MacDonald left Lough early in 1892 to pursue a career as a journalist, writer and lecturer. He represented Central Finsbury on the London County Council 1901–04. With his wife he travelled abroad, to the USA in 1897 and to South Africa in 1902.

Other posts 1894–1900, member of the Executive Committee of the Fabian Society; 1912–15, member of the Royal Commission on Indian Public Services headed by Lord Islington; Nov 1920, Joint Secretary of the Second International.

HONOURS

Freedom of cities 1929, City of London; 1929, City of New York; 1930, Inverness

Academic 1924, LLD Glasgow; 1925, LLD Edinburgh; 1926, LLD Wales; 1929, LLD McGill, Canada. 1931, LLD Oxford. (In 1926 it was proposed at Cambridge that an honorary degree should be conferred upon him but he refused to accept one which at that time was unlikely to have been passed unanimously.)

Other than peerage 26 Jun 1930, Fellow of the Royal Society

CLUBS

Moray Golf Club until 1915; Athenaeum

HOBBIES AND SPORTS

MacDonald was a keen golfer but he never played on the Lossiemouth links again after members of the Moray Golf Club, to which he belonged, passed a resolution in 1915 declaring that his opposition to the war had endangered the character and interests of the club.

He was a great walker and traveller and his two collections *Wanderings and Excursions* (1925) and *At Home and Abroad* (1936) contain many of his experiences in this area.

He read widely, and in his leisure time enjoyed the work of Thomas Hardy, Joseph Conrad and the classics of the 18th and early 19th centuries by Gibbon, Defoe, Boswell, Addison and Sir Walter Scott.

MacDonald, with the help of his friend Alec Martin, a buyer at Christie's, enjoyed buying pictures and fine furniture.

FINANCES

MacDonald struggled to make a living from journalism and lecturing in the early 1890s. Marriage to Margaret Gladstone in 1896 brought a degree of financial independence but bringing up six young children and not having a parliamentary salary until 1911 was a strain. The loss of his seat in 1918, at a time when payments from his wife's estate were reduced, caused MacDonald financial difficulty. However, the support of Henry Markwald, an eccentric businessman who had admired MacDonald's stand during the war and who subsequently bought insurance policies for him, enabled him to afford foreign travel and to buy pictures and fine furniture in the early 1920s. In 1924 a loan of £40,000 from Alexander Grant enabled MacDonald to invest the money, mainly in McVitie and Price, and draw an income. He returned the shares at the end of 1924, however.

Income From journalism and lecturing. Parliamentary salary of £400 p.a. from 1911. Income from his wife's trust fund. Income from money loaned to him in 1924. From 1927 £800 from the National Executive to meet his expenses as party leader.

Spouse's finances Margaret MacDonald's private income after her marriage in 1896 was about £460 p.a. The capital sum in her trust fund was eventually about £30,000.

Legacies A legacy from Henry Markwald in 1925 enabled MacDonald to move from Howitt Road to Upper Frognal Lodge, Hampstead, and also to travel abroad.

Will MacDonald's estate was valued at £25,418. He left £250 to the Margaret MacDonald and Mary Middleton Baby Clinic and £50 to the Children's Hospital at Harpenden. All his papers were left to his son Malcolm and 'trusted to his discretion as to their use by publication or otherwise'.

ANECDOTES

'We travelled up in the train with Ramsay MacDonald, who spent the time telling long stories of pawky Scotch humour so dull that it was almost impossible to be aware when the point had been reached.' (Bertrand Russell, *Autobiography 1914–1944*, 1968)

'Ramsay MacDonald attended a big concert one Sunday afternoon at the Palladium. Gladys Faber and I went round to his box and she asked him if there were any of the artists on the bill he would care to meet. He said, "Your husband, and Mr. Charles Coburn who sang 'The Man Who Broke the Bank at Monte Carlo' if it wouldn't inconvenience him at all" Gladys told him she was very proud, and all the artists were very proud to have him at the concert.

"Miss Faber, please, you musn't say that," he said, "it makes me terribly humble, and—no one really likes to feel humble, whatever they may tell you".' (Naomi Jacob, *A Chronicle about Other People*, 1933)

QUOTATIONS

3 May 1926, With the discussion of general strikes and Bolshevism and all that kind of thing, I have nothing to do at all. I respect the constitution as much as Sir Robert Horne. (Speech in the House of Commons)

9 Nov 1929, The League of Nations grows in moral courage. Its frown will soon be more dreaded than a nation's arms, and when that happens you and I shall have security and peace. (Speech at the Guildhall, London)

4 May 1930, We hear war called murder. It is not: it is suicide. (*Observer* magazine)

If God were to come to me and say 'Ramsay, would you rather be a country gentleman than a prime minister?' I should reply, 'Please God, a country gentleman'. (In H. Nicholson, *Diaries and Letters*, 1966, p. 57)

Yes, tomorrow every Duchess in London will be wanting to kiss me! (After forming the National Government in 1931, in Viscount Snowden *Autobiography*, 1934, vol. 2, p. 957)

RESIDENCES

Isabella Ramsay's cottage in Lossiemouth, Morayshire
Allan Lane, Lossiemouth
Doughty Street, London
3 Lincoln's Inn Fields, London
The Hillocks, Lossiemouth
9 Howitt Road, Hampstead, London
10 Downing Street
Upper Frognall Lodge, Hampstead, London

MEMORIALS

STATUES AND BUSTS

1926, bust by Sir Jacob Epstein, House of Commons, London; 1931, bust by Sir Jacob Epstein; 1934, bronze cast of 1926 bust by Sir Jacob Epstein, National Portrait Gallery; *c.* 1936, by Felix Joubert.

PORTRAITS

1889, by William Small, Scottish National Portrait Gallery, Edinburgh; *c.* 1910, by Solomon J. Solomon, National Portrait Gallery; 1923, by Sir William Rothenstein, Manchester City Art Gallery; *c.* 1926, by Ambrose McEvoy, Scottish National Portrait Gallery; 1929, by E. J. Walters, National Museum of Wales, Cardiff; 1930, by Sir William Hutchison, Palace of Westminster, London; 1931, by Sir John Lavery, National Portrait Gallery; 1931, by Sir Max Beerbohm, National Portrait Gallery

BIBLIOGRAPHIC INFORMATION

LETTERS AND PERSONAL PAPERS

The Ramsay MacDonald papers, including his diary, are in the Public Record Office in London.

A Singular Marriage: a Labour Love Story in Letters and Diaries: Ramsay and Margaret MacDonald, edited by Jane Cox, 1988 contains his letters to his wife.

PUBLICATIONS

1895, *How to Lose and How to Win an Election*, Fabian Tract 64; *c.* 1902, *What I saw in South Africa*; 1903, *The Zollverein and British Industry*; 1905, *Socialism and Society*; 1907, *Labour and the Empire*; 1909, *Socialism and Government*; 1910, *The Awakening of India*; 1911, *The Socialist Movement*; 1912, *Margaret Ethel MacDonald*; 1917, *National Defence*; c. 1918, *Socialism after the War*; 1919, *Parliament and Revolution*; 1921, *Socialism: Critical and Constructive*; 1925, *Wanderings and Excursions*; 1936, *At Home and Abroad.*

Articles in *The Socialist*, *Seedtime*, the *Ethical World* and the *New Age* (pre-1900); the *Echo*, the *Leicester Pioneer* and the *Socialist Review* c. 1900–1914; *Forward*, the *Labour Leader*, the *New Leader*, the *Socialist Review* c. 1914–1929. Articles for the *Dictionary of National Biography.*

FURTHER READING

Elton, Lord. *The Life of James Ramsay MacDonald (1866–1919)*. London, 1939.

Hamilton, M. A. *J. Ramsay MacDonald.* London, 1929.

Marquand, D. *Ramsay MacDonald.* Manchester, 1987.

Morgan, A. *J. Ramsay MacDonald.* Manchester, 1987.

Tiltman, H. H. *James Ramsay MacDonald: Labour's Man of Destiny.* London, 1929.

Weir, L. MacN. *The Tragedy of Ramsay MacDonald: A Political Biography.* London, 1938.

H.H.

Bettmann

Neville Chamberlain

Lived 1869–1940
Political Party Conservative
Prime Minister 28 May 1937–10 May 1940
Government Conservative
Reigning Monarch George VI

Je tiens ferme I stand fast

CHAMBERLAIN AS PRIME MINISTER

Chamberlain was 49 when he first entered Parliament as a successful Birmingham businessman from a family with strong political and public service traditions. A respected and creative Minister of Health under Baldwin, later he helped negotiate arrangements for a National Government in 1931. He served more than five years as Chancellor of the Exchequer under MacDonald and subsequently Baldwin. Good at detailed planning and forceful execution his forte was domestic rather than foreign affairs. He could be stubborn and righteous, but his organizing abilities, which he applied to the Conservative Party itself at Baldwin's request, could be impressive. When Baldwin retired in 1937, although aged 68 Chamberlain was the obvious successor. His problems centred on foreign affairs, where a rational, clear-minded Prime Minister was faced by dictators whose aggressive policies were supported by appeals to mass emotion. He needed time to rearm and secured widespread Parliamentary support for his policy of 'appeasement', except from the Labour Party. Finally, in March 1939 he promised British support for Poland should Germany intervene. Thus when Germany invaded Poland, war was declared and Churchill joined Chamberlain's Government. The opening months of the war were quiet but Chamberlain was not suited to being a war leader and his unimaginative approach to the national crisis failed to kindle support. The first serious British defeat was the unsuccesssul Norway campaign in the spring of 1940. When it was debated the majority support for Chamberlain was so reduced that after much discussion he resigned to make way for Churchill.

PERSONAL INFORMATION

Names Arthur Neville Chamberlain
Nicknames The Coroner
Born 18 Mar 1869
Birthplace Edgbaston, Birmingham
Religion Unitarian
Ancestry Chamberlain's father, Joseph, was born and brought up in London where the family had a successful shoemaking business. He moved to Birmingham and built up Nettlefold and Chamberlain, screw manufacturers, before entering public life, first as Mayor of Birmingham then as a Birmingham MP and a Minister. Chamberlain's mother's family came originally from Wales and had prospered in Birmingham.
Date and place of marriage 5 Jan 1911, St. Paul's Church, Knightsbridge, London
Age at marriage 41 years, 291 days
Years married 29 years, 309 days
First entered Parliament 14 Dec 1918
Date appointed PM 28 May 1937
Age at appointment 68 years, 71 days
Date ceased to be PM 10 May 1940
Total time as PM 2 years, 348 days
Ceased to be MP 9 Nov 1940
Lived after last term as PM 183 days
Date and place of death 9 Nov 1940, Highfield Park, Heckfield, near Reading, Hampshire
Age at death 71 years, 246 days
Last words 'Approaching dissolution brings relief'. (to Halifax who visited him two days before his death)
Place of funeral Westminster Abbey, London
Place of burial Ashes interred in Westminster Abbey, London
Zodiac sign Pisces

FATHER

Joseph Chamberlain
Date and place of birth 8 Jul 1836, 3 Camberwell Grove (later re-numbered 118), Camberwell, London
Occupation Manufacturer of screws in Birmingham. Three times Mayor of Birmingham. An MP—Liberal, Jun 1876 until Mar 1886; Liberal Unionist from Mar 1886. Sat for Birmingham, 1876–85, West Birmingham 1885–1914. President of the Board of Trade, Apr 1880–May 1885; President of the Local Government Board, Jan–Mar 1886; Chief Commissioner to settle the North American Fisheries Dispute 1887; Chairman of the Coal Dust Commission, 1891–94; Member of the Aged Poor Commission 1893–95; Secretary of State for the Colonies 1895–1903.
Dates of marriages 1) 1861, Harriet Kenrick (d. 1863); 2) 1868, Florence Kenrick (d. 1875); 3) 1888, Mary Endicott
Date of death 2 Jul 1914
Place of burial Key Hill Cemetery, Birmingham

MOTHER

Florence Kenrick
Date of marriage 1868
Date of death 14 Feb 1875

BROTHERS AND SISTERS

Neville Chamberlain was the only son of his father's second marriage and the third of six children.
From his father's first marriage:
Beatrice, d. 1918
Sir (Joseph) Austen, b. 16 Oct 1863; m. 21 Jul 1906, Ivy Dundas, GBE; MP East Worcestershire, 1892–1914, West Birmingham, 1914–37; various Cabinet posts including Chancellor of the Exchequer, Secretary of State for India, Foreign Secretary and Leader of the House of Commons; d. 16 Mar 1937
From his father's second marriage:
Ida, b. 1870; unm.; a county councillor and alderman in Hampshire; an authority on rural housing; d. 1942
Hilda, unm.; a local school governor in Hampshire
Ethel, m. Lio Richards
From his father's third marriage:
None

WIFE

Anne de Vere Cole
Mother Mary de Vere (later Mrs. Herbert Studd)
Father Major William Utting Cole
Father's occupation Officer in 3rd Dragoon Guards
Number of children 2
Profile After her father died of cholera in India, she was raised at West Woodhay, the home of her Cole grandparents in Berkshire. The Chamberlains were delighted with the match, when they became engaged, but the de Veres and the Coles thought the Chamberlain family too stuffy for Anne, who had a military and a county background, rather than a business one. In fact, theirs was a love match. Chamberlain said after each of his successes, 'I'd never have done it without Annie'.

Although she had a reputation for insouciance and was chronically late and had spells of nervousness and depression, she was a fiercely loyal and loving wife, wrapped up in her husband's political career almost to the point of neglecting her children. She believed Chamberlain could do no wrong.

CHILDREN

1 son, 1 daughter
Dorothy, b. 25 Dec 1911; m. Dr. Stephen Lloyd; d. 1992
Frank, b. late 1913/early 1914; m. Roma; d. before 1984

LIFE AND CAREER

PARLIAMENTARY ELECTIONS FOUGHT

*(*designates candidate elected)*

DATE Dec 1918. General Election
CONSTITUENCY Birmingham, Ladywood
RESULT A.N. Chamberlain* (Con) 9,405; J.W. Kneeshaw (Lab), 2,572; Mrs. M.I.C. Ashby (Lib), 1,552

DATE 15 Nov 1922. General Election
CONSTITUENCY Birmingham, Ladywood
RESULT A. N. Chamberlain* (Con) 13,032; Dr. R. Dunstan (Lab) 10,589

DATE 6 Dec 1923. General Election
CONSTITUENCY Birmingham, Ladywood
RESULT A. N. Chamberlain* (Con), 12,884; Dr. R. Dunstan (Lab) 11,330

PARLIAMENTARY ELECTIONS FOUGHT—*Continued*

DATE 29 Oct 1924. General Election
CONSTITUENCY Birmingham, Ladywood
RESULT A. N. Chamberlain* (Con) 13,374; O.E. Mosley (Lab) 13,297; A.W. Bowkett (Lib), 539

DATE 30 May 1929. General Election
CONSTITUENCY Birmingham, Edgbaston
RESULT A. N. Chamberlain* (Con) 23,350; W.H.D. Caple (Lab) 8,590; P.R.C. Young (Lib) 4,720

DATE 27 Oct 1931. General Election
CONSTITUENCY Birmingham, Edgbaston
RESULT A. N. Chamberlain* (Con) 33,085; W.W. Blaylock (Lab) 5,157

DATE 14 Nov 1935. General Election
CONSTITUENCY Birmingham, Edgbaston
RESULT A. N. Chamberlain* (Con) 28,243; J. Adshead (Lab), 6,381

PARTY ACTIVITY

Party Leadership Leader of the Conservative Party 31 May 1937–4 Oct 1940
Other offices Jun 1930–Apr 1931, Chairman of the Conservative Party; 1930–40, Chairman, Conservative Research Department.
Membership of group or faction During his first four years in Parliament Chamberlain supported the Coalition Government. After the Carlton Club meeting on 19 Oct 1922 Chamberlain followed Bonar Law and other Conservatives who withdrew their support from Lloyd George's Coalition Government.

PARLIAMENTARY AND MINISTERIAL EXPERIENCE

Maiden Speech 12 Mar 1919, spoke during Committee stage of the Increase of Rent and Mortgage Interest (Restrictions) Bill. (*HC Deb*, vol 113, col 1176–77, 1192)
Opposition offices Spokesman on health and housing, Jan–Oct 1924
Privy Counsellor 2 Nov 1922
Ministerial Offices Minister of National Service, 19 Aug 1916–8 Aug 1917; Postmaster-General, 31 Oct 1922–7 Mar 1923; Paymaster General, 5 Feb 1923–15 Mar 1923; Minister of Health, 7 Mar 1923–27 Aug 1923, 6 Nov 1924–7 Jun 1929, 25 Aug–5 Nov 1931; Chancellor of the Exchequer, 27 Aug 1923–22 Jan 1924, 5 Nov 1931–28 May 1937; First Lord of the Treasury and Leader of the House of Commons 28 May 1937–10 May 1940; Lord President of the Council, 11 May–3 Oct 1940
Opposition leader while PM Neville Chamberlain as Prime Minister headed a National Government.

GOVERNMENTS FORMED

Administration (National Government) 28 May 1937–10 May 1940

GENERAL ELECTION RESULT
14 NOV 1935: Conservative 429; Labour 154; Liberal 21; Others 11. Total 615
National Government majority 242 (excl. the Speaker)

CABINET
Prime Minister and First Lord of the Treasury N. Chamberlain
Lord President Viscount Halifax (May 1937–Mar 1938); Viscount Hailsham (Mar–Oct 1938); Viscount Runciman (Oct 1938–Sep 1939); Earl Stanhope (Sep 1939–May 1940)
Lord Chancellor Viscount Hailsham (May 1937–Mar 1938); Lord Maugham (Mar 1938–Sep 1939); Viscount Caldecote (Sep 1939–May 1940)
Lord Privy Seal Earl De La Warr (May 1937–Oct 1938); Sir J. Anderson (Oct 1938–Sep 1939); †Sir S. Hoare (Sep 1939–Apr 1940); Sir K. Wood (Apr–May 1940)
Chancellor of the Exchequer †Sir J. Simon
Foreign Secretary A. Eden (May 1937–Feb 1938) Viscount Halifax (Feb 1938–May 1940)
Home Secretary Sir S. Hoare (May 1937–Sep 1939); Sir J. Anderson (Sep 1939–May 1940)
First Lord of the Admiralty A. D. Cooper (May 1937–Oct 1938); Earl Stanhope (Oct 1938–Sep 1939);†W. Churchill (Sep 1939–May 1940)
Minister of Agriculture W. Morrison (May 1937– Jan 1939); Sir R. Dorman-Smith (Jan 1939–May 1940)
Secretary of State for Air Sir P. Cunliffe-Lister (Viscount Swinton) (May 1937–May 1938); †Sir K. Wood (May 1938–Apr 1940) Sir S. Hoare (Apr–May1940)
Secretary of State for the Colonies W. Ormsby-Gore (May 1937–May 1938); M. MacDonald (May 1938–May 1940)
Minister for the Coordination of Defence Sir T. Inskip (May 1937–Jan 1939); †Lord Chatfield (Jan 1939–Apr 1940, when office was abolished)
Secretary of State for Dominion Affairs M. MacDonald (May 1937–May 1938); Lord Stanley (May– Oct 1938); M. MacDonald, (Oct 1938–Jan 1939); Sir T. Inskip (Viscount Caldecote) (Jan–Sep 1939) A. Eden (Sep 1939–May 1940)
President of the Board of Education Earl Stanhope (May 1937–Oct 1938); Earl De La Warr (Oct 1938–Apr 1940); H. Ramsbotham (Apr–May 1940)
*Minister of Food** Lord Woolton (Apr–May 1940)
Minister of Health Sir K. Wood (May 1937–May 1938); W. Elliot (May 1938–May 1940)
Secretary of State for India and for Burma Marquess of Zetland
*Minister of Information** Lord Macmillan (Sep 1939–Jan 1940); Lord Reith (Jan–May 1940)
Minister of Labour E. Brown (Sep 1939 *Labour and National Service*)
Chancellor of the Duchy of Lancaster (Office not in Cabinet) Earl Winterton (Mar 1938–Jan 1939); W. Morrison (Jan 1939–May 1940) (Sep 1939–Apr 1940 combined with Ministry of Food)
Minister without Portfolio Lord Burgin (Apr–Jul 1939) †Lord Hankey (Sep 1939–May 1940)
Secretary of State for Scotland W. Elliot (May 1937–May 1938); J. Colville (May 1938–May 1940)
*Minister of Shipping** Sir J. Gilmour (Oct 1939–Apr 1940); R. Hudson (Apr–May 1940)
*Minister of Supply** Lord Burgin (Jul 1939–May 1940)
President of the Board of Trade O. Stanley (May 1937–Jan 1940); Sir A. Duncan (Jan–May 1940)
Minister of Transport Lord Burgin (May 1937–Apr 1939); E. Wallace (Apr 1939–May 1940)
Secretary of State for War Lord Hore-Belisha (May 1937–Jan 1940); O. Stanley (Jan–May 1940)
[*Office not previously established]
†Following the British declaration of war against Germany on 3 Sep 1939, all members of the Cabinet formally

surrendered their portfolios to the Prime Minister; in the evening of the same day the formation of a War Cabinet was announced.

IMPORTANT DATES IN PERSONAL AND POLITICAL LIFE

1886–88 Chamberlain studies metallurgy and engineering design at Mason College (later University of Birmingham).

1889 He is apprenticed to a firm of chartered accountants in Birmingham.

1890 He goes to the island of Andros in the Bahamas to manage a sisal plantation on land bought by his father. The enterprise is not a success and the Andros Fibre Company is wound up in 1897.

1897 Chamberlain returns to Birmingham to take charge of two firms, Elliott's Metal Company and Hoskins and Sons.

5 JAN 1911 Marries Anne de Vere Cole.

1911 Elected to Birmingham City Council as Liberal Unionist Councillor for All Saints ward.

2 JUL 1914 Death of his father, Joseph.

4 AUG 1914 Britain declares war on Germany.

1915 Chamberlain is appointed a member of the Central Control Board (Liquor Traffic). He becomes Lord Mayor of Birmingham for the first time.

19 AUG 1916 He is made Director General of National Service to organise and direct the work of recruiting labour for the war industries. It is a ministerial post, although he is not an MP.

14 DEC 1918 Elected as Coalition Conservative Member for Birmingham, Ladywood, at the General Election.

12 MAR 1919 Makes his maiden speech during the Committee stage of the Increase of Rent and Mortgage Interest (Restrictions) Bill.

19 OCT 1922 Carlton Club meeting at which Bonar Law and a number of Conservatives withdraw their support from the Coalition Government. Chamberlain, on his way back from holiday in Canada at the time, soon follows suit.

31 OCT 1922 He is appointed Postmaster-General by Bonar Law.

15 NOV 1922 Returned as Conservative Member for Birmingham, Ladywood, at the General Election.

7 MAR 1923 He becomes Minister of Health and passes an important housing Bill.

27 AUG 1923 Appointed Chancellor of the Exchequer by Stanley Baldwin, who has succeeded Bonar Law as Prime Minister. Chamberlain is not able to present a Budget before Baldwin calls a General Election in December.

6 DEC 1923 Again returned for Birmingham, Ladywood.

JAN–OCT 1924 Ramsay MacDonald having formed the first Labour Government, Chamberlain becomes Opposition spokesman on health and housing.

29 OCT 1924 Again returned for Birmingham, Ladywood, at the General Election but with a majority of only 77. Baldwin forms a Government and Chamberlain is appointed Minister of Health.

1925 He pilots the Widows', Orphans' and Old Age Pensions Bill through the House, and takes the Rating and Valuation Bill through the House. This measure paves the way for a massive programme of house building.

27 MAR 1929 The Local Government Act, which reforms the Poor Law and recasts the financial relations of central government and the local authorities is passed.

30 MAY 1929 Returned for Birmingham, Edgbaston. Ramsay MacDonald again becomes Prime Minister.

JUN 1930 Chamberlain is appointed Conservative Party Chairman and is involved in the reorganisation of Central Office, the setting up of the Research Department and the review of the party leadership.

AUG 1931 During the financial crisis Chamberlain represents the Conservative Party (in Baldwin's absence abroad on holiday) in negotiations preceding the formation of the National Government, in which he becomes Minister of Health again.

27 OCT 1931 Again returned for Birmingham, Edgbaston. He continues to serve in the National Government now as Chancellor of the Exchequer, a post he is to hold for the next five and half years.

4 FEB 1932 Moves in the House that with effect from 1 Mar there should be charged a duty of 10 per cent on all goods imported into the United Kingdom, with certain specific exceptions.

19 APR 1932 Chamberlain presents his first Budget which sets up an Exchequer Equalisation Fund to hold reserves of gold and foreign exchange.

17 JUN 1932 He attends the Lausanne Conference at which the question of German war debts and reparations is settled.

7 JUN 1935 Stanley Baldwin becomes Prime Minister in place of Ramsay MacDonald.

OCT 1935 Italy invades Abyssinia.

14 NOV 1935 General Election. Chamberlain again returned for Birmingham, Edgbaston.

MAR 1936 Hitler occupies the demilitarised zone of the Rhineland.

JUL 1936 Outbreak of the Spanish Civil War.

28 MAY 1937 Baldwin resigns as Prime Minister and is succeeded by Chamberlain.

20 FEB 1938 The Foreign Secretary, Anthony Eden, unable to support Chamberlain's intention to negotiate with Mussolini's Italy, resigns. He is succeeded by Lord Halifax.

12 MAR 1938 Hitler invades Austria.

24 MAR 1938 Chamberlain, in a statement to the House of Commons, sets out Britain's foreign policy aims.

16 APR 1938 Anglo-Italian Agreement signed in Rome. Britain recognises Italian supremacy in Abyssinia and undertakes not to intervene in the Spanish Civil War.

15 SEP 1938 Chamberlain meets Hitler in Berchtesgaden in an attempt to prevent the outbreak of a general European war over Hitler's demand that Czechoslovakia cede the Sudetenland to Germany.

22 SEP 1938 Chamberlain again meets Hitler, this time in Godesberg, to discuss the situation in Czechoslovakia.

28 SEP 1938 During Chamberlain's statement to the House of Commons on his meeting, he receives an invitation from Hitler to a conference in Munich on the following day. Mussolini and Daladier, the French Prime Minister, are also invited.

30 SEP 1938 By the Munich Agreement, Chamberlain and Daladier grant almost all of Hitler's demands and leave Czechoslovakia defenceless. Chamberlain returns to London a popular hero.

3–6 OCT 1938 The Labour Party and a small group of Conservatives including Winston Churchill criticise the Agreement during four days' debate in the House of Commons. At the end of the debate, by 366 votes to 144, the House of Commons declares its confidence in the Government.

10–16 MAR 1939 Hitler seizes the rest of Czechoslovakia. Chamberlain repudiates appeasement and publishes

IMPORTANT DATES IN PERSONAL AND POLITICAL LIFE—*Continued*

Anglo-French guarantees of armed support for Poland, Romania and Greece in the event of similar attacks.

APR 1939 A measure of compulsory military service is introduced.

23 AUG 1939 The Soviet-German Non-Aggression Treaty is signed.

24 AUG 1939 An Anglo-Polish pact is concluded.

1 SEP 1939 Germany attacks Poland.

3 SEP 1939 Britain declares war on Germany.

SEP 1939 Chamberlain forms his War Cabinet, which includes Winston Churchill. The Labour leaders and the Liberals return to join the Government.

7 AND 8 MAY 1940 After the failure of a British expedition to Norway in April Chamberlain loses the support of many Conservatives in the House of Commons. In the division at the end of a dramatic debate, the Government's majority, normally around 240, falls to 81.

10 MAY 1940 Chamberlain resigns as Prime Minister, the day of the German invasion of Holland, Belgium and Luxembourg.

30 SEP 1940 In Churchill's coalition Government Chamberlain serves as Lord President until ill health forces him to resign that office and the Conservative Party leadership.

9 NOV 1940 Chamberlain dies at Highfield Park, Heckfield, near Reading, Hampshire.

BACKGROUND

PHYSICAL CHARACTERISTICS AND HEALTH

Neville Chamberlain was a slightly built man of medium height (about 5'10") with sharp features, dark brown hair and a heavy moustache. Apart from occasional attacks of gout he enjoyed good health and possessed the energy and stamina necessary for public life.

Soon after he resigned as Prime Minister in May 1940 it became clear that he was seriously ill. Bowel cancer was diagnosed and he died within a few months, on 9 Nov 1940.

EDUCATION

Primary 1) 1877, boarding school near Southport, Lancashire; 2) Preparatory school for Rugby School.

Secondary Rugby School, Warwickshire

University Mason College (later became the University of Birmingham). Studied commerce, metallurgy and engineering design.

Cultural and vocational background In 1889 after his studies at Mason College Chamberlain joined a large family party to visit Paris, his first trip abroad. Later in the year much the same group spent about three months travelling in Egypt.

Languages Good reading and some speaking knowledge of French.

NON-PARLIAMENTARY CAREER

Early occupations In 1889 he was apprenticed to a firm of chartered accountants. Between 1890 and 1897 Chamberlain lived on the island of Andros in the Bahamas, managing an estate bought by his father and attempting in vain to grow sisal. On his return to Birmingham he became a director of two firms, Elliott's Metal Company, manufacturers of copper, brass and yellow metal, and Hoskins and Sons, makers of metal cabin berths.

He was active in public life on the management boards of local hospitals, on the governing body of the new university, on the committee for territorial army units and in the Chamber of Commerce.

Other posts Sep 1911, elected to Birmingham City Council as Liberal Unionist Councillor for All Saints; 1914, became an alderman; 1915, member of Central Control Board (Liquor Traffic); 1915–16, Lord Mayor of Birmingham.

HONOURS

Freedom of cities 1932, Birmingham; 1941, City of London (Chamberlain was unable to accept the freedom of the City of London because of his illness; the scroll was presented to Mrs. Chamberlain after his death.)

Academic LLD, Birmingham; LLD, Bristol; LLD, Cambridge; LLD, Leeds; DCL, Oxford; D.Litt, Reading

Other than peerage 16 Jun 1938, Fellow of the Royal Society; Chamberlain declined the offer of a GBE in 1917 and an Earldom and the Garter in 1940

CLUBS

Carlton; Athenaeum

HOBBIES AND SPORTS

Throughout his life Chamberlain had a great love of and interest in birds, butterflies, insects, flowers and trees. He made a particular study of the trees at Chequers, writing a monograph on the subject.

In middle and later life he became an increasingly expert fisherman for trout and salmon and an excellent shot.

His main indoor relaxations were music and reading. In literature, he had wide but well-defined tastes. Among novelists, Conrad remained his favourite; he loved almost all the works of Dickens, Mark Twain, Thackeray and George Eliot. He knew Shakespeare's works intimately. His library included much history, natural history, travel, everything by Darwin and much about him, biographies, books on porcelain, music, shooting, fishing, gardening, India and Birmingham.

Chamberlain loved the music of the later 18th and early 19th centuries, above all Beethoven. He also enjoyed the works of Mendelssohn, Handel, Mozart and Haydn. He liked the paintings of Turner and the Impressionists and Augustus John.

FINANCES

Chamberlain depended heavily upon his holdings in Hoskins and Elliott's. Hoskins, in particular, did less well after World War I and showed a loss in 1923. Chamberlain's income, therefore, fell at this time.

Legacies His bachelor uncle, George Kenrick, left him a substantial legacy when he died.

ANECDOTES

Aneurin Bevan said of him 'Listening to a speech by Chamberlain is like paying a visit to Woolworths; everything is in its place and nothing above sixpence'. (*Tribune*)

'He was a meticulous housemaid, great at tidying up'. (A.J.P. Taylor, *English History 1914–1945*)

Harold Nicholson wrote: 'I think it is the combination of real religious fanaticism with spiritual trickiness which makes one dislike Mr. Chamberlain so much. He has all the hardness of a self-righteous man, with none of the generosity of those who are guided by durable moral standards'. (*Diary* 26 Apr 1939)

The Penguin Dictionary of Modern Quotations attributes the following to Adolf Hitler: 'Well, he seemed such a nice old gentleman, I thought I would give him my autograph as a souvenir'.

Chamberlain hated war and had wished to supply the people with housing and better food and education, not armaments. He wrote to the Archbishop of Canterbury in 1940, 'I simply can't bear to think of those gallant fellows who lost their lives last night in the RAF attack and of their families . . . . Indeed, I must put such thoughts out of my mind if I am not to be unnerved altogether'. He was upset by the destruction of U-boats, feeling that the crews would be friends if it were not war time. 'And we have to kill one another just to satisfy that accursed madman. I wish he could burn in Hell for as many years as he is costing lives'. (Iain Macleod, *Neville Chamberlain*, London, 1961)

QUOTATIONS

3 Jul 1938, In war, whichever side may call itself the victor, there are no winners, but all are losers. (Speech at Kettering, in *The Times*, 4 Jul 1938)

27 Sep 1938, How horrible, fantastic, incredible it is that we should be digging trenches and trying on gas masks here because of a quarrel in a far away country between people of whom we know nothing. (On Germany's annexation of the Sudetenland; radio broadcast, in *The Times*, 28 Sep 1938)

30 Sep 1938, This is the second time in our history that there has come back from Germany to Downing Street peace with honour. I believe it is peace for our time. (Speech from 10 Downing Street, in *The Times*, 1 Oct 1938)

4 Apr 1940, Whatever may be the reason—whether it was that Hitler thought he might get away with what he had got without fighting for it, or whether it was that after all the preparations were not sufficiently complete—however, one thing is certain—he missed the bus. (Speech at Central Hall, Westminster, in *The Times*, 5 Apr 1940)

RESIDENCES

Southbourne, Augustus Road, Edgbaston, Birmingham
Highbury, Moor Green, Birmingham
Westbourne, Edgbaston, Birmingham
37 Eaton Square, London (Plaque)
11 Downing Street
10 Downing Street
Highfield Park, Heckfield, near Reading, Hampshire

MEMORIALS

STATUES AND BUSTS

1936, bust by Lady Kathleen Kennet, Birmingham City Art Gallery

PORTRAITS

Date not known, by Sir William Orpen; *c.* 1933, by Sir Oswald Birley, Birmingham City Art Gallery; *c.* 1939, by Sir James Gunn, Carlton Club, London; c. 1939, by Henry Lamb, National Portrait Gallery

OTHER MEMORIALS

Stone plaque erected to his memory in Heckfield, near Reading, Hampshire, village church (Highfield Park, where Chamberlain died, is nearby) with these words on it: 'Write me as one that loves his fellow-men'. (From Leigh Hunt's poem *Abou Ben Adhem and the Angel*)

BIBLIOGRAPHIC INFORMATION

LETTERS AND PERSONAL PAPERS

Neville Chamberlain's private papers, together with those of his elder half-brother Austen and their father Joseph, are in the University of Birmingham Library.

PUBLICATIONS

1922, *Norman Chamberlain: A Memoir*, privately printed (Based on the letters and papers of his cousin, who was killed in action in Flanders in Dec 1917); 1939, *The Struggle for Peace.*

FURTHER READING

Charmley, J. *Chamberlain and the Lost Peace*. London, 1989.
Dilks, D. *Neville Chamberlain: Volume One: Pioneering and Reform, 1869–1929*. Cambridge, 1984.
Elletson, D. H. *The Chamberlains*. London, 1966.
Feiling, K. *The Life of Neville Chamberlain*. London, 1970.
Fuchser, L.W. *Neville Chamberlain and Appeasement*. New York, 1982.
Hyde, H. M. *Neville Chamberlain*. London, 1976.
Macleod, I. *Neville Chamberlain*. London, 1961.

H. H.

Bettmann

Winston Churchill

Lived 1874–1965

Political Party 1900–1904 Conservative
1904–1924 Liberal
1924–1965 Conservative

Prime Minister 10 May 1940–26 July 1945; 26 October 1951–5 April 1955

Governments Coalition; Conservative Caretaker; Conservative

Reigning Monarchs George VI; Elizabeth II

Fiel pero desdichado Faithful, though unfortunate

CHURCHILL AS PRIME MINISTER

Churchill, who came from a famous political family, had formidable strength and energy, as well as a sometimes abrasive manner, great courage, and an impish sense of humour. As a political leader he was described as 'original rather than reliable.' A soldier and journalist in his early years, he entered Parliament as a Conservative in the Khaki Election of 1900, then switched to the Liberals, serving in Asquith's and Lloyd George's administrations. He rejoined the Conservatives in 1924, becoming Baldwin's Chancellor of the Exchequer until 1929, then passed from the centre of the political stage for a decade. At the outbreak of the 1939–1945 war, after having warned of the Nazi threat for years, he joined Chamberlain's Government and succeeded him as the natural wartime leader. For five years he prodded, challenged and inspired the nation and the free world, his celebrated broadcasts having a significant impact on morale. Despite his concentration on the British war effort, he supported steps taken for the future, such as the Beveridge Plan for social insurance (1942), the Butler Education Act (1944) and the establishment of a Ministry of Town and Country Planning. All were to be of importance in post-war Britain. With peace at hand, Churchill was rejected at the 1945 General Election, when the country turned to Labour. In 1951, he formed his third administration, which, apart from denationalising steel, left most of the Labour government changes in place. He returned to the world stage, serving as his own Foreign Secretary during Eden's illness, finally resigning as Prime Minister in 1955.

PERSONAL INFORMATION

Names Winston Leonard Spencer Churchill
Nickname Winnie
Born 30 Nov 1874
Birthplace Blenheim Palace, Oxfordshire
Religion Anglican
Ancestry English. Descended from the Dukes of Marlborough. The 7th Duke was his grandfather.
Date and place of marriage 12 Sep 1908, St. Margaret's, Westminster, London
Age at marriage 33 years, 287 days
Years married 56 years, 135 days
First entered Parliament 3 Oct 1900
Dates appointed PM 1) 10 May 1940; 2) 26 Oct 1951
Age at appointments 1) 65 years, 163 days; 2) 76 years, 331 days
Dates ceased to be PM 1) 26 Jul 1945; 2) 5 Apr 1955
Total time as PM 1) 5 years, 78 days; 2) 3 years, 162 days; a total of 8 years, 240 days
Ceased to be MP 25 Sep 1964
Lived after last term as PM 9 years, 295 days
Date of death 24 Jan 1965
Place of death 28 Hyde Park Gate, London
Age at death 90 years, 56 days
Place of funeral Lay in state, Westminster Hall 27–30 Jan 1965; St. Paul's Cathedral, London
Place of burial Bladon Church, Oxfordshire
Zodiac sign Sagittarius

FATHER

Lord Randolph Churchill
Date and place of birth 13 Feb 1849, Blenheim Palace, Oxfordshire
Occupation Politician; MP Woodstock 1874–85, South Paddington 1885–95
Date of marriage 15 Apr 1874
Date and place of death 24 Jan 1895, 50 Grosvenor Square, London
Place of burial Bladon Church, Oxfordshire

MOTHER

Jennie Jerome
Date and place of birth 9 Jan 1854, Brooklyn, New York
Profile She was famous as a great and extravagant hostess.
Dates of marriages 1) 15 Apr 1874, Lord Randolph Churchill; 2) Jul 1900, George Cornwallis-West; 3) 1 Jun 1918, Montagu Phippen Porch
Date of death 29 Jun 1921
Place of burial Bladon Church, Oxfordshire

BROTHERS AND SISTERS

Winston Churchill was the elder of two sons

John Strange Spencer ('Jack'), b. 4 Feb 1880; m. 4 Aug 1908; his daughter Clarissa married Anthony Eden (*q.v.*); d. 23 Feb 1947

WIFE

Clementine Hozier, created Baroness Spencer-Churchill 17 May 1965
Date and place of birth 1 Apr 1885; 75 Grosvenor Street, London
Mother Lady Blanche Ogilvy
Father Col. Sir Henry M. Hozier
Father's occupation Secretary of Lloyds, London
Age at marriage 23 years, 165 days
Number of children 5
Date and place of death 12 Dec 1977, 7 Princes Gate, London
Place of burial Bladon Church, Oxfordshire
Years younger than PM 11 years, 121 days
Education Berkhamstead Grammar School; Studied French and German at the Sorbonne
Profile Tall, stately and handsome she enjoyed social life and stood out in company. A practical person, she was quite shy by nature. Inclined to worry about financial matters, but very supportive to her husband with a very active and demanding career and lifestyle. Her advice on personal matters was usually followed by Churchill, and many observers noted that her political judgements were often wiser and steadier than her husband's.

CHILDREN

1 son, 4 daughters
Diana, b. 11 Jul 1909, m. 1) 12 Dec 1932, John Milner Bailey (div. 1935; d.1963) 2) 16 Sep 1935, Duncan Sandys (d. 1987) (MP Norwood 1935–45, Streatham 1950–74); d. 19 Oct 1963
Randolph, b. 28 May 1911, m. 1) 4 Oct 1939, Hon. Pamela Digby (dis. 1946); 2) 2 Nov 1948, June Osborne (dis. 1961; d. 1980.) MP Preston 1940–45; served in Yugoslavia during World War II; an irascible and difficult man, he started the great biography of his father; d. 6 Jun 1968
Sarah, b. 7 Oct 1914, m. 1) 25 Dec 1936, Vic Oliver (div. 1945; d. 1964), 2) 18 Oct 1949, Anthony Beauchamp Entwistle (d. 1957); 3) 26 Apr 1962, Henry, Baron Audley (d. 1963); actress; d. 23 Sep 1982
Marigold, b. 15 Nov 1918; d. 23 Aug 1921
Mary, b. 15 Sep 1922; m. 11 Feb 1947, Hon. Christopher Soames (MP Bedford 1950–66); d. 1987

LIFE AND CAREER

PARLIAMENTARY ELECTIONS FOUGHT

*(*designates candidate elected)*

DATE 6 Jul 1899. By-election caused by death of R. Ashcroft and resignation of J.F. Oswald

PARLIAMENTARY ELECTIONS FOUGHT—*Continued*

CONSTITUENCY Oldham
RESULT A. Emmott* (Rad) 12, 976; W. Runciman* (Rad) 12,770; W. Churchill (Con) 11,477; J. Mawdsley (Con) 11,449

DATE Oct 1900. General Election
CONSTITUENCY Oldham
RESULT A. Emmott* (Lib) 12,947; W. Churchill* (Con L.) 12,931; W. Runciman (Lab) 12,709; C.B. Crisp (Con) 12,522

DATE Jan 1906. General Election
CONSTITUENCY Manchester North-west
RESULT W. Churchill* (Lib) 5,639; W. Joynson-Hicks (Con) 4,398

DATE 24 Apr 1908. By-election caused by Churchill's appointment as President of the Board of Trade
CONSTITUENCY Manchester North-west
RESULT W. Joynson-Hicks* (Con) 5,417; W. Churchill (Lib) 4,988; D.D. Irving (S.D.F.) 276

DATE 9 May 1908. By-election caused by E. Robertson becoming Lord Lochie of Gowrie
CONSTITUENCY Dundee
RESULT W. Churchill* (Lib) 7,079; Sir. G. W. Baxter (L.U.) 4,370; G.H. Stewart (S.L.P.) 4,014; E. Scrymgeour (S.P.P.) 655

DATE Jan 1910. General Election
CONSTITUENCY Dundee
RESULT W. Churchill* (Lib) 10,747; A. Wilkie (Lab) 10, 365; J.H.S. Lloyd (Con) 4,552; J. Glass (L.U.) 4,339; E. Scrymgeour (S.P.P.) 1,512

DATE Dec 1910. General Election
CONSTITUENCY Dundee
RESULT W. Churchill (Lib)* 9,246; A. Wilkie (Lab) 8, 957; Sir. G.W. Baxter (L.U.) 5,685; J.H.S. Lloyd (Con) 4,914; E. Scrymgeour (S.P.P.) 1,825

DATE 30 Jul 1917. By-election caused by Churchill's appointment as Minister of Munitions
CONSTITUENCY Dundee
RESULT W. Churchill (Lib)* 7,302; E. Scrymgeour (S. P.P.) 2,036

DATE 14 Dec 1918. General Election
CONSTITUENCY Dundee
RESULT W. Churchill* (Con Lib) 25,788; A. Wilkie (Lab) 24,822; E. Scrymgeour (S.P.P.) 10,423; J.S. Brown (Lab) 7,769

DATE 15 Nov 1922. General Election
CONSTITUENCY Dundee
RESULT E. Scrymgeour* (S.P.P.) 32,578; E.D. Molel* (Lab) 30,292; D.J. Macdonald (Nat. Lib) 22,244; W. Churchill (Nat. Lib) 20,466; R.R. Pilkington (Lib) 6, 681; W. Gallacher (Com) 5,906

DATE 6 Dec 1923. General Election
CONSTITUENCY West Leicester
RESULT F. Pethic-Lawrence* (Lab) 13,634; W. Churchill (Lib) 9,236; A. Instone (Con) 7,696

DATE 19 Mar 1924. By-election caused by death of J.S. Nicholson
CONSTITUENCY Westminster, Abbey
RESULT O. W. Nicholson* (Con) 8,187; W. Churchill (Ind.) 8, 144; F. Brockway (Lab) 6,156; S. Duckers (Lib) 291

DATE 29 Oct 1924. General Election
CONSTITUENCY Epping
RESULT W. Churchill* (Constitutionalist) 19,843; G. G. Sharp (Lib) 10,080; J.R. McPhie (Lab) 3,768

DATE 30 May 1929. General Election
CONSTITUENCY Epping
RESULT W. Churchill* (Con) 23,972; G.G. Sharp (Lib) 19,005; J.T. Newbold (Lab) 6,475

DATE 27 Oct 1931. General Election
CONSTITUENCY Epping
RESULT W. Churchill* (Con) 35,956; A.S. Comyns Carr (Lib) 15, 670; J. Ranger (Lab) 4,713

DATE 14 Nov 1935. General Election
CONSTITUENCY Epping
RESULT W. Churchill* (Con) 34,849; G.G. Sharp (Lib) 14,430; J. Ranger (Lab) 9,758

DATE 5 Jul 1945. General Election
CONSTITUENCY Woodford
RESULT W. Churchill* (Con) 27,688; A. Hancock (Ind.) 10,488

DATE 23 Feb 1950. General Election
CONSTITUENCY Woodford
RESULT W. Churchill* (Con) 37,239; S. Hills (Lab) 18, 740; H. Davies (Lib) 5,664; W. Brooks (Com.) 827

DATE 25 Oct 1951. General Election
CONSTITUENCY Woodford
RESULT W. Churchill* (Con) 40,938; W.P. Archer (Lab) 22,359; J. Campbell (Com.) 871; A. Hancock (Ind.) 851

DATE 26 May 1955. General Election
CONSTITUENCY Woodford
RESULT Sir W. Churchill* (Con) 25,069; A. Milner (Lab) 9,261

DATE 8 Oct 1959. General Election
CONSTITUENCY Woodford
RESULT Sir W. Churchill* (Con) 24,815; A. Latham (Lab) 10,018

PARTY ACTIVITY

Party Leadership Leader of Conservative Party 7 Oct 1940–5 Apr 1955
Other offices 1943–65 Grand Master of the Primrose League

PARLIAMENTARY AND MINISTERIAL EXPERIENCE

Maiden Speech 18 Feb 1901, He spoke in the debate on the King's Speech on the Boer War, of which he had had personal experience. (*HC Deb*, vol 89, 18 Feb 1901, col 407–415
Opposition offices Leader of the Opposition 26 Jul 1946–26 Oct 1951
Privy Counsellor 1 May 1907
Ministerial Offices Under-Secretary for the Colonies 15 Dec 1905–12 Apr 1908; President of the Board of Trade 12 Apr 1908–14 Feb 1910; Home Secretary 14 Feb 1910–23 Oct 1911; First Lord of the Admiralty 13 Oct 1911–25 May 1915, 3 Sep 1939–10 May 1940; Chancellor of the Duchy of Lancaster 25 May–25 Nov 1915; Minister of Munitions 17 Jul 1917– 10 Jan 1919; Secretary of State for War 10 Jan 1919–13 Feb 1921; Secretary of State for the Colonies 13 Feb 1921–24 Oct 1922; Chancellor of the Exchequer 6 Nov 1924–7 Jun 1929;

First Lord of the Treasury and Minister of Defence 10 May 1940 -26 Jul 1945, 28 Oct 1951-1 Mar 1952
Opposition Leader while PM Churchill's first Administration was a war-time National Government so there was no Opposition leader; Clement Attlee May-Jul 1945; 1951-55.
Father of the House 8 Oct 1959-25 Sep 1964

GOVERNMENTS FORMED

First Administration 10 May 1940-23 May 1945

GENERAL ELECTION RESULT
14 NOV 1935: Conservative 429; Labour 154; Liberal 21; Others 11. Total 615
National Government majority 242 (excl. the Speaker)
Coalition Government formed after the resignation of Neville Chamberlain

CABINET
War Cabinet
Prime Minister, First Lord of the Treasury and Minister of Defence W. Churchill
Lord President of the Council N. Chamberlain (May-Oct 1940); Sir J. Anderson (Oct 1940-Sep 1943); C. Attlee (Sep 1943-May 1945)
*Lord Privy Seal** C. Attlee (May 1940-Feb 1942); Sir S. Cripps (Feb-Nov 1942);
*Chancellor of the Exchequer** Sir K. Wood (Oct 1940-Feb 1942); Sir J. Anderson (Sep 1943-May 1945)
Foreign Secretary Lord Halifax (May-Dec 1940); A. Eden (Dec 1940--May 1945)
*Minister of State** Lord Beaverbrook (May-Jun 1941); O. Lyttelton (Jun 1941-Mar 1942)
Minister of Production O. Lyttelton (Mar 1942-May 1945)
*Home Secretary** H. Morrison (Nov 1942-May 1945)
*Minister of Aircraft Production** Lord Beaverbrook (Aug 1940-May 1941)
*Secretary of State for the Dominions** C. Attlee (Feb 1942-Sep 1943)
*Minister of Labour and National Service** E. Bevin (Oct 1940-May 1945)
*Minister Resident in Middle East** O. Lyttelton (Feb -Mar 1942); R. Casey (Mar 1942-Dec 1943)
*Minister without Portfolio** A. Greenwood (May 1940-Feb 1942)
Minister of Reconstruction Lord Woolton
Minister of Supply Lord Beaverbrook (Jun 1941-Feb 1942)
[*office not always in War Cabinet]

Second Administration 23 May 1945-26 Jul 1945 (Caretaker Government)

GENERAL ELECTION RESULT
14 NOV 1935: Conservative 429; Labour 154; Liberal 21; Others 11. Total 615
National Government majority 242 (excl. the Speaker)

CABINET
Prime Minister, First Lord of the Treasury and Minister of Defence W. Churchill
Lord President of the Council Lord Woolton
Lord Privy Seal Lord Beaverbrook
Chancellor of the Exchequer Sir J. Anderson
Foreign Secretary A. Eden
Home Secretary Sir D. Somervell
First Lord of the Admiralty B. Bracken
Minister of Agriculture and Fisheries R. Hudson
Secretary of State for Air H. Macmillan
Colonial Secretary O. Stanley
Secretary of State for the Dominions Viscount Cranborne
Secretary of State for India and Burma L. Amery
Minister of Labour and National Service R. Butler
Minister of Production and President of the Board of Trade O. Lyttelton
Secretary of State at the War Office Sir J. Grigg
Secretary of State for Scotland Lord Rosebery

Third Administration 26 Oct 1951-6 Apr 1955

GENERAL ELECTION RESULT
25 OCT 1951: Conservative 321; Labour 295; Liberal 6; Others 3. Total 625
Conservative majority 16

CABINET
Prime Minister and First Lord of the Treasury W. Churchill
Lord Chancellor Lord Simonds (Oct 1951-Oct 1954); Viscount Kilmuir (Oct 1954-1955)
Lord President of the Council Lord Woolton (Oct 1951-Nov 1952); Lord Salisbury (Nov 1952-1955)
Lord Privy Seal Lord Salisbury (Oct 1951-May 1952); H. Crookshank (May 1952-1955)
Chancellor of the Exchequer R. Butler
Foreign Secretary A. Eden
Home and Welsh Affairs Secretary Sir D. Maxwell Fyfe (Oct 1951- Oct 1954); G. Lloyd-George (Oct 1954-1955)
Minister of Agriculture and Fisheries† Sir T. Dugdale (Sep 1953- Jul 1954); D. Heathcoat Amory (Jul 1954-1955)
Colonial Secretary O. Lyttelton (Oct 1951-Jul 1954); A. Lennox-Boyd (Jul 1954-1955)
Commonwealth Relations Secretary Lord Ismay (1951-Mar 1952); Lord Salisbury (Mar-Nov 1952); Viscount Swinton (Nov 1952-1955)
Secretary of State for Coordination of Transport Fuel and Power Lord Leathers (Oct 1951-Sep 1953); Office abolished
Minister of Defence W. Churchill (Oct 1951-Mar 1952); Earl Alexander (Mar 1952-Oct 1954); H. Macmillan (Oct 1954-1955)
Minister of Education† Miss F. Horsbrugh (Sep 1953-Oct 1954); Sir D. Eccles (Oct 1954-1955)
*Minister of Food** G. Lloyd-George (Sep 1953-Oct 1954)
*Agriculture Fisheries and Food combined 18 Oct 1954
Minister of Health H. Crookshank (Oct 1951- May 1952)
Minister of Housing and Local Government H. Macmillan (Oct 1951- Oct 1954); D. Sandys (Oct 1954-1955)
Minister of Labour and National Service Sir W. Monckton
Chancellor of the Duchy of Lancaster† Lord Woolton (Nov 1952-1955)
Paymaster General† Lord Cherwell (Oct 1951-Nov 1953)
Minister of Pensions and National Insurance† O. Peake (Oct 1954-1955)
Secretary of State for Scotland J. Stuart
President of the Board of Trade P. Thorneycroft
[† office not always in Cabinet]

IMPORTANT DATES IN PERSONAL AND POLITICAL LIFE

1888–93 He has a not very academically successful career at Harrow School, of which he is very fond, returning there regularly all his life.

1893–94 He attends the Royal Military College (for officers) at Sandhurst.

MAR 1895 He is commissioned into the 4th Hussars and a break in service permits him to visit Cuba, where the Spanish are putting down a revolt. Being his father's son enables him to obtain 5 guineas per article from the *Daily Graphic* for dispatches. He is on the side of Spain, the colonialist power.

1895–99 Churchill continues to combine the role of soldier and journalist in India and the Sudan, where he fights in the battle of Omdurman. In the Boer War, he is a journalist, having resigned his commission, but he is captured by the Boers and sent to a prisoner-of-war camp. During this period he writes his first three books, including *Savrola*, a novel.

12 DEC 1899 He escapes from a prison camp in Pretoria and makes his way to the coast after many adventures.

1899–1900 He returns to England to fight a by- election, unsuccessfully, at Oldham, but wins the seat in the General Election in October 1900. He continues to work on the biography of his father, whose independence and unorthodox stands he echoes.

31 MAY 1904 He leaves the Conservative Party on the issue of free trade and joins the Liberal Party, in which he is to remain until 1924.

15 DEC 1905 Churchill appointed to his first ministerial post as Under-Secretary for the Colonies in Campbell-Bannerman's administration.

12 APR 1908 Asquith promotes him to a Cabinet post: President of the Board of Trade.

12 SEP 1908 Marries Clementine Hozier at St. Margaret's, Westminster, the church of the House of Commons.

14 FEB 1910 He is promoted to the post of Home Secretary in which he advocates old age pensions and labour exchanges.

11 OCT 1911 He exchanges the post of Home Secretary for that of First Lord of the Admiralty, a position better suited to his military interests and pugnacious nature.

25 MAY 1915 He resigns as First Lord of the Admiralty after the failed expedition to capture the Dardanelles, the strategic waterway in Turkey, which he had promoted. He takes up painting.

1915–16 He rejoins the army and goes on active service in the army with the Grenadier Guards in France.

FEB 1917 The Dardanelles Commission investigating the losses in Turkey exonerates Churchill.

17 JUL 1917 He joins Lloyd George's Government as Minister of Munitions.

10 JAN 1919 Appointed Secretary of State for War, responsible for the Army and the Royal Air Force.

13 FEB 1921 Appointed Colonial Secretary, in which post he negotiates the treaty for the Irish Free State, but is unsuccessful in dealing with Turkey under Kemal Ataturk.

15 NOV 1922 A General Election returns the Conservatives to power, and Churchill is not re-elected. He uses the time to finish *The World Crisis*, a major work, published 1923–31.

29 OCT 1924 He fails to get re-elected to the House of Commons at a by-election in March, but is elected for Epping as a Constitutionalist in the General Election, and sits for the next 40 years as a Conservative for Epping and Woodford.

6 NOV 1924 Appointed Chancellor of the Exchequer in Baldwin's Government, in which position he reintroduces the gold standard for the first time since World War I. The ensuing lowering of coal prices and attempted lowering of miners' wages results in a coal miners' strike led by Ernest Bevin and, ultimately, the General Strike of 1926.

MAY 1926 General Strike. Churchill militantly opposes it and puts out his own newspaper, the *British Gazette*. He loses the support of the working class for his stand until the 1939–1945 war.

JUN 1929 A Labour Government under Ramsay MacDonald comes to power and Churchill is no longer Chancellor.

JAN 1931 Resigns from the Shadow Cabinet in protest at its support for the Simon Commission's report on the future of India. He begins work on *Marlborough: His Life and Times*.

1932 Churchill campaigns for preparedness to meet the threat of Germany under Hitler, as a backbencher, regarded as a maverick, he has little success.

3 SEP 1939 On the outbreak of War, he is appointed First Lord of the Admiralty for the second time.

10 MAY 1940 Churchill appointed Prime Minister, replacing Chamberlain, who has lost the confidence of the House of Commons. He appoints a Coalition War Cabinet with Clement Attlee as his deputy.

JUN–SEP 1940 The Battle of Britain: Germany attempts to force British surrender by saturation bombing. Churchill's rhetoric, broadcast to the nation, stiffens British resistance and maintains morale in the face of terrible losses, including the evacuation of British forces from Dunkirk in France by a flotilla of small boats piloted largely by civilians. 'Their finest hour', Churchill declares it, speaking of the British people.

11 MAR 1941 Lend-Lease Bill passed: Churchill calls it 'A monument of generous and far-reaching statemanship'.

22 JUN 1941 Germany invades Russia.

AUG 1941 Churchill and Franklin D. Roosevelt, the U.S. President, meet for the first time during the war and agree on the Atlantic Charter.

7 DEC 1941 Japanese attack US at Pearl Harbor, and UK declares war on Japan the next day. Churchill finally regards the US as an active ally in the war.

23 FEB 1942 A new Lend-Lease agreement is signed with the US.

JUL 1942 After a visit by Churchill to Washington, Roosevelt sends General Marshall and others to London to plan the invasion of North Africa.

1942 A scheme of social insurance against ' interruption and destruction of earning power' and 'for special expenditure arising at birth, marriage or death' is proposed, based on a report by Lord Beveridge, 'Social Insurance and Allied Services'.

23–24 OCT 1942 Battle of El Alamein at which British and Commonwealth allies defeat the previously very successful German North African offensive under Rommel.

8 NOV 1942 Anglo/US invasion of North Africa.

14 JAN 1943 Churchill and Roosevelt meet at Casablanca and agree to accept only 'unconditional surrender' as an acceptable conclusion to the war.

9 JUL 1943 Allied forces invade Italy, beginning in Sicily. The landing at Anzio follows in Jan 1944.

16 JUL 1943 A paper on post-war education policy is issued whose proposals include raising the school leaving age to 15.

28 NOV–1 DEC 1943 Churchill meets with Roosevelt and Stalin at Teheran, Iran. Stalin demands a Second Front in which the Allies are to invade France by May 1944. Agreement is reached on an invasion of France to be led by Eisenhower.

6 JUN 1944 Allies land in Normandy.

SEP 1944 Most of France liberated from the Germans.

FEB 1945 Roosevelt, Stalin and Churchill confer at Yalta, where Roosevelt attempts to enlist Stalin's help against Japan. The Soviet forces report successes in the field and Churchill tells the War Cabinet that Stalin is sincere, especially about Poland.

MAR 1945 Central Burma is liberated from the Japanese.

5 APR 1945 Roosevelt dies. During the war Churchill has had 9 meetings with him, covering 120 days, and sent him over 1,700 messages.

8 MAY 1945 VE (Victory in Europe) Day.

23 MAY 1945 Churchill resigns and the King invites him to form a Caretaker (Conservative) Government. Preparations are put in hand for the first General Election in 10 years.

26 JUL 1945 General Election results in a Labour victory. Attlee replaces Churchill at Potsdam Conference of the Allied leaders. No permanent post-war friendship between east and west is established. Churchill resigns and becomes Leader of the Opposition, a post in which he is not very effective, although his party slowly adapts to the Labour Government's idea of a welfare state.

5 MAR 1946 Churchill speaks at Fulton, Mo., in the presence of Truman, indicating that the 'splendid comradeship-in- arms' of the war has ended and that 'from Stettin in the Baltic to Trieste in the Adriatic an *iron curtain* has descended across the Continent'.

19 SEP 1946 Churchill speaks at Zurich, promoting a Council of Europe: 'We must build a kind of United States of Europe. This must start with a partnership of France and Germany'. In opposition Churchill's Conservative Party slowly adapts to and accepts the idea of a welfare state as introduced by Attlee's Labour Government.

23 FEB 1950 General Election. Attlee re-elected with a much reduced majority.

JUN 1950 Korean War starts.

25 OCT 1951 General Election. Churchill becomes Prime Minister for the third time the following day.

JAN 1952 Churchill visits Truman and addresses US Congress.

6 FEB 1952 Death of King George VI and accession of Queen Elizabeth II.

27 MAY 1952 European Defence Community Treaty signed, as Churchill wishes.

25 JUL 1952 European Coal and Steel Community established.

5 MAR 1953 Stalin dies, leaving Churchill the last survivor of the wartime Big Three.

4 DEC 1953 Churchill meets Eisenhower in Bermuda.

29 JUL 1954 Parliament approves Suez Canal Agreement with Egypt, which was to result in a debacle for Churchill's successor, Eden.

8 SEP 1954 South-East Asia Defence Treaty signed.

28 SEP 1954 Western European Union established as part of the allied structure to balance the growing military might of the Soviet Union.

23 OCT 1954 The Paris Agreements, ending the postwar allied occupation of Germany, are signed.

5 APR 1955 Churchill resigns, pressured to do so by his own Cabinet.

26 MAY 1955 General Election in which Eden increases the Conservative majority in the House of Commons. Churchill is to retain his seat until 1964, and he writes the monumental *History of the English-speaking Peoples.*

9 APR 1963 President Kennedy signs a bill 'to proclaim Sir Winston Churchill an honorary citizen of the United States of America'. Churchill responds: 'I have received many kindnesses from the United States of America, but the honour which you accord me is without parallel. I accept it with deep gratitude and affection'. This unique award can be seen in his former home, Chartwell, Kent.

27 JUL 1964 Churchill makes last visit to the House of Commons at the age of 89.

24 JAN 1965 Churchill dies in his London home.

BACKGROUND

PHYSICAL CHARACTERISTICS AND HEALTH

Churchill was a short (5 feet 6 1/2 inches), muscular man with russet tinged hair in his youth, wide-set blue eyes and a 'bulldog' mouth. He was not immune from standard ailments but was resilient. He was a competitive sportsman, especially at polo. He worked himself and others very hard late into the night. His constitution had not only to withstand work but also the demands of a bon viveur.

EDUCATION

Primary 1882–84, St. George's School, Ascot; 1884–88, Misses Thomson, Brighton

Secondary 1888–93, Harrow

University Sep 1893–94, Royal Military College, Sandhurst

Cultural and vocational background Very widely read with great knowledge of British literature and history.

Languages Elementary French with a schoolboy accent that caused amusement.

NON-PARLIAMENTARY CAREER

Early occupations War correspondent in Cuba and later in the Boer War 1899–1902

Military service Feb 1895 joined Fourth Hussars. Served in other regiments. Saw action in: 1895, Cuba; 1896–98, India; 1898, Nile; 1899, left the Army; 1915–16, France with Oxford Hussars; numerous military awards

Other posts 1914–18, Lord Rector of Aberdeen University; 1929–32, Lord Rector of Edinburgh University; 1929, Chancellor of Bristol University; 1941–65, Warden of the Cinque Ports; 1959, Chairman of Trustees, Churchill College, Cambridge

HONOURS

Freedom of cities About 50 cities gave him their freedom, including: 1941, Oldham; 1942, Edinburgh; 1943, City of London; 1945, Wanstead and Woodford, Brussels, Antwerp; 1946, Aberdeen, City of Westminster, Luxembourg, Blackpool; 1947, Darlington, Ayr, Woodstock, Brighton, Manchester; 1948, Eastbourne, Perth,

HONOURS—*Continued*

Cardiff; 1949, Kensington, Strasbourg; 1950, Bath, Worcester, Wimbledon, Portsmouth; 1951, Sheffield, Aberystwyth, Deal, Dover; 1953, Leeds; 1954, Poole; 1955, Rochester, Londonderry, Belfast, Harrow; 1957, Douglas (I.O.M.) Margate, Hastings

Academic 1925, D.C.L., Oxford; 1926, Doctor of Law, Queen's, Belfast; 1929, Bristol; 1941, Rochester, NY; 1943, Harvard; 1944, McGill, Canada; 1945, Brussels, Louvain; 1946, Miami, Westminster College, U.S.; 1948, St. Andrew's; 1949, Liverpool; 1948, D. Phil and Hist, Oslo; Litt. D. Cambridge, D. Litt London; 1950, D. Phil., Copenhagen; 1950, Royal Academician Extraordinary; 1953, Nobel prize for Literature; 1954, State University of New York

Foreign 1955, Freedom House Award (US); 1955, Williamsburg Award (US); 1956, Charlemagne prize; 1956, Franklin Medal of City of Philadelphia (US); 1956, Grand Seigneur of the Hudson Bay Company; 1963, Honorary Citizen of US (a unique award); 1964, Theodor Herzl Award

Other than peerage 1922, Companion of Honour; 24 May 1941, Fellow of the Royal Society; 1 Jan 1946, Order of Merit; 1954, Knight of the Garter

CLUBS

Other Club, a dining club founded in 1911 by Churchill and F.E. Smith; Jockey Club; Athenaeum; Boodle's; Buck's; Carlton

HOBBIES AND SPORTS

He enjoyed polo (he was a fine horseman) and also shooting and fishing. Indoor hobbies included bezique, chess, gin rummy, and bridge.

He took up painting in 1915 and painted until the age of 85, exhibiting regularly in the 1940s–1950s at the Annual Exhibition of the Royal Academy.

FINANCES

Although he had no great inheritance he was throughout his life a remarkably successful journalist, lecturer and author commanding very high fees, e.g. *Daily Telegraph* paid him £60,000 for the first volume of his war memoirs in 1951. His lifestyle was quite extravagant and always generous.

Income By the age of 26 (1901) he had earned himself £10,000. He stopped his allowance of £500 a year from his mother. In 1906 he secured a £5,000 advance on his biography of his father and £500 for his book *My African Journey*. As a Minister during the first World War and later his salary was £4-5,000 p.a. As Prime Minister 1940–45 and 1951–55 his salary was £10,000 p.a.

Spouse's finances Clementine Hozier did not come from a wealthy family. In her will (1979) she left £150,000.

Pensions 1955–65 Prime Minister's pension £2,000 a year

Legacies 1921, He inherited about £50,000 from Lord Herbert Vane-Tempest. In 1951 created family trust of the royalties of his war memoirs.

Will Left £266,000, most of it divided between his wife and his 3 surviving children.

ANECDOTES

17 Nov 1935, Baldwin wrote: 'I feel we should not give him (Churchill) a post at this stage. Anything he undertakes he puts his heart and soul into. If there is going to be a war—and no one can say that there is not—we must keep him fresh to be our War Prime Minister.' (Gilbert M.: *Winston S. Churchill* vol. v. p. 687)

'I think that the first time I ever deeply disliked Winston and realised the depths of selfish brutality to which he could sink was when he told me not only that he was getting rid of Wavell from the Middle East but why. "I wanted to show my power".' (Thompson R. W. ed. *Churchill and Morton*)

Churchill to General Alexander: 'I envy you the command of armies on the field. That is what I should have liked.' (Lord Moran. *The Struggle for Survival*, 1966)

Churchill to Richard Stokes MP, an implacable opponent: 'Such hatred as I have left in me, and it is not much, I would rather reserve for the future than the past.' (Herbert, A.P. *Independent Member*, 1950)

QUOTATIONS

9 Nov 1914, The maxim of the British people is 'Business as usual'.

1 Oct 1939, I cannot forecast to you the action of Russia. It is a riddle wrapped in a mystery inside an enigma.

13 May 1940, I would say to the House (of Commons) 'I have nothing to offer but blood, toil, tears, and sweat'.

4 Jun 1940, . . . We shall never surrender.

18 Jun 1940, Let us therefore brace ourselves to our duties and so bear ourselves that if the British Empire and its Commonwealth last for a thousand years men will still say 'This was their finest hour'.

20 Aug 1940, Never in the field of human conflict was so much owed by so many to so few.

9 Feb 1941, Give us the tools and we will finish the job. (to President Roosevelt)

24 Dec 1941, What kind of people do they (the Japanese) think we are? (to US Congress)

5 Mar 1946, 'An iron curtain has descended across the continent.' (To Westminster College, Fulton, MO., USA)

30 Nov 1954, It was the nation and the race dwelling all around the globe that had the lion's heart. I had the luck to be called upon to give the roar. (To Parliament on his 80th birthday).

RESIDENCES

12 Bolton Street, London
33 Eccleston Square, London
Admiralty House, London
41 Cromwell Road, London (his brother's house)
Hoe Farm, Godalming, Surrey
Lullenden, East Grinstead, Sussex
Chartwell, Westerham, Kent. Bought in 1922 for £5,000. Sold to National Trust in 1946 for £43,800. Friends of Churchill raised the money and the Churchills retained use for their lifetime.
10 Downing Street
27–28 Hyde Park Gate, London (plaque)
Open to the public

Chartwell, Kent (National Trust) Churchill was very found of Chartwell. He put a great deal of thought and work into its development including building a great garden wall and it remains very much the Churchill home.

MEMORIALS

STATUES AND BUSTS

By Oscar Nemon, Windsor Castle; by Oscar Nemon, Guildhall, London; by David McFall, Woodford Green, London; by Oscar Nemon, Members Lobby, House of Commons; by Ivor Roberts-Jones, Parliament Square, London; by Oscar Nemon, Chartwell, Kent, also Kansas City, USA

PORTRAITS

1927, by Walter Richard Sickert, National Portrait Gallery; 1942, by F.O. Salisbury (in siren suit), Chartwell; 1954, by Graham Sutherland, presented by the House of Commons on his 80th birthday, destroyed 1956; by Bernard Hailstone, National Portrait Gallery; 1956, by Sir Oswald Birley, House of Commons

OTHER MEMORIALS

1950, Attlee named the arch at the entrance to the House of Commons, preserved from the pre-bombed House of Commons 'Churchill Arch'; 1950–62, Churchill Gardens, London 1964, Churchill College, Cambridge; 1966, Winston Churchill Memorial Trust Travelling Scholarships; 1970, Churchill Hotel, Portman Square, London; 1971, Churchill Theatre, Bromley, Kent; Churchill Homes for Elderly People; British Rail named a locomotive after him. In 1965 Mount Churchill and the Churchill Peaks, Arkansas were named after him.

BIBLIOGRAPHIC INFORMATION

LETTERS AND PERSONAL PAPERS

His papers are in three groups. 1) Chartwell Trust papers—1945, Churchill College, Cambridge (open to the public); 2) Churchill papers 1945—Churchill College, Cambridge (papers in the Churchill College Archives Unit are not yet open to the public); 3) Prime Ministerial papers—Public Record Office, London (open to the public, in the PREM series). In addition, Martin Gilbert is publishing the documentation used for his biography, including: *Churchill. Companion Volumes 1876–1939,* 13 Vols. London, 1967–1982; *Churchill. War Papers September 1939–May 1940.* London, 1993.

PUBLICATIONS

His extensive writings are listed in the bibliography: Woods, F. *A Bibliography of the Works of Sir Winston Churchill*, 2nd ed, 1969. 'A major new Bibliography of the works of Sir Winston Churchill compiled by Ronald Cohen is due for publication in 1996'.

In addition, Churchill was a painter: Coombs, D. *Churchill: His Paintings*, 1967 includes catalogue of his paintings.

Churchill received the Nobel Prize for Literature in 1953. His major works include: 1898, *The Story of the Malakand Field Force*; 1899, *The River War*; 1906, *Lord Randolph Churchill*, 2 Vols.; 1923–31, *The World Crisis*, 4 Vols.; 1933–38, *Marlborough: His Life and Times*, 4 Vols.; 1948–54, *War Memoirs*, 6 Vols.; 1948, *Painting as a Pastime*; 1956–58, *History of the English Speaking Peoples*, 4 Vols.

Speeches published: 1938, 'Arms and the Covenant'; 1941, 'Into Battle': 1942, 'The Unrelenting Struggle'; 1943, 'The End of the Beginning'; 1944, 'Onwards to Victory'; 1945, 'The Dawn of Liberation'; 1946, 'Victory'; 1948, 'The Sinews of Peace'; 1950, 'Europe Unite'; 1951, 'In the Balance'; 1953, 'Stemming the Tide'; 1961, 'The Unwritten Alliance'; Cannadine, D., ed. *Blood, Toil, Tears and Sweat: The Speeches of Winston Churchill.* Boston, 1989.

FURTHER READING

Bardens, D. *Churchill in Parliament.* London, 1967.

Blake, R. and W.R. Lewis, eds. *Churchill. A Major New Assessment of His Life in Peace and War.* Oxford, 1993.

Gilbert, M. (ed.) *Churchill Companion Volumes 1876–1939.* 13 vols. London, 1967–1982.

Gilbert, M. *Winston S. Churchill.* 8 Vols. London, 1966–88 (Vols. 1 and 2 by Randolph Churchill)

Gilbert, M. *Churchill: A Photographic Portrait.* 2nd ed. London, 1988.

Gilbert. M. *Churchill: A Life.* London, 1991.

Gilbert, M. *Churchill War Papers September 1939–May 1940.* London, 1993. (*NB* Further volumes of Churchill War Papers to follow)

Hough, R. *Winston and Clementine: The Triumph of the Churchills.* London, 1990.

Kimball, W., ed. *Churchill and Roosevelt: The Complete Correspondence.* Three vols. Princeton, 1984.

Manchester, W. *The Caged Lion: Winston Spencer Churchill 1932–1940.* London, 1988.

Lord Moran. *Winston Churchill: The Struggle for Survival 1940–65.* London, 1966.

D.J.T.E.

Bettmann

Clement Attlee

Lived 1883–1967
Political Party Labour
Prime Minister 26 July 1945–26 October 1951
Government Labour
Reigning Monarch George VI

Sursum corda Lift up your hearts

ATTLEE AS PRIME MINISTER

Coming from a late Victorian professional background, Attlee took to politics for moral reasons. He was educated to service rather than leadership and saw himself as a steady builder with an economic approach to solving problems—preferably without argument. Elected Member of Parliament in 1922 and leader of the Labour Party in 1935, his strong patriotism ensured that his party joined Churchill's National Government of 1940. He served in the War Cabinet throughout the war, acting as a perfect foil to Churchill and learning the rigours of Cabinet government which included acting as chairman during Churchill's absences abroad. He made his mark in the House of Commons by incisive and revelant contributions. As Prime Minister for six remarkable years, he oversaw the national recovery and introduced many far-reaching socialist measures, from nationalising railways and the coal industry, to reforming education, health and housing, many of which became accepted practice, and led to further development. The postwar Labour Party had a wide range both of talents and political views, but Attlee managed to sustain the momentum of change, at least throughout his first Government when he had a comfortable majority. His second administration, formed in 1950, enjoyed a far smaller majority and less momentum. In October 1951 he was dismissed by the electorate. The development of the welfare state is his lasting contribution.

PERSONAL INFORMATION

Names Clement Richard Attlee
Peerages 1st Earl Attlee and Viscount Prestwood of Walthamstow, 7 Dec 1955.
Nickname Clem
Born 3 Jan 1883
Place of birth Putney, London
Religion Anglican
Ancestry English. His family were millers and corn merchants in Surrey
Date and place of marriage 10 Jan 1922, Christ Church, Hampstead, London
Age at marriage 39 years, 7 days
Years married 42 years, 151 days
First entered Parliament 15 Nov 1922
Date appointed PM 26 Jul 1945
Age at appointment 63 years, 205 days
Date ceased to be PM 26 Oct 1951
Total time as PM 6 years, 92 days
Ceased to be MP 7 Dec 1955
Lived after last term as PM 15 years, 347 days
Date and place of death 8 Oct 1967, Westminster Hospital, London
Age at death 84 years, 279 days
Place of funeral Temple Church, London
Place of burial Westminster Abbey, London
Zodiac sign Capricorn

FATHER

Henry Attlee
Date and place of birth 23 Dec 1841, Dorking, Surrey
Occupation Solicitor. President of the Law Society 1906.
Date of marriage 11 Aug 1870
Date of death 19 Nov 1908
Place of burial Putney Vale Cemetery, London

MOTHER

Ellen Bravery Watson
Date of birth 4 Jul 1847
Profile An aesthetic cultured woman, well-read and conservative in disposition, she spoke French and some Italian. Her mother died early and as the eldest daughter she helped bring up younger brothers and sisters
Date of marriage 11 Aug 1870
Date of death 19 May 1920
Place of burial Putney Vale Cemetery, London

BROTHERS AND SISTERS

Clement Attlee was the fourth son and the seventh of eight children
Robert, b. 7 Jul 1871; d. 14 May 1953
Bernard, b. 6 May 1873; d. 27 Mar 1943
Mary, b. 28 Feb 1875; d. 6 Sep 1956
Dorothy, b. 1877; d. 1920
Margaret, b. 10 Dec 1878; unm.; Mayoress of Stepney 1919–20 when Attlee was Mayor; d. 8 Mar 1964
Thomas, b. 18 Oct 1880; d. 11 Oct 1960
Laurence, b. 6 Nov 1884; d. 3 May 1969

WIFE

Violet Helen Millar
Date and place of birth 20 Nov 1895, Hampstead, London
Mother Ada Margaret France
Father Henry Edward Millar
Father's occupation Merchant, especially exports and imports
Age at marriage 26 years, 52 days
Number of children 4
Date and place of death 7 June 1964, Amersham, Buckinghamshire
Place of burial Cremated Ruislip Crematorium
Years younger than PM 12 years, 321 days
Education St. Felix, Southwold, Sussex
Profile She was very loyal to her husband but not deeply interested in politics. She enjoyed sports, gardening and her family, resenting the public life which drew Attlee away from her. More conventionally religious than her husband, she played an important role in charitable work after he became Prime Minister.

CHILDREN

1 son, 3 daughters
Janet, b. 25 Feb 1923; m. 15 Nov 1947, Harold Shipton; Commissioned in the Womens Auxiliary Air Force during the Second World War
Felicity, Lady Harwood, b. 22 Aug 1925; m. 2 Apr 1955, John Keith Harwood; nursery school teacher
Martin Richard (2nd Earl Attlee) b. 10 Aug 1927; m. 16 Feb 1955, Anne Barbara Henderson; Politician (S.D.P., House of Lords); d. 27 Jul 1991
Alison Elizabeth, b. 14 Apr 1930; m. 8 Mar 1952, Richard Lionel Lance Davis

LIFE AND CAREER

PARLIAMENTARY ELECTIONS FOUGHT

*(*designates candidate elected)*
DATE 15 Nov 1922. General Election
CONSTITUENCY Stepney, Limehouse
RESULT C.R. Attlee*(Lab) 9,688; Sir W. Pearce (N.L.) 7,789

DATE 6 Dec 1923. General Election
CONSTITUENCY Stepney, Limehouse
RESULT C.R. Attlee (Lab)* 11,473; T. Millar-Jones (Con) 5,288

DATE 29 Oct 1924. General Election
CONSTITUENCY Stepney, Limehouse
RESULT C.R. Attlee* (Lab) 11,713; T. Millar-Jones (Con) 5,692; H. Marks (Lib.) 2,869

DATE 30 May 1929. General Election
CONSTITUENCY Stepney, Limehouse

PARLIAMENTARY ELECTIONS FOUGHT—*Continued*

RESULT C.R. Attlee* (Lab) 13,872; Hon. E.F. Morgan (Con) 6,584; J.J.J. Addis (Lib) 4,116; W.T.L. Tapsell (Com) 245

DATE 27 Oct 1931. General Election
CONSTITUENCY Stepney, Limehouse
RESULT C.R. Attlee* (Lab) 11,354; R. Girouard (Con) 10,803; H.L. Lodge (N.P.) 307

DATE 14 Nov 1935. General Election
CONSTITUENCY Stepney, Limehouse
RESULT C.R. Attlee* (Lab) 14,600; C.J. Busby (Con) 7, 355

DATE 5 Jul 1945. General Election
CONSTITUENCY Stepney, Limehouse
RESULT C.R. Attlee* (Lab) 8,348; A.N.P. Woodward (Con) 1,618

DATE 23 Feb 1950. General Election
CONSTITUENCY West Walthamstow
RESULT C.R. Attlee* (Lab) 21,095; J.A. Paul (Con) 8,988; A.W. Pim (Lib) 4,102; H.L. Hutchinson (I Lab) 704

DATE 25 Oct 1951. General Election
CONSTITUENCY West Walthamstow
RESULT C.R. Attlee* (Lab) 23,021; E.D.L. du Cann (Con) 11,447

DATE 26 May 1955. General Election
CONSTITUENCY West Walthamstow
RESULT C.R. Attlee* (Lab) 19,327; R.P. Hornby (Con) 10,077

PARTY ACTIVITY

Party Leadership 1935–55, Leader of Labour Party.
Other offices 1931–35, Deputy Leader of Labour Party; 1940–45 Chairman of the House of Commons Committee of Privileges.
Membership of group or faction Oct 1907, Joined the Fabian Society; Mar 1931, Chairman of the New Fabian Bureau.

PARLIAMENTARY AND MINISTERIAL EXPERIENCE

Maiden Speech 23 Nov 1922, In the debate on the King's speech, he spoke on the waste created by post-war unemployment. (*HC Deb* vol 159 col 92–96)
Opposition offices 1935–40, 1945, 1951–55, Leader of the Opposition
Privy Counsellor 1 Jun 1935
Ministerial Offices Under-Secretary of State for War, 23 Jan–3 Nov 1924; Chancellor of the Duchy of Lancaster, 23 May 1930–13 Mar 1931; Postmaster General, 3 Mar 1931–3 Sep 1931; Lord Privy Seal, 11 May 1940–19 Feb 1942; Secretary of State for the Dominions, 19 Feb 1942–24 Sep 1943; Lord President of the Council, 24 Sep 1943–23 May 1945; Deputy Prime Minister, 19 Feb 1942–23 May 1945; First Lord of the Treasury, 26 Jul 1945–26 Oct 1951; Minister of Defence, 27 Jul 1945–20 Dec 1946
Opposition Leader while PM Winston Churchill

GOVERNMENTS FORMED

First Administration 26 Jul 1945–23 Feb 1950

GENERAL ELECTION RESULT
5 JUL 1945: Labour 393; Conservative 210; Liberal 12; Others 25. Total 640
Labour majority 147 (excl. the Speaker)

CABINET
Prime Minister and First Lord of the Treasury C.R. Attlee
Lord Chancellor Lord Jowitt
Lord President of the Council H. Morrison
Lord Privy Seal A. Greenwood (Jul 1945–Apr 1947); Lord Inman (Apr–Oct 1947); Viscount Addison (Oct 1947–Feb 1950)
Chancellor of Exchequer H. Dalton (Jul 1945–Nov 1947); Sir S. Cripps (Nov 1947–Feb 1950)
Minister of Economic Affairs Sir S. Cripps (Sep–Nov 1947) (Then combined with Chancellor of Exchequer)
Foreign Secretary E. Bevin
Home Secretary C. Ede
*First Lord of the Admiralty** A. Alexander (Aug 1945–Oct 1946)
Minister of Agriculture and Fisheries T. Williams
*Secretary of State for Air** Viscount Stansgate (Aug 1945–Oct 1946)
Colonial Secretary G. Hall (Aug 1945–Oct 1946); A.C. Jones (Oct 1946–Feb 1950)
Commonwealth Relations Secretary Viscount Addison (Jul–Oct 1947); P. Noel-Baker (Oct 1947–Feb 1950)
Minister of Defence C.R. Attlee (Jul 1945–Dec 1946); A. Alexander (Dec 1946–Feb 1950)
Secretary of State for the Dominions Viscount Addison (Aug 1946– Jul 1947) (Became Commonwealth Relations Office Jul 1947)
Minister of Education Miss E. Wilkinson (Aug 1945–Feb 1947); G. Tomlinson (Feb 1947–Feb 1950)
*Minister of Fuel and Power** E. Shinwell (Jul 1945–Oct 1947)
Minister of Health A. Bevan
Secretary of State for India and Burma Lord Pethick-Lawrence (Jul 1945–Apr 1947); Lord Listowel (Apr 1947–Jan 1948) (Office abolished)
Minister of Labour and National Service G. Isaacs
President of the Board of Trade Sir S. Cripps (Sep 1945–Sep 1947); H. Wilson (Sep 1947–Feb 1950)
Secretary of State for Scotland J. Westwood (Jul 1945–Oct 1947); A. Woodburn (Oct 1947–Feb 1950)
*Secretary of State for War** J. Lawson (Aug 1945–Oct 1946)
*Paymaster General** A. Greenwood (Jul 1946–Mar 1947)
Chancellor of the Duchy of Lancaster H. Dalton (May 1948–Feb 1950)
Minister without Portfolio A. Alexander (Oct–Dec 1946); A. Greenwood (Apr–Sep 1947)
[* Office not always in Cabinet]

Second Administration 23 Feb 1950–26 Oct 1951

GENERAL ELECTION RESULT
23 FEB 1950: Labour 315; Conservative 298; Liberal 9; Others 3. Total 625
Labour majority 6 (excl. the Speaker)

CABINET
Prime Minister and First Lord of the Treasury C.R. Attlee
Lord Chancellor Lord Jowitt
Lord President of the Council H. Morrison (Feb 1950–Mar 1951); Lord Addison (Mar–Oct 1951)
Lord Privy Seal Lord Addison (Feb 1950–Mar 1951); E. Bevin (Mar–Apr 1951); R. Stokes (Apr–Oct 1951)

Chancellor of the Exchequer Sir S. Cripps (Feb–Oct 1950); H. Gaitskell (Oct 1950–Oct 1951)
Foreign Secretary E. Bevin (Feb 1950–Mar 1951); H. Morrison (Mar–Oct 1951)
Home Secretary C. Ede
Minister of Agriculture and Fisheries T. Williams
Chancellor of the Duchy of Lancaster Lord Alexander
Colonial Secretary J. Griffiths
Commonwealth Relations Secretary P. Gordon-Walker
Minister of Defence E. Shinwell
Minister of Education G. Tomlinson
*Minister of Health** A. Bevan (Feb 1950–Jan 1951)
Minister of Labour and National Service G. Isaacs (Feb 1950– Jan 1951); A. Bevan (Jan–Apr 1951); A. Robens (Apr–Oct 1951)
President of the Board of Trade H. Wilson (Feb 1950–Apr 1951); Sir H. Shawcross (Apr–Oct 1951)
Secretary of State for Scotland H. McNeil
Minister of Town and Country Planning (from Jan 1951 *Local Government and Planning*) H. Dalton
[* office not always in Cabinet]

IMPORTANT DATES IN PERSONAL AND POLITICAL LIFE

1896–1901 Attlee is a successful student at Haileybury, for which he retains a lifelong affection.

1901–04 Reads history at University College, Oxford.

1906 Attlee called to the Bar by the Inner Temple. Becoming involved in practical socialism, he joins the Fabian Society and then becomes secretary of Toynbee Hall, a Universities Settlement in East London, studying the development of trade unions and immersing himself in working class problems.

1914–18 Serves in the army in World War I, at Gallipoli, Mesopotamia and France. He acquires a gallant record and is severely wounded.

1919 Becomes mayor of Stepney, a working-class area in East London where unemployment causes widespread suffering.

10 JAN 1922 Marries Violet Helen Millar.

15 NOV 1922 Elected MP for Stepney, Limehouse, which he is to represent until 1948.

23 JAN 1924 The first Labour Government although a minority in the House of Commons, gives Attlee his first ministerial experience, when MacDonald makes him Under- Secretary for War.

1927–29 Appointed to the Simon Commission, formed to consider the future of India: his first experience with Indian affairs, and important in view of the fact that India achieves independence under his premiership in 1948.

30 MAY 1929 MacDonald forms the second Labour Government; Attlee becomes Chancellor of the Duchy of Lancaster from 1930–31 and then Postmaster-general.

OCT 1931 Becomes Deputy Leader of the Labour Party after the General Election.

OCT 1935 Becomes Leader of the Labour Party on Lansbury's resignation, and opposes rearming until nearly the end of the decade.

11 MAY 1940 During the crisis after Chamberlain's failure, Attlee, favouring Halifax for PM, declines to serve under Chamberlain, but joins Churchill's War Cabinet, becoming the only member besides Churchill himself to serve throughout the war.

1940–45 Attlee serves as Churchill's deputy during the war years, taking responsibility for many domestic matters and chairing the War Cabinet, with crisp expedition, during Churchill's frequent absences.

19 FEB 1942 Appointed Deputy Prime Minister.

1943–45 Plays leading role in preparation for social reform after the war, planting the seeds of the Welfare State which, as Prime Minister, he is later able to introduce.

MAY 1945 Attends with Eden, the Foreign Secretary, the foundation conference of the United Nations in San Francisco.

MAY 1945 The Labour Party executive refuses to accept the idea that only a Coalition with Attlee as Deputy PM should govern until the end of the war with Japan, which looks as though it will continue for a long time.

23 MAY 1945 Churchill forms a Caretaker Government without Attlee and Parliament is dissolved on 15 Jun when a General Election is called.

26 JUL 1945 After Labour's sweeping election victory, Attlee becomes PM, establishing the first majority Labour Government, which will enact a huge programme of social change.

28 JUL 1945 Attlee flies to Potsdam to complete the work of the Conference, which Churchill had been attending as PM. Returns to the opening of Parliament on 1 Aug.

AUG 1945 Atomic bombs dropped on 6 Aug on Hiroshima and on 9 Aug on Nagasaki; Japanese surrender on 14 Aug. Attlee broadcasts news of the end of the war to the nation.

23 AUG 1945 Parliament approves Charter of the United Nations.

24 AUG 1945 President Truman terminates Lease-Lend agreement.

NOV 1945 Attlee visits Truman to discuss implications of the atomic bomb in the post-war world.

1945 Attlee's Government faces postwar domestic difficulties including fuel shortages and problems of the coal industry, financial problems requiring an American loan, and enacting the legislation for the social Welfare State.

7 DEC 1945 US loan to UK agreed. UK accepts the Bretton Woods Agreements for international monetary co-operation to promote trade and to establish the International Monetary Fund (IMF).

10 JAN 1946 First meeting of the United Nations is held at Central Hall, Westminster, London.

24 JAN 1946 National Insurance Bill introduced, fulfilling promises made in the Beveridge Report of 1942.

29 JAN 1946 Coal (Nationalisation) Bill introduced.

21 MAR 1946 National Health Service Bill introduced.

7 JUL 1946 Bread rationing is introduced in an attempt to cope with serious persistent post-war food shortages. A loan by the U.S. to the U.K. is approved by the U.S. Congress.

28 NOV 1946 Transport (Nationalisation) Bill introduced.

JAN–FEB 1947 Severe winter weather and a coal shortage result in electricity cuts; 2 million workers are laid off.

1 JAN 1947 Coal mines nationalised.

20 FEB 1947 UK agrees to relinquish power in India in 1948, some 20 years after the recommendations of the Simon Commission on which Attlee had served.

18 MAR 1947 Attlee makes his first BBC 'Party Political Broadcast'.

1 APR 1947 School leaving age raised from 14 to 15.

MID 1947 Economic crisis necessitates drastic import cuts. Emigration grows with an offering of £10 one-way tickets to Australia.

5 JUN 1947 Marshall Speech on Europe is delivered at Harvard. Marshall Plan signed 22 Sep for post-war aid to Europe, helping to stave off drastic reductions in the nation's standards of living.

IMPORTANT DATES IN PERSONAL AND POLITICAL LIFE—*Continued*

OCT 1947 Food rationing made more stringent.

30 OCT 1947 General agreement on Tariffs and Trade (GATT) signed by 23 countries.

20 NOV 1947 Partition of Palestine rejected by Arabs.

1 JAN 1948 Railways nationalised under British Rail, eliminating the previous four main railway companies.

17 MAR 1948 Treaty of Brussels: UK, France, Belgium, Netherlands and Luxemburg agree to fortify principles of democracy.

5 JUL 1948 National Insurance Act comes into force, firmly establishing the Welfare State and completing the work of Lord Beveridge.

10 JUL 1948 Berlin blockaded by Soviet Union; air- lift by Allies later effective in countering Soviet threat.

2 NOV 1948 Truman re-elected President of US.

29 JAN 1949 UK recognises Israel.

MAR 1949 Attlee visits Berlin to check on air-lift and to boost morale.

APR 1949 Attlee hosts Commonwealth Conference as several major countries achieve independence and helps work out a formula by which those wishing to be republics can remain in the Commonwealth and recognise George VI as head of the Commonwealth, the formula still in effect.

4 APR 1949 UK joins North Atlantic Treaty Organisation (NATO).

18 SEP 1949 £1 devalued from US $4.03 to US $2.80. Serious economic problems continue to dog Attlee's government at a time when it will soon be necessary to hold a General Election.

6 JAN 1950 UK recognizes Communist government of China.

23 FEB 1950 General Election and formation of second Attlee administration; Labour majority reduced to less than 12 and Attlee rearranges the Cabinet.

19 APR–1 MAY A London dock strike adds to economic dificulties.

JUL 1950 North Korea invades South Korea. British army and naval resources put at the disposal of UN. Rising prices of raw materials and arms spending increase economic problems. Charges imposed for some National Health Service facilities lead to resignation of Aneurin Bevan (architect of the NHS) and Harold Wilson (President of Board of Trade) because of their belief that health services should be free.

13 SEP 1950 National military service extended to 2 years because of Korean War at an emergency session of Parliament.

26 SEP 1950 North Atlantic Council is set up to integrate European Defence Force.

4 DEC 1950 Attlee visits President Truman to discuss mutual world problems.

9 MAR 1951 Ernest Bevin resigns as Foreign Secretary and dies 14 Apr.

3 MAY 1951 George VI opens the Festival of Britain, an event that puts the seal on Attlee's administration.

25 OCT 1951 General Election results in Labour defeat; Attlee remains Labour Party Leader and becomes Opposition Leader when Churchill becomes Prime Minister for the third time.

6 FEB 1952 George VI dies at the age of 56, and Attlee pays an unusually emotional tribute to him, speaking as Opposition Leader of the House of Commons.

1954 *As It Happened*, his autobiography—showing an unassuming, upright and contented man of principle—published.

AUG 1954 Attlee leads Labour Party delegation to China.

5 APR 1955 Anthony Eden succeeds Churchill as PM.

26 MAY 1955 Conservative majority rises to 60 seats in General Election. Although he is 72, Attlee has campaigned actively.

AUG 1955 Attlee suffers a slight stroke from which he completely recovers.

6 DEC 1955 Attlee steps down after 20 years as Leader of the Parliamentary Party and 4 as Leader of the Opposition. The Queen confers an earldom on him.

1956 Attlee becomes a writer and embarks on lecture tours, especially in the US, and also throughout the world.

1961 He becomes president of the Campaign for Democratic Socialism and remains critical of Britain's application to join the European Community.

7 JUN 1964 Lady Attlee dies.

8 OCT 1967 Clement Attlee dies.

BACKGROUND

PHYSICAL CHARACTERISTICS AND HEALTH

Old-fashioned in appearance with a prominent moustache and dome-shaped head, he was small in stature but had a resilient constitution. Fighting the Turks at Gallipoli in World War I, he contracted dysentery and was later wounded.

He suffered ulcer attacks in 1948 and 1951, and had a slight stroke in 1955.

EDUCATION

Primary 1892–96, Northaw Place, Potters Bar, Herts.

Secondary 1896–1901, Haileybury.

University 1901–04, University College, Oxford

Qualifications Second class honours, modern history, 1904; called to the Bar, Inner Temple 1906.

Cultural and vocational background A serious reader, Attlee said he came from 'a typical family of the professional class brought up in the atmosphere of Victorian England.' One brother was a solicitor, another a clergyman and several of the family were involved in teaching and social work.

Languages Working French.

NON-PARLIAMENTARY CAREER

Early occupations 1906–09, Barrister at Law; 1907–10, Manager of Haileybury House, Limehouse, London; 1913–23, Lecturer, London School of Economics; 1919–20, Mayor of Stepney.

Military service 1914–18, Inns of Court regiment followed by the 6th South Lancashire regiment. Fought at Gallipoli 1915, in Mesopotamia 1916, where he was wounded, and later in France.

Other posts 1927–29, Member of the Statutory Commission on India (Simon Commission).

HONOURS

Freedom of cities 1946, Merthyr Tydfil; 1947, Birmingham; 1948, Dartford; 1948, Stepney; 1948, Greenwich;

1951, Leeds; 1953, London; 1954, Manchester; 1956, Oxford; 1956, Aberdeen; 1959, Bristol

Academic 1946, Oxford D.C.L.; 1946, Cambridge LL.D.; 1947, London LL.D.; 1948, Reading D.Lit.; 1949, Wales LL.D.; 1951, Glasgow LL.D.; 1953, Nottingham LL.D.; 1956, Aberdeen LL.D.; 1957, Madras LL.D.; 1961, Ceylon LL.D.; Hull LL.D.; Bristol LL.D.; Honorary Fellow, University College Oxford; Queen Mary College, London; London School of Economics; Honorary Fellow of R.I.B.A.

Other than peerage May 1945, Companion of Honour; 15 May 1947, Fellow of the Royal Society; 5 Nov 1951, Order of Merit; Jun 1956, Knight of the Garter.

CLUBS

Atheneum, Oxford and Cambridge

HOBBIES AND SPORTS

A practical man who enjoyed making things with his hands and gardening, he enjoyed ball games (especially tennis) and was a billiards ½ Blue for Oxford. He was especially fond of cricket and enjoyed playing chess doing crossword puzzles.

FINANCES

He lived modestly, preferring a quiet life. After retirement he wrote articles and undertook lecture tours to supplement his pension.

Income As Haileybury Club Manager £50 p.a.; After the death of his father in 1908, a private income of about £400 p.a.; 1922–37 MP £400 p.a.; 1937–40 Leader of the Opposition £2,000 p.a.; 1940–45 Minister £5,000 p.a.; 1945–51 Prime Minister £10,000 p.a.; 1951–55 Leader of the Opposition £2,000 p.a.

Spouse's finances Lady Attlee left £52,658 in 1964.

Pensions Prime Minister's Pension from 1955 £2,000 p.a.

Legacies Sufficient from his father to give a small private income. His father left £70,000 in 1908.

Debts Lived modestly within his means.

Will He left a little more than £6,700 in 1967. He left his Garter flag to Haileybury.

ANECDOTES

'He was always completely master (as Prime Minister) and in his quiet way impressed his personality not merely on his colleagues but on all parties in the House of Commons'. (H. Macmillan)

'Mr. Attlee was Deputy Prime Minister during the war, and played a great part in winning the war. Mr. Attlee is a great patriot'. (Winston Churchill)

'I once happened to be in Herbert Morrison's company shortly after we had finished a meeting with Clem Attlee. "I've known Attlee for twenty-five years" he said, "but I still don't understand him"—and he never did'. (J. Callaghan)

'Advice from Attlee on being appointed a Minister: "Remember you will be playing for the first Cricket Eleven in future: if you intend to negotiate with someone tomorrow, don't insult him today." It took him ninety seconds to appoint me'. (J. Callaghan)

'He was genuine. We didn't always follow what he said, mind you (he's a bit highbrow for some of us) but we knew he meant what he said'. (Comment by an old docker about Attlee after his first parliamentary election in 1922, quoted in C. Clemens, *The Man from Limehouse: CRA*, 1946)

In his autobiography, Attlee described being invited, along with several Labour MPs, to dinner by Robert Bingham, the American ambassador. Although Attlee thought it was an 'unlikely recreation' for Labour MPs, when asked whether any of them had done any big game hunting, he answered Yes, he had. When asked what he shot, he replied laconically, 'Germans'.

When asked on an American lecture tour, after his term as Prime Minister, what he expected to be remembered for, Attlee replied 'Don't know. If anything India, possibly'. (K. Harris, *Attlee*, 1982)

On another American tour, the question, 'How is your Socialist medicine getting on'? came up. Attlee's reply: 'First class. How's your Socialist sewage system getting on or do you stick to the old bucket?' (Harris, 1982)

QUOTATIONS

Having now exceeded the age of three score years and ten I would say that up to the present I have been a very happy and fortunate man . . . (*As it Happened* 1954)

1935, On the League of Nations in Parliament, 'If you turn and run away from the aggressor you kill the League . . . and you kill all faith in the word of honour of this country'.

Few thought he was even a starter
There were many who thought themselves smarter
But he ended PM
CH and OM
An earl and a knight of the garter (On being made a Knight of the Garter, 1956)

RESIDENCES

Westcott, 18 Portinscale Rd. Putney, London
Haileybury House, Stepney, London
Toynbee Hall, Whitechapel, London
Commercial Rd., Limehouse, London
17 Monkhams Avenue, Woodford Green, Essex (plaque)
Heywood, Stanmore, Hertfordshire
10 Downing Street
Cherry Cottage, Great Missenden, Buckinghamshire
Westcott, Great Missenden, Buckinghamshire
1 King's Bench, Temple, London

MEMORIALS

STATUES AND BUSTS

1965, by David McFall, National Portrait Gallery; 1980, by Ivor Roberts-Jones, Members' Lobby, House of Commons.

PORTRAITS

1946, by G. Harcourt, National Portrait Gallery; 1948, by Rodrigo Moynihan, Oxford and Cambridge Club, London; 1946, by C. Dobson, Haileybury, Hertfordshire; 1963, by Lawrence Gowing, Haileybury, Hertfordshire

OTHER MEMORIALS

Attlee Foundation, Commercial Road, Whitechapel, London. Financed through a national appeal after

MEMORIALS—*Continued*

Lord Attlee's death, it provides practical help for young people with problems including drugs. Attlee House was opened 18 Nov 1971 by the Queen.

BIBLIOGRAPHIC INFORMATION

LETTERS AND PERSONAL PAPERS

Letters to his brother Tom 1913–1960 unpublished. The originals in the possession of Mrs. Margaret Attlee, Tom's daughter-in-law.

Attlee papers 1939–1951. Bodleian Library, Oxford (University College papers).

Attlee papers, Churchill College, Cambridge (Correspondence between Churchill and Attlee, 1941–45).

PUBLICATIONS

1920, *The Social Worker*; 1920, *Metropolitan Borough Councils* (Fabian Tract 190); 1920, *Borough Councils* (Fabian Tract 191); 1925, (with W. A. Robson) *The Town Councillor*; 1935, *The Will and the Way to Socialism*; 1937, *The Labour Party in Perspective*; 1947, *Purpose and Policy* (speeches); 1949, *The Labour Party in Perspective and Twelve Years Later*, 1954, *As it Happened* (autobiography); 1961, *Empire into Commonwealth* (Chichele Lectures); 1961, *Future of United Nations and Democracy* (3rd Azad Memorial Lecture of Indian Council for Cultural Relations, Delhi).

FURTHER READING

Burridge, T. *Clement Attlee*. London, 1985.
Jenkins, R. *Mr. Attlee*. London, 1961.
Granada Historical Records Interview: Clem Attlee. London, 1967.
Harris, K. *Attlee*, London, 1982.
—*Attlee as I Knew Him (essays)* London, 1983.
The Attlee Memorial Statue in the House of Commons. London: House of Commons Library Public Information Office Series No 2 1980.
Royal Society: Clement Richard Attlee, First Earl Attlee 1883–1967, London, 1968.
Tiratsoo, N. *The Attlee Years*. London, 1991.
Williams, F. *A Prime Minister Remembers*. London, 1961.

D.J.T.E.

Bettmann

Anthony Eden

Lived 1897–1977
Political Party Conservative
Prime Minister 6 April 1955–9 January 1957
Government Conservative
Reigning Monarch Elizabeth II

Si sit prudentia If there be prudence

EDEN AS PRIME MINISTER

A Member of Parliament at 26 and Foreign Secretary at 38, Eden enjoyed a meteoric rise that contrasted with the careers of most future Prime Ministers of the 20th century. An exponent of internationalism, he served as Great Britain's representative to the League of Nations. He resigned from Chamberlain's Government because of its appeasement of the Nazis. During the 1939–1945 war he was effective as Foreign Secretary and as Leader of the House of Commons. In 1951, Churchill's third administration led to Eden's most impressive period as Foreign Secretary during many world crises, including the Cold War, the Korean War, and British withdrawal from Egypt and the Middle East. He was kept waiting in the wings a long time before Churchill resigned. In the 1955 General Election, he tripled the Conservatives' small majority, but once in office, Eden took too detailed an interest in the work of his Cabinet colleagues at a time when the need was for firm leadership and a clear strategy. When he did act strongly, after Colonel Nasser's Egyptian government nationalised the Suez Canal in 1956, his decision to join with France and Israel in a military intervention failed to secure US or Commonwealth support and led to a humbling withdrawal. Extra pressure on his weakened health led to his resignation less than two years after he had succeded Churchill.

PERSONAL INFORMATION

Names Robert Anthony Eden
Peerages 1st Earl of Avon and Viscount Eden of Royal Leamington Spa, 12 Jul 1961
Born 12 Jun 1897
Place of birth Windlestone Hall, Bishop Auckland, Durham
Religion Anglican
Ancestry An old county Durham landed family with a long history of public service
Dates and places of marriages 1) 5 Nov 1923, St. Margaret's, Westminster; 2) 14 Aug 1952, Caxton Hall, London
Age at marriages 1) 26 years, 147 days 2) 55 years, 64 days
Years married 1) 26 years, 215 days; 2) 24 years, 154 days
First entered Parliament 6 Dec 1923
Date appointed PM 6 Apr 1955
Age at appointment 57 years, 299 days
Date ceased to be PM 9 Jan 1957
Total time as PM 1 year, 279 days
Ceased to be MP 9 Jan 1957
Lived after last term as PM 20 years, 5 days
Date and place of death 14 Jan 1977, Manor House, Alvediston, Salisbury, Wiltshire
Age at death 79 years, 216 days
Place of funeral and burial St. Mary's at Alvediston, Salisbury, Wiltshire
Zodiac sign Gemini

FATHER

Sir William Eden, 7th Baronet
Date of birth 4 Mar 1849
Occupation Landowner, sportsman and accomplished painter
Date of marriage 20 Jul 1886
Date of death 20 Feb 1915
Place of burial Windlestone Chapel, Bishop Auckland, Durham

MOTHER

Sybil Francis Grey
Date and place of birth c.1867, India
Profile An outstanding beauty with a steady and tranquil temperament, she was extravagant and generous which created financial problems for the family. Her children found her difficult, but she was very popular with the local people in Durham.
Date of marriage 20 Jul 1886
Date of death 19 Jun 1945

BROTHERS AND SISTERS

Anthony Eden was the third son and fourth of five children.

Elfrida Marjorie, b. 1887; m. 5th Earl of Warwick; Mayor of Warwick 1929–30, 1931; d. 10 Feb 1943
John, b. 9 Oct 1888; d. 17 Oct 1914 in military action
Sir Timothy, (8th Bt.) b. 3 May 1893; d. 13 May 1963
Nicholas. b. 1900; d. 31 May 1916 Battle of Jutland

FIRST WIFE

Beatrice Beckett
Date of birth 1905
Mother Queenie Faversham
Father Hon. Sir Gervase Beckett, 1st Bart.
Father's occupation MP Whitby 1906–22, North Leeds 1923–29; banker; proprietor of the *Yorkshire Post* newspaper
Age at marriage 18 years
Number of children 2
Date and place of death 29 Jun 1957, New York
Years younger than PM c. 8 years
Profile High spirited and attractive, she was not an intellectual and not interested in politics. She was very young and rather immature when she married. She went to New York, was divorced in 1950, and remarried.

SECOND WIFE

Clarissa Anne Spencer-Churchill
Date of birth 28 Jun 1920
Mother Lady Gwendolene Spencer-Churchill
Father John Strange Spencer- Churchill (brother of Winston Churchill (*q.v.*)
Age at marriage 32 years, 47 days
Number of children none
Years younger than PM 23 years, 16 days
Profile From a political family, she was deeply committed not only to her husband but also to his career. She frequently travelled with him when he was still active. She was a great gardener and encouraged him during his retirement to write *Another World* about his early life.

CHILDREN

2 sons
By his first wife, Beatrice:
Simon Gascoign, b. 13 Nov 1924; Pilot officer (navigator) Royal Air Force; d. 20 Jul 1945, confirmed killed in action.
Nicholas (2nd Earl of Avon) b. 3 Oct 1930; politician; d. 17 Aug 1985
By his second wife, Clarissa:
None

LIFE AND CAREER

PARLIAMENTARY ELECTIONS FOUGHT

*(*designates candidate elected)*

DATE 15 Nov 1922. General Election
CONSTITUENCY Spennymore
RESULT J. Batey* (Lab) 13,766; A. Eden (Con) 7,567; T. Wing (Lib) 6,046

DATE 6 Dec 1923. General Election
CONSTITUENCY Warwick and Leamington
RESULT A. Eden* (Con) 16,337; G. Nicholls (Lib) 11, 134; Lady Warwick (Lab) 4,015

DATE 29 Oct 1924. General Election
CONSTITUENCY Warwick and Leamington
RESULT A. Eden* (Con) 19,575; G. Nicholls (Lib) 12,966

DATE 30 May 1929. General Election

CONSTITUENCY Warwick and Leamington
RESULT A. Eden* (Con) 23,045; W. L. Dingley (Lib) 17,585; C. G. Garton (Lab) 7,741

DATE 27 Oct 1931. General Election
CONSTITUENCY Warwick and Leamington
RESULT A. Eden* (Con) 38,584; C.G. Garton (Ind. Lab.) 9,261

DATE 14 Nov 1935. General Election
CONSTITUENCY Warwick and Leamington
RESULT A. Eden* (Con) 35,746; J. Perry (Lab) 10,930

DATE Jul 1945. General Election
CONSTITUENCY Warwick and Leamington
RESULT A. Eden* (Con) 37,110; D. Chesworth (Lab) 19,476; W. Dingley (Lib) 3,908

DATE 23 Feb 1950. General Election
CONSTITUENCY Warwick and Leamington
RESULT A. Eden* (Con) 26,326; H. Bithell (Lab) 17,512

DATE 25 Oct 1951. General Election
CONSTITUENCY Warwick and Leamington
RESULT A. Eden* (Con) 28,282; W. Wilson (Lab) 18,479

DATE 26 May 1955. General Election
CONSTITUENCY Warwick and Leamington
RESULT Sir A. Eden* (Con) 29,979; W. Wilson (Lab) 16,513

PARTY ACTIVITY

Party Leadership Leader of the Conservative Party 22 Apr 1955– 9 Jan 1957

PARLIAMENTARY AND MINISTERIAL EXPERIENCE

Maiden Speech 19 Feb 1924 A short speech emphasising preparedness against air attack. (*HC Deb* 5th ser, vol 169, col 1678–79)
Opposition offices Deputy Leader of the Opposition 1945–51
Privy Counsellor 3 Jun 1934
Ministerial Offices Parliamentary Under Secretary, Foreign Office 3 Sep 1931–31 Dec 1933; Lord Privy Seal 31 Dec 1933–7 Jun 1935; Minister for League of Nations Affairs 7 Jun 1935–22 Dec 1935; Foreign Secretary 22 Dec 1935–21 Feb 1938, 22 Dec 1940–26 Jul 1945, 26 Oct 1951–6 Apr 1955; Dominions Secretary 3 Sep 1939–11 May 1940; Secretary of State for War 11 May–22 Dec 1940; Leader of the House 22 Nov 1942–26 Jul 1945; First Lord of the Treasury 6 Apr 1955–9 Jan 1957
Opposition Leaders while PM C. Attlee 6 Apr 1955–14 Dec 1955; H. Gaitskell 14 Dec 1955–9 Jan 1957

GOVERNMENTS FORMED

Administration 6 Apr 1955–9 Jan 1957

GENERAL ELECTION RESULT
25 OCT 1951: Conservative 321; Labour 295; Liberal 6; Others 3. Total 625
Conservative majority 16
26 MAY 1955: Conservative 345; Labour 277; Liberal 6; Others 2. Total 630
Conservative majority 59 (excl. the Speaker)

CABINET
Prime Minister and First Lord of the Treasury A. Eden
Chancellor of the Exchequer R. Butler (Apr–Dec 1955); H. Macmillan (Dec 1955–Jan 1957)
Home and Welsh Affairs Secretary G. Lloyd-George
Foreign Secretary H. Macmillan (Apr–Dec 1955); S. Lloyd (Dec 1955–Jan 1957)
Colonial Secretary A. Lennox-Boyd
Secretary of State for Scotland J. Stewart
Minister of Labour and National Service Sir W. Monckton (Apr– Dec 1955); I. Macleod (Dec 1955–Jan 1957)
Lord Chancellor Lord Kilmuir
Lord Privy Seal H. Crookshank (Apr–Dec 1955); R. Butler (Dec 1955–Jan 1957)
Lord President of the Council Lord Salisbury
President of the Board of Trade P. Thorneycroft
Chancellor of the Duchy of Lancaster Lord Woolton (Apr –Dec 1955); Lord Selkirk (Dec 1955–Jan 1957)
Minister of Agriculture Fisheries and Food D. Heathcoat-Amory
Paymaster General Sir. W. Monckton (Oct 1956–Jan 1957)
Minister of Defence S. Lloyd (Apr– Dec 1955); Sir W. Monckton (Dec 1955–Oct 1956); A. Head (Oct 1956–Jan 1957)
Commonwealth Relations Secretary Earl of Home
Minister of Education Sir D. Eccles
Minister of Housing and Local Government D. Sandys
*Minister of Pensions and National Insurance** O. Peake (Apr– Dec 1955)
*Minister of Works** P. Buchan-Hepburn (Dec 1955–Jan 1957)
[*Office not always in Cabinet]

IMPORTANT DATES IN PERSONAL AND POLITICAL LIFE

1911–1915 Attends Eton College.
1915 Gazetted 2nd Lieutenant in the army, where he remains until the end of the war, becoming youngest Brigade-Major.
4 JUN 1917 Receives Military Cross after risking his life to rescue his platoon sergeant from behind German lines.
1919 Attends Christ Church College Oxford; secures a first-class degree in Persian and Arabic.
15 NOV 1922 Stands for Parliament unsuccessfully at a by-election at Spennymore, Co. Durham.
5 NOV 1923 Marries Beatrice Beckett at St. Margaret's, Westminster.
6 DEC 1923 Elected MP for Warwick and Leamington, a constituency he will represent for over 30 years.
28 JUL 1926 Appointed Parliamentary Private Secretary to the Foreign Secretary, beginning a life-long association with foreign affairs.
3 SEP 1931 Promoted to Parliamentary Under-Secretary at the Foreign Office in the National Government.
NOV 1932 Attends Disarmament Conference in Geneva as UK delegate, starting his long association with the League of Nations.
1933 Germany now under Hitler leaves both the Disarmament Conference and the League of Nations.
FEB 1934 First meeting with Hitler in Berlin: 'Dare I confess it? I rather liked him.' Within a year, however, Eden would develop quite different views.
26 FEB 1934 First meeting with Mussolini in Rome; calls him, 'Lively, friendly, vigorous and entertaining'.
OCT 1934 King Alexander of Yugoslavia murdered. Eden asked by League of Nations to mediate and act as rapporteur in the crisis.
5 DEC 1934 He makes proposals to the League of Nations for peacekeeping forces to cover the Saar plebiscite.

IMPORTANT DATES IN PERSONAL AND POLITICAL LIFE—*Continued*

MAR 1935 Second meeting in Berlin with Hitler, whom he now describes as 'Negative and shifty'. Eden goes on to make the first visit to the Soviet Union by a British minister since 1917. Stalin is 'Well-informed at all points that were of concern to him . . . prudent but not slow', Eden says.

7 JUN 1935 Baldwin replaces Ramsay MacDonald as Prime Minister and Eden is promoted to become Minister for League of Nations Affairs, a new post, with, for the first time, a seat in the Cabinet.

8 DEC 1935 Mussolini pursues aggression in Abyssinia. Samuel Hoare, the Foreign Secretary, and Pierre Laval, the French premier, make concessions which are 'leaked', forcing Hoare to resign.

22 DEC 1935 Eden appointed Foreign Secretary, the youngest in the 20th century.

7 MAR 1936 Eden is forced to deal with Hitler's invasion of the Rhineland, which meets no resistance; Mussolini's conquest of Abyssinia; the outbreak of the Spanish Civil War and Japan's intervention in China, foreshadowing World War II.

20 FEB 1938 Eden resigns as Foreign Secretary after clashing with Chamberlain over his policy of appeasing the Nazis.

3 SEP 1939 Eden appointed Dominions Secretary, returning him to a position in the Government.

11 MAY 1940 Churchill, now Prime Minister, appoints Eden Secretary of State for War. Halifax, who had succeeded Eden as Foreign Secretary remains in post.

11 JUN 1940 Eden, heavily involved in the evacuation from Dunkirk and now Under-Secretary of Defence, accompanies Churchill to France to meet Prime Minister Paul Reynaud and Charles de Gaulle, who occupies a position equivalent to Under-Secretary of Defence.

22 DEC 1940 Eden appointed Foreign Secretary, replacing Halifax, now ambassador to the US. Eden is to remain in the War Cabinet until 1945.

FEB 1941 Eden visits Greece, which is engaged in resistance to an Italian invasion from Albania; he remains preoccupied by the situation of Turkey and by the crisis in Yugoslavia, which is invaded by Germany in Mar 1941.

JUN 1941 Germany invades Russia, bringing an entirely new dimension to the war and international situation.

15 DEC 1941 Travelling by sea via Murmansk, Eden arrives in Moscow for talks with Stalin, who insists that the Baltic states and half of Poland be part of the Soviet Union after the war.

JUN 1942 Churchill, aged 64, advises the King that Eden, aged 45, should lead the Government as Prime Minister should anything befall him.

12 MAR 1943 Eden visits President Roosevelt.

27 NOV 1943 Eden goes to Teheran conference with Churchill, Roosevelt and Stalin; Eden is growing more concerned about Soviet aspirations in Eastern Europe.

3 FEB 1945 Eden attends the Yalta conference with Churchill, Roosevelt and Stalin.

12 APR 1945 President Roosevelt dies, and Eden is chosen to represent the UK at his funeral.

APR/MAY 1945 Eden leads the UK delegation to San Francisco to prepare the United Nations Charter. He is accompanied by Attlee, the Deputy Prime Minister.

23 JUN 1945 His elder son Simon posted missing in Burma. Courageous in the face of this tragedy, Eden is, nevertheless, deeply affected by his loss.

5–26 JUL 1945 General Election. Churchill defeated and Attlee forms Labour Government. Eden, now out of office, is a serious candidate to be first Secretary-General of the UN, but lacks support of the new Labour Government. Exhausted by the war years and with his domestic life broken up, he plays a reduced role during six years of Opposition, but remains a popular and successful constituency MP.

8 JUN 1950 Eden wins a divorce decree on the grounds of his wife's desertion.

25 OCT 1951 General Election returns Churchill to office as Prime Minister of a Conservative Government with Eden as Foreign Secretary.

NOV 1951 Eden attends the sixth session of the United Nations, the first such meeting in his experience.

MAY 1952 Eden goes to Paris to sign the European Defence Community agreement, although he has made it clear in Cabinet that he does not support the idea of a European federation.

14 AUG 1952 Marries Clarissa Spencer-Churchill, the Prime Minister's niece.

JAN 1953 Eisenhower, an old friend, inaugurated as President of the US.

4 MAR 1953 Eden flies to Washington to work with John Foster Dulles, the American Secretary of State, on the problems of Iran.

APR 1953 Seriously ill, Eden has two operations, and is forced to undergo a third in Boston, Massachusetts, Churchill takes on duties of Foreign Secretary for the six months of Eden's illness.

25 JAN 1954 Berlin Conference of Foreign Ministers regarding the future of Germany attended by Bidault, Dulles, Eden and Molotov. Molotov objects to the 'Eden Plan', which proposes free elections in both halves of divided Germany.

APR–JUL 1954 Eden works hard with France to achieve an Indo-China ceasefire, a remarkable feat, considering how seriously ill he had been the previous year.

SEP 1954 A Nine Power Conférence called by Eden in London at which he announces that the UK will not withdraw its forces from Europe is a great personal success for him.

19 OCT 1954 Eden signs an agreement for the withdrawal of British troops from the Suez Canal.

6 APR 1955 Churchill resigns and Eden, aged 57, finally becomes Prime Minister. He appoints Harold Macmillan Foreign Secretary.

26 MAY 1955 General Election: Conservatives are re-elected with an increased majority, now 60. Eden becomes the first Prime Minister to campaign effectively on television; he uses the theme of 'property-owning democracy'.

JUL 1955 Eden participates in a summit meeting in Geneva with Bulganin, Eisenhower and Fauré. The cordial spirit of the meeting, which had been proposed by Eden, comes to be known as 'the spirit of Geneva'.

26 OCT 1955 Butler's Budget raises indirect taxation and curbs public expenditure, both unpopular measures.

26 JAN 1956 With his new Foreign Secretary, Selwyn Lloyd, Eden visits Eisenhower and Dulles to discuss Soviet anti-colonialism and the situation in the Middle East, but nothing concrete emerges from the talks.

1 MAR 1956 King Hussein of Jordan dismisses Sir John Glubb as commander of the Arab legion. Eden decides on 'tolerant restraint', viewed by some as appeasement, but Eden believes Glubb's dismissal was instigated by Nasser whom Eden wishes to see 'destroyed'.

9 MAR 1956 Archbishop Makarios deported from Cyprus by the British and sent to the Seychelles.

18 APR 1956 Eden hosts a 10-day visit by Khrushchev and Bulganin to Britain, warning his Soviet guests that the UK will fight for their oil supplies from the Middle East.

26 JUL 1956 President Nasser of Egypt nationalises Suez Canal Company. Eden sees this move as a challenge to international legality.

1 AUG 1956 Dulles flies to London and expresses a cautious view on the Suez Canal affair to Eden.

16–18 AUG 1956 The 22-nation London Conference on Suez Canal recommends that the Canal be placed under the control of an international board. Menzies of Australia sent to explain the proposal to President Nasser.

7 SEP 1956 Menzies-Nasser talks break down. Eden wants the Security Council to take up the matter, but Dulles refuses to support this idea and suggests a User Club to sail their ships through the canal.

12 SEP 1956 Dulles refuses US agreement to sanction force to back up the User Club. Eden and the French think military force is necessary.

24 SEP 1956 Eden endorses Israeli attack on Egypt, to be followed by an Anglo-French ultimatum to both sides.

29 OCT 1956 Israel invades Egypt; Eden announces the object of the ultimatum to the House of Commons: 'to separate the belligerents and to guarantee freedom of transit through the Suez Canal to all ships'. The Labour Opposition turns against Eden's Government on the Suez question.

5 NOV 1956 Anglo-French paratroopers land at Port Said, Egypt, leading an allied amphibious force aiming to seize the Canal.

6 NOV 1956 Eden announces cease-fire to the House of Commons.

9 NOV 1956 He defends his conduct of the Suez affair with great vigour at the annual Lord Mayor's Banquet.

23 NOV 1956 Eden, now ill again, goes to Jamaica for three weeks' rest, but continues to feel the strain of being Prime Minister.

5 DEC 1956 Anglo-French force begins withdrawal, which is completed by 22 Dec 1956.

20 DEC 1956 Eden tells the House of Commons there was no foreknowledge of Israeli attack on Egypt.

9 JAN 1957 Eden resigns as Prime Minister and two days later resigns the seat he has held in the House of Commons for 33 years.

12 JUL 1961 Created 1st Earl of Avon and Viscount Eden of Royal Leamington Spa.

26 JUL 1961 Takes his seat in the House of Lords as Earl of Avon, having retired to Wiltshire to farm and live the life of a country gentleman.

1960–65 Publishes three long volumes of political memoirs, starting with the final volume detailing his version of the Suez affair.

14 JAN 1977 Dies at Alvediston, Salisbury, Wiltshire.

BACKGROUND

PHYSICAL CHARACTERISTICS AND HEALTH

Tall, slim and elegant with conventional good looks, he had a rather tense and sometimes irascible temperament. He was not clubbable in the House of Commons sense of the word. He was a very hard worker and demanding on others, but suffered from ill health, including ulcers, frequently, although he was resilient and usually recovered quickly.

EDUCATION

Primary 1907–11, Sandroyd School, Cobham, Surrey
Secondary 1911–15, Eton College
University 1919–22, Christchurch College, Oxford
Prizes and awards Divinity Prize at Eton
Qualifications First class degree in Oriental Studies
Cultural and vocational background Founded Uffizi Society at Oxford in 1920; interested in modern art when young and collected Impressionist paintings; widely read
Languages French, German, Persian, Arabic

NON-PARLIAMENTARY CAREER

Military service 1915, gazetted 2nd Lieutenant King's Royal Rifle Corps; 1916, took company to France; 1917, awarded MC for bravery; 1918, Brigade-Major (youngest in the British Army); 1919, left the army
Other posts 1958–66, President of the Royal Shakespeare Theatre, Stratford-on-Avon.

HONOURS

Freedom of cities 1935, Leamington Spa; 1944, Athens; 1945, Durham; 1947, Warwick; 1956, Perth
Academic 1936, DCL Oxford; 1937 DCL, Durham University; Chancellor of Birmingham University 1945–73; 1952, Hon. Degree Columbia University; President of Royal Shakespeare Theatre, Stratford-on-Avon 1958–66
Foreign 1954 Wateler Peace Prize
Other than peerage 20 Oct 1954, Knight of the Garter

CLUBS

He did not appreciate men's clubs and refused honorary membership of the Athenaeum. He was a member of Carlton and Buck's.

HOBBIES AND SPORTS

He built up a small but distinctive collection of modern paintings described in *Apollo Magazine* Jun 1969. He played a good game of tennis and enjoyed shooting. He bred Hereford cattle in retirement and very much enjoyed life in the country.

FINANCES

Because his parents were free-spending and he was not an elder son, he inherited only about £8,000 from his father in 1921. During 1939–45 he calculated he overspent about £1,000 p.a. but when in Opposition 1945–51 he took city directorships. After retirement (1957) he was not at all well off but then was made a large offer (over £100,000) for his memoirs, which, in time, solved the problem. By 1970 they had earned him £185,000.

Income £120 p.a. as second lieutenant in the army from 1915; £400 p.a. as a MP from 1924; total income in 1924 £1200; £700 p.a. investment income from 1921; a small amount from writing until his retirement, when the sums became substantial; £5,000 p.a. as Foreign Secretary and £10,000 as PM.

FINANCES—*Continued*

Pensions Small pensions as an MP and as Prime Minister

Legacies *c.* £8,000 from his father in 1921

Debts He was careful about financial matters and did not live seriously beyond his means.

Will He left £82,670.

ANECDOTES

In France during World War I, Eden faced a German company on the other side of the Oise, a member of which was Hitler, then a corporal. Later, when Hitler had become the Nazi leader, a French diplomat told Eden he should have been shot for missing Hitler in 1918. (S. Aster *Anthony Eden*, NY, 1976)

Eden's political mentor was Baldwin, who taught him that a Conservative PM should be left of centre, enabling him thus to influence the floating vote to his left. (Aster)

Eden took a conciliatory stand toward the Soviet Union. He was not as strongly anti-Bolshevik as Churchill. When Churchill delivered his famous 'Iron Curtain' speech in Fulton, Missouri, Eden was silent. He thought Churchill's characterisation of the Soviet Union somewhat too harsh, but would not engage in intrigue against Churchill, as he knew he could not win. (D. Carlton *Anthony Eden*, London, 1981)

'Many of his good ideas came to him in his bath.' (*Times* of London Obituary, 15 Jan 1977)

QUOTATIONS

Sep 1937, There are those who say that at all costs we must avoid being brought into opposition with Germany, Japan and Italy. This is certainly true, but it is not true that the best way to avoid such a state of affairs is continually to retreat before all three of them. (In a dictated note)

Sep 1956, It would be hard to imagine a statement more likely to cause maximum allied disunity and disarray. (Commenting on a statement by Dulles that the US 'did not intend to shoot its way' through the Suez Canal)

1956, I thought and think that failure to act would have brought the worst of consequences just as I think the world would have suffered less if Hitler had been resisted on the Rhine. (On the Suez Crisis)

RESIDENCES

2 North Street, Westminster, London
Mulberry Walk, Chelsea, London
Binderton House, near Chichester, Sussex
10 Downing Street
Fyfield Manor, Pewsey, Wiltshire
Manor House, Alvediston, Salisbury, Wiltshire

MEMORIALS

STATUES AND BUSTS

1994, bust by Roy Noakes, Members' Lobby, House of Commons (copy in Foreign Office)

PORTRAITS

1935, by Edmond Xavier Kapp, National Portrait Gallery; by Sir William Coldstream, Christchurch College, Oxford; 1942, by W. Stoneman, National Portrait Gallery

BIBLIOGRAPHIC INFORMATION

LETTERS AND PERSONAL PAPERS

Eden's papers are mainly found in the University of Birmingham Library

PUBLICATIONS

1926, *Places in the Sun: Foreign Affairs*; 1966, *Towards Peace in Indo-China*;

Memoirs

1962, *Facing the Dictators (1923–1938)*; 1965, *The Reckoning (1939–1945)*; 1960, *Full Circle (1951–1957)*; 1976, *Another World 1897–1917* (autobiography)

Speeches

1939, *Foreign Affairs*; 1947, *Freedom and Order*; 1949, *Days for Decision.*

FURTHER READING

Bardens, D. *Portrait of a Statesman*. London, 1955
Carlton, D. *Anthony Eden: A Biography*. London, 1981.
James, R. R. *Anthony Eden*. London, 1986.
Peters, A. *Anthony Eden at the Foreign Office 1931–38*. New York, 1986.
Lamb, R. *The Failure of the Eden Government*. London, 1987.
Young, J.W. ed. *The Foreign Policy of Churchill's Peacetime Administration 1951–55*. Leicester, 1988.

D.J.T.E.

Bettmann

Harold Macmillan

Lived 1894–1986
Political Party Conservative
Prime Minister 10 January 1957–18 October 1963
Government Conservative
Reigning Monarch Elizabeth II

Miseris succurrere disco I learn to relieve the wretched

MACMILLAN AS PRIME MINISTER

Born to a wealthy publishing family and married to the daughter of a duke, Harold Macmillan took his first Cabinet position as Churchill's Minister of Housing, where he was instrumental in the postwar rebuilding of Britain. After serving as Eden's Chancellor of the Exchequer and Foreign Secretary, he became Prime Minister in January 1957 immediately following the Suez crisis and Eden's resignation. He had to restore confidence in the Government both at home and abroad and in particular Great Britain's 'special relationship' with the United States. He quickly asserted domination of the House of Commons and ran his Cabinet firmly. His re-election in 1959 was a personal triumph and showed his 'actor-manager' skills at using the media. He was strong in foreign affairs and the world stage suited him. He was aided in sustaining relations with the United States through his friendship with President John Kennedy. He accepted the demise of the Central African Federation and his 'Wind of Change' speech in 1960 presaged the end of colonial domination in Africa. He was dismayed by De Gaulle's veto of the UK joining the European Communities. He worked hard with Kennedy and Khruschev to establish the Test Ban treaty in 1963 but his administration was weakened by a scandal involving one of his junior ministers, leading to investigations of lax internal security in the face of Cold War spying. He resigned while ill in hospital. In 1984, on his ninetieth birthday, he became Earl of Stockton. His maiden speech in the House of Lords, which was made at the height of the miners' strike, was considered a brilliant reflection on change and tradition in his long lifetime, a summation of his broad vision.

PERSONAL INFORMATION

Names Maurice Harold Macmillan
Peerage 1st Earl of Stockton and Viscount Macmillan of Ovenden, 10 Feb 1984
Nicknames Supermac; Macwonder; MacBlunder, the Mothball Prime Minister; Mac the Knife; The Old Poseur
Born 10 Feb 1894
Birthplace 52 Cadogan Place, London
Religion Anglican
Ancestry English. Macmillan, the great grandson of a Scottish crofter, became son-in-law to a Duke. His grandfather moved to Cambridge and co-founded Macmillan publishers. His father, born into strong Christian Socialist tradition, married an American. Family politics evolved—through prosperity and education—from Radical Liberal to Liberal Unionist, and later, generally to Conservative opinion.
Date and place of marriage 21 Apr 1920, St. Margaret's, Westminster, London
Age at marriage 26 years, 71 days
Years married 46 years, 31 days
First entered Parliament 29 Oct 1924
Date appointed PM 10 Jan 1957
Age at appointment 62 years, 335 days
Date ceased to be PM 18 Oct 1963
Total time as PM 6 years, 281 days
Ceased to be MP 25 Sep 1964
Lived after last term as PM 23 years, 72 days
Date of death 29 Dec 1986
Place of death Birch Grove House, Chelwood Gate, near Haywards Heath, Sussex
Age at death 92 years, 322 days
Last words I think I will go to sleep now.
Place of funeral and burial 5 Jan 1987, St. Giles Parish Church, Horsted Keynes, West Sussex
Zodiac sign Aquarius

FATHER

Maurice Crawford Macmillan
Date and place of birth 19 Apr 1853, Cambridge
Occupation Publisher, Macmillan and Company. Before entering the field of publishing he was a classics master for six years at St. Paul's School, London.
Date of marriage 1884
Date of death 30 Mar 1936
Place of burial St. Giles Parish Church, Horsted Keynes, West Sussex

MOTHER

Helen Artie Tarleton Belles (Nellie)
Date and place of birth 1856, Spencer, Indiana, USA
Profile A competent singer, she spoke fluent French and some Italian. Studied music and sculpture in Paris and exhibited at the Salon and sang at the Madeleine. An excellent hostess, she was involved in much philanthropic work, particularly a charity school for orphaned boys. Member of the Women's Liberal Unionist Association, Victoria League & Ladies Working Guild.
Dates of marriages 1) Jun 1874, John Bayliss Hill who died five months later; 2) 1884, Maurice Crawford Macmillan
Date of death 26 Oct 1937
Place of burial St. Giles Parish Church, Horsted Keynes, West Sussex

BROTHERS AND SISTERS

Macmillan was the youngest of three sons.
Daniel de Mendi, b. 1 Feb 1886; m. 1918, Margaret (Betty) Matthews; publisher, Macmillan and Company; invalided out of the army and 'worked with distinction' in Paris while the Treaty of Versailles was drafted; d. 6 Dec 1965
Arthur Tarleton, b. 1890; m. Margaret (Peggy) Macmillan; barrister from 1921; 1944, published 'What is Christian Marriage', 1961, an abridged translation of a biography of Abbé Fernaud Portal; d. 1968

WIFE

Lady Dorothy Cavendish
Date and place of birth 28 Jul 1900, Holker Hall, Carnforth, North Lancashire
Mother Lady Evelyn Emily Mary Fitzmaurice
Father Victor William Christian Cavendish, 9th Duke of Devonshire
Father's occupation MP West Derbyshire, 1891–1908; Chancellor, Leeds University; Treasurer of H.M. Household, 1900–03; Financial Secretary of the Treasury, 1903–05; Chief Conservative Whip, House of Lords, 1911; Civil Lord of the Admiralty, 1915–16; Secretary of State, Colonial Department, 1922–24; Governor General of Canada, 1916–21; Privy Counsellor, 1905.
Age at marriage 19 years, 268 days
Number of children 4
Date and place of death 22 May 1966, Birch Grove House, Sussex
Place of burial St. Giles Parish Church, Horsted Keynes, West Sussex
Years younger than PM 6 years, 169 days
Profile She was taught by several English, French and German governesses, 6 hours a day during the week and 3 hours on Saturdays. Said to be neither clever nor intellectual, she was a shrewd judge of character and according to a niece, 'free of any kind of snobbery'. She had a keen sense of humour, as well as warmth and charm. One of her children's friends said that whenever she was expected to stay, 'you knew there was going to be fun—she lit up the room'. Lady Dorothy gave considerable help to Macmillan, in canvassing and as a hostess. She never let him down when called on to assist in his political life. She was extremely protective of his ambitions, to the extent of encouraging her unmarried daughter Sarah to have an abortion, lest her pregnancy ruin Macmillan's career.

She worked for the National Society for Prevention of Cruelty to Children (NSPCC) and the East Sussex

Nursery Association. She was awarded the GBE in 1964 for her charity work.

CHILDREN

1 son, 3 daughters

Maurice Victor (Viscount Macmillan of Ovenden) b. 27 Jan 1921; m. 22 Aug 1942, Hon. Katharine Margaret Alice Ormsby-Gore; Publisher and Chair Macmillan Ltd; Member of Kensington Borough Council, 1948–51; MP Halifax, 1955–64; Farnham, 1966–83; Economic Secretary, Treasury, 1963–64; Chief Secretary, Treasury, 1970–72; Secretary of State, Employment, 1972–73; Paymaster General, 1973–74; Delegate: Council of Europe, 1960–63; Political Committee Rapporteur, 1962; Delegate WEU, 1960–63; Founder, Chair, Wider Share Ownership Council; Privy Counsellor, 1972; d. 10 Mar 1984

Ann Caroline (Carol), b. 1923; m. Apr 1944, Julian Tufnell Faber

Catherine, b. 1926; m. 26 Jan 1950, Baron Amery of Lustleigh (MP Preston North; 1950–66; Brighton Pavilion, 1969–92; Minister of Aviation, 1962–64; Minister of Public Building and Works, Jun–Oct 1970; Minister for Housing and Construction, 1970–72; Minister of State, FCO, 1972–74); d. 1991

Sarah, b. 1930; m. 30 Jul 1953,Andrew Heath; (div. 1966) d. 26 Mar 1970

LIFE AND CAREER

PARLIAMENTARY ELECTIONS FOUGHT

*(*designates candidate elected)*

DATE 6 Dec 1923. General Election
CONSTITUENCY Stockton-on-Tees
RESULT R. S. Stewart* (Lib) 11,734; M.H. Macmillan (Con) 11,661; F.F. Riley (Lab) 10,619

DATE 29 Oct 1924. General Election
CONSTITUENCY Stockton-on-Tees
RESULT M.H. Macmillan* (Con) 15,163; F.F. Riley (Lab) 11,948; R.S. Stewart (Lib) 8,971

DATE 30 May 1929. General Election
CONSTITUENCY Stockton-on-Tees
RESULT F.F. Riley* (Lab) 18,961; M.H. Macmillan (Con) 16,572; J.C. Hayes (Lib) 10,407

DATE 27 Oct 1931. General Election
CONSTITUENCY Stockton-on-Tees
RESULT M.H. Macmillan* (Con) 29,199; F.F. Riley (Lab) 18,168

DATE 14 Nov 1935. General Election
CONSTITUENCY Stockton-on-Tees
RESULT M.H. Macmillan* (Con/Ind Con) 23,285; A.S. Lawrence (Lab) 19,217; G.L. Tossell (Lib) 5,158

DATE 5 Jul 1945. General Election
CONSTITUENCY Stockton-on-Tees
RESULT G.R. Chetwynd* (Lab) 27,128; M.H. Macmillan (Con) 18,464; G.P. Evans (Lib) 3,718

DATE 16 Nov 1945. By-election caused by death of Sir Edward Campbell
CONSTITUENCY Bromley
RESULT M.H. Macmillan* (Con) 26,367; A. Bain (Lab) 20,810; J.C. Sayer (Lib) 5,990

DATE 23 Feb 1950. General Election
CONSTITUENCY Bromley
RESULT M.H. Macmillan* (Con) 23,042; J.R. Elliott (Lab) 12,354; P.W. Grafton (Lib) 4,847

DATE 25 Oct 1951. General Election
CONSTITUENCY Bromley
RESULT M.H. Macmillan* (Con) 25,710; T.E.M. McKitterick (Lab) 13,585

DATE 26 May 1955. General Election
CONSTITUENCY Bromley
RESULT M.H. Macmillan* (Con) 24,612; G.B. Kaufman (Lab) 11,473

DATE 8 Oct 1959. General Election
CONSTITUENCY Bromley
RESULT M.H. Macmillan* (Con) 27,055; A.J. Murray (Lab) 11,603

PARTY ACTIVITY

Party Leadership Leader of the Conservative Party 22 Jan 1957–11 Nov 1963

Other offices Member of the United Europe Movement, a non-party committee founded by Churchill in 1947; Delegate to the Council of Europe, 1949–52.

Membership of group or faction 1924, Young Conservatives, a radical Tory group, nicknamed 'YMCA', which was led by Noel Skelton and included Bob Boothby, John Loder and Oliver Stanley; 1924, Group led by Colonel Spender-Clay which was, 'neither Right nor Left . . . mainly social in character . . . it nevertheless had considerable importance'; 1931, The Northern Group, around 40 Government supporters who held seats in the north of England, led by Sir Nicholas Grattan-Doyle; Successor to the YMCA, a group of between 18 and 20 members, including Robert Bernays, Anthony Crossley and Geoffrey Ellis; 1934–37, The Next Five Years, a radical group of around 150 political and professional people who supported a planned economy, inspired by Lord Allen of Hurtwood, included Will-Arnold Foster, Geoffrey Crowther and Arthur Salter; 1934, Eden Group, known as the 'Glamour Boys', a group of anti-appeasement Tories, divided into the Eden Group and the Churchill Group, (nicknamed the Old Guard). Macmillan was part of the Eden Group but also maintained contact with Churchill, acting as a link between the two groups.

PARLIAMENTARY AND MINISTERIAL EXPERIENCE

Maiden Speech 30 Apr 1925, Budget debate (*HC Deb*, vol 183, col 403–406)

Opposition offices 1945–51, no specific portfolio but generally spoke on industrial and economic affairs

Privy Counsellor 5 Feb 1942

Ministerial Offices Parliamentary Secretary, Ministry of Supply 12 May 1940–Feb 1942, Parliamentary Under Secretary for the Colonies 5 Feb–Dec 1942; Minister Resident, Allied Headquarters 22 Dec 1942–May 1945; Minister for Housing and Local Government, 28 Oct 1951–Oct 1954; Minister of Defence, 18 Oct 1954–Apr 1955; Secretary of State for Foreign Affairs, 7 Apr–Dec 1955; Chancellor of the Exchequer, 21 Dec 1955–Jan

PARLIAMENTARY AND MINISTERIAL EXPERIENCE—*Continued*

1957; First Lord of the Treasury, 10 Jan 1957–18 Oct 1963

Opposition Leaders while PM Hugh Gaitskell (Dec 1955–18 Jan 1963); Harold Wilson (14 Feb 1963–Apr 1976)

GOVERNMENTS FORMED

First Administration 10 Jan 1957–8 Oct 1959

GENERAL ELECTION RESULT

26 MAY 1955: Conservative 345; Labour 277; Liberal 6; Others 2. Total 630

Conservative majority 59 (excl. the Speaker)

CABINET

Prime Minister and First Lord of the Treasury H. Macmillan

Chancellor of the Exchequer P. Thorneycroft (Jan 1957–Jan 1958); D. Heathcoat Amory (Jan 1958–Oct 1959)

Home Secretary R. A. Butler

Foreign Secretary S. Lloyd

Secretary of State for Commonwealth Relations Earl of Home

Secretary of State for the Colonies A. Lennox-Boyd

Secretary for Scotland J. Maclay

Minister of Defence D. Sandys

*Paymaster General** R. Maudling (Sep 1957–Oct 1959)

Lord Chancellor Viscount Kilmuir

Lord Privy Seal R. A. Butler

Lord President of the Council Marquess of Salisbury (Jan–Mar 1957); Earl of Home (Mar–Sep 1957); Viscount Hailsham (Sep 1957–Oct 1959)

President of the Board of Trade D. Eccles

Minister of Agriculture Fisheries and Food D. Heathcoat Amory (Jan 1957–Jan 1958); J. Hare (Jan 1958–Oct 1959)

Minister of Labour and National Service I. Macleod

Minister of Housing & Local Government and Minister for Welsh Affairs H. Brooke

Minister of Education Viscount Hailsham (Jan–Sep 1957); G. Lloyd (Sep 1957–Oct 1959)

Minister of Power Lord Mills

Minister of Transport and Civil Aviation H. Watkinson

Chancellor of the Duchy of Lancaster C. Hill

[* Office not always in Cabinet]

Second Administration 8 Oct 1959–18 Oct 1963

GENERAL ELECTION RESULT

8 OCT 1959: Conservative 365; Labour 258; Liberal 6; Others 1. Total 630

Conservative majority 100

CABINET

Prime Minister and First Lord of the Treasury H. Macmillan

First Secretary of State R. A. Butler (Jul 1962–Oct 1963)

Home Secretary R. A. Butler (Oct 1959–Jul 1962); H. Brooke (Jul 1962–Oct 1963)

Lord Chancellor Viscount Kilmuir (Oct 1959–Jul 1962); Lord Dilhorne (Jul 1962–Oct 1963)

Foreign Secretary S. Lloyd (Oct 1959 –Jul 1960); Earl of Home (Jul 1960–Oct 1963)

Chancellor of the Exchequer D. Heathcoat Amory (Oct 1959–Jul 1960); S. Lloyd (Jul 1960–Jul 1962); R. Maudling (Jul 1962– Oct 1963)

Lord President of the Council and Secretary of State for Commonwealth Relations Earl of Home (Oct 1959–Jul 1960)

Lord President of the Council and Minister for Science Viscount Hailsham (Jul 1960–Oct 1963) (Minister for Science, 14 Oct 1959)

Secretary of State for Scotland J. Maclay (Oct 1959–Jul 1962); M. Noble (Jul 1962–Oct 1963)

Lord Privy Seal Viscount Hailsham (Oct 1959–Jul 1960) (also Minister of Science, Oct 1959–Oct 1963); E. Heath (Jul 1960–Oct 1963)

*Minister of Aviation** D. Sandys (Oct 1959–Jul 1960); P. Thorneycroft (Jul 1960–Jul 1962)

Secretary of State for the Colonies I. Macleod (Oct 1959–Oct 1961); R. Maudling (Oct 1961–Jul 1962); D. Sandys (Jul 1962–Oct 1963) (Joint Minister with Commonwealth Relations Office, 13 Jul 1962)

Minister of Defence H. Watkinson (Oct 1959–Jul 1962); P. Thorneycroft (Jul 1962–Oct 1963)

Minister of Housing and Local Government and Minister for Welsh Affairs H. Brooke (Oct 1959–Oct 1961); C. Hill (Oct 1961–Jul 1962); K. Joseph (Jul 1962–Oct 1963)

Minister of Education D. Eccles (Oct 1959–Jul 1962); E. Boyle (Jul 1962–Oct 1963)

Paymaster General Lord Mills (Oct 1959–Oct 1961); H. Brooke (Oct 1961–Jul 1962); J. Boyd-Carpenter (Jul 1962–Oct 1963)

President of the Board of Trade R. Maudling (Oct 1959–Oct 1961); F. Erroll (Oct 1961–Oct 1963)

Minister of Agriculture Fisheries and Food J. Hare (Oct 1959–Jul 1960); C. Soames (Jul 1960–Oct 1963)

Minister of Labour E. Heath (Oct 1959–Jul 1960); J. Hare (Jul 1960–Oct 1963)

Chancellor of the Duchy of Lancaster C. Hill (Oct 1959–Oct 1961); I. Macleod (Oct 1961–Oct 1963)

Minister of Transport E. Marples (Oct 1959–Oct 1963)

*Minister of Health** E. Powell (Jul 1962–Oct 1963)

*Minister without Portfolio** Lord Mills (Oct 1961–Jul 1962); W. Deedes (Jul 1962–Oct 1963)

[* Office not always in Cabinet]

IMPORTANT DATES IN PERSONAL AND POLITICAL LIFE

JUN 1914 Macmillan obtains a First in Preliminary Moderations at Balliol College, Oxford.

1914–1916 Serves in France during the war, bringing him into contact with the working classes for the first time, later a great help to him in his constituency work.

15 SEP 1916 Seriously wounded at the Battle of the Somme.

1920 Joins Macmillan & Co. the family publishing business.

21 APR 1920 Marries Lady Dorothy Cavendish, daughter of the Duke of Devonshire.

6 DEC 1923 First stands for Parliament in Stockton-on-Tees, but loses by 73 votes. He is deeply affected by the unemployment in Stockton, and the poverty he witnesses influences his approach to domestic politics for the rest of his career.

29 OCT 1924 First elected to Parliament for Stockton-on-Tees.

30 APR 1925 Makes his maiden speech.

1927 Publishes *Industry and the State*—'a manifesto of the progressive wing of our party'.

28 NOV 1927 Votes against his party over a Bill designed to revise the Poor Law because he feels it lacks humani-

ty. He gains a reputation as a radical through articles demanding housing and rating reform. His speeches stress the need for progressive social reform and industrial reorganisation.

30 MAY 1929 Defeated at Stockton in General Election but returned in 1931.

1929 His wife Dorothy falls in love with Robert Boothby, MP. The relationship is to last until her death in 1966. Boothby is believed to have been Sarah's father.

1930 Macmillan briefly considers joining Oswald Mosley's New Party.

1932 Publishes *The State and Industry* and *The Next Step*. In 1933 publishes *Reconstruction* and in 1935, *Planning for Employment* and *The Next Five Years*.

1936 Macmillan's father, uncle Frederick, and cousin George die. All had been senior partners in Macmillan, and greater responsibility for the firm now passes to Harold and his brother Daniel.

29 JUN 1936–JUL 1937 Macmillan resigns as Tory Whip over the party's foreign policy towards Abyssinia.

1938 Publishes *The Middle Way*.

12 MAY 1940 Churchill appoints him Parliamentary Secretary to Herbert Morrison, Minister of Supply.

5 FEB 1942 Macmillan becomes Under Secretary at the Colonial Office and a Privy Counsellor, unusual advancement for only a junior Minister.

22 DEC 1942 Appointed Minister, Resident Allied Force Headquarters.

1943 Builds strong relationship with U.S. President Dwight D. Eisenhower and his personal political adviser, Robert Murphy. The initial meeting is aided by Macmillan's reference to his mother's Indiana origins.

21 FEB 1943 Suffers serious burns in an air crash at Algiers airport.

1943 Macmillan is instrumental in gaining British and American recognition of de Gaulle as de facto Prime Minister of the French Provincial Government.

1943 Churchill sends Macmillan a formal instruction to carry out the same advisory role to Eisenhower and Alexander in Italian affairs as he has done with the French. He is briefed to report to Eisenhower's successor, General Wilson, on all countries under his control except Turkey. Macmillan establishes an exceptionally close working liaison with General Alexander. He amasses huge personal power and becomes in John Wyndham's words, 'Viceroy of the Mediterranean by stealth'.

1944 Macmillan works to establish stability within Yugoslavia. His main achievement is to maintain Anglo-American harmony, strained by British support of Tito. Later he is to assist in the resolution of the Greek civil war.

MAY 1945 Macmillan is involved in the controversial decision to repatriate about 40,000 Cossacks and White Russians who have been captured by the Germans during the war; he is accused later of being a war criminal by Nikolai Tolstoy in *The Minister and the Massacres*.

21 MAY 1945 Churchill offers him the Air Ministry and the Ministry of Labour. He chooses the Air Ministry.

5 JUL 1945 Loses Stockton at the General Election.

16 NOV 1945 Elected for Bromley in by-election caused by the death of Sir Edward Campbell.

17 AUG 1949 Macmillan is an enthusiastic supporter of European unity, and tables an amendment in the Council of Europe Assembly, proposing that 'the Committee of Ministers shall be an executive authority with supranational powers'.

28 OCT 1951 Appointed Minister of Housing, taking on a campaign pledge to build 300,000 houses a year. He is later to reflect that his assistant Ernest Marples 'made me Prime Minister—I was never heard of before housing'.

MAR 1952 He considers resigning because of conflict with Churchill and Eden in relation to the Government's anti-European attitude.

18 OCT 1954 Moves from Housing to be Minister of Defence.

DEC 1954 Macmillan acts as spokesman for his Cabinet colleagues in asking Churchill to resign.

7 APR 1955 Eden appoints Macmillan Foreign Secretary.

10 MAY 1955 Macmillan appears on television as part of the election campaign.

JUL 1955 He helps to set up a summit in Geneva between America, Britain, France and the Soviet Union. Around the same time, however, he refuses to participate in a meeting at Messina which is to lay the foundations for the EEC.

7 NOV 1955 Macmillan forced to answer a parliamentary question on Kim Philby, which effectively clears Philby of being the 'Third Man' in the Burgess and Maclean spy scandal. Burgess and Maclean, were discovered to be spying for the Soviet Union and defected to Moscow before they could be tried. Philby is later to defect as well, proving him indeed the 'Third Man'.

21 DEC 1955 Macmillan becomes Chancellor of the Exchequer. His Budget in April 1956 is judged uncontroversial except for the introduction of Premium Bonds.

JUL–NOV 1956 Suez Crisis. Macmillan misjudges the US attitude to Britain's part in the conflict. He thinks, wrongly, that America will support UK intervention against Egypt.

9 JAN 1957 Eden resigns. Macmillan chosen by Cabinet colleagues to be Prime Minister.

21–24 MAR 1957 Macmillan meets Eisenhower in Bermuda. Strains in the special relationship are healed and the US agrees to supply the UK with guided weapons.

25 MAR 1957 Treaty of Rome signed.

APR 1957 Macmillan strongly supports the British nuclear deterrent. The issue is to cause numerous problems internationally—particularly with France—and at home, when the Campaign for Nuclear Disarmament is launched.

25 JUL 1957 Chancellor Thorneycroft announces a Council on Prices, Productivity and Incomes. Macmillan makes 'never had it so good' speech.

23–25 OCT 1957 Macmillan and Eisenhower meet in Washington and set up two Anglo-American committees to deal with collaboration on weapons and nuclear cooperation, signalling the end of the McMahon Act, which had barred nuclear cooperation.

6 JAN 1958 Thorneycroft, the Chancellor of the Exchequer, and his two financial secretaries, Nigel Birch and Enoch Powell, resign when they are unable to restrict Government expenditure. Macmillan describes the resignations as 'little local difficulties'.

17 FEB 1958 Campaign for Nuclear Disarmament launched by Bertrand Russell and Canon Collins. In March Bulganin, the Soviet Premier, criticises Macmillan for allowing US missile bases in Britain.

APR 1958 Anti-nuclear protestors march from the Aldermaston nuclear weapons establishment to a CND rally in London.

30 APR 1958 Life Peerages Bill receives Royal Assent.

30 AUG 1958 Notting Hill race riots. The legacy of an imperial past, the riots were allegedly caused by a reaction

IMPORTANT DATES IN PERSONAL AND POLITICAL LIFE—*Continued*

against increasing numbers of black Commonwealth immigrants, particularly West Indians, entering the UK in the 1950s.

2 FEB 1959 Macmillan involved in lengthy negotiations which lead to an agreement between Greece and Turkey for the independence of Cyprus.

FEB 1959 Visits Khrushchev in the USSR and agrees to a summit conference to discuss a nuclear test ban. Macmillan then sees de Gaulle in France, Adenauer in West Germany, Diefenbaker in Canada and Eisenhower in the US. In April Khrushchev sends Macmillan a secret letter asking him to abandon the special relationship with the US and sign a non-aggression treaty with Russia. Macmillan reluctantly reveals the letter to Eisenhower.

8 OCT 1959 General Election: Conservatives increase majority to 100. First media-dominated election. Macmillan is accused of exploiting his friendship with Eisenhower for electoral advantage.

20 NOV 1959 European Free Trade Association (EFTA) established.

5 JAN 1960 Macmillan departs for a tour of Africa. In a speech to the Houses of Parliament in Cape Town, South Africa he reflects on the spirit of self-determination which is evident throughout Africa. 'The wind of change is blowing through this continent and, whether we like it or not, this growth of national consciousness is a political fact'. He expressly rejects 'the idea of the inherent superiority of one race over another'.

5 MAR 1960 Made Chancellor of Oxford University.

16–19 MAY 1960 Paris summit collapses when Soviets walk out over United States U2 spy plane incident. Macmillan calls the break up of the summit, 'the most tragic moment of my life'.

8 NOV 1960 John F. Kennedy wins the US presidency. He and Macmillan build up an extremely strong 'special relationship'. Kennedy's late sister Kathleen ('Kick') was married to Lady Dorothy Macmillan's nephew, the Marquess of Hartington. Macmillan prepares 'the grand design', for Kennedy.

17 APR 1961 'Bay of Pigs' invasion by the US of Cuba. Although disappointed at not being consulted over the operation, Macmillan offers his support. Kennedy becomes more receptive to advice from Macmillan when the operation fails.

5 APR 1962 Radcliffe Committee reports on security. Macmillan has to deal with various security scandals during his premiership: a conspiracy to obtain secret submarine information at Portland Hill (1961); security service employee George Blake being found guilty of espionage; Kim Philby admitting to being the 'Third Man'; civil servant John Vassall being found guilty of spying (1962); John Profumo's involvement with Christine Keeler, her simultaneous affair with a Soviet naval attache and Profumo's subsequent lying to Parliament (Mar–Jun 1963). Macmillan is severely criticised for his handling of the Vassall and Profumo affairs.

13 JUL 1962 Economic insecurity, including an unpopular Pay Pause, breeds several by-election defeats for the Conservatives. Macmillan sacks seven Cabinet ministers in a reshuffle dubbed 'the night of the long knives'.

22–28 OCT 1962 Cuban missile crisis: when Soviets install missiles in Cuba Kennedy turns to Macmillan for advice, at times telephoning him up to three times a day.

21 DEC 1962 US Skybolt missile system is abandoned. At Nassau Macmillan successfully negotiates for the UK to have Polaris instead.

29 JAN 1963 De Gaulle vetoes UK application to the EEC, accusing Britain of being insular and differing too profoundly with other EC states. He feels the UK is too closely tied to the US, particularly objecting to Anglo-American nuclear cooperation and the independent British deterrent.

25 JUL 1963 Macmillan works with Kennedy to secure partial test ban treaty with USSR.

18 OCT 1963 Macmillan resigns as Prime Minister for health reasons and retires from the House at the General Election of 1964. He returns to Macmillan publishing.

22 NOV 1963 President Kennedy assassinated.

22 MAY 1966 Lady Dorothy Macmillan dies.

10 FEB 1984 Macmillan becomes Earl of Stockton. Unusually, in recent times, this is a hereditary peerage. Makes maiden speech in the House of Lords on 13 Nov 1984 on economic and industrial affairs.

29 DEC 1986 Macmillan dies after a short illness. Dean Rusk, former US Secretary of State, 1961–69, under Presidents Kennedy and Johnson calls Macmillan: 'One of the greatest Prime Ministers. . . . President Kennedy looked on him as a sort of uncle and adviser. The relationship was very warm and constructive. . . . He will be remembered with gratitude on this side of the Atlantic'. (*The Times*, 30 Dec 1986)

7 FEB 1987 Memorial service: University Church of St. Mary the Virgin, Oxford.

10 FEB 1987 Memorial service: Westminster Abbey, London.

BACKGROUND

PHYSICAL CHARACTERISTICS AND HEALTH

Macmillan's contemporaries at Oxford remembered him as an attractive man—elegant with striking good looks. He has been described as 'tall, willowy and languid' with enormous eyes and a full sensitive mouth. Later, however, he is recorded as having unstylish clothes, gold-rimmed glasses, an unappealing bushy moustache and a toothy, diffident half smile. Yet by the time he became Prime Minister a change had been effected. Alistair Horne notes that, 'The baggy trousers had been replaced by spruce new suits from Saville Row. Gone were the commissar-like spectacles; the Colonel Blimp moustache had been ruthlessly pruned; the disarrayed teeth fixed. The hair assumed a more sophisticated shapeliness. There was a new almost dapper figure'.

Throughout his life Macmillan had a tendency towards hypochondria over small ailments. He was prone to periodic bouts of depression (the 'Black Dog'). Several members of the family suffered a drinking problem.

Macmillan was unathletic and shy as a boy. He was in poor health at Eton where he suffered pneumonia. In 1909 heart trouble was diagnosed and he left Eton a semi-invalid. He was wounded several times in the First World War; in particular his hand and pelvis were injured which contributed to the limp handshake and shuffling walk for which he was sometimes criticised.

In 1931 he suffered a nervous breakdown and there were rumours of a suicide attempt. He was diagnosed as having neurasthenia.

During the Second World War he was knocked over by a taxi but was only bruised. In 1943 he suffered serious burns in an air accident at Algiers. This contributed to an attack of eczema on his hands which necessitated a month's leave. In Jul 1953 he needed an operation to remove a gallstone.

According to his memoirs he seriously considered resigning after he contracted a virus in Jun 1961. From 1962 his health visibly declined. He wore a corset to counteract the pain from his war wounds. At this time were the first signs of the 'old man's disease'—inflamed prostate—that was to lead to his resignation. Macmillan did not inform his doctor of the problems he was having. If he had, something might have been done to limit the prostate trouble and thus avert his resignation at that time. On 8 Oct 1963, he was taken seriously ill. He told colleagues of his decision to resign the following day. By 1984 his eyesight had deteriorated so much that he could no longer enjoy reading and shooting. He had cataracts and inoperable degeneration of the retina.

In 1985 he was seriously ill with pleurisy. Then in Jul 1986 he suffered pneumonia. He died after a short illness on 29 Dec 1986.

EDUCATION

Primary 1900–03, Mr. Gladstone's Day School, near Sloane Square, London; also taught by French governess; 1903–06, Summerfields boarding preparatory school, Oxford

Secondary 1906–09, Eton (Scholar). Left Eton because of heart trouble. Series of tutors including A. B. Ramsay and Ronald Knox, to prepare for Oxford scholarship

University 1912–14, Balliol College, Oxford, where he was awarded an Exhibition, an allowance/scholarship for academic merit. He left before graduating, however, and did not return, due to outbreak of war.

Prizes and awards Third Scholarship to Eton; Williams Classical Exhibition to Oxford

Qualifications 1914, First in Preliminary Moderations, the first public examination before the bachelor's degree

Cultural and vocational background 1913, During the summer Macmillan joined a reading party organised by Oxford don, F. F. Urquhart. He travelled through Paris and stayed in Urquhart's chalet in the French Alps.

Languages Macmillan was fluent in French. He taught himself Italian through reading Dante.

NON-PARLIAMENTARY CAREER

Early occupations 1920, Junior partner in Macmillan and Co., publishers. Macmillan continued in publishing after becoming a Member of Parliament. Initially he would work from 9:30–1:00 and then go to the House. He came into contact with many well-known authors, including Hardy, Kipling, W. B. Yeats and Maynard Keynes. He worked for the firm from 1920–40 until he joined the Government and again while in Opposition between 1945–51. He returned after his resignation as Prime Minister in 1963 and was instrumental in rationalising the company and increasing sales. He was chairman until 1967, when his son Maurice took over. In 1970 he became the first president of the company and continued to play an active role until his death.

Military service 1914, Joined the King's Royal Rifle Corps as Second Lieutenant. In Mar 1915 he transferred to the Grenadier Guards Reserve Battalion. In July the Guards formed a 4th Battalion which selected him and on 15 Aug 1915 he left for Flanders. He was injured in the head and hand at the Battle of Loos on 27 Sep 1915. He convalesced in London and was then given routine duties in the Reserve Battalion at Chelsea Barracks. He was posted back to France with the 2nd Battalion in Apr 1916. At Ypres he was injured and received a second wound stripe and a commendation from his Brigadier. By September he was a captain and had joined the Battle of the Somme. On 15 Sep he was severely injured by bullet fragments in the thigh and pelvis and eventually returned to England. In his memoirs he maintained that but for the intervention of his mother to ensure adequate treatment he would have died from his wounds. He spent much of the following two years in hospital. In 1919 he was ADC to the Governor General of Canada, Victor, 9th Duke of Devonshire, and Macmillan's future father-in-law.

Other posts 1929–40, 1945–47, Board Member Great Western Railway; 1934–36, President Institute of Industrial Administration; 1955, Vice President Franco-British Society; 1957, Trustee Historic Churches Preservation Fund; 1960, President Game Research Association; 1960, Chancellor of Oxford University; 1979, President for Life Carlton Club; 1979, Honorary Life Patron Young Conservatives

HONOURS

Freedom of cities 1957, City of London (Stationers' and Newspaper Makers' Company 1957); Bromley, Kent; 1961, Hon. Freedom of City of London; 1962, Toronto; 1968, Stockton-on-Tees

Academic 1956, Hon. degree University of Indiana; 1957, Hon. Fellow Balliol College, Oxford; 1958, Hon. DCL Oxford; 1960, DCL Oxford (by diploma); 1961, LLD Cambridge; 1963, LLD Sussex; 1976, Benjamin Franklin Medal Royal Society of Arts; 1979, Olympia Prize; 1981, Hon. FBA Oxford

Foreign 1943, Tunisian 'medal to be proud of' First Class; 1945, Red armlet given by leader of Italian Partigiani.

Other than peerage 31 May 1962, Fellow of the Royal Society; 2 Apr 1976, Order of Merit

CLUBS

Athenaeum; Beefsteak; Buck's; Carlton; Guards; Pratt's; Turf; MCC

HOBBIES AND SPORTS

One of Macmillan's greatest pleasures throughout his life was reading. He particularly enjoyed Trollope, Austen, Dickens, Disraeli and Thackeray. While at Oxford he played cricket and tennis. Macmillan was a member of the Marylebone Cricket Club (MCC) from 1929. Later he developed his love of shooting grouse and pheasant. When time allowed he would go fishing or sometimes share a round of golf with his wife Dorothy.

FINANCES

In his official biography, Alistair Horne refers to Macmillan as a millionaire publisher, author and landowner. He was by inheritance and marriage a man of wealth and privilege. When Frank Pakenham, later Lord Longford, tried to persuade him to join Labour in 1938, Macmillan replied 'When I consider the prospect of associating with your wild men of the Left, I have to remember that I am a very rich man!'

At the time of his engagement in January 1920, Macmillan's father wrote to him that he would receive £3,000 a year but 'would be able to get more'.

Income In 1963 Macmillan and Co.'s sales were worth £12.5 million; by 1983, £40 million. By the time he retired from politics, ownership of the company was transferred to the Macmillan Trust which owned almost all the 370,000 company shares.

Spouse's finances Diana Farr notes, 'The Macmillan riches paid for servants and a stable background. . . . Dorothy gained a good deal materially from her marriage'. She died intestate, leaving £62,441 of which £5, 000 eventually went to Macmillan, along with her belongings and the rest in trust to her children. Dorothy was co-director of Birch Grove Estates Ltd. which owned the house and £94,000 in preference shares in the firm, which was in turn owned by Macmillan Trust.

Legacies Birch Grove House: Macmillan's mother persuaded his father to leave it entirely to Harold, ruling out his brothers Daniel and Arthur. (In 1988 it was put up for sale for £5 million.); Partnership Macmillan and Co.; £5,000 from Dorothy.

Will Macmillan was said to have arranged his tax affairs so well within the family that when he died his will for probate totalled only £37,000.

ANECDOTES

'By far the most radical man I've known in politics wasn't on the Labour side at all—Harold Macmillan. If it hadn't been for the war he'd have joined the Labour Party. If that had happened Macmillan would have been Labour Prime Minister and not me'. (Clement Attlee, quoted in James Margach, *The Abuse of Power*, 1981)

When he became Prime Minister Macmillan's appointment took second place on the front page of his local paper in Sussex to a report of a Brighton and Hove Albion football match. He used to keep the cutting on his desk at No. 10 in order, he said, to prevent himself from the impulse towards self-importance. (*The Times*, 31 Dec 1986)

'Harold Macmillan was one of the best-read British Prime Ministers in living memory. He was addicted to Trollope and during the Suez crisis he re-read the whole of George Eliot. "It was the only thing that kept me from going barmy. I didn't mention this in my memoirs because I thought that a Chancellor should be better employed".' (Alistair Horne, *Sunday Times*, 4 Jan 1987)

Macmillan had a relaxed response to the satirical television programme, 'That Was the Week That Was' when it began in 1962. 'I hope you will not, repeat not, take any action about TWTWTW without consulting me' he told his Postmaster-General, Reginald Bevins, in an urgent personal minute. 'It is a good thing to be laughed over. It is better than to be ignored'. (*Guardian* 2 Jan 1993)

QUOTATIONS

Sep 1925, Housing is not a question of Conservatism or Socialism. It is a question of humanity. (Article, used in slogan 1951)

Mar 1929, Modernisation at Home, Markets Abroad (Memo to Churchill arguing that the means to industrial revival was through modernisation and research rather than tariffs and protection.)

20 Jul 1957, Indeed let us be frank about it: most of our people have never had it so good. (Speech at Bedford)

3 Feb 1960, The wind of change is blowing through this continent and whether we like it or not, this growth of national consciousness is a political fact. (Speech to South African Parliament in Cape Town.)

30 Jan 1963, What happened at Brussels yesterday was bad, bad for us, bad for Europe and bad for the whole free world. (Broadcast following French veto of UK application to the EEC.)

8 Nov 1985, In the ordinary working of the economy we are practically bankrupt save for oil. . . . Unity . . . is the only way to meet our burden. It is not by scrimping and saving here and there, not by selling off national assets here and there . . . first of all the Georgian silver goes and then all that nice furniture that used to be in the saloon. Then the Canalettos go. (Speech to tenth anniversary dinner of the Tory Reform Group.)

RESIDENCES

52 Cadogan Place, London

Birch Grove House, Chelwood Gate, Haywards Heath, Sussex. Birch Grove House was split down the middle between East Sussex and West Sussex and rates had to be paid to both councils. During the war the house was used for evacuees. The Macmillans moved into a small house on the estate called *Pooks Cottage*. They stayed there until 1952.

14 Chester Square, London

90 Piccadilly, London, bombed during the war

1 Carlton Gardens, official residence of the Foreign Secretary

11 Downing Street

10 Downing Street

Admiralty House, while Downing Street was being renovated, 1961–63

MEMORIALS

STATUES AND BUSTS

1959, by Oscar Nemon, Oxford University Union; 1973, by Angela Conner, National Portrait Gallery

PORTRAITS

1929, by Philip de Laszlo, Birch Grove; 1954, photograph by Arnold Newman, National Portrait Gallery; 1960, by James Gunn, of Macmillan in his robes as Chancellor of Oxford University, Balliol College, Oxford; 1960, by A. R. Thomson of the debate on the Address featuring Macmillan at the Despatch Box; 1980, diptych by Bryan Organ, commissioned by the

University to commemorate his 20 years as Chancellor, offices of Oxford University

OTHER MEMORIALS

St. Giles School, Horsted Keynes named a classroom extention the Macmillan Memorial Wing, July 1994.

British Rail named a locomotive after him.

BIBLIOGRAPHIC INFORMATION

LETTERS AND PERSONAL PAPERS

British Library; Birch Grove Library

PUBLICATIONS

1927, *Industry and the State*; 1932, *The State and Industry*; *The Next Step*; 1933, *Reconstruction: A Plea for a National Policy*; 1935, *Planning for Employment*; 1935, *The Next Five Years*; 1936, *New Outlook*; 1938, *The Middle Way*, (re-issued 1966); 1938, *The Price of Peace*; 1939, *Economic Aspects of Defence*; 1947, *The Industrial Charter*; 1949, *The Right Road for Britain*; Memoirs: 1966, *Winds of Change*, Vol. I; 1967, *The Blast of War*, Vol. II; 1969, *Tides of Fortune*, Vol. III; 1971, *Riding the Storm*, Vol. IV; 1972, *Pointing the Way, 1959–1961*, Vol. V; 1973, *At the End of the Day, 1961–1963*,, Vol. VI; 1975, *Past Masters*; 1983, *A Life in Pictures*; 1984, *War Diaries: Politics and War in the Mediterranean, January 1943–May 1945*

FURTHER READING

Davenport-Hines, R. *The Macmillans*. London, 1992.
Dickson, L. *The House of Words*. London, 1963.
Edwards, R. D. *Harold Macmillan: A Life in Pictures*. London, 1983.
Fisher, N. *Harold Macmillan: A Biography*. London,.
Horne, A. *Macmillan: The Official Biography*, 2 Vols. (Vol. I: 1894–1956; Vol. II: 1957–1986). London, 1988.
Sampson, A. *Macmillan: A Study in Ambiguity*. London, 1967.

Z.S.

Bettmann

Sir Alec Douglas-Home

Lived 1903–
Political Party Conservative and Unionist
Prime Minister 19 October 1963–16 October 1964
Government Conservative
Reigning Monarch Elizabeth II

True to the end

DOUGLAS-HOME AS PRIME MINISTER

Douglas-Home was an MP from 1931 to 1945 and again in 1950–1951. He went to the House of Lords on the death of his father. He had served under Chamberlain, accompanying the PM to Munich to meet Hitler in 1938. He was appointed Secretary of State for the Commonwealth in 1955 and Foreign Secretary in 1960. In the Conservative Party crisis of 1963 following Macmillan's illness and resignation, a reluctant Douglas-Home agreed to be drafted as a compromise candidate to lead the party, becoming the first person to disclaim his peerage in order to be elected to the House of Commons after taking up his Prime Ministership. He was not especially successful as Prime Minister possibly because as a recent peer, he was said to be out of touch with ordinary people and, particularly, their economic problems. Indeed his adequacy in economic affairs generally was questioned. Despite this he was only just beaten by Wilson at the General Election in 1964. In 1965, he was replaced as leader of the Conservative party by Edward Heath who appointed Douglas-Home spokesman on foreign affairs and, when Heath became Prime Minister in 1970, Foreign Secretary. In modern times it is unusual for a former Prime Minister to take up a ministerial post. In 1975 he returned to the House of Lords as a life peer.

PERSONAL INFORMATION

Names Alexander Frederick Douglas-Home Known as Lord Dunglass 1918–51; Earl of Home 1951–63; Sir Alec Douglas-Home 1963–74; Lord Home of the Hirsel since 1974.
Peerages Earl of Home (disclaimed 23 Oct 1963); Baron Home of the Hirsel, 7 Nov 1974
Born 2 Jul 1903
Birthplace 28 South Street, Mayfair, London
Religion Anglican
Ancestry Scottish. His father's family had owned lands around the Scottish lowlands since the 13th century. His mother was the daughter of the 4th Earl of Durham. Her great-grandfather, the 1st Earl, had campaigned in favour of electoral reform and Dominion status for Canada.
Date and place of marriage 3 Oct 1936, Durham Cathedral
Age at marriage 33 years, 93 days
Years married 53 years, 335 days
First entered Parliament 27 Oct 1931
Date appointed PM 19 Oct 1963
Age at appointment 60 years, 109 days
Date ceased to be PM 16 Oct 1964
Total time as PM 362 days
Ceased to be MP 1) 11 Jul 1951 on the death of his father, when he succeeded to the Earldom; 2) 18 Sep 1974
Zodiac sign Cancer

FATHER

Charles Cospatrick Archibald Douglas-Home, 13th Earl of Home
Date and place of birth 29 Dec 1873, Coldstream, Berwickshire
Occupation A landowner. He was an officer in the British Army during World War I. Lieutenant Colonel, Lanarkshire Yeomanry Cavalry; Governor of the British Linen Bank; Lord Lieutenant of Berwickshire and Vice-Lieutenant of Lanarkshire.
Date of marriage 14 Jul 1902
Date of death 11 Jul 1951
Place of burial Lennel Church, near Coldstream, Berwickshire

MOTHER

Lady Lilian Lambton
Date and place of birth 8 Dec 1881, London
Date of marriage 14 Jul 1902
Age when PM took office 81 years, 317 days
Date of death 26 Sep 1966
Place of burial Lennel Church, near Coldstream, Berwickshire

BROTHERS AND SISTERS

Sir Alec Douglas-Home was the eldest son and first of seven children.
Lady Bridget, b. 4 May 1905
Hon. Henry Montagu, b. 21 Nov 1907; m. 1) 7 Jul 1931, Lady Margaret Spencer (diss. 1947); 2) 1947, Vera Johansen (d. 1965); 3) 1966, Felicity Wills; a British Army officer and also a well-known ornithologist and broadcaster; d. 19 Jul 1980
Lady Rachel, b. 10 Apr 1910; m. 27 Apr 1937, Lt. Col. Lord William Walter Montagu-Douglas-Scott (d. 1958)
Hon. William, b. 3 Jun 1913; m. 26 Jul 1951, Rachel Brand (later Baroness Dacre); a British Army officer in World War II, he was court-martialled and jailed for refusing to endanger the lives of civilians by attacking the German-held town of Le Havre; author and playwright; d. 28 Sep 1992
Hon. Edward, b. 1 Mar 1920; m. 24 Jul 1946, Nancy Rose Straker-Smith; a career officer in the Royal Artillery
Hon. George, b. 2 Sep 1922; a flying officer in the RAF, he was killed while on active service during World War II; d. 14 Jun 1943

WIFE

Elizabeth Hester Alington
Date and place of birth 6 Nov 1909, Shrewsbury
Mother Hon. Hester Lyttleton
Father Rt. Rev. Cyril Alington
Father's occupation Successively headmaster of Shrewsbury and Eton schools, then Dean of Durham Cathedral.
Age at marriage 26 years, 332 days
Number of children 4
Date and place of death 3 Sep 1990, Lanarkshire
Place of burial Coldstream, Berwickshire
Years younger than PM 6 years, 127 days
Profile A tireless and imperturbable hostess she was of invaluable assistance and support to Home, not least by allegedly having to remind her notoriously forgetful husband of the name of the country he was visiting while he was on official foreign visits.

CHILDREN

1 son, 3 daughters
(Lavinia) Caroline, b. 11 Oct. 1937; Woman of the bedchamber (temp) to Queen Elizabeth, the Queen Mother 1963–65; Lady in waiting (temp) to the Duchess of Kent 1966–67; Trustee National Museum of Antiquities of Scotland 1982–85. Deputy Lieutenant for Berwickshire since 1983
Meriel Kathleen, b. 27 Nov. 1939; m. 30 Mar 1964, Adrian Darby; Acupuncturist
Diana Lucy, b. 18 Dec 1940; m. 1963, James Wolfe-Murray (diss. 1972)
David Alexander Cospatrick (Lord Dunglass), b. 20 Nov 1943; m. 10 Oct 1972, Jane Margaret Williams-Wynne; Chairman, Morgan Grenfell (Scotland) 1986– ; Chairman, Committee for Middle East Trade, 1986–92; Governor, Ditchley Foundation, 1977–

LIFE AND CAREER

PARLIAMENTARY ELECTIONS FOUGHT

*(*designates candidate elected)*
DATE 30 May 1929. General Election
CONSTITUENCY Coatbridge
RESULT J. C. Walsh* (Lab) 16,879; Lord Dunglass (Con) 9,210; R. Irvine (Lib) 4,610
DATE 27 Oct 1931. General Election
CONSTITUENCY Lanark

PARLIAMENTARY ELECTIONS FOUGHT—*Continued*

RESULT Lord Dunglass* (Con) 20,675; J. Gibson (Lab) 11,815.
DATE 14 Nov 1935. General Election
CONSTITUENCY Lanark
RESULT Lord Dunglass* (Con) 17,759; J. Gibson (Lab) 10,950; W. Carlin (I.L.P.) 2,583.
DATE 5 Jul 1945. General Election
CONSTITUENCY Lanark
RESULT T. Steele* (Lab) 17,784; Lord Dunglass (Con) 14,900
DATE 23 Feb 1950. General Election
CONSTITUENCY Lanark
RESULT Lord Dunglass* (Con) 19,890; T. Steele (Lab) 19,205
DATE 7 Nov 1963. By-election caused by the death of the sitting Conservative MP. The Tory candidate who had been selected to fight the constituency withdrew in order to allow Home to stand in a fairly safe Conservative seat.
CONSTITUENCY Kinross and West Perthshire
RESULT Sir A. Douglas-Home* (Con) 14,147; A. Millar (Lib) 4,819; A. Forrester (Lab) 3,752; A. Donaldson (Scot Nat) 1,801; I. Smith (Ind Tory) 78; W. Rushton (Ind) 45; R. Wort (Ind) 23
DATE 15 Oct 1964. General Election
CONSTITUENCY Kinross and West Perthshire
RESULT Sir A. Douglas-Home* (Con) 16,659 A. Forrester (Lab) 4,687; A. Donaldson (Scot Nat) 3,522; C. M. Grieve (Com) 127
DATE 31 Mar 1966. General Election
CONSTITUENCY Kinross and West Perthshire
RESULT Sir A. Douglas-Home*
DATE 18 Jun 1970. General Election 14,466; A. Donaldson (Scot Nat) 4,884; B. K. Parnell (Lab) 4,461
CONSTITUENCY Kinross and West Perthshire
RESULT Sir A. Douglas-Home* (Con) 14,434; E.Y. Whitley (Scot Nat) 4,670; D.F. Leach (Lab) 3,827; J.M. Calder (Lib) 2,228.
DATE 28 Feb 1974. General Election
CONSTITUENCY Kinross and West Perthshire
RESULT Sir A. Douglas-Home* (Con) 14,356; D.C. Murray (Scot Nat) 6,274; D. Barrie (Lib) 3,807; D.G. Skene (Lab) 2,694.

PARTY ACTIVITY

Party Leadership Leader of Conservative Party 1963–65
Other offices 1986, Patron of Hughenden Foundation; 1978, Chairman of Conservative Party committee on the reform of the House of Lords; 1970, Chairman of Conservative Party 'Scottish Constitutional Committee' on Scottish devolution; 1963, President of National Union of Conservative and Unionist Associations.

PARLIAMENTARY AND MINISTERIAL EXPERIENCE

Maiden Speech 15 Feb 1932. He spoke in support of the Second Reading of the Imports Bill, a measure designed to protect British industries by imposing duties on a range of imported goods. (*HC Deb.* vol 261, col 1381–1388)
Opposition offices Leader of Opposition, 1964–65; Spokesman on External Affairs, 1965–66; Spokesman on Foreign Affairs, 1966–70 and 1974
Privy Counsellor 14 Nov 1951
Ministerial Offices Joint Under-Secretary of State for Foreign Affairs, 29 May– 5 Jul 1945; Minister of State for Scotland, Oct 1951–Apr 1955; Secretary of State for Commonwealth Relations, 7 Apr 1955–Jul 1960; Lord President of the Council, 29 Mar–Sep 1957; Leader of House of Lords, 29 Mar 1957–27 Jul 1960; Secretary of State for Foreign Affairs, 27 Jul 1960– 19 Oct 1963, 21 Jun 1970– 4 Mar 1974; First Lord of the Treasury 19 Oct 1963–16 Oct 1964
Opposition Leader While PM Harold Wilson

GOVERNMENTS FORMED

Administration 19 Oct 1963–16 Oct 1964

GENERAL ELECTION RESULT
8 OCT 1959: Conservative 365; Labour 258; Liberal 6; Others 1. Total 630
Conservative majority 99

CABINET
Prime Minister and First Lord of the Treasury Sir A. Douglas-Home
Foreign Secretary R.A. Butler
Lord President of the Council and Minister for Science (from 1 Apr 1964 *Secretary of State for Education and Science*) Viscount Hailsham;
Lord Chancellor Lord Dilhorne
Chancellor of the Exchequer R. Maudling
Home Secretary H. Brooke
Secretary of State for Commonwealth Relations and the Colonies D. Sandys
Secretary of State for Industry, Trade and Regional Development and President of the Board of Trade E. Heath
Secretary of State for Defence P. Thorneycroft
Lord Privy Seal S. Lloyd
Chancellor of the Duchy of Lancaster Viscount Blakenham
Minister of Agriculture, Fisheries and Food C. Soames
Minister of Transport E. Marples
Chief Secretary to the Treasury and Paymaster-General J. Boyd Carpenter
Secretary of State for Scotland M. Noble
Minister of Education (later Minister of State for Education and Science) Sir E. Boyle
Minister of Labour J. Godber
Minister of Housing and Local Government and Minister for Welsh Affairs Sir K. Joseph
Minister of Health A. Barber
Minister of Power F. Erroll
Minister of Public Building and Works G. Rippon
Ministers without Portfolio W. Deedes; Lord Carrington

IMPORTANT DATES IN PERSONAL AND POLITICAL LIFE

30 APR 1918 His father becomes 13th Earl of Home and he becomes Lord Dunglass (courtesy title accorded to the eldest son of the Earl of Home).
1925 Graduates from Oxford University
30 MAY 1929 General Election. He stands as Conservative candidate for Coatbridge, but is defeated by sitting Labour MP.
27 OCT 1931 General Election. Elected as MP for Lanark.
15 FEB 1932 Makes maiden speech in support of the Second Reading of the Imports Bill.
27 MAY 1935 Speaks at Church of Scotland Assembly and warns of the dangers of 'a pagan revival'. Emphasises the importance of passing on Christian values to the young.

14 NOV 1935 General Election. Re-elected. Later becomes Parliamentary Private Secretary to Neville Chamberlain MP, Chancellor of the Exchequer.

3 OCT 1936 Marries Elizabeth Alington.

28 MAY 1937 Chamberlain becomes Prime Minister.

29 SEP 1938 Flies to Munich with Chamberlain for meeting with Hitler held in order to preserve peace.

3 SEP 1939 Britain declares war on Germany following the Nazi invasion of Poland.

DEC 1939 Visits British Expeditionary Force in France with Chamberlain.

10 MAY 1940 Chamberlain resigns and Churchill becomes Prime Minister. Home returns to Scotland and volunteers for military service with his regiment. He is rejected on medical grounds and is diagnosed as suffering from spinal tuberculosis. He undergoes an operation and spends two years encased in plaster recovering from his illness.

AUTUMN 1943 He returns to Westminster and becomes one of the first members of the Progress Trust, a non-party research group into socio-political subjects.

FEB 1945 In a debate in the House of Commons on the Yalta agreement, Dunglass condemns Soviet expansionism and speaks for Polish independence.

26 MAY 1945 Home is appointed joint Under-Secretary for Foreign Affairs in the Conservative caretaker Government.

5 JUL 1945 General Election. Home is defeated in Lanark and the Labour Party wins a landslide victory nationally.

1948 He becomes President of the Scottish Unionist Party.

1949 He sits on a Conservative committee of Scottish MPs and Peers which issues 'Scottish Control of Scottish Affairs', a report proposing the devolution of certain powers to Scotland.

23 FEB 1950 General Election. Home elected in Lanark.

9 MAR 1950 In a Commons debate he opposes the nationalisation of the iron and steel industry.

JUN 1950 He speaks in favour of British intervention in Korea.

29 NOV 1950 He again attacks Soviet expansionism and in particular its attempts to control Germany.

11 JUL 1951 His father dies and he becomes the 14th Earl of Home, thereby ceasing to be an MP.

2 NOV 1951 He becomes Minister of State for Scotland.

14 NOV 1951 He becomes a Privy Counsellor.

7 APR 1955 Appointed Secretary of State for the Commonwealth by the new Conservative Prime Minister Anthony Eden.

26 JUL 1956 President Nasser of Egypt announces his plans to nationalise the Suez Canal, which provokes an international political crisis.

29 OCT 1956 Israeli troops invade Egypt and advance towards the Suez Canal.

5–6 NOV 1956 British and French soldiers land in the Suez area.

8 NOV 1956 Home defends the Government's behaviour in a speech in the House of Lords.

9 JAN 1957 Harold Macmillan becomes PM.

29 MAR 1957 When Salisbury resigns as Leader of the House of Lords, Home takes over.

MAR 1958 He holds clandestine talks with Eamon de Valera, PM of the Republic of Ireland. De Valera suggests that Ireland would rejoin the Commonwealth if the British would support reunification, but De Valera is soon to become President of the Republic (a purely figurehead position), so that this change is not put into effect.

8 OCT 1959 General Election. The Conservatives win with a majority of 100.

3 FEB 1960 Macmillan's 'wind of change' speech in Capetown, in which he accepts the fact that the days of imperialist rule in Africa are numbered.

28 MAR 1960 In a House of Lords speech, Home declares that the kind of 'racialism which claims Africa for the Africans can equally imply an attempt to dominate'.

27 JUL 1960 Home is appointed Foreign Secretary. The Opposition objects because Home is a peer. A motion of no confidence is proposed, but defeated. Home's appointment is confirmed.

28 DEC 1961 In a speech to the Berwick-on-Tweed United Nations Association he criticises communist manipulation of the UN and what he sees as the double standards of newly independent countries. He feels the British are accused of imperialism, yet the expansionism of the Soviet Union is ignored.

OCT 1962 The Cuban Missile Crisis. The Soviet Union places nuclear missiles in Cuba. President Kennedy threatens war unless they are removed. Macmillan and Home support Kennedy's actions. The missiles are withdrawn after a period of tension.

AUGUST 1963 Home goes to Moscow to sign the nuclear test ban treaty on behalf of Britain.

9 OCT 1963 As the Conservative Party Conference gathers in Blackpool, Macmillan is rushed into hospital for an operation. He tells Home he is resigning because of ill-health.

10 OCT 1963 Home reads Macmillan's resignation message to the Conference. In the following days he is persuaded to stand for the leadership as a compromise figure between the favoured candidates of the left and right wings of the Party.

18 OCT 1963 Macmillan tenders his resignation as PM and suggests that the Queen appoint Lord Home as his successor. Home is called to the Palace and asked to form a government. He requests time to consult his colleagues and ask for their support. Only two of his fellow Cabinet members refuse to serve under him—Iain Macleod and Enoch Powell.

19 OCT 1963 After another audience with the Queen he accepts the post of PM.

23 OCT 1963 Home disclaims his peerage and becomes Sir Alec Douglas-Home.

7 NOV 1963 He wins a by-election at Kinross and West Perthshire.

12 NOV 1963 Home is formally adopted as leader of the Conservative Party.

29 NOV 1963 Speaking in Grantham he declares, 'It seems to have gone out of fashion to be proud of our national flag, but patriotism in the twentieth century is still a noble thing if we think of our flag not as a symbol of conquest but as a banner proclaiming the image of the kind of life and the values in which the British people believe . . . '

JAN 1964 He holds inconclusive talks on independence with the PM of Southern Rhodesia, Winston Field.

4 FEB 1964 In a speech at Bury he claims, 'The bomb is a deterrent and it has in fact deterred'.

25 FEB 1964 Resale Prices Bill published. This measure, designed to stop suppliers of goods from fixing a price at or below which goods cannot be sold, causes much discontent among Conservative backbenchers. The Government is forced to amend the Bill in order to placate dissenting Conservatives.

IMPORTANT DATES IN PERSONAL AND POLITICAL LIFE—*Continued*

19 JUN 1964 In a speech in Leeds he states that the following elements are the basics of Conservative philosophy: work, the home, education, value for money, thrift and service.

16 JUL 1964 The Resale Prices Bill is enacted.

15 OCT 1964 General Election. After a campaign in which there had been concern about the slowing rate of growth of the economy, together with an increasing sense that people simply wanted a change after 13 years of Tory rule, the Conservative share of the vote is significantly reduced.

16 OCT 1964 Home acknowledges defeat.

FEB 1965 Rumblings of discontent with Douglas-Home's leadership of the Conservative Party grow. The process of electing the leader of the Party is reformed.

22 JUL 1965 At a meeting of the backbench 1922 Committee he announces his resignation as party leader. The new leader, Edward Heath, appoints Douglas-Home foreign spokesman in the Shadow Cabinet.

11 NOV 1965 Rhodesia unilaterally declares independence from Britain.

19 JAN 1966 Speaking in New York to the Economic Club he claims, 'Majority rule in Rhodesia today or tomorrow would bring collapse and ruin'.

OCT 1969 Makes speech at the Conservative Party Conference in favour of British entry to Common Market.

MAR 1970 'Scottish Constitutional Committee' chaired by Home issues its report, 'Scotland's Government', advocating limited devolution of powers to an assembly at Edinburgh.

21 JUN 1970 Home is appointed Foreign and Commonwealth Secretary in the new Conservative Government.

20 SEP 1974 Parliament is dissolved as a General Election is called. Home does not stand for re-election.

22 JAN 1975 He returns to the House of Lords as a life peer, Baron Home of the Hirsel (peerage conferred on 7 Nov 1974).

7 OCT 1976 Home's autobiography *The Way the Wind Blows* is published.

MAR 1978 A Conservative committee of MPs and Peers chaired by Home publishes proposals on the reform of the House of Lords.

14 FEB 1979 Home advises Scots to vote No in the referendum for Scottish devolution.

JUL 1986 He becomes patron of the Hughenden Foundation, a Conservative Party think tank which aims to strengthen links between industry and politics.

4 DEC 1989 In the House of Lords, Home speaks against proposals to prosecute in Britain any war criminals found to be resident.

3 SEP 1990 His wife dies following a stroke.

NOV 1990 Lord Home suffers a stroke from which he slowly recovers.

18 MAY 1992 In a letter to *The Scotsman* Home maintains that support for the union between Scotland and England is growing.

BACKGROUND

PHYSICAL CHARACTERISTICS AND HEALTH

Home's tall (6'1"), somewhat gaunt appearance gave rise to a few unkind remarks from his political opponents. The Labour politician George Brown once described him as looking 'like a refugee from Madame Tussaud's'. The *Evening Standard* (London) was more generous, describing him as 'tall and thin with a slight stoop, charming manners, a mop of fair hair and a romantic appearance' (29 Sep 1938), (noted in *Sir Alec Douglas-Home* by K. Young).

In his autobiography, Home drily recounts a conversation he had with a makeup lady while he was being prepared for a public appearance as Prime Minister: 'Can you not make me look better than I do on television?' 'No.' 'Why not?' 'Because you have a head like a skull.' 'Does not everyone have a head like a skull?' 'No'. 'So that was that.' (*The Way the Wind Blows*, p. 203)

From 1940–42, Home suffered from an extremely painful attack of spinal tuberculosis which necessitated his withdrawal from political life. After an operation he had to remain immobile for two years while he recuperated.

When he was asked to stand for the Tory leadership in 1963 he first had to check with his doctor to see if he was well enough to perform the office.

In Jan 1964 he punctured a lung after slipping on some ice.

In Nov 1990 he suffered a stroke from which he slowly recovered.

EDUCATION

Primary Ludgrove Preparatory School, Hertfordshire

Secondary 1917–22, Eton

University 1922–25, Christ Church College, Oxford University

Qualifications 1925, Degree in Modern History (3rd)

NON-PARLIAMENTARY CAREER

Military service Volunteered for military service in 1940 but was turned down on grounds of ill-health. Major in Lanarkshire Yeomanry (Territorial Army Reserve).

Other posts 1960, Deputy Lieutenant of Lanarkshire; 1963, Honorary Master of the Bench, Inner Temple; 1966–67, President of Marylebone Cricket Club, 1966–84, Grand Master, Primrose League; 1966–77, Captain, Royal Company of Archers, Queen's Body Guard for Scotland; 1973, Honorary President, NATO Council; 1973, Chancellor, Order of the Thistle; 1985, President of Peace through NATO

HONOURS

Freedom of cities 1969, Edinburgh

Academic 1960, DCL Oxford University; 1962, Hon. Student of Christ Church College, Oxford; 1961, DDL Harvard; 1962, DDL Edinburgh; 1966, DDL Aberdeen; 1967, DDL Liverpool; 1968, DDL St. Andrews; 1966, DSC Heriot Watt

Other than peerage 1962, Knight of the Thistle (Chancellor of the Order from 1973)

CLUBS

Carlton, Travellers, New (Edinburgh), MCC, Buck's

HOBBIES AND SPORTS

His hobbies were shooting and fishing for most of his life. He wrote a book on the subject in 1979.

He was also a keen flower arranger. R. A. Butler once remarked, 'whenever things became most tense he would go away on his own for half an hour and arrange a vast bowl of flowers'.

A fine cricketer, he played several games for Middlesex at County level and took part in the Marylebone Cricket Club (MCC) tour of South America in 1926–27. He was President of the MCC 1966–67.

FINANCES

In 1913, according to an article by Bernard Harris in the *Sunday Express* (27 Oct 1963, quoted by Emrys Hughes in his biography of Douglas-Home), the Home estates covered 134,000 acres and produced an annual rental return of £98,035. In addition to this, the family drew royalties from the coal mines on its land. When the coal industry was nationalised in 1947, the Home family was paid compensation.

In 1937 the family's landholdings were transferred to a private company. At the time, the estates were valued at £445,000. When the 13th Earl (Sir Alec's father) died in 1951, there were death duties amounting to about £350,000. In his 1963 article, Harris estimated that Home was a millionaire by the time he became PM.

Income Apart from income from his estates, Home earned £360 p.a. as an MP in 1931 rising to £4,500 in 1974. As Under-Secretary of State for Scotland he earned £1,500 p.a. (although he only held this office from May–Jul 1945). As Secretary of State for Commonwealth Relations from 1955–60 he earned £5,000 p.a. While he was Secretary of State he earned £5,000 p.a. from 1960 to 1963 and £12,000 p.a. As PM from 1963–64 he earned £10,000. As Leader of the Opposition from 1964–65 he earned £2,000 p.a.. From 1991, he received an allowance of approximately £30,000 p.a. to help with his office/secretarial costs.

ANECDOTES

Although his political opponents loathed his politics, most of them found it impossible to dislike Home personally. James Maxton, one of the most famous left-wing Labour MPs of the 1930s, once said to him in the House of Commons tearoom, 'Alec, I had been thinking that, come the revolution, I'll have you strung up on a lamp post, but I think instead I'll offer you a cup of tea'. (from *Sir Alec Douglas-Home* by K. Young)

While he was Foreign Secretary Home commented to Humphrey Berkeley that Africans were not yet ready for self-government because they hadn't discovered electric light or the wheel. Berkeley asked him if he could have invented either. Home thought this question a little 'offside'. (Humphrey Berkeley in *The Times* 7 Oct 76)

When he had recovered from his bout of spinal tuberculosis which had necessitated an operation in which flakes of his shin bones were grafted onto his vertebrae, he told the medical team who had looked after him that they had 'achieved what had hitherto been thought impossible, namely put backbone into a politician.' (from *The Way the Wind Blows*)

In a newspaper interview in 1962 Home remarked that he needed to use matchsticks to help him with his economic calculations.

During his 1963 by-election campaign in Kinross and West Perthshire, he was asked if he intended to live in the constituency. Douglas-Home replied that he had more houses than he could live in already. (from *Sir Alec Douglas-Home: Modern Conservative* by E. Hughes)

QUOTATIONS

When he learned that the Conservative Party had chosen the Earl of Home to lead the Party and the country, the Labour leader Harold Wilson remarked scathingly, 'after half a century of democratic advance . . . the whole process has ground to a halt with a 14th Earl.' In response, Home commented: 'As far as the 14th Earl is concerned, I suppose Mr. Wilson, when you come to think of it, is the 14th Mr. Wilson.' (quoted by K. Young in *Sir Alec Douglas-Home*)

RESIDENCES

Springhill House, near Coldstream, Berwickshire
The Hirsel, near Coldstream, Berwickshire
Castlemains, Douglas, Lanarkshire
Chester Square, London
10 Downing Street
24 Roebuck House, Palace Street, London

MEMORIALS

STATUES AND BUSTS

1983, by Michael Black, Norman Porch, House of Lords

PORTRAITS

1988, by Avigdor Arikha, Scottish National Portrait Gallery; 1993, by Henry Mee, House of Commons.

BIBLIOGRAPHIC INFORMATION

LETTERS AND PERSONAL PAPERS

Stored at *The Hirsel*, near Coldstream, Berwickshire.

PUBLICATIONS

1961, *Great Britain's Foreign Policy*; 1969, *Britain's Place in the World*; 1970, *Scotland's Government: The report of the Scottish constitutional committee*; 1971, *Great Britain in the 70's*: 1971, *Our European Destiny*; 1971, *The Modern Commonwealth*; 1974, *Britain's Changing Role in World Affairs*; 1976, *Diplomacy, Detente and the Democracies* ; 1976, *The Way the Wind Blows: An Autobiography*; 1978, *The House of Lords—The Report of the Conservative Review Committee* ; 1979, *Border Reflections Chiefly on the Arts of Shooting and Fishing*; 1981, *Peace with Honour*; 1983, *Letters to a Grandson*

FURTHER READING

Butler, D. and King, A. *The British General Election of 1964.*

BIBLIOGRAPHIC INFORMATION—*Continued*

Hughes, E. *Sir Alec Douglas-Home: Modern Conservative.* London, 1964.

Young, K. *Sir Alec Douglas-Home.* London, 1970.

F.C.

Bettmann

Harold Wilson

Lived 1916–
Political Party Labour
Prime Minister 16 October 1964–19 June 1970; 4 March 1974– 5 April 1976
Government Labour
Reigning Monarch Elizabeth II

Tempus rerum imperator Time the ruler of all things

WILSON AS PRIME MINISTER

With a background as an economist and civil servant, Wilson, first elected to Parliament in 1945, rose rapidly through the ministerial ranks to become a remarkably young President of the Board of Trade in 1947. Successful in opposition from 1951, he was elected Labour Party leader in February 1963. A great foil to his predecessor Douglas-Home, he sought to introduce a scientific and technological revolution in the country. At the same time he promoted greater cooperation between the Labour Party and the trade unions, together with a number of socialist measures. He fought off devaluation of sterling until November 1967. The Northern Ireland crisis started towards the end of his first administration, and he secured all-party support for sending British troops to assume responsibility for maintaining law and order in Northern Ireland. Probably his greatest single achievement was holding the Labour party together, especially in government, despite its wide range of views and personalities. Although the Cold War caused anxiety, Wilson's relationship with American President Johnson was workmanlike, and the Soviet leader visited London in 1967. When the white regime in Rhodesia declared independence in 1965 he was unsuccessful in negotiating with them. Leader of the opposition from 1970 to 1974 while Heath was PM Wilson returned to power in

1974. Partly because of deep divisions in his own party, he held a referendum which confirmed UK membership of the European Communities. During his second administration he had to maintain good relations with the trade unions and tried to prevent crippling industrial strikes. A foreign crisis was the invasion of Cyprus by Turkey, when he unsuccessfully tried to mediate between the Greek and Turkish Cypriots. He resigned April 1976 to give Callaghan, his elected successor, time to develop fresh policies for the next election but also left him serious economic problems and a small majority.

PERSONAL INFORMATION

Names James Harold Wilson
Peerage Baron Wilson of Rievaulx, of Kirklees in the county of West Yorkshire, 21 Jul 1983
Born 11 Mar 1916
Birthplace 4 Warneford Road, Cowlersley, Huddersfield, Yorkshire
Religion Congregationalist
Ancestry English. The Wilsons came originally from the lands surrounding the Abbey of Rievaulx, in the North Riding of Yorkshire. They lived as yeomen and craftsmen until the 19th century.
Date and place of marriage 1 Jan 1940, Mansfield College Chapel, Oxford
Age at marriage 23 years, 296 days
First entered Parliament 5 Jul 1945
Dates appointed PM 1) 16 Oct 1964 2) 4 Mar 1974
Age at appointments 1) 48 years, 219 days 2) 57 years, 358 days
Dates ceased to be PM 1) 19 Jun 1970; 2) 5 Apr 1976
Total time as PM 1) 5 years, 246 days; 2) 2 years, 33 days; a total of 7 years, 279 days
Ceased to be MP 13 May 1983
Zodiac sign Pisces

FATHER

James Herbert Wilson
Date and place of birth 12 Dec 1882, Chorlton-upon-Medlock, Lancashire
Occupation Trained at Manchester Technical College and qualified as an industrial chemist. Worked in the dyestuffs industry first in Manchester then Huddersfield. In the 1930s he was made redundant twice, necessitating the family's move to Cheshire in 1932 (he became chief chemist at Brotherton's chemical works in Bromborough), and to Cornwall in 1938.
Date of marriage 14 Mar 1906
Age when PM took office 81 years, 309 days
Date and place of death 8 Nov 1971, Australia
Place of cremation Truro, Cornwall

MOTHER

Ethel Seddon
Date and place of birth Apr 1882, Manchester
Profile Became a pupil teacher, probably at elementary level, in the late 1890s. After her marriage she was involved in community activities, as founder and organiser of the Women's Guild, a Guide captain and Sunday school teacher.
Date of marriage 14 Mar 1906
Date and place of death 1958, Cornwall
Place of cremation Truro, Cornwall

BROTHERS AND SISTERS

Harold Wilson is the only son and younger of two children.
Marjorie, b. 12 Mar 1909; studied chemistry at Leeds University then trained as a teacher, becoming headmistress of a primary school in Cornwall

WIFE

Gladys Mary Baldwin
Date and place of birth 12 Jan 1916, Diss, Norfolk
Mother Sarah Bentley
Father Rev. Daniel Baldwin
Father's occupation Congregational minister
Age at marriage 23 years, 354 days
Number of children 2
Years older than PM 59 days
Profile She boarded at Milton Mount College, Crawley, Sussex until 1932 then attended a secretarial course in Cumbria from 1932–34. She was employed as a shorthand-typist at Lever Brothers in Port Sunlight from 1934 until shortly before her marriage. She shared her husband's non-conformist, radical liberal background and beliefs but was ill-at-ease in the political limelight, preferring to concentrate on their family life. In a newspaper interview in 1964 she said 'My job is to keep the home going and look after the boys. I don't think too much about 10 Downing Street. I'm not ambitious. I'm interested in the broad picture of politics but not who's in, who's out.' However, this disguised the depth of her loyalty and support for her husband's career and her perceptive observations of political life. Her candour and lack of pretence endeared her to contemporary observers and the public. The publication of her work *Selected Poems* in 1971 was an immediate popular success.

CHILDREN

2 sons
Robin James, b. 5 Dec 1943; m. 7 Aug 1968, Margaret Elizabeth Joy Crispin; read mathematics at Balliol College, Oxford (MA) and studied further at the University of Pennsylvania and the Massachusetts Institute of Technology; head of the mathematics department at the Open University
Giles Daniel John, b. 7 May 1948; studied at Brighton College of Education and The Open University (BA); a schoolteacher in London.

LIFE AND CAREER

PARLIAMENTARY ELECTIONS FOUGHT

*(*designates candidate elected)*

DATE 5 Jul 1945. General Election
CONSTITUENCY Ormskirk

RESULT J.H. Wilson* (Lab) 30,126; A.C. Greg (Con) 23, 104; W.S.R. King-Hall (Nat Ind) 11,848

DATE 23 Feb 1950. General Election
CONSTITUENCY Huyton
RESULT J.H. Wilson* (Lab) 21, 536, S. Smart (Con) 20, 702; H.G. Edwards (Lib) 1,905; L.J. McGree (Com) 387

DATE 25 Oct 1951. General Election
CONSTITUENCY Huyton
RESULT J.H. Wilson* (Lab) 23,582; F.L. Neep (Con) 22, 389

DATE 26 May 1955. General Election
CONSTITUENCY Huyton
RESULT J.H. Wilson* (Lab) 24,858; W.G.O. Morgan (Con) 22,300

DATE 8 Oct 1959. General Election
CONSTITUENCY Huyton
RESULT J.H. Wilson* (Lab) 33,111; G.B. Woolfenden (Con) 27,184

DATE 15 Oct 1964. General Election
CONSTITUENCY Huyton
RESULT J.H. Wilson* (Lab) 42,213; H. Tucker (Con) 22, 940; M.C.W. Baker (Ind Com) 899

DATE 31 Mar 1966. General Election
CONSTITUENCY Huyton
RESULT J.H. Wilson* (Lab) 41,132; Dr. T.L. Hobday (Con) 20,182; D.E. Sutch (Nat Teenage) 585

DATE 18 Jun 1970. General Election
CONSTITUENCY Huyton
RESULT J.H. Wilson* (Lab) 45,583; J.N.M. Entwistle (Con) 24,509; J.W.G. Sparrow (Dem) 1,232; J.I. Kenny (Com) 890

DATE 28 Feb 1974. General Election
CONSTITUENCY Huyton
RESULT J.H. Wilson* (Lab) 31,767; T.Y. Benyon (Con) 16,462; N.F.E. Snowden (Lib) 7,584; H. Smith (Campaign For a More Prosperous Britain) 234

DATE 10 Oct 1974. General Election
CONSTITUENCY Huyton
RESULT J.H. Wilson* (Lab) 31,750; W. Peters (Con) 15, 517; M.P. Braham (Lib) 4,956

DATE 3 May 1979. General Election
CONSTITUENCY Huyton
RESULT Sir J.H. Wilson* (Lab) 27,449; G. Harrison (Con) 19,939; D.P. Cottier (Lib) 5,476

PARTY ACTIVITY

Party Leadership 1963–76, Leader of the Labour Party
Other offices 1952–76, Member, Labour Party Executive Committee; 1955, Chairman, Labour Party Executive Committee Inquiry on Party Organisation; 1955, Chairman, Labour Party Executive's Financial and Economic Policy Committee; 1960–61, Vice-chairman, Labour Party; 1961–62, Chairman, Labour Party; 1961, Chairman, Labour Party Executive's Home Policy Committee.
Membership of group or faction c. 1951–52, The Bevanites. Wilson wrote later, 'I disliked the word Bevanite as much as Nye [Bevan] did. I was a co-belligerent, not a satellite.'

PARLIAMENTARY AND MINISTERIAL EXPERIENCE

Maiden Speech 9 Oct 1945. He spoke for the Government as Parliamentary Secretary to the Ministry of Works in a debate on the amenities and facilities provided for Members of Parliament. (*HC Deb*, vol 414, col 186–191)
Opposition offices 1955, Opposition spokesman on trade; 1956–61, Shadow Chancellor; 1959–63, Chairman, Public Accounts Committee; 1961–63, Shadow Foreign Secretary; 1963–64, 1970–74, Leader of the Opposition
Privy Counsellor 14 Oct 1947
Ministerial Offices Parliamentary Secretary, Ministry of Works 6 Aug 1945–5 Mar 1947; Secretary for Overseas Trade 5 Mar –14 Oct 1947; President of the Board of Trade 14 Oct 1947–23 Apr 1951; First Lord of the Treasury 16 Oct 1964–19 Jun 1970, 4 Mar 1974–5 Apr 1976; Minister for the Civil Service 1 Nov 1968–19 Jun 1970, 4 Mar 1974–5 Apr 1976
Opposition Leaders while PM 1964–65 Sir Alec Douglas-Home; 1965–70, 1974–75 Edward Heath; 1975–76 Margaret Thatcher

GOVERNMENTS FORMED

First Administration 16 Oct 1964–31 Mar 1966

GENERAL ELECTION RESULT
15 OCT 1964: Labour 317; Conservative 304; Liberal 9. Total 630
Labour majority 5 (excl. the Speaker)

CABINET
Prime Minister and First Lord of the Treasury H. Wilson
First Secretary of State and Secretary of State for Economic Affairs G. Brown
Lord President of the Council H. Bowden
Lord Chancellor Lord Gardiner
Lord Privy Seal Earl of Longford (Oct 1964–Dec 1965); Sir F. Soskice (Dec 1965–Mar 1966)
Chancellor of the Exchequer J. Callaghan
Foreign Secretary P. Gordon Walker (Oct 1964–Jan 1965); M. Stewart (Jan 1965–Mar 1966)
Home Secretary Sir F. Soskice (Oct 1964–Dec 1965); R. Jenkins (Dec 1965–Mar 1966)
Minister of Agriculture, Fisheries and Food F. Peart
Secretary of State for the Colonies A. Greenwood (Oct 1964–Dec 1965); Earl of Longford (Dec 1965–Mar 1966)
Secretary of State for Commonwealth Relations A. Bottomley
Secretary of State for Defence D. Healey
Secretary of State for Education and Science M. Stewart (Oct 1964–Jan 1965); A. Crosland (Jan 1965–Mar 1966)
Minister of Housing and Local Government R. Crossman
Minister of Labour R. Gunter
Chancellor of the Duchy of Lancaster D. Houghton
Minister of Overseas Development Mrs. B. Castle (Oct 1964–Dec 1965); A. Greenwood (Dec 1965–Mar 1966)
Minister of Power F. Lee
Secretary of State for Scotland W. Ross
Minister of Technology F. Cousins
President of the Board of Trade D. Jay
Minister of Transport T. Fraser (Oct 1964–Dec 1965); Mrs. B. Castle (Dec 1965–Mar 1966)
Secretary of State for Wales J. Griffiths

Second Administration 31 Mar 1966–19 Jun 1970

GENERAL ELECTION RESULT

31 MAR 1966: Labour 364; Conservative 253; Liberal 12; Others 1. Total 630
Labour majority 97 (excl. the Speaker)

CABINET

Prime Minister and First Lord of the Treasury H. Wilson
First Secretary of State G. Brown (Mar–Aug 1966) (office linked to Ministry of Economic Affairs 16 Oct 1964–29 Aug 1967); B. Castle (Apr 1968–Jun 1970) (office linked to Ministry of Employment)
Lord President of the Council H. Bowden (Mar–Aug 1966); R. Crossman (Aug 1966–Oct 1968); F. Peart (Oct 1968–Jun 1970)
Lord Chancellor Lord Gardiner
Lord Privy Seal Earl of Longford (Mar 1966–Jan 1968); Lord Shackleton (Jan–Apr 1968); F. Peart (Apr–Oct 1968); Lord Shackleton (Oct 1968–Jun 1970)
Chancellor of the Exchequer J. Callaghan (Mar 1966–Nov 1967); R. Jenkins (Nov 1967–Jun 1970)
Chief Secretary to the Treasury J. Diamond (Nov 1968–Jun 1970)
Secretary of State for Economic Affairs G. Brown (Mar–Aug 1966); M. Stewart (Aug 1966–Aug 1967); P. Shore (Aug 1967–Oct 1969) (office abolished in 1969).
Foreign Secretary M. Stewart (Mar–Aug 1966); G. Brown (Aug 1966–Mar 1968); M. Stewart (Mar 1968–Jun 1970) (merged with Commonwealth Office 17 Oct 1968)
Home Secretary R. Jenkins (Mar 1966–Nov 1967); J. Callaghan (Nov 1967–Jun 1970)
Minister of Agriculture, Fisheries and Food F. Peart (Mar 1966–Apr 1968); C. Hughes (Apr 1968–Jun 1970)
Secretary of State for the Colonies F. Lee (Mar 1966– Jan 1967) (came under Dept. of Commonwealth Affairs 1 Aug 1966. Office abolished 7 Jan 1967)
Secretary of State for Commonwealth Relations (renamed *Commonwealth Affairs* 1 Aug 1966) A. Bottomley (Mar–Aug 1966); H. Bowden (Aug 1966–Aug1967); G. Thomson (Aug 1967–Oct 1968) (merged with Foreign Office 17 Oct 1968).
Secretary of State for Defence D. Healey
Secretary of State for Education and Science A. Crosland (Mar 1966–Aug 1967); P. Gordon Walker (Aug 1967–Apr 1968); E. Short (Apr 1968–Jun 1970)
Secretary of State for Employment and Productivity Mrs. B. Castle (Apr 1968–Jun 1970)
Secretary of State for Health and Social Security R. Crossman (Nov 1968–Jun 1970)
*Minister of Housing and Local Government** R. Crossman (Mar–Aug 1966); A. Greenwood Aug 1966–Oct 1969)
Minister of Labour R. Gunter (Mar 1966–Apr 1968) (reorganised as Ministry of Employment and Productivity 6 Apr 1968)
Chancellor of the Duchy of Lancaster G. Thomson (Oct 1969–Jun 1970)
Secretary of State for Local Government and Regional Planning A. Crosland (Oct 1969–June 1970) (office created 6 Oct 1969).
*Minister of Overseas Development** A. Greenwood (Mar–Aug 1966); A. Bottomley (Aug 1966–Aug 1967)
Paymaster General Lord Shackleton (Apr 1968–Nov 1968); J. Hart (Nov 1968–Oct 1969); H. Lever (Oct 1969–Jun 1970)
Minister without Portfolio D. Houghton (Mar 1966–Jan 1967); P. Gordon Walker (Jan–Aug 1967); G. Thomson (Oct 1968–Oct 1969); P. Shore (Oct 1969–Jun 1970)
Minister of Power R. Marsh (Mar 1966–Apr 1968); R. Gunter (Apr–Jul 1968); R. Mason (Jul 1968–Oct 1969) (office abolished 6 Oct 1969).
Secretary of State for Scotland W. Ross
Minister of Technology F. Cousins (Mar–Jul 1966); T. Benn (Jul 1966–Jun 1970)
President of the Board of Trade D. Jay (Mar 1966–Aug 1967); A. Crosland (Aug 1967–Oct 1969); R. Mason (Oct 1969–Jun 1970)
*Minister of Transport** Mrs. B. Castle (Mar 1966–Apr 1968); R. Marsh (Apr 1968–Oct 1969)
Secretary of State for Wales C. Hughes (Mar 1966–Apr 1968); G. Thomas (Apr 1968–Jun 1970)
[* Office not always in Cabinet]

Third Administration 4 Mar 1974–10 Oct 1974

GENERAL ELECTION RESULT

28 FEB 1974: Labour 301; Conservative 297; Liberal 14; Others 23. Total 635
No overall majority

CABINET

Prime Minister, First Lord of the Treasury and Minister for the Civil Service H. Wilson
Lord President of the Council E. Short
Lord Chancellor Lord Elwyn Jones
Lord Privy Seal Lord Shepherd
Chancellor of the Exchequer D. Healey
Parliamentary Secretary to the Treasury R. Mellish (Jul–Oct 1974)
Foreign Secretary J. Callaghan
Home Secretary R. Jenkins
Minister of Agriculture, Fisheries and Food F. Peart
Secretary of State for Defence R. Mason
Secretary of State for Education and Science R. Prentice
Secretary of State for Employment M. Foot
Secretary of State for Energy E. Varley
Secretary of State for the Environment A. Crosland
Secretary of State for Social Services Mrs. B. Castle
Secretary of State for Industry T. Benn (also Minister of Posts and Telecommunications 7 Mar–29 Mar 1974)
Chancellor of the Duchy of Lancaster H. Lever
Secretary of State for Northern Ireland M. Rees
Secretary of State for Prices and Consumer Protection Mrs. S. Williams
Secretary of State for Scotland W. Ross
Secretary of State for Trade and President of the Board of Trade P. Shore
Secretary of State for Wales J. Morris

Fourth Administration 10 Oct 1974–5 Apr 1976

GENERAL ELECTION RESULT

10 OCT 1974: Labour 319; Conservative 277; Liberal 13; Scottish National Party 11; Plaid Cymru 3; Others 12. Total 635
Labour majority 4 (excl. the Speaker)

CABINET

Prime Minister, First Lord of the Treasury and Minister for the Civil Service H. Wilson
Lord President of the Council E. Short
Lord Chancellor Lord Elwyn Jones
Lord Privy Seal Lord Shepherd
Chancellor of the Exchequer D. Healey
Parliamentary Secretary to the Treasury R. Mellish
Foreign Secretary J. Callaghan

Home Secretary R. Jenkins
Minister of Agriculture, Fisheries and Food F. Peart
Secretary of State for Defence R. Mason
Secretary of State for Education and Science R. Prentice (Oct 1974–Jun 1975); F. Mulley (Jun 1975–Apr 1976)
Secretary of State for Employment M. Foot
Secretary of State for Energy E. Varley (Oct 1974–Jun 1975); T. Benn (Jun 1975–Apr 1976)
Secretary of State for the Environment A. Crosland
Minister for Planning and Local Government J. Silkin
Secretary of State for Social Services Mrs. B. Castle
Secretary of State for Industry T. Benn (Oct 1974–Jun 1975); E. Varley (Jun 1975–Apr 1976)
Chancellor of the Duchy of Lancaster H. Lever
Secretary of State for Northern Ireland M. Rees
Minister of Overseas Development R. Prentice (Jun 1975–Apr 1976)
Secretary of State for Prices and Consumer Protection Mrs. S. Williams
Secretary of State for Scotland W. Ross
Secretary of State for Trade and President of the Board of Trade P. Shore
Secretary of State for Wales J. Morris

IMPORTANT DATES IN PERSONAL AND POLITICAL LIFE

JUN 1937 Graduates with an outstanding first-class degree in Philosophy, Politics and Economics from Jesus College, Oxford.

OCT 1937 Research assistant to Sir William Beveridge. Their work on the trade cycle and unemployment is interrupted by the outbreak of war.

1 JAN 1940 Marries Mary Baldwin, daughter of a Congregational Minister.

JUN 1942 Appointed Joint Secretary of the Board of Investigation into wages in the coal industry, resulting in a national minimum wage for mineworkers.

JUL 1944 As Director of Economics and Statistics at the Ministry of Fuel and Power he prepares a statistical white paper on the coal industry.

JUL 1945 *New Deal For Coal*, a plan for the nationalisation of the coal industry, published.

5 JUL 1945 Elected Labour Member of Parliament for Ormskirk, Lancashire.

6 AUG 1945 Appointed Parliamentary Secretary to the Ministry of Works with responsibility for the post-war housing programme.

9 OCT 1945 Makes his maiden speech in the House of Commons.

OCT 1946 Appointed by Attlee to head the United Kingdom delegation to a commission of the Food and Agriculture Organisation in Washington; opens an adjournment debate on the commission's report on 6 Feb 1947, his first major speech in the House.

5 MAR 1947 Appointed Secretary for Overseas Trade. He visits Moscow on three occasions during 1947 as head of the Board of Trade delegation to negotiate supplies of timber and grain. The talks are successfully concluded in Dec 1947.

14 OCT 1947 Made a Privy Counsellor and President of the Board of Trade. Aged 31, he is the youngest cabinet minister of the 20th century.

FEB 1948 He negotiates an agreement to limit the export earnings of US film producers from American films shown in the United Kingdom and introduces a range of measures to assist the British film industry, including the Eady levy on cinema tickets and the establishment of the National Film Finance Corporation (1949).

4 NOV 1948 Wilson announces measures aimed at the removal of wartime rationing and production controls, referring to them the following day as a 'bonfire.'

23 FEB 1950 Elected Labour Member of Parliament for Huyton, Lancashire. He had chosen to be selected for Huyton after the parliamentary boundary proposals of 1948 radically altered the nature of the Ormskirk constituency.

23 APR 1951 Resigns as President of the Board of Trade over the Government's proposed defence budget.

APR 1951 Shortly after his resignation from the Cabinet Wilson accepts the position of part-time economic adviser to the timber firm of Montague L. Meyer.

4 DEC 1951 Becomes chairman of the 'Keep Left' group of Labour backbenchers, generally known as 'Bevanites' after the Cabinet resignations of Apr 1951. The group is formally disbanded in 1952 but continues unofficially until 1955.

6 FEB 1952 Death of King George VI, succeeded by Queen Elizabeth II.

APR 1954 Wilson is co-opted onto the Shadow Cabinet after Aneurin Bevan's resignation over proposals for a South East Asia Treaty Organisation (SEATO).

22 JUN 1955 Appointed Chairman of the Labour Party inquiry into party organisation following the 1955 election defeat.

JUL 1955 Following elections to the Shadow Cabinet Wilson becomes Opposition Spokesman on Trade.

NOV 1955 Government's Finance Bill is lost, due to a motion introduced by Wilson, a procedural triumph that enhances his standing with the Party leadership.

JAN 1956 Appointed Shadow Chancellor. In the years that follow, his speeches in the annual budget debates are widely acclaimed for their expertise and wit.

OCT 1956 Marcia Williams becomes his political secretary.

1958 Death of his mother, Ethel.

DEC 1959 Appointed Chairman of the Public Accounts Committee. At the same time he gives up his consultancy with Montague L. Meyer to avoid any perceived conflict of interest.

3 NOV 1960 Wilson's challenge for the leadership of the Labour Party fails. Hugh Gaitskell is re-elected by 166 votes to 81.

NOV 1961 Appointed Shadow Spokesman on Foreign Affairs.

8 NOV 1962 Defeated in the election for deputy leadership of the Labour Party, losing to George Brown by 103 votes to 133.

18 JAN 1963 Hugh Gaitskell, Leader of the Labour Party since 1955, dies suddenly after a brief illness.

14 FEB 1963 Wilson elected Leader of the Labour Party having defeated George Brown by 144 votes to 103.

1 APR 1963 During a visit to Washington to meet President Kennedy, Wilson also addresses the National Press Club, the first major presentation of Labour's policies to an American audience.

8 SEP 1963 In a speech in Glasgow he makes his first public reference to a 'University of the Air', later to become the Open University.

1 OCT 1963 At Scarborough Wilson makes his first speech to the annual party conference as Leader on the theme of Labour and the scientific revolution. He expounds a vision of Britain's economic revival through 'the white heat of this revolution' and technological advance.

IMPORTANT DATES IN PERSONAL AND POLITICAL LIFE—*Continued*

16 OCT 1964 With the victory of the Labour Party in the General Election Wilson becomes Prime Minister and is immediately faced with a balance of payments crisis. The option of devaluation is rejected in favour of import surcharges.

16 SEP 1965 The Department of Economic Affairs publishes the National Plan, a statement of the Government's proposals to achieve growth in a planned economy. The Plan is effectively abandoned after the sterling crisis of 1966.

11 NOV 1965 The Rhodesian Government issues a Proclamation of Independence, the first rebellion by a British dependency since the 18th century. Despite sanctions and Wilson's attempts to reach a settlement, Ian Smith's regime will survive until 1979.

16 DEC 1965 Wilson visits Washington for talks with President Johnson on Vietnam and Rhodesia. In return for American participation in sanctions and support of sterling the United Kingdom agrees to adhere to its foreign policy east of Suez.

31 MAR 1966 The General Election results in a greatly increased parliamentary majority for the Labour Party.

16 MAY 1966 A national strike by the Seamen's Union begins and lasts until 1 Jul, precipitating a sterling crisis.

3 JUL 1966 Frank Cousins, Minister of Technology, resigns over the Government's proposed incomes policy and returns to the Transport and General Workers Union. His resignation ends the informal concordat between the Government and the trade unions.

20 JUL 1966 In the House of Commons Wilson announces a package of deflationary measures to relieve pressure on sterling.

6 FEB 1967 Soviet Premier Kosygin arrives in London for talks. Wilson acts as intermediary between Kosygin and President Johnson in an attempt to contain the scale of fighting in Vietnam, but no agreement is reached.

2 MAY 1967 Wilson announces the Government's decision to apply for membership of the European Economic Community. The House of Commons endorses the proposals after a three-day debate but Britain's application is vetoed by General de Gaulle on 16 May and again in November.

4 NOV 1967 A new sterling crisis begins, precipitated by the increased cost of imported oil after the Arab-Israeli Six Day War and dock strikes in London and Liverpool.

13 NOV 1967 Wilson and James Callaghan, Chancellor of the Exchequer, decide to devalue the pound.

19 NOV 1967 Wilson makes a television broadcast to explain the consequences of devaluation to the British public.

15 MAR 1968 George Brown resigns as Foreign Secretary over the conduct of Government business. He believed that he had been excluded from discussions prior to an emergency meeting of the Privy Council and he later criticised the apparent tendency for Government policy to be determined by the Prime Minister rather than by the collective decisions of the Cabinet.

16 JAN 1969 *In Place of Strife*, the Government's white paper on industrial relations, published. Its proposals, incorporated in the Industrial Relations Bill, include the principle of legal sanctions against the Trades Union Congress to control industrial disputes. The Bill is abandoned due to widespread opposition.

19 AUG 1969 Wilson and the Cabinet meet Ulster politicians and agree on the 'Downing Street Declaration,' whereby British troops assume responsibility for law and order in Northern Ireland at Stormont's request.

19 JUN 1970 Wilson resigns as Prime Minister after the victory of the Conservative Party in the General Election.

29 JUN 1970 He is re-elected unopposed to the leadership of the Labour Party but ceases, at his own suggestion, to be Chairman of the Parliamentary Labour Party.

26 JUL 1971 Publication of *The Labour Government 1964–1970: A Personal Record.*

8 NOV 1971 Death of his father, Herbert Wilson, while visiting the Seddon family in Australia.

23 FEB 1973 The Trades Union Congress (TUC)-Labour Party Liaison Committee, of which Wilson is a member, publishes its statement 'Economic Policy and The Cost of Living.' It is later to be referred to as the 'social contract' between government and industry.

28 FEB 1974 The result of the General Election is inconclusive. Neither the Labour Party nor the Conservatives can achieve a parliamentary majority without the support of the minority parties.

4 MAR 1974 After the breakdown of negotiations between the Conservative Party and the Liberals, Wilson agrees to form a government.

25 MAY 1974 In a ministerial broadcast Wilson underlines the Government's support for the Northern Ireland Executive in the face of Loyalist disturbances. The Executive collapses the following day and the Northern Ireland Assembly is prorogued.

10 OCT 1974 After the second General Election of the year Wilson is able to form a government with a narrow overall majority in Parliament. It had been generally accepted since the formation of a minority administration in March that another election would be necessary to provide a firm mandate for the Labour Government's legislative programme.

5 JUN 1975 In a referendum, 67 per cent of the electorate support the Government's policy to remain in the European Economic Community. Wilson's political contemporaries acknowledge his achievement in keeping Britain in Europe and his party in power, yet undivided.

11 JUL 1975 Against a background of increasing inflation he announces details of an agreement between the Government and the TUC of a voluntary limit on pay increases of £6 per week.

16 MAR 1976 Wilson makes the unexpected announcement of his resignation as Prime Minister to take effect on 5 Apr. Many in the Cabinet are surprised and shocked, a reaction shared by the Parliamentary Party and the public. He gives four reasons for his decision: his length of service in government and opposition; his desire not to deny others the opportunity to seek election to the post; the need to give his successor time to settle in before the next election; and the need for a fresh approach.

14 JUN 1976 Invested as Knight of the Garter in a ceremony at Windsor Castle.

5 JAN 1977 Appointed Chairman of the Committee to Review the Functioning of Financial Institutions.

3 MAY 1979 Returned as Member of Parliament for Huyton for the last time.

JUN 1980 Report of the Committee on Financial Institutions published. Its recommendations include a Note of Dissent, signed by Sir Harold and others, calling for a special fund jointly financed by the City and the Government to aid industrial investment. The report is debated in the House of Commons on 23 Jan 1981.

27 FEB 1981 He announces that he will not seek renomination for the seat at Huyton. His decision is influenced by the strength of the Conservative majority in the House of Commons after the 1979 General Election and the likelihood of the new Government's surviving for a full parliamentary term.

21 JUL 1983 Made a life peer in the Dissolution Honours.

14 MAR 1984 Makes his maiden speech in the House of Lords in a debate on higher education.

14 JUL 1987 Peter Wright publishes *Spycatcher* in the USA. Its revelations about the British secret services cause an international sensation. The book appears to confirm Wilson's complaint of Aug 1977 about secret service surveillance in the 1970s.

1990 Unveils a plaque to commemorate the twenty-first anniversary of the Open University.

BACKGROUND

PHYSICAL CHARACTERISTICS AND HEALTH

In *The New Anatomy of Britain* Anthony Sampson wrote the following description of Wilson in 1965: 'His face is round and unobtrusive, with still a hint of the chubby look of his youth, but now looking older than his forty-nine years (he is the youngest prime minister since Lord Rosebery, and third youngest member of his cabinet, but that would not be guessed from his looks). His hair greyed before he was forty, and his shape in the last few years has become more paunchy and hunched. His pale eyes have always looked distant, giving no clue to what he is thinking. His mouth has looked sceptical since he was a baby, now emphasised by his perpetual pipe which, with all the lighting, relighting, scraping, cleaning and tapping, provides an additional smokescreen. His clothes add to the greyness—grey suits bought from Burtons, and dark patterned ties. And the picture is corroborated by the voice—clipped, dry, matter-of-fact, and still with a definite though modified Yorkshire accent'.

As a child in 1923 he underwent an operation for appendicitis and seven years later he contracted typhoid fever after drinking milk on a Scouts' outing. Both illnesses were followed by long periods of convalescence but he recovered to lead an active life and was renowned for his energy and capacity for work. From his father he inherited an exceptional memory and from his mother a calm temperament and low blood pressure. A smoker, he adopted the pipe that was to become his trademark in 1947. His legendary energy appeared to waver in the mid-1970s but rumours of serious ill health were unfounded. On the eve of the General Election in Oct 1974 he said 'According to the rumours, I have had three strokes, two heart attacks and I am suffering from leukaemia and I am going blind . . . I did strain my knee last November and I thought I was suffering from housemaid's knee. My knee is now better'. He underwent a successful operation for bowel cancer in Jun 1980.

EDUCATION

Primary 1920–27, New Street Council School, Milnsbridge

Secondary 1927–32, Royds Hall Secondary School, Huddersfield; 1932–34, Wirral Grammar School, Bebington

University 1934–37, Jesus College, Oxford. At the beginning of 1935 he changed his degree from history to Philosophy, Politics and Economics (PPE).

Prizes and awards 1927, County Minor Scholarship; 1934, Open Exhibition in Modern History to Jesus College, Oxford; 1936, Gladstone Memorial Prize; 1936, George Webb Medley Junior Economics Scholarship; 1937, George Webb Medley Senior Scholarship

Qualifications 1937, BA Hons (First Class)

Cultural and vocational background Religious observance had been of central importance throughout his life. As a boy, his family's social activities took place within the framework of the local Baptist church and he continued to attend church regularly in adulthood.

His cultural interests included the ballet and music, especially the work of Gilbert and Sullivan.

Languages He excelled academically in French, Latin and Italian.

NON-PARLIAMENTARY CAREER

Early occupations From 1937–39 he pursued an academic and teaching career at Oxford, first as a Lecturer in Economics at New College then as Research Fellow at University College teaching economic history. During these years he was also research assistant to Sir William Beveridge.

His civil service career began in Apr 1940 in London as a Research Statistician to the secretariat of the Anglo-French Co-ordinating Committee. In Jul 1940 he was transferred to the Economic Section of the Cabinet Secretariat to work on forward estimates of industrial manpower requirements. He joined the Ministry of Power as Head of the Manpower, Statistics and Intelligence Branch early in 1941. Later that year he accepted the post of Head of Statistics in the Department of Mines and acted as Joint Secretary of the Board of Investigation into wages and conditions in the coal industry. In Jun 1942 the Department of Mines merged into the Ministry of Fuel and Power and Wilson became its Director of Economics and Statistics from 1943–44.

Once adopted as a parliamentary candidate Wilson was obliged to resign from the civil service. He returned to University College, Oxford as Praelector in Economics and Domestic Bursar before his election as a Member of Parliament in July 1945.

Military service He volunteered for military service at the outbreak of war in 1939. Categorised as a specialist, he was drafted into the civil service instead. Call-up was slow and he remained at Oxford, officially assigned to the Potato Marketing Board as an economist, and continuing to work for Beveridge, until moving to London in 1940.

Other posts 1966–85, Chancellor of Bradford University; 1968, Elder Brother of Trinity House; 1972–73, President, Royal Statistical Society; 1976–85, President, Royal Shakespeare Theatre Company; 1976, Chairman, British Screen Advisory Council; 1976, Honorary President, Great Britain-USSR Association

HONOURS

Freedom of cities 1966, Sheffield; 1968, Huddersfield; 1969, Merthyr Tydfil; 1975, City of London

HONOURS—*Continued*

Academic 1963, Fellow, Jesus and University Colleges, Oxford; 1964, LLD Lancaster; 1965, DCL Oxford; 1965 LLD, Liverpool; 1966 LLD, Nottingham, Sussex; 1966, DTech Bradford; 1967, DUniv Essex; 1974, DUniv Open; 1993, Hon Member, Open University Graduates' Association

Other than peerage 1 Jan 1945, Officer, Order of the British Empire; 12 Jun 1969, Fellow of the Royal Society; 14 Jun 1976, Knight of the Garter

CLUBS

Athenaeum

HOBBIES AND SPORTS

In his youth he was a keen Boy Scout and long-distance runner. He captained the Wirral junior team in the Merseyside Championships and represented Oxford University at cross-country running. Later in life he took up golf.

The family pets included a labrador called Paddy and a Siamese cat.

FINANCES

Wilson's studies at Oxford were financed by the value of his Open Exhibition (£60), £50 from his father and a county grant of £190. The George Webb Medley Scholarships amounted to £400 and enabled him to become financially independent.

The Wilsons purchased their first home in 1948 for £5,100 with the help of a loan from his father and the rest raised on a mortgage. Future homes were also bought with mortgages or acquired leasehold. In 1971 he estimated the value of their three homes to be £60, 000.

From 1971–74 the cost of running his private office was independently estimated to be £25,000 p.a. To help him meet these costs friends contributed to a trust fund and the Labour Party made an allowance of £6, 000. However, only the serialisation of his memoirs in the *Sunday Times* in 1971 for an estimated £224,000 enabled him to meet the full cost of staff salaries and make financial provision for his future.

In 1991 it was announced that as a former Prime Minister he would receive nearly £30,000 p.a. towards the continuing additional office costs incurred as a result of his special position in public life.

Income As Research Fellow at University College, Oxford in 1938 his stipend was £400 p.a. During the war his civil service salary rose from £550 p.a. to approximately £1,200 p.a. From 1945–47 his ministerial salary as a Junior Minister was £1,500 p.a. and as President of the Board of Trade, £5,000 p.a. During the 1950s his MP's salary of between £1,000–£1,750 p.a. was supplemented by an allowance from Montague L. Meyer estimated at £1,500 p.a. As Leader of the Opposition his salary was £3,000 p.a. from 1963–64 and £4,500 from 1970–74 in addition to his parliamentary salary. As Prime Minister his salary was £10,000 p.a. in 1964, £14, 000 p.a. from 1965–70 and £20,000 p.a. from 1974–76. His parliamentary salary as a backbencher rose from £6,062 p.a. in 1976 to £15,308 p.a. in 1983.

Pensions Prime Minister's pension

Legacies His father Herbert Wilson died leaving £212 in 1971.

Debts In a newspaper interview in 1971 he said he had a bank overdraft of £4,739.

ANECDOTES

1951, When Hugh Dalton reported to Gaitskell that John Strachey was considering joining Aneurin Bevan and Harold Wilson in resigning, the reply was 'We shall be well rid of all three of them.'

1965, In July Sir Alec Douglas-Home announced his resignation as Leader of the Opposition. The Prime Minister and Secretary of State for Economic Affairs, George Brown, were together in the Cabinet Room when they heard the news. Lord Kennet, a junior minister, was in attendance: he remembers that the two men clasped each other and did a celebratory jig around the cabinet table singing 'There Will Never Be Another You.'

1966, During the election campaign he was struck in the eye by a stink bomb thrown by a schoolboy. His eye was slightly damaged and the police cautioned the assailant but Wilson said 'With an aim like that he ought to be in the English eleven' (a reference to the national cricket team).

1969, On Thursday 17 Jul Richard Crossman, Secretary of State for Health and Social Security, made the following entry in his diary: ' . . . I must refer to the Prime Minister's Questions this afternoon, because I think they were one of the most brilliant parliamentary occasions I have ever attended. We shall never understand Harold's hold on the Parliamentary Labour Party until we understand this. If you look at today's Hansard you will see his elegant answer to Sydney Bidwell on the announcement of the resignation of John Davies from the C.B.I. Then the P.M. switched to rather a delicate Question about the nationalisation of the pharmaceutical industry and then to another on nuclear weapons. On health he just put things in their place, on nuclear weapons he was serious and gave nothing away. Eldon Griffiths asked a snide Question on whether the Prime Minister had received representations on parliamentary boundaries from residents of Huyton. Harold waited, making little interludes, and then said with tremendous effect, "The total number of communications about the Government's Bill which I have received in both my capacity as Prime Minister and as constituency M.P. from constituents—the total number—is not one, Sir. With regard to the number received from the whole of Britain, the answer is about twenty." Then he rebuked Geoffrey Rippon and scored off our friend Jeremy Thorpe.

'It was the most deft and brilliant exhibition of parliamentary lightweight boxing. Harold prepares it all carefully in advance, working on all these quips and quiddities and interesting facts. As he sat down he said, "That was fun".'

1970, Joe Haines, Wilson's Press Secretary, remembered how, after the election defeat, the Wilsons had left Huyton in the early hours of the morning for London. Sometime after dawn a *Sun* photographer, in a car following Wilson's on the motorway, obtained a picture of the Prime Minister sleeping with his head on Mary's shoulder. 'It said all that there was to say.'

QUOTATIONS

1956, Traders and financiers all over the world had been listening to the Chancellor. For months he had said that if he could not stop the wage claims, the country was 'facing disaster'. . . . Rightly or wrongly these people believed him. For them, 5th September—the day that the Trades Union Congress unanimously rejected the policy of wage restraint—marked the end of an era. And all these financiers, all the little gnomes in Zurich and the other financial centres about whom we keep on hearing, started to make their dispositions in regard to sterling. (Speech to the House of Commons)

1962, This Party is a moral crusade or it is nothing. (Speech at the Labour Party annual conference)

1963, We are re-defining and we are re-stating our socialism in terms of the scientific revolution. . . . The Britain that is going to be forged in the white heat of this revolution will be no place for restrictive practices or outdated methods on either side of industry. (Speech at the Labour Party annual conference)

1964, A week is a long time in politics. (Attributed; probably first used in a Lobby briefing in the wake of the sterling crisis shortly after he became Prime Minister)

1967, From now the pound abroad is worth 14 percent or so less in terms of other currencies. It does not mean, of course, that the pound here in Britain, in your pocket or purse or in your bank, has been devalued. (Ministerial broadcast)

1970, Referring to the meeting of the Conservative policy-making committee at Selsdon Park, Croydon: 'Selsdon Man is designing a system of society for the ruthless and the pushing, the uncaring . . . his message to the rest is: you're out on your own.' (Speech in London)

c. 1970, You don't need to worry about the outside left—they've got nowhere else to go: it's the inside left that you must worry about. (Attributed, in *The New Anatomy of Britain* by Anthony Sampson, 1971)

c. 1970–74, Whichever party is in office, the Treasury is in power. (Attributed, in *The Changing Anatomy of Britain* by Anthony Sampson, 1981)

RESIDENCES

10 Southway, Hampstead Garden Suburb, London
12 Southway, Hampstead Garden Suburb, London
Lowenva, Hugo Town, Scilly Isles
10 Downing Street
5 Lord North Street, Westminster, London
Grange Farm, near Little Missenden, Buckinghamshire

MEMORIALS

PORTRAITS

c. 1974, by Ruskin Spear, National Portrait Gallery, London; 1991, by Henry Mee, House of Commons, 1 Parliament Street, London

OTHER MEMORIALS

1950, Huyton Council named Wilson Road on Huyton's industrial estate after him in recognition of his efforts to bring new industry to the area; 1990, The Harold Wilson Building at the Open University, Milton Keynes, Buckinghamshire.

BIBLIOGRAPHIC INFORMATION

LETTERS AND PERSONAL PAPERS

Lord Wilson's private papers are held by the Bodleian Library, Oxford. Many letters and memoranda are cited in *The Labour Government 1964–1970: A Personal Record* (1971).

State papers are available at the Public Record Office, Kew, for the Second World War, when Wilson was a temporary civil servant, and for his period of ministerial office up to 1951 but not—under the thirty-year rule—for his period as Prime Minister from 1964. 1964, *The New Britain-Labour's Plan: Selected Speeches*; 1964, *Purpose in Politics: Selected Speeches*; 1966, *Purpose of Power: Selected Speeches.*

PUBLICATIONS

1945, *New Deal for Coal*; 1950, *We Accuse: Labour's Indictment of Tory Economic Policy* (co-author); 1952, *In Place of Dollars*; 1953, *Today They Die: The Case for World Co-operation*; 1953, *Two Out of Three: The Problem of World Poverty*; 1953, *The War on World Poverty: An Appeal to the Conscience of Mankind*; 1954, *It Need Not Happen: the Alternative to German Rearmament* (co-author); 1957, *Remedies for Inflation*; 1964, *The Relevance of British Socialism*; 1971, *The Labour Government 1964–1970: A Personal Record*; 1976, *The Governance of Britain*; 1977, *A Prime Minister on Prime Ministers*; 1979, *Final Term: The Labour Government 1974–1976*; 1981, *Chariots of Israel: Britain, America and the State of Israel*; 1986, *Memoirs: The Making of a Prime Minister 1916–1964.*

FURTHER READING

Morgan, A. *Harold Wilson.* London, 1992.
Noel, G. E. *Harold Wilson and the New Britain: The Making of a Modern Prime Minister.* 2nd ed. London, 1964.
Pimlott, B. *Harold Wilson.* London, 1992.
Smith, L. *Harold Wilson: The Authentic Portrait.* London, 1964.
Ziegler, P. *Wilson: The Authorised Life of Lord Wilson of Rievaulx.* London, 1993.

E.J.J.

Bettmann

Edward Heath

Lived 1916–
Political Party Conservative
Prime Minister 19 June 1970–4 March 1974
Government Conservative
Reigning Monarch Elizabeth II

Plus fait douceur que violence Gentleness achieves more than violence

HEATH AS PRIME MINISTER

Heath was a successful Chief Whip under Churchill and Eden and spent much of the time between 1960 and 1963 trying to negotiate terms for Britain to join the European Communities. In 1965 he became the first elected leader of the Conservative party and continued to press for British membership in the European Communities, which he achieved as Prime Minister. His other goals were to bring increased law and order to the nation, to restrict immigration, to promote free trade and to restrict the power of trade unions, which he confronted when a prices and income policy was introduced. In 1973 the administration was partly blown off course by an increase in the price of oil and further economic deterioration, culminating in the 'three day week' during the winter of 1973–1974. He succeeded in passing the necessary legislation for Britain to join the European Communities during the parliamentary session of 1971–72. Negotiations with striking miners failed and violence was renewed in Northern Ireland, leading Heath to call a General Election in spring 1974, where the result was almost a dead heat between the two major parties. Failing to strike a deal with the Liberal party he resigned as Prime Minister. He was defeated by Wilson in a further General Election in October 1974 and by Mrs. Thatcher for the party leadership in February 1975.

PERSONAL INFORMATION

Names Edward Richard George Heath
Born 9 Jul 1916
Birthplace 2 Holmwood Villas, Albion Road, St. Peter's, Kent
Religion Anglican
Ancestry English. Early generations of the Heath family were variously craftsmen and mariners living in Devon and then, from the early 19th century, in the adjoining Kent towns of Ramsgate and Broadstairs.
First entered Parliament 23 Feb 1950
Date appointed PM 19 Jun 1970
Age at appointment 53 years, 335 days
Date ceased to be PM 4 Mar 1974
Total time as PM 3 years, 259 days
Zodiac sign Cancer

FATHER

William George Heath
Date and place of birth 11 Oct 1888, Ramsgate, Kent
Occupation He worked as a carpenter for local builders in Broadstairs and, from 1916–23, at the Vickers aircraft factory in Crayford. After the death of his employer in 1930 he was able first to rent, then buy, work premises and thus established his own small building firm in Broadstairs.
Dates of marriages 1) 10 May 1913, Edith Anne Pantony (d. 15 Oct 1951); 2) 18 Jul 1953, Doris Lewis (d. 15 Jun 1963); 3) 10 Oct 1964, Ethel Mary Emes (d. 21 Aug 1984)
Age when PM took office 81 years, 251 days
Date of death 15 Oct 1976
Place of cremation Charing, Kent

MOTHER

Edith Anne Pantony
Date and place of birth 6 Jun 1889, St. Peter's, near Broadstairs, Kent.
Profile After leaving school at 14 she entered domestic service as a lady's maid to a family with homes in London and Broadstairs.
Date of marriage 10 May 1913
Date and place of death 15 Oct 1951, Broadstairs, Kent
Place of burial St. Peter's, Kent

BROTHERS AND SISTERS

Edward Heath is the elder of two sons.
From his father's first marriage:
John Ronald, b. 26 Aug 1920; m. 1) 25 Oct 1947, Marian Lucy Easton, 2) 13 Dec 1958, Muriel Constance Jackson; apprenticed to the family business then joined the Army in 1939 serving with the British Expeditionary Force, Royal Army Ordnance Corps and the Royal Electrical and Mechanical Engineers; after the war qualified as a building inspector and worked in local government; d. 20 Aug 1984
There were no children from his father's later marriages.

MARRIAGE

Heath is unmarried.

LIFE AND CAREER

PARLIAMENTARY ELECTIONS FOUGHT

*(*designates candidate elected)*

DATE 23 Feb 1950. General Election
CONSTITUENCY Bexley
RESULT E.R.G. Heath* (Con) 25,854; E.A. Bramall (Lab) 25, 721; Miss M.E. Hart (Lib) 4,186; C.C. Job (Com) 481

DATE 25 Oct 1951. General Election
CONSTITUENCY Bexley
RESULT E.R.G. Heath* (Con) 29,069; E.A. Bramall (Lab) 27,430

DATE 26 May 1955. General Election
CONSTITUENCY Bexley
RESULT E.R.G. Heath* (Con) 28,610; R.J. Minney (Lab) 24,111

DATE 8 Oct 1959. General Election
CONSTITUENCY Bexley
RESULT E.R.G. Heath* (Con) 32,025; E.A. Bramall (Lab) 23,392

DATE 15 Oct 1964. General Election
CONSTITUENCY Bexley
RESULT E.R.G. Heath* (Con) 25,716; L.L. Reeves (Lab) 21,127; P.L. McArthur (Lib) 6,161; J.A. Paul (Ind) 1, 263

DATE 31 Mar 1966. General Election
CONSTITUENCY Bexley
RESULT E.R.G. Heath* (Con) 26,377; R.L. Butler (Lab) 24,044; R.F. Lloyd (Lib) 4,405

DATE 18 Jun 1970. General Election
CONSTITUENCY Bexley
RESULT E.R.G. Heath* (Con) 27,075; J.C. Cartwright (Lab/Co-op) 19,017; E.P.G. Harrison (Lib) 3,222; E.J. R.L. Heath (Ind Con) 938; M.P. Coney (Ind Con) 833

DATE 28 Feb 1974. General Election
CONSTITUENCY Sidcup
RESULT E.R.G. Heath* (Con) 20,448; C.F. Hargrave (Lab) 10,750; O.C.N. Moxon (Lib) 9,847; D.C.T. Bennett (Ind) 613

DATE 10 Oct 1974. General Election
CONSTITUENCY Sidcup
RESULT E.R.G. Heath* (Con) 18,991; W.J. Jennings (Lab) 11,448; I.R.P. Josephs (Lib) 6,954; D.H. Jones (Ind/Cons) 174; M.J. Norton (Ind) 61

DATE 3 May 1979. General Election
CONSTITUENCY Sidcup
RESULT E.R.G. Heath* (Con) 23,692; F. Keohane (Lab) 10,236; P. Vickers (Lib) 4,980; A. D. Webb (Nat Front) 774

DATE 9 Jun 1983. General Election
CONSTITUENCY Old Bexley and Sidcup
RESULT E.R.G. Heath* (Con) 22,422; P. Vickers (Lib) 9, 704; C.A. Kiff (Lab) 5,116

DATE 11 Jun 1987. General Election
CONSTITUENCY Old Bexley and Sidcup
RESULT E.R.G. Heath* (Con) 24,350; T.H. Pearce (Lib) 8,076; Dr. H.G.A. Stoate (Lab) 6,762

DATE 9 Apr 1992. General Election
CONSTITUENCY Old Bexley and Sidcup

PARLIAMENTARY ELECTIONS FOUGHT—*Continued*

RESULT Sir E.R.G. Heath* (Con) 24,450; Ms. D. Brierly (Lab) 8,751; D.J. Nicolle (Lib Dem) 6,438; B. Rose (Ind/ Con) 733; R. Stephens (Natural Law Party) 148

PARTY ACTIVITY

Party Leadership 1965–75, Leader of the Conservative Party

Other offices 1964–70, Chairman, National Advisory Committee on Policy; 1964–70, Chairman, Future Economic Policy Sub-Committee; 1974, President, Conservative Commonwealth & Overseas Council; 1975, President, Greater London Young Conservatives; 1980, President, Conservative Group for Europe

Membership of group or faction 1950–51, One Nation Group, so called to underline their attachment to Disraeli's conception of a united people.

PARLIAMENTARY AND MINISTERIAL EXPERIENCE

Maiden Speech 26 Jun 1950. He spoke in favour of the Schuman Plan for a European Coal and Steel Community (*HC Deb*, vol 476, col 1959–1964)

Opposition offices 1951, Assistant Whip; 1964, Shadow Spokesman on Economic Affairs; 1965, Shadow Chancellor; 1965–70, 1974–75, Leader of the Opposition

Privy Counsellor 30 Dec 1955

Ministerial Offices Junior Lord of the Treasury and Senior Government Whip 7 Nov 1951–28 May 1952; Joint Deputy Chief Whip 28 May 1952–3 Jul 1953; Deputy Chief Whip 3 Jul 1953–20 Dec 1955; Parliamentary Secretary to the Treasury and Government Chief Whip 30 Dec 1955–14 Oct 1959; Minister of Labour 14 Oct 1959–27 Jul 1960; Lord Privy Seal 27 Jul 1960–20 Oct 1963; Secretary of State for Industry, Trade and Regional Development and President of the Board of Trade 20 Oct 1963–15 Oct 1964; First Lord of the Treasury and Minister for the Civil Service 19 Jun 1970–4 Mar 1974

Opposition Leader while PM 1970–74, Harold Wilson

Father of the House 9 Apr 1992–

GOVERNMENTS FORMED

Administration 19 Jun 1970–4 Mar 1974

GENERAL ELECTION RESULT

18 JUN 1970: Conservative 330; Labour 288; Liberal 6; Others 6. Total 630
Conservative majority 31 (excl. the Speaker)

CABINET

Prime Minister, First Lord of the Treasury and Minister for the Civil Service E. Heath

Lord President of the Council W. Whitelaw (Jun 1970–Apr 1972); R. Carr (Apr–Nov 1972); J. Prior (Nov 1972–Mar 1974)

Lord Chancellor Lord Hailsham

Lord Privy Seal Earl Jellicoe (Jun 1970–May 1973); Lord Windlesham (Jun 1973–Mar 1974)

Chancellor of the Exchequer I. Macleod (Jun–Jul 1970); A. Barber (Jul 1970–Mar 1974)

Foreign Secretary Sir A. Douglas-Home

Home Secretary R. Maudling (Jun 1970–Jul 1972); R. Carr (Jul 1972–Mar 1974)

Minister of Agriculture, Fisheries and Food J. Prior (Jun 1970–Nov 1972); J. Godber (Nov 1972–Mar 1974)

Secretary of State for Defence (and Minister of Aviation Supply from 1 May 1971) Lord Carrington (Jun 1970–Jan 1974); Sir I. Gilmour (Jan–Mar 1974)

Secretary of State for Education and Science Mrs. M. Thatcher

Secretary of State for Employment (and Productivity till 12 Nov 1970) R. Carr (Jun 1970–Apr 1972); M. Macmillan (Apr 1972–Dec 1973); W. Whitelaw (Dec 1973–Mar 1974)

Secretary of State for Energy Lord Carrington (Jan -Mar 1974)

Secretary of State for the Environment P. Walker (Oct 1970–Nov 1972); G. Rippon (Nov 1972–Mar 1974)

Secretary of State for Social Services Sir K. Joseph

Minister of Housing and Local Government P. Walker (Jun -Oct 1970) (office reorganised under Environment 15 Oct 1970)

Chancellor of the Duchy of Lancaster (with special responsibility for Europe) A. Barber (Jun–Jul 1970); G. Rippon (Jul 1970–Nov 1972); J. Davies (Nov 1972–Mar 1974)

Secretary of State for Northern Ireland W. Whitelaw (Apr 1972–Dec 1973); F. Pym (Dec 1973–Mar 1974)

Paymaster General M. Macmillan (Dec 1973–Mar 1974)

Secretary of State for Scotland G. Campbell

Minister of Technology G. Rippon (Jun–Jul 1970); J. Davies (Jul–Oct 1970) (office reorganised under Trade and Industry 15 Oct 1970)

President of the Board of Trade M. Noble (Jun -Oct 1970) (office reorganised under Trade and Industry 15 Oct 1970)

Secretary of State for Trade and Industry and President of the Board of Trade J. Davies (Oct 1970–Nov 1972); P. Walker (Nov 1972–Mar 1974)

Minister for Trade and Consumer Affairs Sir G. Howe (Nov 1972–Mar 1974)

Secretary of State for Wales P. Thomas

IMPORTANT DATES IN PERSONAL AND POLITICAL LIFE

1939 Heath elected President of the Oxford Union on an anti-appeasement platform. He had been a successful debater, notably winning the motion against Chamberlain's policy of appeasement in Oct 1938 and defeating an earlier motion to approve the Labour Party's economic programme, which had been supported by Hugh Dalton MP in Nov 1937.

JUN 1939 Graduates with a second-class degree in Philosophy, Politics and Economics from Balliol College, Oxford.

1945 Appointed Major of 334 Battery of the 107th HAA Regiment then stationed in Belgium. The Battery is to take part in the crossing of the Rhine under his command.

8 NOV 1945 Mentioned in despatches and awarded the MBE in 1946 for war service.

1947 Placed joint first in the administrative class examination for the civil service and is assigned to the Ministry of Civil Aviation's Directorate of Long-Term Planning.

MAR 1947 Appointed Lieutenant-Colonel of the 2nd Regiment of the HAC (HAA), a Territorial regiment, reformed in May 1947. Heath remains their commanding officer until 1951.

23 FEB 1950 Elected Conservative Member of Parliament for Bexley, Kent.

26 JUN 1950 Makes his maiden speech in the House of Commons.

OCT 1950 Publication of the pamphlet *One Nation—a Tory Approach to Social Problems* by the One Nation Group, of which Heath was a founder member. It advocates an improved Britain with better housing, education, physical health and reformed industrial relations.

15 OCT 1951 Death of his mother, Edith, at the family home in Broadstairs.

7 NOV 1951 Appointed a Lord Commissioner of the Treasury and Government Whip.

30 DEC 1955 Made a Privy Counsellor upon his appointment as Parliamentary Secretary to the Treasury and Government Chief Whip.

26 JUL 1956 President Nasser of Egypt nationalises the Anglo-French Suez Canal Company and seizes control of the Canal. An Anglo-French ultimatum to the Egyptians to overthrow Nasser is followed by the bombing of Egyptian airfields on 31 October.

1 NOV 1956 In the face of widespread hostility the Government survives a censure motion on its decision to use military force. The fact that all the Conservative MPs present vote against the censure motion, despite deep divisions within the Party, is widely attributed to Heath's skill and professionalism as Chief Whip. Similarly, on 8 Nov, another censure motion is defeated with only 6 Conservative abstentions instead of the 20 that had been feared.

11 JAN 1957 Harold Macmillan succeeds Sir Anthony Eden as Prime Minister and Leader of the Conservative Party. Heath's favourable report as Chief Whip on the attitude of the Parliamentary Party towards Macmillan had helped to secure his victory. Their celebratory dinner at the Turf Club that evening is discovered by the press and widely publicised.

14 OCT 1959 Following the Conservative victory in the General Election Heath becomes Minister of Labour and a member of the Cabinet. He helps to avert a national railway strike in Feb 1960 and urges more Conservative voters to join the trade union movement.

27 JUL 1960 Appointed Lord Privy Seal at the Foreign Office, responsible for the negotiation of terms for Britain's entry into the European Economic Community. To this end, he flies 100,000 miles touring the capitals of Europe from 1961–63 trying to reach an economic agreement.

29 JAN 1963 France vetoes Britain's application to join the EEC because of the perceived threat to the Community of her political and military connections with the USA. Heath returns to London, deeply disappointed, but his work is the subject of widespread tributes at home and overseas and is recognised by the award of the Charlemagne Prize of the City of Aachen for 'the most notable achievement in the service of encouraging international understanding and co-operation in Europe'. De Gaulle predicts that it will be Heath who will eventually enable Britain to enter Europe.

20 OCT 1963 Appointed Secretary of State for Industry, Trade and Regional Development and President of the Board of Trade in Sir Alec Douglas-Home's administration.

10 MAR 1964 The Second Reading of Heath's Bill to repeal Resale Price Maintenance (the selling of goods at the prices fixed by manufacturers) provokes the greatest internal revolt within the Conservative Party since the war, and the Government's majority falls to one in the vote on 11 March. The Bill survives to become the Resale Prices Act in Jul 1964.

23 OCT 1964 Heath, out of office after the defeat of the Conservatives in the General Election, becomes a Director of Brown, Shipley, merchant bankers, until Aug 1965.

24 OCT 1964 Appointed Shadow Spokesman on Economic Affairs and Chairman of the Conservative Party's Policy Advisory Committe.

8 FEB 1965 Appointed Chief Shadow Spokesman on Economic Affairs (Shadow Chancellor). His organisation of the opposition to the Labour Governement's Finance Bill, a lengthy and complex Bill which requires over 100 divisions between May and July, contributes to his emergence as a potential Party Leader.

22 JUL 1965 Sir Alec Douglas-Home suddenly announces his resignation.

27 JUL 1965 In the first ballot for the Leadership of the Conservative Party, a method newly adopted in Feb 1965, Heath secures 150 votes, Reginald Maudling 133 and Enoch Powell 15. Although Heath has not received the 15 per cent overall majority required to avoid a second ballot, Maudling and Powell withdraw from the contest.

2 AUG 1965 Formally adopted as Leader of the Conservative Party. At 49 Heath is the youngest Leader since the office was created—for Disraeli—in 1868, and the first to be elected.

6 OCT 1965 Heath launches his new policy statement *Putting Britain Right Ahead*, a collation of the work of the various policy groups that he supervised as Chairman of the Policy Advisory Committee.

31 MAR 1966 Despite the Conservative defeat in the General Election, Heath remains Leader of the Party. His performance in the campaign is considered to have been better than that of any of his potential rivals and there is no enthusiasm for another leadership battle.

20 APR 1968 In a speech in Birmingham on immigration, Enoch Powell, a member of the Shadow Cabinet, describes his fears for the future of race relations in Britain: 'Like the Roman, I seem to see the river Tiber foaming with much blood'. Heath dismisses him the following day for delivering a speech which he considers 'racialist' in tone and only avoids an open split within the Conservative Party by reaffirming a policy of rigorous immigration control.

31 DEC 1969 Heath and his crew win the Sydney to Hobart ocean race on his yacht *Morning Cloud*—the first British team to win since 1945.

30 JAN 1970 Heath holds a weekend meeting of his senior parliamentary colleagues and their advisers at the Selsdon Park Hotel, Croydon, to determine the broad lines of their election strategy. They reaffirm their determination to give priority to the enforcement of law and order, to reduce the level of direct taxation, to reform trade union laws and to restrict immigration. Several years later, on 19 Sep 1973, the Selsdon Group is launched at the same hotel. Formed by those Conservatives who regarded the Government's industrial and economic policies as a reversal of the 1970 manifesto commitments, the Group aims to promote the philosophy of the free market economy within the Conservative Party.

19 JUN 1970 The Conservative Party wins the General Election, contrary to the predictions of the opinion polls, and Heath becomes Prime Minister.

20 JUL 1970 Iain Macleod, the Chancellor of the Exchequer, suffers a heart attack and dies. At 56, he has been the most formidable and experienced member of the Cabinet and the driving force behind the post-1964 re-

IMPORTANT DATES IN PERSONAL AND POLITICAL LIFE—*Continued*

assessment of Conservative policy. He is succeeded by Anthony Barber.

10 OCT 1970 In his first speech to the Conservative Party conference as Prime Minister, Heath promises 'a change so radical, a revolution so quiet and yet so total that it will go beyond the programme for a Parliament'. The Government's economic strategy will be to leave more to individual or to corporate effort and to make savings in Government expenditure. He identifies excessive wage claims as the cause of inflation and stresses that the Government will not assist employers in the private sector who accede to such demands.

FEB 1971 The Cabinet agrees to rescue part of Rolls-Royce after its sudden financial collapse in Jan 1971. The key aeroplane, gas turbine and marine engine segments are nationalised as Rolls-Royce Ltd. in order to safeguard the livelihood of many thousands of workers in Britain and the USA where the Lockheed Aircraft Corporation is dependent on Rolls-Royce engines for the TriStar aircraft. Heath's actions save the industrial heart of the company but appear contrary to the Government's earlier stated purpose.

19–21 MAY 1971 At the start of two days of talks in Paris on the EEC Heath says: ' . . . We are living an historic moment comparable to that 20 years ago' [when six European nations agreed to pool their coal and steel resources]. He reaches an understanding with President Pompidou of France on the remaining obstacles to British entry and clears the way for the final round of negotiations.

5 AUG 1971 The Industrial Relations Bill becomes law despite considerable trade union opposition. Its proposals, similar in intent to those of the previous Labour Government, seek to control industrial disputes through union registration and the establishment of the Industrial Relations Court.

22 JAN 1972 In Brussels Heath signs the Treaty of Accession, formally establishing Britain's membership of the European Economic Community. The long battle to get the enabling legislation through the House of Commons begins, against the great majority of Labour MPs and a substantial block of Conservatives, led by Enoch Powell.

30 JAN 1972 In Londonderry the army opens fire on demonstrators taking part in an illegal civil rights march, killing 13 people. 'Bloody Sunday' has a dramatic and far-reaching effect on the British Government's thinking about the Ulster crisis and the Prime Minister orders a complete reappraisal of the political and military issues involved.

17 FEB 1972 The Government secures the Second Reading of the European Communities Bill by a majority of only 8 votes. Although 15 Conservative MPs had voted with the Opposition, the victory nonetheless represents a political triumph for the Prime Minister.

18 FEB 1972 Following a strike by coal miners in support of a pay claim and the subsequent disruption to energy supplies, Heath holds talks with the National Union of Mineworkers and their employers, the National Coal Board, at 10 Downing Street. The dispute is settled in the miners' favour and work resumes on 28 Feb, but many supporters of the Conservative Party regard the outcome as a surrender to militant trade unionism.

24 MAR 1972 After talks with Brian Faulkner, the Ulster Premier, Heath announces the suspension of the Stormont Parliament, the introduction of direct rule, the phasing-out of internment and provision for periodic plebiscites concerning the border. These measures are intended to win the confidence of the Catholic minority in Northern Ireland but are opposed by Unionist MPs and their Conservative allies at Westminster.

24 MAY 1972 As a result of parliamentary boundary proposals which would make Bexley a marginal seat, Heath agrees to contest Sidcup instead at the next General Election.

18 JUL 1972 Reginald Maudling resigns from the Cabinet because of a conflict of interest between his role as Home Secretary and the police investigation into the involvement of civil servants and local government officials in the Poulson affair.

9 AUG 1972 The Industry Act 1972 represents one of the most dramatic reversals of Heath's administration. By 1972 he has become convinced that the Government must intervene to revive industry and that only an incomes policy can curb inflation. The Act provides large funds to the Department of Trade and Industry and constructs a statutory incomes policy.

26 SEP 1972 Heath puts forward counter-inflationary proposals during tripartite talks between the Government and trades union and employers' representatives at Chequers.

6 NOV 1972 After further meetings fail to produce an agreement Heath announces a three-phase statutory control of prices and incomes beginning with a pay, price, rent and dividend freeze. Phases 2 and 3 follow in Apr and Nov 1973, in which pay increases are limited and price controls retained.

1 JAN 1973 Britain formally joins the European Economic Community.

23 MAY 1973 Earl Jellicoe, Lord Privy Seal, resigns from the Cabinet over rumours of his involvement in 'call-girl scandals'. An enquiry exonerates him from any breach of security.

6 OCT 1973 The outbreak of the Middle East war is followed by a cut-back in oil supplies from the region and the quadrupling of world oil prices. The subsequent effect on transport and industrial costs and the cost of living threatens Phase 3 of the Government's prices and incomes policy before it can be brought into effect.

9 DEC 1973 An agreement is reached on the creation of a Council of Ireland after 4 days of tripartite talks between the London and Dublin Governments and the party leaders from Northern Ireland at Sunningdale, Berkshire. The new Northern Ireland Executive takes office at midnight on 31 Dec 1973, ending 21 months of direct rule.

13 DEC 1973 In response to the worsening energy crisis Heath announces restrictions in the use of electricity by the bulk of industry and commerce to 3 days per week from 31 Dec 1973. The crisis in oil supplies has been compounded since November by industrial disputes involving the coal miners, power engineers and train drivers.

14 JAN 1974 Talks between Heath and Trades Union Congress leaders fail to resolve the miners' overtime ban which had begun on 12 Nov 1973. An early General Election appears imminent.

28 FEB 1974 The General Election results in a delicate balance of power between the Labour Party (301 seats), the Conservatives (296) and the Liberals (14). Heath does not resign immediately but remains in office over the weekend of 1–3 Mar to try to form a coalition with the Liberals.

4 MAR 1974 Liberal MPs reject Heath's offer of a coalition because it does not include a commitment to proportional representation. Heath resigns as Prime Minister that evening and Harold Wilson forms a Labour Government.

10 OCT 1974 After the second General Election the Labour Government is returned to power with an overall majority of 3 seats.

14 NOV 1974 In a written message to the 1922 Committee of Conservative backbench MPs, Heath indicates that he will submit himself for re-election as Party Leader as soon as new procedures can be devised. (The 1965 rules had made no provision for the Leader's formal removal.)

17 DEC 1974 The changes recommended by a Committee under Lord Home of Hirsel include the regular election of the Party Leader at the beginning of a new Parliament and annually thereafter.

23 JAN 1975 Heath announces his acceptance of the Committee's recommendations and the date of the first ballot.

4 FEB 1975 Heath is defeated in the first ballot for the Leadership and immediately stands down from the contest. Margaret Thatcher secures 130 votes, Heath 119 and Hugh Fraser 16. New contenders emerge and on the second ballot on 10 Feb Margaret Thatcher gains a clear overall majority to become the new Leader of the Conservative Party.

15 OCT 1976 Death of his father, William George Heath.

29 NOV 1977 Appointed a member of the Independent Commission on International Development Issues (Brandt Commission). In Feb 1980 Heath helps to launch the Commission's report *North-South: A Programme for Survival.*

14 MAY 1979 Offered the post of Ambassador to the United States but declines, saying that he wishes to remain in the House of Commons.

9 JUN 1983 Heath's constituency renamed Old Bexley and Sidcup following parliamentary boundary proposals.

3 FEB 1985 Publication of an interview with the *Sunday Times* in which Heath describes the Government's policies as '1860 laissez-faire liberalism that never was' rather than true Conservatism.

23 OCT 1990 Following talks with President Saddam Hussein of Iraq, Heath secures the unconditional release of 33 British hostages.

23 APR 1992 Appointed Knight of the Garter and invested in a ceremony at Windsor Castle on 15 June.

27 APR 1992 As Father of the House he presides over the election of the new Speaker of the House of Commons, Betty Boothroyd, the first woman to hold the office.

15 SEP 1992 A gala concert is held at the Guildhall, City of London, to celebrate his achievements.

BACKGROUND

PHYSICAL CHARACTERISTICS AND HEALTH

Shortly before his election as Leader of the Conservative Party in 1965 he was described thus: 'Heath has a blank, boyish face, smooth grey hair, an intense manner which gives way suddenly and disconcertingly to a bright smile and shaking laughter . . . ' (A. Sampson. *Anatomy of Britain Today*, 1965, p. 77.) and in 1970: 'Today, with his "comfortable" yet compact figure, a good and usually sun-tanned colour, clear blue eyes and strong grey hair, he looks just what he is—a man of middle years in excellent physical condition. He stands 5 ft. 10½ in. and he weighs, in his own words, 165 lb. . . . ' (G. Hutchinson. *Edward Heath, A Personal and Political Biography*, 1970, p. 152.)

He suffered the usual childhood ailments of whooping cough, chicken pox and measles but was otherwise considered to be an exceptionally healthy, if rather chubby, child. At his army medical in 1939 he was declared 'fit for every kind of service' and during the war senior officers commented on his stamina. He emerged relatively unscathed apart from an operation to remove his appendix and a scalp wound sustained during the defence of Nijmegen in Dec 1944. In 1959 he was hospitalized with jaundice. A non-smoker, his moderate and discerning tastes in food and drink and regular exercise have enhanced a strong constitution. In 1981 he received medical treatment for a glandular complaint, followed by a brief period of convalescence.

EDUCATION

Primary 1920–23, Crayford Infants School; 1923–26, St Peter's Church of England School, Broadstairs

Secondary 1926–35, Chatham House Grammar School, Ramsgate

University 1935–39, Balliol College, Oxford. Read Philosophy, Politics and Economics (PPE)

Prizes and awards 1926, Scholarship to Chatham House Grammar School; 1934, Belasco Prize (inter-house piano competition); 1935, Leslie and Douglas Prize (for character; shared with the captain of school, J. E. Hobbs); 1935, Balliol organ scholarship; 1939, Scholarship to Gray's Inn

Qualifications 1939, BA Hons (Second Class)

Cultural and vocational background His musical talent was fostered at an early age by his family and the parish church. He began to play the piano at the age of 9 and the organ at 14. He made a notable contribution to the musical life of Balliol as organ scholar, creator of the Balliol Choir and conductor, and briefly considered music as a career before leaving university. A keen traveller, he visited Germany, Spain and Poland as a student and witnessed the political upheaval of the pre-war years.

Languages French and some German

NON-PARLIAMENTARY CAREER

Early occupations In 1939, his final year at university, Heath had been elected to a scholarship at Gray's Inn, but the outbreak of war disrupted his plans to train for the Bar. He joined the civil service in 1947 and was appointed to the Ministry of Civil Aviation. Assigned to the Directorate of Long-Term Planning and Projects, he represented the Director-General on the London Airport Planning Committee and the Informal Light Aircraft Committee. In Nov 1947 he resigned from the civil service after his adoption as prospective parliamentary candidate for Bexley. In 1948 he became news editor for the *Church Times* leaving in 1949 to join merchant bankers Brown, Shipley & Co. as a management

NON-PARLIAMENTARY CAREER—*Continued*

trainee. This last position continued until the end of 1951, coinciding with the beginning of his parliamentary career.

Military service A few days after the outbreak of war in September 1939 Heath volunteered to the Oxford Recruiting Board and was allocated to the Royal Artillery, but was not called up until August 1940. In Mar 1941 after a period of officer training, he was posted as Second-Lieutenant to the 107th Heavy Anti-Aircraft Regiment, then engaged in the defence of Merseyside. He was made Adjutant of the Regiment with the rank of Captain in March 1942 and was stationed in various parts of the country for the next two years. On 3 Jul 1944 the regiment was sent to the Normandy front to support the 6th Airborne Division attacking Caen. It took part in the relief of Antwerp and the defence of Nijmegen. In 1945 Heath was posted as commander of 334 Battery with the rank of Major. Arriving in Hanover to take over occupation duties in June 1945 he witnessed the Nuremberg trials. In September 1945 he was posted as second in command of the 86th Heavy Anti-Aircraft Regiment and, on the demobilisation of his commanding officer in October, became acting-Lieutenant Colonel for 3 months. Mentioned in despatches in November 1945, he was demobilised in May 1946 and returned to England the following month. In 1947 Heath was promoted to Lieutenant Colonel to become the commanding officer (until 1951) of a Territorial regiment, the 2nd Regiment of the Honourable Artillery Company (Heavy Anti-Aircraft).

Other posts 1937, President, Oxford University Conservative Association; 1938, Chairman, Federation of University Conservative Associations; 1939, President, Oxford Union; 1951–54, Master Gunner within the Tower of London; 1959–77, President, Federation of University Conservative Associations; 1961–70, Member, Council of the Royal College of Music; 1963–1970, Chairman, London Symphony Orchestra Trust; 1964–65, Director, Brown, Shipley & Co.; 1970– , Vice President, Bach Choir; 1970–74, Chairman, Commonwealth Parliamentary Association; 1971, Elder Brother of Trinity House; 1974, Honorary Member, London Symphony Orchestra and Trustee, 1975– ; 1976– , Director, Dumpton Gap Company; 1977–79, Member, Independent Commission on International Development Issues; 1977–80, President, European Community Youth Orchestra; 1978– , Member, Public Review Board, Arthur Andersen & Co.; 1979–88, Joint President, St Stephen's Constitutional; 1981–83, Chairman, Advisory Council, International Reporting Information Systems; 1991– , Member, Board of Governors of the Centre for Global Energy Studies; 1992– , Development Adviser to the China Investment and Development Fund Ltd. and to Kleinwort Benson China Management Ltd.; 1992– , Adviser to the China Ocean Shipping Company

HONOURS

Academic 1962–70, Visiting Fellow, Nuffield College, Oxford; 1969, Hon Fellow, Balliol College, Oxford; 1969, Hon Fellow, Queen Mary and Westfield College; 1969, Hon Fellow, Institute of Development Studies, University of Essex; 1970, Hon Fellow, Nuffield College, Oxford; 1971, DCL Oxford; 1971, DTech Bradford; 1980, Montgomery Fellow, Dartmouth College; 1985, DCL Kent

Foreign 1953, Smith-Mundt Fellowship, USA; 1963, Charlemagne Prize; 1971, Estes J Kefauver Prize; 1971, Stresseman Gold Medal; 1972, Freiherr Von Stein Foundation Prize; 1975, Visiting Chubb Fellow, Yale; 1975, LLD Westminster College, Salt Lake City; 1976, Dr *honoris causa* University of Paris, Sorbonne; 1978, Gold Medal of the City of Paris; 1979, European Peace Cross; 1980, World Humanity Award; 1981, Gold Medal, European Parliament; 1981, Dr of Public Administration, Wesleyan College, Macon, Georgia; 1982, DL Westminster College, Fulton, Missouri; 1990, Deroy Professor, University of Michigan; 1993, Great Cross of Merit with Star and Sash, Germany

Other than peerage 24 Jan 1946, Member, Order of the British Empire; 19 Nov 1965, Hon Member and Hon Fellow, Royal College of Organists; 20 Apr 1966, Liveryman, Worshipful Company of Goldsmiths; 12 Dec 1966, Hon Fellow, Royal College of Music; 8 Jul 1970, Hon Bencher, Gray's Inn; 3 Oct 1973, Hon Freeman, Musician's Company; 1977–1 Apr 1985, Hon Life Patron, Federation of University Conservative and Unionist Associations; 15 Jun 1992, Knight of the Garter

CLUBS

Coningsby; Royal Yacht Squadron; Buck's; Carlton; St. Stephen's Constitutional; Marylebone Cricket Club

HOBBIES AND SPORTS

Music and sailing have been his two main interests outside politics. He has conducted orchestras all over the world including the European Community Youth Orchestra, of which he was co-founder and president.

A successful and accomplished yachtsman, he did not take up the sport until he was 50. Only 3 years later in 1969, he won the Sydney to Hobart race on his yacht *Morning Cloud.*

He also captained the British Admiral's Cup team in 1971 and 1979, and the Sardinia Cup team in 1980.

As a boy he had a brown mongrel terrier called Erg (after his initials), and in later life a beagle called Maggie May.

FINANCES

Heath was able to accept the offer of Common Entrance to Balliol College with a loan from Kent Education Committee of £90 p.a. and a further £130 p.a. from his parents. In his first term he won the Balliol Organ Scholarship, worth £80 p.a., and thereby spared his family a considerable financial commitment. He also supplemented his student income by tutoring at Broadstairs during the university vacations.

During the 1950s and early 1960s he lived in modest accommodation and allowed his savings to be invested. In 1969 he purchased the first of several racing cruisers to be named *Morning Cloud* at an estimated cost of £7,000. *Morning Cloud V*, launched in 1977, was thought to have cost in the region of £70,000.

He is the director and major shareholder of the Dumpton Gap Company, formed in 1976 as a holding company for his earnings from books, lectures and concerts.

In 1991 it was announced that, as a former Prime Minister, he would receive nearly £30,000 p.a. towards the continuing additional office costs incurred as a result of his special position in public life.

A member of Lloyds, he maintains homes in Belgravia, and Salisbury, Wiltshire.

Income His civil service salary from 1946–47 was £450 p.a.; as news editor for the *Church Times* he earned £650 p.a. from 1948–49 and £200 p.a. as a trainee at Brown, Shipley from 1949–51. His salary as a Member of Parliament was £1,000 from 1951, £1,250 from 1954 and £1,750 from 1957. In addition to this he received a ministerial allowance of £500 as a Government Whip from 1952 onwards. His salary as a member of the Cabinet between 1959–64 was £5,000 p.a. In Opposition from 1964–65 he supplemented his parliamentary salary of £3,250 with a directorship at Brown, Shipley. As Leader of the Opposition from 1965–70 his salary was £3,000 p.a. and from 1974–75 £4,500 p.a. in addition to his parliamentary salary. As Prime Minister in 1970 his salary was £14,000 p.a. rising to £20,000 p.a. from 1972–74. His parliamentary salary as a backbencher rose from £4,500 p.a. in 1975 to £30,854 in 1992. From 1981–83 his salary as Chairman of the Advisory Council of International Reporting Information Systems was estimated to be £50,000 p.a.

Pensions Prime Minister's pension

Legacies His father William Heath left £47,712 in his will in 1976.

ANECDOTES

c. 1942, During the war Heath conducted the Battery band but transport was sometimes difficult to arrange, and on one occasion a RAMC doctor provided an ambulance to take them to an engagement in Chester. On the journey it was held up at a bridge, when a rather grand commanding officer pulled up behind in his staff car and was dumbfounded to hear the beat of dance music from the back of the regimental ambulance. 'Typically', said a colonel later, 'Heath had got the band rehearsing to avoid wasting time.'

1955, At Heath's adoption meeting in his constituency prior to the General Election, the Conservative Chairman was in full flight pointing to his 'truly remarkable' voting record. Of the 730 parliamentary divisions since entering the House, he had voted in 720 and had been paired in 6. Came a harsh growl from the back of the hall, 'What about the other four?'

1963, When de Gaulle announced that Britain would not be allowed to enter the European Economic Community he also made the following prediction: 'The Labour Party will come to power for a short and disastrous period, to be followed by the Conservatives with Heath at their head. It is he who will enable Britain to enter Europe'.

1965, When news of Heath's election as Leader of the Conservative Party was published, he received a congratulatory telegram from the *patron* of the best and most expensive restaurant in Brussels, *Comme Chez Soi.*

1966, Jim Prior, Parliamentary Private Secretary to Heath from 1965–70, recalled in his book *A Balance of Power*: 'Ted's first task after the election defeat was to form a new Shadow Cabinet. The election had been imminent from the moment he had become Leader and there had therefore been no opportunity to introduce new faces. But with a full Parliament now ahead of us, it was time to rebuild.

'This was a task primarily for Ted and his Chief Whip, Willie Whitelaw. My advice was asked on only one aspect. We still thought in terms of appointing a "statutory woman". "Who should she be?" asked Ted. "Margaret Thatcher," was my immediate reply. There was a long silence. "Yes," he said, "Willie agrees she's much the most able, but he says once she's there we'll never be able to get rid of her. So we both think it's got to be Mervyn Pike".'

QUOTATIONS

1950, Yes, I owe everything to my mother really. (In conversation with a friend. Quoted by M. Laing in *Edward Heath: Prime Minister*, 1972)

1962, No one knows better than a former patronage secretary [Chief Whip] the limitations of the human mind and the human spirit. (In conversation. Quoted by A. Sampson in *The New Anatomy of Britain, 1971.)*

1966, In an interview for the *Observer* newspaper he was asked if he would make a better Prime Minister if he were married and he replied, 'I don't know. It would depend to some extent on the woman, wouldn't it? What I do know is that a man who got married in order to be a better Prime Minister wouldn't be either a good Prime Minister or a good husband'.

1970, On the Conservative's proposals to cut taxation and curb nationalised industries' prices: 'This would, at a stroke reduce the rise in prices, increase production and reduce unemployment'. (In a signed statement to reporters at a press conference, 16 Jun)

1970, We will have to embark on a change so radical, a revolution so quiet and yet so total, that it will go far beyond the programme for a Parliament . . . (Speech to the Conservative Party Conference.)

1973, It is the unpleasant and unacceptable face of capitalism but one should not suggest that the whole of British industry consists of practices of this kind. (Replying in the House of Commons to a question about the activities of the Lonrho international trading group.)

1973, From 31 December, they will be limited to three specified days each week. (In the House of Commons, announcing restrictions on the use of electricity by most industrial and commercial premises)

1974, I am the servant of the Party. (In a written message to backbench Conservative MPs when he volunteered to open discussions for a review of the Party's leadership election procedures)

1989, There are a lot of people I've encouraged and helped to get into the House of Commons. Looking at them now, I'm not at all sure it was a wise thing to do. (Interview for the *Evening Standard* newspaper)

RESIDENCES

H.A.C headquarters, Armoury House, City Road, London
Artillery Mansions, Victoria, London
88 Petty France, Westminster, London
F2, Albany, Piccadilly, London
10 Downing Street
Cathedral Close, Salisbury, Wiltshire
House in Belgravia, London

MEMORIALS

STATUES AND BUSTS

A bust made for the Oxford Union

PORTRAITS

1971, by Terence Cuneo, St Stephen's Constitutional Club, London; 1975, by Peter Greenham RA, Carlton Club, London; 1992, by Graham Jones, House of Commons

OTHER MEMORIALS

Heath House, Chatham House School; the Edward Heath Charitable Trust (established 1972)

BIBLIOGRAPHIC INFORMATION

LETTERS AND PERSONAL PAPERS

Sir Edward Heath has not yet identified an archive for his private papers. State papers are available at the Public Record Office, Kew, for the period up to 1963. 1970, *Old World, New Horizons: Britain, the Common Market and the Atlantic Alliance* (Godkin Lectures); 1976, *A British Approach to European Foreign Policy* (33rd Montague Burton Lecture on international relations); 1980, *North-South: A Programme for Survival* (University of Essex Noel Buxton Lecture); 1980, *Third Hoover Address* (University of Strathclyde); 1982, *An Atlantic Approach to North-South Relations* (Second David Bruce Memorial Lecture); 1982, *The Brandt Report: Restoring the Health of the World Economy.* (Stevens Lectures for the Laity).

PUBLICATIONS

1950, *One Nation—A Tory Approach to Social Problems.* (co-author); 1960, *Parliament and People*; 1965, *Putting Britain Right Ahead*; 1966, *The Conservative Goal: A Call to Action*; 1968, *Keeping the Peace: A New Look at the Role of the United Nations*; 1975, *Sailing. A Course of My Life*; 1976, *Music. A Joy for Life*; 1977, *Travels. People and Places in My Life*; 1977, *Carols: The Joy of Christmas*; 1977, *Our Community*

FURTHER READING

Campbell, J. *Edward Heath. A Biography.* London, 1993.
Evans, M. *Ted Heath. A Family Portrait.* London, 1970.
Hutchinson, G. *Edward Heath. A Personal and Political Biography.* London, 1970.
Laing, M. *Edward Heath. Prime Minister.* London, 1972.
Roth, A. *Heath and The Heathmen.* 1972

E.J.J.

Bettmann

James Callaghan

Lived 1912–
Political Party Labour
Prime Minister 5 April 1976–4 May 1979
Government Labour
Reigning Monarch Elizabeth II

Malo laborare quam languere Better to work than to be idle

CALLAGHAN AS PRIME MINISTER

From 1964–1970 and again from 1974–1976 Callaghan held in succession before becoming Prime Minister the three most senior ministerial posts of Chancellor of the Exchequer, Home Secretary and Foreign Secretary—a unique distinction. After Wilson's resignation he was elected leader of the Labour Party and hence Prime Minister. He inherited only a small majority in the House of Commons, which, by early 1977, disappeared because of by-election results, forcing him to reach an agreement with the Liberal Party, 'The Lib-Lab Pact,' in order to stay in power. Difficulties with the trade unions, in particular about pay restraint, made deciding on a date for a General Election a problem. In September 1978 he opted to postpone an election but disputes and strikes undermined both his administration and, eventually, his majority in the House of Commons where, in March 1979, he lost a vote of confidence in his Government by one vote. The subsequent General Election brought Mrs. Thatcher to power. Callaghan was already aged 64 when he became Prime Minister and his relaxed and avuncular style appealed to many. After he resigned as party leader in 1980, he became an impressive elder statesman, welcomed in 1987 to the House of Lords for his experience and wisdom.

PERSONAL INFORMATION

Names Leonard James Callaghan
Peerage Baron Callaghan of Cardiff, of the City of Cardiff in the county of South Glamorgan, 30 Jul 1987
Nicknames Big Jim; Sunny Jim
Born 27 Mar 1912
Birthplace 38 Funtington Road, Portsmouth, Hampshire
Religion Baptist
Ancestry English/Irish. Early details of his paternal ancestors are unclear but the family name was Garoghan when his grandfather worked as a silversmith in Sheffield and Birmingham. His father enlisted in the Navy under the name Callaghan in the early 1890s.
Date and place of marriage 28 Jul 1938, the Baptist Chapel, Maidstone, Kent
Age at marriage 26 years, 123 days
First entered Parliament 5 Jul 1945
Date appointed PM 5 Apr 1976
Age at appointment 64 years, 9 days
Date ceased to be PM 4 May 1979
Total time as PM 3 years, 29 days
Ceased to be MP 18 May 1987
Zodiac sign Aries

FATHER

James Callaghan (Garoghan)
Date and place of birth 21 Jan 1877, Birmingham
Occupation Chief Petty Officer in the Royal Navy. During the 1890s he served on the battleship HMS *Benbow* and the cruiser HMS *St George* and took part in expeditions to Benin City and Zanzibar. He volunteered to join Scott's expedition to Antarctica in HMS *Discovery* (1901–4) but was persuaded instead to join the crew of the Royal Yacht *Victoria and Albert*, based in Portsmouth. On the outbreak of war he joined the battlecruiser HMS *Agincourt* at Scapa Flow. He was wounded at the Battle of Jutland in 1916 and invalided out of the service in 1919. The family then moved to Brixham in Devon where he became a coastguard.
Date of marriage 10 May 1903
Date and place of death 13 Oct 1921, Plymouth, Devon
Place of burial Brixham, Devon

MOTHER

Charlottey Gertrude Cundy
Date and place of birth 3 Aug 1879, Devonport, Plymouth, Devon
Profile Deeply religious and fundamentalist.
Dates of marriages 1) 16 Apr 1900, Daniel Philip Speare (d. 1901); 2) 10 May 1903, James Callaghan
Date of death 4 Jul 1961
Place of cremation Worthing, Sussex

BROTHERS AND SISTERS

James Callaghan is the only son and younger of two children.
Dorothy, b. 15 Jul 1904; teacher; d. Apr 1982

WIFE

Audrey Elizabeth Moulton
Date and place of birth 28 Jul 1913, Maidstone, Kent
Mother Clara Kempton
Father Frank Moulton
Father's occupation Managing Director, Lead Wool Co.; Church Deacon and Sunday School Superintendent.
Age at marriage 25 years
Number of children 3
Years younger than PM 1 year, 123 days
Education During the 1930s she qualified as a domestic science teacher and completed an external London University course in economics, specialising in the causes of children's malnutrition and its remedies.
Profile Politically active with a lifelong interest in children's welfare, she was a member of the London County Council from 1959 and Alderman of the Greater London Council from 1964–70. She was also Chairman of the South East London Children's Committee, which was responsible for the welfare of some 3,000 children in the care of the GLC; Chairman of the Board of Governors of Great Ormond Street Hospital for Sick Children from 1969–83 and Chairman of the Board of Trustees from 1983–91. Lady Callaghan was named Vice-President in 1989 of the National Children's Bureau.

CHILDREN

1 son, 2 daughters
Margaret Ann, b. 18 Nov 1939; m. 16 Sep 1961, Peter Jay (diss. 1986); Somerville College, Oxford, BA; a journalist for the BBC; Director of the National AIDS Trust (1988–92); created Baroness Jay of Paddington in 1992; a Labour Whip and spokesman on health issues in the House of Lords
Julia Elizabeth, b. 21 Oct 1942; m. 9 Sep 1967, Ian Hamilton Hubbard; attended Kidbrooke Comprehensive School, south London; travelled in America; secretary to a Danish architect
Michael James, b. 29 Sep 1945; m. 7 Dec 1968, Jennifer Mary Morris; attended Dulwich College, University College Cardiff and Manchester Business School; corporate strategy planner for Ford of Europe

LIFE AND CAREER

PARLIAMENTARY ELECTIONS FOUGHT

*(*designates candidate elected)*
DATE 5 Jul 1945. General Election
CONSTITUENCY Cardiff, South
RESULT L.J. Callaghan* (Lab) 17,489; Sir H.A. Evans (Con) 11,545

DATE 23 Feb 1950. General Election
CONSTITUENCY Cardiff, South-East
RESULT L.J. Callaghan* (Lab) 26,254; Dr. J.J. Hayward (Con) 20,359; P.A.T. Furnell (Lib) 4,080

DATE 25 Oct 1951. General Election
CONSTITUENCY Cardiff, South-East
RESULT L.J. Callaghan* (Lab) 28,112; H. West (Con) 23,613

DATE 26 May 1955. General Election
CONSTITUENCY Cardiff, South-East
RESULT L.J. Callaghan* (Lab) 25,722; M.H.A. Roberts (Con) 22,482

DATE 8 Oct 1959. General Election
CONSTITUENCY Cardiff, South-East

RESULT L.J. Callaghan* (Lab) 26,915; M.H.A. Roberts (Con) 26,047

DATE 15 Oct 1964. General Election
CONSTITUENCY Cardiff, South-East
RESULT L.J. Callaghan* (Lab) 30,129; E.R. Dexter (Con) 22,288

DATE 31 Mar 1966. General Election
CONSTITUENCY Cardiff, South-East
RESULT L.J. Callaghan* (Lab) 29,313; N. Lloyd-Edwards (Con) 18,476; G.W. Parsons (Lib) 3,829

DATE 18 Jun 1970. General Election
CONSTITUENCY Cardiff, South-East
RESULT L. J.Callaghan* (Lab) 26,226; N. Lloyd-Edwards (Con) 20,771; R.B. Davies (Plaid Cymru) 2,585; G.W. Parsons (Nat Front) 982

DATE 28 Feb 1974. General Election
CONSTITUENCY Cardiff, South-East
RESULT L.J. Callaghan* (Lab) 20,641; S. Terlezki (Con) 13,495; C.H. Bailey (Ind Lib) 3,800; B.M. Christon (Lib) 2,978; K. Bush (Plaid Cymru) 1,254

DATE 10 Oct 1974. General Election
CONSTITUENCY Cardiff, South-East
RESULT L.J. Callaghan* (Lab) 21,074; S. Terlezki (Con) 10,356; C. H. Bailey (Lib) 8,066; K. Bush (Plaid Cymru) 983; B.C.D. Harris (Communist Party of England) 75

DATE 3 May 1979. General Election
CONSTITUENCY Cardiff, South-East
RESULT L.J. Callaghan* (Lab) 23,871; I.A.S. Jones (Con) 15,170; E.R. Roberts (Plaid Cymru) 628; R.W. Aldridge (Ind) 375; Miss M.P. Arrowsmith (Ind Soc) 132; R.H. Spencer (Com) 112

DATE 9 Jun 1983. General Election
CONSTITUENCY Cardiff, South and Penarth
RESULT L.J. Callaghan* (Lab) 17,448; D.A.S. Tredinnick (Con) 15,172; G.W. Roddick (Lib) 8,816; Miss S.A. Edwards (Plaid Cymru) 673; B.T. Lewis (Ind) 165

PARTY ACTIVITY

Party Leadership 1976–80, Leader of the Labour Party
Other offices 1945, Chairman, Parliamentary Labour Party's Defence and Services Committee; 1956, Vice-Chairman Labour Party Executive's Commonwealth Committee; 1957–61, 1963–80, Member, Labour Party Executive Committee; 1967–76, Treasurer, Labour Party; 1970–72, Chairman, Labour Party Executive's Home Policy Committee; 1972–73, Vice-Chairman, Labour Party; 1973–74, Chairman, Labour Party.

PARLIAMENTARY AND MINISTERIAL EXPERIENCE

Maiden Speech 20 Aug 1945. He spoke in the Debate on the Address about the situation in the Pacific following the Japanese surrender. (*HC Deb*, vol 413, col 351–54)
Opposition offices 1951–53, Opposition Spokesman on Transport; 1953–55, Opposition Spokesman on Fuel and Power; 1956–61, Opposition Spokesman on Colonial Affairs; 1961–64, Shadow Chancellor; 1970–71, Shadow Home Secretary; 1971–72, Opposition Spokesman on Employment; 1972–74, Shadow Foreign Secretary; 1979–80, Leader of the Opposition
Privy Counsellor 16 Oct 1964
Ministerial Offices Parliamentary Secretary, Ministry of Transport 7 Oct 1947–2 Mar 1950; Parliamentary and Financial Secretary, Admiralty 2 Mar 1950–25 Oct 1951; Chancellor of the Exchequer 16 Oct 1964–30 Nov 1967; Secretary of State for the Home Department 30 Nov 1967–18 Jun 1970; Secretary of State for Foreign and Commonwealth Affairs 5 Mar 1974–5 Apr 1976; First Lord of the Treasury and Minister for the Civil Service 5 Apr 1976–4 May 1979
Opposition Leader while PM 1976–79, Margaret Thatcher
Father of the House 9 Jun 1983–18 May 1987

GOVERNMENTS FORMED

Administration 5 Apr 1976–4 May 1979

GENERAL ELECTION RESULT
10 OCT 1974: Labour 319; Conservative 277; Liberal 13; Scottish National Party 11; Plaid Cymru 3; Others 12. Total 635
Labour majority 4 (excl. the Speaker)

CABINET
Prime Minister, First Lord of the Treasury and Minister for the Civil Service J. Callaghan
Lord President of the Council M. Foot
Lord Chancellor Lord Elwyn-Jones
Lord Privy Seal Lord Shepherd (Apr–Sep 1976); Lord Peart (Sep 1976–May 1979)
Chancellor of the Exchequer D. Healey
*Chief Secretary to the Treasury** J. Barnett (Feb 1977–May 1979)
Foreign Secretary A. Crosland (Apr 1976–Feb 1977); D. Owen (Feb 1977–May 1979)
Home Secretary R. Jenkins (Apr –Sep 1976) M. Rees (Sep 1976–May 1979)
Minister of Agriculture, Fisheries and Food F. Peart (Apr–Sep 1976) J. Silkin (Sep 1976–May 1979)
Secretary of State for Defence R. Mason (Apr–Sep 1976); F. Mulley (Sep 1976–May 1978)
Secretary of State for Education and Science F. Mulley (Apr–Sep 1976); Mrs. S. Williams (Sep 1976–May 1979)
Secretary of State for Employment A. Booth
Secretary of State for Energy T. Benn
Secretary of State for the Environment P. Shore
Minister for Planning and Local Government J. Silkin (Apr –Sep 1976) (office abolished 10 Sep 1976)
Secretary of State for Social Services D. Ennals
Secretary of State for Industry E. Varley
Chancellor of the Duchy of Lancaster H. Lever
Secretary of State for Northern Ireland M. Rees (Apr –Sep 1976); R.Mason (Sep 1976–May 1979)
*Minister of Overseas Development** R. Prentice (Apr –Dec 1976)
Secretary of State for Prices and Consumer Protection Mrs. S. Williams (Apr–Sep 1976) R. Hattersley (Sep 1976–May 1979)
Secretary of State for Scotland B. Millan
Minister for Social Security S. Orme (Sep 1976–May 1979)
Secretary of State for Trade E. Dell (Apr 1976–Nov 1978); J. Smith (Nov 1978–May 1979)
Secretary of State for Transport W. Rodgers (Sep 1976–May 1979)
Secretary of State for Wales J. Morris
[* Office not always in Cabinet]

IMPORTANT DATES IN PERSONAL AND POLITICAL LIFE

28 JUL 1938 Marries Audrey Moulton, daughter of a Kent businessman.

IMPORTANT DATES IN PERSONAL AND POLITICAL LIFE—*Continued*

5 JUL 1945 Elected Labour Member of Parliament for Cardiff, South.

AUG 1945 Invited by John Parker, Under-Secretary of State for Dominion Affairs, to become his Parliamentary Private Secretary.

20 AUG 1945 Makes his maiden speech in the House of Commons.

14 DEC 1945 Resigns as Parliamentary Private Secretary after voting against the Government's proposals to accept a new US loan in place of Lend Lease and to join the Bretton Woods Agreement.

7 OCT 1947 Appointed Parliamentary Secretary for Transport. As Chairman of the Ministry's Road Safety Committee, his recommendations lead to the introduction of zebra crossings and the extension of catseyes to trunk roads.

23 FEB 1950 Elected Labour Member for Cardiff, South East. The boundaries of the Cardiff constituencies had been adjusted as part of a much wider redistribution following the Representation of the People Act 1948.

2 MAR 1950 Appointed Parliamentary and Financial Secretary to the Admiralty. As a delegate to the early Council of Europe meetings in Strasbourg he furthers his Ministry's policies by successfully resisting an attempt in Aug 1950 to establish a European Army.

25 OCT 1951 In Opposition following the General Election defeat, Callaghan begins to build a broad base of support within the Labour Party. His success is reflected in his election to the Shadow Cabinet each year from 1951–63 and to the National Executive Committee from 1957.

OCT 1955 He takes up a paid position as Parliamentary Advisor to the Police Federation and becomes the principal negotiator for the police force with local authorities during the late 1950s. He wins considerable popularity among policemen for his skillful lobbying for an increase in their pay, his recommendation for which is to be endorsed by a Royal Commission in 1960.

4 OCT 1960 He challenges George Brown and Frederick Lee for the deputy leadership of the Labour Party on an anti-unilateral disarmament platform. Brown is the main candidate for the right wing of the Party, but Callaghan subsequently polls 55 votes and forces the contest to a second ballot which Brown wins.

30 NOV 1961 In a Shadow Cabinet reshuffle Callaghan becomes Shadow Chancellor. During this period he attends informal, private seminars on economics arranged by Nuffield College, Oxford (of which he had been made a visiting fellow in 1959).

7 FEB 1963 He stands against Harold Wilson and George Brown for the leadership of the Labour Party following the death of Hugh Gaitskell in January. In the first ballot he polls 41 votes compared to 115 for Wilson and 88 for Brown. As Brown's and Callaghan's votes total more than Wilson's the contest goes to a second ballot, which Wilson wins on 14 Feb.

16 OCT 1964 Appointed Privy Counsellor and Chancellor of the Exchequer in Wilson's administration. The formulation of Government economic policy in the following years is dominated by the need to correct the balance of payments deficit and to defend sterling.

26 OCT 1964 In the knowledge that devaluation has been ruled out as a means of dealing with the immediate crisis, Callaghan announces the preferred mechanism of import surcharges at a press conference.

11 NOV 1964 Callaghan brings in a mildly deflationary Budget and indicates tax reforms to follow in the spring. Speculation against sterling continues, only to be halted by an announcement on 25 Nov of a $3 billion credit arranged with other central banks to save the pound.

6 APR 1965 Against a background of a weak pound and the prospect of the balance of payments deficit continuing throughout 1965 and 1966, Callaghan introduces a Budget designed to deflate the economy further with the introduction of a capital gains tax and a corporation tax. The debates on the Bill continue through May and July.

5 AUG 1965 The provisions of the Budget become law in the Finance Act despite hundreds of amendments and a Government defeat on 7 Jul relating to unit trusts.

27 JUL 1965 Callaghan introduces still further deflationary measures to the Commons, including tighter hire purchase restrictions and the postponement of some public spending projects. Between autumn 1965 and spring 1966 the balance of payments improves and economic growth continues.

3 MAY 1966 His first Budget of the new Parliament includes the introduction of the selective employment tax, designed to raise revenue and encourage the redistribution of labour from service to manufacturing industries.

9 JUL 1966 At a Cabinet meeting Callaghan votes with Wilson against devaluation as a policy to relieve the sterling crisis of the summer. The following day Wilson announces deflationary measures to the House of Commons, including a six- month standstill on all wage and dividend increases.

JUL–AUG 1967 Callaghan chairs the meetings of the Group of Ten (Finance Ministers of industrial countries) at which agreement is reached on the introduction of a new currency reserve asset to be called the 'Special Drawing Right' (SDR). This becomes an internationally recognised asset for settling inter-governmental debts.

3 OCT 1967 He is elected Labour Party Treasurer at the annual Conference and each year thereafter until 1976. The post is the only office filled by election from all sections of the Conference and reflects his broad support within the Party.

13 NOV 1967 Wilson and Callaghan decide to devalue the pound against a background of an economy weakened by the costs of the Middle East crisis and dock strikes in Britain and further speculation against sterling in November.

18 NOV 1967 On the day that the pound is devalued, Callaghan writes to the Prime Minister to offer his resignation. He states that because of his earlier commitments not to devalue, his position has become insupportable. His resignation is not announced immediately and he remains in office to make a statement on the devaluation to the House of Commons on 22 Nov.

30 NOV 1967 Appointed Home Secretary in place of Roy Jenkins, who becomes Chancellor.

22 FEB 1968 In response to the mass exodus of Kenyan Asians to the United Kingdom caused by the hostile attitude of the Kenyan authorities, Callaghan announces the Government's decision to introduce emergency legislation to bring them under the same restrictions as other Commonwealth citizens. The Commonwealth Immigrants Bill receives the Royal Assent on 1 Mar but is criticised for introducing a distinction between UK citizens on grounds of race alone.

27 OCT 1968 A demonstration against the war in Vietnam takes place in Grosvenor Square, London without the violence that has been anticipated. Afterwards Callaghan is praised for having resisted considerable pressure to ban the demonstration.

13 MAY 1969 Callaghan is dropped from Wilson's inner Cabinet for his opposition to the Industrial Relations Bill, the Government's proposals to control industrial disputes. The Bill is abandoned in June in exchange for a voluntary agreement with the TUC, and Callaghan is readmitted to the inner Cabinet in October after his handling of the crisis in Northern Ireland.

14 AUG 1969 He authorises the intervention of British troops in Ulster at Stormont's request. His visits to the province for talks with Ministers and other representatives at the end of August and October are successful in ensuring the progress of social reforms foreshadowed in the Downing Street Declaration of 19 Aug.

22 MAY 1970 The Cricket Council accedes to a written request from the Home Secretary to cancel the planned South African tour of Britain. By offering to accept responsibility for the cancellation the Government averts the threatened anti-apartheid demonstrations and boycott of the Commonwealth Games.

2 OCT 1972 Callaghan presents the National Executive's statement, *Labour's Programme for Britain* to the annual conference, containing the idea of a 'social contract' with the Trades Union Congress as an alternative to the disputes between the Conservative Government and the trade unions.

MAY 1973 He allows his name to go forward as the British candidate for the post of Managing Director of the International Monetary Fund. His candidature is vetoed by the French Government, however.

SEP 1973 Publication of *A House Divided: The Dilemma of Northern Ireland*, his account of his role as Home Secretary in the events of 1969–70.

5 MAR 1974 He is appointed Secretary of State for Foreign and Commonwealth Affairs in Wilson's minority administration.

1 APR 1974 In a speech to the EEC Council of Ministers in Luxembourg he announces that the Labour Government opposes continued membership on the terms which the Conservatives have negotiated. From Jun 1974 to Mar 1975 he leads the team of Ministers responsible for re-negotiation, securing concessions on the Community budget, agricultural policy and terms for Commonwealth producers.

20 JUL 1974 Turkish forces make a preliminary landing on Cyprus which precipitates the collapse of a five-day-old junta backed by the Greek Government. From 25 Jul Callaghan chairs talks in Geneva with the Turkish and Greek Foreign Ministers in an attempt to maintain the ceasefire of 22 Jul and to prepare the ground for a settlement between Greek and Turkish Cypriots. The talks break down on 14 Aug and the Turkish invasion continues until 40 per cent of the island is occupied.

10 OCT 1974 The General Election results in a narrow overall majority in Parliament for the Labour Party and Callaghan remains as Foreign Secretary in Wilson's fourth administration.

9 APR 1975 Callaghan makes the closing speech in a debate in the House of Commons on membership of the European Community in which the Government wins approval for its re-negotiated terms. In a referendum in June 1975 the British electorate vote in favour of remaining in the Community.

11 MAR 1976 Wilson warns Callaghan of the impending announcement of his resignation as Prime Minister, and to make preparations for the leadership contest.

22 MAR 1976 The House of Commons indicates its general approval of Callaghan's statement regarding Rhodesia, which includes the offer of funds for reconstruction if the Rhodesians concede the principle of early majority rule. Despite international support, the proposals are rejected by the Government in Salisbury.

25 MAR 1976 In the first ballot to elect a new Leader of the Parliamentary Labour Party, Michael Foot leads with 90 votes; followed by Callaghan with 84; Roy Jenkins, 56; Tony Benn, 37; Denis Healey, 30 and Anthony Crosland, 17. Further rounds are necessary under Labour's rules of voting by exhaustive ballot. Crosland, with the lowest vote, is eliminated; Benn withdraws in favor of Foot and Jenkins also withdraws.

30 MAR 1976 Jenkins' decision is crucial to Callaghan's eventual victory. After the second ballot he had taken the lead with 141 votes to Foot's 133 and Healey's 38.

5 APR 1976 On the third ballot most of Healey's votes transfer to Callaghan who defeats Foot by 176 votes to 137, to become Leader of the Party. After Wilson's resignation a few hours later Callaghan becomes the new Prime Minister and the first person to have held all four major Offices of State.

8 APR 1976 Callaghan asks four Ministers from the previous administration—Barbara Castle, Robert Mellish, William Ross and Edward Short— to place their portfolios at his disposal, and brings into the Cabinet Albert Booth, Edmund Dell, David Ennals and Bruce Millan.

10 SEP 1976 Roy Jenkins, the Home Secretary, resigns to become the EEC's new Commissioner in Brussels in Jan 1977. He is replaced by Merlyn Rees.

28 SEP 1976 In a watershed speech to the annual Party Conference Callaghan argues that the pattern of public expenditure pursued by post-war British governments is no longer appropriate.

29 SEP 1976 The Treasury announces the Government's decision to apply to the International Monetary Fund for a stand-by credit of £2.3 billion, to partially fund the expected £3 billion deficit in the balance of payments. However, the terms of the loan are to engender lengthy and bitter conflicts in the Cabinet.

18 OCT 1976 In a speech at Ruskin College, Oxford, Callaghan questions 'progressive' teaching methods and argues the need for a core curriculum of basic subjects in all schools. His speech leads to the 'Great Debate' on education in a series of regional conferences organised by Shirley Williams, the Secretary of State for Education and Science.

21 DEC 1976 Reginald Prentice, Minister of Overseas Development, resigns in protest against public expenditure cuts. His successor, Frank Judd, does not become a member of the Cabinet.

19 FEB 1977 Anthony Crosland, the Foreign Secretary, dies in office. He had been considered a creative thinker and an able administrator but had not succeeded in winning the support of the Party in the 1976 leadership contest. He is succeeded by David Owen.

23 MAR 1977 The Government is placed in an overall minority in the House of Commons by the spring of 1977, following the loss of three by-elections. With a debate imminent on a motion of no confidence in the Government, Callaghan reaches an agreement with David Steel, the Leader of the Liberal Party, which comes to be known as the 'Lib-Lab Pact'. The Liberals agree to support the Government on any confidence issue in re-

IMPORTANT DATES IN PERSONAL AND POLITICAL LIFE—*Continued*

turn for the inclusion of such measures as direct elections to the European Parliament and devolution for Scotland and Wales in the Government's legislative programme. The agreement continues for another 18 months.

1 JAN 1978 In his New Year Broadcast Callaghan expresses his hope for an inflation rate of no more than 5% for the year 1979. By July the Cabinet has agreed to support a 5% norm for pay increases, but the guidelines are rejected in the autumn by the Labour Party Conference and the TUC's General Council.

7 SEP 1978 Callaghan announces his decision to carry on as a minority Government and not call an election until 1979. The decision is taken in the belief that a further successful period of wage restraint and economic growth will best ensure the return of a Labour Government with an effective parliamentary majority.

14 NOV 1978 The TUC's General Council narrowly rejects the Government's proposed pay restraint package and effectively gives sanction to member unions to return to free collective bargaining. Strike action in the private sector widens during Jan–Mar 1979 to include disputes involving low-paid government workers, which impinge directly on the public and result in the breakdown of essential services. This period, known as the 'winter of discontent', leads to a rapid slump in opinion poll support for the Government.

1 MAR 1979 Referenda in Scotland and Wales fail to attract sufficient support to enable devolution measures to become law. Scottish Nationalist MPs then withdraw the support which has maintained the Callaghan administration since September 1978.

28 MAR 1979 The Government is defeated by 311 votes to 310 at the end of a Commons debate on an Opposition motion of no confidence, the first such defeat since 1924. Following a Cabinet meeting on 29 Mar to set a date for the General Election, Callaghan goes immediately to Buckingham Palace to seek a dissolution of Parliament.

4 MAY 1979 After the defeat of the Labour Party by the Conservatives in the General Election, Callaghan resigns and Margaret Thatcher becomes Prime Minister.

15 OCT 1980 Callaghan informs the Shadow Cabinet that he will not stand for re-election as Leader of the Party. Instead he hopes to devote his time as a backbencher to the problems of unemployment and nuclear proliferation. He is succeeded by Michael Foot.

9 JUN 1983 Returned as Member of Parliament for Cardiff South and Penarth. The addition of the seaside resort of Penarth to industrial south Cardiff had created a seat of social and economic variety. In the new Parliament he also becomes Father of the House, as the Member with the longest period of continuous service.

18 OCT 1985 At a meeting in his constituency he announces that he will not contest the seat again. His reasons include his age, as he will be nearly 80 if he serves for the full length of another Parliament, and his intention to visit other countries in pursuit of international co-operation.

DEC 1985 Callaghan is named Back-Bencher of the Year by a panel of political correspondents in the *Spectator*'s 1985 Parliamentary Awards.

APR 1987 Publication of his autobiography *Time and Chance*.

23 APR 1987 Appointed Knight of the Garter and invested in a ceremony at Windsor Castle on 15 Jun.

30 JUL 1987 Made a life peer in the Dissolution Honours.

9 DEC 1987 Makes his maiden speech in the House of Lords in a debate on the progress of disarmament negotiations and the improvement in East-West relations.

18 OCT 1991 In a speech at the University College of Swansea, 15 years after he launched the 'Great Debate' on education at Ruskin College, he speaks of his fears of widening social divisions as a result of the Government's pursuit of choice and competition in education and sets out instead new priorities for more nursery schools, better education and training for 16-19-year-olds and a broad system for adult re-training and education.

BACKGROUND

PHYSICAL CHARACTERISTICS AND HEALTH

In *Anatomy of Britain Today*, published in 1965, the author Anthony Sampson included the following description of Callaghan: 'He is a big, relaxed, handsome man with . . . an enthusiastic manner, and boyish expressions like "Oh boy!" and "My Goodness!" which sound strange and refreshing in the Treasury building. His background is very naval, and he still has the swinging stride of a man on a quarterdeck.'

Tall and smartly dressed, his hair greyed and he adopted large, square-rimmed spectacles during the 1970s. He is most frequently described as having a kindly expression and an avuncular manner. During the war a medical examination revealed tuberculosis, although he did not recall feeling unwell. After hospital treatment he was ordered to spend a further six months ashore. He enjoyed good health throughout middle age and made a full recovery from a prostate gland operation in December 1971. A non-smoker and very moderate drinker (he gave up alcohol completely in 1974) he cited his feeling of fitness as one of the reasons why he was still active in politics in 1983. At the beginning of 1985 he underwent an operation to remove his gall-bladder and in June 1988 he was detained in hospital for a few days after suffering a mild heart attack.

EDUCATION

Primary 1916–23, Elementary schools in Portsmouth and Brixham

Secondary 1923–29, Portsmouth Northern Secondary School

Qualifications 1929, Senior Oxford School Leaving Certificate

Cultural and vocational background In his autobiography *Time and Chance* Callaghan acknowledged ' . . . the immense debt I owe to a Christian upbringing, nor have I ever escaped its influence'. The Baptist community provided moral and practical support for the family. He attended Sunday School and its numerous community activities throughout his youth and, as a young man in Maidstone, he became a Sunday School teacher. At that time he also joined evening classes in social history and economics organised by the Workers' Educational Association.

Languages French, which he improved while attending Council of Europe meetings at Strasbourg in 1950.

NON-PARLIAMENTARY CAREER

Early occupations Callaghan joined the Inland Revenue as a clerk at the Maidstone office in 1929 and was promoted to the tax inspectorate two years later. He played a leading role in the regional affairs of his trade union, the Association of Officers of Taxes (AOT), and was elected to the union's national executive committee annually from 1934–36. In 1936 he resigned from the Inland Revenue following his appointment as Assistant Secretary of the Inland Revenue Staff Federation (the successor to the AOT), a post which he held, with the exception of his period of war service, until 1947. His work for the Federation brought him into contact with Professor Harold Laski, a leading Labour Party intellectual, who encouraged him to enter politics. While on leave from the Navy in 1943 he was adopted as prospective parliamentary candidate for Cardiff South.

Military service He volunteered and was accepted for service in the Royal Navy in 1940 but was not released by the IRSF until the beginning of 1943. He joined the Royal Navy Patrol Service. A subsequent medical examination revealed tuberculosis and he remained on shore for a further six months, assigned to the Admiralty. During this period he wrote *The Enemy Japan*, a report widely distributed to the fleet as background information in preparation for the war in the Far East. Eventually he took passage in HMS *Activity* to join the East Indies Fleet in Ceylon. In June 1944 he was sent by Naval Intelligence to Iceland as a liaison officer with the Icelandic Government. On VE day in May 1945 he was aboard the battleship HMS *Queen Elizabeth* chasing Japanese cruisers across the Indian Ocean. As a parliamentary candidate he was authorised to return home for the last weeks of the election campaign.

Other posts 1963, President, Advisory Committee on Oil Pollution of the Sea (Chairman, 1952–63); 1963–76, President, United Kingdom Pilots Association; 1971–76, Honorary President, International Maritime Pilots Association; 1972–73, Director, Commercial Bank of Wales; 1972–74, Director, Italian International Bank; 1981–, Chairman, Hubert Humphrey Institute (London), University of Minnesota; 1982–, Governor, Rajaji Institute, Delhi; 1983–, Joint President, Royal Institute of International Affairs; 1986–, President, University College Swansea.

HONOURS

Freedom of cities 1974, Cardiff; 1979, Sheffield; 1991, Portsmouth

Academic 1967, Life Fellow, Nuffield College, Oxford (Visiting Fellow, 1959–67); 1976, LLD University of Wales; 1978, Fellow, University College Cardiff; 1978, LLD Sardar Patel University, India; 1981, Fellow, Portsmouth Polytechnic; 1981, LLD Birmingham University; 1984 LLD Meisei University, Japan; 1988, LLD Sussex University; 1991, Fellow, Cardiff Institute of Higher Education.

Foreign 1978, Hubert H. Humphrey International Award; 1979, Grand Cross 1st class Order of Merit of Federal Republic of Germany.

Other than peerage 9 Mar 1976, Hon Bencher, Inner Temple; 23 Apr 1987, Knight of the Garter.

CLUBS

Athenaeum

HOBBIES AND SPORTS

He played rugby and tennis as a young man, and sailed with fellow MPs, but his main hobby has been farming. He realised a long-held ambition when he became co-owner of a 137-acre arable and livestock farm in 1967 and has played an active part in its management. He won the Challenge Cup for growing the best field of corn in the district of the local Agricultural Society.

FINANCES

After her husband's death Charlottey Callaghan struggled to raise her family in a succession of rented rooms until the introduction of the widow's pension in 1924. Their circumstances improved but still precluded any thought of a university education for Callaghan, who instead left school at 17 to become a clerk for the Inland Revenue. James and Audrey Callaghan rented their first home after their marriage for £1 a week in Norwood, South London. Some years later, after he had entered Parliament, their home in Blackheath was built at a reported cost of £8,000. In 1967 they sold their London home and arranged a new mortgage to become co-owners, with a family friend, of a farm in Sussex. In 1991 it was announced that, as a former Prime Minister, he would receive nearly £30,000 p.a. towards the continuing additional office costs incurred as a result of his special position in public life.

Income £52 p.a. as a clerk with the Inland Revenue in 1929 and £350 p.a. as Assistant Secretary of the Inland Revenue Staff Federation in 1936. From 1947–51 his ministerial salary was £1,500 p.a. From 1955–64 his MP's salary of between £1,000-£1,750 p.a. was supplemented by his salary as a consultant to the Police Federation estimated at £1,500 p.a. As Chancellor of the Exchequer his ministerial salary rose from £5,000 p.a. in 1964 to £8,500 p.a. in 1965 and remained at that level while he was Home Secretary from 1967–70. His parliamentary salary in Opposition from 1970–74 ranged between £3,250 p.a. to £4,500 p.a. As Foreign Secretary his ministerial salary was £13,000 p.a. from 1974–76; as Prime Minister £20,000 p.a. from 1976–78 and £22,000 p.a. in 1979; as Leader of the Opposition £16,225 p.a. to £20,950 from 1979–80. His parliamentary salary as a backbencher rose from £11,750 p.a. in 1980 to £18,500 p.a. in 1987.

Spouse's finances A £2,000 legacy to Audrey Callaghan helped towards the cost of their home in Blackheath.

Pensions Prime Minister's pension

ANECDOTES

1944, In December Callaghan went as the prospective candidate for Cardiff South to the annual Conference of the Labour Party. He spoke in favour of Ian Mikardo's resolution which committed the Party to an election programme that included extensive nationalisation. After the debate, one Labour luminary, Herbert Morrison, went up to Mikardo and Callaghan and said: 'Do you realise you have just lost us the next general election'?

1969, During a visit to Northern Ireland while Home Secretary, Callaghan hosted a dinner attended

ANECDOTES—*Continued*

by both Catholic and Protestant dignitaries. In his book *A House Divided: The Dilemma of Northern Ireland* he recalled: ' . . . I was treading on eggshells. Two matters of protocol in particular concerned me, which I thought might wreck the whole proceedings. One was who should say grace; the second was should we have the loyal toast? In the end I decided we would pay our respects to God, and hoped the Sovereign would forgive a certain informality at the end of dinner. But who to choose between Cardinal Conway, the Catholic Primate; Dr. Simms, the Archbishop of Armagh; and Dr. Carson, Moderator of the Presbyterian Church? I settled the issue by myself saying the simple grace that we used to repeat before meals at home when I was a boy, and the distinguished clerics all solemnly intoned "Amen".'

1976, In her diaries, Barbara Castle (Secretary of State for Social Services, 1974–76) recorded her dismissal from the Cabinet and her protest that she was about to introduce the Health Services Bill to Parliament. In a footnote she added: 'Some months later I was chatting in the Commons to Merlyn Rees, one of Jim Callaghan's strongest backers, and he recalled how much Jim had hated dismissing me. "He told me it spoilt his day", he remarked apologetically. "It spoilt my session", I retorted'.

1979, After Callaghan had tendered the Government's resignation to the Queen on 4 May, he went to the Labour Party's headquarters at Transport House to thank Party workers. When asked what he would miss most from his office as Prime Minister, he said, smiling, 'I will tell you what I am going to gain. During the last two or three days of the campaign Audrey was talking to my second daughter in Cumbria where all the children have been distributing handbills. My four-year-old grandson said "I hope grandad does not win because he does not come to see us enough". That's what I'm going to gain'.

1979, In its coverage of the Labour Party Conference in October the *Daily Telegraph* included the following: 'Does Mr. Callaghan need enemies when he has friends like Mr. Terry Duffy, president of the AUEW? Mr. Callaghan told his host at the Trades Union Conference dinner that he would have to leave as soon as he had finished speaking as he had other engagements. Mr. Duffy rose to his feet and said loudly: "Jim must go". A few moments later, he put his foot in it again when he said: "We all make mistakes, but Jim gets blamed for his mistakes". The Party Leader reproved him, saying: "I would have liked you to phrase that in rather a different way". And then he left. . . . '

1983, When Roy Hattersley, a member of the Shadow Cabinet, reviewed Callaghan's autobiography *Time and Chance* in 1987 he recalled: 'Four years ago—in the middle of the Labour Party's leadership election the *Sunday Times* asked the candidates in that election to give their opinion of past leaders. I described Jim Callaghan in language which was meant to keep just on the respectable side of idolatry. 'Three quarters a great Prime Minister—very brave, very tough, very clever; but not quite ideological enough for my taste'. The next day I received a handwritten note from the great man himself. Could I, it asked, help him to solve a constitutional dilemma? He had intended to support my candidature, but could he cast three-quarters of a vote? If not, he might have to reconsider his position'.

QUOTATIONS

1967, I sum up the prospects for 1967 in three short sentences. We are back on course. The ship is picking up speed. The economy is moving. Every seaman knows the command at such a moment, 'Steady as she goes'. (In the House of Commons, at the end of his Budget Statement)

1972, We say that what Britain needs is a new social contract. That is what this document [*Labour's Programme for Britain*] is about. (Speech at the Labour Party annual Conference)

1976, We used to think that you could spend your way out of a recession, and increase employment by cutting taxes and boosting Government spending. I tell you in all candour that that option no longer exists, and that in so far as it ever did exist, it only worked on each occasion since the war by injecting a bigger dose of inflation into the economy, followed by a higher level of unemployment as the next step . . . That is the history of the last 20 years. (Speech at the Labour Party annual Conference)

1976, A lie can be half-way around the world before truth has got his boots on. (In the House of Commons, in a debate on the appointment of a select committee to inquire into the conduct and activities of Members)

1978, I have promised nobody that I shall be at the altar in October, nobody at all. (Speech at the annual meeting of the Trades Union Congress, when he had been widely expected to announce the date of the General Election)

1979, I don't think that other people in the world would share the view that there is mounting chaos. (Speaking at London Airport on return from the Guadaloupe summit during widespread strikes. The following day the *Sun* headlined its report: 'Crisis? What Crisis?')

1979, I trust that there will be a return to some co-operation in these matters, as distinct from, I was going to say free collective bargaining, but it would be more true to say the free collective vandalism that is now taking place. (In the House of Commons, in answer to a question on the negotiation of pay settlements)

RESIDENCES

17 Montpelier Row, Blackheath, London
11 Downing Street
Upper Clayhill Farm, Ringmer, East Sussex
Carrick Court, Kennington Park Road, London
10 Downing Street
Temple West Mews, West Square, London

MEMORIALS

PORTRAITS

1983, by Bryan Organ, National Portrait Gallery, London; 1989, by Harry Holland, County Hall, Cardiff; 1991, by Graham Jones, House of Commons, London

BIBLIOGRAPHIC INFORMATION

LETTERS AND PERSONAL PAPERS

Lord Callaghan's papers are to go to either the London School of Economics and Political Science or the Bodleian Library, Oxford, upon completion of his official biography by Kenneth Morgan, scheduled for 1997. State papers are available at the Public Record Office, Kew, for his period of ministerial office up to 1951 but not—under the thirty-year rule—for his period in government from 1964.

PUBLICATIONS

1947, *Czechoslovakia. Six Studies in Reconstruction.* (co-author); 1953, *Whitleyism: A Study of Joint Consultation in the Civil Service*; 1973, *A House Divided: The Dilemma of Northern Ireland*; 1975, *Challenges and Opportunities for British Foreign Policy*; 1987, *Time and Chance.*

FURTHER READING

Kellner, P. and Hitchens. C. *Callaghan: The Road to Number Ten.* London, 1976.

Mackintosh, J. P. (ed). *British Prime Ministers in the Twentieth Century.* Vol 2: Churchill to Callaghan. London, 1978.

Morgan, K. O. *Labour People: Leaders and Lieutenants, Hardie to Kinnock.* Oxford, 1992.

E.J.J.

Bettmann

Margaret Thatcher

Lived 1925–
Political Party Conservative
Prime Minister 4 May 1979–28 November 1990
Government Conservative
Reigning Monarch Elizabeth II

Cherish freedom

THATCHER AS PRIME MINISTER

The first woman Prime Minister, Margaret Thatcher, despite being the longest-serving PM in the 20th century, was the first PM removed from office through losing a party leadership election. Entering Parliament in 1959, she immediately made her mark by piloting through a limited freedom of information bill. She held junior and Cabinet posts in the early 1960s and early 1970s before defeating Heath for the Conservative leadership in 1975. Her three administrations, starting in 1979, were marked by her strong ideological and personal character; 'Thatcherism,' a blend of free-market economics, strong defence and nationalism, was a deliberate break with post-war consensus politics. Her leadership during the 1982 Falklands War transformed her public image and helped rescue what was becoming a beleaguered administration. A divided and poorly led Opposition helped ensure her a landslide election victory in 1983 which, despite further crises, she repeated in 1987. Further splits in her party and Government over economic and European policies, plus the introduction of the disastrous 'poll tax' led to further resignations and finally a challenge to her leadership in 1990. Failing to secure an adequate majority she resigned, thus ending one of the most eventful and controversial premierships. She became a member of the House of Lords in 1992 where she has remained active—especially concerning British membership of the European Union.

PERSONAL INFORMATION

Names Margaret Hilda Thatcher (née Roberts)
Peerage Baroness Thatcher of Kesteven, 29 June 1992
Nicknames Milk Snatcher, The Iron Lady
Born 13 Oct 1925
Birthplace 1, North Parade, Grantham, Lincolnshire
Religion Methodist
Ancestry English. Her father came from Northamptonshire, her mother from Lincolnshire. Her father's ancestry was Welsh on his father's side and Irish on his mother's side, while her mother's family was Irish. Her paternal grandfather was a bootmaker, her maternal grandfather a railway cloakroom attendant.
Date and place of marriage 13 Dec 1951, Wesley's Chapel, London
Age at marriage 26 years, 62 days
First entered Parliament 8 Oct 1959
Date appointed PM 4 May 1979
Age at appointment 53 years, 204 days
Date ceased to be PM 28 Nov 1990
Total time as PM 11 years, 209 days
Ceased to be MP 16 Mar 1992
Zodiac sign Libra

FATHER

Alfred Roberts
Date and place of birth 18 Apr 1892, Ringstead, Northamptonshire
Occupation He ran his own grocer's shop in Grantham, Lincolnshire. Active in community affairs—councillor, alderman, JP, mayor, local Methodist preacher, trustee to several local churches, school governor, Rotarian, President of local Grocers' Association and head of local National Savings movement.
Dates of marriages 1) 28 May 1917, Beatrice Ethel Stephenson; 2) 26 Nov 1965, Cissie Miriam Hubbard
Date of death 10 Feb 1970
Place of cremation Grantham

MOTHER

Beatrice Ethel Stephenson
Date and place of birth 24 Aug 1888, 10 South Parade, Grantham, Lincolnshire
Profile An accomplished dressmaker, she had her own business before her marriage. She was also musical.
Date of marriage 28 May 1917
Date of death 7 Dec 1960
Place of cremation Leicester

BROTHERS AND SISTERS

Margaret was the younger of two daughters.
Muriel Joyce, b. 24 May 1921; m. William Cullen (a Scottish farmer); trained in Birmingham to be a physiotherapist; settled in Essex

HUSBAND

Sir Denis Thatcher, Bart.
Date and place of birth 10 May 1915, 26 Southbrook Road, Lee, London
Mother Lilian Kathleen Bird
Father Thomas Herbert Thatcher
Father's occupation Head of the family business, Atlas Preservative Co., which his father had founded
Age at marriages 1) 28 Mar 1942, Margaret Kempson (div. 1946) 26 years, 322 days; 2) 13 Dec 1951, Margaret Roberts, 36 years, 217 days.
Number of children 2
Years older than PM 10 years 157 days
Profile He attended preparatory school in Bognor Regis, Sussex, then Mill Hill School, London. After obtaining accountancy training, he joined his grandfather's firm, Atlas Preservative Co., in 1934. After war service with the Royal Artillery, during which he was awarded an MBE and twice mentioned in despatches, he continued with the company, becoming Managing Director. In 1965, it was sold to Castrol, whose board he joined. When Burmah Oil took it over, he became a board member there, too, retiring in 1975, but retaining several non-executive directorships. He served as Chairman of the London Association of Paint and Varnish Manufacturers for a term, and he was the co-author of *Accounting and Costing in the Paint Industry.* He became a Liveryman of the Worshipful Company of Painters and Stainers. He was the subject of the satirical 'Dear Bill' letters in *Private Eye* magazine, and of the West End comedy, *Anyone for Denis?* His interests include golf and rugby (he was a rugby referee for many years), and in 1980 he became a member of the Lord's Taverners, which organises cricket and other matches for charity.

CHILDREN

1 son, 1 daughter (twins)
Mark, b. 15 Aug 1953; m. 14 Feb 1987, Diane Burgdorf of Texas; failing to qualify as an accountant, he became involved in motor racing and rallying; engaged in public relations or promotion work; pursues business interests in the United States and elsewhere
Carol Jane, b. 15 Aug 1953; unm.; a solicitor; journalist and broadcaster at, among other organisations, the *Sydney Morning Herald*, a Sydney commercial television station in Australia, the London Broadcasting Company, the *Daily Telegraph* and TV-AM in the UK; author of *Diary of an Election: With Margaret Thatcher on the Campaign Trail* (1983), and contributor to *Lloyd on Lloyd*, about tennis players Chris (Evert) and John Lloyd,(1985) and *Switzerland: Through the Eyes of Others* (1992)

LIFE AND CAREER

PARLIAMENTARY ELECTIONS FOUGHT

*(*designates candidate elected)*
DATE 23 Feb 1950. General Election
CONSTITUENCY Dartford
RESULT N.N. Dodds* (Lab/Co) 38,128; M.H. Roberts (Con) 24,490; A.H. Giles (Lib) 5,011

DATE 25 Oct 1951. General Election
CONSTITUENCY Dartford

PARLIAMENTARY ELECTIONS FOUGHT—*Continued*

RESULT N.N. Dodds* (Lab/Co) 40,094; M.H. Roberts (Con) 27,760

DATE 8 Oct 1959. General Election
CONSTITUENCY Finchley
RESULT M.H. Thatcher* (Con) 29,697; E.P. Deakins (Lab) 13,437; H.I. Spence (Lib) 12,701

DATE 15 Oct 1964. General Election
CONSTITUENCY Finchley
RESULT M.H. Thatcher* (Con) 24,591; J.W. Pardoe (Lib) 15,789; A.E. Tomlinson (Lab) 12,408

DATE 31 Mar 1966. General Election
CONSTITUENCY Finchley
RESULT M.H. Thatcher* (Con) 23,968; Y. Sieve (Lab) 14,504; F. Davis (Lib) 13,070

DATE 18 Jun 1970. General Election
CONSTITUENCY Finchley
RESULT M.H. Thatcher* (Con) 25,480; M.L. Freeman (Lab) 14,295; G.D. Mitchell (Lib) 7,614

DATE 28 Feb 1974. General Election
CONSTITUENCY Finchley
RESULT M.H. Thatcher* (Con) 18,180; M.J. O'Connor (Lab) 12,202; L.S. Brass (Lib) 11,221

DATE 10 Oct 1974. General Election
CONSTITUENCY Finchley
RESULT M.H. Thatcher* (Con) 16,498; M.J. O'Connor (Lab) 12,587; L.S. Brass (Lib) 7,384

DATE 3 May 1979. General Election
CONSTITUENCY Finchley
RESULT M.H. Thatcher* (Con) 20,918; R.G. May (Lab) 13,040; A.J. Paterson (Lib) 5,254

DATE 9 Jun 1983. General Election
CONSTITUENCY Finchley
RESULT M.H. Thatcher* (Con) 19,616; L.G. Spigel (Lab) 10,302; M.J. Joachim (Lib) 7,763

DATE 11 Jun 1987. General Election
CONSTITUENCY Finchley
RESULT M.H. Thatcher* (Con) 21,603; J.R.M. Davies (Lab) 12,690; D. Howarth (Lib) 5,580

PARTY ACTIVITY

Party Leadership 1975–90, Leader of Conservative Party
Other offices 1979–90, Chairman, UK Branch, Commonwealth Parliamentary Association; 1979–90, President, British Group, Inter-Parliamentary Union
Membership of group or faction Conservative Philosophy Group; President, No Turning Back Group of Conservative MPs; President, Conservative Way Forward; President, Bruges Group (a body set up to oppose creation of a federal Europe); Patron, Maastricht Referendum Campaign

PARLIAMENTARY AND MINISTERIAL EXPERIENCE

Maiden Speech 5 Feb. 1960. Unusually, her maiden speech was made at the second reading of her Private Member's Bill, the Public Bodies (Admission of the Press to Meetings) Bill. (*HC Deb*, vol 616, col 1350–8). Its scope was widened and the Public Bodies (Admission to Meetings) Act received Royal Assent on 27 Oct 1960.

Opposition offices 1964–65, Opposition spokesman on Pensions; 1965–66, Opposition spokesman on Housing and Land; 1966–67, Opposition spokesman on Treasury affairs (Deputy to Shadow Chancellor); 1967–68, Entered Shadow Cabinet as Shadow Minister of Fuel and Power; 1968–69, Shadow Minister of Transport; 1969–70, Shadow Minister of Education; 1974, Shadow Environment Secretary; 1974–75, Shadow spokesman on Treasury affairs (Deputy to Shadow Chancellor); 1975–79, Leader of the Opposition
Privy Counsellor 20 Jun 1970
Ministerial Offices Joint Parliamentary Secretary, Ministry of Pensions and National Insurance 9 Oct 1961–18 Oct 1964; Secretary of State for Education and Science 20 Jun 1970–5 Mar 1974; First Lord of the Treasury and Minister for the Civil Service 4 May 1979–28 Nov 1990
Opposition Leaders while PM 1979–80, James Callaghan; 1980–83, Michael Foot; 1983–90, Neil Kinnock

GOVERNMENTS FORMED

First Administration 4 May 1979–9 Jun 1983

GENERAL ELECTION RESULT
3 MAY 1979: Conservative 339; Labour 269; Liberal 11; Scottish National Party 2; Plaid Cymru 2; Others 12. Total 635
Conservative majority 44 (excl. the Speaker)

CABINET
Prime Minister, First Lord of the Treasury and Minister for the Civil Service M. Thatcher
Lord President of the Council Lord Soames (May 1979–Sep 1981); F. Pym (Sep 1981–Apr 1982); J. Biffen (Apr 1982–Jun 1983)
Lord Chancellor Lord Hailsham
Lord Privy Seal Sir I. Gilmour (May 1979–Sep 1981); H. Atkins (Sep 1981–Apr 1982); Baroness Young (Apr 1982–Jun 1983)
Chancellor of the Exchequer Sir G. Howe
Chief Secretary to the Treasury J. Biffen (May 1979–Jan 1981); L. Brittan (Jan 1981–Jun 1983)
Foreign Secretary Lord Carrington (May 1979–Apr 1982); F. Pym (Apr 1982–Jun 1983)
Home Secretary W. Whitelaw
Minister of Agriculture, Fisheries and Food P. Walker
Secretary of State for Defence F. Pym (May 1979–Jan 1981); J. Nott (Jan 1981–Jan 1983); M. Heseltine (Jan–Jun 1983)
Secretary of State for Education and Science M. Carlisle (May 1979–Sep 1981); Sir K. Joseph (Sep 1981–Jun 1983)
Secretary of State for Employment J. Prior (May 1979–Sep 1981); N. Tebbit (Sep 1981–Jun 1983)
Secretary of State for Energy D. Howell (May 1979–Sep 1981); N. Lawson (Sep 1981–Jun 1983)
Secretary of State for the Environment M. Heseltine (May 1979–Jan 1983); T. King (Jan–Jun 1983)
Secretary of State for Social Services P. Jenkin (May 1979–Sep 1981); N. Fowler (Sep 1981–Jun 1983)
Secretary of State for Industry Sir K. Joseph (May 1979–Sep 1981); P. Jenkin (Sep 1981–Jun 1983)
Chancellor of the Duchy of Lancaster and Minister for the Arts N. St-John Stevas (May 1979–Jan 1981); (designated *Minister for the Arts*); F. Pym (Jan–Sep 1981); Baroness Young (Sep 1981–Apr 1982); C. Parkinson (Apr 1982–Jun 1983)

Secretary of State for Northern Ireland H. Atkins (May 1979–Sep 1981); J. Prior (Sep 1981–Jun 1983)
*Paymaster General** A. Maude (May 1979–Jan 1981); F. Pym (Jan–Sep 1981); C. Parkinson (Sep 1981–Jun 1983)
Secretary of State for Scotland G. Younger
Secretary of State for Trade J. Nott (May 1979–Jan 1981); J. Biffen (Jan 1981–Apr 1982); Lord Cockfield (Apr 1982–Jun 1983)
*Secretary of State for Transport** N. Fowler (Jan –Sep 1981; D. Howell (Sep 1981–Jun 1983)
Secretary of State for Wales N. Edwards
[* Office not always in Cabinet]

Second Administration 9 Jun 1983–11 Jun 1987

GENERAL ELECTION RESULT

9 JUN 1983: Conservative 397; Labour 209; Liberal 17; Social Democratic Party 6; Scottish National Party 2; Plaid Cymru 2; Others 17. Total 650 Conservative majority 144

CABINET

Prime Minister, First Lord of the Treasury and Minister for the Civil Service Mrs. M. Thatcher
Lord President of the Council and Leader of the House of Lords Viscount Whitelaw
Lord Chancellor Lord Hailsham
Lord Privy Seal J. Biffen
Chancellor of the Exchequer N. Lawson
Chief Secretary to the Treasury P. Rees (Jun 1983–Sep 1985); J. MacGregor (Sep 1985–Jun 1987)
Foreign Secretary Sir G. Howe
Home Secretary L. Brittan (Jun 1983–Sep 1985); D. Hurd (Sep 1985–Jun 1987)
Minister of Agriculture, Fisheries and Food M. Jopling
Secretary of State for Defence M. Heseltine (Jun 1983–Jan 1986); G. Younger (Jan 1986–Jun 1987)
Secretary of State for Education and Science Sir K. Joseph (Jun 1983–May 1986); K. Baker (May 1986–Jun 1987)
Secretary of State for Employment N. Tebbit (Jun–Oct 1983); T. King (Oct 1983–Sep 1985); Lord Young of Graffham (Sep 1985–Jun 1987)
Secretary of State for Energy P. Walker
Secretary of State for the Environment P. Jenkin (Jun 1983–Sep 1985); K. Baker (Sep 1985–May 1986); N. Ridley (May 1986–Jun 1987)
Secretary of State for Social Services N. Fowler
Chancellor of the Duchy of Lancaster Lord Cockfield (Jun 1983–Sep 1984); Earl of Gowrie (Sep 1984–Sep 1985) (designated as *Minister for the Arts*); N. Tebbit (Sep 1985–Jun 1987)
Secretary of State for Northern Ireland J. Prior (Jun 1983–Sep 1984); D. Hurd (Sep 1984–Sep 1985); T. King (Sep 1985–Jun 1987)
Paymaster General and Minister for Employment K. Clarke (Sep 1985–Jun 1987)
Secretary of State for Scotland G. Younger (Jun 1983–Jan 1986); M. Rifkind (Jan 1986–Jun 1987)
Secretary of State for Trade and Industry C. Parkinson (Jun–Oct 1983); N. Tebbit (Oct 1983–Sep 1985); L. Brittan (Sep 1985–Jan 1986); P. Channon (Jan 1986–Jun 1987)
Secretary of State for Transport T. King (Jun–Oct 1983) N. Ridley (Oct 1983–May 1986); J. Moore (May 1986–Jun 1987)
Secretary of State for Wales N. Edwards
Minister without Portfolio Lord Young of Graffham (Sep 1984–Sep 1985)

Third Administration 11 Jun 1987–28 Nov 1990

GENERAL ELECTION RESULT

11 JUNE 1987: Conservative 376; Labour 229; Liberal 17; Social Democratic Party 5; Scottish National Party 3; Plaid Cymru 3; Others 17. Total 650 Conservative majority 101 (excl. the Speaker)

CABINET

Prime Minister, First Lord of the Treasury and Minister for the Civil Service Mrs. M. Thatcher
Lord President of the Council Viscount Whitelaw (Jun 1987–Jan 1988); J. Wakeham (Jan 1988–July 1989); Sir G. Howe (Jul 1989–1 Nov 1990); J. MacGregor (2–28 Nov 1990)
Lord Chancellor Lord Havers (Jun–Oct 1987); Lord Mackay of Clashfern (Oct 1987–Nov 1990)
Lord Privy Seal J. Wakeham (Jun 1987–Jan 1988); Lord Belstead (Jan 1988–Nov 1990)
Chancellor of the Exchequer N. Lawson (Jun 1987–Oct 1989); J. Major (Oct 1989–Nov 1990)
Chief Secretary to the Treasury J. Major (Jun 1987–Jul 1989); N. Lamont (Jul 1989–Nov 1990)
Foreign Secretary Sir G. Howe (Jun 1987–Jul 1989); J. Major (Jul–Oct 1989); D. Hurd (Oct 1989–Nov 1990)
Home Secretary D. Hurd (Jun 1987–Oct 1989); D. Waddington (Oct 1989–Nov 1990)
Minister of Agriculture, Fisheries and Food J. MacGregor (Jun 1987–Jul 1989); J. Gummer (Jul 1989–Nov 1990)
Secretary of State for Defence G. Younger (Jun 1987–Jul 1989); T. King (Jul 1989–Nov 1990)
Secretary of State for Education and Science K. Baker (Jun 1987–Jul 1989); J. MacGregor (Jul 1989–1 Nov 1990); K. Clarke (2–28 Nov 1990)
Secretary of State for Employment N. Fowler (Jun 1987–Jan 1990); M. Howard (Jan–Nov 1990)
Secretary of State for Energy C. Parkinson (Jun 1987–Jul 1989); J. Wakeham (Jul 1989–Nov 1990)
Secretary of State for the Environment N. Ridley (Jun 1987–Jul 1989); C. Patten (Jul 1989–Nov 1990)
Secretary of State for Social Services J. Moore (Jun 1987–Jul 1988) (Office split into separate Departments of Health and of Social Security, Jul 1988)
Secretary of State for Health K. Clarke (Jul 1988–1 Nov 1990); W. Waldegrave (2–28 Nov 1990)
Secretary of State for Social Security J. Moore (Jul 1988–Jul 1989); A. Newton (Jul 1989–Nov 1990)
Chancellor of the Duchy of Lancaster and Minister of Trade and Industry K. Clarke (Jun 1987–Jul 1988); A. Newton (Jul 1988–Jul 1989)
Chancellor of the Duchy of Lancaster K. Baker (Jul 1989–Nov 1990)
Secretary of State for Northern Ireland T.King (Jun 1987–Jul 1989); P. Brooke (Jul 1989–Nov 1990)
Secretary of State for Scotland M. Rifkind
Secretary of State for Trade and Industry Lord Young of Graffham (Jun 1987–Jul 1989); N. Ridley (Jul 1989–Jul 1990); P. Lilley (Jul–Nov 1990)
Secretary of State for Transport P.Channon (Jun 1987–Jul 1989); C. Parkinson (Jul 1989–Nov 1990)
Secretary of State for Wales P. Walker (Jun 1987–May 1990); D. Hunt (May–Nov 1990)

IMPORTANT DATES IN PERSONAL AND POLITICAL LIFE

OCT 1943 Margaret Roberts goes up to Somerville College, Oxford, to read Chemistry.

23 FEB 1950 She contests Dartford at the General Election. Although she loses by almost 14,000 votes, she obtains almost half as many votes again as the Conservative candidate in the previous (1945) General Election.

25 OCT 1951 Contests Dartford at the General Election. She loses again, but obtains 3,000 more votes than in 1950.

13 DEC 1951 Marries Denis Thatcher, Managing Director of the Atlas Preservative Co.

15 AUG 1953 Margaret Thatcher gives birth to twins, Mark and Carol.

8 OCT 1959 Elected Conservative Member of Parliament for Finchley, London.

5 FEB 1960 Makes her maiden speech in the House of Commons, introducing a Private Member's Bill, the Public Bodies (Admission of the Press to Meetings) Bill. She is reported to have spoken fluently for 27 minutes, without reference to notes.

7 DEC 1960 Death of her mother, Beatrice Roberts, in Grantham, Linconshire.

9 OCT 1961 Thatcher is appointed Joint Parliamentary Secretary for Pensions and National Insurance in Harold Macmillan's administration, her first ministerial post.

2 AUG 1965 Edward Heath formally adopted as leader of the Conservative Party.

OCT 1967 Thatcher enters the Shadow Cabinet as Shadow Minister of Fuel and Power.

10 FEB 1970 Death of her father, Alfred Roberts, in Grantham, Lincolnshire. His influence on Margaret was substantial and long-lasting.

20 JUN 1970 Appointed Secretary of State for Education and Science in Edward Heath's administration. She is made a Privy Counsellor.

1972 Free school milk withdrawn from 8 to 11-year-old children. The ensuing national row leads to Thatcher's being dubbed 'Milk Snatcher' and (by *The Sun* newspaper) 'The most unpopular woman in Britain'.

1974 Together with Sir Keith Joseph, Thatcher founds the Centre for Policy Studies, a Conservative think-tank.

11 FEB 1975 Thatcher is elected leader of the Conservative Party and, therefore, Leader of the Opposition.

JAN 1976 In Thatcher's Kensington Town Hall speech, she attacks the Russians, claiming they are 'bent on world domination'. In response, Tass, the official Soviet news agency, labels her the 'Iron Lady'. Although this is not the first ever use of the nickname, it is to become much more familiar from now on.

16 MAR 1976 Harold Wilson announces his resignation as Prime Minister. He is succeeded on 5 Apr by the Foreign Secretary, James Callaghan.

28 MAR 1979 In the House of Commons, the Labour Government loses, by a single vote, a motion of no confidence. The Prime Minister, James Callaghan, calls a General Election.

30 MAR 1979 Airey Neave, Conservative spokesman on Northern Ireland, is killed by a bomb under his car as he is leaving the House of Commons car park. A longstanding friend, he had organised Thatcher's party leadership campaign in 1975.

3 MAY 1979 General Election. The Conservative Party wins, with a majority of 43 seats.

4 MAY 1979 Margaret Thatcher becomes Prime Minister, the first woman ever to hold that office.

29–30 NOV 1979 Dublin summit of European Heads of Government. In seeking to renegotiate the United Kingdom's contribution to the European Community's budget, Thatcher is reported to have banged the table and said 'I want my money'.

21 DEC 1979 Agreement on the future of Zimbabwe-Rhodesia signed at Lancaster House, London. A ceasefire takes effect from 28 Dec, and Zimbabwe becomes fully independent in Apr 1980.

4 NOV 1980 Ronald Reagan elected President of the United States. He is to become a close friend and in Feb 1985 Mrs. Thatcher says that she feels 'no inhibitions about describing the relationship as very, very special'.

APR 1981 Thatcher's official visit to Oman is followed by a contract being awarded to Cementation International, a company for which her son Mark is working. When it is revealed that Mark was in Oman at the same time as his mother, there is controversy in Parliament and the media.

JAN 1982 Mark Thatcher is reported lost in the Sahara Desert during the Paris-Dakar motor rally. His mother is visibly upset in public when there is no news. Eventually, he is located and his father flies out to meet him.

2 APR 1982 Argentina invades the Falkland Islands. The House of Commons meets in emergency session on 3 Apr (a Saturday) and a British naval task force is despatched to the South Atlantic.

5 APR 1982 Lord Carrington, the Foreign Secretary, and Humphrey Atkins, Lord Privy Seal (and chief foreign affairs spokesman in the House of Commons), along with Richard Luce, a junior Foreign Office minister, resign from the Government over Argentina's invasion of the Falkland Islands.

14 JUN 1982 Argentina surrenders, and the Falkland Islands are restored to British control.

24 JUN 1983 Margaret Thatcher is instrumental, along with Ronald Reagan and others, in founding the International Democrat Union, an international forum intended to promote democracy and broadly conservative values.

14 OCT 1983 Cecil Parkinson, Secretary of State for Trade and Industry, resigns from the Cabinet after public disclosure of an affair with his former secretary, Sara Keays. Mrs. Thatcher has been aware of the affair since 9 Jun (the day of the General Election), and she is anxious not to lose him.

25 OCT 1983 The United States invades Grenada, without reference to the United Kingdom, after a coup and the murder of the Prime Minister, Maurice Bishop. Thatcher is reportedly furious with President Reagan over the lack of consultation.

25 JAN 1984 A controversial ban on trade union membership at Government Communications Headquarters (GCHQ) is announced by the Foreign Secretary, following strike action there.

6 MAR 1984 A national miners' strike (technically, a series of regional strikes which spread across the country) begins. It continues until March 1985 in an atmosphere of bitterness and violence, dividing some communities, and even families, into strikers and non-strikers. Thatcher, mindful of the defeat of Edward Heath's government in February 1974, is determined not to give in to Arthur Scargill, the left-wing miners' leader.

25–26 JUN 1984 At the Fontainebleau summit of European Heads of Government, a permanent settlement of arrangements for United Kingdom contributions to the

European Community budget is reached, resulting from Thatcher's persistent demand for more equitable treatment for the UK.

12 OCT 1984 In the early hours, a bomb explodes at the Grand Hotel, Brighton, where leading figures in the Conservative Party are staying during the annual party conference. Five people are killed, including Sir Anthony Berry, MP for Enfield, Southgate. Thatcher, who has escaped injury, with Norman Tebbit, who has been injured, is to attend the reopening of the hotel on 28 Aug 1986.

19 DEC 1984 A treaty agreeing on the transfer of sovereignty over Hong Kong from the UK to China in 1997 is signed by Thatcher in Peking.

29 JAN 1985 Oxford University academics vote (by 738 to 319) to refuse Thatcher an honorary doctorate in civil law. This is the first time the university has snubbed an Oxford-educated Prime Minister.

15 NOV 1985 The Anglo-Irish Agreement is signed, allowing the Republic of Ireland a consultative role in Northern Ireland affairs, but affirming that no change in the status of Northern Ireland will occur without majority consent. Ian Gow, Minister of State at the Treasury and Margaret Thatcher's Parliamentary Private Secretary from 1979 to 1983, resigns from the Government in protest.

9 JAN 1986 Michael Heseltine, Secretary of State for Defence, resigns from the Cabinet over the 'Westland Affair'. The basic issue is whether the future ownership of Westland Helicopters should be American or European, but there are complex political ramifications, including the leak of a confidential letter from the Solicitor-General, Heseltine's position regarding the doctrine of collective Cabinet responsibility in decision-making and the Prime Minister's role in the sequence of events. Thatcher is said to come close to resignation.

24 JAN 1986 Leon Brittan, Secretary of State for Trade and Industry, resigns from the Cabinet, also over Westland.

14 APR 1986 A Government Bill to liberalise Sunday shopping hours is defeated in the House of Commons by 296 to 282 votes. Thatcher had voted in favour of the proposed changes.

14–15 APR 1986 The United States bombs Libya overnight, using aircraft stationed at British bases, following a terrorist attack for which Colonel Gaddafi, the Libyan head of state, is blamed. Margaret Thatcher is widely criticised for accommodating President Reagan's wishes.

17 NOV 1986 The 'Spycatcher' trial begins in Australia. *Spycatcher* is the title of the memoirs of Peter Wright, a former British intelligence officer now retired and living in Australia. Believing that Wright's revelations of Security Service activities breached his duty of confidentiality to his former employers, the British Government attempts to ban publication of the book in the UK and Australia. However, it is already available elsewhere and the Government loses the case.

28 MAR–1 APR 1987 Thatcher's first official visit to the Soviet Union.

11 JUN 1987 General Election. The Conservative Party wins, with a majority of 102 seats. Margaret Thatcher becomes the first Prime Minister in the 20th century to win three successive elections.

26 OCT 1987 Lord Havers, the Lord Chancellor, resigns from the Cabinet on health grounds.

3 JAN 1988 Margaret Thatcher becomes the longest-serving Prime Minister of the 20th century.

10 JAN 1988 Viscount Whitelaw, Lord President of the Council and Leader of the House of Lords, and a close friend and trusted adviser to Thatcher, resigns from the Cabinet on health grounds.

20 SEP 1988 Thatcher's speech to the College of Europe in Bruges, Belgium, (subsequently referred to simply as the 'Bruges speech') outlines her views on Europe. She objects to the idea of 'a European superstate' and warns against trying to fit individual countries 'into some sort of identikit European personality'.

1 APR 1989 The Community Charge, or 'Poll Tax', is introduced in Scotland, as a replacement for the previous system of local government finance. It proves very unpopular and its introduction in England and Wales on 1 Apr 1990 is preceded by violence in Trafalgar Square, London.

24 JUL 1989 In a controversial Cabinet reshuffle, Sir Geoffrey Howe is sacked as Foreign Secretary. He is unwilling to go and his new post as Lord President of the Council and Leader of the House of Commons is accompanied (allegedly at his insistence) by the title Deputy Prime Minister. John Major is unexpectedly appointed Foreign Secretary in his place.

26 OCT 1989 Nigel Lawson, Chancellor of the Exchequer, resigns from the Cabinet over conflict with Sir Alan Walters, the Prime Minister's personal economic adviser. He is replaced by John Major.

5 DEC 1989 Sir Anthony Meyer, a backbench MP with no chance of success, challenges Margaret Thatcher for leadership of the Conservative Party. Although party rules allow, in theory, for an annual contest, this is the first actual challenge to a serving Prime Minister since the system for choosing Conservative Party leaders was changed in the 1960s. In the ballot held on that day, Thatcher obtains 314 votes and Sir Anthony 33; there are 27 abstentions or spoilt papers.

3 JAN 1990 Norman Fowler, Secretary of State for Employment, resigns from the Cabinet for personal reasons.

4 MAY 1990 Peter Walker, Secretary of State for Wales, resigns from the Cabinet for personal reasons, of which Thatcher had been forewarned.

14 JUL 1990 Nicholas Ridley, Secretary of State for Trade and Industry, resigns from the Cabinet over remarks about Germany which he made in an interview with *The Spectator* magazine.

30 JUL 1990 Ian Gow, Conservative MP for Eastbourne, is killed in a car bomb explosion at his home. A close friend of Margaret Thatcher, he had been her Parliamentary Private Secretary from 1979 to 1983.

2 AUG 1990 Iraq invades Kuwait. Thatcher encourages President Bush to take firm action against Saddam Hussein, the Iraqi leader.

3 OCT 1990 The reunification of Germany takes effect.

8 OCT 1990 Sterling joins the Exchange Rate Mechanism of the European Monetary System. Thatcher has long been against this, but has apparently been persuaded to agree to it.

1 NOV 1990 Sir Geoffrey Howe, Lord President of the Council, Leader of the House of Commons and Deputy Prime Minister, resigns from the Cabinet over differences with the Prime Minister, attacking Thatcher in his resignation speech to the House on 13 Nov.

19 NOV 1990 Conventional Forces in Europe agreement signed in Paris.

20 NOV 1990 Michael Heseltine, a much more serious contender than Sir Anthony Meyer had been, challenges Margaret Thatcher for leadership of the Conservative

IMPORTANT DATES IN PERSONAL AND POLITICAL LIFE—*Continued*

Party. On the first ballot, Thatcher obtains 204 votes and Heseltine 152, with 16 abstentions. By Conservative Party rules, Thatcher is 4 votes short of outright victory.

22 NOV 1990 Margaret Thatcher announces her resignation, to take effect when a new leader of the Conservative Party has been elected. Two new candidates, John Major and Douglas Hurd, enter the contest.

27 NOV 1990 Second ballot for leadership of the Conservative Party. Major obtains 185 votes, Heseltine 131 and Hurd 56. Heseltine and Hurd withdraw from the contest.

28 NOV 1990 Margaret Thatcher's resignation becomes effective. John Major becomes Prime Minister.

16 MAR 1992 Margaret Thatcher ceases to be an MP, on dissolution of Parliament for a General Election.

30 JUN 1992 She is introduced into the House of Lords as Baroness Thatcher of Kesteven.

2 JUL 1992 Makes her maiden speech in the House of Lords, on Europe.

7 JUN 1993 She speaks again on this subject, to an exceptionally full House of Lords, during passage of the European Communities (Amendment) Bill, known as the 'Maastricht' Bill.

BACKGROUND

PHYSICAL CHARACTERISTICS AND HEALTH

From her schooldays onwards, Margaret Thatcher always displayed a determination to achieve what she wanted, irrespective of the obstacles in her way. As Prime Minister, this showed itself in her single-minded concentration on work—she could work very long hours during the day, with little sleep at night. She tended to regard holidays as a waste of time and she was not known for a sense of humour.

According to Airey Neave in 1979, 'she is self-critical, likes accuracy, enjoys a well-reasoned argument and respects people who know their facts—she has immense powers of concentration and a quite exceptional memory . . . [She has] great personal courage' (quoted in Andrew Thomson, *Margaret Thatcher*, p. 244).

Always concerned with her appearance, she has inspired opposing reactions. President Mitterrand of France allegedly once described her as having 'the eyes of Caligula, but the mouth of Marilyn Monroe', while Dr. Josef Luns, former Secretary-General of NATO, described her as 'sexy'.

In general, Margaret Thatcher's health has been strikingly good, in spite of her punishing schedules. According to one of her biographers, Penny Junor (in *Margaret Thatcher: Wife, Mother, Politician*), ' She fainted in the House once; she caught mumps from the twins; and during her first ten years in Parliament, she suffered quite acutely at times from hay fever. She also suffered from bad posture'.

As Prime Minister, absences from work were very rare. In the first ten years of her premiership, there were three such absences, due to operations on varicose veins, an eye and a hand.

EDUCATION

Primary 1930–36, Huntingtower Elementary School, Grantham

Secondary 1936–43, Kesteven and Grantham Girls' School, Grantham (joint head girl in her last term)

University 1943–47, Somerville College, Oxford (Chemistry); 1953, Passed Bar final examinations; 1954, Called to the Bar, Lincoln's Inn

Prizes and awards County scholarship to Kesteven and Grantham Girls' School; Joint winner of the Kirkauldy Essay Prize while at Oxford.

Qualifications 1949, B.Sc; 1950, MA

Cultural and vocational background 1935, Messenger and runner of errands in Grantham during the General Election campaign; 1945, Canvassed for Conservative Party candidates in Oxford and Grantham during General Election campaign. The Oxford candidate was Quintin Hogg, later Lord Hailsham, who was to serve Thatcher as Lord Chancellor in her first two administrations; 1946, President of Oxford University Conservative Association; 1948, Attended Conservative Party Conference on behalf of Oxford University Graduates' Association.

Languages She took an intensive course in Latin in order to meet Oxford University entrance requirements. While Secretary of State for Education and Science she took Foreign Office French courses.

NON-PARLIAMENTARY CAREER

Early occupations Between 1947 and 1951, after leaving Oxford, she was employed as a research chemist, first by British Xylonite Plastics of Manningtree, Essex, and then by J. Lyons and Co. of London. After unsuccessfully standing for Dartford in the General Elections of 1950 and 1951, she married Denis Thatcher and began law studies. In Dec 1953 she passed her Bar exams and went on to specialise in taxation law.

Other posts 1951, Personal assistant to Director of the Joint Iron Council; 1955–57, Member of Executive Committee, Society of Conservative Lawyers; 1970–74, Co-Chairman, Women's National Commission; 1992, International political consultant to Philip Morris, Inc.

HONOURS

Freedom of cities 1979, Royal Borough of Kensington and Chelsea; 1980, London Borough of Barnet; 1983, Falkland Islands; 1989, City of London; 1990, City of Westminster

Academic 1970, Hon. Fellow, Somerville College, Oxford; 1975, Hon. Bencher, Lincoln's Inn; 1983, Hon. Master of the Bench, Gray's Inn; 1986, LL.D, Buckingham University; 1992, Chancellor, Buckingham University

Foreign 1981, Donovan Award (USA); 1981, Hon. doctorate, Georgetown University, Washington, DC; 1983, Winston Churchill Foundation Award (USA); 1990, Aspen Institute Statesman's Award (USA); 1991, Presidential Medal of Freedom (USA); 1991, Order of Good Hope (South Africa); 1991, Hon. doctorate, Rand Afrikaans University (South Africa); 1992, Hon. degree,

Weizmann Institute of Science (Israel); 1993, Hon. doctorate, Louisiana State University, Baton Rouge; 1993, Chancellor, William and Mary College, Williamsburg, Virginia (the first woman ever to hold this honorary post and the first British subject to do so since American independence); 1993, Hon. degree, Mendeleyev Chemical University, Moscow

Other than peerage 20 Jul 1979, Fellow, Royal Institute of Chemistry and Chemical Society; 16 Jan 1980, Hon. Freeman, Worshipful Company of Grocers; 1983, Liveryman, Worshipful Company of Glovers; 30 Jun 1983, Fellow, Royal Society; 7 Dec 1990, Order of Merit

CLUBS

Carlton (first woman member); St. Stephen's; Variety Club of Great Britain (first woman member)

HOBBIES AND SPORTS

She has skiied regularly and played tennis occasionally. Interests include music, especially opera; reading; decorating; and collecting porcelain, Chinese art, military mementoes, photography and the works of Rudyard Kipling. No pets, but she is said to have reprieved the 10 Downing Street cat and taken in a stray cat at Chequers.

FINANCES

Margaret Thatcher inherited her father's cautious approach to money and has consistently striven to avoid being in debt. Not wealthy in her own right originally, she has freely acknowledged the role of her husband's substantial income in enabling her to pursue her legal studies, and, subsequently, a political career. As Prime Minister, she forewent considerable income by opting to take the salary of a Cabinet Minister, rather than the higher Prime Ministerial one to which she was entitled. Since leaving office, she has become much wealthier, chiefly by means of lectures given all over the world, but also through business interests.

Income On taking office as Prime Minister in 1979, she received a salary of £22,000 plus a Parliamentary salary of £3,529. Subsequently, however, she refused a Prime Ministerial salary in favour of a lower Cabinet Minister one. In 1990, therefore, she earned £35,120 (instead of £46,750), plus a Parliamentary salary of £20,101.

Spouse's finances Denis Thatcher was a relatively wealthy businessman when he met Margaret. He sold his company, Atlas Preservative Co., to Castrol in 1965 for at least £530,000, and he is generally acknowledged to be a millionaire.

Pensions She receives an index-linked former Prime Minister's pension. In addition, she is entitled, as an ex-Prime Minister, to an annual allowance to assist with office and secretarial expenses incurred in her public duties.

Legacies Her father left her a small legacy.

ANECDOTES

Shortly after she was elected Conservative Party leader in Feb 1975, Margaret Thatcher called for Ronald Millar, who had been a speechwriter for her immediate predecessor, Edward Heath. In an atmosphere of mutual suspicion, he was told to prepare a speech for a party political broadcast. He returned later and read the speech to her. It ended with a quotation sometimes (but falsely) attributed to Abraham Lincoln: 'You cannot bring about prosperity by discouraging thrift. You cannot strengthen the weak by weakening the strong. You cannot help small men by tearing down big men. You cannot help the wage-earner by pulling down the wage-payer. You cannot further the brotherhood of man by encouraging class hatred. You cannot help the poor by destroying the rich. You cannot establish sound security on borrowed money. You cannot keep out of trouble by spending more than you earn. You cannot build character and courage by taking away man's initiative and independence. You cannot help men permanently by doing for them what they could and should do for themselves.'

Margaret Thatcher is said to have listened in stony silence. When Millar had finished, she said nothing but bent down and, from inside her handbag, produced a piece of paper which she handed to him. It was the quotation he had just read to her. 'I never go anywhere without it', she said.

As Prime Minister, Margaret Thatcher never liked to relax for too long and kept holidays to a bare minimum. In the summer of 1979, she was invited to the home of Lord Margadale on the Scottish island of Islay. According to Wapshott and Brock (*Thatcher*, 1983), this was 'a country retreat often used by Tory leaders, who would enjoy the rough shooting during the day and the archaic playing of rowdy house-party games in the evening'. However, Mrs. Thatcher did not enjoy the entertainment and, after two nights, she announced that she would return to work in her room which, unfortunately, was directly over the source of the noise. On one occasion, she is said to have thumped several times on the floor, but to no avail. Instead, she went outside for a walk.

Mrs. Thatcher's personal concern for individuals, often not appreciated, is illustrated by an incident which occurred at Chequers, the Prime Minister's official country residence. A meal was being served, and 'Wrens' (members of the Women's Royal Naval Service) were waiting at table. One of them accidentally spilt food over Sir Geoffrey Howe, then Chancellor of the Exchequer. The Prime Minister is reported to have jumped up and rushed instinctively to the Wren's side, putting an arm around her and comforting her at a time of obvious embarrassment.

Margaret Thatcher inherited her father's desire to avoid personal debt. In Mar 1987, when she was opening a new supermarket in North London, she realised that she would need meat for the weekend. She bought three pounds of mince, but only then discovered that she had no money in her handbag and asked the meat counter manager to send her the bill. According to her constituency agent, Andrew Thomson, for months afterwards she kept asking her constituency secretary if the mince bill had been paid. Explanations that the company regarded the mince as a gift, or that the cost of providing the account would exceed the cost of the mince, failed to move her.

QUOTATIONS

1974, It will be years before a woman either leads the (Conservative) Party or becomes Prime Minister. I don't see it happening in my time. (To a reporter from the *Liverpool Daily Post*)

1975, What's right for the family is right for Britain. (Interview in the *Sunday Express*, 29 Jun)

QUOTATIONS—*Continued*

1980, No one would have remembered the Good Samaritan if he'd only had good intentions. He had money as well. (Interview on *Weekend World*, 6 Jan)

1980, You turn if you want to. The lady's not for turning. (Speech at Conservative Party Conference, 10 Oct)

1982, Failure? The possibilities do not exist. (On the risks of sending a naval task force to recapture the Falkland Islands from Argentina)

1984, I like Mr. Gorbachev. We can do business together. (At Chequers, after his visit to the UK as a member of a Soviet delegation)

1985, The West could have no better or braver champion. [ie, than Ronald Reagan] (Speech at Conservative Party Conference, 11 Oct)

1987, I hope to go on and on and on. (Interview with John Cole of the BBC, 12 May, before the General Election of 11 Jun)

1987, There is no such thing as society. (Interview in *Woman's Own* magazine, 31 Oct)

1992, A treaty too far (Describing the Maastricht Treaty on European Union, in the *Independent*, 29 Jun)

RESIDENCES

1 North Parade, Grantham, Lincolnshire (plaque)
St. George's Square Mews, Pimlico, London
Swan Court, Chelsea, London
Dormers, Locks Bottom, Farnborough, Kent
Westminster Gardens, Marsham Street, London
The Mount, Lamberhurst, Kent
19 Flood Street, Chelsea, London
Court Lodge, Lamberhurst, Kent
Scotney Castle, Lamberhurst, Kent
10 Downing Street
Chequers, Buckinghamshire
11 Hambledon Place, Dulwich Gate, London
Eaton Square, London
Open to the public Scotney Castle Garden (owned by the National Trust). The ruined 14th century castle and surrounding garden are open to the public, but the 19th century house in which the Thatchers rented a flat is not.

MEMORIALS

STATUES AND BUTSTS

1979, by Oscar Nemon, Carlton Club, London; 1983, by Oscar Nemon, Somerville College, Oxford

PORTRAITS

1975, by Andre de Moller, Carlton Club, London; 1981, by Roger Birchall (Copies were given away free with *Punch* magazine); 1982, by Leonard Boden, Carlton Club, London; 1984, by Rodrigo Moynihan, National Portrait Gallery; 1985, by John Anthony, retained by Baroness Thatcher; 1986, by David Donaldson, Scottish National Portrait Gallery, Edinburgh; 1989, by June Mendoza, Lincoln's Inn, London; 1990, by Michael Noakes, Worshipful Co. of Grocers, London; 1992, by Henry Mee, 1 Parliament Street, London; 1993, by Sergei Chepik, retained by Baroness Thatcher

OTHER MEMORIALS

There is a plaque at Kesteven and Grantham Girls' School. There is a Thatcher Street in Kuwait City and a Thatcher Drive in Port Stanley (Falkland Islands). A Thatcher Peninsula on South Georgia in the South Atlantic is named after her, and 10 Jan is known as Thatcher Day in the Falkland Islands. The Thatcher Foundation was established after she left office, as a means of marking her influence on the international political scene. Its first meeting of trustees and advisers took place on 22 Nov 1991. Its first grant was to Enterprise Europe, a programme of training placements in the United Kingdom for young business people from Eastern and Central Europe. The Thatcher Award is given annually by Aims of Industry, a free-market industrial body. Thatcher Court, a sheltered housing scheme for the elderly in Dartford, Kent, is also named after her.

BIBLIOGRAPHIC INFORMATION

LETTERS AND PERSONAL PAPERS

1977, *Let Our Children Grow Tall: Selected Speeches 1975–1977*; 1986, *In Defence of Freedom: Speeches on Britain's Relations with the World 1976–86* Foreword by Ronald Reagan; 1989, *Speeches to the Conservative Party Conference 1975–1988*; *The Revival of Britain: Speeches on Home and European Affairs 1975–1988. Compiled by Alistair B. Cooke. London, 1989.*

PUBLICATIONS

1952, 'Wake up, Women!' (Article in the *Sunday Graphic*); 1967, 'Parliament and Money Matters' (Article in *Shades of Blue*); 1968, 'What's Wrong with Politics?' (Annual Conservative Political Centre lecture to the party conference); 1975, 'How to Fight and Survive' (Article in the *Sunday Express*); 1978, *The Right Angle: Three Studies in Conservatism* (jointly with Sir Geoffrey Howe and Sir Keith Joseph); 'The Sinews of Foreign Policy' (Address to Les Grandes Conferences Catholiques, Brussels); 1979, 'Europe: The Obligations of Liberty' (The Winston Churchill Memorial Lecture, Luxembourg); 1984, Contributor to: *Challenges to the Western Alliance: An International Symposium on the Changing Political, Economic and Military Setting*; 1990, *Our Threatened Environment: The Conservative Response*; 1990, Preface to *Christianity and Conservatism*; 1991, 'A Grand Finale: Rt Hon Margaret Thatcher's last speech as Prime Minister'; 1991, 'Europe's Political Architecture' (Speech to the Global Panel, The Hague, 15 May); 1992, Foreword to *A Treaty Too Far*; 1993, *The Downing Street Years*

FURTHER READING

Abse, L. *Margaret, Daughter of Beatrice: A Politician's Psycho-biography of Margaret Thatcher*. London, 1989.
Arnold, B. *Margaret Thatcher: A Study in Power*. London, 1984.
Bruce-Gardyne, J. *Mrs. Thatcher's First Administration: The Prophets Confounded*. London, 1984.
Clarke, P. *A Question of Leadership: Gladstone to Thatcher*. London, 1992.
Cole, J. *The Thatcher Years: A Decade of Revolution in British Politics*. London, 1987.
Cosgrave, P. *Thatcher, The First Term*. London, 1985.

Daly, M. & George, A. (eds.) *Margaret Thatcher in Her Own Words*. London, 1987.
Gardiner, G. *Margaret Thatcher: From Childhood to Leadership*. London, 1975.
Garfinkel, B. *Margaret Thatcher*. London, 1988.
Geelhoed, E. B. *Margaret Thatcher in Victory and Downfall, 1987 and 1990*. New York, 1992.
Harris, K. *Thatcher*. London, 1988.
Ionescu, G. *Leadership in an Interdependent World: The Statesmanship of Adenauer, De Gaulle, Thatcher, Reagan and Gorbachev*. London, 1991.
Junor, P. *Margaret Thatcher: Wife, Mother, Politician*. London, 1983.
Levin, A. *Margaret Thatcher*. London, 1981.
Lewis, R. *Margaret Thatcher: A Personal and Political Biography*. Revised ed. London, 1984.
Little, G. *Strong Leadership: Thatcher, Reagan and an Eminent Person*. Oxford, 1988.
McFadyean, M. & Renn, M. *Thatcher's Reign: A Bad Case of the Blues*. London, 1984.
Maitland, Lady O. *Margaret Thatcher: The First 10 Years*. London, 1989.
Mayer, A. J. *Madam Prime Minister: Margaret Thatcher and Her Rise to Power*. New York, 1979.
Millar, R. *A View from the Wings: West End, West Coast, Westminster*. London, 1993.
Money, E. *Margaret Thatcher: First Lady of the House*. London, 1975.
Murray, P. *Margaret Thatcher*. London, 1980.
Ogden, C. *Maggie: An Intimate Portrait of a Woman in Power*. New York, 1990.
Ranelagh, J. *Thatcher's People: An Insider's Account of the Politics, the Power and the Personalities*. London, 1991.
Riddell, P. *The Thatcher Era and Its Legacy*. Oxford, 1991.
Smith, G. *Reagan and Thatcher*. London, 1990.
Smith, R. A. *The Premier Years of Margaret Thatcher*. London, 1991.
Stephenson, H. *Mrs. Thatcher's First Year*. London, 1980.
Thatcher, C. *Diary of an Election: With Margaret Thatcher on the Campaign Trail—A Personal Account*. London, 1983.
Thomson, A. *Margaret Thatcher: The Woman Within*. London, 1989.
Wapshott, N. & Brock, G. *Thatcher*. London, 1983.
Watkins, A. *A Conservative Coup: The Fall of Margaret Thatcher*. London, 1991.
Webster, W. *Not a Man to Match Her*. London, 1990.
Young, H. *One of Us: A biography of Margaret Thatcher*. Final ed. London, 1991.
Young, H. & Sloman, A. *The Thatcher Phenomenon*. London, 1986.

A.D.P.

Bettmann

John Major

Lived 1943–
Political Party Conservative
Prime Minister 28 November 1990–
Government Conservative
Reigning Monarch Elizabeth II

MAJOR AS PRIME MINISTER

On appointment he was the youngest Prime Minister in the 20th century. He was the first Conservative to become PM simply by virtue of winning a party leadership election and the only 20th century PM to achieve office without ever having been a member of the Opposition. First elected for a safe seat in 1979, he soon held junior posts and entered the Cabinet after the 1987 General Election. He was Foreign Secretary briefly and then Chancellor of the Exchequer in which post he had disagreements with Prime Minister Thatcher over European policy. He supported Thatcher in the first round of the Conservative party leadership contest in 1990 and entered the second round following her withdrawal. Although his appointment as PM coincided with an economic recession, the electorate reaffirmed him as PM at the General Election in 1992. His administration survived sterling dropping out of the Exchange Rate Mechanism in September 1992 and subsequent Tory party divisions over the Maastricht Treaty and the European Union. Major is a strong chairman and able negotiator. His presidency of the EC Council was regarded as a success, in particular his handling of the Edinburgh meeting in December 1992. Despite continuing divisions in his party concerning Europe he continued to receive Cabinet support. The electorate however at the local government and the European Parliament elections in 1994, voiced strong criticism of him as did the public opinion polls.

PERSONAL INFORMATION

Names John (Roy) Major (He was christened and baptised John Roy, but only John appears on the birth certificate).
Born 29 Mar 1943
Birthplace Surrey County Hospital, St. Helier, Carshalton, Surrey
Religion Anglican
Ancestry English. His father was born in Staffordshire, but spent his early years in the United States, where his grandfather, Abraham Ball, a master bricklayer, helped to build blast furnaces for Andrew Carnegie's steel plants in Pennsylvania. His paternal grandmother, Sarah O'Mara, was of Irish descent. His maternal grandfather was an insurance agent.
Date and place of marriage 3 Oct 1970, St. Matthew's Church, Brixton, London
Age at marriage 27 years, 189 days
First entered Parliament 3 May 1979
Date appointed PM 28 Nov 1990
Age at appointment 47 years, 245 days
Zodiac sign Aries

FATHER

Abraham Thomas Ball (stage name Tom Major, also known as Thomas Major-Ball)
Date and place of birth 18 May 1879, New Street, Bloxwich, Staffordshire
Occupation He spent his teenage years in the United States, where he won (but did not take up) a Girard Scholarship to West Point Military Academy, and he played baseball for a Philadelphia junior team. On his return to the UK, after a short spell in building, he worked as a theatrical artist in many capacities, including on the circus trapeze, touring the country. He later ran his own garden ornaments business.
Dates of marriages 1) 1 Jun 1910, Kate Edith Grant (stage name Kitty Drum, d. 1928); 2) 4 Apr 1929, Gwendoline Minnie Coates
Date of death 27 Mar 1962
Place of burial Streatham, London

MOTHER

Gwendoline Minnie Coates
Date and place of birth 12 Apr 1905, 35 St. John's Terrace, Gainsborough, Lincolnshire
Profile She was a dancer in Tom Major's travelling show, performing as one half of a two-person act, 'Glade and Glen'.
Date of marriage 4 Apr 1929
Date of death 17 Sep 1970
Place of burial Streatham, London

BROTHERS AND SISTERS

John Major is the third son and fourth of four children.
Thomas Aston, b. 20 Jun 1929; d. 20 Jun 1929
Patricia June, b. 3 Jun 1930, Gainsborough, Lincolnshire; m. 1959, Peter Dessoy (d. 1972); studied dress design at art school in Wimbledon; worked in various capacities taking responsibility for paying off a family debt incurred by her father's garden ornament business
Terry (Registered as Terry Major Ball), b. 2 Jul 1932, Old Malden Surrey; m. Shirley Wilson; worked for the electricity board, Philips Services and later ran his father's garden ornaments business, continuing to work for David's Rural Industries, which bought it; active in retirement in researching his father's theatrical career. His book *Major Major* was published in 1994.

WIFE

Norma Christina Elizabeth Johnson (née Wagstaff—her mother reverted to her maiden name of Johnson after being widowed)
Date and place of birth 12 Feb 1942, Lady Forester Hospital, Much Wenlock, Shropshire
Mother Edith Johnson
Father Norman Wagstaff
Father's Occupation By profession a printer, he was also a talented pianist. Serving in the Royal Artillery, he was killed in a motorcycle accident a few days after the end of World War II.
Age at marriage 28 years, 234 days
Number of children 2
Years older than PM 1 year, 46 days
Profile She attended boarding school at Bexhill-on-Sea, Sussex; then Oakfield School, Dulwich, London and Peckham School for Girls, London, where she was head girl. An accomplished dressmaker, she trained as a teacher and taught Domestic Science in South London for a while, first at St. Michael & All Angels Church of England School, Camberwell, and later as a supply teacher at Norwood School. She has strong interests in arts and music, with a particular passion for opera. She has worked as a nanny for the soprano June Bronhill, and in 1987 published a biography of the Australian opera singer Joan Sutherland. She is writing a book about *Chequers*, the Prime Minister's official country residence. She is a longstanding supporter of charities, especially MENCAP (the Royal Society for Mentally Handicapped Children & Adults). She is also involved in the Meals on Wheels Service.

CHILDREN

1 son, 1 daughter
Elizabeth Christina, b. 13 Nov 1971, veterinary nurse trainee
James Edward, b. 16 Jan 1975; left school in 1993

LIFE AND CAREER

PARLIAMENTARY ELECTIONS FOUGHT

DATE 28 Feb 1974. General Election
CONSTITUENCY St. Pancras North
RESULT A.W. Stallard* (Lab) 14,761; J.R. Major, (Con), 7,926; P.J. B. Medlicott, (Lib), 4,825
DATE 10 Oct 1974. General Election
CONSTITUENCY St. Pancras North
RESULT A.W. Stallard* (Lab) 14,155; J.R. Major, (Con) 6,602; P.J. B. Medlicott (Lib), 3,428
DATE 3 May 1979. General Election
CONSTITUENCY Huntingdonshire
RESULT J.R. Major* (Con) 40,193; J.G.H. Fulbrook, (Lab), 18,630; D.G. Rowe (Lib), 12,812
DATE 9 Jun 1983. General Election

PARLIAMENTARY ELECTIONS FOUGHT—*Continued*

CONSTITUENCY Huntingdon
RESULT J. R. Major* (Con) 34,254; S. J. Gatiss (Lib), 13,906; M. Slater (Lab), 6,317
DATE 11 Jun 1987. General Election
CONSTITUENCY Huntingdon
RESULT J.R. Major* (Con) 40,530; A.J. Nicholson (SDP), 13,486; D. M. Brown (Lab), 8,883
DATE 9 Apr 1992. General Election
CONSTITUENCY Huntingdon
RESULT J.R. Major* (Con) 48,662; H.A. Seckleman (Lab), 12,432; A. N. Duff (Lib Dem), 9,386

PARTY ACTIVITY

Party Leadership 1990– Leader of the Conservative Party
Other offices 1960–64 Treasurer, Vice-Chairman, Political Officer, Chairman, of Brixton Young Conservatives; 1965, Founder Chairman, Lambeth Young Conservatives; 1965–67 Chairman, Brixton Conservative Association CPC Committee; 1968, Constituency Treasurer; 1968, Member, Conservative Central Office Speakers' Panel; 1969, Constituency Vice-Chairman; 1970–71, Constituency Chairman up to dissolution of the Association following a Boundary Commission report; 1975, Branch Chairman, Beckenham Constituency Association; 1979–81, Joint Secretary, Conservative Party Parliamentary Environment Committee; 1983–85, President, Eastern Area Young Conservatives; 1988–89, President, Association of Conservative Clubs; 1990–, Chairman, U.K. Branch, Commonwealth Parliamentary Association; President, British Group, Inter-Parliamentary Union
Membership of group or faction One Nation Group; Guy Fawkes Group; Blue Chip Group; Patron, European Movement; Patron, Centre for Policy Studies

PARLIAMENTARY AND MINISTERIAL EXPERIENCE

Maiden Speech 13 Jun 1979, on Government economic policy during the debate on the first Budget of the new Thatcher administration. (*HC Deb* vol 968, col 519-26)
Privy Counsellor 13 Jun 1987
Ministerial Offices Assistant Whip, 14 Jan 1983–3 Oct 1984; Lord Commissioner of the Treasury, 3 Oct 1984–2 Sep 1985; Parliamentary Under Secretary of State, Department of Health & Social Security, 2 Sep 1985–10 Sep 1986; Minister of State, Department of Health & Social Security, 10 Sep 1986– 13 Jun 1987; Chief Secretary to the Treasury, 13 Jun 1987– 24 Jul 1989; Secretary of State for Foreign & Commonwealth Affairs, 24 Jul–26 Oct 1989; Chancellor of the Exchequer, 26 Oct 1989–28 Nov 1990; First Lord of the Treasury & Minister for the Civil Service, 28 Nov 1990–
Opposition Leaders while PM 1990–92, Neil Kinnock; 1992–94, John Smith; 1994, Margaret Beckett; Jul 1994– Tony Blair

GOVERNMENTS FORMED

First Administration 28 Nov 1990–9 Apr 1992

GENERAL ELECTION RESULT
11 JUN 1987: Conservative 376; Labour 229; Liberal 17; Social Democratic Party 5; Scottish National Party 3; Plaid Cymru 3; Others 17. Total 650
Conservative majority 101 (excl. the Speaker)

CABINET
Prime Minister, First Lord of the Treasury and Minister for the Civil Service J. Major
Lord President of the Council J. MacGregor
Lord Chancellor Lord Mackay of Clashfern
Lord Privy Seal Lord Waddington
Chancellor of the Exchequer N. Lamont
Chief Secretary to the Treasury D. Mellor
Foreign Secretary D. Hurd
Home Secretary K. Baker
Minister of Agriculture, Fisheries & Food J. Gummer
Secretary of State for Defence T. King
Secretary of State for Education and Science K. Clarke
Secretary of State for Employment M. Howard
Secretary of State for Energy J. Wakeham
Secretary of State for the Environment M. Heseltine
Secretary of State for Health W. Waldegrave
Chancellor of the Duchy of Lancaster C. Patten
Secretary of State for Northern Ireland P. Brooke
Secretary of State for Scotland I. Lang
Secretary of State for Social Security A. Newton
Secretary of State for Trade and Industry P. Lilley
Secretary of State for Transport M. Rifkind
Secretary of State for Wales D. Hunt

Second Administration 9 Apr 1992–

GENERAL ELECTION RESULT
9 APR 1992: Conservative 336; Labour 271; Liberal Democrats 20; Plaid Cymru 4; Scottish National Party 3; Others 17. Total 651
Conservative majority 21

CABINET
Prime Minister, First Lord of the Treasury and Minister for the Civil Service J. Major
Lord President of the Council A. Newton
Lord Chancellor Lord Mackay of Clashfern
Lord Privy Seal Lord Wakeham(Apr 1992–Jul 1994); Viscount Cranborne (Jul 1994–)
Chancellor of the Exchequer N. Lamont (Apr 1992–May 1993); K. Clarke (May 1993–)
Chief Secretary to the Treasury M. Portillo (Apr 1992–Jul 1994); J. Aitken (Jul 1994–)
Foreign Secretary D. Hurd
Home Secretary K. Clarke (Apr 1992–May 1993); M. Howard (May 1993–)
Minister of Agriculture, Fisheries and Food J. Gummer (Apr 1992–May 1993); Mrs. G. Shephard (May 1993–Jul 1994); W. Waldegrave (Jul 1994–)
Secretary of State for Defence M. Rifkind
Secretary of State for Education (Education and Science until 5 Jul 1992) J. Patten (Apr 1992–Jul 1994); G. Shephard (Jul 1994–)
Secretary of State for Employment G. Shephard (Apr 1992–May 1993); D. Hunt (May 1993–Jul 1994); M. Portillo (Jul 1994–)
Secretary of State for the Environment M. Howard (Apr 1992–May 1993); J. Gummer (May 1993–)
Secretary of State for Health V. Bottomley
Chancellor of the Duchy of Lancaster and Minister of Public Service and Science W. Waldegrave (Apr 1992–Jul 1994); D. Hunt (Jul 1994–)
Secretary of State for National Heritage D. Mellor (Apr–Sep 1992); P. Brooke (Sep 1992–Jul 1994); S. Dorrell (Jul 1994–)
Secretary of State for Northern Ireland Sir P. Mayhew

Secretary of State for Scotland I. Lang
Secretary of State for Social Security P. Lilley
President of the Board of Trade (Secretary of State for Trade and Industry) M. Heseltine
Secretary of State for Transport J. MacGregor (Apr 1992–Jul 1994); Dr. B. Mawhinngy (Jul 1994–)
Secretary of State for Wales D. Hunt (Apr 1992–May 1993); J. Redwood (May 1993–)
Minister Without Portfolio J. Hanley (Jul 1994–)

IMPORTANT DATES IN PERSONAL AND POLITICAL LIFE

1959 Leaves school to work as a clerk for Price Forbes, a firm of insurance brokers in the City of London.

27 MAR 1962 His father dies two days before John Major's nineteenth birthday.

1964 Begins his banking career at the District Bank, subsequently moving to the Standard Bank which, in 1970, merges with the Chartered Bank to form Standard Chartered. He remains there until 1979, and then becomes a Parliamentary Consultant to the bank.

1964 Contests (unsuccessfully) elections to Lambeth Borough Council.

8 MAY 1967 Major is involved in a serious car accident in Nigeria, where he had been sent by his employers. After initial treatment locally, he returns to Britain and spends many months in hospital in Croydon, Surrey.

MAY 1968 Elected to Lambeth Borough Council, representing Ferndale Ward. He becomes Chairman of the Accounts Sub-Committee of the Housing Committee and goes on to become Vice-Chairman, and then Chairman, of the Housing Committee, losing his seat in 1971.

17 SEP 1970 His mother, Gwen, dies in hospitol.

3 OCT 1970 Marries Norma Johnson, whom he had met earlier in the year during elections to the Greater London Council.

28 FEB 1974 Contests St. Pancras North at the General Election. He loses, but works very hard and is surprised that his vote is neither more nor less than the national average for the Conservatives.

10 OCT 1974 Contests St. Pancras North at the General Election. He loses again to the same Labour candidate, Jock Stallard, by a slightly greater margin.

3 MAY 1979 Elected Conservative Member of Parliament for Huntingdonshire. He more than doubles (to 21,563) the majority of his long-serving and well-known predecessor, Sir David Renton.

13 JUN 1979 Makes his maiden speech in the House of Commons during the debate on the first Budget of Margaret Thatcher's first administration.

26 JAN 1981 Appointed Parliamentary Private Secretary to both Home Office Ministers of State, Patrick Mayhew and Timothy Raison.

14 JAN 1983 Appointed Assistant Whip.

9 JUN 1983 General Election. The Conservative Party wins, with a majority of 144 seats. John Major's seat now known as Huntingdon.

3 OCT 1984 Appointed Lord Commissioner of the Treasury (i.e., Whip with responsibility for Treasury affairs).

2 SEP 1985 Appointed Parliamentary Under Secretary of State, Department of Health and Social Security.

10 SEP 1986 Appointed Minister of State, Department of Health and Social Security.

13 JUN 1987 Appointed Chief Secretary to the Treasury, under the Chancellor, Nigel Lawson. Made Privy Counsellor.

24 JUL 1989 Appointed Foreign Secretary, after Sir Geoffrey Howe is moved, controversially, to become Lord President of the Council and Leader of the House of Commons.

26 OCT 1989 Appointed Chancellor of the Exchequer, following Nigel Lawson's resignation.

20 MAR 1990 John Major's first (and only) Budget, which encourages personal saving. It is also the first Budget to be televised.

8 OCT 1990 With John Major as Chancellor, sterling joins the Exchange Rate Mechanism of the European Monetary System.

20 NOV 1990 First ballot for leadership of the Conservative Party. Margaret Thatcher obtains 204 votes and Michael Heseltine 152 votes, with 16 abstentions. By Conservative Party rules, Thatcher is 4 votes short of outright victory. At this stage, Major supports Thatcher (he later signs her nomination paper for the second ballot).

22 NOV 1990 Margaret Thatcher announces her resignation, to take effect when a new leader of the Conservative Party has been elected. John Major and Douglas Hurd enter the contest.

27 NOV 1990 Second ballot for leadership of the Conservative Party. John Major obtains 185 votes, Michael Heseltine 131 and Douglas Hurd 56. Heseltine and Hurd then withdraw from the contest.

28 NOV 1990 Mrs. Thatcher's resignation takes effect and John Major becomes Prime Minister, the youngest (at age 47) to reach that office since Lord Rosebery in 1894.

17 JAN 1991 Following Iraq's invasion of Kuwait in Aug 1990, the Gulf War commences, with air attacks by coalition forces on Iraq.

7 FEB 1991 Mortar attack by the IRA on 10 Downing Street. The Gulf War 'War Cabinet' is meeting at the time, and John Major's reaction is to suggest that the group reconvene in another room.

21 MAR 1991 Government announcement of the replacement of the very unpopular Community Charge ('Poll Tax') by a new system of local government finance. This comes to be known as the Council Tax, becoming effective in England, Wales and Scotland on 1 Apr 1993.

5 JUL 1991 The Bank of Credit and Commerce International (BCCI) is closed down, after allegations of fraud. It is argued that John Major, during his term of office as Chancellor, might have been aware of the problems. A judicial inquiry is ordered, reporting on 22 Oct 1992.

22 JUL 1991 John Major announces his 'Citizen's Charter' scheme, to improve public services and make them more accountable to the public.

19 AUG 1991 Attempted coup in the Soviet Union against President Gorbachev. It fails, and he is restored to power on 21 Aug.

9–10 DEC 1991 Maastricht summit on European Community political and monetary union. Agreement is reached on the political treaty and the economic and monetary union treaty, while a protocol on social and employment policy is agreed on by all member states except the UK. John Major regards this 'social chapter' exemption for the UK as a triumph.

21 DEC 1991 The Soviet Union, in effect, ceases to exist. A Commonwealth of Independent States comes into being, but this does not cover all the former Soviet states. Four days later, Mikhail Gorbachev resigns as President.

3 MAR 1992 Bosnia-Herzegovina, a former republic of Yugoslavia, declares its independence, following a referen-

IMPORTANT DATES IN PERSONAL AND POLITICAL LIFE—*Continued*

dum, which is largely boycotted by Serb residents. Tension between the ethnic communities leads to violence and, gradually, to full-scale civil war.

9 APR 1992 John Major's first General Election as Prime Minister. The Conservative Party wins, with a sharply reduced majority of 21 seats. It is also 22 years to the day since Major first met Norma Johnson, his wife.

24 APR 1992 Chris Patten, close friend of John Major and Conservative campaign chief for the 1992 General Election, during which he lost his parliamentary seat, appointed Governor of Hong Kong from July 1992. He is intended to be the last British Governor before Hong Kong reverts to Chinese rule in 1997.

30 JUN 1992 Margaret Thatcher enters the House of Lords as Baroness Thatcher of Kesteven.

1 JUL 1992 UK presidency of the European Community Council of Ministers begins. Lasting until 31 Dec 1992, it gives John Major a key leadership role among European heads of government.

1 JUL 1992 Sir Geoffrey Howe enters the House of Lords as Lord Howe of Aberavon.

6 JUL 1992 Nigel Lawson enters the House of Lords as Lord Lawson of Blaby.

16 SEP 1992 'Black Wednesday'—Sterling suspended from the Exchange Rate Mechanism. The Prime Minister recalls Parliament to discuss the currency crisis and other matters, for 24 and 25 Sep.

13 OCT 1992 Michael Heseltine, President of the Board of Trade, announces that 31 coal mines are to be closed, with the loss of 30,000 jobs. The announcement is followed by a nationwide storm of protest. On 19 Oct the Government announces a moratorium on pit closures and a review of UK energy policy and the potential market for coal. The Trade and Industry Select Committee announces an inquiry into the same issue. On 21 Dec, after a review, the High Court rules that British Coal's pit closure announcement is illegal, as certain procedures had to be followed.

4 NOV 1992 The European Communities (Amendment) Bill (Maastricht) 'paving' motion and an Opposition amendment to it are debated in the House of Commons. The Prime Minister stakes his authority on Government success. The Opposition amendment is defeated by only six votes, and the Government motion carried by an even narrower three votes.

10 NOV 1992 John Major announces a judicial inquiry under Lord Justice Scott into the 'Arms to Iraq' affair, in which several British companies are alleged to have exported items to Iraq with a potential military use, contravening Government guidelines. Ministerial knowledge, or lack of it, is one of the issues involved.

11-12 DEC 1992 European Council meeting at Edinburgh, chaired by John Major. Agreement is reached on two issues: the means of enabling Denmark to ratify the Maastricht Treaty on European Union, and European Community finances. Major's credibility is enhanced by his handling of the summit.

19 FEB 1993 Death of Judith Chaplin, Conservative MP for Newbury and John Major's former political secretary in 10 Downing Street and special adviser to him as Chancellor.

25 MAR 1993 Heseltine's White Paper on the coal industry, taking into account the judicial review, is published.

6 MAY 1993 The Conservatives lose the Newbury by-election (the Liberal Democrats achieve a massive 22, 000 majority) and perform disastrously in the local government elections, losing control of every English county council except one.

20 JUL 1993 The European Communities (Amendment) Bill (the 'Maastricht Bill') finally receives Royal Assent.

22 JUL 1993 In a debate on the 'Social Chapter' (Protocol on Social Policy) of the European Communities (Amendment) Act, the Government is defeated by 8 votes, due to opposition from a determined group of Conservative MPs opposed to the Maastricht Treaty as a whole. John Major announces a vote of confidence for the next day in an effort to bring the 'rebels' into line.

23 JUL 1993 Vote of confidence on the motion 'that this House has confidence in the policy of Her Majesty's Government on the adoption of the Protocol on Social Policy.' The Government wins by 40 votes.

17 JAN 1994 Gives evidence in public to the Scott inquiry into the supply of arms to Iraq, the first serving Prime Minister to appear at a public inquiry.

12 MAY 1994 Sudden death of the Leader of the Opposition, John Smith, after a heart attack.

22 FEB 1995 Issues with Irish PM John Bruton Framework Document outlining comprehensive peace proposals for Northern Ireland.

BACKGROUND

PHYSICAL CHARACTERISTICS AND HEALTH

John Major's ordinary appearance has earned him the adjective 'grey'. *The Observer* newspaper has described him as 'lanky, thin, bespectacled and greying at the temples, classless in speech'. Although he has a reputation for amiability and remarkably few political enemies, he is determined and is highly effective at getting results, more by persuasion than by order. He has a capacity for hard work and long hours, a good memory and the ability to grasp often complex details quickly. One of his biographers, Nesta Wyn Ellis, quotes him as saying, 'Nothing makes me more determined to do something than someone telling me I can't.' (*John Major*, p. 187).

Major's mother was recovering from double pneumonia and pleurisy when she gave birth. Although John was healthy when he was born, he became seriously ill in hospital from an infection and was given several blood transfusions, the scars from which still show on his ankles. He was healthy as a child and young man, but a serious car accident in Nigeria in 1967 caused him to lose his left kneecap. As well as putting paid to his playing cricket, this has limited his ability to walk beyond a certain distance. He underwent a wisdom tooth operation only a few days before becoming Prime Minister, but in general, his health is good.

EDUCATION

Primary Cheam Common Primary School
Secondary 1954–59, Rutlish Grammar School, Wimbledon

Professional 1964–66, Banking Diploma (by correspondence course); 1971, Associate, Institute of Bankers

Prizes and awards Scholarship to Rutlish Grammar School

Qualifications He appears to have left school originally without qualifications, but he subsequently obtained at least 6 '0' Levels (English language, English literature, History, Mathematics, British Constitution and Economics), some by correspondence course.

Cultural and vocational background 1956, Visited the House of Commons with Colonel Marcus Lipton, then Labour MP for Brixton. This aroused in him an intense determination to enter politics. In 1957 he began speaking for the Young Conservatives from a soapbox in Brixton Market. In 1959 he joined Brixton Young Conservatives.

NON-PARLIAMENTARY CAREER

Early occupations After leaving school in 1959, at the age of 16, Major worked briefly for Price Forbes, a firm of insurance brokers, in the City of London. This was followed by a spell as a labourer at David's Rural Industries, which had taken over the garden gnomes (and other ornaments) business belonging to his father and (later) his brother. When this closed in the early 1960s, John Major took short-term labouring jobs, but then came a period of unemployment, initially because he was looking after his dying father and unwell mother. After a short time at the London Electricity Board, he joined the District Bank and, subsequently, Standard Bank, which posted him to Nigeria in late 1966. After a serious car accident there, he returned to the UK in 1967 and spent many months in hospital. However, he remained with the bank which, in 1970, merged with Chartered Bank to become Standard Chartered, and he went on to hold a number of senior positions there.

Other posts 1968–70, School governor; 1968–71, represented Ferndale Ward, Lambeth Borough Council; 1975, President, Fulham Taverners Cricket Club; 1975–83, Board member, Warden Housing Association; 1976, Personal assistant to Lord Barber at the International Monetary Fund Conference, Manila, The Philippines; 1979–83, Parliamentary consultant to the Guild of Glass Engravers; 1979–83, Parliamentary consultant to Standard Chartered Bank

HONOURS

Other than peerage 22 Apr 1991, Hon. Fellow, Chartered Institute of Bankers

CLUBS

Carlton

HOBBIES AND SPORTS

A great cricket enthusiast, he belongs to the Marylebone Cricket Club (MCC) and supports Surrey County Cricket Club. He also enjoys football, supporting Chelsea Football Club. Other interests include opera and reading, especially the novels of Anthony Trollope and Jane Austen. He plays chess. The family has had a pet hamster called Psycho.

FINANCES

From the age of 12, John Major lived in an atmosphere where money was tight, a fact caused by the failure of his father's business and subsequent move from Worcester Park to Brixton. His earliest earnings helped support the family. This awareness of the value of money has remained with him since his marriage, and both he and his wife have been able to make good use of a relatively modest income. This has increased in recent years to reflect his rapidly developing political career.

Income His income as Prime Minister is £53,007, plus a Parliamentary salary of £23,227 (total £76,234). This reflects the salary he is entitled to, and he has not continued Margaret Thatcher's practice of taking a reduced salary.

ANECDOTES

On the night of his election to Ferndale Ward of Lambeth Borough Council in 1968, John Major was determined to convey the result to an elderly woman activist who had not been at the count and who, apparently, had no telephone in her house. According to Bruce Anderson in his biography, Major and a friend went round to her home in the early hours of the morning. Major climbed a lamp-post and was throwing gravel at the woman's window when a policeman appeared. The explanation that he was the Conservative victor of what was normally (both before and since) a solidly Labour ward did not, initially, convince the policeman.

While John Major was Chairman of Lambeth Council Housing Committee, a visit to a local housing estate was scheduled for 3 Oct 1970. This turned out to be Major's wedding day, but he was determined to keep the appointment, albeit in formal morning dress, and did so. The action of Clive Jones, Major's best man and fellow Housing Committee member, in alerting a local newspaper in advance ensured good publicity.

At a dinner of Government business managers in London in July 1985, John Major was trying to convey to the Prime Minister, Margaret Thatcher, the views of Conservative MPs on a particular point of economic policy. She reacted as if he were expressing his own personal opposition to it. The argument intensified and the atmosphere became increasingly heated. Afterwards, Major feared that his political career was ruined. However, Denis Thatcher came up to him and said, 'She rather enjoyed that, you know.' Two months later, Major was promoted.

Major's sense of humour is illustrated by an incident said to have occurred shortly after he became Chancellor of the Exchequer. He and David Mellor, a close friend and former Cabinet Minister, went to watch Chelsea Football Club play one Sunday afternoon. The club's manager introduced them to the team. Major told them: 'Any win bonus you get today is tax free'. Unfortunately, it didn't work out like that.

QUOTATIONS

1989, The harsh truth is that if the [economic] policy isn't hurting, it isn't working. (Speech at Northampton, 27 Oct)

1990, I believe in the next ten years we will have to continue to make changes that will genuinely produce across the whole of this country a genuinely classless society . . . .(Treasury Press Conference, 23 Nov)

QUOTATIONS—*Continued*

1990, I'm not running as son of Margaret Thatcher, I'm running as myself, on my own priorities and my own programme. (Interview on *Walden* television programme, 25 Nov)

1990, You can't influence Europe's future from the terraces. You have to be on the pitch and playing hard. (Speech at Altrincham, 29 Nov)

1991, Gentlemen, I think we had better start again, somewhere else. (At a Gulf War Cabinet meeting, after a mortar attack on 10 Downing Street, 7 Feb)

1991, My aim for Britain in the [European] Community can be simply stated. I want us to be where we belong. At the very heart of Europe. (Speech in Bonn, 11 Mar)

1993, I'm fit, I'm well, I'm here and I'm staying. (Speech to Conservative Women's Conference, London, 4 Jun, during media speculation on his future as Prime Minister)

1995, These are our ideas, but the future is up to you. (Announcing Framework Document containing peace proposals for Northern Ireland)

RESIDENCES

260 Longfellow Road, Worcester Park, Surrey
144 Coldharbour Lane, Brixton, London
80 Burton Road, Brixton, London
Binney Street, Westminster, London
9 Templar Street, Brixton, London
24 Primrose Court, Hydethorpe Road, Streatham, London
26 West Oak, The Avenue, Beckenham, Kent
6 De Vere Close, Hemingford Grey, Cambridgeshire
Kennington Road, London
35 Durand Gardens, Stockwell, London
Chevening, Sevenoaks, Kent
1 Carlton House Terrace, London
11 Downing Street
Dorneywood, Buckinghamshire
10 Downing Street
Chequers, Buckinghamshire
Great Stukeley, Cambridgeshire.

MEMORIALS

STATUES AND BUSTS

1993, by Shenda Amery, Huntingdon

PORTRAITS

1991, Photograph by Yousuf Karsh, at the National Portrait Gallery; 1992, Photograph by Sally Soames, approved by Downing Street as an 'official' picture; 1993, by Diccon Swan, Carlton Club, London; 1993, by Peter Deighan, retained by Mr. Major

BIBLIOGRAPHIC INFORMATION

LETTERS AND PERSONAL PAPERS

1991, *The Power to Choose: The Right to Own*, selected speeches during his first year as Prime Minister, compiled by Alistair B. Cooke; 1992, *Trust the People* keynote speeches of the 1992 General Election campaign, compiled by Alistair B. Cooke.

PUBLICATIONS

1991, 'The Evolution of Europe', speech to the Konrad Adenauer Foundation, Bonn on 11 Mar 1991; 1992, 'Scotland in the United Kingdom', speech in Glasgow to a Conference of Scottish Conservatives; 1992, 'The Next Phase of Conservatism: The Privatisation of Choice', a speech to the Adam Smith Institute; 1993, 'Conservatism in the 1990s: Our Common Purpose', 5th Carlton Club lecture

FURTHER READING

Anderson, B. *John Major*. London, 1992.
Critchley, J. *Some of Us: People Who Did Well Under Thatcher*. London, 1992. (Includes chapter on John Major).
Ellis, N. W. *John Major*. London, 1991.
Jenkin, J. *John Major: Prime Minister*. London, 1990.
Junor, P. *The Major Enigma*. London, 1993.
Major-Ball, T. *Major Major: Memories of an Older Brother*. London, 1994.
Pearce, E. *The Quiet Rise of John Major*. London, 1991.
—. *The Shooting Gallery*. London, 1989.
Walker, T. *Norma: A Biography*. London, 1993.

A.D.P.

Comparative Data

COMPARATIVE DATA

CHRONOLOGY, NAMES AND FAMILY HISTORY

BIRTH AND DEATH DATES

Walpole is generally considered to have been the first British Prime Minister, which makes John Major the 50th Prime Minister. The PMs, with their birth and death dates, are listed here in chronological order and under the name by which they were usually known while they were in office. There is a separate section that lists all of the names by which they were known throughout their career (see Names and Peerages, page 360).

1. Sir Robert Walpole	26 Aug 1676–18 March 1745
2. Earl of Wilmington	1673– 2 Jul 1743
3. Henry Pelham	25 Sep 1694– 6 Mar 1754
4. Duke of Newcastle	21 Jul 1693–17 Nov 1768
5. Duke of Devonshire	1720– 2 Oct 1764
6. Earl of Bute	25 May 1713–10 Mar 1792
7. George Grenville	14 Oct 1712–13 Nov 1770
8. Marquess of Rockingham	13 May 1730– 1 Jul 1782
9. Earl of Chatham	15 Nov 1708–11 May 1778
10. Duke of Grafton	28 Sep 1735–14 Mar 1811
11. Lord North	13 Apr 1732– 5 Aug 1792
12. Earl of Shelburne	2 May 1737– 7 May 1805
13. Duke of Portland	14 Apr 1738–30 Oct 1809
14. William Pitt	28 May 1759–23 Jan 1806
15. Henry Addington	30 May 1757–15 Feb 1844
16. Lord Grenville	24 Oct 1759–12 Jan 1834
17. Spencer Perceval	1 Nov 1762–11 May 1812
18. Earl of Liverpool	7 Jun 1770– 4 Dec 1828
19. George Canning	11 Apr 1770– 8 Aug 1827
20. Viscount Goderich	30 Oct 1782–28 Jan 1859
21. Duke of Wellington	1 May 1769–14 Sep 1852
22. Earl Grey	13 Mar 1764–17 Jul 1845
23. Lord Melbourne	15 Mar 1779–24 Nov 1848
24. Sir Robert Peel	5 Feb 1788– 2 Jul 1850
25. Lord John Russell	18 Aug 1792–28 May 1878
26. Earl of Derby	29 Mar 1799–23 Oct 1869
27. Earl of Aberdeen	28 Jan 1784–14 Dec 1860
28. Viscount Palmerston	20 Oct 1784–18 Oct 1865
29. Benjamin Disraeli	21 Dec 1804–19 Apr 1881
30. William Ewart Gladstone	29 Dec 1809–19 May 1898
31. Marquess of Salisbury	3 Feb 1830–22 Aug 1903
32. Earl of Rosebery	7 May 1847–21 May 1929
33. Arthur James Balfour	25 Jul 1848–19 Mar 1930
34. Sir Henry Campbell-Bannerman	7 Sep 1836–22 Apr 1908
35. H. H. Asquith	12 Sep 1852–15 Feb 1928
36. David Lloyd George	17 Jan 1863–26 Mar 1945
37. Andrew Bonar Law	16 Sep 1858–30 Oct 1923
38. Stanley Baldwin	3 Aug 1867–14 Dec 1947
39. Ramsay MacDonald	12 Oct 1866– 9 Nov 1937
40. Neville Chamberlain	18 Mar 1869– 9 Nov 1940
41. Winston Churchill	30 Nov 1874–24 Jan 1965
42. Clement Attlee	3 Jan 1883–8 Oct 1967
43. Anthony Eden	12 Jun 1897–14 Jan 1977
44. Harold Macmillan	10 Feb 1894–29 Dec 1986
45. Sir Alec Douglas-Home	2 Jul 1903–
46. Harold Wilson	11 Mar 1916–
47. Edward Heath	9 Jul 1916–
48. James Callaghan	27 Mar 1912–
49. Margaret Thatcher	13 Oct 1925–
50. John Major	29 Mar 1943–

NAMES: ALPHABETICAL LIST

The Prime Ministers are listed below in alphabetical order of last name or title together with their chronological rank as PM. (The only exception is Lloyd George, who has never been known as George, so he is listed at L.)

Aberdeen	27
Addington	15
Asquith	35
Attlee	42
Baldwin	38
Balfour	33
Bute	6
Callaghan	48
Campbell-Bannerman	34
Canning	19
Chamberlain	40
Chatham	9
Churchill	41
Derby	26

Devonshire	5
Disraeli	29
Douglas-Home	45
Eden	43
Gladstone	30
Goderich	20
Grafton	10
Grenville, G	7
Grenville, Lord	16
Grey	22
Heath	47
Law	37
Liverpool	18
Lloyd George	36
MacDonald	39
Macmillan	44
Major	50
Melbourne	23
Newcastle	4
North	11
Palmerston	28
Peel	24
Pelham	3
Perceval	17
Pitt	14
Portland	13
Rockingham	8
Rosebery	32
Russell	25
Salisbury	31
Shelburne	12
Thatcher	49
Walpole	1
Wellington	21
Wilmington	2
Wilson	46

NAMES AND PEERAGES

Variations in names can cause a great deal of confusion. Those who become peers are then known by their title. It is quite common for someone to be given a peerage, and later to be given a higher degree of peerage, so that their title would change after each conferment.

Peers are not entitled to sit in the House of Commons, so if a Member of Parliament becomes a peer he or she is automatically disqualified from the House of Commons but becomes entitled to sit in the House of Lords.

Eldest sons of peers are known by a courtesy title during their father's lifetime, such as the Marquess of Hartington, which is the title by which the eldest son of the Duke of Devonshire is known. If they are Members of Parliament, however, it may look as if they are peers sitting in the House of Commons. Similarly, younger sons of dukes and marquesses take the courtesy title 'Lord' before their forename and surname. Lord John Russell was in fact the third son of the 6th Duke of Bedford, but he and his brother George both used the title 'Lord'.

The eldest son inherits his father's peerage when his father dies. Not all peerages, however, are hereditary. Since the Life Peerages Act of 1958 it has been possible to create life peers, whose titles cannot be passed on to their children. A hereditary peerage may also be disclaimed, as the Earl of Home did in 1963 to become Sir Alec Douglas-Home so that he could stand for election to the House of Commons.

One group of peers who may sit in the House of Commons are Peers of Ireland, since an Irish peerage does not entitle its holder to sit in the United Kingdom Parliament's House of Lords. Similarly, until the Peerage Act of 1963 a Scottish peerage did not entitle its holder to sit in the House of Lords. Scottish peers had to elect sixteen of their number to represent them in the House of Lords. They were known as Scottish Representative Peers, of whom Bute and Aberdeen were two.

This list gives all the variant names by which the Prime Ministers have been known throughout their lives, followed by the name that we have used in the book.

Viscount **Amberley** of Amberley & of Ardsalla—Lord John Russell

Herbert Henry **Asquith**—H. H. Asquith

Clement Richard **Attlee**—Clement Attlee

Earl **Attlee**—Clement Attlee

Earl of **Avon**—Anthony Eden

Earl **Baldwin** of Bewdley—Stanley Baldwin

Earl of **Balfour**—Arthur James Balfour

Earl of **Beaconsfield**—Benjamin Disraeli

William Henry Cavendish **Bentinck**—Duke of Portland

Leonard James **Callaghan**—James Callaghan

Baron **Callaghan** of Cardiff—James Callaghan

Viscount **Calne** and Calstone—Earl of Shelburne

Henry **Campbell**—Sir Henry Campbell-Bannerman

William **Cavendish**—Duke of Devonshire

Lord **Cavendish** of Hardwick—Duke of Devonshire

Baron **Cecil** of Essendom—Marquess of Salisbury

Arthur Neville **Chamberlain**—Neville Chamberlain

Winston Leonard Spencer **Churchill**—Winston Churchill

Baron **Cirencester**—Duke of Portland

Earl of **Clare**—Duke of Newcastle

Marquess of **Clare**—Duke of Newcastle

Spencer **Compton**—Earl of Wilmington

Viscount **Corvedale**—Stanley Baldwin

Viscount **Cranborne**—Marquess of Salisbury

Lord **Dalmeny** & Primrose—Earl of Rosebery

Alexander Frederick **Douglas-Home**—Sir Alec Douglas-Home

Baron **Douro** of Wellesley—Duke of Wellington

Marquess of **Douro**—Duke of Wellington

Lord **Dunglass**—Alec Douglas-Home

Baron **Dunkeron**—Earl of Shelburne

Robert Anthony **Eden**—Anthony Eden

Viscount **Eden** of Royal Leamington Spa—Anthony Eden

Baron **Epsom**—Earl of Rosebery

Earl of **Euston**—Duke of Grafton

Viscount **Fitzmaurice**—Earl of Shelburne

William **Fitzmaurice**—Earl of Shelburne

Augustus Henry **Fitzroy**—Duke of Grafton

Robert Arthur Talbot **Gascoyne-Cecil**—Marquess of Salisbury

Viscount **Goderich** of Nocton—Viscount Goderich

George **Gordon**—Earl of Aberdeen

Viscount **Gordon** of Aberdeen—Earl of Aberdeen

Baron **Grenville** of Wotton-under-Bernewood—Lord Grenville

William Wyndham **Grenville**—Lord Grenville

Baron **Grey** of Howick—Earl Grey

Charles **Grey**—Earl Grey

Baron **Guilford**—Lord North

Earl of **Guilford**—Lord North

Viscount **Gwynedd**—David Lloyd George

George **Hamilton-Gordon**—Earl of Aberdeen

Marquess of **Hartington**—Duke of Devonshire

Viscount **Haughton**—Duke of Newcastle

Baron **Hawksbury**—Earl of Liverpool

Viscount **Higham**—Marquess of Rockingham

Thomas **Holles-Newcastle**—Duke of Newcastle

Baron **Home** of the Hirsel—Sir Alec Douglas-Home

Earl of **Home**—Sir Alec Douglas-Home

Baron **Houghton**—Sir Robert Walpole

Viscount **Howick**—Earl Grey

Viscount **Hughenden**—Benjamin Disraeli

Viscount of **Inverkeithing**—Earl of Rosebery

Robert Banks **Jenkinson**—Earl of Liverpool

William **Lamb**—Viscount Melbourne

Marquess of **Lansdowne**—Earl of Shelburne

Earl **Lloyd-George** of Dwyfor—David Lloyd George

James **MacDonald**— Ramsay MacDonald

Maurice Harold **Macmillan**—Harold Macmillan

Viscount **Macmillan** of Ovenden—Harold Macmillan

John Roy **Major**—John Major

Earl of **Malton**—Marquess of Rockingham

Baron **Melbourne**—Viscount Melbourne

Lord **Melbourne**—Viscount Melbourne

Viscount **Melbourne** of Kilmore—Viscount Melbourne

Viscount **Mentmore**—Earl of Rosebery

Earl of **Midlothian**—Earl of Rosebery

Duke of **Newcastle** under Lyme—Duke of Newcastle

Duke of **Newcastle** upon Tyne—Duke of Newcastle

Frederick **North**—Lord North

Lord **North** of Kirtling—Lord North

Earl of **Orford**—Sir Robert Walpole

Earl of **Oxford** & Asquith—H. H. Asquith

Baron **Pelham** of Laughton—Duke of Newcastle

Baron **Pelham** of Stanmer—Duke of Newcastle

Thomas **Pelham-Holles**—Duke of Newcastle

William **Petty**—Earl of Shelburne

Viscount **Pevensey**—Earl of Wilmington

Viscount **Pitt** of Burton Pynsent—Earl of Chatham

William **Pitt**—William Pitt; Earl of Chatham

Earl of **Portland**—Duke of Portland

Viscount **Prestwood** of Walthamstow—Clement Attlee

Archibald Philip **Primrose**—Earl of Rosebery

Baron **Primrose**—Earl of Rosebery

Lord **Primrose** & Dalmeny—Earl of Rosebery

James McDonald **Ramsay**— Ramsay MacDonald

Earl of **Ripon**—Viscount Goderich

Frederick John **Robinson**—Viscount Goderich

Lord **Rosebery**—Earl of Rosebery

Viscount of **Rosebery**—Earl of Rosebery

Earl **Russell** of Kingston Russell—Lord John Russell

Earl of **Salisbury**—Marquess of Salisbury

Viscount **Sidmouth**—Henry Addington

NAMES AND PEERAGES—*Continued*

Edward George Geoffrey Smith **Stanley**—Earl of Derby

Lord **Stanley** of Bickerstaffe—Earl of Derby

Earl of **Stockton**—Harold Macmillan

John **Stuart**—Earl of Bute

Baron **Temple** of Mount Temple—Viscount Palmerston

Henry John **Temple**—Viscount Palmerston

Baroness **Thatcher** of Kesteven—Margaret Thatcher

Earl of **Titchfield**—Duke of Portland

Viscount **Trapain** of Whittingehame—Arthur James Balfour

Viscount **Walpole**—Sir Robert Walpole

Charles **Watson-Wentworth**—Marquess of Rockingham

Arthur **Wellesley**—Duke of Wellington

Earl of **Wellington**—Duke of Wellington

Marquess of **Wellington**—Duke of Wellington

Viscount **Wellington** of Talavera & of Wellington—Duke of Wellington

Arthur **Wesley**—Duke of Wellington

Baron **Wilmington**—Earl of Wilmington

Baron **Wilson** of Rievaulx—Harold Wilson

Viscount **Woodstock**—Duke of Portland

Earl **Wycombe** of Chipping Wycombe—Earl of Shelburne

Lord **Wycombe**—Earl of Shelburne

DATES OF OFFICE

The Prime Ministers are listed below in chronological order of their term of office. A term of office is defined as an unbroken period of time as Prime Minister, irrespective of the governments formed within it. The first date is the date on which the Prime Minister kissed the hand of the monarch, the symbolic seal on the commencement of that term of office. The second date is that on which the Prime Minister's resignation was accepted, and usually announced, or the date of their death. Prime Ministers who died in office are shown with an asterisk .

There have been 72 Prime Ministerial terms of office altogether since Walpole, 16 of which began in the 18th century, 33 in the 19th century, and 23 so far in the 20th century.

Gladstone had a record four terms of office; Baldwin, Derby and Salisbury had three each; and thirteen Prime Ministers had two terms each: Newcastle, Rockingham, Pitt, Portland, Wellington, Melbourne, Peel, Russell, Palmerston, Disraeli, MacDonald, Churchill and Wilson.

Walpole	3 Apr 1721–11 Feb 1742
Wilmington*	16 Feb 1742– 2 Jul 1743
Pelham*	27 Aug 1743– 6 Mar 1754
Newcastle	16 Mar 1754–11 Nov 1756
Devonshire	16 Nov 1756–29 Jun 1757
Newcastle	29 Jun 1757–26 May 1762
Bute	26 May 1762–8 Apr 1763
Grenville, G	16 Apr 1763–10 Jul 1765
Rockingham	13 Jul 1765–30 Jul 1766
Chatham	30 Jul 1766–14 Oct 1768
Grafton	14 Oct 1768–28 Jan 1770
North	28 Jan 1770–27 Mar 1782
Rockingham*	27 Mar 1782– 1 Jul 1782
Shelburne	4 Jul 1782–26 Mar 1783
Portland	2 Apr 1783–18 Dec 1783
Pitt	19 Dec 1783–14 Mar 1801
Addington	17 Mar 1801–10 May 1804
Pitt*	10 May 1804–23 Jan 1806
Grenville, Lord	11 Feb 1806–25 Mar 1807
Portland	31 Mar 1807– 4 Oct 1809
Perceval*	4 Oct 1809–11 May 1812
Liverpool	8 Jun 1812– 9 Apr 1827
Canning*	12 Apr 1827– 8 Aug 1827
Goderich	31 Aug 1827– 8 Jan 1828
Wellington	22 Jan 1828–16 Nov 1830
Grey	22 Nov 1830– 9 Jul 1834
Melbourne	16 Jul 1834–14 Nov 1834
Wellington	17 Nov 1834– 9 Dec 1834
Peel	10 Dec 1834– 8 Apr 1835
Melbourne	18 Apr 1835–30 Aug 1841
Peel	30 Aug 1841–29 Jun 1846
Russell	30 Jun 1846–21 Feb 1852
Derby	23 Feb 1852–17 Dec 1852
Aberdeen	19 Dec 1852–30 Jan 1855
Palmerston	6 Feb 1855–19 Feb 1858
Derby	20 Feb 1858–11 Jun 1859
Palmerston*	12 Jun 1859–18 Oct 1865
Russell	29 Oct 1865–26 Jun 1866
Derby	28 Jun 1866–25 Feb 1868
Disraeli	27 Feb 1868–1 Dec 1868
Gladstone	3 Dec 1868–17 Feb 1874
Disraeli	20 Feb 1874–21 Apr 1880
Gladstone	23 Apr 1880–9 Jun 1885
Salisbury	23 Jun 1885–28 Jan 1886
Gladstone	1 Feb 1886–20 Jul 1886
Salisbury	25 Jul 1886–11 Aug 1892
Gladstone	15 Aug 1892–2 Mar 1894
Rosebery	5 Mar 1894–22 Jun 1895
Salisbury	25 Jun 1895–11 Jul 1902
Balfour	12 Jul 1902–4 Dec 1905

Campbell-Bannerman	5 Dec 1905–5 Apr 1908
Asquith	5 Apr 1908–5 Dec 1916
Lloyd George	6 Dec 1916–19 Oct 1922
Bonar Law	23 Oct 1922–20 May 1923
Baldwin	22 May 1923–22 Jan 1924
MacDonald	22 Jan 1924–4 Nov 1924
Baldwin	4 Nov 1924–4 Jun 1929
MacDonald	5 Jun 1929–7 Jun 1935
Baldwin	7 Jun 1935–28 May 1937
Chamberlain	28 May 1937–10 May 1940
Churchill	10 May 1940–26 Jul 1945
Attlee	26 Jul 1945–26 Oct 1951
Churchill	26 Oct 1951–5 Apr 1955
Eden	6 Apr 1955–9 Jan 1957
Macmillan	10 Jan 1957–18 Oct 1963
Douglas-Home	19 Oct 1963–16 Oct 1964
Wilson	16 Oct 1964–19 Jun 1970
Heath	19 Jun 1970–4 Mar 1974
Wilson	4 Mar 1974–5 Apr 1976
Callaghan	5 Apr 1976–4 May 1979
Thatcher	4 May 1979–28 Nov 1990
Major	28 Nov 1990

Liverpool was the only Prime Minister to be appointed by a Regent. Asquith kissed hands in Biarritz, France, where the King was staying at the time. This is the only occasion on which this ceremony has taken place outside the United Kingdom.

PLACE OF BIRTH

Of the 45 Prime Ministers whose place of birth is known, 37 were born in England (16 of these in London); 5 were born in Scotland and 2 were born in Ireland. Only 1 was born outside the British Isles: Bonar Law, who was born in Canada.

Bute was the first Scottish-born Prime Minister and MacDonald was the latest. No Prime Minister has been born in Wales.

(Place of birth is not known for Devonshire, Rockingham, Grafton, Portland and Goderich.)

Prime Ministers Born in London:

Newcastle	Melbourne
George Grenville	Russell
Chatham	Palmerston
North	Disraeli
Addington	Rosebery
Perceval	Attlee
Liverpool	Macmillan
Canning	Douglas-Home

Prime Ministers Born in Scotland:

Edinburgh:	Bute, Aberdeen
Whittingehame, East Lothian:	Balfour
Kelvinside, near Glasgow:	Campbell-Bannerman
Lossiemouth, Morayshire:	MacDonald

Prime Ministers Born in Ireland:

Dublin:	Shelburne Wellington

Prime Ministers Born in England, By County and City (Excluding London)

Buckinghamshire, Wotton House:	Lord Grenville
Durham, Bishop Auckland:	Eden
Hampshire, Portsmouth:	Callaghan
Hertfordshire, Hatfield House:	Salisbury
Kent, Hayes:	Pitt
St Peter's:	Heath
Lancashire, Chamber Hall, nr Bury:	Peel
Knowsley Park:	Derby
Liverpool:	Gladstone
Manchester:	Lloyd George
Morley:	Asquith
Lincolnshire, Grantham:	Thatcher
Norfolk, Houghton:	Walpole
Northumberland, Fallodon:	Grey
Oxfordshire, Blenheim Palace:	Churchill
Surrey, Carshalton:	Major
Sussex, Laughton:	Pelham
Warwickshire, Birmingham:	Chamberlain
Compton Wynyates:	Wilmington
Worcestershire, Bewdley:	Baldwin
Yorkshire, Huddersfield:	Wilson

PLACE OF BIRTH—*Continued*

Prime Minister Born Outside the British Isles:

Canada
Kingston, N.B.: Bonar Law

ANCESTRY

Prime Ministers who came from English families—33:

Walpole	Peel
Wilmington	Russell
Pelham	Derby
Newcastle	Palmerston
Devonshire	Salisbury
George Grenville	Asquith
Rockingham	Baldwin
Chatham	Chamberlain
Grafton	Churchill
North	Attlee
Pitt	Eden
Addington	Macmillan
Lord Grenville	Wilson
Liverpool	Heath
Goderich	Thatcher
Grey	Major
Melbourne	

Families of of landowners or peers produced 21 of these. Chatham came from a family of civil servants; Addington from a farming family; Melbourne's ancestors were lawyers and Peel's were textile manufacturers. Asquith's family were in the wool trade and Baldwin's were ironmasters. The ancestors of Chamberlain were shoemakers; Attlee's were millers and corn merchants; Macmillan came from a publishing background, and Wilson's and Heath's forbears were craftsmen.

Prime Ministers from Scottish families—8:

Bute	Balfour
Aberdeen	Campbell-Bannerman
Gladstone	MacDonald
Rosebery	Douglas-Home

Bute, Aberdeen, Rosebery, Balfour and Douglas-Home all came from landowning families; Gladstone and Campbell-Bannerman's families were in commerce and MacDonald came from a farming family.

Prime Ministers from Irish families—4:

Shelburne	Bonar Law
Perceval	
Canning	

Shelburne, Perceval and Canning all came from landowning families.

Prime Ministers Wellington and Callaghan came from Anglo-Irish families.

Lloyd George came from a family of Welsh farmers; Portland's family originally came to England with William of Orange in 1688 from Oversijssel in the Netherlands, and Disraeli's family was of Italian Sephardi Jewish origin.

FATHER'S OCCUPATION

The sons of MPs—28 Prime Ministers:

Walpole	Liverpool
Wilmington	Goderich
Pelham	Wellington*
Newcastle	Melbourne
Devonshire	Peel
George Grenville	Russell
Rockingham	Derby
Chatham	Palmerston
Grafton	Gladstone
North	Rosebery
Shelburne	Balfour
Pitt	Baldwin
Lord Grenville	Chamberlain
Perceval	Churchill

(*Wellington's father was an MP in the Irish Parliament.)

The sons or grandsons of Peers—24 Prime Ministers:

Wilmington	Perceval
Pelham	Liverpool
Newcastle	Goderich
Devonshire	Wellington
Bute	Grey
Rockingham	Melbourne
Grafton*	Russell
North	Derby
Shelburne	Aberdeen*
Portland	Palmerston
Pitt	

Salisbury	Douglas-Home
Rosebery*	

*Grafton, Aberdeen and Rosebery all inherited their titles from their grandfathers because of the early deaths of their fathers. (See Age at Death of Father, page 373).

Prime Ministers whose fathers were both MPs and later Peers—16:

Wilmington	Perceval
Pelham	Liverpool
Newcastle	Goderich
Devonshire	Wellington
Rockingham	Melbourne
North	Russell
Shelburne	Derby
Pitt	Palmerston

Prime Ministers whose fathers were businessmen or involved in the manufacturing industries—6:

Peel	Baldwin
Gladstone	Chamberlain
Campbell-Bannerman	

Prime Ministers whose fathers were farmers—2:

Walpole	Lloyd George

MacDonald's father was a ploughman. Grafton and Callaghan's fathers were in the Royal Navy; Grey was the son of a soldier who reached the rank of General. Canning and Attlee were the sons of lawyers and Goderich's father was Ambassador to Spain.

Other occupations are listed below:

Father's Occupation	Prime Minister
Doctor	Addington
Composer/musician	Wellington
Scholar and author	Disraeli
Chairman of the North British Railway	Balfour
Teacher (then farmer)	Lloyd George
Presbyterian minister	Bonar Law
Publisher	Macmillan
Industrial chemist	Wilson
Carpenter and builder	Heath
Grocer	Thatcher
Theatrical artist (then small businessman)	Major

POSITION IN FAMILY

This table excludes siblings from fathers' other marriages.

		Number of Brothers and Sisters
only child	Liverpool	—
only child	Baldwin	—
only child	MacDonald	—
1st of 2	North	1s
1st of 2	Churchill	1b
1st of 2	Heath	1b
1st of 4	Chamberlain	3s
1st of 5	Shelburne	1b 3s
1st of 5	Palmerston	1b 3s
1st of 7	Aberdeen	5b 1s
1st of 7	Douglas-Home	4b 2s
1st of 8	Derby	3b 4s
2nd of 2	Wilson	1s
2nd of 2	Callaghan	1s
2nd of 2	Thatcher	1s
2nd of 3	Grafton	2b
2nd of 3	Canning	1b 1s
2nd of 3	Goderich	2b
2nd of 5	Disraeli	3b 1s
2nd of 5	Asquith	1b 3s
2nd of 6	Melbourne	3b 2s
2nd of 7	Devonshire	3b 3s
2nd of 7	George Grenville	5b 1s
2nd of 8	Bute	2b 5s
2nd of 9	Grey	6b 2s
3rd of 3	Russell	2b
3rd of 3	Macmillan	2b
3rd of 4	Rosebery	1b 2s
3rd of 4	Lloyd George	1b 2s
3rd of 6	Portland	1b 4s
3rd of 8	Balfour	4b 3s
3rd of 9	Lord Grenville	3b 5s
3rd of 11	Peel	5b 5s
4th of 4	Major	2b 1s
4th of 5	Pitt	2b 2s
4th of 5	Bonar Law	3b 1s
4th of 5	Eden	3b 1s

POSITION IN FAMILY—*Continued*

		Number of Brothers and Sisters
4th of 6	Addington	1b 4s
4th of 7	Chatham	1b 5s
5th of 6	Gladstone	3b 2s
5th of 6	Salisbury	3b 2s
5th of 9	Perceval	2b 6s
5th of 17	Walpole	9b 7s
6th of 6	Wilmington	3b 2s
6th of 6	Campbell-Bannerman	1b 4s
6th of 9	Newcastle	2b 6s
6th of 9	Wellington	6b 2s
7th of 8	Attlee	4b 3s
7th of 9	Pelham	2b 6s
8th of 10	Rockingham	4b 5s

Only Children

3:

Liverpool
Baldwin
MacDonald

Eldest Sons

22:

Devonshire	Disraeli
Bute	Rosebery
North	Balfour
Shelburne	Asquith
Portland	Lloyd George
Addington	Chamberlain
Canning	Churchill
Peel	Douglas-Home
Derby	Wilson
Aberdeen	Heath
Palmerston	Callaghan

Eldest Children

9:

North	Chamberlain
Churchill	Shelburne
Heath	Palmerston
Aberdeen	Derby
Douglas-Home	

Second Sons

10:

Newcastle	Perceval
George Grenville	Goderich
Chatham	Grey
Grafton	Melbourne
Pitt	Campbell-Bannerman

Youngest Children

8:

Wilmington	Wilson
Russell	Callaghan
Campbell-Bannerman	Thatcher
Macmillan	Major

SIZE OF FAMILY

Walpole came from the largest family; he had sixteen brothers and sisters. Peel had ten brothers and sisters, Rockingham had nine and Pelham, Newcastle, Lord Grenville, Perceval, Wellington and Grey had eight.

Siblings From Fathers' Other Marriages

Of the Prime Ministers, 12 had siblings from their fathers' other marriages:

Wilmington	5 (2b 3s)
Pelham	2 (2s)
Newcastle	2 (2s)
North	4 (1b 3s)
Perceval	7 (5b 2s)
Liverpool	2 (1b 1s)
Canning	9 (5b 4s)
Russell	4 (4b)
Palmerston	1 (1s)
Salisbury	5 (3b 2s)
Bonar Law	2 (2s)
Chamberlain	2 (1b 1s)

PM's overall position in family

Wilmington	11th of 11	5b 5s
Pelham	9th of 11	2b 8s
Newcastle	8th of 11	2b 8s
North	1st of 6	1b 4s
Perceval	12th of 16	7b 8s

Liverpool	1st of 3	1b 1s
Canning	2nd of 12	6b 5s
Russell	3rd of 7	6b
Palmerston	2nd of 6	1b 4s
Salisbury	5th of 11	6b 4s
Bonar Law	4th of 7	3b 3s
Chamberlain	3rd of 6	1b 4s

MARRIAGE

Wilmington, Pitt, Balfour and Heath were unmarried.

Prime Ministers married twice—10:

Walpole	(widowed)
Grafton	(divorced)
Shelburne	(widowed)
Addington	(widowed)
Liverpool	(widowed)
Russell	(widowed)
Aberdeen	(widowed)
Asquith	(widowed)
Lloyd George	(widowed)
Eden	(divorced)

Only 2 Prime Ministers were divorced: Grafton and Eden. The average age at first or only marriage is 29 years 266 days.

	PM's age years, days	**Spouse's age years, days**
Grafton (1)	20, 123	c.18, —
Aberdeen (1)	21, 181	21, 199
Rockingham	21, 289	16, —
Bute	23, 91	18, c.177
Newcastle	23, 255	c.16, —
Wilson	23, 296	23, 354
Walpole (1)	24, 4	c.18, —
Campbell-Bannerman	24, 6	c.28, —
North	24, 37	c.16, —
Addington (1)	24, 110	21, 126
Liverpool (1)	24, 291	28, 34
Asquith (1)	24, 345	23, 44
Lloyd George (1)	25, 7	21, 81
Baldwin	25, 40	22, 237
Thatcher	26, 62	36, 217
Macmillan	26, 71	19, 268
Melbourne	26, 80	19, 202
Derby	26, 81	20, 45
Callaghan	26, 123	c.25, —
Eden (1)	26, 147	c.18, —
Salisbury	27, 158	30, 96
Major	27, 189	28, 234
Shelburne (1)	27, 275	19, 162
Perceval	27, 283	20, 35
Devonshire	c.28, —	16, 152
Portland	28, 208	16, 73
Gladstone	29, 208	27, 200
MacDonald	30, 42	26, 126
Canning	30, 88	24, 116
Grey	30, 250	18, 259
Rosebery	30, 317	c.27, —
Aberdeen (2)	31, 161	23, 30
Goderich	31, 306	21, 191
Pelham	32, 34	c.26, —
Peel	32, 124	24, 202
Bonar Law	32, 188	c.24, —
Grenville, Lord	32, 268	c.19, —
Douglas-Home	33, 93	26, 332
Churchill	33, 287	23, 165
Disraeli	34, 250	46, 240
Grenville, G	c.36, —	c.32, —
Wellington	36, 345	c.34, —
Attlee	39, 7	26, 52
Asquith (2)	41, 232	30, 105
Grafton (2)	41, 263	23, 235
Chamberlain	41, 291	n.k., —
Shelburne (2)	42, 78	c.24, —
Russell (1)	42, 236	27, 211
Chatham	46, 1	34, 8
Russell (2)	48, 336	25, 247
Liverpool (2)	52, 109	45, 92
Palmerston	55, 57	52, 239
Eden (2)	55, 64	32, 47
Walpole (2)	c.62, —	c.36, —
Addington (2)	66, 60	c.40, —
Lloyd George (2)	80, 279	55, 16

n.k. not known

MARRIAGE—*Continued*

The oldest Prime Minister to marry for the first time was Palmerston at 55 years and 57 days. The oldest Prime Minister to marry was Lloyd George who was 80 years and 279 days old when he married for the second time.

The youngest Prime Minister to marry for the first time was Grafton, who was 20 years and 123 days.

WIVES

Of the Prime Ministers 39 married women younger than themselves. The biggest age gap is about 26 years; this was between Addington and his second wife whom he married when he was 66 and she was 40. Walpole married Molly Skerratt when he was 62 and she was 36, a gap of 25 years and 330 days. Lloyd George married Frances Stevenson when he was 80 and she was 55, an age difference of 25 years and 264 days.

Wives Younger than Prime Ministers:

PM	Age difference years, days
Addington (2)	*c.*26, —
Walpole (2)	25, 330
Lloyd George (2)	25, 264
Russell (2)	23, 89
Eden (2)	23, 16
Palmerston	22, 183
Shelburne	*c.*18, —
Russell (1)	15, 25
Lord Grenville	12, 322
Attlee	12, 321
Asquith	12, 154
Portland	12, 135
Chatham	11, 358
Grey	11, 357
Churchill	11, 121
Devonshire	*c.*11, —
Goderich	10, 115
Grafton (2)	10, 3
Aberdeen (2)	8, 132
Shelburne (1)	8, 116
Bonar Law	*c.*8, —
Eden (1)	*c.*8, —
Newcastle	*c.*8, —
North	*c.*8, —
Peel	7, 288
Liverpool	7, 17
Perceval	6, 248
Melbourne	6, 241
Macmillan	6, 169
Douglas-Home	6, 127
Pelham	*c.*6, —
Rockingham	*c.*6, —
Walpole (1)	*c.*6, —
Derby	5, 355
Canning	5, 341
Bute	*c.*5, —
George Grenville	*c.*4, —
Lloyd George (1)	3, 291
MacDonald	3, 281
Wellington	*c.*3, —
Rosebery	*c.*3, —
Addington (1)	2, 349
Asquith (1)	2, 31
Gladstone	2, 8
Baldwin	1, 169
Callaghan	1, 123

(Numbers in brackets after name of PM indicate first or second wife)

Wives Older Than Prime Ministers

Prime Ministers married to women older than themselves—8. The greatest age difference was between Disraeli and his wife Mary Anne, who was 12 years and 40 days his senior.

PM	Age Difference years, days
Disraeli	12, 40
Campbell-Bannerman	*c.*4, —
Liverpool (1)	3, 108
Grafton (1)	*c.*3, —
Salisbury	2, 303
Major	1, 46
Wilson	—, 59
Aberdeen (1)	—, 18

Margaret Thatcher has not been included in these tables. Her husband, Denis, is 10 years and 157 days older than she. Chamberlain is also excluded, as his wife's date of birth is not known.

Prime Ministers Whose Wives Had Been Married Before

Prime Ministers who married widows—5:

Addington
Russell (1)
Aberdeen (2)
Palmerston
Disraeli
Wellington
Grey
Palmerston
Macmillan

Only 1 Prime Minister has married a spouse who has been divorced, Margaret Thatcher.

Wives' Names

Wives called Mary—6:	Bute Rockingham Addington (2) Liverpool Grey Wilson
Wives called Catherine—5:	Walpole (1) Pelham Wellington Aberdeen (1) Gladstone
Wives called Anne—4:	Grafton (1) North Lord Grenville Chamberlain
Wives called Elizabeth—3:	George Grenville Grafton (2) Douglas-Home
Wives called Charlotte—2:	Devonshire Campbell-Bannerman
Wives called Dorothy—2:	Portland Macmillan
Wives called Frances—2:	Russell (2) Lloyd George (2)
Wives called Harriet—2:	Aberdeen (2) Newcastle
Wives called Margaret—2:	Lloyd George (1) MacDonald
Second wives called Frances—2:	Russell Lloyd George

Wives' fathers

Prime Ministers married to the daughters of peers—6:

Devonshire
Shelburne (1)
Melbourne
Russell (2)
Derby
Aberdeen (1)

Prime Ministers married to the daughters of peers who had formerly been MPs—12:

Pelham
Newcastle
Grafton (1)
Shelburne (2)
Portland
Addington (2)
Lord Grenville
Goderich

Prime Ministers married to the daughters of MPs—10:

Bute
George Grenville
Chatham
Grafton (2)
North
Perceval
Canning
Rosebery
Asquith (2)
Eden (1)

The first Prime Minister to marry the daughter of an MP or peer was Pelham; the last was Macmillan. Two Prime Ministers married the daughters of the Dukes of Devonshire; Portland married Lady Dorothy Cavendish, daughter of the 4th Duke and Macmillan married Lady Dorothy Cavendish, daughter of the 9th Duke.

CHILDREN

Grey and Grafton had the largest number of children, 17 and 16 respectively, while 11 PMs had none. Grey also had an illegitimate daughter by Georgiana, Duchess of Devonshire. Perceval had 12 children and Bute 11. At least 29 Prime Ministers had 4 or more children.

Prime Ministers Who Had No Children—11:

Wilmington
Newcastle
Rockingham
Pitt
Lord Grenville
Liverpool
Palmerston
Disraeli
Balfour
Campbell-Bannerman
Heath

Prime Minister Who Had 1 child:

Melbourne

Prime Ministers Who Had 2 children—6:

Wellington
Chamberlain
Eden
Wilson
Thatcher
Major

Prime Ministers Who Had 3 Children—3:

Goderich
Derby
Callaghan

Prime Ministers Who Had 4 Children—7:

Devonshire
Shelburne
Canning
Rosebery
Attlee
Macmillan
Douglas-Home

Prime Ministers Who Had 5 Children—2:

CHILDREN—*Continued*

Chatham

Churchill

Prime Ministers Who Had 6 Children—6:

Walpole	Lloyd George
Portland	Bonar Law
Russell	MacDonald

Prime Ministers Who Had 7 Children—5:

Pelham	Asquith
North	Baldwin
Peel	

Prime Ministers Who Had 8 Children—4:

Addington	Gladstone
Aberdeen	Salisbury

Prime Minister Who Had 9 Children:

George Grenville

Prime Minister Who Had 11 Children:

Bute

Prime Minister Who Had 12 Children:

Perceval

Prime Minister Who Had 16 Children:

Grafton

Prime Minister Who Had 17 Children:

Grey

CHILDREN WHO BECAME MPS

Prime Ministers who had children who became MPs—27. Bute and Grafton both had 4 sons who became MPs. George Grenville, Peel and Aberdeen each had 3 sons who were MPs. Megan Lloyd George was the first and only daughter of a Prime Minister to become an MP. The first Prime Minister to have a child who became an MP was Walpole and the latest was Macmillan.

	Number of Children Who Became MPs
Walpole	1
Devonshire	2
Bute	4
George Grenville	3
Grafton	4
North	2
Shelburne	2
Portland	2
Chatham	1
Perceval	1
Canning	1
Goderich	1
Wellington	2
Grey	2
Peel	3
Russell	1
Derby	2
Aberdeen	3
Gladstone	2
Salisbury	2
Rosebery	2
Lloyd George	2
Bonar Law	1
Baldwin	1
MacDonald	1
Churchill	1
Macmillan	1

Children of Prime Ministers Who Became Prime Ministers

Two Prime Ministers had sons who also became Prime Ministers:

Chatham was the father of Pitt.

George Grenville was the father of Lord Grenville.

PRIME MINISTERS WHO WERE RELATED TO EACH OTHER

Of the Prime Ministers, 2 were the sons of Prime Ministers and 2 were brothers. These were the closest relations.

Other relations: 4 brothers-in-law, 3 uncles, 3 nephews, 2 cousins and 1 father-in-law. Other Prime Ministers' families (4) were linked less closely by marriage.

Father and Son

Pitt was the son of Chatham.

Lord Grenville was the son of George Grenville.

Brothers

Pelham and Newcastle were brothers.

Father-In-Law and Son-In-Law

Devonshire's daughter Lady Dorothy Cavendish married Portland.

Brothers-In-Law

George Grenville's sister Hester married Chatham.

Melbourne's sister Emily married Palmerston.

Uncles and Nephews

George Grenville's sister Hester was the mother of Pitt.

Chatham's wife Hester was the aunt of Lord Grenville.

Salisbury's sister, Lady Blanche Gascoyne-Cecil, was the mother of Balfour.

Cousins

George Grenville's sister Hester married Chatham, thus making George Grenville's son Lord Grenville and Chatham's son Pitt, cousins.

Other Prime Ministers' Families Linked By Marriage:

Pelham and Newcastle's sister Elizabeth married Charles, 2nd Viscount Townshend who later married Walpole's sister, Dorothy.

Devonshire's sister Rachel married Horatio Walpole, 2nd Baron Walpole of Wolterton, Sir Robert Walpole's nephew.

Russell's daughter Lady Georgiana Adelaide married Archibald Peel, nephew of Sir Robert Peel.

Churchill's niece, Clarissa Anne Spencer-Churchill, daughter of his brother John, married Eden.

ZODIAC SIGNS

More Prime Ministers were born under the signs of Aries and Libra than any other signs.

Aries:	6	North, Portland, Canning, Derby, Callaghan, Major
Taurus:	3	Shelburne, Wellington, Rosebery
Gemini:	5	Bute, Pitt, Addington, Liverpool, Eden
Cancer:	3	Newcastle, Douglas-Home, Heath
Leo:	3	Russell, Balfour, Baldwin
Virgo:	4	Walpole, Campbell-Bannerman, Asquith, Bonar Law
Libra:	6	Pelham, George Grenville, Grafton, Palmerston, MacDonald, Thatcher
Scorpio:	4	Chatham, Lord Grenville, Perceval, Goderich
Sagittarius:	2	Disraeli, Churchill
Capricorn:	3	Gladstone, Lloyd George, Attlee
Aquarius:	4	Peel, Aberdeen, Salisbury, Macmillan
Pisces:	5	Rockingham, Grey, Melbourne, Chamberlain, Wilson

(Exact dates of birth not known for Wilmington and Devonshire.)

AGE AND PHYSICAL APPEARANCE

AGE

Four Prime Ministers were born in the 17th century, 24 in the 18th, 16 in the 19th, and 6 in the 20th century. Two Prime Ministers were born in the same year in 1759, 1770, 1784 and 1916; two died in the same year in 1792.

Since 1730, a Prime Minister has been born on average every 5 years and 69 days. This means that the Prime Minister after John Major will probably have been born around 6 June 1948.

Prime Ministers are listed in order of their birth, followed by their age in years and days.

	years, days
Walpole	60, 204
Wilmington	*c.* 70, —
Newcastle	75, 119
Pelham	59, 161
Chatham	69, 177
Grenville, G	58, 30
Bute	78, 290
Devonshire	*c.* 44, —
Rockingham	52, 49
North	60, 114
Grafton	75, 167
Shelburne	68, 5
Portland	71, 199
Addington	86, 261
Pitt	46, 240
Grenville, Lord	74, 80
Perceval	49, 193
Grey	81, 126

AGE—*Continued*

	years, days
Wellington	83, 136
Canning	57, 119
Liverpool	58, 180
Melbourne	69, 255
Goderich	76, 90
Aberdeen	76, 321
Palmerston	81, 363
Peel	62, 147
Russell	85, 273
Derby	70, 208
Disraeli	76, 119
Gladstone	88, 141
Salisbury	73, 200
Campbell-Bannerman	71, 228
Rosebery	82, 14
Balfour	81, 237
Asquith	75, 163
Bonar Law	65, 44
Lloyd George	82, 68
MacDonald	71, 28
Baldwin	80, 133
Chamberlain	71, 246
Churchill	90, 56
Attlee	84, 279
Macmillan	92, 322
Eden	79, 216
Douglas-Home	
Callaghan	
Wilson	
Heath	
Thatcher	
Major	

LONGEVITY

The Prime Minister who survived to the greatest age was Macmillan, who was 92 years, 322 days old when he died in 1986; although Douglas-Home is already second in the table. He will equal Macmillan's age on 19 May 1996. The youngest to die was Devonshire, at the age of 44.

As of January 1995 6 Prime Ministers were still alive: Douglas-Home, Callaghan, Wilson, Heath, Thatcher and Major. Leaving these out of account, on average, a Prime Minister can expect to live to the age of 73 years and 79 days. Calculations ignore the two for whom exact ages are not available.

Prime Ministers in order of their longevity, listed by years and days:

	years, days
Macmillan	92, 322
Churchill	90, 56
Gladstone	88, 141
Addington	86, 261
Russell	85, 273
Attlee	84, 279
Wellington	83, 136
Lloyd George	82, 68
Rosebery	82, 14
Palmerston	81, 363
Balfour	81, 237
Grey	81, 126
Baldwin	80, 133
Eden	79, 216
Bute	78, 290
Aberdeen	76, 321
Disraeli	76, 119
Goderich	76, 90
Grafton	75, 167
Asquith	75, 163
Newcastle	75, 119
Grenville, Lord	74, 80
Salisbury	73, 200
Chamberlain	71, 246
Campbell-Bannerman	71, 228
Portland	71, 199
MacDonald	71, 28
Derby	70, 208
Wilmington	*c.* 70
Melbourne	69, 255
Chatham	69, 177
Shelburne	68, 5
Bonar Law	65, 44
Peel	62, 147
Walpole	60, 204
North	60, 114
Pelham	59, 161
Liverpool	58, 180
Grenville, G	58, 30
Canning	57, 119
Rockingham	52, 49
Perceval	49, 193
Pitt	46, 240
Devonshire	*c.* 44, —

AGE AT DEATH OF FATHER

Almost half of all Prime Ministers lost their fathers before reaching the age of 21.

	years, days
Canning	1, —
Lloyd George	1, 142
Rosebery	3, 261
Goderich	3, 263
Grafton	5, 242
Balfour	7, 213
Aberdeen	7, 247
Asquith	7, 262
Wilmington	*c.*8, —
Perceval	8, 33
Callaghan	9, 200
Bute	9, 248
Grenville, Lord	11, 21
Wellington	12, 21
Grenville, George	14, 126
Pelham	17, 151
Palmerston	17, 178
Eden	17, 253
Chatham	18, 187
Newcastle	18, 217
Pitt	18, 348
Major	18, 363
Churchill	20, 55
Rockingham	20, 215
Shelburne	24, 8
Portland	24, 17
Bonar Law	24, 20
Walpole	24, 84
Attlee	25, 321
Addington	32, 296
Devonshire	*c.* 35, —
Salisbury	38, 69
Liverpool	38, 193
Campbell-Bannerman	40, 3
Baldwin	40, 140
Gladstone	41, 343
Macmillan	42, 49
Peel	42, 92
Disraeli	43, 29
Grey	43, 246
Thatcher	44, 120
Chamberlain	45, 106
Russell	47, 63
Douglas-Home	48, 9
Melbourne	49, 129
Derby	52, 93
Wilson	55, 242
North	58, 113
Heath	60, 98

MacDonald's father's date of death is not known.

AGE AT DEATH OF MOTHER

Before they were 21, 13 Prime Ministers lost their mothers and Aberdeen became an orphan before he was 12.

	years, days
Liverpool	—, 30
Bonar Law	*c.*2, —
North	2, 24
Chamberlain	5, 333
Pelham	5, 354
Newcastle	7, 54
Russell	9, 54
Salisbury	9, 254
Grenville, Lord	10, 42
Aberdeen	11, 253
Peel	15, 327
Derby	18, 79
Palmerston	20, 92
Addington	21, 161
Perceval	21, 223
Bute	23, 137
Balfour	23, 296
Gladstone	25, 298
Major	27, 172
Chatham	27, 341
Rockingham	31, 17
Lloyd George	33, 154
Thatcher	35, 55
Heath	35, 98

Asquith	36, *c.*79
Attlee	37, 137
Melbourne	39, 22
Grenville, G	39, 358
Wilson	*c.*42, —
Disraeli	42, 121
MacDonald	43, 122
Shelburne	43, 163
Macmillan	43, *c.*171
Pitt	43, 310
Wilmington	*c.*46, —
Churchill	46, 211
Goderich	47, 69
Portland	47, 94
Eden	48, 7
Callaghan	49, 99
Grafton	53, 84
Rosebery	54, 11
Canning	56, 333
Devonshire	*c.*57, —
Baldwin	57, 286
Grey	58, 74
Walpole	61, 282
Wellington	62, 132
Douglas-Home	63, 86

Campbell-Bannerman's mother's date of death is not known.

PHYSICAL APPEARANCE

Height

More than half of all Prime Ministers (27) are described as 'tall', in other words 5 feet 9 inches or over. Twelve are described as of medium height, and 6 as short, but in many cases these are based on subjective assessments rather than facts about actual height. Information is lacking for 5. Salisbury was probably the tallest at 6 feet 4 inches.

Tall:

Walpole, Wilmington, Newcastle, Devonshire, Bute, Rockingham, Chatham, Portland, Pitt, Addington, Liverpool, Wellington, Grey, Melbourne, Peel, Palmerston, Gladstone, Salisbury, Balfour, Bonar Law, MacDonald, Chamberlain, Eden, Macmillan, Douglas-Home, Heath, Callaghan, Major.

Medium Height:

Grafton, North, Shelburne, Lord Grenville, Derby, Aberdeen, Rosebery, Asquith, Baldwin, Wilson, Thatcher.

Short:

Perceval, Canning, Russell, Lloyd George, Churchill, Attlee.

Eyes

Information is available for few Prime Ministers, but of the 22 we have data for, 13 have blue eyes: Pelham, Goderich, Peel, Rosebery, Campbell-Bannerman, Lloyd George, Bonar Law, Baldwin, Churchill, Macmillan, Heath, Callaghan, Thatcher.

Other colours are:

brown	Walpole, Balfour, Chamberlain, Major
black	Disraeli, Gladstone
grey	Newcastle, North
pale	Wilson

Facial Hair

Two Prime Ministers had beards and moustaches: Disraeli and Salisbury. Salisbury's was much thicker and fuller than Disraeli's, which portraits show as rather wispy.

Four Prime Ministers wore bushy side whiskers: Melbourne, Russell, Palmerston and Gladstone.

Nine Prime Ministers, all in the 20th century, have worn a moustache (Wilson wore one early in his career, but not by the time he became Prime Minister): Balfour, Campbell-Bannerman, Lloyd George, Bonar Law, MacDonald, Chamberlain, Attlee, Eden, Macmillan.

CULTURAL AND VOCATIONAL BACKGROUND

RELIGION

All the Prime Ministers have been Protestants. From 1678 to 1829 Roman Catholics were excluded from sitting in either House of Parliament. Even after the Emancipation Act of 1829 some disabilities of the Catholics remained. It was not until an Act of 1926 that most of these were finally removed. Disraeli was born into the Jewish faith but he was baptised into the Church of England at the age of twelve.

The majority of Prime Ministers were Anglicans—37; Balfour and Campbell-Bannerman belonged to the Church of Scotland; Bute was a Scottish Episcopalian and Bonar Law and MacDonald, Presbyterians. Shelburne was a Dissenter, and the other 7 Prime Ministers were non-conformists. Lloyd George and Callaghan were Baptists; Grafton and Chamberlain Unitarians; Wilson was a Congregationalist; Thatcher a Methodist.

EDUCATION

As the table suggests, various secondary schools have links with particular Oxford or Cambridge colleges.

	Secondary School	University
Walpole	Eton College	Cambridge, King's College
Wilmington	St Paul's School	Oxford, Trinity College
Pelham	Westminster School	Oxford, Hart Hall
Newcastle	Westminster School	Cambridge, Clare College
Devonshire	Tutors/Privately	—
Bute	Eton College	Leiden
Grenville G	Eton College	Oxford, Christchurch College
Rockingham	Westminster School	—
Chatham	Eton College	Oxford, Trinity College
Grafton	Westminster School	Cambridge, Peterhouse College
North	Eton College	Oxford, Trinity College
Shelburne	not known	Oxford, Christchurch College
Portland	Westminster School	Oxford, Christchurch College
Pitt	Tutors/Privately	Cambridge, Pembroke College
Addington	Winchester College	Oxford, Brasenose College
Grenville, Lord	Eton College	Oxford, Christchurch College
Perceval	Harrow School	Cambridge, Trinity College
Liverpool	Charterhouse School	Oxford, Christchurch College
Canning	Eton College	Oxford, Christchurch College
Goderich	Harrow School	Cambridge, St John's College
Wellington	Eton College	—
Grey	Eton College	Cambridge, Trinity College
Melbourne	Eton College	Cambridge, Trinity College
Peel	Harrow School	Oxford, Christchurch College
Russell	Westminster School	Edinburgh; Cambridge, St John's College
Derby	Eton College	Oxford, Christchurch College
Aberdeen	Harrow School	Cambridge, St John's College
Palmerston	Harrow School	Edinburgh: Cambridge, St John's College
Disraeli	Higham Hall School, Walthamstow	—
Gladstone	Eton College	Oxford, Christchurch College
Salisbury	Eton College	Oxford, Christchurch College
Rosebery	Eton College	Oxford, Christchurch College
Balfour	Eton College	Cambridge, Trinity College
Campbell-Bannerman	Glasgow High School	Glasgow; Cambridge, Trinity College
Asquith	City of London School	Oxford, Balliol College
Lloyd George	Tutors/Privately	—
Bonar Law	Glasgow High School	—
Baldwin	Harrow School	Cambridge, Trinity College

EDUCATION—*Continued*

	Secondary School	University
MacDonald	Drainie School, Morayshire	—
Chamberlain	Rugby School	—
Churchill	Harrow School	—
Attlee	Haileybury	Oxford, University College
Eden	Eton College	Oxford, Christchurch College
Macmillan	Eton College	Oxford, Balliol College
Douglas-Home	Eton College	Oxford, Christchurch College
Wilson	Wirral Grammar School	Oxford, Jesus College
Heath	Chatham House Grammar School, Ramsgate	Oxford, Balliol College
Callaghan	Portsmouth Northern Secondary School	—
Thatcher	Kesteven and Grantham Girls' School	Oxford, Somerville College
Major	Rutlish Grammar School, Wimbledon	—

SECONDARY EDUCATION

In recent years well over 90% of the population of Great Britain has attended state schools while nearly all the remainder has attended what are now called Independent and were formerly called Public Schools. Despite that, Harold Wilson, when he became Prime Minister in 1964 was, with the exception of MacDonald, the first Prime Minister to have been educated through the state system. Since that date all Prime Ministers have been similarly educated.

The school that has been attended by the greatest number of future Prime Ministers is Eton College (18) which is followed by Harrow School (7) and Westminster School (6).

Eton College:	Walpole, Bute, G Grenville, Chatham, North, Lord Grenville, Canning, Wellington, Grey, Melbourne, Derby, Gladstone, Salisbury, Rosebery, Balfour, Eden, Macmillan, Douglas-Home
Harrow School:	Perceval, Goderich, Peel, Aberdeen, Palmerston, Baldwin, Churchill
Westminster School:	Pelham, Newcastle, Rockingham, Grafton, Portland, Russell
Tutors/Privately:	Devonshire, Shelburne, Pitt, Lloyd George
Glasgow High School:	Campbell-Bannerman, Bonar Law
St Paul's School:	Wilmington
Winchester College:	Addington
Charterhouse School:	Liverpool
Higham Hall School:	Disraeli
City of London School:	Asquith
Drainie School:	MacDonald
Rugby School:	Chamberlain
Haileybury:	Attlee
Wirral Grammar School	Wilson
Chatham House Grammar School, Ramsgate:	Heath
Portsmouth Northern Secondary School:	Callaghan
Kesteven and Grantham Girls' School:	Thatcher
Rutlish Grammar School, Wimbledon:	Major

UNIVERSITY EDUCATION

All but 11 Prime Ministers attended university and nearly all of them have been either to Oxford (24) or to Cambridge (11). There were, of course, only these two universities in England until the foundation of University College, London (1826) and Durham University (1832). Scottish Universities educated 3 PMs and 2 of these went on to Cambridge.

At Oxford, Christ Church College predominates, having educated 13 Prime Ministers and at Cambridge, Trinity College, which has educated 5 Prime Ministers. One future Prime Minister attended a European continental university.

Prime Ministers who did not attend university:

Devonshire, Rockingham, Wellington, Disraeli, Lloyd George, Bonar Law, MacDonald, Chamberlain, Churchill, Callaghan, Major.

Prime Ministers who attended Oxford University:

Christ Church College:	George Grenville, Shelburne, Portland, Lord Grenville, Liverpool, Canning, Peel, Derby, Gladstone, Salisbury, Rosebery, Eden, Douglas-Home
Trinity College:	Wilmington, Chatham, North
Balliol College:	Asquith, Macmillan, Heath
Brasenose College:	Addington
Hart Hall:	Pelham
Jesus College:	Wilson
Somerville College:	Thatcher
University College:	Attlee

Prime Ministers who attended Cambridge University:

Trinity College:	Perceval, Grey, Melbourne, Balfour, Campbell-Bannerman, Baldwin
St John's College:	Goderich, Aberdeen, Palmerston
Clare College:	Newcastle
King's College:	Walpole
Pembroke College:	Pitt
Peterhouse College:	Grafton

Prime Ministers who attended Scottish Universities:

Edinburgh:	Russell, Palmerston (later St John's College, Cambridge)
Glasgow:	Campbell-Bannerman (later Trinity College, Cambridge)

Prime Minister who attended another university:

Leiden:	Bute

EARLY OCCUPATIONS

Of those who had careers before their political ones, 17 of the Prime Ministers either contemplated a legal career or actively pursued one, and 9 were barristers before they became Prime Minister:

Wilmington	Melbourne
George Grenville	Asquith
Pitt	Attlee
Addington	Thatcher
Perceval	

Other occupations are listed below:

Farm Manager:	Walpole
Ambassador:	Aberdeen
Army:	Wellington
Business:	Campbell-Bannerman, Bonar Law
Journalist/Writer:	MacDonald, Churchill
Estate Manager:	Chamberlain
Publisher:	Macmillan
Civil Servant:	Wilson, Heath
Banker:	Bonar Law, Major
Research Chemist:	Thatcher
Tax Inspector:	Callaghan

A number of Prime Ministers—21—came from families of landowners or Peers and many of them combined a political career with that of running a large estate.

OCCUPATIONS AFTER LEAVING OFFICE

Wilmington, Pelham, Rockingham, Pitt, Perceval, Canning and Palmerston all died in office.

Prime Ministers who continued as Peers or were elevated to the peerage after leaving office—33:

Walpole	Derby
Newcastle	Aberdeen
Devonshire	Disraeli
Bute	Salisbury
Chatham	Rosebery
Grafton	Balfour
North	Asquith*
Shelburne	Lloyd George*
Portland	Baldwin
Addington	Attlee*
Lord Grenville	Eden
Liverpool	Macmillan
Goderich	Douglas-Home*
Wellington	Wilson*
Grey	Callaghan
Melbourne	Thatcher*
Russell	

(*PM continued as MP before being elevated to the peerage.)

Prime Ministers who continued as MPs after leaving office and did not become, or have not yet become, Peers—9:

OCCUPATIONS AFTER LEAVING OFFICE—*Continued*

George Grenville	MacDonald
Peel	Chamberlain
Gladstone	Churchill
Campbell-Bannerman	Heath
Bonar Law	

Wellington continued his army career as Commander in Chief after leaving office. Macmillan returned to work for the Macmillan Publishing company.

MILITARY SERVICE

Fewer than half of the Prime Ministers have undertaken military service and less than that number have seen real military action. These include:

Pelham	Captain	Brigadier Dormer's regiment Jacobite rising, 1715
Devonshire	Colonel	Volunteer against Jacobite rising, 1745
Rockingham	Colonel	Volunteer against Jacobite rising, 1745
Chatham	Cornet	King's Own Regiment of Horse, 1731-36
Shelburne	Colonel	20th then 3rd Regiment of Foot Guards, 1757-61
Pitt	Colonel	Cinque Ports and Trinity House Volunteers, 1803-06
Addington	Commander	Woodley Cavalry, Berkshire, 1798-1806
Perceval	Not known	London and Westminster Light Horse Volunteers, 1794-1803
Liverpool	Colonel	Cinque Ports regiment, 1794-
Goderich	Captain	Yorkshire Hussar regiment of Yeomanry, 1803-14
Wellington	Commander in Chief	Various regiments in the army
Melbourne	Major	Hertfordshire voluntary infantry, 1803-
Russell	Captain	Bedfordshire Militia
Palmerston	Lt. Colonel	Hampshire Militia
Campbell-Bannerman	Company Commander	First Lanarkshire Rifle Volunteers
Churchill	Lieutenant	Fourth Hussars, 1895-99 2nd Grenadier Guards, 1915-
	Lt. Colonel	6th Royal Scots Fusiliers, 1916
Attlee	Major	6th Battalion of South Lancashire Regiment, 1914-18
Eden	Brigade Major	King's Royal Rifle Corps, 1915-19
Macmillan	Captain	King's Royal Rifle Corps, 1914-15 Grenadier Guards, 1915-19
Heath	Major	Royal Artillery, 1940-46
Callaghan	Sub-Lieutenant	Royal Navy, 1939-45

MEMBERSHIP OF CLUBS

Most Prime Ministers have been members of clubs and indeed the House of Commons and the House of Lords are often described as clubs and have many of their features, namely libraries, dining rooms, bars, a chess room etc. Club membership was most likely to be White's in the early period and the Atheneum, or, for the Tory Prime Ministers, the Carlton more recently. The date after the name of a club indicates the date of its founding (and sometimes its demise). Wellington and Macmillan were members of at least eight clubs, while Bute, the Grenvilles, Derby and Chamberlain were not members of any club.

Army and Navy (1837)	Wellington
Atheneum (1824)	Wellington, Disraeli, Balfour, Campbell-Bannerman, Asquith, Baldwin, MacDonald, Churchill, Attlee, Macmillan, Wilson, Callaghan
Boodles (1762)	Shelburne, Churchill
Brooks (1764)	Grafton, North, Portland, Pitt, Melbourne, Campbell-Bannerman
Buck's (1919)	Churchill, Eden, Macmillan, Heath
Carlton (1832)	Wellington, Peel, Disraeli, Gladstone, Salisbury, Balfour, Bonar Law, Baldwin, Churchill, Eden, Macmillan, Heath, Thatcher, Major
City of London (1832)	Wellington

Crockfords (1828-*c.*1845)	Wellington, Disraeli
Guards (1810)	Macmillan
Kit-Cat (1700-20)	Walpole, Wilmington, Newcastle
Marylebone Cricket Club (1787)	Baldwin, Eden, Macmillan, Douglas-Home, Heath, Major
National Liberal (1882)	Lloyd George
Oriental (1824)	Wellington
Oxford and Cambridge (1830)	Gladstone, Campbell-Bannerman, Attlee
Pratts (1841)	Macmillan
Reform (1836)	Russell, Gladstone, Campbell-Bannerman, Asquith, Lloyd George
St. Stephen's Constitutional (1870)	Heath, Thatcher
Travellers (1819)	Balfour, Baldwin
Turf (1868)	Macmillan
Union (1799-1964)	Peel
United Services (1815-1976)	Wellington
United University (1921-72)	Baldwin
White's (1693)	Walpole, Pelham, Newcastle, Devonshire, Rockingham, Chatham, Grafton, North, Portland, Pitt, Addington, Perceval, Liverpool, Canning, Goderich, Wellington, Grey, Melbourne, Peel, Aberdeen, Palmerston, Rosebery, Balfour

SPORTS AND HOBBIES

The most popular pastimes were hunting and shooting, which 14 Prime Ministers enjoyed.

Walpole — Aberdeen
Grafton — Palmerston
Pitt — Rosebery
Goderich — Churchill
Grey — Eden
Melbourne — Macmillan
Peel — Douglas-Home

Prime Ministers who were interested in cricket—8:

Chatham — Peel
Addington — Douglas-Home
Baldwin — Major
Attlee
Macmillan

Tennis—6:

Balfour — Attlee
Bonar Law — Macmillan
Baldwin — Callaghan

Horseracing—4:

Rockingham — Palmerston
Grafton — Rosebery

Fishing—2:

Chamberlain — Churchill

Prime Ministers who enjoyed gardening, planting trees or botany—11:

Wilmington — Goderich
Newcastle — Aberdeen
Bute — Disraeli
Chatham — Chamberlain
Pitt — Attlee
Lord Grenville

Prime Ministers who actively pursued farming—4:

Canning — Callaghan
Aberdeen — Eden

Many of the Prime Ministers had a passion for collecting.

Books—9:

Newcastle — Disraeli
Grafton — Rosebery
Shelburne — Balfour
Liverpool — Thatcher
Peel

Paintings—8:

Walpole — Peel
Bute — Gladstone
Lord Grenville — Asquith
Wellington — Eden

Prime Ministers who enjoyed music and opera—8:

Newcastle — Wellington

SPORTS AND HOBBIES—*Continued*

Balfour	Chamberlain
Lloyd George	Heath
Baldwin	Thatcher

Prime Ministers who enjoyed travelling—4:

Russell	Lloyd George
Campbell-Bannerman	MacDonald

Prime Ministers who played chess—10:

Rockingham

Pitt

Peel

Disraeli

Gladstone

Balfour

Asquith

Bonar Law

Churchill

Attlee

Derby, Gladstone and Salisbury were classical scholars; Disraeli and Campbell-Bannerman were both gourmets. More unusually, North enjoyed dancing, Baldwin and Thatcher skiing and Douglas-Home flower-arranging.

DEATH AND BURIAL

CAUSE OF DEATH

Only 1 Prime Minister was assassinated: Perceval, who was shot in the lobby of the House of Commons

Only 1 Prime Minister died as the direct result of an accident: Peel fell from his horse while riding on Constitution Hill in London; the horse stumbled on top of him aggravating his injuries, from which he died 3 days later.

Prime Ministers Who Died After Suffering a Stroke—9:

Newcastle	Wellington
Devonshire	Melbourne
Chatham	Rosebery
Lord Grenville	Asquith
Liverpool	

Prime Ministers Who Died From Cancer—4:

Gladstone	Bonar Law
Chamberlain	Lloyd George

Prime Ministers Who Died From Influenza—3:

Rockingham

Addington

Goderich

Prime Ministers Who Died From Heart Attacks—2:

Campbell-Bannerman

Baldwin

Walpole died as a result of kidney stones, Pitt died from kidney failure. Derby had suffered chronic gout and George Grenville succumbed to a blood disorder. North died of dropsy, Disraeli died of bronchitis, Palmerston of a chill and Macmillan of pneumonia. Grey had erisypelas, Balfour suffered circulatory failure and Portland died of an apoplectic seizure. Information is not available for the causes of death for the other Prime Ministers but nearly all of them were over 70 when they died.

DAYS OF THE WEEK BORN AND DIED

Births

More Prime Ministers were born on a Wednesday than on any other day.

Sunday:	3	Walpole, Asquith, Heath
Monday:	7	Pitt, Addington, Perceval, Wellington, Melbourne, Churchill, Major
Tuesday:	8	Bute, Chatham, Grafton, Shelburne, Grey, Peel, Balfour, Thatcher
Wednesday:	10	Pelham, George Grenville, Lord Grenville, Canning, Goderich, Aberdeen, Palmerston, Salisbury, Campbell-Bannerman, Callaghan
Thursday:	6	Rockingham, Liverpool, Bonar Law, Chamberlain, Attlee, Douglas-Home

Friday:	6	North, Derby, Disraeli, Gladstone, Rosebery, MacDonald
Saturday:	8	Newcastle, Portland, Russell, Lloyd George, Baldwin, Eden, Macmillan, Wilson

(Exact dates of birth are not known for Wilmington and Devonshire.)

Deaths

More Prime Ministers died on a Tuesday than on any other day.

Sunday:	5	North, Lord Grenville, Baldwin, Churchill, Attlee
Monday:	8	Walpole, Wilmington, Rockingham, Chatham, Portland, Perceval, Lloyd George, Macmillan
Tuesday:	10	Devonshire, George Grenville, Shelburne, Wellington, Peel, Russell, Disraeli, Rosebery, Bonar Law, MacDonald
Wednesday:	6	Pelham, Canning, Palmerston, Balfour, Campbell-Bannerman, Asquith
Thursday:	7	Newcastle, Grafton, Pitt, Addington, Liverpool, Grey, Gladstone
Friday:	4	Goderich, Melbourne, Aberdeen, Eden
Saturday:	4	Bute, Derby, Salisbury, Chamberlain

(Six Prime Ministers are still living.)

Eight Prime Ministers were born and died on the same day of the week.

Monday:	1	Perceval
Tuesday:	2	Shelburne, Peel
Wednesday:	4	Pelham, Canning, Palmerston, Campbell-Bannerman
Thursday:	1	Liverpool

MONTHS OF THE YEAR BORN AND DIED

In the months of March, May and October, 20 Prime Ministers were born. 18 died in the same 3 months. Shelburne and Rosebery were both born and died in May; Palmerston was born and died in October. No Prime Minister has died in the month of June.

Births

January:	3	Aberdeen, Lloyd-George, Attlee
February:	3	Peel, Salisbury, Macmillan
March:	7	Grey, Melbourne, Derby, Chamberlain, Wilson, Callaghan, Major
April:	3	North, Portland, Canning
May:	7	Bute, Rockingham, Shelburne, Pitt, Addington, Wellington, Rosebery
June:	2	Liverpool, Eden
July:	4	Newcastle, Balfour, Douglas-Home, Heath
August:	3	Walpole, Russell, Baldwin
September:	5	Pelham, Grafton, Campbell-Bannerman, Asquith, Bonar Law
October:	6	George Grenville, Lord Grenville, Goderich, Palmerston, MacDonald, Thatcher
November:	3	Chatham, Perceval, Churchill
December:	2	Disraeli, Gladstone

(Exact dates of birth are not known for Wilmington and Devonshire.)

Deaths

January:	5	Pitt, Lord Grenville, Goderich, Churchill, Eden
February:	2	Addington, Asquith
March:	6	Walpole, Pelham, Bute, Grafton, Balfour, Lloyd George
April:	2	Disraeli, Campbell-Bannerman
May:	6	Chatham, Shelburne, Perceval, Russell, Gladstone, Rosebery
June:	0	
July:	4	Wilmington, Rockingham, Grey, Peel
August:	3	North, Canning, Salisbury
September:	1	Wellington
October:	6	Devonshire, Portland, Derby, Palmerston, Bonar Law, Attlee
November:	5	Newcastle, George Grenville, Melbourne, MacDonald, Chamberlain
December:	4	Liverpool, Aberdeen, Baldwin, Macmillan

(Six Prime Ministers are still living.)

MONTHS OF THE YEAR BORN AND DIED—*Continued*

Same Birthday

Only two Prime Ministers share the same birthday, Derby and Major, who were born on 29 March.

Same Dates of Death

15 February:	Addington, Asquith
11 May:	Chatham, Perceval
2 July:	Wilmington, Peel
30 October:	Portland, Bonar Law
9 November:	MacDonald, Chamberlain
14 December:	Aberdeen, Baldwin

PLACE OF BURIAL

Of the 44 Prime Ministers deceased 38 are buried in England; 5 are buried in Scotland and 1 in Wales.

Ten Prime Ministers are buried in London; 8 in Westminster Abbey, 1 in St. Paul's Cathedral and 1 in St Marylebone. Chatham was the first to be buried in Westminster Abbey and Attlee the last. Wellington is the only Prime Minister to have been buried in St Paul's Cathedral. In Buckinghamshire, 5 Prime Ministers are buried; in Oxfordshire 3; in Sussex 3 and in Hertfordshire 2.

The only Prime Ministers to be buried in the same place outside London are Pelham and Newcastle who are both buried at Laughton in Sussex, and Melbourne and Salisbury who are buried at Hatfield in Hertfordshire.

Only 1 Prime Minister, Rockingham, is buried in York Minster.

Prime Ministers Buried in London:

Westminster Abbey:	Chatham Pitt Canning Palmerston Gladstone Bonar Law Chamberlain Attlee
St. Paul's Cathedral:	Wellington
St. Marylebone:	Portland

Prime Ministers Buried in Scotland:

Dalmeny:	Rosebery
Meigle, Perthshire:	Campbell-Bannerman
Rothesay:	Bute
Spynie, nr Lossiemouth:	MacDonald
Whittingehame, East Lothian:	Balfour

Prime Minister Buried in Wales:

Ty Newydd, Llanystumdwy, Caernarvonshire:	Lloyd George

Prime Ministers Buried in England, by County (excluding London):

Buckinghamshire, Burnham: Chenies: High Wycombe: Hughenden: Wotton:	 Lord Grenville Russell Shelburne Disraeli George Grenville
Derbyshire, Derby:	 Devonshire
Gloucestershire, Hawksbury:	 Liverpool
Hertfordshire, Hatfield:	 Melbourne Salisbury
Kent, Charlton:	 Perceval
Lancashire, Knowsley:	 Derby
Lincolnshire, Nocton:	 Goderich
Middlesex, Great Stanmore:	 Aberdeen
Norfolk, Houghton:	 Walpole
Northumberland, Howick:	 Grey
Oxfordshire, Bladon: Sutton Courtney: Wroxton:	 Churchill Asquith North
Staffordshire, Drayton Bassett:	 Peel
Suffolk, Euston:	 Grafton
Surrey, Mortlake:	 Addington
Sussex, Laughton: Horsted Keynes:	 Pelham Newcastle Macmillan
Warwickshire, Compton Wynyates:	 Wilmington
Worcestershire, Worcester:	 Baldwin
Wiltshire, Alvediston:	 Eden
Yorkshire, York Minster:	 Rockingham

MISCELLANY

HONOURS OTHER THAN PEERAGE

All Prime Ministers, with the exception of MacDonald, were members of the Privy Council before they became PM. This means they are entitled to be addressed as 'The Right Honourable' although if they are a Peer then, as such, they are 'Right Honourable'. After the name there will follow 'PC'.

The orders of chivalry and their dates of origin most usual for Prime Ministers are:

KG	The Most Noble Order of the Garter (1348)
KT	The Most Ancient and Most Noble Order of the Thistle (revived 1687)
OM	Order of the Merit (1902, limited to 24)
CH	Companion of Honour (1917, limited to 65)
GCVO	Knight Grand Cross of the Royal Victorian Order (1896)
KCMG	Knight Commander of St Michael and St George (1818)
GCB	Knight Grand Cross of the Order of the Bath (1725, enlarged 1815)
KB	Knight of the Bath (1399, revived 1725)
OBE	Officer of the Most Excellent Order of the British Empire (1917)
FRS	Fellow of the Royal Society (1660)

The most usual honour for a Prime Minister has been KG (27) while only two Prime Ministers, Churchill and Attlee, have been Companions of Honour during the last 77 years.

Walpole	KG; KB
Wilmington	KG; KB
Pelham	FRS
Newcastle	KG; FRS
Devonshire	KG; FRS
Bute	KG; KT
Grenville G	—
Rockingham	KG; FRS
Chatham	FRS
Grafton	KG
North	KG
Shelburne	KG
Portland	KG; FRS
Pitt	—
Addington	—
Grenville Lord	FRS
Perceval	—
Liverpool	KG; FRS
Canning	FRS
Goderich	FRS
Wellington	KG; KB; GCB; FRS
Grey	KG; FRS
Melbourne	FRS
Peel	FRS
Russell	KG; KCMG; FRS
Derby	KG; KCMG; FRS
Palmerston	FRS
Disraeli	KG; FRS
Gladstone	FRS
Salisbury	KG; GCVO; FRS
Rosebery	KG; KT; FRS
Balfour	KG; OM; FRS
Campbell-Bannerman	GCB
Asquith	KG; FRS
Lloyd- George	OM
Bonar Law	—
Baldwin	KG; FRS
MacDonald	FRS
Chamberlain	FRS
Churchill	KG; OM; CH; FRS
Attlee	KG; OM; CH; FRS
Eden	KG
Macmillan	OM; FRS
Douglas-Home	KT
Wilson	KG; OBE; FRS
Heath	KG; OBE

Callaghan	KG
Thatcher	OM; FRS
Major	—

RESIDENCES

A number of Prime Ministers have lived in interesting and sometimes distinguished houses. Some of these can be visited and often contain mementoes of great interest in understanding the personal side of their lives.

Walpole	Houghton Hall*, Norfolk
Wilmington	Compton Wynyates, Warwickshire
Devonshire	Chatsworth House*, Derbyshire
Bute	Kenwood House*, London; Luton Hoo*, Bedfordshire
Grenville, G	Wotton House, Buckinghamshire
Grafton	Euston Hall*, Suffolk
Shelburne	Bowood House*, Wiltshire
Grenville, Lord	Wotton House, Buckinghamshire
Wellington	Stratfield Saye House, Hampshire; Apsley House*, London; Walmer Castle*, Kent
Grey	Howick Hall*, Northumberland (Gardens only open)
Melbourne	Melbourne Hall*, Derbyshire
Aberdeen	Haddo House*, Aberdeenshire, Scotland (NTS)
Palmerston	Broadlands*, Hampshire
Disraeli	Hughenden Manor*, Buckinhamshire (NT)
Salisbury	Hatfield House*, Hertfordshire
Rosebery	Mentmore*, Buckinghamshire
Lloyd George	Highgate*, Llanystumdwy, Criccieth, Gwynedd (Memorial Museum)
Churchill	Chartwell*, Kent (NT)

* open to the public; (NT) National Trust; (NTS) National Trust Scotland

DUELS

Four Prime Ministers fought duels.

Shelburne—	wounded in a duel on 22 Mar 1780
Pitt—	fought a duel with a fellow MP on 27 May 1798 but was unhurt
Canning—	wounded in a duel on 21 Sep 1809 with Castlereagh, a fellow member of the Cabinet
Wellington—	fought a duel on 21 Mar 1829 but was unhurt

The Irish agitator, Daniel O'Connell, was almost involved in duels with two Prime Ministers. In 1815 he challenged Peel to a duel in Ostend, but was arrested before he arrived. Disraeli challenged Daniel O'Connell to a duel in May 1835 but the police intervened before it could take place.

ACCIDENTS

Riding Accidents

Five Prime Ministers were injured in riding accidents, Peel so seriously that it led to his death.

North broke his arm in 1776 after a fall from his horse; Chatham fell off his horse in 1777 after a stroke; Portland suffered a dislocated collar bone and a fractured rib in 1782; Canning injured his leg in 1804.

Other Accidents

Bute fell down some cliffs while collecting plants.

Grey was injured when his wife's picture fell off the wall and hit him on the head.

Gladstone lost the top joint of his left forefinger in a shooting accident.

MacDonald was knocked down by a bicycle and Macmillan by a taxi.

Major injured his knee in a car acccident.

ELECTIONS

FIRST ELECTION TO PARLIAMENT

Three Prime Ministers (Newcastle, Rockingham and Rosebery) were Peers, who did not therefore fight any elections. Two others (Bute and Aberdeen) were Scottish Representative Peers, which means that although peers they did not automatically have the right to sit in the House of Lords. They were among 16 of their number, elected to represent them in the House of Lords. Since these were not parliamentary elections in the true sense, Bute and Aberdeen are excluded from the following tables.

By winning a by-election, 18 Prime Ministers first became Members of the House of Commons. In some cases, this by-election would have been deliberately engineered so as to create a vacancy, although it is difficult to be precise about when this happened. In the 20th century the trend is very much against by-elections: only two (Lloyd George and Baldwin) having begun their parliamentary careers that way. Baldwin was the last Prime Minister to come in to the House of Commons originally at a by-election, although Douglas-Home came in for the second time at a by-election, having been appointed Prime Minister while still in the House of Lords, and having renounced his peerage after 4 days. He was then Prime Minister for 15 days without being a member of either House until the by-election took place.

Came in at a By-Election

Wilmington	Wellington*
Pelham	Grey
Chatham	Melbourne
Grafton	Peel
Shelburne*	Russell
Pitt	Derby
Grenville, Lord	Salisbury
Perceval	Lloyd George
Canning	Baldwin

Came in at a General Election

Walpole	Bonar Law
Devonshire	MacDonald
Grenville, G	Chamberlain
North	Churchill
Portland	Attlee
Addington	Eden
Liverpool	Macmillan
Goderich	Douglas-Home
Palmerston	Wilson
Disraeli	Heath
Gladstone	Callaghan
Balfour	Thatcher
Campbell-Bannerman	Major
Asquith	

*Had previously been elected to the Irish Parliament, which was abolished in 1800.

ELECTORAL DEFEATS

Not everyone was elected to the House of Commons on the first attempt. Callaghan was the last to achieve this. Disraeli failed 4 times over (2 by-elections, 2 General Elections); Palmerston failed 3 times (2 General Elections, 1 by-election); MacDonald, Thatcher and Major tried twice before getting in; and Wilmington, Pitt, Campbell-Bannerman, Baldwin, Churchill, Eden, Macmillan, and Douglas-Home won election at their second attempt. No serving Prime Minister has ever lost his or her seat.

Elected at First Attempt	Defeated Later
Walpole	1710*
Pelham	no
Devonshire	no
Grenville, G	no
Chatham	no
Grafton	no
North	no
Shelburne	no
Portland	no
Addington	no
Grenville, Lord	no
Perceval	no
Liverpool	no
Canning	no
Goderich	no
Wellington	no
Grey	no
Melbourne	no
Peel	1829
Russell	1826*, 1830, 1835
Derby	1830
Gladstone	1837*, 1865*, 1868*
Salisbury	no
Balfour	1906
Asquith	1918, 1924
Lloyd George	no
Bonar Law	1906, 1910
Chamberlain	no
Attlee	no
Wilson	no
Heath	no
Callaghan	no

*But also elected for another seat at the same election.

NUMBER OF ELECTIONS FOUGHT

Before 1926 the number of by-election contests is inflated by those caused by Ministers having to seek reelection after appointment to a paid office. This requirement was abolished by the Re-election of Ministers Acts of 1919 and 1926.

Polling in General Election contests before 1918 took place over several days, and sometimes several weeks. It was possible for a candidate to stand in two seats at the same election, and to be elected for both, one of which was then chosen. These are known as double returns, and are included in the figures below marked with an asterisk.

NUMBER OF ELECTIONS FOUGHT—*Continued*

By-Election Contests

11—Palmerston

9—Russell

8—Canning; Gladstone

7—Walpole; Peel

6—Pelham; Chatham; Disraeli

5—Grenville, G; North; Pitt; Melbourne; Derby; Churchill

4—Perceval; Goderich; Balfour; Campbell-Bannerman

3—Grenville, Lord; Liverpool; Wellington; Grey

2—Grafton; Addington; Salisbury; Bonar Law; Baldwin; MacDonald

1—Wilmington; Shelburne; Asquith; Lloyd George; Macmillan; Douglas-Home

***General Election Contests**

19—Palmerston

16—Churchill

15—Gladstone

13—Walpole; Wilmington; Russell; Lloyd George; Heath

12—Peel; MacDonald; Callaghan

11—Disraeli; Balfour; Asquith; Wilson; Thatcher

10—Baldwin; Attlee; Eden; Macmillan

9—Campbell-Bannerman; Douglas-Home

8—Canning

7—North; Derby; Chamberlain

6—Pelham; Goderich; Grey; Bonar Law; Major

5—Grenville, G; Pitt

4—Chatham; Addington; Perceval; Liverpool; Melbourne

3—Salisbury

2—Devonshire; Grenville, Lord; Wellington

1—Shelburne; Portland

MOST ELECTIONS FOUGHT

Excluding the 5 peers, who did not fight any parliamentary elections, 45 Prime Ministers have fought 508 election contests between them. Palmerston holds the record with 30 contests; Portland fought only 1.

30—Palmerston

23—Gladstone

22—Russell

21—Churchill

20—Walpole

19—Peel

17—Disraeli

16—Canning

15—Balfour

14—Wilmington; Lloyd George; MacDonald

13—Campbell-Bannerman; Heath

12—Pelham; North; Derby; Asquith; Baldwin; Callaghan

11—Macmillan; Wilson; Thatcher

10—Grenville, G; Chatham; Pitt; Goderich; Attlee; Eden; Douglas-Home

9—Grey; Melbourne

8—Perceval; Bonar Law

7—Liverpool; Chamberlain

6—Addington; Major

5—Grenville, Lord; Wellington; Salisbury

2—Devonshire; Grafton; Shelburne

1—Portland

ELECTORAL SUCCESS RATE

Of 50 Prime Ministers, 24 won all the elections that they fought. Of the remainder (excluding the five peers) Walpole was the most successful, losing only one of the 20 contests he fought. MacDonald was the least successful, losing 5 out of the 9 at which he was a candidate.

	Attempts–Losses	Percentage won
Walpole	20–1	95.0%
Peel	18–1	94.7%
Balfour	14–1	93.3%
Wilmington	13–1	92.9%
Campbell-Bannerman	12–1	92.3%
Derby	11–1	91.7%
Baldwin	11–1	91.7%
Pitt	9–1	90.0%
Eden	9–1	90.0%
Gladstone	20–3	87.0%
Russell	19–3	86.4%
Asquith	10–2	83.3%
Thatcher	9–2	81.8%
Palmerston	24–6	80.0%

Douglas-Home	8–2	80.0%
Disraeli	13–4	76.5%
Churchill	16–5	76.5%
Bonar Law	6–2	75.0%
Macmillan	8–3	72.7%
Major	4–2	66.7%
MacDonald	9–5	64.3%

(totals: 460-48; 90.6% overall success rate)

ELECTORAL CAREERS

Many Prime Ministers have spent most of their political careers in the House of Commons, fighting elections. The following table calculates the span of their electoral careers, from their first contest to their last. They are ranked in order of the length of their career.

Portland only fought 1 election, so he is not included below. Heath and Major are still in the Commons, so they are also omitted, as are the 5 peers.

Many short electoral careers will be accounted for by the subject's elevation to the House of Lords, and, indeed, the 5 Prime Ministers with the shortest electoral careers continued their political careers in the House of Lords without a break.

	First Election	Last Election	Career Span years, days
Churchill	6 Jul 1899	8 Oct 1959	60, 92
Gladstone	14 Dec 1832	24 Aug 1892	59, 254
Palmerston	7 Feb 1806	13 Jul 1865	59, 156
Russell	4 May 1813	27 Jun 1859	46, 54
Lloyd George	10 Apr 1890	14 Nov 1935	45, 218
Douglas-Home	30 May 1929	28 Feb 1974	44, 274
Disraeli	26 Jun 1832	17 Mar 1874	41, 264
MacDonald	18 Jul 1895	31 Jan 1936	40, 197
Walpole	11 Jan 1701	4 May 1741	40, 113
Asquith	9 Jul 1886	29 Oct 1924	38, 112
Peel	14 Apr 1809	28 Jul 1847	38, 105
Callaghan	5 Jul 1945	9 Jun 1983	37, 339
Campbell-Bannerman	30 Apr 1868	16 Jan 1906	37, 261
Thatcher	23 Feb 1950	11 Jun 1987	37, 108
North	15 Apr 1754	18 Jun 1790	36, 64
Macmillan	6 Dec 1923	8 Oct 1959	35, 306
Balfour	30 Jan 1874	14 Dec 1918	34, 318
Wilson	5 Jul 1945	3 May 1979	33, 302
Canning	28 Jun 1793	20 Apr 1827	33, 296
Eden	15 Nov 1922	26 May 1955	32, 192
Attlee	15 Nov 1922	26 May 1955	32, 192
Wilmington	19 Nov 1695	17 Aug 1727	31, 271
Pelham	28 Feb 1717	6 Jul 1747	30, 128
Baldwin	15 Jan 1906	14 Nov 1935	29, 303
Grenville, G	4 May 1741	17 Mar 1768	26, 318
Chatham	18 Feb 1735	27 Mar 1761	26, 37
Pitt	9 Sep 1780	17 May 1804	23, 251
Bonar Law	6 Oct 1900	15 Nov 1922	22, 40
Melbourne	31 Jan 1806	7 May 1827	21, 96
Grey	6 Jul 1786	20 Jul 1807	21, 14
Goderich	13 Nov 1806	12 Jun 1826	19, 211
Derby	30 Jul 1822	21 Sep 1841	19, 53
Addington	5 Apr 1784	5 Jul 1802	18, 91
Chamberlain	14 Dec 1918	14 Nov 1935	16, 335
Salisbury	22 Aug 1853	12 Jul 1866	12, 324
Liverpool	18 Jun 1790	6 Jul 1802	12, 18
Perceval	9 May 1796	5 May 1807	10, 361
Grenville, Lord	19 Feb 1782	22 Jun 1790	8, 123

ELECTORAL CAREERS—*Continued*

	First Election	Last Election	Career Span years, days
Devonshire	19 May 1721	6 Jul 1747	6, 48
Wellington	1 Apr 1806	21 May 1807	1, 50
Shelburne	2 Jun 1760	28 Mar 1761	—, 299
Grafton	10 Dec 1756	21 Dec 1756	—, 11

The 2 Scottish Representative Peers are exceptions in that they did not fight parliamentary elections in the usual sense. Nevertheless, they did have to go through an election process in order to be eligible to sit in the House of Lords, so their 'electoral' careers are detailed below.

Bute	14 Apr 1737– 15 Nov 1774	37, 215
Aberdeen	4 Dec 1806– 13 Nov 1812	5, 345

AGE WHEN FIRST ELECTED

Liverpool and Russell were returned at elections before they were 21 years of age, although they were not eligible to sit in Parliament until they attained the age of majority at 21.

Apart from Liverpool and Russell, Peel, Grafton and Devonshire were the youngest to be elected to Parliament. Chamberlain was by far the oldest at 49 years 271 days. Balfour was the youngest to be elected in the 20th century. In general the trend is to be elected older and older: 9 of the 10 oldest are 20th century Prime Ministers.

This table excludes those who never fought a parliamentary election (i.e. the 3 peers; Newcastle, Rockingham and Rosebery), but includes the 2 Scottish Representative Peers, Bute and Aberdeen*.

	years, days
Liverpool	20, 11
Russell	20, 259
Devonshire	*c.*21, —
Peel	21, 69
Grafton	21, 73
Pitt	21, 225
North	22, 2
Grey	22, 115
Grenville, Lord	22, 118
Pelham	22, 157
Palmerston	22, 200
Aberdeen	22, 310*
Portland	22, 348
Gladstone	22, 351
Shelburne	23, 31
Canning	23, 78
Derby	23, 123
Salisbury	23, 200
Bute	23, 324*
Goderich	24, 14
Walpole	24, 138
Wilmington	*c.*25, —
Balfour	25, 189
Churchill	26, 3
Chatham	26, 85
Eden	26, 177
Addington	26, 311
Melbourne	26, 322
Lloyd George	27, 83
Douglas-Home	28, 117
Grenville, G	28, 202
Wilson	29, 116
Macmillan	30, 262
Campbell-Bannerman	32, 74
Disraeli	32, 217
Callaghan	33, 70
Perceval	33, 190
Heath	33, 229
Asquith	33, 300
Thatcher	33, 360
Major	36, 35
Wellington	36, 335
MacDonald	39, 96
Attlee	39, 316
Baldwin	40, 212
Bonar Law	42, 18
Chamberlain	49, 271

CONSTITUENCIES REPRESENTED

As peers, 5 Prime Ministers entered Parliament by going straight into the House of Lords. All the others entered Parliament by winning an election to the House of Commons for a particular constituency. 16 sat for the same constituency throughout their Commons career: Lloyd George for a record 54 years 266 days. The 3 longest tenures are all for non-English seats, although Callaghan's seat underwent a number of minor boundary changes over the years.

The Prime Ministers who are still in the Commons, Heath and Major, will have to represent the same constituency until 15 Nov 2004 and 24 Jan 2033 respectively, if they wish to equal Lloyd George's record, although both of their seats have already undergone major boundary changes. Heath has already passed Callaghan's total, putting him in second place.

This table ranks those who have represented the same seat continuously throughout their Commons career.

Name	Constituency	Time years, days
Lloyd George	Caernarvon District of Burghs (10 Apr 1890– 1 Jan 1945)	54, 266
Callaghan	Cardiff South Cardiff South-East Cardiff South & Penarth (5 Jul 1945– 18 May 1987)	41, 317
Campbell-Bannerman	Stirling District of Burghs (20 Nov 1868– 22 Apr 1908)	39, 154
North	Banbury (15 Apr 1754– 4 Aug 1790)	36, 111
Eden	Warwick & Leamington (6 Dec 1923– 9 Jan 1957)	33, 34
Thatcher	Finchley (8 Oct 1959– 16 Mar 1992)	32, 160
Grenville, G	Buckingham (4 May 1741– 13 Nov 1770)	29, 193
Baldwin	Bewdley (2 Mar 1908– 8 Jun 1937)	29, 98
Addington	Devizes (5 Apr 1784– 11 Jan 1805)	20, 281
Perceval	Northampton (9 May 1796– 11 May 1812)	16, 2
Salisbury	Stamford (22 Aug 1853– 12 Apr 1868)	14, 234
Liverpool	Rye (7 Jun 1791– 15 Nov 1803)	12, 161
Devonshire	Derbyshire (19 May 1741– 13 Jun 1751)	10, 25
Portland	Weobley (28 Mar 1761– 1 May 1762)	1, 34
Shelburne	Chipping Wycombe (2 Jun 1760– 10 May 1761)	—, 342
Grafton	Bury St Edmunds (10 Dec 1756– 6 May 1757)	—, 147

4 other Prime Ministers have represented the same constituency for over 30 years, although they have sat for more than 1 during their careers: Pelham (Sussex); Palmerston (Tiverton); Asquith (Fife Eastern); and Wilson (Huyton).

At the opposite end of the spectrum, Canning sat for a record 8 different constituencies during his career in the House of Commons; Melbourne and Russell sat for 7 different constituencies each.

GEOGRAPHICAL AREAS REPRESENTED

Of the 45 Prime Ministers who were elected to the House of Commons, all but 5 represented English constituencies at some time in their careers. 3 of these, (Campbell-Bannerman, Asquith, Douglas-Home) sat only for Scottish constituencies, and 2 (Lloyd George and Callaghan) only for Welsh seats. On the other hand, Melbourne and MacDonald were the only Prime Ministers who sat for constituencies in 3 out of the 4 countries of the United Kingdom. Melbourne never sat for a Welsh seat; MacDonald never for an Irish one. No Prime Minister has sat for seats in all four countries.

Scottish constituencies have sent 8 of the Prime Ministers to Westminster, 5 of whom represented Scottish seats while they were Prime Minister. Wales has only produced 3, but all three sat for Welsh seats as Prime Minister. Ireland, which was represented in the United Kingdom Parliament between 1800 and 1920, produced in that time 5 future Prime Ministers, in addition to the two future PMs (Shelburne and Wellington) who were actually elected to the pre-1800 Irish Parliament.

Until 1832 the majority of constituencies were either the historic shire counties such as Devon, Sussex and Yorkshire; or centres of historic significance such as Bath or Shrewsbury. Since then constituency boundaries have been changed from time to time in an effort to maintain electorates of approximately equal size. Names have also changed, so that tracing the history of a particular seat is a complicated exercise. In the list that follows, constituencies have been arranged under their historic county names, but otherwise the contemporary constituency names have been kept.

Lancashire has sent more Prime Ministers to Parliament than any other county (7), closely followed by London and Sussex (6 each), and Buckinghamshire and Hampshire (5 each). Newport, Isle of Wight, in Hampshire, has been represented by 4 Prime Ministers (Canning, Wellington, Melbourne and Palmerston), and Seaford in Sussex by 3 (Pelham, Chatham and Canning).

GEOGRAPHICAL AREAS REPRESENTED—*Continued*

England

BERKSHIRE

Windsor	Derby

BUCKINGHAMSHIRE

the county	Grenville, Lord; Disraeli*
Buckingham	Grenville, G*; Grenville, Lord
Chipping Wycombe	Shelburne
Wendover	Canning

CAMBRIDGESHIRE

Cambridge University	Pitt*; Palmerston

CORNWALL

Mitchell	Wellington

DERBYSHIRE

the county	Devonshire

DEVON

the county	Russell
Devon, Southern	Russell
Okehampton	Chatham
Tavistock	Grey; Russell
Tiverton	Palmerston*

DURHAM

Seaham	MacDonald
Stockton-on-Tees	Macmillan

ESSEX

Epping	Churchill*
Harwich	Canning
West Walthamstow	Attlee*
Woodford	Churchill*

GLOUCESTERSHIRE

Stroud	Russell

HAMPSHIRE

Hampshire, Southern	Palmerston
Newport, Isle of Wight	Canning; Wellington; Melbourne; Palmerston
Newtown, Isle of Wight	Canning
Stockbridge	Derby

HEREFORDSHIRE

Leominster	Melbourne
Weobley	Portland

HERTFORDSHIRE

the county	Melbourne
Hertford	Balfour

HUNTINGDONSHIRE

the county	Russell; Major
Huntingdon	Major*

KENT

Bexley	Heath*
Bromley	Macmillan*
Maidstone	Disraeli
Old Bexley & Sidcup	Heath
Sidcup	Heath

LANCASHIRE

Bootle	Bonar Law
Huyton	Wilson*
Lancashire, Northern	Derby
Lancashire, Southern	Gladstone
Liverpool	Canning
Manchester East	Balfour*
Manchester North West	Churchill
Oldham	Churchill
Ormskirk	Wilson
Preston	Derby

LEICESTERSHIRE

Leicester	MacDonald

LINCOLNSHIRE

Stamford	Salisbury

LONDON

City of London	Russell*; Balfour
Camberwell, Dulwich	Bonar Law
Finchley	Thatcher*
Greenwich	Gladstone*
Stepney, Limehouse	Attlee*

NORFOLK

Castle Rising	Walpole
King's Lynn	Walpole*

NORTHAMPTONSHIRE

Northampton	Perceval*
Peterborough	Melbourne

NORTHUMBERLAND

the county	Grey
NOTTINGHAMSHIRE	
Newark-on-Trent	Gladstone
OXFORDSHIRE	
Banbury	North*
Oxford University	Peel; Gladstone
SHROPSHIRE	
Shrewsbury	Disraeli
SOMERSET	
Bath	Chatham*
STAFFORDSHIRE	
Tamworth	Peel*
SUFFOLK	
Bury St Edmunds	Grafton
Eye	Wilmington
SURREY	
Bletchingley	Melbourne; Palmerston
SUSSEX	
the county	Wilmington; Pelham*
East Grinstead	Wilmington
Hastings	Canning
Rye	Liverpool; Wellington
Seaford	Pelham; Chatham; Canning*
WARWICKSHIRE	
Birmingham, Ladywood	Chamberlain
Birmingham, Edgbaston	Chamberlain*
Warwick & Leamington	Eden*
WESTMORELAND	
Appleby	Pitt*; Grey
WILTSHIRE	
Chippenham	Peel
Devizes	Addington*
Old Sarum	Chatham
Westbury	Peel
WORCESTERSHIRE	
Bewdley	Baldwin*
YORKSHIRE	
Aldborough	Chatham
Ripon	Goderich

Wales

CARNARVONSHIRE	
Caernarvon	Lloyd George*
GLAMORGAN	
Aberavon	MacDonald*
Cardiff South	Callaghan
Cardiff South-East	Callaghan*
Cardiff South & Penarth	Callaghan

Scotland

Combined Scottish Universities	MacDonald
ANGUS	
Dundee	Churchill
EAST LOTHIAN	
Haddington Burghs	Melbourne
EDINBURGHSHIRE	
the county	Gladstone*
FIFE	
Fife Eastern	Asquith*
KINROSS & WEST PERTHSHIRE	
the county	Douglas-Home*
LANARKSHIRE	
Glasgow Blackfriars & Hutchesontown	Bonar Law
Glasgow Central	Bonar Law*
Lanark	Douglas-Home
RENFREWSHIRE	
Paisley	Asquith
STIRLINGSHIRE	
Stirling District of Burghs	Campbell-Bannerman*

Ireland

CARLOW	
Carlow	Goderich
CORK	
Bandon	Russell
KERRY	
the county	Shelburne (Irish Parliament)
Tralee	Canning
MEATH	
Trim	Wellington (Irish Parliament)

GEOGRAPHICAL AREAS REPRESENTED—*Continued*

OFFALY

Portarlington	Melbourne

TIPPERARY

Cashel	Peel

* Represented while Prime Minister

ELECTORAL CURIOSITIES

Of the Prime Ministers 32 were members of the House of Commons while they were Prime Minister; 5 Prime Ministers (Pitt, Gladstone, MacDonald, Churchill, Attlee) represented different constituencies at some point during their premierships, but Attlee was the only one to change his constituency during the same term of office.

Russell's first ministry was the first time that a Prime Minister had sat for a London seat either while Prime Minister or at any point in their career, but 5 out of the last 10 PMs have sat as Prime Minister for constituencies in what is now Greater London: Churchill, Attlee, Macmillan, Heath, Thatcher.

A record 4 Prime Ministers in a row, from Campbell-Bannerman to Bonar Law, represented seats outside England while Prime Minister. From 1905 to 1923, this is the longest ever such period.

In 1722 and 1727 both Wilmington (as Spencer Compton) and Pelham were elected for Sussex, a two-member seat. In 1722 Wilmington decided to sit for East Grinstead, where he had also been elected, but in 1727 they sat together for the county.

In 1807 both Palmerston and Wellington sat for Newport, Isle of Wight.

Baldwin was the only Prime Minister to succeed to his father's constituency.

Shelburne was the only Prime Minister to have been elected for an Irish constituency (to the Irish Parliament) and for an English constituency (to the British Parliament) at the same time.

'GLITTERING ELECTIONS': PMs CONTESTING GENERAL ELECTIONS

There have been 63 General Election since the premiership can be said to have begun in 1721. In 41 of these, the serving Prime Minister personally sought election to the House of Commons; in the other cases, the Prime Minister was a peer. After the 1802 election, no serving Prime Minister personally contested a General Election until the 1847 election, a gap of 12 elections or 45 years. Before 1721 there were 10 General Elections personally contested by a future Prime Minister, the first being the 1695 election by Wilmington.

9 Prime Ministers have contested the same General Election on 7 occasions; 8 on 3 occasions, 7 on 6 occasions and 6 on 11 occasions. Excluding the pre-1721 General Elections, the only occasion on which only 1 Prime Minister personally contested an election was 1774 (North).

The following table lists, for each General Election since 1695, the serving Prime Minister (those in parentheses did not personally contest it) and the number of Prime Ministers who contested it.

Election	Serving PM	No. of PMs Contesting
1695	—	1
1698	—	1
1701 (Jan)	—	2
1701 (Oct)	—	2
1702	—	2
1705	—	2
1708	—	2
1710	—	1
1713	—	2
1715	—	2
1722	Walpole	3
1727	Walpole	3
1734	Walpole	2
1741	Walpole	5
1747	Pelham	4
1754	(Newcastle)	3
1761	(Newcastle)	5
1768	(Chatham)	2
1774	North	1
1780	North	2
1784	Pitt	4
1790	Pitt	6
1796	Pitt	6
1802	Addington	6
1806	(Grenville, Ld)	6
1807	(Portland)	7
1812	(Liverpool)	4
1818	(Liverpool)	5
1820	(Liverpool)	5
1826	(Liverpool)	6
1830	(Wellington)	4
1831	(Grey)	4
1832	(Grey)	6
1835	(Melbourne)	6
1837	(Melbourne)	6
1841	(Melbourne)	6

1847	Russell	5
1852	(Derby)	4
1857	Palmerston	5
1859	(Derby)	5
1865	Palmerston	4
1868	Disraeli	3
1874	Gladstone	4
1880	Disraeli	3
1885	(Salisbury)	3
1886	Gladstone	4
1892	(Salisbury)	5
1895	(Salisbury)	5
1900	(Salisbury)	7
1906	Campbell-Bannerman	8
1910 (Jan)	Asquith	7
1910 (Dec)	Asquith	7
1918	Lloyd George	8
1922	Bonar Law	9
1923	Baldwin	9
1924	MacDonald	9
1929	Baldwin	9
1931	MacDonald	9
1935	Baldwin	9
1945	Churchill	7
1950	Attlee	9
1951	Attlee	8
1955	Eden	7
1959	Macmillan	6
1964	Douglas-Home	5
1966	Wilson	5
1970	Wilson	5
1974 (Feb)	Heath	6
1974 (Oct)	Wilson	5
1979	Callaghan	5
1983	Thatcher	4
1987	Thatcher	3
1992	Major	2

During the period of the premiership(s), 35 Prime Ministers had General Elections:

4: Walpole*, Liverpool*, Salisbury**

3: Pitt*, Melbourne*, Baldwin*, Wilson**

2: Newcastle*, North*, Grey*, Derby, Palmerston, Disraeli**, Gladstone, Asquith*, MacDonald, Attlee*, Thatcher*

1: Pelham, Chatham, Addington, Grenville Lord, Portland, Wellington, Russell, Campbell-Bannerman, Lloyd George, Bonar Law, Churchill, Eden, Macmillan, Douglas-Home, Heath, Callaghan, Major

* consecutive

** Salisbury: 3 consecutively; Wilson: 2 consecutively; Disraeli: 1 as a Peer

Of the 50 Prime Ministers, 15 (9 Peers, 6 MPs) never had a General Election during their premiership:

Peers: Wilmington, Devonshire, Bute, Rockingham, Grafton, Shelburne, Goderich, Aberdeen, Rosebery

MPs: Grenville G., Perceval, Canning, Peel, Balfour, Chamberlain

PARLIAMENTARY SERVICE

ENTERED PARLIAMENT: CHRONOLOGICAL

Of the Prime Ministers, 45 began their Parliamentary careers by election to the House of Commons at the date shown below. The dates for Liverpool and Russell are the dates on which they came of age, as they were elected before they were 21. Of the 5 who first entered Parliament as Peers in the House of Lords, 2 (Bute and Aberdeen) did so by election as Scottish Representative Peers, and 3 (Newcastle, Rockingham and Rosebery) by coming of age after inheriting their peerages.

Wilson and Callaghan were the only Prime Ministers to become MPs for the first time on the same day, although Wilson can be regarded as the more senior because he took the oath as an MP first. Liverpool came of age 1 day after Grey's first election, and George Grenville and Devonshire (1741) and Bonar Law and Churchill (1900) were elected for the first time at the same General Election. Goderich and Aberdeen were elected at the start of the same Parliament; Goderich at the General Election, and Aberdeen as a Scottish Representative Peer. Four Prime Ministers entered Parliament for the first time in 1806; no other year had more than 2 Prime Ministerial entrants.

Wilmington	3 Jun 1698
Walpole	11 Jan 1701
Newcastle	21 Jul 1714
Pelham	28 Feb 1717

ENTERED PARLIAMENT: CHRONOLOGICAL—*Continued*

Chatham	18 Feb 1735
Bute	14 Apr 1737
Grenville, G	4 May 1741
Devonshire	19 May 1741
Rockingham	13 May 1751
North	15 Apr 1754
Grafton	10 Dec 1756
Shelburne	2 Jun 1760
Portland	28 Mar 1761
Pitt	8 Jan 1781
Grenville, Lord	19 Feb 1782
Addington	5 Apr 1784
Grey	6 Jul 1786
Liverpool	7 Jun 1791
Canning	28 Jun 1793
Perceval	9 May 1796
Melbourne	31 Jan 1806
Wellington	1 Apr 1806
Goderich	13 Nov 1806
Aberdeen	4 Dec 1806
Palmerston	8 May 1807
Peel	15 Apr 1809
Russell	18 Aug 1813
Derby	30 Jul 1822
Gladstone	14 Dec 1832
Disraeli	27 Jul 1837
Salisbury	22 Aug 1853
Rosebery	7 May 1868
Campbell-Bannerman	20 Nov 1868
Balfour	30 Jan 1874
Asquith	9 Jul 1886
Lloyd George	10 Apr 1890
Churchill	3 Oct 1900
Bonar Law	4 Oct 1900
MacDonald	16 Jan 1906
Baldwin	2 Mar 1908
Chamberlain	14 Dec 1918
Attlee	15 Nov 1922
Eden	6 Dec 1923
Macmillan	29 Oct 1924
Douglas-Home	27 Oct 1931
Wilson	5 Jul 1945
Callaghan	5 Jul 1945
Heath	23 Feb 1950
Thatcher	8 Oct 1959
Major	3 May 1979

LEFT PARLIAMENT: CHRONOLOGICAL

The following table lists the date at which each Prime Minister's parliamentary service ended. Of these, 31 were in the House of Lords at that point (including Lloyd George, who never took his seat), and, as peers are members of that House for life: the date at which they ceased their service is their date of death.

While an MP in the Commons, 11 died: Pelham, George Grenville, Pitt, Perceval, Canning, Peel, Palmerston, Campbell-Bannerman, Bonar Law, MacDonald and Chamberlain. Only 2 (Gladstone and Churchill) ended their parliamentary careers by retiring at the dissolution of a Parliament. None departed from the Commons during the lifetime of a Parliament, or has died as a life peer in the Lords. 6 Prime Ministers are at present in Parliament; 2 (Heath and Major) as MPs, and 4 (Douglas-Home, Wilson, Callaghan and Thatcher) as life peers in the Lords. The year 1792 is the only one in which 2 Prime Ministers' service ended (Bute and North).

Wilmington	2 Jul 1743
Walpole	18 Mar 1745
Pelham	6 Mar 1754
Devonshire	2 Oct 1764
Newcastle	17 Nov 1768
Grenville, G	13 Nov 1770
Chatham	11 May 1778
Rockingham	1 Jul 1782
Bute	10 Mar 1792
North	5 Aug 1792
Shelburne	7 May 1805
Pitt	23 Jan 1806
Portland	30 Oct 1809
Grafton	14 Mar 1811
Perceval	11 May 1812
Canning	8 Aug 1827
Liverpool	4 Dec 1828
Grenville, Ld	12 Jan 1834
Addington	15 Feb 1844
Grey	17 Jul 1845

Melbourne	24 Nov 1848
Peel	2 July 1850
Wellington	14 Sep 1852
Goderich	28 Jan 1859
Aberdeen	14 Dec 1860
Palmerston	18 Oct 1865
Derby	23 Oct 1869
Russell	28 May 1878
Disraeli	19 Apr 1881
Gladstone	8 Jul 1895
Salisbury	22 Aug 1903
Campbell-Bannerman	22 Apr 1908
Bonar Law	30 Oct 1923
Asquith	15 Feb 1928
Rosebery	21 May 1929
Balfour	19 Mar 1930
MacDonald	9 Nov 1937
Chamberlain	9 Nov 1940
Lloyd George	26 Mar 1945
Baldwin	14 Dec 1947
Churchill	25 Sep 1964
Attlee	8 Oct 1967
Eden	14 Jan 1977
Macmillan	29 Dec 1986

PARLIAMENTARY SERVICE SPAN

This table ranks the total span of each Prime Minister's parliamentary service, derived from the two preceding tables. As such it does not take into account broken service (see 'Parliamentary service before first appointment'). It excludes the six Prime Ministers still in Parliament, of whom Douglas-Home passed Gladstone's 3rd-ranking span of 62 years and 158 days on 22 May 1994.

Name	Span years, days
Russell	64, 283
Churchill	63, 358
Gladstone	62, 206
Macmillan	62, 61
Rosebery	61, 14
Addington	59, 316
Grey	59, 11
Palmerston	58, 10
Balfour	56, 48
Lloyd George	54, 350
Bute	54, 331
Newcastle	54, 119
Grafton	54, 94
Aberdeen	54, 10
Eden	53, 39
Goderich	52, 76
Grenville, Ld	51, 327
Salisbury	50, —
Portland	48, 216
Derby	47, 85
Wellington	46, 166
Wilmington	45, 29
Shelburne	44, 339
Attlee	44, 327
Walpole	44, 66
Disraeli	43, 266
Chatham	43, 82
Melbourne	42, 298
Asquith	41, 221
Peel	41, 78
Baldwin	39, 287
Campbell-Bannerman	39, 154
Liverpool	37, 180
Pelham	37, 6
Canning	34, 41
MacDonald	31, 297
Rockingham	31, 49
Grenville, G	29, 193
North	28, 112
Pitt	25, 15
Devonshire	23, 136
Bonar Law	23, 26
Chamberlain	21, 331
Perceval	16, 2

PARLIAMENTARY SERVICE BEFORE BECOMING PM

The first table in this section measures the span of time between the dates on which a future Prime Minister first entered Parliament and on which he or she was appointed Prime Minister for the first time.

PARLIAMENTARY SERVICE BEFORE BECOMING PM—*Continued*

In the case of Members of the House of Commons, the date of first entering Parliament is the official date on which the result of their first successful election was declared. Until 1929 this was printed in an official Return to the House of Commons after each election. Since 1918, however, polling has taken place on a single day, and this date has been taken as the day on which a successful candidate became a Member of Parliament.

Members of the House of Lords, i.e. Peers, are assumed to have entered Parliament on the date on which they became eligible to do so. This may be the date on which they inherited a peerage, or were created a new Peer.

In a few cases Members were elected to the House of Commons, or sons inherited a peerage, before the age of majority (21 years of age). In these cases the date used is that on which they are deemed to have become eligible to take their seat (their 21st birthday). Liverpool and Russell are the only Prime Ministers to have been elected to the House of Commons for the first time before the age of 21. Three Prime Ministers inherited their peerages before the age of 21: Newcastle, Rockingham and Rosebery, but they took their seats very soon after their 21st birthdays.

Pitt had the fastest rise to the office of Prime Minister, being appointed just under three years after his first entry to the House of Commons. He is also the youngest ever PM. Major was the fastest appointment this century, just 11 years and 209 days after his first election success, and also the youngest Prime Minister in the century.

The average span of time between first entering Parliament and being appointed Prime Minister for the first time is 25 years and 225 days.

	Entered Parliament	Appointed PM years, days
Pitt	8 Jan 1781	2, 345
Addington	5 Apr 1784	6, 346
Major	3 May 1979	11, 209
Grafton	10 Dec 1756	11, 309
Perceval	9 May 1796	13, 148
Rockingham	13 May 1751	14, 61**
Baldwin	2 Mar 1908	15, 81
Devonshire	19 May 1741	15, 181
North	15 Apr 1754	15, 288
MacDonald	16 Jan 1906	18, 6
Chamberlain	14 Dec 1918	18, 165
Wilson	5 Jul 1945	19, 103
Thatcher	8 Oct 1959	19, 208
Walpole	11 Jan 1701	20, 82*
Heath	23 Feb 1950	20, 116
Goderich	13 Nov 1806	20, 291
Liverpool	7 Jun 1791	21, 1**
Asquith	9 Jul 1886	21, 271*
Wellington	1 Apr 1806	21, 296
Grenville, G	4 May 1741	21, 347
Portland	28 May 1761	22, 5
Bonar Law	4 Oct 1900	22, 19*
Shelburne	2 Jun 1760	22, 32
Attlee	15 Nov 1922	22, 253
Grenville, Lord	19 Feb 1782	23, 357
Bute	14 Apr 1737	25, 42*
Peel	15 Apr 1809	25, 239*
Rosebery	7 May 1868	25, 302**
Pelham	28 Feb 1717	26, 180
Lloyd George	10 Apr 1890	26, 240
Balfour	30 Jan 1874	28, 163*
Melbourne	31 Jan 1806	28, 166*
Derby	30 Jul 1822	29, 208*
Disraeli	27 Jul 1837	30, 215
Callaghan	5 Jul 1945	30, 275
Eden	6 Dec 1923	31, 121
Chatham	18 Feb 1735	31, 162
Salisbury	22 Aug 1853	31, 305
Douglas-Home	27 Oct 1931	31, 357*
Macmillan	29 Oct 1924	32, 73*
Russell	18 Aug 1813	32, 316*,**
Canning	28 Jun 1793	33, 288
Gladstone	14 Dec 1832	35, 355
Campbell-Bannerman	30 Nov 1868	37, 5
Churchill	3 Oct 1900	39, 220*
Newcastle	21 Jul 1714	39, 238**
Wilmington	3 Jun 1698	43, 258*
Grey	6 Jul 1786	44, 139
Aberdeen	4 Dec 1806	46, 15
Palmerston	8 May 1807	47, 274*

*Not continuous service
**Not eligible to take seat until 21 years of age

CONTINUOUS SERVICE IN THE HOUSE OF COMMONS

In the House of Commons, 22 Prime Ministers served continuously before being appointed Prime Minister for the first time. They are ranked in order of their length of service, shortest to longest.

	Entered Parliament	Appointed PM years, days
Pitt	8 Jan 1781	2, 345
Addington	5 Apr 1784	6, 346
Major	3 May 1979	11, 209
Perceval	9 May 1796	13, 148
Baldwin	2 Mar 1908	15, 81
North	15 Apr 1754	15, 288
MacDonald	16 Jan 1906	18, 6
Chamberlain	14 Dec 1918	18, 165
Wilson	5 Jul 1945	19, 103
Thatcher	8 Oct 1959	19, 208
Heath	23 Feb 1950	20, 116
Grenville, G	4 May 1741	21, 347
Attlee	15 Nov 1922	22, 253
Pelham	28 Feb 1717	26, 180
Lloyd George	10 Apr 1890	26, 240
Disraeli	27 Jul 1837	30, 215
Callaghan	5 Jul 1945	30, 275
Eden	6 Dec 1923	31, 121
Chatham	18 Feb 1735	31, 162
Canning	28 Jun 1793	33, 288
Gladstone	14 Dec 1832	35, 355
Campbell-Bannerman	30 Nov 1868	37, 5

Walpole, Peel, Palmerston, Balfour, Asquith, Bonar Law, Churchill and Macmillan, were out of the House of Commons for a period before their first Prime Ministerial appointment.

CONTINUOUS SERVICE IN THE HOUSE OF LORDS

Four Prime Ministers sat continuously in the House of Lords before being appointed Prime Minister for the first time, and three of these inherited their peerages before the age of 21. The fourth, Aberdeen, was a Scottish Representative Peer.

The other Scottish Representative Peer, Bute, was out of the House of Lords for over 20 years before his appointment as Prime Minister.

	Entered Parliament	Appointed PM years, days
Rockingham	13 May 1751	14, 61
Rosebery	7 May 1868	25, 302
Newcastle	21 Jul 1714	39, 238
Aberdeen	4 Dec 1806	46, 15

CONTINUOUS SERVICE IN BOTH HOUSES OF PARLIAMENT

Ten Prime Ministers spent time first in the House of Commons and then in the House of Lords before their first term of office.

	Commons yrs, days	Lords yrs, days	Total yrs, days
Grafton	0, 147	11, 162	11, 309
Devonshire	10, 25	5, 156	15, 181
Goderich	20, 166	0, 125	20, 291
Liverpool	12, 161	8, 206	21, 1
Wellington	3, 156	18, 140	21, 296
Portland	1, 34	20, 336	22, 5
Shelburne	—, 342	21, 55	22, 32
Grenville, Lord	8, 279	15, 78	23, 357
Salisbury	14, 233	17, 72	31, 305
Grey	21, 131	23, 8	44, 139

Wilmington, Melbourne, Russell, Derby and Douglas-Home spent time in both Houses of Parliament before their first term of office, but were also out of Parliament for a period during that time.

BROKEN SERVICE

Fifteen Prime Ministers had periods before their first appointment as PM when they were out of Parliament, for a variety of reasons. The most common reason was a defeat at the polls, although some Prime Ministers simply decided not to stand for re-election.

If someone was defeated at an election, or decided not to stand, their period out of the House is calculated from the date of the dissolution of the last Parliament to the date on which they were re-elected.

If Members of the House of Commons wish to resign between elections, they have to make themselves ineligible by applying for a disqualifying office, usually the Stewardship of the Chiltern Hundreds (see Glossary, page XXXIII). Several Prime Ministers have 'taken the Chiltern Hundreds', and in these cases the date used for the calculations is the date on which a by-election was announced to fill their vacancy.

Bute had by far the longest period out of the House, being away for just over 20 years; 3 Prime Ministers: Melbourne, MacDonald and Douglas-Home were out of Parliament for over 4 years each. Wilmington, Churchill and Macmillan had periods of over 2 years

BROKEN SERVICE—*Continued*

out of Parliament, but the other periods of broken service were around a year or less.

Periods of Broken Service Before First Appointment as PM

Name	Reason	Length of Gap years, days
Walpole	(1) expelled from House, 1712	—, 24
	(2) election declared void, 1712	1, 178
Wilmington	failed to find a seat, 1710	2, 341
Bute	did not stand, 1741	20, 8
Melbourne	(1) did not stand, 1812	3, 200
	(2) took Chiltern Hundreds, 1819	—, 5
	(3) did not stand, 1826	—, 326
	(4) took Chiltern Hundreds, 1828	—, 5
Peel	defeated, 1829	—, 10
Russell	(1) defeated, 1830	—, 290
	(2) defeated, 1835	—, 31
Derby	defeated, 1830	—, 73
Palmerston	(1) took Chiltern Hundreds, 1811	—, 2
	(2) defeated, 1831	—, 86
	(3) defeated, 1835	—, 154
Balfour	defeated, 1906	—, 50
Asquith	defeated, 1918	1, 79
Bonar Law	(1) defeated, 1906	—, 127
	(2) defeated, 1910	—, 119
MacDonald	(1) defeated, 1918 and 1921	3, 355
	(2) defeated, 1935	—, 98
Churchill	(1) defeated, 1908	—, 27
	(2) defeated, 1922, 1923, 1924	2, 3
Macmillan	(1) defeated, 1929	2, 170
	(2) defeated, 1945	—, 154
Douglas-Home	(1) defeated, 1945	4, 253
	(2) renounced peerage 1963	—, 15

ACTUAL SERVICE BEFORE FIRST APPOINTMENT AS PRIME MINISTER

The following table ranks Prime Ministers in order of the length of their actual parliamentary service before their first appointment as Prime Minister. In other words, it subtracts any periods out of the House to give the actual length of parliamentary experience, rather than the span.

PM	Actual Parliamentary Service years, days
Pitt	2, 345
Bute	5, 34
Addington	6, 346
Major	11, 209
Grafton	11, 309
Perceval	13, 148
MacDonald	13, 283
Rockingham	14, 61
Baldwin	15, 81
Devonshire	15, 181
North	15, 288
Chamberlain	18, 165
Walpole	18, 245
Wilson	19, 103
Thatcher	19, 208
Heath	20, 116
Asquith	20, 192
Goderich	20, 291
Liverpool	21, 1
Bonar Law	21, 138
Wellington	21, 296
Grenville, G	21, 347
Portland	22, 5
Shelburne	22, 32
Attlee	22, 253
Grenville, Lord	23, 357
Melbourne	23, 360
Peel	25, 229
Rosebery	25, 302
Douglas-Home	26, 89
Pelham	26, 180
Lloyd George	26, 240
Balfour	28, 113
Macmillan	29, 114

Derby	29, 135
Disraeli	30, 215
Callaghan	30, 275
Eden	31, 121
Chatham	31, 162
Salisbury	31, 305
Russell	31, 360
Canning	33, 288
Gladstone	35, 355
Campbell-Bannerman	37, 5
Churchill	37, 190
Newcastle	39, 238
Wilmington	40, 282
Grey	44, 139
Aberdeen	46, 15
Palmerston	47, 32

MAIDEN SPEECHES

A maiden speech is a special occasion as it marks a Member's Parliamentary debut. By convention it should be uncontroversial and listened to without interruption. Before 1909 the reporting of debates was not verbatim, which has made finding the text of early maiden speeches very difficult. In some cases contemporary sources note that a maiden speech was made on a particular date, but it has proved impossible to locate an account of the speech itself. In cases where we could not find the text of a speech that could be identified as a maiden speech, we have noted the first speech that could be found, and referred to it as the first recorded speech.

The following table shows the time that elapsed between the date of entering Parliament for the first time and the date of making the maiden speech. An asterisk indicates cases where it has not proved possible to identify a maiden speech, but only the first one that was recorded. The times are calendar, whether Parliament was sitting or not.

Attlee holds the record for the shortest time between entering Parliament and making his maiden speech. Apart from Balfour, the gap has been getting shorter throughout the twentieth century.

Nine Prime Ministers made their maiden speeches in the House of Lords (indicated by HL): the five who never sat in the House of Commons (Newcastle, Bute, Rockingham, Aberdeen, Rosebery), together with Wilmington, Grafton, Shelburne and Portland, who sat in the Commons, but apparently without saying a word.

Time Before Making Maiden Speech

	years, days	
Attlee	—, 8	
Wellington	—, 21	
Major	—, 41	
Pitt	—, 44	
MacDonald	—, 46	
Callaghan	—, 46	
Lloyd George	—, 64	
Chatham	—, 71	
Eden	—, 75	
Chamberlain	—, 88	
Wilson	—, 96	
Douglas-Home	—, 111	
Baldwin	—, 112	
Thatcher	—, 120	
Heath	—, 123	
Aberdeen	—, 130	(HL)
Disraeli	—, 133	
Bonar Law	—, 138	
Churchill	—, 138*	
Gladstone	—, 171	
Macmillan	—, 183	
Campbell-Bannerman	—, 209	
Canning	—, 217	
Salisbury	—, 228	
Grey	—, 230	
Asquith	—, 258	
Liverpool	—, 258	
Russell	—, 267	
Palmerston	—, 271	
Peel	—, 283	
Grenville, Lord	—, 304	
Melbourne	—, 322	
Perceval	1, 11	
Goderich	1, 150	
Devonshire	1, 212	
Grenville, G	1, 220	
Derby	1, 244	
Shelburne	1, 248	(HL)
Newcastle	1, 268*	(HL)
Addington	1, 294	
Balfour	2, 193	
Rosebery	2, 278	(HL)
Walpole	3, 6*	
Pelham	3, 68*	

MAIDEN SPEECHES—*Continued*

North	3, 230	
Grafton	5, 361	(HL)
Rockingham	15, 15	(HL)
Wilmington	16, 287*	(HL)
Portland	22, 11*	(HL)
Bute	24, 297*	(HL)

Subjects of Maiden Speeches

The occasion on which most maiden speeches are made is during the debate on the Queen's (or King's) Speech, sometimes called the Debate on the Loyal Address (meaning the address by Parliament in reply to the Sovereign). The Queen's Speech, which occurs at the beginning of each Parliament and/or parliamentary session, sets out the Government's forthcoming legislative programme, and the debate may therefore range over many diverse subjects. It is also the first opportunity for newly elected Members to speak. Ten Prime Ministers have made their maiden speeches during this debate. Devonshire and Melbourne actually moved the Address, and North, Addington, Peel and Rosebery made their speeches as seconders of the Address. Attlee and Callaghan spoke during the course of the debate. Bonar Law and Churchill, who were elected to Parliament on consecutive days, made their maiden speeches on consecutive days of the same debate in 1901.

Of the remainder, 10 spoke in debates about defence matters, including war or peace; a further 5 about other foreign affairs, and 3 more about Ireland.

10 spoke in debates about economic subjects, including 2 (Macmillan and Major), who spoke during a debate on the Budget. 3 others spoke during debates about industry.

Wilmington made his first recorded speech when he was chosen Speaker in 1715.

The first recorded speeches attributed to the Marquess of Rockingham and the Duke of Portland were after they had become Prime Minister. Portland was noted as a very infrequent speaker.

Wilson made his maiden speech when he was already a Minister. He spoke on the ever-popular topic of amenities and facilities for Members of Parliament. The first recorded speech of the Earl of Bute was also after he had become a Minister.

Thatcher was unique in making her maiden speech introducing a Private Member's Bill, on the admission of the press to meetings of public bodies, which eventually became law.

DATE OF FIRST MINISTERIAL POST

Two Prime Ministers held ministerial office before they had entered Parliament: Palmerston, who was elected very soon after his appointment date, and Chamberlain, who was appointed during the First World War as Minister of National Service.

The fastest rise to ministerial office was made by Wilson, who became a junior Minister just over a month after his election to Parliament. This is even more remarkable since the results of the General Election were not announced until 3 weeks after polling day, on 26 Jul 1945. Other swift appointments after World War II were enjoyed by Heath, Thatcher, Callaghan and Major.

Bute holds the record for the longest time before his appointment to Ministerial office, but this is largely accounted for by the long period he spent out of Parliament.

Speed of Appointment

Name	First Ministerial Appointment Date	Gap years, days
Chamberlain	19 Aug 1916	-2, 117
Palmerston	6 Apr 1807	—, -32
Wilson	6 Aug 1945	—, 32
Grenville, Ld	15 Aug 1782	—, 177
Wellington	3 Apr 1807	1, 2
Peel	Jun 1810	*c.*1, 46
Pitt	13 Jul 1782	1, 186
Heath	7 Nov 1951	1, 257
Bonar Law	8 Aug 1902	1, 308
Thatcher	9 Oct 1961	2, 1
Gladstone	26 Dec 1834	2, 12
Liverpool	28 Jun 1793	2, 21
Callaghan	7 Oct 1947	2, 94
Goderich	27 Apr 1809	2, 165
Canning	6 Jan 1796	2, 192
Newcastle	14 Apr 1717	2, 267
Shelburne	20 Apr 1763	2, 322
Campbell-Bannerman	15 Nov 1871	2, 360
Pelham	25 May 1720	3, 87
Grenville, G	27 Dec 1744	3, 237
Major	14 Jan 1983	3, 256
Portland	12 July 1765	4, 106
Walpole	Jun 1705	*c.*4, 141
Derby	Apr 1827	*c.*4, 244
Perceval	14 Jan 1801	4, 250
North	2 Jun 1759	5, 48
Churchill	15 Dec 1905	5, 73
Asquith	18 Aug 1892	6, 40
Attlee	23 May 1930	7, 189
Eden	3 Sep 1931	7, 271

Grafton	12 Jul 1765	8, 214
Wilmington	26 Apr 1707	8, 323
Baldwin	29 Jan 1917	8, 333
Devonshire	Jul 1751	c.10, 42
Chatham	22 Feb 1746	11, 4
Balfour	24 Jun 1885	11, 145
Salisbury	6 Jul 1866	12, 318
Rosebery	8 Aug 1881	13, 93
Douglas-Home	29 May 1945	13, 214
Rockingham	13 Jul 1765	14, 61
Disraeli	27 Feb 1852	14, 215
Macmillan	12 May 1940	15, 196
Lloyd George	11 Dec 1905	15, 245
Addington	21 Mar 1801	16, 350
Russell	16 Dec 1830	17, 120
MacDonald	22 Jan 1924	18, 6
Grey	11 Feb 1806	19, 220
Aberdeen	22 Jan 1828	21, 49
Melbourne	29 Apr 1827	21, 88
Bute	25 Mar 1761	23, 345

CABINET POSTS

Rockingham, Addington and MacDonald became Prime Minister without any previous ministerial experience. Ten others went straight into the Cabinet:-

Name	Cabinet Post
Devonshire	Master of the Horse
Bute	Secretary of State, Northern Department
Grafton	Secretary of State, Northern Department
Pitt	Chancellor of the Exchequer
Grey	First Lord of the Admiralty
Aberdeen	Chancellor of the Duchy of Lancaster
Disraeli	Chancellor of the Exchequer
Salisbury	Secretary of State for India
Asquith	Home Secretary
Lloyd George	President of the Board of Trade

The most popular Department as the first rung on the ladder to the top seems to be the Treasury, where 11 Prime Ministers started their careers (8 excluding the three who began as First Lord, or Prime Minister). Foreign affairs (including India and the Colonies) have provided a springboard for 8 careers, followed by the Royal Household and the War Office with 5 each.

MINISTERIAL EXPERIENCE BEFORE FIRST APPOINTMENT AS PRIME MINISTER

Three Prime Ministers, Rockingham, Addington, and MacDonald, had no previous ministerial experience before being appointed Prime Minister. Bute, Pitt, and Disraeli had only held 1 post before their appointments, while on the other hand Goderich had held 11 posts and Churchill 9.

No. of Posts Held Before First Appointment as PM

0	Rockingham, Addington, MacDonald
1	Bute, Pitt, Disraeli
2	Devonshire, Grafton, Portland, Wellington, Grey, Melbourne, Salisbury, Asquith, Thatcher
3	Newcastle, Chatham, North, Shelburne, Peel, Russell, Aberdeen, Wilson
4	Pelham, Perceval, Derby, Palmerston, Rosebery, Balfour, Campbell-Bannerman, Lloyd George, Bonar Law, Baldwin
5	Grenville, G, Chamberlain, Douglas-Home, Heath, Callaghan
6	Walpole, Wilmington, Liverpool, Canning, Gladstone, Attlee, Eden
7	Macmillan, Major
8	Grenville, Lord
9	Churchill
11	Goderich

All posts prior to first appointment as Prime Minister are included in the list that follows, in which posts in similar areas have been grouped together. First ministerial posts are indicated by an asterisk.

Admiralty

Walpole	Member of the Council of the Lord High Admiral*; Treasurer of the Navy
Grenville, G	Lord of the Admiralty*; Treasurer of the Navy; First Lord of the Admiralty
Canning	Treasurer of the Navy
Goderich	Lord of the Admiralty; Treasurer of the Navy
Grey	First Lord of the Admiralty*
Palmerston	Lord of the Admiralty*
Campbell-Bannerman	Parliamentary and Financial Secretary to the Admiralty
Churchill	First Lord of the Admiralty
Callaghan	Parliamentary and Financial Secretary to the Admiralty

MINISTERIAL EXPERIENCE BEFORE FIRST APPOINTMENT AS PRIME MINISTER—*Continued*

Chancellor of the Duchy of Lancaster

Perceval	
Aberdeen*	
Churchill	
Attlee	

Colonies

Russell	Colonial Secretary
Gladstone	Under-Secretary of State for the Colonies; Colonial Secretary
Bonar Law	Colonial Secretary
Churchill	Under-Secretary of State for the Colonies*; Colonial Secretary
Attlee	Secretary of State for the Dominions
Eden	Secretary of State for the Dominions
Macmillan	Under-Secretary of State for the Colonies
Douglas-Home	Secretary of State for Commonwealth Relations

Education and Science

Thatcher	Secretary of State for Education and Science

Employment

Heath	Minister of Labour

Environment

Rosebery	First Commissioner of Works
Macmillan	Minister for Housing and Local Government
Wilson	Parliamentary Secretary, Ministry of Works*

Foreign Service

Newcastle	Secretary of State, Northern Department
Bute	Secretary of State, Northern Department*
Grenville, G	Secretary of State, Northern Department
Grafton	Secretary of State, Northern Department*
Grenville, Ld	Foreign Secretary
Liverpool	Foreign Secretary
Canning	Under-Secretary of State for Foreign Affairs*; Foreign Secretary
Grey	Foreign Secretary
Aberdeen	Foreign Secretary
Palmerston	Foreign Secretary
Salisbury	Foreign Secretary
Rosebery	Foreign Secretary
Eden	Parliamentary Under-Secretary, Foreign Office*; Minister for League of Nations Affairs; Foreign Secretary
Macmillan	Foreign Secretary
Douglas-Home	Joint Under-Secretary of State, Foreign Office*; Foreign Secretary
Callaghan	Secretary of State for Foreign and Commonwealth Affairs
Major	Secretary of State for Foreign and Commonwealth Affairs

Health and Social Services

Balfour	President of the Local Government Board*
Chamberlain	Minister of Health
Thatcher	Joint Parliamentary Secretary, Ministry of Pensions and National Insurance*
Major	Parliamentary Under-Secretary of State, Department of Health and Social Security; Minister of State, Department of Health and Social Security

Home Office

Newcastle	Secretary of State, Southern Department
Chatham	Secretary of State, Southern Department
Shelburne	Secretary of State, Southern Department; Secretary of State for Home, Irish and Colonial Affairs
Grenville, Ld	Home Secretary
Liverpool	Home Secretary
Melbourne	Home Secretary
Peel	Home Secretary
Russell	Home Secretary
Palmerston	Home Secretary
Rosebery	Under-Secretary of State, Home Office*
Asquith	Home Secretary*
Churchill	Home Secretary

Callaghan	Home Secretary

India

Grenville, Ld	Commissioner of the Board of Control; President of the Board of Control
Liverpool	Commissioner of the Board of Control*
Canning	Commissioner of the Board of Control; President of the Board of Control
Goderich	Commissioner for the Affairs of India
Salisbury	Secretary of State for India*

Ireland

Devonshire	Lord Treasurer of Ireland
Chatham	Joint Vice-Treasurer of Ireland*
Portland	Lord Lieutenant of Ireland
Grenville, Ld	Chief Secretary for Ireland*
Wellington	Chief Secretary for Ireland*
Melbourne	Chief Secretary for Ireland*
Peel	Chief Secretary for Ireland
Derby	Chief Secretary for Ireland
Balfour	Chief Secretary for Ireland
Campbell-Bannerman	Chief Secretary for Ireland

Law Officers

Perceval	Solicitor General*; Attorney General

Lord President of the Council

Wilmington

Attlee

Douglas-Home

Lord Privy Seal

Wilmington

Rosebery

Bonar Law

Attlee

Eden

Heath

Paymaster General

Chamberlain

Postmaster General

Chamberlain

Attlee

Royal Household

Wilmington	Paymaster of the Queen's Pensions*; Treasurer to Prince George of Denmark; Treasurer to the Prince of Wales
Pelham	Treasurer of the Chamber*
Newcastle	Lord Chamberlain*
Devonshire	Master of the Horse*
Portland	Lord Chamberlain*

Scotland

Balfour	Secretary of State for Scotland
Douglas-Home	Minister of State for Scotland

Trade and Industry

Shelburne	President of the Board of Trade*
Grenville, Ld	Member of the Board of Trade; Vice-President of the Board of Trade
Liverpool	Member of the Board of Trade
Goderich	Member of the Board of Trade; Vice-President of the Board of Trade; President of the Board of Trade
Gladstone	Vice President of the Board of Trade; President of the Board of Trade
Lloyd George	President of the Board of Trade*
Bonar Law	Parliamentary Secretary, Board of Trade*
Baldwin	President of the Board of Trade
Churchill	President of the Board of Trade
Macmillan	Parliamentary Secretary, Ministry of Supply*
Wilson	Secretary for Overseas Trade; President of the Board of Trade
Heath	Secretary of State for Industry, Trade and Regional Development and President of the Board of Trade

Transport

Callaghan	Parliamentary Secretary, Ministry of Transport*

Treasury (including Government Whips)

Walpole	First Lord of the Treasury and Chancellor of the Exchequer
Pelham	Lord of the Treasury
Grenville, G	Lord of the Treasury
Grafton	First Lord of the Treasury
North	Lord of the Treasury*; Chancellor of the Exchequer

MINISTERIAL EXPERIENCE BEFORE FIRST APPOINTMENT AS PRIME MINISTER—*Continued*

Pitt	Chancellor of the Exchequer*
Perceval	Chancellor of the Exchequer
Liverpool	Master of the Mint
Goderich	Lord of the Treasury; Chancellor of the Exchequer
Derby	Junior Lord of the Treasury*
Disraeli	Chancellor of the Exchequer*
Gladstone	Junior Lord of the Treasury*; Chancellor of the Exchequer
Balfour	First Lord of the Treasury
Asquith	Chancellor of the Exchequer
Lloyd George	Chancellor of the Exchequer
Bonar Law	Chancellor of the Exchequer
Baldwin	Junior Lord of the Treasury*; Financial Secretary to the Treasury; Chancellor of the Exchequer
Chamberlain	Chancellor of the Exchequer
Churchill	Chancellor of the Exchequer
Macmillan	Chancellor of the Exchequer
Heath	Junior Lord of the Treasury; Parliamentary Secretary to theTreasury
Callaghan	Chancellor of the Exchequer
Major	Assistant Government Whip; Junior Lord of the Treasury; Chief Secretary to the Treasury; Chancellor of the Exchequer

War Office

Walpole	Secretary at War; Paymaster General of the Forces
Wilmington	Paymaster General of the Forces
Pelham	Secretary at War; Paymaster General of the Forces
Chatham	Paymaster General of the Forces
North	Joint Paymaster General of the Forces
Grenville, Ld	Joint (and sole) Paymaster General of the Forces
Liverpool	Secretary of State for War and the Colonies
Canning	Joint Paymaster General of the Forces
Goderich	Under-Secretary of State for War and the Colonies*; Joint Paymaster General of the Forces; Secretary of State for War and the Colonies
Wellington	Master General of the Ordnance
Peel	Under-Secretary of State for War and the Colonies*
Russell	Paymaster General of the Forces*
Derby	Under-Secretary of State for War and the Colonies; Secretary of State for War and the Colonies
Aberdeen	Secretary of State for War and the Colonies
Palmerston	Secretary at War
Campbell-Bannerman	Financial Secretary, War Office*; Secretary of State for War
Lloyd George	Minister of Munitions; Secretary of State for War
Chamberlain	Minister of National Service*
Churchill	Minister of Munitions; Secretary of State for War; Under-Secretary of State for War
Attlee	Under-Secretary of State for War
Eden	Secretary of State for War
Macmillan	Minister Resident, Allied Headquarters; Minister of Defence

Callaghan is unique in being the only Prime Minister to have held the 3 highest offices of state before he became Prime Minister: Chancellor of the Exchequer, Home Secretary and Foreign Secretary. Of the Prime Ministers, 16 became Prime Minister without having held any of these 3 posts.

Walpole, Grafton and Balfour held the post of First Lord of the Treasury before they were appointed Prime Minister. In Walpole's case this is because the term 'Prime Minister' is not applied before his second term of office, 1721-42. Grafton served as First Lord of the Treasury under Chatham, and Balfour was First Lord of the Treasury in Salisbury's third term of office.

'GLITTERING POSTS': MINISTERIAL EXPERIENCE OF MOST PMs

The following ranking of the most popular areas of experience generally reflects the relative importance of the major offices of state. Nearly half of all Prime Ministers, for example, (23 out of 50) had experience of working in the Treasury before they became Prime Minister.

Area of Experience	No. of PMs Who Have Held Posts
Treasury	23
War Office	22
Foreign Office	17
Home Office	13
Trade and Industry	12
Ireland	10
Admiralty	9

Colonies	8
Lord Privy Seal	6
India	5
Royal Household	5

'GLITTERING POSTS': MINISTERIAL POSTS HELD BY MOST PMs

This list ranks the most popular senior ministerial offices held by PMs. It omits junior posts such as 'Under-Secretary of State'. Because the titles and functions of posts and Departments change from time to time, it combines posts with different names under the same heading. Foreign Secretary, for example, includes Secretary of State for the Northern Department, and Home Secretary includes Secretary of State for the Southern Department.

Ministerial Office	No. of PMs Who Have Held It
Foreign Secretary	17
Chancellor of the Exchequer	16
Home Secretary	12
Paymaster General of the Forces	9
President of the Board of Trade	8
Secretary of State for War/War and Colonies	8
Colonial Secretary	7
Chief Secretary for Ireland	7
Lord Privy Seal	6
Chancellor of the Duchy of Lancaster	4

MINISTERIAL POSTS HELD AFTER BEING PRIME MINISTER

Fourteen Prime Ministers have come back after their terms of office to take ministerial office in a later administration. Three of them, Portland, Russell and Baldwin, held ministerial posts in later administrations before coming back for a further term as Prime Minister.

Addington and Goderich held a record 4 different posts, Russell and Balfour 3 each, and Portland, Wellington and Baldwin 2 each. The last Prime Minister to return to ministerial office was Douglas-Home, who was Foreign Secretary under Heath.

The most popular offices, perhaps not surprisingly, are the ones less burdened by heavy departmental responsibilities: Lord President of the Council and Lord Privy Seal. These would be most appropriate for an 'elder statesman'. They are listed below in the order of the number of office-holders.

Lord President of the Council

Portland (between terms)	Baldwin (between terms)
Addington	MacDonald
Russell (between terms)	Chamberlain
Balfour	

Lord Privy Seal

Newcastle	Goderich
Grafton	Baldwin (between terms)
Addington	

Foreign Secretary

Wellington

Russell (between terms)

Balfour

Douglas-Home

Home Secretary

North

Portland (between terms)

Addington

Minister Without Portfolio

Addington

Wellington

Lord Chamberlain

Devonshire

First Lord of the Admiralty

Balfour

President of the Board of Control

Goderich

Secretary of State for War and the Colonies

Goderich

President of the Board of Trade

Goderich

Colonial Secretary

Russell (between terms)

PARLIAMENTARY SERVICE AFTER BEING PRIME MINISTER

The following table ranks Prime Ministers in order of their parliamentary service after they ceased to be Prime Minister for the last time. It calculates the length of time between the date on which the PM left office for the last time and their leaving Parliament. In the case of the House of Commons this can be death, retirement or defeat at an election. In the House of

PARLIAMENTARY SERVICE AFTER BEING PRIME MINISTER—*Continued*

Lords, Peers are assumed to remain in the House of Lords until death.

Seven Prime Ministers died in office: Wilmington, Pelham, Rockingham, Pitt, Perceval, Canning and Palmerston.

Grafton, Addington (Viscount Sidmouth), Rosebery and Goderich each spent over 30 years in the House of Lords after their terms of office. Service in the House of Commons tends to be shorter because Prime Ministers are normally offered a peerage, and go to the Lords. The longest time spent in the Commons (all of it on the back benches) was by Lloyd George (22 years, 74 days). Balfour spent over 16 years in the Commons before going to the Lords. Churchill had the third longest Commons service, with 9 years, 173 days.

Douglas-Home will equal Goderich's post-Prime Ministerial length of service on 10 Mar 1996. Heath will equal Shelburne's on 15 April 1996, while it will take Wilson until 19 Nov 1998 to reach the same point. Callaghan will equal Eden's length of service on 10 May 1995. Thatcher equalled Macmillan's length of service on 18 Jan 1995 and Peel's on 27 Mar in the same year. It will take her until 2 Apr 2022 to equal Goderich's length of service after his last term as Prime Minister.

	Length of service years, days	**House**
Grafton	41, 75	Lords
Addington	39, 281	Commons —, 247 Lords 39, 34
Rosebery	33, 333	Lords
Goderich	31, 20	Lords
Grenville, Lord	26, 293	Lords
Balfour	24, 55	Commons 16, 102 Lords 7, 313
Lloyd George	22, 158	Commons 22, 74 Lords —, 84*
Shelburne	22, 42	Lords
Wellington	17, 280	Lords
Bute	17, 146	Lords
Attlee	15, 347	Commons 4, 42 Lords 11, 305
Eden	15, 188	Commons —, 2 Lords 15, 186
Russell	11, 336	Lords
Grey	11, 8	Lords
Baldwin	10, 200	Commons —, 11 Lords 10, 189
North	10, 131	Commons 8, 130 Lords 2, 1
Asquith	9, 236	Commons 6, 230 Lords 3, 6
Chatham	9, 209	Lords
Churchill	9, 173	Commons
Devonshire	7, 95	Lords
Melbourne	7, 86	Lords
Newcastle	6, 175	Lords
Aberdeen	5, 319	Lords
Grenville, George	5, 126	Commons
Peel	4, 3	Commons
Macmillan	3, 300	Commons —, 343 Lords 2, 322
Walpole	3, 35	Lords
MacDonald	2, 58	Commons —, 141 Lords 1, 282
Derby	1, 240	Lords
Liverpool	1, 239	Lords
Gladstone	1, 128	Commons
Salisbury	1, 42	Lords
Disraeli	—, 363	Lords
Chamberlain	—, 183	Commons
Bonar Law	—, 163	Commons
Portland	—, 26	Lords
Campbell-Bannerman	—, 17	Commons

*Lloyd George did not take his seat in the Lords.

LENGTH OF SERVICE AS AN MP

Of the Prime Ministers, 5 were only Peers, never serving in the House of Commons. Of the remainder, 14 were out of the House for a period of time, so they had what is known as 'broken' service. Gladstone holds the record for the longest unbroken service as an MP with 62 years 206 days. Churchill has a longer total period of service (63 years, 358 days), but he was out of the House for a time.

The following table lists Prime Ministers in order of their length of service in the House of Commons, those with broken service being indicated by asterisks. As of January 1995, Heath was the Father of the House because he had the longest unbroken service, over 44 years, giving him the third longest unbroken service of all Prime Ministers.

	Service years, days
Churchill	63, 358*
Gladstone	62, 206
Palmerston	58, 163*
Lloyd George	54, 265

Balfour	48, 95*
Russell	47, 346*
Douglas-Home	42, 326*
Callaghan	41, 317
Peel	41, 78*
Walpole	41, 26*
Macmillan	39, 332*
Campbell-Bannerman	39, 154
Disraeli	39, 16
Asquith	38, 92*
Wilson	37, 312
Pelham	37,7
North	36, 111
Canning	34, 41
Eden	33, 34
Attlee	33, 22
Thatcher	32, 160
MacDonald	31, 317*
Chatham	31, 167
Wilmington	29, 219*
Grenville, G	29, 193
Baldwin	29, 128
Pitt	25, 15
Bonar Law	23, 26*
Melbourne	22, 173*
Derby	22, 97*
Chamberlain	21, 331
Grey	21, 131
Addington	20, 281
Goderich	20, 156
Salisbury	14, 234
Liverpool	12, 161
Devonshire	10, 25
Grenville, Lord	8, 279
Perceval	6, 2
Wellington	3, 156
Portland	1, 34
Shelburne	—, 342
Grafton	—, 147

OFFICE OF PRIME MINISTER

AGE AT APPOINTMENT AS PM

The top 20 youngest Prime Ministers were under 50 years of age when they were first appointed, Pitt being by far the youngest at just 24. Liverpool was the youngest Prime Minister of the 19th century. Major and Wilson are notable as 20th century Prime Ministers who were as young as most of the 18th and early 19th century ones, Major being the youngest 20th century Prime Minister.

The oldest Prime Minister was Gladstone, when he was appointed for a fourth term of office in 1892 at the age of 82 years, 230 days. The oldest to be appointed for the first time was Palmerston, who was 71 years, 109 days old when he was appointed in 1855. The oldest Prime Minister of the 20th century was Churchill, 76 years, 331 days old when he was appointed for the second time in 1951. Campbell-Bannerman was the next oldest this century, being 69 years, 89 days old at his appointment in 1905.

	Age years, days	**Year of Appointment**
Pitt (1)	24, 205	1783
Grafton	33, 16	1768
Rockingham (1)	35, 61	1765
Devonshire	*c.*36, —	1756
North	37, 290	1770
Liverpool	42, 1	1812
Addington	43, 291	1801
Walpole	44, 107	1721
Goderich	44, 305	1827
Pitt (2)	44, 348	1804
Portland (1)	44, 353	1783
Shelburne	45, 63	1782
Grenville, Lord	46, 110	1806
Rosebery	46, 302	1894
Peel (1)	46, 308	1834
Perceval	46, 338	1809
Major	47, 245	1990
Pelham	48, 336	1743
Wilson (1)	48, 219	1964
Bute	49, 1	1762
Grenville, G	50, 184	1763
Rockingham (2)	51, 318	1782
Derby (1)	52, 331	1852

AGE AT APPOINTMENT AS PM—*Continued*

	Age years, days	Year of Appointment
Thatcher	53, 204	1979
Peel (2)	53, 206	1841
Russell (1)	53, 316	1846
Lloyd George	53, 325	1916
Heath	53, 335	1970
Balfour	53, 352	1902
Melbourne (1)	55, 123	1834
Salisbury (1)	55, 140	1885
Asquith	55, 198	1908
Baldwin (1)	55, 292	1923
Melbourne (2)	56, 34	1835
Salisbury (2)	56, 172	1886
Canning	57, 1	1827
Baldwin (2)	57, 93	1923
MacDonald (1)	67, 102	1924
Chatham	57, 257	1766
Eden	57, 299	1955
Wilson (2)	57, 358	1974
Wellington (1)	58, 267	1828
Derby (2)	58, 328	1858
Gladstone (1)	58, 340	1868
Douglas-Home	60, 109	1963
Newcastle (1)	60, 238	1754
MacDonald (2)	62, 236	1929
Macmillan	62, 335	1957
Disraeli (1)	63, 68	1868
Attlee	63, 205	1945
Newcastle (2)	63, 344	1757
Callaghan	64, 9	1976
Bonar Law	64, 37	1922
Salisbury (3)	65, 142	1895
Churchill (1)	65, 163	1940
Wellington (2)	65, 200	1834
Grey	66, 254	1830
Derby (3)	67, 91	1866
Baldwin (3)	67, 308	1935
Chamberlain	68, 71	1937
Aberdeen	68, 326	1852
Wilmington	c.69, —	1742
Disraeli (2)	69, 61	1874
Campbell-Bannerman	69, 89	1902
Portland (2)	69, 351	1807
Gladstone (2)	70, 116	1880
Palmerston (1)	71, 109	1855
Russell (2)	73, 72	1865
Palmerston (2)	75, 235	1859
Gladstone (3)	76, 34	1886
Churchill (2)	76, 331	1951
Gladstone (4)	82, 230	1892

LENGTH OF SERVICE AS PRIME MINISTER

Walpole holds the record as the longest serving Prime Minister with 20 years 314 days, which is also the longest single term of office. His 20 years 309 days in the Commons is the longest amount of time spent as Prime Minister in a single House. Canning had the shortest length of service as Prime Minister with 119 days, although Wellington's second term of office was the shortest at 22 days. The shortest amount of time spent as Prime Minister in any one House was Douglas-Home's 4 days in the House of Lords before he renounced his peerage. Gladstone was appointed Prime Minister a record 4 times, although Salisbury, Baldwin and Derby had 3 terms each.

Prime Ministers serving only in the House of Lords (18) were: Wilmington, Newcastle, Devonshire, Bute, Rockingham, Grafton, Shelburne, Portland, Lord Grenville, Liverpool, Goderich, Wellington, Grey, Melbourne, Derby, Aberdeen, Salisbury, and Rosebery, who was the last to do so. Of these, Liverpool holds the record as longest serving Prime Minister with 14 years 305 days, which is also the longest single term of office in the Lords.

Only 26 have served their terms solely in the House of Commons. Russell served his first term in the House of Commons, but his second in the House of Lords, the only Prime Minister to do so. Walpole, Chatham, Disraeli and Douglas-Home were translated from one House to the other while serving as Prime Minister, although Douglas-Home was the only one to renounce his peerage and leave the House of Lords in order to fight a by-election to get into the House of Commons. He is also unique in being the only Prime Minister to have served while being out of Parliament altogether, for the 15 days between the renunciation of his peerage and his re-election to the House of Commons at the by-election.

	Commons yrs, days	Lords yrs, days	Total yrs, days
Walpole	20, 309	—, 5	20, 314
Pitt	(1) 17, 85	—	
	(2) 1, 258	—	18, 243
Liverpool	—	14, 305	14, 305

Salisbury	(1) — (2) — (3) —	0, 219 6, 17 7, 16	13, 252
Gladstone	(1) 5, 76 (2) 5, 47 (3) —, 169 (4) 1, 199	— — — —	12, 126
North	12, 58	—	12, 58
Thatcher	11, 209	—	11, 209
Pelham	10, 191	—	10, 191
Palmerston	(1) 3, 13 (2) 6, 128	— —	9, 141
Asquith	8, 244	—	8, 244
Churchill	(1) 5, 78 (2) 3, 162	— —	8, 240
Wilson	(1) 5, 246 (2) 2, 33	— —	7, 279
Newcastle	(1) 2, 240 (2) 4, 330	— —	7, 205
Baldwin	(1) —, 245 (2) 4, 212 (3) 1, 355	— — —	7, 82
Disraeli	(1) —, 278 (2) 2, 172	— 3, 253	6, 338
MacDonald	(1) —, 287 (2) 6, 2	— —	6, 289
Macmillan	6, 281	—	6, 281
Melbourne	(1) — (2) —	—, 121 6, 134	6, 255
Russell	(1) 5, 236 (2) —	— —, 240	6, 111
Attlee	6, 92	—	6, 92
Lloyd George	5, 317	—	5, 317
Peel	(1) —, 119 (2) 4, 303	— —	5, 57
Derby	(1) — (2) — (3) —	—, 292 1, 111 1, 242	3, 280
Heath	3, 259	—	3, 259
Grey	—	3, 229	3, 229
Balfour	3, 145	—	3, 145
Portland	(1) — (2) —	—, 260 2, 187	3, 82
Addington	3, 54	—	3, 54
Callaghan	3, 29	—	3, 29
Chamberlain	2, 348	—	2, 348
Wellington	(1) — (2) —	2, 298 —, 22	2, 320
Perceval	2, 221	—	2, 221
Campbell-Bannerman	2, 122	—	2, 122
Grenville, G	2, 85	—	2, 85
Chatham	—, 5	2, 71	2, 76
Aberdeen	—	2, 42	2, 42
Eden	1, 279	—	1, 279
Wilmington	—	1, 136	1, 136
Rockingham	(1) — (2) —	1, 17 —, 96	1, 113
Rosebery	—	1, 109	1, 109
Grafton	—	1, 106	1, 106
Grenville, Lord	—	1, 42	1, 42
Douglas-Home	—, 344	—, 4	—, 363*
Bute	—	—, 317	—, 317
Shelburne	—	—, 266	—, 266
Devonshire	—	—, 225	—, 225
Bonar Law	—, 209	—	—, 209
Goderich	—	—, 130	—, 130
Canning	—, 119	—	—, 119

*Includes 15 days when he was in neither House, between the time he renounced his peerage and the date on which the by-election was held.

LONGEST TERM OF OFFICE

	years, days	House
Walpole	20, 314	HC, HL
Pitt	(1) 17, 85	HC
Liverpool	14, 305	HL
North	12, 58	HC
Thatcher	11, 209	HC
Pelham	10, 191	HC
Asquith	8, 244	HC
Salisbury	(3) 7, 16	HL
Disraeli	(2) 6, 338	HC, HL
Macmillan	6, 281	HC
Melbourne	(1) 6, 134	HL
Palmerston	(2) 6, 128	HC
Attlee	6, 92	HC
Salisbury	(2) 6, 17	HL
MacDonald	(2) 6, 2	HC
Wilson	(1) 5, 246	HC
Russell	(1) 5, 236	HC
Lloyd George	5, 137	HC
Churchill	(1) 5, 78	HC

LONGEST TERM OF OFFICE—*Continued*

	years, days	House
Gladstone	(1) 5, 76	HC
Gladstone	(2) 5, 47	HC
Newcastle	(2) 4, 330	HL
Peel	(2) 4, 303	HL
Baldwin	(2) 4, 212	HC
Heath	3, 259	HC
Grey	3, 229	HL
Churchill	(2) 3, 162	HC
Balfour	3, 145	HC
Addington	3, 54	HC
Callaghan	3, 29	HC
Palmerston	(1) 3, 13	HC
Chamberlain	2, 348	HC
Wellington	(1) 2, 298	HL
Newcastle	(1) 2, 240	HL
Perceval	2, 221	HC
Portland	(2) 2, 187	HL
Campbell-Bannerman	2, 122	HC
Grenville, G	2, 85	HC
Chatham	2, 76	HC, HL
Aberdeen	2, 42	HL
Wilson	(2) 2, 33	HC
Baldwin	(3) 1, 355	HC
Eden	1, 279	HC
Pitt	(2) 1, 258	HC
Derby	(3) 1, 242	HL
Gladstone	(4) 1, 199	HC
Wilmington	1, 136	HL
Derby	(2) 1, 111	HL
Rosebery	1, 109	HL
Grafton	1, 106	HL
Grenville, Lord	1, 42	HL
Rockingham	(1) 1, 17	HL
Douglas-Home	—, 363	HL, HC
Derby	(1) —, 292	HL
MacDonald	(1) —, 287	HC
Disraeli	(1) —, 278	HC
Shelburne	—, 266	HL
Portland	(1) —, 260	HL
Baldwin	(1) —, 245	HC
Russell	(2) —, 240	HL
Devonshire	—, 225	HL
Salisbury	(1) —, 219	HL
Bonar Law	—, 209	HC
Gladstone	(3) —, 169	HC
Goderich	—, 130	HL
Melbourne	(1) —, 121	HL
Canning	—, 119	HC
Peel	(1) —, 119	HC
Rockingham	(2) —, 96	HL
Wellington	(2) —, 22	HL

INTERVALS BETWEEN APPOINTMENTS

Gaps between the departure of one Prime Minister and the appointment of the next in the 20th century have rarely been more than a day. The longest interval this century was 4 days in October 1922, between Lloyd George and Bonar Law. The 4 longest intervals have followed cases where the Prime Minister died in office: Wilmington, Perceval, Canning and Pitt.

Year	Interval days	Outgoing PM	Incoming PM
1743	56	Wilmington	Pelham
1812	28	Perceval	Liverpool
1827	23	Canning	Goderich
1806	19	Pitt	Grenville, Lord
1885	14	Gladstone	Salisbury
1828	14	Goderich	Wellington
1865	11	Palmerston	Russell
1835	10	Peel	Melbourne
1754	10	Pelham	Newcastle
1763	8	Bute	Grenville, G
1855	7	Aberdeen	Palmerston
1834	7	Grey	Melbourne
1783	7	Shelburne	Portland
1807	6	Grenville, Ld	Portland
1886	5	Gladstone	Salisbury
1830	5	Wellington	Grey
1756	5	Newcastle	Devonshire
1742	5	Walpole	Wilmington
1892	4	Salisbury	Gladstone
1886	4	Salisbury	Gladstone
1895	3	Rosebery	Salisbury
1894	3	Gladstone	Rosebery

1874	3	Gladstone	Disraeli
1834	3	Melbourne	Wellington
1827	3	Liverpool	Canning
1801	3	Pitt	Addington
1782	3	Rockingham	Shelburne
1765	3	Grenville, G	Rockingham
1880	2	Disraeli	Gladstone
1868	2	Disraeli	Gladstone
1868	2	Derby	Disraeli
1866	2	Russell	Derby
1852	2	Derby	Aberdeen
1852	2	Russell	Derby
1859	1	Derby	Palmerston
1858	1	Palmerston	Derby
1846	1	Peel	Russell
1834	1	Wellington	Peel
1783	1	Portland	Pitt
1841	0	Melbourne	Peel
1809	0	Portland	Perceval
1804	0	Addington	Pitt
1782	0	North	Rockingham
1770	0	Grafton	North
1768	0	Chatham	Grafton
1766	0	Rockingham	Chatham
1762	0	Newcastle	Bute
1757	0	Devonshire	Newcastle

DATES OF ADMINISTRATIONS

The following table lists, in chronological order, each prime ministerial administration. An 'administration' differs from a 'term of office' in that a Prime Minister can have more than one administration during a term of office. Events giving rise to a new administration are (1) a change of Prime Minister, (2) a General Election (the date of which is taken here as polling day, or, pre-1918, last polling day), whether or not it leads to a change of Prime Minister, or (3) a change in the party composition of the Government, such as the creation or reformulation of a coalition (*eg* Asquith 1915, MacDonald 1931). However where a General Election took place almost immediately after the appointment of a new Prime Minister (*eg* Eden 1955) or where a Government remained in office for a brief time after an unsuccessful General Election in order to meet the new Parliament (*eg* Baldwin 1923-24), such short periods cannot be regarded as an administration in any meaningful sense. A reconstruction or reshuffle of a Government, however major, which does not otherwise meet any of the three stated criteria, is not regarded as an event giving rise to a new administration.

This definition of an administration has only been used for the period from 1900. Thus for earlier periods an administration equates to a term of office. Before the 20th century a General Election which did not result in a change of Prime Minister or Government did not appear to have been regarded as a necessary or usual occasion for a significant reconstruction of a Government, or as a break in the continuity of a Government. Such reconstructions usually occurred with a change of Prime Minister or during the lifetime of a particular Government.

Walpole	1st	3 Apr 1721–11 Feb 1742
Wilmington	1st	16 Feb 1742–2 Jul 1743
Pelham	1st	27 Aug 1743–6 Mar 1754
Newcastle	1st	16 Mar 1754–11 Nov 1756
Devonshire	1st	16 Nov 1756–29 Jun 1757
Newcastle	2nd	29 Jun 1757–26 May 1762
Bute	1st	26 May 1762–8 Apr 1763
Grenville, G	1st	16 Apr 1763–10 Jul 1765
Rockingham	1st	13 Jul 1765–30 Jul 1766
Chatham	1st	30 Jul 1766–14 Oct 1768
Grafton	1st	14 Oct 1768–28 Jan 1770
North	1st	28 Jan 1770–27 Mar 1782
Rockingham	2nd	27 Mar 1782–1 Jul 1782
Shelburne	1st	4 Jul 1782–26 Mar 1783
Portland	1st	2 Apr 1783–18 Dec 1783
Pitt	1st	19 Dec 1783–14 Mar 1801
Addington	1st	17 Mar 1801–10 May 1804
Pitt	2nd	10 May 1804–23 Jan 1806
Grenville, Ld	1st	11 Feb 1806–25 Mar 1807
Portland	2nd	31 Mar 1807–4 Oct 1809
Perceval	1st	4 Oct 1809–11 May 1812
Liverpool	1st	8 Jun 1812–9 Apr 1827
Canning	1st	12 Apr 1827–8 Aug 1827
Goderich	1st	31 Aug 1827–8 Jan 1828
Wellington	1st	22 Jan 1828–16 Nov 1830
Grey	1st	22 Nov 1830–9 Jul 1834
Melbourne	1st	16 Jul 1834–14 Nov 1834
Wellington	2nd	17 Nov 1834–9 Dec 1834
Peel	1st	10 Dec 1834–8 Apr 1835
Melbourne	2nd	18 Apr 1835–30 Aug 1841
Peel	2nd	30 Aug 1841–29 Jun 1846
Russell	1st	30 Jun 1846–21 Feb 1852
Derby	1st	23 Feb 1852–17 Dec 1852
Aberdeen	1st	19 Dec 1852–30 Jan 1855

DATES OF ADMINISTRATIONS—*Continued*

Palmerston	1st	6 Feb 1855–19 Feb 1858
Derby	2nd	20 Feb 1858–11 Jun 1859
Palmerston	2nd	12 Jun 1859–18 Oct 1865
Russell	2nd	29 Oct 1865–26 Jun 1866
Derby	3rd	28 Jun 1866–25 Feb 1868
Disraeli	1st	27 Feb 1868–1 Dec 1868
Gladstone	1st	3 Dec 1868–17 Feb 1874
Disraeli	2nd	20 Feb 1874–21 Apr 1880
Gladstone	2nd	23 Apr 1880–9 Jun 1885
Salisbury	1st	23 Jun 1885–28 Jan 1886
Gladstone	3rd	1 Feb 1886–20 Jul 1886
Salisbury	2nd	25 Jul 1886–11 Aug 1892
Gladstone	4th	15 Aug 1892–2 Mar 1894
Rosebery	1st	5 Mar 1894–22 Jun 1895
Salisbury	3rd	25 Jun 1895–24 Oct 1900
Salisbury	4th	24 Oct 1900–11 Jul 1902
Balfour	1st	12 Jul 1902–4 Dec 1905
Campbell-Bannerman	1st	5 Dec 1905–5 Apr 1908
Asquith	1st	5 Apr 1908–9 Feb 1910
Asquith	2nd	9 Feb 1910–19 Dec 1910
Asquith	3rd	19 Dec 1910–25 May 1915
Asquith	4th	25 May 1915–5 Dec 1916
Lloyd George	1st	6 Dec 1916–14 Dec 1918
Lloyd George	2nd	14 Dec 1918–19 Oct 1922
Bonar Law	1st	23 Oct 1922–20 May 1923
Baldwin	1st	22 May 1923–22 Jan 1924
MacDonald	1st	22 Jan 1924–4 Nov 1924
Baldwin	2nd	4 Nov 1924–4 Jun 1929
MacDonald	2nd	5 Jun 1929–24 Aug 1931
MacDonald	3rd	24 Aug 1931–27 Oct 1931
MacDonald	4th	27 Oct 1931–7 Jun 1935
Baldwin	3rd	7 Jun 1935–14 Nov 1935
Baldwin	4th	14 Nov 1935–28 May 1937
Chamberlain	1st	28 May 1937–10 May 1940
Churchill	1st	10 May 1940–23 May 1945
Churchill	2nd	23 May 1945–26 Jul 1945
Attlee	1st	26 Jul 1945–23 Feb 1950
Attlee	2nd	23 Feb 1950–26 Oct 1951
Churchill	3rd	26 Oct 1951–5 Apr 1955
Eden	1st	6 Apr 1955–9 Jan 1957
Macmillan	1st	10 Jan 1957–8 Oct 1959
Macmillan	2nd	8 Oct 1959–18 Oct 1963
Douglas-Home	1st	19 Oct 1963–16 Oct 1964
Wilson	1st	16 Oct 1964–31 Mar 1966
Wilson	2nd	31 Mar 1966–19 Jun 1970
Heath	1st	19 Jun 1970–4 Mar 1974
Wilson	3rd	4 Mar 1974–10 Oct 1974
Wilson	4th	10 Oct 1974–5 Apr 1976
Callaghan	1st	5 Apr 1976–4 May 1979
Thatcher	1st	4 May 1979–9 Jun 1983
Thatcher	2nd	9 Jun 1983–11 Jun 1987
Thatcher	3rd	11 Jun 1987–28 Nov 1990
Major	1st	28 Nov 1990–9 Apr 1992
Major	2nd	9 Apr 1992–

NUMBER OF ADMINISTRATIONS

4– Gladstone, Salisbury, Asquith, MacDonald, Baldwin, Wilson (6)

3– Derby, Churchill, Thatcher (3)

2– Newcastle, Rockingham, Portland, Pitt, Wellington, Melbourne, Peel, Russell, Palmerston, Disraeli, Lloyd George, Attlee, Macmillan, Major (14)

1– Walpole, Wilmington, Pelham, Devonshire, Bute, George Grenville, Chatham, Grafton, North, Shelburne, Addington, Lord Grenville, Perceval, Liverpool, Canning, Goderich, Grey, Aberdeen Rosebery, Balfour, Campbell-Bannerman, Bonar Law, Chamberlain, Eden, Douglas-Home, Heath, Callaghan (27)

The most Prime Ministers in a calendar year was 4 in 1834. They were Grey, Melbourne, Wellington and Peel.

PARTY IN GOVERNMENT

Political parties have become increasingly significant in Parliament since Walpole's time, but even in the 18th century they represented a description of a political point of view, although there was very little central party organisation. Many were simply factions that gathered around personalities. Governments in the 18th century often included ministers from different political parties, but this practice has died out as party affiliations have become more rigid, except in the case of coalition governments. Nevertheless, it is possible to give broad party labels to all governments.

The main parties in the 18th century were the Tories, who supported the monarchy, and the Whigs, who wanted to increase the power of Parliament and limit the power of the monarchy. From the 1830s to the 1850s shifting allegiances gradually transformed the old parties into what became known as the Conservative Party and the Liberal Party respectively. The Labour Party was formed in the early 1900s.

Period	Party in Government	Prime Minister
1721-1762	Whig	Walpole, Wilmington, Pelham, Newcastle, Devonshire
1762-1763	Tory	Bute
1763-1770	Whig	Grenville, G, Rockingham, Chatham, Grafton
1770-1782	Tory	North
1782-1783	Whig	Rockingham, Shelburne
1783	Whig/Tory Coalition	Portland
1783-1806	Tory	Pitt, Addington
1806-1807	Whig	Grenville, Lord
1807-1827	Tory	Portland, Perceval, Liverpool
1827-1828	Whig/Tory Coalition	Canning, Goderich
1828-1830	Tory	Wellington
1830-1834	Whig	Grey, Melbourne
1834	Tory	Wellington
1834-1835	Con	Peel
1835-1841	Whig	Melbourne
1841-1846	Con	Peel
1846-1852	Lib	Russell
1852	Con	Derby
1852-1855	Coalition	Aberdeen
1855-1858	Lib	Palmerston
1858-1859	Con	Derby
1859-1866	Lib	Palmerston, Russell
1866-1868	Con	Derby, Disraeli
1868-1874	Lib	Gladstone
1874-1880	Con	Disraeli
1880-1885	Lib	Gladstone
1885-1886	Con	Salisbury
1886	Lib	Gladstone
1886-1892	Con	Salisbury
1892-1895	Lib	Gladstone, Rosebery
1895-1905	Con	Salisbury, Balfour
1905-1915	Lib	Campbell-Bannerman, Asquith
1915-1922	Coalition	Asquith, Lloyd George
1922-1924	Con	Bonar Law, Baldwin
1924	Lab	MacDonald
1924-1929	Con	Baldwin
1929-1931	Lab	MacDonald
1931-1937	National	MacDonald, Baldwin
1937-1940	Con	Chamberlain
1940-1945	Coalition	Churchill
1945	Con Caretaker	Churchill
1945-1951	Lab	Attlee
1951-1964	Con	Churchill, Eden, Macmillan, Douglas-Home
1964-1970	Lab	Wilson
1970-1974	Con	Heath
1974-1979	Lab	Wilson, Callaghan
1979–	Con	Thatcher, Major

The longest period of single-party government was the 41 years of Whig rule between 1721 and 1762. The Tories were in power for 23 years between 1783 and 1806, but since then periods of one-party domination have been rarer. In the 20th century the Conservative Party has had two long spells of government: the 13 years between 1951 and 1964, and the period since 1979.

MINISTERIAL OFFICES COMBINED WITH PRIME MINISTERSHIP

The office of Prime Minister is not itself a ministerial post, so it must be combined with a ministerial office. This is now, but has not always been, the post of First Lord of the Treasury. Two Prime Ministers, Chatham and Salisbury, were not also First Lord of the Treasury, although Salisbury did combine the office of Prime Minister with that of First Lord of the Treasury in his second term of office.

Five Prime Ministers have combined the office of Prime Minister with that of First Lord of the Treasury alone: Bute, Lloyd George, Eden, Macmillan and Douglas-Home.

Until the early years of the 20th century Prime Ministers were always the Leader of the House in which they sat. The only exception to this was during the Duke of Portland's second term of office, from 1807-1809, when Liverpool was Leader of the House of Lords. If a Prime Minister becomes a Peer during his period as Prime Minister, he automatically becomes Leader of the House of Lords. Since 1916, however, the Prime Minister has not always been the Leader of the House in which he sits, and since 1942 this has never been so.

MINISTERIAL OFFICES COMBINED WITH PRIME MINISTERSHIP—*Continued*

The following offices have been combined with the office of Prime Minister, though not necessarily all at the same time.

Chancellor of the Duchy of Lancaster

Perceval

Chancellor of the Exchequer

Walpole, Pelham, G Grenville, North, Pitt, Addington, Perceval, Canning, Peel, Gladstone, Baldwin

Commissioner of the Treasury for Ireland

Perceval

Foreign Secretary

Wellington, Salisbury, MacDonald

Lord Chamberlain

Devonshire

Lord President of the Council

Rosebery

Lord Privy Seal

Chatham, Disraeli, Gladstone, Salisbury, Balfour

Lord Treasurer for Ireland

Devonshire

Minister for the Civil Service

Wilson, Heath, Callaghan, Thatcher, Major

Minister of Defence

Churchill, Attlee

Secretary of State, Northern Department

Walpole

Secretary of State for War

Asquith

Perceval held most offices at the same time as being Prime Minister, (3): Chancellor of the Exchequer, Chancellor of the Duchy of Lancaster and Commissioner of the Treasury for Ireland.

'GLITTERING CABINETS' FORMER PMs IN LATER CABINETS

Fourteen former Prime Ministers served in Cabinets in a later Administration of another Prime Minister. Devonshire was the first to do so, and Douglas-Home the latest. This total includes three (Portland, Russell and Baldwin) who later became Prime Minister again (noted * in the following list). Three former Prime Ministers (Grafton, Addington and Balfour) each served under three other Prime Ministers. Baldwin served in four later Administrations, the most of any of the 14 in this list.

Former PM	Later administration served in
Devonshire	Newcastle (2nd); Bute.
Newcastle	Rockingham (1st).
Grafton	North; Rockingham (2nd); Shelburne.
North	Portland (1st).
Portland	Pitt (1st)*; Pitt (2nd)*; Addington*.
Addington	Grenville, Ld; Perceval; Liverpool.
Goderich	Grey; Peel (2nd).
Wellington	Peel (1st); Peel (2nd).
Russell	Aberdeen*; Palmerston (1st)*; Palmerston (2nd)*.
Balfour	Asquith (4th); Lloyd George (1st); Lloyd George (2nd); Baldwin (2nd).
MacDonald	Baldwin (3rd); Baldwin (4th).
Baldwin	MacDonald (3rd)*; MacDonald (4th)*.
Chamberlain	Churchill (1st).
Douglas-Home	Heath.

'GLITTERING CABINETS': OTHER PRIME MINISTERS IN THEIR CABINETS

Only 4 Prime Ministers (George Grenville, Balfour, Callaghan and Major) have had no former or future Prime Ministers in their Cabinet. In addition, there have been 8 other Administrations containing no former or future Prime Minister (Wellington's 2nd; Disraeli's 1st; Gladstone's 1st; Salisbury's 1st; MacDonald's 1st & 2nd and Thatcher's 1st & 2nd) making 12 administrations in total.

Grey and Peel are the only 2 Prime Ministers to have had 5 former or future Prime Ministers in their Cabinet at the same time.

This list sets out the number of different former or future Prime Ministers each Prime Minister had in the Cabinets of one or more of their Administrations.

5– Liverpool, Grey, Peel, Baldwin

4– Newcastle, Portland, Pitt, Asquith, Churchill

3– Walpole, Pelham, Rockingham, Perceval, Wellington, Aberdeen, Gladstone, Lloyd George

2– Wilmington, Devonshire, Bute, Chatham, Grafton, Shelburne, Addington, Lord Grenville, Canning, Melbourne, Russell, Derby, Palmerston, Rosebery, Campbell-Bannerman, MacDonald, Chamberlain, Eden, Macmillan, Heath

1– North, Goderich, Disraeli, Salisbury, Bonar Law, Attlee, Douglas-Home, Wilson, Thatcher

0– George Grenville, Balfour, Callaghan, Major

'GLITTERING CABINETS': OTHER PRIME MINISTERS SERVED UNDER

Only two Prime Ministers (Walpole and Rockingham) did not serve as a Minister in any other Prime Minister's Cabinet. Palmerston served in the Cabinets of 8 other Prime Ministers (Perceval, Canning, Goderich, Wellington, Grey, Melbourne, Russell and Aberdeen), twice the number of any other Prime Minister, and all before he became Prime Minister.

The following list sets out the number of other Prime Ministers in whose Cabinets each Prime Minister served.

8– Palmerston

4– Newcastle, Addington, Liverpool, Goderich, Russell, Gladstone, Balfour, Churchill

3– Devonshire, George Grenville, Chatham, Grafton, North, Shelburne, Asquith, Chamberlain, Eden, Douglas-Home

2– Pelham, Portland, Canning, Wellington, Peel, Derby, Aberdeen, Salisbury, Campbell-Bannerman, Lloyd George, Bonar Law, Baldwin, Macmillan, Heath

1– Wilmington, Bute, Pitt, Lord Grenville, Perceval, Grey, Melbourne, Disraeli, Rosebery, MacDonald, Attlee, Wilson, Callaghan, Thatcher, Major

0– Walpole, Rockingham

FORMER PMs ALIVE WHEN PM TOOK OFFICE

As of January 1995, there are five former Prime Ministers alive at the same time. There have been many occasions in the past when this has happened. The following table details the five former Prime Ministers who have been alive at the date on which another has taken office.

Grafton– Newcastle; Bute; Grenville, G.; Rockingham; Chatham

North– Bute; Grenville, G.; Rockingham; Chatham; Grafton

Pitt (1st)– Bute; Grafton; North; Shelburne; Portland

Melbourne (2nd)– Addington; Goderich; Wellington Grey; Peel

Peel (1st)– Addington; Goderich; Wellington; Grey; Melbourne

Peel (2nd)– Addington; Goderich; Wellington; Grey; Melbourne

Baldwin (1st)– Rosebery; Balfour; Asquith; Lloyd George; Bonar Law

Baldwin (2nd)– Rosebery; Balfour; Asquith; Lloyd George; MacDonald

MacDonald (2nd)– Rosebery; Balfour; Asquith; Lloyd George; Baldwin

Wilson (1st)– Churchill; Attlee; Eden; Macmillan; Douglas-Home

Callaghan– Eden; Macmillan; Douglas-Home; Wilson; Heath

Thatcher– Macmillan; Douglas-Home; Wilson; Heath; Callaghan

Major– Douglas-Home; Wilson; Heath; Callaghan; Thatcher

Addington holds the record for having to live through most successors. After his own term of office, he saw nine Prime Ministers follow in his footsteps before he died: Lord Grenville, Perceval, Liverpool, Canning, Goderich, Wellington (both terms), Grey, Melbourne (both terms) and Peel (both terms).

MISCELLANY

THE PRIVY COUNCIL

The Privy Council is an ancient body which originally carried out the Sovereign's business, although in its modern form its functions are largely formal, mainly to advise the Sovereign and to exercise certain limited statutory responsibilities. Appointment to the Privy Council follows the assumption of high office, such as a Cabinet post, and is a great honour.

A Privy Counsellor is required to take a special Privy Counsellor's oath, and there is a difference between the date of appointment and the date on which someone is sworn of the Privy Council. We have preferred the appointment date, but the section on Important Dates in Part 1 should always make clear which date is being used. Appointment is for life, although members can be dismissed by the Sovereign. Devonshire is the only Prime Minister ever to have been dismissed.

Only 10 Prime Ministers have been appointed to the Privy Council before the age of 30. Pitt was the youngest, at 23 years, 43 days. The youngest appointments in the 20th century were Wilson, at 31 years, 217 days; Churchill, at 32 years, 152 days; and Eden, at 37 years, 142 days.

	Date Appointed PC	Age yrs, days
Pitt	10 Jul 1782	23, 43
Newcastle	16 Apr 1717	23, 269
Grenville, Lord	15 Sep 1782*	23, 326
Peel	13 Aug 1812	24, 190
Palmerston	1 Nov 1809	25, 12
Shelburne	20 Apr 1763	25, 353
Portland	10 Jul 1765	27, 87
Liverpool	13 Mar 1799	28, 279
Grafton	10 Jul 1765	29, 285
Goderich	13 Aug 1812	29, 288

* Privy Council of Ireland

MacDonald was not only the oldest PM to be appointed a Privy Counsellor appointed at the age of 57 years, 102 days, he was also appointed both Prime Minister and a member of the Privy Council on the same day, 22 Jan 1924. Apart from MacDonald, only 8 Prime Ministers have become Prime Minister less than 5 years after their appointment as Privy Counsellors: Rockingham, Pitt, Bute, Perceval, Baldwin, North, Grafton and Major. Palmerston, who became a Privy Counsellor at the young age of 25 years, 12 days, had the longest wait. He became Prime Minister 45 years and 97 days after his appointment to the Privy Council.

	Date Appointed PC	Gap Before Appointed PM yrs, days
Rockingham	10 Jul 1765	—, 3
Pitt	10 Jul 1782	1, 162
Bute	27 Oct 1760	1, 211
Perceval	26 Mar 1807	2, 192
Baldwin	11 Jun 1920	2, 345
North	10 Dec 1766	3, 49
Grafton	10 Jul 1765	3, 96
Major	13 Jun 1987	3, 168

7 Prime Ministers were also members of the Privy Council of Ireland: Devonshire (appointed but not sworn), Lord Grenville, Melbourne, Peel, Derby, Balfour, and Asquith. The Privy Council of Ireland ceased to exist when the Irish Free State was established in 1922.

Baldwin is the only Prime Minister to have been a member of the Privy Council of Canada.

SPEAKERS OF THE HOUSE

3 Prime Ministers have also served as Speaker of the House of Commons, although this has not happened since the 18th century.

Speaker		yrs, days
Wilmington	17 Mar 1715–17 Jul 1727	12, 122
Addington	8 Jun 1789–10 Feb 1801	11, 247
Grenville, Lord	5 Jan 1789–5 Jun 1789	—, 151

Wilmington served as Speaker at the same time as holding ministerial office, a practice which was subsequently discontinued to avoid any possible conflicts of interest.

FATHERS OF THE HOUSE

The senior Member of Parliament in the House of Commons is known by the affectionate name of Father of the House. This unofficial title is bestowed on the Member with the longest unbroken service in the House of Commons. Its use can be traced back to the 19th century, although the modern qualification for the title has not been used consistently throughout that time.

Five Prime Ministers have stayed in the House of Commons long enough to become Father of the House. They are listed below in order of the length of time that they remained as Father. The first date is either the polling date of the relevant General Election or the date of death of the previous Father. The final date is the date on which they ceased to be a Member of the House of Commons.

Father of the House		yrs, days
Lloyd George	18 Nov 1929–1 Jan 1945	16, 44
Churchill	8 Oct 1959–25 Sep 1964	4, 353
Callaghan	9 Jun 1983–18 May 1987	3, 343
Heath	9 Apr 1992–	
Campbell-Bannerman	22 May 1907–22 Apr 1908	—, 335

Campbell-Bannerman was the only one to be Prime Minister and Father of the House at the same time.

Index

INDEX